SQL SERVER 7

SQL Server 7 Developer's Guide

Michael Otey is Senior Technical Editor for *Windows NT Magazine* and *SQL Server Magazine.*

Paul Conte is a database expert and the author of several computer books, including *Database Design and Programming for DB2/400* and *Common Sense C.* He is the president of Picante Software.

SQL SERVER 7

SQL Server 7 Developer's Guide

Michael Otey
Paul Conte

Osborne **McGraw-Hill**

Berkeley   New York   St. Louis   San Francisco
Auckland   Bogotá   Hamburg   London   Madrid
Mexico City   Milan   Montreal   New Delhi   Panama City
Paris   São Paulo   Singapore   Sydney
Tokyo   Toronto

Osborne **McGraw-Hill**
2600 Tenth Street
Berkeley, California 94710
U.S.A.

For information on translations or book distributors outside the U.S.A., or to arrange bulk purchase discounts for sales promotions, premiums, or fund-raisers, please contact Osborne/**McGraw-Hill** at the above address.

SQL Server 7 Developer's Guide

1234567890 DOC DOC 90198765432109

ISBN 0-07-882548-2

Publisher
   Brandon A. Nordin
Editor-in-Chief
   Scott Rogers
Acquisitions Editor
   Wendy Rinaldi
Project Editor
   Emily Rader Perez
Editorial Assistant
   Monika Faltiss
Technical Editor
   Gil Milbauer
Proofreaders
   Linda Medoff
   Paul Medoff

Copy Editors
   Kimberly Torgerson
   Judy Ziajka
   Dennis Weaver
   Claire Splan
   William McManus
Indexer
   David Heiret
Computer Designers
   Jani Beckwith
   Ann Sellers
Illustrator
   Beth Young
   Brian Wells
Series Design
   Peter Hancik

To the honor and glory of God and to the memory of my father
—Michael Otey

To Hazel and Jim Hynds, wonderful people
who embraced me as one of their family
—Paul Conte

CONTENTS

Foreword xix
Acknowledgments xxi
Introduction. xxiii

Part I
Managing SQL Server

▼ 1   An Essential Overview of SQL Server   3
SQL Server's Networked Architecture   4
SQL Server's Basic Components   7
Transact-SQL   8
SQL Server Database Architecture   9
      Servers.   9
      Databases   10
      Database Objects   12
Administrative Components   19
      SQL Server Enterprise Manager   19
      Administrative Wizards.   22
      Distributed Transaction Coordinator   22
      Query Analyzer   22

SQL Server Profiler 23
SQL Performance Monitor 23
Data Transformation Services 24
Distributed Management Objects 25
Command-Line Utilities. 26
Conclusion 26

▼ 2   SQL Server Administration. 27
Overview of a SQL Server Installation. 28
Directories and Databases. 28
Tools. 30
Setting Enterprise Manager Properties. 39
Registering and Unregistering a Server 41
Stopping, Starting, Pausing, and Continuing a Server 47
Setting Server Properties 48
Managing Databases and Database Objects 65
Creating and Modifying a Database 65
Enterprise Manager Database Folders. 74
Server Logins and Roles. 90
Working with SQL Server Agent. 90
Displaying Event Logs 105
Viewing and Creating SQL Server Messages 106
Working with Linked Servers 108
Creating a Database Maintenance Plan 110
Other Enterprise Manager Facilities 115
Conclusion 116

▼ 3   SQL Server Security 117
Security Basics 118
Logging On to NT Server 118
Logging In to SQL Server 119
Groups and Roles 123
System Administrator 126
Database Owner 126
Database Guest. 127
SQL Server Security Modes. 127
Setting Up Database Users 128
Step 1: Plan Your Application Databases, User Names,
Database Owners, and Logical Roles. 128
Step 2: Plan Your NT Server Users and Groups
and Your SQL Server Logins, Roles, and
Database Users 131
Step 3: Set the SQL Server Security Mode. 135
Step 4: Create NT Server Groups. 135
Step 5: Create NT Server Users and Add Them
to NT Server Groups 137

Step 6: Create SQL Server Logins for NT Server
Users and Groups That Will Be Members of
SQL Server Fixed Server Roles   140
Step 7: Create SQL Server Application Databases   141
Step 8: Set Up User-Defined Database Roles   143
Step 9: Set Up the Login Names and Database User Names
for NT Users and Groups That Will Be SQL
Server Application Users.   143
What You've Accomplished   147
Removing Users   148
Managing Database Users.   151
Managing Logins.   152
Managing Roles   153
Managing Database User Names.   153
Using Stored Procedures   154
Permissions   158
Restricted Statements   159
Statement Permissions.   161
Object Permissions.   162
Role Permissions   167
Application Roles   167
Stored Procedures and Permissions   168
Ownership Chain.   168
Database Security Principles and Guidelines   170
Conclusion   171

▼ 4   SQL Server Backup and Recovery.   173
Why Back Up the Database?   174
Backing Up Database Objects   175
Backup Devices.   176
Checking the Database   177
Backing Up a Database   178
Backing Up Only the Transaction Log.   181
Scheduling a Backup.   182
Truncating the Transaction Log   182
Organizing Backups   183
Database Recovery   188
Recovery for a Damaged Database.   188
Recovering the master Database   194
Restoring a File or Filegroup   195
Restoring from a Backup Device   196
Backup and Recovery Server Options   196
Using a Standby Server   197
Conclusion   198

▼ **5** Data Replication and Data Warehousing 199
  Database Replication. 200
    SQL Server Replication Components 201
    Types of SQL Server Replication 202
    Setting Up a Simple Merge Replication 204
  Data Warehousing 221
    Types of OLAP 222
    Microsoft Data Warehousing Framework. 222
    SQL Server Components for Data Warehousing 224
    Installing SQL Server OLAP Services 225
    Using the Microsoft OLAP Manager. 225
    Using the Cube Wizard 226
  Conclusion 231
  Additional Resources 231

▼ **6** Database Performance. 233
  Selecting the Appropriate Tool 235
  SQL Server Profiler. 238
    Creating a Trace Definition 242
    Running a Trace 263
    Trace Defaults 264
    Using SQL Scripts 265
    Replaying a Trace 266
    The Create Trace Wizard 266
    Using Trace Data to Monitor Performance 268
  SQL Server Performance Monitor 269
    Running the Performance Monitor. 277
    Using the Performance Monitor Data 289
  Enterprise Manager Current Activity Categories 289
    Process Info Category 289
    Locks / Process ID Category 290
    Locks / Object Category 291
  Index Tuning Wizard 292
    Preparing a Workload 293
    Running the Index Tuning Wizard 294
  Showplan 299
    Using Showplan with the Set Statement. 301
    Using Graphical Showplan 304
  Other Performance Tools 306
    The DBCC Statement 306
    Trace Flags 307
    Query Analyzer Index Analysis 308
    Transact-SQL Functions and Stored Procedures 308
  SQL Statement Hints. 310
    Query Hints. 310

Join Hints 310
Table Hints 312
Conclusion 315

▼ 7   Advanced Management Using SQL-DMO 317
Distributed Management Object Hierarchy 318
Distributed Management Framework 318
SQL-DMO Core Object Hierarchy 319
SQL-DMO Files 327
Using SQL-DMO 327
Adding SQL-DMO Objects to Visual Basic 328
Creating the SQLServer Object 329
Connecting to SQL Server 330
Using SQL-DMO Properties 331
SQL-DMO Property Collections 332
Putting SQL-DMO to Work 335
Conclusion 344

Part II

Database Development with SQL Server

▼ 8   Introduction to the Relational Database Model 347
Background: Database Management Systems 348
Conventional File System Versus DBMSs 349
Defining Data 350
Enforcing Data Integrity 351
Manipulating Data 352
Database Models 353
The Relational Database Model 354
Relational Model: Data Structure 354
Normal Forms 358
Relational Model: Data Integrity 365
Relational Model: Data Manipulation 367
Introduction to Entity Relationship Diagrams (ERDs) 377
Basic ERD Concepts and Symbols 377
Adding Properties to ERDs 380
Multivalued Properties 381
Representing Associations 382
Exclusive Relationships 384
Entity Subtypes 384
When to Use ERDs 386
Conclusion 388
Additional Resources 388

▼ 9   SQL Primer: Data Definition Language   389

Introduction to SQL   390
    A SQL Preview   392
    Benefits of SQL   393
    Entering SQL Statements   394
    Alternatives to SQL Statements for Creating
       Database Objects   397
    Setting ANSI-Standard Behavior   397
Creating a Database   397
    Specifying the Database File Locations and Sizes   398
    Altering a Database   399
    Defining Filegroups   400
Creating a Table   401
    SQL Naming Conventions   403
    Column Definitions   404
    Constraints   412
    Creating a Table on a Specific Filegroup   415
    Adding, Dropping, and Disabling Constraints   416
    Adding, Dropping, and Altering Table Columns   417
Creating a View   418
    Defining the View Contents   419
    Read-Only and Updateable Views   423
    With Check Option   424
    Encrypted View Definitions   425
    More View Examples   425
Creating an Index   428
    Clustered Indexes   431
    Other Index Options   431
Dropping Databases, Tables, Views, and Indexes   433
Granting and Revoking Table and View Privileges   433
    Object Permissions   434
    Column-Level Security   437
    Statement Permissions   438
The SQL Catalog   438
DDL Coding Suggestions   439
Conclusion   442
Additional Resources   442

▼ 10   SQL Primer: Data Manipulation Language   443

Introduction to DML   444
Retrieving Rows with the Select Statement   445
    Search Conditions   448
    SQL Conditions and Three-Valued Logic   450

Retrieving Data from Views 451
Specifying the Columns to Retrieve 452
Eliminating Duplicate Rows 452
Constants, Functions, and Expressions 453
Date and Time Arithmetic 469
Aggregate Functions. 471
Group By Clause 474
Having Clause 475
Using a Where Clause Versus a Having Clause 477
The Order By Clause. 478
Complex Select Statements 479
Conditions and Subqueries 487
Using a Case Expression 497
Using a Subquery as a Scalar Value 498
Using a Select Expression in the From Clause 499
Additional Select Statement Features 500
The Rollup and Cube Options of the Group By Clause 502
The Compute Clause 505
The Into Clause. 506
Using DML to Modify Table Data 507
The Insert Statement. 507
The Update Statement. 510
The Delete and Truncate Table Statements 513
Concurrent Updates and Table Locks 515
Transaction Integrity and the Commit and
Rollback Statements 516
Stored Procedures 519
Altering and Deleting Stored Procedures 520
Displaying Information About Stored Procedures 520
Stored Procedure Parameters 521
Returning Result Sets 522
Status Return Value 523
Fundamental Programming Techniques 524
Using Cursors 528
Sending Error Messages. 534
Triggers 536
Checking for Specific Column Changes 539
Altering and Deleting Triggers. 540
Working with Triggers 540
Displaying Information About Triggers. 541
Trigger Programming 542
DML Coding Suggestions 544
Conclusion 545
Additional Resources 545

▼ **11** Developing SQL Server Database Applications with Access 547

The Difference Between Multiple-User Access and
   SQL Server Database Implementations 549
Using Access as a Front-End Development Tool 552
Microsoft Access Networking Architecture 552
Connecting to SQL Server 553
   Installing the SQL Server ODBC Driver 554
   Configuring a Data Source 555
   Linking Tables 561
Using the Query Designer 567
Using the Forms Designer 570
Using the Report Designer 573
Using Macros 577
Using VBA Code Modules to Build
   SQL Server Applications 580
   Using a DAO Recordset 581
   Using Parameterized Queries 582
   Using SQL Server Stored Procedures 584
   Error Handling 588
Tips 589
Conclusion 590

▼ **12** Developing SQL Server Database Applications with DAO and
   ODBCDirect 591

DAO Files 594
DAO Architecture 594
   An Overview of Using DAO 596
Adding the DAO 3.5 Reference to Visual Basic 597
Using DAO Objects with Visual Basic 598
   Creating the DBEngine Object 598
   Creating the Workspace Object 598
   Connecting to SQL Server 599
   Retrieving Data with DAO 607
   Limiting Data in a Recordset 619
   Closing a Recordset 623
   Executing Dynamic SQL Using SQLPassThrough 623
   Modifying Data Using Recordsets and SQLPassThrough . . . 624
   Working with QueryDefs 631
   Error Handling 645
Ending the Jet Engine 647
General Performance Tips for DAO and ODBC 647
ODBCDirect 648
ODBCDirect Files 650
ODBCDirect Architecture 650
   An Overview of Using ODBCDirect 651
Creating the DBEngine Object 652

Creating an ODBCDirect Workspace Object   652
   Using the CreateWorkspace Method   652
   Setting the Default Workspace Type.   652
   Connecting to SQL Server.   653
   Retrieving Data with ODBCDirect.   657
   Modifying Data with ODBCDirect.   663
   Executing Dynamic SQL with ODBCDirect.   668
   Executing Stored Procedures with QueryDef Objects   669
   Error Handling   671
Advanced Database Functions Using ODBCDirect   672
   Working with Multiple Result Sets   672
   Asynchronous Operations   674
   Using Transactions.   676
Conclusion   679
Additional Resources   679

▼ 13   Developing NT Database Applications with the ODBC API   681
ODBC Architecture.   683
   The ODBC Application   683
   The ODBC Driver Manager.   684
   The ODBC Driver   684
   The Data Source   685
Configuring an ODBC Data Source   685
   Basic Use of the ODBC API   693
   ODBC Initialization Functions   696
   Retrieving Data Using the ODBC API   702
   Updating Data Using ODBC   708
   Calling Stored Procedures   714
   ODBC Error Handling and SQLGetDiagRec   716
Conclusion   718
Additional Resources   718

▼ 14   Developing NT Database Applications with RDO   719
RDO Files   721
RDO Architecture   721
An Overview of Using RDO   723
Adding RDO 2.0 Objects to Visual Basic.   723
Using the RDO Objects with Visual Basic   724
   Creating the RDO Engine and Environment   724
   Closing the rdoEnvironment   727
   Working with RDO Connections.   727
   Closing an RDO Connection   729
   Retrieving Data Using RDO   729
   Using Dynamic SQL and RDO Execute   736
   Modifying Data with RDO Cursors   737

Modifying Data with RDO Using SQL 741
Error Handling 747
Advanced Topics 748
Working with Multiple Result Sets 748
Asynchronous Queries 750
Server-Side Cursors 752
Managing Data Concurrency 753
Conclusion 755
Additional Resources 755

▼ **15** Developing SQL Server Database Applications with OLE DB and ADO 757

OLE DB and Universal Data Access 758
OLE DB Architecture Overview 758
ADO (ActiveX Data Objects) 761
OLE DB and ADO Files **762**
ADO Architecture 763
An Overview of Using ADO 764
Adding the ADO 2 Reference to Visual Basic 764
Using ADO Objects with Visual Basic 765
Connecting to SQL Server. 766
Retrieving Data with the ADO Recordset 772
Closing a Recordset 783
Executing Dynamic SQL with the ADO Command Object . . 786
Modifying Data with ADO 787
Executing Stored Procedures with Command Objects. 796
Error Handling 799
Advanced Database Functions Using ADO 800
Batch Updates 800
Working with Multiple Result Sets 802
Using Transactions. 804
Storing Binary Data 806
Conclusion 810
Additional Resources 810

▼ **16** Developing Database Applications with DB-Library 811

An Overview of Using DB-Library 814
Adding vbsql.ocx to Visual Basic 814
Using the DB-Library for Visual Basic 816
DB-Library Initialization 818
Enumerating SQL Server Systems 818
Connecting to SQL Server. 820
Retrieving Data with DB-Library. 824
Executing Dynamic SQL 831
Modifying Data with Dynamic SQL 832
Working with Cursors. 836
Executing Stored Procedures 847

Error Handling 850
Advanced Techniques 852
Using Multiple Result Sets 853
Using Transactions 855
Conclusion 856
Additional Resources 857

▼ **17** Web Integration and ASP Development 859
Web Integration Using the Web Assistant Wizard 860
Building a Simple Web Wizard Query 861
Calling a Stored Procedure with the Web Wizard 871
Web and Database Integration Using ASP 875
The ASP Object Model 878
ASP Basics 879
Using ADO Objects with ASP 882
Web-Database Development with Visual InterDev 921
Conclusion 925
Additional References 925

Part III

Appendixes

▼ **A** Migrating from SQL Server 6.x to 7 929
Migration Overview **930**
Prerequisites 931
Using the Version Upgrade Wizard 931
Conclusion 939

▼ **B** Maximum Capacities 941
Database Capacities 942
SQL Capacities 943

Index 945

FOREWORD

've been privileged to know and work with Paul Conte and Mike Otey for nearly a decade. During that time we've seen a number of operating systems, database products, and programming paradigms come and go. Throughout this time both Paul and Mike have demonstrated an uncanny ability to see through the hype and identify significant trends and important products in the market. I can't tell you how many times I've turned to them for their opinion on new database technology or new programming models.

Paul's understanding of database architecture and programming structures is legendary (at least in my mind). His books and articles on these topics have undoubtedly inspired tens of thousands of database administrators and programmers to create more organized databases and write cleaner database access code. It is rare to find someone who can so easily translate complex computer theories into practical actions.

Mike, on the other hand, is one of the most practical, down-to-earth gentlemen I've ever met. Mike's understanding of database structure, storage, and retrieval is clearly comprehensive; however, Mike never loses focus on solving real problems. To Mike, a database product or programming interface is of no value unless it can be harnessed to solve a customer need or a business problem. Mike's problem-solving focus is a breath of fresh air in an industry more obsessed with features than solutions.

I was thrilled when I learned that Paul and Mike came together to work on this book about SQL Server 7, and I'm even more thrilled about the result. In this book, Paul and Mike provide a 360-degree perspective of SQL Server; they look at theoretical and administrative aspects of SQL Server, practical applications for SQL Server, and more. More important, they deliver this information to you in a way that is both easily understood and practical.

In closing, this is not a book with which you curl up in front of a fireplace and ponder the many realms of database applications. Instead, this is a practical, hands-on book that you keep by your side as you strive to deliver or administer high-quality database solutions for your company.

John Enck
Director of Technology and Research
Windows NT Magazine

ACKNOWLEDGMENTS

Every book starts with someone who plants the seed for what eventually grows into the published work. We were lucky to have Wendy Rinaldi at Osborne plant the seed for a book on SQL Server 7 and ask us to help it grow. She nourished the idea and was a wonderful source of encouragement as we plowed through the sometimes-daunting task of understanding and explaining a major new version of SQL Server.

We got essential technical reviews and assistance along the way from Gil Milbauer at Microsoft. Gil's substantial and unflagging effort as we poured out more and more pages on the new and rapidly evolving version of SQL Server was essential to delivering an accurate and comprehensive developer's guide. To the degree this book meets our goal of technical excellence, we owe a lot to Gil. Of course, we take responsibility for any errors that may remain in the final version. We also appreciate the help provided by Tom Kreyche at Microsoft in getting early releases of SQL Server and in obtaining technical help from SQL Server developers. Bob Vogt, one of the SQL Server developers, provided lots of valuable information on performance-related topics.

Emily Rader at Osborne juggled a hectic schedule and a steady stream of new material, revisions, and questions from two authors as she managed the copy editing and layout of the book. We are also thankful for the efforts of copy editor Kim Torgerson; Proofreaders Linda Medoff and Paul Medoff; Typesetters Jean Butterfield, Ann Sellers, and Jani Beckwith; and Illustrators Beth Young and Brian Wells.

We appreciate John Enck at *Windows NT Magazine* giving us encouraging feedback on the manuscript and providing the book's foreword. In addition to the Osborne and Microsoft staff we've mentioned by name, we'd like to thank all those others who contributed to the book along the way.

This book was a *large* endeavor that spanned almost two years, and we made it only with the help of two great families. Special thanks to our wives, Denielle Otey and Janice Gotchall, and to "Team TECA" (Tyson Marty, Eric Otey, Cory Marty, and Alex Otey).

INTRODUCTION

The SQL Server 7 Developer's Guide is intended as a guide and reference for both SQL Server application development and common SQL Server administrative tasks. We feel that the *SQL Server 7 Developer's Guide* is unique in that it provides vital information about both developing applications for SQL Server and administering and managing SQL Server in an enterprise environment. Most other SQL Server books either concentrate on the administrative issues or on the developer details, forcing the reader to go to other sources to find the missing essential information. This typical dichotomy assumes that developers have no need for administrative information and that administrators don't need to know about development issues. However, years of enterprise-level database management and development experience have shown us that isn't the case. Database developers certainly do need to understand administrative issues such as setting up security or database replication to write optimal database applications. Likewise, administrators must understand how to build SQL queries, as well as understand the issues involved in writing well-performing database applications.

PART 1

Part 1 of this book covers the administrative aspects of SQL Server 7. Chapter 1 provides an introduction to SQL Server's fundamental concepts, including an overview of SQL Server's system architecture and the different SQL Server database objects. Chapter 2 shows you how to manage SQL Server using the SQL Server Enterprise Manager and the Microsoft Management Console (MMC). The SQL Server Enterprise Manager operates as a "snap-in" to MMC and allows you to work with SQL Server's server and database configurations for both local and remote SQL Server systems. Chapter 3 moves forward into the topic of setting up SQL Server security. Database security is a fundamental part of SQL Server, and Chapter 3 provides you with a set of guidelines that you can use to understand how to set up security for end users, developers, and administrators. Chapter 3 also gives you tips on how to integrate SQL Server's security with the security provided by NT Server. Chapter 4 covers backup and recovery issues. It will give you an understanding of how to establish a backup plan to handle database recovery, as well as how to implement online backups. Chapter 5 shows you how to set up database replication. In this chapter, you see how to set up data replication between local SQL Servers, as well as how to set up merge replications between a local SQL Server system and remote SQL Server systems in branch offices. Chapter 6 covers the basics on how to tune SQL Server. In this chapter, you see how to run SQL Server's Performance Monitor and trace a database application using SQL Server's Profiler. Part 1 wraps up by showing you how to build custom SQL Server management tools using SQL Server's Distributed Management Objects (SQL-DMO).

PART 2

Part 2 focuses on developing SQL Server database applications. It begins with an introduction to the concepts of relational database systems in Chapter 8 and then proceeds with a SQL tutorial in Chapters 9 and 10. This fundamental SQL information is another feature that sets this book apart from other developer references. Most references focus solely on using the different database APIs but ignore the fact that these APIs are SQL-based and that an understanding of SQL is implicit in their use. Indeed, a solid understanding of SQL is essential to writing efficient database applications. From here, the remaining chapters illustrate how to use each of the different data access APIs. Chapter 11 shows how you can use Access as a front-end development platform for building SQL Server database applications. Chapter 12 follows this up by showing you how to use Visual Basic's Data Access Objects (DAO) and its newer ODBC-based cousin, ODBCDirect, to build SQL Server database applications. Chapter 13 shows you how to build high-performance applications by coding directly to the ODBC 3.x APIs from Visual Basic. In Chapter 14, you see how to connect to SQL Server using the Remote Data Objects (RDO) that are a part of the Visual Basic Enterprise Edition. Chapter 15 dives into ADO and OLE DB, the newest data access APIs that are provided with SQL Server 7. Chapter 16 wraps up the data access APIs by presenting an example of the use of the DB-Library OCX. Finally, Chapter 17 describes how to tie SQL Server into Web-based applications using the SQL Server Web Assistant Wizard and shows you how to build Web applications with ActiveX Server Pages (ASP).

WHAT'S ON THE CD?

All of the code presented in Part 2 is provided on the CD that accompanies this book. For each of the example chapters, a wizard-style program is provided that guides you through the running of all of the different code examples while you are connected to your own SQL Server system. Cutting and pasting from these examples can give you a head start in developing your SQL Server applications.

You can install the example programs onto your hard drive or access the source code and executable programs directly on the CD itself. The CD installation program will autoplay when the CD is first inserted into your CD-ROM drive. Alternatively, you can run the setup.exe program that's located in the CD's root directory.

To run the example program, you must be connected to a SQL Server 7 system, and the respective database access components must be installed on your PC. For example, you must have installed the ADO library on your computer. All of the example programs make use of the example pubs database that is shipped with SQL Server. Because some of the example programs create tables and stored procedures, you must have both object creation and access authority to the pubs database.

SQL SERVER 7

SQL Server release 7 was two years in the making, and it is probably the most significant release of SQL Server since the product's initial introduction. According to the Microsoft SQL Server development team, this release focused on three main areas: ease of use, scalability, and data warehousing. A little later in this introduction, you'll get an overview of the most significant enhancements in SQL Server 7; but first, here's see a brief history of the development of SQL Server.

The History of SQL Server

SQL Server 7 is the latest version of a product that has been evolving since the late 1980s. Microsoft SQL Server originated as Sybase SQL Server in 1987. In 1988, Microsoft, Sybase, and Ashton-Tate ported the product to OS/2. Later, Ashton-Tate dropped out of the SQL Server development picture, and Microsoft and Sybase signed a codevelopment agreement to port SQL Server to Windows NT. The codevelopment effort cumulated in the release of SQL Server 4 for Windows NT. After the version 4 release, Microsoft and Sybase split on the development of SQL Server; Microsoft moved forward with future releases targeted for the Windows NT platform, and Sybase moved forward with releases targeted for the UNIX platform. SQL Server 6 was the first release of SQL Server that was developed entirely by Microsoft. In 1996, Microsoft updated SQL Server with the 6.5 release. After a two-year development cycle, Microsoft released the vastly updated SQL Server 7 release in 1998. The following timeline summarizes the developmental history of SQL Server:

1987 - Sybase releases SQL Server for UNIX
1988 - Microsoft, Sybase, and Ashton-Tate port SQL Server to OS/2
1989 - Microsoft, Sybase, and Ashton-Tate release SQL Server 1 for OS/2
1990 - SQL Server 1.1 is released with support for Windows 3 clients
     - Ashton-Tate drops out of SQL Server development

1991 - Microsoft and IBM end joint development of OS/2
1992 - Microsoft SQL Server 4.2 for 16-bit OS/2 1.3 is released
    - Microsoft and Sybase port SQL Server to Windows NT
1993 - Windows NT 3.1 is released
    - Microsoft and Sybase release version 4.2 of SQL Server for Windows NT
1994 - Microsoft and Sybase codevelopment of SQL Server officially ends
    - Microsoft continues to develop the NT version of SQL Server
    - Sybase continues to develop the UNIX version of SQL Server
1995 - Microsoft releases version 6 of SQL Server
1996 - Microsoft releases version 6.5 of SQL Server
1998 - Microsoft releases version 7 of SQL Server

What's New with SQL Server 7

The enhancements to SQL Server 7 were primarily focused on ease of use, scalability, and data warehousing. To that end, SQL Server 7 has undergone both fundamental changes to the core database engine as well as cosmetic changes to its user interface and management utilities. From a database engine standpoint, the enhancement that required the most fundamental change was probably the introduction of dynamic row-level locking. All of the previous versions of SQL Server relied on page-level locking, which is implemented in a fundamentally different manner than row-level locking. This change, along with additional scalability enhancements, required alterations to the page size and underlying database engine management structures used internally by SQL Server. For new users this isn't an issue, but for existing SQL Server users this means that migration to SQL Server 7 requires reloading all of the existing SQL Server 6.5 databases into SQL Server 7. To make this migration path easier, Microsoft has provided a Version Upgrade Wizard that guides the administrator through several different possible migration scenarios. Appendix A of this book shows you how to use the Version Upgrade Wizard. Next, let's take a more detailed look at some of the major enhancements that are found in SQL Server 7.

Dynamic Self-Management

In the area of ease of use, probably the biggest enhancement was the introduction of dynamic self-management. SQL Server 7's dynamic self-management eliminates the need to preallocate a given amount of NT's memory and disk space for SQL Server. With SQL Server 6.5, you needed to manually configure both of these settings. The memory allocated to SQL Server was set during SQL Server's installation and was modified using the configuration parameters. SQL Server 6.5's disk allocation was set up using devices. A device contained multiple databases and was built at a given size. As your system grew, you had to manually alter the configuration settings for these resources to keep SQL Server operating optimally.

Using dynamic self-management, SQL Server 7 is able to automatically increase and decrease the amount of memory and disk space required. SQL Server 7 is tightly integrated with the operating system and, depending on the competing system requirements, can automatically increase the amount of memory it is using to handle an increase in database activity. Likewise, SQL Server 7 will dynamically shrink, giving unused memory back to the operating system when its activity level decreases. For dynamic disk storage, SQL Server 7 now uses operating system files instead of devices to contain databases. When a SQL Server 7 database is defined, you can specify a growth limit and a maximum size. When the database becomes full, it is automatically expanded by the size of the growth increment. SQL Server 7 databases can be expanded dynamically up to the limit of available disk space or until the maximum configured size has been reached.

While primarily targeted at ease of use, the benefits of dynamic self-management stretch into the areas of scalability and performance as well. Dynamic self-management allows SQL Server 7 to scale from small, desktop-sized systems where resources are scarce to large, enterprise-scale systems. Dynamic self-management also greatly facilitates unattended operations and helps to autotune SQL Server 7, allowing it to adjust to changing conditions automatically.

Multisite Management Using the Microsoft Management Console

With SQL Server 7, Microsoft has adopted the use of the Microsoft Management Console (MMC) for SQL Server administration. This simplifies management by making MMC the common management console for all of the Microsoft BackOffice products. The following illustration shows the new MMC using the SQL Server Enterprise Manager:

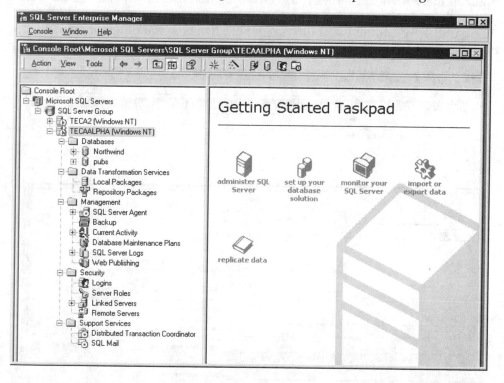

The SQL Server Enterprise Manager is a "snap-in" to MMC, and it facilitates centralized management for multiple SQL Server systems. MMC and the SQL Server Enterprise Manager can be run on either Windows 9x or Windows NT systems, and the

Enterprise Manager provides the ability to access all of the SQL Server 7 server and database configuration options.

Wizard-Based Management Tools

SQL Server 7 also introduces a set of new administrative wizards to help perform many of the common database management tasks. Some of the more commonly used wizards are used to register servers, create a database, create tables, create indexes, create stored procedures, create alerts, create Web pages, set up user security, schedule backups, create database maintenance plans, import data, export data, tune indexes, and set up database replication. These wizards replace the need to rely extensively on stored procedures to perform many of the common SQL Server database administration tasks. While they are primarily designed to help the new SQL Server administrator to be immediately productive, the new wizards also enable experienced administrators to quickly perform common tasks.

Graphical Query Analyzer

SQL Server 7's new Graphical Query Analyzer is a vastly updated version of the old ISQL/w utility that was a part of SQL Server 6.5. Like the old ISQL/w utility, the new Graphical Query Analyzer allows you to type in SQL statements and immediately see the results of those statements. However, Graphical Query Analyzer goes well beyond the ISQL/w utility by adding the ability to graphically show the different steps that SQL Server uses to process a query. Here is a brief preview of the Graphical Query Analyzer:

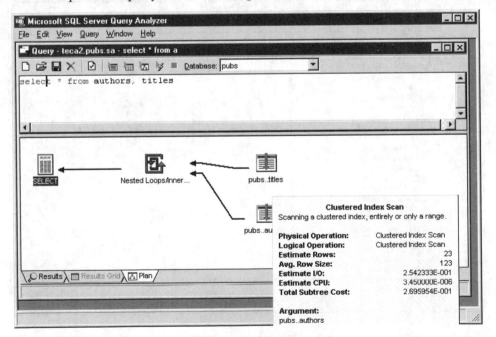

In this illustration you can see a sample of the output produced by the Graphical Query Analyzer. You read the results of the Graphical Query analyzer from right to left. On the far right-hand portion of the screen, the Graphical Query Analyzer presents the tables that are accessed. In the center of the screen, you can see the type of processing performed by SQL Server's query engine. On the far left, you can see the results that are produced. Moving the mouse pointer over each of the objects shown in the Plan window displays a pop-up window that contains additional information about the SQL Server object, how it was accessed, and the cost as determined by the query processor. The information presented by the Graphical Query Analyzer can help you to determine how to optimize your queries and whether your queries will benefit by creating indices.

Windows 9*x* Support

Another a major enhancement of SQL Server 7 is its support for Windows 95 and 98. All of the previous versions of SQL Server ran only on the Windows NT platform. Support for Windows 9*x* allows SQL Server applications to be scaled down to single desktop applications, as well as into the small branch-office scenario. For instance, many businesses consist of a main office with many small remote offices. These offices typically perform a variety of independent tasks such as order entry during the day and sending a summary of their activity to the main office at night. Being small operations, they usually opt for Windows 95 or 98 instead of Windows NT. Earlier versions of SQL Server required the use of the NT platform, which would have kept SQL Server out of this small-office type environment. SQL Server 7's support for Windows 9*x* allows it to be used as the database for the day's activity, and the new distributed merge replication can be used to batch that day's activity back to a central location.

SQL Server 7 on Windows 9*x* uses a working memory set of approximately 5MB, and while it uses the same code as SQL Server under Windows NT, it does have some limitations that are imposed by the operating system. For instance, Windows 9*x* doesn't provide asynchronous I/O and doesn't support SMP, integrated security, or non-Intel hardware platforms. Naturally, SQL Server running under Windows 9*x* will share these same limitations.

Mobile Offline Support Using Merge Replication

Closely related to its support for Windows 9*x* is SQL Server 7's improved support for offline and distributed databases. Windows 9*x* support enables high-powered laptops to be used as database platforms for mobile users just as it enables small, remote offices to use one or two Windows 9*x* desktops as a database platform. Many modern laptops support 233MHz and higher processors and are quite capable of functioning as database platforms for mobile users. Unlike most of the other competing database products, SQL Server 7 is the same product for Windows 9*x* systems and laptop systems as it is for high-end SMP or Alpha NT Server systems. This ensures that there are no unexpected incompatibilities in mobile and remote database applications. In conjunction with this low-end platform support, SQL Server 7's new merge replication feature enables mobile and offline users to work autonomously and then merge all of the offline data into a single database. Merge replication can take place using RAS connections or across the Internet. More detailed information on setting up SQL Server database replication is presented Chapter 5.

Improved Very Large Database Support

To better support high-end scalability, SQL Server 7 has several new features aimed at improving support for very large databases (VLDBs). One of the main improvements in this area is the new high-performance online backup. SQL Server 7 is able to run the database backup as a background job with minimal performance impact on the system. Typical results show that the online backup incurs only a five percent performance degradation. Another VLDB improvement is the introduction of incremental database backup and restore features. With SQL Server 7, you can use the new incremental backup feature to back up just database changes and not the entire database. Another VLDB enhancement is the improved performance for index creation. SQL Server 7 creates indexes roughly twice as fast as SQL Server 6.5. The Database Consistency Checker (DBCC) has also received significant speed improvements. With SQL Server 7, DBCC is 5 to 100 times faster than the version of DBCC that was shipped with SQL Server 6.5.

Improved symmetrical multiprocessing (SMP) support is another of the SQL Server enhancements that is clearly aimed at high-end scalability. While SQL Server 6.5 was able to take advantage of multiple processors, several independent benchmarks have shown that it wasn't able to really take advantage of more than four processors. Improvements to SQL Server 7 allow it to take advantage of more processors. In fact, Microsoft labs have tested SQL Server 7 on eight-way systems. In addition to these performance improvements, SQL Server 7 also increases the amount of memory that it can utilize. When run with NT 5 over the DEC Alpha processor, SQL Server 7 is able to directly address up to 32GB of memory using 64-bit addressing.

Dynamic Row-Level Locking

Dynamic row-level locking was probably the enhancement that required the most extensive changes to SQL Server's core database engine. All of the previous versions of SQL Server relied on page-level locking. While page-level locking tends to provide good performance because of its low overhead, it doesn't offer the most granular control. In an online transaction processing (OLTP)–type system, page-level locking can result in multiple users being locked out of a given row because another user has locked the page—even though that user may be on a completely different row. Row-level locking solves that problem, but its higher locking overhead tends to make it perform worse than it does with page-level locking. SQL Server 7 addresses this issue by implementing a locking scheme based on cost, where cost is a predetermined value of a combination of required CPU and I/O resources. For OLTP-type single-row transactions, SQL Server uses its internal cost calculation to take a row-level lock; but for batch-type transactions involving multiple rows, SQL Server 7 uses the cost to take a page-level lock. The following illustrating shows two different scenarios in which SQL Server uses different types of locks depending on the cost.

Dynamic Row-Level Locking

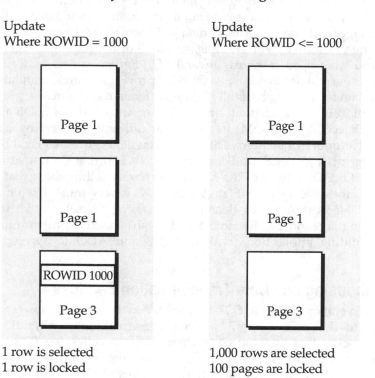

Update
Where ROWID = 1000

Update
Where ROWID <= 1000

1 row is selected
1 row is locked

1,000 rows are selected
100 pages are locked

On the left, you can see where the SQL Update statement is operating on a single row in the database. In this instance, SQL Server 7's dynamic record locking will place a lock on just that specific row. The surrounding rows and pages are not locked and can be accessed by other users. On the right, you can see where the SQL Update statement will potentially update a thousand rows. In this instance, rather than placing locks on the thousand records that would need to be locked, SQL Server's cost formula determines that it is better to use page locks, which allow much better performance. In this instance, if the row size were 800 bytes, there would be 10 rows per page. Updating a thousand records would require only 100 locks to be established and released.

Support for OLE DB and Heterogeneous Queries

Microsoft's inclusion of a native OLE DB provider for SQL Server 7 provides several new capabilities for the SQL Server database developer. OLE DB, along with the ADO (ActiveX Data Objects) object model, opens up the ability to perform heterogeneous queries that incorporate data from both relational databases like SQL Server and nonrelational source-like spreadsheets, ISAM (Indexed Sequential Access Method) databases, and even mail or document management data sources.

Unlike ODBC (Open Database Connectivity), which was strongly oriented toward relational databases, OLE DB can potentially access data from any source that can present data in a tabular (rows and columns) form. This allows the database developer to build queries that have the capability of joining data from a variety of different resources. This is important because most businesses do not maintain all of their data together with their database management system. Instead, data is dispersed throughout the enterprise in a variety of different sources. For example, to get all of the required data about a given customer, you may need to access several SQL Server tables, as well as an Excel spreadsheet or even Word documents. OLE DB provides a single standard data access interface that can be used to access all of those different data sources.

ADO is the object model that sits on top of OLE DB. OLE DB is a low-level Component Object Model (COM) interface that can only be used by languages that provide direct support for pointers. This means languages such as Visual Basic, Java, VB Script, Java Script, and Windows Scripting Host (WSH) that do not support pointers cannot use the OLE DB interface. The ADO object library is the vehicle that allows access to OLE DB for these development languages. ADO is very much like its predecessors, Data Access Objects (DAO) and Remote Data Objects (RDO), in that it provides an easy-to-use, language-independent interface that can be used to programmatically access databases. Building applications with OLE DB and ADO is covered in detail in Chapter 15.

Data Warehousing and Data Transformation Services

The other main enhancements to SQL Server 7 are in the area of data warehousing. The query engine used by SQL Server 7 has been redesigned to better handle the large and complicated queries that are required by Decision Support Systems (DSS). SQL Server's improved query support is closely tied to its support for the new Microsoft OLAP Services, which is bundled with SQL Server. Microsoft OLAP Services provides the multidimensional data navigation and query capabilities required by a DSS, with SQL Server providing the database engine and repository.

In addition, the new Data Transformation Service (DTS) has been added to facilitate the transfer of data between SQL Server and a variety of other database systems. DTS is built using an OLE DB architecture, which allows it to work with both relational and nonrelational data sources. DTS can be used from the graphical user interface supplied with SQL Server, or it can be used procedurally from any language that supports COM (Visual Basic, VBScript, JavaScript, PERL, or WSH).

While DTS is primarily oriented toward importing and exporting data to SQL Server, it supports 100 percent of both the source and target data sources. This means that it can also be used to transfer data between other external data sources without going to SQL Server. For example, DTS can be used to move data directly between an Access database and an Oracle database.

Microsoft English Query

The introduction of the Microsoft English Language Query product allows users to submit database queries without understanding SQL or other developer-oriented data access methods. With this product, the developer uses the built-in authoring tool to map the database schema to the English syntax. This enables the end user to submit a database query using a more natural, language-type statement. English Language Query then takes this statement and converts it into its SQL equivalent before submitting the query to SQL server and returning the results to the end user.

PART I

Managing SQL Server

CHAPTER 1

An Essential Overview of SQL Server

In this chapter, you'll get an overview of the essential elements of Microsoft's SQL Server. I'll begin by providing you with the big picture of SQL Server. In this first section, you'll see how SQL Server is used and how it fits into both small business and enterprise-level computing. Next, this chapter will cover SQL Server's networked architecture. SQL Server is built using a modular architecture that is made up of a collection of core components. This section will introduce you to these major objects that make up SQL Server and show you how they are related. After that, I'll provide an overview of SQL Server's database architecture followed by its major administrative components.

Microsoft SQL Server 7 is a relational database system that is scaleable from small departmental networks to enterprise-wide networks. SQL Server maintains the core database files for use by custom database applications using development languages such as Visual Basic and Visual C++, or by desktop applications such as Microsoft Word, Excel, and Access.

SQL Server is a native 32-bit Windows database that benefits from its tight integration with the Windows NT operating system. For small-scale databases, SQL Server runs on simple Windows 9x systems with as little as 32MB of RAM. For high-end databases, SQL Server can take advantage of NT's support for high-performance RISC-based systems such as the DEC Alpha, in addition to symmetric multiprocessing (SMP) systems.

SQL SERVER'S NETWORKED ARCHITECTURE

SQL Server's distributed architecture splits the database access application from the database engine. SQL Server's core database server runs on an NT Server system that is typically connected to multiple client systems via an Ethernet or Token Ring local area network (LAN). The client systems are typically PCs that are running SQL Server client software. SQL Server supports the following client systems:

Windows for Workgroups
Windows 9x
Windows NT
Remote Access Server (RAS)
Macintosh
DOS
OS/2
UNIX

Figure 1-1 illustrates the networked database access that SQL Server provides. You can see that the client side of SQL Server is separate from the server portion. The SQL Server database engine runs on either a Windows NT or a Windows 9x server, but data is not generally accessed from the server system. Instead, users typically access the SQL Server database from the networked client systems. In other words, the SQL Server client component runs on each of the networked clients, while the database server component only runs on the SQL Server system.

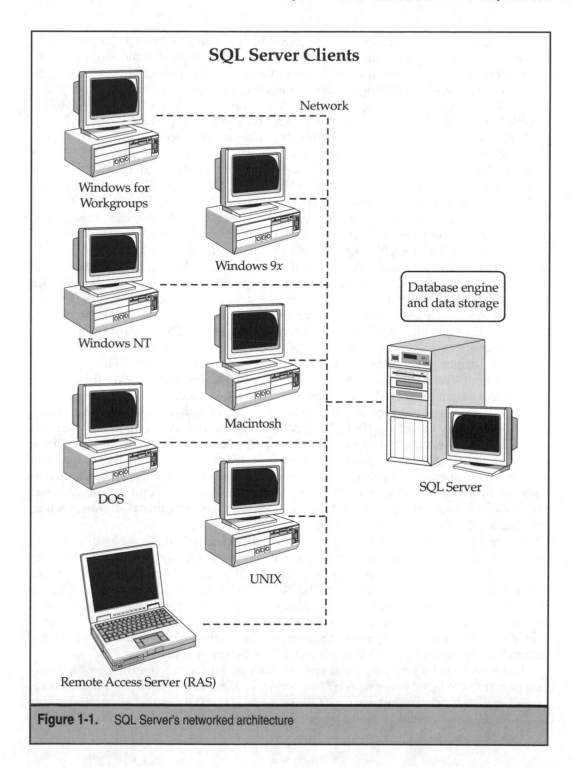

Figure 1-1. SQL Server's networked architecture

The network is essential for connecting the client systems to the SQL Server system. Instead of using a proprietary cabling scheme like a typical mainframe-terminal connection, SQL Server network connection makes use of popular network topologies such as Ethernet and Token Ring. SQL Server also provides protocol independence and is compatible with all of the popular network protocols, including TCP/IP, NetBEUI, IPX/SPX, Banyan VINES, DEC PATHWORKS, and Apple's AppleTalk.

SQL Server's client/server foundation gives it many advanced features that are not shared by traditional mainframe databases. Data access is not restricted to an existing set of host database application programs. Instead, one of the primary advantages of SQL Server is its tight integration with both leading edge client/server development tools and desktop applications such as Microsoft Word, Access, and Excel. SQL Server's database can be accessed using a variety of methods. For example, you can access a SQL Server database from custom client/server applications built using Visual Basic, Visual C++, PowerBuilder, Delphi, SQL Windows, Visual FoxPro, and many other PC development environments. For custom database development, SQL Server is compatible with several data access interfaces that can be used by the popular development tools. SQL Server databases can be accessed using the Microsoft JET Engine and Data Access Objects (DAO), Remote Data Objects (RDO), ActiveX Data Objects (ADO), OLE DB, ODBC, SQL Server's built-in DB-Library, and other third-party tools.

For seamless desktop database access, SQL Server comes with an OLE DB driver and an ODBC driver that enable SQL Server data access from any ODBC- or OLE DB–compliant desktop application. OLE DB and ODBC database access opens up the SQL Server database for ad hoc queries, data analysis, and custom reporting from shrink-wrapped desktop applications. While OLE DB is still a new data access method, there are currently more than 180 ODBC-enabled desktop applications such as Microsoft Word, Excel, and Access that are capable of using SQL Server's ODBC driver for database access. Desktop integration reduces the need for custom programming that is typically required by host environments for every new report or query. Instead, users can access database information using the desktop tool that they are already familiar with. Support for ODBC also enables SQL Server databases to be accessed by other platforms, such as the Macintosh or various UNIX systems.

Figure 1-2 provides a more detailed look at SQL Server's client/server architecture. In the top portion of the figure, you can see how the various client applications use the data access application programming interfaces (APIs) that SQL Server provides. SQL Server's four primary data access APIs are OLE DB, ODBC, the DB-Library, and Transact- SQL. For Windows clients, all of these APIs are implemented as dynamic link libraries (DLLs) and they communicate to SQL Server via the client network library. The client network library uses a networked IPC (interprocess communication) method to communicate across the network to the Server network libraries on the SQL Server system.

The server's network libraries receive the data packets sent from the client systems and pass them to SQL Server's Open Data Services (ODS), a server-side API that consists of a set of C++ functions and macros. SQL Server itself is an ODS application that accepts the ODS calls, processes them, and passes the results back to ODS. While it is possible to

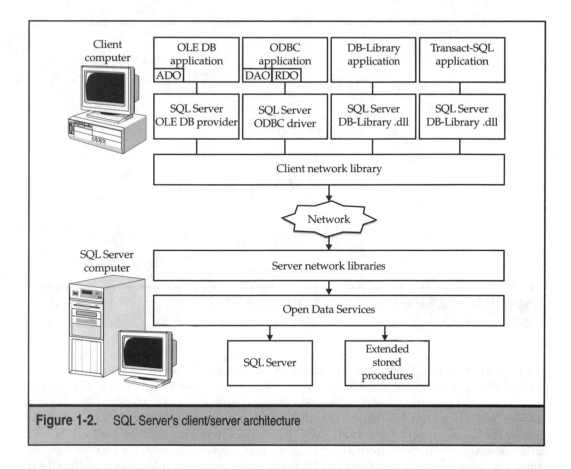

Figure 1-2. SQL Server's client/server architecture

develop applications using the ODS API, it is typically only used to provide custom gateways to other database systems. The heterogeneous database support provided by the much-easier-to-use ODBC and OLE DB APIs has largely eliminated the need to develop applications using ODS.

SQL SERVER'S BASIC COMPONENTS

Figure 1-3 presents a high-level view of SQL Server's four basic server components. As you saw earlier, SQL Server's Open Data Services component provides an interface between the server's network libraries and the SQL Server engine (MSSQLServer). The MSSQLServer service manages all of the files that comprise the SQL Server database. It is also responsible for processing SQL statements and allocating system resources. The SQLServerAgent service is responsible for scheduling SQL Server's jobs and alerts. In SQL Server terminology, a *job* is a predefined object consisting of one or more steps,

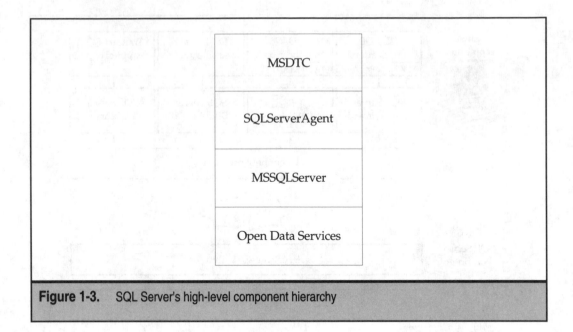

Figure 1-3.   SQL Server's high-level component hierarchy

where each step is a Transact-SQL statement and an alert is an action that is taken in response to a specific event. An alert can be set up to perform a variety of tasks such as running jobs or sending e-mail. The Microsoft Distributed Transaction Coordinator (MSDTC) is a transaction manager that is responsible for coordinating database transactions across multiple servers. MSDTC can be invoked either by the SQL Server database engine or directly from a client application. On Windows NT, these components are implemented as NT services. On Windows 9x, they are implemented as standard executable programs.

TRANSACT-SQL

Structured Query Language (SQL) is a high-level language that was originally developed to provide access to the data contained in relational databases. Since its origin, SQL has been widely adopted and now almost all modern databases can be accessed using SQL. With its widespread adoption, the SQL language has been standardized by the American National Standards Institute (ANSI). SQL Server uses a dialect of SQL called Transact-SQL. Transact-SQL is compliant with most ANSI SQL standards, but it also provides several extensions and enhancements. For instance, Transact-SQL contains several flow-control keywords that facilitate its use for developing stored procedures.

Transact-SQL is commonly used for database management tasks such as creating and dropping tables and columns, as well as for writing triggers and stored procedures. You can also use Transact-SQL to change SQL Server's configuration, or you can even use it interactively with SQL Server's Graphical Query Analyzer utility to perform ad hoc queries. Transact-SQL provides three categories of SQL support: Data Definition

Language (DDL), Data Manipulation Language (DML), and Data Control Language (DCL). SQL DDL commands are used for database management tasks such as creating tables and views. SQL DML commands are used to query and update the data that's contained in the database. SQL DCL commands are used to control the database operations. Chapter 9 provides more detailed information on DDL, while Chapter 10 provides detailed information on DML.

SQL SERVER DATABASE ARCHITECTURE

Now that you've had a high-level look at SQL Server's basic components, let's take a closer look at the database architecture. Figure 1-4 presents SQL Server 7's database architecture.

Servers

The core of SQL Server's database architecture is the server, or database engine. The SQL Server database engine is a true 32-bit Windows NT program that is responsible for processing the incoming database requests and returning the appropriate results to the client systems. SQL Server takes full advantage of preemptive multitasking, virtual memory, and asynchronous I/O that are a part of the Windows NT operating system. Windows NT's hardware independence enables the SQL Server database engine to run on a variety of different hardware platforms, including Intel Pentium, Pentium Pro, Pentium II, Xeon processors, and high-performance RISC systems such as the DEC Alpha.

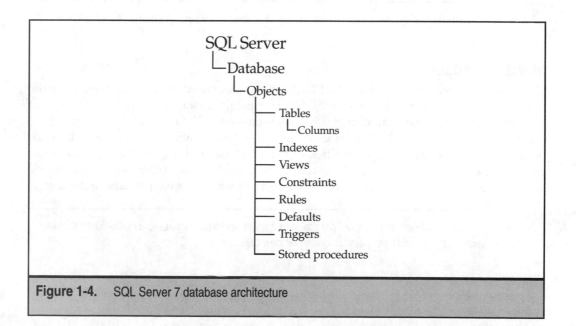

Figure 1-4.   SQL Server 7 database architecture

Beyond utilizing the basic Windows NT operating environment, the SQL Server database engine is built on a multithreaded kernel that allows it to provide high performance for multiple transactions. For scaleability, SQL Server uses a parallel symmetric architecture that allows it to automatically distribute the workload among multiple CPUs. Support for symmetric multiprocessing (SMP) allows separate tasks to run simultaneously on separate processors. SQL Server automatically detects the number of processors that are available on startup and can immediately begin using them with no additional configuration.

Databases

Each SQL Server contains multiple databases, where each database is maintained in one or more operating system (OS) files. Unlike the old devices that were part of SQL Server 6.5, multiple databases cannot use the same file. Keeping each database in a separate OS file is the key attribute that allows SQL Server databases to dynamically grow and shrink. By default the SQL Server installation process creates four system databases (master, model, msdb, and tempdb) and two user databases (pubs and Northwind). Each database has a corresponding log file that contains database transactions. Table 1-1 shows SQL Server's databases and the OS files that they use.

master Database

The master database keeps track of all data values that affect operation of SQL Server. It contains information about the login accounts, the existence of all of the other SQL Server databases, and all of the server's configuration settings.

TIP: Never manually alter the master database, and always be sure to keep a recent backup of it.

model Database

The model database is a template that SQL Server uses to create new databases. Since the tempdb database is created each time SQL Server is initialized, the model database must always be present. When a new user database is created, SQL Server makes a copy of the model database. The model database contains the system tables that are used by each database. The system tables keep track of the database options, including the default settings, user authorities, and database rules. Changing the model database affects all the new created databases. The model database is created in the master database device.

TIP: You can customize the model database to automatically propagate your custom set of defaults, referential integrity, and user permissions to all new databases.

Database	NT Operating System File	Description
master	Mssql7/Data/master.mdf	Database file
	Mssql7/Data/mastlog.ldf	Log file
model	Mssql7/Data/model.mdf	Database file
	Mssql7/Data/modellog.ldf	Log file
msdb	Mssql7/Data/msdbdata.mdf	Database file
	Mssql7/Data/msdblog.ldf	Log file
tempdb	Mssql7/Data/tempdb.mdf	Database file
	mssql7/Data/templog.ldf	Log file
pubs	Mssql7/Data/pubs.mdf	Database file
	Mssql7/Data/pubs_log.ldf	Log file
Northwind	Mssql7/Data/northwind.mdf	Database file
	Mssql7/Data/northwind.ldf	Log file

Table 1-1.   SQL Server Default Databases and OS Files

msdb Database

The msdb database contains information about scheduling jobs and alerts, as well as tracking the operators that receive alerts. It is used internally by the SQLServerAgent component responsible for SQL Server's scheduling processes.

tempdb Database

The tempdb database is used to store temporary tables built by SQL Server. It is re-created each time SQL server is started. The tempdb database is a global resource, and all users must have permission to use it. All of the temporary tables created in tempdb are automatically dropped when the user disconnects from SQL Server.

pubs Database

The pubs database is an example database that is supplied with SQL Server. It is intended to be used as a learning tool, and several of the examples in this book make use of it.

TIP: You can delete the pubs database if you don't need it as a training database. However, it's best to leave it intact since it is quite small and many sources (including this book) use it as an example database.

Northwind Database

Like the pubs database, the Northwind database is a sample database that's supplied with SQL Server. The Northwind database that comes with SQL Server 7 is essentially the same as the Northwind database that is shipped with Microsoft Access. It is a larger and more realistic database than the pubs database.

Database Objects

Each SQL Server database consists of other objects that are used for data storage and organization. SQL Server database objects consist of Tables, Columns, Indexes, Views, Constraints, Rules, Defaults, Triggers, Stored Procedures, and Extended Stored Procedures.

Tables

Each SQL Server database contains one or more tables. Table objects are SQL Server's primary data storage component. A *table* is essentially an organized set of columns. Each set of columns is typically referred to as a row. SQL Server has two basic types of tables: system tables and user tables. As you would expect, system tables contain information about SQL Server and its various objects, while user tables contain user data. SQL Server's system tables are named with the prefix sys. The different system tables that are maintained in each of SQL Server's databases are listed in Tables 1-2 through 1-4.

sysallocations	sysdevices	sysperfinfo
sysaltfile	syslanguages	sysprocesses
syscharsets	syslockinfo	sysremotelogins
sysconfigures	syslogins	sysservers
syscurconfigs	sysmessages	
sysdatabases	sysoledbusers	

Table 1-2.   System Tables in the master Database

syscolumns	sysforeignkeys	syspermissions
syscomments	sysfulltextcatalogs	sysprotects
sysconstraints	sysindexes	sysreferences
sysdepends	sysindexkeys	systypes
sysfilegroups	sysmembers	sysusers
sysfiles	sysobjects	

Table 1-3.   System Tables in User Databases

sysalerts	sysjobschedules	systargetservergroup-members
syscategories	sysjobservers	systargetservergroups
sysdownloadlist	sysjobsteps	systargetservers
sysjobhistory	sysnotifications	systaskids
sysjobs	sysoperators	

Table 1-4.   System Tables in the msdb Database

Generally, each table represents some type of object. For example, the sample pubs database contains a set of tables where each table contains data about the different aspects of a fictitious publishing organization. The sample user tables that make up the pubs database are listed in Table 1-5.

As you can see in the table, each SQL Server table contains a set of related information where each table represents a different object in the publishing business. For instance, the authors table contains the related information pertaining to a set of authors. Similarly, the sales table contains a set of columns that are related to book sales information.

Table	Description
authors	Author information
discount	Book discount levels
employee	Publishing employee information
jobs	Publishing job descriptions
pub_info	Publishing logos
roysched	Royalty schedules
sales	Sales information
stores	Store information
titleauthor	A listing of each author's book titles
title	A listing of all book titles

Table 1-5.   Sample User Tables That Make Up the pubs Database

Columns

Each table consists of a set of related columns. *Columns* are the data items that represent a property of the table. In traditional systems terminology, a column is also known as a *field*. For example, the authors table in the pubs database contains the following columns:

Column	Description
au_id	Author ID
au_lname	Author's last name
au_fname	Author's first name
phone	Author's phone number
address	Author's address
city	Author's city
state	Author's state
contract	Author's contract ID

Each column must have a given data type. The following is a summary of the data types used by SQL Server:

binary	**binary** data type, length 0 to 8,000 bytes
binary	**binary** data type
bit	**bit** data type
bit null	**bit** data type, null values allowed
char	**character** data type, length 0 to 8,000 bytes
datetime	8-byte **datetime** data type
datetime null	**smalldatetime** or **datetime** data type, null values allowed
decimal	**decimal** data type
decimal null	**decimal** data type, null values allowed
float	8-byte **float** data type
image	**image** data type
int	4-byte **int** data type
money	8-byte **money** data type
money null and smallmoney null	**money** or **smallmoney** data type, null values allowed
nchar	Unicode **character** data type
ntext	Unicode **text** data type
numeric	**numeric** data type
numeric null	**numeric** data type, null values allowed
nvarchar	Unicode variable-length **character** data type
real	4-byte **real** data type
real null and float null	**real** or **float** data type, null values allowed
smalldatetime	4-byte **smalldatetime** data type
smallint	2-byte **smallint** data type
smallmoney	4-byte **smallmoney** data type
text	**text** data type
tinyint	1-byte **tinyint** data type

tinyint null, smallint null, and int null	**tinyint**, **smallint**, or **int** data type, null values allowed
varbinary	Variable-length **binary** data type, length 0 to 8,000 bytes
varchar	Variable-length **character** data type, length 0 to 8,000 bytes

You can refer to Chapter 9 for more information about SQL Server data types.

Indexes

SQL Server indexes are used to optimize SQL Server's data access speed. Without indexes, every time a user selected a set of rows from a table, the entire table would need to be scanned in order to complete the request. Obviously, this would not result in good performance—especially for large tables. Indexes eliminate the need to perform time-consuming table scans by presenting the data in various alternative and more efficient organizations. Indexes are made using a given set of columns that uniquely identify a subset of data. An index is created as a separate database object from the original table. SQL Server uses two basic types of indexes, clustered and nonclustered:

▼ *Clustered indexes* force SQL Server to store the data in the base table using the same organization as the clustered index. Depending upon the data access method, physically storing the data in a sorted order can result in significant performance improvements. There can be only one clustered index per table.

▲ *Nonclustered indexes* do not alter the way the data is stored in the base table. A nonclustered index consists of one or more columns along with a pointer to the data contained in the base table. Nonclustered indexes are SQL Server's default index type. There can be up to 250 nonclustered indexes per table, although in practice you would never want to use this many indexes.

Figure 1-5 illustrates the difference between clustered and nonclustered indexes.

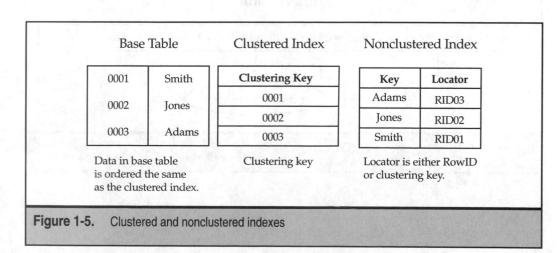

Figure 1-5.   Clustered and nonclustered indexes

Views

A SQL Server view is a virtual table. A view does not actually exist as a separate table but rather is stored as a Select statement that references one or more base tables. A view can be used for a number of different functions. Views can be queried just like base tables. They can also be updated, as long as the update operation only affects a single table. Some of the more common uses for views include selecting a subset of rows or columns from a table, joining columns from different tables, and summarizing the data from one or more columns. Figure 1-6 illustrates how a view can be used to filter the columns in the authors table in the pubs database.

Constraints

Constraints ensure data integrity for SQL Server tables and columns. Constraints are generally added when a table is created, and they can be specified at the table or column level. SQL Server supports five types of constraints:

▼ **Primary Key**   You use Primary Key constraints for entity integrity. A Primary Key constraint ensures that all rows in a table have a unique key that is not null. Using a Primary Key constraint also creates a unique index over the table.

■ **Foreign Key**   The Foreign Key constraint is used for referential integrity. Foreign Key constraints are sometimes referred to as *declarative referential integrity (DRI)*. A Foreign Key constraint associates one or more columns in a table with a Primary Key that has been defined in another table. Foreign Key constraints ensure that a specified relationship exists between two files. For instance, you might use a Foreign Key constraint to make sure that all rows in an order detail table have a matching row in an order header table.

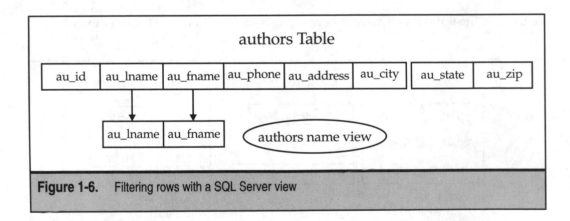

Figure 1-6.   Filtering rows with a SQL Server view

■ **Unique Key** The Unique Key constraint prevents any column from having a duplicate value. A Unique constraint can't be defined on a column that's part of a Primary Key. Like a Primary Key constraint, using a Unique Key constraint ensures entity integrity and also results in the creation of an index. However, unlike a Primary Key constraint, a Unique Key constraint allows null values.

■ **Check** A Check constraint enforces domain integrity by restricting the range of values that can be entered into a column. For example, you might use a Check constraint to ensure that a column accepts only data values between 1 and 100. A column can have one or more Check constraints.

▲ **Not Null** You use a Not Null constraint to ensure that a column will not contain any null values.

The following listing shows a sample of Transact-SQL that is used to create the employee table in the pubs database.

```
Create Table [dbo].[authors] (
    [au_id] [id] Not Null ,
    [au_lname] [varchar] (40) Not Null ,
    [au_fname] [varchar] (20) Not Null ,
    [phone] [char] (12) Not Null Constraint
        [DF__authors__phone__09DE7BCC] Default ('UNKNOWN'),
    [address] [varchar] (40) Null ,
    [city] [varchar] (20) Null ,
    [state] [char] (2) Null ,
    [zip] [char] (5) Null ,
    [contract] [bit] Not Null ,
    Constraint [UPKCL_auidind] Primary Key  Clustered
    (
        [au_id]
    ),
    Check (([au_id] Like '[0-9][0-9][0-9]-[0-9][0-9]-[0-9][0-9][0-9]
            [0-9]')),
    Check (([zip] Like '[0-9][0-9][0-9][0-9][0-9]'))
)
```

This example illustrates the use of several different constraints. First, a Primary Key constraint is used with the au_id column. This ensures that all rows will be identified by a unique au_id that is not null. Next you can see the Not Null constraint is also used on the au_lname, au_fname, and contract columns to prohibit any null values from being entered in these columns. You can also see that a Default constraint is used on the phone column to substitute the value of UNKNOWN where a row is inserted but there is no value explicitly supplied for the phone number. Finally, you can see that Check constraints are used on the au_id and zip columns. In both cases, the Check constraint is used to force the column to accept only numeric values.

Rules

Rules are very similar to Check constraints in that they restrict the values that can be entered into a column. However, unlike a Check constraint, which is a relatively simple value test, a rule can restrict data values based on a condition expression or list of values. Also unlike a Check constraint, you can have only one rule per column and SQL Server rules are stored as separate database objects. While a column can be associated with a single rule only, a rule can be bound to multiple columns. Rules can be applied also to user-defined data types.

TIP: While you can have only one rule per column, you can have multiple Check constraints on that same column. As a general rule of thumb, when you have a choice, it is better to use constraints instead of a rule.

Defaults

A default specifies the value that is used automatically for a given column when no data values are explicitly assigned to the column and a new row is inserted. The default value can be a constant, a built-in function, an expression, or a global variable. Defaults are typically applied when a table is created.

Triggers

A *trigger* is a stored procedure that is automatically executed when a SQL Server table is modified using the Update, Insert, or Delete operations. Like a stored procedure, a trigger contains a set of Transact-SQL statements. Triggers are generally used to enforce database referential integrity rules that are more sophisticated than the table-based DRI (declarative referential integrity) rules that can be enforced by SQL Server. For example, using DRI you can specify that all order details rows must be related to a corresponding row in the order header table. Triggers can go beyond this basic level of entity relationships by taking action based on specific data values. For instance, a trigger can be used to write out rows to a log file for data records that do not meet a given set of validity tests.

Stored Procedures

Stored procedures are a group of Transact-SQL statements that are compiled into a single execution plan at the time the stored procedure is created. Stored procedures are powerful and flexible tools that are used to perform various administrative and data-manipulation functions such as creating tables, granting authorities, or performing multistep database updates. While SQL itself is a nonprocedural language, SQL Server's Transact-SQL dialect contains several SQL extensions, including the use of flow-control keywords. This enables SQL Server stored procedures to contain complex logic and perform a wide variety of tasks.

When the stored procedure is compiled, SQL Server optimizes the data access plan that the stored procedure will use. This optimization gives stored procedures very good performance. Stored procedures can return parameters, result sets, and codes, or create cursors. A single stored procedure is shared for multiple users. Stored procedures can accept up to 1,024 parameters, and they can be executed on local or remote SQL Server systems.

Extended Stored Procedures

Extended Stored Procedures are DLLs that can be loaded and run just like standard stored procedures that are written using Transact-SQL. Extended stored procedures are written and debugged using programming languages such as Visual Basic or Visual C++. Each function exported in an extended stored procedure must be registered in SQL Server using the sp_addextendedproc stored procedure.

ADMINISTRATIVE COMPONENTS

Now that you've had an overview of the database concepts and architecture used by SQL Server, the next part of this introduction to the essential components of SQL Server presents the administrative tools and utilities. SQL Server 7 includes a set of graphical administrative tools that makes it easy to perform most of the SQL Server administrative functions.

SQL Server Enterprise Manager

The SQL Server Enterprise Manager is a graphical client/server administration and management tool that allows you to perform database management and backup and restore operations, as well as set up security and database replication. The SQL Server Enterprise Manager is a snap-in to the Microsoft Management Console that allows you to perform centralized management for one or more SQL Server systems. The SQL Server Enterprise Manager is a native 32-bit program that runs on the SQL Server system or on 32-bit client systems such as Windows 9x or Windows NT. Because of its graphical user interface, the SQL Server Enterprise Manager makes it easy to perform SQL Server Administrative functions by simply pointing and clicking.

Figure 1-7 shows you the SQL Server Enterprise Manager. As you can see, the SQL Server Enterprise Manager allows you to view and work with all of the different SQL Server components using a hierarchical tree view. At the top level are the different SQL Server Groups, which contain one or more SQL Server systems. The next level of the hierarchy displays the individual SQL Server components, including Databases, Data Transformation Services, Management, Replication, Security, and Support Services. Each node of the tree showing a plus sign can be expanded to show the objects it contains. For instance, the level under Databases lists all of the SQL Server databases. Each database node in turn expands to show a list of Database Users, Database Roles, Tables, SQL Server Views, Rules, Defaults, User Defined Datatypes, and Database Diagrams.

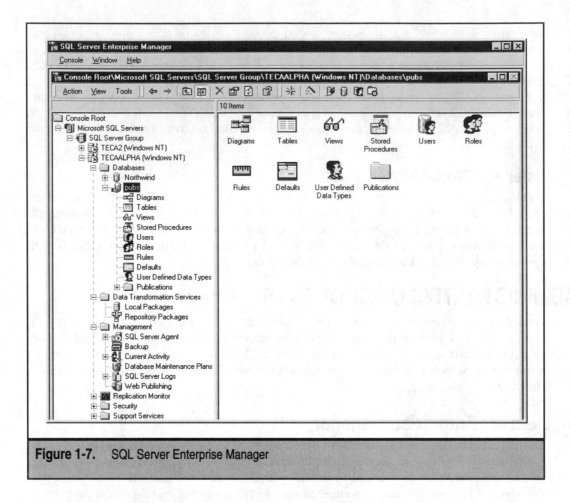

Figure 1-7.   SQL Server Enterprise Manager

In addition to viewing the different database objects, the SQL Server Enterprise Manager allows you to control these objects. The object tree displayed by the SQL Server Enterprise Manager is context sensitive and right-clicking each object in the tree view displays a different pop-up menu that allows you to work with that type of object. For instance, right-clicking the SQL Server object at the top of the list displays a pop-up menu that allows you to start and stop the SQL Server service. Likewise, right-clicking the Database object allows you to create a new database. Right-clicking the SQL Agent allows you to schedule tasks, as well as start and stop SQL Server's built-in job scheduler. In addition to working with the specific objects, right-clicking the different nodes in the tree also allows you to add new objects of the appropriate type. Chapter 2 goes into more detail on using the SQL Server Enterprise Manager to perform the common administrative tasks.

The SQL Server Enterprise Manager also allows you to set up security. Right-clicking the Logins object in SQL Server Enterprise Manager displays a pop-up menu that allows you to bring up the New Login Properties dialog box, shown in Figure 1-8.

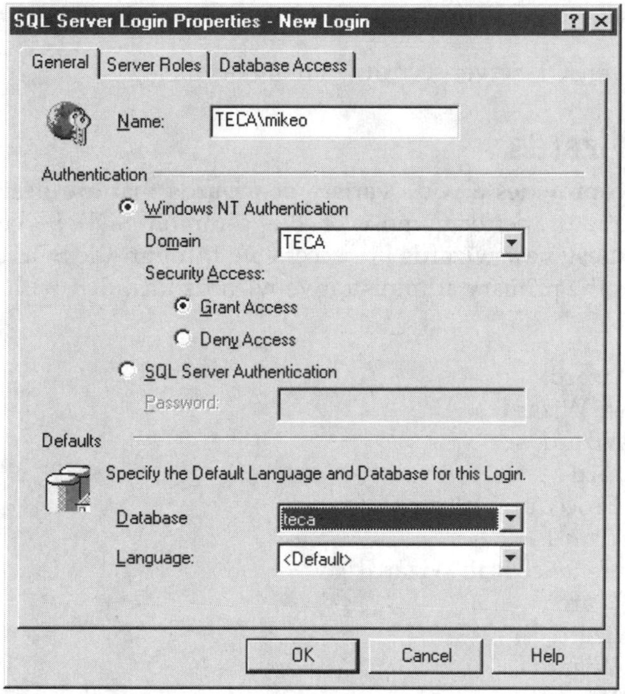

Figure 1-8.   SQL Server Login Properties - New Login dialog box

SQL Server logins can be set up to have one of two different types of SQL Server security: Windows NT authentication mode or mixed mode:

▼ **Windows NT authentication**   Windows NT authentication mode allows you to have a single login for both Windows NT and SQL Server. Users are initially authenticated when they log into Windows NT. When the user is connected over a trusted connection, SQL Server trusts the login and does not independently validate the user account or password. Using Windows NT Authentication mode allows SQL Server's security to be tightly integrated with Windows NT security. Any changes made to the rights of a connected user's NT accessibility rights will automatically become effective the next time the user establishes a connection with SQL Server.

▲ **Mixed**   As the name suggests, mixed mode security allows users to connect using either Window NT authentication or SQL Server's authentication. With mixed mode security, if the user is connected over a trusted connection, then Windows NT authentication can be used. If the user is connected over a connection that is not trusted, then SQL Server's authentication is used and the user account is validated using SQL Server's security. Mixed security is needed for Internet and non-Windows NT connections.

Chapter 3 covers SQL Server security in more detail.

Administrative Wizards

SQL Server 7 also provides a wide variety of wizards that are designed to help the database administrator perform most of the common SQL Server administrative functions. All of these new wizards are accessible through the SQL Server Enterprise Manager. Some of the primary administrative wizards included with SQL Server 7 are listed here:

Create Alert Wizard
Create Database Wizard
Create Index Wizard
Create Job Wizard
Create Stored Procedures Wizard
Create View Wizard
Database Maintenance Plan Wizard
DTS Export Wizard
DTS Import Wizard
Index Tuning Wizard
ODBC Driver Wizard
Register Server Wizard
Security Wizard
Version Upgrade Wizard
Web Assistant Wizard

Distributed Transaction Coordinator

The Distributed Transaction Coordinator manages distributed updates that occur across multiple SQL Server systems. Using the Distributed Transaction Coordinator, you can ensure that transactions across multiple systems are recoverable. This ability is known as a two-phase commit. The Distributed Transaction Coordinator is managed using the SQL Server Enterprise Manager and can be programmatically accessed using Transact-SQL, ODBC, DB-Library, and the XA-compliant transaction monitors such as Encina.

Query Analyzer

The Query Analyzer is a multipurpose tool that allows you to create Transact-SQL stored procedures, and interactively enter and execute SQL statements, as well as analyze queries and view the statistics of a query plan using Showplan. Figure 1-9 shows the initial screen of the Query Analyzer.

For entering Transact-SQL stored procedures, the Query Analyzer provides color-coded editing and context-sensitive help. The results of interactive SQL queries are

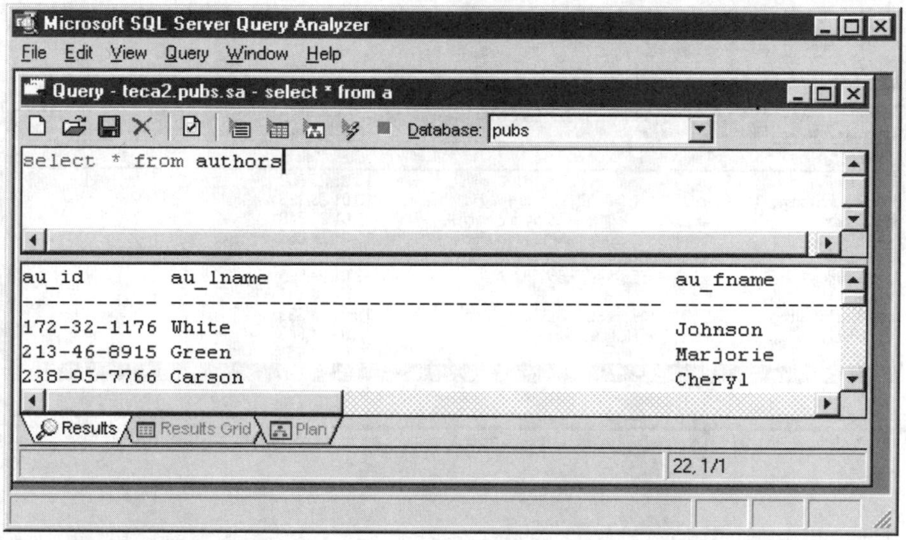

Figure 1-9.   Query Analyzer

displayed in the integrated grid that is accessed by the Results tab. More information about using the Query Analyzer's Showplan option to tune queries is presented in Chapter 6.

SQL Server Profiler

The SQL Server Profiler is a query analysis and trace tool that captures a period of server activity. It records all of the SQL Server events, including the Transact-SQL statements executed, the database objects that are accessed, the object locks that are maintained, and any errors that occur. The SQL Server Profiler allows you filter the type of events that you want to trace and then allows you to replay the recorded activity. You can replay the trace using the same SQL Server system or you can even replay the trace on a different system. The SQL Server Profile is run from the SQL Server Enterprise Manager. Figure 1-10 presents the main windows of the SQL Server Profiler. More information about using the SQL Server Profiler to tune queries is presented in Chapter 6.

SQL Performance Monitor

The SQL Performance Monitor provides a snapshot of the server's current activity level. Figure 1-11 shows the selected set of SQL Server performance counters that are tracked by the SQL Performance Monitor.

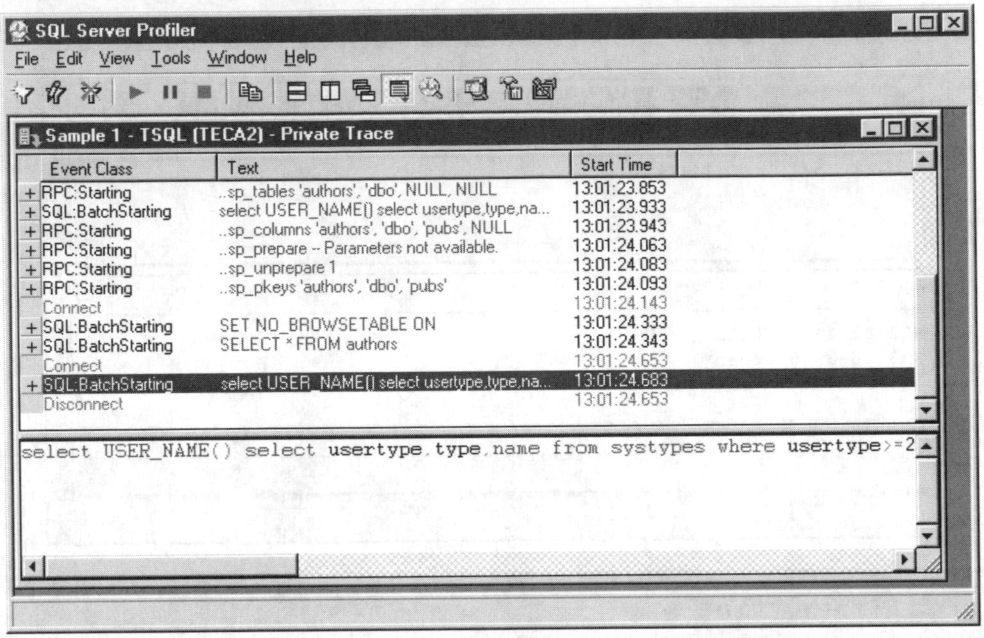

Figure 1-10. SQL Server Profiler

By default the SQL Performance Monitor takes a three-second server snapshot. This snapshot records the percentage of time a request was found in the cache (as opposed to needing to go to disk), the number of Transact-SQL commands executed per second, the number of physical pages read per second, the number of pages written per second, and the current number of connected users. More information about using the SQL Performance Monitor is presented in Chapter 6.

Data Transformation Services

Data Transformation Services (DTS) allows you to copy data and database schema between databases. SQL Server 7 provides a DTS wizard that allows you to create DTS packages for importing and exporting data from SQL Server. DTS packages can be used with OLE scripting languages such as VB Script, or they can be scheduled to run at a predetermined time using the SQL Server Agent. DTS uses OLE DB to access heterogeneous databases; and, while DTS is obviously geared toward integrating SQL Server with other external databases, it can also be used as a generic data transfer tool

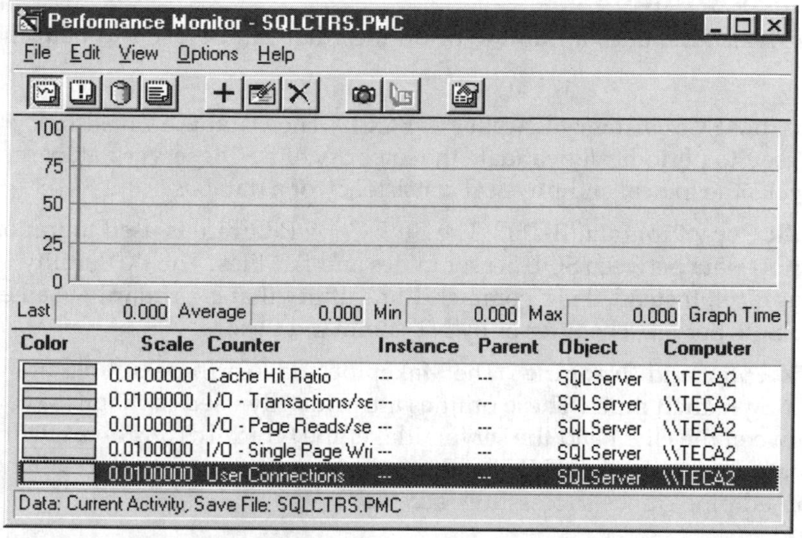

Figure 1-11. Performance Monitor

without requiring a connection to SQL Server. More information about DTS is presented in Chapter 5.

Distributed Management Objects

SQL-DMO (SQL Distributed Management Objects) is another feature that sets SQL Server apart from other database engines. SQL-DMO is a collection of 32-bit COM (Component Object Model) objects that allow you to easily write applications to programmatically administer and manage SQL Server from the distributed client systems. The SQL-DMO interface provides access to virtually the entire range of functionality provided by the SQL Server Enterprise Manager. You can use SQL-DMO from any development language that is able to make use of Object Linking and Embedding (OLE) COM objects, including Visual Basic and Visual C++. Since SQL-DMO is implemented using OLE, there's no need to master a complex set of APIs or to declare and call functions from a set of DLLs. Instead, you can simply make an instance of the SQL-DMO object and call its methods. You can use SQL-DMO to provide a custom interface to some of the SQL Server Enterprise Manager functions; to extend the capabilities provided by the SQL Server Enterprise Manager; or to perform a wide variety of other programming tasks, such as reverse engineering your database schema. Chapter 7 covers SQL-DMO in detail and shows you how it can be used from Visual Basic.

Command-Line Utilities

SQL Server 7 also includes a number of utilities that can be used to help manage the server:

▼ **Database Consistency Checker (DBCC)** The Database Consistency Checker is used to periodically validate the integrity of a SQL server database. DBCC checks the logical and physical consistency of a database.

■ **Bulk Copy Program (BCP)** The Bulk Copy Program is used to import and export data between SQL Server tables and flat files. The BCP utility is not graphical. Instead, it is a command-line utility that is primarily used either by the SQL Server scheduler or by NT command files.

▲ **Makepipe and Readpipe** The Makepipe and Readpipe utilities are used for testing named pipes. These utilities are primarily used to diagnose connections between the client and the server. Makepipe typically runs on a client system to create a named pipe, while Readpipe runs on the server to test if that client's named pipe can be successfully accessed.

CONCLUSION

As you have seen in this chapter, SQL Server 7 is a client/server-based database system. The database engine and data storage are both maintained on the SQL Server system. Network clients access the database using the appropriate network protocol and the client network libraries. A SQL Server system itself is comprised of a collection of related database objects, including tables, views, indexes, and stored procedures. You've also seen that the SQL Server system is managed using either the SQL Server Enterprise Manager or through Transact-SQL. Chapter 2 will provide a more detailed look at managing SQL Server 7 using the SQL Sever Enterprise Manager.

CHAPTER 2

SQL Server
Administration

We start our look at SQL Server administration by exploring several key elements of a SQL Server installation, to see what there is to administer and what database tools are available. Then we'll dive into the most important administration tasks that you can perform with the SQL Server Enterprise Manager. We cover setting server properties, managing database objects, working with SQL Server Agent, and other tasks that are important for a developer to understand.

OVERVIEW OF A SQL SERVER INSTALLATION

After SQL Server has been installed, your Windows NT system has a variety of files installed, including programs, system and sample databases, online documentation, and other files. In this section, we provide you an overview of the installation so you know what tools and other elements are available in SQL Server.

Directories and Databases

A standard SQL Server installation creates the directories shown in Table 2-1. You should use caution before deleting any directory used by SQL Server; Table 2-1 indicates which directories are essential for SQL Server operation. When you create database tables, SQL Server creates additional Windows NT files for the table data and transaction logs. When you create a new table, you can specify whether the table's files are created in the \Data default subdirectory or a different location.

SQL Server also has a set of databases, listed in Table 2-2, that are installed along with the program and other files. The Windows NT files for these databases are stored in the \Data subdirectory.

Directory	Required for SQL Server Operation	Contents
\Mssql7\Backup		Backup files
\Mssql7\Binn	Yes	Executable files, online Help files, and dynamic link libraries (DLLs) for extended stored procedures
\Mssql7\Books		Books Online files
\Mssql7\Data	Yes	System and sample database files

Table 2-1. SQL Server Installed Directories

Directory	Required for SQL Server Operation	Contents
\Mssql7\DevTools\Include		Object Linking and Embedding database (OLE DB) include (*.h) files
\Mssql7\DevTools\Lib		OLE DB library (*.lib) files
\Mssql7\DevTools\Samples		Sample Open Database Connectivity (ODBC), DB-Library, Open Data Services, SQL Distributed Management Objects (SQL-DMO), Embedded SQL for C, and Microsoft Distributed Transaction Coordinator (MSDTC) files
\Mssql7\FtData	Yes	Full-text catalog files
\Mssql7\Html	Yes	Microsoft Management Console (MMC) and SQL Server HTML files
\Mssql7\Install		Setup scripts and the .out files produced by setup
\Mssql7\Jobs		Temporary job output files
\Mssql7\Log		Error log files
\Mssql7\ReplData		Working directory for replication tasks
\Mssql7\Upgrade		Files used during an upgrade from SQL Server version 6.x to SQL Server 7

Table 2-1.   SQL Server Installed Directories (*continued*)

NOTE: The master, model, msdb, and tempdb system databases do not appear in the Enterprise Manager list of databases unless you select the Show system databases and system objects option on the Registered SQL Server Properties dialog box. Registered server properties are discussed in the "Registering and Unregistering a Server" section, later in this chapter.

Database	Contents
master	All system-level information
model	Tables, views, stored procedures, and other objects that are copied to a new database whenever you create a database
msdb	SQL Server Agent alert, job, operator, and scheduling information
Northwind	Sample database with information about a hypothetical import-export company
pubs	Sample database with information about a hypothetical book publishing company
tempdb	Temporary tables and stored procedures

Table 2-2.   Installed Databases

Tools

SQL Server provides a variety of tools for administering servers and clients and for developing databases and applications. Table 2-3 lists the most important tools and describes how to run each tool. The Enterprise Manager is perhaps the most commonly used tool for many administration and development purposes. The Enterprise Manager provides a graphical interface with dialog boxes for tasks such as setting server configuration options, managing logins and database users, and creating databases and database objects. The Query Analyzer is another frequently used tool because it lets you execute SQL statements through a graphical interface.

Tool	How to Run	Purpose and Notes
Bulk Copy	Execute bcp.exe from a command prompt.	Import and export data to and from SQL Server database tables.
Books Online	Choose Start | Programs | Microsoft SQL Server 7.0 | Books Online.	Browse online, HTML-based documentation.

Table 2-3.   Major SQL Server Tools

Tool	How to Run	Purpose and Notes
Client Configuration	Choose Start	Programs	Microsoft SQL Server 7.0	Client Network Utility; or execute the SQL Server Client Configuration application in the Windows Control Panel.	Create and manage client connections to SQL Server servers and manage client network libraries.
Data Transformation Services (DTS)	Choose Tools	Data Transformation Services from the Enterprise Manager menu; or execute dtswiz.exe or dtarun.exe from a command prompt.	Import and export data to and from SQL Server database tables.
Database Diagrammer	Right-click the Diagrams folder under a database in the Enterprise Manager tree and select New Database Diagram from the pop-up menu; or double-click an existing diagram icon displayed in the Diagrams folder.	Create and edit entity-relationship (ER) diagrams for the tables in a database. (See Chapter 8 for a discussion of ER diagrams.)
Enterprise Manager	Choose Start	Programs	Microsoft SQL Server 7.0	Enterprise Manager.	Perform server and database administration and development tasks using a graphical interface.
Full-Text Indexing	Right-click the Full-Text Search item under a server's Support Services folder in the Enterprise Manager tree and select Start or Stop from the pop-up menu; or execute sqlftwiz.exe from a command prompt; or use the Full-Text Catalogs folder under a specific database.	Start and stop the full-text search engine and create and manage full-text search catalogs.

Table 2-3.   Major SQL Server Tools (*continued*)

Tool	How to Run	Purpose and Notes
Microsoft English Query	Choose Start	Programs	Microsoft English Query	Microsoft English Query.	Retrieve information from a database using an English language–like query.
Microsoft Management Console	Runs automatically when you run the Enterprise Manager.	Standard graphical interface for Microsoft BackOffice applications such as SQL Server Enterprise Manager.
MSDTC	Choose Start	Programs	Microsoft SQL Server 7.0	MSDTC Administrative Console; or right-click the Distributed Transaction Coordinator item under the Support Services folder for a server in the Enterprise Manager tree and select Start or Stop from the pop-up menu.	Provide transaction integrity for transactions that involve multiple Windows NT and Windows 9x systems.
Network Library Configuration	Choose Start	Programs	Microsoft SQL Server 7.0	Server Network Utility.	View, add, remove, or edit a server network library.
OSQL	Execute osql.exe from a command prompt.	Enter and execute SQL statements using a command-line interface. (Note: OSQL replaces the ISQL utility, which is also available for backward compatibility.)
Performance Monitor	Choose Start	Programs	Microsoft SQL Server 7.0	Performance Monitor.	Use Windows NT Performance Monitor to monitor server and database resource use (for example, page requests or memory).

Table 2-3. Major SQL Server Tools (*continued*)

Tool	How to Run	Purpose and Notes
Profiler	Choose Start | Programs | Microsoft SQL Server 7.0 | Profiler; or choose Tools | SQL Server Profiler from the Enterprise Manager menu.	Capture a continuous record of server and database activity (for example, deadlocks, fatal errors, and connections).
Query Analyzer	Choose Start | Programs | Microsoft SQL Server 7.0 | Query Analyzer; or choose Tools | SQL Server Query Analyzer from the Enterprise Manager menu.	Enter SQL statements and execute stored procedures. For Select statements, Query Analyzer also displays the results. For any statement, Query Analyzer can also display the execution plan created by the optimizer, as well as an analysis of indexes that may be used in the query.
Registry Backup/ Restore	Execute regrebld.exe from a command prompt.	Back up and restore SQL Server entries in the Windows NT registry.
Replication Conflict Viewer	Right-click a database folder in the Enterprise Manager tree and select View Conflicts from the pop-up menu; or right-click a publication item under the Publishers folder in the Replication Monitor container for a server in the Enterprise Manager tree and select View Conflicts from the pop-up menu.	View and resolve replication conflicts.

Table 2-3.   Major SQL Server Tools (*continued*)

Tool	How to Run	Purpose and Notes
Replication Distribution Agent	Right-click a publication item under the Distribution Agents folder in the Replication Monitor container for a server in the Enterprise Manager tree and select Start or Stop from the pop-up menu; or execute distrib.exe from a command prompt.	Start and stop an agent for moving replicated data from the distribution databases to subscribers
Replication Log Reader Agent	Right-click a publication item under the Log Reader Agents folder in the Replication Monitor container for a server in the Enterprise Manager tree and select Start or Stop from the pop-up menu; or execute logread.exe from a command prompt.	Start and stop an agent for moving replicated transactions to the distribution database
Replication Merge Agent	Right-click a publication item under the Merge Agents folder in the Replication Monitor container for a server in the Enterprise Manager tree and select Start or Stop from the pop-up menu; or execute replmerg.exe from a command prompt.	Start and stop an agent for merging snapshot-replicated data into the subscriber databases

Table 2-3.   Major SQL Server Tools (*continued*)

Tool	How to Run	Purpose and Notes
Replication Snapshot Agent	Right-click a publication item under the Snapshot Agents folder in the Replication Monitor container for a server in the Enterprise Manager tree and select Start or Stop from the pop-up menu; or execute snapshot.exe from a command prompt.	Start and stop an agent for preparing snapshot files of replicated databases
Service Manager	Choose Start	Programs	Microsoft SQL Server 7.0	Service Manager; or right-click the server icon on the Windows taskbar and select Open SQL Server Service Manager from the pop-up menu.	Start, stop, pause, or continue a SQL Server server or the SQL Server Agent, MSDTC service, or Microsoft Search service
Setup	Execute setup.exe from the installation CD-ROM.	Install SQL Server components or change installation options
SQL Mail	Right-click the SQL Mail item under the Support Services folder for a server in the Enterprise Manager tree and select Start or Stop from the pop-up menu.	Send and receive Microsoft Exchange mail messages

Table 2-3.   Major SQL Server Tools (*continued*)

Tool	How to Run	Purpose and Notes
SQL Maintenance Utility	Choose Tools | Database Maintenance Planner from the Enterprise Manager menu; or right-click the Database Maintenance Plans item under the Management folder for a server in the Enterprise Manager tree and select New Maintenance Plan from the pop-up menu; or execute sqlmaint.exe from a command prompt.	Perform maintenance operations (for example, run data integrity checks, backup processing, or index rebuilding) on databases
SQL Server Agent	Right-click the SQL Server Agent item under the Management folder for a server in the Enterprise Manager tree and select Start or Stop from the pop-up menu; or right-click the Alerts, Operators, or Jobs items under the SQL Server Agent item for a server; or use the SQL Server Service Manager.	Run scheduled jobs for database operations
Uninstall	Choose Start | Programs | Microsoft SQL Server 7.0 | Uninstall SQL Server 7.0; or in the Control Panel's Add/Remove Programs dialog box, choose to remove Microsoft SQL Server 7.0.	Uninstall SQL Server 7

Table 2-3.   Major SQL Server Tools (*continued*)

Tool	How to Run	Purpose and Notes
Version Upgrade Wizard	Choose Start	Programs	Microsoft SQL Server Switch	SQL Server Upgrade Wizard.	Upgrade from SQL Server version 6.x to SQL Server 7
Version Switch	Choose Start	Programs	Microsoft SQL Server Switch	SQL Server Version 6.x; or execute vswitch.exe from a command prompt.	Switch between SQL Server version 7 and SQL Server 6.x as the active version of SQL Server
Wizards	See Table 2-4.	

Table 2-3.   Major SQL Server Tools (*continued*)

SQL Server also has a number of wizards to step you through various tasks using a series of dialog boxes. Table 2-4 lists the wizards available from within the Enterprise Manager. All of the graphical tools include online help, and the Books Online facility provides comprehensive reference documentation.

Wizard	Purpose
Database Wizards	
Create Database	Steps you through creation of a database
Create Diagram	Steps you through creation of an entity-relationship diagram for a database's tables
Create Index	Steps you through creation of an index
Create Login	Steps you through creation of a login

Table 2-4.   SQL Server Wizards

Wizard	Purpose
Create Stored Procedures	Steps you through creation of one or more stored procedures to insert, update, or delete rows in selected tables
Create View	Steps you through creation of a view
Full-Text Indexing	Steps you through definition of full-text indexing
Data Transformation Services (DTS) Wizards	
DTS Export	Steps you through creation of a DTS package to export data from a SQL Server database
DTS Import	Steps you through creation of a DTS package to import data into a SQL Server database
Management Wizards	
Backup	Steps you through a full or partial database or transaction log backup
Create Alert	Steps you through creation of an alert
Create Job	Steps you through creation of a job
Create New Data Source	Steps you through installation and testing of an ODBC driver and data source
Create Trace	Steps you through creation of a trace
Database Maintenance Plan	Steps you through creation of a database maintenance plan for the SQLMaint utility
Failover	Steps you through failover support setup. Available only with SQL Server Enterprise Edition
Index Tuning	Steps you through index tuning for one or more tables based on a captured workload
Make Master Server	Steps you through setup of a master server
Make Target Server	Steps you through setup of a target server
Register Server	Steps you through server registration

Table 2-4. SQL Server Wizards (*continued*)

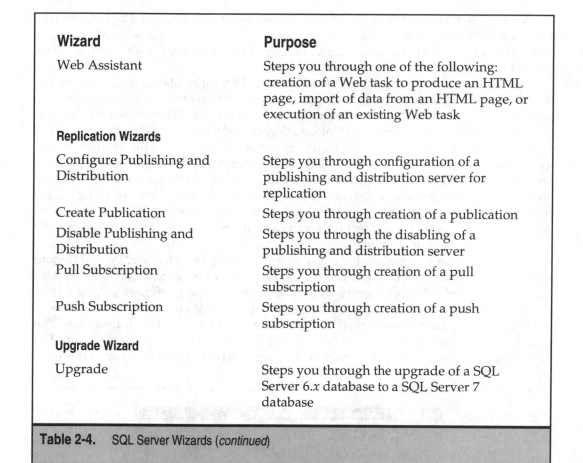

Wizard	Purpose
Web Assistant	Steps you through one of the following: creation of a Web task to produce an HTML page, import of data from an HTML page, or execution of an existing Web task
Replication Wizards	
Configure Publishing and Distribution	Steps you through configuration of a publishing and distribution server for replication
Create Publication	Steps you through creation of a publication
Disable Publishing and Distribution	Steps you through the disabling of a publishing and distribution server
Pull Subscription	Steps you through creation of a pull subscription
Push Subscription	Steps you through creation of a push subscription
Upgrade Wizard	
Upgrade	Steps you through the upgrade of a SQL Server 6.*x* database to a SQL Server 7 database

Table 2-4.   SQL Server Wizards (*continued*)

The rest of this chapter concentrates on the use of the Enterprise Manager to administer servers and create the database objects you need for your applications. Other chapters in this book cover specific utilities and SQL statements in more detail.

SETTING ENTERPRISE MANAGER PROPERTIES

There are several properties of the Enterprise Manager tool that you may want to set when you use this tool to administer one or more SQL Server servers. To set these properties, select Tools | Options from the Enterprise Manager main menu to display the SQL Server Enterprise Manager Properties dialog box shown in Figure 2-1. The General tab lets you specify how frequently (if at all) the Enterprise Manager application should check the current states of SQL Server, SQL Server Agent, SQL Mail, and MS Distributed Transaction Coordinator. For normal operations, leave this option selected. You can change the polling interval for each individual service by selecting it from the drop-down list and entering the desired Poll interval value.

The SQL Server registration information used by Enterprise Manager can be stored in the Windows NT registry of a local or central system. When stored on a local system, the SQL Server registration information can be shared or private. When stored on a central system, the SQL Server registration information can be shared among other connected systems. To store the Enterprise Manager's SQL Server registration information on the local system, select the Store locally option in the Server registration information panel. If you want to let other local or remote users share this registration information, deselect the Store user independent check box; otherwise, select this check box to have private, local registration information. To use existing registration information on a remote system, select the Read from remote option and enter the remote server name where the registration information is stored.

The SQL Server Enterprise Manager Properties dialog box's Connection tab (Figure 2-2) has three options. The Login time-out value is the number of seconds the system waits for a successful connection (for the Enterprise Manager) before returning with a failed login attempt error. The Query time-out value specifies the maximum number of seconds a query that you execute on a remote server can take before it times out. The default of 0 specifies that there's no limit to how long your remote queries can run. The Packet size value is the number of bytes in each network packet used for your connection.

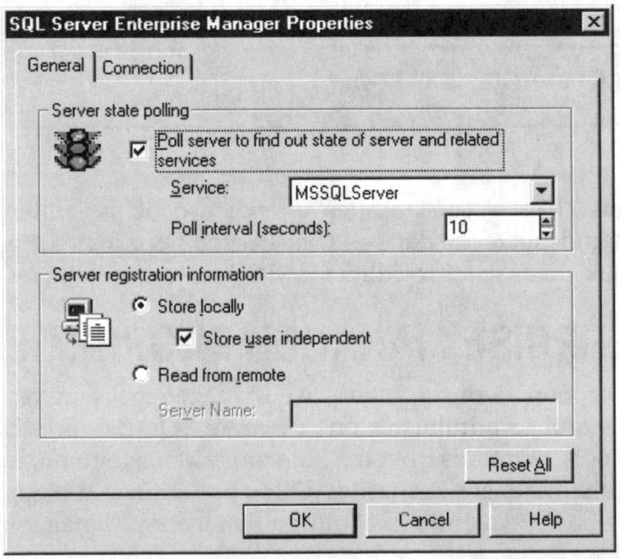

Figure 2-1.   SQL Server Enterprise Manager Properties dialog box – General tab

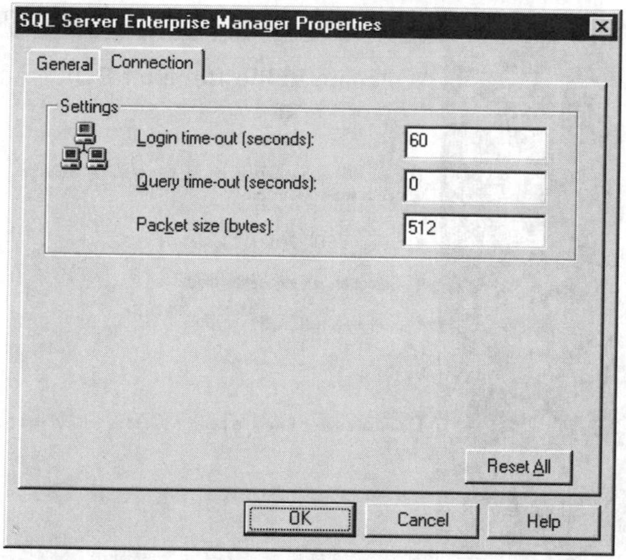

Figure 2-2. SQL Server Enterprise Manager Properties dialog box – Connection tab

NOTE: Don't be confused by the three categories for which you can set properties: the Enterprise Manager *application,* the *registration* for a specific server managed through the Enterprise Manager, and the properties of a *server* itself. The first category is discussed in this section; the other two categories are discussed in the following section, "Registering and Unregistering a Server," and "Setting Server Properties," later in this chapter.

REGISTERING AND UNREGISTERING A SERVER

To be able to manage a local or remote SQL Server installation with the Enterprise Manager, you must *register* the server with Enterprise Manager on the systems you plan to use for administering servers. When you run Enterprise Manager for the first time, the local server is automatically registered. You can register additional servers using the Register SQL Server Wizard or the SQL Server Properties dialog box. To register a new server with the wizard, right-click a server group item (for example, SQL Server Group) in the Enterprise Manager tree and select New SQL Server Registration from the pop-up menu. On the Welcome dialog box (Figure 2-3), you can specify whether to use this wizard or the Properties dialog box to register additional servers in the future.

Click Next to display a list of the available servers (Figure 2-4). Select each server you want to register and click Add to place the servers in the Added servers list.

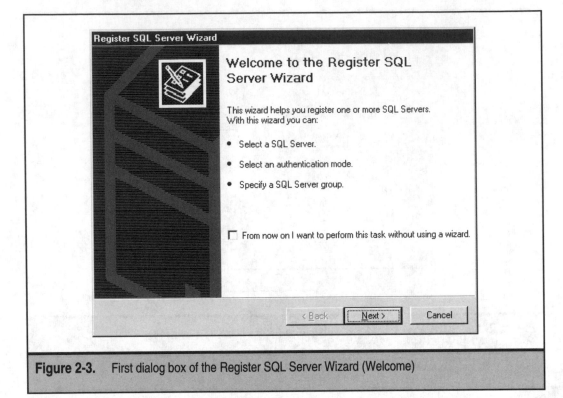

Figure 2-3. First dialog box of the Register SQL Server Wizard (Welcome)

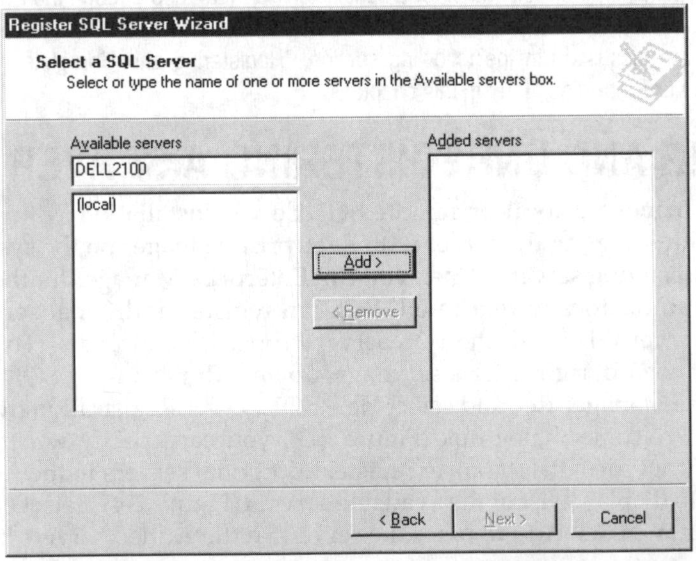

Figure 2-4. Second dialog box of the Register SQL Server Wizard (Select servers)

Click Next to specify how you want to connect to the added server (Figure 2-5). Generally, you should select the Windows NT account information option, which will use your Windows NT user name as the SQL Server login (user names and logins are explained more fully in Chapter 3).

NOTE: This item does *not* specify the overall authentication mode for the SQL Server server (which is set on the SQL Server Properties dialog box's Security tab, as explained in the "Setting Server Properties" section, later in this chapter).

Click Next to select an existing or new SQL Server group to add the server to (Figure 2-6).

Click Next to display the confirmation dialog box (Figure 2-7) and click Finish to complete the registration. After registering a server, you should see a Register SQL Server Messages dialog box with either a "Registered successfully" message or error messages. After a server is registered successfully, it appears as an entry in the Enterprise Manager navigation tree.

NOTE: For many tasks, the Enterprise Manager provides a variety of ways to execute a wizard or to display the appropriate dialog boxes. For example, you can also run the Register SQL Server Wizard by clicking the Register Server icon on the Enterprise Manager's toolbar or by right-clicking a Microsoft server group on the Enterprise Manager tree and selecting New SQL Server Registration from the Enterprise Manager Action menu. This chapter usually describes one or two simple ways to accomplish each task. We encourage you to explore the available Enterprise Manager menus and tools to discover the alternatives that you find most convenient.

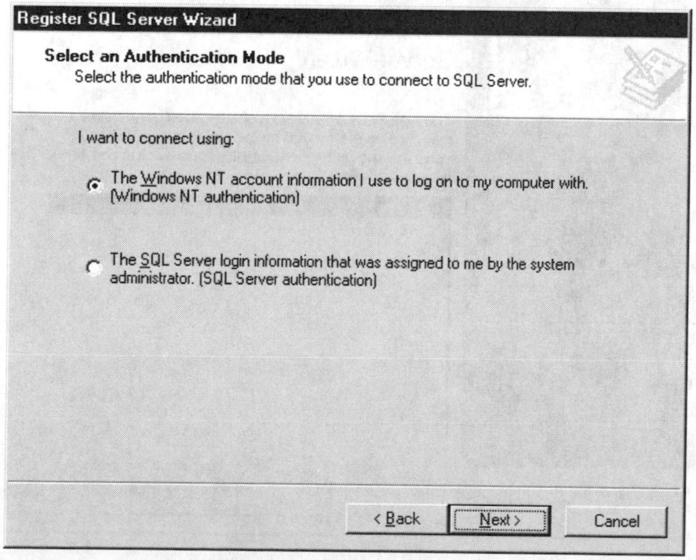

Register SQL Server Wizard

Select an Authentication Mode
Select the authentication mode that you use to connect to SQL Server.

I want to connect using:

○ The Windows NT account information I use to log on to my computer with. (Windows NT authentication)

○ The SQL Server login information that was assigned to me by the system administrator. (SQL Server authentication)

< Back   Next >   Cancel

Figure 2-5. Third dialog box of the Register SQL Server Wizard (Authentication mode)

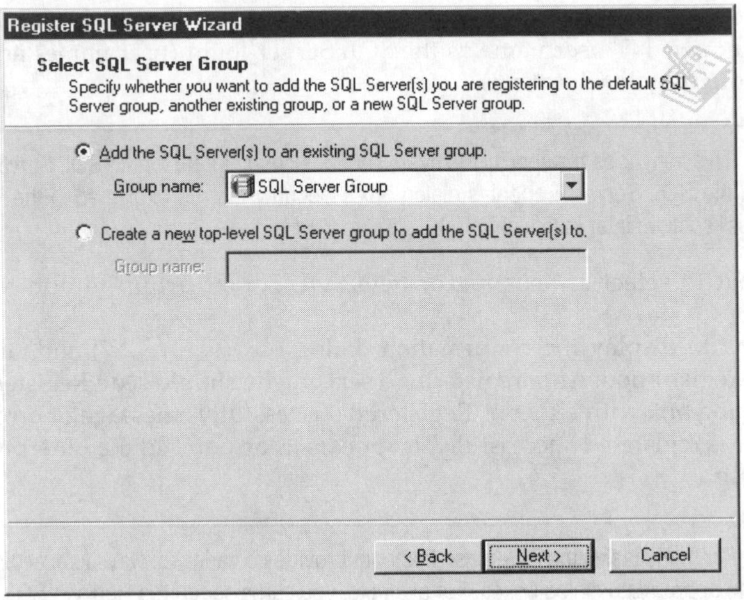

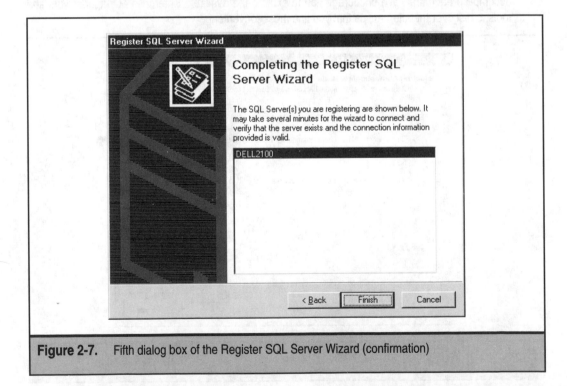

Figure 2-6. Fourth dialog box of the Register SQL Server Wizard (Server group)

Figure 2-7. Fifth dialog box of the Register SQL Server Wizard (confirmation)

For any registered server, you can click the ⊞ icon to expand a server entry, displaying categories of the server's objects and services, as shown in Figure 2-8.

After registering a server, you can change how you connect to the server and the server group it belongs to by right-clicking the server entry and selecting Edit SQL Server Registration properties from the pop-up menu to display the Registered SQL Server Properties dialog box, shown in Figure 2-9.

In this dialog box, you can also set several other SQL Server Enterprise Manager options. For most purposes, you should select both the Display SQL Server state in console and the Automatically start SQL Server when connecting options. These make it somewhat more convenient to use the Enterprise Manager.

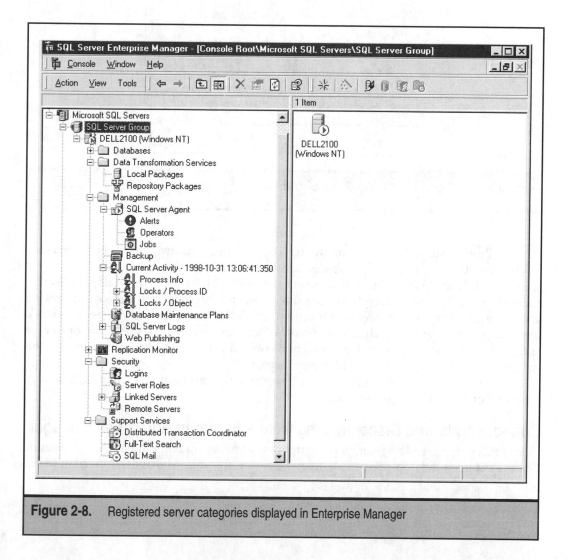

Figure 2-8.   Registered server categories displayed in Enterprise Manager

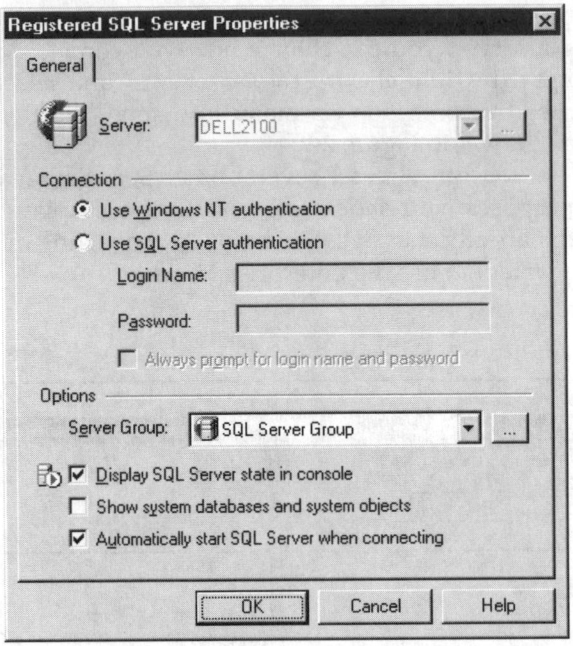

Figure 2-9. Registered SQL Server Properties dialog box

The Show system databases and system objects option controls whether the master, model, msdb, and tempdb databases are shown under the Enterprise Manager's Databases folder. Also, if this option is selected, each database's SQL catalog tables (for example, syscolumns; catalog tables are discussed in Chapter 9) are shown along with user-defined tables. You can leave this option unselected except when you need to work with one of the system databases or tables. When you select or deselect this option, it takes effect immediately; you don't need to reconnect Enterprise Manager to change the tables included in the Enterprise Manager display.

To unregister a server, right-click the server entry and select Delete SQL Server Registration from the pop-up menu.

Connecting to and Disconnecting from a Server in Enterprise Manager

Once you've registered a server, you can right-click the server entry and select Connect or Disconnect from the pop-up menu to manage your Enterprise Manager connection to the server.

STOPPING, STARTING, PAUSING, AND CONTINUING A SERVER

You can right-click a server entry and select Stop, Start, Pause, or Continue from the pop-up menu to control a server's execution. When you pause a server, current connections are allowed to continue working, but new connections aren't allowed. Stopping a server immediately terminates all connections.

NOTE: To broadcast a message to all users informing them that you're shutting down a server, run the NT Server Manager, select the server from the list of computers, and select Computer I Send Message from the main menu. If you're already connected to the server, you can execute a command such as the following from the Windows NT command prompt:

```
net send /users "SQL Server will shut down in 30 minutes."
```

As an alternative to using the Enterprise Manager, you can select Programs I Microsoft SQL Server 7.0 I Service Manager from the Start menu to display the SQL Server Service Manager dialog box, shown in Figure 2-10. On this dialog box, you can select a server and specific service to stop, start, pause, or continue. The Service Manager can also be accessed by right-clicking the server icon on the Windows NT taskbar and selecting Open SQL Server Service Manager from the pop-up menu.

Figure 2-10.   SQL Server Service Manager dialog box

The Shutdown Transact-SQL statement (which you can enter using either the Query Analyzer or OSQL utility) also shuts down the server on which the command is executed. You can use this command in a stored procedure to automate other tasks before shutting down the server. The optional With NoWait clause of the Shutdown command terminates all transactions immediately and stops the server without performing other cleanup actions. Using the With NoWait clause can lengthen the recovery time when you restart the server.

SETTING SERVER PROPERTIES

Once you've registered a server, you can set the most commonly used server properties by right-clicking the server entry in the Enterprise Manager tree and selecting Properties from the pop-up menu. Alternatively, select a server group and double-click a server's icon in the contents pane to display the SQL Server Properties dialog box. The SQL Server Properties dialog box has seven tabs, which are discussed in the following sections. After changing values on a tab, you can click the OK or Apply button to accept the changes. For changes that require restarting SQL Server, a dialog box is displayed that asks whether you want to stop and restart the server immediately. Select Yes only if there are no active users and the server is prepared for stopping.

Although the Enterprise Manager offers the most convenient way to change server configuration options, you can also execute the sp_configure system stored procedure (for example, by using Query Analyzer) for many of the options available on the SQL Server Properties dialog box. There are also some less frequently used options that can be set with the sp_configure stored procedure, but which aren't on the SQL Server Properties dialog box. Table 2-5 lists all the sp_configure stored procedure options.

Option	SQL Server Properties Tab (or Alternative)	Self-Configuring	Requires Restarting SQL Server	Minimum	Maximum	Default
Standard Options						
Allow updates	Server Settings			0	1	0
Default language	Server Settings			0	9999	0
Fill factor	Database Settings		Yes	0	100	0
Language in cache			Yes	3	100	3

Table 2-5. Available Options for sp_configure System Stored Procedure

Option	SQL Server Properties Tab (or Alternative)	Self-Configuring	Requires Restarting SQL Server	Minimum	Maximum	Default
Max async IO			Yes	1	255	32
Max text repl size				0	2147483647	65536
Max worker threads	Processor			10	1024	255
Nested triggers	Server Settings			0	1	1
Network packet size	(Tools | Options: Connection)			512	32767	4096
Recovery interval	Database Settings	Yes		0	32767	0
Remote access	Connections		Yes	0	1	1
Remote proc trans	Connections		Yes	0	1	0
Show advanced options				0	1	0
User options	Connections			0	4095	0
Advanced Options						
Affinity mask	Processor		Yes	0	2147483647	0
Cost threshold for parallelism	Processor			0	32767	5
Cursor threshold				–1	2147483647	–1
Default sortorder id			Yes	0	255	52
Index create memory				704	1,600,000	1216
Lightweight pooling				0	1	0
Locks		Yes	Yes	5000	2147483647	0

Table 2-5.   Available Options for sp_configure System Stored Procedure (*continued*)

Option	SQL Server Properties Tab (or Alternative)	Self-Configuring	Requires Restarting SQL Server	Minimum	Maximum	Default
Max degree of parallelism	Processor			0	32	0
Max query wait				0	2147483647	600
Max server memory	Memory	Yes		0	2147483647	2147483647
Media retention	Database Settings		Yes	0	365	0
Min memory per query	Memory			0	2147483647	1024
Min server memory	Memory	Yes		0	2147483647	0
Open objects		Yes	Yes	0	2147483647	500
Priority boost	Processor		Yes	0	1	0
Query governor cost limit	Server Settings		Yes	0	2147483647	0
Remote login timeout				0	2147483647	5
Remote query timeout	Connections			0	2147483647	0
Resource timeout				5	2147483647	10
Scan for startup procs			Yes	0	1	0
Set working set size	Memory		Yes	0	1	0
Spin counter			Yes	0	2147483647	0 (single processor) 10000 (multi-processor)
Time slice			Yes	50	1000	100
Unicode comparison style	SQL Server Setup		Yes	0	2147483647	0

Table 2-5.   Available Options for sp_configure System Stored Procedure (*continued*)

Option	SQL Server Properties Tab (or Alternative)	Self-Configuring	Requires Restarting SQL Server	Minimum	Maximum	Default
Unicode locale id	SQL Server Setup		Yes	0	2147483647	1033
User connections	Connections	Yes	Yes	0	32767	0
VLM size	Alpha versions of NT only			0	2147483647	0

Table 2-5.   Available Options for sp_configure System Stored Procedure (*continued*)

To execute the sp_configure stored procedure, enter a statement such as the following using the Query Analyzer or OSQL utility:

```
sp_configure 'remote access', 1
```

To access the options in the Advanced Options category in Table 2-5, you must first execute the following statement:

```
sp_configure 'show advanced options', 1
```

Configuration changes take effect when you restart SQL Server. For all options other than those that Table 2-5 indicates require a restart, you can execute a Reconfigure statement after executing the sp_configure stored procedure to make the option take effect immediately.

NOTE: The Allow updates, Recovery interval, and Time slice options require you to use a Reconfigure With Override statement if you're setting the option to a nonrecommended value (for example, if you set Allow updates to 1).

To use the Enterprise Manager to change a configuration option, display the SQL Server Properties dialog box and select the appropriate tab.

General Tab

The General tab (Figure 2-11) shows product information and basic hardware and operating system information.

You can select three options on this tab:

▼ **Autostart SQL Server**   Start SQL Server whenever Windows NT starts.

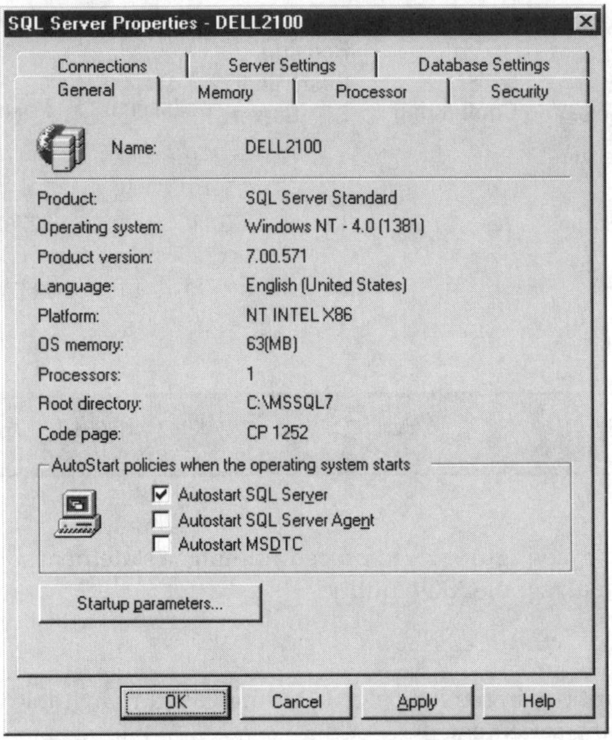

2

SQL Server 7 Developer's Guide

Figure 2-11. SQL Server Properties dialog box – General tab

- **Autostart SQL Server Agent** Start SQL Server Agent whenever Windows NT starts. (You must also specify that SQL Server autostarts.)
- ▲ **Autostart MSDTC** Start Microsoft Data Transformation Services whenever Windows NT starts.

Clicking the Startup Parameters button displays the Startup Parameters dialog box (Figure 2-12), where you can add and remove startup parameters for the sqlservr.exe program. Table 2-6 lists the available parameters.

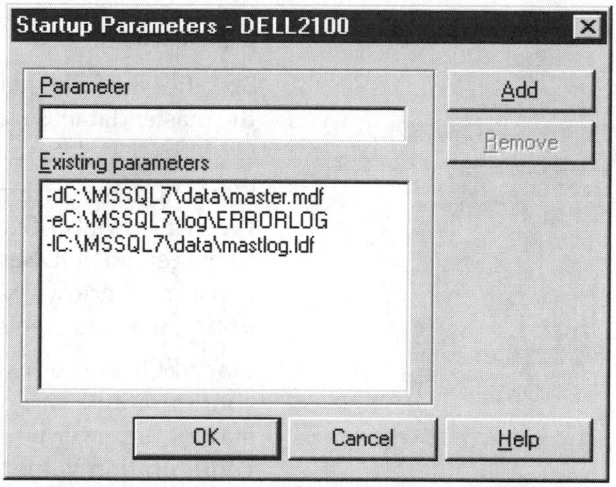

Figure 2-12. Startup Parameters dialog box

Parameter	Default	Explanation
–d*master_file_ path*	Yes	Specifies the fully qualified path for the Master database file (typically, C:\MSSQL7\data\master.mdf). When this parameter is not specified, the existing registry value is used.
–e*error_log_ path*	Yes	Specifies the fully qualified path for the error log file (typically, C:\MSSQL7\log\Errorlog). When this parameter is not specified, the existing registry value is used.

Table 2-6. sqlservr.exe Program Parameters

Parameter	Default	Explanation
−l*master_log_path*	Yes	Specifies the fully qualified path for the master database log file (typically, C:\MSSQL7\data\mastlog.ldf).
−c		Starts SQL Server independently of the Windows NT Service Control Manager, so SQL Server does not run as a Windows NT service. (This option may shorten startup time.)
−f		Starts SQL Server using the minimal configuration. This option lets you start SQL Server when a configuration value setting (for example, overcommittment of memory) otherwise prevents the server from starting. This option also enables the sp_configure allow updates option.
−m		Starts SQL Server in single-user mode, which allows only a single user to connect. In addition, the checkpoint process is not started. This option is required to restore the master database and may be necessary to repair other system databases. This option also enables the sp_configure allow updates option.
−n		Does not use the Windows NT application event log to log SQL Server events. Generally, you should use the −e parameter along with −n so that SQL Server events are logged.

Table 2-6.   sqlservr.exe Program Parameters (*continued*)

Parameter	Default	Explanation
–p*precision-level*		Specifies the maximum precision (from 1 to 38) supported for decimal and numeric data types. By default, SQL Server has a maximum precision of 28. If no *precision-level* value is supplied with this parameter, a maximum precision of 38 is used.
–s*registry-key*		Starts SQL Server using the startup parameters stored in the registry under *registry-key*. This option, which can be used only from a command prompt, lets you select a previously defined startup configuration.
/T*trace-flag*		Starts SQL Server with the specified *trace-flag* value in effect. Trace flags control the execution behavior of SQL Server.
–x		Disables collection of CPU time and cache-hit ratio statistics. Selecting this option may improve performance.

Table 2-6.   sqlservr.exe Program Parameters (*continued*)

Memory

The Memory tab (Figure 2-13) lets you specify whether to dynamically allocate memory within a range or to use a fixed amount of memory for SQL Server execution. In most cases, you should accept the default dynamic memory settings. With these settings, SQL Server will allocate memory for its own use when memory is available and will relinquish memory for other applications as needed. If you're running other applications on the same NT Server and want to limit the maximum memory SQL Server can allocate, you can adjust the Maximum (MB) setting.

The Reserve physical memory for SQL Server check box lets you lock physical memory for use by SQL Server. This may improve SQL Server performance when other

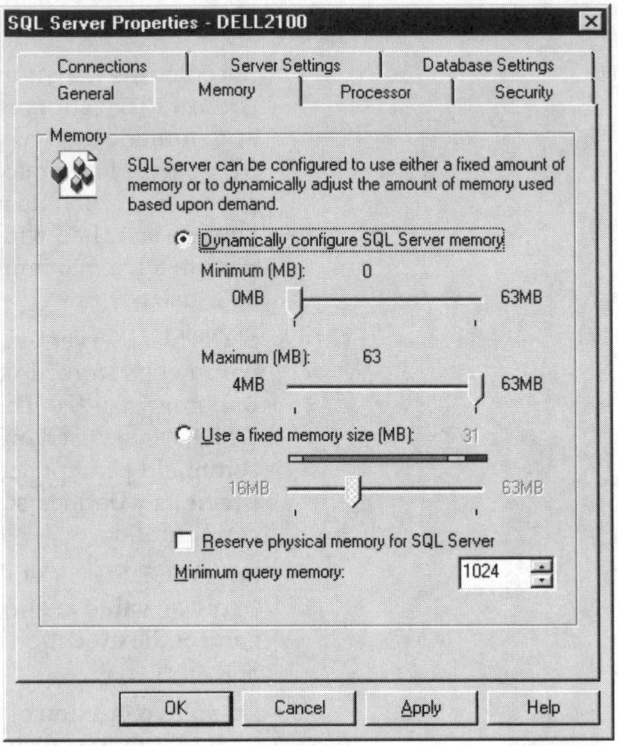

Figure 2-13. SQL Server Properties dialog box – Memory tab

applications are running on the same server, but you should be cautious with this option because it may cause out-of-memory errors in other applications.

The Minimum query memory value specifies in kilobytes the minimum amount of memory that will be allocated for execution of a query. Increasing this value may improve performance for queries that use hashing and sorting operations, but it may decrease performance for other concurrent queries.

▼

NOTE: The minimum and maximum server memory settings correspond to the min server memory and max server memory sp_configure options, respectively. Selecting Use a fixed memory size on the Memory tab corresponds to setting min server memory and max server memory to the same value. The Reserve physical memory for SQL Server check box corresponds to the set working set size sp_configure option, and the Minimum query memory setting corresponds to the min memory per query sp_configure option.

Processor

On the Processor tab (Figure 2-14), you can specify how SQL Server uses single-processor and multiprocessor platforms. For a symmetric multiprocessing (SMP) environment, you can select which processors SQL Server can use. Normally, you can let NT Server manage the assignment of work to individual processors; however, deselecting a processor that has been assigned a particular (non-SQL Server) application workload may improve the performance of that application. Selecting processors for an SMP environment corresponds to specifying the affinity mask sp_configure option.

The Maximum worker threads value specifies how many Windows NT threads will be available to handle connections. When there are no more connections than threads, each connection is handled by its own thread. When there are more connections than threads, the connections share the threads in a pool. The default of 255 is fine for most systems; however, depending on your system configuration, adjusting this value may improve performance. This value can also be set with the max worker threads sp_configure option.

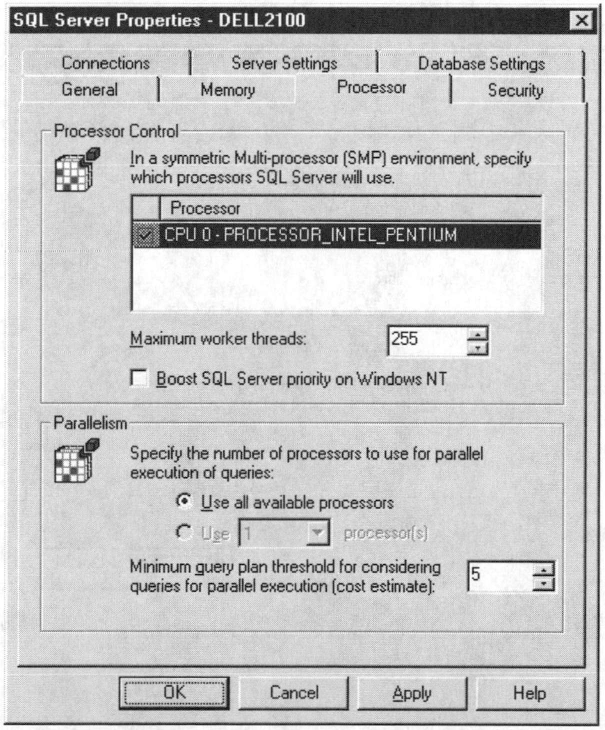

Figure 2-14. SQL Server Properties dialog box – Processor tab

The boost SQL Server priority on Windows NT option should normally *not* be selected. Select this option only when you are running SQL Server on a dedicated system in an SMP environment, and be careful you don't degrade other system functions such as the handling of network connections. This check box corresponds to the priority boost sp_configure option.

In an SMP environment, you can limit the number of CPUs used for a parallel query. Select either Use all available processors or Use ... processor(s) and enter the maximum number. Also for SMP environments, you can specify that SQL Server not use parallel query execution unless a query is estimated to take more than a minimum number of elapsed seconds for serial (that is, nonparallel) execution. You can also set these two values with the max degree of parallelism and cost threshold for parallelism sp_configure options.

Security

The Security tab (Figure 2-15) lets you specify the authentication mode (as explained in Chapter 3). In brief, *Windows NT authentication mode* uses the Windows NT user name to determine the login name for all SQL Server login attempts, and *mixed authentication mode*

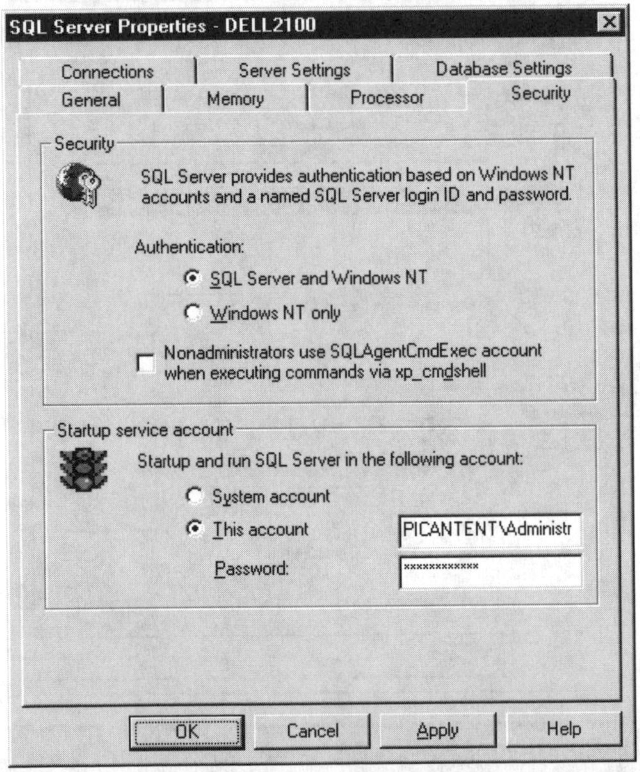

Figure 2-15. SQL Server Properties dialog box – Security tab

allows Windows NT authentication where possible (that is, over trusted connections). Otherwise, mixed authentication mode requires a user to explicitly log in to SQL Server by providing a login name and (usually) a password. If you want to use mixed authentication mode, select the SQL Server and Windows NT option on this dialog box.

The Nonadministrators use SQLAgentCmdExec account when executing commands via xp_cmdshell option should generally be checked if you grant anyone other than the system administrator Execute permission to the xp_cmdshell system stored procedure. With this option selected, a nonadministrator who calls xp_cmdshell executes operating system commands with the permissions of the SQLAgentCmdExec Windows NT user. Otherwise, anyone who calls xp_cmdshell executes operating system commands with the permissions of the local Windows NT administrator—a potential security exposure.

The Startup service account option lets you choose whether to run SQL Server under the built-in local Windows NT administrator account or under a specified Windows NT account. If you specify an account, you must also enter the account's password.

Connections

The Connections tab (Figure 2-16) provides options for client and remote server connections. The Connections panel lets you set the maximum number of concurrent

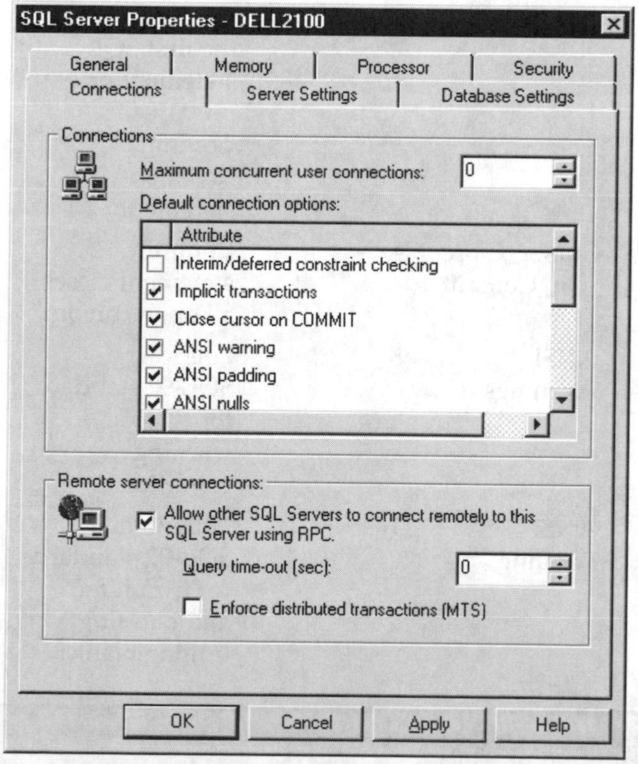

Figure 2-16.   SQL Server Properties dialog box – Connections tab

client connections. This number is dynamically managed by SQL Server and should normally not be changed. You can also set this value with the user connections sp_configure option.

Table 2-7 lists the Default connection options available on the Connections tab, the corresponding Transact-SQL Set command keywords, and the corresponding values for the user options sp_configure option. Table 2-7 also indicates which options you should set to maximize SQL Server's compliance with the ANSI SQL-92 standard, a practice we generally recommend.

Connections Tab Check Box	Set Command Keyword	sp_configure User Options Value	Purpose	Set for ANSI SQL-92 Standard
Interim/ deferred constraint checking	Disable_Def_ Cnst_Chk	1	For version 6.5 compatibility.	
Implicit transactions	Implicit_ Transactions	2	Begin a new transaction with the first SQL statement or previous Commit or Rollback statement.	Yes
Close cursor on COMMIT	Cursor_Close _On_Commit	4	Commit statement closes all open cursors.	Yes
ANSI warning	ANSI_ Warnings	8	Follow the SQL-92 standard for error and warning conditions.	Yes
ANSI padding	ANSI_ Padding	16	Follow the SQL-92 standard for trimming and padding trailing blanks.	Yes

Table 2-7.   Connection (User) Options

Connections Tab Check Box	Set Command Keyword	sp_configure User Options Value	Purpose	Set for ANSI SQL-92 Standard
ANSI nulls	ANSI_Nulls	32	Follow the SQL-92 standard for comparison with nulls.	Yes
Arithmetic abort	ArithAbort	64	Terminate a query when an arithmetic overflow or divide-by-zero error occurs.	
Arithmetic ignore	ArithIgnore	128	Do not emit an error message when an arithmetic overflow or divide-by-zero error occurs.	
Quoted identifier	Quoted_ Identifier	256	Follow the SQL-92 standard for quoted identifiers and string literals.	Yes
No count	NoCount	512	Do not emit a message indicating the number of rows affected by an SQL statement.	
ANSI null defined	ANSI_Null_ Dflt_On	1024	Assume Null when a new column is defined without the Null or Not Null keyword.	Yes

Table 2-7. Connection (User) Options (*continued*)

Connections Tab Check Box	Set Command Keyword	sp_configure User Options Value	Purpose	Set for ANSI SQL-92 Standard
ANSI null defined OFF	ANSI_Null_D flt_Off	2048	Assume Not Null when a new column is defined without the Null or Not Null keyword.	

Table 2-7.   Connection (User) Options (*continued*)

For maximum SQL-92 compatibility, you also need to execute a system stored procedure such as the following after you create a new database:

```
sp_dboption AppDta, 'concat null yields null', true
```

This command specifies that string concatenation follows the SQL-92 standard.

NOTE: For some applications, you may want to execute a Set Cursor_Close_On_Commit Off statement so that cursors aren't closed on every transaction. See the "Using Cursors" section of Chapter 10 for a discussion of cursors.

The Connections tab's Remote server connections panel lets you specify whether remote SQL Servers can log in to this SQL Server and execute calls to remote stored procedures. If you select this option, you can also set the maximum elapsed seconds a remote query takes to process before it times out. Also, if you allow remote server connections, you can specify that the Microsoft Distributed Transaction Coordinator must be used to provide all-or-none transaction integrity for distributed transactions (transactions are discussed further in the "Transaction Integrity and the Commit and Rollback Statements" section of Chapter 10). These three settings correspond to the remote access, remote query timeout, and remote proc trans sp_configure options, respectively.

Server Settings

The Server Settings tab (Figure 2-17) includes several miscellaneous items. You can select a default language for server messages, which can also be set by the default language sp_configure option.

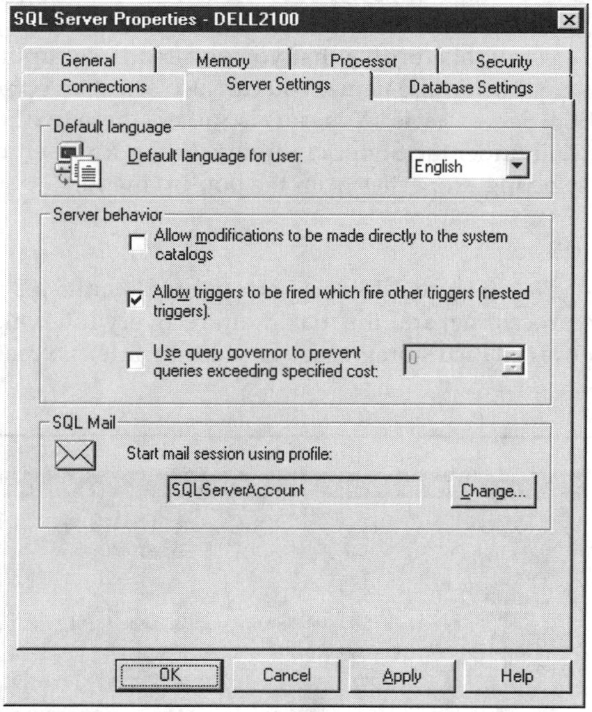

Figure 2-17.   SQL Server Properties dialog box – Server Settings tab

In the Server behavior panel, you can allow direct modifications to the tables in the system catalog. You should *never* leave this option permanently selected. The only time you should use this option is when there's no other way to correct a problem in the catalog. (The SQL Server catalog is discussed in the section "The SQL Catalog" in Chapter 9.) If you encounter a situation where it's necessary to modify the catalog directly, we recommend you stop SQL Server and reexecute it in single-user mode (using the –m parameter; see Table 2-6), which also enables catalog updates. This setting corresponds to the allow updates sp_configure option.

Another Server behavior option allows nested triggers (triggers are explained in the "Triggers" section of Chapter 10). You can also allow nested triggers with the nested triggers sp_configure option. To block any query that is estimated to run longer than a specified number of elapsed seconds, you can specify that SQL Server use the *query governor*. Setting the option on this dialog box or using an sp_configure query governor cost limit statement sets the limit across *all* connections. You can use the Set Query_Governor_Cost_Limit statement to set the limit for a specific connection.

The SQL Mail panel options let you specify a Microsoft Exchange Server mail profile to use for sending mail from SQL Server. Click the Change button and enter the name, such as SQLServerAccount, of a profile that you've already set up in Exchange Server. When you set or change the profile name, you can also select an option to start the SQL Mail service when SQL Server starts. (You can also access these two SQL Mail options by right-clicking SQL Mail under the Support Services folder for a server in the Enterprise Manager and then selecting Properties from the pop-up menu.)

Database Settings

The Database Settings tab (Figure 2-18) lets you specify defaults for rebuilding indexes, backup and restore processing, and the maximum recovery interval. The default index fill factor specifies how full each storage page is when an index is created or rebuilt if you

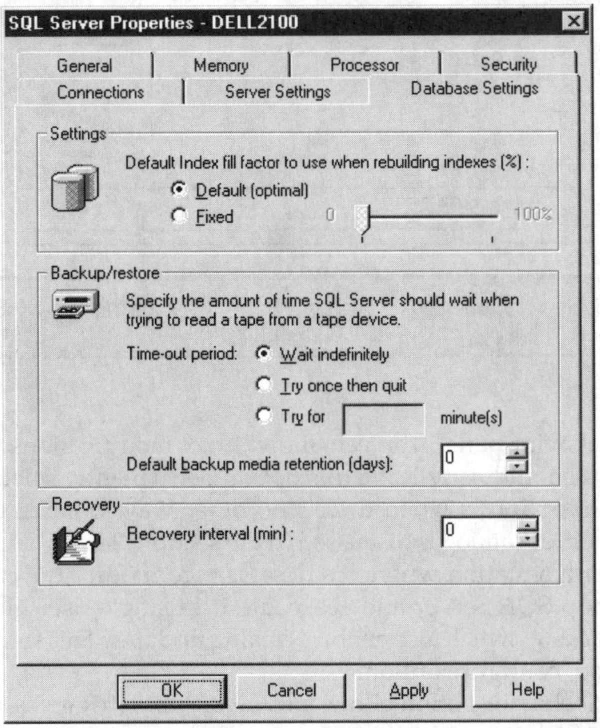

Figure 2-18. SQL Server Properties dialog box – Database Settings tab

don't specify an explicit fill factor in the Create Index statement. (Indexes are explained in the "Creating an Index" section of Chapter 9.) You can also set this default with the fill factor sp_configure option.

In the Backup/restore panel, you can select a tape device time-out period for backup and recovery operations. You can also set a default media retention period on this dialog box or by executing an sp_configure statement with the media retention option.

The Recovery interval setting controls how SQL Server writes changed data from the transaction log to database tables and flushes modified memory pages to disk. A setting of 0 lets SQL Server automatically adjust this value. For values greater than zero, lower values cause more frequent checkpoints, which may reduce performance.

MANAGING DATABASES AND DATABASE OBJECTS

The Enterprise Manager provides convenient dialog boxes for many database management tasks, such as the creation of databases, tables, and views. The following sections explore many of the important dialog boxes that you're likely to use in developing database applications. The focus here is on the creation and management of databases, tables, and views. Other chapters of this book explain in detail how to use the Enterprise Manager for additional functions: Chapter 3 discusses security; Chapter 4 discusses backup and recovery; Chapter 5 discusses replication; and Chapter 6 discusses performance. This introduction to the Enterprise Manager interface for managing databases and database objects doesn't go into all the details you'll want to know about database objects–you'll find that information in Chapters 9 and 10, which describe how to use the Transact-SQL language to define and manipulate database objects.

Creating and Modifying a Database

To create a new database with Enterprise Manager, right-click a Databases folder and select New Database from the pop-up menu. The Database Properties dialog box (Figure 2-19) has three tabs on which you enter information for the new database. On the General tab, enter the database name. As you enter the name, SQL Server will fill in default values for the Windows NT file where the database data is stored. You can revise the name, directory location, and initial file size. You can add files to store database contents and, for these, you can specify a different file group name as well. (Consult Chapter 9 for details on various database and database object options.) The File properties panel lets you select whether to limit the Windows NT file size (and consequently, the size of the database) or to let SQL Server increase the file size as you add data to tables in the database. We recommend you leave the Automatically grow file option selected. For

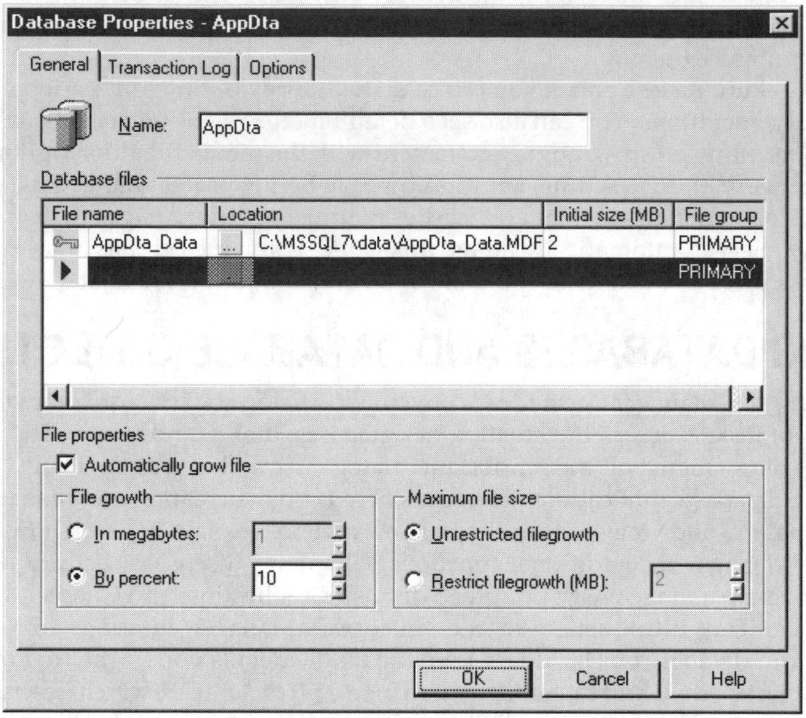

Figure 2-19. Database Properties dialog box – General tab

automatic file growth, you can specify the increment of each increase (in megabytes or as a percentage) and an optional maximum size.

NOTE: The Create Database Wizard, which you can access by selecting Tools | Wizards, offers another way to enter the information shown on the Database Properties dialog box.

The Transaction Log tab (Figure 2-20) provides similar specifications for the Windows NT file that holds transaction log entries for the database.

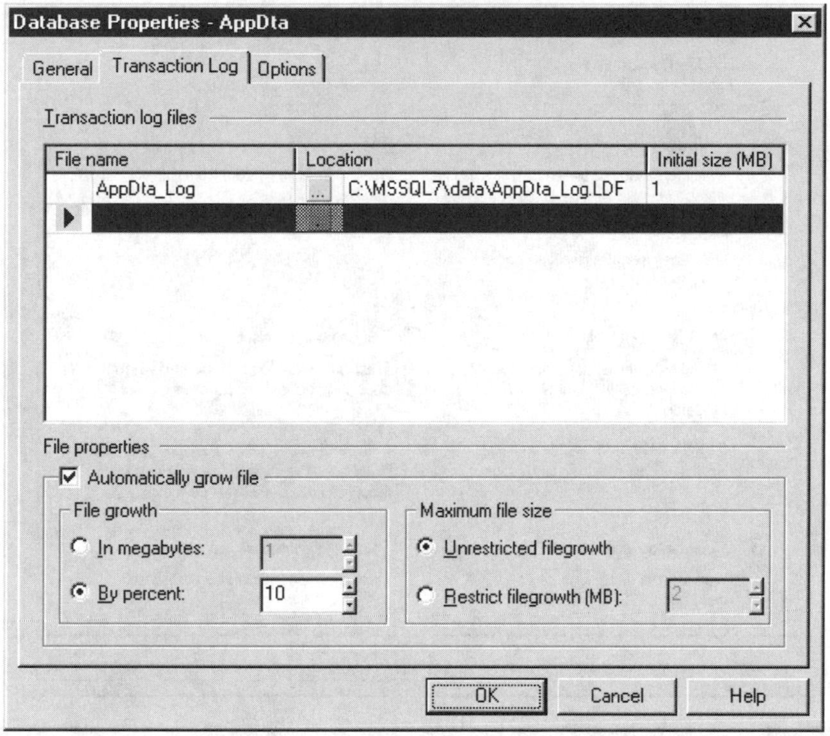

Figure 2-20.   Database Properties dialog box – Transaction Log tab

The Options tab (Figure 2-21) has nine check boxes for database options. Table 2-8 lists these options and the corresponding sp_dboption system stored procedure keywords.

As indicated in Table 2-8, we generally recommend that several of the options be selected. Others are primarily for temporary use: for example, when recovering from errors or performing other database maintenance operations.

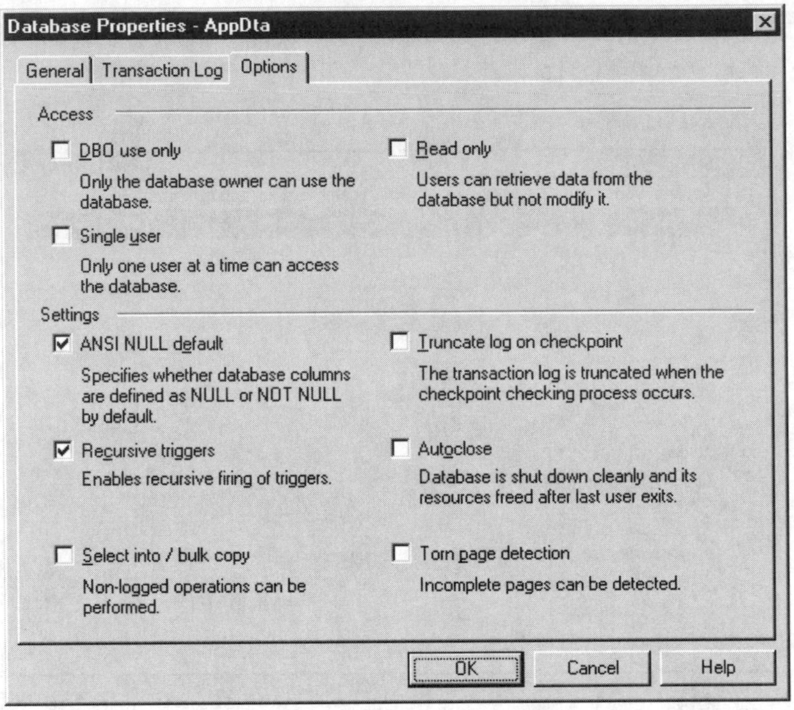

Figure 2-21. Database Properties dialog box – Options tab

Database Property Check Box	sp_dboption Keyword	Purpose	Recommended Setting
DBO use only	dbo use only	Only the database owner can use the database.	Temporary, as needed
Read only	read only	Only read (that is, Select) operations are allowed.	Temporary, as needed

Table 2-8. Database Properties Dialog Box Options

Database Property Check Box	sp_dboption Keyword	Purpose	Recommended Setting
Single user	single user	Only one user at a time can access the database.	Temporary, as needed
ANSI NULL default	ANSI null default	When selected, a table column created without a Null or Not Null clause is treated as Not Null.	Selected for ANSI SQL-92 compatibility
Truncate log on checkpoint	trunc. log on chkpt.	A checkpoint operation truncates the transaction log.	Not selected
Recursive triggers	recursive triggers	A trigger can be invoked recursively.	Selected
Autoclose	autoclose	The database is shut down and resources freed when the last user exits SQL Server.	Unselected
Select into/bulk copy	select into/bulkcopy	Allows bulk copy (bcp) utility operations, Select Into statements, and other nonlogged operations.	Temporary, as needed
Torn page detection	torn page detection	Enables detection of incomplete writes of a database page to disk.	Selected unless your system has battery-backed disk caches

Table 2-8.   Database Properties Dialog Box Options (*continued*)

The Enterprise Manager doesn't allow you to set all the important options for a database, so in many cases you may want to execute one or more sp_dboption statements after creating the database. Table 2-9 lists additional sp_dboption options and the settings we recommend.

sp_dboption Keyword	Purpose	Recommended Setting
ANSI nulls	All comparisons to null evaluate to unknown (instead of true or false).	Set on for ANSI SQL-92 compatibility.
ANSI warnings	Emit ANSI-standard warnings and error messages.	Set on for ANSI SQL-92 compatibility.
auto create statistics	Create statistics as needed during query optimization.	Optional.
auto update statistics	Update statistics as needed during query optimization.	Optional.
autoshrink	SQL Server periodically reduces the size of the Windows NT files for a database and its transaction log.	Optional.
concat null yields null	Any concatenation operation with a null operand yields null.	Set on for ANSI SQL-92 compatibility.
cursor close on commit	Open cursors are closed when a transaction is committed.	Selected for ANSI SQL-92 compatibility; however, you may want to set this off for some application connections.
default to local cursor	When a cursor declaration does not specify the Global keyword, the cursor is created with a local scope.	Set on.

Table 2-9. Additional sp_dboption Options

sp_dboption Keyword	Purpose	Recommended Setting
merge publish	The database can be used for merge replication publications.	As needed for data replication.
offline published	Database tables can be published for replication.	As needed for data replication.
quoted identifier	Use ANSI-standard rules for quoting strings and reserved words used as identifiers.	Set on for ANSI SQL-92 compatibility.
subscribed	The database can be subscribed for replication.	As needed for data replication.

Table 2-9. Additional sp_dboption Options (continued)

For a number of database-related properties, SQL Server checks a series of settings to determine the behavior of a specific connection. The process boils down to the following sequence of checks, using the first value that's set:

▼ The setting specified in an explicit Set statement in the current connection

■ The setting specified with sp_configure user options as the default for all connections

▲ The setting specified with sp_dboption as the default for the database

Thus, a setting for a connection overrides a database's setting, and a Set statement overrides a default connection setting.

Setting Maximal ANSI SQL-92 Compatibility

Specifying all the relevant SQL Server options so you achieve as close to ANSI-standard behavior as possible for all your SQL Server databases can be a bit tricky because there's no single setting for that behavior. You also can't set all the relevant properties with the Enterprise Manager's server or database properties dialog boxes. In fact, you can't even set everything you need to with just the sp_configure or sp_dboption stored procedure. Table 2-10 lists all the properties that you need to set for maximal ANSI compatibility. You can achieve maximal ANSI compatibility by setting the listed sp_configure user options (also available on the SQL Server Properties dialog box's Connections tab; see

Figure 2-16) and by executing the sp_dboption command on the model database for each listed database option, as in the following:

```
sp_dboption model, 'ANSI null default', true
sp_dboption model, 'ANSI nulls', true
sp_dboption model, 'ANSI padding', true
sp_dboption model, 'ANSI warnings', true
sp_dboption model, 'concat null yields null', true
sp_dboption model, 'cursor close on commit', true
sp_dboption model, 'quoted identifier', true
```

Once you change the model database properties, any new database you create will inherit the same properties unless you explicitly change them.

NOTE: You can use this technique for *all* database properties, not just those related to ANSI-standard behavior.

Displaying and Changing Database Properties

Right-click a database in the Enterprise Manager tree and select Properties from the pop-up menu to display or change database properties. The database Properties dialog box has the same tabs as when you create a new database (see Figures 2-19 through 2-21) plus an additional tab for setting statement permissions for database users (Figure 2-22). This tab lists all current database users and provides a check box for granting, denying, or revoking permission to Create Table and other statements, as explained in the "Managing Statement Permissions" section of Chapter 3.

Property	sp_dboption Keywords	sp_configure User Option Value
ANSI null default	ANSI null default	1024
ANSI nulls	ANSI nulls	32
ANSI padding	n/a	16
ANSI warnings	ANSI warnings	8
Concatenation of nulls	concat null yields null	n/a
Cursor close on commit	cursor close on commit	4
Implicit transactions	n/a	2
Quoted identifier	quoted identifier	256

Table 2-10.   Database and Connection Properties Related to the ANSI SQL-92 Standard

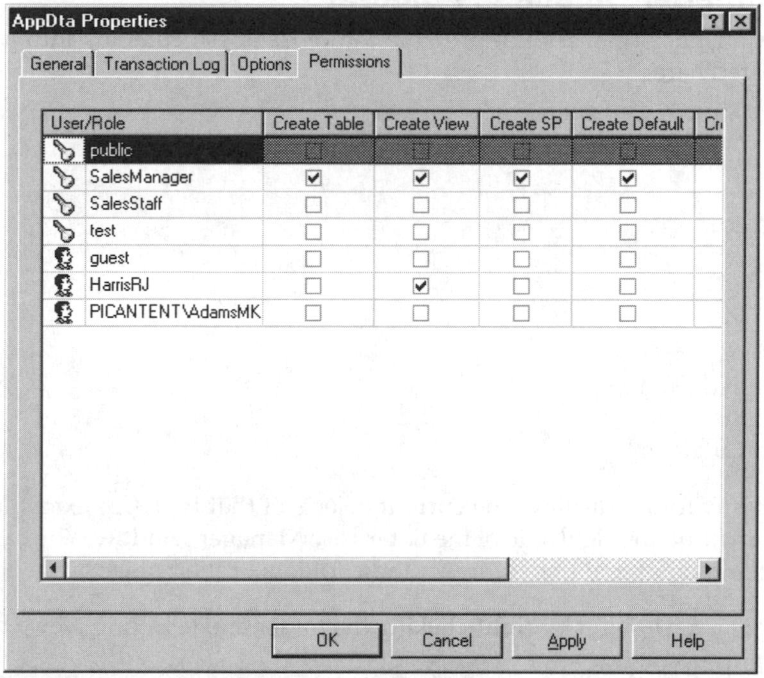

Figure 2-22. Database Properties dialog box – Permissions tab

Other Database Operations

Enterprise Manager lets you perform several database operations by right-clicking a database entry and selecting All Tasks from the pop-up menu. From the tasks menu, you can do the following:

▼ Back up a database (see Chapter 4).

■ Restore a database (see Chapter 4).

■ Shrink the Windows NT files used for a database.

■ Truncate the contents of the database transaction log.

■ Import data into database tables using DTS.

■ Export data from database tables using DTS.

■ Define a database maintenance plan for backup, optimization, and integrity check operations.

■ Generate SQL scripts to create and drop existing database objects.

▲ View data replication conflicts.

Enterprise Manager Database Folders

Enterprise Manager organizes the presentation of database contents into a number of folders, as listed here:

Diagrams
Tables
Views
Stored Procedures
Users
Roles
Rules
Defaults
User Defined Data Types
Publications
Full-Text Catalogs

Selecting any folder displays the current objects of that type (for example, tables) in the contents pane on the right side of the Enterprise Manager window. You can perform a number of common operations on any of these folders or their objects:

▼ Create a new object by right-clicking the folder and selecting New *object* from the pop-up menu.

■ Display or change an object's properties by double-clicking the object or by right-clicking the object and selecting Properties from the pop-up menu.

■ Copy a database table, view, or diagram by right-clicking the object and selecting Copy from the pop-up menu.

■ Rename a database table, view, stored procedure, rule, default, or user-defined data type by right-clicking the object and selecting Rename from the pop-up menu.

■ Delete an object by right-clicking the object and selecting Delete from the pop-up menu or by selecting the object and pressing the DELETE key.

▲ Display the online documentation "Creating and Maintaining Databases" by right-clicking the object and selecting Help from the pop-up menu or by selecting the object and pressing the F1 key.

Chapter 3 explains how to use Enterprise Manager to create database users and roles. The following sections discuss other types of database objects.

Table Tasks

The New Table dialog box (Figure 2-23) provides a grid where you can define the table columns and each of the column attributes (as described in the "Creating a Table" section of Chapter 9). To specify primary-key columns, position the cursor on the line for the

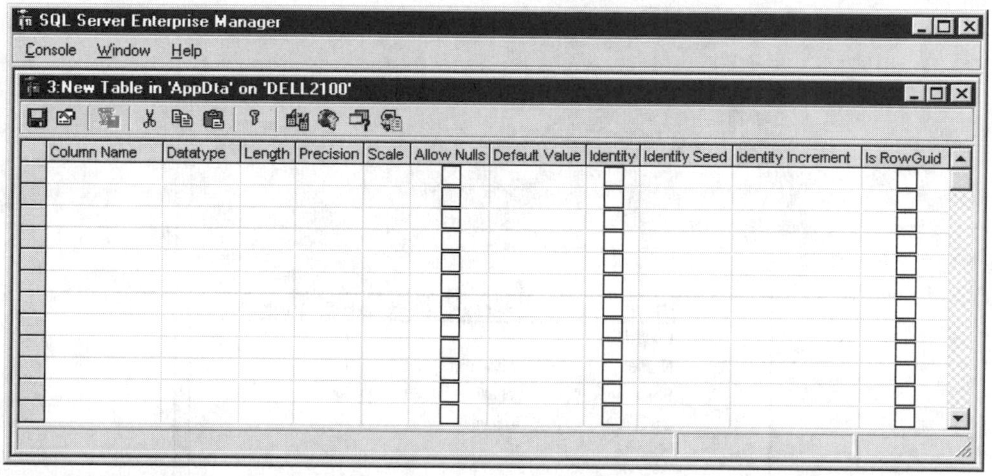

Figure 2-23.   New Table dialog box

appropriate column and click the Set primary key toolbar icon (the key, the icon seventh from the left). Alternatively, you can right-click a column entry and select Set Primary Key from the pop-up menu.

Clicking the Table and Index Properties toolbar icon (second from the left) on the New Table dialog box displays a three-tab dialog box where you can enter foreign key and check constraints and other properties for the new table or create an index for the table. You can also display this dialog box by right-clicking a column entry and selecting Properties from the pop-up menu. Other toolbar icons and pop-up menu items let you create a trigger for the table, manage permissions for the table, show interdependencies between the table and other database objects (for example, views), and generate a Transact-SQL script for the Create Table (and other) statements used to create the table.

When you double-click a table entry in the Enterprise Manager window to display its properties, you see the dialog box in Figure 2-24, which lists basic information for the table and its columns. You can get more information, as well as alter the table definition, by right-clicking the table and selecting Design Table from the pop-up menu. The Design Table dialog box, shown in Figure 2-25, is identical to the New Table dialog box and lets you change column definitions, as well as work with other table-related objects, such as triggers.

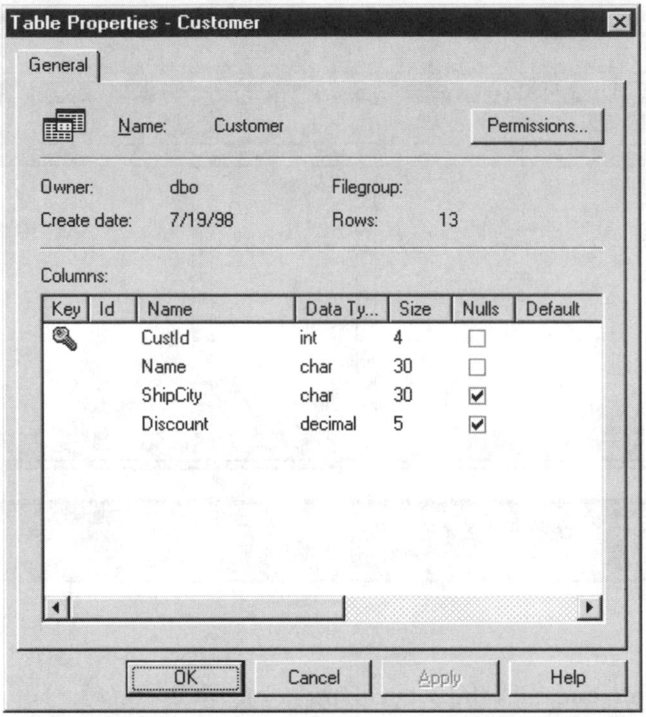

Figure 2-24. Table Properties dialog box

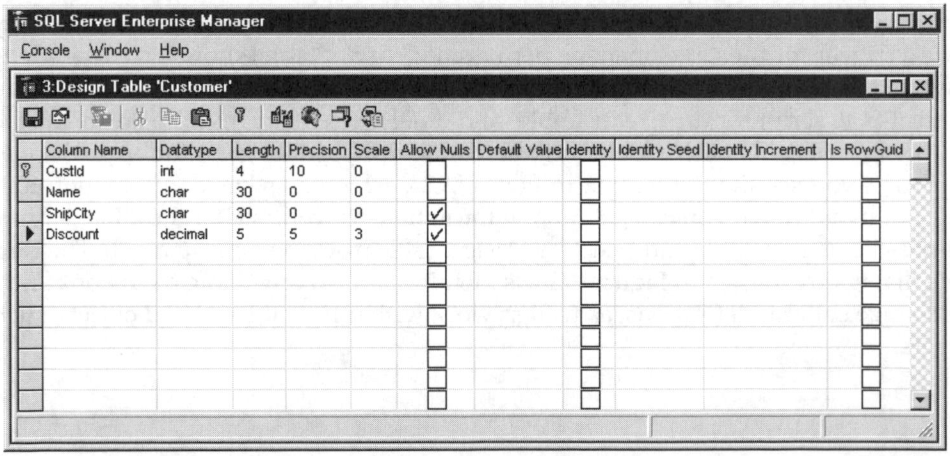

Figure 2-25. Design Table dialog box

NOTE: On the New Table and Design Table dialog boxes, you must save a newly entered or changed table definition by clicking the Save toolbar icon (the diskette, the leftmost icon) to enable the Triggers, Show permissions, Show dependencies, and Generate SQL scripts toolbar icons.

By clicking an appropriate toolbar icon on either the New Table or Design Table dialog box or by right-clicking a table and selecting All Tasks from the pop-up menu, you can display several dialog boxes to work with table-related objects.

The Manage Indexes icon or menu option displays the Manage Indexes dialog box, shown in Figure 2-26. This dialog box lets you delete or edit an existing index, or create a new index by clicking the New button to display the Create New Index dialog box, shown in Figure 2-27.

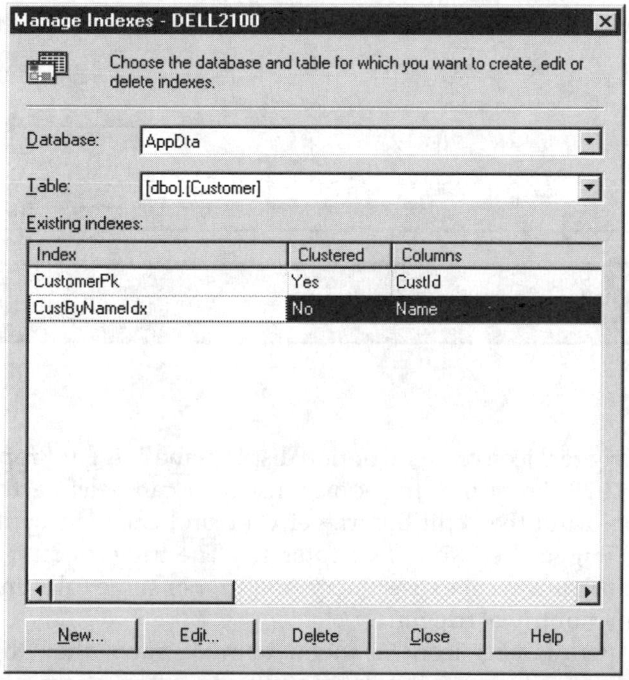

Figure 2-26.   Manage Indexes dialog box

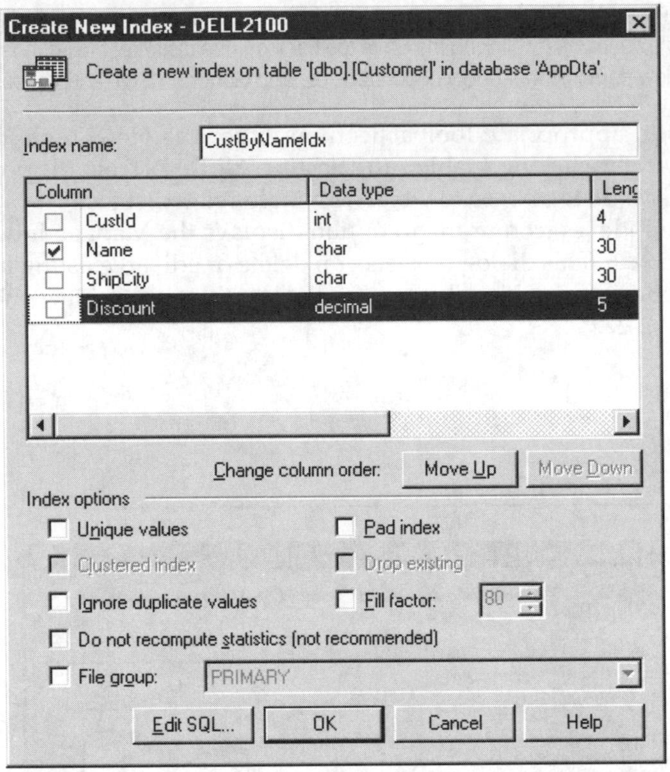

Figure 2-27. Create New Index dialog box

The Manage Triggers icon or menu option displays the Trigger Properties dialog box, shown in Figure 2-28. From the drop-down list, you can select a trigger that's been created for the table and then edit the trigger code and check its syntax. (Triggers are discussed in the "Triggers" section of Chapter 10.) The trigger editor is such a limited editor that you'll probably want to use Query Analyzer or some full-function source code editor to create any nontrivial trigger.

The Manage Permissions icon or menu item displays the Object Properties – Permissions dialog box (Figure 2-29), where you can grant, deny, or revoke database users' permissions to read or update the table contents, as discussed in Chapter 3.

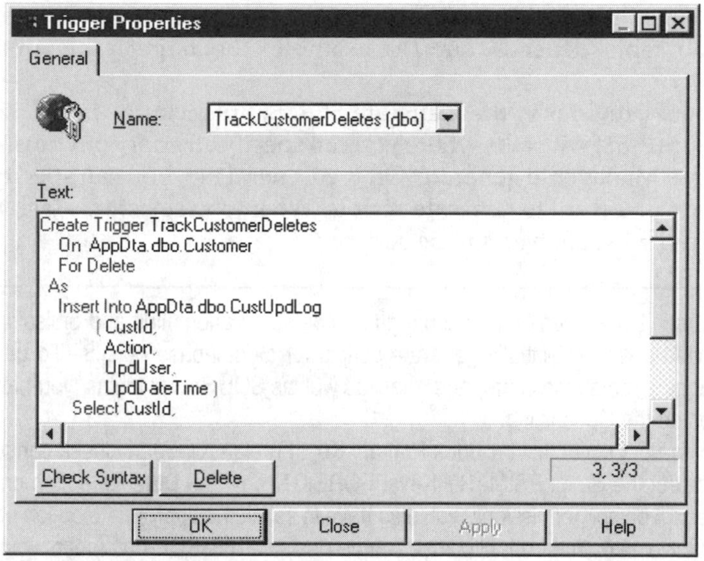

Figure 2-28. Trigger Properties dialog box

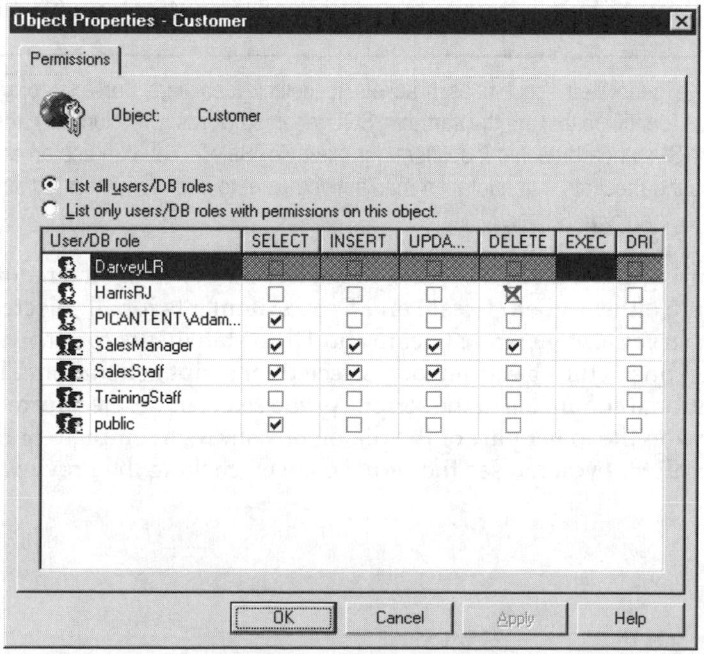

Figure 2-29. Object Properties – Permissions dialog box

The Display Dependencies icon or menu item displays the Dependencies dialog box (Figure 2-30), which lists all objects (for example, views) that depend on the table and all objects that the table depends on (for example, the target table of a foreign-key constraint).

As mentioned previously, the Generate SQL Scripts icon or menu item displays a dialog box (Figure 2-31) with tabs where you can specify a variety of Transact-SQL scripts for the Enterprise Manager to generate. On the General tab, you can specify the database objects for which you want to generate scripts. When you select this task for a table, the table appears in the list of objects to be scripted.

NOTE: The initial version of the scripting tool has some anomalies and omissions. The Script All Objects option does *not* actually generate scripts for all database objects. To generate scripts for indexes, triggers, database users, and roles, as well as SQL Server logins, you have to select those object types on the Options tab.

Also, to generate a script that includes Primary Key, Foreign Key, and Check constraints for a table, you must select the Script PRIMARY Keys, FOREIGN Key and Defaults option on the Options tab. Finally, to script object permissions, you also have to select the appropriate option on the Options tab. In Chapter 9, we recommend that you use source files for all the SQL statements you use to create and alter database objects, a practice that's more reliable than using the scripting tool.

To see the Transact-SQL source code that will be generated (Figure 2-32), you can click the Preview button. The Object Scripting Preview dialog box has an editing window where you can make additional modifications before saving the source code. This dialog box also has a Save As button to save the source code in a Windows NT file.

NOTE: The generated script uses brackets to delimit identifiers (for example, [Sale]) to avoid conflicts with identifiers that are the same as SQL reserved words. Unfortunately, there's no option to generate ANSI-standard *quoted identifiers* (for example "Sale"). You can use an editor to search for and replace the brackets with quotation marks if you want to use the generated script with a DBMS product other than SQL Server.

The Formatting tab (Figure 2-33) lets you select the types of statements to generate. You can generate either or both Create and Drop statements for all selected objects. You can have SQL Server also generate Create and Drop statements for any database object that depends on one of the objects already selected for script generation. The final option generates additional comments in the script. As you select or deselect formatting options, the text window in the lower part of the dialog box shows a template of the script to be generated. (Recall that you can see the actual code by clicking the Preview button on the General tab.)

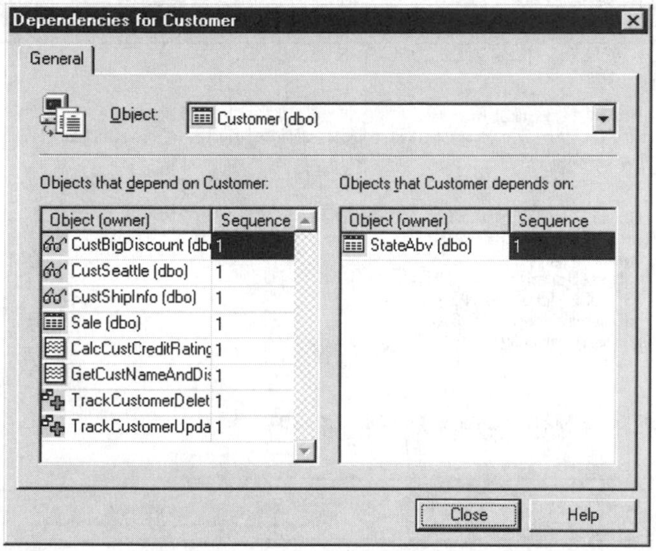

Figure 2-30.   Dependencies dialog box

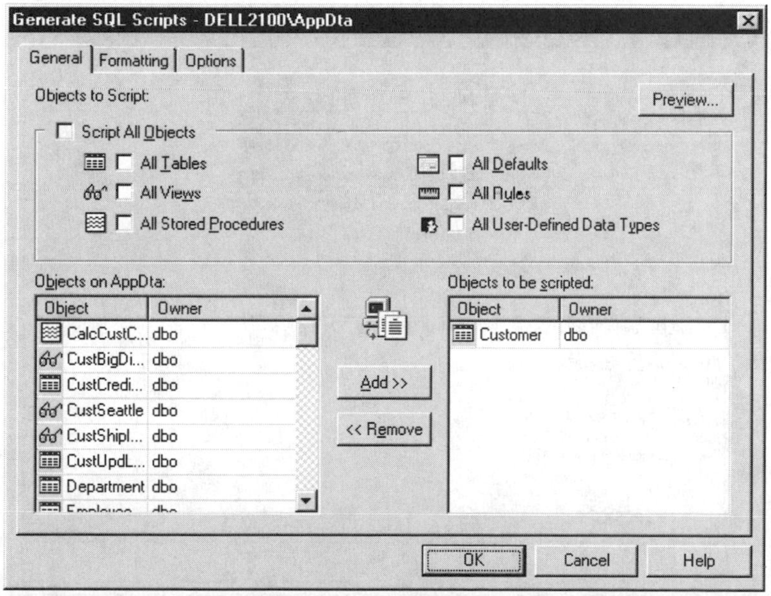

Figure 2-31.   Generate SQL Scripts dialog box – General tab

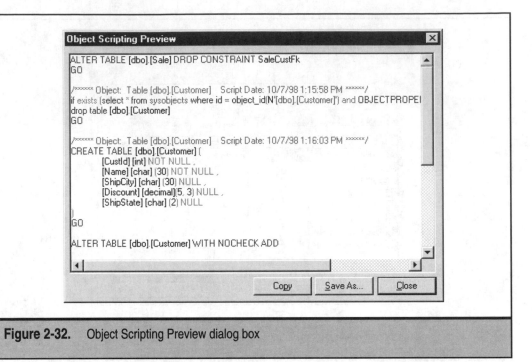

Figure 2-32. Object Scripting Preview dialog box

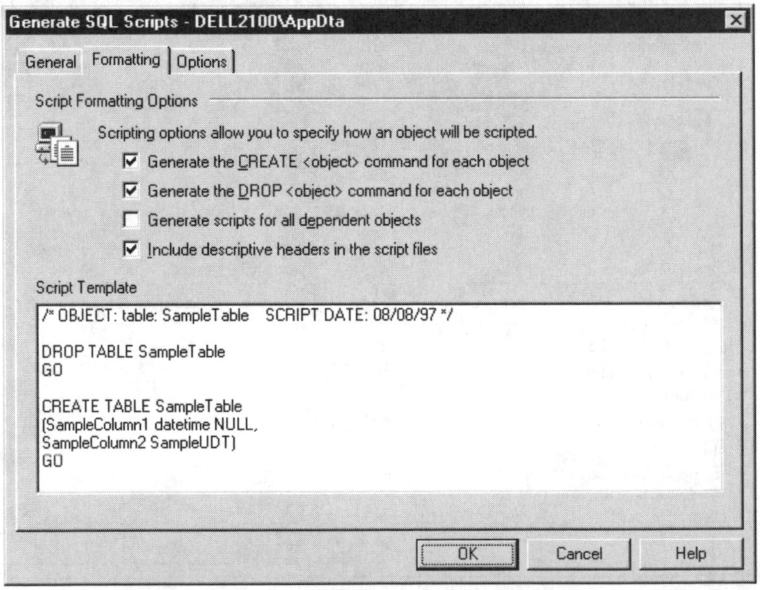

Figure 2-33. Generate SQL Scripts dialog box – Formatting tab

On the Options tab (Figure 2-34), you can select options to generate scripts for several database objects not listed on the General tab, including database users, roles, SQL Server logins, indexes, full-text indexes, and triggers. In addition, you can generate scripts for all permissions to the objects. You should always select the Script PRIMARY Keys, FOREIGN Keys, and Defaults option when you generate scripts for one or more tables, unless you're intentionally creating a script for a table without these important constraints. In the file options, you can select the character set to use and specify whether to create a single text file or one file for each object's statements.

One other tool available for tables is a grid-oriented retrieval and update tool for accessing data. To use this tool, right-click a table object and select either Open Table | Return all rows or Open Table | Return top from the pop-up menu. Both options display the Data in Table dialog box (Figure 2-35); the first choice includes all rows in the display, and the second choice prompts for the maximum number of rows to display.

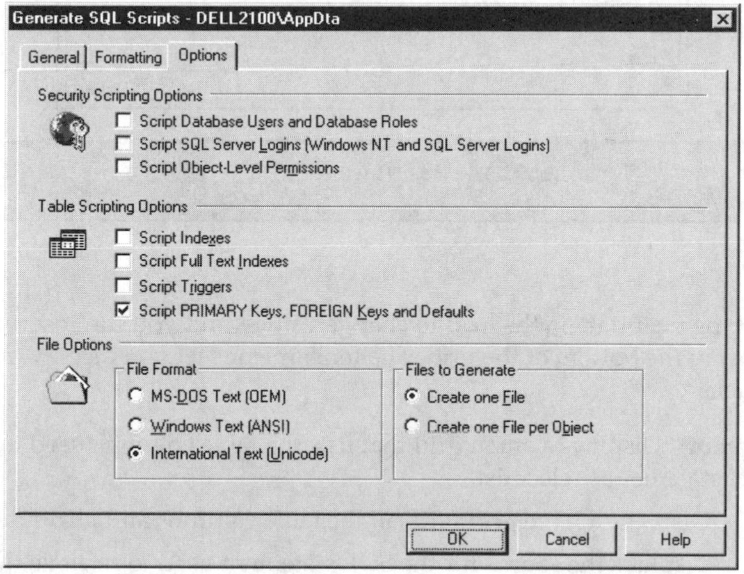

Figure 2-34.   Generate SQL Scripts dialog box – Options tab

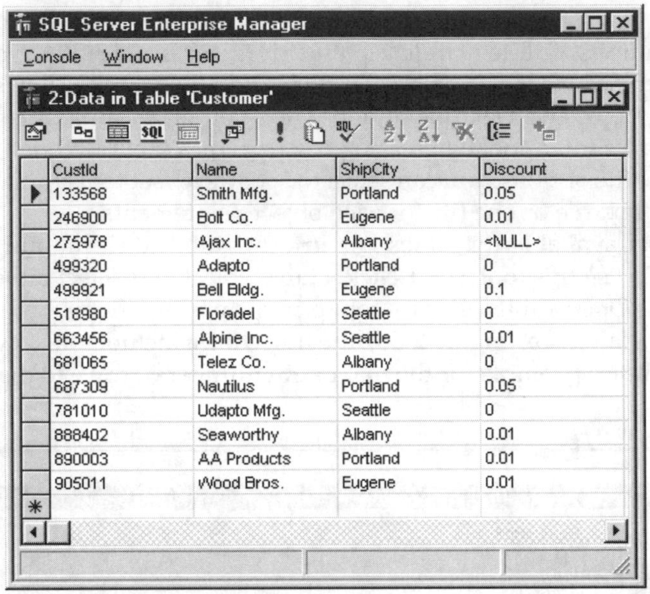

Figure 2-35. Data in Table dialog box – Results pane

You can type over data in the grid to change values, and you can insert new rows in the empty row at the bottom of the grid. The toolbar icons let you display or hide any or all of four panes:

▼ **Diagram** Displays a small grid that lists the table columns used in the SQL Select statement's select list.

■ **Grid** Displays a large grid with all the table columns and attributes.

■ **SQL** Displays the source for the SQL statement used to retrieve the displayed results (see Figure 2-36).

▲ **Results** Displays the retrieval results (as in Figure 2-35).

You can edit the source code in the SQL pane or select columns in the Diagram and Grid panes to change the query used to produce the contents of the Results pane. The Change Query type tool lets you also enter Insert, Update, Delete, or Create Table statements. Other toolbar icons let you construct Where, Group By, and Order By clauses for the underlying SQL statement. These SQL capabilities are discussed in detail in Chapter 10.

View Tasks

Right-clicking the icon for a view displays a pop-up menu with several options similar to those discussed for tables, such as designing a view, managing permissions, displaying dependencies, generating SQL scripts, and accessing data through a view.

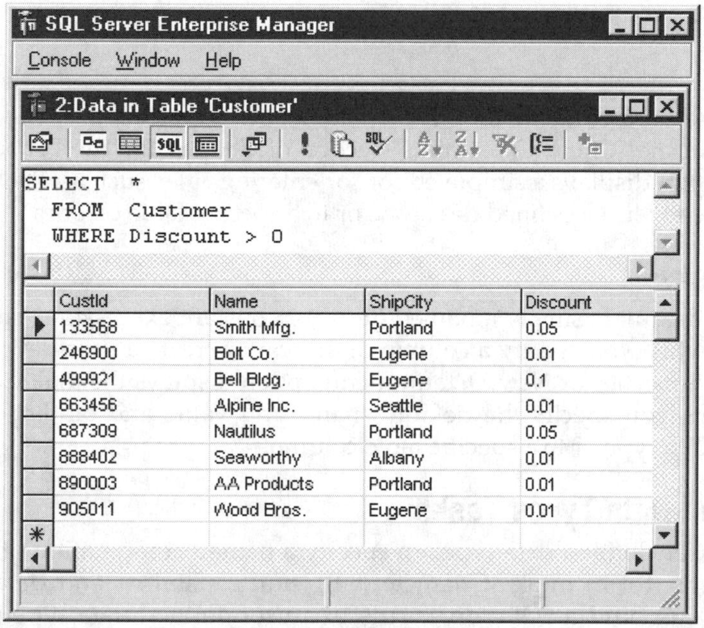

Figure 2-36.   Data in Table dialog box – SQL and Results panes

Stored Procedure Tasks

Right-clicking the icon for a stored procedure displays a pop-up menu with several options similar to those discussed for tables, such as managing permissions, displaying dependencies, and generating SQL scripts. Selecting the New Stored Procedure menu item displays a limited-function editor where you can enter the source code for a SQL Create Procedure statement. As mentioned with regards to the trigger editor, you'll probably want to use Query Analyzer or some full-function source code editor to create any nontrivial stored procedure. Double-clicking the icon for a stored procedure displays this same editor for changing existing code.

NOTE: If you attempt to display the source code for a stored procedure created with the Create Procedure statement's With Encryption clause, the Enterprise Manager displays the source code as exec(decrypt(0x...)), where the argument of the decrypt function is a hexadecimal constant that represents the encrypted source code.

Rules Tasks

Rules are a backward-compatibility feature that's been superseded by check constraints (as explained in the "Check Constraints" section of Chapter 9). The Properties or New Rule menu option displays a simple editor for entering rules such as @col > 0. You can also bind a rule to a user-defined data type or to a specific table column.

Defaults Tasks

A SQL Server default is simply a named literal or constant expression. You can use the default name when you specify a column definition or create a user-defined data type. Selecting the Properties or New Default menu option displays the dialog box in Figure 2-37, which lets you specify the default's name and value and bind the default to a user-defined data type or to a specific table column.

User-Defined Data Types Tasks

You can use user-defined data types to specify a named combination of column data type and length (for example, Character(50)), null capability, and default value. In addition, you can bind a SQL Server rule to a user-defined data type. Selecting the Properties or New User Defined Data Type menu option displays the dialog box in Figure 2-38, which lets you select the column data type from a drop-down list, specify the length (if appropriate), and bind a default value and rule. For an existing user-defined data type, click the Where Used button to display a list of columns that are defined using the data type.

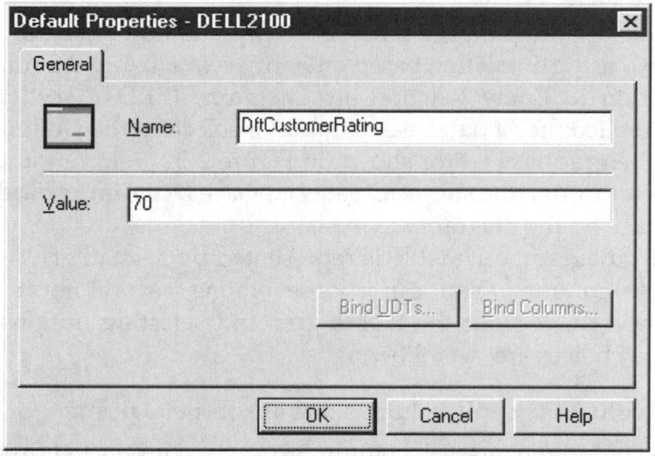

Figure 2-37.   Default Properties dialog box

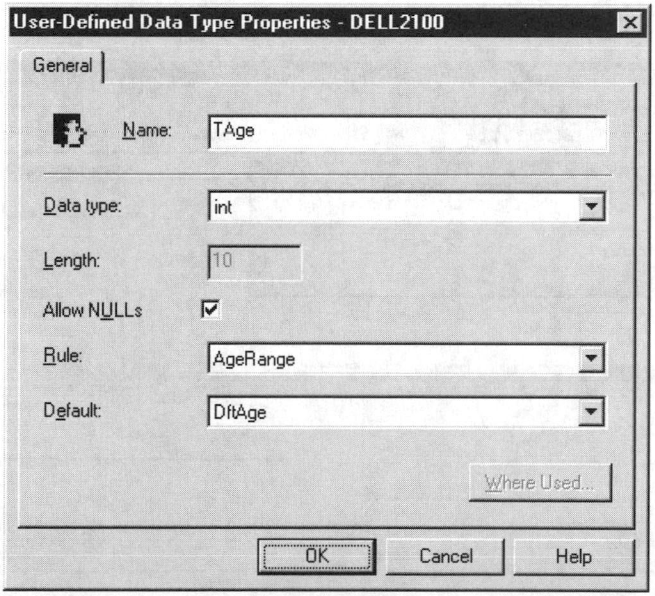

Figure 2-38.   User-Defined Data Type Properties dialog box

Database Diagrams Tasks

A SQL Server database diagram is a graphical representation of one or more tables and their relationships, using a notation based on entity-relationship diagrams, as described in the "Introduction to Entity Relationship Diagrams (ERDs)" section of Chapter 8. Double-clicking the icon for a database diagram or selecting the Design Diagram menu option displays the graphical editor shown in Figure 2-39. Selecting the New Database Diagram steps you through the simple Create Database Diagram Wizard dialog boxes to select tables to place on the diagram.

On a database diagram, each table is represented by a small grid with one row for each of the table columns. You can choose among several formats for a table's representation by right-clicking the table's grid and selecting options on the pop-up menu. Among the choices are the following:

▼ Show all columns or only columns that are part of a primary or foreign key.

▲ Show just column names, all column properties, or selected properties.

Pop-up menu options and toolbar icons also let you perform tasks on tables, views, and relationships; for example, you can add new columns to a table, define new foreign keys, and so on.

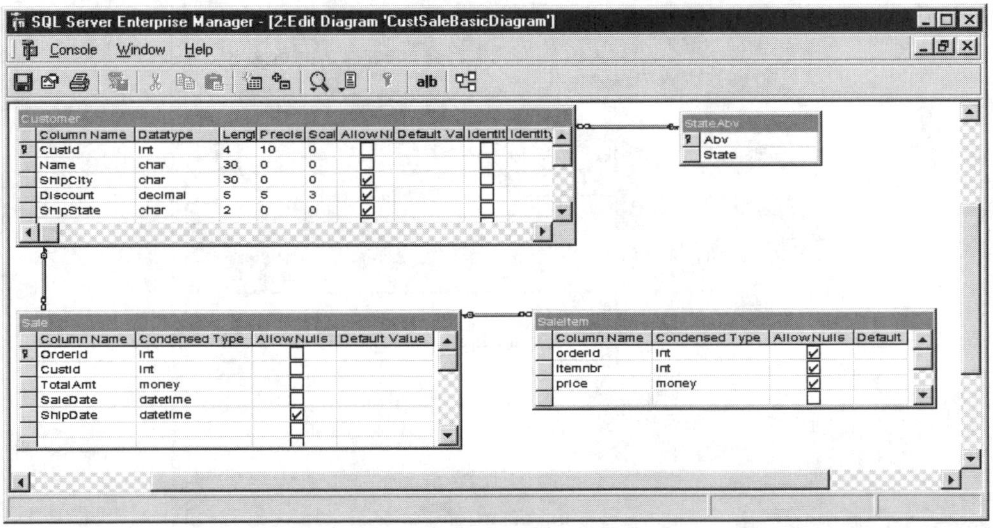

Figure 2-39.   Edit Diagram dialog box

Full-Text Catalogs Tasks

SQL Server's full-text search facility lets you create indexes on all the words in one or more character columns. Columns that have a type of Character, VarCharacter, NCharacter, NVarCharacter, Text, or NText can be indexed for use in full-text searches. You can then use extended search facilities to look for rows containing text information. If you've installed the full-text search facility, you can start and stop the full-text service by right-clicking the Full-Text Search entry under a server's Support Services folder and selecting the Start or Stop menu option.

Each database has a Full-Text Catalogs container where you can create and manage the full-text catalog objects that contain information used by the full-text search facility. To create a new full-text catalog, right-click the Full-Text Catalogs container under a database and select New Full-Text Catalog from the pop-up menu. On the New Full-Text Catalog Properties dialog box (Figure 2-40), enter a name and a Windows NT directory for the catalog data.

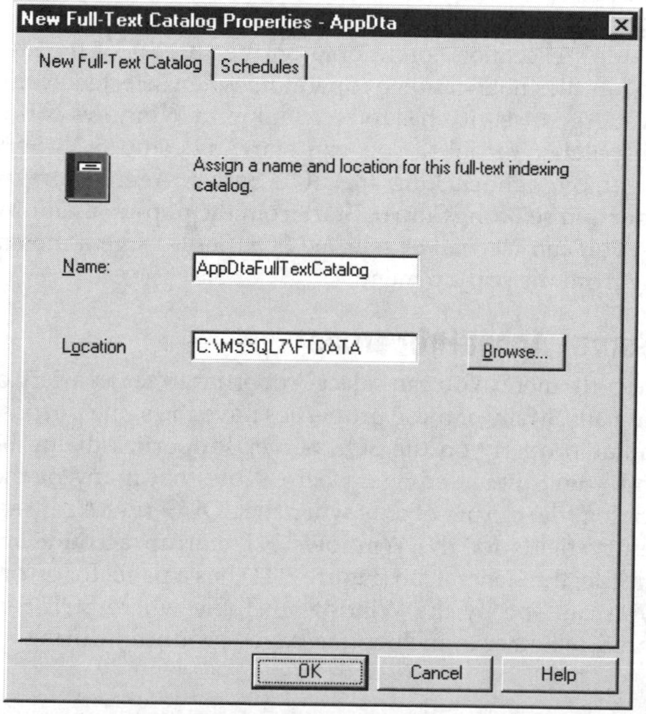

Figure 2-40. New Full-Text Catalog Properties dialog box

On the Schedules tab (not shown), you can create a schedule for the jobs that populate the catalog with information, such as the special full-text indexes used by the search facility.

Server Logins and Roles

Under a server's Security folder are Logins and Server Roles containers that contain security-related objects. The Logins container has all the logins you create for accessing the server. The Server Roles container has the seven fixed system roles defined for SQL Server. Chapter 3 explains how to use Enterprise Manager menu options and dialog boxes to manage logins and roles.

Working with SQL Server Agent

SQL Server Agent runs jobs based on a specific request, a predefined schedule, or the occurrence of an event. A job consists of one or more steps, and each job step contains one or more statements or commands. Each step has only one type of statement or command: Transact-SQL statements, Windows NT commands, ActiveScript statements, or replication agent actions. In many cases, a job might consist of a single step with one Execute SQL statement to call a stored procedure. Other jobs might involve multiple steps, with each step's execution conditional on the success of the step before it. SQL Server Agent also handles notification of operators when selected events occur.

The SQL Server Agent service has to be running in Windows NT and serves as the scheduler and dispatcher for jobs. You can start and stop SQL Server Agent from Enterprise Manager by right-clicking the SQL Server Agent entry under a server's Management folder and selecting Stop or Start from the pop-up menu. When SQL Server Agent is running, you can view all or selected SQL Server Agent messages by selecting Display Error Log from the pop-up menu.

Setting SQL Server Agent Properties

From this same pop-up menu, you can select Properties to set a variety of aspects of how SQL Server Agent runs. Many of these properties have the same purpose for SQL Server Agent as the similar property on the SQL Server Properties dialog box (Figures 2-11 through 2-18) and aren't discussed again here. Note that many of the properties (for example, the error log file) can be set only when the SQL Server Agent service is stopped. In addition to entry fields for the Windows NT startup account and the Microsoft Exchange mail profile, the General tab (Figure 2-41) has a panel for error log information. On this panel, you can specify the Windows NT file where SQL Server Agent error messages are stored, whether to include messages produced during execution tracing,

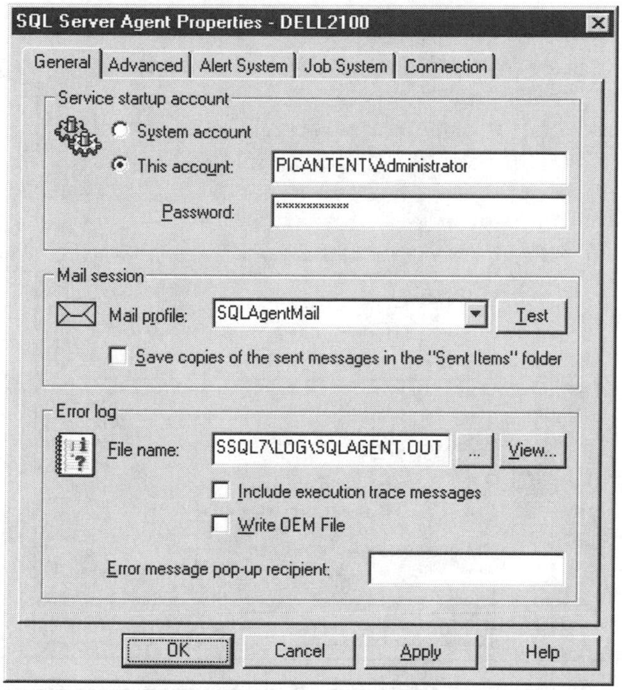

Figure 2-41. SQL Server Agent Properties dialog box – General tab

and which character set to use (Unicode or OEM). If you want a pop-up message to appear whenever a SQL Server Agent error is logged, you can supply a user name on this panel.

On the Advanced tab (Figure 2-42), you can specify automated restart of SQL Server Agent if either SQL Server or SQL Server Agent stops unexpectedly. You can also have SQL Server forward to a remote server all or selected Windows NT application events that occur on a local server. This lets the remote server take action (for example, by defining an alert, as discussed in the section "Creating an Alert," later in this chapter) based on events on the local server. The final panel on this tab specifies when SQL Server Agent should consider the CPU to be idle based on a percentage of usage over a period of time.

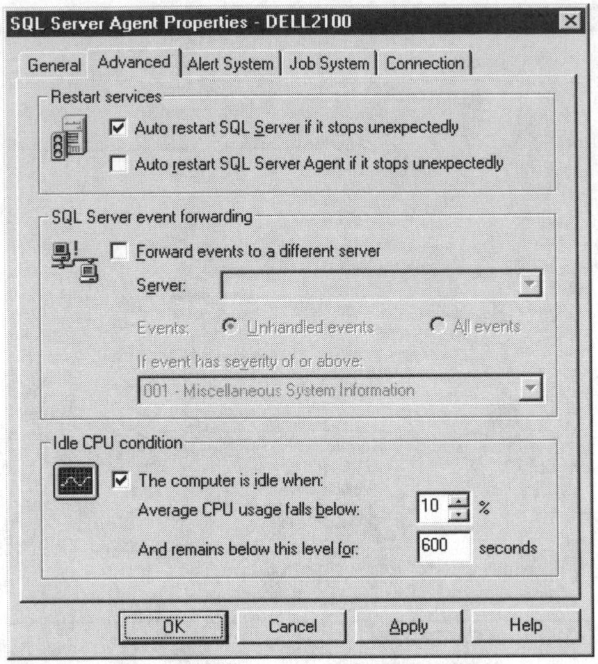

Figure 2-42.   SQL Server Agent Properties dialog box – Advanced tab

The Alert System tab (Figure 2-43) lets you specify how to notify an operator of an alert. After selecting an operator, you can have alerts sent by e-mail, pager, or a net send message. For pager e-mail, you use this tab to define the appropriate e-mail header fields (To, CC, and Subject).

You can use the Job System tab (Figure 2-44) to limit the size of the job history log or to clear the current log. The Shutdown time-out interval value specifies how long SQL Server lets a running job execute after SQL Server is shut down. To limit who can run job steps that include Windows NT commands or ActiveScripts, you can select the corresponding option on the Job System tab. If you allow nonsystem administrators to run CmdExec and ActiveScript job steps (the dialog check box is not selected), you can

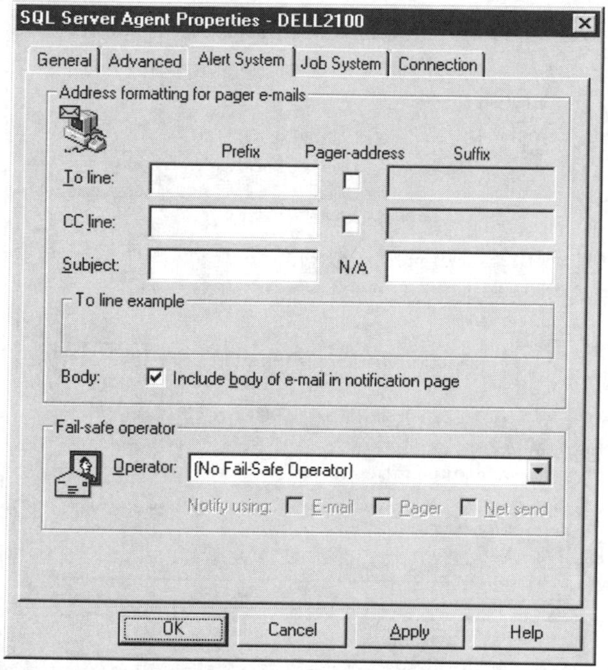

Figure 2-43.   SQL Server Agent Properties dialog box – Alert System tab

click the Reset Proxy Account and Reset Proxy Password buttons to reinstate the original nonsystem administrator proxy account.

The Connection tab (Figure 2-45) specifies how SQL Server Agent connects to SQL Server (see the discussion of similar information for Enterprise Manager in the section "Registering and Unregistering a Server," earlier in this chapter). On this tab, you can also specify an optional alias for the local server.

Creating an Operator

A SQL Server operator is basically a named object with e-mail, pager, or net send contact information. You supply an operator name whenever you want SQL Server Agent to automatically send an alert message (that is, a message sent about some event). To create

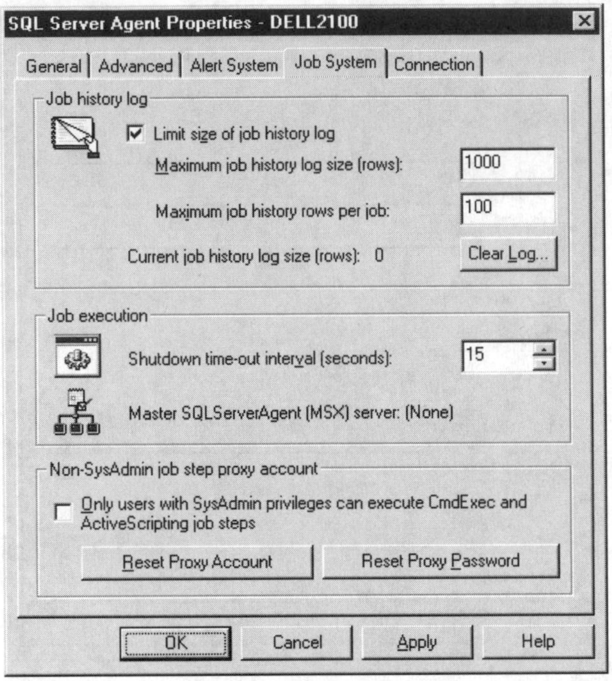

Figure 2-44. SQL Server Agent Properties dialog box – Job System tab

a new operator, right-click the Operators container under SQL Server Agent in the Enterprise Manager and select New Operator from the pop-up menu. The Operator Properties dialog box (Figure 2-46) is displayed for this menu selection or when you double-click an existing operator to display its properties.

On the operator Properties dialog box's General tab, enter any name up to 128 characters. An operator name doesn't have to be the same as a SQL Server login or database user name, although you may want to follow this practice. Enter specifications for at least one of the three means of sending a message to an operator:

▼ A MAPI-1–compliant e-mail client (for example, Microsoft Exchange or Microsoft Outlook)

■ An e-mail address with a pager address as specified by third-party pager software

▲ A Windows NT user's net send address

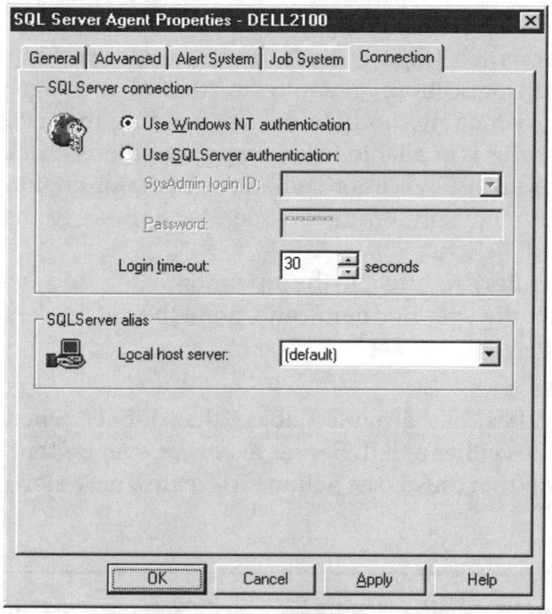

Figure 2-45.   SQL Server Agent Properties dialog box – Connection tab

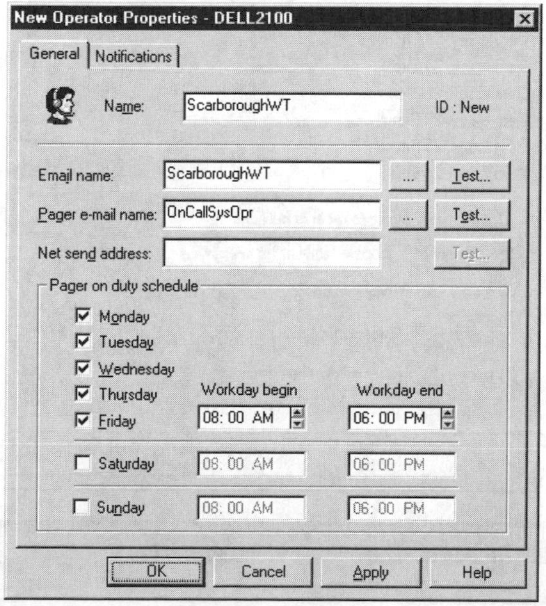

Figure 2-46.   Operator Properties dialog box – General tab

If you supply a pager e-mail address, you can also specify when the operator is monitoring the pager.

On the Notifications tab (Figure 2-47), you can specify for which defined alerts (discussed in the following section, "Creating an Alert") a message will be sent. For each alert, you can specify which methods to use for sending the message. Normally, you should leave the Operator is available to receive notifications check box selected, except for temporary periods such as vacation, when the operator is unavailable. Clicking the Send E-mail button immediately sends the operator a message that advises him or her that alert messages will be sent.

To delete an operator, right-click the operator name and select Delete from the pop-up menu or select the operator name and press the DELETE key.

Creating an Alert

A SQL Server alert is basically a named object that defines when some action should occur. An alert specifies either a SQL Server event (or events) that cause the action or a performance condition that causes the action. To create a new alert, right-click the Alerts

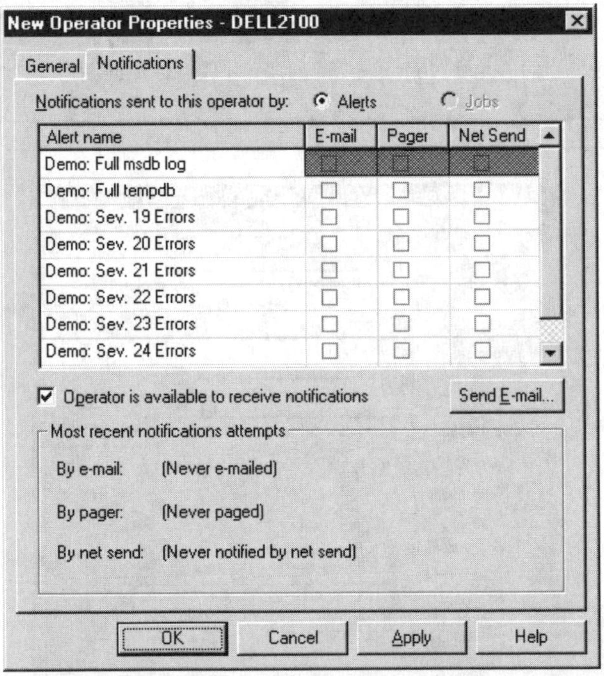

Figure 2-47.   Operator Properties dialog box – Notifications tab

container under SQL Server Agent in the Enterprise Manager and select New Alert from the pop-up menu. The Alert Properties dialog box (Figure 2-48) is displayed for this menu selection or when you double-click an existing alert to display its properties.

On this dialog box, provide an alert name of up to 128 characters. From the Type drop-down list, select either SQL Server event alert or SQL Server performance condition alert. Use the Enabled check box to enable or disable the alert. For an event alert, you can either specify an individual error number or select for events that have a particular severity level. The alert can be defined so that it covers errors that occur in any database or a specific database. You can further restrict the errors that cause the alert by specifying a string that must be contained in the error message text. The General tab also reports when this alert last occurred and the number of times it has occurred since it was created or since you clicked the Reset Count button to zero out the count.

When you select a performance type of event, the General tab lets you define a comparison (falls below, equals, or rises above) between a particular counter for one of SQL Server's performance categories and a specified value, as shown in Figure 2-49. The

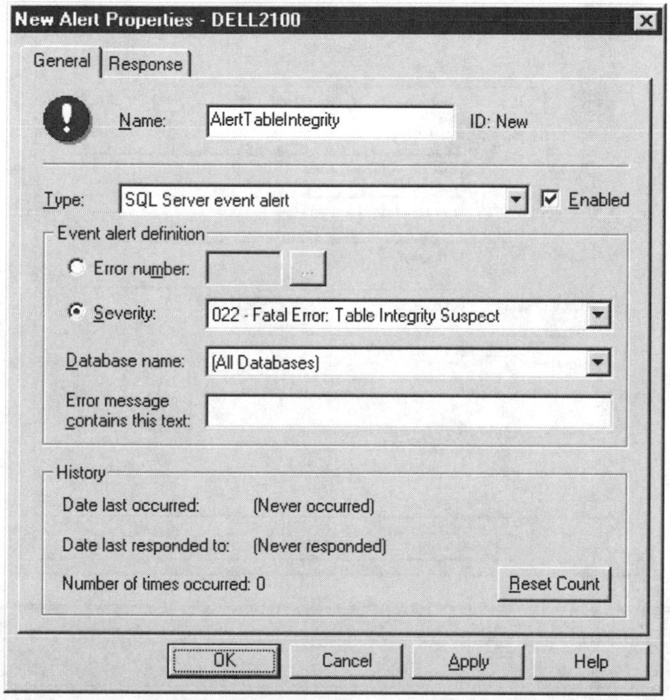

Figure 2-48.   Alert Properties dialog box – General tab (event alert)

"SQL Server Performance Monitor" section in Chapter 6 explains performance-related objects, counters, and instances.

The Response tab (Figure 2-50) lets you execute a SQL Server job or notify an operator. You can optionally include the error message text and your own customized text in any operator notifications. For alerts that may occur in close succession, you can avoid unnecessary (in some cases) multiple responses by setting a delay between alert responses. If the same alert condition is repeated within this interval, only one response will occur.

Creating a Job

As mentioned previously, a SQL Server job is a sequence of steps that perform various operations. To create a new job, right-click the Jobs container under SQL Server Agent in the Enterprise Manager and select New Job from the pop-up menu. The Job Properties

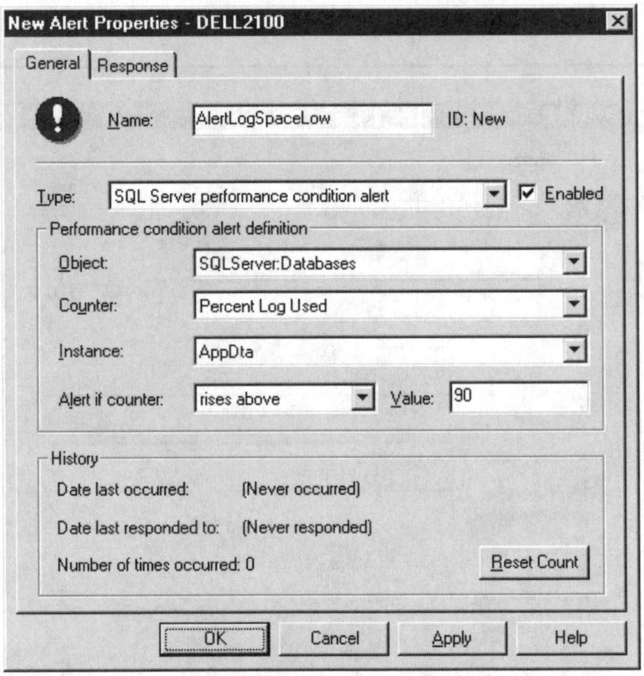

Figure 2-49.   Alert Properties dialog box – General tab (performance alert)

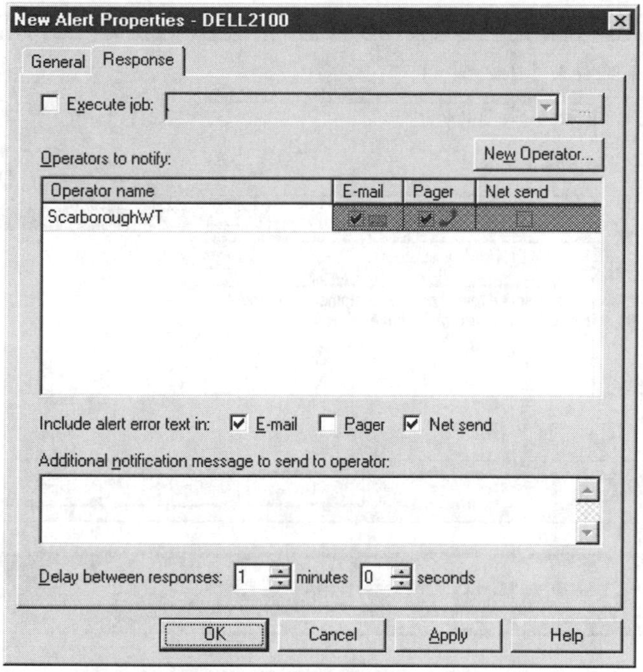

Figure 2-50.   Alert Properties dialog box – Response tab

dialog box (Figure 2-51) is displayed for this menu selection or when you double-click an existing job to display its properties.

On the General tab, assign a job name of up to 128 characters. You can enable or disable jobs with the check box provided. Select one of the job categories and an owner from the respective drop-down lists. For improved documentation, you can add a description for the job, as well. If this is the master server, you can select the Target multiple servers option and specify which remote servers should run the job; otherwise, the job runs on the local server.

The Steps tab (Figure 2-52) is where you define the actual work a job does. This tab has buttons to add, delete, and edit job steps, as well as adjust their relative order. You can also select the step at which a job starts, although this is normally the first step unless you're running only part of a job that didn't complete on its previous run.

Clicking the New, Insert, or Edit button displays a dialog box such as Figure 2-53 for editing the step.

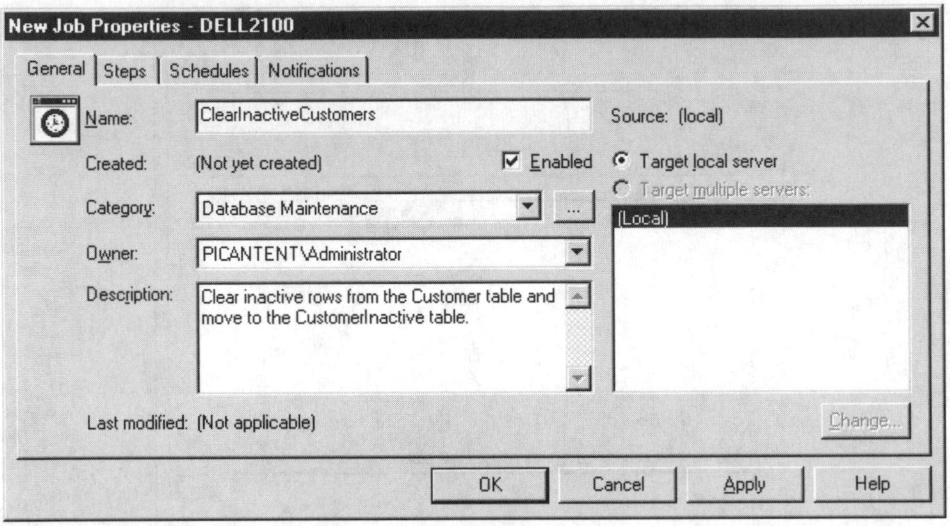

Figure 2-51.   Job Properties dialog box – General tab

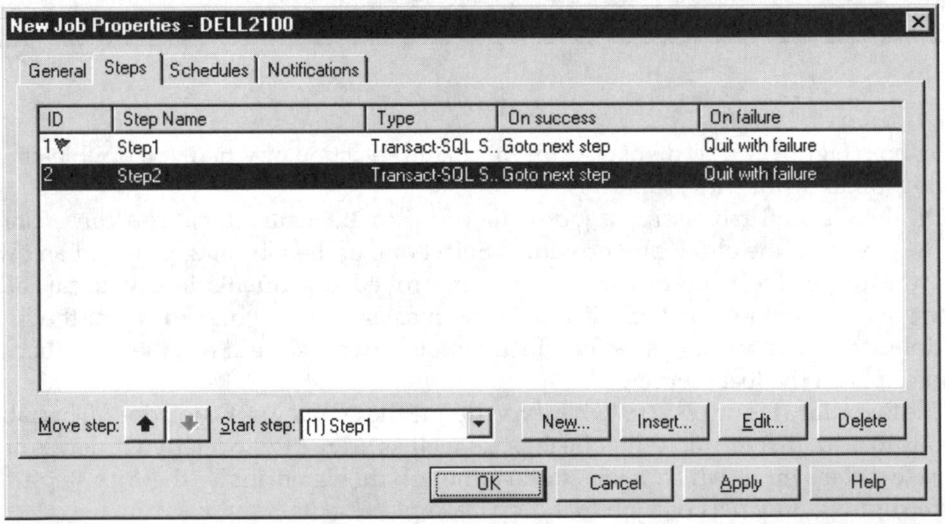

Figure 2-52.   Job Properties dialog box – Steps tab

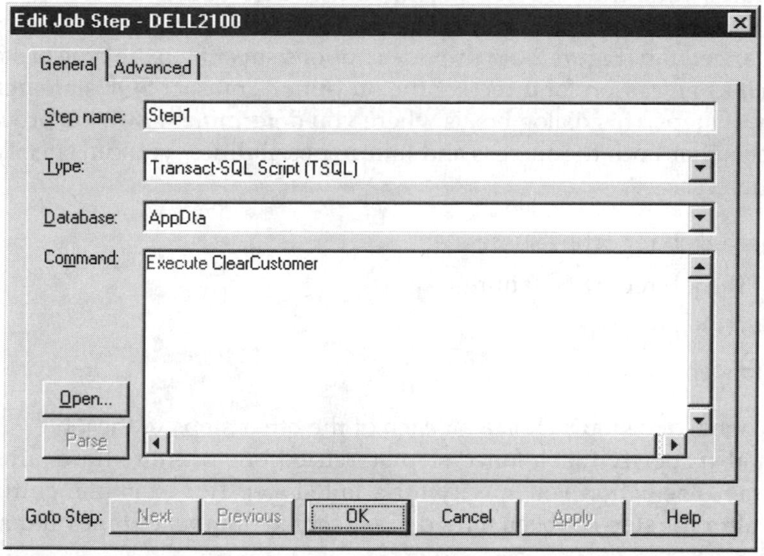

Figure 2-53.   Edit Job Step dialog box – General tab

On the Edit Job Step dialog box's General tab, you can provide a step name and select the type of executable statements that the step contains. The choices in the drop-down list are as follows:

▼ ActiveScript

■ Operating System Command (CmdExec)

■ Replication Distributor

■ Replication Transaction-Log Reader

■ Replication Merge

■ Replication Snapshot

▲ Transact-SQL Script (TSQL)

You can enter only one type of statement in each step, but a multiple-step job can contain different types of statements in different steps. Next you select a database from the drop-down list to be used as the current database (discussed in Chapter 10) when the step runs. The actual statements are entered in the Command text box. If you have some existing Transact-SQL or ActiveScript in a source file, you can click the Open button to read that source code into the step's commands. After you enter or make changes to Transact-SQL or ActiveScript, you can click the Parse button to check your code.

The Advanced tab (Figure 2-54) provides options specific to the type of statements in the step, such as an option for directing the output of Transact-SQL statements to a file. For all types of steps, this dialog box is where you determine how a job proceeds after a step completes. For both the success and failure possibilities, you can specify one of the following choices:

▼ Quit the job reporting success

■ Quit the job reporting failure

■ Go to the next step

▲ Go to step *n*

There is one Go to step *n* choice for each of the other steps in the job.

You can also specify that a failed step be retried one or more times after waiting a period of time. The action you specify for a failed step (for example, quitting the job) occurs only after the step has been retried the specified number of times and has failed on all attempts.

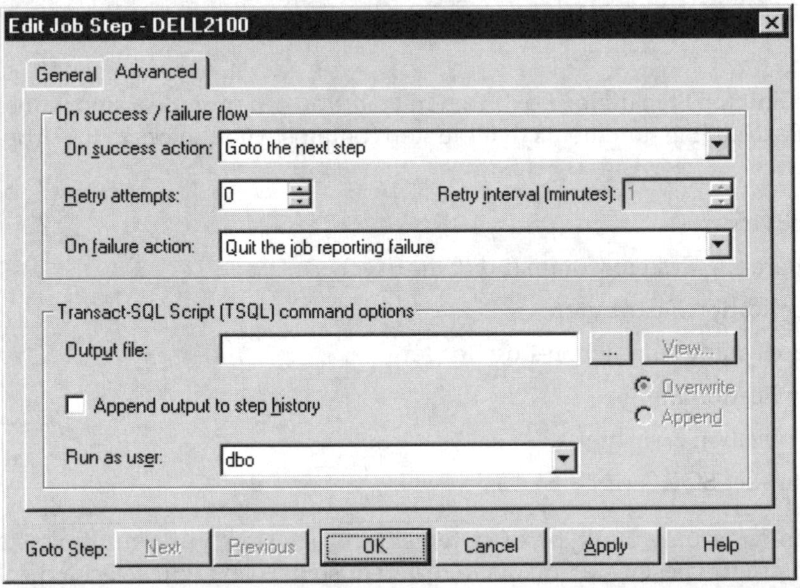

Figure 2-54.   Edit Job Step dialog box – Advanced tab

The Schedules tab on the Job Properties dialog box (Figure 2-55) is where you define when a prescheduled job runs. The Schedules tab lets you enter multiple schedules for cases where the options available for a single schedule don't cover all the times you need the job to run (for example, once every week and once on the first of the month). The list of schedules also displays any alert you've created with a response to execute this job. The New Alert button displays the Alert Properties dialog box (Figures 2-48 through 2-50), discussed previously, to create a new alert to run this job.

The New schedule or Edit button displays the Edit Job Schedule dialog box (Figure 2-56), where you define the schedule. You can define a schedule as *once* whenever SQL Server Agent starts; *repeatedly* whenever the CPU becomes idle (as defined on the SQL Server Agent Properties – Advanced tab; see Figure 2-42); *once* at a specified time; or *recurring*, based on your specification of a schedule.

If you select the Recurring option, click the Change button to set the schedule using the Edit Recurring Job Schedule dialog box shown in Figure 2-57. This dialog box provides hourly, daily, weekly, and monthly options for specific days or days of the week. You can also specify the range of dates for which this schedule is in effect.

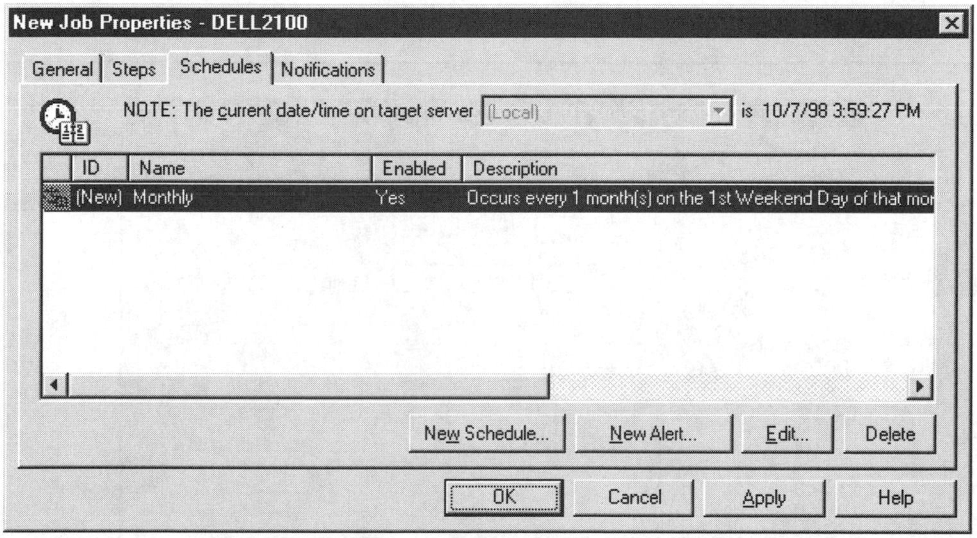

Figure 2-55. Job Properties dialog box – Schedules tab

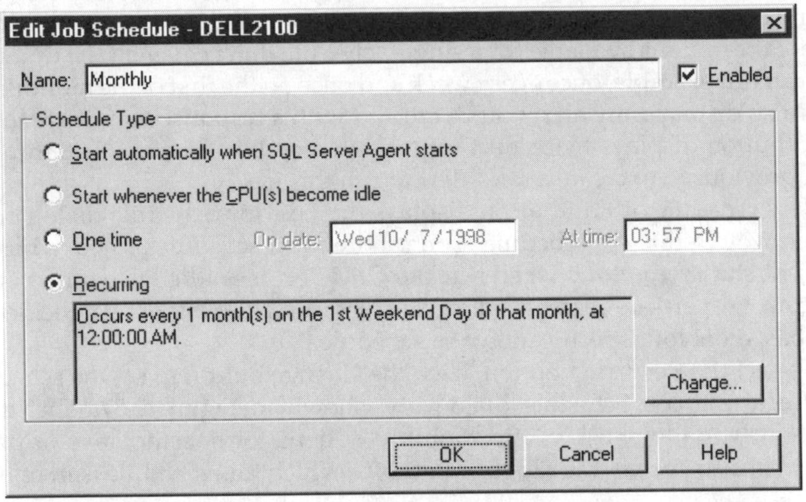

Figure 2-56.   Edit Job Schedule dialog box

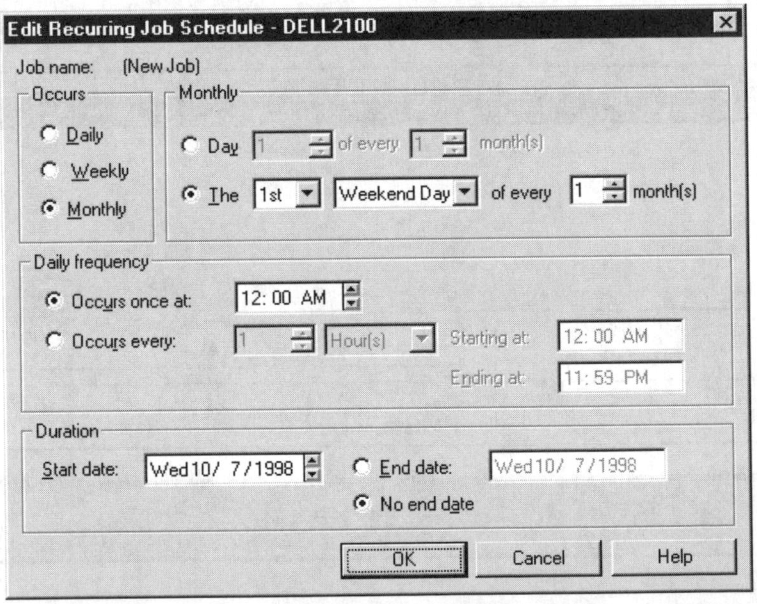

Figure 2-57.   Edit Recurring Job Schedule dialog box

On the Notifications tab of the Job Properties dialog box (Figure 2-58), you can specify that e-mail, pager, or net send messages be sent to selected operators based on one of three outcomes of the job:

▼ Successful completion

■ Unsuccessful completion

▲ Successful or unsuccessful completion

You can also have a completion entry placed in the Windows NT application log. For one-time jobs, you can have the job definition automatically deleted when the job completes.

Displaying Event Logs

SQL Server writes entries for various events in the SQL Server error log, as well as in the Windows NT application log. The SQL Server error log has entries for backup and restore operations, automatic recovery messages, and many of the other important activities of the database server. SQL Server creates a new error log each time you start a server. To view log entries, expand the SQL Server Logs container under a server's Management folder, and select one of the log entries displayed in the tree. The panel on the right of the Enterprise Manager displays that log's entries.

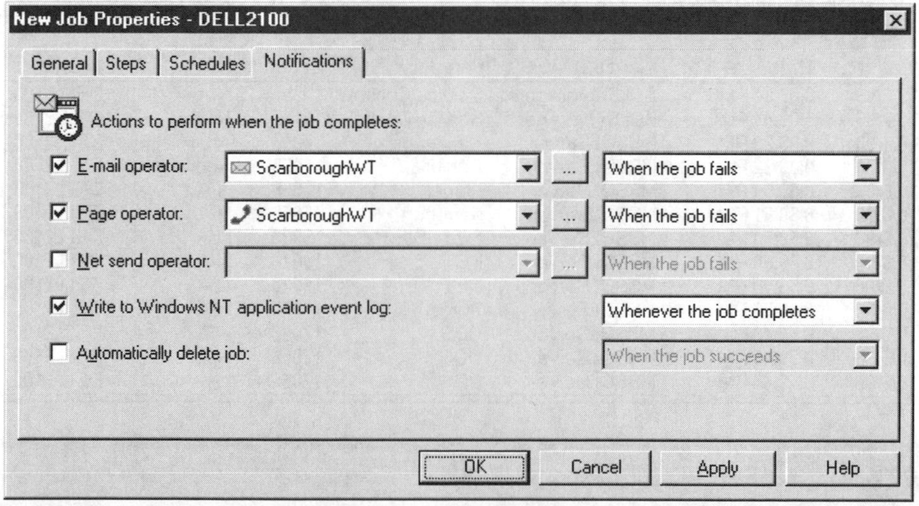

Figure 2-58.   Job Properties dialog box – Notifications tab

To view the Windows NT application log, select Programs | Administrative Tools | Event Viewer from the Windows Start menu. From the Event Viewer's main menu, select Log | Application to see application log entries (Figure 2-59). SQL Server entries have the name MSSQLServer in the Event Viewer's Source column.

Viewing and Creating SQL Server Messages

When an application performs database operations, SQL Server sends both informational and error messages to the connection. User-written stored procedures (covered in the "Stored Procedures" section of Chapter 10) also can send messages. The Tools | Manage SQL Server Messages option on the Enterprise Manager main menu lets you view and create messages in the sysmessages table using the dialog box shown in Figure 2-60. On the Manage SQL Server Messages dialog box's Search tab, you can specify which messages are displayed on the Messages tab (Figure 2-61). First enter a string to be found in the message text or an error number, or select one or more entries in the Severity list. Then click the Find button to display the list of matching messages.

On the Messages tab, you can click the New or Edit buttons to display a dialog box such as the one in Figure 2-62 for defining the message number, severity, text, language, and Windows NT logging.

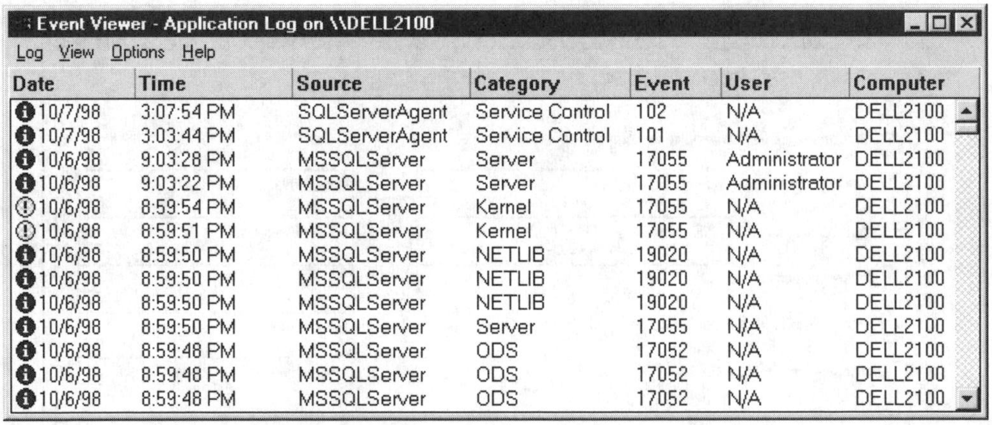

Figure 2-59.   NT Server Event Viewer

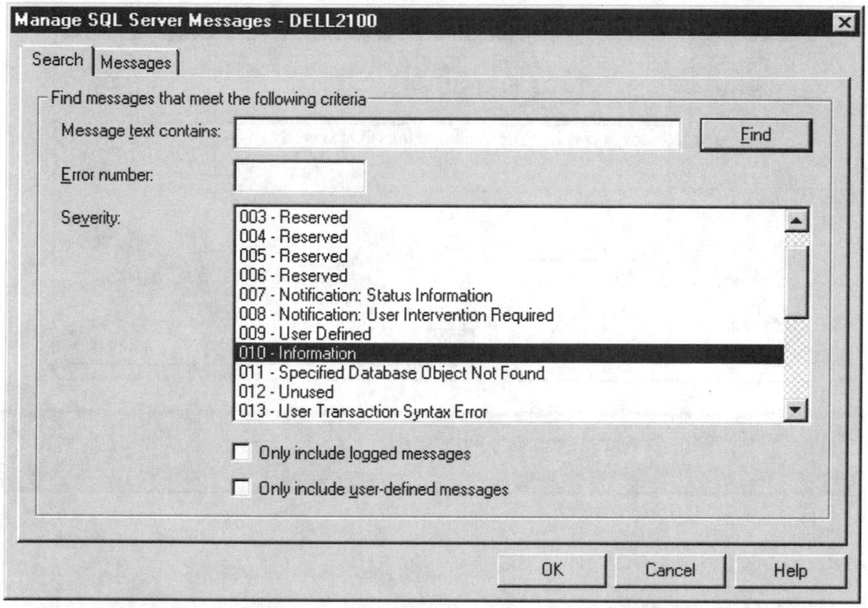

Figure 2-60.   Manage SQL Server Messages dialog box – Search tab

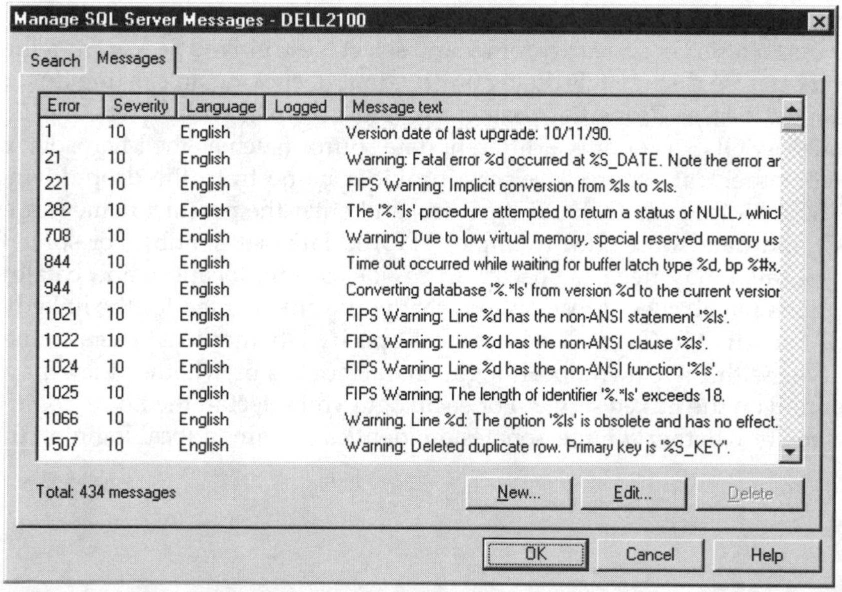

Figure 2-61.   Manage SQL Server Messages dialog box – Messages tab

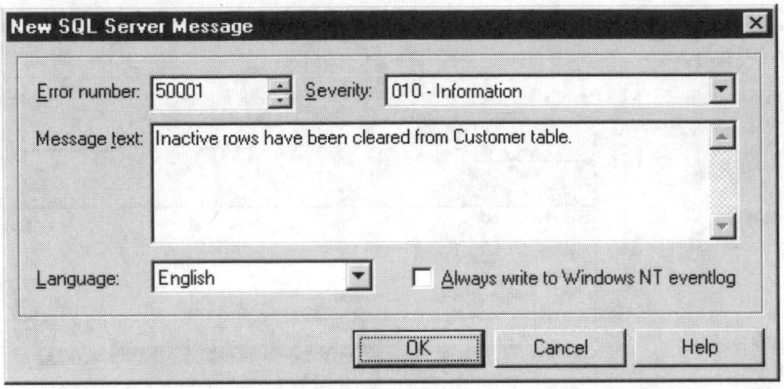

Figure 2-62. New SQL Server Message dialog box

Working with Linked Servers

A linked server is a *remote* server on which a client of the *local* server can execute SQL statements and stored procedures without having to explicitly connect to the remote server. The operation is routed to the linked server by the local server. A linked server specification includes an OLE DB provider and an OLE DB source (see Chapter 15 for information on OLE DB). To create a linked server, right-click the Linked Servers container under a server's Security folder and select New Linked Server from the pop-up menu. You can also display this dialog box by double-clicking an existing linked server. On the Linked Server Properties dialog box (Figure 2-63), specify whether the linked server is also a SQL Server or is a different data source (such as the Microsoft Access Jet engine). For other data sources, select a provider name from the drop-down list (for example, Microsoft Jet 4.0 OLE DB Provider) and enter the product name (for example, Access 97) and data source (for example, C:\proddata\sales.mdb). For some OLE DB sources, you also may need to specify a provider string, location, and catalog. In the Server options panel, check those options that you want enabled for the linked server.

On the Security tab (Figure 2-64), you can specify whether local users connect to the linked server with their own (local) login characteristics or whether they map to local logins defined on the linked server. For each login you select in the Local Login column, you can specify whether it impersonates an identically named local login on the linked

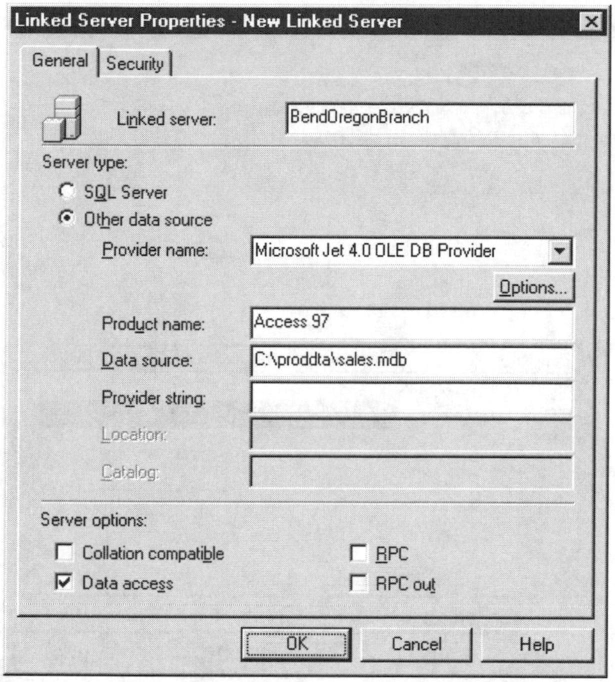

Figure 2-63.   Linked Server Properties dialog box – General tab

server, or you can specify a different local login name and password on the linked server to which the local login on this server is mapped.

For users who aren't listed in the Local Login column, you can specify the following: they can only connect without a security context provided by a login on the linked server, they must impersonate an identically named local login on the linked server, they all map to a specified login name and password on the linked server, or they can't connect at all. Once you've successfully created a linked server, you can expand it in the Enterprise Manager tree and see table entries when the linked server is connected.

Executing a query against a linked server uses a linked server qualifier for object names, in addition to the database and owner qualifiers, as discussed in Chapters 9 and 10.

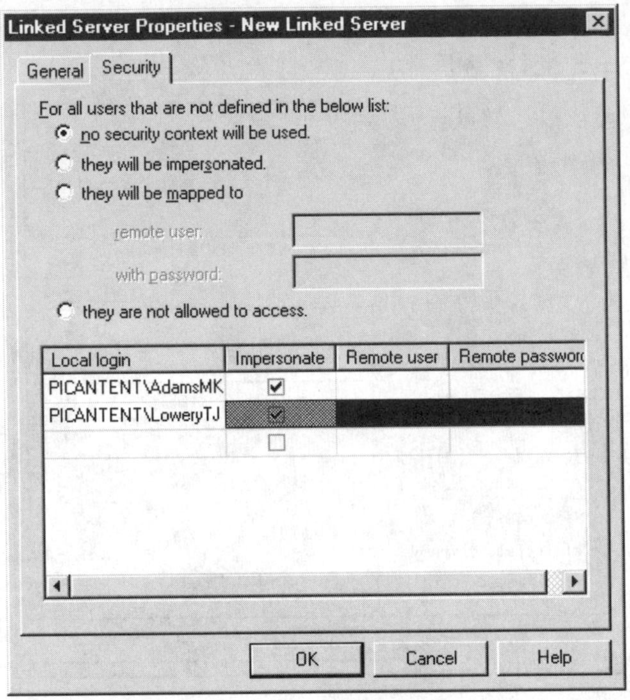

Figure 2-64. Linked Server Properties dialog box – Security tab

The following is an example of a query that accesses the Sale table on the linked server named BendOregonBranch:

```
Select *
  From BendOregonBranch.AppDta.dbo.Sale
```

Creating a Database Maintenance Plan

SQL Server has a Database Maintenance Plan Wizard to simplify the setup of scheduled jobs for backup and other operations. To run the wizard, right-click the Database Maintenance Plans container in a server's Management folder and select New Maintenance Plan from the pop-up menu. After the Welcome dialog box appears, the wizard lets you specify for which databases you want to create a maintenance plan (Figure 2-65).

When you click Next on this dialog box, a dialog box is displayed for any optimization actions you want taken when this plan runs. On the optimization dialog box (Figure 2-66), you can reorganize the Windows NT files used to store database data and

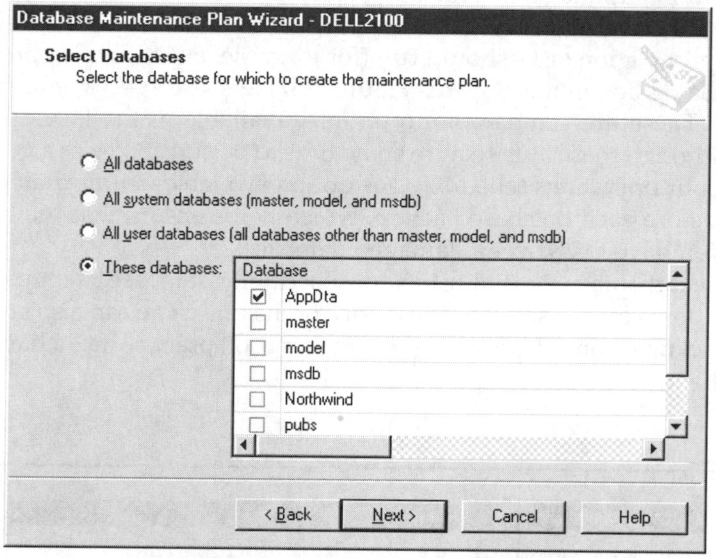

Figure 2-65.   Database Maintenance Plan Wizard dialog box (databases)

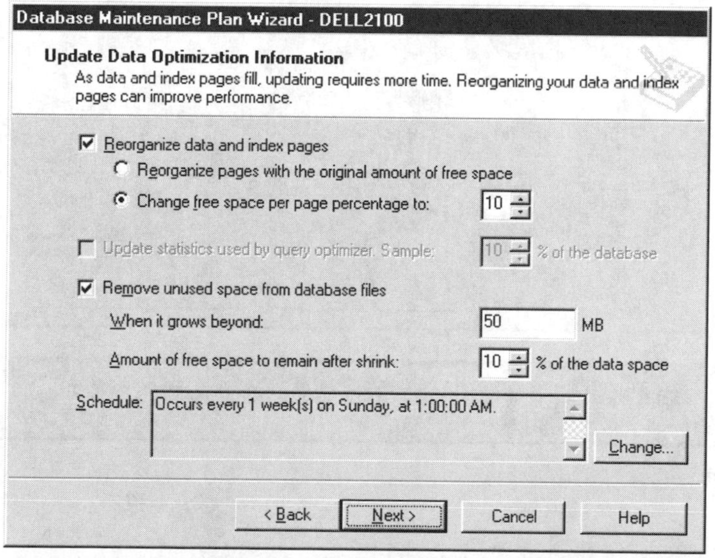

Figure 2-66.   Database Maintenance Plan Wizard dialog box (optimization)

index information, update the database statistics used by the query optimizer, or compress the size of the database file. On this dialog box, you can also specify a schedule of when the optimization tasks should run (for example, every Sunday at 1:00 A.M.).

The next dialog box in this wizard (Figure 2-67) lets you specify integrity checks on the database. (These are comparable to options available in the DBCC Transact-SQL statement.) Although these tests require some time to perform, they're a good idea if you have time in your operations schedule. One option available on this dialog box lets you run the tests before each database backup, which helps ensure that the backup can be used should you have to recover a damaged database.

Clicking Next displays the dialog box for scheduling database backups (Figure 2-68). On this dialog box, you can select a tape device or disk file. You can also specify whether to verify the backup upon completion—generally a good practice if you have time in your operations schedule.

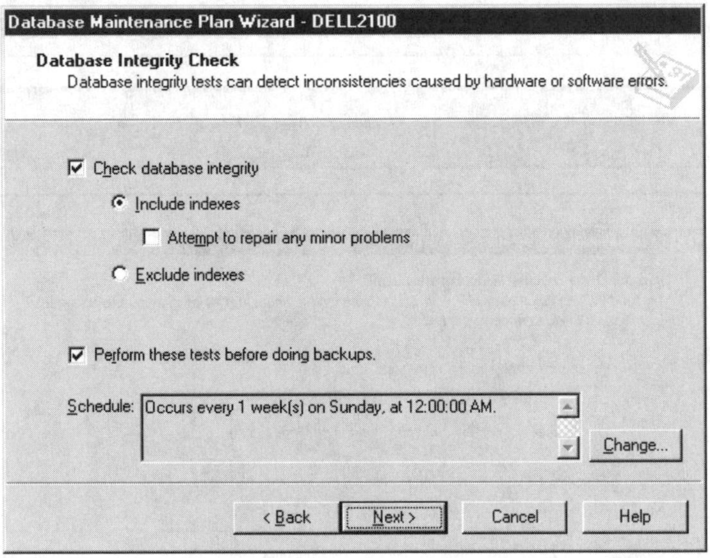

Figure 2-67.   Database Maintenance Plan Wizard dialog box (integrity checks)

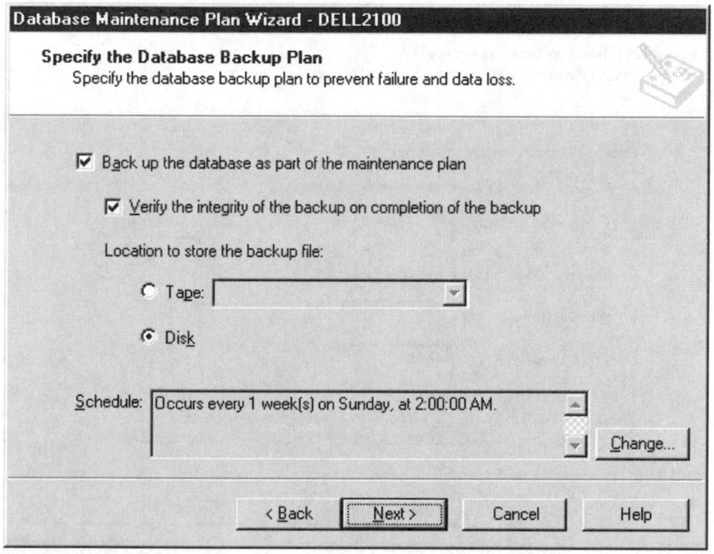

Database Maintenance Plan Wizard - DELL2100

Specify the Database Backup Plan
Specify the database backup plan to prevent failure and data loss.

☑ B̲ack up the database as part of the maintenance plan

☑ V̲erify the integrity of the backup on completion of the backup

Location to store the backup file:

○ Ta̲pe:

● Dis̲k

Schedule: Occurs every 1 week(s) on Sunday, at 2:00:00 AM.   Change...

< B̲ack   Next >   Cancel   Help

Figure 2-68.   Database Maintenance Plan Wizard dialog box (database backup)

If you select Disk as the backup location, when you click Next, the dialog box in Figure 2-69 is displayed so you can specify the location and extension of the Windows NT file that will contain the backup copy.

The next two dialog boxes (not shown) have fields similar to those in Figures 2-68 and 2-69 for specifying a backup of the transaction log. After the transaction log dialog boxes appear, a dialog box is displayed for producing reports about actions taken by the maintenance plan (Figure 2-70).

The next dialog box (Figure 2-71) lets you specify whether history data should be written to the local or a remote server. The final dialog box is a confirmation dialog box that lets you review your maintenance plan and give it a name.

Once you've generated a maintenance plan, you'll see one or more jobs listed in the Jobs folder under SQL Server Agent. You can manage these jobs (for example, you can change the schedule) using the Jobs Properties dialog box, as described previously.

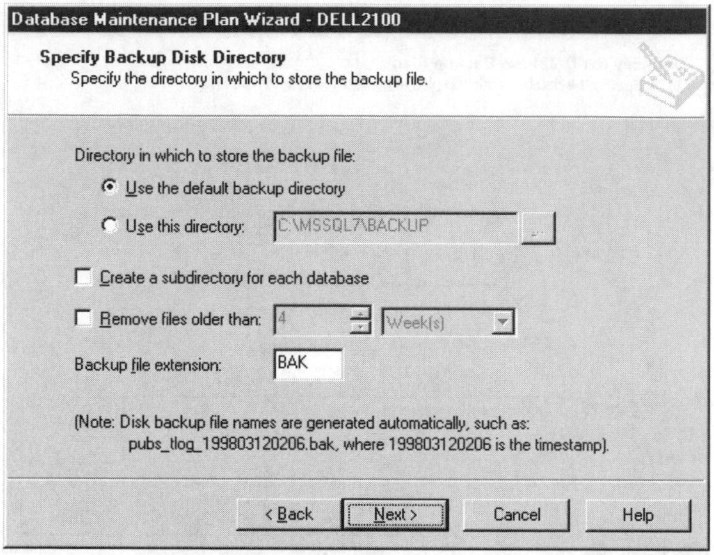

Figure 2-69.   Database Maintenance Plan Wizard dialog box (backup disk file)

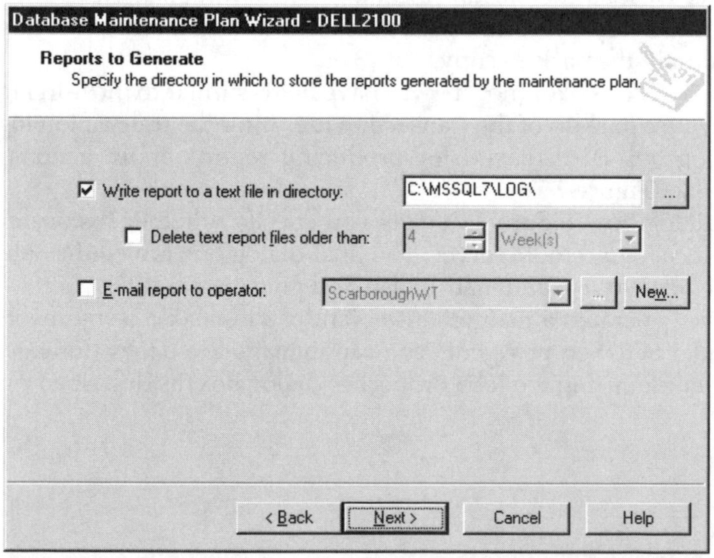

Figure 2-70.   Database Maintenance Plan Wizard dialog box (reports)

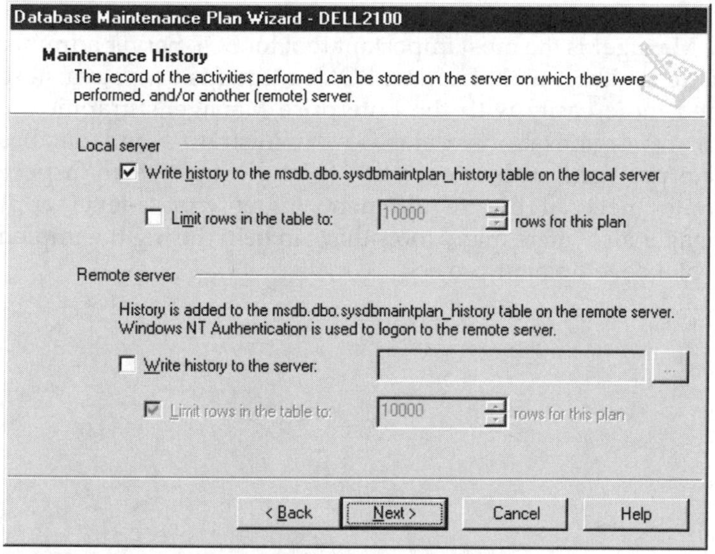

Figure 2-71.   Database Maintenance Plan Wizard dialog box (history data)

Other Enterprise Manager Facilities

The Enterprise Manager provides several additional facilities beyond those covered in this chapter:

▼ **Remote Servers container in the Security folder**   Supports a SQL Server facility available in previous versions but now superseded by linked servers. A remote server allows a client connection to execute stored procedures on a connected system; however, remote servers don't support distributed queries.

■ **Data Transformation Services folder**   Lets you manage DTS packages to import data to and export data from SQL Server databases.

■ **Backup container in the Management folder**   Lets you create and delete disk and tape database backup devices and view their contents, as explained in Chapter 4.

■ **Replication Monitor container**   Lets you manage replication publishers, subscribers, and agents, as explained in Chapter 5.

■ **Current Activity container in the Management folder**   Lets you display and manage SQL Server processes and locks, as explained in Chapter 6.

▲ **Web Publishing folder**   Lets you create, delete, and manage jobs that produce HTML pages from SQL Server database contents or that import data into a database from a Web page, as explained in Chapter 17.

CONCLUSION

The Enterprise Manager is the most important tool for SQL Server administration. Many functions that are available with Transact-SQL statements or system stored procedures can be managed more easily with the Enterprise Manager's graphical user interface. Although in many organizations, database administrators and database developers occupy separate positions, a developer has to understand many aspects of database administration to meet all the requirements of enterprise-level applications. The Enterprise Manager also offers many tools that can help during the implementation and testing phases of a development project.

CHAPTER 3

SQL Server Security

S QL Server, along with NT Server, provides a wide variety of security mechanisms to control access to the contents of a database. This chapter introduces the way NT Server and SQL Server implement security and how you can set up logins, database users, roles, and permissions to control the types of database operations people can perform.

SECURITY BASICS

Effective system security requires that people who use the system identify themselves when they log on to the system. A password is generally also required at logon to verify that the person is authorized to use the system. After logging on, a person's identity controls the type of access allowed. The system administrator or other person with proper authority grants or revokes different types of access permission to users based on their identity. For example, John Q. Smith might be granted read-only access to the Employee table. A user's identity also can be recorded in audit logs to track which actions the user takes.

Logging On to NT Server

Typically, when a person who's not already authorized to use an NT Server installation needs access to data and other resources, here's what happens. The organization's security officer or authorized representative uses the NT User Manager application to create a new *user* object with the person's user name, full name, description, password, and other properties.

> **NOTE:** A user object provides access to an NT domain or an individual computer. A *domain* is a set of computers that are treated collectively for security purposes. One computer within an NT 4 domain is identified as the *primary domain controller (PDC)* and maintains the security information for the entire domain. One or more computers can optionally be designated as a *backup domain controller*— one that maintains a backup copy of the security information and that can become the PDC if the original PDC is unavailable. The PDC and SQL Server can (and often do) run on separate computers.

A *user name* is the system identifier for a person, in NT Server terminology. For example, the user name for John Q. Smith might be SmithJQ. A user name and password are typically associated with a single person, so that you know who's responsible for any actions performed by someone logged on under a particular user name.

> **NOTE:** Some organizations may provide a person with two (or more) distinct user names and passwords so the person can log on under different user names and have correspondingly different kinds of access. For example, a person who works half-time as a payroll clerk and half-time as a computer operator might log on with SmithJQPayroll for one set of job responsibilities and log on with SmithJQSysOpr for the other set of job responsibilities. Although the NT Server group facility (discussed below) lets a single user name have multiple sets of permissions (for example, as a payroll clerk and as a computer operator), using a distinct user name for each set of responsibilities may reduce the possibility of inadvertent operations. For example, when logged on as SmithJQPayroll, the user couldn't accidentally perform operations that are permitted only to a computer operator.
>
> Some organizations also provide for "anonymous" access by creating one or more user objects (for example, with user name Guest) that don't require a password and which can be used by anyone with physical access to the system.

When someone logs on to NT Server, he or she must generally supply a valid combination of user name and password. After a person has logged on with a particular user name, that user name governs all access to other objects, including applications such as SQL Server. SQL Server itself has another layer of security, which can be managed separately or in conjunction with NT Server security.

Logging In to SQL Server

SQL Server has an approach to security similar to NT Server; however, there are differences between NT Server's and SQL Server's specific mechanisms and terminology. This inconsistency between NT Server and SQL Server can be confusing and requires some forethought when you set up security to keep security management simple. Table 3-1 lists various terms for NT Server and SQL Server security.

NT Server Term	SQL Server Term	Purpose	Notes
User (also referred to as user account)	Login	The object that contains the identity, password, and other attributes representing a user.	Note that a SQL Server *login* represents a user of SQL Server database services. A SQL Server *user* represents a user of a specific database.

Table 3-1. NT Server and SQL Server Security Terminology

NT Server Term	SQL Server Term	Purpose	Notes
User name	Login name (also referred to as login ID)	The identifier for the user or login.	NT Server user names can be 20 characters long, and contain any characters except " / \ [ ] : ;	= , + ? < and >. A user name can't be all spaces or periods. SQL Server login names can be 128 characters long, and can contain any characters except \.
Password	Password	A string that a user must provide in addition to the user name or login name when attempting to log on.	
N/A	User (also referred to as user account)	The identifier for the user of a database. When a user logs into SQL Server, the login name determines the corresponding user name(s) that the user is known by in individual databases.	SQL Server user names can be 128 characters long and can contain any characters except \.

Table 3-1.   NT Server and SQL Server Security Terminology (*continued*)

NT Server Term	SQL Server Term	Purpose	Notes
Group	Role	The object that contains the identity and other attributes representing a set of users.	An NT user can belong to an arbitrary number of NT groups. A SQL Server role may be one of the following: *Fixed server role (system-defined) *Fixed database role (system-defined) *User-defined database role A user-defined role is specific to a database (the same role name can be used in multiple databases, but the role memberships and permissions are not necessarily the same). A SQL Server user can be a member of an arbitrary number of roles.

Table 3-1. NT Server and SQL Server Security Terminology (*continued*)

NT Server Term	SQL Server Term	Purpose	Notes
Group name	Role name	The identifier for a group or role.	NT Server local group names can be 256 characters long and contain any characters except \. Global group names are limited to 20 characters.
			SQL Server role names can be 128 characters long, and can contain any characters except \.

Table 3-1. NT Server and SQL Server Security Terminology *(continued)*

Like NT Server, SQL Server requires a person to log in with a specific identity. You can configure SQL Server to automatically derive the login information from the NT Server user name or to require the user to explicitly enter login information. SQL Server uses the term *login name* (or *login ID*) for the identifier a user must explicitly or implicitly supply when logging in to SQL Server. The person responsible for SQL Server security (who may be the same person responsible for overall NT Server security) creates a *login* object for each NT Server user who should have access to SQL Server. (SQL Server also provides an option to create a single login for a group of users.) A SQL Server login is the object that contains the login name, password, full name, and other attributes that control access to SQL Server databases. Login names must be unique for each server.

NOTE: NT Server uses the terminology "log *on* to NT Server" whereas SQL Server uses "log *in* to SQL Server." They mean essentially the same kind of action: identify yourself and gain access to the available services and resources.

When an NT Server user logs in to SQL Server, SQL Server provides the NT Server user access to databases in which the login name is known. The system administrator or database owner makes a login name known to a specific database by creating a SQL Server *user account* in the database and associating the database user with an existing login name. A SQL Server user name must be unique within a database, and the same user name (for example, SmithJQ) in different databases can be associated with different login names, although this is not a recommended practice.

NOTE: A SQL Server user account is *not* the same as an NT Server user. This confusing terminology can trip you up when reading NT Server or SQL Server documentation. Keep in mind that an NT Server user name is the identifier for a user of NT Server, and is supplied along with a password when a user logs on to NT Server. A SQL Server user name is the identifier by which a SQL Server login name is known in a specific database.

So, to access a database, a user logs on to NT Server and then logs in to SQL Server. At that point, the user can access any database with a user name that has been associated with the login name. To control the specific types of database access a user has, the system administrator, database object owner, or other authorized user grants and revokes *permissions* to a database user (or role, discussed in the next section) in a specific database. This may sound a bit complex, but if you follow the guidelines to come, you can simplify NT Server and SQL Server security and most users can have a single identifier for NT Server, SQL Server, and all the databases they use.

Groups and Roles

Before we look at how to set up security, we need to cover a few other concepts, including *groups* and *roles*, similar features available in NT Server and SQL Server. NT Server has two kinds of groups: *global groups* and *local groups*. A global group is an object that has a set of NT Server user objects as members. A local group is similar, but can have global groups, as well as user objects, as members. For both types of groups, only users within the same domain as the group can be immediate members of the group.

A user object implicitly has all permissions that the groups it belongs to have. If a user belongs to multiple groups, the user has the union of all the groups' permissions. If a user belongs to a global group and the global group belongs to one or more local groups, the user also has the permissions of all the local groups of which the user is indirectly a member.

Thus, groups provide a way to simplify security management because you can create groups to reflect job responsibilities and authority and make users members of the appropriate groups. Then you can grant permissions to a group to indirectly grant the permissions to the group members. When you remove a user from an NT Server group, that user loses the permissions granted to the user as a consequence of membership in the group. An NT Server user can be a member of an arbitrary number of groups; however, groups can't be arbitrarily nested. Only one type of nesting is allowed: a global group can be a member of a local group. This restriction limits group membership to a maximum of three levels: a user at the lowest level as a member of a global group that is a member of a local group.

NOTE: In addition to providing limited group nesting, global groups provide a mechanism to grant permissions to users in a different domain. You can define a global group whose members are users within the same domain that the global group is defined in. That global group can then be a member of a local group in a *different* domain. By granting permissions to the local group, you indirectly grant the same permissions to users in the global group that's a member of the local group.

SQL Server roles have a corresponding purpose—simplifying security management—but operate differently than NT Server groups. There are three kinds of SQL Server roles:

▼ Fixed server role (system-defined)

■ Fixed database role (system-defined)

▲ User-defined database role

SQL Server provides seven *fixed server roles*, as listed in Table 3-2. Each of these roles has specific statement permissions that provide the capability for server-wide actions, such as managing logins and creating databases. You can't change the permissions granted a fixed server role, and you can't delete any of these roles or create new server roles. The system administrator or other authorized person can add and remove logins as members of each of the server roles. A login has all the permissions of all the server roles to which the login belongs.

For each database, SQL Server provides ten *fixed database roles*, as listed in Table 3-3. Each of these roles has specific statement and object permissions that provide the capability for database-wide actions, such as managing database users and creating tables. As with the system-defined server roles, all system-defined database roles, except public, have *fixed* permissions—you can't change the permissions of these roles. The database owner or other authorized user can change the public role's permissions. You can't delete any of these ten roles.

Role Name	Capabilities
dbcreator	Can create and alter databases
diskadmin	Can manage disk files
processadmin	Can manage the processes running in SQL Server
securityadmin	Can manage the logins for a server
serveradmin	Can configure server-wide settings
setupadmin	Can install replication and manage extended procedures
sysadmin	Can perform any operation for a server

Table 3-2.   Fixed Server Roles

Role Name	Capabilities
db_accessadmin	Can add or remove users to or from the database
db_backupoperator	Can back up the database
db_datareader	Can read all data from all user tables in the database
db_datawriter	Can insert, update, or delete data in all user tables in the database
db_ddladmin	Can create, alter, or drop objects in the database
db_denydatareader	Cannot read any data in the database
db_denydatawriter	Cannot modify any data in the database
db_owner	Can perform all operations on the database
db_securityadmin	Can manage roles and the members of roles in the database, and can grant and revoke statement and object permissions for the database
public	Can perform only those operations for which explicit permission has been granted

Table 3-3. Fixed Database Roles

The owner of a database, or other authorized user, can also create *user-defined database roles* and grant statement and object permissions to the role.

Each user added to a database is automatically a member of the system-defined public role, and the database owner can add the user name to any other roles in the database. User-defined roles also can be nested; that is, you can add a user-defined database role to another user-defined or fixed role in the same database. However, you cannot add any of the fixed database roles to another role, either user-defined or fixed.

The system administrator, database owner, or other authorized user can grant and revoke database permissions to SQL Server roles as a way to indirectly grant and revoke permissions to the role members. A user has all the permissions of all the database roles to which the user belongs, directly or indirectly, through a chain of nested roles. We'll look more closely at using SQL Server roles later in the chapter. For now the important thing to know is that both NT Server and SQL Server have a feature to group users, but the rules for NT groups and SQL Server roles are different.

System Administrator

NT Server has a user with the user name Administrator that can do *anything* with the system. Among other things, this "super user" can be used by an organization's security officer or other authorized person to create other NT Server groups and users, to add and remove members of groups, and to grant and revoke permissions.

NOTE: The Administrator user's capabilities and permissions can be granted to another user by making the user a member of the Domain Admins global group that ships with NT Server. The Domain Admins global group is a member of the Administrators local group, which has complete NT Server permissions.

SQL Server has a comparable system administrator login with the login name sa. The sa login is a member of the sysadmin fixed server role, which has all access to all SQL Server objects. You can add other logins or roles to the sysadmin role, but you can't remove the sa login from this role. Note that logging in to SQL Server with the sa login name doesn't in itself provide any special authority to NT Server objects not under the control of SQL Server.

NOTE: SQL Server ships with no password assigned for the sa login name. This allows anyone to log in as the system administrator. One of the first things you should do is assign a password to the sa login name.

Database Owner

In SQL Server, the login that creates or is given ownership of a database is known as the *database owner*. Within a database, the user name dbo is always associated with the login name of the database owner. Thus, if AppOwner is the login name of the login that owns the AppDta database, you'll see dbo listed as one of the database user names. You can't add a user name that's associated with the login name of the database owner. For example, in a database owned by the AppOwner login name, there's no way to add an AppOwner user name and associate it with the AppOwner login name. In other databases, not owned by the AppOwner login name, you can add an AppOwner user name and associate it with the AppOwner login name.

NOTE: In complex, multidatabase installations, the fact that SQL Server doesn't allow any user name but dbo for the database owner can be a bit cumbersome because it prevents using a single user name (for example, AppOwner) as the qualifier for *all* database objects owned by a particular login name. A better solution would have been for SQL Server to treat dbo as a synonym for the actual user name of the database owner, allowing qualification by either dbo or the actual user name.

The dbo user is always a member of the db_owner database role, and you can't remove dbo from this role.

Database Guest

When you create a new database, SQL Server initially creates a user named guest in the database. SQL Server lets any login access the database as this user name if there's not another user name in the database associated with the login name. The guest user name is *not* associated with any login name (not even a login named guest, if one exists). The guest user name is a member of the public role and can be added to other fixed or user-defined database roles, as well.

NOTE: You can delete the guest user to prevent anonymous access of the database. If you subsequently want to add the guest user to a database, you can use the Enterprise Manager, as described in the "Managing Database User Names" section later in this chapter, or you can use the following stored procedure to add a guest user name to the current database.

```
sp_adduser guest
```

SQL Server Security Modes

You can configure SQL Server to operate in either of two security modes:

▼   Windows NT authentication mode

▲   Mixed authentication mode

These modes determine how SQL Server uses the NT Server user objects when a user attempts to log in to SQL Server. Once a user is logged in to SQL Server, there's no difference between the modes, except that for Windows NT authentication mode, SQL Server can use NT Server groups to determine permissions, as discussed later.

Windows NT authentication mode uses the NT Server user name to determine the login name for all SQL Server login attempts. This mode requires that all clients have a *trusted connection* to the computer running SQL Server. SQL Server supports named pipes and multiprotocol as the network protocols for trusted connections. Trusted connections are available with clients running the following: Windows NT Server, Windows NT Workstation, Windows for Workgroups, Windows 9*x*, Microsoft LAN Manager MS-DOS and Windows 3.*x* clients, and Novell Windows 3.1 clients. If all of your SQL Server connections will use trusted connections, Windows NT authentication mode is a good choice.

Mixed authentication mode allows Windows NT authentication when possible, that is, over trusted connections. Otherwise, mixed authentication mode requires a user to log in with *SQL Server authentication*—that is, to explicitly log in to SQL Server by providing a login name and (usually) a password. If you may have nontrusted connections, configure SQL Server to use mixed authentication mode.

SETTING UP DATABASE USERS

Now that we've covered the basics, let's look at the steps involved in setting up the various security objects for your databases and people who will access the databases. After these objects are set up, you can grant specific database access permissions so people can work with the database according to your organization's security policies.

The steps required are

1. Plan your application databases, user names, database owners, and logical roles.

2. Plan your NT Server users and groups and your SQL Server logins, roles, and database users.

3. Set the SQL Server security mode.

4. Create NT Server groups.

5. Create NT Server users and add them to NT Server groups.

6. Create SQL Server logins for NT Server users and groups that will be members of SQL Server fixed server roles.

7. Create SQL Server application databases.

8. Set up user-defined database roles.

9. Set up the login names and database user names for NT Server users and groups who will be SQL Server application users.

Some of these steps are iterative; that is, you may repeat a sequence of steps when you add a database or additional roles.

Step 1: Plan Your Application Databases, User Names, Database Owners, and Logical Roles

It's very important with SQL Server to carefully plan which application databases, user names, database owners, and logical roles you'll use *before* you begin creating various NT Server and SQL Server objects. If you don't have a well-planned approach to your database organization, you may subsequently find it difficult to maintain a coherent set of users, tables, and other objects in the database.

NOTE: As you work through the next sections to plan various NT Server and SQL Server objects, you'll need to give names to many of these objects. You can make administration and application development much simpler by using only letters to form names and by keeping names to 20 characters or less. Names formed according to these guidelines will be recognizable everywhere with no special character mappings required.

Single or Multiple Databases

The first decision is whether to have a single application database or multiple application databases. For small- to medium-size organizations with closely related applications, a single database named AppDta will work. For larger organizations, or in situations where applications and their databases are supplied by different application software vendors, you may need separate databases, such as HRDta (human resources) and SalesDta (sales). Database names should be brief, clearly understandable, and use consistent abbreviations.

Identifying Users

For each person who should have database access, plan a unique identifier that will serve as the person's NT Server user name and SQL Server login name. As with other names, use only letters and limit the name to 20 characters. You can use any naming system you prefer, as long as it provides for unique names. One common system is to use the last name and initials, or as much of the rest of the name as is necessary to form a unique name. For example, for John Q. Smith, you can use SmithJQ.

SQL System Administrators

For a person that you want to allow access as the SQL system administrator, you may want to plan a second user name in addition to the person's normal user name. One user name (for example, SmithJQ) is used for normal database access. The other user name (for example, SmithJQSysAdm) is used for system administrator access. This allows a person to log in with the more limited capabilities of a normal user name, which can help prevent accidental use of operations that require a login with system administrator capabilities. When system administrator authority is required, the user can use the more powerful user name.

Database Owners

If you use a single application database, you need one special user name, such as AppOwner, defined just for the purpose of owning the database and all shared objects in it. For multiple application databases, you can use one or more special user names as owners. A single user name that owns all application databases simplifies management; and, by using SQL Server roles, you can allow different people to manage individual databases once the databases are created. On the other hand, separate database owners provide complete separation of responsibilities, for both creating and managing databases. Whichever approach you select, do *not* share a single user name and password among several people who manage databases, because this violates an important security principle—controlling and tracking access on an individual basis.

In most cases, a user name you create as a database owner should not be the user name for any individual person because the person responsible for a database may change from time to time. The database owner user name should remain constant. Use user names such as AppOwner, HROwner, SalesOwner, and so on, for the database owners. You can then use SQL Server roles (discussed next) to allow an individual to log in with his or her own user name and yet work as the db_owner (or other role) for a particular database.

Logical Roles

In any organization there's a distinction between individuals and their roles. For example, John Smith—the person—might have the following roles: "personnel department manager," "employee database administrator," and "annual company meeting committee member." There may be other individuals who have some of the same roles, for example, Betty Jones may also be an "annual company meeting committee member." The vast majority of a company's security policies are best expressed as a combination of roles people have and the permissions granted to roles. For a few exceptional cases, you may need to grant some permissions to a specific person.

Logical roles can be nested. For example, all "department managers" are "employees," and all "training section employees" are also "personnel department employees." A policy that grants permissions to a role such as "personnel department employee" implicitly grants the same permissions to a nested role, such as "training section employee."

The advantage to using logical roles is that you can make a person a member of a role or remove them from a role to control the person's permissions. This is a simpler way to manage security than having to grant and revoke complex sets of permissions each time you hire a person or he or she changes jobs.

As you plan your databases and database security, lay out the logical roles that are part of your organization's structure and security policies. As part of this documentation, include the nesting of roles, as illustrated with the previous examples. You should also plan for a few roles, discussed next, that are directly related to managing your databases.

System Administrator and Database Creator Logical Roles

Plan to have a SQLSysAdmin logical role that represents the responsibility for overall management of your SQL Server databases. People who perform this role will be given SQL Server system administrator authority. Also plan to have a SQLDbCreator logical role for database owners (discussed previously).

List the Members of Each Logical Role

Once you have your users and logical roles identified, document which roles a user has. This will result in a list of members of each role. Of course, this isn't a task you do only once. As people are hired and change jobs, you keep their role memberships up-to-date. You may also need to change the roles you've defined and their nestings to reflect organizational or security policy changes.

Step 2: Plan Your NT Server Users and Groups and Your SQL Server Logins, Roles, and Database Users

After you've identified users and logical roles, you're ready to plan the actual NT Server and SQL Server objects to represent them. Ideally, you should have a single, consistent NT Server and SQL Server implementation for users and logical roles. Unfortunately, this can be challenging because NT Server and SQL Server have separate and somewhat inconsistent security mechanisms. For small systems with simple security policies, an ad hoc approach may work satisfactorily. However, for more complex systems, you should make one key decision: whether or not to use NT Server groups. The basic tradeoff is that NT Server groups require more work, but they are the only way to incorporate your organization's logical roles into the security for NT Server resources other than the database. SQL Server roles are more flexible than NT Server groups, but they can't be used to define NT Server security. In the following sections, we'll provide you with guidelines for both alternatives. Later sections describe the steps to implement your choice.

Without Using NT Server Groups

If you don't use NT Server groups, all you need to do in NT Server is to create a user for each person and special user, such as a database owner. Then, in SQL Server, create a login for each of these NT Server users. For each login, create a database user in each database that the login should have access to.

To implement your organization's logical roles, use SQL Server's fixed server and database roles and create your own user-defined database roles, as needed. Finally, add logins to fixed server roles and add database users to fixed and user-defined database roles, based on the logical roles you've defined in Step 1.

> **NOTE:** SQL Server has an idiosyncrasy that makes this type of security setup more cumbersome than it should be when you have multiple databases. There is no simple way to define a person's role memberships in a single place. Instead, you have to add the person's login to fixed server roles, and you have to add the person's database user name(s) to fixed and/or user-defined database roles in every database that the person should have access to. It would be simpler if SQL Server let you define one object for each user and each role outside of any specific database. Then you could define role membership in a single place, rather than repeatedly in multiple databases. The use of NT Server groups (discussed next) can avoid some of this complexity; however, NT Server groups have their own complexities, as well.

Using NT Server Groups

If you decide to use NT Server groups to represent logical roles, you may have to compensate for the fact that NT Server groups—unlike SQL Server user-defined roles—can't be arbitrarily nested. You can only make a global group a member of a local group, which limits the depth of nesting to three levels: user–global group–local group.

How you use global and local groups also depends on whether your enterprise has multiple NT Server domains that may require authorization of users in one domain to functions in another domain. If you have only a single domain or you don't require cross-domain access, you can use global and local group nesting to implement nested logical roles. Otherwise, you should use global and local group nesting only to implement cross-domain access.

The simplest case is when you don't require cross-domain access and your logical role structure, defined in Step 1, has no more than three levels. If you're certain these conditions won't change in the future, you can use a direct mapping of your logical role structure to global and local groups. For nonnested logical roles, create an NT Server local group and add users to it; for nested logical roles, create an NT Server global group, add users to it, and then add the global group to the appropriate local group.

In the second case, when you don't require cross-domain access but your logical role structure, defined in Step 1, has more than three levels, you can use global and local group nesting for one layer of logical role nesting (as described for the previous case). Deeper layers of nesting, however, have to be implemented with a workaround, as you'll see.

In the third and final case, when you require cross-domain access, you should not use global and local group nesting for any logical role nesting. Instead, follow these four guidelines:

▼ For each logical role, create both an NT Server global group and an NT Server local group. NT Server requires unique group names, so adopt a convention such as adding the prefix "Domain" to the beginning of global group names.

■ Add each global group as a member of its corresponding local group.

■ Add users as members of global groups, not local groups.

▲ Grant and revoke permissions to local groups, not global groups.

These steps provide for cross-domain access. Putting users only in global groups lets you give any group of users permissions in a different domain by exporting the global group. Granting and revoking permissions only to local groups lets you grant these permissions to any global group imported from a different domain by making the global group a member of the local group. Note that you won't have these two general capabilities if you add some users only to a local group or if you grant some permissions only to a global group. To effectively grant permissions to users, this approach requires the second guideline listed above, which is to add global groups to corresponding local groups.

NOTE: It might seem that creating a global group and a local group for each logical role is extra work. However, because NT Server only lets you export a global group for subsequent import as a member of a local group, you have to create one of each type to enable full cross-domain access. If your enterprise doesn't require complete cross-domain access, you may want to use a simpler, ad hoc approach. But be careful to plan for ways that your enterprise requirements may change in the future, because restructuring group membership and permissions isn't a trivial task.

Implementing Nested Logical Roles with NT Server Groups

The second case in the previous section requires additional techniques to implement more than three levels of user and logical role nesting, and the third case requires similar techniques to implement any level of nested roles. In either case, when you cannot represent a nested logical role by using a nested group, you can add all members of the group for the *nested* role to the group for the *containing* role. Consider the case where the SmithJQ user is a member of the Manager logical role, and the Manager logical role is a member of the Staff logical role. Thus, Manager is the nested role, and Staff is the containing role. To implement the example user and role relationships, create a Manager group and a Staff group and add the SmithJQ user to both groups. These actions give the SmithJQ user the combined permissions of both groups. To manage permissions, you grant those permissions appropriate to all staff (including managers) to the Staff group, and you grant only those permissions appropriate to managers (but not staff) to the Manager group.

NOTE: An alternative approach is to make a user a member only of the group(s) corresponding to the most specific logical role(s) they have. In the example above, SmithJQ would be a member only of the Manager group. Then, for any group that's logically a member of another group, explicitly grant all the containing group's permissions to the member group. For example, grant all the Staff group's permissions to the Manager group (in addition to those permissions granted only to the managers). With this approach, you make an NT Server user a member of whichever group(s) provide the full range of permissions that the user should have.

However you handle nested logical roles, you should have an NT Server group for each logical role you've defined. In the first two cases above, you subsequently create a SQL Server login for each NT Server global or local group. In the third case, you create a SQL Server login for each NT Server local group only. (Recall that in the third case, every global group is a member of one or more local groups.) In all cases, you optionally create a login for each NT Server user, as well. You need a SQL Server login for an individual user if the user will own any database objects (for example, a table) or if the user is a member of multiple NT Server groups and the logins for those groups have different default databases (a login property that's discussed later).

For each login that maps to an NT Server group, create a database user in each database that the login (that is, the logical role that the login represents) should have access to. Finally, add these logins for groups to SQL Server fixed server roles (if appropriate), and add database users to fixed database roles, as appropriate. Other than for special cases, you don't need to create database users for logins that map to NT Server users (as opposed to groups), nor do you need to add database users to user-defined database roles. With the approach outlined here, you control most database access via logins for NT Server groups.

> **NOTE:** As we've outlined here, if you want to implement your organization's logical role structure in both NT Server and SQL Server, you must use NT Server groups as the implementation mechanism for your logical roles. This approach is necessary, because SQL Server can use NT Server users and groups, but NT Server can't use SQL Server logins and roles. This one-way relationship makes SQL Server's nested roles a somewhat superfluous feature for a comprehensive approach to NT Server and SQL Server security. Once you've granted permissions to NT Server groups and added NT Server users to NT Server groups, you need only SQL Server logins that correspond to the NT groups to represent all logical roles in SQL Server. If you define SQL Server roles, you'll just duplicate what you've already achieved with the NT Server group specifications. This is true, despite the fact that it's easier to implement nested logical roles with SQL Server user-defined roles than it is with NT Server groups, which have very limited nesting.

Plan the NT Server Group Membership for Each NT Server User

If you're using NT groups, list which NT Server groups you'll add each NT Server user to. Depending on how you implement NT Server groups to correspond to nested database roles, as noted in the prior discussion, you may need to add a user to more than one NT Server group for each logical role. For example, you may need to add a user to both the Staff and Manager NT Server groups if the user is a member of the Manager logical role, which is in turn a member of the Staff logical role.

Plan the SQL Server Role Membership for Each Login Name

For each SQL Server login name you've planned for an NT Server group or user, plan which SQL Server roles it will be a member of. If a login name should have permission for any of the server-wide operations, such as configuring the server, it should be a member of one or more of the fixed server roles that were listed in Table 3-2. If a login name should have access to a database, you should plan a corresponding database user, which implicitly adds the user to the database's public role. You can also plan to add the user to one or more of the database's fixed or user-defined roles if appropriate.

Plan the Default Database for Each Login Name

When people log in to SQL Server, they start out with the current database set to the default database associated with their login name or one of the logins associated with the NT Server groups to which they belong. For each login name, you need to plan which database will be the default. This is the database used for operations that don't specify an explicit database name. Be sure to plan for the login name to have an associated user name in the login's default database; otherwise, SQL Server will report an error during the login process.

NOTE: For Windows NT authentication of a login, SQL Server first searches for a login name that matches the NT Server user name. If a match is found, the default database specified for this login is used. If there's no match, SQL Server searches the logins associated with an NT Server group name to find a group that contains the NT Server user name. When one is found, the default database specified for the NT Server group name login is used. SQL Server searches the NT Server group name logins in the order the logins were originally added to SQL Server, so it's nearly impossible to control a specific person's default database when his or her NT Server user name belongs to multiple NT Server groups that have corresponding logins. For this reason, it's a good idea to create a login for each NT Server user who is a member of multiple groups, if the SQL Server logins for the groups have different default databases. Once you've created a login for the NT Server user, you can set the person's default database on this login.

Step 3: Set the SQL Server Security Mode

The previous two steps covered the planning for database security. With Step 3, you begin the implementation. You start by setting the SQL Server security mode either to Windows NT authentication or to mixed authentication, as described previously. Run the SQL Server Enterprise Manager and connect to SQL Server using the sa login name. From the main window, right-click the tree entry for the server and then select Properties from the pop-up menu. On the Security tab of the SQL Server Properties dialog box, select the appropriate Security item, as shown in Figure 3-1. For Windows NT authentication mode, select Windows NT only; for mixed authentication mode, select SQL Server and Windows NT.

Step 4: Create NT Server Groups

If you are using NT Server groups to implement logical roles or for cross-domain access, you need to create the groups at this point. If you're not using NT Server groups, you can skip this step. Log on to NT Server with the Administrator user name (or a user name in either the Administrators or Domain Admins group). Run the User Manager to create new NT Server groups. From the main window (Figure 3-2) you can browse users and groups. Double-clicking a user name or group name displays the entry's properties.

Create the NT Server groups (if any) that you planned in Step 2, including

▼ SQLSysAdmin, SQLDbCreator, and additional groups for any other fixed server roles that you plan to add members to (see Table 3-2)

■ For each database, one group for users (other than the database owner) who have database owner permissions; for example, SalesDtaDb_Owner

■ Groups for any other fixed database roles that you plan to add members to (see Table 3-3)

■ Groups for all user-defined database roles that you planned in Step 2

▲ Groups for other logical roles not covered by one of the previous categories

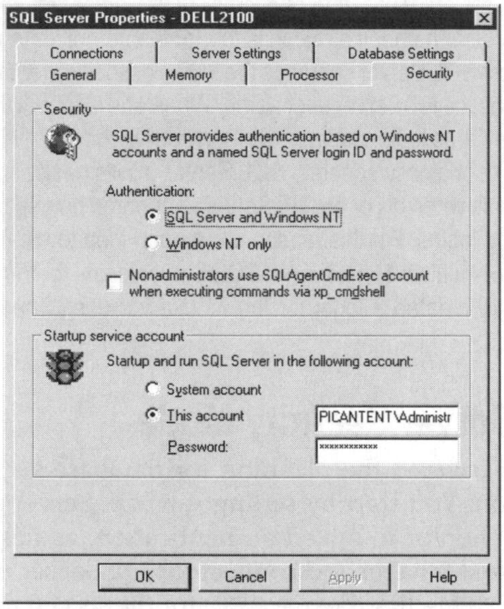

Figure 3-1. SQL Server Properties dialog box

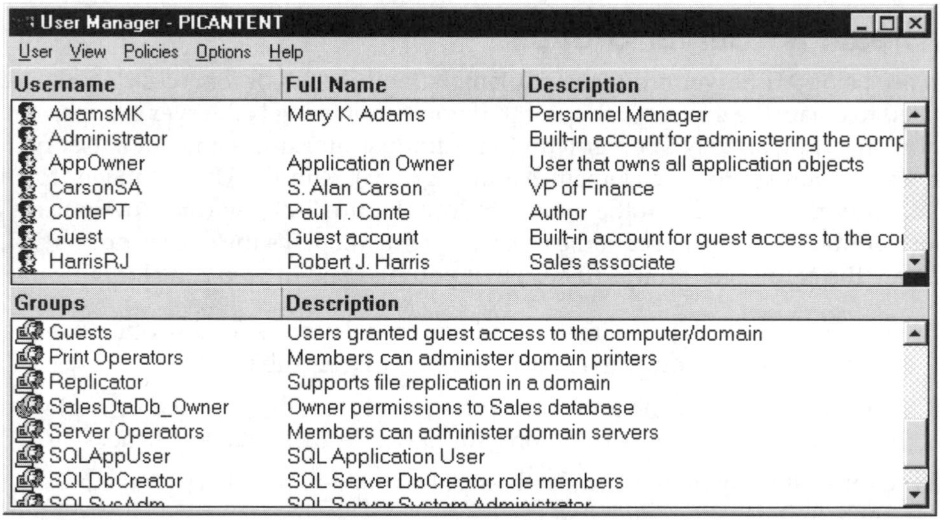

Figure 3-2. NT User Manager window

To create an NT Server local group, first select any group name in the Groups list. Then select the User | New Local Group menu item to display the New Local Group dialog box shown in Figure 3-3.

Enter a group name and description and click OK to create the group.

NOTE: If you click the User | New Local Group menu option while a user name is selected in the User Manager's user name list, the New Local Group dialog box will have that user name already entered in the Members list. This "helpful" feature can lead to unexpected group members if you're not careful. If you select any group name before you click the User | New Local Group menu option, the initial Members list will be empty.

To create an NT Server global group, follow a similar process, but select the User | New Global Group menu item to display the New Global Group dialog box.

Step 5: Create NT Server Users and Add Them to NT Server Groups

Once you've set up your NT Server groups (if you're using them), you can create NT users for people, and special users such as database owners, who are authorized to access the system. To create a new user, log on to NT Server with the Administrator user name, and run the User Manager. From the main menu, select User | New User to display the New User dialog box shown in Figure 3-4.

Enter a user name and password, along with the other attributes. The NT Server user name should be the identifier you planned in Step 1. If you are using NT Server groups,

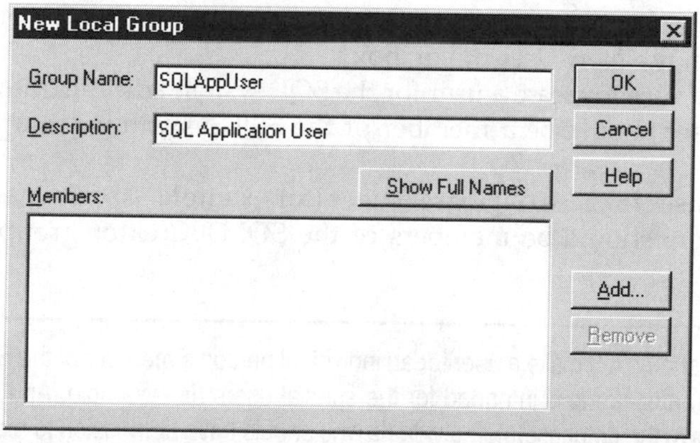

Figure 3-3.   New Local Group dialog box

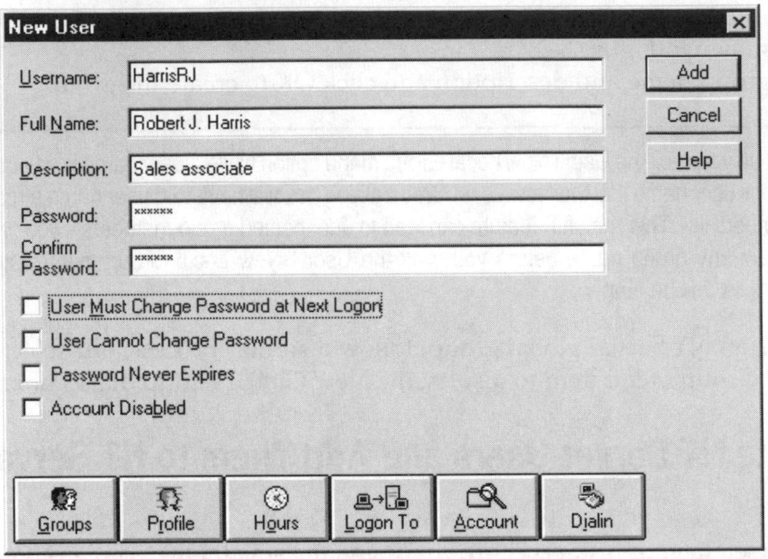

Figure 3-4. New User dialog box

you can add a new user to one or more NT Server groups by clicking the Groups button to display the Group Memberships dialog box shown in Figure 3-5.

On this dialog box, you can select from the groups listed under Not member of:, and click the Add button to make the user a member of the selected group. When you've finished adding the user to groups, click OK. To complete the creation of a new user, click the Add button on the New User dialog box.

In this step, be sure to create a user for the SQL system administrator(s) you planned in Step 1. This user should be a member of the SQLSysAdmin group (if you're using groups).

Also create a user for each database owner (for example, AppOwner) you planned in Step 1. These users should be members of the SQLDbCreator group (if you're using groups).

NOTE: You should not make a user for an individual person a member of the SQLDbCreator group. The SQLDbCreator group is intended for the special users (for example, AppOwner) you create to permanently own the database(s). Individuals who should have permission to manage a database will get the necessary authority via membership in the group (for example, SalesDtaDb_Owner) corresponding to the db_owner role for the respective database.

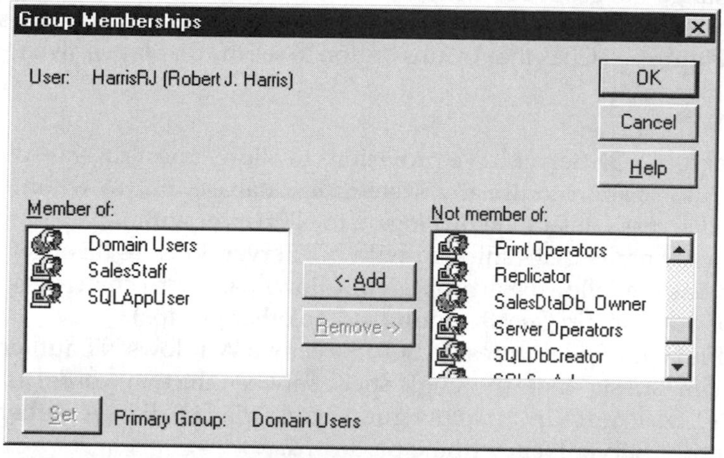

Figure 3-5.   Group Memberships dialog box

For all individuals and other special users you planned in Step 1, be sure to create NT Server user objects and make them members of the appropriate groups.

After you've added your original NT Server groups and users, you can add or remove members of a group by double-clicking a group in the User Manager main window to edit the group's properties (see Figure 3-6).

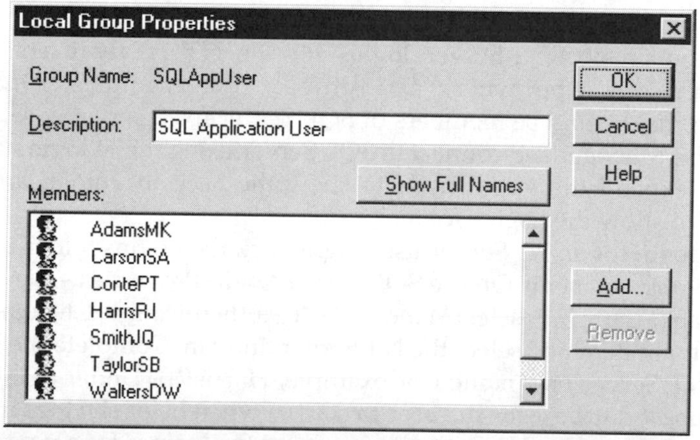

Figure 3-6.   Local Group Properties dialog box

You can change the groups to which a user belongs by double-clicking a user in the User Manager main display to edit the user's properties with a dialog box similar to the one shown in Figure 3-4. Click the Groups button to see the display shown in Figure 3-5.

Guest Users

Both NT Server and SQL Server have provisions to allow "guest" users—people without any explicit authorization to use the system or database, but to whom you want to provide limited access. To let someone log on to NT Server without a password, you can use the Guest user name that's shipped with NT Server. Be sure this user name has no password and has the following attributes: disallows password changes, is enabled, and is a member of the Domain Guests group (and no other groups).

To allow this type of guest access to SQL Server via Windows NT authentication, you can add "Domain Guests" (note the single space between the two words) as a SQL Server login for the NT Server group. To allow guest access via SQL Server authentication, just create a Guest SQL Server login with no password.

> **NOTE:** The name "Guest" has no special significance as an NT Server user name or SQL Server login name, but is a widely followed convention.

At the database level, recall that by default SQL Server lets any login access a database as the guest user name if there's not another user name in the database associated with the particular login name.

Step 6: Create SQL Server Logins for NT Server Users and Groups That Will Be Members of SQL Server Fixed Server Roles

In this step, you create SQL Server logins for the NT Server users (for example, SmithJQSysAdm and AppOwner) and groups (for example, SQLSysAdm and SQLDbCreator) that should be members of SQL Server fixed server roles. Run the SQL Server Enterprise Manager and connect to SQL Server using the sa login name. From the main window, expand the server node to show the Security folder, and expand the Security folder to show the Logins folder.

To create a login for an NT Server user, right-click the Logins folder and select New Login from the pop-up menu. On the SQL Server Login Properties – New Login dialog box's General tab (Figure 3-7), select Windows NT Authentication. Click the button to the right of the Domain field and select the NT Server domain. Complete the Name field by typing in the NT Server user name (for example, HarrisRJ). Under defaults, select the appropriate default database for the user to start in when he or she logs in.

Also, if you are not using NT Server groups, and the login is for a person who should be a member of one of the SQL Server fixed server roles, you need to add the login to the role(s) at this point. Click the Server Roles tab to display the list of fixed server roles

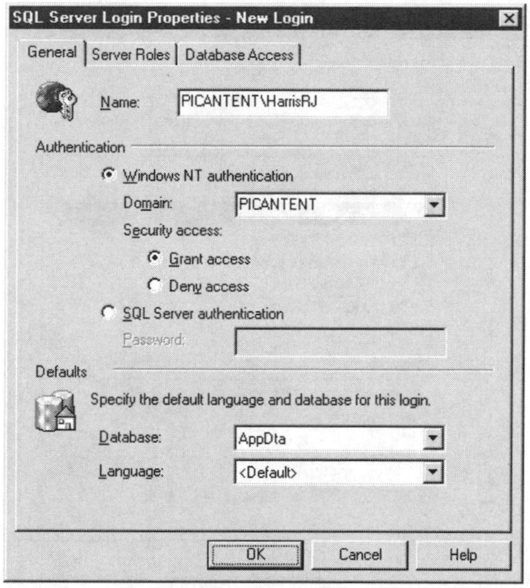

Figure 3-7. SQL Server Login Properties – New Login dialog box's General tab

shown in Figure 3-8. Then check the appropriate box(es) to make the login a member of one or more of the roles. Click OK to complete the creation of the login.

If you're using NT groups, you'll want to have logins for at least the SQLSysAdmin and SQLDbCreator groups, and possibly other groups that correspond to SQL Server fixed server roles. To create a login for an NT Server group, follow a similar process, except type in the group name to complete the Name field. Use the Server Roles tab to make the login a member of one or more fixed server roles. When you make this login a member of a fixed server role, all members of the corresponding NT Server group will then have the permissions of the role. For example, you should select the Database Creators check box for the SQLDbCreator login so that members of the SQLDbCreator NT Server group can create new databases. Once you've added the login to the appropriate roles, click OK to complete the creation of the login.

Step 7: Create SQL Server Application Databases

At this point, you should create the application databases you plan to use. The specific steps to create a database are covered in Chapter 9. Each database should be owned by the respective special user (for example, AppOwner) that you planned in Step 1. Because in Step 6 you made the logins for database owners members of the dbcreator role (either directly or via the SQLDbCreator NT Server group), these database owners can log in to

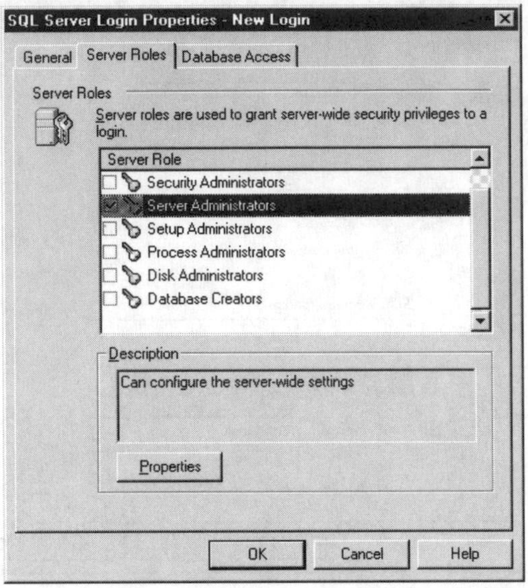

Figure 3-8.   SQL Server Login Properties – New Login dialog box's Server Roles tab

SQL Server and create a new database. This approach requires that a person actually log in under the special user name to create the database. Alternatively, the SQL Server system administrator (the sa login) can create a database and transfer ownership to a direct or indirect member of the dbcreator role. To transfer ownership of a database, run SQL Server Query Analyzer, set the current database to the database you want to transfer to another owner, and execute an sp_changedbowner stored procedure such as the following:

```
sp_changedbowner AppOwner
```

Either way you create the database, it will initially have the public and db_owner roles containing the dbo user name as a member. The dbo user name will be associated with the login name of the database owner. The public role will also have the guest user name as a member.

After a database has been created, the NT Server administrator should change the password for the database owner's NT Server user object (for example, the AppOwner user name). Once a database has been created, the person responsible for managing the database doesn't need to be a member of the dbcreator fixed server role to manage the database; all management of the database can be handled via membership in the db_owner fixed database role.

If you need to create additional databases after your initial round of setting up SQL Server, you should follow the sequence of steps that is presented here. The essential requirement is that a database must exist before you can add roles and user names to it.

With the approach outlined here, either the SQL Server system administrator must create a database and transfer ownership to the appropriate database owner login name, or a person must log in to SQL Server using the database owner login name (for example, AppOwner) and password and create the database. After a database is created, the person who manages the database should *not* use either the sa or database owner login name. Instead, the person should log in with his or her personal login name, which is a direct or indirect (for example, via the AppDtaDb_Owner NT Server group) member of the database's db_owner fixed database role, as explained next.

When a person is no longer responsible for managing a database, and thus should no longer have database owner permissions, the SQL Server system administrator should remove the user name from the database's db_owner fixed database role (and possibly other roles), if the user name was a member of the role. Also, the NT Server administrator should remove the person's NT Server user from NT Server groups (such as the group AppDtaDb_Owner) that provide indirect membership in the database's db_owner fixed database role.

Step 8: Set Up User-Defined Database Roles

If you aren't using NT Server groups to implement logical roles, you need to create the user-defined database roles at this point. Either the sa or a user with db_owner authority can create user-defined roles for a database. From SQL Server Enterprise Manager's main window, expand the server node and the Databases folder; then expand the specific database's folder to show the Roles folder.

To create a user-defined role, right-click the Roles folder and select New Database Role from the pop-up menu. On the Database Role Properties - New Role dialog box (Figure 3-9), enter a role name, leave Standard Role selected, and click OK.

To add a user-defined database role as a member of one of the fixed database or other user-defined roles in the same database, view the contents of the database's Roles folder and double-click the role that will contain the nested role. On the containing role's Database Role Properties dialog box (Figure 3-10), click the Add button. Select the role(s) that you want to add from the Add Role Members dialog box and click OK on both dialog boxes to complete the role nesting.

Step 9: Set Up the Login Names and Database User Names for NT Users and Groups That Will Be SQL Server Application Users

Now you're ready to use SQL Server Enterprise Manager to create login names for the remaining NT Server groups and (optionally) users that should have access to SQL Server.

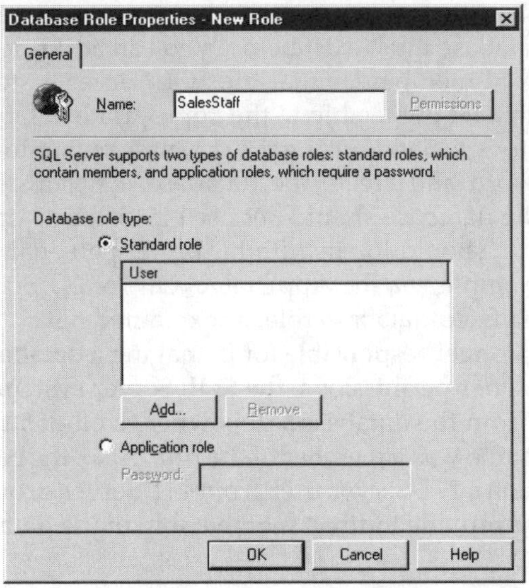

Figure 3-9. Database Role Properties – New Role dialog box

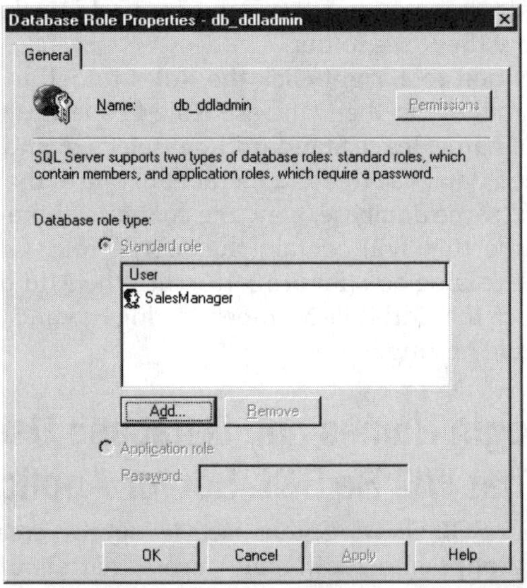

Figure 3-10. Database Role Properties dialog box

Run the SQL Server Enterprise Manager and connect to SQL Server using the sa login name. From the main window, expand the server node to show the Security folder and expand the Security folder to show the Logins folder. Follow the process described in Step 7 to add logins for the remaining NT Server groups that should have database access. If you are not using NT Server groups, you should also add logins for the remaining NT Server users who should have database access. Also, you should add logins for any NT Server user who will own database objects or who's a member of multiple NT Server groups that have different default databases. Be sure to specify the default database for each login for an NT Server user. The logins you add in this step shouldn't require any fixed server permissions. (Those types of logins were added in Step 6.)

As you add the logins, you can create the corresponding database users to add to the databases you created in Step 7. If you use NT Server groups to implement logical roles, for the most part you only have to add database users for the logins for the NT Server groups—NT Server users will get access to databases through their group(s). In this approach, you generally won't have user-defined database roles to deal with either, but you might still add some database users to fixed database roles because this is a convenient way to give the members of an NT Server group the same permissions as a fixed database role.

If you don't use NT Server groups to implement logical roles, you have to add database users for logins for NT Server users and then add the database users to appropriate database roles. Either the sa or a user who's a member of the db_owner role can add users to each database.

To add a database user as you create a login, on the SQL Server Login Properties dialog box, select the Database Access tab. This displays a list of databases, as shown in Figure 3-11. Check the box in the Permit column beside each database that you want to provide access to. Although you can change the name in the User column, it's better to leave it the same as the login name. A list of the roles in the currently selected database is displayed at the bottom of this dialog box. You can check the boxes for those roles the database user should be a member of. Be careful that you have the intended database selected as you select roles—this dialog box has a layout that's easy to make mistakes on.

You can also create a database user by working with the specific database. Expand the SQL Server Enterprise Manager hierarchy to show the folders under the database you want to work with. Right-click the Users folder and select New Database User from the pop-up menu. On the Database User Properties – New User dialog box (Figure 3-12), select a login name from the dropdown list and that name will appear in the User Name field. Generally, you should leave this name unchanged. Next, check the boxes for any fixed or user-defined database roles of which the user should be a member. Click OK to complete the addition of the new user.

Updating SQL Server Login Names

Whenever you add a new NT Server user who needs to access SQL Server, also add a SQL Server login for this person if the user will own database objects or is a member of multiple NT Server groups and the SQL Server logins for these groups have different

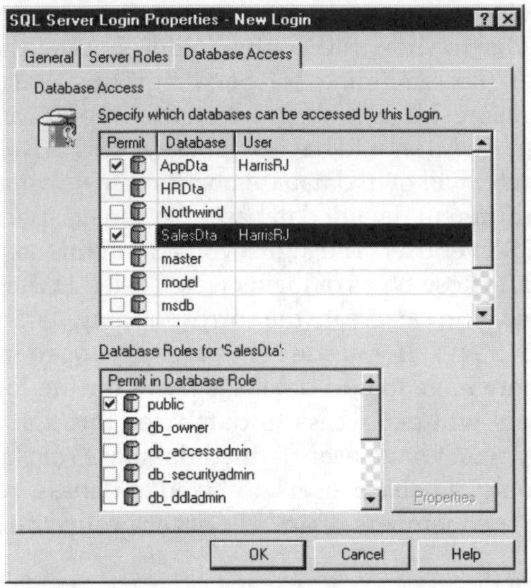

Figure 3-11. SQL Server Login Properties dialog box—Database Access tab

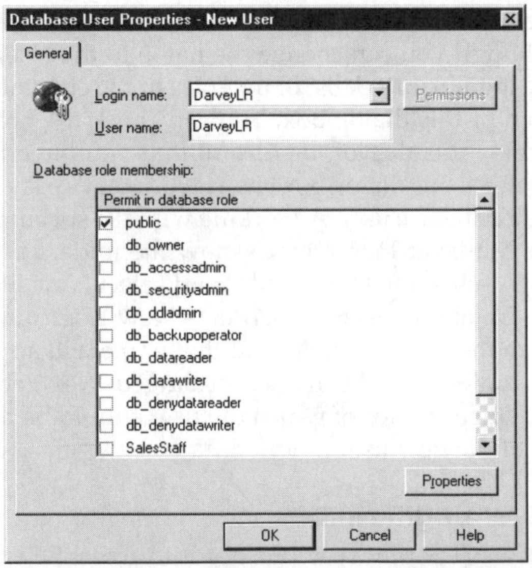

Figure 3-12. Database User Properties – New User dialog box

default databases. And, if you aren't using NT Server groups to implement logical roles, add a corresponding user to the appropriate databases, as described previously.

When you no longer want a person authorized to SQL server, you have to cover three areas:

▼   Deny access to the login for the user (if a login exists).

■   Remove the NT Server user name from any NT Server groups that have SQL Server logins.

▲   If the person also shouldn't be able to log on to NT Server, disable the NT Server user name.

You can deny access to a SQL Server login for an NT Server user or group by displaying the login properties in the SQL Server Enterprise Manager and selecting the Deny access option. For a SQL Server authentication login, simply change the password (and don't provide the new password to the user) to prevent access.

Use the NT User Manager to remove a user from one or more groups. Double-click the user name and click the Groups button to display the groups that a user belongs to. In the Member of list, select one or more groups and click the Remove button.

You can also use NT User Manager to disable an NT Server user. Double-click the user entry to display the user properties and check the Account Disabled box.

What You've Accomplished

By following the previous steps, you'll have set up SQL Server security so it's consistent with your NT Server security. Your system will be easier to manage than if you independently create NT Server users and groups and SQL Server logins and roles on an ad hoc basis. Here are the key elements of this recommended structure:

▼   For each person, the same identifier is used for the NT Server user name, the SQL Server login name, and all database user names.

■   Each database has a SQL Server login name (and a corresponding NT Server user name) that's the permanent owner, and this login name isn't the login name for any individual person.

■   Each database has one or more people who can operate as the database owner while logged in under their individual login names. You use SQL Server Enterprise Manager to add and remove database users, either for individuals or NT Server groups, from the db_owner fixed database role to control who can operate as a database owner.

▲   One or more people are able to log on to NT Server as a user who can log in to SQL Server and operate as the SQL Server system administrator. You manage who has this capability by adding and removing logins to the sysadmin fixed server role. You can either add and remove logins for NT Server users, or you can indirectly manage who has this capability through membership in a SQLSysAdmin NT Server group that has a corresponding SQL Server login that's a member of the sysadmin fixed server role.

Once you have your initial setup, you can add new users, logins, roles, and so on, by following the steps in this chapter. You also will need to remove some of these entries from time to time, as explained in the next sections.

Removing Users

Removing a Member from a Group

Use the NT User Manager application to remove an NT Server user from a group. From the main display, you can double-click a user name and then click the Groups button to display the Group Membership dialog box (Figure 3-13), from which you can add the user to or remove the user from selected groups. Alternatively, you can double-click a group name to display the Local (or Global) Group Properties dialog box (Figure 3-14), from which you can add users to and remove users from the selected group's members.

Removing a user from an NT Server group eliminates any indirect SQL Server permissions the user had because of the group membership. However, if there is a SQL Server login for the NT Server user, and the login is explicitly a member of any SQL Server roles, removing the user from an NT Server group doesn't remove the login or associated database user name(s) from any SQL Server role.

Use the SQL Server Enterprise Manager to remove a login from a fixed server role or a database user name from a fixed or user-defined database role. From the main window's tree list, you can display the contents of the Server Roles folder or any database's Roles folder. Double-click a role to display its Properties dialog box, as shown in Figure 3-15. From this dialog box, you can remove one or more users from the selected role.

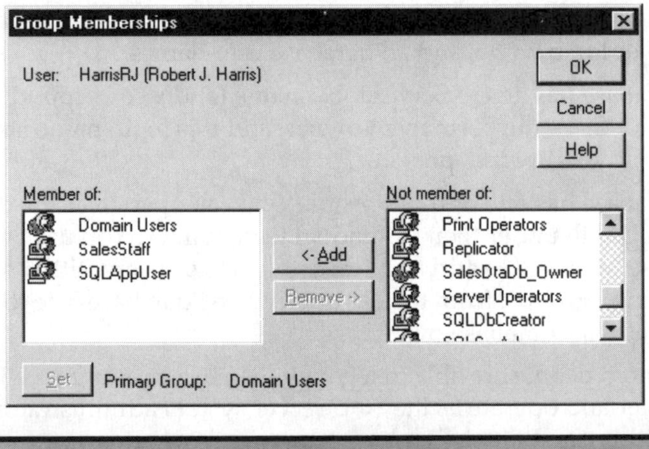

Figure 3-13. Group Membership dialog box

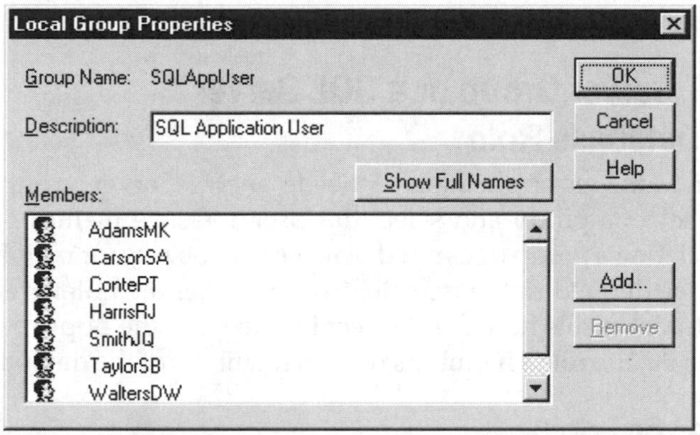

Figure 3-14.   Group Properties dialog box

Alternatively, from SQL Server Enterprise Manager's tree list, you can display the contents of the Logins folder or any database's Users folder. Double-click a login or

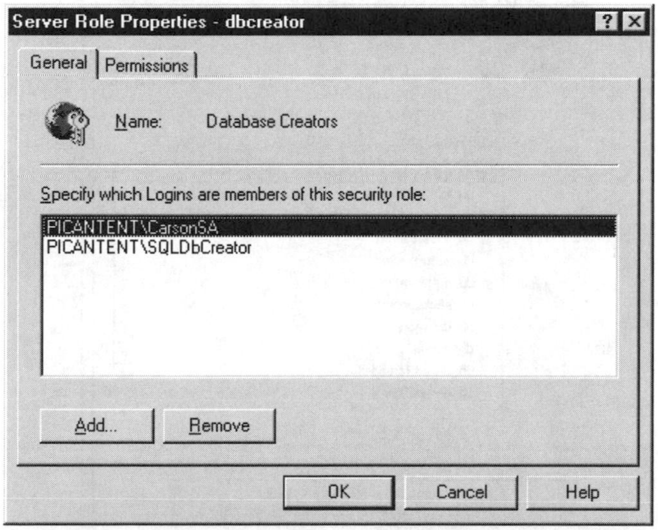

Figure 3-15.   Role Properties dialog box

database user to display the item's Properties dialog box, as in Figure 3-16. From this dialog box, you can remove a login or database user from one or more roles.

Deleting an NT Server Group or a SQL Server User-Defined Database Role

Use the NT User Manager application to delete an NT Server group. From the main display, you can select a group and select the User | Delete menu option to delete the selected group. Deleting a group does not delete the user objects for members of the group.

To delete a user-defined database role, from SQL Server Enterprise Manager's tree list, you can right-click a role name and select Delete from the pop-up menu. When you delete a database role, the role's members remain members of the database's public role.

Deleting a User or Login

Use the NT User Manager application to delete an NT Server user. From the main window, you can select a user and select the User | Delete menu option to delete the selected user. Deleting a user removes the user from all groups that the user was a member of. Deleting an NT Server user does not delete the corresponding SQL Server login name.

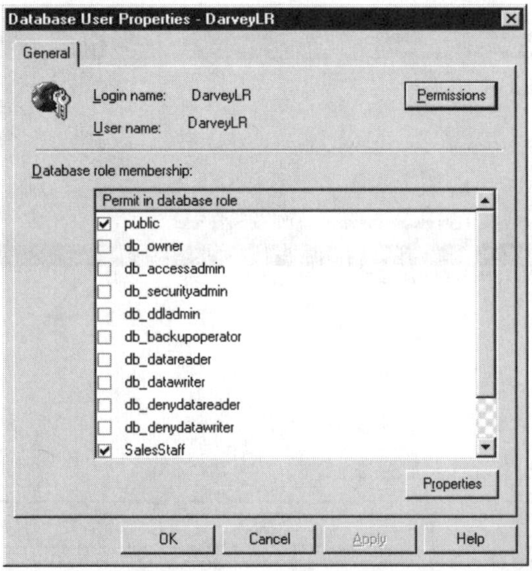

Figure 3-16.   Database User Properties dialog box

NOTE: As a preferable alternative to deleting a user, you can *disable* the user instead. To disable a user, double-click the user name in the NT User Manager and check the Account Disabled check box in the User Properties dialog box. The advantage of disabling, rather than deleting, a user is that you'll preserve a record of the user's full name and description, as well as prevent accidentally reusing the same user name for a different person.

To delete a SQL Server login name, open the Logins folder in the SQL Server Enterprise Manager's tree list, and then right-click a login name and select Delete from the pop-up menu. Deleting a login implicitly deletes all database user names associated with the login.

NOTE: You can't delete a user name that owns any database objects. You must use the sp_changeobjectowner stored procedure to change an object's owner. Generally, permanent database objects, such as tables and views, should not be owned by user names associated with a login name for an individual person. Otherwise, when the person is no longer authorized to access the database, you have to transfer the objects to a new owner before you can delete the user's user name(s) and login name.

Like NT Server, SQL Server lets you effectively disable a login name when it's defined as using NT authentication. Double-click the login name and select the Deny access option.

MANAGING DATABASE USERS

The previous section provides a recommended approach to setting up and managing SQL Server logins and database users in conjunction with NT Server users. With mixed security mode, you'll also have to set up some database login names, roles, and user names on an individual basis using SQL Server authentication. The SQL Server Enterprise Manager provides the most convenient way to perform these actions. Keep in mind the following requirements and guidelines:

▼ If you're creating new databases and new login names for the databases' users, create the databases first. Then create user-defined roles in the databases. Finally, create the login names. That way, you'll be able to create associated user names and assign them to roles at the same time you create a new login name. You'll also be able to set a default database for each login name when you create it.

■ You must create a login name before a database user name that's associated with the login name. (Both steps can be done from one SQL Server Enterprise Manager dialog box.)

■ You must create a database before you can create roles and user names in the database.

■ Create roles in a database before creating user names in the database. That way, you can add the user name to a role when you create the user name.

■ As far as possible, use the same name for the login name and all database user names associated with it. This is a simple, workable approach and avoids confusion. Even though SQL Server allows it, don't use the same user name in different databases and associate them with different login names.

▲ Use only letters in login, role, and user names, and limit the names to no more than 20 characters.

The following sections describe how to use SQL Server Enterprise Manager to perform various actions on login names, roles, and user names.

Managing Logins

To manage logins, select a server from the SQL Server Enterprise Manager tree list, expand the Security folder, and select the Logins folder to display the existing logins. You can double-click any login to display the Properties dialog box for it. Right-click the Logins folder and select New Login to display the Properties dialog box for entering a new login (Figure 3-17). To create a login that isn't based on an NT Server user or group name, enter a unique login name, select the SQL Server Authentication option, and enter a password. The rest of the creation process is the same as described previously for logins based on NT Server users.

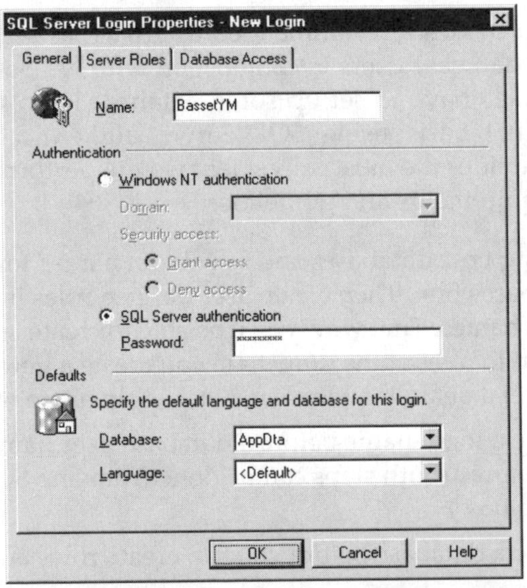

Figure 3-17.   SQL Server Login Properties – New Login dialog box

Managing Roles

To add and remove members of a fixed server role, select a server from the SQL Server Enterprise Manager tree list, expand the Security folder, and select the Server Roles folder to display the fixed server roles. You can double-click any role to display its Properties dialog box, in which you can add and remove logins as members.

To manage roles in a database, expand a database folder from the SQL Server Enterprise Manager tree list and select the Roles folder to display the fixed and user-defined database roles. You can double-click any role to display its Properties dialog box, in which you can add and remove database users as members. Right-click the Roles folder and select New Database Role to display the Database Role Properties – New Role dialog box for entering a new user-defined database role (Figure 3-18). In this dialog box, enter a role name and click the Add button to select members to add to the role. To delete a user-defined database role, first remove all members from it, and then right-click its entry in the Enterprise Manager and select Delete from the pop-up menu.

Managing Database User Names

To manage users in a database, expand a database folder from the SQL Server Enterprise Manager tree list and select the Users folder to display the database users. You can double-click any user name to display its Properties dialog box, in which you can add and

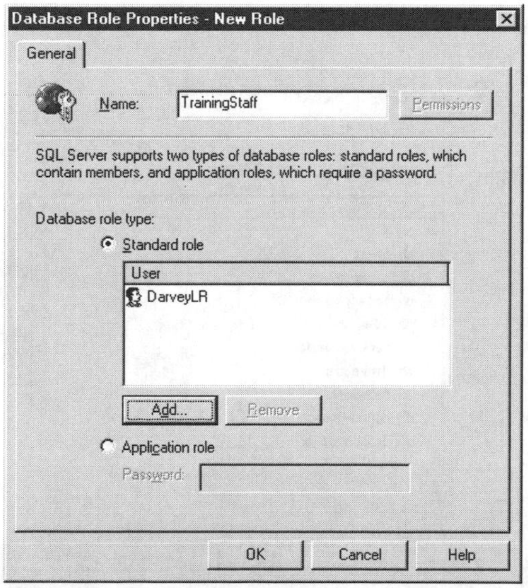

Figure 3-18.   Database Role Properties – New Role dialog box

remove the user as a member of the fixed and user-defined database roles. Right-click the Users folder and select New Database User to display the Database User Properties - New User dialog box for entering a new user (Figure 3-19). In this dialog box, select a login name from the drop-down list and leave the suggested user name (which is the same as the login name) unchanged. Select the database roles that the user should be a member of. You can click the Permissions button to display and set all statement and object permissions for the user.

NOTE: As discussed earlier in this chapter, it's generally better to manage permissions via logins for NT Server groups or via SQL Server roles.

To delete a user, right-click it in the SQL Server Enterprise Manager and select Delete from the pop-up menu.

USING STORED PROCEDURES

In the previous sections, we looked at using SQL Server Enterprise Manager to manage logins, roles, and database users. In most cases, the described techniques are the easiest way to work interactively with database security. At some point, however, you may want to write your own stored procedures that provide security management functions.

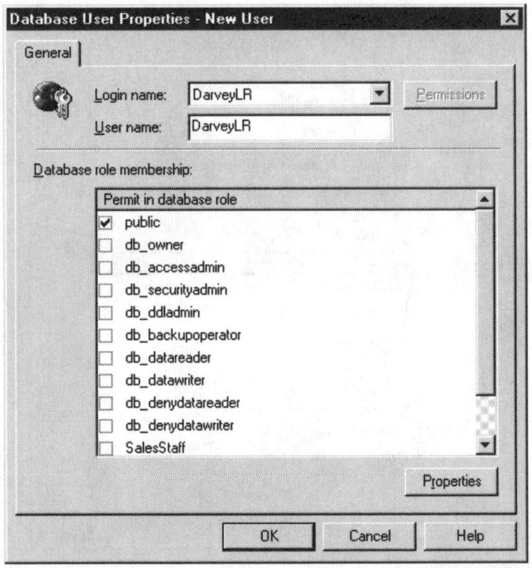

Figure 3-19.   Database User Properties – New User dialog box

Table 3-4 provides a list of available SQL Server stored procedures related to security, which you can use either interactively with SQL Server Query Analyzer or call from your own stored procedures. Full documentation of these stored procedures is in the *Microsoft Transact-SQL Reference* manual.

Stored Procedure	Purpose
sp_addapprole	Add an application role to the current database.
sp_addlogin	Add a login.
sp_addremotelogin	Add a remote login.
sp_addrole	Add a role to the current database.
sp_addrolemember	Add a user or role as a member of a role in the current database.
sp_addsrvrolemember	Add a user or role as a member of a fixed server role.
sp_approlepassword	Change an application role password.
sp_change_users_login	Change the relationship between a login and a user in the current database.
sp_changedbowner	Change the owner of the current database.
sp_changeobjectowner	Change the owner of an object in the current database.
sp_column_privileges	List column privileges (permissions) for a table.
sp_column_privileges_ex	List column privileges (permissions) for a table on a linked server.
sp_databases	List existing databases.
sp_dbfixedrolepermission	List permissions for a fixed database role.
sp_defaultdb	Change the default database for a login name.
sp_defaultlanguage	Change the default language for a login name.
sp_denylogin	Prevent an NT Server user or group from logging in to SQL Server.
sp_dropapprole	Drop an application role from the current database.
sp_droplogin	Drop a login.
sp_dropremotelogin	Drop a remote login.

Table 3-4.   SQL Server Security-Related Stored Procedures

Stored Procedure	Purpose
sp_droprole	Drop a role from the current database.
sp_droprolemember	Drop a user or role as a member of a role in the current database.
sp_dropsrvrolemember	Drop a user or role as a member of a fixed server role.
sp_grantdbaccess	Add a user in the current database for the specified login.
sp_grantlogin	Allow an NT Server user or group to log in to SQL Server.
sp_helpdb	Report information on one or more databases.
sp_helpdbfixedrole	Report the fixed roles in the current database.
sp_helplogins	Report information on logins.
sp_helpntgroup	Report information on NT Server groups with corresponding users in the current database.
sp_helpremotelogin	Report information on remote logins.
sp_helprole	Report information on roles in the current database.
sp_helprolemember	Report information on a role's members in the current database.
sp_helpsrvrole	Report information on fixed server roles.
sp_helpsrvrolemember	Report information on a fixed server role's members.
sp_helpuser	Report information on users in the current database.
sp_password	Change the password for a login name.
sp_revokedbaccess	Remove a database user from the current database.
sp_revokelogin	Remove an NT Server user or group login from SQL Server.
sp_setapprole	Activate the permissions associated with an application role in the current database.
sp_srvrolepermission	Report the permissions for a fixed server role.

Table 3-4. SQL Server Security-Related Stored Procedures (*continued*)

Stored Procedure	Purpose
sp_table_privileges	Report the privileges (permissions) associated with tables in the specified database.
sp_table_privileges_ex	Report the privileges (permissions) associated with tables in the specified database on a linked server.
sp_validatelogins	Report NT Server users and groups that are in SQL Server system tables but no longer exist in the NT Server environment.
xp_enumgroups	List NT Server groups.
xp_loginconfig	Report SQL Server and NT Server login configuration information.
xp_logininfo	Report information about an NT Server user or group.

Table 3-4. SQL Server Security-Related Stored Procedures (*continued*)

There are also several Transact-SQL functions that you can use in Select and other statements for information about the database users. SQL statements and the functions listed in Table 3-5 are discussed more fully in Chapters 9 and 10.

Function	Purpose
Current_User Session_User User	The database user name of the user executing the statement.
IsMember(*NTgroup-or-SQLrole*)	Returns 1 if current user is a member of the specified NT Server group or the SQL Server role; returns 0 if the user is not a member.
IsSrvRoleMember(*fixed-server-role*, *login*)	Returns 1 if specified login is a member of the specified fixed server role; returns 0 if the login is not a member. The *login* is optional; the default is the login for the current user.

Table 3-5. Transact-SQL Security-Related Functions

Function	Purpose
Permissions(*object-id, column*)	Returns a bitmap indicating the current user's permissions for the specified object and (optionally) column.
SUser_SID(*login*)	Returns the internal security ID (SID) of the specified server *login*. The *login* is optional; the default is the login for the current user.
SUser_SName(*security-id*)	Returns the login name of the specified internal *security-id* (SID). The *security-id* is optional; the default is the security ID of the login for the current user.
System_User	Returns the login name of the user executing the statement.
User_ID(*user-name*)	Returns the internal ID of the specified database *user-name*. The *user-name* is optional; the default is the current user.
User_Name(*user-id*)	The database user name of the specified internal database *user-id*. The *user-id* is optional; the default is the internal ID of the current user.

Table 3-5. Transact-SQL Security-Related Functions (*continued*)

PERMISSIONS

All SQL Server operations are controlled by the *permissions* granted or denied to a user name or role. There are two kinds of permissions:

▼ Statement permissions

▲ Object permissions

Statement permissions allow the execution of specific SQL statements, such as Create Database. Object permissions allow different types of access (for example, update access) to specific database objects, such as tables and stored procedures.

> **NOTE:** The sa login name and other members of the sysadmin fixed server role can do *anything* within SQL Server, essentially working outside the SQL Server permissions system.

It's important to realize that permissions are always granted to a user name or role—not to a login name. Thus, if a person has user names in several databases, all corresponding to his or her login name, you must grant permission to one or more of the user names, rather than the login name. You can, of course, add a login as a member of a fixed system role to indirectly grant the role's permissions to all database user names associated with the login.

Restricted Statements

Many SQL Server statements are restricted. This means they can be used only by the system administrator, members of certain roles, or by user names that have been granted explicit statement permission.

Table 3-6 shows statements that only members of certain fixed server roles have permission to execute.

Table 3-7 lists statements that can be used only by the user name that owns the affected object or by certain fixed database roles. Statement permissions for these statements can't be directly granted to other user names; however, you can make a

Statement	dbcreator	processadmin	securityadmin	serveradmin	sysadmin
Create Database	Yes				Yes
Grant, deny, or revoke permission to the Create Database statement			Yes		Yes
Kill		Yes			Yes
Reconfigure				Yes	Yes
Shutdown				Yes	Yes

Table 3-6. Statements Restricted to Specific Fixed Server Roles

Statement	Object Owner	db_owner	db_ddladmin	db_backup-operator	db_securityadmin
Alter Database		Yes	Yes		
Alter Procedure	Procedure owner	Yes	Yes		
Alter Table	Table owner	Yes	Yes		
Alter Trigger	Table owner	Yes	Yes		
Alter View	View owner	Yes	Yes		
Backup		Yes		Yes	
Checkpoint		Yes		Yes	
Create Index	Table owner	Yes	Yes		
Create Trigger	Table owner	Yes	Yes		
DBCC		Yes		Yes	
Deny *statement permission*		Yes			Yes
Drop *object*	Object owner	Yes	Yes		
Grant *statement permission*		Yes			Yes
Restore		Yes			
Revoke *statement permission*		Yes			Yes
SetUser		Yes			
Truncate Table	Table owner	Yes			
Update Statistics	Object owner	Yes	Yes		

Table 3-7. Statements Restricted to Object Owner and Fixed Database Roles

database user a member of an appropriate role (for example, db_owner) to indirectly give the user the role's permissions. Note also that the Alter Database statement can be used by members of the dbcreator fixed server role.

Statement Permissions

Table 3-8 lists statements for which statement permissions can be granted, denied, and revoked using the Grant, Deny, and Revoke statements. Notice that only members of the sysadmin and securityadmin fixed server roles can grant or deny permission to the Create Database statement, and then only to user names or role names that are in the master database. The most common way to provide permission for the Create Database statement is to make a login a member of the dbcreator fixed server role.

The dbo user name and other members of the db_owner fixed database role can grant or deny permissions for the other restricted statements to user names and role names in the same database. When any statement permission is granted to a user name or role name in a database, the permission applies only to using that statement on objects in the *same* database.

Managing Statement Permissions

To manage statement permissions, right-click a database entry in the SQL Server Enterprise Manager tree list and select Properties from the pop-up menu to display the database Properties dialog box. Select the Permissions tab to see the dialog box shown in Figure 3-20. From this dialog box you can grant, revoke, or deny statement permissions for the statements listed in Table 3-8.

Statement	Statement Permission Can Be Granted by Members of sysadmin and securityadmin Roles	Statement Permission Can Be Granted by Members of db_owner Role
Create Database (also includes Alter Database permission)	Yes	
Create Default	Yes	Yes
Create Procedure	Yes	Yes
Create Rule	Yes	Yes
Create Table	Yes	Yes
Create View	Yes	Yes
Backup Database	Yes	Yes
Backup Log	Yes	Yes

Table 3-8. Statements for Which Permissions Can Be Granted

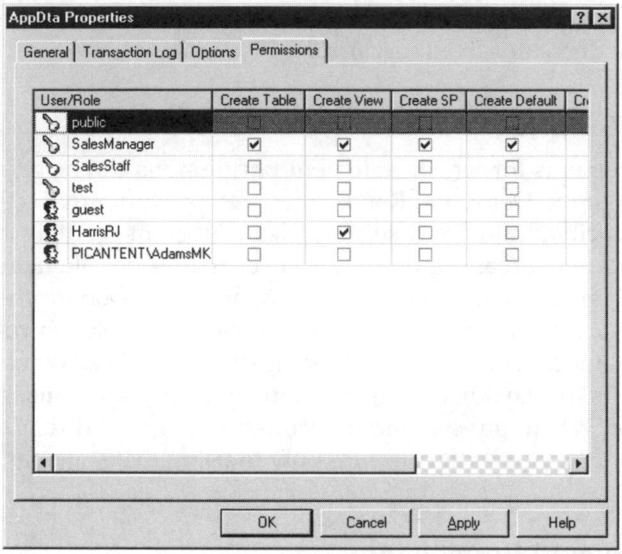

Figure 3-20. Database Properties dialog box—Permissions tab

Each check box controls the permission for a specific combination of user name or role name and statement. A check box has three states: blank—permission neither granted nor denied; checked—permission granted; or X'd—permission denied. Clicking a check box cycles its setting through the three states. You can also use the Grant, Revoke, and Deny Transact-SQL statements to grant, revoke, or deny permission for these statements, as explained in Chapter 9.

Object Permissions

Statements that access the contents of database tables or that execute stored procedures are controlled on an object-by-object basis. For example, any user name can execute a Select statement, but only for a table or view to which the user name has the Select object permission. You can only grant a database user object permissions to objects in the same database. If a person needs access to objects in multiple databases, you must create a user for him or her in each database.

NOTE: The terminology may seem a little confusing at first—the Select permission is an object permission, even though "Select" is the name of a SQL statement. Just remember that the Select permission controls which objects you can execute the Select statement on.

Table 3-9 shows the available object permissions. The second column shows which users can grant a permission. In addition to the users listed in Table 3-9, any user who has been granted the With Grant Option along with a permission may in turn grant other users that permission. The With Grant Option clause is available on the Transact-SQL Grant statement, discussed in Chapter 9. Note that the References permission is required to reference a table as the parent table in a foreign key constraint. Chapter 9 also explains foreign key constraints.

Managing Object Permissions

To manage object permissions, display the contents of the folder containing the object (for example, the Tables folder). Right-click the object in the list of contents and select All Tasks | Manage Permissions from the pop-up menu to display the Permissions tab of the Object Properties dialog box, shown in Figure 3-21. Each check box controls the permission for a specific combination of user name or role name and object. A check box has three states: blank—permission neither granted nor denied; checked—permission granted; or X'd—permission denied. Clicking a check box cycles its setting through the three states. After you've changed any permissions, click the Apply or OK button to complete the action.

Statement	Can Be Granted By
Delete	Table or view owner
Execute	Stored procedure owner
Grant *object permission*	Object owner (can only be granted using the Transact-SQL Grant statement's With Grant Option clause)
Insert	Table or view owner
References	Table owner (appears as "DRI" on Permissions dialog box)
Select	Table or view owner (also includes permission for the ReadText statement)
Update	Table or view owner (also includes permission for the UpdateText and WriteText statements)

Table 3-9.   Object Permissions

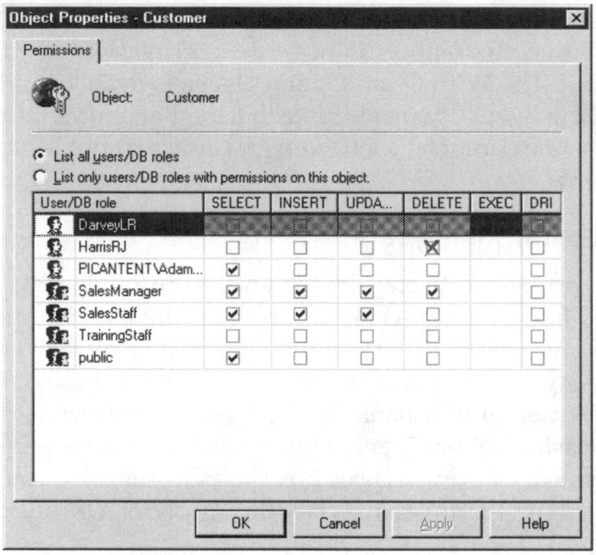

Figure 3-21.   Object Properties – Permissions dialog box

You can also manage a specific database user's permissions by displaying the contents of a database's Users folder and then right-clicking a user in the list of folder contents. Select All Tasks | Manage Permissions from the pop-up menu to display the Database User Properties - Permissions dialog box, shown in Figure 3-22. This dialog box shows lots of objects potentially accessible by the user; you'll find tables and views towards the end of the list. To grant, revoke, or deny a permission, you can blank, check, or X a check box (as described previously) for a specific combination of object and object permission. After you've changed any permissions, click the Apply or OK button to complete the action.

Column-Level Permissions

Normally, when you grant Select permission to a table or view, a user name can retrieve all the table or view columns. Similarly, the Update permission normally lets a user name change the value of all columns. For finer-grained control, SQL Server lets you specify *column-level* permissions for Select and Update object permissions. With this feature, you specify a subset of columns that the user name can retrieve or update. You must use the SQL Grant, Revoke, or Deny statement to grant, revoke, or deny column-level permissions, as explained in Chapter 9.

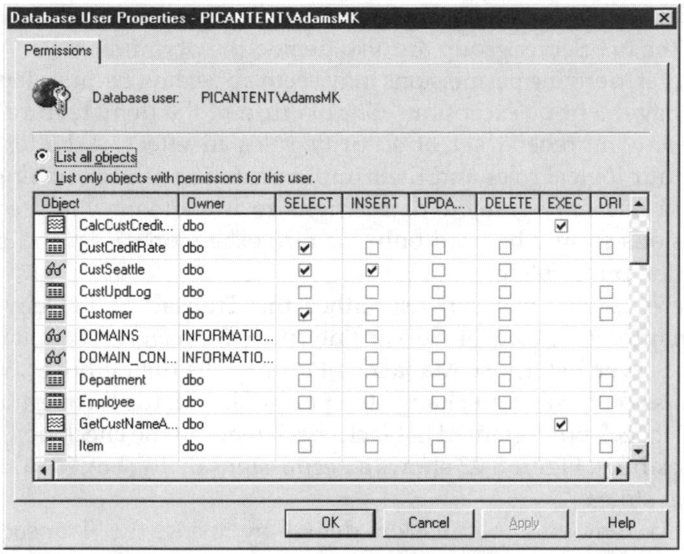

Figure 3-22. Database User Properties – Permissions dialog box

NOTE: With the SQL Grant statement's With Grant Option clause, you can permit the user name being granted the object permission to grant the same permission to other user names. This feature isn't available through SQL Server Enterprise Manager.

Deny Permissions and Permission States

Normally, you grant permissions to a database user or role and the database user has the sum of all permissions granted explicitly or granted to any role the database user is directly or indirectly a member of. SQL Server also lets you *deny* permissions. For example, you can deny the SmithJQ database user Update permission to the Employee table. When you deny a database user a permission, the deny feature blocks the specified access, regardless of any indirect permission that the database user might inherit from being a member of one or more roles. Similarly, if you deny a permission to a role, all direct or indirect members of the role are blocked from the specified access, regardless of their other explicit or inherited permissions. In summary, a denied permission anywhere in a database user's explicit or inherited permissions blocks the specified access.

The deny mechanism also works through NT Server groups. That is, if you deny a permission to a database user that's associated with a login for an NT Server group, then all members of the NT Server group are also denied the permission.

On the face of it, denying permissions may seem appealing because it provides a kind of "security management by exception." But overuse of the deny feature can result in a complex, hard-to-comprehend set of security rules in effect. A better strategy is to carefully plan your logical roles and their implementation as NT Server groups or SQL Server roles and use only granted permissions to implement your security policies. Denied permissions should be used only for rare exception cases, and should be well documented when put in place.

To deny permissions, you can use either the Transact-SQL Deny statement, as explained in Chapter 9, or the SQL Server Enterprise Manager. As explained earlier, on any of the SQL Server Enterprise Manager's Permissions dialog boxes, when you click one of the permission boxes, you change the permission status through three states: not granted (a blank check box), granted (a black check mark in the check box), and denied (a red X in the check box). Figure 3-23 shows a Permissions dialog box for a table that has all three permission states.

You can also remove a permission denial by using the Transact-SQL Revoke statement.

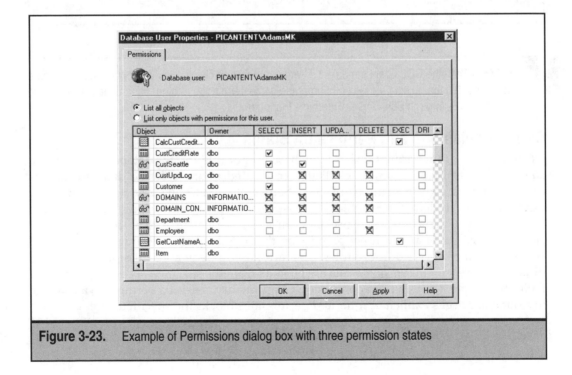

Figure 3-23.   Example of Permissions dialog box with three permission states

ROLE PERMISSIONS

You can grant statement or object permissions to a role name, as well as a user name. A user name that's a member of a role effectively has the combined permissions of the user name and the role. Because all user names are members of the public role, all user names also have the public role's permissions, too.

When you revoke permission from public or other role name, you revoke only those permissions for the role itself. This means that members of the role will no longer inherit the permission from the role. However, revoking a permission from a role doesn't revoke the permission from a user name that's a member of the role if the permission was granted directly to the user name.

Application Roles

In addition to standard, user-oriented database roles, SQL Server has *application roles*. You create an application role in a database using the same dialog box as described previously for creating a standard role (see Figure 3-18). However, you select the Application role option and enter a password. Like standard roles, application roles can be granted permissions. Unlike standard roles, application roles don't have members.

To use an application role, the user (or the application he or she is running) must directly execute a Transact-SQL statement such as the following:

```
sp_setapprole EmpUpdRole, thepassword
```

The sp_setapprole stored procedure can't be executed from within another stored procedure or from within a user-defined transaction.

Once the correct application role name and password are supplied, the user operates with exactly the permissions granted to the application role. All of the user's normal permissions, including those directly granted and ones inherited from standard roles, are dropped. The only way to deactivate an application role is to disconnect from SQL Server.

NOTE: It's hard to see much usefulness in application roles. They work outside normal database user and standard role permissions, creating potential security exposures. If a client application on a desktop PC executes an sp_setapprole stored procedure, there is no way to guarantee that the only statements executed by the client are those you intend. A malicious user can circumvent the client application logic (for example, by using a debugger) to execute statements under the permissions of the application profile. In addition, application roles are clumsy to activate and deactivate. They're included in this chapter mainly for completeness.

STORED PROCEDURES AND PERMISSIONS

The system administrator, dbo, or stored procedure owner can grant, revoke, or deny the Execute object permission to a stored procedure. Any user name with Execute permission can execute a stored procedure. A stored procedure can directly access any object that's owned by the stored procedure owner, regardless of the permissions of the person calling the stored procedure. Consider the following example:

▼   The dbo user name owns the P1 stored procedure and the T1 table.

■   The P1 stored procedure performs an Update statement on the T1 table.

■   The dbo grants the SmithJQ user name Execute permission to the P1 stored procedure.

▲   The SmithJQ user name has no permissions to the T1 table.

In this scenario, SmithJQ can execute the P1 stored procedure and consequently update the T1 table, via the stored procedure.

You can use this capability to control access to data with more complex security policies than simple "all-or-none" or column-level object permissions on tables and views. For example, a stored procedure can use the current user name (namely, the Current_User function) to determine the maximum discount that can be assigned to rows in the Customer table. With this technique, a row for each employee would be stored in an Employee table and have one column for the employee's user name and another column that indicates the employee's level of authority to give customer discounts. The stored procedure would retrieve this value to constrain updates to the Customer table.

Notice that this example illustrates how you can use stored procedures to provide additional access to user names that don't have adequate permission via their user name or role object permissions. In this case, you would normally have at least some employees who couldn't update the Customer table's Discount column except by executing the stored procedure. To grant this type of controlled access, you'd grant a user name Execute permission to the stored procedure.

OWNERSHIP CHAIN

In many cases, the owner of a view owns all the tables and/or views over which the view is defined. Likewise, in many cases, the owner of a stored procedure owns all the tables, views, and other stored procedures referenced by the stored procedure. To avoid the run-time cost of checking permissions, SQL Server stores information about the *ownership chain* of objects that a view or stored procedure references. At run time, SQL Server checks permission to a referenced object only when the object is not owned by the same owner as the referencing object, or when a referenced object is not in the same database as the referencing object.

Consider the set of dependencies depicted in Figure 3-24. (Assume that all objects are in the same database.) These are the dependencies:

▼   Procedure P1 references the V1 view and T1 table.

■   View V1 references the V2 view and T2 table.

▲   View V2 references the T3 table.

The user name in parentheses beside each object name is the owner, as follows:

▼   SmithJQ owns P1, V1, and T2

■   JonesLR owns T1

▲   AllenTW owns V2 and T3

When any user executes the P1 stored procedure, SQL Server checks that the user name has Execute permission to P1 and checks the user name's object permissions to T1 (at A in Figure 3-24) and V2 (at B in Figure 3-24). Access to V1 and T2 is not independently checked and is allowed if the user name has Execute permission to P1. Likewise, access to T3 is governed implicitly by the user name's permissions to V2.

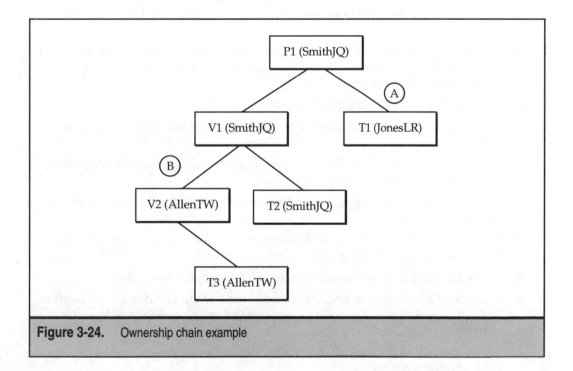

Figure 3-24.   Ownership chain example

DATABASE SECURITY PRINCIPLES AND GUIDELINES

Database security is an important and extensive topic. This section provides a summary of some principles and guidelines to help you lay a solid foundation for your SQL Server database security.

▼ Security is a business function of protecting an organization's resources and operations; computer system security should be designed within the context of the organization's overall security plan.

■ Security rules cover different levels of threat—the more vital a security policy is to your organization's well being, the more thoroughly you must enforce the policy.

■ Assume that people who will intentionally try to breach your security understand the technical aspects of NT Server and SQL Server as well as you do. Don't rely on an attacker's ignorance to protect your system. What they shouldn't know are the passwords.

▲ If the implementation of a security mechanism fails, the error should result in unintended restrictions on access rather than unintended additional access.

Here are some security guidelines specific to SQL Server:

▼ Don't associate the same SQL Server user name in different databases with different login names.

■ Establish a good standard for user names (letters only, unique across the entire system and all databases) and use these for NT Server user name, SQL Server login name, and database user names.

■ Use Windows NT authentication mode, if feasible.

■ Assign a unique NT Server user name and password to each individual who uses your system.

■ Carefully consider how much public permission each application table, view, and stored procedure should have.

■ Organize user names into logical roles that can be granted identical authority for many objects.

■ Be aware of how SQL Server adds together permissions for a user name and the roles to which it belongs.

■ Grant the minimum permissions necessary for any required access.

■ Use stored procedures to provide limited access when you don't want to give the full capabilities of a specific permission (for example, Update) to a user name.

▲ Have special-purpose user names (not programmer or end-user user names) own application objects.

CONCLUSION

Planning and implementing security are essential parts of enterprise-level database application development. As this chapter emphasizes, you should begin with a well-thought-out logical structure for your security, based on identifying users and roles. This logical structure provides the basis for using NT Server and SQL Server facilities—which are related but not quite identical—to implement your organization's security policies. The techniques we've described offer an effective way to have database security that is both thorough and manageable.

CHAPTER 4

SQL Server Backup and Recovery

This chapter describes SQL Server's facilities for backing up database tables and transaction logs and for restoring a database if it becomes lost or damaged because of a hardware or software failure or due to a human error. We also look at several approaches to saving database-related objects that can reduce the amount of time needed for daily backups and provide redundant backup copies for a subsequent recovery process.

WHY BACK UP THE DATABASE?

If nothing ever went wrong with computer hardware or software, we wouldn't have to worry about database backup and recovery. But things do sometimes go wrong; among the potential problems are

▼ A power failure that causes the system to halt

■ A disk drive or other piece of hardware that fails

■ A system software failure

■ An application error

▲ A mistake by a user

When one of these events happens, database tables may be lost or corrupted and need to be recovered. The most basic means of recovery is to use a backup copy of data to restore tables to a valid state. In the simplest terms, a *backup* consists of a complete copy of a database written to magnetic tape or other media. When recovery is necessary, the copy is rewritten to disk to completely restore the lost or corrupted database. Figure 4-1 shows this simple cycle of backup and restore operations. Keep in mind that in typical

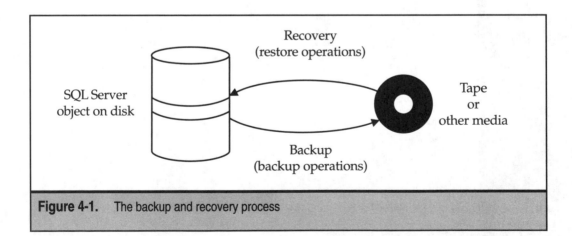

Figure 4-1.   The backup and recovery process

operations backups are made regularly so the tape copies of database tables are relatively current, but the need to restore a database is usually a rare event.

NT Server has extensive facilities for backing up everything on the system, including the operating system, user accounts and permissions, device configurations, programs, files, and all the other vendor-supplied and user objects. In this chapter, we look only at the SQL Server facilities for backing up and restoring databases and transaction logs. In SQL Server, you can use the SQL Server Enterprise Manager or Transact-SQL statements to perform backup and restore operations.

NOTE: In previous versions of SQL Server, the term "dump" was used for backup, and "load" was used for restore.

BACKING UP DATABASE OBJECTS

A full backup and recovery strategy must periodically back up everything on the system, including vendor-supplied software, user programs, database objects, and other types of user-created objects. The NT Server manuals provide step-by-step instructions for a complete system backup and recovery plan. The database-related objects that you need to back up (and possibly restore) are

▼   Databases

■   Transaction logs

▲   Files or filegroups

A database contains table data, stored procedures, and other objects. A transaction log contains complete information for each logged database operation, such as updating a row. SQL Server writes the data for an operation to the transaction log and subsequently updates the actual database tables on disk. The transaction log enables SQL Server to roll back (undo) an uncommitted transaction and to redo transactions during a recovery process. SQL Server provides backup and restore facilities for databases and transaction logs.

SQL Server stores each database's data and transaction log contents on separate operating system files—one (or more) files for the database data and one (or more) other files for the transaction log. By default, database data files are considered part of the system-defined *default filegroup*. You can create *user-defined filegroups* that consist of one or more database data files (transaction log files are never in a filegroup). When you create a database table, you can optionally specify that it be stored on the file(s) in a specific filegroup that you've defined for the database. SQL Server provides options to back up and restore specific files or filegroups, rather than the entire database. (Chapter 9 explains how to use filegroups when you create database objects.)

SQL Server can back up a database while it's in use. When a database backup begins, SQL Server notes a starting entry in the transaction log. This entry is the earliest of the following:

▼ The entry after the most recent checkpoint that has written to the database files all committed transactions in the transaction log.

■ The earliest Begin Transaction entry for an uncompleted transaction (one that hasn't been committed or rolled back).

▲ The earliest Begin Transaction entry for a published transaction that hasn't yet been replicated.

After identifying this transaction log entry, SQL Server begins copying database pages to the backup device(s). Once the database is fully backed up, SQL Server backs up the transaction log, beginning with the starting entry identified earlier and ending with the last transaction log entry made while the database backup was in progress. The combination of a complete copy of the database, plus a copy of the transaction log entries for any changes made during the backup, allows SQL Server to subsequently restore the database to the state it was in at the end of the backup.

Even with the optimization techniques used by SQL Server to improve backup performance, making a backup consumes processor and device resources and can slow normal transaction processing. For that reason, backups are generally scheduled during a period when database activity is at a minimum, such as the evening or weekend.

Backup Devices

Before you can back up anything from a SQL Server database, you need a backup device (also referred to as a *dump device*). A *backup device* is usually a local or network disk file or a tape drive. SQL Server also lets you create and use a named pipe as a backup device.

> **NOTE:** SQL Server Enterprise Manager supports only disk and tape backup devices. Named pipes are generally used by third-party utilities. If you want to use diskettes for small databases, you should first back up to a disk file and then copy the file to diskette.
>
> Also note that the NT Server account under which the MSSQLSERVER service runs (see Chapter 2) must have appropriate NT Server permissions to the backup device.

Creating a Backup Device

To create a backup device, run the SQL Server Enterprise Manager and right-click the Backup entry in the Management folder.

Select New Backup Device from the pop-up menu to display the Backup Device Properties – New Device dialog box shown in Figure 4-2. Enter a backup device name and select whether you want to create a disk file or tape backup device. Enter the full path and filename for the location of this backup device.

Table 4-1 shows sample entries for different types of backup devices. Click the OK button to complete the operation.

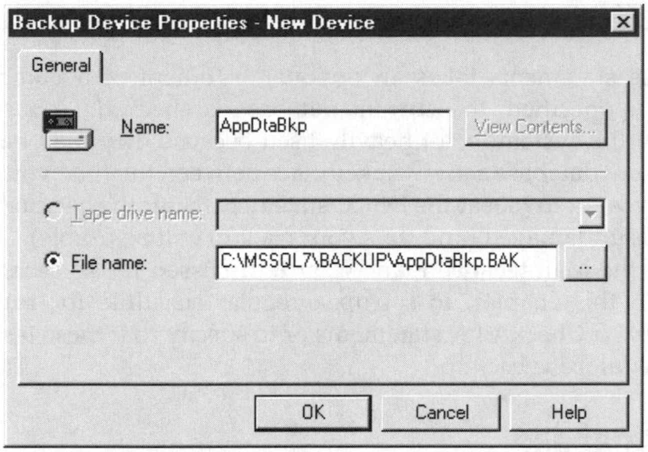

Figure 4-2.   Backup Device Properties – New Device dialog box

You can also create a backup device using an sp_addumpdevice stored procedure such as the following:

```
sp_addumpdevice 'disk', 'AppDtaBkp', 'C:\MSSQL7\BACKUP\AppDtaBkp.bak'
```

Checking the Database

Prior to backing up a database, you may want to verify that the database contents are valid. This assures that the backup you create will be usable should you need it for a subsequent restore operation. The Transact-SQL DBCC statement has several options to check the database:

▼   **DBCC CheckDB**   Checks all tables in the database to see that data pages are correctly linked, indexes are in proper order, all pointers are consistent, and other control structures are valid. Includes all the checks provided by the DBCC CheckAlloc statement.

Backup Device Type	Sample Name	Sample Location
Local disk	AppDtaBkp	C:\MSSQL7\BACKUP\AppDtaBkp.bak
Network disk	ServerBkp	\\SERVERA\BACKUP\SqlDtaBkp.bak
Tape	TapeBkp	\\.\TAPE1

Table 4-1.   Sample Entries for Backup Devices

- ■ **DBCC CheckAlloc**   Validates the allocation of all data pages.
- ▲ **DBCC CheckCatalog**   Checks consistency among system catalog tables.

Each of these statements takes an optional argument of a database name; if no database name is specified, the current database is checked. You should run these statements when the system is not heavily used because they may have an impact on performance. If any database activity takes place between the time you run DBCC and a backup, you may want to repeat the DBCC statements after the backup to verify that the database remains undamaged (and thus your backup will be usable).

You can use the Maintenance Plan Wizard, discussed in the section "Scheduling a Backup," later in this chapter, to set up a regular schedule for running the DBCC CheckDB and DBCC CheckAlloc statements or to specify that these tests should always be run prior to a database backup.

Backing Up a Database

The simplest way to back up a database is to right-click the database entry in the SQL Server Enterprise Manager main window, and select All Tasks | Backup Database from the pop-up menus. On the SQL Server Backup dialog box shown in Figure 4-3, enter a backup set name and description, select the Database – complete option to create a *full backup*, and select one of the entries listed under Destination. The Add and Remove buttons let you add and remove backup devices or disk files in this list. If you're not sure what's on a backup device, click the Contents button before choosing the Append to media or Overwrite existing media option.

Select Append to media or Overwrite existing media, depending on whether you want to preserve what's already on the device or overwrite it. If you haven't ever used the device, the options are equivalent.

To create a scheduled SQL Server Agent job, select the Schedule check box and click the button to the right to edit the schedule. As explained in Chapter 2, you can use the Jobs Properties dialog box to define more complex schedules and to specify other job attributes.

On the Options tab shown in Figure 4-4, you can select options to reread the tape after the backup to verify the media integrity and/or to check the identity and expiration date of the media before overwriting it. If you selected the Overwrite existing media option on the General tab, you can enter an expiration date and time or number of days, as well as a media set name and description on the Options tab. When you've completed the SQL Server Backup dialog box, click OK to begin the backup or create the SQL Server Agent job. When the backup runs (immediately or as scheduled in the job), SQL Server copies the entire contents of the specified database and the necessary transaction log entries (as described previously in the section "Backing Up Database Objects") to the backup device. Should the database subsequently be damaged, you can restore the database from this backup copy.

Generally, it's a good idea to have backup copies on tape or other removable media so the backup data can be stored in a separate location from the computer on which the database resides. This practice offers protection not only against a failed hard drive, but also against an event, such as a fire, that damages the entire system. You can create a tape

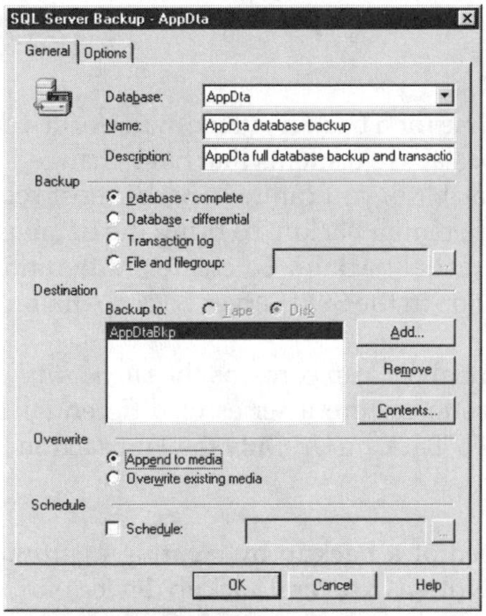

Figure 4-3.   SQL Server Backup dialog box – General tab

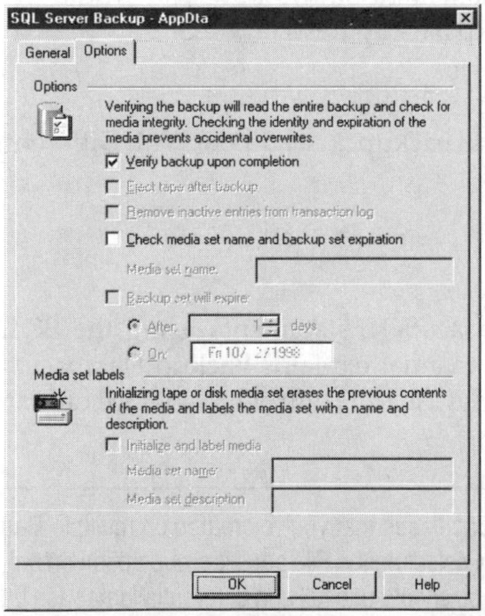

Figure 4-4.   SQL Server Backup dialog box – Options tab

backup copy either by using a tape backup device or by using a disk backup device and then copying the disk backup file to tape using NT Server commands.

Differential Backups

To reduce the amount of time for a backup, you can perform a *differential backup*. This is a backup that copies all the database contents that have changed since the last full backup. If you need to restore a database, you can restore the most recent full backup and then restore the most recent differential backup to bring the database to the point that it was when you made the differential backup. To create a differential backup, just select the Database – differential option in the SQL Server Backup dialog box shown previously in Figure 4-3.

Note that each differential backup contains the *cumulative* changes since the last full backup, so you don't have to restore a series of differential backups, as you do with transaction log backups (see "Backing Up Only the Transaction Log" later in this chapter).

Striped Backups

You can improve the speed of a backup by creating a *striped backup*. This is a full or differential backup that's written to several backup devices simultaneously. If the backup devices are on separate physical devices, SQL Server can more quickly transfer the complete contents of the database. To create a striped backup, just add multiple devices to the backup devices list in the SQL Server Backup dialog box (Figure 4-3).

The Backup Database Statement

Transact-SQL provides the Backup Database statement for full or differential database backups. The following statement shows how you would back up the entire AppDta database to the AppDtaBkp backup device:

```
Backup Database AppDta To AppDtaBkp
```

To perform a differential backup, just add the With Differential clause to the following statement:

```
Backup Database AppDta To AppDtaBkp
  With Differential
```

You can execute Transact-SQL statements using the SQL Server Query Analyzer utility. The Transact-SQL manual explains Backup Database statement options that let you create a new backup device and control tape device operations when you perform a backup.

NOTE: For very large databases that you've created on multiple files, you can back up one or more of the files or filegroups by selecting the File and filegroup option on the SQL Server Backup dialog box (Figure 4-3). Generally, you should use full and differential database backups, rather than this feature, to ensure that you can restore the entire database. Even with full or differential database backups, you can restore a selected file or filegroup to speed recovery when you know that a specific file has been damaged, and other files used by the database are undamaged.

Backing Up Only the Transaction Log

You can use a backup operation to make a copy of only the part of the current transaction log that hasn't yet been backed. The reason to back up just the transaction log is to save time and storage space, since the transaction log contains only database changes, not the entire database content. As long as you have a full backup of the database and an unbroken chain of transaction log backups made after the full backup (or after a differential backup made since the full backup), you can use SQL Server's recovery tools to recover the database up to the point of the most recent transaction log backup.

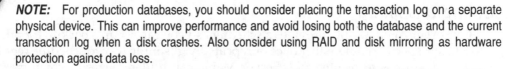

NOTE: For production databases, you should consider placing the transaction log on a separate physical device. This can improve performance and avoid losing both the database and the current transaction log when a disk crashes. Also consider using RAID and disk mirroring as hardware protection against data loss.

There are several guidelines to follow for successful transaction log backups:

▼   Do not set the "Truncate log on checkpoint database" option (discussed in Chapter 2). This option removes transaction log entries whenever the checkpoint process occurs, which means the transaction log won't necessarily contain complete transaction data for transactions that occur after the last database backup.

■   Back up the full database at least once to provide the starting point for recovery.

▲   You should not have performed any unlogged operation, such as a bulk copy or a Truncate Table statement, since the most recent full or differential database backup. The transaction log doesn't include the information necessary to recover these operations.

To back up the transaction log, follow the same steps as explained previously for backing up the entire database, except check the Transaction log option on the SQL Server Backup dialog box, shown previously in Figure 4-3.

By default, each time you back up the transaction log, SQL Server *truncates* the transaction log by removing the backed up log entries for completed transactions. SQL Server does not truncate the transaction log when you perform a full or differential database backup. In order to have a complete copy of all the transaction data since the last database backup, you need an unbroken chain of successive transaction log backups taken since the database backup. There are several operations that break a chain of transaction logs:

▼   A Select Into or bulk copy operation with the select into/bulk copy database option set on. The data for these operations isn't written to the transaction log.

■   A nonlogged modification to a text, ntext, or image column.

▲ A Backup Log statement with the Truncate_Only or No_Log option. This operation removes transaction log entries without backing them up.

The Backup Log Statement

Transact-SQL provides the Backup Log statement for transaction log backups. The following statement shows how you would back up the AppDta database's transaction log to the AppDtaLogBkp backup device:

```
Backup Log AppDta To AppDtaLogBkp
```

Scheduling a Backup

The SQL Server Agent facility provides a scheduler so you can set up a backup (or other) job to run at a specified time, either once or repeatedly. A simple way to schedule regular database backups is to use the SQL Server Maintenance Plan Wizard, which creates appropriate Agent jobs. The "Creating a Database Maintenance Plan" section in Chapter 2 explains how to use this wizard.

NOTE: The Maintenance Plan Wizard generates one or more jobs to run the SQLMAINT program, which is documented in SQL Server Books On-line. You can create more sophisticated, multistep Agent jobs and use SQLMAINT features to perform the operations.

Truncating the Transaction Log

When you back up the transaction log and do not specify No_Truncate, inactive transaction log entries are removed from the transaction log, freeing storage space for future transactions. In SQL Server, the term for removing inactive transaction log entries is *truncating* the transaction log. You can leave the inactive part of the transaction log when you back up the transaction log by using the No_Truncate option of the Backup Log statement:

```
Backup Log AppDta To AppDtaLogBkp
  With No_Truncate
```

NOTE: Although the No_Truncate option leaves backed up entries in the transaction log, subsequent Backup Log operations will *not* backup these inactive entries. Thus, the No_Truncate option does not support a cumulative backup of the transaction log. The main purpose of the No_Truncate option is to enable a Backup Log operation when the database has been damaged, as discussed in the section "Backing Up the Transaction Log," later in this chapter.

You can also truncate the transaction log *without making a backup copy*, using the Truncate_Only or No_Log option (which are equivalent):

```
Backup Log AppDta With Truncate_Only
```

For production databases, it's not a good idea to truncate the transaction log without making a backup of the log. If you do truncate the log without a backup, be sure to immediately do a full or differential database backup so you can recover up to the most recent committed transactions.

Organizing Backups

To have adequate backups for your databases, you need to plan for backups after certain events, as well as periodic and archival backups. The following guidelines cover the events that should be followed by a backup.

Events Requiring a System Database Backup

For the master database, perform a full database backup after you execute any statement that changes system tables. These include statements that

- ▼ Add, modify, or drop logins
- ■ Create, alter, or drop a database
- ■ Create, alter, or drop a filegroup or backup device
- ■ Change any server-wide or database configuration options
- ▲ Add or drop a linked server

You can use the SQL Server Enterprise Manager or a Transact-SQL Backup Database statement to back up the master database. Generally, you should do a full backup of the master database, rather than depend on differential database or transaction log backups.

> **NOTE:** To show system databases in the SQL Server Enterprise Manager database list, right-click a server entry and select Edit SQL Server Registration from the pop-up menu. On the Registered SQL Server Properties dialog box, check the Show system databases and system objects option.

The msdb database holds system-generated scheduling and backup/restore history information. You should perform a full database backup of msdb after you perform any operation that changes this information, including

- ▼ Configuring replication
- ■ Adding, modifying, or dropping scheduled jobs
- ■ Storing Data Transformation Services packages
- ▲ Maintaining online backup and restore history during a backup or restore operation

Because the msdb database is usually fairly small, frequent full database backups are the recommended approach.

The model database is used when you create a new database. Any object in model is replicated in the new database. You should perform a full database backup of model whenever you add, modify, or drop any object in it. Because the model database is usually fairly small, frequent full database backups are the recommended approach.

Events Requiring a User Database Backup

For all user databases, perform a full or differential database backup after you change its structure. Among the operations that should be followed by a full or differential database backup are

▼ Creating the database

■ Adding or altering tables

▲ Creating an index

You should also perform a full or differential backup after a nonlogged operation, such as a Truncate Table, Select Into, or a bulk copy.

Periodic Backups

In addition to the events already listed, you should generally schedule regular periodic backups of the master, msdb, model, and distribution databases. The distribution database holds system-generated replication information that's updated by a variety of replication utilities and operations. Because the distribution database is usually fairly small, full database backups are the recommended approach.

Planning a periodic backup schedule for user databases is a balancing act among three goals:

▼ Minimize the impact of backups on normal system operations

■ Maximize the ability to recover databases through the most recent committed transaction

▲ Minimize the time required for recovery

To see how these three goals interact, consider an admittedly extreme approach to achieving the second and third goals—taking a full database backup after every transaction. With this approach, if the database becomes damaged, you need only restore the most recent backup and resume operations. Of course, performing a full backup takes time and machine resources, so this approach isn't practical because it could significantly reduce your ability to process transactions.

You could still fully achieve the second goal (100 percent recovery) if you backed up the transaction log after every transaction. This would reduce the time to make backups but might still impact transaction processing more than you'd like. In addition, recovery could involve processing lots of separate transaction logs, significantly lengthening recovery time.

Most organizations find that a mix of full and differential database backups and more frequent transaction log backups offers the optimal solution. For example, you might back up the full database once a month, do differential database backups every weekend, and back up the transaction log every night. The specific frequency of each type of backup depends on the size and volatility of the database and the recovery requirements.

Archival Backups

Depending on your organization's accounting and other systems, you may need to make full database backups for archival purposes. For example, you may need to create a backup of the accounting tables at the end of each quarter and at the end of the year. It's often a good idea to back up the master database at the same time you create archival backups that will be retained for a long time. Then, if necessary, you can temporarily re-create all database definitions that existed when the database was backed up for the archive.

Your company's policies determine what the retention period is for archival backups, as well as how many copies of each backup you need to make. Be sure to use high-quality tapes or other media for archival backups and to store them in a secure location and a properly maintained environment.

Backup Copies and Retention Period

In addition to setting up a backup schedule, you must decide whether to make multiple copies and how long to retain backup copies. You should always have at least two relatively current backups from which you can restore the database; many organizations always have three or more backups available. The idea is that if one backup gets damaged—perhaps if the tape gets mangled during a recovery attempt—there's still a way to recover.

There are several ways to keep multiple backups available. One technique is to use NT Server utilities to make additional disk or tape copies of backups. Another approach provides multiple backups by rotating sets of tapes (or other media) so that a set isn't overwritten until some number of backups have been made to other sets of tapes.

A very common system of tape rotation is known as the "grandfather" system because three "generations" of tapes are used: "son" (most recent), "father" (second most recent), and "grandfather" (oldest). The easiest way to understand how this system works is to look at an example.

Consider an approach in which a full database backup is done every Sunday and a transaction log backup is done every day. For simplicity's sake, assume that each backup fits on a single tape. If your goal is to always have a way to recover the database, even if any two tapes are damaged, the schedule shown in Table 4-2 will achieve the goal.

You can see that a separate set of tapes is used for each week; and after three weeks, a set gets reused. To see how this system provides redundant protection, consider what happens when the database and transaction log are damaged on the Sunday of Week 4 before any backups are made.

Week 1

Day	Tape Name	Type of Backup(s)
Sunday	L1SU01	1. Transaction log
	D1SU01	2. Full database
Monday	L1MO01	Transaction log
Tuesday	L1TU01	Transaction log
Wednesday	L1WE01	Transaction log
Thursday	L1TH01	Transaction log
Friday	L1FR01	Transaction log
Saturday	L1SA01	Transaction log

Week 2

Day	Tape Name	Type of Backup(s)
Sunday	L2SU01	1. Transaction log
	D2SU01	2. Full database
Monday	L2MO01	Transaction log
Tuesday	L2TU01	Transaction log
Wednesday	L2WE01	Transaction log
Thursday	L2TH01	Transaction log
Friday	L2FR01	Transaction log
Saturday	L2SA01	Transaction log

Week 3

Day	Tape Name	Type of Backup(s)
Sunday	L3SU01	1. Transaction log
	D3SU01	2. Full database
Monday	L3MO01	Transaction log

Table 4-2. "Grandfather" Tape Rotation Example

Day	Tape Name	Type of Backup(s)
Tuesday	L3TU01	Transaction log
Wednesday	L3WE01	Transaction log
Thursday	L3TH01	Transaction log
Friday	L3FR01	Transaction log
Saturday	L3SA01	Transaction log

Week 4

Day	Tape Name	Type of Backup(s)
Sunday	L1SU01 D1SU01	1. Transaction log 2. Full database
Monday	L1MO01	Transaction log

Table 4-2. "Grandfather" Tape Rotation Example (*continued*)

Let's suppose two tapes are damaged:

▼ *Case 1: Tapes D2SU01 and D3SU01 are damaged.* To fully recover, you could restore the full database from tape D1SU01 and process all the transaction log backups starting with L1MO01 and ending with L3SA01. Although this would be tedious, it would still provide full recovery up to the day of the database damage.

▲ *Case 2: Tapes D3SU01 and L2MO01 damaged.* This is the worst case for losing two tapes. The most recent full database backup is on tape D2SU01, and we can't recover beyond that point because we've lost the transaction log backup taken the day after this full database backup. This points out an important aspect of SQL Server transaction log backups—they are *not* cumulative.

Although this approach leaves us with a recovered database that is almost two weeks old, it avoids losing the database in its entirety. With this schedule of rotation, three tapes (all the D*x*SU01 tapes) must be lost before the database can't be recovered at all.

You can create a variety of alternative backup strategies using full and differential database backups and transaction log backups. When you plan your own backup schedule and tape rotation, be sure to examine what the worst case is from losing one, two, three, or more tapes.

Using Striped Backups in a Restore Operation

If you created a striped backup using multiple backup devices, you should normally specify the same devices on the restore operation. However, if you only have one backup device available because, for example, a tape drive isn't available, you can still restore from a single device.

DATABASE RECOVERY

Several situations can arise that require database recovery. The simplest case is when SQL Server abnormally terminates in the middle of a transaction leaving a potentially inconsistent, but undamaged, database. In this case, when SQL Server restarts, it uses the transaction log to automatically recover to the last consistent database state. Effectively, SQL Server makes sure that all committed transactions found in the transaction log are written to the database and rolls back database changes caused by any uncommitted transactions. No user action is required for SQL Server's automatic recovery.

Recovery for a Damaged Database

A hardware or software failure may damage a database so that the database can't be recovered by SQL Server's automatic recovery process. When the database is damaged, recovery involves the following steps:

1. Attempt to back up the transaction log.
2. Restore the database from the most recent backup (full backup only or full and differential backups).
3. Restore from the entire chain of transaction log backups (including the backup you make in step 1) taken after the database backup used in step 2.
4. Manually reenter any update operations that weren't committed.

If all goes well, this sequence of operations will bring the database back to the point of the last committed transaction just before the database damage occurred.

Backing Up the Transaction Log

As long as the transaction log is undamaged, you can use a statement such as the following to back up the transaction log:

```
Backup Log AppDta To AppDtaLogBkp
  With No_Truncate
```

This step makes sure you have the log records for the most recent completed transactions, which you'll use later in the recovery process. Note that SQL Server requires the No_Truncate option to back up the transaction log when the database isn't accessible.

Restoring the Database

Prior to restoring a database, locate the backup file(s) for the most recent full database backup. If you also have a more recent differential database backup, locate the backup file(s) for it as well. Finally, locate the backup file(s) for all transaction log backups made after the most recent full or differential backup. You can display the contents of a backup device by selecting the Backup entry in the Management folder of the SQL Server Enterprise Manager tree, and double-clicking a backup device in the Results pane to display the Backup Device Properties dialog box shown in Figure 4-5. Click the View Contents button to display the View Backup Media Contents dialog box shown in Figure 4-6.

You can restore a database with the SQL Server Enterprise Manager. First be sure that no one, including yourself, is using the database. From the SQL Server Enterprise Manager main window, right-click the database you want to restore and select All Tasks | Restore database from the pop-up menu. Fill in the Restore database dialog box shown in Figure 4-7.

Make sure the database you want to restore is selected in the Restore as database drop-down list.

NOTE: You can restore a database to a different name as a way to make a copy of the database.

Select Database for the Restore option. In the Parameters panel, select the same database name in the Show backups of database drop-down list. Then, from the First

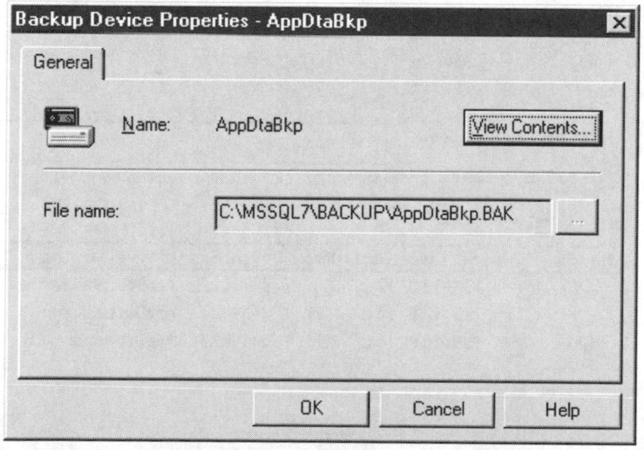

Figure 4-5.   Backup Device Properties dialog box

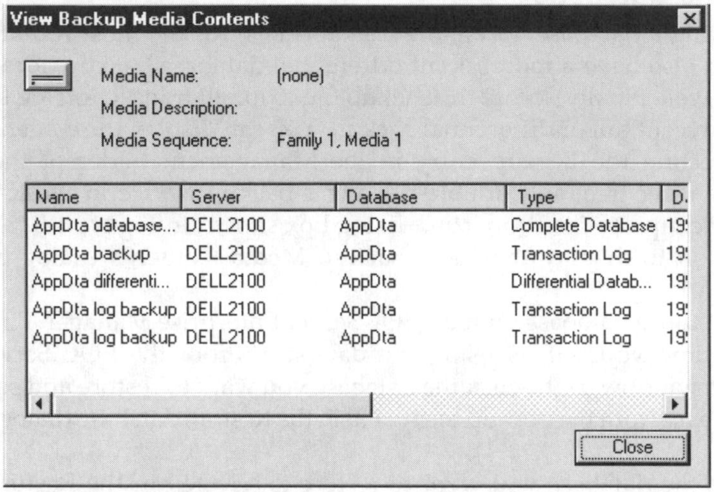

Figure 4-6.   View Backup Media Contents dialog box

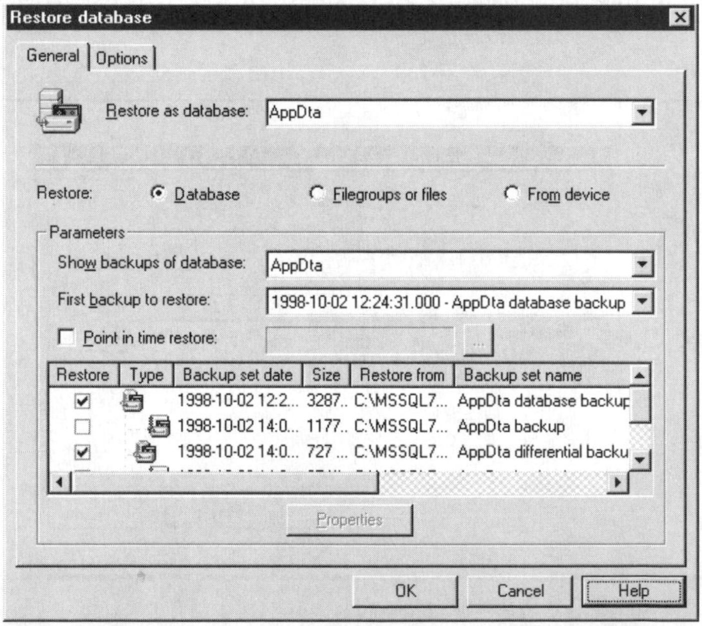

Figure 4-7.   Restore database dialog box – General tab

backup to restore drop-down list, select the appropriate backup set to use. This should generally be the backup set for the most recent full database backup.

Once you've selected the backup set, the list at the bottom of the Parameters panel shows the sequence of full database, differential database, and transaction log backups that have been made since the selected backup set. By default, the check boxes under this list's Restore column are selected for the backup copies required to fully restore the database. You can optionally select and deselect entries in this list to control which backup copies are restored.

NOTE: To restore a database that no longer exists on the server, first use Enterprise Manager (Chapter 2) or a Create Database SQL statement (Chapter 9) to create the database using default values for the database properties. This will add the database to the drop-down list on the Restore Database dialog box. The restore operation will replace the "dummy" database you create with the database on the backup copy.

On the Options tab (Figure 4-8), you can select options to eject tapes after they are used, prompt for confirmation before each restore operation, or force a restore over an existing database that doesn't have the same name as the backup copy you're using.

The Options tab also shows a list of the Windows NT filenames on the backup and the default names that will be used for the database and its log when they're restored. You can edit the target filenames if you want to use different files for the restored database.

The Recovery completion state panel has three choices, which correspond to the Restore statement's options as shown in Table 4-3. When you're doing a full recovery at

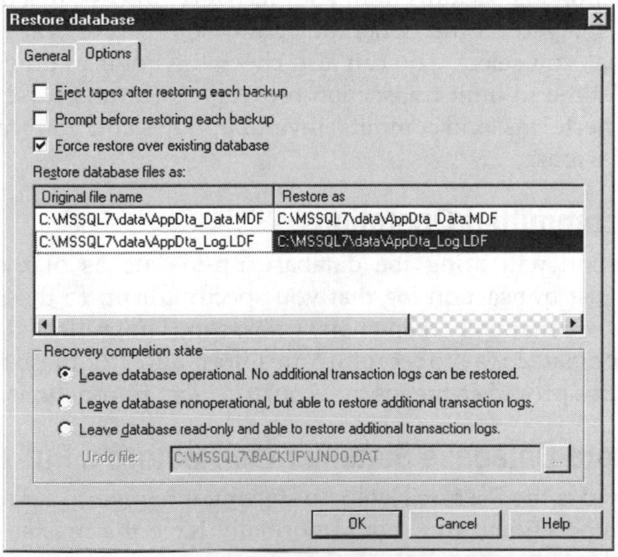

Figure 4-8. Database Restore dialog box – Options tab

Restore Database Dialog Box Option	Tape Name
Leave database operational. No additional transaction logs can be restored.	With Recovery or Neither With NoRecovery nor Standby is specified.
Leave database nonoperational, but able to restore additional transaction logs.	With NoRecovery
Leave database read-only and able to restore additional transaction logs.	With Standby = *undo-filename*

Table 4-3. Database Recovery Options

one time, select the first option. If you plan to recover additional differential database backups or transaction log backups, select the second option for normal servers and the third option for standby ("warm backup") servers.

Limiting the Transactions That Are Recovered

If you don't want to recover all backed up transactions, you can omit one or more of the most recent transaction log backups from your recovery process. Just deselect those logs in the list that's displayed on the General tab, and SQL Server will restore only those transaction logs that you select. You can also check the Point in time restore option to specify a date and time to limit transaction recovery. You might use this feature if an errant application performs (and commits) invalid updates and you want to go back to a prior state of the database.

Reentering Uncommitted Operations

The restore operation will bring the database up-to-date as of the last committed transaction in the last transaction log that you specify (or up to the point in time you specify). You'll have to manually reenter any transactions not reflected in the transaction logs. There's no automated way to recapture the information for these transactions, so be sure your procedures provide a means to reconstruct lost transactions.

Using the Restore Database Statement to Restore a Full Backup

Transact-SQL provides the Restore Database statement to restore a database. When you perform recovery operations, you should normally have the master database as your current database. The following statement shows how you would restore the AppDta database from the AppDtaBkp backup device:

```
Restore Database AppDta From AppDtaBkp
```

This simple form of the statement is appropriate if all you plan to do is to restore the last full backup.

Using Restore Database Statements to Restore Full and Differential Backups

If you have a differential backup in addition to a full backup, you can use statements such as the following to restore the database:

```
Restore Database AppDta From AppDtaFullBkp
  With NoRecovery
Restore Database AppDta From AppDtaDifBkp
```

In this example, the full backup was saved to the AppDtaFullBkp backup device, and the differential backup was saved to the AppDtaDifBkp backup device. If you append backups to the same device, you would use statements such as the following:

```
Restore Database AppDta From AppDtaBkp
  With NoRecovery, File = 2
Restore Database AppDta From AppDtaBkp
  With File = 5
```

The File argument specifies which backup set to use from the backup device.

Note that there are several important aspects of restoring a differential backup. First, you must restore a full backup before you can restore a differential backup. Second, when you restore the full backup, specify With NoRecovery so the process doesn't roll back uncommitted transactions that are in the portion of the log saved with the full backup. Don't specify the NoRecovery option when you restore the differential database backup, unless you're going to also restore the transaction log, as discussed next.

Restoring Full Backups, Differential Database, and Transaction Log Backups

If you have one or more transaction log backups in addition to a full and (optionally) a differential backup, you can use statements such as the following to restore the database:

```
Restore Database AppDta From AppDtaFullBkp
  With NoRecovery
Restore Database AppDta From AppDtaDifBkp
  With NoRecovery
Restore Log AppDta From AppDtaLogBkp
  With NoRecovery, File = 1
Restore Log AppDta From AppDtaLogBkp
  With File = 2
```

In this example, the full backup was saved to the AppDtaFullBkp backup device, and the differential backup was saved to the AppDtaDifBkp backup device. The transaction log backups were saved as a series of backup sets to the AppDtaLogBkp backup device.

To restore transaction log backups, you must start by restoring from a full backup (and, optionally, restoring a differential backup after restoring the full backup). Then you must restore an unbroken chain of transaction log backups that begin with the first log backup taken after the full (or differential) database backup. Each Restore statement, except the last one, must specify With NoRecovery. The last Restore statement must *not* specify NoRecovery.

> **NOTE:**   If you get a message such as "Database 'AppDta' cannot be opened—it is in the middle of a load." after restoring a database, it's probably because you specified NoRecovery on the last Restore statement. You can recover from this situation by entering a statement such as Restore AppDta With Recovery (don't specify a From clause).

The Transact-SQL manual explains additional Restore Database and Restore Log statement options that let you control tape device operations when you perform a restore operation.

Recovering the master Database

If you lose the master database and cannot start SQL Server, you have to run the SQL Server Setup program to recover it. These are the steps required:

1. Rebuild the master database.

   a. Have the SQL Server installation CD (or shared network directory) loaded.

   b. Run the rebuildm.exe program (found in the \Mssql7\Binn directory), click the Browse button, select the \Data folder from the installation CD, and click OK.

   c. Click the Settings button and verify or change the character set, sort order, and Unicode collation options to use for all databases. Click OK.

   Note: In rebuildm.exe, the initial setting values are the installation *defaults*, not necessarily your current SQL Server installation's settings. Be sure to set these correctly.

   d. Click the Rebuild button to create a fresh copy of the master database.

2. Start SQL Server in single-user mode using a command such as the following:

   ```
   sqlservr.exe -m
   ```

   Then use SQL Server Enterprise Manager to add the backup device that was used when you did the most recent master database backup.

3. Restore the master database using the steps described previously under "Recovery for a Damaged Database." You must be running SQL Server in single-user mode to restore the master database.

4. Manually reenter any master database changes that weren't reflected in the backup used to restore the master database.

5. Restore the msdb database, which the rebuilding step destroys, using the steps described previously for recovering a database (see "Recovery for a Damaged Database").

6. If you have previously changed the model database, you need to restore it, too.

7. If you are using replication, you need to restore the distribution database, too.

8. Restore any unusable user databases.

9. Verify that your security (that is, logins, users, and permissions) are properly set up after the Restore operations; reenter any necessary operations.

> **NOTE:** It's very important to make a backup of the master database after every change that affects tables in the master database. This allows you to fully recover all information about the rest of your database objects.

Restoring a File or Filegroup

If you know that only some of the files or filegroups (as discussed in Chapter 9) used for a large database have been damaged, you may be able to reduce recovery time by restoring just the files or filegroups, instead of the entire database. To restore a file or filegroup, however, you *must* also have an unbroken transaction log chain that spans from the *oldest* transaction on the *earliest* file or filegroup you restore through the *most recent* transaction on the *latest* file or filegroup you restore. On the Restore Database dialog box's General tab (Figure 4-7), select "Filegroups or files" for the Restore option. In the Parameters panel, select each file or filegroup entry that you want to restore. On the Options tab (Figure 4-8), select the Recovery completion state option labeled "Leave database nonoperational, but able to restore additional transaction logs. "Selecting this option lets you subsequently apply the transaction logs." The rest of the steps are the same as for restoring a database. After restoring the files or filegroups, restore the transaction logs that span the files or filegroups you restore.

Specifying Files and Filegroups on the Restore Database Statement

The Restore Database statement also lets you specify one or more files or filegroups to restore, rather than restoring the entire database. The following statement shows how you would restore the SalesFileGroup filegroup in the AppDta database from the AppDtaBkp backup device:

```
Restore Database AppDta..Customer
  FileGroup = 'SalesFileGroup'
  From AppDtaBkp
  With No Recovery
```

Use the File keyword instead of the FileGroup keyword to specify a file, and separate multiple file and filegroup entries with commas. After you restore a file or filegroup, you should also restore the appropriate transaction log backups that were made after the database backup.

Restoring from a Backup Device

Another approach to restoring a database is to select From device for the Restore option on the Restore Database dialog box's General tab (see Figure 4-9). When this option is chosen, you can click the Select Devices button to add a previously defined database backup device(s), or Windows NT disk file(s) or tape device(s) as the source of the backup set. After selecting devices, you can identify which type of backup set to use (for example, Database-complete) and click the View contents button to select a specific backup set from the devices. These steps identify the source of the database and transaction log backups used for the restore operation. After selecting any options on the Options tab, click OK to run the restore.

BACKUP AND RECOVERY SERVER OPTIONS

SQL Server has several configuration options that relate to backup and recovery. (Configuration options are discussed more fully in Chapter 2.) To display or change backup configuration options, you can use SQL Server Enterprise Manager. From the main window, expand the tree and right-click a server. Select Properties from the pop-up menu, and select the Database Settings tab to display the SQL Server Properties dialog box shown in Figure 4-10.

In this dialog box, you can set the default amount of time to wait for a tape to be ready, the media retention period, and the recovery interval. The media retention period

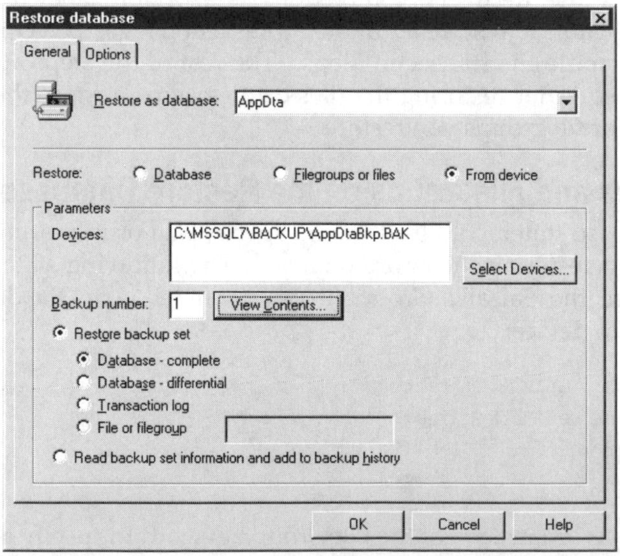

Figure 4-9.   Restore Database dialog box – General tab (restore from device)

specifies the number of days to retain a backup copy before allowing it to be overwritten. The recovery interval specifies the desired maximum number of minutes for SQL Server to automatically recover each database in case of a failure that doesn't damage the database. Setting this number lower will reduce the maximum recovery time, but it will cause data to be written more frequently, which may reduce the overall transaction processing rate.

You can use the sp_configure stored procedure to specify the latter two properties, as in the following examples:

```
sp_configure 'media retention', '180'
sp_configure 'recovery interval', '10'
```

USING A STANDBY SERVER

You can significantly reduce recovery time by maintaining a second NT system as a *standby server* (or *warm backup*). All this means is that the backup system is kept nearly up-to-date with the primary system. To set up a standby server, you create the same logins, devices, and databases as you have on your primary system. Then, every time you back up a database or transaction log on the primary system, you immediately restore the database or transaction log onto the standby server. If the primary system fails, the standby server is ready to use, although it may be missing the most recent transactions that haven't been backed up from the primary system.

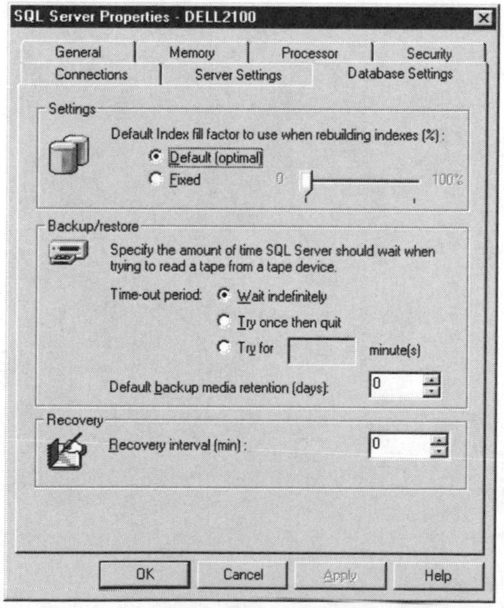

Figure 4-10. SQL Server Properties dialog box – Database Settings

NOTE: You can use SQL Server Agent jobs (discussed in Chapter 2) to automate the steps to maintain a standby server.

CONCLUSION

The ability to fully recover from damage to your database is critical to production databases. Be sure that you plan, document, and faithfully carry out a backup schedule that provides a reliable basis for recovery. It's also a good idea to use only high-quality tape drives and tapes because they become critical elements in your recovery process. SQL Server Enterprise Manager provides an easy-to-use interface for most backup and restore operations. The Transact-SQL Backup and Restore statements provide an alternative means of performing these operations.

CHAPTER 5

Data Replication and Data Warehousing

D ata replication and data warehousing are two of the hottest database technologies, and SQL Server 7 brings a lot of new features to the table in both of these areas. SQL Server database replication enables you to distribute your database information to multiple systems across your network. Replication enables your business to share its vital data between different departments and even different company locations. Starting with release 6, SQL Server includes tools that allow both push and pull models of data replication. To this, SQL Server 7 adds the new *distributed merge replication* capability that enables disconnected and mobile users to run their applications offline and then periodically synchronize with the main database. As you'll see later in this chapter, SQL Server database replication is a powerful and flexible tool for distributing information across your enterprise.

Data warehousing technology is intended to help you analyze and better understand the data that's contained within your databases. Data warehousing and decision-support applications help you to see the trends and relationships that exist with the data that's contained in your databases. Prior to SQL Server 7, data warehousing required the use of third-party tools. SQL Server 7 encompasses a primary part of the *Microsoft Data Warehousing Framework*, a set of tools that is designed to enable you to build data warehousing applications using SQL Server. At the heart of the Data Warehousing Framework is the new *OLAP Services*, which enables you to use SQL Server databases as a data source for data warehousing applications. The first part of this chapter explains SQL Server's database replication and presents an example of how to implement distributed merge replications. The second part of this chapter covers data warehousing and shows how you can use the new SQL Server OLAP Services to build a data warehouse using SQL Server.

DATABASE REPLICATION

Database replication enables you to distribute copies of data automatically from a single source to one or more target systems. SQL Server's database replication is based on a push-pull model of data replication. In this model, the replication process can be initiated either by a source server "pushing" the replicated data to a target server or by a target server "pulling" the data from a source server. In SQL Server terminology, the source system is typically referred to as the *Publisher*, while the target system is referred to as the *Subscriber*. With *push replication*, the Publisher replicates the data to the Subscriber without waiting for the Subscriber to request the data. Conversely, with *pull replication*, the Subscriber must request the information, to prompt the Publisher to deliver the data to the Subscriber.

The need for transactional consistency and site autonomy are two of the primary factors that govern how replication should be set up. *Transactional consistency* refers to the need for a given database transaction to remain as a unit, even if it is distributed across multiple locations. *Site autonomy* refers to the ability of a location to function even if it is not currently connected to the central or primary database. These two factors tend to be at odds with each other. Full transactional consistency across multiple locations requires that sites be well connected, to establish the two-phase commit protocol that is required for all database transactions to have atomicity. On the other hand, site autonomy requires that a particular site be capable of functioning regardless of the status of the connection to other locations.

SQL Server Replication Components

The basic components of SQL Server replication are articles, Distributors, publications, Publishers, and Subscribers. Figure 5-1 presents an overview of the basic SQL Server replication components.

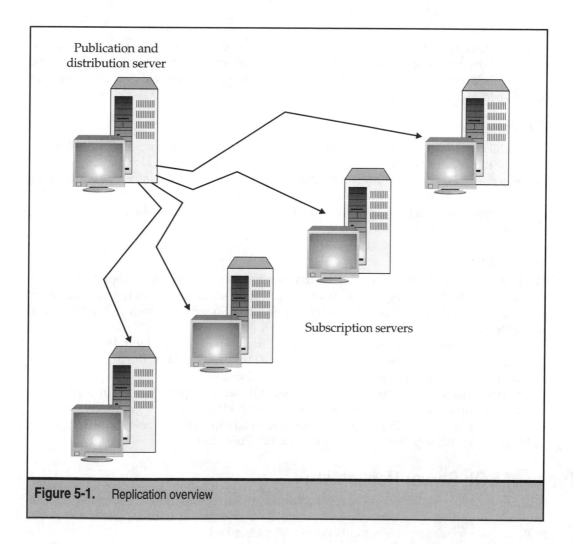

Figure 5-1.   Replication overview

Article

An article is the basic replication unit. In other words, the article represents what is being published. An article can be data from a table or a database object, such as an entire table or even a stored procedure. All articles must belong to a publication.

Distributor

The Distributor is the SQL Server system that is responsible for transferring the replicated data between the Publisher and the Subscriber. For small-scale replication, the Distributor and the Publisher are usually parts of the same system. For large-scale replication, the Distributor often is implemented as a separate system.

Publication

A publication represents a group of articles, which consists of the data that will be replicated from the Publisher to the Subscriber. A Subscriber subscribes to a publication, not to individual articles. The concept of the publication enables related data and objects to be grouped together for replication.

Publisher

The Publisher is responsible for making data available for replication. The Publisher contains the master replication database. SQL Server replication always has just one Publisher. The SQL Server Publisher extracts from its database the information that will be replicated and then forwards that information to the Distributor, which is often on the same system. Although exceptions exist, typically, only the Publisher can modify the data that's being replicated.

Subscriber

The Subscriber is a SQL Server system that receives the data that is updated and made available by the Publisher. A SQL Server replication scenario has only one Publisher, but can have multiple Subscribers. Normally, the Subscriber does not update the replicated data.

As you may have noticed, SQL Server replication is based on a hierarchical structure. It is not a peer-to-peer arrangement. Instead, the Publisher contains the master database and makes the publication available to the Subscribers.

At first, this structure seems to imply that SQL Server replication is quite limited—forcing the replication to flow in one direction only. However, that's not the case. Each SQL Server system is able to function simultaneously in multiple roles. For instance, a Publisher can also subscribe to one or more other Publishers.

Types of SQL Server Replication

SQL Server supports four types of replication: snapshot, transactional, transactional with immediate-updating Subscribers, and merge. Each of these types of replication uses the SQL Server replication components previously described.

Snapshot Replication

As its name suggests, *snapshot replication* makes a copy of the data being replicated at a specific point in time. The entire copy is then published to the Subscribers. Snapshot replication is particularly well suited to situations that do not need a high degree of data consistency. For instance, you might use snapshot replication when you have one SQL Server system functioning as a primary online transaction processing (OLTP) system, and a second SQL Server system functioning as a decision-support system. The decision-support system doesn't require the absolutely latest data and can function just fine by using the data from the end of the preceding day. In this case, snapshot replication can be used to perform a nightly replication of the OLTP database to the query database.

Transactional Replication

Transactional replication uses the SQL Server transaction log to replicate individual transactions between the Publisher and the Subscriber. The Publisher's transaction log captures the Publisher's database modifications, which then are applied to the Subscriber(s) transaction log in the same order that they occurred. With transactional replication, the exchange of data between the Publisher and the Subscriber can happen either continuously, almost in real time, or at predefined intervals. Transaction replication is designed to handle cases in which two databases require a high degree of data consistency. For instance, transactional replication is a good choice to handle a situation in which two different locations take orders from a shared inventory database, and both locations need frequent database updates that reflect the activity of all the locations.

Transactional Replication with Immediate-Updating Subscribers

Transactional replication with immediate-updating Subscribers builds on standard transactional replication by enabling Subscribers to modify the replicated data. With immediate-updating Subscribers, the replicated transaction can be modified as long as the Subscriber can establish a two-phase commit connection with the Publisher. Updates to the replicated data made by the Subscriber can then be posted back to the Publisher, using the two-phase commit protocol. Transactional replication with immediate-updating Subscribers ensures a very high degree of enterprise-wide database consistency, but it also requires a network connection always to be available between the Publisher and the Subscriber. In a well-connected network, the update latency typically is only a few seconds when using transactional replication with immediate update.

Merge

Merge replication tracks the changes made in both the source and target databases, and then synchronizes the changes to both the Subscriber and Publisher when the database is replicated. Merge replication is designed to handle branch-office situations that require a very high degree of autonomy. For instance, by using merge replication, a branch office can function while fully disconnected from a primary centralized database that is located at corporate headquarters. During the day, the branch office can use its own database to perform all the tasks that it may need to. At the end of the day, the branch office can connect to the central office and merge with the central corporate database any sales summary, order, or new customer information that has been generated during the day. Likewise, any changes that have been made to the corporate customer or credit databases can be merged with the databases in the branch office. If changes in the Publisher and the Subscriber conflict with each other, the conflict is resolved by using a set of rules that govern the merge replication.

As implied in the preceding explanation, the type of replication that you choose depends on the degree and site autonomy that you need, as well as the degree of enterprise transaction consistency that you require. Figure 5-2 lays out a scale of the replication types and shows how they relate to the factors of data consistency and site autonomy. You can see that merge replication provides the highest degree of site autonomy, and transaction replication with immediate-updating Subscribers provides the highest degree of data consistency. Snapshot replication and standard transactional replication fall in the middle of the scale.

NOTE: You can achieve an even higher degree of enterprise data consistency by building distributed applications using the Microsoft Distributed Transaction Coordinator (MSDTC).

Setting Up a Simple Merge Replication

The first part of this chapter presented an overview of the basic SQL Server data-replication concepts and shows how the different SQL Server replication types interact with the factors of site autonomy and enterprise database consistency. Now, you'll see how to set up a simple SQL Server replication task by using the replication wizards

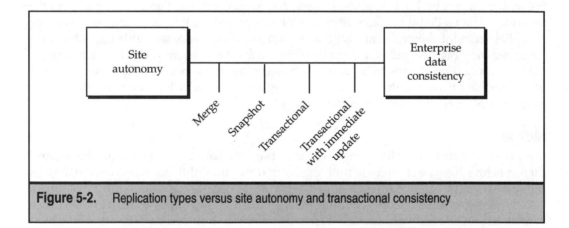

Figure 5-2. Replication types versus site autonomy and transactional consistency

provided with SQL Server 7. The first step to set up replication is to create a new publication. Then the Distributors and Subscribers are defined.

Creating a New Publication

You can start the SQL Server Create Publication Wizard from the SQL Server Enterprise Manager by selecting the Replication option on the Tools menu. A screen similar to the one shown in Figure 5-3 is displayed.

As mentioned, your first step to set up replication is to create a publication. After you create a publication, you can add articles to the publication and select the replication method. To create a new publication, first select the Create and Manage Publications option from the Replication menu, which displays a window that enables you to select the SQL Server system and database that you want to act as the replication Publisher. After you select the replication database, click OK, and the Create Publication Wizard Welcome dialog box appears, as shown in Figure 5-4.

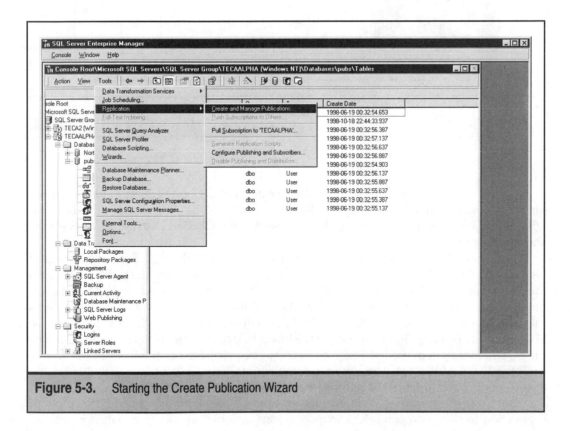

Figure 5-3.   Starting the Create Publication Wizard

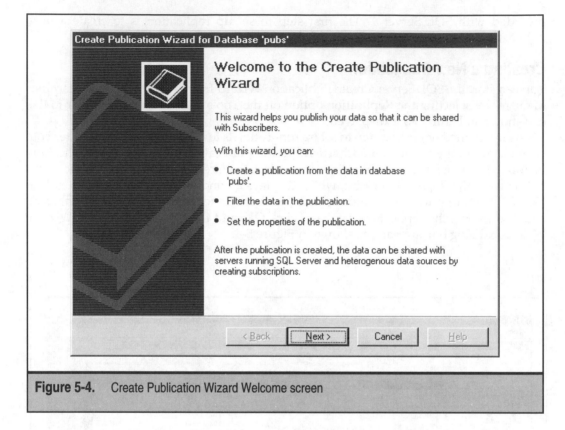

Figure 5-4. Create Publication Wizard Welcome screen

The title bar and the first bullet on the Create Publication Wizard Welcome screen display the name of the database that will be the *master database*, the source of the data that will be replicated. Click the Next button to display the Choose Distributor dialog box, shown in Figure 5-5.

The Choose Distributor dialog box enables you to select the SQL Server system that will act as the Distributor. The Distributor is responsible for sending the publication from the Publisher to the Subscribers. By default, the Publisher is selected as the Distributor, but you can select another system to act as the Distributor. The other SQL Server systems that can function as a Distributor and that are registered in the SQL Server Enterprise Manager are displayed in the list box in the lower half of the screen. As Figure 5-5 shows, the SQL Server system named TECAALPHA has been selected as the Distributor. In this case, the TECAALPHA system is also the Publisher. Click the Next button to display the Create Publication Wizard dialog box, shown in Figure 5-6.

The Create Publication Wizard dialog box enables you to specify the type of replication to use. You can select snapshot, transactional, or merge replication. Merge replication has been selected in Figure 5-6. Merge replication provides a high degree of data independence and is suitable for branch office applications or for use in mobile and

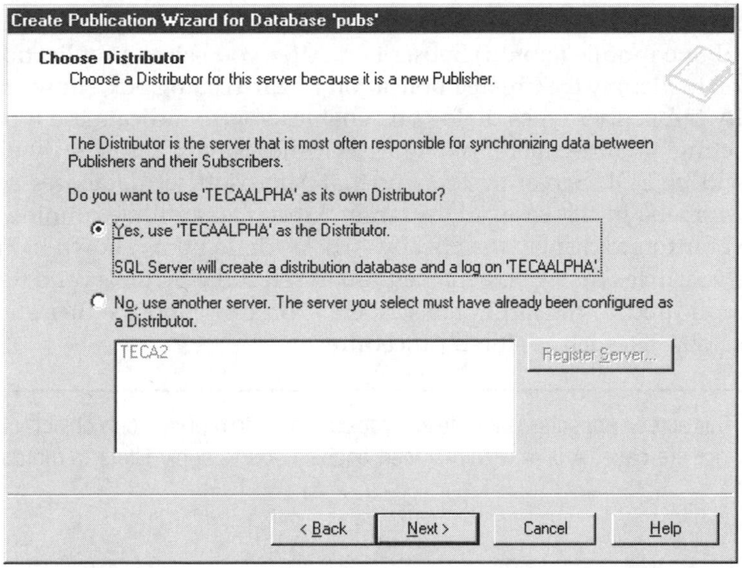

Create Publication Wizard for Database 'pubs'

Choose Distributor
Choose a Distributor for this server because it is a new Publisher.

The Distributor is the server that is most often responsible for synchronizing data between Publishers and their Subscribers.

Do you want to use 'TECAALPHA' as its own Distributor?

- Yes, use 'TECAALPHA' as the Distributor.

  SQL Server will create a distribution database and a log on 'TECAALPHA'.

- No, use another server. The server you select must have already been configured as a Distributor.

  TECA2   Register Server...

< Back   Next >   Cancel   Help

Figure 5-5.   Create Publication Wizard – Choose Distributor

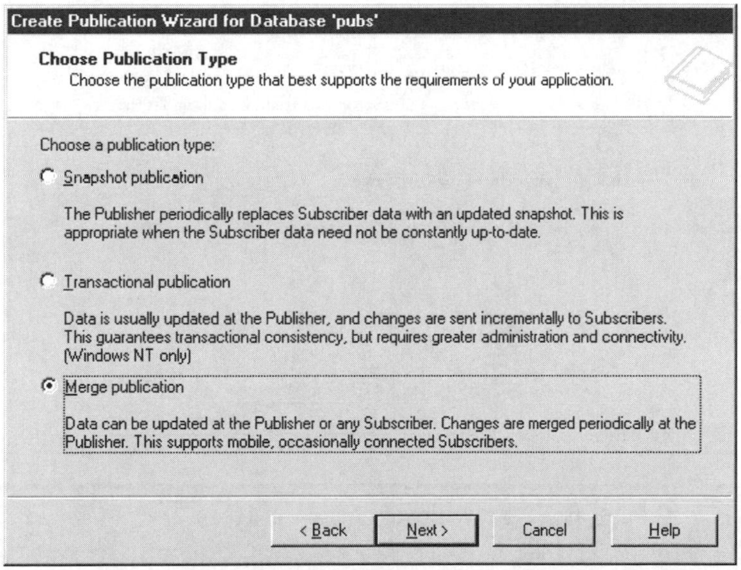

Create Publication Wizard for Database 'pubs'

Choose Publication Type
Choose the publication type that best supports the requirements of your application.

Choose a publication type:

- Snapshot publication

  The Publisher periodically replaces Subscriber data with an updated snapshot. This is appropriate when the Subscriber data need not be constantly up-to-date.

- Transactional publication

  Data is usually updated at the Publisher, and changes are sent incrementally to Subscribers. This guarantees transactional consistency, but requires greater administration and connectivity. (Windows NT only)

- Merge publication

  Data can be updated at the Publisher or any Subscriber. Changes are merged periodically at the Publisher. This supports mobile, occasionally connected Subscribers.

< Back   Next >   Cancel   Help

Figure 5-6.   Create Publication Wizard – Choose Publication Type

disconnected database applications. In this example, merge replication is selected because the data replication is intended to flow to two Subscribers: one well-connected Subscriber and one mobile (laptop) Subscriber. After you select a replication type, click the Next button to display the Create Publication Wizard dialog box, shown in Figure 5-7.

The Specify Subscriber types dialog box enables you to indicate the type of systems that will be acting as Subscribers. As Figure 5-7 shows, you can specify either that all Subscribers will be SQL Server systems or that Microsoft Jet databases could also be acting as Subscribers. In this case, all the target Subscribers will be running SQL Server. Click the Next button to display the Specify Articles dialog box, shown in Figure 5-8.

The Specify Articles dialog box enables you to select the SQL Server database objects that will be replicated to the target Subscribers. You can choose either entire tables or other database objects, such as stored procedures.

NOTE: This screen appears to indicate that you can select to replicate only objects at the table level, but that's not the case. A later wizard screen enables you to apply filters to the data that's being replicated.

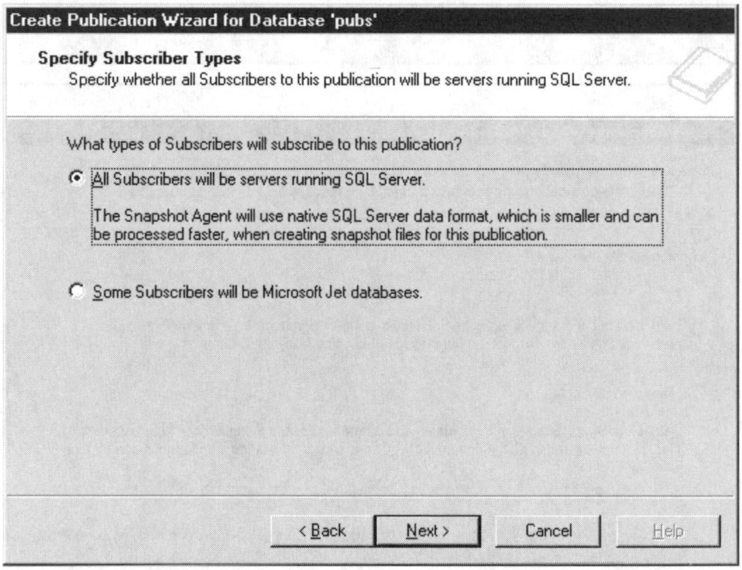

Figure 5-7.   Create Publication Wizard – Specify Subscriber Types

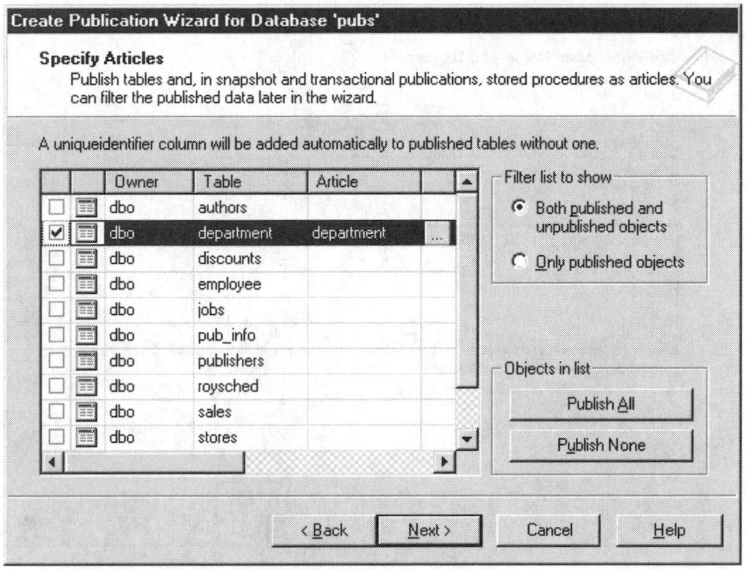

Figure 5-8. Create Publication Wizard – Specify Articles

The radio buttons on the right side of this screen enable you to filter the database objects that are included in the list. You can choose to see either the unpublished database objects only or all of the database objects in the list. The example shown in Figure 5-8 selects for replication just the department table in the pubs database. After you select the articles to include in the publication, click the Next button to assign a name to the publication.

NOTE: The department file is not a standard part of the pubs database. It is an example table that is created for use with several of the examples in this book. This table illustrates data modification and replication without modifying the original tables in the pubs database.

The Choose Publication Name and Description dialog box, shown in Figure 5-9, enables you to name the publication that was created using the Replication Wizard. By default, the Create Publication Wizard assigns the name of the database that's being replicated. The name of the sample table that's being replicated has been added to the figure. This dialog box also enables you to enter an additional text description for the

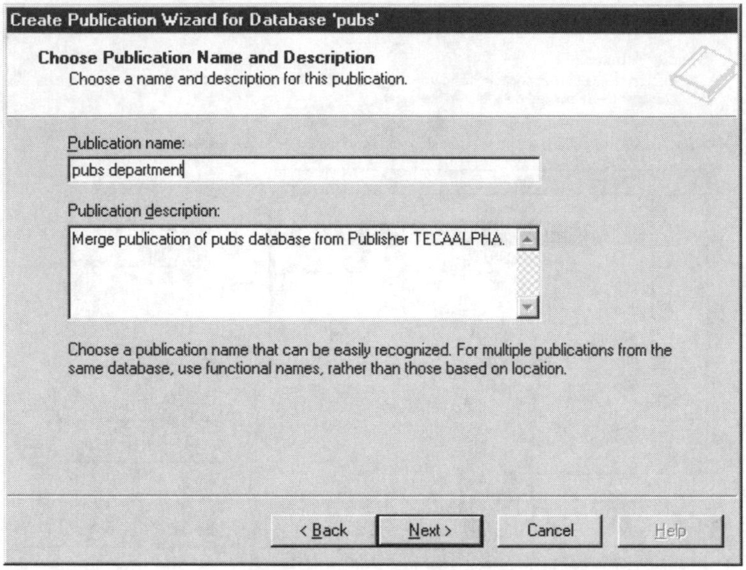

Figure 5-9. Create Publication Wizard – Choose Publication Name and Description

publication. Click the Next button to display the Use Default Properties dialog box, shown in Figure 5-10.

The Use Default Properties dialog box enables you to set any data filters that you want to apply to the replicated data, and to confirm the settings that you made on the prior wizard dialog boxes. Data filters allow you to select from the tables the columns and rows that are being used as publication articles. The example in Figure 5-10 shows that no data filters are being used, which means that all the changes in the department table will be replicated to the Subscribers. Click the Next button to display the final Create Publication Wizard dialog box, shown in Figure 5-11.

This completes the steps required to create a new SQL Server publication by using the Create Publication Wizard. At this point, you can click either the Back button, to modify any of the settings that you entered on the previous dialog boxes, or the Next button, to create the new publication. After the publication has been created, a new Replication Monitor icon is added to the SQL Server Enterprise Manager.

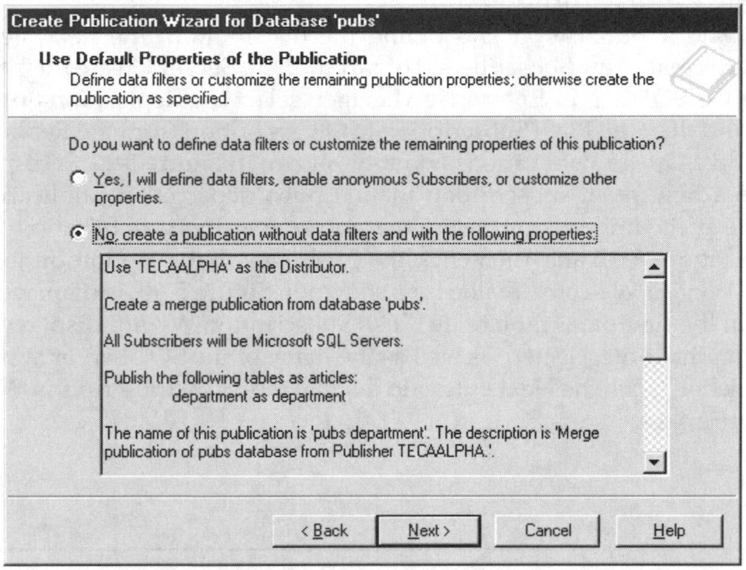

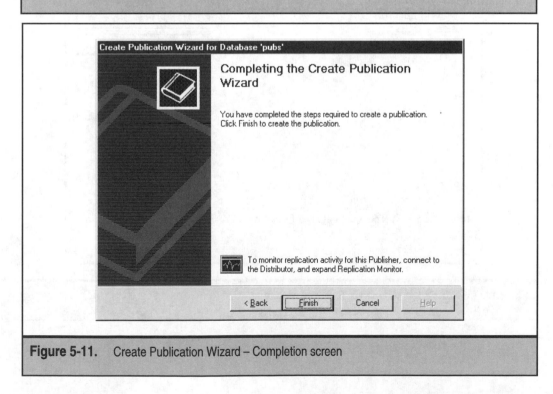

Figure 5-10.   Create Publication Wizard – Use Default Properties of the Publication

Figure 5-11.   Create Publication Wizard – Completion screen

Creating New Subscriptions

After you create a publication and define the distribution, the next step to set up replication is to create new Subscribers. To start the SQL Server Create Push Subscription Wizard from the SQL Server Enterprise Manager, select the Replication option from the Tools menu and then the Push Subscription to Others option from the Replication menu. The Create and Manage Publications window, shown in Figure 5-12, is displayed.

To create a new push subscription for the pubs department publication that was created in the preceding section, select the pubs department publication from the list displayed in Figure 5-12 and then click the Push New Subscription button. The Push Subscription Wizard Welcome dialog box, shown in Figure 5-13, is displayed.

The text in the first paragraph of the Push Subscription Wizard displays the name of the publication that you selected, as well as the name of the SQL Server system that will serve as Publisher. Click the Next button to display the Push Subscription Wizard screen shown in Figure 5-14.

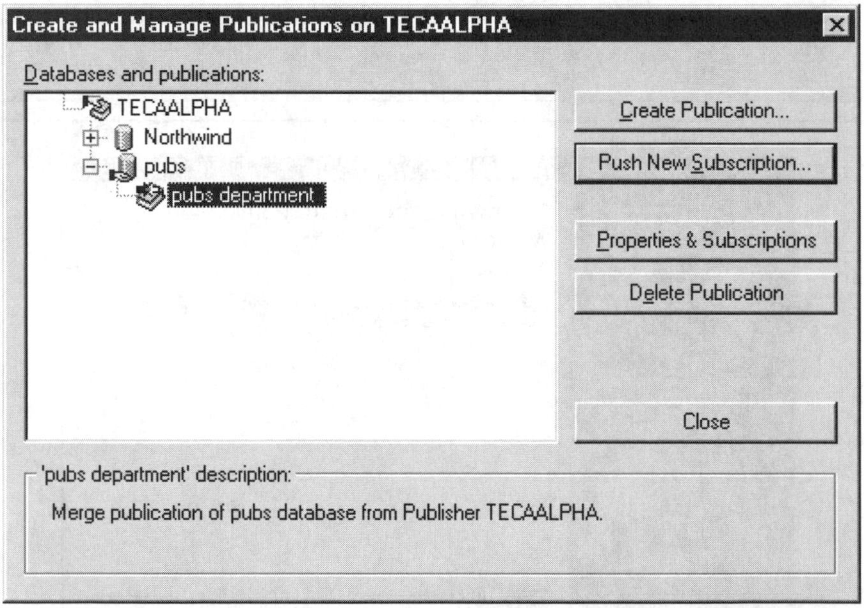

Figure 5-12. Create and Manage Publications screen

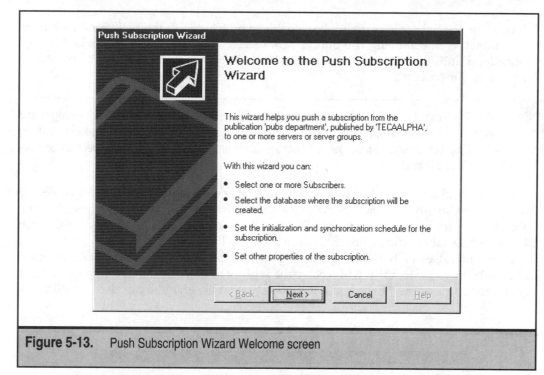

Figure 5-13.   Push Subscription Wizard Welcome screen

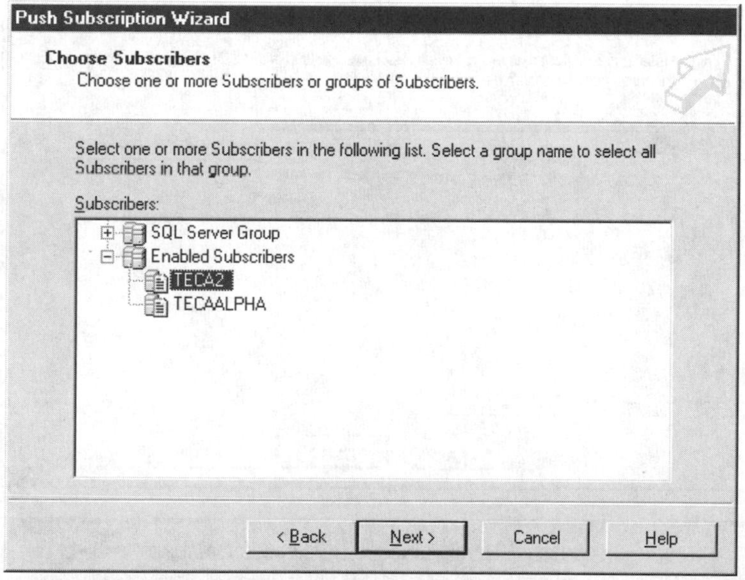

Figure 5-14.   Push Subscription Wizard – Choose Subscribers

The Choose Subscribers dialog box enables you to specify the SQL Server systems that will act as Subscribers. The Subscribers receive the data that is published by the replication Publisher. Figure 5-14 shows the two SQL Server systems that can potentially function as Subscribers.

TIP: The Push Subscription Wizard sees only the SQL Server systems that have been registered using the SQL Server Enterprise Manager. If a System is not listed, you can either register it by using the SQL Server Enterprise Manager or select the Configure Publishing and Subscribers option from the Replication menu.

To specify the systems that will act as Subscribers, select them in the list. In Figure 5-14, you can see that the SQL Server system named TECA2 has been selected as the Subscriber. After you select the Subscribers, click the Next button to display the Choose Destination Database dialog box, shown in Figure 5-15.

The Choose Destination Database dialog box enables you to select the database on the target Subscriber system that will receive the replicated data. By default, this value is set to the same name as the database that is used as the Publisher, but it can also be a different

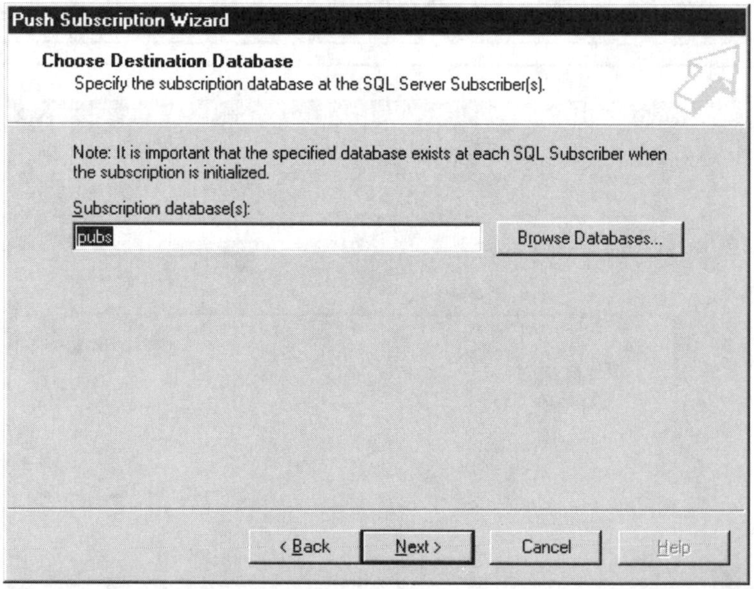

Figure 5-15. Push Subscription Wizard – Choose Destination Database

name. However, while the name can be different, the named database must exist on the Subscriber. If you want to use a different database name, you can enter it in the text box or use the Browse Databases button to view the databases that exist on the Subscription. Click the Next button to display the Set Merge Agent Schedule dialog box, shown in Figure 5-16.

The Set Merge Agent Schedule dialog box enables you to indicate how frequently the data should be replicated from the Publisher to the Subscriber. You can choose to replicate the data either continuously or at a predetermined interval. As you might expect, continuous replication is best suited for local connections that are always available, and scheduled replication is best suited for WAN connections that are not well connected. The default setting schedules the push replication to occur once an hour. Click the Change button to adjust the scheduled replication frequency. The Change button displays the Edit Recurring Job Schedule dialog box, shown in Figure 5-17.

The Edit Recurring Job Schedule dialog box allows you to set all the variables that control how frequently the publication is pushed to the Subscriber. Most of the settings are straightforward; however, note that you must select the Daily option even if you want the replication to occur on a more frequent basis. For instance, the Daily option must be

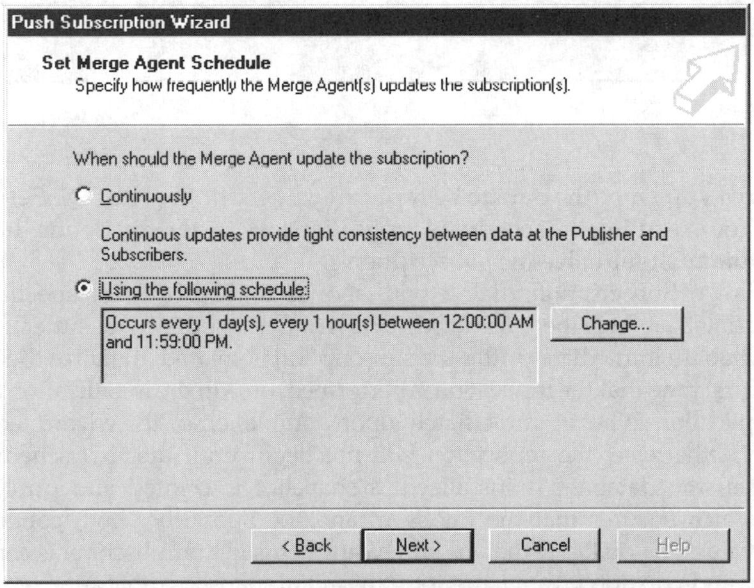

Figure 5-16. Push Subscription Wizard – Set Merge Agent Schedule

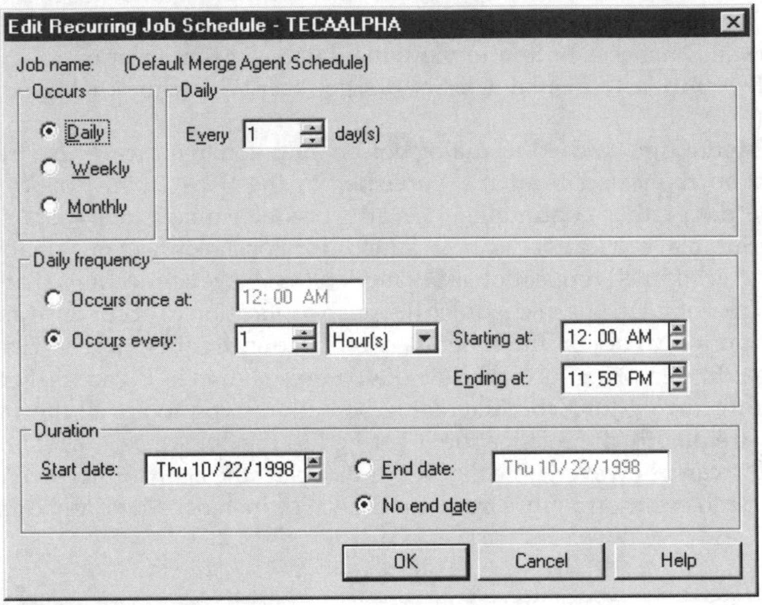

Figure 5-17. Push Subscription Wizard – Edit Recurring Job Schedule

selected even if you want the data to be replicated every hour. The SQL Server Agent is responsible for executing the scheduled replication jobs. After you define the replication frequency, you must initialize the subscription.

The Initialize Subscription dialog box, shown in Figure 5-18, specifies how the Subscriber's database will be initialized. You have the option to either initialize the Subscriber database immediately after the subscription is created, initialize the subscription database the first time that the replication is performed, or skip the initialization altogether. If you want replication to begin immediately upon completion of the wizard, check the first radio button. Otherwise, the replication will not begin until the first scheduled time is reached. When the database is initialized, a snapshot is created and published to the Subscriber, which ensures that the Publisher and the Subscriber both contain the same schema and values. If you know that the database schema in the Subscriber is consistent with the Publisher, and you don't want to perform the initial snapshot replication, you can bypass the initialization. However, if the replication targets do not exist or their schema is different from the schema used in the Publisher, then the replication will fail. After you select the subscription initialization option, click the Next button to display the Set Subscription Priority dialog box, shown in Figure 5-19.

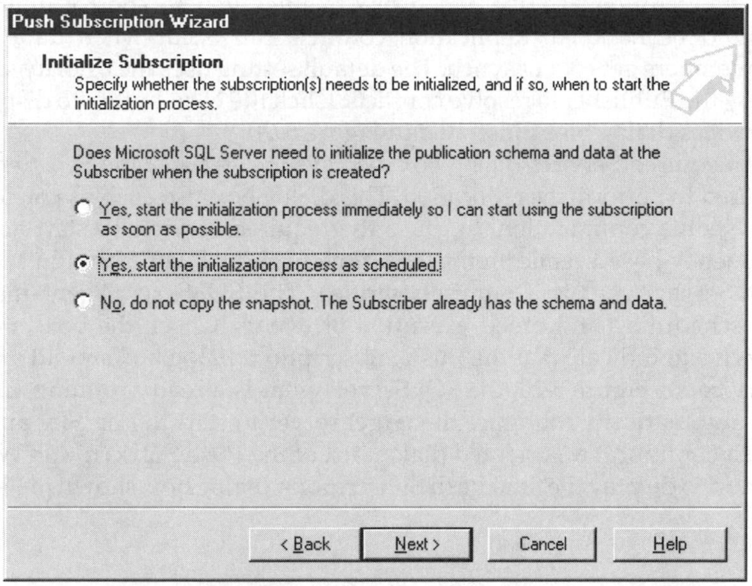

Figure 5-18.   Push Subscription Wizard – Initialize Subscription

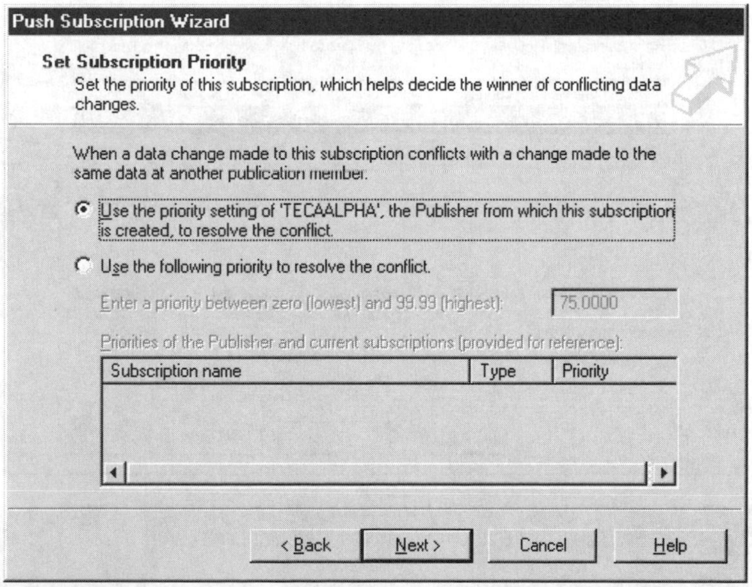

Figure 5-19.   Push Subscription Wizard – Set Subscription Priority

The Set Subscription Priority dialog box enables you to control how replication conflicts should be handled. Replication conflicts can occur when data in different publication members gets out of synch. The default setting uses the priority setting that is maintained by the Publisher to resolve conflicts. Click the Next button to display the Start Required Services dialog box, illustrated in Figure 5-20.

The Start Required Services dialog box displays the status of the SQL Server services that are required to perform the replication. This dialog box also enables you to update the Subscriber system's configuration, to cause the required services to start automatically. Because frequency-based replication uses a timed interval, you shouldn't be surprised that the SQLServerAgent is a required service. The SQLServerAgent manages SQL Server's job scheduling and timed execution of events. Check the box in front of the specified service to indicate that the Push Subscription dialog box should automatically start this service. In Figure 5-20, the SQLServerAgent is already running, and the Push Wizard will automatically configure the target server to start this service automatically. This is the last configuration-oriented dialog box of the Push Subscription Wizard. Click the Next button to display the final Push Subscription dialog box, shown in Figure 5-21.

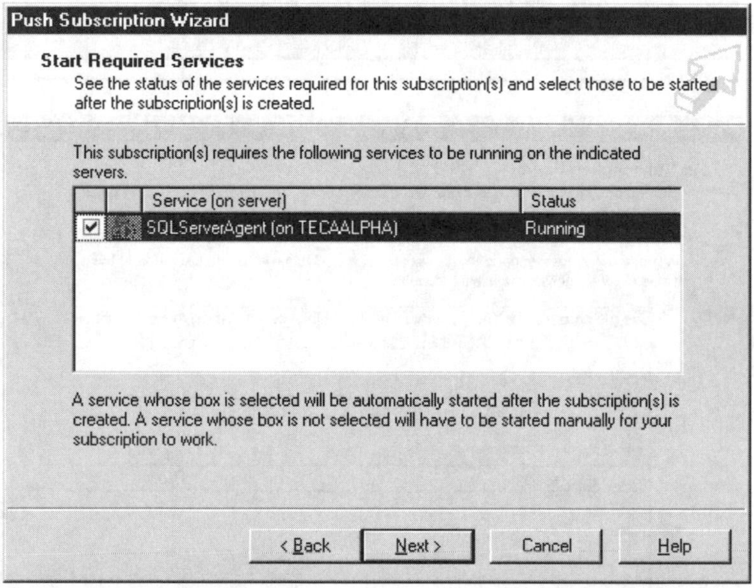

Figure 5-20.   Push Subscription Wizard – Start Required Services

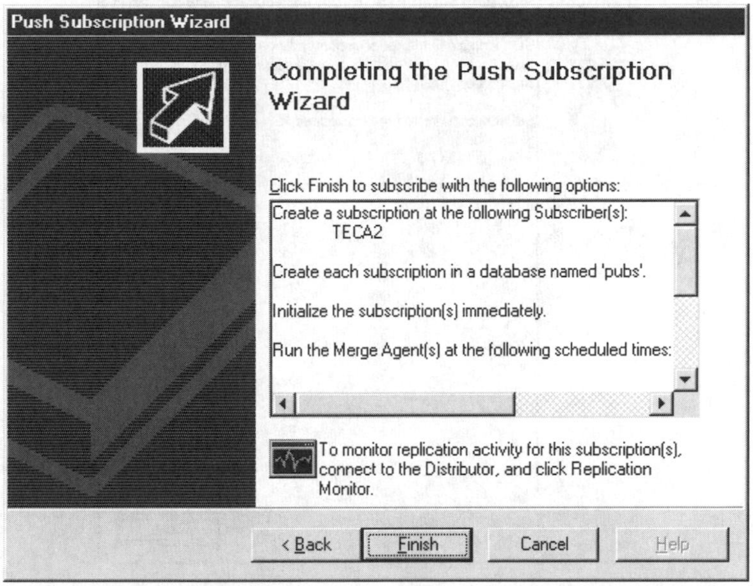

Figure 5-21. Push Subscription Wizard – Completion screen

This completes the steps required to create a new SQL Server subscription by using the Push Subscription Wizard. This dialog box summarizes the push subscription setting that you created in the earlier dialog boxes. At this point, you can click either the Back button, to modify any of the settings that you entered in the previous dialog boxes, or the Next button, to create the new subscription on the target SQL Server system.

After you create the publication, the dialog box shown in Figure 5-22 is displayed by the SQL Server Enterprise Manager. This dialog box confirms the creation of the subscription on the remote SQL Server system. If you selected the option to initialize the Subscriber immediately, the replication process can begin immediately. Otherwise, the replication will not start until the first replication trigger event is fired.

After you establish the replication, you can check the status of the replication by selecting the publication, using the SQL Server Enterprise Manager. Right-click the Merge Publication Agent, shown in the right pane of the SQL Server Enterprise Manager, to display a pop-up menu that contains the Agent History option. Select the Agent History option to display a status window similar to the one shown in Figure 5-23.

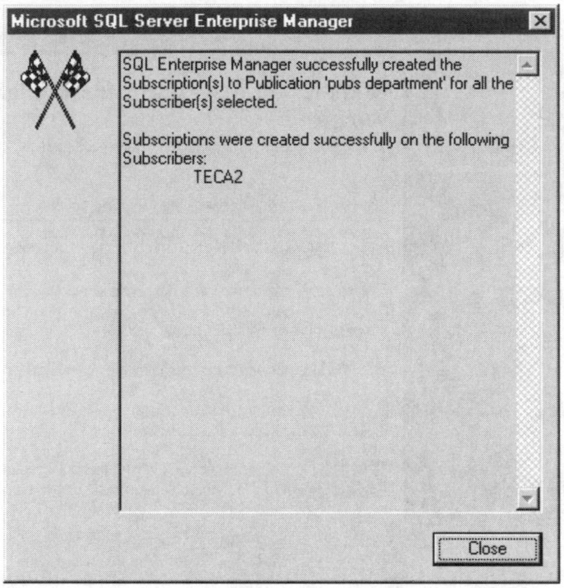

Figure 5-22. Subscription completion message

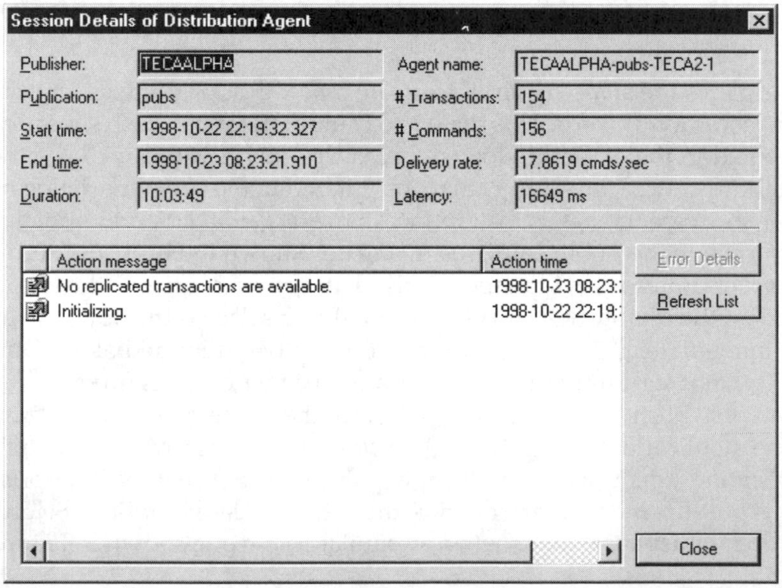

Figure 5-23. Displaying the Replication agent history

The upper-left portion of the window shows the Publisher's name and the database that contains the publication. Displayed beneath these items are the start time, end time, and elapsed time of the Replication agent. The upper-right portion of the screen shows some summary statistics for the replication process, including the total number of commands and transactions, as well as the delivery rate and average latency of the replication, in milliseconds.

SQL Server replication is relatively simple to set up, and it is also very flexible. That flexibility allows it to be used in a variety of situations, but it also makes it impossible to cover the entire spectrum of its capabilities in one chapter. You can refer to the "Additional References" section, later in this chapter, for a pointer to additional SQL Server data replication resources. The next section of this chapter covers SQL Server data warehousing.

DATA WAREHOUSING

Data warehousing involves taking the data stored in a relational database and processing that data to make it a more effective tool for queries and decision-support analysis. The most current buzzword for this process of data transformation and analysis is *business intelligence*. In other words, data warehousing is a technology that aims to transform collected data into meaningful information. Data warehousing is performed by using a multistep process that includes collecting data, cleansing data, and storing data for use in analyses and reporting applications. The data can originate from a variety of different sources, including different database systems and even different operating systems. The primary goal of the data analysis is to identify patterns and trends, to help you make better decisions about the operation of your enterprise.

As you might guess, collecting and summarizing the data stored in a variety of locations and formats across the enterprise is no small undertaking. That's where *data marts* enter the picture. Whereas a data warehouse refers to an enterprise-level store of standardized and summarized information, a data mart refers to a targeted subset of that information. A data mart contains just the information that addresses one particular aspect of the enterprise. For example, one common use of a data mart is to store the analytical information that's related to just one specific business unit.

The information in a data warehouse or data mart is processed by using *online analytical processing (OLAP)*. OLAP essentially views data as cubes that consist of dimensions and measures. A *dimension* is a descriptive category. For instance, a dimension might be a geographical location or a product type. A *measure* is a quantitative value, such as sales dollars, inventory amount, or total expenses. Aggregates derived from the original data source are stored in each cube cell. This method of organizing data makes filtering data easy, and makes subsequent queries fast and efficient. However, a trade-off does exist: although OLAP aggregations are a key to the query performance attainable in data warehouse queries, the cost of storing the aggregate data is disk storage. In fact, the number of aggregations can easily exceed the number of original detail rows. Additionally, the required OLAP data storage increases dramatically as the number of dimensions and aggregates increases. This dramatic increase in storage requirement is typically termed *data explosion*.

Types of OLAP

The following three primary methods, used to store the dimensional data used in data warehousing, are supported by SQL Server 7. Each of these methods varies with respect to its data storage requirements and its data retrieval speed.

▼ **MOLAP**   Multidimensional OLAP stores dimension and fact data in a persistent data store that uses compressed indexes. Aggregations are stored to facilitate fast data access. MOLAP query engines are usually proprietary and optimized for the storage format used by the MOLAP data store. MOLAP offers faster query processing than ROLAP and usually requires less storage. However, it doesn't scale as well and requires a separate database for storage.

■ **ROLAP**   Relational OLAP stores aggregations in relational database tables. ROLAP's use of the relational database enables it to take advantage of existing database resources, and allows ROLAP applications to scale well. However, ROLAP's use of tables to store aggregates usually requires more disk storage than MOLAP, which generally is not as fast.

▲ **HOLAP**   As its name suggests, Hybrid OLAP is a cross between MOLAP and ROLAP. Like ROLAP, HOLAP leaves the primary data stored in the source database. Like MOLAP, HOLAP stores aggregates in a persistent data store that's separate from the primary relational database. This mix enables HOLAP to offer the advantages of both MOLAP and ROLAP. However, unlike MOLAP and ROLAP, which follow well-defined standards, no uniform implementation exists for HOLAP.

Microsoft Data Warehousing Framework

Building a data warehouse traditionally required complex and often costly third-party products that could work with the data stored in your relational database system. SQL Server 7 significantly lowers the hurdles required to implement a data warehouse by bundling its OLAP Services with SQL Server. Code-named *Plato*, SQL Server's OLAP Services includes support for MOLAP, ROLAP, and HOLAP data stores and provides a set of wizards and management tools that drastically lower the entry level to data warehousing technology. SQL Server's OLAP Services is a part of Microsoft's overall data warehousing strategy, known as the *Microsoft Data Warehousing Framework*. Figure 5-24 presents Microsoft's Data Warehousing Framework.

The Microsoft Data Warehousing Framework is an extensible COM-based architecture that's intended as a guideline for building data warehouses on the Windows NT platform. The Microsoft Data Warehousing Framework includes the components required to build, manage, and use a data warehouse. Not surprisingly the majority of these components are features of the OLAP Services product. SQL Server's *Data Transformation Services (DTS)* provides the data transformation and cleansing function. DTS provides the ability to both import and export data from SQL Server. In the data warehousing scheme, DTS is used to load the data warehouse and perform any required data transformations. Microsoft's OLAP Services is a middle-tier server that allows users

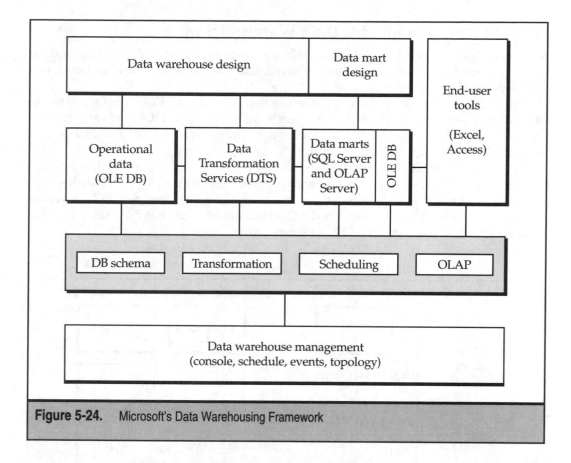

Figure 5-24.   Microsoft's Data Warehousing Framework

to perform decision-support queries on large volumes of data, with a high level of performance. OLAP Services includes the *Data Cube Service* and a client-side caching and query engine called the *PivotTable Service*. The Data Cube Service provides client-side access to OLAP data. It enables portions of the OLAP database to be sliced and stored on the client system for disconnected data analysis. The PivotTable Service essentially enables client systems to connect to the OLAP server, and enables users to conduct analysis while disconnected from the server. Application support for OLAP applications is provided by the Microsoft OLE DB for OLAP interface and the ADO-MD interface. The PivotTable Service provides end-user access, and the Microsoft Repository provides a persistent store for metadata.

In addition to these data warehousing features found in the new OLAP Services, many of the enhancements to the SQL Server 7 storage engine are designed expressly to improve support for the data warehousing and data mart type of applications. For example, SQL Server 7's support for Very Large Databases (VLDB), new hash join algorithms, new merge replication support, and intra-query parallelism support are all intended to improve the performance of large-scale query and decision-support applications used in data warehousing applications.

SQL Server Components for Data Warehousing

SQL Server's OLAP Services consists of tools that are provided on both the client and the server. Figure 5-25 presents an overview of the data warehousing components used by SQL Server's OLAP Services.

The data used by OLAP Services comes either from the MOLAP data store or the ROLAP data store. The MOLAP store is a persistent object on the OLAP server that is not part of the SQL Server database. The ROLAP data store consists of relational tables that are included in the SQL Server database.

The heart of Microsoft's OLAP Services is the *DSS Analysis Server*. This function operates as a Windows NT Service and provides the core data warehousing and computation functions. Programmatic access to the DSS Analysis Server is provided through the Decision Support Objects (DSO) object model. The OLAP Manager uses the DSO object model to control the DSS Analysis Server.

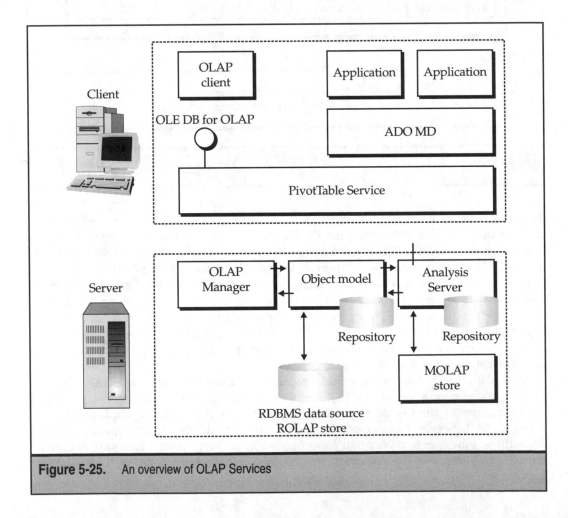

Figure 5-25. An overview of OLAP Services

End-user access is provided by the PivotTable service. Both the OLE DB provider for OLAP and the ADO MD interfaces connect to the OLAP server by using the PivotTable Service.

Installing SQL Server OLAP Services

OLAP Services is not installed as part of the standard installation for SQL Server 7. To install OLAP Services for SQL Server, you must first run the autoplay.exe file from the SQL Server installation CD-ROM, and then select the option to install the OLAP Servers from the main SQL Server installation screen.

Using the Microsoft OLAP Manager

After you install the OLAP Services, you can manage it by using the Microsoft OLAP Manager, shown in Figure 5-26. Like the SQL Server Enterprise Manager, the Microsoft OLAP Manager is a Microsoft Management Console (MMC) snap-in. Being based on

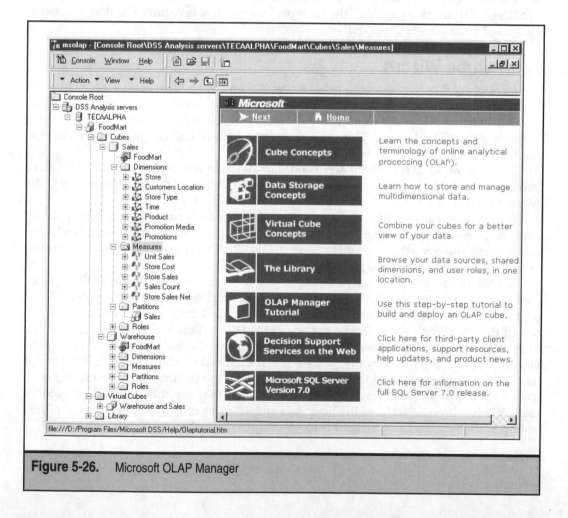

Figure 5-26.   Microsoft OLAP Manager

MMC gives the OLAP Manager the same look and feel as the SQL Server Enterprise Manager and the other BackOffice products.

The left pane of the OLAP Manager contains the different OLAP Server objects, while the right pane contains the OLAP Manager online help. The DSS Analysis Server is at the root of the tree. The defined data warehouses are found at the next level, beneath the DSS Analysis Server. OLAP Services comes with one predefined data warehouse example named FoodMart, shown in Figure 5-26, that has two cubes: Sales and Warehouse. The cube attributes are located beneath each cube. These attributes include the cube's defined dimensions, measures, partitions, and roles. The dimensions and measures define the data values that can be queried in the cube. Figure 5-26 shows the seven dimensions and five measures defined in the Sales cube. The partitions indicate the ways the cube can be split, and the roles indicate the users who have authority to use the cube.

Figure 5-26 also shows the virtual cubes and library that are used in the example FoodMart data warehouse. The Library contains the data source's shared dimensions and user roles that are used by the data warehouse. Virtual cubes are similar to SQL Server views for OLAP cubes—they enable you to combine the dimensions and measures found in different cubes, without the storage overhead that is required to store the actual additional cube dimensions in either of the original cubes.

Using the Cube Wizard

The Microsoft OLAP Manager is a graphical management tool that makes it easy to work with the different components of OLAP Services. OLAP Services also includes several wizards that are designed to help you build a data warehouse. The most central of these wizards is the Cube Wizard. This section shows how you can use the Cube Wizard to create a new OLAP cube.

To create an OLAP cube for the FoodMart data warehouse, right-click the OLAP Manager to display the pop-up menu, and then select the Cube Wizard option. The Cube Wizard Welcome dialog box, shown in Figure 5-27, is displayed.

The Cube Wizard enables you to specify the dimensions and measures that you can later use to analyze your data. The data that's used to populate the cube is derived from the columns and rows that are contained in an OLE DB data source. Click the Next button to display the Cube Wizard screen shown in Figure 5-28.

The Select a fact table dialog box enables you to select the basic fact table that will be used as the source for the OLAP cube. Fact tables contain the basic underlying details that represent a business transaction. The fact table is the fundamental element on which the rest of the OLAP cube is built. The list box in the left portion of the screen contains the data sources and tables that are contained in the data warehouse's Library. You select the fact table by clicking the entry that you want in the list of data sources and tables. The list box on the right portion of the dialog box displays the columns of the selected data source. In the example in Figure 5-28, you can see that the table named inventory_fact_1998 has been selected as the basic fact table for this example cube. Click the Next button to display the Cube Wizard Select Measures dialog box, shown in Figure 5-29.

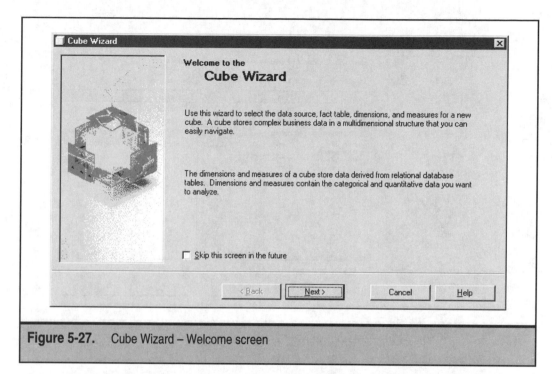

Figure 5-27. Cube Wizard – Welcome screen

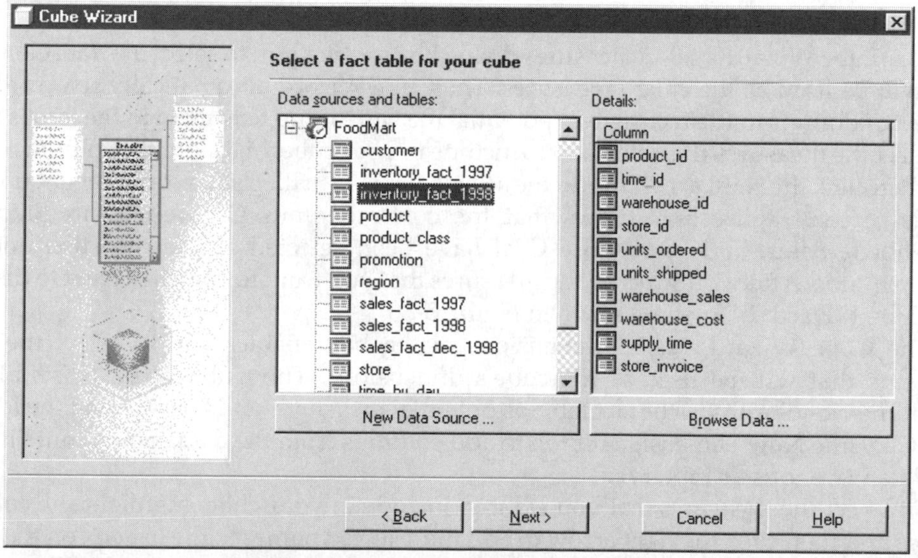

Figure 5-28. Cube Wizard – select fact table

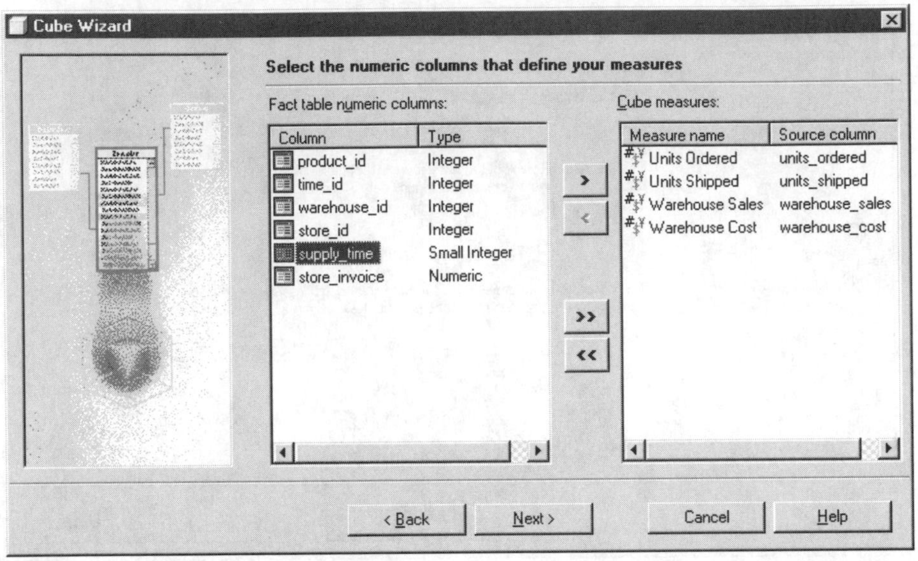

Figure 5-29. Cube Wizard – select measures

The Cube Wizard's select measures dialog box enables you to select the data elements that will be used as the cube's measures. The Cube Wizard automatically selects all the numeric columns in the fact table as potential measures, and lists them in the left list box. To select the measures that you want to include in your cube, highlight the column names and then click the right arrow to add the selected names to the list box on the right portion of the screen. Figure 5-29 shows that the columns Units Ordered, Units Shipped, Warehouse Sales, and Warehouse Cost have been selected as the measures for the example cube. After you select all the measures that you want to use, click Next to display the Cube Wizard dialog box shown in Figure 5-30.

The Cube Wizard's select dimensions dialog box enables you to select the data elements that will be used as the cube's dimensions. The Cube Wizard lists all the non-numeric columns in the fact table as potential measures, and lists them in the left list box. Click the New Dimension button to add columns from the data source contained in the data warehouse's Library.

To select the measures that you want to include in your cube, highlight the column names and then click the right arrow to add the selected names to the list box on the right portion of the screen. Figure 5-30 shows that the columns Customer Gender, Customers Location, Product, Promotion Media, and Promotions will be used as cube dimensions. This is the last configuration-oriented dialog box of the Cube Wizard. Click the Next button to display the final Cube Wizard completion dialog box, shown in Figure 5-31.

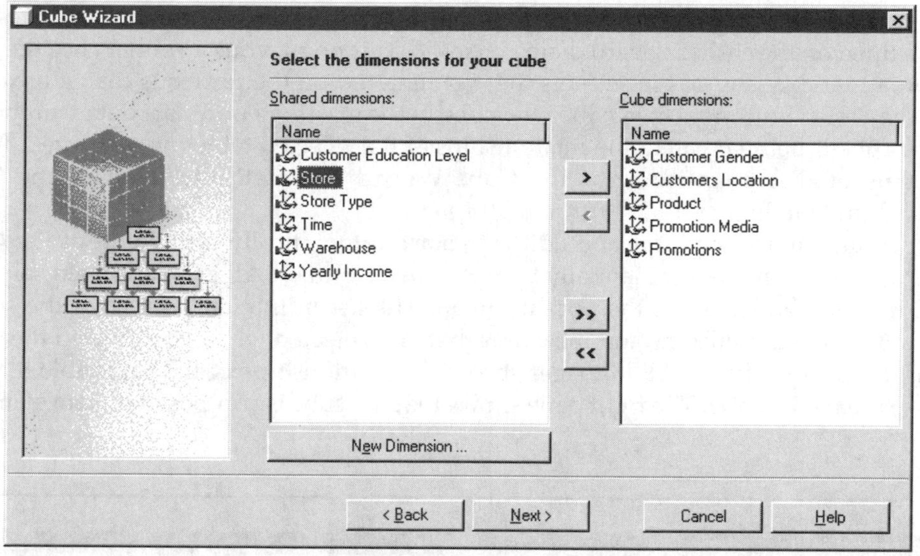

Figure 5-30. Cube Wizard – select dimensions screen

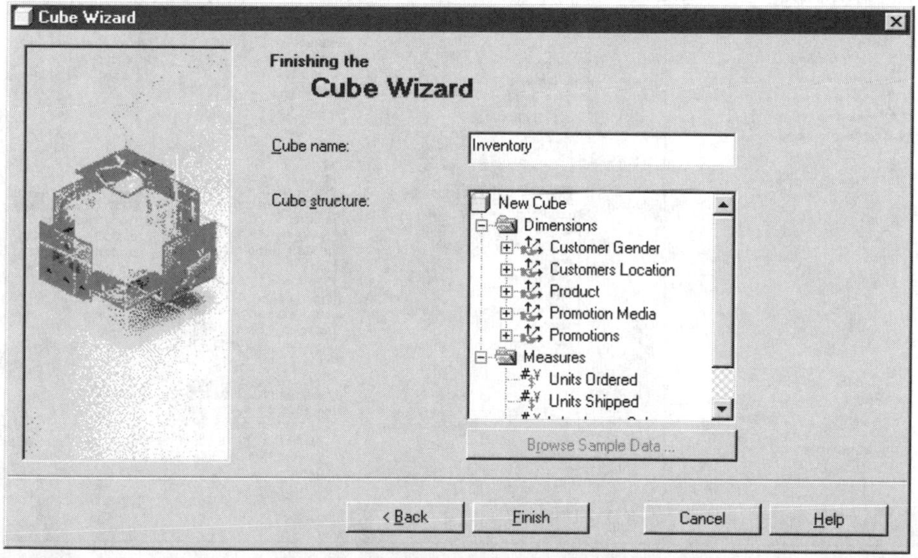

Figure 5-31. Cube Wizard – completion screen

This completes the steps required to create a new OLAP cube by using the Cube Wizard. The Finishing the Cube Wizard dialog box summarizes the cube attributes that you defined on the earlier wizard dialog boxes. At this point, you can either click the Back button, to modify any of the settings that you entered on the previous dialog boxes, or click the Finish button, to create the new cube in the existing FoodMart data warehouse. As the cube is being created, the relationships of the selected tables are analyzed. If any problems or discrepancies exist, the Cube Wizard automatically displays the Cube Editor, shown in Figure 5-32.

You can choose for the Cube Editor to start automatically at the end of the Cube Wizard, or you can start it manually by right-clicking an OLAP cube and then selecting the Edit Cube option from the pop-up menu. The list in the left portion of the screen shows the cube dimensions and measures that you selected when you created the cube. The right pane of the OLAP Manager shows the relationships of the base table that are used to create the cube. The right pane shows that the cube is composed of data elements

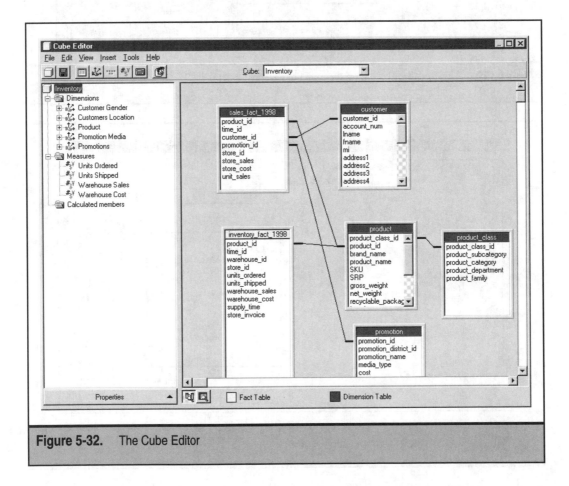

Figure 5-32.   The Cube Editor

that originate from the inventory_fact_1998 table, the sales_fact_1998 table, the customer table, the sales table, the product table, the product_class table, and the promotions table. To add tables to this collection, right-click the table relationship pane and then select the Insert tables option from the pop-up menu. In addition, you can edit and change the data relationships of the tables that are displayed onscreen. To delete a relationship, click the relationship line that you want to delete and then press the DELETE key. To create relationships, click and drag from one column to another.

CONCLUSION

The data replication and data warehousing features included in SQL Server 7 enable SQL Server to better scale both upward and downward through the enterprise. Data replication enables SQL Server to be used for distributed applications, as well as implementing branch office and mobile computing. SQL Server 7's new OLAP Services enables SQL Server to be used for decision-support applications that are aimed at turning raw data into business intelligence. Although both of these technologies can be complex, the new wizards included with SQL Server 7 make it easy to get started. Likewise, you can take advantage of the wizards' COM interfaces for more-sophisticated program control.

ADDITIONAL RESOURCES

Both data replication and data warehousing are topics that are too big to cover adequately in a single chapter. This chapter is intended to provide an overview of each of the topics and show you how to use some of the primary tools that SQL Server provides in each respective area. You can find more-detailed information about data replication and data warehousing by using the following resources.

▼ Microsoft's SQL Server replication Web page:

http://premium.microsoft.com/msdn/library/techart/msdn_sqlrepl.htm

■ Microsoft's data warehousing strategy:

www.microsoft.com/sql/dss

■ Microsoft's Data Warehousing White Paper, "The Microsoft Data Warehousing Strategy" (part number 098-80704):

http://www.microsoft.com/directaccess/prodinfo/sql/whtpprs.htm

If this link becomes outdated, go to www.microsoft.com and search for "SQL white papers."

▲ *The Data Warehouse Toolkit,* by Ralph Kimball (New York: John Wiley & Sons, 1996)

CHAPTER 6

Database Performance

Database performance is an important component of overall application performance. Generally, database performance addresses how quickly data can be retrieved from a database table and provided to a connection or how quickly changes to the database can be received from a connection and reflected in the database. In addition to database performance, the overall performance of an application will depend on factors such as computational efficiency, speed in presenting the user interface, and network communication costs. The two most important overall measures of performance are *average response time* and *throughput*.

Average response time applies most commonly to interactive applications—for example, where a user is entering transactions or retrieving information. In this context, average response measures the average elapsed time from the point at which the user takes an action to initiate a transaction or retrieval (for example, clicking the OK button on a dialog box) to the point at which the transaction is complete or the initial information for a retrieval is displayed. The average can be calculated across any appropriate time interval and group of applications or users. Of course, when comparing different values for this measure, it's important to identify exactly what time interval, applications, and users the average reflects.

Throughput applies to both interactive and noninteractive (or "batch") work. Throughput measures how much total work can get done in a particular time interval. A measure of throughput can be system wide or limited to specific applications. For example, you might measure how many orders can be entered between 8:00 A.M. and 5:00 P.M. and calculate the average hourly throughput of orders for the normal work day.

Response time and throughput fulfill different business requirements. The required or desirable response time for an application is based on how quickly you need to be able to retrieve or update information. For example, to provide good customer service, your customer inquiry applications would generally need to retrieve and display customer information within seconds, or at least tens of seconds. A "heads down" transaction entry application, as a different example, might require subsecond response time to keep data entry operators working at full capacity.

Throughput requirements are often determined by the length of the "window" available to get work done. For example, a batch account aging job may need to complete in a two-hour period each evening before the system is dedicated to other tasks. Or, more commonly, you may have a sequence of dependent jobs (or job steps) that have to all complete within an eight-hour shift. Obviously, this requires each job or step in the sequence to complete quickly enough so the entire sequence is finished in the available time.

Response time and throughput can be, but aren't necessarily, tightly related. For example, with an order entry application, you may be able to get excellent response time as long as only one person is entering orders. This may not provide adequate throughput to handle all of a company's orders, however. By adding more people to enter orders, the average response time may worsen (either a little or a lot) while throughput increases. As you tackle performance-related issues, be sure to carefully identify the business reason for specific performance criteria, and be sure to consider both parts of the equation: response time and throughput.

In addition to response time and throughput, there are some other important principles of performance management. A key principle is that you measure relevant performance characteristics before and after making adjustments. Comparable before and after measures are essential so you *know* what the quantitative impact is of changing a configuration option, adding hardware, or changing an application design or implementation.

Also, be sure you measure both application-level performance and system-wide performance. It's not uncommon for configuration or design and implementation changes that improve the performance of one application to worsen the performance of other applications. This may be acceptable for your overall performance objectives, but you don't want to inadvertently exchange one set of performance problems for another.

In many cases, you can meet performance objectives by buying hardware (for example, more memory), changing your system configuration (for example, adjusting process priorities), changing an application's design or implementation (such as by adding an index), or by a combination of these actions. Adding hardware has a direct cost, as well as indirect costs for such things as the time required to install the hardware. Changing the system configuration or an application usually involves only indirect costs. A common mistake is to choose only one strategy based on preconceived notions of the "best" way to improve performance. Over time, however, you're likely to find that the most cost-effective approach to improving performance is sometimes to add hardware, sometimes to change the configuration or an application, and sometimes a combination of all of these. Any major effort to improve performance should include an estimate of both direct and indirect costs, as well as good and bad side-effects. That is, buying hardware may improve the performance of applications other than the one you're focusing on, or changes to an application may make application maintenance more complex in the future.

In this chapter, we concentrate on SQL Server tools to monitor events and resources related to database performance. We also look at how the information these tools provide can help you improve database performance. As mentioned, the topic of application performance is broader than just database performance, so be sure to consider the other areas we've mentioned in this introduction. In particular, be sure to learn about NT Server performance tools and techniques.

SELECTING THE APPROPRIATE TOOL

SQL Server provides the following performance-related tools:

▼ **SQL Server Profiler**   Records and analyzes specific events, such as the opening of a database table.

■ **SQL Server Performance Monitor**   Records and analyzes resource usage, such as how busy a processor is.

■ **Enterprise Manager Current Activity categories**   Display current SQL Server activity, such as current processes.

■ **Index Tuning Wizard**   Analyzes a workload and recommends indexes that may improve performance for the workload.

■ **Showplan**   Displays the execution plan steps that the optimizer will produce to implement a query.

- ■ **DBCC statement**   Displays information about resource usage.
- ■ **Trace flags**   Capture additional information on events and resource usage.
- ■ **Query Analyzer Index Analysis**   Analyzes a single SQL statement and suggests indexes that may improve the statement's performance.
- ■ **Transact-SQL functions and stored procedures**   Return information about resource usage.
- ▲ **SQL statement hints**   Control the optimization, lock granularity, and transaction isolation level for a single statement.

Although there is some overlap in the information and control provided by these tools, each one has specific capabilities that suit it to a particular aspect of performance management. In the sections that follow, we'll cover how to use the tools, as well as the situations for which each is best suited. Table 6-1 provides an overview of the tools' characteristics.

Tool	Purpose, Features, and Limitations	Graphical Interface	Use from Your Own Application
SQL Server Profiler	*Records database events. *Allows selective capture of specific types of events and data. *Allows data to be captured to SQL table for analysis with a query tool. *Allows replay of captured events.	Yes	Yes (with extended stored procedures)
SQL Server Performance Monitor	*Records Windows NT and SQL Server resource usage. *Displays current activity as line graph, histogram, or formatted report. *Generates performance alerts to display exceptional conditions, send a message, or run a program. *Captures performance data to a log file for subsequent analysis.	Yes	

Table 6-1. SQL Server Performance Tools

Tool	Purpose, Features, and Limitations	Graphical Interface	Use from Your Own Application
SQL Server Enterprise Manager Current Activity categories	*Provide ad hoc view of current resource usage. *Displays information about current database processes, users, and locks.	Yes	
Index Tuning Wizard	*Analyzes a set of queries and recommends indexes to improve performance. *Allows workload to be a SQL Server Profiler trace or SQL source code. Produces reports on index usage.	Yes	
Showplan	*Displays information on the steps in the execution plan produced by the SQL Server optimizer. *Outputs results in text or graphical form, as well as in a result table.	Yes	Yes
DBCC statement	*Returns various database performance statistics. *Can be coded in user-written stored procedures.		Yes
Trace flags	*Control SQL Server behavior. *Can be set with DBCC statement or as SQL Server startup option.		Yes
Query Analyzer Index Analysis	*Analyzes a single SQL statement and recommends indexes that may improve the statement's performance. *Limited to analyzing one statement at a time.		

Table 6-1. SQL Server Performance Tools (*continued*)

Tool	Purpose, Features, and Limitations	Graphical Interface	Use from Your Own Application
Transact-SQL functions and stored procedures	*Returns various database performance statistics. *Can be coded in user-written stored procedures.		Yes
SQL statement hints	*Control various aspects of the execution plan created by the SQL Server optimizer for Select, Insert, Update, and Delete statements. *Control optimization algorithms, locking, and transaction analysis.		Yes

Table 6-1.   SQL Server Performance Tools (*continued*)

SQL SERVER PROFILER

SQL Server Profiler is a tool that records SQL Server events and provides options to analyze the captured data or to replay the data. You can use the Profiler through a graphical user interface or by calling extended stored procedures. Using the graphical tool is a much easier approach; however, the stored procedures let you embed Profiler functions in your own applications.

NOTE: In the current implementation of the Profiler, the graphical interface supports only client-side performance trace queues. The extended stored procedures use server-side performance trace queues. In most cases, you can just pick the appropriate interface based on whether you want to use a graphical interface or process Profiler performance in your own application. There are a few things you can only do with the extended stored procedures, however. These include using the NT Server event log as a destination for captured data, autostarting a trace when SQL Server starts, and forwarding performance events captured on one server to be traced on another server.

In this section, we describe the Profiler capabilities and how to use the graphical interface. Table 6-2 provides a list of the Profiler extended stored procedures for reference. You can find details about these procedures in the online documentation.

NOTE: To use the Profiler graphical interface on a SQL Server system, you must register the server. The "Registering and Unregistering a Server" section in Chapter 2 explains how to register a server using the SQL Server Enterprise Manager. You can also register a server directly from the Profiler by selecting Tools | Register SQL Server from the Profiler menu and following the steps described in Chapter 2.

Extended Stored Procedure	Purpose
xp_trace_addnewqueue	Adds new trace queue and sets trace configuration values
xp_trace_deletequeuedefinition	Deletes trace queue definition
xp_trace_destroyqueue	Deletes trace queue
xp_trace_enumqueuedefname	Lists trace queue definition names
xp_trace_enumqueuehandles	Lists active trace queue handle values
xp_trace_eventclassrequired	Returns event classes being captured by a trace queue
xp_trace_flushqueryhistory	Flushes SQL Server events into a file
xp_trace_generate_event	Adds a user-defined event to all trace queues
xp_trace_getappfilter	Retrieves the current application filter value
xp_trace_getconnectionidfilter	Retrieves the current connection ID filter value
xp_trace_getcpufilter	Retrieves the current CPU filter value
xp_trace_getdbidfilter	Retrieves the current database ID filter value
xp_trace_getdurationfilter	Retrieves the current duration filter value
xp_trace_geteventfilter	Retrieves the current event filter value

Table 6-2.   Profiler Extended Stored Procedures

Extended Stored Procedure	Purpose
xp_trace_geteventnames	Lists event class names
xp_trace_getevents	Returns events from a trace queue
xp_trace_gethostfilter	Retrieves the current host filter value
xp_trace_gethpidfilter	Retrieves the current host process ID filter value
xp_trace_getindidfilter	Retrieves the current index ID filter value
xp_trace_getntdmfilter	Retrieves the current NT Server domain filter value
xp_trace_getntnmfilter	Retrieves the current NT Server computer name filter value
xp_trace_getobjidfilter	Retrieves the current object ID filter value
xp_trace_getqueueautostart	Retrieves the autostart setting for a trace queue
xp_trace_getqueuedestination	Retrieves the destination setting for a trace queue
xp_trace_getqueueproperties	Retrieves all filters currently set for a trace queue
xp_trace_getreadfilter	Retrieves the current read filter value
xp_trace_getserverfilter	Retrieves the current server filter value
xp_trace_getseverityfilter	Retrieves the current severity filter value
xp_trace_getspidfilter	Retrieves the current system process ID filter value
xp_trace_getsysobjectsfilter	Retrieves the current system objects filter value
xp_trace_gettextfilter	Retrieves the current text filter value
xp_trace_getuserfilter	Retrieves the current user filter value
xp_trace_getwritefilter	Retrieves the current write filter value
xp_trace_loadqueuedefinition	Loads a saved trace queue definition
xp_trace_pausequeue	Pauses a trace queue
xp_trace_restartqueue	Restarts a trace queue
xp_trace_savequeuedefinition	Saves a trace queue definition
xp_trace_setappfilter	Sets the application filter value for a trace queue

Table 6-2. Profiler Extended Stored Procedures (*continued*)

Extended Stored Procedure	Purpose
xp_trace_setconnectionidfilter	Sets the connection ID filter value for a trace queue
xp_trace_setcpufilter	Sets the CPU filter value for a trace queue
xp_trace_setdbidfilter	Sets the database ID filter value for a trace queue
xp_trace_setdurationfilter	Sets the duration filter value for a trace queue
xp_trace_seteventclassrequired	Sets the event classes to be captured by a queue
xp_trace_seteventfilter	Sets the event filter value for a trace queue
xp_trace_sethostfilter	Sets the host filter value for a trace queue
xp_trace_sethpidfilter	Sets the host process ID filter value for a trace queue
xp_trace_setindidfilter	Sets the index ID filter value for a trace queue
xp_trace_setntdmfilter	Sets the NT Server domain filter value for a trace queue
xp_trace_setntnmfilter	Sets the NT Server computer name filter value for a trace queue
xp_trace_setobjidfilter	Sets the object ID filter value for a trace queue
xp_trace_setqueryhistory	Enables or disables query history
xp_trace_setqueueautostart	Sets the autostart setting for a trace queue
xp_trace_setqueuecreateinfo	Sets trace queue properties
xp_trace_setqueuedestination	Sets the trace queue destination
xp_trace_setreadfilter	Sets the read filter value for a trace queue
xp_trace_setserverfilter	Sets the server filter value for a trace queue
xp_trace_setseverityfilter	Sets the severity filter value for a trace queue
xp_trace_setspidfilter	Sets the system process ID filter value for a trace queue
xp_trace_setsysobjectsfilter	Sets the system objects filter value for a trace queue
xp_trace_settextfilter	Sets the text filter value for a trace queue
xp_trace_setuserfilter	Sets the user filter value for a trace queue
xp_trace_setwritefilter	Sets the write filter value for a trace queue
xp_trace_startconsumer	Starts the trace queue consumer

Table 6-2. Profiler Extended Stored Procedures (*continued*)

Creating a Trace Definition

To use the Profiler, you first have to create a *trace definition*, which is a named entry stored in the NT Server registry that specifies the following elements:

▼ Trace name

■ Whether shared or private

■ Which SQL Server to record events for

■ A database table or operating system file to store event data in

■ A list of events to trace

■ Which data columns to capture for each event

▲ Filter conditions to further limit which events are captured

Once you've defined the trace, you can start, stop, pause, and continue it. When the trace is running, the Profiler monitors SQL Server events on the specified server and captures the data you specify for the selected events that satisfy the filter conditions. This trace data can be displayed interactively as it's captured, as well as stored in a specified table or file.

You can create a trace by filling in the Profiler's Trace Properties dialog box or by using the Create Trace Wizard. We'll look first at using the Trace Properties dialog box to understand all the elements of defining a trace, and then we'll explore the Create Trace Wizard.

To run the Profiler, select Programs | Microsoft SQL Server 7.0 | Profiler from the Windows Start menu or select Tools | SQL Server Profiler from the SQL Server Enterprise Manager menu. In the Profiler window, click the New Trace toolbar icon (leftmost icon) or select File | New | Trace from the main menu. Either action displays the Trace Properties dialog box (Figure 6-1).

General Tab

On the General tab, enter a descriptive name for the trace you're creating. For Trace Type, select either Shared or Private, depending on whether you want other users or just yourself to be able to use the trace.

Next, select the server that you want to trace. You can change several server settings by clicking the server icon to the right of the server name. On the Source Server dialog box (Figure 6-2), you can set the following:

▼ The maximum number of rows buffered in the trace queue (a temporary storage area for trace data)

■ The timeout period before a trace queue stops accepting new event entries

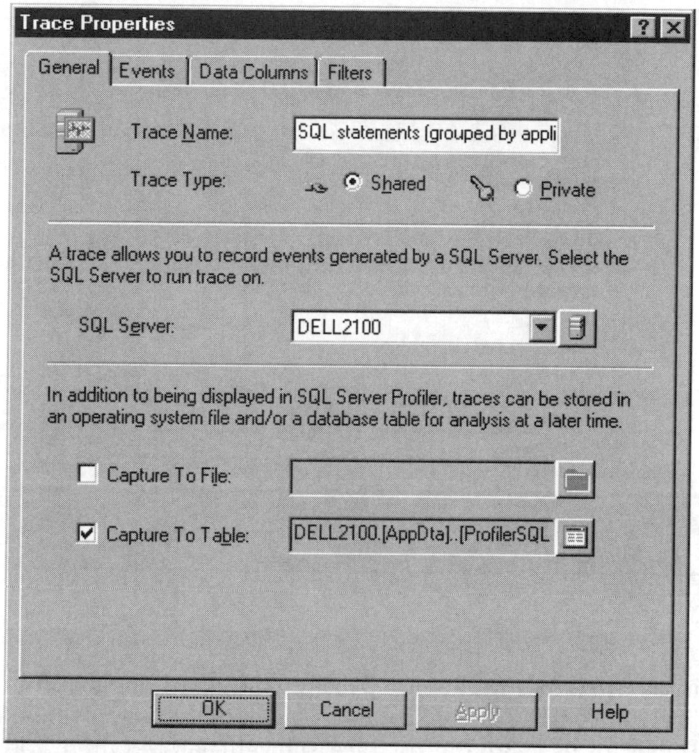

Figure 6-1.   Trace Properties dialog box—General tab

- How full the queue must be to boost the runtime priority of the Profiler task that's consuming (that is, reading and removing) event entries from the queue

▲ At what level to reduce the queue consumer task's priority

You can capture trace data to a SQL table, a Windows NT file, or both. Capturing data to a table lets you subsequently work with the data using Query Analyzer or other query tools.

Events Tab

On the Events tab (Figure 6-3), you add and remove events that you want to capture with the trace. Individual events belong to one of the defined *event classes*. Event classes are in

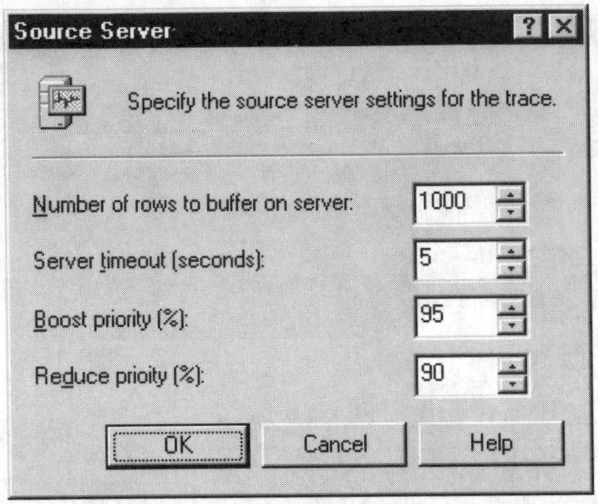

Figure 6-2. Source Server dialog box

turn grouped into *event categories*. Table 6-3 lists all the event categories and event classes available on the Events tab. The last column in this table provides the corresponding event mask number for use with the xp_trace_seteventclassrequired stored procedure.

NOTE: The default configuration of the Profiler doesn't show all event classes in the Events tab's list. To see the complete set of event classes, select Tools I Options from the Profiler menu and select the All event classes option on the Trace Options dialog box. Also, there are a number of Profiler-related events that are not in this list (to avoid the Profiler tracing its own actions), which are shown in Table 6-4. The Profiler-related events can be traced with the xp_trace_*xxx* extended stored procedures.

Data Columns Tab

For each event that you trace, the Profiler captures particular pieces of information, known as *data columns*. To limit the amount of captured data, you can add and remove data columns on the Trace Properties dialog box's Data Columns tab (Figure 6-4). Table 6-5 lists the available data columns, including the name shown on the Data Columns tab and the SQL table column name used when you capture trace data to a table. The SQL column names are what you use with Query Analyzer or other query tools. The last column in this table provides the corresponding column mask number for use with the xp_trace_addnewqueue stored procedure.

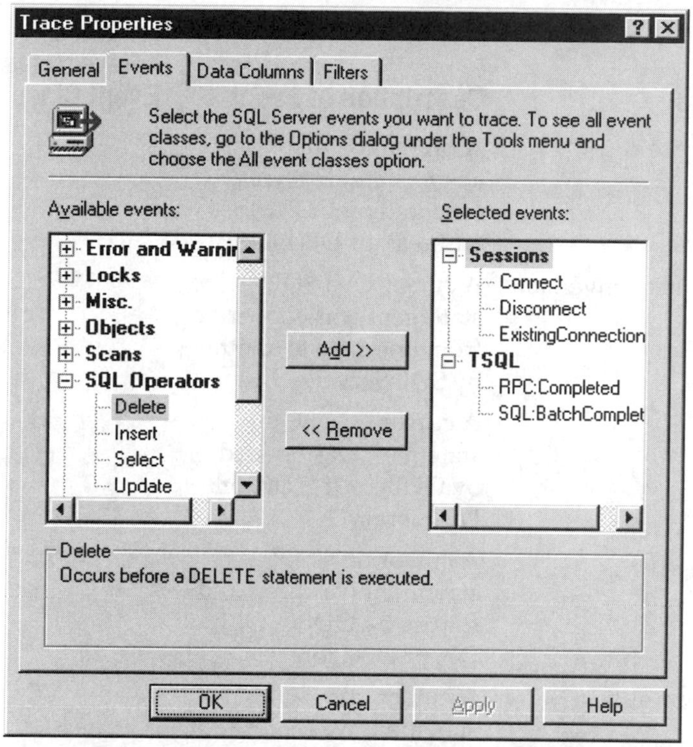

Figure 6-3. Trace Properties dialog box—Events tab

Event Class	Description of Event	xp_trace_ seteventclassrequired Event Class Number
Cursors Event Category		
CursorClose	A cursor on a SQL statement was closed by ODBC, OLE DB, or DB-Library.	78

Table 6-3. SQL Server Profiler Event Classes (Available on Trace Properties Dialog Box)

Event Class	Description of Event	xp_trace_ seteventclassrequired Event Class Number
CursorExecute	A prepared cursor on a SQL statement was executed by ODBC, OLE DB, or DB-Library.	74
CursorImplicitConversion	A cursor on a SQL statement was converted from one type to another by SQL Server.	76
CursorOpen	A cursor on a SQL statement was opened by ODBC, OLE DB, or DB-Library.	53
CursorPrepare	A cursor on a SQL statement was prepared for use by ODBC, OLE DB, or DB-Library.	70
CursorRecompile	A cursor on a SQL statement was recompiled.	75
CursorUnprepare	A cursor on a SQL statement was unprepared by ODBC, OLE DB, or DB-Library.	77
Error and Warning Event Category		
ErrorLog	Error event logged in the SQL Server error log.	22
EventLog	Event logged in the Windows NT application event log.	21
Exception	Exception occurred in SQL Server.	33

Table 6-3. SQL Server Profiler Event Classes (Available on Trace Properties Dialog Box) (*continued*)

Event Class	Description of Event	xp_trace_ seteventclassrequired Event Class Number
Execution Warnings	Warning occurred during execution of a SQL Server statement or stored procedure.	67
Hash Warnings	Warning occurred during execution of a hashing operation.	55
Missing Column Statistics	Column statistics were not present.	79
Missing Join Predicate	Predicate for joining two tables was not present.	80
OLEDB Errors	An OLE DB error occurred.	61
Sort Warnings	A sort operation did not fit into memory.	69
Locks Event Category		
Lock:Acquired	A resource lock was acquired.	24
Lock:Cancel	A requested resource lock acquisition was canceled.	26
Lock:Deadlock	Two concurrent transactions deadlocked each other.	25
Lock:Deadlock Chain	Indicates an event leading up to a deadlock.	59
Lock:Escalation	A finer-grained lock was converted to a coarser-grained lock.	60
Lock:Released	A resource lock was released.	23

Table 6-3.   SQL Server Profiler Event Classes (Available on Trace Properties Dialog Box) (*continued*)

Event Class	Description of Event	xp_trace_ seteventclassrequired Event Class Number
Lock:Timeout	A requested resource lock acquisition timed out.	27
Misc. Event Category		
Attention	An attention event occurred (e.g., a client-interrupt request).	16
Auto-UpdateStats	An event associated with the automatic updating of index statistics occurred.	58
Exec Prepared SQL	A prepared SQL statement was executed by ODBC, OLE DB, or DB-Library.	72
Execution Plan	The plan tree of a SQL statement that has been executed.	68
LoginFailed	A login attempt to SQL Server from a client failed.	20
Prepare SQL	A SQL statement was prepared for use by ODBC, OLE DB, or DB-Library.	71
Server Memory Change	SQL Server memory usage increased or decreased.	81
ServiceControl	A server control event occurred (e.g., a server paused).	18
Unprepare SQL	A SQL statement was unprepared by ODBC, OLE DB, or DB-Library.	73

Table 6-3.   SQL Server Profiler Event Classes (Available on Trace Properties Dialog Box) (*continued*)

Event Class	Description of Event	xp_trace_ seteventclassrequired Event Class Number
Objects Event Category		
Object:Closed	An open object was closed.	49
Object:Created	An object was created.	46
Object:Deleted	An object was deleted.	47
Object:Opened	An object was opened.	48
Scans Event Category		
Scan:Started	A table or index scan was started.	51
Scan:Stopped	A table or index scan was stopped.	52
Sessions Event Category		
Connect	A connection event occurred (e.g., a client requested a connection).	14
Disconnect	A disconnect event occurred (e.g., a client issued a disconnect command).	15
ExistingConnection	A user connected before the trace started.	17
SQL Operators Event Category		
Delete	A Delete statement was executed.	30
Insert	An Insert statement was executed.	28
Select	A Select statement was executed.	31

Table 6-3.   SQL Server Profiler Event Classes (Available on Trace Properties Dialog Box) (*continued*)

Event Class	Description of Event	xp_trace_ seteventclassrequired Event Class Number
Update	An Update statement was executed.	29
Stored Procedures Event Category		
SP:CacheHit	A stored procedure was found in the cache.	38
SP:CacheInsert	An item was inserted into the stored procedure cache.	35
SP:CacheMiss	A stored procedure was not found in the stored procedure cache.	34
SP:CacheRemove	An item was removed from the stored procedure cache.	36
SP:Completed	A stored procedure completed.	43
SP:ExecContextHit	The context of the local state for a stored procedure that has started.	39
SP:Recompile	A stored procedure was recompiled.	37
SP:Starting	A stored procedure started.	42
SP:StmtCompleted	A statement within a stored procedure completed.	45
SP:StmtStarting	A statement within a stored procedure started.	44
Transactions Event Category		
DTCTransaction	An MS DTC coordinated transaction event has occurred between two or more databases.	19

Table 6-3. SQL Server Profiler Event Classes (Available on Trace Properties Dialog Box) (*continued*)

Event Class	Description of Event	xp_trace_ seteventclassrequired Event Class Number
SQLTransaction	A Begin Transaction, Commit, Save Transaction, or Rollback Transaction statement was executed.	50
TransactionLog	A transaction was written to the transaction log.	54
TSQL Event Category		
RPC:Completed	An RPC completed.	10
RPC:Starting	An RPC started.	11
SQL:BatchCompleted	A SQL batch completed.	12
SQL:BatchStarting	A SQL batch started.	13
SQL:StmtCompleted	A SQL statement within a batch completed.	41
SQL:StmtStarting	A SQL statement within a batch started.	40
User Configurable Event Category		
UserConfigurable:1	A user-defined event occurred.	82
UserConfigurable:2	A user-defined event occurred.	83
UserConfigurable:3	A user-defined event occurred.	84
UserConfigurable:4	A user-defined event occurred.	85
UserConfigurable:5	A user-defined event occurred.	86

Table 6-3. SQL Server Profiler Event Classes (Available on Trace Properties Dialog Box) (*continued*)

Event Class	Description of Event	xp_trace_ seteventclassrequired Event Class Number
TraceStart	A trace has been started.	0
TracePause	A trace has been paused.	1
TraceRestart	A trace has been restarted.	2
TraceAutoPause	A trace has been paused automatically.	3
TraceAutoRestart	A trace has been restarted automatically.	4
TraceStop	A trace has stopped.	5
EventRequired	A trace event to trace has been changed.	6
FilterChanged	A trace filter has been changed.	7
8	Reserved.	8
9	Reserved.	9
Connection being killed	A connection that's being traced is being killed.	32
56	Reserved.	56
57	Reserved.	57
Replay Error	Error occurred during trace replay.	62
Replay Internal Error	Internal error occurred during trace replay.	63
Replay Result Set	Replay produced result set.	64
Replay Result Row	Replay produced result row.	65
66	Reserved	66

Table 6-4. SQL Server Profiler Event Classes (Not Available on Trace Properties Dialog Box)

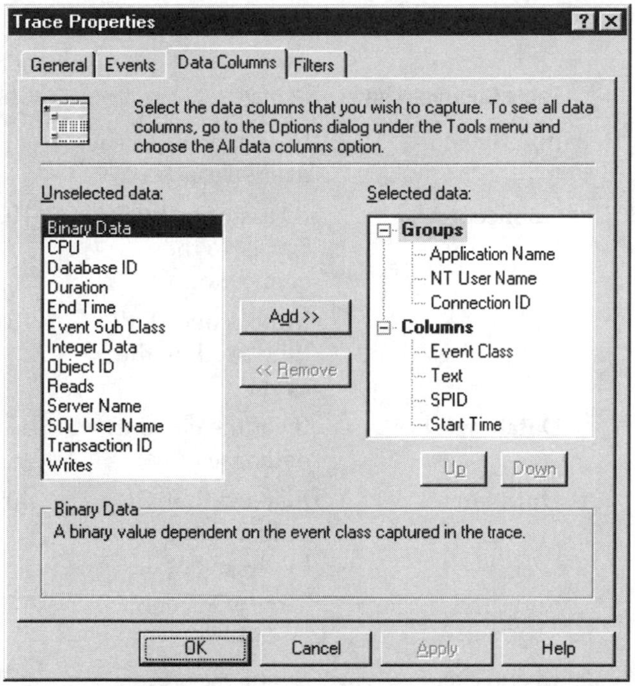

Figure 6-4.   Trace Properties dialog box—Data Columns tab

NOTE: The default configuration of the Profiler doesn't show all data columns in the Data Columns tab's list. To see the complete set of data columns, select Tools | Options from the Profiler menu and select the All data columns option on the Trace Options dialog box.

Data Column	Table Column Name	Contents	xp_trace_ addnewqueue Column Mask
Application Name	ApplicationName	Name of the client application that created the connection (as passed by the application)	512

Table 6-5.   SQL Server Profiler Trace Data Columns

Data Column	Table Column Name	Contents	xp_trace_ addnewqueue Column Mask
Binary Data	BinaryData	Data specific to each event class	2
Connection ID	ConnectionID	ID assigned by SQL Server to the connection	1024
CPU	CPU	Milliseconds CPU time used by the event	131072
Database ID	DatabaseID	ID of the current database	4
Duration	Duration	Elapsed time in milliseconds taken by the event	4096
End Time	EndTime	Time that event ended	16384
Event Class	EventClass	Event class name (e.g., Object:Opened)	67108864
Event Sub Class	EventSubClass	Event subclass name (e.g., SystemTable)	1048576
Host Name	HostName	Name of the computer on which the client is running	128
Host Process ID	HostProcessID	Process ID assigned by the host to the client's process	256
Index ID	IndexID	Internal ID of any index on the object that's affected by the event	8388608
Integer Data	IntegerData	Data specific to each event class	16777216

Table 6-5. SQL Server Profiler Trace Data Columns (*continued*)

Data Column	Table Column Name	Contents	xp_trace_ addnewqueue Column Mask
NT Domain Name	NTDomainName	NT Server domain name of the NT Server user	64
NT User Name	NTUserName	NT Server user name	32
Object ID	ObjectID	Internal ID of object	2097152
Reads	Reads	Count of physical disk reads done for the event	32768
Server Name	ServerName	SQL Server server name	33554432
Severity	Severity	Severity level of an exception	524288
SPID	SPID	Process ID assigned by SQL Server to the process associated with the client	2048
SQL User Name	SQLUserName	SQL Server database user name	16
Start Time	StartTime	Time that event started	8192
Text	TextData	Data specific to each event class	1
Transaction ID	TransactionID	Internal ID of the transaction	8
Writes	Writes	Count of physical disk writes done for the event	65536

Table 6-5.   SQL Server Profiler Trace Data Columns (*continued*)

Four of the data columns are overloaded with different contents, depending on the type of event. Table 6-6 shows the contents of the Event Sub Class, Binary Data, Integer Data, and Text data columns for each event that has data for one of these data columns.

The Selected data list on the Data Columns tab has two nodes: Groups and Columns. The data columns under either of these nodes are the ones that are captured. The difference is that data columns under the Groups node are used to group the events in the Profiler's interactive display of captured data.

NOTE: If you include the Object ID, Server Name, and Database ID data columns, the Profiler displays the object name, rather than its internal ID.

Event Class	Event Sub Class Data Column	Binary Data Data Column	Integer Data Data Column	Text Data Column
Cursors Event Category				
CursorClose	Cursor handle			
CursorExecute	Cursor handle	Prepared cursor handle	Cursor type	
CursorImplicit-Conversion	Cursor handle	Resulting cursor type	Requested cursor type	
CursorOpen	Cursor handle		Cursor type	
CursorPrepare	Prepared cursor handle			
CursorUnprepare	Prepared cursor handle			

Table 6-6. SQL Server Profiler Event-Specific Data Column Contents

Event Class	Event Sub Class Data Column	Binary Data Data Column	Integer Data Data Column	Text Data Column
Error and Warning Event Category				
ErrorLog	Error number			Error message
EventLog	Error number	Error binary data (if available)		Error message
Exception	Server state		Error number	
Execution Warnings	Query status		Query wait time	
Hash Warning	Type of hash operation		Hash recursion level	
Missing Column Statistics				List of columns with missing statistics
OLEDB Errors				Error message
Sort Warnings	Single/multipass			
Locks Event Category				
Lock:Cancel	Lock mode	Resource ID		
Lock:Deadlock	Lock mode	Resource ID	Deadlock number	
Lock:Deadlock Chain	Lock mode	Resource ID	Deadlock number	
Lock:Released	Lock mode	Resource ID		
Lock:Timeout	Lock mode	Resource ID		

Table 6-6. SQL Server Profiler Event-Specific Data Column Contents (*continued*)

Event Class	Event Sub Class Data Column	Binary Data Data Column	Integer Data Data Column	Text Data Column
Misc. Event Category				
Auto-UpdateStats	Success/failure			
Exec Prepared SQL	Prepared statement handle			
Execution Plan		Estimated cost	Estimated number of rows returned	Execution plan tree
LoginFailed				Error message
Prepare SQL	Prepared statement handle			
Server Memory Change	Increase/decrease		New memory size	
ServiceControl	Action			
Unprepare SQL	Prepared statement handle			
Objects Event Category				
Object:Closed	Object type			
Object:Created	Object type			
Object:Deleted	Object type			
Object:Opened	Object type			
Scans Event Category				
Scan: Started	Scan mode			
Scan: Stopped	Scan mode			
Sessions Event Category				
Connect		Session level settings		
ExistingConnection		Session level settings		

Table 6-6.   SQL Server Profiler Event-Specific Data Column Contents (*continued*)

Event Class	Event Sub Class Data Column	Binary Data Data Column	Integer Data Data Column	Text Data Column
SQL Operators Event Category				
Delete	Number of CPUs used for parallel processing			
Insert	Number of CPUs used for parallel processing			
Select	Number of CPUs used for parallel processing			
Update	Number of CPUs used for parallel processing			
Stored Procedures Event Category				
SP:CacheHit	Nesting level			
SP:CacheInsert	Nesting level			
SP:CacheMiss	Nesting level			
SP:CacheRemove	Nesting level			
SP:Completed	Nesting level			Stored procedure source
SP:ExecContextHit	Nesting level			
SP:Recompile	Nesting level			
SP:Starting	Nesting level			Stored procedure source
SP:StmtCompleted	Nesting level		Rows returned by statement	Statement source
SP:StmtStarting	Nesting level			Statement source
Transactions Event Category				
DTCTransaction	DTC state	GUID (hex)		GUID (character)
SQLTransaction	Type of event			Transaction name
TransactionLog	Type of event			

Table 6-6.   SQL Server Profiler Event-Specific Data Column Contents (*continued*)

Event Class	Event Sub Class Data Column	Binary Data Data Column	Integer Data Data Column	Text Data Column
TSQL Event Category				
RPC:Completed				RPC text
RPC:Starting				RPC text
SQL:BatchCompleted				Batch source
SQL:BatchStarting				Batch source
SQL:StmtCompleted			Rows returned by statement	Statement source
SQL:StmtStarting				Statement source

Table 6-6.   SQL Server Profiler Event-Specific Data Column Contents (*continued*)

Filters Tab

You can further limit which events are captured by specifying event *filters*. A filter is a condition on one of the data columns that must be satisfied for the event to be captured. For example, you can use a filter on the Database ID data column to limit a trace to events for a specific database. There are three types of filters:

▼ **ID value**   Specifies an ID value that must be matched by the specified data column

■ **Range**   specifies a range (minimum and maximum integer values) in which the specified data column's value must fall

▲ **Include/Exclude**   specifies one or more strings that must be matched or one or more strings that must be unmatched (or both kinds of strings) by the specified data column

You can specify only one type of filter for a particular column, as listed in Table 6-7. For an Include/Exclude filter, you can specify multiple values by separating the values with a semicolon (;). If you specify multiple filters, they're ANDed—that is, all the conditions must be met for an event to be captured.

Data Column	Type of Filter
Application Name	Include/Exclude
Binary Data	n/a
Connection ID	ID value
CPU	Range
Database ID	ID value
Duration	Range
End Time	n/a
Event Class	n/a
Event Sub Class	n/a
Host Name	Include/Exclude
Host Process ID	ID value
Index ID	ID value
Integer Data	n/a
NT Domain Name	Include/Exclude
NT User Name	Include/Exclude
Object ID	ID value
Reads	Range
Server Name	Include/Exclude
Severity	Range
SPID	value
SQL User Name	Include/Exclude
Start Time	n/a
Text	Include/Exclude
Transaction ID	n/a
Writes	Range

Table 6-7. Profiler Data Column Filters

NOTE: There's no way to specify multiple ID values or ranges for a column. If you need this type of selected data, use the selection capabilities of a query tool.

To add a filter, select a data column (for example, Application Name) in the Trace event criteria list on the Filters tab (Figure 6-5). Below the list, one or two entry fields are displayed for the appropriate values:

▼   Value field

■   Minimum and Maximum fields

▲   Include and Exclude fields

Enter the value(s) for the filter and the filter specification appears under the data column node in the Trace event criteria list. To remove a filter, select the data column name and delete the value in the entry field.

When you've completed the properties for the new trace, click the OK button. The Profiler saves your trace definition and (by default) starts it running. As events are captured, the Profiler displays them in a trace window, as shown in Figure 6-6.

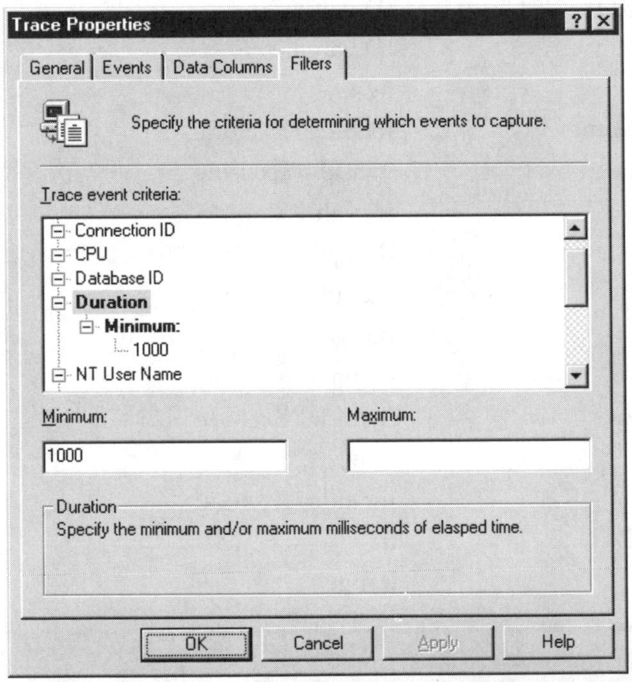

Figure 6-5.   Trace Properties dialog box—Filters tab

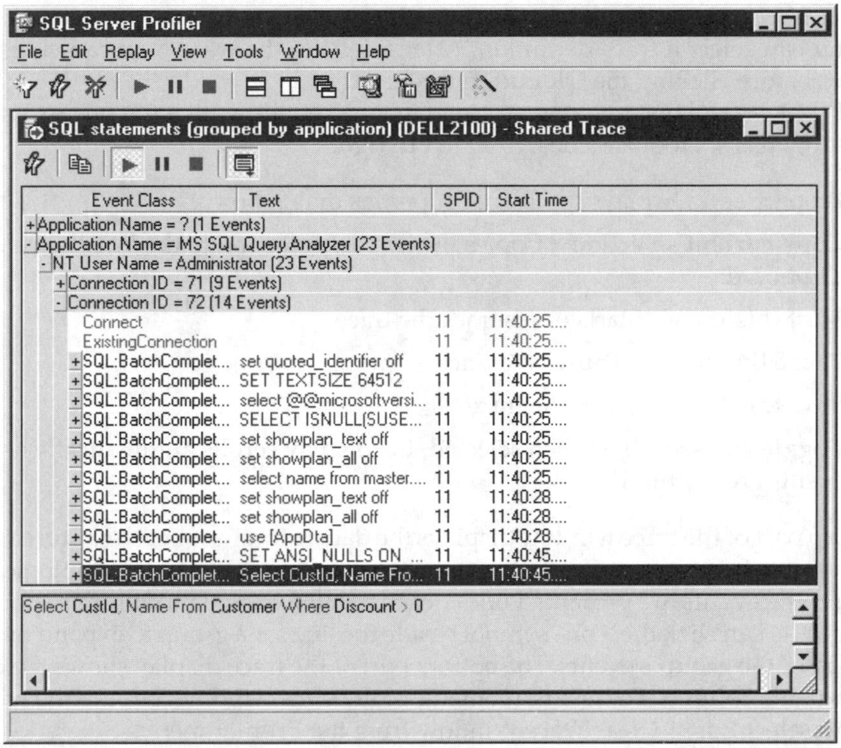

Figure 6-6.   Profiler trace window

You can delete a trace definition by selecting the File | Delete Traces menu option and double-clicking the trace name in the displayed list.

Exporting and Importing Trace Definitions

To transfer a trace definition to another system, you can select the File | Export Trace menu item, select a trace definition from the displayed list, and specify a Windows NT file to export the definition to. Copy the Windows NT file to the other system where you want to use the trace definition, and then run the Profiler and select File | Import Trace from its menu. Select the Windows NT file to import and the Profiler will create a new trace definition from it.

Running a Trace

You can start a previously defined trace by selecting File | Run Traces from the Profiler's menu to display a list of trace definitions. Double-click a trace name to start it. Alternatively, select File | Open | Trace Definition from the Profiler's menu to display a

Trace Properties dialog box similar to the one in Figures 6-1 through 6-5. When you're opening a trace, this dialog box's General tab has a Trace Name drop-down list from which you can select a trace definition. After selecting the trace, you can change other properties before clicking the OK button to start it.

The Profiler displays each open trace in its own window, like the one in Figure 6-6. This window has six toolbar icons, from left to right:

▼ **Properties**   Displays the Trace Properties dialog box

■ **Copy current selection**   Copies the current selection to the Windows Clipboard

■ **Start this trace**   Starts or resumes the trace

■ **Pause this trace**   Pauses the trace

■ **Stop this trace**   Stops the trace

▲ **Toggle auto-scroll**   When selected, the display scrolls automatically as new events are captured

The top part of the trace window displays the data columns for each captured event. If you didn't specify any grouping for the trace, the events are listed in chronological order. Otherwise, the events are presented under each value for the data columns specified for grouping. You can click the + or − symbol beside the line for a group to expand or contract the display of the group's events. The bottom part of the trace display shows the contents of the Text data column. To clear the contents of the trace window, be sure the window is active and select Edit | Clear Trace Window from the Profiler menu.

When you pause a trace, no additional events are captured until you resume the trace; however, entries that have already been captured are not deleted from the trace. When you stop a trace, no more entries are captured and, when you restart the trace, the previously captured entries are deleted. You can, of course, capture trace data to different tables or files to keep permanent copies. In addition, you can select the File | Save As | Trace Table or File | Save As | Trace File menu option to save the current trace data to a SQL table or Windows NT file.

To close a trace in the Profiler, click the Close button (the X in the upper-right corner) on the trace's window. Closing a trace also stops it.

If you save trace data to a table or file, you can subsequently open it for viewing by selecting File | Open | Trace Table or File | Open | Trace File from the Profiler menu.

Trace Defaults

In addition to controlling whether all or only commonly traced events and data columns are displayed on the Trace Properties dialog box, you can select Tools | Options to set several other defaults, including

▼ The default server

■ Whether new traces are created as shared or private

■ Whether to automatically start a new trace when it's created
■ The maximum number of lines to display in a trace window
■ Number of items to buffer for the display
▲ The font size for the trace window

Using SQL Scripts

One use of the Profiler is to run one or more SQL statements and see what exceptional events occur. To create a SQL script for the Profiler, select File | New | SQL Script from the menu to display the Profiler's SQL Script editing window shown in Figure 6-7. In the lower pane, type in (or copy and paste from another source) the SQL statements you want to run. The first statement should be a Use statement that identifies the current database for the script. For example, the following statements

```
Use AppDta
Select *
  From Customer
  Where Discount > .01
```

will trace events that occur during execution of the Select statement.

You can use the Replay menu items or the toolbar icons to start, stop, and pause execution, and to single-step and run to the cursor position, thus providing a few simple

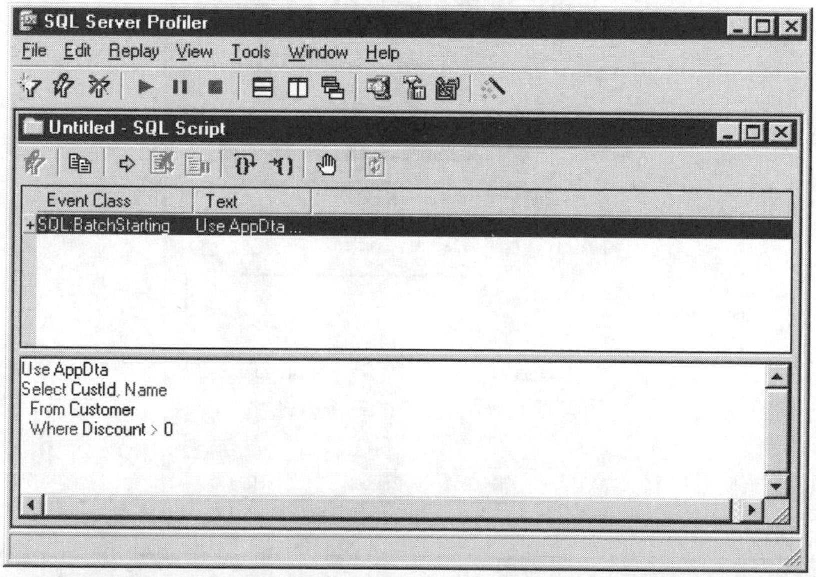

Figure 6-7.   Profiler SQL Script editing window

debugging functions for SQL statements. When you run a SQL script, the Profiler captures and displays exception events, as well as the results of any statements. You can select Replay | Settings from the Profiler menu to control several execution and trace options.

Replaying a Trace

Similar to the way you can execute SQL Scripts, you can open a previously captured trace table or file (the data, not the definition) and replay it. Select File | Open | Trace Table or File | Open | Trace File from the Profiler menu and select a table or file to open. A Replay dialog box, such as the one in Figure 6-8, lets you use the same features that are available for SQL scripts (for example, single-stepping). This feature is most useful when you have trace data from a specific set of application operations that you're trying to analyze. For example, you might capture a trace for a series of queries, and rerun the trace table after making adjustments to improve performance.

The Create Trace Wizard

The Create Trace Wizard provides several prepackaged trace definitions to get you started quickly with the Profiler. To run the wizard, select Tools | Create Trace Wizard from the Profiler menu. Click the Next button on the Welcome dialog box to display the

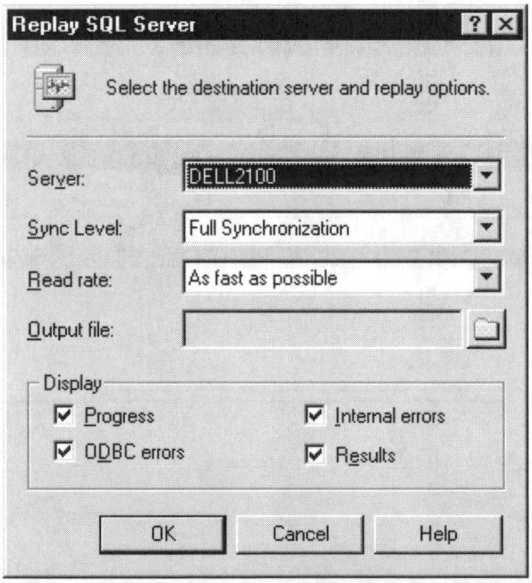

Figure 6-8.   Profiler Replay dialog box

dialog box shown in Figure 6-9. Select a server and then select one of the items from the Problem list. The available prepackaged trace definitions include

▼ Find the worst performing queries

■ Identify scans of large tables

■ Identify the cause of a deadlock

■ Profile the performance of a stored procedure

■ Trace Transact-SQL activity by application

▲ Trace Transact-SQL activity by user

Depending on which trace definition you select, the subsequent dialog boxes prompt for appropriate filter information. For example, when you select the Trace Transact-SQL activity by user trace and click Next, the dialog box shown in Figure 6-10 displays a list of users from which you can select the users whose activity you want to trace. After completing the appropriate dialog boxes, click the Finish button on the final wizard dialog box. On this last dialog box, you can also change the name of the trace from the default. When you click the Finish button, the wizard generates a trace definition, which you can then modify and run as needed.

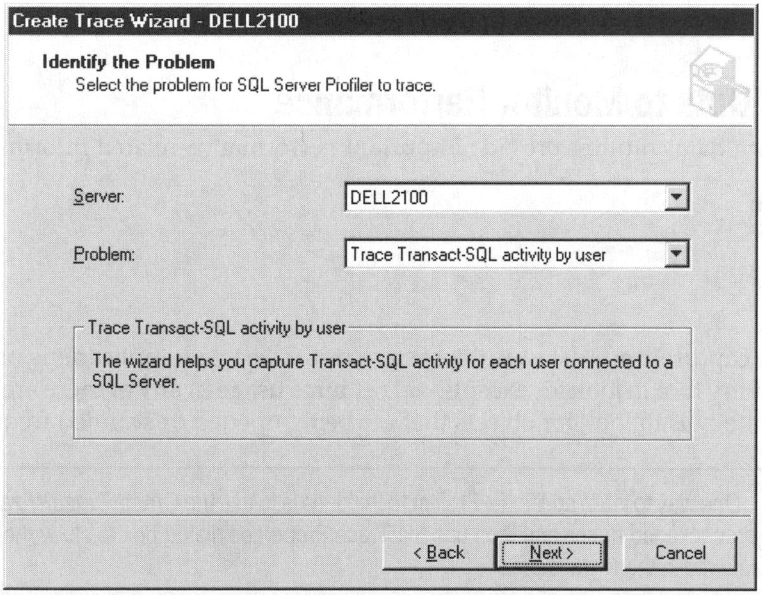

Figure 6-9. Create Trace Wizard dialog box to select prepackaged trace definition

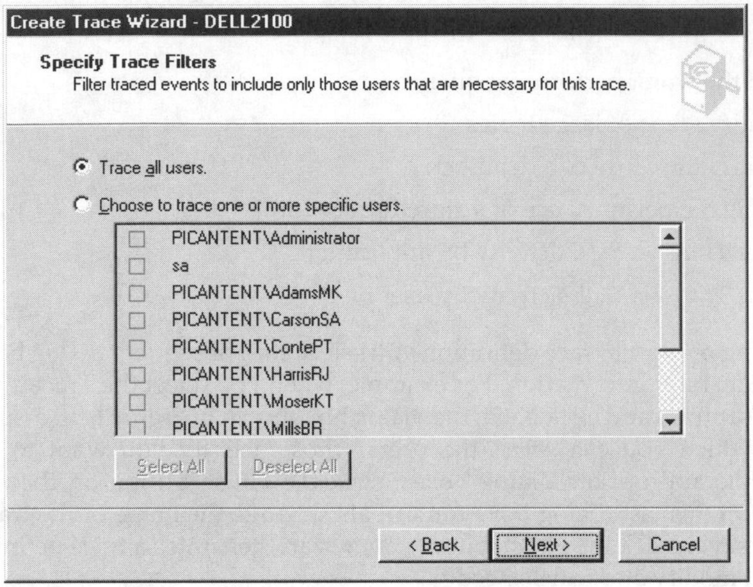

Figure 6-10. Create Trace Wizard dialog box to select users

Using Trace Data to Monitor Performance

The following data columns provide important performance-related information:

Duration
CPU
Reads
Writes

You can capture trace data for the system or for selected applications or users, and then use a query tool to look for exceptional resource usage in any of these areas. Another valuable strategy is to look for objects that are being opened or scanned frequently.

NOTE: One way to learn additional Profiler techniques is to use the Create Trace Wizard to generate various prepackaged traces and then use the Trace Properties dialog box to study the data columns and filters used in these traces.

SQL SERVER PERFORMANCE MONITOR

The SQL Server Performance Monitor is essentially the NT Server Performance Monitor (that is, the perfmon.exe program) executed with the sqlctrs.pmc file, which specifies a number of SQL Server–related performance objects. As NT Server and applications run, the Performance Monitor increments a variety of counters that track system and application activity and usage of resources such as memory and disk. You can use the Performance Monitor's graphical interface to view this information in several different ways, including graphs, lists, and summary reports. You can also have the Performance Monitor send a network message or run a program when a counter goes above or below a specified value.

Every resource that the Performance Monitor tracks is represented by a *performance object*. Here is a list of the NT Server Performance Monitor object types:

Browser	NetBEUI Resource
Cache	Objects
FTP Server	Paging File
Gopher Service	PhysicalDisk
HTTP Service	Process
Internet Information Services Global	Processor
LogicalDisk	RAS Port
Memory	RAS Total
Microsoft Gatherer	Redirector
Microsoft Gatherer Projects	Server
Microsoft Search	Server Work Queues
Microsoft Search Catalogs	System
Microsoft Search Indexer Catalogs	Telephony
NBT Connection	Thread
NetBEUI	

Table 6-8 lists the additional Performance Monitor object types added for SQL Server, along with a description of the database resources these object types represent. If your system has multiple resources of the same type, there is one performance object of the appropriate type for each of the resources. For example, a typical system has multiple Process objects, each one representing a different running process.

> **NOTE:** Some Performance Monitor dialog boxes and documentation use *object* instead of *object type*, and *instance* instead of *object*.

Each object type defines a set of *counters*, which are simply information fields for performance data. Table 6-9 lists the counters available for each of the SQL Server performance object types.

Performance Monitor Object Type	Database Resources Represented
SQL Server:Access Methods	Database objects
SQL Server:Backup Device	Backup devices
SQL Server:Buffer Manager	Memory buffers
SQL Server:Cache Manager	Cache memory
SQL Server:Databases	Database transaction objects, such as transaction log space and active transactions
SQL Server:General Statistics	General server-wide activity, such as the number of currently connected users
SQL Server:Latches	Latches on internal resources
SQL Server:Locks	Locks
SQL Server:Memory Manager	Memory
SQL Server:Replication Agents	Replication agents
SQL Server:Replication Dist.	Replication distribution agent commands and transactions
SQL Server:Replication Logreader	Replication logreader agent commands and transactions
SQL Server:Replication Merge	Merge replication activity and errors
SQL Server:Replication Snapshot	Snapshot replication activity
SQL Server:SQL Statistics	SQL queries
SQL Server:User Settable	User-defined

Table 6-8.   SQL Server Performance Monitor Object Types

NOTE: The Performance Monitor graphical interface displays lists of the available counters and their descriptions for all object types.

To use the Performance Monitor, you identify which objects and which of their counters you want to monitor. You then use the Performance Monitor graphical interface to observe the selected information for the current server activity or you capture the selected information to a performance *log file* for subsequent viewing. As mentioned, you can also define a performance *alert* that sends a network message or runs a program when a counter goes above or below a certain value.

Counter Name	Description
Access Methods Counters	
Extent Deallocations/sec	Extents deallocated
Extents Allocated/sec	Extents allocated to database objects for storing index or data records
Forwarded Records/sec	Records fetched through forwarded record pointers
FreeSpace Page Fetches/sec	Pages returned by free space scans to satisfy requests to insert record fragments
FreeSpace Scans/sec	Scans initiated to search for free space in which to insert a new record fragment
Full Scans/sec	Unrestricted, full base table or index scans
Index Searches/sec	Index searches
Mixed page allocations/sec	Pages allocated from mixed extents
Page Deallocations/sec	Pages deallocated
Page Requests	Logical page requests issued by access methods modules
Page Splits/sec	Page splits that occur as the result of index pages overflowing
Pages Allocated/sec	Pages allocated to database objects for storing index or data records
Probe Scans/sec	Probe scans to directly find a row in an index or base table
Range Scans/sec	Qualified range scans through indexes
Scan Point Revalidations/sec	Revalidations of scan points
Skipped Ghosted Records/sec	Ghosted records skipped
Table Lock Escalations/sec	Table locks that were escalated
Workfiles Created/sec	Work files created
Worktables/sec	Work tables created
Worktables From Cache Ratio	Percent of new work tables with initial pages in the work table cache

Table 6-9. SQL Server Object Counters

Counter Name	Description
Backup Device Counters	
Device Throughput Bytes/sec	Read/write throughput for a device
Buffer Manager Counters	
Buffer Cache Hit Ratio	Percentage of pages found in the buffer cache without having to read from disk
Cache Size (pages)	Cache size in pages
Checkpoint Writes/sec	Pages flushed by a checkpoint operation
Committed Pages	Buffer pages committed
ExtendedMem Cache Hit Ratio	Percentage of page requests that were satisfied from the extended memory cache
ExtendedMem Cache Migrations/sec	Pages migrated into the extended memory cache
ExtendedMem Requests/sec	Requests for pages from large memory region
Free Buffers	Free buffers available
Lazy Writer Buffers/sec	Buffers examined by the buffer manager's lazy writer
Lazy Writes/sec	Buffers written by the buffer manager's lazy writer
Page Reads/sec	Reads of a buffer page
Page Requests/sec	Requests for buffer page
Page Writes/sec	Writes of a buffer page
Readahead Pages/sec	Requests to asynchronously prefetch pages before they're actually encountered
Reserved Page Count	Buffer cache reserved pages
Stolen Page Count	Buffer cache pages that have been stolen to satisfy other server memory requests

Table 6-9.   SQL Server Object Counters (*continued*)

Counter Name	Description
Cache Manager Counters	
Cache Hit Ratio	Ratio of cache hits to lookups
Cache Object Counts	Objects in the cache
Cache Pages	Cache pages used
Cache Use Counts/sec	Times each cache object has been used
Databases Counters	
Active Transactions	Active transactions for the database
Backup/Restore Throughput/sec	Read/write throughput for backup and restore operations
Bulk Copy Rows/sec	Rows copied
Bulk Copy Throughput/sec	Kilobytes copied
Data File(s) Size (KB)	Total size of all data files in a database
DBCC Logical Scan Bytes/sec	Logical read scan rate for DBCC commands
Log Bytes Per Flush	Bytes in log buffer when it's flushed
Log Cache Hit Ratio	Percentage of log cache reads that were satisfied from the log cache
Log Cache Reads/sec	Reads performed through the log manager cache
Log File(s) Size (KB)	Total size of all log files in a database
Log Flush Wait Time	Total wait time in milliseconds
Log Flush Waits/sec	Commits waiting on log flush
Log Flushes/sec	Log flushes
Log Growths	Log growths
Log Shrinks	Log shrinks
Log Truncations	Log truncations
Percent Log Used	Percentage of space used in the transaction log
Repl. Pending Xacts	Pending replication transactions
Repl. Trans. Rate	Replicated transactions/second

Table 6-9.   SQL Server Object Counters (*continued*)

Counter Name	Description
Shrink Data Movement Bytes/sec	Bytes moved by autoshrink, DBCC ShrinkDatabase, or DBCC ShrinkFile
Transactions/sec	Cumulative number of transactions started for the database
General Statistics Counters	
Logins/sec	Logins started
Logouts/sec	Logouts started
User Connections	Users connected to the system
Latches Counters	
Average Latch Wait Time (ms)	Average latch wait time, in milliseconds
Latch Waits/sec	Latch requests that could not be granted immediately and had to wait
Total Latch Wait Time (ms)	Total latch wait time (in milliseconds)
Locks Counters	
Average Wait Time (ms)	Average amount of wait time (in milliseconds) for each lock request
Lock Requests/sec	New locks and lock conversions requested from the lock manager
Lock Timeouts/sec	Lock requests that timed out, including internal requests for NOWAIT locks
Lock Wait Time (ms)	Total lock wait time, in milliseconds
Lock Waits/sec	Lock requests that could not be granted immediately and had to wait
Number of Deadlocks/sec	Lock requests that resulted in a deadlock
Memory Manager Counters	
Connection Memory (KB)	Total dynamic memory used for connections

Table 6-9. SQL Server Object Counters (*continued*)

Counter Name	Description
Granted Workspace Memory (KB)	Total memory granted to executing processes
Lock Blocks	Lock blocks in use
Lock Blocks Allocated	Lock blocks allocated
Lock Memory (KB)	Total dynamic memory used for locks
Lock Owner Blocks	Lock owner blocks in use
Lock Owner Blocks Allocated	Lock owner blocks allocated
Maximum Workspace Memory (KB)	Maximum available workspace memory
Memory Grants Outstanding	Number of processes that have acquired workspace memory
Memory Grants Pending	Number of processes waiting to acquire workspace memory
Optimizer Memory (KB)	Total dynamic memory used for query optimization
SQL Cache Memory (KB)	Total dynamic memory used for dynamic SQL cache
Target Server Memory (KB)	Total dynamic memory the server is willing to use
Total Server Memory (KB)	Total dynamic memory the server is using
Replication Agents Counters	
Running	Instances of a given replication agent that are currently running
Replication Dist. Counters	
Delivered Commands	Distribution commands delivered in the last batch
Delivered Transactions	Distribution transactions delivered in the last batch
Delivery Latency	Distribution latency in seconds
Delivery Rate	Distribution commands delivered per second

Table 6-9.   SQL Server Object Counters (*continued*)

Counter Name	Description
Replication Log Reader Counters	
Delivered Commands	Log reader commands delivered in the last batch
Delivered Transactions	Log reader transactions delivered in the last batch
Delivery Latency	Log reader latency in seconds
Delivery Rate	Log reader commands inserted per second
Replication Merge Counters	
Conflicts	Conflicts that occurred in the Publisher/Subscriber upload and download changes
Download Changes	Changes sent from the Publisher to the Subscriber
Merge Rate	Changes sent from the Publisher to the Subscriber divided by the duration of the merge run
Upload Changes	Changes sent from the Subscriber to the Publisher
Replication Snapshot Counters	
Bulk Copy Rate	Rows bulk copied per second
Rows Bulk Copied	Rows bulk copied
SQL Statistics Counters	
Auto-Param Attempts/sec	Auto-parameterization attempts
Batch Requests/sec	SQL batch requests
Failed Auto-Params/sec	Failed auto-parameterizations
Safe Auto-Params/sec	Safe auto-parameterizations
SQL Compilations/sec	SQL compilations
SQL Re-Compilations/sec	SQL recompiles
Unsafe Auto-Params/sec	Unsafe auto-parameterizations
User Settable Counters	
Query	User-defined

Table 6-9. SQL Server Object Counters (*continued*)

Running the Performance Monitor

To run the Performance Monitor from the Windows Start menu, select Programs | Microsoft SQL Server 7.0 | Performance Monitor. The Performance Monitor has the following four views:

▼ **Chart**   A line graph or histogram of the selected counters

■ **Alert**   A list of the alerts in effect and a log of any alert that's occurred

■ **Log**   The current performance logging status

▲ **Report**   A formatted text display of the selected counters' current value

You can select a view from the Performance Monitor's View menu or by clicking the appropriate toolbar icon (they're arranged left to right in the same order as the list above).

Each view has its own settings, including which counters are used in the view. This enables you to log a comprehensive set of counters with the log view while you watch selected sets of counters in a graph or report view. At the same time, you can have performance alerts defined for counters that you may or may not also be logging or viewing.

The Chart View

The chart view (Figure 6-11) displays current activity or previously logged information. The top part of the window is a line graph or histogram. For a graph, the horizontal

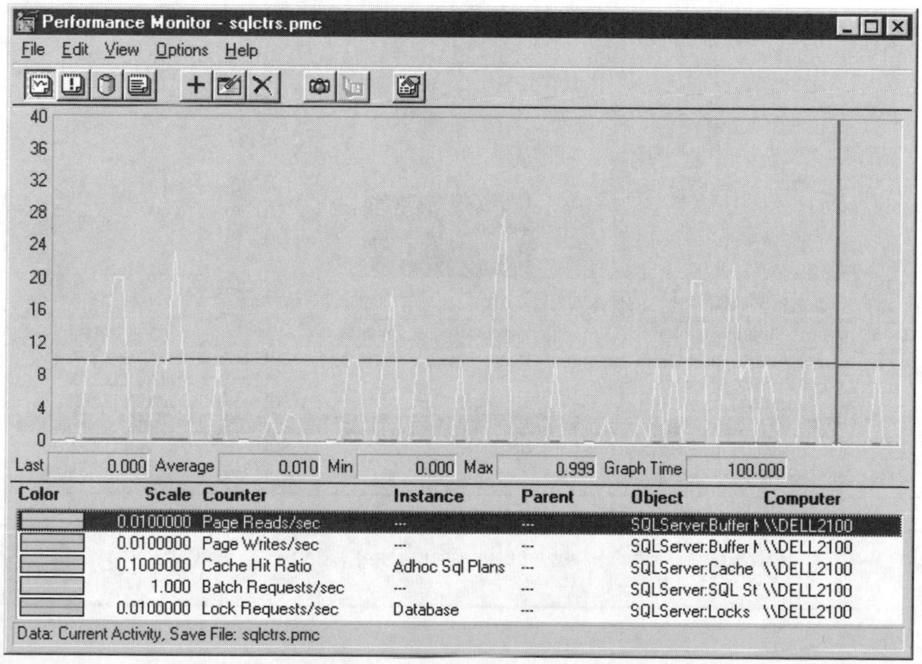

Figure 6-11.   Performance Monitor—chart view (line graph)

dimension is time and the vertical dimension is the value of the monitored counters. A color-coded line represents each counter's value over time. For a histogram (Figure 6-12), a separate, color-coded vertical bar represents each of the monitored counter's value.

Along the lower side of the graph or histogram is information (including last, average, minimum, and maximum values) for a single counter that's been selected from the list of counters displayed in the legend at the bottom of the window.

NOTE: Use the BACKSPACE key to toggle the currently selected counter's graph color between its normal color and white.

The legend for the graph or histogram appears in the bottom part of the window. For each counter being displayed, the legend shows the line or bar color and the scale used to plot points on the graph or to size the vertical bar on the histogram.

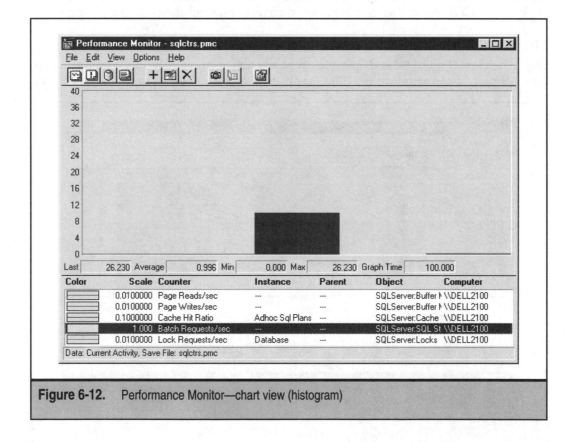

Figure 6-12.   Performance Monitor—chart view (histogram)

When you're monitoring current activity using a graph, a vertical red line advances from left to right (and repeats after reaching the right side of the window) with each sampling of the counters. The vertical bars in a histogram adjust their height with each sampling.

You can clear the currently displayed contents of a chart, alert, or report view (without deleting any of the selected counters) by selecting Edit | Clear Display from the Performance Monitor menu.

To add a counter to a chart view, select Edit | Add To Chart from the Performance Monitor menu. On the Add to Chart dialog box, shown in Figure 6-13, select an object type (for example, Processor) from the Object drop-down list. For object types that have more than one instance, select one or more instances from the Instance list; otherwise, selecting the object type implicitly selects the single object of that type. Next, select one or more counters from the Counter drop-down list. To see the definition of the currently selected Counter drop-down list item, click the Explain button. You can optionally set a counter's line or bar color, scale, line width, and line style on this dialog box.

▼

NOTE: Use SHIFT+click or CTRL+click to select multiple instances or counters on the Add to Chart dialog box.

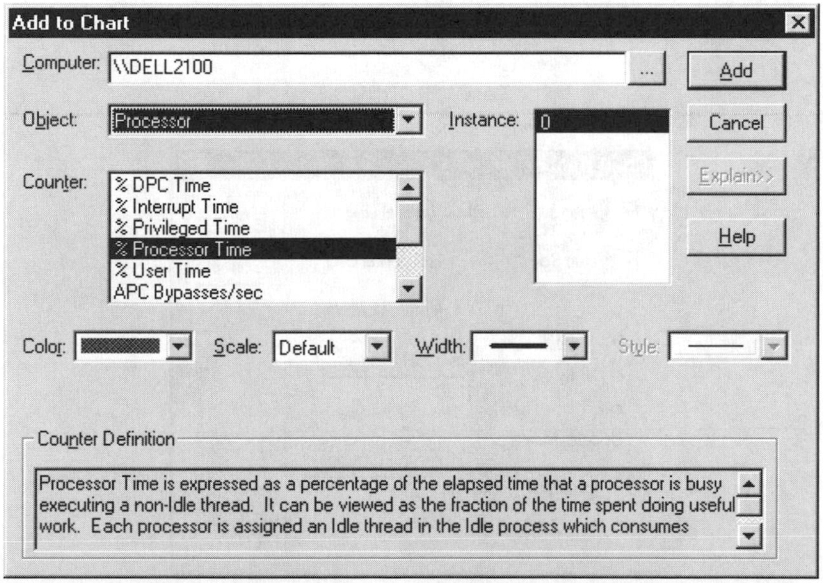

Figure 6-13.   Add to Chart dialog box

The Performance Monitor supports monitoring multiple systems, too. To add counters for objects on another system, click the "..." button beside the Computer entry field and select a system from the displayed list. Then use the process described above to add counters to the chart view.

After you've selected one or more counters (and instances, if necessary) and optionally set the counters' graph and histogram display properties, click the Add button. The counters are added to the chart view graph or histogram and legend.

NOTE: Avoid clicking the Add button repeatedly just because you don't see any confirmation in the Add to Chart dialog box. The chart view is where you'll see the results of adding a counter.

To delete a counter from the chart view, select the counter in the legend and select Edit | Delete from Chart from the main menu. To change the graph and histogram display properties of a counter, double-click it in the legend to display the Edit Chart Line dialog box (similar to the one in Figure 6-13).

You can set several chart options from the Options menu. Selecting the Options | Chart menu item displays the Chart Options dialog box in Figure 6-14. This dialog box lets you select whether to display a graph or histogram, as well as set several display properties. You also can set the periodic sampling interval or specify that the graph or histogram should be updated only when you manually request updated counter information. To update the displayed values immediately, select Update Now from the Options menu.

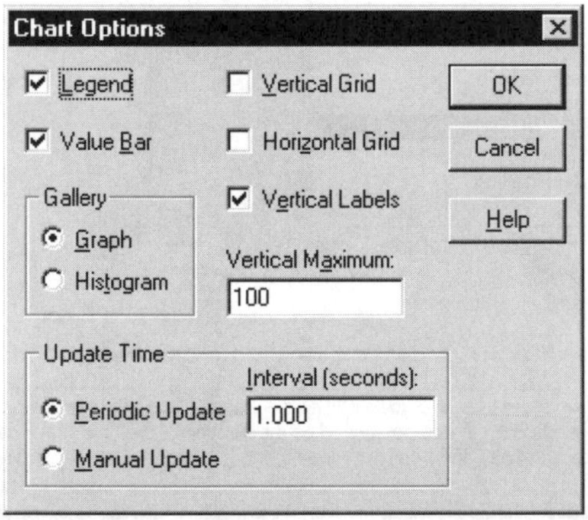

Figure 6-14. Chart Options dialog box

To save the settings for a chart view, select Save Chart Settings or Save Chart Settings As from the File menu and (for a new file) specify a filename. The default extension for chart view definition files is .pmc. Alternatively, you can save all the current workspace definitions, including chart, agent, log, and report view definitions, into a single file by selecting Save Workspace from the File menu. Performance Monitor workspace definition files have a default extension of .pmw. The File menu also provides a New Chart menu item to create a new chart definition and an Open menu item to open a previously saved chart (or other) view definition file.

You can also export counter data to an NT Server file by selecting File | Export Chart. On the Export As dialog box (not shown) enter a filename and select either TSV (tab-delimited values) or CSV (comma-delimited values) for the file type. Exported counter information can subsequently be imported into a spreadsheet or other analysis tool. The first few lines in a chart export file contain chart specifications. These are followed by a line with comma- or tab-delimited headings for the counter, date, and time columns. The remaining lines have the counter, date, and time values for each sampling.

Viewing a Chart of a Log File

The previous discussion covered the chart view of current activity. You can also use the chart view with performance data that was previously captured to a log file, as described in the section "The Log View," later in this chapter. To display log data, rather than current activity, select Options | Data From from the Performance Monitor menu. On the Data From dialog box (Figure 6-15) select the Log File option and enter or select a log file.

NOTE: The status bar at the bottom of the Profile Monitor window displays either "Current Activity" or the name of the log file that you're viewing.

Viewing a log file is similar to viewing current activity, except the performance information isn't periodically updated. You can add and delete counters (as long as they were captured in the log file) and change display characteristics. You can also limit the

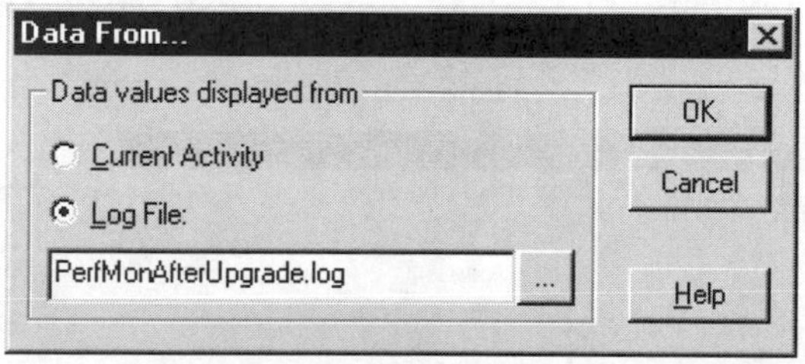

Figure 6-15. Data From dialog box

time interval that's displayed by selecting Edit | Time Window. The Input Log File Timeframe dialog box (Figure 6-16) displays a horizontal bar representing the entire time interval covered by the log file. Above this bar, the endpoints are labeled with the start and stop dates and times for the entire log contents. Below the bar, the left value indicates the start date and time of the interval you want to view, and the right value indicates the stop date and time of the interval you want to view. You can adjust these two boundaries by dragging the left or right end of the bar. As you drag either end, the area of the bar *outside* the viewing limits turns blue and the lower date and time values change to reflect the new viewing limits.

An alternative way to set a start or stop value for the viewed interval is to select a bookmark (discussed in the section "The Log View," later in this chapter) from the displayed list and click either the Set As Start or Set As Stop button. Setting the start or stop point with a bookmark also adjusts the time interval bar so it reflects the date and time of the bookmark. Once you've set the time window, click the OK button.

NOTE: When viewing data from a log file, the time window affects all four views. In most cases, it's easiest to set the time window while displaying the chart view because the chart view adjusts to reflect the time window as you change the start and stop points.

The Alert View

In the lower part of the alert view (Figure 6-17) there's a legend with a list of all performance alerts that you've defined for the view. In the upper part of the alert view there's a log of all performance alerts that have fired. When you're monitoring current activity, new entries are added to the alert log display as an alert fires. When you're

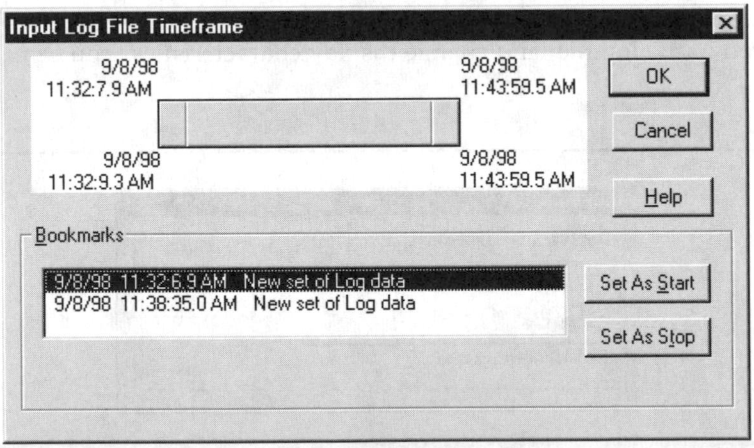

Figure 6-16. Input Log File Timeframe dialog box

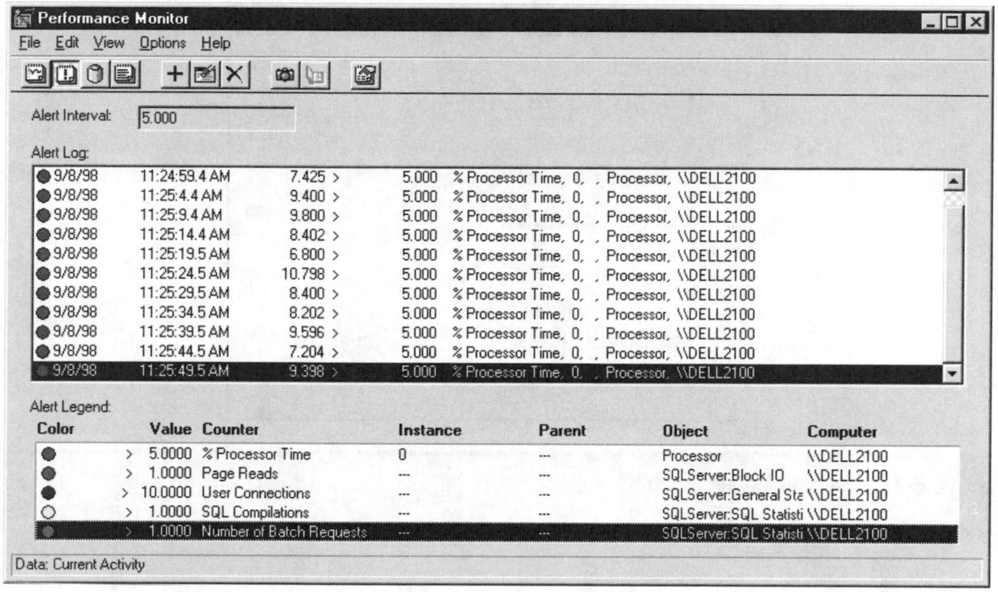

Figure 6-17.   Performance Monitor—alert view

viewing data from a log file, the alert log shows alerts that *would have fired* during the time interval, based on the current alert definitions. To select whether to work with alerts for current activity or a log file, select Options | Data From on the Performance Monitor menu, and specify the performance data source, as described previously for the chart view.

NOTE: When viewing a log file, it doesn't matter which alerts were defined when the log was captured. When you add, delete, and change alert definitions in the alert view, the alert view of a log file changes to reflect the way the alert log would appear if the current alert view definitions had been in effect at the time the log was captured. However, you can only define alerts for counters that were captured in the log file.

You can set several options by selecting Options | Alert to display the Alert Options dialog box shown in Figure 6-18. Select the Switch to Alert View check box if you want the alert view to be displayed whenever an alert occurs while viewing current activity in a different view. Without this option selected, an alert icon (a ball with an exclamation point) appears on the right side of the status bar in the chart, log, and report views whenever an alert occurs.

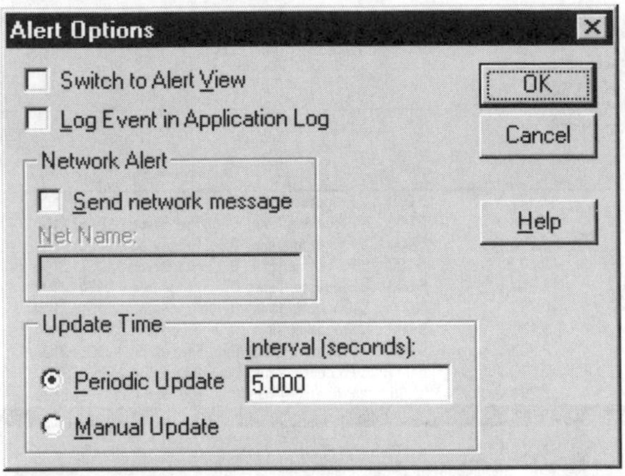

Figure 6-18. Alert Options dialog box

The Log Event in Application Log option logs an event for the performance alert in the Windows NT application log. The Send network message option sends a message to the specified network name whenever an alert occurs; and, as explained for chart views, you can specify that counter values should be manually or periodically updated. Performance alert conditions are tested whenever the counters are updated.

To add an alert, select Edit | Add To Alert from the Performance Monitor menu. The Add to Alert dialog box (Figure 6-19) provides similar Computer, Object, Instance, Counter, and Color selection fields, as well as the Add and Explain buttons, as previously described for the Add to Chart dialog box. For an alert you also have to select whether the alert should fire when the counter has a value that's over or under a specified value. See Table 6-9 (or use the Explain button) for the meaning of each counter value. You can optionally specify the filename of a Windows NT program to run either the first time an alert fires or every time it fires.

NOTE: Use values in the range 0 to 100 (not 0 to 1.0) for counters that hold percentages.

To delete an alert, select it in the legend and select Edit | Delete Alert from the Performance Monitor menu. To clear the alert log display (without deleting alerts), select Edit | Clear Display from the main menu. To change the comparison value, color, or optional program to run for an alert, double-click the alert in the legend.

You can save or export alert view definitions or open previously saved alert definitions by using the File menu, as explained for chart views. The default extension for alert view definition files is .pma.

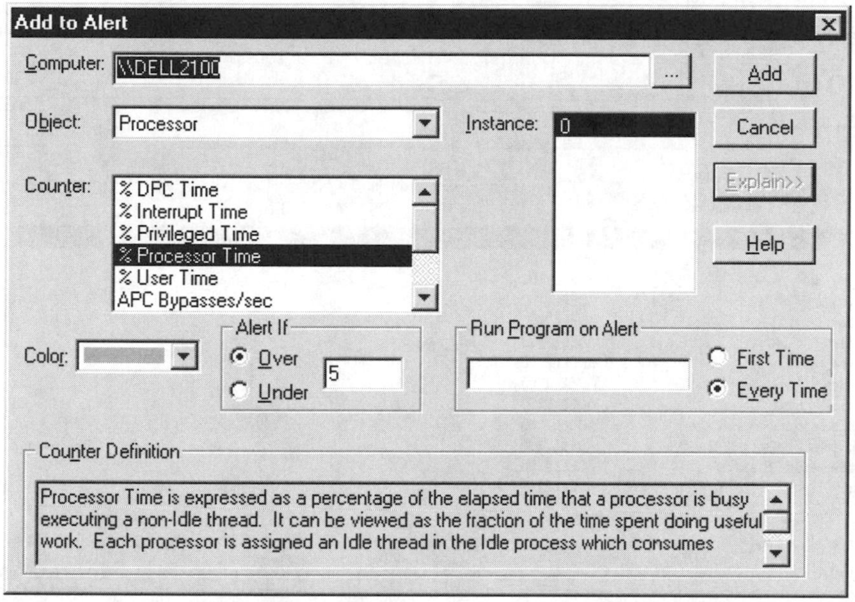

Figure 6-19. Add to Alert dialog box

NOTE: When you export an alert view, the export file contains the alert definitions, not the alert log.

The Log View

The log view (Figure 6-20) lets you control the capturing of performance counter data to a performance log file. You use the chart, alert, and report views to actually look at the contents of a performance log file. As explained under the sections covering these views, the Data From dialog box lets you select a performance log file for viewing, and the Input Log File Timeframe dialog box lets you select all or part of the time interval covered by a log.

To create a new log definition, select Options | Log from the Performance Monitor menu. On the Log Options dialog box (Figure 6-21), enter or select a Windows NT file for the log to be stored in. The default extension for performance log files is .log. Set either the periodic update interval or specify manual update. Click the Save button to complete this step.

After identifying the log file, select Edit | Add to Log from the Performance Monitor menu to display the Add To Log dialog box shown in Figure 6-22. You can capture performance data from multiple systems into a single log by clicking the "..." button beside the Computer entry field and selecting a system from the displayed list. Unlike the chart and alert views discussed previously, you don't add individual instances or counters to a log. Instead, you add object types, and for each object type in the log, all

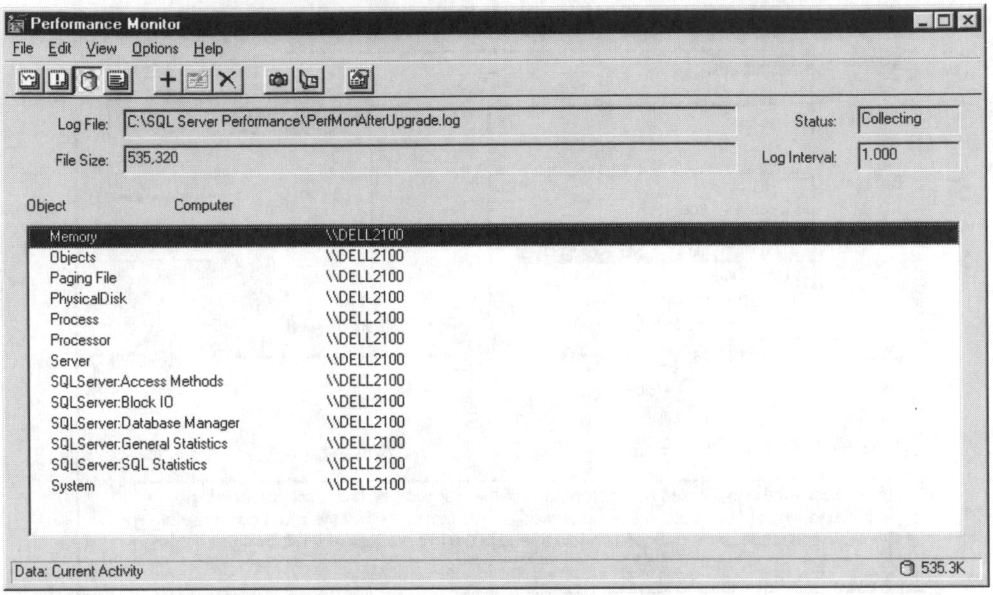

Figure 6-20. Performance Monitor—log view

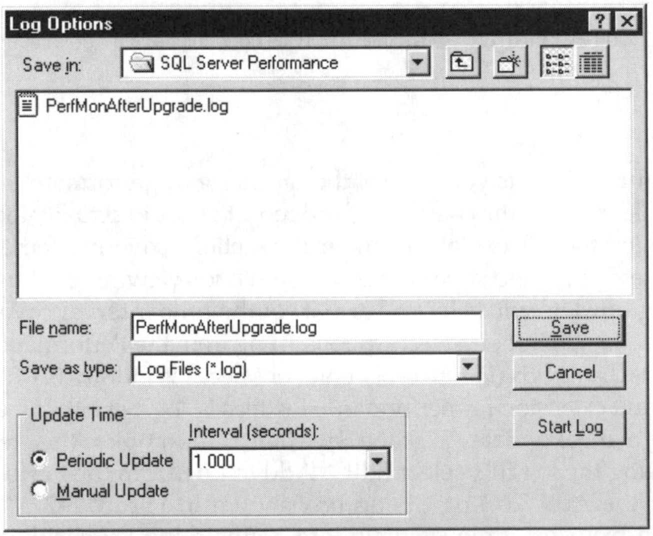

Figure 6-21. Log Options dialog box

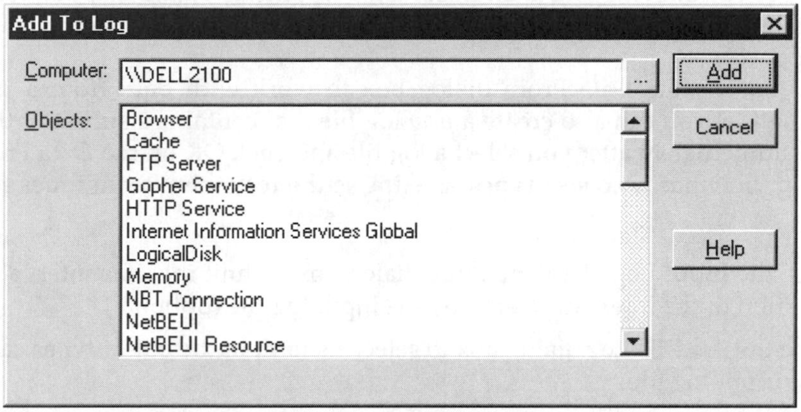

Figure 6-22.   Add To Log dialog box

counters for all instances are captured. When you subsequently work with the logged data using a chart, alert, or report view, you can select which counters are displayed. To add an object type, select it in the Objects list and click Add. After adding object types to a log, they're listed in the log view. To delete an object type, select it in the log view and select Edit | Delete From Log from the Performance Monitor menu.

To start and stop the capturing of data to a log, select Options | Log from the Performance Monitor menu and click the Start or Stop button. The log view displays the log file and status (Closed or Collecting), current log file size, and the sampling interval. When data is being captured to a log (that is, the status is Collecting), a small disk drive icon appears on the right side of the Performance Monitor status bar.

As with other view definitions, you can save and open log file definitions, which have a default extension of .pml. When you open a previously saved log definition file, the Performance Monitor immediately begins logging to the log file that was specified in the definition. You can also export a log view definition, which contains the view specifications, not any log data.

NOTE: Don't confuse the performance log file, which has an extension of .log and contains the counter data, and the performance log definition file, which has an extension of .pml and contains the specifications for which counters are logged, the sampling interval, and the name of the log file.

A performance log file can contain *bookmarks*, entries with the date and time and some system- or user-defined message, rather than counter data. To add your own bookmark to a log that's capturing data, select Options | Bookmark from the Performance Monitor menu and enter a bookmark comment. The Performance Monitor may also add bookmarks, for example, when a remote system that you're monitoring shuts down or reconnects.

Whenever you start logging to an existing log file, the new data is appended. To clear an old log file, you must stop logging to it and then use Windows NT facilities to delete or clear the file.

When you use the Data From dialog box to work with data from a previously captured log file, you can also create a *new* log file that contains a subset of the old log file's data. Immediately after you select a log file and click OK on the Data From dialog box, the log view has no object types listed. Use the following techniques to create a new log:

▼ Use the Input Log File Timeframe dialog box to limit the time interval to a portion of the interval covered by the input log file (optional).

■ Use the Add To Log dialog box to select a subset of the object types captured in the input log file.

▲ Use the Log Options dialog box to specify a new output log file.

The Report View

The report view (Figure 6-23) provides a "listing" style display that corresponds to the information shown on a chart view histogram. Select Edit | Add To Report from the Performance Monitor menu to display the Add to Report dialog box (not shown) to add

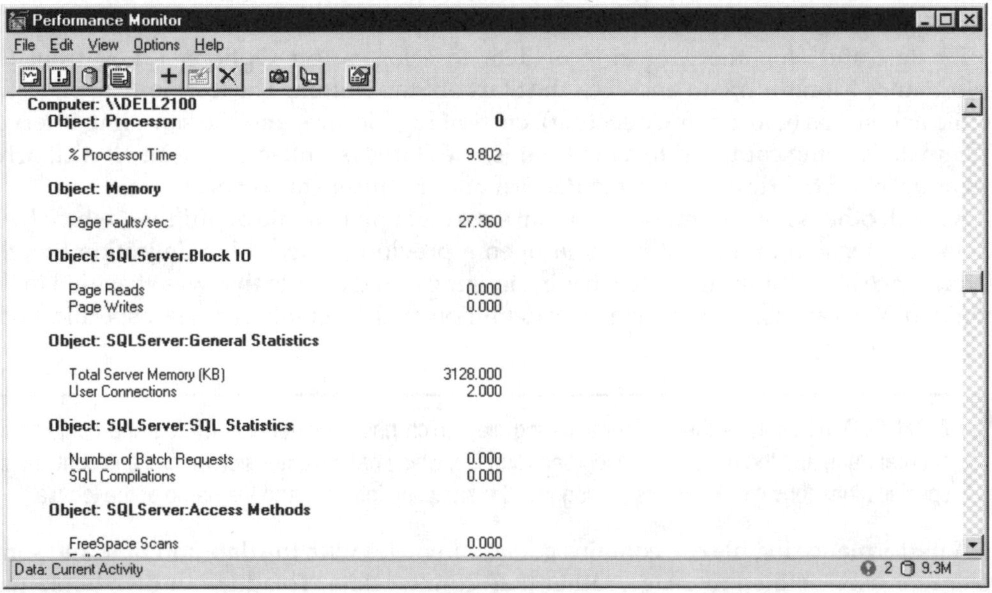

Figure 6-23.   Performance Monitor—report view

counters. This dialog box is identical to the Add to Chart dialog box shown in Figure 6-13, except there aren't fields for the line or bar display style and scale. The only option available by selecting Options | Report from the main menu is the sampling interval. Report view definition files, which have a default extension of .pmr, can be saved and opened. You can also export a report, which produces a text file with the actual lines of the report, including labels and data values, although not with the same layout that you see in the report view.

Using the Performance Monitor Data

The Performance Monitor chart view provides an excellent real-time display to monitor critical resources. Adding performance alerts further enhances your ability to watch for performance problems as they occur. The Performance Monitor logging capabilities let you capture periodic data for subsequent analysis either with the chart view or by exporting the chart view of the data and using a query tool to analyze the data. Combining the Performance Monitor and a query tool in this fashion is a good way to compare system-wide performance over intervals before and after you make changes that may affect performance.

ENTERPRISE MANAGER CURRENT ACTIVITY CATEGORIES

To get a quick glimpse of SQL Server activity, you can expand a server entry in the SQL Server Enterprise Manager's navigation tree and select one of the following three Current Activity categories under the Management folder:

Process Info
Locks / Process ID
Locks / Object

Process Info Category

The Process Info category shows the process ID, the current user or database (or both), and the status. Depending on the type of process, the following information may also be shown:

Open transactions
Command
Application
Wait time
Wait resource
CPU time
Physical I/O
Memory usage

Login time
Last batch
Host name
Network library
Network address
Blocked by (process)
Blocking (process)

Locks / Process ID Category

When you expand the Locks / Process ID category, Enterprise Manager displays one entry for each lock that a process holds. The lock information includes the following:

System process ID (SPID)
Lock type (see list in Table 6-10)
Lock mode (see list in Table 6-11)
Lock status
Lock owner
Index ID of locked index
Resource (object) ID of locked object

Displayed Lock Type	Meaning
DB	Database
EXT	Extent
FIL	File
IDX	Index
KEY	Key
NUL	None of above
PG	Page
RID	Row identifier
TAB	Table

Table 6-10.   Object Lock Types

Displayed Lock Mode	Meaning
IS	Intent shared
IX	Intent exclusive
S	Shared
Sch-M	Schema modification
Sch-S	Schema stability
SIX	Share with intent exclusive
U	Update
X	Exclusive

Table 6-11.   Object Lock Modes

Locks / Object Category

The Locks / Object category is similar to the Locks / Process ID category; however, the list is organized by locked objects rather than by processes holding locks.

For all three categories, you can right-click a category or item and select Refresh from the pop-up menu to update the displayed information. Or, right-click a Process Info or Locks / Process ID item and select Detailed Information from the pop-up menu to display the Process Details dialog box shown in Figure 6-24. This dialog box shows the last Transact-SQL statement and the cumulative CPU and disk resource usage. The Send Message button presents a dialog box that lets you send a message to a connected user or computer.

To end a process immediately, click the Kill Process button on the Process Details dialog box or right-click a Process Info or Locks / Process ID item in the Enterprise Manager tree and select Kill Process from the pop-up menu. Only members of the sysadmin role can use this feature. (Chapter 4 explains SQL Server roles.)

Although the SQL Server Performance Monitor, discussed previously in the section "SQL Server Performance Monitor," provides more comprehensive information, the Current Activity categories provide an easy-to-use tool for getting a quick picture of what's going on in your system. You can use these two features in combination to keep an ongoing watch over database activity and performance.

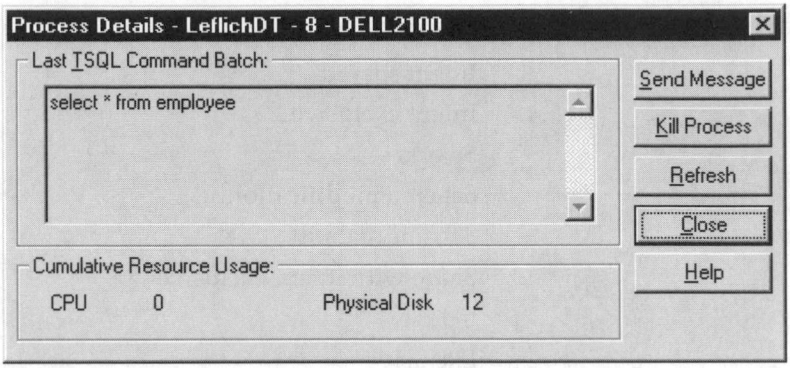

Figure 6-24. Process Details dialog box

INDEX TUNING WIZARD

The Index Tuning Wizard is a tool that analyzes a set of database queries and provides recommendations for a set of database indexes that will maximize the overall performance of the queries. For an analysis, you specify the following items:

▼ The set of queries that represents the workload to optimize

■ The database that contains the tables over which indexes may be created to improve performance

■ The specific tables in the specified database to consider in the analysis

▲ Constraints on the analysis (for example, maximum disk space used by indexes)

The workload can be specified either by capturing a trace with the SQL Server Profiler (as explained previously in the section "Running a Trace") or by providing a file that contains SQL statements. If you use a trace, the index analysis uses the queries that are captured in the trace. A trace should capture at least the following events:

▼ SQL:BatchStarting or SQL:BatchCompleted

▲ RPC:Starting or RPC:Completed

The trace data should also include at least the Text data column.

NOTE: The Create Trace Wizard provides the "Find the worst performing queries" prepackaged trace that you can use as the basis for a trace to provide a workload for the Index Tuning Wizard. After running the Create Trace Wizard, you may want to remove the Duration filter from this trace (or reduce this filter's threshold value) so that all queries are traced. Another way to create a suitable trace for the Index Tuning Wizard is to open the Sample 1 - TSQL trace in the Profiler. This trace definition is shipped with SQL Server and captures the necessary events and data columns.

Essentially, the Index Tuning Wizard calls on the SQL Server query optimizer to assess the hypothetical performance of each query in the workload using each of the possible combinations of indexes over columns used in the queries. The Index Wizard then recommends the set of indexes that produce the best *overall* performance for the entire set of queries in the workload. (The Index Tuning Wizard may take some shortcuts in this process, but the basic approach is as we describe.)

It's important to understand that the Index Tuning Wizard's recommendations are always based on a defined workload. If this workload doesn't reflect your normal operations, the recommended indexes may not be the ones that produce the best performance under real workloads. The crucial step in getting good results from the wizard is capturing a meaningful workload.

NOTE: In general, this means that using a file of SQL statements to define your workload has limited value. This might be useful for single SQL statements or batches of SQL statements that can be run in isolation; but for mixed loads, a profile trace is a better way to define the workload.

After the Index Tuning Wizard runs its analysis, you can view a variety of reports. You can also have the Index Tuning Wizard create the recommended set of indexes immediately or as a scheduled job, or produce a source file with the SQL statements to create the indexes. You can subsequently edit this file and run it using the Query Analyzer or OSQL tools.

Preparing a Workload

To prepare a workload before running the Index Tuning Wizard, run the SQL Server Profiler and capture an appropriate trace file, as described previously in the section "Running a Trace." Or, use the Query Analyzer or other tool to produce a source file with SQL statements that represent the workload.

NOTE: A SQL script for the Index Tuning Wizard doesn't require a Use statement; however, because a Use statement must be the first statement in a SQL script for the SQL Server Profiler, it's good practice to include one anyway. We also recommend you end the script with a Go statement and use Go statements to "batch" groups of statements in scripts that have lots of statements.

Running the Index Tuning Wizard

You can run the Index Tuning Wizard from either the SQL Server Enterprise Manager or the SQL Server Profiler. From the SQL Server Enterprise Manager, select a server, then select Tools | Wizards from the main menu. On the Select Wizard dialog box, expand the Management category and double-click Index Tuning Wizard. From the SQL Server Profiler, select Tools | Index Tuning Wizard from the main menu. Click the Next button on the Index Tuning Wizard's Welcome dialog box to display the dialog box shown in Figure 6-25, in which you can select a server and database.

Click the Next button and select I have a saved workload file on the dialog box shown in Figure 6-26.

> **NOTE:** If you don't already have a workload file, you can select the I will create the workload file on my own option and click the Finish button. This ends the Index Tuning Wizard and runs SQL Server Profiler.

Click the Next button to display the dialog box shown in Figure 6-27, in which you can specify your workload file or table. To use trace data saved to a Windows NT file or to use a SQL script file, select the My workload file option, and select the file from the Open dialog box (not shown). To use trace data saved to a SQL table, select the SQL Server table option and select the database table from the Source Table dialog box (not shown).

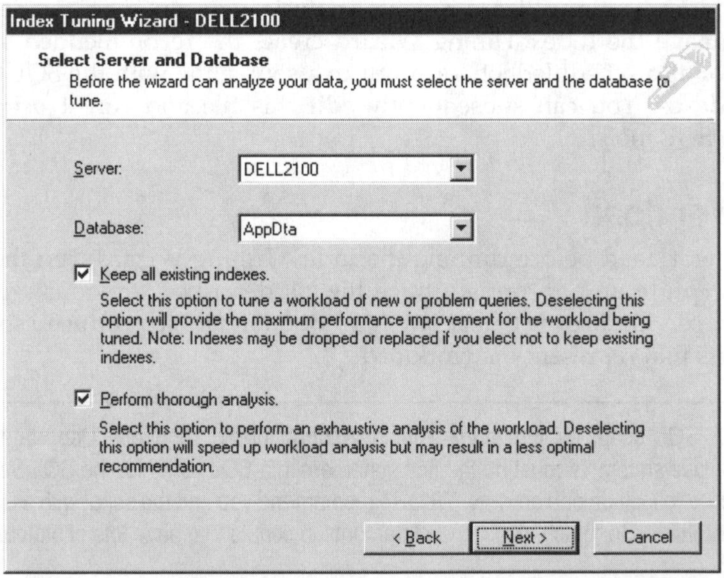

Figure 6-25.   Index Tuning Wizard dialog box to select a server and database

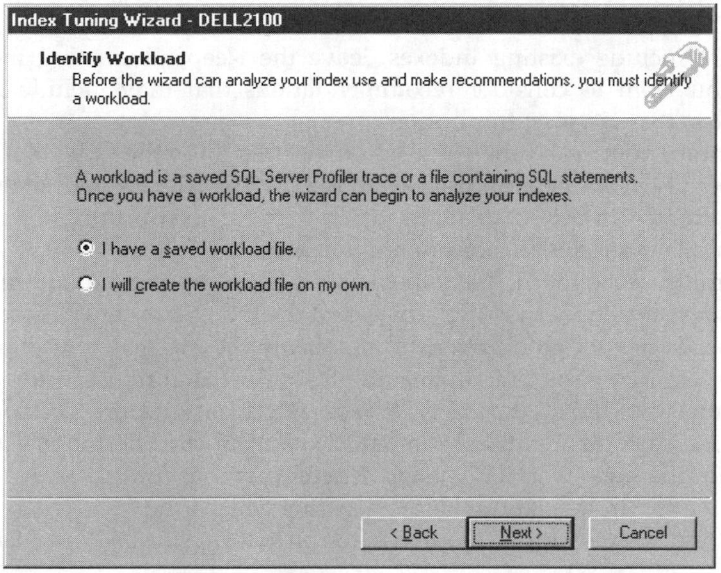

Figure 6-26.   Index Tuning Wizard dialog box to select the type of workload

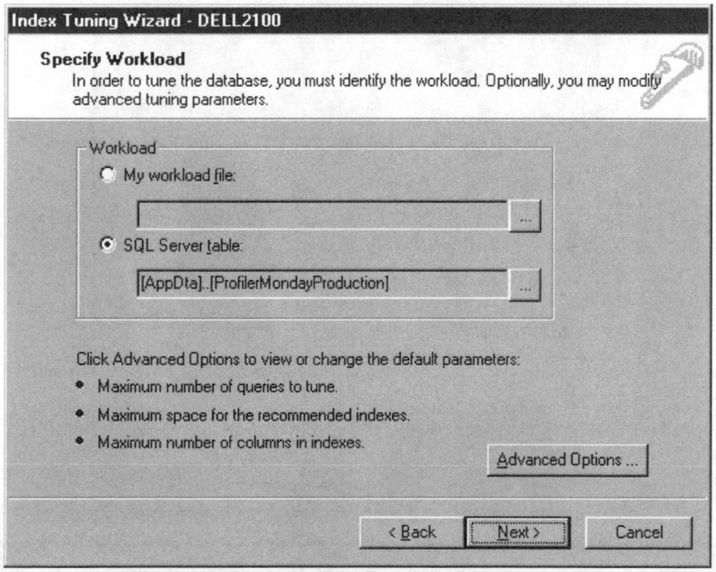

Figure 6-27.   Index Tuning Wizard dialog box to specify the workload

On the wizard's Workload dialog box, you can click the Advanced Options button to display the dialog box shown in Figure 6-28. If you want the analysis to consider only index sets that include existing indexes, leave the Keep all existing indexes option selected. If you want to consider recommendations that may include *deleting* some existing indexes, then deselect this option.

The Maximum queries to tune value limits the breadth of the Index Tuning Wizard's analysis. Generally, you shouldn't limit the number of queries you analyze with this value (so use a high number). Instead, capture a trace for an appropriate workload as the way to control what queries are considered in the analysis.

The Maximum space for the recommended indexes and the Maximum columns per index options also constrain the alternatives that the Index Tuning Wizard considers. Be sure you use a large enough number for the maximum space so you don't restrict the analysis unnecessarily. The default maximum of 16 columns per index is probably adequate for most workloads; however, for some decision support workloads, you may also want to increase this number. Remember, you can run the Index Tuning Wizard repeatedly over the same workload, using different settings for these advanced options, and compare the recommendations before deciding which indexes to create. After setting the advanced options, click the OK button to return to the wizard's Workload dialog box.

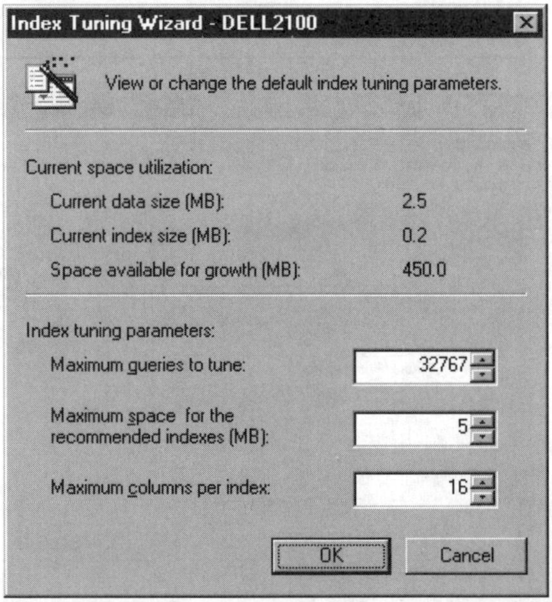

Figure 6-28. Index Tuning Wizard dialog box to specify advanced options

Click the Next button to display the dialog box in Figure 6-29, in which you select which tables to consider in the analysis. You can use the four buttons to add and remove tables from the Tables to tune list. Generally, you should include all tables that are accessed in the workload. Although eliminating some tables may reduce the time required for the Index Tuning Wizard to perform the analysis, you may miss important alternatives by excluding some tables.

When you click the Next button on this dialog box, the Index Tuning Wizard begins its analysis and displays a status dialog box during the process. When the analysis is complete, the Index Tuning Wizard displays a dialog box with index recommendations (Figure 6-30). This dialog box shows information on existing and recommended new indexes. You can click the Analysis button to choose any of the following reports:

Index Usage Report (Recommended Configuration)
Index Usage Report (Current Configuration)
Table Analysis Report
Query Cost Report
Workload Analysis Report

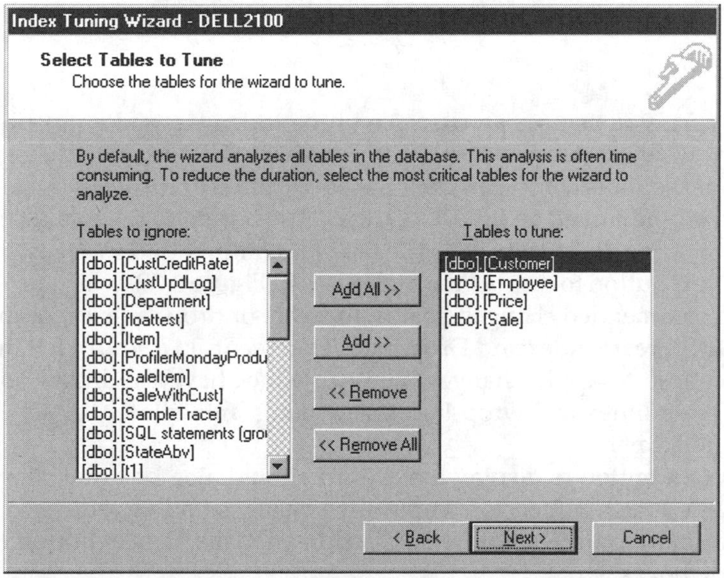

Figure 6-29. Index Tuning Wizard dialog box to specify the tables

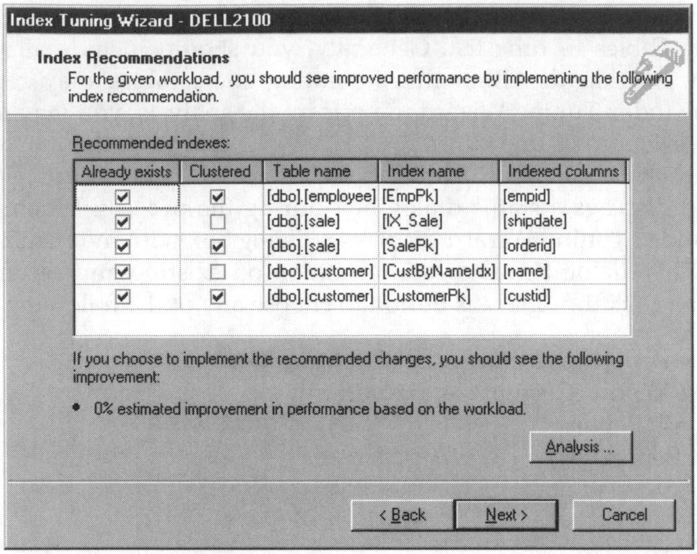

Figure 6-30.   Index Tuning Wizard dialog box with index recommendations

In Figure 6-31, you can see an example of the Index Usage Report (Recommended Configuration). As you select a report, the bottom part of the analysis dialog box displays a description of the report. You can click the Save button and specify a filename to save the report as a tab-delimited text file. Click the Close button to remove the report dialog box and return to the dialog box with the list of recommended indexes (Figure 6-30).

Click the Next button to display the dialog box in Figure 6-32, which provides options to apply the recommended changes (that is, to create or drop indexes) or to generate the appropriate SQL Create Index and Drop Index statements in a source file that can be run later. If you choose to apply changes, you can either have the Index Tuning Wizard execute the Create Index and Drop Index statements immediately or schedule them to run at a specified time.

Click the Next button to display the confirmation dialog box (not shown) on which you can click the Finish button to complete the changes you've requested. If you don't want to make changes or generate a SQL script, click the Cancel button on any of the wizard's dialog boxes.

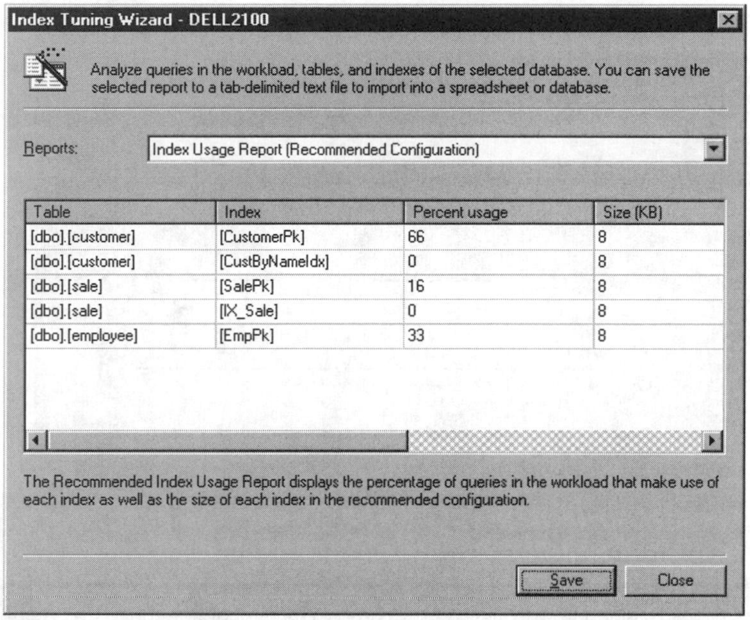

Figure 6-31.   Index Tuning Wizard dialog box with analysis reports

You should consider running the SQL Server Performance Monitor before and after using the Index Tuning Wizard to see how changes affect your normal workloads. Also, you can use the Showplan tool (discussed in the next section) to see how new indexes affect the execution plan for individual queries.

SHOWPLAN

When SQL Server executes a SQL statement, it uses the query optimizer to construct an *execution plan* for the statement. An execution plan is a series of steps that produces the desired result for the query. For example, a simple query such as

```
Select    *
  From    Sale
  Order By CustId
```

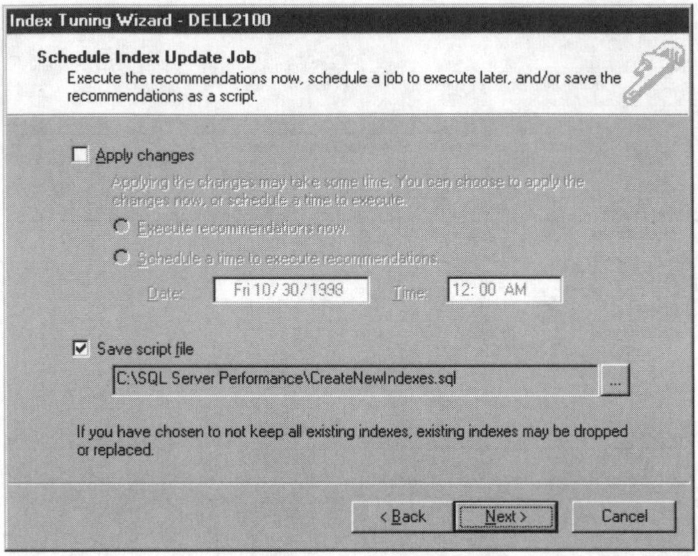

Figure 6-32. Index Tuning Wizard dialog box to apply changes or generate SQL script

might result in the following execution plan steps:

1. Scan the clustered index for the Sale table's primary key.
2. Sort the results from step 1 by the CustId column.
3. Return the results from step 2 to the application.

The optimizer uses statistical information stored with database tables and indexes to evaluate alternative ways to produce the final results. For example, a Select statement's Order By clause might be satisfied by using an available or temporary index or by physically sorting rows. The query optimizer attempts to produce a "least cost"—that is, most efficient—execution plan for a query.

SQL Server's Showplan feature lets you see the execution plan that the optimizer creates for a specific statement. You can use this information to help decide how a statement's performance might be improved, either by changing the query or by adding a database index. Keep in mind that using Showplan information to improve an individual statement's performance can have positive or negative impacts on overall system performance, so don't use it as your only performance tool. Tools such as the Index Tuning Wizard (discussed in the section "Index Tuning Wizard") often provide a better way to decide on changes that will have system-wide impact, such as which indexes to create.

Using Showplan with the Set Statement

There are two Transact-SQL statements you can use to see a SQL query statement's execution plan:

```
Set Showplan_Text On
```

or

```
Set Showplan_All On
```

Both these statements cause SQL Server to *not* execute subsequent SQL statements for the connection until you execute another Showplan_Text or Showplan_All command with Off as the new setting. When Showplan_Text or Showplan_All is in effect, SQL Server returns information about the execution plan for each subsequently executed statement. Showplan_Text causes basic information to be returned in a format suitable for you to read directly, whereas Showplan_All returns more comprehensive information in a result table suitable for processing by an application program.

As an example of using Showplan_Text, executing the following three statements in Query Analyzer produces the results shown in Figure 6-33.

```
Set Showplan_Text On
Go
Select   *
  From   Sale
  Order By CustId
```

```
StmtText
-----------------------------------
Select * from sale order by custid
(1 row(s) affected)

StmtText
-------------------------------------------------------
  |--Sort(ORDER BY: ([Sale].[CustId] ASC))
       |--Clustered Index Scan([AppDta].[dbo].[Sale].[SalePk])
(2 row(s) affected)
```

Figure 6-33.   Sample output for Showplan_Text

The first part of the output just repeats the statement; the second part of the output shows the execution plan steps. This part of the output is structured as a tree, with steps whose results are used in other steps, shown indented under the later step. In this example, the first execution step is the clustered index scan, and the results of this step are used in a sort step. The results of the sort step are returned to the application.

NOTE: You cannot execute Set Showplan_Text or Set Showplan_All inside a stored procedure.

When you use Set Showplan_All, a result set is returned with the columns listed in Table 6-12.

Column Name	Used Only in Rows with Type of PLAN_ROW	Contents
Argument	Yes	Supplemental information about the operation, depending on the physical operator.
AvgRowSize		Estimated average row size (in bytes) of rows processed by this operator.
DefinedValues		Comma-delimited list of values introduced by this operator.
EstimateCPU	Yes	Estimated CPU cost for this operation.
EstimateIO	Yes	Estimated I/O cost for this operation.
EstimateRows	Yes	Estimated number of output rows from this operation.
LogicalOp	Yes	Relational algebraic operator this node represents.

Table 6-12. Showplan_All Column Definitions

Column Name	Used Only in Rows with Type of PLAN_ROW	Contents
NodeId		Node (execution step) ID within the current query.
OutputList		Comma-delimited list of columns projected by this operation.
Parent		Node ID of the parent step.
PhysicalOp	Yes	Physical implementation algorithm for the node.
StmtId		Statement ID within the current batch.
StmtText		Transact-SQL statement. (For rows of PLAN_ROW type, a description of the operation.)
TotalSubtreeCost		Estimated cumulative cost of this operation and all operations it depends on (i.e., child nodes).
Type		Node type: For the parent node of each query, the SQL statement type: Select, Insert, Execute, etc. For subnodes representing an execution plan step, the type is PLAN_ROW.
Warnings		Comma-delimited list of warning messages for the current operation.

Table 6-12.   Showplan_All Column Definitions (*continued*)

Using Graphical Showplan

The Query Analyzer tool has a feature that displays a graphical representation of a statement's execution plan. To run the Query Analyzer, select Programs | SQL Server 7.0 | Query Analyzer from the Windows Start menu, or select Tools | SQL Server Query Analyzer from the Enterprise Manager menu or the SQL Server Profiler menu. (Chapter 9 provides additional information on using the Query Analyzer to execute SQL statements.)

To see the execution plan for a statement, enter the statement in the query pane (the upper part of a query window) and select Display Estimated Execution Plan from the Query menu. Alternatively, you can click the similarly titled toolbar icon or press CTRL+L. The statement does not execute, but the Estimated Execution Plan tab in the lower part of the query window displays a flow diagram for the execution plan. Figure 6-34 shows the graphical plan for the following statement:

```
Select   *
  From   Sale
  Order By CustId
```

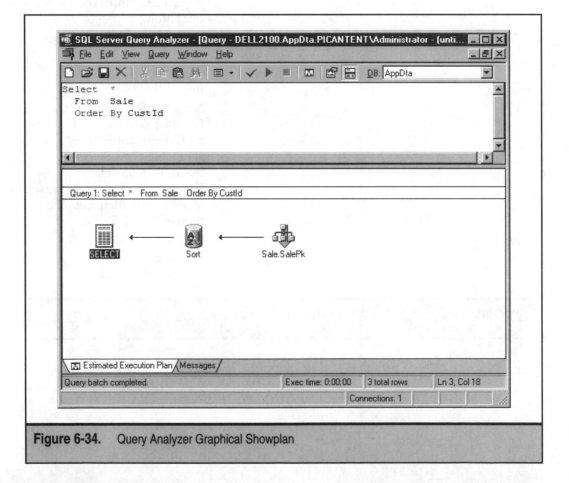

Figure 6-34. Query Analyzer Graphical Showplan

NOTE: You do not need to execute a Set Showplan_Text or Set Showplan_All statement in Query Analyzer to use the Graphical Showplan feature.

Each icon represents a step in the execution plan. You can move the cursor over an icon to display the details for the step, as shown in Figure 6-35. The displayed information is the same as listed in Table 6-12 for the Set Showplan_All statement. You can also move the cursor over an arrow between icons to display the estimated row count and estimated average row size of rows that are passed from one step to the next. To print the graphical plan, click the cursor in the SQL Execution Plan pane to make it active and select Print from the File menu.

By displaying a SQL Statement's execution plan in table or graphic form without actually executing a query, you can experiment with different query structures to see how they affect the execution plan. Among other variations, you can try using table, query, and join hints, as discussed later in this chapter in the section "SQL Statement Hints."

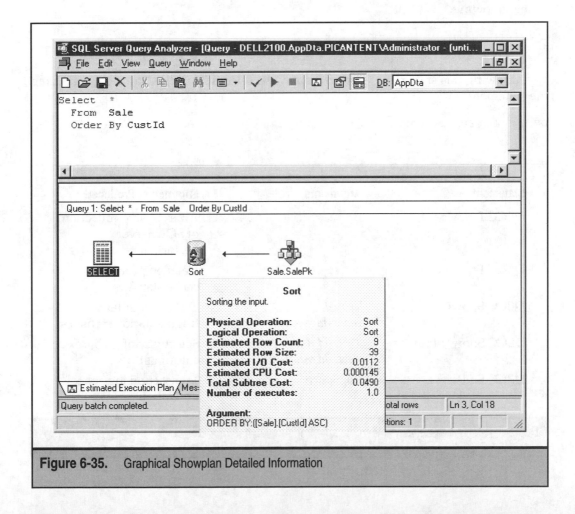

Figure 6-35. Graphical Showplan Detailed Information

OTHER PERFORMANCE TOOLS

There are several other tools that you can use to obtain performance information. These are more specialized than the tools covered in the previous sections, and we cover them only briefly in this book. However, for some situations, they may provide the information you need to improve database performance.

The DBCC Statement

The Transact-SQL DBCC statement has several variations to obtain performance statistics. Table 6-13 lists the performance-related statements, arguments for the statements, and the information produced.

DBCC Show_Statistics

To use the DBCC Show_Statistics statement on columns that aren't already part of an index, you first have to create a *statistics collection* using a Create Statistics statement such as the following:

```
Create Statistics CustomerStats
  On Customer ( Name )
```

Following this statement, you can display the selectivity of the Name column using the statement

```
DBCC Show_Statistics ( Customer, CustomerStats )
```

Statement	Arguments	Information Produced
DBCC PerfMon		An extensive collection of SQL Server performance statistics
DBCC ProcCache		Detailed procedure cache statistics
DBCC ShowContig	*Table-Id* *Index-Id*	Table and index fragmentation statistics
DBCC Show_Statistics	*Table-Id, Index-Name* *Table-Id, Statistics-Name*	Selectivity of an index or column(s)
DBCC SqlPerf	LogSpace	Transaction log space utilization

Table 6-13. DBCC Statements to Produce Performance Information

DBCC UpdateUsage

There are also several DBCC statements that can affect SQL Server performance. The DBCC UpdateUsage statement reports and corrects incorrect space usage information in the sysindexes system table. The following example checks and corrects this information for all indexes in the AppDta database:

```
DBCC UpdateUsage AppDta
```

You can optionally limit the checks to a specific table's indexes or to a specific index. The following statement checks just the CustomerByNameIdx index, which has an index ID of 3:

```
DBCC UpdateUsage AppDta, Customer, 3
```

DBCC PinTable

You can specify that SQL Server should never flush a table's pages from memory once they've been loaded—an action referred to as *pinning* a table. The following statement pins the StateAbv table (ID of 67) in the AppDta database (ID of 101):

```
DBCC PinTable 101, 67
```

Use the DBCC UnpinTable statement to disable pinning for a table.

You should generally consider pinning only very small tables with very high access rates from multiple connections. Even then, you may not gain much over NT Server and SQL Server default memory management.

Trace Flags

Trace flags are an ad hoc mechanism in SQL Server to customize server behavior. Many of the flags control behavior that should rarely be changed, but are available for special circumstances. The performance-related trace flags are listed in Table 6-14.

Flag	Purpose
325	Prints performance cost of using a nonclustered index or sort for an Order By clause
326	Prints performance cost of using a sort
330	Enables additional join information for the Set Showplan_All statement
1704	Prints information when a temporary table is created or dropped

Table 6-14.   SQL Server Performance-Related Trace Flags

You can set one or more trace flags on with a statement such as the following:

```
DBCC TraceOn ( 325, 330 )
```

You can set one or more trace flags off with a statement such as the following:

```
DBCC TraceOff ( 325, 330 )
```

You can use a statement such as the following to determine the status of one or more trace flags:

```
DBCC TraceStatus ( 325, 330 )
```

You can also set trace flags when you start SQL Server, as explained in the "Setting Server Properties" section of Chapter 2. The following example shows the NT Server command line to start SQL Server with a trace flag set:

```
SqlServer /T325
```

Query Analyzer Index Analysis

You can enter a SQL statement in the Query Analyzer and select Perform Index Analysis from the Query menu to have the Query Analyzer recommend new indexes that may improve the performance of the statement. Generally, the Index Tuning Wizard provides a more powerful tool for index analysis. You should be careful not to rely on the Query Analyzer recommendations without considering the negative performance impact that additional indexes may have on update operations.

Transact-SQL Functions and Stored Procedures

Transact-SQL has several built-in functions you can call in stored procedures to get performance-related information. Table 6-15 lists the most commonly used functions. The section "Constants, Functions, and Expressions," in Chapter 10, provides a complete

Function	Return Value
@@Connections	Number of attempted connections since SQL Server was last started
@@Cpu_Busy	Milliseconds CPU has spent doing work since SQL Server was last started
@@Idle	Milliseconds SQL Server has been idle since it was last started

Table 6-15. Transact-SQL Performance-Related Functions

Function	Return Value
@@IO_Busy	Milliseconds SQL Server has spent doing I/O operations since it was last started
@@Pack_Received	Number of network input packets SQL Server has received since it was last started
@@Pack_Sent	Number of network output packets SQL Server has sent since it was last started
@@Packet_Errors	Number of network packet errors on SQL Server connections since SQL Server was last started
@@RowCount	Number of rows affected by the last statement
@@Total_Errors	Number of disk read/write errors encountered by SQL Server since it was last started
@@ Total_Read	Number of disk reads by SQL Server since it was last started
@@ Total_Write	Number of disk writes by SQL Server since it was last started

Table 6-15. Transact-SQL Performance-Related Functions (*continued*)

list of Transact-SQL functions, and the "Stored Procedures" section explains how to write stored procedures.

There are also several system stored procedures, listed in Table 6-16, that provide performance information. For the most part, the SQL Server Profiler, SQL Server Performance Monitor, and SQL Server Enterprise Manager Current Activity categories discussed previously provide the information returned by these stored procedures (and more) through graphical interfaces that are easier to use. However, the system stored procedures can be used in your own applications to capture performance data.

Stored Procedure	Information Returned
sp_lock	Database lock information for all or selected processes
sp_monitor	Basic CPU and I/O resource usage information
sp_spaceused	Number of rows and disk space usage for all tables or a selected table in a database
sp_who	Basic process information for all or selected logins

Table 6-16. Transact-SQL Performance-Related System Stored Procedures

SQL STATEMENT HINTS

Generally, the SQL Server optimizer creates an execution plan, as described previously in the section "Showplan," that provides optimal performance. If, however, you find that the optimizer has not created the best execution plan for a particular Select, Insert, Delete, or Update statement, you can add *hints* to the statement to influence how the optimizer creates the execution plan. You should always carefully measure before and after performance when considering hints, as well as use Showplan to inspect the resulting execution plan with and without hints. Also, be sure to consider the impact that changes to one statement may have on other concurrent database activity. There are three types of hints:

> Query hints
> Join hints
> Table hints

You specify a hint by coding it on a SQL Select, Insert, Delete, or Update statement. Chapter 10 explains how to use these statements, and the following discussion covers only the use of the SQL syntax related to hints.

Query Hints

A query hint governs the execution plan for the entire statement. You specify a query hint by adding the Option clause at the end of the SQL statement, as in the following example:

```
Select  *
  From  Customer
  Where Discount > 0
  Option ( Fast 25 )
```

You can specify multiple query hints, separated by commas, after the Option keyword. Table 6-17 lists the available query hints.

Join Hints

A join hint specifies how a join operation should be implemented. As explained more fully in Chapter 10, a join combines rows from two tables, usually based on some conditional expression that involves columns in the two tables. For example, the following statement combines rows from the Customer and Sale tables that have matching CustId columns:

```
Select  Customer.CustId,
        Customer.Name,
        Sale.SaleDate
  From  Customer
        Inner Join
        Sale
        On Customer.CustId = Sale.CustId
```

Query Hint	Purpose
Hash Group Order Group	Use hashing or ordering to produce aggregates for the Group By or Compute clauses (use only one or the other of these hints).
Merge Union Hash Union Concat Union	Use merging, hashing, or concatenation for Union operations. You can specify more than one of these hints, and SQL Server will use the least-cost alternative from the choices specified.
Fast *n*	Minimize the time to return the first *n* rows for the query.
Force Order	Use the exact order of tables specified in Join operations to join tables.
MaxDop *n*	Use a maximum of *n* processors for parallel execution of the query.
Robust Plan	Attempt to create an execution plan that will work for the maximum possible row size for a query that uses rows with variable-length columns. If a robust plan can't be created, return an error.

Table 6-17. SQL Server Query Hints

This join can be carried out in several ways:

▼ **Loop** Execute a loop to read rows from the first table and, for each row in the first table, loop to get all matching rows in the second table.

■ **Hash** For each row in the first table, compute a hash value on the column(s) used in the join and store an entry in a hash table. For each row in the second table, compute a hash value on the column(s) used in the join and look up the matching row(s) in the hash table.

▲ **Merge** Process rows from both tables in order of the join columns, using a "match/merge" algorithm.

When you don't specify a join hint (as in this example), the optimizer will select the method that appears to be most efficient. Also, when no join hints are specified, the optimizer may rearrange the order of the tables and, if there is more than one join operation, the order of the operations.

To specify a joint hint, add one of the four keywords—Loop, Hash, Merge, or Remote—before the Join keyword, as in the following example:

```
Select  Customer.CustId,
        Customer.Name,
        Sale.SaleDate
```

```
From   Customer
       Inner Hash Join
       Sale
       On Customer.CustId = Sale.CustId
```

The Loop, Hash, and Merge keywords specify the join algorithm to use; the Remote keyword specifies that the join process occurs on the system in which the table on the right side of the Join operator resides. The Remote hint is useful only when the tables reside on different systems.

When you specify a join hint, the optimizer enforces both the order of multiple join operations (if more than one) and the order of tables specified on each join. When you have multiple join operations in the From clause, you can use any one of the three keywords (or no keyword) for each join.

NOTE: When you don't specify a join hint for an inner join, the Inner keyword is optional. However, the Inner keyword is required when you specify a join hint for an inner join.

Table Hints

A table hint specifies access characteristics for a single base table used in a query. You specify a table's hints by adding a With (*hints*) clause after the table name. If you use an As clause to specify a correlation name (also known as an *alias*) for the table, code the With (*hints*) clause after the correlation name. The following example shows how to place a shared lock on the Customer table until the end of the statement or transaction:

```
Select   *
  From   Customer With ( TabLock )
  Where Discount > 0
```

You can use a With (*hints*) clause anywhere that a table name appears in a Select, Insert, Update, or Delete statement. The following example shows how to code an Update statement that places an exclusive lock on the Customer table during the update process:

```
Update Customer With ( TabLockX )
  Set    Discount = 1.001 * Discount
  Where Discount > 0
```

For multiple hints, separate adjacent keywords with a comma or space, as in the following example:

```
Select   *
  From   Customer With ( Serializable, TabLock )
  Where Discount > 0
```

Table 6-18 lists the available table hints. The Index hint lets you direct the optimizer to use a specific index (or indexes) to access a table. In rare cases, the optimizer may not use a particular index in the execution plan, and you may determine by experimentation that you can improve performance by adding an Index hint.

Table Hint	Purpose
Optimization Hint	
FastFirstRow	Minimize the time to return the first row from this table for the query. (Equivalent to the Option(Fast 1) query hint.)
Index Hint	
Index(*index-name*, ...) Index(*index-ID*, ...)	Specifies the index name(s) or ID(s) of indexes that should be used to access the table.
Row Lock Type Hint	
UpdLock	Uses update row locks instead of shared row locks.
Lock Granularity Hints	*Note that only one hint from this category is allowed.*
NoLock ReadUncommitted	Query does not obtain shared locks and ignores exclusive locks by other processes. The two keywords are equivalent. (Allowed only in Select statement.)
PagLock	Uses shared data page locks instead of a shared table lock.
RowLock	Uses shared row locks instead of a shared page or table lock.
TabLock	Obtains shared table lock. The lock is held until the end of the statement, unless Holdlock or Serializable is specified, in which case the lock is held until the end of the transaction.
TabLockX	Obtains an exclusive table lock.

Table 6-18. SQL Server Table Hints

Table Hint	Purpose
Transaction Isolation Level Hints	*Note that only one hint from this category is allowed.*
HoldLock Serializable	Holds shared locks until the end of the transaction, rather than releasing them when the table or data page is no longer needed in the query. The two keywords are equivalent.
NoLock ReadUncommitted	See definition under "Lock Granularity Hints" category. The two keywords are equivalent.
ReadCommitted	Holds shared locks until the end of the statement, but allows data to be changed by other processes after being read, so the read may not be repeatable.
RepeatableRead	Holds locks to prevent other processes from changing data used in the query.
Skip Rows Hint	
ReadPast	Skips changed but uncommitted rows. (Allowed only in a Select statement, and takes effect only when the statement is executed with the ReadCommitted transaction isolation level.)

Table 6-18.   SQL Server Table Hints (*continued*)

The lock granularity table hints serve two purposes: increasing concurrency and increasing protection from conflicts with concurrent access of the same table. The NoLock, RowLock, and PagLock hints may allow more concurrent processing of the table by multiple processes. Be careful when using NoLock because it lets you read data that's been changed but not committed—if the transaction that changed the data is rolled back (that is, undone), the data read by your query won't represent the actual database contents. The RowLock and PagLock hints cause a finer-grained lock to be used in some cases, which can improve system-wide performance when concurrent queries access different data in the same table and they don't place a large number of locks; in other cases, using either of these options may degrade performance because of the additional lock overhead.

NOTE: The ReadPast hint also provides for increased concurrency, but generally shouldn't be used by normal application programs.

The TabLock and TabLockX hints provide a way to explicitly hold a table lock to prevent conflicting access, as discussed in the "Concurrent Updates and Table Locks" section of Chapter 10.

The transaction isolation level hints let you set the locking protocol used for the individual statement, regardless of what the connection's current transaction isolation level is (that is, as set by the Set Transaction Level statement). The four levels, from least protective and highest concurrency to most protective and highest concurrency are

ReadUncommitted
ReadCommitted
RepeatableRead
Serializable

SQL Server's default level is ReadCommitted unless you specify a different table hint or Set Transaction Level statement value.

CONCLUSION

With SQL Server's many performance tools, you can get a good handle on how your system and applications are performing, as well as where the critical resource usage or bottlenecks are occurring. You can anticipate and plan for increasing workloads by using the SQL Server Profiler and SQL Server Performance Monitor to regularly capture ongoing performance statistics. The SQL Server Performance Monitor's alert capability provides a feature that can inform you when exceptional performance conditions occur, for example, when CPU utilization becomes exceptionally high.

Many of the tools covered in this chapter also have capabilities that let you improve the performance of queries used in your application. Be sure to familiarize yourself with these tools so that applications you deliver will provide optimal performance. Likewise, it pays to know how to use these tools to monitor and tune system-wide performance so your applications deliver adequate response and throughput.

CHAPTER 7

Advanced Management Using SQL-DMO

In this chapter, you'll learn how you can manage SQL Server programmatically from Visual Basic or other OLE-compliant development languages by taking advantage of SQL-DMO (Distributed Management Objects). SQL-DMO enables you to easily develop custom SQL Server management applications that are tailored to your environment. Using SQL-DMO, you can use Visual Basic or any other OLE-compliant language to create custom SQL Server management interfaces that allow you to streamline the functions that SQL Server's Enterprise Manager provides. SQL-DMO allows your applications to perform the same set of functions that you can do manually through SQL Server's Enterprise Manager. In fact, SQL-DMO is the foundation for SQL Server's Enterprise Manager. Using SQL-DMO, you can list databases and tables, add logins, control replication, import data, export data, and perform many other administrative tasks. SQL-DMO opens up SQL Server to a number of custom programs that can both display and manipulate SQL Server itself.

First, you'll get an overview of SQL-DMO as well as a look at its underlying architecture. Then, you'll see how to use SQL-DMO from Visual Basic. In this section you'll see how to add the SQL-DMO type library to the Visual Basic Integrated Development Environment. You'll also see how to perform some common tasks with SQL-DMO. Finally, this chapter finishes by presenting a sample utility that's built using Visual Basic and SQL-DMO.

DISTRIBUTED MANAGEMENT OBJECT HIERARCHY

DMO is a set of 32-bit OLE COM (Component Object Model) objects that enable application access to SQL Server's management functions. SQL Server's DMO was first introduced in SQL Server 6, and the set has continued to be enhanced in SQL Server 7. Having over 60 different objects and more than 1,000 different properties and methods, SQL Server's DMO provides far-reaching access into the capabilities of SQL Server. SQL-DMO connects to the SQL Server using the SQL Server ODBC 3.x driver. As its name suggests, SQL Server's DMO is intended to facilitate using SQL Server in a distributed environment. The DMO set does this by extending the power of SQL Server's management function to all of the clients in the network. While SQL-DMO can be used to access data, that's not its real purpose. Other application programming interfaces (APIs) like Active Data Objects (ADO), Data Access Objects (DAO), Open Database Connectivity (ODBC), and Remote Data Objects (RDO) are better data access mechanisms. The real strength of SQL-DMO is to programmatically manage networked SQL Server systems.

DISTRIBUTED MANAGEMENT FRAMEWORK

SQL Server 7 is managed using an integrated collection of objects and components known as the SQL Distributed Management Framework (SQL-DMF). The SQL-DMF enables you to manage SQL Server interactively using the Microsoft Management Console (MMC) and the SQL Server Enterprise Manager or programmatically through the use of SQL-NS, SQL-DMO, and DTS. Figure 7-1 illustrates the main components of SQL-DMF.

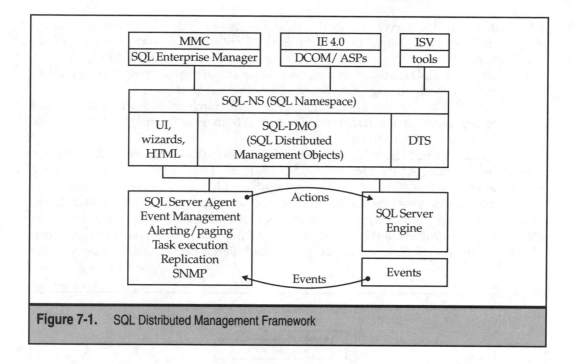

Figure 7-1. SQL Distributed Management Framework

At the top level of the SQL-DMF architecture, you can see the different end-user applications that are used to manage SQL Server 7. While the SQL Server Enterprise Manager is provided as a part of SQL Server 7, the same underlying components that are used by the SQL Server Enterprise Manager are also available to custom management tools. The SQL Namespace (SQL-NS) exposes the user interface elements of the SQL Server Enterprise Manager to application programs. The SQL Distributed Management Objects (SQL-DMO) exposes an OLE interface that can be used to control virtually all aspects of the SQL Server Engine and SQL Server Agent. Data Transformation Services (DTS) provides the ability to transfer and transform the data contained in SQL Server databases for use in data marts and data warehousing applications. You can learn more about DTS in Chapter 5.

SQL-DMO Core Object Hierarchy

The Distributed Management Objects (DMO) are a set of 32-bit OLE COM (Component Object Model) objects that enable application access to SQL Server's management functions. SQL Server's Distributed Management Objects were first introduced in SQL Server 6, and they have continued to be enhanced in SQL Server 7. Having over 60 different objects and more than a 1000 different properties and methods, SQL Server's Distributed Management Objects provides far-reaching access into the capabilities of SQL Server. SQL-DMO connects to the SQL Server using the SQL Server ODBC 3.0 driver. As its name suggests, SQL Server's Distributed Management Objects is intended to facilitate using SQL Server in a distributed environment. It does this by extending the power of SQL Server's management function to all of the clients in the network. While SQL-DMO can be used to access data, that's not is real purpose. Other APIs like ADO, DAO, ODBC, and RDO are better data access mechanisms. The real strength of SQL-DMO is to programmatically manage networked SQL Server systems.

The SQL-DMO Core objects are organized in a hierarchical order that follows the same basic organization of SQL Server's Enterprise Manager. The hierarchy of the core SQL-DMO objects is shown in Figure 7-2.

As you can see in Figure 7-2, SQL Server's Distributed Management Objects use a layered architecture. At the top level of SQL Server's DMO object framework is the SQLServer object. The SQLServer object represents a physical SQL Server system. The various object collections beneath the SQLServer object allow you to work with different aspects of the SQL Server system. For instance, the RemoteServers object collection allows you to create and manage remote servers. Likewise, the JobServer object collection allows you to control SQL Server tasks, jobs, and alerts. Each Database object in the

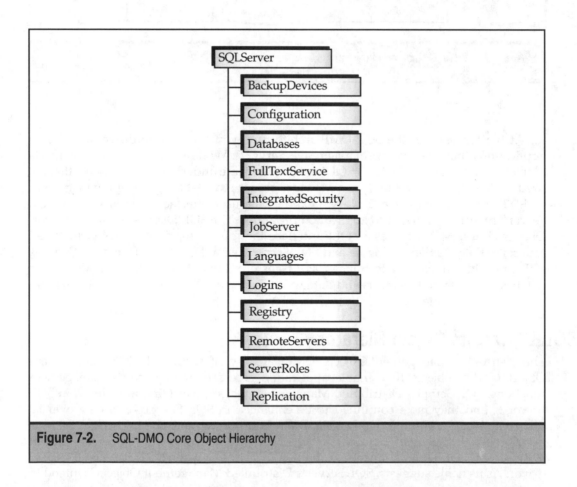

Figure 7-2. SQL-DMO Core Object Hierarchy

Databases collections represents a physical SQL Server database, and, as you would expect, each database object contains one or more table objects, as well as other types of SQL Server objects like triggers, views, and stored procedures. Similarly, the Table object level includes column, trigger, and key and index objects. Finally, the Replication objects allow you to set up and control SQL Server database replications. The following section explores each of these areas in more detail.

SQL-DMO SQLServer Object Hierarchy

The SQLServer object is the primary SQL-DMO object. All other SQL-DMO objects are accessed using an instance of the SQLServer object.

▼ **SQLServers**   The SQLServers object is a collection of SQLServer objects where each object represents a physical SQL Server system.

■ **BackupDevices**   The BackupDevices object is a collection of BackupDevice objects where each object represents a file that contains a database or transaction log.

■ **Configurations**   The Configurations object contains the ConfigValue collection. Each ConfigValue object contains a configuration value that controls SQL Server.

■ **FullTextService**   The FullTextService object exposes the full-text indexing service to the SQL-DMO application.

■ **IntegratedSecurity**   The IntegratedSecurity object contains the information about the mapping of SQL Server logins and NT users and groups.

■ **Logins**   The Logins object is a collection Login objects where each object contains a database login ID and password.

■ **Languages**   The Languages object is a collection of Language objects where each object represents a language that is supported by the local SQL Server system.

■ **Registry**   The Registry object contains all of the SQL Server information that is stored in the local system's registry.

■ **RemoteServers**   The RemoteServers object is a collection of the remote SQL Server systems where each RemoteServer object represents a remote SQL Server system that is connected to the local SQL Server system.

▲ **ServerRoles**   The ServerRoles object is a collection of ServerRole objects where each object contains all of the SQL Server system's roles.

SQL-DMO Database Object Hierarchy

The SQL-DMO Database objects allow you to work with the various SQL Server database objects like defaults, rules, tables, and stored procedures. Figure 7-3 illustrates the SQL-DMO Database object hierarchy.

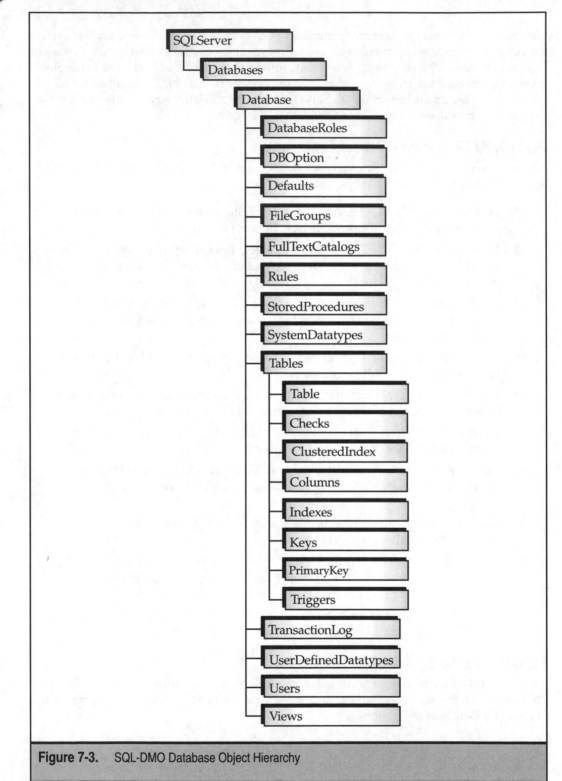

Figure 7-3. SQL-DMO Database Object Hierarchy

The Database object hierarchy falls beneath the primary SQLServer object. The primary object of the SQL-DMO Database objects is the Database object. The following SQL-DMO objects are contained in the SQL-DMO Database object hierarchy:

▼ **Databases**   The Databases object is a collection of Database objects where each object contains all of the information that relates to a single SQL Server database.

■ **DatabaseRoles**   The DatabaseRoles collection consists of DatabaseRole objects where each object represents a group of users that have similar security attributes.

■ **DBOption**   The DBOption object contains a SQL Server database options property. Database options include properties like allowing Nulls and DBO owner usage.

■ **Defaults**   The Defaults object is a collection of Default objects where each object contains a default value that will be used by a column or data type when no other value has been supplied.

■ **FileGroups**   The FileGroups object is a collection of FileGroup objects. Each FileGroup object contains information about a database's file groups.

■ **FullTextCatalogs**   The FullTextCatalogs object exposes the properties of a Microsoft Search catalog.

■ **Rules**   The Rules object is a collection of Rule objects where each object specifies the valid data that can be stored in a database column or in a data type.

■ **StoredProcedures**   The StoredProcedures object is a collection of StoredProcedure objects where each object is either a set of Transact-SQL statements or an extended stored procedure contained by a dynamic link library (DLL).

■ **SystemDatatypes**   The SystemDatatypes object is a collection of SystemDatatype objects. Each SystemDatatype object represents a system-supplied data type.

■ **TransactionLog**   The TransactionLog object represents a database transaction log.

■ **UserDefinedDatatypes**   The UserDefinedDatatypes object is a collection of UserDefinedDatatype objects. Each UserDefinedDatatype object represents a user-defined data type.

■ **Users**   The Users object is a collection of User objects where each object represents a separate database login.

▲ **Views**   The Views object is a collection of View objects where each object represents a Select statement that includes rows from one or more tables.

TABLE OBJECTS

▼ **Tables**   The Tables object is a collection of Table objects where each object contains the information that relates to a single table that is contained within a SQL Server database.

■ **Checks**   The Checks object is a collection of Check objects where each object represents a single table check constraint.

■ **ClusteredIndex**   The ClusteredIndex object represents a clustered index that's associated with the given table.

■ **Columns**   The Columns object is a collection of Column objects where each object represents a single column in a table.

■ **Indexes**   The Indexes object is a collection of Index objects where each object represents a single index for a table.

■ **Keys**   The Keys object is a collection of Key objects where each object represents a table's foreign, primary, or unique keys.

■ **Permissions**   The Permissions object is a collection of Permission objects where each object represents the table's access rights.

■ **PrimaryKey**   The PrimaryKey object represents a primary key that's associated with the given table.

▲ **Triggers**   The Triggers object is a collection of Trigger objects where each object represents a set of Transact-SQL statements that are executed when a table is updated.

SQL-DMO JobServer Object Hierarchy

The SQL-DMO JobServer objects allow you to control SQL Server's Agent functions such as tasks, jobs, and alerts. Figure 7-4 illustrates the SQL-DMO JobServer object hierarchy.

The primary object of the SQL-DMO Agent objects is the JobServer object. The JobServer object controls SQL Server's tasks and scheduling functions.

▼ **JobServer**   The JobServer object is a collection of JobServer objects where each object represents a SQL Server scheduling engine.

■ **Alerts**   The Alerts object is a collection of Alert objects where each object represents a SQL Server alert. An alert is an event that requires operator notification.

■ **AlertSystem**   The AlertSystem object contains information about the alert engine.

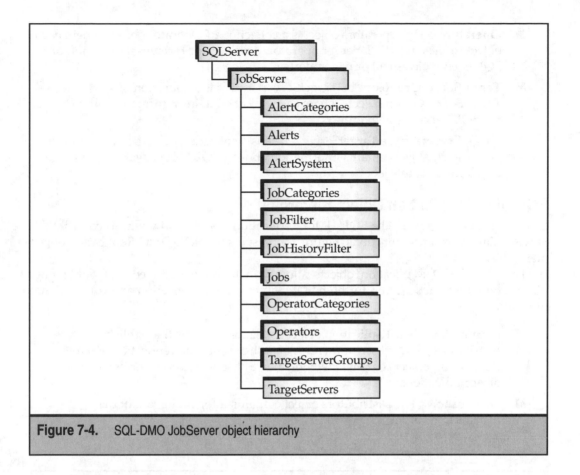

Figure 7-4.   SQL-DMO JobServer object hierarchy

- **JobCategories**   The JobCategories collection contains Category objects exposing a SQL Server Agent job-organizing method.

- **JobFilter**   The JobFilter object contains information that limits the types of jobs that will be monitored.

- **JobHistoryFilter**   The JobHistoryFilter object specifies the jobs history records that will be purged.

- **Jobs**   The Job object is a collection of Job objects where each object contains information about a scheduled SQL Server job and its associated job steps.

- **OperatorCategories**   The OperatorCategories collection contains Category objects referencing a classification method for SQL Server Agent operators.

- **Operators** The Operators object is a collection of Operator objects where each object represents a SQL Server operator. An operator receives notification of SQL events via e-mail or pager alerts.

- **TargetServerGroups** The TargetServerGroups is a collection of TargetServerGroup objects where each object contains information about the SQL Server system group.

▲ **TargetServers** The TargetServer object is a collection of TargetServer objects where each object contains information about a SQL Server system that is the target for a remote job.

SQL-DMO Replication Object Hierarchy

Like their name suggests, the SQL-DMO Replication objects allow you to control SQL Server's data replication functions. Figure 7-5 presents the SQL-DMO Replication object hierarchy.

The SQL-DMO Replication objects allow you to set up and control publishing, distribution, and subscription for both SQL Server merge replication and transactional replication.

▼ **Replication** The Replication object collection controls the publishing, distribution, and subscription roles of SQL Server data replication. Each Replication object contains the Publisher, Subscriber, and Distributor object collections.

- **Distributor** The Distributors object contains information about the distribution server.

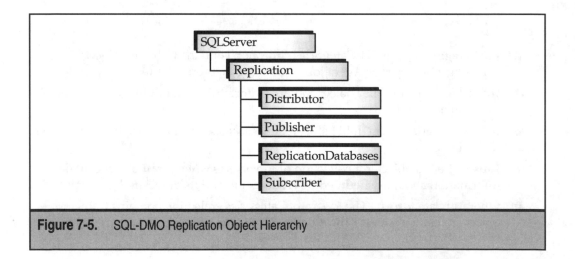

Figure 7-5.   SQL-DMO Replication Object Hierarchy

- **Publisher**   The Publisher object contains information about the publishing server.

- **ReplicationDatabases**   The ReplicationDatabases is a collection of ReplicationDatabase objects where each object contains information about the databases that are replicated.

▲ **Subscriber**   The Subscriber object contains information about the subscribing server.

SQL-DMO FILES

The following table summarizes the client files that are used to implement SQL-DMO on SQL Server 7.

SQLDMO.HLP	Help file containing an online reference to the SQL-DMO objects
SQLDMO.DLL	SQL-DMO in-process COM server and Type Library
SQLDMO.SQL	Transact-SQL script to create SQL-DMO stored procedures
SQLDMO.H	SQL-DMO header file for C++ function prototypes
SQLDMOID.H	SQL-DMO header file for C++ interface IDs

USING SQL-DMO

To get programmatic access to management functions of other database platforms, you might need to master low-level networking and system interfaces—if a system interface is available at all. SQL-DMO provides an OLE foundation that makes SQL Server's database management functions easy to access. Since the SQL-DMO is implemented as a set of OLE objects, the objects can only be used from 32-bit client applications. SQL Server's SQL-DMO functions can be used by any 32-bit, OLE-compliant development tool including Visual Basic, Visual C++, Delphi, and many others.

To use SQL-DMO from Visual Basic, you need to follow some basic steps:

1. Include the SQL-DMO Type Library (SQLDMO).
2. Create a SQL Server object.
3. Connect the SQL Server object to SQL Server.
4. Use the SQL-DMO Server objects.
5. Disconnect from SQL Server.

Adding SQL-DMO Objects to Visual Basic

Before you can begin to use the SQL-DMO objects in Visual Basic's development environment, you need to install them. The files that provide the basic support for DMO are copied to your client system when you first install the SQL Server 32-bit client. However, you still need to set a reference to them in Visual Basic's development environment to enable their use from Visual Basic. To add SQL-DMO support to Visual Basic 4, you need to reference the SQL-DMO Type Library from Visual Basic by selecting the References option from Visual Basic's Tools menu. To add the SQL-DMO reference to Visual Basic 5 or 6, you must select the References option from the Project menu. This action displays the References dialog box that you can see in Figure 7-6.

Scroll through the References dialog box until you see the selection Microsoft SQLDMO Object Library. Clicking the checkbox next to this entry adds the SQL-DMO OLE Object Library file to Visual Basic's Interactive Development Environment (IDE). When you add a reference to Visual Basic's IDE, no visual objects are added to the Visual Basic Toolbox, as would happen when you add ActiveX controls, for example. In order to

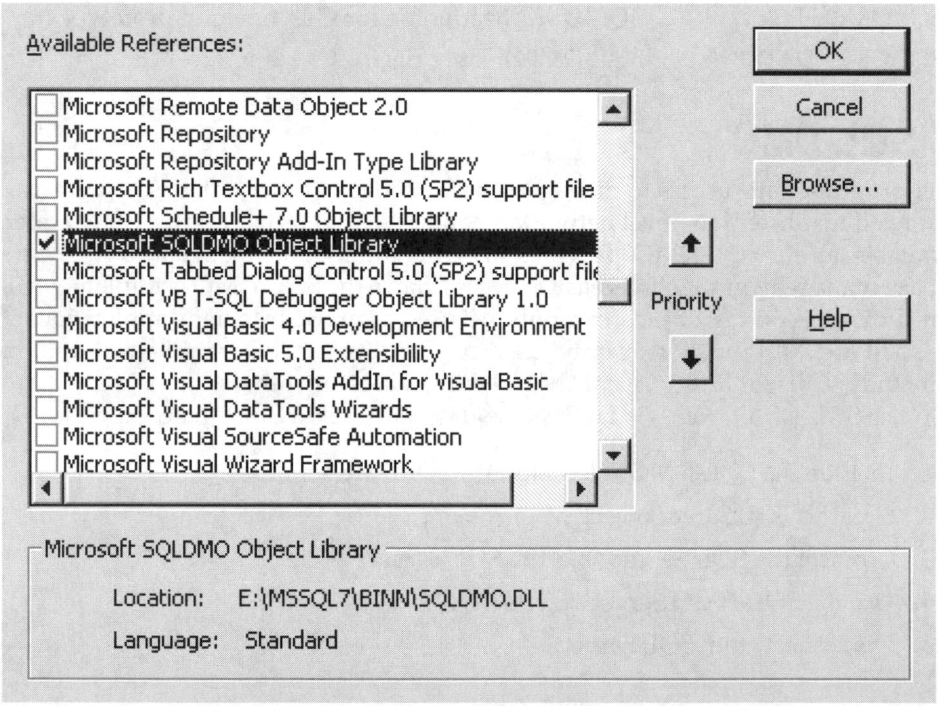

Figure 7-6. Setting a reference to the SQL-DMO Type Library

see the SQL-DMO properties and methods, you must use Visual Basic's Object Browser, shown in Figure 7-7.

Creating the SQLServer Object

Before you can use any of the SQL-DMO methods, you must create an instance of the SQLServer object, which is the most basic object in the SQL-DMO set and must be present in all SQL-DMO applications. Using Visual Basic, you can create an instance of the SQLServer object in three different ways: using the New keyword, using the CreateObject function, or using the generic object type.

The preferred method to create a new SQLServer object is to use the New keyword, as shown here:

```
Dim oSQLServer As New SQLDMO.SQLServer
```

This method creates a new SQLServer object named oSQLServer. It also creates an instance of the SQLServer object.

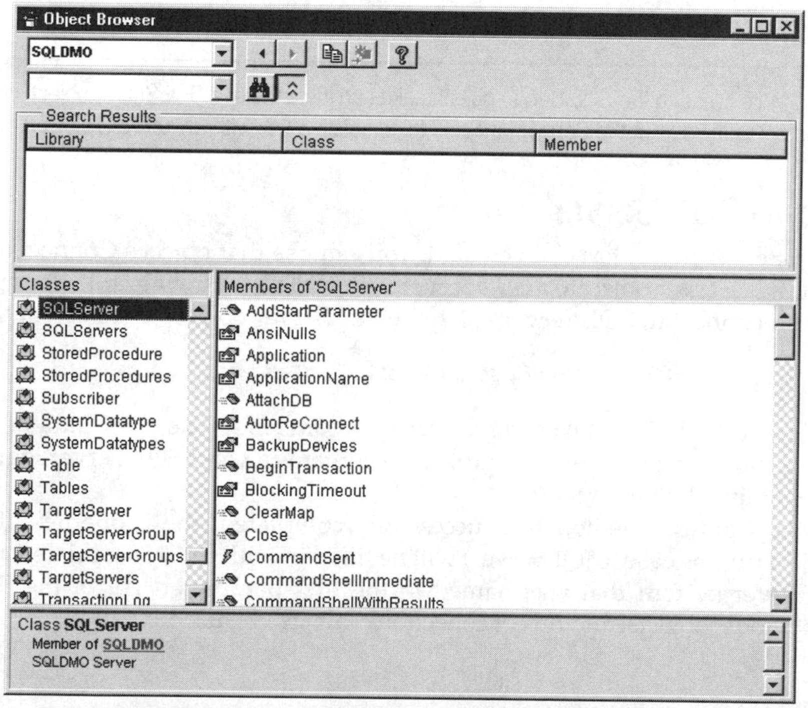

Figure 7-7.   Viewing the SQL-DMO Library from the Object Browser

NOTE: A common naming convention for OLE objects is to prefix the name with a lowercase o, which signifies that the variable is an object.

Alternatively, you also can create an instance of the SQLServer object by using the CreateObject function, as shown in this code example:

```
Dim oSQLServer as SQLDMO.Server
Set oSQLServer = CreateObject("SQLDMO.SQLServer")
```

This method creates a SQLServer variable called oSQLServer and then uses the CreateObject function to instantiate the object. Typically you would only use this method with older versions of Visual Basic that do not support the New keyword.

Alternatively, you also can create a new SQLServer object using Visual Basic's generic object type as shown here:

```
Dim oSQLServer as Object
Set oSQLServer = CreateObject("SQLDMO.SQLServer")
```

This method is supported by all versions of Visual Basic; however, its use is not as clear as using the CreateObject function. In addition, the generic object type is the slowest of the three methods because it relies on late binding using OLE IDispatch.

TIP: While creating the SQL Server object makes an instance of a SQLServer object, you can't use that object until you run the Connect method to establish a link with an active SQL Server system.

Connecting to SQL Server

After a SQLServer object has been created, you can use that object's Connect method to connect the SQLServer object to a SQL Server system. The following code example shows how you can connect to SQL Server using the SQLServer object's Connect method:

```
oSQLServer.Connect sSQLServer$, sUserID$, sPassword$
```

This Connect method takes three string parameters. The first parameter string contains the name of a SQL Server, the second contains a valid SQL Server login ID, and the third contains the password.

After the Connect method has successfully completed, the properties of the SQL Server object (in this case, oSQLServer) will be filled in with the appropriate values from the SQL Server system that was named in the first parameter. All of the SQLServer object's methods, objects, and object collections can also be used.

TIP: While all of the SQLServer objects and collections can be used after the Connection method has successfully executed, the actual SQLServer values are not retrieved until you first access each object. After the objects are first accessed, the SQLServer object retains them in a local cache. Using the Refresh method causes the SQLServer object to update all of the objects that are locally cached.

Using SQL-DMO Properties

A SQLServer object has more than 1,000 different properties that can be accessed from your application. All of the SQLServer properties can be read, but only a small subset of these properties can be written to. The SQL Server Distributed Management Object Help (sqldmo.hlp) online help file lists all of the SQL-DMO object properties and notes if they are read-only or read-write.

TIP: You can use the Visual Basic Object Browser to list the properties for each SQLServer object from Visual Basic's IDE.

Getting Property Values

You can retrieve the property values for all of the properties that are standard data types using the Visual Basic assignment operator (=), as shown here:

```
Dim sHostName As String
sHostName = oSQLServer.HostName
```

In the previous example you can see that a string named sHostName is first declared using the Visual Basic Dim statement. Then the Visual Basic assignment operator is used to fill the sHostName string variable with the contents of the oSQLServer. HostName property. This technique works for all of the standard Visual Basic data types like String, Long, and Integer. However, object properties are treated a little differently, as you can see in the following example:

```
Dim oExecutive As SQLDMO.Executive
Set oExecutive = oSQLServer.Executive
```

To retrieve the contents of SQL-DMO object properties, you must use the Visual Basic Set statement. The Set statement is used to assign an object reference to a variable. In this case the Dim statement is used to declare an object of the SQLDMO.Executive data type named oExecutive. Then the Set statement is used to assign the contents of the oSQLServer.Executive object to the oExecutive object.

TIP: The system resources associated with an object are normally released when the object goes out of scope. However, if you set an object reference in a global function then you must explicitly set the object to nothing in order to release the system memory and resources used by the object.

Setting Property Values

You can set the value of SQL-DMO read-write properties from Visual Basic by using the assignment operator (=). The following example shows how to set the SQLServer object's ApplicationName property:

```
Dim sApplicationName as String
sApplicationName = "MyApp"
oSQLServer.ApplicationName = sApplicationName
```

In this example you can see that the oSQLServer.ApplicationName property is set using the Visual Basic assignment operator to the value of "MyApp", which is contained in the sApplicationName String variable.

TIP: You cannot set any object properties of SQL-DMO objects. The object properties are read-only. You can only set properties that use standard data types such as String, Boolean, or Long.

SQL-DMO Property Collections

Ealier in Figure 7-2, you saw that SQL-DMO's Core object hierarchy made extensive use of *object collections*, which are basically groups of related objects. For instance, the Databases collection in the SQLServer object is a collection of Database objects.

TIP: Collection objects typically end with an "s". For instance, Databases indicates a collection of Database objects.

Table 7-1 lists the object collections that are a part of the SQLServer object.

Databases	Listing of databases
Languages	Listing of supported languages
Logins	Listing of login IDs
RemoteServers	Listing of remote SQL Servers
ServerRoles	Roles of SQL Servers

Table 7-1. SQLServer Object Collections

Like objects, collections are all contained within a parent object. In the case of the object collections shown in Table 7-1, all of the object collections belong to the SQLServer Core objects.

A collection is actually a collection object that has its own set of properties and methods. The following list shows the different properties and methods contained in the Databases collection:

Application
Count
Item
ItemByID
Parent
Refresh
Remove
TypeOf
UserData

You can see that the properties of the Databases collection object are all oriented toward working with the group of databases. For instance, the Count property reports on the number of Database objects that are contained in the collection, while the ItemByID property identifies a specific Database object in the Databases collection. Since all collection objects contain and manage multiple objects, the properties and methods for all collections are very similar.

In contrast, the following list shows a selection of some of the properties of an individual Database object:

Application
CreateDate
DataSpaceUsage
Defaults
FileGroups
Name
Owner
Permissions
Rules
SpaceAvailable
StoredProcedures
Tables
Views

You can see that the properties of the Database object are all directly related to a SQL Server database. For instance, the Size property reports the space that the database consumes on the disk, while the Owner property contains the name of the database owner. Notice that some of the Database object properties are also other collection objects. For instance, the StoredProcedures property is a collection of the stored procedures that are in the database. Likewise, the Tables property is a collection of the tables that are contained in the database. You can refer back to Figures 7-2, 7-3, and 7-4 to see the complete object and collection hierarchy that SQL-DMO uses.

Iterating Through Collections

To use SQL-DMO effectively, one of the first things that you need to know is how to work with the collection objects. Iterating though a collection can be accomplished using the following code:

```
For Each oDatabase in oSQLServer.Databases
    Debug.Print oDatabase.Name
Next
```

Visual Basic's For Each statement automatically loops through all of the objects in a collection. This example will print a list of all the database names that are contained in the Databases collection of the oSQLServer object. The code within the For Each block refers to the current object in the collection.

Getting a Specific Collection Object

You also need to understand how to reference a specific object that's in a collection. You can refer to individual objects that are within a collection either by the object name or by the ordinal value within the collection. For example, to refer to a Database object by name you would use one of the following:

```
oSQLServer.Databases("model")
```

or

```
oSQLServer.Databases.Item("model")
```

Both of these examples are equivalent. They both reference the database named "model" in the oSQLServer object. Since the Item method is the default, you can optionally omit the use of the Item method. In other words, to reference an individual collection object by name, you pass the Item method a string containing the object's name.

> **NOTE:** This code implicitly uses the Item method of the collection object. The Item method is the default method in a collection; therefore, you don't need to explicitly code oSQLServer.Databases.Item("model"). The Item method can accept either a string or an ordinal number.

To refer to the first database object by ordinal number, you would use the following code:

```
oSQLServer.Databases(1)
```

Again, this code implicitly uses the Item method of the Databases collections. In this case the Item method is passed the first ordinal value instead of a string containing the name of the database. The ordinal value of 1 will return the name first database in the oSQLServer object. Similarly, the ordinal value of 2 will return the name of the second database and so on.

Putting SQL-DMO to Work

In the first part of this chapter you had an overview of the SQL-DMO object hierarchy, followed by a brief tutorial showing you how to use some of the most important SQL-DMO collections, methods, and properties. In this part of the chapter, you'll see how you can actually put SQL-DMO to work in a sample Visual Basic program. Figure 7-8 presents the main screen of an example SQL-DMO application that was built using Visual Basic.

This sample application will demonstrate many of the essential techniques that are required to utilize SQL-DMO, including

▼ Creating the SQLServer object

■ Connecting to a SQL Server system

■ Using the SQL-DMO object hierarchy

■ Using collections

■ Getting specific objects from a collection

▲ Disconnecting from a SQL Server system

The sample application connects to the specified SQL Server system after you fill out the prompts for SQL Server name, Login ID, and Password and then click on the Connect button. Following a successful connection, the sample application lists all of the databases that the user is authorized to use. Lists showing the tables and columns for the first database in the list are automatically filled in. The Columns list is automatically filled in with the column names from the first table. Likewise, the Attributes list is filled in with the attributes of the first column in the list.

Double-clicking on any of the list items updates all of the dependent lists. For instance, double-clicking on a different database name causes the list of tables, columns, and column attributes to be updated with information from the newly selected database. Similarly, double-clicking on a different item in the Tables list causes the Columns and Attributes lists to be updated with the column names and attributes of the selected table. However, double-clicking on an item in the Tables list will not update the Databases list because the collections of tables falls beneath databases in the SQL Server object hierarchy. You may want to refer back to Figure 7-2 for an overview of the SQL Server system object and collection hierarchy.

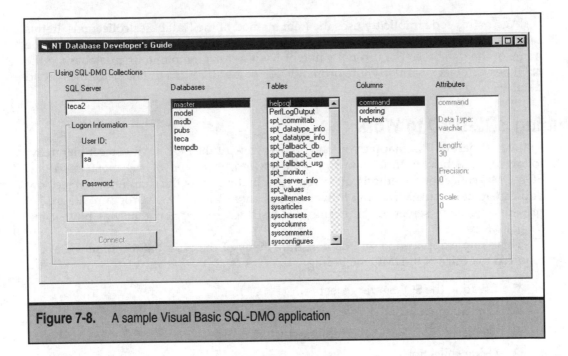

Figure 7-8. A sample Visual Basic SQL-DMO application

Creating the SQLServer Object and Connecting to SQL Server

The first thing that the sample application needs to do is to create a SQLServer object and then connect to the SQL Server system. In the sample application, the SQLServer object is shared by all of the objects on the form so it has been created using the following code in the Declarations section of the main Visual Basic form:

```
Option Explicit

Dim oSQLServer As New SQLDMO.SQLServer
```

After the oSQLServer object is created, you can use the object's Connect method to establish a connection to a SQL Server system. In the sample application, the SQL Server connection is started after the user fills in the name of the appropriate SQL Server along with a login ID and password for that SQL Server and then clicks on the Connect button. Clicking on the Connect button executes the following code that's in the Command_Connect_Click subroutine:

```
Private Sub Command_Connect_Click()

    Dim oDatabase As SQLDMO.Database
```

```
    On Error GoTo ConnectError

    Screen.MousePointer = vbHourglass

    oSQLServer.Connect Text_SQLServer.Text, Text_ID.Text, _
    Text_Pwd.Text

Command_Connect.Enabled = False

    For Each oDatabase In oSQLServer.Databases
        If oDatabase.Status <> SQLDMODBStat_Inaccessible Then
          List_Databases.AddItem oDatabase.Name
        End If
    Next oDatabase

    List_Databases_DblClick

    Screen.MousePointer = vbDefault
    Exit Sub

ConnectError:
    SQLDMOError
    Screen.MousePointer = vbDefault

End Sub
```

The Connect method of the oSQLServer object establishes the connection to the SQL Server system. As you can see in the Command_Connect_Click subroutine, the Connect method is using three parameters: the SQL Server system name, the login ID, and the password. These values are all supplied by the text boxes that you can see in Figure 7-7. The SQL Server name is contained in the Text_SQLServer.Text property; the login ID comes from the Text_ID.Text property; and the password is supplied by the Text_Pwd.Text property.

The Connect method could fail if the user enters an invalid SQL Server name or other invalid login information. If the Connect method fails, a run-time error will be generated and Visual Basic's error handler will be invoked. This causes control of the Command_Connect_Click subroutine to jump to the ConnectError tag, where the SQLDMOError function is executed. Handling SQL-DMO errors and the SQLDMOError subroutine is discussed later in this chapter.

If the Connect method is successful, the Command_Connect_Click subroutine continues and the Command_Connect button is disabled, preventing the user from attempting to connect a second time. Next, the Command_Connect_Click subroutine will fill the Database list with the database names from the SQL Server system.

Listing Databases

The Databases property of the oSQLServer object contains a collection of the database names for the connected SQL Server. In the Command_Connect_Click subroutine, you can see that Visual Basic's For Each operation is used to loop through the collection of database names and add each name to the list of databases. Each iteration of the For Each loop addresses a different Database object in the Databases collection. For instance, the first time the For Each loop is executed, the first Database object in the Databases collection will be the current object. The second time the For Each loop is executed, the second Database object in the Databases collection will be the current object. Within the For Each loop, the database name contained in the Name property of the current oDatabase object is added to the List_Databases list using the AddItem method. The For Each loop executes once for each object contained in the Databases collection.

To automatically fill out the Tables list, the Columns list, and the Columns attributes, the Command_Connect_Click subroutine then executes the List_Databases_DblClick subroutine, which retrieves a list of tables contained in a given database.

Listing Tables

The code that retrieves the database table information for the sample application is executed either automatically at the end of the Command_Connect_Click subroutine or when the user double-clicks on one of the database names in the list of databases. Both cases execute the List_Databases_DblClick subroutine shown here:

```
Private Sub List_Databases_DblClick()
    Dim oTable As SQLDMO.Table
    Dim sDatabaseName As String

    On Error GoTo DatabaseError

    If List_Databases.ListIndex >= 0 Then
        sDatabaseName = List_Databases.List(List_Databases.ListIndex)
    Else
        sDatabaseName = oSQLServer.Databases(1).Name
    End If

    List_Tables.Clear

    List_Columns.Clear
    Text_Column.Text = vbNullString

    For Each oTable In oSQLServer.Databases(sDatabaseName).Tables
        List_Tables.AddItem oTable.Name
    Next oTable
```

```
      List_Tables_DblClick
      Exit Sub

DatabaseError:
      SQLDMOError

End Sub
```

At the top of the List_Databases_DblClick subroutine, you can see where an instance of the SQLDMO table object is created. Next, the Visual Basic error handler is set up to transfer control to the DatabaseError tag and the SQLDMOError function to trap any run-time errors. Next, the ListIndex property of the List_Databases list is checked to determine if this subroutine was evoked automatically by the Command_Connect_Click subroutine or by the user double-clicking one of the database names in the list of databases. If the value of the List_Databases.ListIndex property is 0 or greater, then the user double-clicked one of the database list items, and the program should display the tables for the selected database. The List method of the List_Databases list returns a string that contains the name of the selected list item. Otherwise, if the List_Databases.ListIndex property value is less than 0 (actually –1), then no user selection was made. The List_Databases_DlbClick subroutine was called from the Command_Connect_Click subroutine, and the program should display the tables from the first database in the list of databases.

Next, all of the information currently displayed in the dependent interface objects is cleared. If you refer back to the SQL-DMO object hierarchy, you can see that the column object is dependent on the table object; which is in turn dependent on the database object; which is dependent on the SQLServer object. When a new database item is selected, the information that was contained in the Tables, Columns, and Attributes lists will be replaced with data that's based on the new database selection.

Again, as with the Databases collection, Visual Basic's For Each operation is used to list the members of the Tables collection. The For Each operation loops through the collection of SQL Server table names that are contained in a specific member of the Databases collection of the oSQLServer object. The name of the specific Database object is contained in the sDatabase string variable which is passed to Item method of the oSQLServer.Databases object. (Remember, the Item method is the default method of the Database object and, as such, it does not need to be expressly coded). Inside the For Each loop, the name of each member of the Tables collection is added to the List_Tables list using the AddItem method.

After all of the table names have been added to the list of tables, the List_Tables_DblClick subroutine is executed to refresh the list of column names.

Listing Columns

The code that retrieves the names of the columns contained in a given table is executed either automatically at the end of the List_Tables_DblClick subroutine or when the user double-clicks one of the table items displayed in the Tables list. In both instances, the List_Tables_DblClick subroutine shown here is executed:

```
Private Sub List_Tables_DblClick()
    Dim oColumn As SQLDMO.Column
    Dim sDatabaseName As String
    Dim sTableName As String

    On Error GoTo TableError

    If List_Tables.ListIndex >= 0 Then
        sDatabaseName = List_Databases.List(List_Databases.ListIndex)
        sTableName = List_Tables.List(List_Tables.ListIndex)
    Else
        If List_Databases.ListIndex < 0 Then
        List_Databases.ListIndex = 0
        sDatabaseName = List_Databases.List(List_Databases.ListIndex)

        If List_Tables.ListIndex < 0 Then List_Tables.ListIndex = 0
        sTableName = List_Tables.List(List_Tables.ListIndex)
    End If

    List_Columns.Clear
    Text_Column.Text = vbNullString

    For Each oColumn In _
            oSQLServer.Databases(sDatabaseName).Tables(sTableName) _
            .Columns
        List_Columns.AddItem oColumn.Name
    Next oColumn

    List_Columns_DblClick
    Exit Sub

TableError:
    SQLDMOError

End Sub
```

The List_Tables_DblClick subroutine is structured very much like the List_Databases_DblClick subroutine. The first thing that the List_Tables_DblClick subroutine does is to make an instance of the SQLDMO Columns object named oColumns. Next, the List_Tables_Click subroutine sets up the Visual Basic error handler to jump to the TableError tag and subsequently execute the SQLDMOError function.

Then the List_Tables.ListIndex property is tested to determine if this subroutine has been evoked automatically from the List_Databases_DblClick subroutine, or if this subroutine has been evoked by the user double-clicking one of the items in the List_tables list. If the List_tables_DblClick subroutine was called by the user double-clicking an entry in the List_Tables list, then the sDatabase and sTables string variables are assigned the value of the selected list items. Otherwise, the sDatabase and sTable variables are set to the first entry in each of their respective lists.

After the variables containing the parent Database and Table names have been set, the old values in the List_Columns list and Text_Column text box interface objects are cleared. This ensures that the List_Columns list and the Text_Columns text box will contain the values from the user's new selection.

Like the Databases and Tables collections, a For Each loop is used to iterate through the collection of Column objects. As the For Each loop progresses, the name of each current Column object is added to the List_Columns list. The primary difference that you can see in working with the Columns collection and the Tables collection that you saw earlier is that the Columns collection is one level deeper in the SQL-DMO object hierarchy. To work with the Columns collection, you must specify both a specific member of the Tables collection and a specific member of the Databases collection.

After all the names from the Columns collection have been added to the List_Columns list, the List_Columns_DblClick subroutine is called to retrieve some of the specific attributes of a selected column.

Retrieving Column Attributes

The code that retrieves the attributes of a specific column is executed either automatically at the end of the List_Column_DblClick subroutine or when the user double-clicks an item in the Columns list. The List_Columns_DblClick subroutine shown here is executed for both of these actions:

```
Private Sub List_Columns_DblClick()
    Dim oColumn As SQLDMO.Column
    Dim sDatabaseName As String
    Dim sTableName As String
    Dim sColumnName As String

    On Error GoTo ColumnError

    If List_Columns.ListIndex >= 0 Then
        sDatabaseName = List_Databases.List(List_Databases.ListIndex)
        sTableName = List_Tables.List(List_Tables.ListIndex)
        sColumnName = List_Columns.List(List_Columns.ListIndex)
    Else
        If List_Databases.ListIndex < 0 Then
        List_Databases.ListIndex - 0
        sDatabaseName = List_Databases.List(List_Databases.ListIndex)
```

```
      If List_Tables.ListIndex < 0 Then List_Tables.ListIndex = 0
      sTableName = List_Tables.List(List_Tables.ListIndex)

      If List_Columns.ListIndex < 0 Then List_Columns.ListIndex = 0
      sColumnName = List_Columns.List(List_Columns.ListIndex)
   End If


   Text_Column.Text = vbNullString

   Text_Column.Text = _
       oSQLServer.Databases(sDatabaseName).Tables(sTableName). _
       Columns(sColumnName).Name & CRLF & CRL _
       & "Data Type:" & CRLF _
       & oSQLServer.Databases(sDatabaseName).Tables(sTableName). _
       Columns(sColumnName).Datatype & CRLF & CRLF _
       & "Length:" & CRLF _
       & oSQLServer.Databases(sDatabaseName).Tables(sTableName). _
       Columns(sColumnName).Length & CRLF & CRLF _
       & "Precision:" & CRLF _
       & oSQLServer.Databases(sDatabaseName).Tables(sTableName). _
       Columns(sColumnName).NumericPrecision & _
       CRLF & CRLF _
       & "Scale:" & CRLF _
       & oSQLServer.Databases(sDatabaseName).Tables(sTableName). _
       Columns(sColumnName).NumericScale

   Exit Sub

ColumnError:
   SQLDMOError

End Sub
```

Again, the List_Columns_DblClick subroutine starts by declaring an instance of the SQLDMO.Columns object along with several working variables and the Visual Basic error handler.

Also like the other subroutines, the List_Columns_DblClick subroutine then determines if the user has double-clicked an entry in the List_Columns List or if the List_Columns_DblClick subroutine was called automatically from the List_Tables_DblClick subroutine. If the user has double-clicked one of the List_Column items, then the sDatabase, sTable, and sColumn variables are assigned the names of the selected list items. Otherwise, the sDatabase, sTable, and sColumn variables are assigned the name of the first item in each of the respective lists.

Next, the Text_Columns.Text property is cleared. You might notice that unlike the other subroutines, the List_Tables_DblClick subroutine doesn't use a list box, nor does it iterate through a collection. Instead, the List_Columns_DblClick subroutine displays a selection of properties from one specific member of the Columns collection. The following properties of the Column object are displayed:

▼ Name

■ DataType

■ Length

■ NumericPrecision

▲ NumericScale

The Text_Columns text box has the Multiline property enabled, which allows multiple lines to be displayed in the text box. Each line is separated by CR + LF (carriage return + line feed) characters that are represented by the Chr$(10) and Chr$(13) statements.

SQL-DMO Error Handling

Errors that the SQL-DMO methods generate can be trapped using Visual Basic's standard error handling. If an error is raised by one of the SQL-DMO methods and Visual Basic's error handling is not implemented, the user will see a Visual Basic run-time error and the application will be terminated.

TIP: Make use of Visual Basic's built-in error handler to trap any SQL-DMO errors and prevent unsightly application errors.

All of the subroutines presented in the sample SQL-DMO application make use of the common SQLDMOError subroutine shown here:

```
Public Function SQLDMOError()

   Dim sErrorMsg As String

   sErrorMsg = Err.Source & " Error: " & _
             Err.Number - vbObjectError & ": " & Err.Description

   SQLDMOError = MsgBox(sErrorMsg, vbOKOnly, "SQL-DMO Error")

End Function
```

The SQLDMOError function is a relatively simple function. It displays a message box to the user that provides more information about any error conditions that are encountered. SQL-DMO errors can be displayed using the Visual Basic Err object. The

Err.Source property contains the name of the SQL-DMO component that raised the error. Subtracting the vbObjectError constant from the Err.Number property results in the SQL-DMO error number. The Err.Description property contains a text description of the error.

CONCLUSION

As you can see from the code examples, DMO opens up the power of SQL Server's management functions to Visual Basic, and its OLE implementation makes it easy to use from Visual Basic and other OLE-complaint applications. For more information about using SQL-DMO, you can refer to the SQL Server manual, *Programming SQL-DMO Reference*, as well as the Microsoft Developer's Network (MSDN) CD, which contains several articles and programming examples of how to use SQL-DMO.

PART II

Database Development with SQL Server

CHAPTER 8

Introduction to the Relational Database Model

This chapter explores the relational database model, which is the foundation of SQL Server and all other relational database management systems, or DBMSs. With an understanding of the relational model, you'll be able to design flexible and efficient databases, as well as create applications that use SQL to read and update your organization's data. To help you understand why relational databases have become so popular for business applications, this chapter starts with a look at the overall purpose of a DBMS and the advantages a DBMS has over a conventional computer file system. That understanding provides a springboard for discussing the relational model and its three main parts—structure, integrity, and data manipulation. The relational model's approach to data structure and integrity provides a well-organized way to design and implement complex databases, and relational operations offer powerful ways to manipulate data.

The relational model underlies both database design and database implementation. In this chapter, after exploring the fundamentals of the relational model, you'll learn about a helpful and widely used design tool—*entity relationship diagrams* (ERDs). Many software tools for database design use ERDs, and you can use ERDs with informal pad-and-pencil or chalkboard drawings. ERDs give you a simple, but effective, visual technique to document application entities and their interrelationships. Because of their intuitive nature, ERDs are especially helpful when discussing database designs with nontechnical end users. In the next chapter, you'll dive into structured query language (SQL) and learn how to use this relational-based language to implement a database and work with its contents.

BACKGROUND: DATABASE MANAGEMENT SYSTEMS

Although the relational database model underlies both the architecture of relational DBMSs and popular database design methods, its origin was in the research community that was studying how computer systems could better handle application data. Thus, it's appropriate to start with a discussion of the whole problem of computerized data storage and manipulation.

According to some estimates, with traditional file systems, up to 80 percent of a typical business application is taken up with code related to file access (including file definition, record selection, and input/output [I/O]) and the editing of input data for valid values. As little as 20 percent of program code is concerned with calculations and transformations of data after it's read as input and before it's written as output. The large proportion of code required just to get valid data for a computation and then to store the results is an expensive part of traditional application development. When the same file access and editing code is repeated in different programs—as it often is—both coding errors and software maintenance costs increase, too. Taken together, the large proportion of code not directly related to the main business function of an application system and the repetition of this code throughout the system have historically been obstacles to higher productivity in application development.

This problem led computer systems designers around the late 1960s to look for ways to reduce the large chunk of non-problem-oriented application code by having the system software automatically handle many record specification, file access, and field editing functions, thus freeing application programmers to concentrate on the computations and data manipulation. This effort led to what we now call database management systems. In the decades since their first appearance, DBMSs have had a dramatic impact on data processing. As a result, more and more applications are being built on top of DBMSs instead of more primitive conventional file systems. This requires, of course, that applications be designed with the use of DBMS facilities in mind—a subject covered later in this chapter.

Conventional File System Versus DBMSs

Conventional file systems provide a relatively primitive set of facilities to store and retrieve data. A conventional file is either a sequence of bytes (a *stream-oriented* file) or a sequence of records (a *record-oriented* file). In conventional file systems, a record is just some chunk of bytes, either fixed- or variable-length. A conventional file system usually takes care of low-level device operations, such as disk operations, so the programmer can use high-level language (HLL) I/O statements, such as read or write, without being concerned with device-level programming. But conventional file systems don't usually do much more than that. In each program, the programmer has to code the layout of the data, such as field starting positions, lengths, and data types, as well as handle record sequencing and other file-related tasks.

Although using C/C++ #include facilities, or a similar feature in other HLLs, can reduce some of the repetitive coding, it remains the programmer's responsibility to define a file and its contents within each program. Even more costly than the original coding of definitions is the effort required to change the source code in all programs that use a file if any change is made to its physical storage, such as adding a field, changing a field's length, or splitting files. Source code changes may be necessary even if a program doesn't use any of the modified items. For example, a change in one field's length may change the starting position of another field that the program uses.

A DBMS, on the other hand, attempts to free programs from physical data dependence and reduce the amount of code that must be repeated in multiple programs. Central to this goal is the ability to define to the DBMS some construct that represents an application entity type about which you want to store properties. In different types of DBMSs, entity types are represented by different constructs, among them record types, segments, relations, and tables. In SQL Server, a SQL table represents an entity type. Table 8-1 shows some of the terminology you're likely to encounter in various contexts.

What these various constructs have in common is that they represent a set of distinguishable objects of some sort, whether the objects are concrete, such as customers, or abstract, such as NT Server tasks. This is true of conventional file systems, as well—as far as it goes. What's important about DBMSs is that you include as part of a file definition or other construct some representation of the entity type's properties. Properties are usually represented by fields or columns. If you were to define a Customer entity type

Relational Model	Table-Oriented DBMSs	Conventional File Systems	Conceptually Represents
Relation	Table	File	Entity type
Tuple	Row	Record	Entity instance
Attribute	Column	Field	Property
Domain	Column type	Data type	Allowable values and meaning
Element	Column value	Field value	Property value

Table 8-1. Comparative Terminology Used in Different Contexts

(for example, as a table in a SQL Server database) in a DBMS, you would also define CustomerId, Name, Address, and other properties (for example, as columns). Conceptually, a property is simply some piece of information about an entity type.

Defining Data

So far it may appear that a DBMS offers no earth-shattering improvement over the records and fields of an ordinary file. But for a conventional (nondatabase) file, every program must contain the layout of fields in a record while a DBMS provides a *data definition language* (DDL) that's used to define constructs for both entity types and properties including, for example, record layouts and fields, in a system *catalog.* Thus, a DBMS lets a program reference a property by name, for example, Customer.Name, without a programmer-coded specification in the program of how the actual field-level data is physically stored. Defining entity types and their properties in the DBMS is just the first step toward representing more of the logical structure and meaning of application data in a central place.

> **NOTE:** As its name implies, SQL Server uses SQL for the DDL and stores information about database tables in a set of system tables known as the SQL catalog. And, as you'll see in Chapter 9, once you define a SQL Server table, every program that references the table automatically has access to the table's definition.

With most DBMSs, how a property (field) is stored can be changed and programs that use the property continue to execute properly with no revisions. For example, you can change the length or location (within the table definition) of a column in a SQL Server table, and you generally need only to rebind programs that use the file for them to work properly with the changed definition. Removing the physical storage aspects of a property from a program's code removes a significant amount of work, especially in system maintenance; it also removes a significant source of errors.

Enforcing Data Integrity

Besides requiring specification of the record layout in every program, a conventional file system also requires that every file-update program include code to check for legitimate values in the fields before a record is written. This validation is typically implemented by a series of conditional tests (for example, If Age > 21 ..., If ActTyp = 'A' or 'B' or 'C' ...) on values entered on a display for interactive updating or on values in a transaction record handled by a server program. One disadvantage of this approach is that this code may be repeated—possibly with slight variations—in many programs. In addition, when validity tests are directed at input values before any program calculations or transformations, rather than at a record's output values at the time of a file update, it's still possible, due to a program error, to write a record containing invalid data to the file. Thus, most field-editing code in a conventional file system is both cumbersome to maintain and not wholly effective at guaranteeing the integrity of the data.

A DBMS can address this problem by providing DDL features you can use to specify *integrity constraints* in the system catalog. The integrity constraints that can be specified vary among different DBMSs. At a minimum they usually include range checks ("between 1 and 50") or allowable values ("equal to A or B or C"). More complex constraints may be specifiable as well. Examples include relationships between properties for the same entity type (for example, an employee's hire date must be greater than his or her birth date) or interrecord relationships (a customer ID value in an order entity must exist as a customer ID value in exactly one customer entity). The DBMS, which handles all database updating, generally checks these constraints when database records are inserted, updated, or deleted. If a constraint is not met, the DBMS blocks the operation and signals an error. Specifying integrity in a central catalog helps immensely in speeding implementation and in achieving improved quality of the organization's data.

Historically, efficient DBMS support for built-in integrity has been difficult to achieve. Recent developments in hardware power and more efficient DBMS software implementations have prompted a trend toward improved DBMS capabilities for ensuring data integrity. This is an area in which you can expect significant change over the next few years.

At a level above the field level, a conventional file system leaves it to each program to implement relationships between entity types. For example, every program that deals with customers, orders, or both must be aware of the relationship between these two entity types. Thus, a customer file maintenance program must have code to ensure that a customer record isn't deleted if there are still order records for that customer. Likewise, a program that needs an order header record, a customer information record, and a set of order detail records must know which files to access and how to retrieve the related records. Applications implemented over conventional file systems typically use one of two methods to relate records: They use fields to store the relative record numbers (RRNs) or byte offsets of related records, in the same file or in different files, or they use matching values in common fields to associate records as in having, for example, an OrderId field in both the order header record and the order detail record. Whichever method is used in a conventional file system, the access strategy required to retrieve related records is reimplemented in every program that uses or affects a relationship between records.

But in many DBMSs, relationships can be defined in the catalog using the DDL. Thus, an order header entity type might be defined as the parent of an order detail entity type, which is the dependent. Ideally, the implementation details of this relationship are hidden from application programs. A program doesn't know whether RRN pointers or indexes are being used; for that matter, a program doesn't necessarily know whether one, two, or more files are used to store the data. The DBMS provides logical I/O operations such as get all records with a specific property, get first dependent, get next sibling, and update current.

In summary, a DBMS lets you define—independently from individual programs— entity types, properties, integrity constraints, and relationships. The DBMS can then enforce constraints and provide data access methods that hide the physical storage details.

Manipulating Data

DDL capabilities are only part of the story: a DBMS also provides a *Data Manipulation Language (DML)* to retrieve and update the data. The DML may be provided through extensions to HLL I/O facilities, or through a distinct language such as SQL, which SQL Server provides. The DML typically provides a superset of the conventional HLL I/O operations: read, write (or insert), delete, and update. DML operations may operate on one or more records at a time, depending on the DBMS system.

An important distinction between a DBMS DML and conventional file I/O operations is the way in which the target of the action is specified. In a conventional file system, the I/O operation must target a specific record in the file using either an explicit RRN (or relative byte position), an explicit key value for an indexed file, or a read next operation that implicitly targets a record based on the RRN or key of the previous record. Many DBMSs, on the other hand, support access by field contents regardless whether the field is a key (for example, get next course with course status = 'OPEN'). And, based on relationships defined in the catalog, a DBMS can retrieve related records without explicit targeting (for example, get first student for this course, or get all courses joined with enrolled students).

The power, consistency, and ease of use of a particular DBMS's DML helps determine how useful it will be in complex application systems. If the DML is wel implemented in the DBMS, it can significantly reduce the number of source code statements necessary to implement application functions.

Database Models

DBMSs vary in how much they provide the application developer. The best are powerful, highly dynamic, and easy to use; most importantly, they succeed in substantially reducing the proportion of non-problem-oriented code. DBMSs also vary in how they support the definition of entity types, properties, integrity constraints, and relationships between entity types and the types of manipulations that can be performed on the data.

Most commercial DBMSs have been based on one of four major database models:

▼ Hierarchic

■ Network (also known as CODASYL)

■ Inverted list

▲ Relational

In recent years, a fifth model, object-oriented, has become more widespread. However, DBMSs based on the relational model are still the most widely used. Both the hierarchic and network models are based on explicit physical links, such as RRNs, between records of the same type (siblings) or between records of different types, where one is the parent and one is the dependent. The major difference between the two is that the hierarchic model allows a dependent to have only one parent just as in any familiar form of hierarchy, such as an organization chart, while the network model allows a record type to be the dependent of any number of parent record types, as in the case in which a course record type can be the dependent of both an instructor record type and a student record type.

Both the hierarchic and the network DBMS approaches have fallen into disfavor because they, like conventional file systems, require a knowledge of how the entity types are physically structured—that is, which entity types have explicit links to each other. These explicit links not only require that the programmer write procedural code to navigate the database along the link pathways, but they also make the database structure cumbersome to change: new or modified link types are not always easy to incorporate once the database has gone into production.

A third alternative, the inverted list model, is really little more than a conventional file system with enhanced file index facilities to aid in record retrieval. Records in different files are implicitly related by the values in key fields (rather than by pointers), but retrieval is still done by single-record read and write operations. As such, the inverted list is of interest not so much because of its particular approach but rather because a DBMS based on the inverted list model can be extended naturally to a relational DBMS by adding integrity rules and relational operators.

The foundation of most commercial DBMSs today is the relational database model, covered in the next section.

THE RELATIONAL DATABASE MODEL

The relational database model was first introduced in the paper "A Relational Model of Data for Large Shared Data Banks," published by Edgar Codd in June 1970. Since the publication of this paper, the relational model has been developed extensively, and products such as SQL Server provide many of the capabilities covered in the previous section. The relational model has been especially successful for business applications, because relations and their table-like representations are a natural fit for many kinds of business data. In addition, the relational model puts a firm conceptual foundation under both database design and DBMS features, thus aiding the progress of both design techniques and DBMS capabilities.

Relational Model: Data Structure

The relational database model has three main parts: structure, integrity, and data manipulation. The data structure portion defines the form for representing data. Most basic to this form is the concept of a *relation*. Figure 8-1 shows an informal picture of a relation, which looks like what is commonly called a table. That is, a relation can be thought of as having columns that lay out properties (*attributes* in relational nomen-

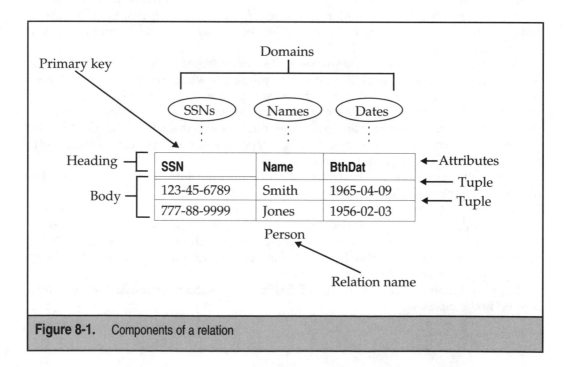

Figure 8-1. Components of a relation

clature) and rows (*tuples* in relational nomenclature) that hold specific instances of the entity type represented by the relation.

This informal table representation is convenient for most purposes and is used in many parts of this book.

But to be more precise for the moment, a relation has two parts—the *relation heading* and the *relation body*. The heading is a set of attribute-and-domain pairs. For the Person relation represented informally by the table in Figure 8-1, the heading is the set of pairs {<SSN:SSNs>, <Name:Names>, <BthDat:Dates>}. Because a set has no specific ordering of its elements, it's just as correct to say the heading is the set of pairs {<BthDat:Dates>, <SSN:SSNs>, <Name:Names>}. The number of attribute-and-domain pairs in a relation is known as its *degree*; for example, the relation in Figure 8-1 is a degree three relation.

The body of the relation is a set of tuples; each tuple is represented as a row in Figure 8-1. Each tuple in the Person relation represents information about a single person; that is, each tuple represents an *instance* of the Person entity type. Formally, each tuple is a set of attribute-and-value pairs. The tuple in the Person relation identified by SSN value 123-45-6789 is actually the following set of pairs: {<SSN:123-45-6789>, <Name:Smith>, <BthDat:1965-04-09>}. Or again, because sets are not ordered, you could also say the tuple is the following set of pairs: {<Name:Smith>, <SSN:123-45-6789>, <BthDat:1965-04-09>}. Because the values in a tuple are not ordered, a value is always paired with the appropriate attribute that serves as a label; thus, you can keep track of the meaning of all the values in all the tuples in a relation. The number of tuples in a relation is known as its *cardinality*. For example, the relation in Figure 8-1 has a cardinality of two.

At this point, you may wonder why something so simple as the row-column structure of a table must become as complex as a "set of attribute-and-value pairs." Because an unordered, labeled representation of data is used, the relational model can reference all values *by name* rather than by some physical mechanism, such as the position of the column in a table. This distinction is not a minor one—it's one of the breakthroughs in modeling data that the relational approach brought about. Nevertheless, in practical use of the relational model, it's perfectly adequate to use a table-like notation or other simplifications. It's important, however, not to make invalid inferences from the informal representation of a relation as a table. For example, although a table is depicted with a particular ordering of rows, relations do not have any particular ordering of tuples.

If tuples have no ordering—and thus can't be identified by row number, how can you refer to a particular tuple? Every tuple in a relation can be referenced by specifying values for *primary key* attributes. For example, in Figure 8-1, a tuple can be referenced by specifying its SSN attribute value; SSN is thus a primary key attribute for the Person relation. This, of course, requires that a unique combination of attribute values exist for each tuple in a relation. This requirement is one of the integrity concepts covered later in this chapter.

Referencing attributes by name and referencing tuples by primary key values provide a data model that has no physical storage concepts associated with the data organization. The same statement cannot be made about the hierarchic, network, or inverted list DBMS approaches. Thus, the relational database model is the only one that achieves complete *physical data independence*. Consider this: as long as the relational DBMS takes care of finding the right data when your program provides entity and attribute names along with primary key values, your program doesn't have to know anything about how the data is stored. The data could even be rearranged between program executions and it wouldn't matter, as long as the DBMS kept track of the data's physical location. Internally, of course, a relational DBMS generally uses RRNs or other physical references to keep track of data. These physical references may or may not be accessible to application programs. The important thing for a relational DBMS is that it must at least allow applications to access data without physical references.

Another fundamental part of data representation in the relational model is the concept of *domain*. Simply put, a domain combines two pieces of information: the set (possibly infinite) of allowable values and the semantics (or meaning) of the values. A domain is not part of a relation, and it stores no particular values. Instead, a domain defines a pool of values that an attribute can have. Every attribute is specified as being "over" a domain. Two or more attributes can be over the same domain. Table 8-2 shows some simplified examples of domains and attributes defined over those domains.

These examples point out some interesting and important facets of domains. First, as just mentioned, domains define allowable values; thus, the attribute EmpSalary can never be negative because it's defined over the domain Salary, which has no negative

Domain Name	Domain Definition	Example Attributes
Color	Values {Red, Orange, Yellow, Green, Blue, Indigo, Violet}	ProductColor HairColor
Salary	Range: [0:100,000,000] Units: Dollars/year	EmpSalary ContractorSalary
Wages	Range: [0:100,000] Units: Dollars/hour	EmpWages ContractorWages
Weight	Range: [0:100,000,000] Units: Pounds	ShippingWeight EmpWeight
Children	Range: Integers ≥ 0 Units: People	ChildCnt
Cars	Range: Integers ≥ 0 Units: Cars	CarCnt
Units	Range: Integers Units: (none)	ItemCnt

Table 8-2.   Examples of Domains and Attributes

values. Second, a domain often specifies the units of measure. Attributes defined over domains with similar units of measure can be compared or added, but attributes defined over domains with dissimilar units of measure cannot be compared or added meaningfully. Thus, a statement such as "If HairColor = ProductColor", while perhaps an unlikely comparison, is at least possible, whereas "If HairColor = EmpSalary" is not allowed. This type of mismatched comparison may seem obvious, but domains help clarify more subtle distinctions in a data model and to the DBMS. For example, in most HLLs and many DBMSs a field used to store the number of children in a household (ChildCnt) will be an integer, as will the field to store the number of cars owned by a household (CarCnt). Neither the C++ nor VB compiler would balk at a statement such as "ItemCnt = ChildCnt + CarCnt". This statement is probably the result of bad coding, not a medieval social philosophy in which children and cars are both merely possessions, and should be prevented. In the relational database model, these two attributes could not be added because they are from different domains.

What if you really do want to add such dissimilar units? In that case, you might use a mapping function—for example a function, UnitCvt, that is defined to convert, or map, any integer value to a unitless value. The required statement then becomes "ItemCnt = UnitCvt(ChildCnt) + UnitCvt(CarCnt)". A more common example of a required mapping would be from annual salary values to hourly wages or vice versa. In this case, the numerator (dollars) for both units of measure is identical, but the denominators (year and hour) are different. This similarity, exacerbated by ambiguous field names, is precisely the cause of a typical HLL programming error in adding fields such as EmpSalary and EmpWages without converting either. The concept of domains allows system detection of invalid or questionable comparisons or computations. Note, however, that current commercial DBMSs generally have only limited support for domains.

Another point to be made about a relation is that a database relation (unlike the more general mathematical notion of relation) cannot have *sets* as values for an attribute. Every attribute value in a tuple must be a single element drawn from the underlying domain (and the domain's values must not be sets).

> **NOTE:** Actually, this restriction is part of the original relational model, but a variation known as the non-first normal form (NFNF) relational model does allow sets as attribute values. The reason for this restriction was that it greatly simplified the mathematical definitions of the relational operators. The NFNF model is also a step toward the object-oriented database model, which allows arbitrarily complex data attribute values.

Figure 8-2 shows in table format the distinction between a mathematical relation and a database relation.

Note that restructuring a mathematical relation that has sets of values into a database relation is a mechanical operation of adding additional tuples that repeat values for some attributes.

Parent	Children
Smith	Bubba
Jones	Billy Susie Fred
Harris	Janice Tommy

Mathematical relation

Parent	Child
Smith	Bubba
Jones	Billy
Jones	Susie
Jones	Fred
Harris	Janice
Harris	Tommy

Database relation

Figure 8-2.   Mathematical versus database relations

Normal Forms

Consideration of repeating values introduces another facet of the relational database model—*normal forms*. By definition, a database relation is in what is called *first normal form (1NF)*, which simply means that there are no sets as attribute values. Because a relation is in 1NF, all the referencing and manipulative operations of the relational model can be performed on it. However, a 1NF relation may not always be the ideal form for representing data. A relation in 1NF may appear to represent information redundantly. And, if a database file or table is subsequently implemented that corresponds directly to the relation, actual redundant data may be updated inconsistently. Figure 8-3 shows a 1NF relation with apparent redundant storage of WarehouseAddress.

Figure 8-4 shows the 1NF relation split into two relations that eliminate the WarehouseAddress redundancy.

The process of splitting relations with redundant information storage into two or more relations without the redundancy is a process often called *normalization*. There are five main normal forms (1NF through 5NF) for relations. Each normal form addresses the potential for a particular type of redundancy.

Before taking a closer look at the various normal forms, it's important to be clear about the meaning of redundancy. First, any nontrivial set of relations will have some values repeated more than once in the database. For example, in the relations in Figure 8-4, the warehouse IDs that appear in the Inventory relation all appear in the Warehouse relation, as well. This is one of the central features of the relational model—tuples are related by values, not pointers or other physical means. So the three instances of warehouse ID 1 and the three instances of warehouse ID 2 don't represent the type of redundancy we're concerned with.

The redundancy to avoid is repeated representation of the same fact. For example, in Figure 8-3, the fact that warehouse 1 is located at 1511 Central Ave. is repeated in two

ItemId	WarehouseId	Qty	WarehouseAddress
167	1	10	1511 Central Ave.
167	2	20	6803 Alder St.
448	1	26	1511 Central Ave.
302	2	18	6803 Alder St.

Inventory

Figure 8-3.   First normal form (1NF) inventory relation

tuples. If you actually created a database file with this structure, you'd have to ensure that any change to the warehouse address was made consistently to all records that stored the address.

ItemId	WarehouseId	Qty
167	1	10
167	2	20
448	1	26
302	2	18

Inventory

WarehouseId	WarehouseAddress
1	1511 Central Ave.
2	6803 Alder St.

Warehouse

Figure 8-4.   Inventory relation split into two relations to eliminate redundancy

> **NOTE:** *Formally, the concept of facts is known as* functional dependence. *In a nutshell, if a relation has two attributes A and B, B is functionally dependent on A if and only if two tuples in the relation having the same value for A necessarily have the same value for B.*

Now, let's look at an example that's not so obvious. Suppose there's an OrderItem relation for the items that are included in customers' orders:

OrderId	ItemId	Qty	Price
9877	73	2	50.00
9878	52	1	10.00
9878	73	5	50.00
9879	73	1	50.00

OrderItem

This relation appears to redundantly represent the fact that the ItemId determines the Price. In many business systems, an item will always be sold for the same price, and the preceding OrderItem relation represents some items' prices (item 73) redundantly. But what if items' prices were negotiated on each order? Then it would be possible for the relation to have the following contents at some point in time:

OrderId	ItemId	Qty	Price
9877	73	2	50.00
9878	52	1	10.00
9878	73	5	45.00
9879	73	1	50.00

OrderItem

For the business model that this relation represents, there is no fact redundancy. The price of an item must be explicitly stored with each record for an order item.

This example brings us to a crucial point in understanding normal forms: If you want to unambiguously represent various facts in a (logical) database model that uses relations, you must structure the relations so they have no redundant representation of facts. The obvious consequence is that there's no mechanical method of normalizing relations. You first must know which facts you want to represent, and then you define the relations accordingly.

Despite these principles, some textbook and other presentations of normal forms convey the misconception that normalization is a process you apply when you implement files or SQL tables. Although informally you might consider some of the ideas related to nonredundant representation of facts when you implement files, normal forms are specifically a *design* concept.

The misunderstanding probably stems from the conventional approach, more or less followed here, of introducing the normal forms in order 1NF to 5NF and using examples that have obvious redundant representation of facts. Keep in mind as you go through the following examples, however, that each relation with apparent redundancy might, in some specific situations, be free of redundancy.

The Main Types of Normal Forms

With that cautionary note, let's look at the main normal forms. To review, first normal form (1NF) requires that each attribute value be atomic; that is, it must not be a set or other composite structure. The database relation in Figure 8-2 and the relation in Figure 8-3 illustrated first normal form. *Second normal form (2NF)*, which is illustrated by the two relations in Figure 8-4, requires that the relation be in at least first normal form and that each non-key attribute depend on the *entire* primary key. The primary key for the Inventory relation includes both the ItemId and WarehouseId; neither alone is unique. Because we assume that a warehouse's address depends only on the WarehouseId attribute, the relation in Figure 8-3 violates the 2NF requirement. Looking at the problem from the other direction, if we assumed incorrectly that Figure 8-3 was already in 2NF, we would think that, for some reason, the WarehouseAddress values could be determined only by knowing both the ItemId and the WarehouseId.

Third normal form (3NF) requires that the relation be in at least second normal form and that each non-key attribute depend *only* on the primary key. In the following relation, each tuple represents a customer order:

OrderId	OrderCustId	CustCity	Amt
601	123	Portland	2,000
602	789	Eugene	50
603	123	Portland	500
604	198	Portland	1,000

Order

If you assume that a customer's city depends only on the customer's ID, the proper 3NF structure is as shown here:

CustId	City
123	Portland
198	Portland
789	Eugene

Customer

OrderId	OrderCustId	Amt
601	123	2,000
602	789	50
603	123	500
604	198	1,000

Order

Fourth normal form (*4NF*) requires that the relation be in (at least) third normal form and that there be no more than one *multivalued* fact in the relation. A multivalued fact is one in which there may be several values for an attribute determined by one value for another attribute; for example, the children of an employee or the courses taken by an employee. The following relation represents two multivalued facts:

EmployeeId	Child	Course
576	Bonnie	Math 101
576	Janice	Psych 203
576	Sam	?
601	Abigail	Art 101

EmployeeChildCourse

Look at the problem in this relation—when an employee has an unequal number of children and courses, what value should be used as a placeholder? You can't use null, discussed later in the chapter, because all three attributes are necessary in the primary key, and primary key attributes can't have null.

The solution is to use two relations:

EmployeeId	Child
576	Bonnie
576	Janice
576	Sam
601	Abigail

EmployeeChild

EmployeeId	Course
576	Math 101
576	Psych 203
601	Art 101

EmployeeCourse

So far, the rules for normal forms are pretty intuitive, which should be no surprise because the intent is to make clear the facts represented by a relation. The final normal form is a bit more involved to explain but also has an intuitive rule: A table in *fifth normal form (5NF)* cannot be split into two or more tables (each having a primary key with a proper subset of the attributes in the original table's primary key) without loss of information. Suppose you know the following rule about sales agents, products, and companies:

If a sales agent sells a certain product and that agent represents a company that makes the product, then the agent sells that product for that company.

You might try to represent this with the following relation:

Agent	Company	Product
Boyd	Ford	Car
Boyd	Ford	Truck
Boyd	GM	Car
Boyd	GM	Truck
Harper	GM	Car

AgentCompanyProduct

But observe that, by definition, this relation isn't in fifth normal form. It can be split into the following three relations with no loss of information because you can determine, with the previously stated rule, exactly what each agent sells by looking at the contents in these three relations:

Agent	Company
Boyd	Ford
Boyd	GM
Harper	GM

AgentCompany

Agent	Product
Boyd	Car
Boyd	Truck
Harper	Car

AgentProduct

Company	Product
Ford	Car
Ford	Truck
GM	Car
GM	Truck

CompanyProduct

But even if you can split the original table, why would you want to? To answer that question, consider how you would store the (new) fact that Harper sells Ford trucks. In the three-relation representation, the answer is simple: insert a <Harper, Ford> tuple into the AgentCompany relation and a <Harper, Truck> tuple into the AgentProduct relation. However, in the single-relation representation, as in AgentCompanyProduct, you would have to add the following tuples:

<Harper, Ford, Truck>
<Harper, Ford, Car>
<Harper, GM, Truck>

What's going on here is that the AgentCompanyProduct relation redundantly stores some of the more elementary facts—which products an agent sells—to satisfy the rule stated earlier. By splitting the relation, as long as you also state the rule about which companies' products an agent sells, you don't redundantly represent the elementary facts. It's important to note, however, that without the rule, you would need a relation like AgentCompanyProduct to know which companies' products an agent sells. Although fifth normal form may be a bit difficult to grasp at first, it illustrates the real purpose of normal forms—establishing a clear meaning for what a set of relations represents. This is especially important when you're designing a database.

In summary, the data structures of the relational model provide data independence (a separation of the conceptual and physical aspects), and when viewed—as they normally are—as tables, relations are easy to understand and work with. Relations also put a firm theoretical footing under any DBMS based on them. This combination of the conceptual simplicity and formal definition of relations forms the foundation for the next two parts of the model: data integrity and data manipulation.

Relational Model: Data Integrity

While the data structure portion of the relational database model defines the form for representing data, the data integrity portion of the model defines mechanisms for ensuring that the stored data is valid. This requires, at a minimum, that the attribute values each be valid, that the set of values in a tuple be unique, and that relations known to be interrelated have consistent values within the tuples.

In the previous section the discussion of the concept of domains essentially covered the first form of data integrity, known as *attribute integrity*—that values for attributes come only from their respective underlying domains. A widely accepted variation of the relational model also permits an attribute to contain a marker, referred to as *null*, that indicates a missing or unknown value. Note that null is not a value per se—it's merely a placeholder.

The domain concept provides for integrity checking comparable to the common HLL implementation technique of testing a value to see that it's within an allowable range or that it's one of a list of allowable values. Domains also extend validation to the meaning of the values, for example, whether units are children or cars. What domains don't address is a large group of integrity constraints that involve other attribute values in the same tuple, such as QtyShip ≤ QtyOrdered, or other tuples, such as Sum(LoanAmt) ≤ 10,000. These more comprehensive aspects of attribute integrity are included as part of extensions to the relational database model that have been developed since its inception. Many DBMSs now support a *check constraint* feature that lets you define a wide variety of intra- and inter-record tests that the DBMS enforces for database updates.

The second form of integrity essential to the relational database model is *entity integrity*. This is a fairly straightforward concept—every tuple in a relation represents an entity (that is, an instance of an entity type) that must exist in the real world; therefore, every tuple must be uniquely identifiable. It follows that there can be no completely duplicate tuples (all attribute values identical) in a relation; otherwise, the unique existence of entities is not represented in the database. From this property of uniqueness is derived the principle that there exists in every relation some set of attributes (possibly all the relation's attributes) whose values are never duplicated entirely in any two tuples in the relation. If you don't include any superfluous attributes—namely, ones not needed to guarantee uniqueness—in the set of attributes, the set of attributes can serve as the relation's primary key. More than one possible set of attributes may meet the criteria for a primary key; each of these is referred to as a *candidate key*, and one is picked arbitrarily as the primary key.

The primary key is a minimal set of attributes whose values are unique for all tuples in a relation. Because of this, the primary-key forms the only means of addressing a specific tuple in the relational database model. A consequence of the requirement for unique primary key values is that none of the values in a tuple's primary key attributes can be null, that is, missing or unknown. None of the primary key attributes can be null because then this tuple's primary key value couldn't be guaranteed to be unequal to some other tuple's primary key value. Recall that in the relational model, null isn't a value in the attribute's domain; null is essentially a placeholder that means "the value of this attribute is unknown—*and it might be any value in the domain.*" Because the actual attribute value, if it were known, could be any domain value, there's no way to know that the value isn't also present in the same primary-key attribute of some other tuple. Thus, if SSN is the attribute serving as the primary key in the Person relation and there exists a tuple with SSN = 123-45-6789, another tuple could not have a null SSN attribute, because you couldn't tell whether the actual SSN value is equal to 123-45-6789. If you can't tell whether the two values are equal, you can't guarantee uniqueness. A similar argument holds for primary keys made up of more than one attribute (composite primary keys), which need all attribute values to guarantee uniqueness and hence cannot have null for any of the attributes in the primary key.

The third, and final, form of integrity fundamental to the relational database model is *referential integrity*. Simply put, referential integrity requires that tuples that exist in separate relations, but that are interrelated, be unambiguously interrelated by corresponding attribute values. Let's look at the warehouse example again to understand referential integrity. In Figure 8-4, two relations are used so a warehouse address can be stored nonredundantly. The WarehouseId is stored as an attribute in both relations, so the WarehouseId value from an Inventory tuple can be used to reference, or look up, the appropriate Warehouse tuple via the Warehouse relation's WarehouseId primary key. Thus, the tuples in the two relations are interrelated, based on matching values in the WarehouseId attributes in the two relations.

As pointed out earlier, the WarehouseId attribute in the Warehouse relation serves as a primary key and can never be null. The WarehouseId attribute in the Inventory relation is referred to as a *foreign key*—it addresses "foreign" tuples that are usually outside the relation with the foreign key. A foreign key value can be all null. That means that its related tuple is unknown. A foreign key value also can exactly match a primary key value in a related tuple. But a foreign key value cannot have some attribute values present (that is, at least one attribute value is not null) and not match the primary key value of an existing tuple in the related relation. This requirement says nothing more than this: if the foreign key points to a related tuple, the tuple must be there. A consequence of this rule is that composite foreign key values cannot be partially null because, by the entity integrity rule, no primary key attribute value can ever be null.

Together, the three integrity rules—attribute, entity, and referential—allow specification of important constraints that a relational DBMS can enforce automatically whenever a database update occurs. These rules protect not only the specific values in attributes, but also the identity and interrelationships of tuples as well. A DBMS that provides this level of integrity support lifts a large coding load off application programmers.

Relational Model: Data Manipulation

As stated earlier, data representation and integrity do not make a complete model. There must be some means of manipulating the data as well. The relational database model defines data manipulations as the relational assignment operation and eight algebraic operations. The assignment operation simply allows the value of some arbitrary expression of relational algebra to be assigned to another relational variable. For example, the expression

RelationC← RelationA JOIN RelationB

allows the relational variable RelationC to take on the value (set of tuples) resulting from the JOIN operation performed over tuples in the RelationA and RelationB relations. This is analogous to arithmetic assignment in HLL computations.

The eight relational algebraic operations include four standard set operations and four operations specific to database relations. The four relational algebraic operations found in conventional set theory (and the syntax of the corresponding operators used in expressions in the examples in this chapter) are

▼ *union* (rel$_1$ UNION rel$_2$)

■ *intersection* (rel$_1$ INTERSECT rel$_2$)

■ *difference* (rel$_1$ MINUS rel$_2$)

▲ *product* (rel$_1$ TIMES rel$_2$)

Figure 8-5 shows Venn diagrams of these operations. The results of these four operations performed on the sample relations in Figure 8-6a are shown in Figures 8-6b through 8-6f.

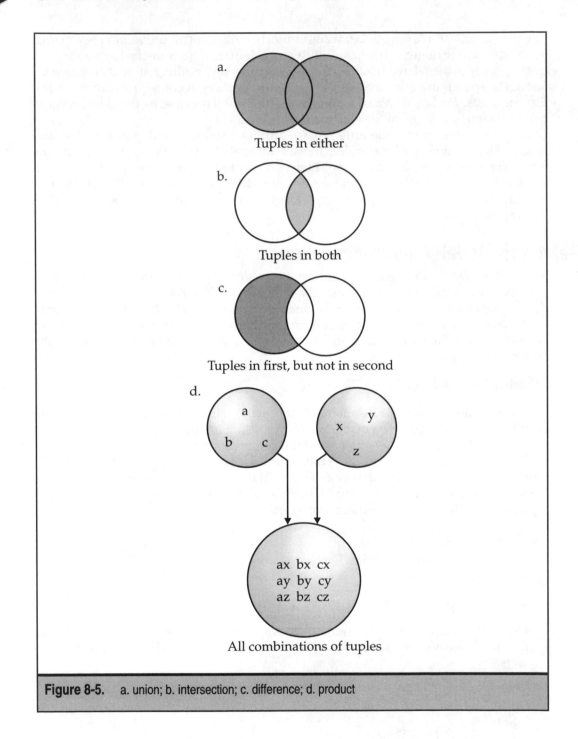

Figure 8-5. a. union; b. intersection; c. difference; d. product

a. Three relations used as operands

SSN	Name
123-45-6789	Smith
601-11-9999	Wilson

RelA

SSN	Name
145-67-8888	Jones
601-11-9999	Wilson

RelB

Course	Instructor
Math 101	Aldridge
Psych 203	Ulrich

RelC

b. RelA UNION RelB

SSN	Name
123-45-6789	Smith
601-11-9999	Wilson
145-67-8888	Jones

(Duplicate tuples are dropped.)

c. RelA INTERSECT RelB

SSN	Name
601-11-9999	Wilson

d. RelA MINUS RelB

SSN	Name
123-45-6789	Smith

Figure 8-6.   Examples of standard set operations on database relations

e. RelB MINUS RelA

SSN	Name
145-67-8888	Jones

(Difference is not commutative.)

f. RelA TIMES RelC

SSN	Name	Course	Instructor
123-45-6789	Smith	Math 101	Aldridge
123-45-6789	Smith	Psych 203	Ulrich
601-11-9999	Wilson	Math 101	Aldridge
601-11-9999	Wilson	Psych 203	Ulrich

Figure 8-6. Examples of standard set operations on database relations (*continued*)

Note that union, intersection, and difference require the two relations to have the same attributes; that is, they must be *union compatible*. The product operation can work on dissimilar relations; if one relation has *m* attributes and the other has *n* attributes, the result is a relation with *m* + *n* attributes. Also, union, intersection, and product are *commutative* operations—the order of operands does not matter; for example, A UNION B is equal to B UNION A. The difference operation is not commutative as Figures 8-6d and 8-6e show.

The four special relational algebraic operations (and the syntax of the corresponding operators used in expressions in the examples in this chapter) are

▼ *projection* (PROJECT rel$_1$ [attribute-list])

■ *selection* (SELECT rel$_1$ WHERE predicate)

■ *division* (rel$_1$ DIVIDEBY rel$_2$)

▲ *join* (rel$_1$ JOIN rel$_2$ WHERE predicate)

Examples of these operations performed on the sample relations in Figure 8-7a are shown in Figures 8-7b through 8-7g.

Projection (Figures 8-7b and 8-7c) eliminates some attributes (columns) from a relation; any resulting duplicate tuples are then eliminated. Selection (Figure 8-7d) eliminates entire tuples (rows) if they don't satisfy a condition. Note that if you specify "WHERE CustId = 123", a specific tuple can be selected by its unique primary-key value. The division operation (Figures 8-7e and 8-7f) results in tuples where all values of an attribute in the first relation match all values (in a different attribute) in the second relation.

a. Sample relations

CustId	City	Status	Credit
123	Portland	00	1,000
456	Portland	20	500
789	Eugene	10	10,000
304	Portland	00	2,000

Customer

OrderId	OrderCustId	Amt
601	123	2,000
602	789	50
603	123	500
604	198	1,000

Order

Company	Vehicle
Ford	Car
Ford	Truck
GM	Car
Nissan	Truck

AutoCompany

Vehicle
Car

CarsOnly

Vehicle
Car
Truck

CarsAndTrucks

Figure 8-7.   Examples of special relational operations on database relations

b. PROJECT Customer [CustId, City]

CustId	City
123	Portland
456	Portland
789	Eugene
304	Portland

c. PROJECT Customer [City, Status]

City	Status
Portland	00
Portland	20
Eugene	10

(Duplicate tuples are dropped.)

d. SELECT Customer WHERE City = "Portland"

CustId	City	Status	Credit
123	Portland	00	1,000
456	Portland	20	500
304	Portland	00	2,000

e. AutoCompany DIVIDEBY CarsOnly

Company
Ford
GM

Figure 8-7.   Examples of special relational operations on database relations (*continued*)

f. AutoCompany DIVIDEBY CarsAndTrucks

Company
Ford

g. Customer JOIN Order WHERE CustId = OrderCustId

CustId	City	Status	Credit	OrderId	OrderCustId	Amt
123	Portland	00	1,000	601	123	2,000
123	Portland	00	1,000	603	123	500
789	Eugene	10	10,000	602	789	50

Figure 8-7.   Examples of special relational operations on database relations (*continued*)

The final special relational algebraic operation is *join*. Join operations are equivalent to the product of two relations from which some tuples are then selected. Join is not a primitive operation; however, its usefulness in interrelating two relations is so great that it's treated as one of the essential set of eight operations. Figure 8-7g provides an example of an *equijoin* in which the two relations (Customer and Order) are interrelated by equal values in the CustId and OrderCustId attributes. Conditions other than equality can be used to join tuples in two relations; for example, values of two attributes can be tested for greater than or unequal. In general, the test used can be any scalar comparison ($=, >, \geq, \leq,$ or $<$). This comparison operator is often referred to by the Greek symbol for theta (θ), and thus the generic version of the operation is often called a *theta-join*.

The result of an equijoin always has two attributes with identical values in every tuple. In Figure 8-7g, these attributes are CustId and OrderCustId. If one of these redundant attributes is dropped from the resulting relation, the equijoin is said to be a *natural join*. The natural join is the join most commonly meant when you see a nonspecific reference to a database join.

Other variants of join are possible. Figure 8-7g shows an *inner join*, one in which unmatched tuples are dropped. If instead of dropping unmatched tuples, you include them and put null in the attributes of the missing tuple, you have an *outer join*. If only the first relation's (the one on the left of the JOIN operator) unmatched tuples are paired with nulls, the result is a *left outer join*; a mirror image *right outer join* is also possible. A *full outer join* extends unmatched tuples from both relations with nulls.

This group of eight relational algebraic operations has the property of algebraic closure, which means that the result of any of the eight operations is a relation. Thus, the operations can be combined into complex, parenthesized expressions similar to the way ordinary arithmetic expressions can be built up; for example,

(RelationA UNION RelationB) TIMES RelationC

is a valid relational algebraic expression. Because the operands and results in relational algebra are relations (not simple values or single tuples, such as rows or records), the manipulations provide a very powerful base for database operations, as well as a means of expressing subsets in complex integrity constraints. To relate this concept to a conventional file system, think of how much you could accomplish with operations that are expressed in algebraic form but that treat entire files or record subsets as the operands.

The eight relational algebraic operations provide a standard by which to measure any DBMS that claims to support relational data manipulations. While a particular DBMS may use a different syntax than that used here, it must provide equivalent power in manipulating relations without iteration (looping) or recursion. In fact, the most widely used relational DML is SQL, and it is based on *relational calculus*, another way of expressing relational operations that is equivalent to the relational algebra.

The relational database model is unique among the various database models in that it provides for manipulations of entire sets of tuples. The following expression provides an example of using a set-at-a-time manipulation:

Update all Customers where AmtDue > 600, setting Status to 'H'

Set-at-a-time operations provide a more powerful means of manipulating data than is possible with the record-at-a-time operations available with conventional file system I/O or with other types of DBMSs. Keep in mind that a set of tuples can contain a single tuple; and, thus, set-at-a-time operations provide both higher-level manipulations and record-at-a-time operations.

Expressions in relational algebra are used not only to retrieve data or create new relations, but also to define a scope for record-at-a-time retrieval and update. The result of a relational algebraic expression can be treated as a *view* relation, rather than a *base* relation—one in which the data is actually stored. Figure 8-8 depicts in table format a view relation and the base relation over which it is defined.

Changes to a tuple in a view are treated as changes to the underlying tuple in the base relation. Thus, the statement

Update all tuples in CustomerHighDebt, setting Status to 'H'

View relation

CustId	AmtDue	InterestRate	Status
663309	1,250.00	0.12	B
802145	630.00	0.55	A
264502	800.00	0.10	B

CustomerHighDebt

SELECT Customer WHERE AmtDue>600.00

Base relation

CustId	AmtDue	InterestRate	Status
123886	500.00	0.07	A
663309	1,250.00	0.12	B
802145	630.00	0.55	A
264502	800.00	0.10	B

Customer

Figure 8-8.   View relation

is equivalent to the statement

Update all tuples in Customers where AmtDue > 600, setting Status to 'H'

because the CustomerHighDebt view defines a subset of the Customer relation for purposes of set-at-a-time operations, and the attribute update operation (setting Status to 'H') is applied to all tuples in the base relation (Customer) that satisfy the view's predicate.

Those attributes in a view relation that are also in the base relation are known as *direct attributes*. Views can also have *virtual* (or *derived*) *attributes*, which are calculated from attribute values in the base relation. Figure 8-9 shows a simple example of a view that has one direct and one virtual attribute.

As you look at SQL views in the next chapter, you'll see more ways to derive the contents of a view, as well as additional operations that use views.

Another important use of the relational algebra is to define complex integrity rules.

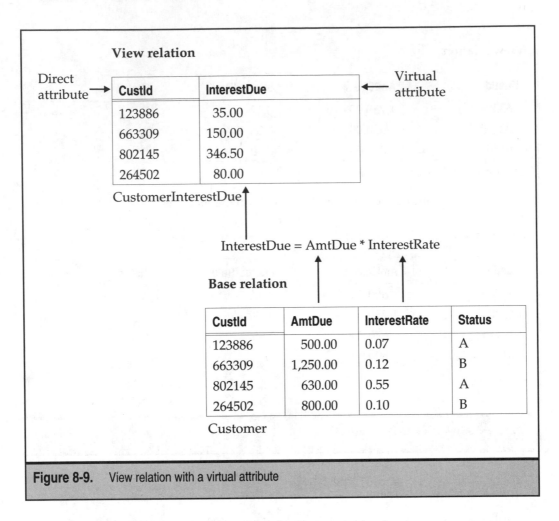

Figure 8-9.   View relation with a virtual attribute

For example, we could specify the constraint

For all Customers where AmtDue > 600, Status = 'H'

to require that the DBMS reject any update to the database that would violate this rule. We can use a full range of aggregation functions, such as SUM or AVERAGE, to specify many other integrity rules. For example, in a financial system we might express a borrower's maximum permissible outstanding debt as follows:

For each BorrowerId X in Borrowers,
(SUM(AmtDue) in Loans where Loans.BorrowerId = X) < 1,000,000

This type of rigorous specification is useful for both database modeling and specifying integrity rules in a DBMS so the DBMS can enforce the rule across all applications.

Taken together, the data structure, data integrity, and data manipulation components of the relational database model provide the foundation for both DBMS facilities and database design methods. In the next chapter, you'll see these concepts brought to life in SQL. Even more immediately, the next sections use some of these relational concepts as part of a practical tool for database design.

INTRODUCTION TO ENTITY RELATIONSHIP DIAGRAMS (ERDs)

During the analysis and design steps that precede setting up database tables, you'll need various means to document the data that the organization requires and how it's structured. Often, this documentation will be reviewed by several people: the person creating the data model, the end user, and the person responsible for creating the actual database tables. Entity relationship diagrams (ERDs) are a technique that can improve the clarity and comprehensibility of a data model.

ERDs describe data with pictures. For simple systems and high-level views of complex systems, an ERD's boxes, lines, and other symbols can be easier to understand than a textual description, which is what makes them a valuable data modeling tool for business systems. ERDs aren't suited for every data modeling task, however, and it's just as important to know when not to use ERDs as it is to know how to use them. You'll come back to that point at the end of the chapter.

There are many flavors of ERD notation and lots of religious wars about method-ologies—most of which you can safely ignore, as this section does. The techniques described in this section are representative of widely used ERD notations.

You can draw ERDs either by hand or using a variety of PC-based software tools. Usually, ER diagramming tools are part of a larger software package that may include other diagramming tools, for example for data flow diagrams, as well as dictionary facilities to store detailed definitions of various other elements of a complete data model. Before looking at some of the advantages of both hand-drawn and tool-drawn ERDs, let's get more familiar with how you construct ERDs.

Basic ERD Concepts and Symbols

In ERDs, boxes represent entity types, and lines connecting boxes represent relationships between entity types—hence the name *entity relationship*. In the rest of this discussion, the common shorthand *entity* is used to refer to entity type. An entity is some object, event, or association of interest in the data model. A relationship represents some dependency between two or more entities. The nature of relationships in an ERD reveals a lot about the structure of an organization's data.

The following illustration shows a simple ERD with Customer and Order entities and a Places relationship between them:

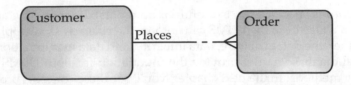

This ERD is a clear, quickly digested depiction of an important aspect of a business: the system under consideration deals with customers and orders. This ERD's clarity and simplicity illustrate why ERDs are a popular technique that business analysts use.

The line representing the relationship in the illustration above indicates two other important aspects of the business model: each order is placed by one customer, and a customer may place zero, one, or multiple orders.

The unbroken, single portion of the line attached to the Customer box specifies that each order has exactly one customer associated with it. The broken, crowsfoot portion of the line attached to the Order box specifies that each customer can have zero, one, or more associated orders. This illustration shows an easy way to remember what the crowsfoot means and on which end of the line you should place it:

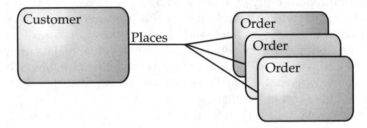

As you can see, the crowsfoot is shorthand for showing multiple boxes.

A break at one end of a relationship line means the entity is optional (there can be zero or more), whereas a solid line on an end means it's required (there must be one or more). You can combine broken- or solid-line endings with single-line or crowsfoot endings to depict four possibilities on each end of a relationship, as shown here:

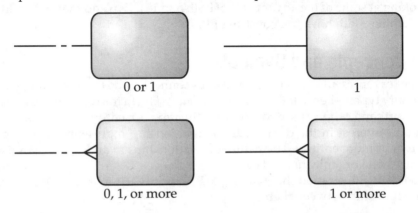

If you encounter a business situation that doesn't fit within these four possibilities, you can add your own annotation for the cardinality of the relationship, that is, how many instances of one entity can be associated with an instance of the other entity. The following example shows one way to specify that an instance of a Team on court, such as a basketball team, must have exactly five instances of Player. The solid line ending next to Player states that Player is required, and the 5 above the crowsfoot specifies the number of Players that a Team on court must have.

You can also specify a range for the cardinality of a relationship, using annotation such as the following:

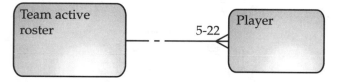

The 5-22 above the crowsfoot specifies that a team has at least 5, but no more than 22, players on the Team active roster.

One final addition completes the basic ERD notation. The line representing the relationship between two entities is often labeled at both ends so it's easier to talk about the relationship from the perspective of either entity. This example adds Shows to the Order end of the relationship.

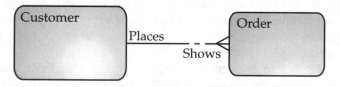

The entity and relationship labels, together with the way the relationship line is drawn, provide the pieces for verbal descriptions of the data model; for example, "Each customer places zero, one, or more orders, and each order shows exactly one customer."

The two relationship labels are just alternatives for stating the same thing—there is still only one relationship—and the second label is completely optional. Don't clutter your diagrams with second labels that are merely passive-voice constructions, such as *is placed by*, for the relationship. While you're working on early versions of ERDs, you often don't need to label a relationship line at all, if the relationship is obvious. For example, in the Customer-Order diagram, it's pretty obvious that customers place orders. In your final diagrams, however, it's a good idea to label all relationship lines, even if the relationship is obvious.

Adding Properties to ERDs

A property is some identifying or descriptive piece of information for an entity. For example, a Customer entity would likely have a Name property, and an Order entity would likely have an OrderDate property. You can list property names either inside an entity's box, as in this entity box,

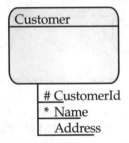

or on an attached list, as shown here:

You place a # before properties that uniquely identify an entity (in relational terminology, the attributes that constitute the primary key). You place a * before properties that must have a value and that are not part of the entity's identifier. Any remaining properties you list are for optional values—in relational terminology, the attribute can be null.

A relationship between two entities implies that one of them has one or more properties that contain identifier values from the other entity (in relational terminology, the foreign key). The following ERD shows that you can think of the box for the Order entity as implicitly specifying a CustomerId property that associates each order with a specific customer.

These properties don't necessarily need to be shown on an ERD because the relationship line implies the logical relationship between the two entities and the required foreign key property. If a foreign key property is shown explicitly on an ERD, you may want to add some notation to indicate for which relationship it serves as a foreign key and with which property in the target entity it is paired, as shown here:

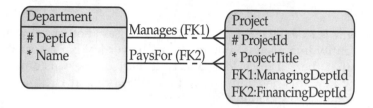

In this example, there are two relationships between the Department and Project entities. The Manages relationship represents which department is responsible for managing specific project(s). The PaysFor relationship represents which department is responsible for funding specific project(s). This ERD shows that a project's managing and funding departments may be different. The FK1 and FK2 annotations specify which Project property is used as the foreign key for each of the respective relationships. Although the property names make this fairly obvious, the FK1 and FK2 annotations remove any doubt.

In practice, you may find that listing all of an entity's properties clutters your ERD and diminishes the value of presenting the data model pictorially. Nothing says you must use only ERDs to describe your entire data model. In fact, that's not likely. It's often easier to record and discuss entity properties with end users using a table—a formatted list—rather than working with all the properties on ERDs. Some computer-based analysis and design tool products let you display properties either way, which is especially helpful if the tool lets you mark a subset of an entity's properties for display on ERDs, helping keep the ERD readable. With hand-drawn ERDs, you should choose the level of detail to put on a diagram, depending on how you're using the diagram, and determine what stage of data model development you are at. Final drawings typically have more detail than early, working drafts.

You may also want to specify the details of foreign key rules—for example, update and delete restrictions—separately from the ERD, using SQL or some other specification language.

Multivalued Properties

A property may be single-valued or multivalued. For example, a customer would typically have a single name but might have several phone numbers. There are two ways to represent multivalued properties on ERDs. You can simply list a multivalued property under an entity and describe the property as permitting a set of values by enclosing the property name in braces ({}), as is done for PhoneNbr in the following ERD.

Customer
CustomerId
* Name
  Address
  { PhoneNbr }

The other way is to show the multivalued property as another entity and associate it with the main entity in a many-to-one relation. The vertical bar across the relationship line indicates that the CustomerId property is part of the CustomerPhoneNumber entity's primary key; this notation is called a *weak entity* and is explained in the next section, "Representing Associations."

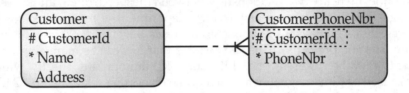

This latter method of specifying multivalued properties illustrates that, in ERDs, an entity can represent some "real" thing, such as a customer, or it can be a design artifact that represents a more abstract notion, such as the multivalued nature of a customer's telephone numbers.

Both techniques for showing multivalued properties can express the same underlying structure of the data. Although the basic, first-normal form (1NF) of the relational model forbids using multivalued attributes, there's really no reason not to use the {} notation on ERDs during your data modeling stage, if doing so makes your model's diagrams easier for the end user to understand. You can rest easy knowing you're on firm theoretical ground, too. There's an extension to the basic relational model, known as *non-first normal form (NFNF)*, that deals with nonatomic attributes, including multivalued attributes. When you start to develop your physical database design, you want to show multivalued properties as separate tables; but remember to adapt various techniques to the situation at hand, and don't get hung up on dogma during the data modeling stage.

Representing Associations

You can also use an entity to represent an *association* between other entities. Take the case of describing a many-to-many association between suppliers and parts. You can show the many-to-many aspect of the association as follows:

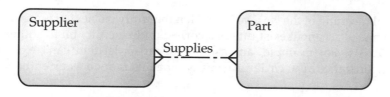

The way this ERD is drawn, a supplier may supply no parts or one or more parts; and a part may have no supplier or one or more suppliers. There's no place on this diagram, however, to place the price that a specific supplier charges for a particular part. This example splits the many-to-many relationship into two one-to-many relationships and adds a new SupplierOfPart entity to represent the association.

This new entity provides a place to list the Price property. This type of entity is sometimes called an *intersection entity*.

In the previous example, the SupplierOfPart entity's identifier consists of properties that contain ID values that match associated Supplier and Part instances' ID values. Remember that these two SupplierOfPart properties don't have to be listed explicitly because such foreign-key properties are implied by the two relationships. However, you do need to specify that these implicit properties are part of the SupplierOfPart entity's identifier. In ERDs, you can explicitly represent the fact that one entity's identifier includes all its foreign-key properties corresponding to the identifier properties of a parent entity by putting a bar across the dependent entity's end of the relationship line. The two bars across the relationship lines close to the crowsfeet connected to the SupplierOfPart entity mean that the identifier for SupplierOfPart contains all the foreign-key properties that reference the identifier properties of the Supplier and Part entities.

The following example shows another case in which the bar notation is helpful:

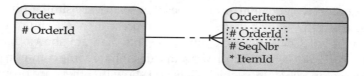

The OrderItem entity, which has a many-to-one relationship with the Order entity, uses an identifier comprising an OrderId property and a sequence number (SeqNbr) unique within each OrderId value. The only OrderItem identifier property that needs to be shown explicitly is SeqNbr.

The formal meaning of the vertical bar is that the entity it's next to is a *weak entity*, one for which an instance cannot exist unless a corresponding entity on the other end of the relationship exists. For example, an instance of an OrderItem can't exist without a corresponding instance of an Order. An entity type that is not a weak entity is known as a *regular entity*.

Exclusive Relationships

There are lots of either-or situations in business, and ERDs provide a notation that helps identify them. The ERD shown next depicts the business situation in which an account is associated with either a person or a company, but not both.

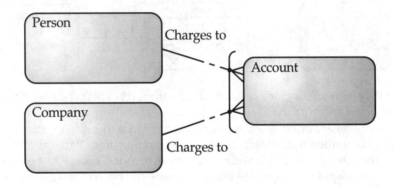

The *exclusive relationship* arc with connector dots (•) specifies that an instance of the entity having multiple relationship lines connected by the arc can participate in one and only one of the alternative relationships. For example, account number 123 might be associated with person Jones, and account 456 might be associated with company Ajax, Inc., but no account could be charged to by more than one person, more than one company, or both a person and a company.

Entity Subtypes

When you encounter two potential entity types that seem very similar but not quite the same, you can use ERD *entity subtype* boxes to represent them. Figure 8-10 shows a Vehicle entity that has Car and Truck subtypes. This diagram shows that all cars are vehicles and all trucks are vehicles, and cars and trucks share some common properties of vehicles, such as color. Subtyping vehicles lets you show that there are properties of cars that don't apply to trucks, and vice versa. You can also show relationships between other entities and a Vehicle, Car, or Truck entity depending on how the organization's data is structured.

An implicit way to represent a subtype is to use a single entity with a "type" property, and specify optional properties for properties that don't apply to all instances of the type. The ERD in Figure 8-11 shows how the Vehicle entity might be represented. The two Has

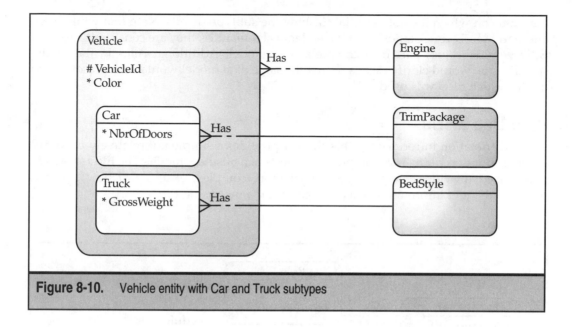

Figure 8-10. Vehicle entity with Car and Truck subtypes

relationships that were connected to Car and Truck, respectively, in the previous example are now shown as exclusive relationships. The explicit depiction of subtypes gives a more precise view on the ERD of the underlying data model, but the simpler style of representing a subtype with a "type" property may be more appropriate for high-level

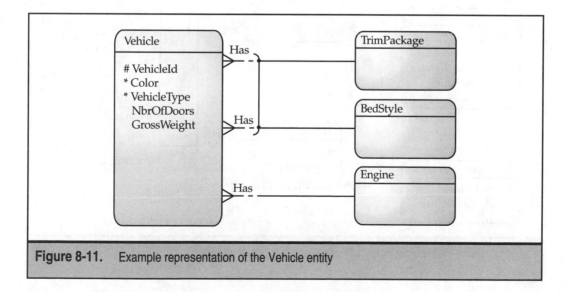

Figure 8-11. Example representation of the Vehicle entity

diagrams on which it's not essential to show the subtype details. Note that while these alternative ERDs in isolation don't have identical semantics, they are consistent and each ERD would be just part of a complete data model. Additional rules in the model specification would clarify details so that the same data model would be represented no matter which ERD was used.

When to Use ERDs

The ERD notation introduced in this chapter provides a simple but relatively powerful language for describing many important aspects of a business model. The ERD shown in Figure 8-12 provides one final, somewhat more complex, example of how you can represent a lot of information in a clear, concise manner using ERDs.

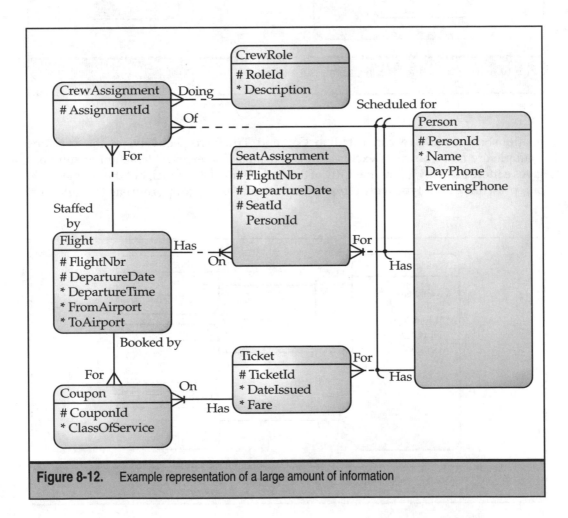

Figure 8-12. Example representation of a large amount of information

Here are a few of the things we know about this part of the business, just by looking at the ERD:

▼ A person either

- *may* be scheduled for *one or more* crew assignments, or

- *may* have *one or more* seat assignments.

■ A person either

- *may* be scheduled for *one or more* crew assignments, or

- *may* have *one or more* seat tickets.

■ A ticket *must* be for *exactly one* person.

■ A ticket *must* have *one or more* coupons.

■ A crew assignment *must* be of *exactly one* person.

■ A crew assignment *must* be for *exactly one* flight.

▲ A crew assignment *must* do *exactly one* crew role.

As you can see, this is an effective method for getting a high-level view of the entities and their interrelationships that are important to an organization.

Additional forms of notation are used in some versions of ERDs. You can explore these using the books listed at the end of the chapter. Keep in mind, however, that ERDs are simply one of many possible means of expressing the structure and rules of your data model. The ERD notation is well suited for simple systems, parts of complex systems, or for high-level views of the most important entities and relationships of interest to a business.

On the other hand, ERDs may not be the best choice for expressing model details, such as the enumeration of all entities' properties, for a complex system. For a system of significant size, ERDs that include all entities, relationships, and properties become very difficult to read. Further, ERDs may provide no way to express some business rules. For example, there's no standard ERD notation to represent a regulation that a construction company must use local subcontractors for projects funded by the local government. Yet you can easily state and understand this business-model rule in natural language, SQL, or some other textual form. Researchers have expended a great deal of effort to add expressive capability to ERDs; but while these efforts may have academic value, practical applications for many of them are limited.

ERDs are almost always accompanied by textual and table-oriented specifications, including details about the entity types and their properties, integrity rules, and individual user's views. Some of this information can also be shown on an ERD, where adding the information enhances comprehensibility.

Remember two basic aspects of ERDs, however, before you go overboard learning dozens of arcane symbols in some extended ERD notation. First, ERD notations are based on formal logic and consequently do not add expressive power but offer an alternative means of expression. Second, ERDs are preferable as a means of expression when they are easier to understand than the alternatives, such as table- or text-oriented representations.

In other words, ERDs are neither the only tool you need nor always the best. Yet when used for the right purpose, ERDs are a useful addition to your collection of analysis and design techniques. The best approach in most practical data modeling tasks is to use a mixture of ERDs, other diagrams, text, and tables to create the specification.

CONCLUSION

Creating effective, enterprise-level databases depends on a solid conceptual foundation. Fortunately, many years of work have gone into creating the relational database model as a logical basis for designing databases. Understanding the relational database concepts presented in this chapter will help you use SQL Server's tools, especially the Transact-SQL language covered in Chapters 9 and 10. As a specific design technique, entity-relationship diagrams can aid communication among end users and developers, resulting in databases that better meet the organization's requirements.

ADDITIONAL RESOURCES

▼ Fleming, Candace, C., and Barbara von Halle. *Handbook of Relational Database Design.* Reading, Mass.: Addison-Wesley Publishing Co., 1989.

This book is an excellent step-by-step guide to practical database design. The authors understand both the formal foundations of the relational model and the practical aspects of business database design.

■ Date, C.J. *An Introduction to Database Systems*, Sixth Edition. Reading, Mass.: Addison-Wesley Publishing Co., 1995.

This book is a must-have for the professional database designer. Date provides a highly readable, comprehensive, technically accurate explanation of the relational database model, as well as other important database topics. Chapters 9, 10, and 11 provide a very good explanation of normal forms.

▲ Barker, Richard. *CASE*Method Entity Relationship Modelling.* Reading, Mass.: Addison-Wesley Publishing Co., 1990.

Barker provides an excellent book on business data modeling. The emphasis is on entity relationship diagrams (ERDs), which can be useful for recording or presenting parts of the data model. The ERD techniques described in this chapter are based on the ERD notation described in Barker's book.

CHAPTER 9

SQL Primer: Data Definition Language

This chapter and Chapter 10 cover Structured Query Language (SQL), specifically the Transact-SQL language provided with Microsoft's SQL Server database. SQL is an industry-standard language for defining and manipulating data contained in a relational database. This chapter introduces SQL and covers the Data Definition Language (DDL) parts of SQL. You learn how to create several kinds of SQL objects: databases, base tables, views, and indexes. Chapter 10 covers the Data Manipulation Language (DML) parts of SQL. Many of the statements covered in these two chapters can be used within high-level language (HLL) programs, such as through ODBC, as well as entered interactively. Chapters 11 through 15 cover techniques for using SQL statements in HLL programs.

INTRODUCTION TO SQL

An IBM research lab developed SQL in the 1970s to explore an implementation of the relational database model. Since that time, SQL has become a widely used language that's included in most relational database management systems (DBMSs), including Microsoft's SQL Server product. Several national and international standards organizations have published SQL standards, which the major relational DBMSs, including SQL Server, follow for their versions of SQL.

NOTE: Version 7 of SQL Server meets most of the entry-level requirements of the following standards: ISO (International Organization for Standardization) 9075-1992, ANSI (American National Standards Institute) X3.135-1992, and FIPS (Federal Information Processing Standards) publication 127-2.

SQL includes Data Definition Language (DDL) statements to create database objects based on the relational model covered in Chapter 8. SQL also includes Data Manipulation Language (DML) statements, which are covered in Chapter 10, to retrieve and update the contents of a database. In addition, there are statements for writing Transact-SQL procedures and a variety of miscellaneous statements to control other aspects of database access. Table 9-1 lists the available Transact-SQL statements, including DDL, DML, programming, and miscellaneous categories. Chapters 9 and 10 cover most of the DDL, DML, and programming statements; Chapter 3 provides additional information on the security-related Grant, Deny, and Revoke statements; and Chapter 4 covers the Backup and Recovery (and the synonyms: Dump and Load) statements. For statements not covered in this book, consult the *Microsoft SQL Server Transact-SQL Reference* manual or online documentation.

Data Definition Language

Alter Database	Create View
Alter Table	Deny
Alter Trigger	Drop Database
Alter View	Drop Default
Create Database	Drop Index
Create Default	Drop Rule
Create Index	Drop Table
Create Rule	Drop Trigger
Create Schema	Drop View
Create Table	Grant
Create Trigger	Revoke

Data Manipulation Language

Begin Distributed Transaction	Open
Begin Transaction	ReadText
Close	Rollback
Commit	Save Transaction
Deallocate	Select
Declare...Cursor	Truncate Table
Delete	Update
Fetch	UpdateText
Insert	WriteText

Programming and Control of Flow

Begin...End	GoTo
Break	If...Else
Case	RaisError
Continue	Return
Declare	WaitFor
FormatMessage	While

Table 9-1.   Available Transact-SQL Statements

	Miscellaneous	
Alter Procedure	Go
Backup	Kill
Bulk Insert	Load (synonym for Restore)
Checkpoint	Print
Create Procedure	ReConfigure
Create Statistics	Restore
DBCC	Set
Drop Procedure	SetUser
Drop Statistics	ShutDown
Dump (synonym for Backup)	Update Statistics
Execute	Use

Table 9-1. Available Transact-SQL Statements (*continued*)

A SQL Preview

We look closely at most of the DDL statements later in this chapter (see "DDL Coding Suggestions"); however, for now a simple example provides a preview of what SQL looks like. The following statement creates a simple base table to contain customer data:

```
Create Table Customer
    ( CustId    Int                Not Null,
      Name      Char    (  30 )    Not Null,
      ShipLine  VarChar ( 100 ),
      ShipCity  Char    (  30 ),
      ShipState Char    (   2 ),
      Status    Char    (   1 ),
  Constraint CustomerPk Primary Key ( CustId ) )
```

NOTE: In SQL terminology, a table is an object, made up of columns and rows, that stores data. A *base table* is a named persistent object created with the Create Table statement. A *result table* is an unnamed temporary set of rows that the DBMS produces from one or more base tables during database retrieval or update operations. In this book, the term "table" is used to mean "base table" when the context makes it clear that the term refers to a permanent object.

The Customer table can be used to store information about customers. Each customer-related item, such as Name, listed in the Create Table statement defines a table *column*—a SQL column in a table is analogous to a field in a nondatabase file.

As mentioned, SQL also includes statements to manipulate data in tables. For example, the following SQL statement inserts a customer's data into the table created in the preceding listing:

```
Insert Into Customer
  Values ( 10001,
           'Ajax Plumbing',
           '12 Main St.',
           'Seattle',
           'WA',
           'A' )
```

Each value supplied on the Insert statement corresponds positionally to a column in the Customer table. This Insert statement adds a new *row* to the Customer table—a SQL row in a table is analogous to a record in a nondatabase file. If you're wondering how you can write application programs with Insert statements that handle a variety of customers and not just specific customers (for example, Ajax Plumbing), don't worry—SQL provides many features that support writing complete Visual Basic, C/C++, and other HLL programs using SQL. There's lots more flexibility than these first examples show. Chapters 11 through 15 cover programming with SQL.

Benefits of SQL

As these simple examples suggest, SQL provides statements that can be used to create tables and views. (A *view* is a SQL mechanism that lets you work with selected rows and columns of base tables.) SQL also provides statements to retrieve, insert, update, and delete individual rows within a table or view. If this were all SQL did, it's only claim to fame would be that it's a widely adopted standard for database definition and manipulation. But SQL also lets you manipulate *sets* of rows. For example, the following statement changes the status of all customers in Seattle that currently have a status of X:

```
Update   Customer
  Set    Status   = 'B'
  Where  ShipCity = 'Seattle'
    And  Status   = 'X'
```

The Where clause selects only those rows that satisfy the specified condition, and the Set clause assigns the new value to the Status column in the selected rows. This statement can be entered interactively (using various SQL Server tools), but just as importantly, it can be placed in an HLL program and can use program variables for the values of the city and the old and new status. This approach provides powerful set-at-a-time data manipulation that's not found in conventional HLL file access. For example, without SQL, a C++ program would require a read-write loop to carry out what SQL can do with a single Update statement.

Another significant capability that SQL offers is the ability to define very complex views. Views don't store data, but they provide an alternative way to access data in one or more underlying base tables. Views can select a subset of a base table's rows or can be defined with a subset of a base table's columns. Views can also derive new columns from other columns. SQL views have a rich language (as we shall see in this chapter, as well as in Chapter 10) for expressing both row selection and column derivation.

Learning SQL has many advantages. For NT Server applications, SQL provides important database capabilities not available with conventional file systems and HLL file I/O operations. Because SQL is an industry standard, programming skills in SQL can also be used with many other relational databases, including Oracle and IBM's DB2 family. This commonality also makes SQL a valuable cross-platform tool, especially with distributed database facilities, such as the widely used Open Database Connectivity (ODBC) interface between Microsoft Windows platforms and other operating systems. For Web-based applications, SQL is also the standard database language and is part of the new Java Database Connectivity (JDBC) standard.

SQL is also a good starting point for expressing many of the definitions, manipulations, and integrity constraints you need to document in the logical data modeling stage of a project. When you use SQL as a modeling language, you can extend it with your own notation to cover conditions that aren't directly supported by any actual SQL implementation. (This use of SQL is sometimes referred to as *pseudo-SQL*.) Then, when you implement tables, views, and application programs, you can use various techniques to handle cases in which SQL Server (or the DBMS facility you use) doesn't provide a direct implementation of your pseudo-SQL design specification. Even though pseudo-SQL as a design language doesn't eliminate implementation challenges, it provides a very capable language for clearly expressing many database design concepts.

Entering SQL Statements

In this chapter, we look at many SQL statements. You can use a variety of means to enter these statements, but for production development, you generally use the Query Analyzer, which is one of the SQL Server utilities. Figure 9-1 shows a typical Query Analyzer window that's used to enter SQL statements.

In the Query pane (the upper pane in Figure 9-1), you can type one or more SQL statements. To execute all the statements in the Query pane, press CTRL+E. To execute a subset of the statements in the Query pane, select them with the mouse, and press CTRL+E. The results are shown in the Results pane (the lower pane in Figure 9-1).

Query Analyzer provides context-sensitive Help for Transact-SQL statements, so it's an especially good tool if you're just learning SQL. To get help on a particular statement, select (highlight) the statement name and press SHIFT+F1. Query Analyzer also has an option to just parse statements without actually executing them; press CTRL+F5 to use this feature. Or, you can set the No execute option on the Current Connection Options dialog

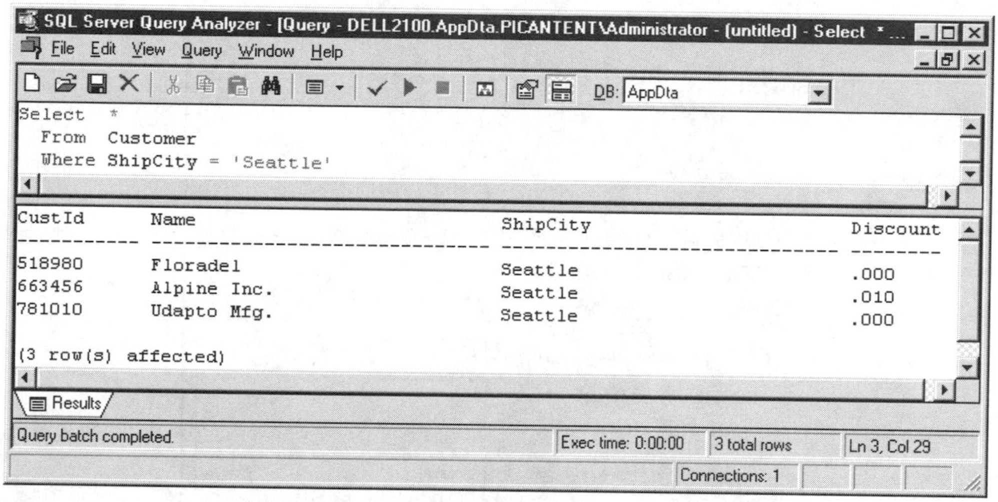

Figure 9-1.   Query Analyzer display

box (Figure 9-2) that is displayed when you select the Query | Current Connection Options menu item.

Once you have the proper syntax for a statement, you can save it (from the Query pane) to a source file. To save the contents of the Query pane in an ASCII text file, select File | Save As and provide an output filename. On the Save File dialog box, select ANSI from the File Format drop-down list. You can subsequently load the saved statements (or statements entered into a source file with any editor) by opening the file with the File | Open menu item. Saved source statements also can be copied to the source file of an HLL program and used as embedded SQL statements.

You can save statements for later execution using the OSQL batch facility. When you save the Query pane, select the current Windows code page (for example, cp 437) for the file format. The OSQL batch facility processes the SQL statements contained in a source file, as in the following example:

```
osql -U SmithJH -P ThePassword -i crtcustomr.sql
```

In this example, the -U and -P options specify the login and password to run the batch job under. The crtcustomr.sql source file might contain a Create Table statement to create a base table. You can find additional information on the OSQL utility under the "Command Prompt Utilities" topic in the SQL Server online documentation.

Putting SQL statements—especially statements to create production tables and views—in a source file is a good idea because you can subsequently revise and rerun the

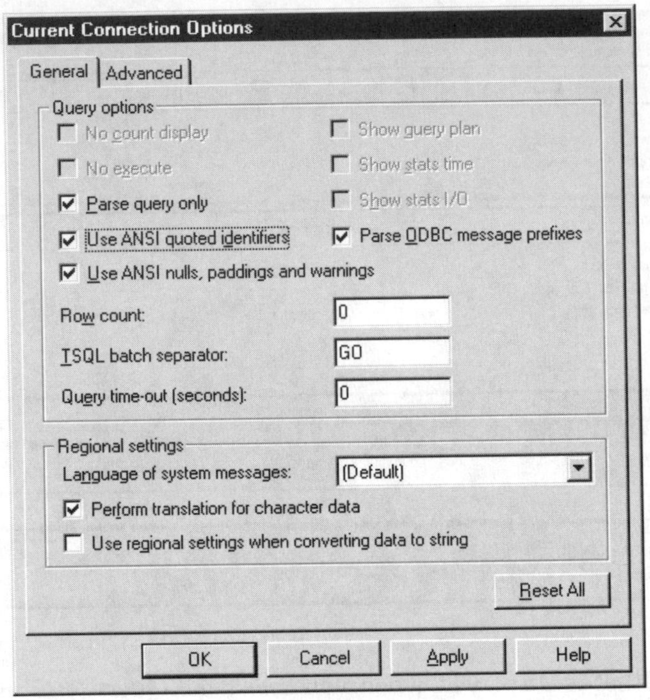

Figure 9-2. Current Connection Options dialog box

statements without having to re-create them. You can put one or more SQL statements in a source file by saving the session log from an interactive SQL session. You can also enter SQL statements in a source file using any source code editor.

You can code comments in a source file that's subsequently processed by the OSQL batch facility. To code a comment, begin the comment with two adjacent dashes (- -) and use the rest of the line for the comment, as in the following example:

```
-- This is a comment in a SQL source file
```

You can also code comments between the /* and */ delimiters, as shown here:

```
/* This is a comment that
   spans multiple lines */
```

Alternatives to SQL Statements for Creating Database Objects

SQL provides the foundation for creating SQL Server database objects. You can enter SQL statements in several ways. You also can create database objects using alternative tools available with SQL Server. As described in Chapter 2, the SQL Server Enterprise Manager provides menus, dialog boxes, and wizards to make it easier to create, alter, and drop database objects. The Enterprise Manager also provides a graphical database diagram editor that lets you create entity-relationship diagrams similar to those described in Chapter 8.

Although the Enterprise Manager provides more user-friendly interfaces to database definition and manipulation, it still helps to have an understanding of SQL for several reasons. First, as already mentioned, you can save SQL source code to be run in batch mode if you need to re-create database objects on the same system or a different system. Of course, making regular backups is also an essential way to provide for recovery, but source files can give you another level of protection. Also, you may need to perform some database operations programmatically, and SQL may be required to implement the necessary function (for example, to write stored procedures or to use ODBC function calls). Another advantage of learning SQL is that you get a good understanding of the foundation on which the visual tools rest, which helps you use those tools more effectively.

Setting ANSI-Standard Behavior

SQL Server can create tables that conform to ANSI SQL-92 standards or that behave according to the way previous versions of SQL Server operated. If you're creating a new database, we generally recommend you create it as an ANSI-standard database. The easiest and most reliable way to ensure ANSI-standard databases is to configure the appropriate SQL Server connection options and change several database options for the model database, as described in the "Setting Maximal ANSI SQL-92 Compatibility" section in Chapter 2. You can also execute sp_dboption system stored procedure calls (also explained in Chapter 2) to set a specific database to operate in an ANSI-standard manner.

CREATING A DATABASE

In SQL terms, a *database* is a container for related base tables, views, indexes, stored procedures, and other objects. Before you can create any of these objects, you must have a database for them. Within a database, objects are further organized as having an *owner*. For some types of objects, such as tables, you can have objects of the same name in the same database, as long as they're owned by different users. For production systems, however, duplicate names aren't a recommended practice. Typically, most production objects are owned by the database owner. Chapter 3 provides guidelines for setting up database and object owners.

To create a database, you must be the system administrator or have been granted the authority to use the Create Database command. The simplest form of the Create Database command is as follows:

```
Create Database AppDta
```

This creates the AppDta database and copies the SQL Server model database object definitions to the new database. That is, an empty copy of each table, as well as views, stored procedures, and so on, in the model database is created in the new database. SQL Server creates two NT Server files for this database: appdta.mdf to hold data and appdta_log.ldf to hold transaction log entries. The default initial sizes of these two files are set to the sizes of the model database's primary and log files, respectively, and SQL Server will expand them automatically if necessary.

Specifying the Database File Locations and Sizes

If you want to specify one or more specific files for the database or transaction log, add an On clause that lists one or more files and an optional value for the amount of space (in megabytes) to allocate for that file:

```
Create Database AppDta
   On    Primary
     ( Name       = AppDta1,
       Filename   = 'c:\production\data\appdta1.mdf',
       Size       = 10MB,
       MaxSize    = 100MB,
       FileGrowth = 10MB ),
     ( Name       = AppDta2,
       Filename   = 'c:\production\data\appdta1.ndf',
       Size       = 10MB,
       FileGrowth = 10MB )
```

The first entry after the On keyword should specify the optional Primary keyword indicating that this is the *primary file*—the one that contains the database's system tables and initialization information. Any additional *secondary files* that you specify are used to hold data in user tables and other objects. The arguments in this example are listed here:

▼ **Name**   The logical name used by SQL Server

■ **Filename**   The fully qualified NT Server filename

■ **Size**   The initial file size; defaults to the size of the model database's primary file (model.mdf)

■ **MaxSize**   The maximum file size; defaults to no maximum

▲ **FileGrowth**   The amount that SQL Server expands the file when necessary; defaults to 10%

A SQL Server database can be over a million terabytes (a *terabyte* is a thousand megabytes) in size.

For potentially greater performance and recovery, you can use a Log On clause to specify that the SQL Server transaction log for a database be stored on a different device than the database objects, as in the following example:

```
Create Database AppDta
   On    Primary
      ( Name          = AppDta1,
        Filename      = 'c:\production\data\appdta1.mdf',
        Size          = 10MB,
        MaxSize       = 100MB,
        FileGrowth =   10MB ),
      ( Name          = AppDta2,
        Filename      = 'c:\production\data\appdta1.ndf',
        Size          = 10MB,
        FileGrowth =   10MB )
   Log On
      ( Name          = AppDtaLog1,
        Filename      = 'd:\production\log\appdtalog1.ldf',
        Size          = 10MB,
        MaxSize       = 100MB,
        FileGrowth =   10MB )
```

This way, if the physical device on which the database resides is damaged, the log may still be usable (if the device it's on is not damaged). With an offline copy of a previous database backup and an undamaged log, you can restore the database to the point where the device holding the database failed. (See Chapter 4 for more information on backup and recovery.) When you specify explicit files, follow the SQL Server convention of using .mdf as the file extension for the database primary file, .ndf for database secondary file(s), and .ldf for transaction log file(s).

Altering a Database

After a database has been created, you can use the Alter Database statement to add new files, drop existing files, or modify the settings for a file. For example, the following statement adds a new file:

```
Alter Database AppDta
   Add File
      ( Name          = AppDta3,
        Filename      = 'c:\production\data\appdta3.ndf',
        Size          = 10MB,
        FileGrowth =   10MB )
```

There's also an Add Log File clause, which has the same format as the Add File clause. The Remove File clause uses just the logical filename that you previously assigned:

```
Alter Database AppDta
  Remove File AppDta2
```

The Modify File clause requires the logical filename that you previously assigned and takes any of the other arguments (for example, FileGrowth):

```
Alter Database AppDta
  Modify File
    ( Name       = AppDta1,
      FileGrowth =  50MB )
```

Defining Filegroups

Database files (but not transaction log files) are grouped into *filegroups*. When you initially create a database, the database's default filegroup contains the primary file and any secondary files that you don't explicitly assign to a user-defined filegroup. In many cases, the default filegroup is adequate. For some systems, you may improve performance or recoverability by creating user-defined filegroups on specific devices. Because you can specify in which filegroup a table or index goes, filegroups provide an indirect means of placing tables and indexes on specific devices. Also, when you use a file group containing multiple files, SQL server proportionally spreads data that is placed in the file group among the files based on the files' available free space. Here's an example of creating a filegroup:

```
Alter Database AppDta
  Add FileGroup AppDtaGroup1
```

After a filegroup has been created, you can use the Alter Database statement to add new files to the filegroup. For files added to a user-defined filegroup, you normally specify a different device than the one on which the database's primary file resides:

```
Alter Database AppDta
  Add File
    ( Name       = AppDta2,
      Filename   = 'd:\production\data\appdta2.ndf',
      Size       =  10MB,
      MaxSize    = 100MB,
      FileGrowth =  10MB ),
    ( Name       = AppDta3,
      Filename   = 'd:\production\data\appdta3.ndf',
      Size       =  10MB,
      MaxSize    = 100MB,
```

```
     FileGrowth =  10MB )
  To FileGroup AppDtaGroup1
```

To remove a filegroup and the files it contains, use statements like the following:

```
Alter Database AppDta
  Remove File AppDta2
Alter Database AppDta
  Remove File AppDta3
Alter Database AppDta
  Remove FileGroup AppDtaGroup1
```

A file or filegroup must be empty before you can remove it.

You can also use the Alter Database statement to change a database's default filegroup, as in the following example:

```
Alter Database AppDta
  Modify FileGroup AppDtaGroup1 Default
```

CREATING A TABLE

In a relational database, a base table contains the actual data. You can create up to about two billion tables in a SQL Server database. To create a table with SQL, you enter a Create Table statement that specifies the following:

▼   The database to contain the table

■   The owner of the table

■   The table name, which must not be the same name as any other base table or view with the same owner and in the same database

■   Specifications for 1 to 1,024 columns

■   A Primary Key constraint (optional)

■   1 to 250 Unique constraints (optional)

■   1 to 253 Foreign Key constraints (optional)

■   1 or more Check constraints that limit what can be inserted in the table (optional)

▲   The filegroup on which the table is stored (optional)

Figure 9-3 shows a more complete version of a Create Table statement for a Customer table.

As you can see from Figure 9-3, the Create Table statement first specifies the table to be created and then lists the column and constraint definitions, separated by commas and enclosed in a set of parentheses. SQL is a free-format language, and you can use multiple

```
Create Table AppDta.dbo.Customer
     ( CustId           Int               Not Null
                                          Check ( CustId > 0 ),
       Name             Char    ( 30 )    Not Null
                                          Check ( Name <> ' ' ),
       ShipLine1        VarChar ( 100 )   Not Null
                                          Default ' ',
       ShipLine2        VarChar ( 100 )   Not Null
                                          Default ' ',
       ShipCity         Char    ( 30 )    Not Null
                                          Default ' ',
       ShipState        Char    (  2 )    Not Null
                                          Default ' ',
       ShipPostalCode1  Char    ( 10 )    Not Null
                                          Default ' ',
       ShipPostalCode2  Char    ( 10 )    Not Null
                                          Default ' ',
       ShipCountry      Char    ( 30 )    Not Null
                                          Default ' ',
       PhoneVoice       Char    ( 15 )    Not Null
                                          Default ' ',
       PhoneFax         Char    ( 15 )    Not Null
                                          Default ' ',
       Status           Char    (  1 )    Not Null
                                          Default ' ',
       CreditLimit      Money             Default Null
                                          Check (
                                              ( CreditLimit Is Null ) Or
                                              ( CreditLimit >= 0     ) ),
       EntryDateTime    DateTime          Not Null
                                          Default Current_Timestamp,
       RowTimeStamp     TimeStamp         Not Null,
  Constraint CustomerPk      Primary Key ( CustId ),
  Constraint CustomerStatus Check ( ( Status <> ' ' ) Or
                                    ( CreditLimit Is Null ) ) )
```

Figure 9-3.   Create Table statement for Customer base table

lines for a statement, as well as blanks between words and symbols to improve readability. The example shows a coding style that begins each column definition and constraint on a separate line and aligns the similar parts of each column definition. Although this columnar style isn't required, it makes the statement much easier to understand than an unaligned stream of text.

SQL keywords aren't case sensitive: Create Table, CREATE TABLE, and CrEaTe TaBlE are all correct. Be aware, however, that the *sort order* you choose when installing SQL Server determines whether or not identifiers and string literals are case sensitive. If you installed SQL Server with a *case-insensitive* sort order (the default installation option), SQL Server treats the table names Customer, customer, and CUSTOMER as identical, and 'x' is considered equal to 'X'. If you installed SQL Server with a *case-sensitive* sort order, SQL Server treats the table names Customer, customer, and CUSTOMER as different identifiers, and 'x' is considered unequal to 'X'.

> **NOTE:** Even with a case-insensitive sort order, table and other object names are stored in the system catalog just the way you enter them (for example, Customer, customer, or CUSTOMER). Thus, if you display a list of the tables in the AppDta database, the table created by the statement shown in Figure 9-3 will be listed as Customer. With a case-insensitive sort order, you can still refer to the table as CUSTOMER or customer in SQL statements.

SQL Naming Conventions

The table name used in Figure 9-3 is a fully qualified name, which includes the database name (AppDta) and owner name (dbo) before the unqualified table name (Customer). You use a period (.) as the separator in qualified names.

It's generally a good idea to code explicit database and owner names when you create database objects. This practice documents the table's database and owner and avoids accidentally creating a table in the wrong database or with the wrong owner. As this example demonstrates, to create a table that's owned by the owner of the database, you use dbo in the qualified name. If you omit the database name, the table is created in the current database. The current database is either the one assigned to your SQL Server account or the one most recently specified in a Use statement, such as the following:

```
Use AppDta
```

The owner name can also be omitted, and SQL Server will use the current username as the owner. Fully qualified table and view names must be unique.

SQL object names can be up to 128 characters long and can include letters, digits, and these special characters: _ (underscore), # (number sign), $ (dollar sign), and @ (at sign). You'll avoid potential naming problems for cross-system or international applications if you use only names that begin with a letter (A–Z), and contain only letters and digits (0–9).

Also be aware that Transact-SQL has many reserved words, such as Create, Table, and Order, that have special meaning. These reserved words are listed in the "Reserved Keywords" topic of the *Microsoft SQL Server Transact-SQL Reference* manual. If you want to use one of these reserved words as the name of a table, column, or other SQL object, you must use double quotation marks around the names when they appear in a SQL statement. The following example shows how you would code a SQL Select statement that retrieves rows from a table named Order:

```
Select *
  From "Order"
  Where CustId = 499320
```

Quoted names can also be used for names that contain special characters, as in the following example:

```
Select *
  From "Order+Detail"
  Where CustId = 499320
```

Generally, avoid using SQL reserved words or special characters for names of SQL objects.

NOTE: You must have SQL Server's "quoted identifier" user option enabled to use quoted identifiers. Transact-SQL also allows the use of square brackets to delimit reserved words; for example, [Order]. This syntax doesn't require the quoted identifier user option.

Column Definitions

On the Create Table statement, after the new table name, you code 1 to 1,024 column definitions. The maximum length for a row is 8,060 bytes, including bytes required for internal data. In practice, the maximum amount of application data per row is somewhat less than 8,060 bytes. For example, a table with ten columns declared as Character data types can hold a maximum of 8,038 bytes of application data.

Each column definition specifies the column name and a data type. Some data types have a length or precision (total number of digits). In addition, the Decimal and Numeric data types can have a scale (number of digits to the right of the decimal point). Table 9-2 lists the SQL column data types.

TimeStamp Columns

A column specification with the TimeStamp data type (or a column specification with the name TimeStamp and no data type) is automatically updated whenever you insert or update a row. SQL Server sets a TimeStamp column to a value that's guaranteed to be unique within a database and greater than any previously assigned value. The value is not the same type as values with the DateTime data type. Never set a TimeStamp column's value directly.

A table can have only one TimeStamp column. You can use the TimeStamp column value to determine whether any other process has updated a row since you last retrieved it. In application programs, checking a TimeStamp column's value provides an efficient way to allow concurrent browsing and updating of a table while protecting against conflicting updates from different processes.

Character and Text	Description
Char (*length*) Character (*length*)	Fixed-length character string with a *length* from 1 to 8,000. (If the *length* is omitted, it defaults to 1.)
nChar (*length*) nCharacter (*length*) National Char (*length*) National Character (*length*)	Fixed-length Unicode character string with a *length* from 1 to 4,000. (If the *length* is omitted, it defaults to 1.)
Char Varying (*max-length*) Character Varying (*max-length*) VarChar (*max-length*)	Variable-length character string with a maximum length from 1 to 8,000. (If *max-length* is omitted, it defaults to 1.)
nChar Varying (*max-length*) nCharacter Varying (*max-length*) nVarChar (*max-length*) National Char Varying (*max-length*) National Character Varying (*max-length*) National VarChar (*max-length*)	Variable-length Unicode character string with a maximum length from 1 to 4,000. (If *max-length* is omitted, it defaults to 1.)
Text	Variable-length character data up to 2,147,483,647 bytes. A pointer to the first page of data is stored with the row; the actual text is stored in a b-tree of data pages.
nText National Text	Variable-length Unicode character data up to 1,073,741,823 characters (or 2,147,483,646 bytes). A pointer to the first page of data is stored with the row; the actual text is stored in a b-tree of data pages.

Table 9-2. SQL Column Data Types

Numeric	Description
Dec (*precision*, *scale*) Decimal (*precision*, *scale*) Numeric (*precision*, *scale*)	Decimal number. The *precision* is the number of digits and can range from 1 to 38. The *scale* is the number of digits to the right of the decimal point and can range from 0 to the value specified for *precision*. You can use Decimal(p) for Decimal(p, 0). You can also use Decimal by itself for Decimal(18, 0); however, using an explicit precision with Decimal provides clearer documentation. Note: SQL Server's default maximum precision for Decimal columns is 28. Start SQL Server with the /p command-line switch to set the maximum to a different value.
TinyInt	One-byte, unsigned, binary integer. Range: 0 to 255
SmallInt	Two-byte, binary integer. Range: −32,768 to 32,767
Int Integer	Four-byte, binary integer. Range: −2,147,483,648 to 2,147,483,647
Float (*mantissa-size-in-bits*)	Floating-point number. The *mantissa-size-in-bits* is the number of bits in the mantissa and can range from 1 to 53. The values 1 through 24 specify single-precision (4 bytes), the values 25 through 53 specify double-precision (8 byte). Note: You can use Float by itself for Float(53).
Real	Equivalent to Float(23). A Real column has 7 digits of precision.
Double Precision	Equivalent to Float.

Table 9-2. SQL Column Data Types (*continued*)

Money	Description
SmallMoney	Four-byte decimal value with four digits to the right of the decimal. Range: −214,748.3648 to 214,748.3647
Money	Eight-byte decimal value with four digits to the right of the decimal. Range: −922,337,203,685,477.5808 to 922,337,203,685,477.5807

Date and Time	Description
SmallDateTime	Four-byte date and time. Date range: 1-1-1900 to 6-6-2079 Time precision: Within 1 minute of elapsed time since midnight.
DateTime	Eight-byte date and time. Date range: 1-1-1753 to 12-31-9999 Time precision: Within 3.33 milliseconds of elapsed time since midnight.

Bit, Binary, and Image	Description
Bit	One bit. Values are 0 or 1.
Binary (*length*)	Fixed-length binary data with a *length* from 1 to 8,000 bytes. (If *length* is omitted, it defaults to 1.)
Binary Varying (*max-length*) VarBinary (*max-length*)	Variable-length binary data with a maximum length from 1 to 8,000 bytes. (If *max-length* is omitted, it defaults to 1.)
Image	Variable-length binary data up to 2,147,483,647 bytes. A pointer to the first page of data is stored with the row; the actual data is stored in a b-tree of data pages.

Table 9-2. SQL Column Data Types (*continued*)

System Types	Description
SysName	Equivalent to nChar Varying (128).
UniqueIdentifier	A unique identification number stored as a 16-byte binary value.
TimeStamp	Unique, 8-byte, time-sequenced value assigned by SQL Server when a row is inserted or updated. Note: A column with the name TimeStamp and no data type is created with the TimeStamp data type.

Table 9-2. SQL Column Data Types (*continued*)

Identity Columns

SQL Server allows you to designate one integral (TinyInt, SmallInt, Integer, Decimal(p,0), or Numeric(p,0)) column in a table as the table's *identity* column. You do this by adding the Identity keyword after the column's data type, as in the following example:

```
...,
RowId Integer Identity, ...
```

When you insert a new row, SQL Server automatically assigns a number to the identity column. By default, this number starts with 1 and increases by 1 for each new row. You can set the start and increment values by specifying either or both after the Identity keyword:

```
RowId Integer Identity(10), ... Start at 10, increment by 1
RowId Integer Identity(100, 2), ... Start at 100, increment by 2
```

Note that an identity column must not allow null (see the following section) and is not guaranteed to be unique unless you specify a Primary Key or Unique constraint, or create a unique index for the column.

Row Global Unique Identifier Columns

SQL Server also allows you to designate one UniqueIdentifier column in a table as a row global unique identifier (GUID) column. You do this by adding the RowGuidCol keyword after the column's data type, as in the following example:

```
...,
RowGuid UniqueIdentifier RowGuidCol, ...
```

A RowGuidCol column isn't updated automatically when you insert a new row, as is an Identity column. However, you can specify the NewId function as the column's default value to achieve a similar effect:

```
RowGuid UniqueIdentifier
        RowGuidCol
        Not Null
        Default NewId()
```

Notice that an Identity column, which contains a system-generated integer, is normally used as a primary key. A RowGuidCol column, which normally contains a value from the NewId function, is generally used for replication or in other cases where you need a unique identifier across all rows in all tables on all systems.

Null and Not Null Columns

SQL supports the concept of a *null* column or expression. When a column is null, it means the actual value is unknown. We'll look more extensively at how you work with nulls in Chapter 10, but when you declare a table you can specify the Null keyword for a column that allows null or the Not Null keywords for a column that should not allow nulls. As shipped, SQL Server treats columns without Null or Not Null as if Not Null were specified. However, this is backward from the ANSI-standard SQL syntax, which treats column definitions without Not Null as if Null were specified. As described in the "Setting Maximal ANSI SQL-92 Compatibility" section in Chapter 2, you can change the server defaults or you can change the default for a specific database to the ANSI standard by executing the sp_dboption stored procedure:

```
sp_dboption AppDta, 'ANSI null default', true
```

The examples shown earlier in Figure 9-3 and elsewhere in this book follow the ANSI standard by specifying Not Null for those columns that should not allow null. In this example, only the CreditLimit column is defined as null capable. For a null-capable column, you can set the column to null when you insert or update a row.

User-Defined Data Types

As we discussed in Chapter 8, in the relational model, every base table column should be defined over a domain. The domain specifies the allowable values and operations for the column. Although the ANSI standard for SQL includes a Create Domain statement to define database domains, version 7 of SQL Server doesn't support this feature. Instead, SQL Server provides a somewhat comparable, nonstandard feature called *user-defined data types*. Essentially, a user-defined data type is a synonym for a built-in data type, length (if appropriate), and null capability.

To create a user-defined data type, use the sp_addtype stored procedure, as in the following example:

```
sp_addtype TDescription, 'Character Varying (50)', 'Not Null'
```

This example creates the TDescription data type as a synonym for a Character Varying (50) data type that doesn't allow null. After creating this data type, you can use it in Create Table column specifications, such as

```
...,
ProductDescription TDescription, ...
```

which is equivalent to

```
...,
ProductDescription Character Varying (50) Not Null, ...
```

User-defined data types provide a nice way to standardize the data types used for primary and foreign keys, as well as frequently repeated column definitions. Data type names must be unique within each database, and you may want to follow a convention of beginning each type name with "T" to distinguish data type names from column names.

If you no longer need a user-defined data type, you can drop it with the sp_droptype stored procedure:

```
sp_droptype TDescription
```

Default Values

On the Create Table statement, you can use a Default clause to define a default value for a column. When you insert a row with an Insert statement that doesn't list all the base table columns or insert a row via a view that doesn't include all the columns in the underlying base table, SQL Server puts a default value in those columns that aren't in the column list or view. You can also use the Default keyword in Insert and Update statements to set a column's value to its default.

In Figure 9-3, earlier in this chapter, most of the character columns have a default of blank. The Name column, however, has no default and doesn't allow null, so a value must always be provided when a new Customer row is inserted. The CreditLimit column has a default of Null. This particular Default clause isn't really necessary because SQL Server assumes Null as the default for a null-capable column without an explicit Default clause. The EntryDateTime column uses the Current_Timestamp niladic function for the default. By specifying the Default keyword for the EntryDateTime column when a new row is inserted, you can have SQL Server place the current system date and time into the column.

The Default clause value must be a valid value for the data type and length of the column you're defining (the Null keyword is also valid if the column is null capable). As mentioned, if the column allows null, and you don't specify a Default clause, SQL Server uses null as the default. If the column doesn't allow null, and you don't specify a Default clause, you cannot insert a row unless you specify an explicit value for the column. You cannot specify a Default clause for a column with a TimeStamp data type or the Identity property.

Instead of a constant value, you can specify a constant expression. The expression can include any of the niladic functions listed in Table 9-3 or the other scalar functions listed in Table 10-2 in Chapter 10.

> **NOTE:** You can also create named *defaults* with the Create Default statement. To associate a named default with a column or user-defined data type, you use the sp_bindefault system stored procedure. Although named defaults provide a way to reuse a default definition, the approach isn't ANSI standard. We recommend you use named defaults only with user-defined data types.

Computed Columns

In addition to columns to hold application data, you can define *computed columns* in a table. A computed column has a column name, but the rest of its definition is simply an expression that uses other columns in the same table (and possibly constants or system functions). The following example shows how to create the FullName computed column by concatenating three other columns:

```
Create Table AppDta.dbo.Employee
    ( EmplId     Int            Not Null
                                Check ( EmplId > 0 ),
    LastName   Char ( 30 )  Not Null,
    FirstName  Char ( 30 )  Not Null,
    MdlInl     Char (  1 )  Not Null,
    ...,
    FullName As FirstName + MdlInl + LastName,
    ...
```

Niladic Function	Value Used
User Current_User Session_User	Database username of the user who executes the SQL Insert or Update statement
System_User	Login ID of the user who executes the SQL statement
Current_Timestamp	Date and time when SQL statement is executed (returns the same value as the GetDate function)

Table 9-3. Niladic Functions Allowed for Create Table Default Clause

You don't directly insert or update computed columns; instead, SQL Server computes the value when you retrieve a row from the table. In a computed column's expression, you cannot reference columns from other tables or use subqueries (a topic covered in Chapter 10). You also cannot use a computed column in a primary, unique, or foreign key or in another column's Default clause. SQL views, discussed in the section "Creating a View" later in this chapter, offer a superset of the capabilities of a computed column, and also a provide a valuable separation between the physical storage of data (in base tables) and the logical perspective of the data (in views). In most cases, a view is a preferable way to implement computed columns.

Constraints

When you create a table, you optionally can specify four types of constraints:

> Primary Key
> Unique
> Foreign Key
> Check

Note that Transact-SQL lets you specify default values and constraints by adding appropriate clauses either as part of a column definition or after the last column definition. The examples in this book observe the following conventions:

▼ Default clauses are coded as part of the column definition.

■ Check constraints that involve a single column are coded as part of that column's definition.

▲ Other constraints are coded after the last column definition, in the following order:

> Primary Key constraints
> Unique constraints
> Foreign Key constraints
> Check constraints

Key Constraints

Primary Key, *Unique*, and *Foreign Key constraints* protect the integrity of data that identifies rows or establishes the relationships among rows. SQL Server enforces these constraints when rows in the table are inserted or updated, and—in the case of a Foreign Key constraint—when rows in the referenced table are updated or deleted. It's a good idea to begin each constraint clause with the Constraint keyword followed by a constraint name:

```
Constraint CustomerPk Primary Key ( CustId )
```

The Constraint keyword and name are optional, but it's good practice to use them. None of the constraints are required, although most base tables will, by design, have a primary key that serves as the unique identifier for rows in the table. For example, in Figure 9-3, the CustId column is the primary key used to identify customers. A constraint name must be unique within a database.

A Primary Key constraint has this basic form:

Constraint *constraint-name* Primary Key [Clustered | NonClustered]
   (*column-name*, ...)
   [On *filegroup*]

A primary key can have up to 16 columns. The definition of each primary key column must not allow null. For a table with a Primary Key constraint, SQL Server blocks any attempt to insert or update a row that would cause two rows in the same table to have identical values for their primary key column(s). A table definition can have no more than one Primary Key constraint.

A Unique constraint is similar to a Primary Key constraint; however, a column listed in a unique key *can* allow null. A unique key can have up to 16 columns, and a table can have up to 250 Unique constraints. The form of the Unique constraint is also similar to a Primary Key constraint:

Constraint *constraint-name* Unique [Clustered | NonClustered]
   (*column-name*, ...)
   [On *filegroup*]

For each Primary Key and Unique constraint, SQL Server creates an internal index. If you specify NonClustered for any constraint, SQL Server creates a nonclustered index for that constraint. If you specify Clustered for any constraint, SQL Server creates a clustered index for that constraint and nonclustered indexes for all other constraints (only one index per table can be clustered). If Clustered is not specified for any other constraint, SQL Server creates a clustered index for a Primary Key constraint that doesn't specify NonClustered. For Unique constraints, SQL Server creates a nonclustered index unless Clustered is specified. A primary or foreign key index can be placed on a specific filegroup using an On clause, which is discussed in the section "Other Index Options," later in this chapter.

Recall from Chapter 8 that a foreign key is a set of columns in one table (the dependent table) whose column values match the values of a primary or unique key in another, usually different, table—the parent (or referenced) table. A Foreign Key constraint specifies the columns of the foreign key (in the same table as the constraint) and the columns of a primary or unique key in the parent table. SQL Server requires that the parent and dependent tables be in the same database, and each foreign key column must be the same data type and size as the corresponding primary or unique key column.

Consider a Sale table that contains rows with information about sales, including a CustId column that contains the customer ID of the customer who placed the order. You might create the Sale table with the following constraints:

```
Create Table AppDta.dbo.Sale
  ( OrderId   Int   Not Null
                    Check ( OrderId > 0 ),
    CustId    Int   Not Null,
  ...,
  Constraint SalePk      Primary Key ( OrderId ),
  Constraint SaleCustFk  Foreign Key ( CustId  )
             References dbo.Customer ( CustId  ),
  ... )
```

This SaleCustFk Foreign Key constraint specifies that the CustId column in the Sale table is a foreign key that references the CustId primary key column in the Customer table. With this constraint, SQL Server does not allow an application to insert a new row in the Sale table unless the row's CustId column contains the value of some existing CustId value in the Customer table. This constraint also blocks any attempt to update the CustId column of a row in the Sale table to a nonnull value that doesn't exist in any row in the Customer table. In other words, a new or updated Sale row must have a parent Customer row. A Foreign Key constraint also prevents parent table deletes or updates that would leave "orphan" rows (ones with unmatched foreign key values) in the dependent table.

NOTE: If any column in a foreign key is null capable, SQL Server allows a row in the dependent table to have a foreign key with one or more of the foreign key columns being null. Generally, foreign key columns should not allow null.

Check Constraints

The final type of constraint is a *Check constraint*, which specifies a condition that a row must satisfy before it can be successfully inserted or updated. A *column-level* Check constraint tests values for a single column and is coded as part of the column specification. In Figure 9-3, shown earlier in this chapter, the CustId, Name, and CreditLimit columns have column-level Check constraints. The Check constraint for the Name column (shown here) requires that a new or updated value be nonblank, as well as nonnull:

```
...
  Name  Char( 30 )  Not Null
                     Check ( Name <> ' ' ),
...
```

There can be only one column-level constraint for each column, but compound conditions are allowed, as in the constraint for the CreditLimit column:

```
...
  CreditLimit   Money   Default Null
                        Check ( ( CreditLimit Is Null ) Or
                                ( CreditLimit >= 0     ) ),
...
```

A *table-level* Check constraint follows the column specifications and, like key constraints, should begin with the Constraint keyword and a constraint name. Then code the Check keyword followed by a logical expression in parentheses:

```
Constraint CustomerStatus Check
        ( ( Status <> ' ' ) Or ( CreditLimit Is Null ) ) )
```

This constraint implements the policy that a Customer must have a nonblank status once the customer has been assigned a credit limit (even zero). You can have multiple table-level Check constraints, which provides a powerful facility for having SQL Server enforce data integrity.

NOTE: You can also create named *rules*, which are similar to Check constraints, with the Create Rule statement. To associate a named rule with a column or user-defined data type, you use the sp_bindrule system stored procedure. Although named rules provide a way to reuse a rule definition, it is not an ANSI-standard approach. Also, a rule can reference only one column, whereas table-level constraints can reference multiple columns. If you use user-defined data types, you might consider binding a rule to a data type, when appropriate, to further define the valid values for the data type. Combining SQL Server user-defined data types and rules comes close to the capabilities of ANSI-standard domains, which are not available in SQL Server.

Disabling Constraints for Replication

You can add the keywords Not For Replication to a Foreign Key or Check constraint, as shown in the following code, so that SQL Server won't enforce the constraint when a replication process modifies rows. The constraint still is enforced for user modifications.

```
Constraint CustomerStatus Check Not For Replication
        ( ( Status <> ' ' ) Or ( CreditLimit Is Null ) )
```

Creating a Table on a Specific Filegroup

As discussed in the section "Defining Filegroups" earlier in this chapter, you can define filegroups that are sets of one or more operating system files on which application data is stored. To place a new table on a user-defined filegroup, you can add an On clause at the end of the Create Table statement:

```
Create Table AppDta.dbo.Customer
    ( CustId           Int                 Not Null
                                            Check ( CustId > 0 ),
      Name             Char(    30  )      Not Null
                                            Check ( Name <> ' ' ),
    ...
    Constraint CustomerStatus Check ( ( Status <> ' ' ) Or
                                      ( CreditLimit Is Null ) ) )
    On AppDtaGroup1
```

The filegroup must have been previously created with an Alter Database statement.

> **NOTE:** SQL also has a Create Schema statement to "batch" together multiple Create Table, Create View, and Grant statements into a single SQL statement. When a Create Schema statement is processed, SQL Server sequences the object creation so that all logical dependencies (for example, for views and foreign keys) are satisfied. Create Schema is generally used by code generators, but the statement also can be used to create two or more tables with mutually dependent foreign keys.

Adding, Dropping, and Disabling Constraints

After you create a table, you may need to add or remove a constraint. The Alter Table statement provides this capability:

```
Alter Table AppDta.dbo.Sale
   Drop Constraint SaleCustFk

Alter Table AppDta.dbo.Sale
   Add Constraint SaleCustFk Foreign Key  ( CustId )
                 References dbo.Customer ( CustId )
```

The first example drops (removes) the table's Foreign Key constraint named SaleCustFk. The second example adds a Foreign Key constraint. The rules for specifying a constraint with the Alter Table statement are the same as those for the Create Table statement.

If you don't want to enforce a new Foreign Key or Check constraint on existing data, you can add the With NoCheck clause after the table name:

```
Alter Table AppDta.dbo.Sale
   With NoCheck
   Add Constraint SaleCustFk Foreign Key ( CustId )
                 References dbo.Customer ( CustId )
```

You can also temporarily disable a constraint (for example to insert a row that doesn't satisfy the constraint):

```
Alter Table AppDta.dbo.Sale
   NoCheck Constraint SaleCustFk
```

When you're ready to enforce the constraint again, use a statement such as the following:

```
Alter Table AppDta.dbo.Sale
   Check Constraint SaleCustFk
```

You can specify the All keyword instead of a constraint name when you disable or enable constraints. By default, when you enable a constraint, the With NoCheck option is in effect, which allows any rows inserted or updated while the constraint was disabled to remain in the database. To check that all rows in the database still satisfy a constraint when you enable it, add a With Check clause:

```
Alter Table AppDta.dbo.Sale
  With Check
  Check Constraint SaleCustFk
```

Be careful when temporarily disabling constraints or using the With NoCheck option as you add or enable a constraint. Both these circumventions of constraints allow data that doesn't satisfy your integrity rules and could lead to problems with applications that expect all data to meet the table's constraints.

Adding, Dropping, and Altering Table Columns

You can add a new column to an existing table with the Alter Table statement. The following example shows how to add a column to the Customer table created in Figure 9-3 earlier in this chapter:

```
Alter Table AppDta.dbo.Customer
  Add Discount Decimal ( 5, 3 ) Default 0
                                Check( Discount Between 0 And 100 )
```

The Alter Table statement provides flexibility for revising a database table without having to manually delete and re-create it. Note, however, that all new columns must either be null capable or have a Default clause so that SQL Server can initialize the column for existing rows. Otherwise, the rules for new columns are the same as described previously in the "Create a Table" section for the Create Table statement.

The Alter Table also lets you change an existing column's data type, size, and nullability. The following statement sets the Discount column's data type and size, as well as disallows nulls:

```
Alter Table AppDta.dbo.Customer
  Alter Column Discount Decimal ( 7, 5 ) Not Null
```

You cannot generally alter Text, nText, Image, or Timestamp columns; computed or replicated columns; or columns that are referenced in a computed column, a constraint, a default, or an index. The exceptions to this rule are that you can increase the length of a variable-length column used in an index, and you can change the length of a variable-length column used in a Unique or Check constraint. In addition, you cannot alter the type, size, or nullability of a column with the RowGuidCol property. You can add or drop the RowGuidCol property for a UniqueIdentifier column with a slightly different form of the Alter Table statement:

```
Alter Table AppDta.dbo.Customer
  Alter Column RowId Add RowGuidCol
```

You can also drop an existing column from a table with the Alter Table statement:

```
Alter Table AppDta.dbo.Customer
   Drop Column Discount
```

Before you can drop a column, you must drop any constraints, default or computed column expressions, or indexes that refer to the column. You cannot drop a replicated column.

NOTE: The Alter Table statement also lets you enable and disable database triggers, which are covered in Chapter 10.

CREATING A VIEW

In SQL terms, a view is an object that appears like a table to someone performing a database query or to application programs; however, a view doesn't contain any data. Instead, a view is defined over one or more base tables (or other views) and provides an alternative way to access the data in the underlying base tables. You can use SQL views to do the following:

▼ Select a subset of the rows in a base table.

■ Include only a subset of a base table's columns.

■ Derive new view columns based on one or more underlying base table columns.

■ Join related rows from multiple base tables into a single row in the view.

▲ Combine sets of rows from multiple tables using a union operation.

Views provide a way to simplify, as well as restrict, access to data. For example, to provide a view that contains only customers with a credit limit of at least $5,000, you would execute the following statement:

```
Create View dbo.CustHighCredit As
   Select  *
     From  AppDta.dbo.Customer
     Where CreditLimit >= 5000
```

When this Create View statement is executed, SQL Server creates the view definition in the database's catalog. Once you create this view, you can use it just like a table in other SQL statements. For example, you could execute the following Update statement to change the Status column for the selected rows:

```
Update  CustHighCredit
   Set    Status  = 'B'
   Where ShipCity = 'Seattle'
     And Status  = 'X'
```

Notice something important about the way this Update over a view works: only those rows that meet all three conditions—CreditLimit >= 5000, ShipCity = 'Seattle', and Status = 'X'—will have their Status set to B. When the Update statement is processed, SQL Server accesses only rows that satisfy the CustHighCredit view's selection criteria. To those rows, SQL Server then applies the Update statement's selection criteria to determine which rows to update. As this example demonstrates, you can think of a view as if it were a table that contained just those rows with the specified criteria.

The Create View statement is the most complex DDL statement in SQL, and the best way to approach it is to look at one part at a time. Following the Create View keywords, you provide the view name, which is best coded as a qualified name that includes the owner of the view. In the Create View statement, you don't qualify a view name with a database name because the view is always created in the current database. The table and view names used in the view's definition can be qualified, however; this lets you create views over tables and views in other databases. A view name must not be the same name as any base table or other view with the same owner and in the same database.

> **NOTE:**   If you don't code a qualifier for the view name, SQL Server uses the current user.

The next part of the Create View statement is an optional list of up to 1,024 column names in the view. If you don't specify a list of names, which is the case in the preceding example, the view has the column names of the result table defined by the *select expression* (an expression that has a similar structure to the Select statement covered in Chapter 10) specified after the As keyword. The select expression's result table determines which columns and rows from one or more underlying tables or views are encompassed by the view being defined. Keep in mind that a result table is a SQL concept, not necessarily a real table stored on disk or in memory. In the following example, the select expression defines a result table with all the columns from the Customer base table and only those rows that have a credit limit of at least 5,000:

```
Select   *
   From   AppDta.dbo.Customer
   Where CreditLimit >= 5000
```

> **NOTE:**   The asterisk (*) following the Select means *all columns.* When the view is created, SQL Server generates a list of the columns in the result table at the time the view is created. If columns are subsequently added to underlying tables, the new columns aren't included in a view that specifies * for the column list until the view is deleted and re-created.

Defining the View Contents

The select expression is probably the most important (and often the most challenging) aspect of the SQL syntax to master. A select expression specifies a result table derived from the base tables and views listed in the From clause and is used in view definitions, SQL Select, Update, Delete, and Insert statements, and SQL cursor declarations. In the following chapter on SQL's DML (Data Manipulation Language), we delve deeply into the structure of select expressions (and some related parts of SQL). For now, we just look at a few of the simpler parts of a select expression to understand the basic way views work.

The Select Expression

A select expression always begins with the Select keyword. For the simplest select expression, you follow the Select keyword with a list of column names (or * to use an implicit list of all columns) and a From clause that specifies a base table or view. The following Create View statements uses a select expression that defines a result table with all the rows from the Customer table but only a subset of the columns:

```
Create View dbo.CustShip As
   Select   CustId,
            ShipLine1,
            ShipLine2,
            ShipCity,
            ShipState,
            ShipPostalCode1,
            ShipPostalCode2,
            ShipCountry
      From  AppDta.dbo.Customer
```

A SQL statement referencing the CustShip view can treat it as if it were a table with just the columns listed and with all the rows in the Customer table.

The From clause can list a view as well as a table:

```
Create View dbo.CustHighCreditSeattle As
   Select  *
     From  AppDta.dbo.CustHighCredit
     Where ShipCity = 'Seattle'
```

SQL Server combines (ANDs) the Where clauses for a view defined over another view. Given the previous definition of the CustHighCredit view, this definition of the CustHighCreditSeattle view includes only rows from Customer that have CreditLimit $\geq$ 5000 and ShipCity = 'Seattle'.

Spanning Multiple Tables

A From clause can also list multiple base tables and views. For example, the following statement defines a view that joins related rows in the Customer and Sale tables:

```
Create View dbo.Custsale As
   Select  Customer.CustId,
```

```
       Customer.Name,
       Sale.OrderId,
       Sale.SaleDate,
       Sale.SaleTotal
From   AppDta.dbo.Customer,
       AppDta.dbo.Sale
Where  Customer.CustId = Sale.CustId
```

NOTE: The maximum number of tables and views in the From clause is 256.

When you specify multiple tables or views in the From clause, conceptually, SQL Server produces an intermediate result table that has all combinations of all rows from all the listed tables and views. Each row has all the columns from all the tables, as well. From this complete set of combinations, only those rows that satisfy the condition specified in the Where clause are included in the select expression result table. And, only those columns listed after the Select keyword are in the result table. In this example, only rows with matching CustId column values are in the result table. Consequently, the result table contains one row for each sale (with a matching customer), and each row has both sale data and customer data. Because an explicit list of columns is specified following the Select keyword, the result table has only the five columns listed.

NOTE: SQL Server usually takes a much more efficient approach to the actual implementation of a select expression that references multiple tables. What's described here is the *logical* definition of how a multitable select expression works.

As an example of joining two tables, look at Table 9-4 (sample Customer data), Table 9-5 (sample Sale data), and Table 9-6 (sample data as seen through the CustSale view defined in the preceding listing).

CustId	Name
10001	Ajax Plumbing
10003	Picante Software
10008	Bubba's Grill

Table 9-4.   Sample Data in Customer Table

OrderId	SaleDate	SaleTotal	CustId
3678	1998-02-29	567.25	10003
3679	1998-03-06	1089.00	10001
3680	1998-03-06	376.50	10008
3681	1998-03-22	2012.90	10001
3682	1998-03-23	1233.00	10001
3683	1998-04-02	440.00	10003

Table 9-5.   Sample Data in Sale Table

Notice how the select expression column names in this example are qualified with the table name from which the column is taken. For example, Customer.CustId specifies that this column in the result table is the CustId column from the Customer table. To qualify a column name, code the table or view name followed by a period (.) before the column name.

In this example, no explicit names are specified for the view's columns, so SQL Server uses the same unqualified names as in the result table (CustId, Name, OrderId, SaleDate, and SaleTotal). If you were subsequently to refer to the CustSale view's column names using qualification, you would use CustSale.CustId, CustSale.Name, and so on. If there are duplicate unqualified column names in the select expression result table (for example, if both Customer.CustId and Sale.CustId were in the result table), you would have to use explicit and unique column names for the view's columns, as described in the "Reordering and Renaming Columns" section, later in this chapter.

CustId	Name	OrderId	SaleDate	SaleTotal
10001	Ajax Plumbing	3679	1998-03-06	1089.00
10001	Ajax Plumbing	3681	1998-03-22	2012.90
10001	Ajax Plumbing	3682	1998-03-23	1233.00
10003	Picante Software	3678	1998-02-29	567.25
10003	Picante Software	3683	1998-04-02	440.00
10008	Bubba's Grill	3680	1998-03-06	376.50

Table 9-6.   Sample Data as Seen Through the CustSale View

The Where clause of a select expression is optional. If a Where clause isn't specified, the select expression includes all the rows from the underlying base table or view if a single table or view is specified on the From clause, or all combinations of rows if multiple tables and views are specified on the From clause. A Where clause can specify a very complex search condition (such as a test), which we explore further in Chapter 10.

Read-Only and Updateable Views

A select expression can also group together rows with a common value (for example, customers in the same city) and calculate an aggregate value, such as a total or average over one or more columns (for example, an average discount). The Group By and Having clauses specify aggregation and are covered in Chapter 10. For now, the main thing you need to know is that any view that has an outer (not nested) select expression that uses Group By or Having is a *read-only* view. For example, the following view contains one row for each city in which there's at least one customer, and each row has the city name and average customer discount for customers in that city:

```
Create View dbo.CustDiscountAvg
    ( ShipCity,
      DiscountAvg )
  As Select      ShipCity,
                 Avg( Discount )
      From       AppDta.dbo.Customer
      Group By ShipCity
```

This view might have rows that look like this:

ShipCity	DiscountAvg
Seattle	00.056
Eugene	00.009
Portland	00.012
Richmond	00.011
Loveland	00.003
Denver	00.024

NOTE: Notice in this example how a view doesn't specify a particular order to the rows. Ordering of rows in SQL is always specified when the rows are retrieved (in other words, on a Select statement), never when a base table or view is defined.

With a view like this, it wouldn't make sense to allow rows to be inserted or updated through the view. If that were possible, which row(s) would SQL Server change in the Customer base table, for example, if you updated the DiscountAvg value of the Eugene row in the CustDiscountAvg view?

A view is also read-only if the first Select (following the As keyword) doesn't contain at least one column that is derived directly (without an expression) from a column of the underlying base table, or the first Select specifies the Distinct keyword or a column function such as Max. A view with a subquery (nested Select, discussed in Chapter 10) is also read-only. You cannot use a read-only view as the target of a SQL Insert, Update, or Delete statement.

There are additional restrictions on Delete, Insert, and Update statements that reference views. For a multitable view, you cannot use a Delete statement, and an Insert or Update must affect only a single underlying base table. Insert statements aren't allowed if the view omits a base table column that has no default and doesn't allow null. An Update statement cannot directly change the value of a computed column. Generally, the best practice for changing database contents is to perform Delete, Insert, and Update operations directly on base tables or simple views based on a single underlying base table. If you use update operations with more complex views, be sure to test them carefully so you get the intended results.

The preceding CustDiscountAvg example also illustrates how to code view column names explicitly. The column list (if any) immediately follows the view name and is enclosed in parentheses, with commas used to separate each column's entry. The view column names correspond positionally to the columns in the select expression result table. In this example, the correspondence is as follows:

View Column Name	Result Table Column
ShipCity	ShipCity
DiscountAvg	Avg(Discount)

You cannot specify column data types, Null or Not Null, default values, key constraints, or the Identity property for views. The data type and other properties of a view column are determined by the based-on result table column (or expression). SQL includes the Convert function to convert from one column data type or length to another in a derived column.

With Check Option

Another option for a Create View statement is With Check Option. This option restricts row insert and update operations through an updateable view that selects a subset of rows. For example, the following view definition will not allow an Insert or Update operation that would create a row with CreditLimit < 5000:

```
Create View dbo.CustHighCredit As
  Select  *
    From  AppDta.dbo.Customer
    Where CreditLimit >= 5000
  With Check Option
```

This prevents so-called "phantom updates" in which a row is inserted or updated through a view, but cannot subsequently be retrieved through the view. When a view specifies With Check Option and another view is defined over the view with the check option, the check option restrictions also apply to the dependent view. For example, to insert a row into the following view, the row must have CreditLimit ≥ 5000, regardless of whether the CustHighCreditSeattle view definition specifies With Check Option:

```
Create View dbo.CustHighCreditSeattle As
  Select  *
    From  AppDta.dbo.CustHighCredit
    Where ShipCity = 'Seattle'
```

If a view defined over another view specifies With Check Option, all the lower-level views' conditions must be met (in addition to the condition, if any, specified on the view being defined), regardless whether the lower-level view definitions specify With Check Option.

Encrypted View Definitions

The full text of a Create View statement is normally stored in the syscomments system table and can be retrieved by anyone with read access to the syscomments table. You can add a With Encryption option to a Create View statement and the syscomments entry for the view will be encrypted:

```
Create View dbo.CustHighCredit
  With Encryption As
  Select  *
    From  AppDta.dbo.Customer
    Where CreditLimit >= 5000
```

Since there is no way to retrieve the source for an encrypted view, be sure you save the Create View statement in a source file if you use the With Encryption option.

More View Examples

Now that we've covered the basics of how you create a SQL view, let's look at some more examples.

Compound Conditions

A view can select rows using compound conditions. This example selects customers not in Richmond with a credit limit between 1000 and 9999 and a status of A, B, or C:

```
Create View dbo.CustSpecialCredit As
  Select  *
    From  AppDta.dbo.Customer
    Where ShipCity <> 'Richmond'
      And CreditLimit Between 1000 And 9999
      And Status In ( 'A', 'B', 'C' )
```

This example uses some SQL syntax features covered in Chapter 10, such as Between and In, that can improve the readability of search conditions.

Reordering and Renaming Columns

You can reorder and rename columns, as in the following example, which provides abbreviated names for the shipping information:

```
Create View dbo.CustShipAbv
    ( CsStrt,
      CsCity,
      CsSt,
      CsZip,
      CsCrRt,
      CsAttn,
      CsCnry,
      CustId )
  As Select  ShipLine1,
             ShipCity,
             ShipState,
             ShipPostalCode1,
             ShipPostalCode2,
             ShipLine2,
             ShipCountry,
             CustId
         From AppDta.dbo.Customer
```

Derived Columns

The following example illustrates how you can derive columns in a SQL view using substring and concatenation (+) operations:

```
Create View dbo.EmpNamePhonePfx
    ( EmpId,
      PfxVoice,
      FullName )
  As Select EmpId,
            SubString( PhoneVoice, 5, 3 ),
            FirstName + MdlInl + LastName
        From AppDta.dbo.Employee
```

SQL also provides a way to strip trailing blanks before you concatenate fixed-length character columns. The following expression strips both leading and trailing blanks and puts a single blank between each part of the name:

```
LTrim( RTrim( FirstName ) ) + ' ' +
LTrim( RTrim( MdlInl   ) ) + ' ' +
LTrim( RTrim( LastName ) )
```

Notice how in this example, the LTrim and RTrim functions are nested to trim blanks from both ends.

Joining a Table to Itself

A SQL view can join a table to itself, as in the following example that produces a view with one row for each employee, including the ID and name of the employee's manager:

```
Create View dbo.EmpMgr
    ( EmpId,
      LastName,
      MgrEmpId,
      MgrLastName )
  As Select   Emp.EmpId,
              Emp.LastName,
              Emp.MgrEmpId,
              Mgr.LastName
       From   AppDta.dbo.Employee Emp,
              AppDta.dbo.Employee Mgr
      Where Emp.MgrEmpId = Mgr.EmpId
```

The From clause for the select expression in this view lists the same Employee table twice. To have unambiguous references to the appropriate role of the table (that is, either the first role, which is as the whole set of employees, or the second role, which is the set from which matching manager rows are retrieved), each Employee table reference in the From clause is followed by a *correlation name* (also known as an *alias*), Emp for the first reference and Mgr for the second reference. The unique correlation names are used as column qualifiers instead of the ambiguous table name. You can use correlation names in any select expression, not just ones that specify a join. For nested or other long, complex select expressions, short correlation names can make the SQL code more readable.

Joining Four Tables

SQL views can be created over a maximum of 256 base tables, including both tables listed directly on the view's From clause, as well as tables on which views listed in the From clause are based. As a final example, consider the Customer table defined in Figure 9-3 and the three tables defined in Figure 9-4.

Based on the Customer table in Figure 9-3, shown earlier in this chapter, and the three tables defined in Figure 9-4, the view in Figure 9-5 provides a join that shows all the parts ordered by all customers.

Tables 9-4 (Customer), 9-5 (Sale), 9-7 (Part), and 9-8 (SaleItem) show sample data for the base tables. When the view defined in Figure 9-5 is used to retrieve this data, the result would appear as in Table 9-9.

As you can see, SQL has many ways to define the contents of a view. We learn more of them when we study the select expression further in Chapter 10. As you work with SQL

```
Create Table AppDta.dbo.Sale
     ( OrderId   Int   Not Null,
       SaleDate  Date  Not Null,
       SaleTotal Money Not Null,
       CustId    Int   Not Null,
  Constraint SalePk     Primary Key ( OrderId ),
  Constraint SaleCustFk Foreign Key ( CustId )
    References Customer ( CustId ) )


Create Table AppDta.dbo.Part
     ( PartId    Int          Not Null,
       PartDesc  VarChar( 50 ) Not Null,
  Constraint PartPk Primary Key ( PartId ) )


Create Table AppDta.dbo.SaleItem
     ( OrderId   Int Not Null,
       PartId    Int Not Null,
       Qty       Int Not Null,
  Constraint SaleItemPk      Primary Key ( OrderId, PartId ),
  Constraint SaleItemOrderFk Foreign Key ( OrderId )
    References Sale ( OrderId ),
  Constraint SaleItemPartFk Foreign Key ( PartId )
    References Part ( PartId ) )
```

Figure 9-4.   Sale, Part, and SaleItem table definitions

views, here's a tip that can help you test them. Using Query Analyzer, enter a statement
such as the following:

```
Select * From CustSalePart
```

This Select statement displays all columns and rows of the specified view. You can
browse the result to see whether it's what you want.

CREATING AN INDEX

Although you don't specify a particular order of rows on either the Create Table or the
Create View statement, SQL Server does use internal indexes for efficient row selection
and ordering. SQL Server automatically selects which indexes to use when a DML
statement, such as Select, is executed or when a SQL cursor is opened. When you specify a

```
Create View dbo.CustSalePart
     ( CustId,
       Name,
       SaleDate,
       PartDesc )
   As Select  Customer.CustId,
              Customer.Name,
              Sale.SaleDate,
              Part.PartDesc
       From   AppDta.dbo.Customer,
              AppDta.dbo.Sale,
              AppDta.dbo.SaleItem,
              AppDta.dbo.Part
       Where Customer.CustId = Sale.CustId
         And Sale.OrderId    = SaleItem.OrderId
         And SaleItem.PartId = Part.PartId
```

Figure 9-5. CustSalePart view definition

Primary Key or Unique constraint, SQL Server creates an internal index for the base table. You can create additional indexes using the SQL Create Index statement.

The required part of the Create Index statement is fairly simple. You code an index name and then specify a single base table and up to 16 columns over which the index should be created. Index names cannot be qualified because they are always owned by the table owner and created in the same database as the table. The index name must be unique within the set of indexes for a table. To avoid confusion, use index names that are also unique within a database, even though SQL Server doesn't require it. You cannot use Text, nText, Image, Bit, or computed columns in an index; and the maximum total length

PartId	PartDesc
2654	Fax machine
3620	Stapler
4101	Desk

Table 9-7. Sample Data for Part Table

OrderId	PartId	Qty
3678	2654	1
3679	3620	10
3679	4101	2
3680	4101	3
3681	2654	2
3682	2654	1
3682	4101	1
3683	3620	5

Table 9-8.　Sample Data for SaleItem Table

of all columns in the index is 900 bytes. The following example creates an index over the ShipCity and CreditLimit columns of the Customer table:

```
Create Index CustCityCreditIx
  On AppDta.dbo.Customer
  ( ShipCity,
    CreditLimit )
```

CustId	Name	SaleDate	PartDesc
10001	Ajax Plumbing	1998-03-06	Stapler
10001	Ajax Plumbing	1998-03-06	Desk
10001	Ajax Plumbing	1998-03-22	Fax machine
10001	Ajax Plumbing	1998-03-23	Fax machine
10001	Ajax Plumbing	1998-03-23	Desk
10003	Picante Software	1998-02-29	Fax machine
10003	Picante Software	1998-04-02	Stapler
10008	Bubba's Grill	1998-03-06	Desk

Table 9-9.　Sample Data as Seen Through the CustSalePart View

Unlike a view, you cannot access a SQL index directly with any SQL DML statement. In SQL, indexes are solely for the internal use of SQL Server, and their purpose is generally related to performance.

> **NOTE:**   You can optionally specify Unique for an index definition, which has the same effect as specifying a Unique constraint on the Create Table statement. You should use a Unique constraint rather than a separate unique index, because it associates the integrity rule with the table definition.

Clustered Indexes

SQL Server allows one clustered index for each base table. A clustered index has the table data stored with the index and keeps the physical order of the rows the same as the index order. This structure can significantly improve access of rows, especially for a set of rows with contiguous key values. If you frequently access rows in a particular sequence (for example, employees by name), retrieve a related set of rows (for example, order items for a specific order ID), or retrieve rows based on a range of values, consider a clustered index on the appropriate columns. If the columns are already listed in a Primary Key or Unique constraint, you can add the Clustered keyword to the constraint clause on the Create Table, as described earlier in this chapter in the "Key Constraints" section. Otherwise, you can add the Clustered keyword to a Create Index statement, as in the following example:

```
Create Clustered Index EmpNameIx
  On AppDta.dbo.Employee
  ( LastName,
    FirstName,
    MdlInl )
```

If you don't specify Clustered, SQL Server creates a nonclustered index.

> **NOTE:**   There is a space/performance tradeoff to using a clustered index for a long key. When a table has a clustered index, SQL Server stores a clustered key value as the "locator" for each entry in the table's nonclustered indexes. For a large table, this can significantly increase the space required for nonclustered indexes. For a short key, the impact is not so great. For a table with no clustered index, SQL Server uses an internal row identifier as the locator stored with each index entry.

Other Index Options

SQL Server supports several other options on the Create Index statement. These are summarized in Table 9-10.

Option	Purpose
FillFactor = *x*	*x* specifies the percent (0 to 100) of each *leaf* (lowest level) index node (page) to fill when creating a new index over a table that already has data in it. The default is 0, which is equivalent to 100. Interior nodes always are created with enough space allocated for at least one or two additional entries. Note: Do not use FillFactor for a table without any data. Generally, FillFactor is useful only when you know the pattern of future changes to the table.
Pad_Index	Can be used with FillFactor to specify that the same effective ratio of free space should be allocated on *interior* (as well as *leaf*) index nodes.
Drop_Existing	Specifies that the table's existing clustered index should be dropped and rebuilt, then all existing nonclustered indexes rebuilt. This can speed up creation of some indexes.
Statistics_NoRecompute	Disables the automatic recomputing of out-of-date index statistics.

Table 9-10.   Create Index Statement Options

NOTE: The Create Index statement also supports the Ignore_Dup_Key option for backward compatibility. Avoid using this option for new indexes.

The following example shows how to create a nonunique, clustered index with a fill factor of 25 percent:

```
Create Clustered Index EmpNameIx
  On AppDta.dbo.Employee
    ( LastName,
      MdlInl,
      FirstName )
  With Fillfactor = 25
```

To enhance performance, you can create a nonclustered index on a different filegroup than the one containing the table data. To place the index on a specific filegroup, code a second On clause following the column list and other options (if any):

```
Create Index CustCityCreditIx
  On AppDta.dbo.Customer
  ( ShipCity,
    CreditLimit )
  On AppDtaGroup2
```

Indexes can have both positive and negative performance impacts on database performance. In brief, indexes can speed data retrieval, but may slow updates that change the value of index columns due to the time SQL Server spends updating the entries in the index(es) over the base table. As a general rule, be cautious about creating an index over any column that is frequently changed after the row is initially inserted in the table. Such indexes should provide substantial retrieval benefits to balance their impact on updates.

DROPPING DATABASES, TABLES, VIEWS, AND INDEXES

To delete a database object, you use one of the following statements:

> Drop Database *database-name*, ...
> Drop Table *table-name*, ...
> Drop View *view-name*, ...
> Drop Index *table-name.index-name*, ...

Be careful with these statements! When you drop a database, all objects in the database are also deleted. When you drop a table, all indexes and constraints that reference the table being dropped are also deleted. And, when you drop a table or view, all dependent views become invalid until you create another table or view with the same name and with appropriate columns for any references by a dependent view.

All the Drop statements allow a list of objects, separated by commas. The table name for a Drop Table statement can be qualified by a database and owner name. The view name for a Drop View statement or the table name for a Drop Index statement can be qualified by an owner name; you can drop views and indexes only in the current database.

GRANTING AND REVOKING TABLE
AND VIEW PRIVILEGES

NT Server and SQL Server have extensive facilities for controlling access to all objects on the system, including database objects. Many of these facilities are best controlled through the Enterprise Manager or stored procedures, as discussed in Chapter 3. Transact-SQL itself has the Grant, Revoke, and Deny statements to provide an additional means to control database access.

In SQL terminology, a *permission* (or *privilege*) is the authorization to use a table, view, or some other database resource in a certain way. If you have the appropriate authority, you can grant, revoke, or deny permissions using the SQL Grant, Revoke, and Deny statements. You grant permissions to a *security account*, which is a database username or role, or a SQL server login, and then anyone who accesses the database under that security account has the authority you've granted. (Chapter 3 explains the SQL Server security architecture in more detail, including how roles work.)

Object Permissions

Let's suppose you've created a Customer table (and thus are the table's owner) and want to grant the username SmithJH the ability to retrieve rows from this table. You could enter a statement such as this:

```
Grant Select
  On  Customer
  To  SmithJH
```

In a Grant statement, you list the permissions (or the All keyword), then the On keyword followed by a single table, view, or stored procedure name, then the To keyword followed by one or more user or role names. Here's a slightly more comprehensive example:

```
Grant Select,
      Insert
  On  Customer
  To  SmithJH,
      JonesRK
```

NOTE: The table, view, or stored procedure must be in the current database; you can optionally qualify the name with an owner and database name.

To revoke permissions, you use a Revoke statement that has a similar syntax to the Grant statement:

```
Revoke Select,
       Insert
  On   Customer
  From SmithJH,
       JonesRK
```

SQL Server also lets you *deny* permissions. When you deny a permission, you guarantee that the security account cannot get the permission indirectly by inheriting it, such as by being a member of a database role. The Deny statement has a similar syntax to the Grant statement. The following example denies the SmithJH username the Update permission to the Customer table:

```
Deny Update
  On Customer
  To SmithJH
```

To revoke a permission denial, use a Revoke statement, just as you would to revoke a normal permission. The following statement revokes (removes) the permission denial that was made by the previous statement:

```
Revoke Update
  On   Customer
  From SmithJH
```

If you execute a Grant statement for a permission that has previously been specified on a Deny statement, the permission denial is removed when the normal permission is granted (a permission and a permission denial are mutually exclusive).

Table 9-11 lists the SQL permissions you can grant, revoke, and deny to tables and views, as well as the meanings of the permission keywords. For stored procedures, the only relevant permissions are Execute and With Grant Option.

The All keyword can be used instead of a list of permissions, and the implicit list contains those permissions that you're authorized to grant and that are relevant to the type of SQL object.

Keyword	SQL Statement Permissions That Are Granted or Revoked for the Object
Delete	Delete
Insert	Insert
References	Add a Foreign Key constraint that references this table as parent
Select	Select Create View
Update	Update
With Grant Option	Grant Revoke

Table 9-11.   SQL Table Permissions

The public role, which is present in every database, is an alternative to a specific username or user-defined role. When you grant or deny permissions to public, you effectively grant or deny them to all users in a database.

The As Clause

Because SQL Server keeps track of the user (or role) that granted a permission, each Grant statement must be associated unambiguously with a "granting" user or role. In cases where the user executing a Grant statement inherits the necessary permissions from more than one role, the As clause is required to identify which role should be considered the granting role. The following statement shows how to specify that the SalesMgt role is the granting role:

```
Grant   Select
   On   Customer
   To   SmithJH
   As   SalesMgt
```

The Revoke statement has a similar As clause, so you can specify the same role that was used in the As clause of the Grant statement that granted the permission.

With Grant Option

On the Grant statement, you can optionally specify With Grant Option following the list of security accounts. This clause permits the security accounts listed on the Grant statement to themselves grant the same permissions on the listed tables and views:

```
Grant   Select
   On   Customer
   To   SmithJH
   With Grant Option
```

Consider making limited use of the With Grant Option feature, because it complicates security management. For one thing, the indirect granting of permissions is hard to track. Also, you cannot remove a username from a database if the username has granted (and not revoked) permission—via the With Grant Option—to another username in the database.

To revoke the With Grant Option permission (but not the object permissions themselves), use a Revoke statement such as the following:

```
Revoke Grant Option For Insert
   On   Customer
   From SmithJH
```

This statement not only removes the SmithJH user's ability to grant the Insert permission for the Customer table (unless SmithJH also has the capability via some other inherited or granted permission), it also revokes any Insert permissions for the Customer table that SmithJH may have granted to other users as a result of the With Grant Option.

The Cascade Keyword

When you're revoking a permission that was granted along with the With Grant Permission, you must specify the Cascade keyword following the list of security accounts on the Revoke statement:

```
Revoke Insert
  On    Customer
  From  SmithJH
  Cascade
```

This statement revokes the specified permission from other users to whom the SmithJH username granted the permission via the With Grant Option permission. SQL Server maintains a record of the entire tree of permissions granted via With Grant Option, and a Revoke statement that specifies Cascade removes the permission from all of the subtree that was granted permission directly or indirectly from the specified security account.

You also must specify Cascade on a Deny statement that names a security account that was previously granted the With Grant Option permission along with the specified permission. The effect is to deny the permission to the specified security account and to revoke (but not deny) the permission for the entire subtree of security accounts that were granted permission directly or indirectly from the specified user.

Column-Level Security

The Grant, Revoke, and Deny statements also support *column-level* security. In addition to a table name, you can specify a list of the table's columns following the list of permissions. The permissions granted can be Select, Update, or References. The following two statements give SmithJH the ability to retrieve five columns and to update two columns in the Customer table:

```
Grant Select
      ( CustId, Name, ShipCity, ShipState, CreditLimit )
  On  Customer
  To  SmithJH

Grant Update
      ( ShipCity, ShipState )
  On  Customer
  To  SmithJH
```

The Revoke and Deny statements support a similar syntax for column lists, as well.

Statement Permissions

The Grant, Revoke, and Deny statements can also be used to control permission to use certain statements. The following Grant statement shows how the owner of a database could allow SmithJH to create views and stored procedures in the database:

```
Grant Create View,
      Create Procedure
  To  SmithJH
```

The SQL statements that can be listed after Grant, Revoke, or Deny are listed here:

Create Database
Create Table
Create View
Create Procedure
Create Default
Create Rule
Backup Database
Backup Log

The Grant statement for statement permissions does not allow the With Grant Option or As clauses.

THE SQL CATALOG

Each SQL Server database has a set of system tables that store descriptive information about the structure of tables, views, and other database objects. This information includes such things as a description of the tables' columns, constraints, and indexes. Table 9-12 lists these tables, which are collectively referred to as the *catalog*.

SQL Server creates one set of these tables for each database. Because the catalog tables are just like any other SQL tables, anyone with the proper permission can retrieve data from the catalog. For example, you can use Query Analyzer to produce a list of all user tables in the database by entering the following statement:

```
Select    Name,
          Uid
  From    SysObjects
  Where   Type = 'U'
  Order By Name
```

This statement produces a display similar to the one shown in Figure 9-6.

The *Microsoft SQL Server Transact-SQL Reference* manual lists all SQL catalog table definitions, as well as system tables for system-wide information such as the names of databases, data replication, and the SQL Server Agent.

Table	Contents
sysallocations	Database file allocations
syscolumns	Column definitions
syscomments	Descriptions of views, rules, defaults, triggers, Check constraint, and stored procedures
sysconstraints	Mapping of constraints to objects
sysdepends	Table, view, stored procedure, and trigger dependencies
sysfilegroups	Information about default and user-defined filegroups
sysfiles sysfiles1	Information about operating system files used by the database
sysforeignkeys	Foreign Key constraint definitions
sysfulltextcatalogs	Names and information for full-text catalogs
sysindexes	Index definitions
sysindexkeys	Index key definitions
sysmembers	Information about role members
sysobjects	Database object entries
syspermissions	Information about permissions
sysprotects	Grant, Deny, and Revoke statement information
sysreferences	Foreign Key constraint column mappings
systypes	System-supplied and user-defined data types
sysusers	Database users and roles

Table 9-12.   SQL Catalog Tables

DDL CODING SUGGESTIONS

When you create database objects, pay attention to the naming, documentation, and other aspects of the process. A little bit of effort as you get started can make it much easier to use and manage your database. The following items provide suggestions that can help you create and maintain SQL Server objects.

▼   Store most DDL statements to create production databases, tables, views, and indexes in source files and execute them by retrieving them into Query Analyzer or by using the OSQL -i command.

```
SQL Server Query Analyzer - [Query - DELL2100.AppDta.PICANTENT\Administrator - [un...   _ □ ×
  File  Edit  View  Query  Window  Help                                                _ 🗗 ×

  □ 🖙 🖫 ✕ | ✂ 🖻 🖺 🏥 | 🗏 ▾ | ✓ ▶ ■ | 🖵 | 🖻 🖩  DB: AppDta                          ▾

Select      Name,                                                                       ▲
            Uid
  From      SysObjects
  Where     Type = 'U'
  Order By  Name                                                                        ▼
◀                                                                                      ▶

Name                                                                      Uid          ▲
--------------------------------------------------------------------      ------
CustCreditRate                                                            1
Customer                                                                  1
CustUpdLog                                                                1
Department                                                                1
dtproperties                                                             1
Employee                                                                 1
Item                                                                     1
Price                                                                    1
Sale                                                                     1
SaleItem                                                                 1            ▼
◀                                                                                      ▶

  ▤ Results

  Query batch completed.                    Exec time: 0:00:00 | 28 total rows | Ln 5, Col 16
                                                          Connections: 1
```

Figure 9-6.   Sample output from querying the SysObjects catalog view

■ Organize your SQL source files in subdirectories for each database (for
   example, \AppDta). For each type of SQL object, use meaningful source
   filenames that contain the object name as well as an indication of which
   statement(s) are included; for example:

Create Database AppDta	SQL statement(s) to create a database
Create Table Customer	SQL statement(s) to create a table
Create Table All	SQL statements to create all tables in a database
Create View CustHighCredit	SQL statement(s) to create a view
Create View All	SQL statements to create all views in a database
Create Index CustCityCreditIx	SQL statement(s) to create an index
Create Index All	SQL statements to create all indexes in database

■ Place comments at the beginning of your SQL source to describe the object(s) being created.

■ Align column names, data types, constraints, and so on, on multiline statements for readability.

■ Establish and follow a good naming convention for all SQL names. Use only letters (A–Z) and digits (0–9) in names of databases, tables, views, indexes, column names, constraints, and other SQL objects. Avoid SQL reserved words (such as Order) as names.

■ Use user-defined data types or standard column definitions to provide consistent definitions of columns that have a similar purpose; for example, use VarChar(50) for all columns that contain short descriptive text. You can create SQL Server rules and defaults and bind them to user-defined data types to create a similar capability as provided by ANSI-standard domains.

■ Use server connection options and the sp_dboption stored procedure to set various default behaviors to the ANSI standard.

■ On the Create Table statement, code the Not Null option for all columns, except columns that should accept the system null value; generally, code Not Null for unique and foreign key fields.

■ On the Create Table statement, code the Default clause for columns that have an acceptable default for Insert operations that don't supply a value. (Generally, use the Create Table's Default clause for a column, rather than the Create Default statement and sp_bindefault system stored procedure.)

■ On the Create Table statement, code a column-level Check constraint for any integrity constraints that apply to a single column. (Generally, use column-level Check constraints rather than the Create Rule statement and sp_bindrule system stored procedure.)

■ For most tables, define one or more fields as a Primary Key constraint, and use the primary key as the main way you identify rows.

■ Code any key or multicolumn Check constraints after all column definitions on the Create Table statement; use a consistent order—for example, Primary Key, followed by Unique, followed by Foreign Key, followed by Check constraints.

■ Use a consistent prefix or suffix (for example, Pk for Primary Key, Uk for Unique, Fk for Foreign Key, and Ck for Check constraint) in constraint names.

■ Use Primary Key or Unique constraints instead of the Create Index statement to enforce unique key values.

▲ Consider update, as well as retrieval, performance implications to decide which indexes to create.

CONCLUSION

Transact-SQL's Data Definition Language (DDL) is the key to implementing SQL Server databases. Whether you enter DDL statements directly, use the Enterprise Manager's graphical interface, or execute DDL via one of the programmatic interfaces, you'll benefit from a thorough understanding of the statements covered in this chapter. Once you've created the appropriate database objects, you're ready to use the SQL Data Manipulation Language covered in Chapter 10.

ADDITIONAL RESOURCES

In addition to the SQL Server Books Online documentation, there are several helpful books you may want to consult as you create and manipulate database objects:

▼ *Microsoft SQL Server Transact-SQL Reference*. Microsoft Corporation.
This manual provides a complete description of the Transact-SQL language. Although it doesn't provide a tutorial, you'll want to have it (or the online version) handy for looking up the finer points of some language elements.

■ *Microsoft SQL Server Database Developer's Companion*. Microsoft Corporation.
This short manual provides a readable introduction to Transact-SQL. It also describes all the available online books.

▲ Date, C. J., *A Guide to the SQL Standard, Fourth Edition*. Reading, MA: Addison-Wesley Publishing Co., 1997.
This book provides a clear description of the ANSI SQL/92 standard. Having this book at hand can help you choose which of several Transact-SQL statements to use for various purposes. For example, Transact-SQL's Check constraints are part of the standard, whereas rules are not. You can also use this reference to see how fully Transact-SQL, as well as other versions of SQL, meets the standard.

CHAPTER 10

SQL Primer: Data Manipulation Language

In Chapter 9, you learned how to use SQL's Data Definition Language (DDL) to create SQL base tables that contain data and SQL views that provide alternative ways to access data in base tables. In this chapter, we study SQL's Data Manipulation Language (DML), which provides data retrieval and update capabilities for a relational database such as SQL Server. The four main DML statements we cover in this chapter are Select, Insert, Update, and Delete. We also delve deeply into SQL select expressions, which are at the heart of SQL's set-at-a-time retrieval and update facilities. This chapter also introduces Transact-SQL facilities for transaction integrity. In the last part of the chapter, we describe how to write stored procedures and triggers that contain multiple SQL statements.

INTRODUCTION TO DML

SQL lets you define and manipulate data represented in table-like form. SQL base tables contain actual data, and SQL views—which are structured like tables, with columns and rows—provide an alternative way to access the data. SQL's data representation and manipulation features are based on the relational model presented in Chapter 8. The relational model—and SQL—provide data manipulation capabilities that include not only row-at-a-time operations, but also set-at-a-time operations. So, for example, you can retrieve and display a specific row using a Select statement such as the following:

```
Select  *
  From  Customer
  Where CustId = 499320
```

Or, you can retrieve and display a set of rows with this statement:

```
Select  *
  From  Customer
  Where ShipCity = 'Seattle'
```

Both examples retrieve a set of rows; however, if CustId values are unique (for example, if CustId is the table's primary key), the first statement never returns more than a single row. (It might return no rows—the empty set—if there's no customer with the specified customer ID value.) The second example might return any of the following results:

▼ No rows—if there are no customers in Seattle

■ One row—if there's exactly one customer in Seattle

▲ Multiple rows—if there are two or more customers in Seattle

As you can see, a set of rows can have zero, one, or more rows. The important thing is that SQL has the ability to express conditions (such as ShipCity = 'Seattle') that define a multirow set and then retrieve or update that set in a single statement.

Another important aspect of SQL is that previously defined column names (for example, ShipCity) are used to identify the specific data that's retrieved, changed, or used in comparisons. With SQL Server, the information about tables and columns, such as a column's name, data type, and size, is stored in the SQL catalog. These stored descriptions enable SQL database routines to determine how to access the appropriate data without requiring further definition in a query utility or high-level language (HLL) program. This same information also supports SQL Server's interactive Query Analyzer facility, so you can execute SQL DML statements without having to write an HLL program. (The SQL catalog and Query Analyzer are described in Chapter 9.)

The four main DML statements are

Select	To retrieve rows from one or more tables
Insert	To add new rows to a table
Update	To update column values in a table's rows
Delete	To delete rows in a table

All four statements can be used with base tables or views, although Insert, Update, and Delete require that a view be updateable (that is, not read-only). The Select statement can retrieve rows from one or more underlying base tables; however, the Insert, Update, and Delete statements can update only one underlying base table in a single statement.

RETRIEVING ROWS WITH THE SELECT STATEMENT

The SQL Select statement retrieves rows from one or more tables or views. If you enter a Select statement using Query Analyzer, the results are displayed in the Results tab window, as shown in Figure 10-1. You can edit and print the results or save them to a nondatabase file.

To use a Select statement, you list the columns you want in the result, identify the tables and views to access, and specify the selection criteria for returned rows. You also can group and order rows. SQL combines the information you specify on the Select statement with information in the catalog to determine what to retrieve and how to carry out the retrieval. The basic structure of a Select statement is shown here:

Select	*select-list*
From	*table-list*
Where	*search-condition*
Group By	*grouping-column-list*
Having	*search-condition*
Order By	*order-by-column-list*

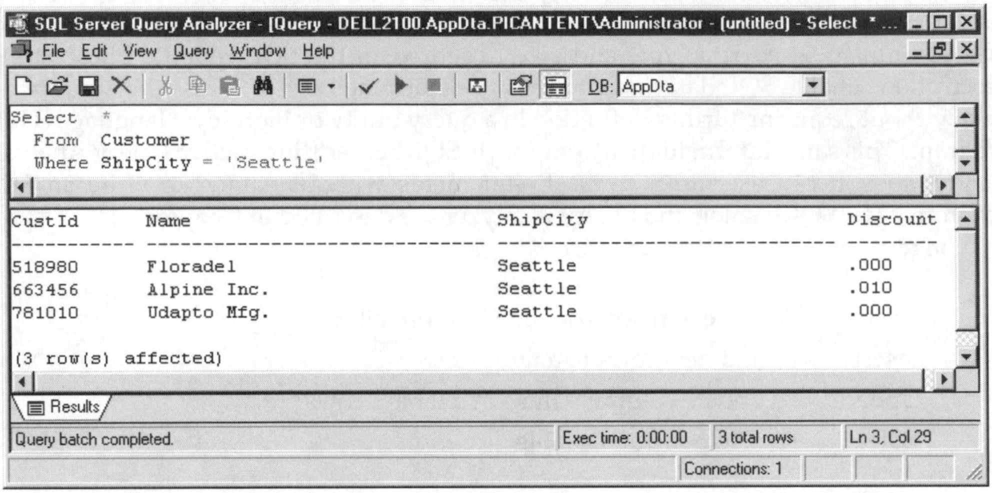

Figure 10-1.   Sample Query Analyzer results

There are several additional clauses that extend the Transact-SQL version of the Select statement, and we'll look at those as well.

Mastering the Select statement, which is powerful and can take quite complex forms, is the key to using SQL successfully. Many of the Select statement's forms are similar to forms of other SQL DML statements, such as Update. And, as we saw in Chapter 9, the select expression (which is part of a complete Select statement) is central to defining SQL views.

The next series of examples work through each part of the Select statement. Many of the examples use the three tables shown in Figures 10-2 through 10-4.

We begin with an example of the simplest form of Select statement:

```
Select *
  From Customer
```

The asterisk (*) that follows the Select keyword means "all columns." The From clause specifies one or more base tables or views to be used—in this case, the Customer table. A table or view name in the From clause can optionally be qualified with a database name and/or owner name (for example, AppDta.dbo.Customer). The examples in this chapter use unqualified table and view names to streamline the code and make it easier to digest. Because in this example no further restrictions are placed on what's retrieved (that is, there is no Where clause), all columns for all rows are retrieved.

```
Create Table Customer
     ( CustId   Int          Not Null,
       Name     Char ( 30 )  Not Null,
       ShipCity Char ( 30 )  Null,
       Discount Dec  ( 5, 3 ) Null,
   Constraint CustomerPk Primary Key ( CustId ) )
```

CustId	Name	ShipCity	Discount
133568	Smith Mfg.	Portland	.050
246900	Bolt Co.	Eugene	.020
275978	Ajax Inc.	Albany	Null
499320	Adapto	Portland	.000
499921	Bell Bldg.	Eugene	.100
518980	Floradel	Seattle	.000
663456	Alpine Inc.	Seattle	.010
681065	Telez Co.	Albany	.000
687309	Nautilus	Portland	.050
781010	Udapto Mfg.	Seattle	.000
888402	Seaworthy	Albany	.010
890003	AA Products	Portland	.010
905011	Wood Bros.	Eugene	.010

Figure 10-2.   Sample Customer base table

NOTE: The * represents all columns that exist at the time the statement is prepared. When a Select statement is executed interactively, it's prepared and executed at essentially the same time. However, in stored procedures or HLL programs, a statement may be prepared during the translation step (as part of program creation) and executed some time later. If a column is added to a table or view after the statement is prepared, the new column will not be included in the implicit column list until the statement is prepared again.

```
Create Table Sale
     ( OrderId  Int      Not Null,
       CustId   Int      Not Null,
       TotalAmt Money    Not Null,
       SaleDate DateTime Not Null,
       ShipDate DateTime Null,
   Constraint SalePk     Primary Key ( OrderId ),
   Constraint SaleCustFk Foreign Key ( CustId  )
     References Customer ( CustId ) )
```

OrderId	CustId	TotalAmt	SaleDate	ShipDate
234112	499320	35.00	1998-05-01	1998-05-15
234113	888402	278.75	1998-05-01	1998-05-04
234114	499320	78.90	1998-05-03	Null
234115	890003	1000.00	1998-05-04	1998-05-10
234116	246900	678.00	1998-05-04	1998-05-08
234117	133568	550.00	1998-05-05	1998-05-08
234118	905011	89.50	1998-05-05	1998-05-10
234119	499320	201.00	1998-05-05	Null
234120	246900	399.70	1998-05-06	1998-05-08

Figure 10-3. Sample Sale base table

Search Conditions

The previous example retrieved all customers, but suppose you want only the customers from Seattle? This can be accomplished by adding a Where clause to restrict the retrieved rows:

```
Select  *
 From  Customer
 Where ShipCity = 'Seattle'
```

The simplest Where clause contains a SQL *search condition* that is a single SQL *simple condition*, as above. All rows for which the search condition is true are retrieved.

When you need to retrieve a single, specific row with a Select statement, you can specify a search condition with a primary key value, as in the following statement:

```
Create Table Employee
    ( EmpId      Int         Not Null,
      FirstName Char( 20 )   Null,
      MdlInl    Char( 1 )    Null,
      LastName  Char( 30 )   Not Null,
      MgrEmpId  Int          Null
  Constraint EmpPk    Primary Key ( EmpId )
  Constraint EmpMgrFk Foreign Key ( MgrEmpId )
    References Employee ( EmpId ) )
```

EmpId	FirstName	MdlInl	LastName	MgrEmpId
104681	Barb	L	Rillens	898613
227504	Greg	J	Waterman	668466
668466	Dave	R	Herbert	Null
898613	Trish	S	Allen	668466
899001	Rick	D	Castor	898613

Figure 10-4. Sample Employee base table

```
Select  *
  From   Customer
  Where CustId = 499320
```

A Where clause with a primary key column lets you use SQL for single-row operations, comparable to an HLL built-in I/O operation (for example, a Cobol Read or Rewrite statement) to read or update a single record.

The Where clause also may contain a search condition that is two or more SQL simple conditions connected with And or Or. The following example shows a search condition with the conjunction (connection by And) of two simple conditions:

```
Select  *
  From   Customer
  Where ShipCity = 'Seattle'
    And Discount > 0
```

To negate a condition, you can specify the Not logical operator at the beginning of any condition or before conditions connected by And or Or. To use Not to negate a compound condition, place parentheses around the condition:

```
Not ( ShipCity = 'Seattle' And Discount > 0 )
```

This condition is true if ShipCity is not Seattle (and not null) or if Discount is ≤ 0 (and not null).

You can also use parentheses to specify the order of evaluation for a compound condition that has both And's and Or's. In the following example:

```
( ShipCity = 'Seattle' Or Discount > 0 ) And TotalAmt > 100
```

SQL Server first evaluates the compound condition ShipCity = 'Seattle' Or Discount > 0. The result of the conditions connected by Or is then And'd with the value of the last condition, TotalAmt > 100. Without parentheses, SQL evaluates negated expressions first; then conditions connected by And; and, finally, conditions connected by Or. Thus, the example

```
ShipCity = 'Seattle' Or Discount > 0 And TotalAmt > 100
```

is evaluated as

```
ShipCity = 'Seattle' Or ( Discount > 0 And TotalAmt > 100 )
```

Note that this is *not* equivalent to the previous example that put parentheses around the conditions connected by Or.

SQL Conditions and Three-Valued Logic

A SQL condition is a logical expression that is true, false, or unknown for a given row. When the ANSI_Null option is set on, as recommended in the "Setting Maximal ANSI SQL-92 Compatibility" section of Chapter 2, a condition is unknown if it involves a comparison and one or both of the values being compared are null. (Recall from the discussion of the Create Table statement in Chapter 9 that a null-capable column—one defined with an implicit or explicit Null property—may be set to null rather than contain a valid value.) For example, the value of the condition ShipCity = 'Seattle' is unknown if ShipCity is null. In general, with ANSI-standard behavior, for any comparison

$$expression_1 = expression_2$$

the result is unknown if $expression_1$, $expression_2$, or both are null. This rule applies whether the comparison operator is not equal, greater than, or any of the other possibilities.

NOTE: When the ANSI_Null option is set off (a practice we do *not* recommend), SQL Server treats null as an actual value. A comparison null = null evaluates to true, and a comparison null = non-null evaluates to false.

To negate a condition with Not or to combine conditions with And and Or, SQL uses three-valued logic (see Table 10-1) rather than conventional two-valued logic.

This somewhat unusual form of logic is necessary to handle a condition whose value may be unknown. As Table 10-1 shows, when you connect two conditions (*p* and *q* in the table) with And, if the value of either condition is unknown, the conjunction is also unknown.

A Select statement's result table contains only those rows for which the Where clause search condition is true. If the search condition is false or unknown, the row is omitted. So, if a row had a null ShipCity column and its Discount column were 0.05, the search condition

```
Where ShipCity = 'Seattle' And Discount > 0
```

would evaluate to unknown, and the row would not be selected. Notice that a row with a null ShipCity column would also be omitted with the following search condition:

```
Where Not ( ShipCity = 'Seattle' And Discount > 0 )
```

Retrieving Data from Views

A Select statement can retrieve rows using views as well as base tables in the From clause (recall that views are SQL objects that define a way to access data from one or more underlying base tables). When you specify a view in a Select statement, SQL Server

p	*q*	Not *p*	*p* And *q*	*p* Or *q*
True	True	False	True	True
True	False	False	False	True
True	Unknown	False	Unknown	True
False	True	True	False	True
False	False	True	False	False
False	Unknown	True	False	Unknown
Unknown	True	Unknown	Unknown	True
Unknown	False	Unknown	False	Unknown
Unknown	Unknown	Unknown	Unknown	Unknown

Table 10-1. SQL Three-Valued Logic

merges the view specifications with the Select statement specifications to produce the result table. For example, consider the view defined by the following Create·View statement:

```
Create View  CustSeattle
   As Select  *
       From  Customer
       Where ShipCity = 'Seattle'
```

The CustSeattle view uses a form of the Select statement (known as a select expression) to specify that the view contains only rows from the underlying Customer table that meet the specified condition: ShipCity = 'Seattle'. You can use this view in a DML Select statement that further restricts the returned rows to customers who get a discount:

```
Select  *
   From  CustSeattle
   Where Discount > 0
```

This Select statement's result table contains only rows from the Customer table for Seattle customers who get a discount. In general, when both the view and the Select statement contain Where clauses, SQL tests the conjunction (effectively using an And operation) of the two search conditions.

Specifying the Columns to Retrieve

Generally, a list of the columns you want in the result table follows the Select keyword. As mentioned earlier, when you specify * following the Select keyword, it means "all columns" in the result table. Rather than specifying *, you can list the columns you want, separated by commas:

```
Select  CustId,
        Name
   From  Customer
   Where ShipCity = 'Seattle'
```

Eliminating Duplicate Rows

When the select list doesn't include the primary key column(s), the result table may contain duplicate rows. For example, the following Select statement returns one row for each customer:

```
Select ShipCity
   From Customer
```

but because only the ShipCity column is in the result table, there may be multiple rows with identical city values. To eliminate duplicate rows from the result table, you can follow the Select keyword with the Distinct keyword, as in the following statement:

```
Select Distinct ShipCity
  From Customer
```

which returns a list of the cities (with no duplicates) in which there is at least one customer.

Constants, Functions, and Expressions

The select list that follows the Select keyword can also include constants, functions, and expressions that use column names, constants, and functions.

> **NOTE:** Transact-SQL also allows the use of the IdentityCol keyword instead of the column name of a column with the Identity property, or the RowGuidCol keyword instead of the column name of a column with the RowGuidCol property.

For example, this Select statement

```
Select  Name,
        ' has a discount of ',
        Discount * 100,
        '%'
  From  Customer
```

uses both constants and an arithmetic expression to retrieve the result table shown here:

Smith Mfg.	has a discount of	5.000	%
Bolt Co.	has a discount of	2.000	%
Ajax Inc.	has a discount of	Null	%
Adapto	has a discount of	.000	%
Bell Bldg.	has a discount of	10.000	%
Floradel	has a discount of	.000	%
Alpine Inc.	has a discount of	1.000	%
Telez Co.	has a discount of	.000	%
Nautilus	has a discount of	5.000	%
Udapto Mfg.	has a discount of	.000	%
Seaworthy	has a discount of	1.000	%
AA Products	has a discount of	1.000	%
Wood Bros.	has a discount of	1.000	%

SQL supports standard four-function arithmetic (+, –, *, and /), as well as modulo or integer remainder (%), for numeric values.

The Transact-SQL string concatenation operator (+) can be used to concatenate (join together) two character strings. If an Employee table has three columns—FirstName, MdlInl, and LastName—to contain different parts of a person's name, the following shows how they might be concatenated into a single string:

```
Select FirstName + MdlInl + LastName
  From Employee
```

This example produces a result table with a single column that is the concatenated result of the three base table columns.

NOTE: Be sure to read the section "Setting Maximal ANSI SQL-92 Compatibility" in Chapter 2. We recommend you always define tables with ANSI-standard padding. With ANSI-standard padding, string values inserted into Char (fixed character) columns are always blank-padded to the size of the column, and trailing blanks on string values inserted into VarChar (variable-length character) columns are never trimmed. Without ANSI-standard padding, padding and trimming are handled differently, depending on the type of column and whether or not it's null capable.

Transact-SQL has four bitwise operators: And (&), Or (|), Exclusive Or (^), and Not (~). The Not operator can be used with the TinyInt, SmallInt, Integer, Bit, Binary, or VarBinary data types; the other operators can be used with the following column data types:

Left Operand	Right Operand
TinyInt SmallInt Integer	TinyInt, SmallInt, Integer, Binary, or VarBinary
Binary VarBinary	TinyInt, SmallInt, or Integer
Bit	Bit, TinyInt, SmallInt, or Integer

SQL also has a variety of scalar functions, listed in Table 10-2, that can be used in expressions.

Data Type Conversion Functions

Function	Description
Cast(*expression* As *datatype*(*length*)) or Cast(*expression* As *datatype*(*precision, scale*))	Converts *expression* to the specified system-defined *datatype* and *length*. The *length* is an optional value in the range 1–8000 for Char, VarChar, Binary, and VarBinary datatypes; and in the range 1–4000 for NChar and NCharVar datatypes. If not specified, 30 is used. Numeric datatypes can have a precision and scale.
Convert(*datatype*(*length*), *expression*) or Convert(*datatype*(*precision, scale*), *expression*) or Convert(*datatype*(*length*), *expression*, *datestyle*)	For character and numeric expressions, the Convert function is equivalent to the Cast function. For converting DateTime and SmallDateTime expressions to character data, *datestyle* specifies the style of date and time representation. Commonly used *datestyle* values are

Parameter Value	Date/Time Format
0 or 100 (default)	mon dd yyyy hh:miAM
1 (USA)	mm/dd/yy
2 (ansi)	yy.mm.dd
10 (USA)	mm-dd-yy
11 (Japan)	yy/mm/dd
12 (ISO)	yymmdd

	Except for 0 and 100, which always return four-digit years, add 100 to a *datestyle* to get a four-digit year (yyyy).
Str(*expression, length, decimal*)	String value representing numeric *expression*. The *length* and *decimal* arguments are optional. The default for *length* is 10. The default *decimal* value is 0.

Table 10-2.   SQL Scalar Functions

Character String Functions

Function	Description
ASCII(*string*)	Returns ASCII integer value (in the range 0–255) of the leftmost character in the specified *string*.
Char(*ascii-code*)	Returns the character for the *ascii-code* value in the range 0–255. Returns Null for values outside this range.
CharIndex(*substring, string*) or CharIndex(*substring, string, start-position*)	Returns the starting position of the *substring* in the *string*. The first position in *string* is 1. If the *substring* is not found, returns 0. An optional *start-position* can be specified, and the search starts with this position.
Difference(*string1, string2*)	Returns a value in the range 0 (worst match) to 4 (best match) representing the difference between two string expressions according to their Soundex values.
Left(*string, length*)	Returns the substring of *string* that is the leftmost *length* characters (i.e., the beginning of the *string* argument).
Len(*string*)	Returns the length of *string*, excluding trailing blanks.
Lower(*string*)	Lowercase of value in *string*.
LTrim(*string*)	Removes leading blanks from *string*.
NChar(*unicode*)	Returns the character for the *unicode* value in the range 0–65535. Returns Null for values outside this range.

Table 10-2. SQL Scalar Functions *(continued)*

Character String Functions

Function	Description
PatIndex(*pattern*, *string*)	Returns the starting position of the *pattern* in the *string*. The first position in *string* is 1. If the *pattern* is not found, returns 0. The pattern must begin and end with %, except when matching the first or last characters. The *string* argument can be Char, VarChar, nChar, nCharVar, or Text datatype. (See the section "Like Condition," later in this chapter, for a description of patterns.)
QuoteName(*string*, *quote-character*)	Returns the *string* as a delimited SQL Server identifier. The quote-character is optional and can be ', ", [, or]. If not specified, the returned string uses [] as delimiters.
Replace(*string*, *match-string*, *replace-string*)	Replaces all occurrences of *match-string* in *string* with *replace-string*.
Replicate(*string*, *count*)	Returns the *string* replicated *count* times. If the *count* is negative, returns Null.
Reverse(*string*)	Returns a string with the characters in the *string* parameter in reverse order.
Right(*string*, *length*)	Returns the substring of *string* that is the rightmost *length* characters (i.e., the end of the *string* argument).
RTrim(*string*)	Removes trailing blanks from *string*.
Soundex(*string*)	Returns a four-character code representing the sound of the *string*.
Space(*count*)	Returns a string containing *count* spaces. If the *count* is negative, returns Null.

Table 10-2. SQL Scalar Functions *(continued)*

Character String Functions

Function	Description
Stuff(*string1*, *start-position*, *length*, *string2*)	Deletes substring of *string* beginning at *start-position* and having specified *length*, and inserts *string2* at *start-position*.
SubString(*string*, *start-position*, *length*)	Returns substring of *string* beginning at *start-position* and having *length* length. The *string* datatype can be any of the character or binary types, as well as Text or Image.
Unicode(*string*)	Returns Unicode integer value (in the range 0–65535) of the leftmost character in the specified *string*.
Upper(*string*)	Uppercase of value in *string*.

Note: Except where specified otherwise, the *string* arguments to the character string functions must be Char, VarChar, nChar, nCharVar, Binary, and VarBinary data types. Constants, column names, and expressions are allowed.

Text and Image Functions

Function	Description
TextPtr(*column-name*)	Returns a VarBinary pointer to the first page of a text column.
TextValid(*qualified-col-name*, *text-ptr*)	Returns 1 if *text-ptr* is a valid pointer to the qualified column name (e.g., Customer.Name). Otherwise, returns 0.

Note: See also the PatIndex character string function and the miscellaneous function DataLength.

Mathematical Functions

Function	Description
Abs(*expression*)	Absolute value of *expression*.
ACos(*expression*)	Arc cosine of *expression* in radians.
ASin(*expression*)	Arc sine of *expression* in radians.

Table 10-2. SQL Scalar Functions *(continued)*

Mathematical Functions

Function	Description
ATan(*expression*)	Arc tangent of *expression* in radians.
ATn2(*expression1, expression2*)	Arc tangent of (*expression1 / expresssion2*) in radians.
Ceiling(*expression*)	Smallest integer $\geq$ *expression*.
Cos(*expression*)	Cosine of *expression* in radians.
Cot(*expression*)	Cotangent of *expression* in radians.
Degrees(*expression*)	Number of degrees in an angle expressed by *expression* radians.
Exp(*expression*)	Exponentiation; natural logarithm (base *e*) raised to power specified by *expression*.
Floor(*expression*)	Largest integer $\leq$ *expression*.
Log(*expression*)	Natural logarithm (base *e*) of *expression*.
Log10(*expression*)	Common logarithm (base 10) of *expression*.
Pi()	Constant value of 3.141592653589793.
Power(*expression1, expression2*)	Result of *expression*[1] raised to the power *expression*[2].
Radians(*expression*)	Number of radians in an angle expressed by *expression* degrees.
Rand(*seed*)	Random number between 0 and 1, optionally specifying an integer expression as the *seed*.
Round(*expression, round-spec*)	Value of *expression* rounded to the specified precision. A positive integer value for *round-spec* specifies the number of positions to the right of the decimal point to round to (e.g., Round(123.456, 2) returns 123.46). A negative value for *round-spec* specifies the number of positions to the left of the decimal point to round off (e.g., Round(123.456, –2) returns 100).

Table 10-2.   SQL Scalar Functions *(continued)*

Mathematical Functions

Function	Description
Sign(*expression*)	Returns −1 when the value of *expression* is negative, zero when *expression* is zero, and 1 when *expression* is positive.
Sin(*expression*)	Sine of *expression* in radians.
Square(*expression*)	Square of *expression*.
Sqrt(*expression*)	Square root of *expression*.
Tan(*expression*)	Tangent of *expression* in radians.

Date, Time, and Timestamp Functions

Function	Description
DateAdd(*date-part*, *number*, *datetime*)	Returns *datetime* plus the interval represented by the *number* of *date-parts*. Only the integral part of *number* is used. The Day, DD, DY, and DW *date-part* values all represent days.
DateDiff(*date-part*, *datetime1*, *datetime2*)	Returns the number of date-part "boundaries" between *datetime1* and *datetime2*. The value is positive if *datetime1* is earlier than *datetime2*; negative if *datetime1* is later than *datetime2*; and zero if the two values are the same.
DateName(*date-part*, *datetime*)	Returns a string that's the name for the *date-part* of the *datetime*. The only *date-parts* with meaningful names are Month and DW. All other *date-part* values return the same value as the DatePart function, converted to a string.

Table 10-2.   SQL Scalar Functions *(continued)*

Date, Time, and Timestamp Functions

Function	Description
DatePart(*date-part*, *datetime*)	Returns an integer value for the *date-part* of the *datetime*. DW values range from 1 to 7. For default (U.S. English) installations, 1 represents Sunday, and 7 represents Saturday; however, you can use the Set DateFirst statement to change the first day of the week from the default of Sunday, and the return value of the DatePart function will adjust accordingly.
Day(*datetime*)	Returns an integer value for the day of the month (1 to 31) in *datetime*.
GetDate() Current_Timestamp	Returns current date and time as a DateTime value. Note that you code Current_Timestamp *without* parentheses.
IsDate(*expression*)	Returns 1 when *expression* contains a valid date string.
Month(*datetime*)	Returns an integer value for the month of the year (1 to 12) in *datetime*.
Year(*datetime*)	Returns an integer value for the year (1753 to 9999) in *datetime*.

Note: For the *datetime* parameters of all of the preceding functions, the value can be a DateTime column or expression value, or a character string in date, time, or date-and-time format. For all *date-part* parameters, the following values and abbreviations are allowed. For each value, the range of return values for the DatePart function is shown. These values aren't case sensitive. Do not use quotes around the values.

Table 10-2.   SQL Scalar Functions *(continued)*

Value/Abbreviation	Range of Return Values
Year or YY	Years (1753–9999)
Quarter or QQ	Quarters (1–4)
Month or MM	Months (1–12)
Day or DY	Days or Day-of-year (1–366)
DD	Day-of-month (1–31)
DW	Day-of-week (1–7; Sun-Sat)
Week or WK	Week-of-year (1–53)
Hour or HH	Hour (0–23)
Minute or MI	Minute (0–59)
Second or SS	Second (0–59)
Millisecond or MS	Millisecond (.0–.999)

User Functions

Function	Description
Current_User Session_User User	Database username of the user executing the statement. Note that you code the Current_User, Session_User, and User niladic functions *without* parentheses.
Is_Member(*role*)	Returns 1 if current user is a member of specified *role*, 0 if not. Returns Null for invalid *role*.
Is_SrvRoleMember(*server-role*, *login*)	Returns 1 if *login* is a member of specified *server-role*, 0 if not. Returns Null for invalid *server-role*. If *login* is not specified, login for current user is used.

Table 10-2. SQL Scalar Functions *(continued)*

User Functions

Function	Description
SUser_SID(*server-login-name*)	Internal security ID (SID) of specified *server-login-name*.
SUser_SName(*security-id*)	Login name of specified internal *security-id* (SID).
System_User	Login name of the user executing the statement. Note that you code the System_User niladic function *without* parentheses.
User_ID(*username*)	ID of specified database *username*.
User_Name(*user-id*)	Database name of specified database *user-id*.

Miscellaneous Functions

Function	Description
@@Connections	Number of attempted connections since SQL Server was last started.
@@Cpu_Busy	Milliseconds CPU has spent doing work since SQL Server was last started.
@@Cursor_Rows	Number of rows in the most recently opened cursor's result set. Returns −1 for dynamic cursors, and for asynchronous cursors returns the current number of rows times −1.
@@DateFirst	The integer value (1 to 7) of the first day of the week (as set by Set DateFirst).
@@DBTS	Current timestamp for the current database.
@@Error	Error number of the last statement executed.
@@Fetch_Status	Status of most recent Fetch statement.
@@Identity	Most recently inserted identity value.

Table 10-2.   SQL Scalar Functions *(continued)*

Miscellaneous Functions

Function	Description
@@Idle	Milliseconds SQL Server has been idle since it was last started.
@@IO_Busy	Milliseconds SQL Server has spent doing I/O operations since it was last started.
@@LangId	Local language ID currently in use.
@@Language	Language name currently in use.
@@Lock_Timeout	Lock timeout setting in milliseconds.
@@Max_Connections	Maximum allowable concurrent connections.
@@Max_Precision	The maximum precision allowed for decimal and numeric data types.
@@NestLevel	Current call nesting (i.e., invocation) level for a stored procedure.
@@Options	Bitmap of current options set by the Set statement.
@@Pack_Received	Number of network input packets SQL Server has received since it was last started.
@@Pack_Sent	Number of network output packets SQL Server has sent since it was last started.
@@Packet_Errors	Number of network packet errors on SQL Server connections since SQL Server was last started.
@@ProcId	Current stored procedure's ID.
@@RemServer	Name of the remote SQL Server database server.
@@RowCount	Number of rows affected by the last statement.
@@ServerName	Name of the local SQL Server database server.

Table 10-2. SQL Scalar Functions *(continued)*

Miscellaneous Functions

Function	Description
@@ServiceName	Name of the registry key of the Windows NT service under which SQL Server is running.
@@SPID	Server process ID of the current user process.
@@TextSize	Maximum length of a Text, NText, or Image value returned by a Select statement (as set by Set TextSize).
@@TimeTicks	Number of microseconds per tick.
@@Total_Errors	Number of disk read/write errors encountered by SQL Server since it was last started.
@@ Total_Read	Number of disk reads by SQL Server since it was last started.
@@ Total_Write	Number of disk writes by SQL Server since it was last started.
@@TranCount	Number of active transactions for the current user.
@@Version	Date, version, and processor type for the current SQL Server installation.
AppName()	Current application name.
Coalesce(*expression1*, *expression2*, ...)	First non-null value from list of *expression*s, or Null if all *expression*s are Null.
Col_Length(*tablename*, *columnname*)	Defined length of *tablename.columnname*.
Col_Name(*table-id*, *column-id*)	Name of specified column in specified table.
ColumnProperty(*table-id*, *column-id*, *property*)	Integer value indicating status of specified *property* (e.g., 'AllowsNull') of specified column in specified table.

Table 10-2.   SQL Scalar Functions *(continued)*

Miscellaneous Functions

Function	Description
Cursor_Status(*name-type, name*)	Status of cursor or result set with specified *name*. The *name-type* can be 'local', 'global', or 'variable' to indicate the type of cursor or variable identified by *name*.
DatabaseProperty(*databasename, property*)	Integer value indicating status of specified *property* (e.g., 'IsAnsiNullDefault') of specified *databasename*.
DataLength(*expression*)	Length in bytes of *expression* value.
Db_Id(*databasename*)	The ID of *databasename*. If no *databasename* is specified, the current database is used.
Db_Name(*database-id*)	Name of specified database. If no *database-id* is specified, the current database is used.
File_Id(*filename*)	The ID of *filename*.
File_Name(*file-id*)	Name of specified file.
FileGroup_Id(*filegroupname*)	The ID of *filegroupname*.
FileGroup_Name(*filegroup-id*)	Name of specified filegroup.
FileGroupProperty(*filegroupname, property*)	Integer value indicating status of specified *property* (e.g., 'IsReadOnly') of specified *filegroupname*.
FileProperty(*filename, property*)	Integer value indicating status of specified *property* (e.g., 'IsReadOnly') of specified *filename*.
FormatMessage(*msg-nbr, parm1, ...*)	Formats message with *msg-nbr* using parameter values *parm1*, etc.
FullTextCatalogProperty(*catalogname, property*)	Integer value indicating status of specified *property* (e.g., 'ItemCount') of specified *catalogname*.
FullTextServiceProperty(*property*)	Integer value indicating status of specified full-text service-level *property* (e.g., 'ResourceUsage').

Table 10-2. SQL Scalar Functions *(continued)*

Miscellaneous Functions

Function	Description
GetAnsiNull(*databasename*)	Returns true if *databasename* is configured to follow the ANSI standard for allowing nulls in columns. If no *databasename* is specified, the current database is used.
Host_Id()	The ID of the current host.
Host_Name()	The name of the current host.
Ident_Incr(*tablename*)	The increment value for the identity column (if any) of *tablename*. Returns Null if the table has no identity column.
Ident_Seed(*tablename*)	The seed value for the identity column (if any) of *tablename*. Returns Null if the table has no identity column.
Index_Col(*tablename*, *index-id*, *key-id*)	Name of specified index column in specified index of specified table.
IndexProperty(*table-id*, *index*, *property*)	Integer value indicating status of specified *property* (e.g., 'IsUnique') of specified *index* in specified table.
IsNull(*expression1*, *expression2*)	Same as Coalesce(*expression1*, *expression2*).
IsNumeric(*expression*)	Returns 1 when *expression* contains a string with a valid representation of an integer, floating point, decimal, or money value.
NewId()	Returns a unique value of type UniqueIdentifier.
NullIf(*expression1*, *expression2*)	Returns Null if *expression1* = *expression2*; otherwise, returns *expression1*.
Object_Id(*objectname*)	The ID of *objectname*.
Object_Name(*object-id*)	Name of specified object.

Table 10-2.   SQL Scalar Functions *(continued)*

Miscellaneous Functions

Function	Description
ObjectProperty(*object-id*, *property*)	Integer value indicating status of specified *property* (e.g., 'IsTable') of specified object.
ParseName(*object-name*, *name-part*)	The *name-part* of the *object-name*. The *name-part* can be 1 – object name 2 – owner name 3 – database name 4 – server name This function simply returns the specified part of the *object-name* string, based on the period (.) as a separator; no validation of the returned value takes place.
Permissions(*object-id*) or Permissions(*object-id*, *column-name*)	Bitmap of the current user's permissions to the specified object or column.
Stats_Date(*table-id*, *index-id*)	Date that statistics were last updated for the specified index in specified table.
TypeProperty(*datatype*, *property*)	Integer value indicating status of specified *property* (e.g., 'Precision') of specified *datatype*.

Table 10-2.   SQL Scalar Functions (continued)

A scalar function takes one or more arguments that can be literals, column names, or expressions. If a column name is used in a function, the function is applied to the column's value in each row in the result table and produces a value for the same row. The following statement shows how you could use the RTrim function to format an Employee name:

```
Select   RTrim( FirstName ) + ' '
     + RTrim( MdlInl   ) + ' '
```

```
         + RTrim( LastName   )
  From Employee
```

This example produces strings like the following:

```
Barb L Rillens
```

Date and Time Arithmetic

Another important use of expressions and scalar functions is to work with date and time values. Externally, SQL represents date values as character strings containing numbers or abbreviations for the year, month, day, and (in some formats) date separators. When you want to enter a literal date, you code the value as a string. The format of the string depends on the language (for example, us_english) and the date format (set with the Set DateFormat statement). For example, with the ymd format, the following string represents May 1, 1998:

```
'1998-05-01'
```

With mdy format, the proper representation is

```
'05/01/1998'
```

SQL provides date addition and subtraction with the + and – operators and the DateAdd and DateDiff functions. The following example uses the DateDiff function to get the number of days between the ShipDate and SaleDate to see how long after a sale the order was shipped:

```
Select  CustId,
        OrderId,
        SaleDate,
        ShipDate,
        DateDiff( Day, SaleDate, ShipDate ) As DaysToShip
  From  Sale
 Where ShipDate Is Not Null
```

This Select statement produces the result table shown here:

CustId	OrderId	SaleDate	ShipDate	DaysToShip
499320	234112	1998-05-01	1998-05-15	14
888402	234113	1998-05-01	1998-05-04	3
890003	234115	1998-05-04	1998-05-10	6

CustId	OrderId	SaleDate	ShipDate	DaysToShip
246900	234116	1998-05-04	1998-05-08	4
133568	234117	1998-05-05	1998-05-08	3
905011	234118	1998-05-05	1998-05-10	5
246900	234120	1998-05-06	1998-05-08	2

Notice how for the first row, the SaleDate is 1998-05-01 and the ShipDate is 1998-05-15, which results in a difference of 14 days between the values for the two columns. If the SaleDate were 1997-05-01 (notice the year) and the ShipDate were 1998-05-15, the difference between the values for the two columns would be 379 days (365 + 14). An alternative way to code this example is this:

```
Select  CustId,
        OrderId,
        SaleDate,
        ShipDate,
        Convert( Int, ShipDate - SaleDate ) As DaysToShip
  From  Sale
 Where  ShipDate Is Not Null
```

This variation uses the minus (–) operator to subtract one date from another, producing a DateTime result. The Convert function converts this to a number of days. Note that if we had just used the expression

```
ShipDate - SaleDate
```

the resulting value for the first row (1998-05-15 – 1998-05-01) would have been

```
1900-01-15 00:00:00.000
```

SQL Server maps the beginning of January 1, 1900, to zero and adds one for each successive day.

The preceding example also shows how the As option can be used to provide a column name for an expression in the select list:

```
DateDiff( Day, SaleDate, ShipDate ) As DaysToShip
```

You can also use As to provide a different name (or *alias*) for a column in the select list.

NOTE: Although you can use this feature to create an alias for a named column, you should avoid a proliferation of aliases because the practice leads to less-consistent names.

Even though you can give a column name to an expression in the select list, SQL doesn't let you use this name in a Where, Group By, or Having clause because column names in these clauses must refer to columns that exist in a table listed in the From clause.

The Query Analyzer interactive utility uses an alias name as a column heading when the query results are displayed. To create column headings that include spaces, enclose the column alias in double quotes:

```
DateDiff( Day, SaleDate, ShipDate ) As "Days To Ship"
```

Note also how the search condition in this example excludes rows with a null ShipDate. Because the Sale table permits the ShipDate column to be null, we must consider the case in which a row has a null ShipDate. For arithmetic expressions, if one of the operands is null, the result of the expression is null. This rule makes sense, as you can see in this example in which the difference between two dates is obviously unknown if one or both of the dates is unknown (null). The Is Not Null search condition lets us eliminate the cases where the ShipDate isn't known because the order hasn't shipped yet.

> **NOTE:** The behavior described here for comparison with a null ShipDate column is based on the recommended setting of ANSI Nulls On (see Chapters 2 and 9). You should never use a comparison operator and the Null keyword (for example, ColA = Null or ColA <> Null), even though Transact-SQL allows it. The ANSI-standard value of any comparison to Null is always unknown, as explained in the section "SQL Conditions and Three-Valued Logic," earlier in this chapter.

Transact-SQL supports time literals and arithmetic similar to the way we've seen for date arithmetic. To code a time value, use a string representation like '13:30:10' for 10 seconds after 1:30 P.M.

Aggregate Functions

Scalar functions work on values from one row at a time. SQL also has *aggregate functions* (or *column functions*) that you can specify in a select list to produce a value from a set of rows. Table 10-3 lists the available SQL aggregate functions. Note that the optional

Function	Description
Avg(*expression*)	Average of non-null expression values.
Count(*) Count(*expression*) Count(Distinct *expression*)	Count(*) returns the number of rows in the result table. (The Distinct keyword cannot be used with this form of the Count function.) Count(*expression*) returns the number of non-null expression values. When Distinct is specified, Count returns the number of unique, non-null expression values.

Table 10-3.   SQL Aggregate Functions

Function	Description
Max(*expression*)	Maximum of non-null expression values. The Distinct keyword can be used, but is meaningless.
Min(*expression*)	Minimum of non-null expression values. The Distinct keyword can be used, but is meaningless.
StDev(*expression*)	Standard deviation of non-null expression values.
StDevP(*expression*)	Standard deviation of the population of all non-null expression values.
Sum(*expression*)	Sum of non-null expression values.
Var(*expression*)	Variance of non-null expression values.
VarP(*expression*)	Variance of the population of all non-null expression values.

Table 10-3.   SQL Aggregate Functions *(continued)*

Distinct keyword can be used with the Avg, Count, Max, Min, and Sum aggregate functions, and causes the function to eliminate duplicate values before aggregation.

As an example, the following Select statement results in a single row with the total number of customers and their average discount:

```
Select 'Average discount for ',
       Count ( * ),
       ' customers is ',
       Avg ( Discount )
  From Customer
```

The aggregate function Count(*) returns the number of rows in a result table. The aggregate function Avg(Discount) returns the numerical average of the set of non-null values for the specified column.

Be careful when you use aggregate functions with columns that allow null. For example, suppose the Discount column allows nulls and that at least one row in the

Customer table has a null Discount column. In this case, the following statement returns surprising results:

```
Select Count( * ),
       Avg( Discount ),
       Sum( Discount )
  From Customer
```

The sum is *not* equal to the average times the count! The Count(*) function includes all rows, but the Avg and Sum functions ignore rows with a null Discount column. There are two solutions to this problem. You can use an alternative form of the Count function, which does eliminate rows with a null Discount column:

```
Select Count( Discount ),
       Avg( Discount ),
       Sum( Discount )
  From Customer
```

Or, you can use a more general solution: use a Where clause to eliminate rows with null columns before the functions are applied:

```
Select  Count( * ),
        Avg( Discount ),
        Sum( Discount )
  From  Customer
 Where Discount Is Not Null
```

When you use an aggregate function in the select list and you don't specify a Group By clause (discussed in the next section, "Group By Clause"), the aggregate function applies to the entire set of rows selected by the Where clause, and the Select statement's result table is always a single row. When you specify a Group By clause, the Select statement's result table contains one row for each group, or—if a Having clause (discussed in the upcoming section "Having Clause") is also specified—one row for each group that satisfies the Having clause's condition.

If the set of rows to which an aggregate function is applied is empty (that is, there are no rows), the result of any aggregate function except Count(*) is null. Count(*) returns zero for an empty set.

You can optionally specify the Distinct keyword immediately after the opening parenthesis of an Avg, Count, Max, Min, or Sum aggregate function to eliminate duplicate expression values (as well as nulls) from the set of values to which the function is applied. The main practical use of this feature is with the Count function, to count the number of different values for a column, as in

```
Select Count( Distinct ShipCity )
  From Customer
```

which produces a one-row, one-column result table that is the number of cities in which there's at least one customer.

Group By Clause

You can use the Group By clause to apply aggregate functions to subgroups of the rows you select. For instance, the statement

```
Select      ShipCity,
            Count( * )      As "Customer Count",
            Avg( Discount ) As "Avg. Discount"
  From      Customer
  Group By ShipCity
```

returns one row for each group of customers in a different city, as shown here:

ShipCity	Customer Count	Avg. Discount
Albany	3	.005000
Eugene	3	.043333
Portland	4	.027500
Seattle	3	.003333

In this example, ShipCity is the *grouping column* that partitions the rows in the Customer table into groups, one group for each different ShipCity value. The aggregate functions Count and Avg are applied to each group in turn and produce one row in the result table for each group. For any null-capable grouping column, all nulls are considered in the same group.

NOTE: In this example, rows with a null Discount column are intentionally *not* excluded, letting the result set have a complete count of the number of customers in each city. The average discount is for the customers with a non-null Discount column.

In the Group By clause, you can list column names or scalar expressions. The following Group By clause creates a separate group for each combination of the calculated DaysToShip and the SaleDate column:

```
Select      SaleDate,
            DateDiff( Day, SaleDate, ShipDate ) As DaysToShip,
            Avg( TotalAmt )                     As AvgAmt
  From      Sale
  Where     ShipDate Is Not Null
  Group By SaleDate,
            DateDiff( Day, SaleDate, ShipDate )
```

Normally, you list grouping columns' names (and expressions) in the select list as well as in the Group By clause so that each row in the final result table has the identifying value(s) for the group. Any other columns that appear in the select list must be used as arguments of an aggregate function.

When you use a Where clause to select rows, you may eliminate all rows for a particular value of the grouping column(s). When no rows are selected for a group, SQL Server normally does not produce a row for the group in the result table. Thus, with the data in Figure 10-2, a statement such as this:

```
Select      ShipCity,
            Count( * ) As "Customer Count"
  From      Customer
  Where     Discount > .01
  Group By ShipCity
```

produces a table that has no row for Albany or Seattle:

ShipCity	Customer Count
Eugene	2
Portland	2

To get a row for *every* grouping value, even those with no rows in the group, use the All keyword immediately after the Group By keywords:

```
Select      ShipCity,
            Count( * ) As "Customer Count"
  From      Customer
  Where     Discount > .01
  Group By All ShipCity
```

This will produce the following result:

ShipCity	Customer Count
Albany	0
Eugene	2
Portland	2
Seattle	0

Having Clause

You can use the Having clause to restrict rows in the result table after aggregate functions have been applied to grouped rows. The Having clause has a form similar to the form of the Where clause, which selects rows before they are grouped. For example, you could enter the following Select statement:

```
Select      ShipCity,
            Count( * )       As "Customer Count",
            Avg( Discount ) As "Avg. Discount"
```

```
From      Customer
Where     Discount Is Not Null
Group By  ShipCity
Having    Avg( Discount ) > .01
```

to retrieve the information shown here for cities with an average discount above one percent.

ShipCity	Customer Count	Avg. Discount
Eugene	3	.043333
Portland	4	.027500

The search condition for a Having clause can include grouping columns such as ShipCity or aggregate functions such as Avg(Discount).

NOTE: Although you can specify a Having clause without a Group By clause, this is very unusual.

There's a conceptual ordering to a select expression (the part of a Select statement that we've been discussing up to this point) that helps clarify when the search conditions of the Where and Having clauses are tested, as well as how the other clauses come into play. Each step produces a hypothetical result table from the intermediate result table of the previous step. The steps are as follows:

1. All combinations of all rows from all tables and views listed in the From clause are included in an intermediate result table produced by this step. (If only one table or view is specified in the From clause, the intermediate result table's columns and rows are the same as those in the specified table or view.)

2. If a Where clause is specified, the search condition is applied to each row in the result table produced by Step 1. Only those rows for which the search condition is true are included in the intermediate result table produced by this step. (If no Where clause is specified, all rows from the result table produced in Step 1 are included.)

3. If a Group By clause is specified, the rows from the result table produced in the previous steps are collected into separate groups such that all the rows in a group have the same values for all grouping columns. (If no Group By clause is specified, all the rows are considered as one group.)

4. If a Having clause is specified, the search condition is applied to each group. Only those groups of rows for which the search condition is true are included in the intermediate result table produced by this step. (If no Having clause is specified, all groups (and rows) from the result table produced in the previous steps are included.)

If a Having clause is specified but no Group By clause is specified, the intermediate result table produced by this step is either empty or contains all rows produced in the previous steps.

5. If neither a Group By nor a Having clause is specified, the intermediate result table produced by this step includes the rows in the result table produced in steps 1 and 2. Each row contains the direct and derived columns specified in the select list.

    If either a Group By or Having clause or both clauses are specified, the intermediate result table produced by this step includes one row for each group of rows produced in steps 1 through 4. (If the previous result table was empty, the result table produced by this step is also empty.) Each row contains any grouping columns included in the select list as well as the result of applying any aggregate function(s) in the select list to the group.

6. If the Distinct keyword is specified for the select list, duplicate rows are eliminated in the result table produced in the previous steps; otherwise, all rows are included in the final result table.

While this sequence of steps provides a way to understand the result of a select expression, it isn't necessarily how SQL Server actually carries out a Select or other statement. The SQL Server optimizer may use indexes or other techniques to produce equivalent results.

Using a Where Clause Versus a Having Clause

Because you can use either a Where clause or a Having clause for selecting rows based on the value of a grouping column, you can choose either of the following statements to retrieve the average discount of customers in Portland or Seattle:

```
Select     ShipCity,
           Avg( Discount )
  From     Customer
  Where    ShipCity In ( 'Portland', 'Seattle' )
  Group By ShipCity
```

or

```
Select     ShipCity,
           Avg( Discount )
  From     Customer
  Group By ShipCity
  Having   ShipCity In ( 'Portland', 'Seattle' )
```

Using a Where clause is a clearer way to code this retrieval, and in some cases putting a test in the Where clause performs significantly faster than putting it in the Having clause because SQL Server can eliminate rows before the grouping step and the calculation of aggregate function values.

The Order By Clause

You can use the Order By clause to sequence a Select statement's result table before it's displayed or returned to your program. An Order By clause specifies a list of columns with ascending or descending (with the Desc keyword) sequence. For an unnamed column in the result table (for example, one specified by an expression or function and not having an alias), you can use a relative column number instead of a column name to specify that the unnamed column is used to sequence the rows.

NOTE: An Order By clause is *not* part of the select expression but is valid only in a Select statement. Thus, you can use an Order By clause when you execute an interactive Select or in an Insert statement, or when you declare a cursor in a program, but you can't use an Order By clause in a view definition.

The following statement retrieves shipped orders sequenced by customer ID and within customer ID, by the number of days (longest interval first) it took to ship the order:

```
Select    CustId,
          OrderId,
          SaleDate,
          ShipDate,
          DateDiff( Day, SaleDate, ShipDate )
   From   Sale
   Where  ShipDate Is Not Null
Order By CustId,
          5 Desc
```

In this case, the unnamed fifth column that results from the DateDiff(Day, SaleDate, ShipDate) expression is used to sequence rows within the same CustId value.

For a more readable version of this statement, code an alias name for a derived column by following an expression or function with the As keyword and a column name. Here's the previous example rewritten to use this technique:

```
Select    CustId,
          OrderId,
          SaleDate,
          ShipDate,
          DateDiff( Day, SaleDate, ShipDate ) As DaysToShip
   From   Sale
   Where  ShipDate Is Not Null
Order By CustId,
          DaysToShip Desc
```

Complex Select Statements

The previous examples illustrate the basic parts of a Select statement. In the next examples, we look at a few more complex variations, starting with the select list. We'll also cover some additional clauses available with Transact-SQL.

Specifying Multiple Tables in the From Clause

The From clause can list up to 256 tables and views. If you list more than one table or view in the From clause, the Select statement executes as if you had specified a single table that has all the columns from the specified tables and all possible combinations of rows from the tables (that is, the Cartesian product of the two tables). This potentially large intermediate table isn't always created when you execute a multitable Select statement, but that's the simplest way to think about what happens. For example, the two tables in Figures 10-2 and 10-3 can be used in the following Select statement:

```
Select *
  From Customer,
       Sale
```

The result, shown in Table 10-4, isn't very useful because some rows combine information from unrelated customers and sales.

Customer table columns   Sale table columns

CustId	Name	ShipCity	Discount	OrderId	CustId	TotalAmt	SaleDate	ShipDate
133568	Smith Mfg.	Portland	.050	234112	499320	35.00	1998-05-01	1998-05-15
133568	Smith Mfg.	Portland	.050	234113	888402	278.75	1998-05-01	1998-05-04
133568	Smith Mfg.	Portland	.050	234114	499320	78.90	1998-05-03	Null
133568	Smith Mfg.	Portland	.050	234115	890003	1,000.00	1998-05-04	1998-05-10
133568	Smith Mfg.	Portland	.050	234116	246900	678.00	1998-05-04	1998-05-08

Table 10-4.   Sample Retrieval Using Cartesian Product

CustId	Name	ShipCity	Discount	OrderId	CustId	TotalAmt	SaleDate	ShipDate
133568	Smith Mfg.	Portland	.050	234117	133568	550.00	1998-05-05	1998-05-08
133568	Smith Mfg.	Portland	.050	234118	905011	89.50	1998-05-05	1998-05-10
133568	Smith Mfg.	Portland	.050	234119	499320	201.00	1998-05-05	Null
133568	Smith Mfg.	Portland	.050	234120	246900	399.70	1998-05-06	1998-05-08
246900	Bolt Co.	Eugene	.020	234112	499320	35.00	1998-05-01	1998-05-15
246900	Bolt Co.	Eugene	.020	234113	888402	278.75	1998-05-01	1998-05-04
246900	Bolt Co.	Eugene	.020	234114	499320	78.90	1998-05-03	Null
246900	Bolt Co.	Eugene	.020	234115	890003	1,000.00	1998-05-04	1998-05-10
246900	Bolt Co.	Eugene	.020	234116	246900	678.00	1998-05-04	1998-05-08
246900	Bolt Co.	Eugene	.020	234117	133568	550.00	1998-05-05	1998-05-08
246900	Bolt Co.	Eugene	.020	234118	905011	89.50	1998-05-05	1998-05-10
246900	Bolt Co.	Eugene	.020	234119	499320	201.00	1998-05-05	Null
246900	Bolt Co.	Eugene	.020	234120	246900	399.70	1998-05-06	1998-05-08
275978	Ajax Inc.	Albany	Null	234112	499320	35.00	1998-05-01	1998-05-15
275978	Ajax Inc.	Albany	Null	234113	888402	278.75	1998-05-01	1998-05-04
275978	Ajax Inc.	Albany	Null	234114	499320	78.90	1998-05-03	Null
275978	Ajax Inc.	Albany	Null	234115	890003	1,000.00	1998-05-04	1998-05-10
275978	Ajax Inc.	Albany	Null	234116	246900	678.00	1998-05-04	1998-05-08
275978	Ajax Inc.	Albany	Null	234117	133568	550.00	1998-05-05	1998-05-08
275978	Ajax Inc.	Albany	Null	234118	905011	89.50	1998-05-05	1998-05-10
275978	Ajax Inc.	Albany	Null	234119	499320	201.00	1998-05-05	Null
275978	Ajax Inc.	Albany	Null	234120	246900	399.70	1998-05-06	1998-05-08
499320	Adapto	Portland	.000	234112	499320	35.00	1998-05-01	1998-05-15

Table 10-4. Sample Retrieval Using Cartesian Product *(continued)*

CustId	Name	ShipCity	Discount	OrderId	CustId	TotalAmt	SaleDate	ShipDate
499320	Adapto	Portland	.000	234113	888402	278.75	1998-05-01	1998-05-04
Omitted rows ...								
890003	AA Products	Portland	.010	234119	499320	201.00	1998-05-05	Null
890003	AA Products	Portland	.010	234120	246900	399.70	1998-05-06	1998-05-08
905011	Wood Bros.	Eugene	.010	234112	499320	35.00	1998-05-01	1998-05-15
905011	Wood Bros.	Eugene	.010	234113	888402	278.75	1998-05-01	1998-05-04
905011	Wood Bros.	Eugene	.010	234114	499320	78.90	1998-05-03	Null
905011	Wood Bros.	Eugene	.010	234115	890003	1,000.00	1998-05-04	1998-05-10
905011	Wood Bros.	Eugene	.010	234116	246900	678.00	1998-05-04	1998-05-08
905011	Wood Bros.	Eugene	.010	234117	133568	550.00	1998-05-05	1998-05-08
905011	Wood Bros.	Eugene	.010	234118	905011	89.50	1998-05-05	1998-05-10
905011	Wood Bros.	Eugene	.010	234119	499320	201.00	1998-05-05	Null
905011	Wood Bros.	Eugene	.010	234120	246900	399.70	1998-05-06	1998-05-08

Table 10-4. Sample Retrieval Using Cartesian Product *(continued)*

But if you use a select list and add a Where clause, you get a very useful table:

```
Select  Sale.OrderId,
        Sale.CustId,
        Customer.Name
```

```
From  Customer,
      Sale
Where Sale.CustId = Customer.CustId
```

The resulting table, shown here, provides a list with the customer ID and name for each sale:

OrderId	CustId	Name
234112	499320	Adapto
234113	888402	Seaworthy
234114	499320	Adapto
234115	890003	AA Products
234116	246900	Bolt Co.
234117	133568	Smith Mfg.
234118	905011	Wood Bros.
234119	499320	Adapto
234120	246900	Bolt Co.

This two-table operation is an *equijoin*, one of the most common and useful relational database operations. An equijoin selects only those rows from the Cartesian product in which related columns from separate tables have identical values; in this example, the equijoin selects columns in which the customer ID of the sale (Sale.CustId) matches the customer ID of the customer (Customer.CustId). In addition to the equijoin, SQL allows tables to be joined using other comparison operators such as greater than (>) or not equal (<>). As this example illustrates, when a column with the same name exists in more than one table, you use a qualified column name of the form *table.column* to avoid ambiguity.

NOTE: As the next example shows, the qualifier can be a correlation name rather than a table name.

You also can join a table to itself. That is, a table can assume several roles in the From clause. To keep clear which table role you mean when you specify a column name in any of the other clauses, you must add a unique *correlation name* (also known as a *table alias*) for any table listed more than once in a From clause. For example, you could enter the following statement

```
Select   Emp.EmpId,
         Emp.LastName,
         Mgr.LastName
  From   Employee As Emp,
         Employee As Mgr
  Where Emp.MgrEmpId = Mgr.EmpId
```

to produce the table shown here, which includes both employees' names and their managers' names:

Emp.EmpId	Emp.LastName	Mgr.LastName
104681	Rillens	Allen
227504	Waterman	Herbert
898613	Allen	Herbert
899001	Castor	Allen

In this example, the Employee table is used in two roles: once to provide the set of employees (correlation name Emp) and once to provide a lookup table to find the corresponding name for each MgrEmpId value (correlation name Mgr). A correlation name follows the table name and optional As keyword. Using a qualified column name such as Emp.LastName makes it clear from which role of the Employee table the column value is drawn.

For simple *inner joins* between two tables (where unmatched rows are dropped from the result), techniques using the From and Where clauses work fine. For more complex *outer joins* (where unmatched rows are retained in the result), or for cases where more than two tables are used in a query that has one or more joins, you can use explicit join syntax in the From clause. The previous example could be coded as follows:

```
Select   Emp.EmpId,
         Emp.LastName,
         Mgr.LastName
  From   Employee As Emp
         Join
         Employee As Mgr
         On Emp.MgrEmpId = Mgr.EmpId
```

SQL Server also has variations of the join syntax to support the left outer, right outer, and full outer join variations described in Chapter 8. The syntax for a left outer join looks like this:

```
Select   Customer.CustId,
         Customer.Name,
         Sale.SaleDate
  From   Customer
         Left Outer Join
         Sale
         On Customer.CustId = Sale.CustId
```

This Select statement's result is shown in Table 10-5.

CustId	Name	SaleDate
133568	Smith Mfg.	1998-05-05
246900	Bolt Co.	1998-05-04
246900	Bolt Co.	1998-05-06
275978	Ajax Inc.	Null
499320	Adapto	1998-05-01
499320	Adapto	1998-05-03
499320	Adapto	1998-05-05
499921	Bell Bldg.	Null
518980	Floradel	Null
663456	Alpine Inc.	Null
681065	Telez Co.	Null
687309	Nautilus	Null
781010	Udapto Mfg.	Null
888402	Seaworthy	1998-05-01
890003	AA Products	1998-05-04
905011	Wood Bros.	1998-05-05

Table 10-5. Sample Retrieval Using Left Outer Join

The syntax for a right outer join uses the Right Outer Join keywords and extends unmatched rows from the table on the right-hand side of the operator with nulls. If you use the Full Outer Join keywords, unmatched rows from both tables are extended as described for the left and right outer joins.

> **NOTE:**   SQL Server also has nonstandard join operators *= (left outer equijoin) and =* (right outer equijoin) for compatibility with previous releases. These operators are not equivalent to the ANSI-standard join keywords described above and shouldn't be used for new queries.

The Union Keyword

You can also derive a left outer join by specifying the union of two sets: the set of matched (and hence joined) rows and the set that is the first (that is, the left) table's unmatched rows extended with null (or any other value) for the column(s) drawn from the second table. For example, you could enter the following Select statement to retrieve the left outer join that contains all customers and their sale dates, if any:

```
Select  Customer.CustId,
        Customer.Name,
        Sale.SaleDate
  From  Customer,
        Sale
 Where Customer.CustId = Sale.CustId
Union
Select  Customer.CustId,
        Customer.Name,
        Null As SaleDate
  From  Customer
 Where Not Exists
       ( Select  *
           From  Sale
          Where Sale.CustId = Customer.CustId )
```

This example uses the SQL Union operator, which combines the rows from two select expressions' result tables into a single result table. The first Select retrieves the Customer rows with at least one matching Sale row (the inner join). The second Select uses a nested Select (explained later in the section "Exists Condition") to return only unmatched rows. Essentially, the second set of rows includes one row for each Customer row where there does not exist any matching row in the Sale table. The result of the complete Select statement (the union of the two select expressions) is the same as for the left outer join example, as shown in Table 10-5.

A Select statement that contains a Union operator can specify a result table as the union of two or more intermediate result tables defined by select expressions. Recall that a select expression is the form of SQL expression that starts with the Select keyword, has a

From clause, and can optionally have Where, Group By, or Having clauses. A select expression (by itself) does not have a Union operator or an Order By clause. A complete Select statement, which can be a simple select expression or the union of two or more select expressions, can have an Order By clause. When the Select statement contains a Union operator, the Order By clause is specified after the last select expression and determines the order of the resulting union of the rows in the select expressions.

To specify the union of two select expressions, the select expressions' result tables must be *union-compatible*, which means they must have the same number of columns and each pair of corresponding columns (by position in the respective select lists) must have compatible column definitions (either the same data type or allowing an implicit conversion). The result table column name is the column name or alias used in the first select expression.

When you specify the Union operator, duplicate rows are normally eliminated from the final result table. Two rows are duplicates if all columns in the result table have identical values. You can specify Union All to include duplicate rows in the result table. The following example illustrates the use of Union All to get the last names of all employees and contractors:

```
Select    LastName
   From   Employee
Union All
Select    LastName
   From   Contractor
```

Another technique you can use is to add a tag column to each row of the result table to show from which select expression the row came. The following Select statement retrieves the names (including people with the same name) of all employees and contractors, ordered by the person's name:

```
Select    'Employee' As Tag,
          FirstName,
          MdlInl,
          LastName
   From   Employee
Union All
Select    'Contractor' As Tag,
          FirstName,
          MdlInl,
          LastName
   From   Contractor
Order By LastName,
          FirstName,
          MdlInl
```

As the sample results here show, each row includes a tag to indicate whether the person is an employee or a contractor.

Tag	FirstName	MdlInl	LastName
Employee	Trish	S	Allen
Employee	Rick	D	Castor
Contractor	Bill	M	Dutcher
Employee	Dave	R	Herbert
Contractor	Cricket	S	Katz
Contractor	Tim	L	Murphy
Employee	Barb	L	Rillens
Contractor	Richard	M	Russle
Employee	Greg	J	Waterman

This example also shows how you code an Order By clause to sequence the rows in a Select statement that's the union of two select expressions.

The previous examples have touched on most parts of the Select statement. In the next section, we delve deeper into the search condition used in Where and Having clauses. The search condition is an important part of the select expression, which is at the heart of SQL's set-at-a-time facilities and must be well understood to make effective use of views; the Select, Insert, Update, and Delete statements; and SQL cursors.

Conditions and Subqueries

As we've seen, the Where and Having clauses of a select expression have a search condition that contains either a simple condition or multiple simple conditions connected by And or Or. Recall that a simple condition specifies a logical expression that evaluates to true, false, or unknown. SQL has several kinds of conditions, including Basic, Null, Between, In, Like, Exists, and Quantified.

> **NOTE:** The Text, NText, and Image data types can be used only in the Like condition and within functions such as PatIndex that allow Text and Image arguments. The Text and Image data types can't be used in the select list of a subquery.

Basic Condition

A basic condition compares two values using one of the comparison operators listed here:

Operator	Meaning
=	Equal
<>	Not equal

Operator	Meaning
<	Less than
<=	Less than or equal
>	Greater than
>=	Greater than or equal

Transact-SQL also allows the following equivalent operators:

Operator	Equivalent to
!=	<>
!<	>=
!>	<=

We've already seen several examples of the simpler form of basic condition, which has the general syntax

$$expression_1 \ \theta \ expression_2$$

where each expression is a column name, literal, or some valid arithmetic, string, or other form of expression; and θ is one of the logical comparison operators shown in the preceding tables. An example of this type of condition is this:

```
Customer.CustId = Sale.CustId
```

A basic condition also can take the following form:

$$expression \ \theta \ (select\text{-}expression)$$

where *expression* and θ have the same meaning as above and the *select-expression* specifies exactly one column and produces a result table with exactly one row. The following Select statement displays all customers who have an above average discount:

```
Select  CustId,
        Name
  From  Customer
  Where Discount > ( Select Avg( Discount )
                       From Customer )
```

A select expression that's used in a search condition is known as a *subquery*. In the preceding example, the subquery is

```
Select Avg( Discount )
  From Customer
```

This particular subquery produces a scalar value—that is, a result table with a single row and one column. In this case, the value is the average discount for all customers. The search condition in the outer Select statement then compares each customer's discount to the average discount and includes in the Select statement's result table only those Customer rows with a Discount column value greater than the average.

Null Condition

Recall that, with ANSI-standard behavior, a comparison between two values is unknown if either or both of the values is null. The Null condition provides a way to test for null or not null, using a syntax such as

```
Where ShipDate Is Null
```

or

```
Where ShipDate Is Not Null
```

Between Condition

SQL also has some shorthand forms for compound conditions. The Between condition is an alternative to two inequality tests. The search condition

```
Where Discount Between 0.01 And 0.02
```

is equivalent to

```
Where Discount >= 0.01
   And Discount <= 0.02
```

You also can use

```
Where Discount Not Between 0.01 And 0.02
```

which is equivalent to

```
Where Discount < 0.01
   Or Discount > 0.02
```

In Condition

To simplify a series of equality tests, you can use the In condition. A search condition such as

```
Where ShipCity In ( 'Eugene', 'Portland', 'Seattle' )
```

is equivalent to

```
Where ShipCity = 'Eugene'
   Or ShipCity = 'Portland'
   Or ShipCity = 'Seattle'
```

Another form of the In condition lets you use a subquery to define the set of values to be compared:

```
Select  CustId,
        Name
  From  Customer
 Where  ShipCity In ( Select Distinct City
                        From Warehouse )
```

In this example, the subquery produces a result table with one row for each city in which there's a warehouse. Each row from the Customer table is then selected only if the row's ShipCity column contains one of the cities in the subquery's result table. The Select statement's final result table has only those customers who are in the same city as a warehouse. Note that an In condition's subquery must specify a result table with just one column. You also can specify the Not keyword before either form of In condition to negate the test.

For those conditions that allow a subquery with multiple rows, you can use the Union operator in the subquery. The following example shows how to code this type of test:

```
Select  CustId,
        Name,
        ShipCity
  From  Customer
 Where  ShipCity In ( Select  ShipCity
                        From  Customer
                       Where CustId = 246900
                      Union
                      Select  ShipCity
                        From  Customer
                       Where CustId = 687309 )
```

With the data in Figure 10-2, this statement produces the following results:

CustId	Name	ShipCity
133568	Smith Mfg.	Portland
246900	Bolt Co.	Eugene
499320	Adapto	Portland
499921	Bell Bldg.	Eugene
687309	Nautilus	Portland
890003	AA Products	Portland
905011	Wood Bros.	Eugene

Like Condition

The Like condition provides string pattern matching. A Select statement with a search condition such as

```
Select   CustId,
         Name
   From  Customer
  Where Name Like '%Steel%'
```

would display customers with the string Steel anywhere in the name. The following names would be included:

> Ajax Consolidated Steel
> Portland Steel Yards
> Steel Fabricators of the Northwest
> John Steeling Grocery Company
> Umpqua Steelhead Fly Fishing Guides

The expression before the Like keyword must identify a string (for example, a character or date/time column or a string function, such as SubString). Following the Like keyword, you code a string literal. This string provides the pattern to be matched. In the pattern, you can use the percent character (%) to represent a substring of zero or more occurrences of any character or the underscore character (_) to represent a substring of exactly one occurrence of any character. The following condition tests for names that are exactly four characters long and end in 'ick':

```
Name Like '_ick'
```

This pattern matches Dick, Rick, Mick, Nick, as well as dick, rick, mick, nick, kick, and !ick. The pattern doesn't match ick (too short), Ricky (too long), or rock (doesn't contain ick).

> **NOTE:** By default, SQL Server uses a sort order that ignores case differences, so the pattern _ick would match DICK, etc. When you install SQL Server, you can specify a sort order that treats uppercase and lowercase characters as distinct for comparison purposes, in which case the pattern '_ick ' would not match the string DICK.

You can also use a pattern such as [aeiou] to match a single character that's in the set of characters within the brackets. Or, you can use a range such as [0-9] to specify the set of characters (in this case, any digit). If you put a ^ at the beginning of a character set or range, it means the set of matching characters contains all characters except those within the brackets. Thus, [^aeiou] means any character except a, e, i, o, and u; and [^0-9] means any character except a digit.

If you need to match a literal %, _, or [character, put the character inside brackets. For example, the following pattern matches any string that is at least two characters long and has an underscore in the second or later character:

```
Name Like '_%[_]%'
```

The first _ matches any one character. The first % matches zero or more of any character. The [_] matches only an _. And the final % matches zero or more of any character.

An alternative way to specify a literal %, _, or [character is to specify an escape character, as in the following pattern, which is equivalent to the previous example:

```
Name Like '_%\_%' Escape '\'
```

This example's Escape clause specifies that any character following a \ character in the pattern will be treated as the literal character.

Exists Condition

The Exists condition is another form of condition that uses a subquery. The syntax is

Exists (*select-expression*)

This condition is true if the select expression's result table contains one or more rows, and false otherwise (the value of the Exists condition is never unknown). The select expression's select list can specify any number of columns, but the column values are ignored, so you can just use * for the column list. You can specify the Not keyword before the Exists condition, and the value of the negated condition will be true only if the select expression's result table is empty. The following condition is true if and only if there is at least one customer in Seattle:

```
Exists ( Select   *
         From   Customer
         Where ShipCity = 'Seattle' )
```

This example may not appear very practical because it just tells us whether there are any customers in Seattle. We saw a more useful form of the Exists condition in the search condition of the example showing how to produce a left outer join:

```
Select  Customer.CustId,
        Customer.Name,
        Null As SaleDate
  From   Customer
  Where Not Exists
```

```
( Select   *
     From   Sale
     Where Sale.CustId = Customer.CustId )
```

The select expression used in this search condition is known as a *correlated subquery* because the inner select expression (the one following the Not Exists condition) refers to Customer.CustId, which is a *correlated reference* to a column of a table specified in the outer select expression. Thus, the evaluation of the inner select expression is correlated to the outer select expression's current row.

A close look at this example can help clarify both correlated subqueries and the usefulness of the Exists condition. The example's Exists condition answers the question, "Do any sales exist for this customer?" If the answer is No, the search condition (Not Exists ...) is true and the customer is selected. (Recall that this Select was the second half of the left outer join and was intended to select unmatched Customer rows.) This Exists condition tests whether the customer has any sales by (essentially) producing a temporary result table that contains all the Sale rows for the customer. If this set of rows isn't empty, the Exists condition is true—the customer has one or more sales.

The temporary result table containing the customer's sales is produced by the following subquery (the nested select expression):

```
Select   *
  From   Sale
  Where Sale.CustId = Customer.CustId
```

Because we're interested only in the number of Sale rows, we use * to specify an implicit list of columns rather than listing explicit column names. The search condition we use for this select expression is quite simple: a Sale row is included in this select expression's result table if its CustId column contains the same customer ID as the current Customer row being tested in the outer select expression. You can think of SQL Server executing the following algorithm for the complete Select statement:

For all Customer rows
> *Set CurCustId = Customer.CustId*
> *Set TmpSaleResultTable to Empty (remove all rows)*
> *For all Sale rows*
>> *If Sale.CustId = CurCustId*
>>> *Add Sale row to TmpSaleResultTable*
>> *EndIf*
> *EndFor*
> *If TmpSaleResultTable is Empty*
>> *Add Customer row to final result table*
> *EndIf*
EndFor

While SQL Server doesn't necessarily use this algorithm to carry out the Select statement, the algorithm provides a logical way to understand a correlated subquery's result.

Subqueries can get quite complex, but they provide enormous power to express different search conditions. We're now ready to look at a more difficult, but practical, use of subqueries. Suppose you want to retrieve the name and city for each customer who has placed any order with a total amount greater than the average total amount of orders placed by customers in the same city. The following Select statement retrieves the desired list of customers:

```
Select  CurCust.Name,
        CurCust.ShipCity
 From   Customer As CurCust
 Where Exists
    ( Select  *
        From  Sale As BigSale
       Where BigSale.CustId = CurCust.CustId
         And BigSale.TotalAmt >
          ( Select  Avg( AvgSale.TotalAmt )
             From   Customer As AvgCust,
                    Sale    As AvgSale
            Where AvgCust.CustId    = AvgSale.CustId
              And AvgCust.ShipCity = CurCust.ShipCity ) )
```

With the data in Figure 10-2, this statement produces the following results:

Name	ShipCity
Smith Mfg.	Portland
Bolt Co.	Eugene
AA products	Portland

A detailed look at how this Select statement is structured illustrates many of SQL's advanced retrieval capabilities.

The first From clause specifies that the result table rows come from the Customer table and that correlation name CurCust is used elsewhere in the statement to qualify columns that come from this particular role of the Customer table.

The first Where clause uses the Exists condition to see whether the customer has any orders that meet the specified criteria. The set of orders to be tested is specified by the first subquery (beginning with the second Select keyword). Remember, when you use a subquery, you can think of SQL Server as executing the subquery for every row defined by the From clause in the outer Select statement. Thus, in this example, consider that for every row in Customer, the subquery is executed and then tested to see whether its result contains any rows.

The first subquery retrieves rows from the Sale table. Because the only test made on the result of this subquery is whether it contains any rows, all columns are retrieved

(Select *). The From clause specifies that the rows from this use of Sale are qualified by the correlation name BigSale. The only rows retrieved in this subquery are those that are for the current customer and that have a total sale amount greater than the average total amount of orders placed by customers in the same city as the current customer.

The Where clause specifies the conjunction of two conditions that must be true for a Sale row to be in the subquery's result. The first condition is that a Sale row must have the same customer ID as the current customer row's customer ID.

The second condition is a basic condition that uses another subquery. The total amount for each sale is compared to the average total amount of a set of sales. In this example, the greater-than (>) test is used, and because both values in a basic condition must be scalar, the set the subquery returns in this example must include no more than one value (one row with one column). By specifying only the Avg aggregate function in the subquery's list of result columns, the subquery retrieves a single row with a single column that has the desired average value. This value is then compared to the column value BigSale.TotalAmt.

The second subquery (that is, the third Select statement) specifies the set of rows from which the average is calculated. The rows come from the equijoin of the Customer and Sale tables (AvgCust.CustId = AvgSale.CustId). But only those rows that have customers from the same city as the current customer are included in the average. To evaluate this condition, the city of each row in the innermost subquery (AvgCust.ShipCity) is compared to the city for the current customer in the main query (CurCust.ShipCity).

Quantified Condition

The final type of condition is a quantified condition, which has the following syntax:

expression θ *quantifier* (*select expression*)

The comparison operator can be any of those listed previously under "Basic Condition." The quantifier can be either of the keywords All or Any.

> **NOTE:** The Some keyword can be used as a synonym for Any.

The following example selects customer rows that have a discount greater than all the Portland customers:

```
Select  CurCust.CustId,
        CurCust.Discount
  From  Customer As CurCust
 Where CurCust.Discount > All
        ( Select  CityCust.Discount
            From  Customer As CityCust
           Where CityCust.ShipCity = 'Portland'
             And CityCust.Discount Is Not Null )
```

This example's > All quantified condition is true if the subquery's result table is empty or if the current customer's discount is greater than all the values in the subquery's result table. With the customers listed in Figure 10-2, only one is selected:

CustId	Discount
499921	0.100

The select expression used in a quantified condition must have only one column, and the comparison test is applied to each value in the select expression's result table.

In general, a condition with the All quantifier is

▼ True if the select expression's result table is empty or the comparison test is true for all values in the result table

■ False if the comparison test is false for at least one value in the result table

▲ Unknown if the comparison test doesn't evaluate to false for at least one value in the result table and the comparison test is unknown for at least one value in the result table

A condition with the Any quantifier is

▼ True if the comparison test is true for at least one value in the result table

■ False if the select expression's result table is empty or the comparison test is false for all values in the result table

▲ Unknown if the comparison test doesn't evaluate to true for at least one value in the result table and the comparison test is unknown for at least one value in the result table

Be careful when you code a quantified condition not to confuse informal ways of expressing a condition in English with the specific meanings of the SQL All and Any quantifiers. For example, you might hear someone ask for a list of "customers who have a bigger discount than *any* of the Portland customers." But if you use the following Select statement, the retrieved list would include all customers who have a discount greater than the *lowest* discount of any Portland customer:

```
Select  CurCust.CustId
  From  Customer As CurCust
  Where CurCust.Discount > Any
      ( Select  CityCust.Discount
          From  Customer As CityCust
          Where CityCust.ShipCity = 'Portland'
            And CityCust.Discount Is Not Null )
```

This list obviously might include some customers in Portland (those who have a discount that isn't the lowest among Portland customers). Using the All quantifier (as in the previous example) retrieves customers who have a discount greater than the highest discount of any Portland customer, which, of course, excludes all Portland customers. A simpler approach to this Select statement would be to use the following basic condition:

```
Select  CurCust.CustId
  From   Customer As CurCust
  Where CurCust.Discount > ( Select  Max( CityCust.Discount )
                             From   Customer As CityCust
                             Where CityCust.ShipCity = 'Portland' )
```

Using a Case Expression

SQL provides a Case structure to *conditionally* return a value. A Case structure has this form:

> Case
> When *condition*$_1$ Then *result-expression*$_1$
> ...
> When *condition*$_n$ Then *result-expression*$_n$
> Else   *result-expression*$_x$
> End

SQL Server evaluates each condition in order, and when the first one that's true is found, SQL Server uses the value of the expression that follows the associated Then keyword. If no condition is true, the expression after the optional Else keyword is used. If no condition is true and there's no Else keyword, the value of the Case expression is null. In the following example, a Case expression is used to create a category value for each customer:

```
Select CustId,
       Name,
       Case
         When Discount > .3 Then 2
         When Discount > .0 Then 1
         Else                  0
       End As Category
  From Customer
```

There's a shorthand form of the Case structure when the series of tests are all for different values of the same expression. For example, to expand a set of character codes, you might use the expression shown next.

```
Select PartId,
       Case PartType
         When 'E' Then 'Electrical'
         When 'M' Then 'Mechanical'
         Else           'Other'
       End
   From Part
```

Each of the When cases tests the condition PartType = *value* for the respective value (which could also be an expression). A Case expression can be used in most places where a scalar value is valid, including in Select, Insert, Update, and Delete statements.

Using a Subquery as a Scalar Value

You can use a subquery that returns a single column and a single row anywhere you can use a scalar value or expression. The following example shows how to retrieve the ratio of each customer's discount to the average discount for all customers:

```
Select      Name,
            Discount,
            Discount / ( Select Avg( Discount ) From Customer )
               As TimesAvg
   From      Customer
   Order By TimesAvg Desc
```

This statement returns the following result:

Name	Discount	TimesAvg
Bell Bldg.	.100	4.615
Nautilus	.050	2.307
Smith Mfg.	.050	2.307
Bolt Co.	.020	0.923
AA Products	.010	0.461
Alpine Inc.	.010	0.461
Seaworthy	.010	0.461
Wood Bros.	.010	0.461
Adapto	.000	0.00
Floradel	.000	0.00
Telez Co.	.000	0.00
Udapto Mfg.	.000	0.00
Ajax Inc.	Null	Null

You can even use correlation names within this type of subquery. This technique, shown in the following example, allows you to retrieve a similar list, but calculate the discount ratio based on the average discount for customers in the same city:

```
Select CurCust.Name,
       CurCust.Discount,
     ( Select Avg( AvgCust1.Discount )
         From Customer As AvgCust1
         Where CurCust.ShipCity = AvgCust1.ShipCity ) As CityAvg,
       CurCust.Discount /
     ( Select Avg( AvgCust2.Discount )
         From Customer As AvgCust2
         Where CurCust.ShipCity = AvgCust2.ShipCity ) As TimesCityAvg
From     Customer As CurCust
Order By TimesCityAvg Desc
```

This statement returns the following result:

Name	Discount	CityAvg	TimesCityAvg
Alpine Inc.	0.01	0.003333	3.0003
Bell Bldg.	0.10	0.043333	2.3077
Seaworthy	0.01	0.005000	2.0000
Smith Mfg.	0.05	0.027500	1.8181
Nautilus	0.05	0.027500	1.8181
Bolt Co.	0.02	0.043333	0.4615
AA Products	0.01	0.027500	0.3636
Wood Bros.	0.01	0.043333	0.2307
Adapto	0.00	0.027500	0.0000
Telez Co.	0.00	0.005000	0.0000
Floradel	0.00	0.003333	0.0000
Udapto Mfg.	0.00	0.003333	0.0000
Ajax Inc.	Null	0.005000	Null

Using a Select Expression in the From Clause

As we saw earlier, the From clause lists one or more tables and/or views from which rows are drawn to produce a Select statement's result set. You can also use a select expression in the From clause, thus creating a temporary table from which rows can be drawn. This feature can be a convenient way to join aggregate values with individual rows, as in the following example, which calculates how much discount would be given each customer if the customer got the average discount for customers in the same city:

```
Select      Customer.CustId,
            CustSaleTotal.SumTotalAmt,
            CityDisc.AvgDisc,
            CustSaleTotal.SumTotalAmt * CityDisc.AvgDisc
              As AvgDiscValue
   From     Customer
            Join
            ( Select      Sale.CustId,
                          Sum( TotalAmt ) As SumTotalAmt
                From      Sale
                Group By CustId ) As CustSaleTotal
            On Customer.CustId = CustSaleTotal.CustId
            Join
            ( Select      ShipCity,
                          Avg( Discount ) As AvgDisc
                From      Customer
                Group By ShipCity ) As CityDisc
            On Customer.ShipCity = CityDisc.ShipCity
```

Note that for many queries, you can use simple or correlated subqueries that produce a scalar value, joins of tables and views, or Where clause subqueries to achieve the same effect as a select expression in a From clause.

Additional Select Statement Features

Transact-SQL offers several other features for select expressions. To limit the size of the result set to a specific number or percent of rows, you can add a Top clause before the select list columns. The following example shows how to specify an exact row count:

```
Select Top 10
            Name,
            Discount
   From     Customer
   Order By Discount Desc
```

This statement returns the following result:

Name	Discount
Bell Bldg.	0.10
Smith Mfg.	0.05
Nautilus	0.05

Name	Discount
Bolt Co.	0.02
Alpine Inc.	0.01
Seaworthy	0.01
AA Products	0.01
Wood Bros.	0.01
Adapto	0.00
Floradel	0.00

In most cases, a Select statement will have an Order By clause along with a Top clause so that the records are the ones with the highest or lowest value for some column(s). To return a specified percentage of the selected rows, use the following form:

```
Select Top 10 Percent
        Name,
        Discount
  From    Customer
  Order By Discount Desc
```

This statement returns the following result:

Name	Discount
Bell Bldg.	0.10
Smith Mfg.	0.05

When there's an Order By clause (as in most cases), you can also specify that all rows having the same Order By column value(s) as the last row included in the Top number or percent be included in the results:

```
Select Top 10 Percent With Ties
        Name,
        Discount
  From    Customer
  Order By Discount Desc
```

This statement returns the following result:

Name	Discount
Bell Bldg.	0.10
Smith Mfg.	0.05
Nautilus	0.05

The With Ties option would be useful, for example, to avoid having some customers with a particular discount included in the results and other customers, with the same discount, excluded.

The Rollup and Cube Options of the Group By Clause

We saw earlier that aggregate functions and the Group By clause provide a way to retrieve aggregate information. These standard SQL features don't provide a way to combine detail rows and summary information, nor do they provide a way to get summary information at multiple levels within the same query. Transact-SQL has two extensions to the Group By clause that provide these capabilities. After a Group By list of columns, and after the Having clause (if any), you can specify either With Rollup or With Cube. With Rollup causes SQL Server to add a subtotal row for each level in the grouping list. For example, the following statement illustrates the use of With Rollup:

```
Select    Customer.CustId,
          Sale.OrderId,
          Avg( SaleItem.Price ) As "Avg. Sale Price"
  From    ( Customer Join Sale
              On Customer.CustId = Sale.CustId )
          Join
          SaleItem
              On Sale.OrderId = SaleItem.OrderId
Group By Customer.CustId, Sale.OrderId
          With Rollup
```

The query result when using Query Analyzer looks like the first three columns shown here:

CustId	OrderId	Avg. Sale Price	Notes
133568	234117	6.5733	Group By row
133568	Null	6.5733	Rollup summary for a CustId
246900	234116	4.0066	Group By row
246900	234120	4.2800	Group By row
246900	Null	4.1160	Rollup summary for a CustId
499320	234112	4.9000	Group By row
499320	234114	8.3400	Group By row
499320	234119	4.2800	Group By row
499320	Null	6.1971	Rollup summary for a CustId
888402	234113	7.2033	Group By row
888402	Null	7.2033	Rollup summary for a CustId

CustId	OrderId	Avg. Sale Price	Notes
890003	234115	3.3066	Group By row
890003	Null	3.3066	Rollup summary for a CustId
905011	234118	5.9000	Group By row
905011	Null	5.9000	Rollup summary for a CustId
Null	Null	5.5221	Rollup summary for all rows

Note how the summary levels work from right to left through the Group By columns. The With Cube option works similarly, but creates a set of summary rows for each possible combination of columns formed by removing one or more columns from the Group By column list. In the previous example, specifying With Cube instead of With Rollup would result in summary rows for each combination of CustId and OrderId, for each CustId value, for each OrderId value, and for all rows. If a Group By list had three columns—C1, C2, and C3—there would be eight sets of summary rows in the result table:

▼ For each unique combination of C1, C2, and C3 values (these are the rows created by the Group By clause with or without the Cube option)

■ For each unique pair of C1 and C2 values

■ For each unique pair of C1 and C3 values

■ For each unique pair of C2 and C3 values

■ For each value of C1

■ For each value of C2

■ For each value of C3

▲ One row for the whole set of selected rows

NOTE: The Cube operator has a puzzling name since it supports more than three dimensions (as a cube solid object has), and the number of sets of summary rows isn't c^3 (the cube of the number of Group By columns) but rather is 2^c.

If none of the Group By columns allow null or you eliminate all rows with a null grouping column, you can tell which result table rows are summary rows added by the Rollup or Cube option by checking for null in a grouping column. Otherwise, a null grouping column may be for the group of rows that have null for this column, leaving you no way to distinguish the two types of summary rows. SQL Server provides the Grouping function to solve this problem. To add result table columns to identify the type of summary row, include a Grouping function for every grouping column in the select list:

```
Select    Grouping( Customer.CustId ) As RollupAllCustId,
          Grouping( Sale.OrderId )    As RollupAllOrderId,
          Customer.CustId,
```

```
          Sale.OrderId,
          Avg( SaleItem.Price )
From      ( Customer Join Sale
              On Customer.CustId = Sale.CustId )
          Join
          SaleItem
              On Sale.OrderId = SaleItem.OrderId
Group By Customer.CustId, Sale.OrderId
          With Rollup
```

The result will look like this:

RollupAllCustId	RollupAllOrderId	CustId	OrderId	Avg. Sale Price
0	0	133568	234117	6.5733
0	1	133568	Null	6.5733
0	0	246900	234116	4.0066
0	0	246900	234120	4.2800
0	1	246900	Null	4.1160
0	0	499320	234112	4.9000
0	0	499320	234114	8.3400
0	0	499320	234119	4.2800
0	1	499320	Null	6.1971
0	0	888402	234113	7.2033
0	1	888402	Null	7.2033
0	0	890003	234115	3.3066
0	1	890003	Null	3.3066
0	0	905011	234118	5.9000
0	1	905011	Null	5.9000
1	1	Null	Null	5.5221

The first column (alias RollupAllCustId) will have a value of 1 for Rollup summary rows that *don't* use CustId values to determine subgroups; in this case, only the summary row for all rows has 1 for this column. The RollupAllCustId column will have 0 for ordinary Group By rows and any Rollup summary row that uses CustId to determine subgroups. Similarly, the second column (alias RollupAllOrderId) will have a value of 1 or 0, depending on the type of summary row. In this example, all Rollup summary rows have 1 for RollupAllOrderId because no Rollup summary rows use OrderId to determine subgroups. OrderId is the lowest-level grouping column and is used only to determine the ordinary Group By groups. Notice that ordinary Group By rows have 0 for all Grouping function columns; whereas Rollup-generated rows have at least one Grouping function column with a value of 1. You can use the Grouping function in a similar way to identify the kind of row in a result table produced using the Cube option.

The Compute Clause

For interactive retrieval, Transact-SQL has another feature that provides subtotaling capabilities. You can follow a Select statement, including one that's the union of several select expressions, with one or more Compute clauses that list aggregate functions as well as columns to be used for one or more levels of aggregation. The following statement produces a list of Sale rows with subtotals for each customer and a grand total:

```
Select     CustId,
           OrderId,
           TotalAmt
  From     Sale
  Order By CustId, OrderId
  Compute  Sum( TotalAmt ) By CustId
  Compute  Sum( TotalAmt )
```

The query result when using Query Analyzer looks like the following:

```
CustId        OrderId       TotalAmt
----------    ----------    --------
133568        234117        550.0000


sum
--------
550.0000


CustId        OrderId       TotalAmt
----------    ----------    --------
246900        234116        678.0000
246900        234120        399.7000


sum
---------
1077.7000


CustId        OrderId       TotalAmt
----------    ----------    --------
499320        234112        35.0000
499320        234114        78.9000
499320        234119        201.0000


sum
--------
314.9000


CustId        OrderId       TotalAmt
----------    ----------    --------
888402        234113        278.7500
```

```
sum
--------
278.7500


CustId       OrderId      TotalAmt
-----------  -----------  ---------
890003       234115       1000.0000


sum
---------
1000.0000


CustId       OrderId      TotalAmt
-----------  -----------  --------
905011       234118       89.5000


sum
-------
89.5000


sum
---------
3310.8500
(16 row(s) affected)
```

A Compute clause can contain any of the aggregate functions listed previously in Table 10-3. The optional By column list for a Compute clause defines the level breaks and must contain one or more columns or expressions listed in the Order By clause. The By columns must start with the first item in the Order By clause and be in the same left-to-right order and not skip any item. As the previous example shows, you can use multiple Compute clauses to get aggregate information at several levels.

The Into Clause

The primary purpose of the Select statement is to retrieve data. Transact-SQL has an extension to let you create a new table from the rows retrieved by a Select Statement. A new table is specified with an Into clause that follows immediately after the Select column list:

```
Select   *
  Into   CustomerSeattle
  From   Customer
  Where ShipCity = 'Seattle'
```

The newly created table has the same columns as you specify in the Select column list and has the rows from the result table, including the effect of row selection or aggregation. The main purpose of this feature is to create a temporary table that can be used for subsequent retrievals during a query session. If you want to add rows to a permanent table using the Select statement, you must turn on the select into/bulkcopy option with the following system stored procedure call:

```
sp_dboption AppDta, 'select into/bulkcopy', true
```

You can also set this option from the SQL Enterprise Manager by right-clicking a database, selecting Properties from the pop-up menu, and checking the Select Into / bulk copy check box on the Options tab.

Note that the new table doesn't have any constraints that may have been defined for a source table. This is one reason you should generally use Create Table, rather than Select, to create new, permanent tables. To copy data from one or more tables to an existing table, use the Insert statement with a subquery (discussed shortly).

USING DML TO MODIFY TABLE DATA

SQL has three main DML statements that can be used to modify table data: Insert, Update, and Delete. All three statements can modify either a single row in a table or a set of rows in a table. None of the statements can modify more than one table in a single statement. You can also modify data through a view; however, a DML statement that operates on a view can update only one underlying base table. All three DML statements let you use a Where clause to specify the set of rows to be inserted, updated, or deleted. The general form of the Where clause in these statements parallels the form in the Select statement.

NOTE: Transact-SQL also has the Bulk Insert statement, which provides a data import facility; however, this isn't a standard SQL data manipulation statement.

The Insert Statement

To add a new row to a table, you use the Insert statement. For example, to add a new customer, you enter the following:

```
Insert Into Customer
          ( CustId,
            Name,
            ShipCity,
            Discount )
   Values ( 678987,
            'Atlas Inc.',
            'Portland',
            Null )
```

A column list in parentheses follows the table or view name, and the Values clause specifies a list of new values, also in parentheses, for the columns that correspond positionally in the column list. You can omit the column list, in which case the implicit column list is all columns in the order they were defined by Create Table, Alter Table, Create View, or Alter View DDL statements. Omitting the column list is generally not a good practice, however, because it's error-prone and provides poor documentation.

In the list of inserted columns, you must include any column for which the system can't determine a value. You can omit a column if it is defined with the Identity keyword, has the Default clause specified on the Create Table or Alter Table statement, is a TimeStamp data type, or allows null. If an omitted column has an explicit default value (as described in Chapter 9), the default value is used; otherwise, SQL Server inserts the next incremental identity value for an Identity column, inserts the current timestamp value for a TimeStamp column, or sets the column to null.

You can use any valid expression for a column's value. As the example above illustrates, you can use the Null keyword to explicitly set a column to null. Of course, a column that is set to null must have been defined without the Not Null clause.

You can also use the Default keyword in the Insert statement's list of values to specify that a column's default value (or null) should be used. Any column for which you specify Default must either have a default (as described previously) or allow null.

A multirow Insert copies data from one table to another and implements the closest SQL equivalent to the relational assignment operation discussed in Chapter 8. The target table for a multirow Insert must already exist (unlike a Select statement with the Into clause, the Insert statement doesn't create a new table). For example, the following Insert copies all rows from an old version of a customer table to a new version that has an additional ShipState column:

```
Insert Into Customer
        ( CustId,
          Name,
          ShipCity,
          ShipState,
          Discount )
   Select CustId,
          Name,
          ShipCity,
          ' ',
          Discount
     From CustOld
```

Initially, all rows in the new table have a blank ShipState column because the result table for the Select includes the ' ' literal as the next-to-last element in its select list.

Although the Insert statement can add rows to only a single table, the inserted rows can be constructed from more than one table. For example, the following Create Table and Insert statements make a copy of combined customer and sale information:

```
Create Table SaleWithCust
     ( OrderId  Int          Not Null,
       TotalAmt Money         Not Null,
       Name     Char ( 30 ) Not Null )

Insert Into SaleWithCust
        ( OrderId,
          TotalAmt,
          Name )
   Select  OrderId,
           TotalAmt,
           Name
     From  Customer, Sale
     Where Customer.CustId = Sale.CustId
```

After the Insert statement is executed, changes to the data in the Customer or Sale tables are not reflected in the SaleWithCust table. A multirow Insert, unlike a view, copies the data from the tables referenced in the From clause.

As the previous two examples show, you can use a form of the Select statement within an Insert statement to specify the rows to be inserted. This nested Select statement can use the From, Where, Having, Group By, Union, and Order By clauses (but not Into or Compute) discussed in the previous section.

Transact-SQL also lets you specify a nested Execute statement that calls a stored procedure to produce the result table for a multirow Insert. If you have a stored procedure named CalcCustCreditRating that uses the Customer and Sale tables to produce a result table with customers' credit ratings, you might use the following statements to create and load this new table:

```
Create Table CustCreditRate
    ( CustId     Int Not Null,
      CreditRate Int )

Insert Into CustCreditRate
        ( CustId,
          CreditRate )
   Execute CalcCustCreditRating
```

The CalcCustCreditRating must produce a result set that has two columns corresponding to the Insert statement's column list. (Stored procedures are discussed later in this chapter.)

Inserting Rows into a View

To insert rows through a view, the view must not contain any columns defined by a literal or expression. The view columns must be simple columns from an underlying base table or insert-capable view. If a view spans multiple base tables (for instance, is a join), an Insert statement can list only view columns defined over a single underlying base table.

When you use a view, any base table column not present as an updateable column in the view must have a default (as discussed previously) or allow null, and the new row gets the default value or null for the omitted column.

> **NOTE:**   Although the Insert rules for views may seem complex, in practice most Insert operations use either a base table or a view over some or all columns of a single base table. For these cases, the main rules to be aware of are the restrictions on omitted columns.

The Update Statement

You can update a specific row by using its primary key value in the Where clause of an Update statement and assigning new values to one or more columns. For example, the following Update statement changes the name and adds two percent to a customer's current discount:

```
Update  Customer
  Set   Name     = 'Wood Products',
        Discount = Discount + .02
  Where CustId = 905011
```

The Set keyword is followed by one or more column assignments of this form:

column-name = expression

You can update a set of rows by using a search condition that specifies more than one row. The following statement gives all Portland customers a ten percent discount:

```
Update  Customer
  Set   Discount = .10
  Where ShipCity = 'Portland'
```

If you don't specify a Where clause, all rows in the specified table are updated.

> **NOTE:**   This type of Update is known as a *searched Update* because SQL Server searches for the rows to be updated. Using a SQL cursor (as discussed under "Stored Procedures," later in this chapter), there's also a *positioned Update*, in which you first retrieve the row you want to update and then specify Where Current Of *cursor-name* to update the current row. Chapters 13 and 14 also cover the use of cursors.

You can set a null-capable column to null, using the Null keyword:

```
Update  Customer
  Set   Discount = Null
  Where ShipCity = 'Portland'
```

Similarly, you can set a column with a default (or a column that allows nulls) to its default (or to null), using the Default keyword:

```
Update   Customer
  Set    Discount = Default
  Where ShipCity = 'Portland'
```

Using Subqueries in Update Statements

The expression on the right-hand side of a column assignment can be a *scalar* subquery—one that returns a single row and a single column. The following example sets all Portland customers' discount to the overall average for all customers:

```
Update   Customer
  Set    Discount = ( Select Avg( Discount ) From Customer )
  Where ShipCity = 'Portland'
```

By using a correlated subquery in the column assignment, you can set the values in one table's rows based on values from related rows in another table. The following example shows how to copy the price of items from a separate Price table to the Item table:

```
Update   Item
  Set    ItemPrice = ( Select   ItemPrice
                       From   Price
                       Where Price.ItemId = Item.ItemId )
  Where Exists (  Select *
                  From   Price
                  Where Price.ItemId = Item.ItemId )
```

Notice how this example uses an Exists condition to limit changes to those rows in the Item table that have a matching row in the Price table. Without this condition, all Item rows would be updated, and those without a matching Price row would have their price set to Null.

NOTE: Transact-SQL has a non-ANSI-standard extension to the Update statement that allows a From clause as part of the Update (not just in a subquery). Using this extension, the previous example could be coded as follows:

```
Update   Item
  Set    ItemPrice = Price.ItemPrice
  From   Item, Price
  Where Price.ItemId = Item.ItemId
```

An Update statement can use a search condition with a subquery to select rows to be updated. The following statement increases to ten percent the discount of customers who currently get less than a ten percent discount and who have placed orders with a grand total amount greater than 1,000:

```
Update  Customer
  Set   Discount = .10
  Where ( Discount < .10 Or Discount Is Null )
    And 1000 < ( Select  Sum( TotalAmt )
                 From    Sale
                 Where Sale.CustId = Customer.CustId )
```

In an Update statement's Where clause, you can use any of the conditions discussed for the Select statement. You can even use the table being updated as the base table of a subquery. Thus, the following Update statement is valid:

```
Update  Customer
  Set   Discount = .10
  Where Discount Is Null
    Or Discount <
      ( Select  Avg( Discount )
          From   Customer
          Where ShipCity = 'Portland' )
```

This Update statement gives a ten percent discount to customers without a discount or with a discount less than the average for customers in Portland. In this case, SQL Server calculates the subquery average once and uses it as the test value for all rows in the Update. Note that although individual updates to Portland customers may change the average, this change doesn't affect the selection of rows in the Update.

Updating Multiple Tables

To update multiple tables, you must use more than one DML statement. For example, to increase the hourly rate of both employees and contractors, you would use two statements:

```
Update Employee
  Set  HourlyRate = HourlyRate * 1.05
Update Contractor
  Set  HourlyRate = HourlyRate * 1.05
```

When you update primary, unique, or foreign key columns, you must consider the key constraints that exist for a table. For example, to change a customer's ID, you must be sure the CustId column value is changed in the Customer table as well as in all tables that use CustId as a foreign key. If no foreign key constraints exist, you can just use multiple Update statements, such as the following:

```
Update Customer
  Set   CustId = 123789
  Where CustId = 888402

Update Sale
  Set   CustId = 123789
  Where CustId = 888402
```

But if the Sale table has a foreign key constraint specified for the CustId column, both statements cause an error because either statement by itself would result in unmatched Sale rows. One solution is to insert a *new* Customer row, change the Sale rows to reference the new Customer row, and then delete the *old* Customer row:

```
Insert Into Customer
        ( CustId,
          Name,
          ShipCity,
          Discount )
  Select  123789,
          Name,
          ShipCity,
          Discount
    From  Customer
    Where CustId = 888402

Update Sale
  Set   CustId = 123789
  Where CustId = 888402

Delete
  From  Customer
  Where CustId = 888402
```

The Delete and Truncate Table Statements

To remove a row from a table, you enter a Delete statement like the following:

```
Delete
  From  Customer
  Where CustId = 905011
```

A set of rows can be deleted from a single table using a search condition that specifies more than one row:

```
Delete
  From  Customer
  Where ShipCity = 'Portland'
```

> **NOTE:** As with the Update statement, this type of Delete is known as a *searched Delete*. SQL also has a *positioned Delete*, discussed in the section on stored procedures and in Chapters 13 and 14.

The search condition for a Delete statement also can contain a subquery like the ones described for the Update statement example. To delete all customers with no associated Sale rows, you would use a Where clause with a Not Exists condition and a correlated subquery:

```
Delete
  From  Customer
  Where Not Exists ( Select  *
                       From  Sale
                       Where Sale.CustId = Customer.CustId )
```

> **NOTE:** Transact-SQL has a non-ANSI-standard extension to the Delete statement that allows a From clause as part of the Delete (not just in a subquery). Generally, a subquery is the preferred technique.

Clearing an Entire Table

You can clear all rows from a table—intentionally, or accidentally—by entering a Delete statement with no Where clause:

```
Delete
  From Customer
```

Note that after you clear all rows from a table, the table still exists; it's just an empty table. A table is cleared and deleted from the catalog using the Drop statement discussed in Chapter 9.

SQL Server provides the Truncate Table statement as a faster method of clearing a table. The following statement is functionally equivalent to the previous Delete statement:

```
Truncate Table Customer
```

NOTE: Unlike a Delete statement, the Truncate Table statement doesn't put entries for deleted rows in the transaction log, and hence can't be rolled back. The Truncate Table statement also doesn't activate a delete trigger on the table. You can't use a Truncate Table statement on a table that's referenced as the "parent" table in a foreign key constraint.

Deleting Rows from Multiple Tables

As discussed for the Update statement, if you want to delete rows from multiple tables, you must execute multiple Delete statements.

Concurrent Updates and Table Locks

When two NT Server processes access the same base table, there's a possibility that one process's row updates might conflict with the other process's retrieval or update. For example, if one process executes the Select statement:

```
Select   Avg( Discount )
  From   Customer
```

while another process is executing this statement to update the Discount column:

```
Update   Customer
  Set    Discount = .10
  Where ShipCity = 'Portland'
```

the first process may get an average based on the old Discount value for some Portland customers and the new Discount value for others. SQL Server (and other DBMS) doesn't automatically do anything to prevent these two processes from interleaving the retrieval and update of individual rows.

Transact-SQL has extensions to the Select and Update statements to provide a way to explicitly lock a base table to prevent conflicting access. In both cases, you code *table hints* using the With keyword after a referenced table name. The following statement would protect the Select statement from conflicting updates:

```
Select   Avg( Discount )
  From   Customer With ( TabLock )
```

On the Select statement, the TabLock hint specifies that a *shared lock* on the entire table should be held for the duration of the Select statement. A shared lock prevents other update access, but allows other read access.

Alternatively, an Update statement can use a From clause with a TabLockX table hint to hold an *exclusive lock*, which prevents any type of access to the table by another process. The following statement would assure that no other access to the Customer table occurred during the Update statement:

```
Update   Customer
  Set    Discount = .10
```

```
From   Customer With ( TabLockX )
Where ShipCity = 'Portland'
```

Generally, you should keep a table locked for the briefest time necessary because a table lock may block other processes from executing their normal access to a table.

Transaction Integrity and the Commit and Rollback Statements

Another consideration when updating a SQL Server database is maintaining a consistent database when multiple rows are being modified. Suppose you enter the following Update statement to increase the discount for all customers with a non-null discount:

```
Update  Customer
  Set   Discount = Discount + 0.001
  Where Discount Is Not Null
```

To execute this statement, SQL Server retrieves, tests, and potentially updates each row. If the process in which this statement is being executed abruptly terminates (for example, because of a power failure) after some—but not all—Customer rows have been processed, the Customer table will be in an inconsistent state. Some rows will have the increase, but others won't. The Update statement can't just be reentered either, because that would add an additional discount to the customers who were updated in the previous, incomplete statement execution.

SQL Server provides a facility for transaction integrity and recovery that guarantees all-or-none execution of multirow transactions. SQL Server assures that all row changes made by an update that fails before completion (and being committed) will automatically be backed out by SQL Server—even if the system is shut down by a power failure. After a failed update, all rows in the table are reset to exactly their values before the update was started.

NOTE: There's no magic to this SQL Server capability. When a table is being updated, SQL Server simply stores in the transaction log (a SQL Server file designed for this purpose) a before image (copy) of each row just before the row is updated. If the whole update doesn't complete normally, SQL Server uses these before images to change each row back to its preupdate values.

By default, SQL Server operates in *autocommit* transaction mode, which treats each individual Insert, Update, or Delete statement as an all-or-none transaction. When the statement completes, the changes are permanent.

When operating in autocommit transaction mode, you can define an *explicit transaction* be executing a Start Transaction statement, followed by the statements you want included in the transaction. You end an explicit transaction with either a Commit statement to make changes permanent or a Rollback statement to undo the changes made in this transaction.

Rather than use autocommit transaction mode (with or without explicit transactions), you can set the transaction mode to *implicit* transaction mode. With implicit transaction mode, the first SQL statement in a session from among those listed here starts the first transaction, and a Commit or Rollback statement that ends a transaction implicitly begins the next transaction.

Alter Table
Create *xxx*
Delete
Drop *xxx*
Fetch
Grant
Insert
Open
Revoke
Select
Truncate Table
Update

Implicit transaction mode follows the ANSI-standard SQL approach. See the section "Setting Full ANSI SQL-92 Compatibility" in Chapter 2 for information on changing the SQL server default to implicit transaction mode. You can use the following statement to change a specific session to implicit transaction mode:

```
Set Implicit_Transactions On
```

Transactions can be used to group multiple update statements into a single operation so that either all database changes for all update statements in the transaction occur or no changes occur. Consider a classic banking transaction in which an amount is transferred from a savings account to a checking account. This transaction requires at least two Update statements, and it's essential that either both complete or neither complete. Using an explicit transaction, the sequence of statements would be as follows:

```
Begin Transaction

Update  Saving
  Set   Balance = Balance - 100.00
  Where AccountId = 123987

Update  Checking
  Set   Balance = Balance + 100.00
  Where AccountId = 123987

Commit
```

If you decide you want to back out updates that have not yet been committed, you simply execute the following Rollback statement:

Rollback

With implicit transaction mode, you wouldn't code the Begin Transaction statement because the beginning of the transaction would be defined by the first statement in a session or a previous Commit or Rollback statement.

Both Commit and Rollback statements are typically used in stored procedures and HLL programs rather than interactively. In particular, a Rollback statement is usually coded to back out uncommitted updates when an error is detected. The basic logic where a Rollback might be used looks like the following:

```
-- Begin transaction (explicitly or implicitly)

Update  Saving
  Set   Balance = Balance - 100.00
  Where AccountId = 123987

If Error
    Rollback
Else
Update  Checking
  Set   Balance = Balance + 100.00
  Where AccountId = 123987

If Error
    Rollback
Else
Commit
  EndIf
EndIf
```

The transaction is committed only if both parts of the funds transfer complete successfully.

NOTE: With explicit transactions, you can optionally specify a transaction name after Begin Transaction, Commit, and Rollback, but this doesn't have any useful effect. You can also nest transactions (for example, in a trigger), and SQL Server ignores all but the outer Commit or Rollback. Nested transactions require balanced pairs of Begin Transaction and Commit/Rollback operations, however, and, if handled improperly cause errors. Generally, transactions should be started and ended at the point in your application where the operation that must occur "all–or–none" is initiated and its completion status determined.

STORED PROCEDURES

In addition to the individual DML statements described above, SQL has a variety of statements to let you write *stored procedures*. A SQL stored procedure is created with the Create Procedure statement and is called with SQL's Execute statement (or a function in one of the other database interfaces, such as ODBC). You can use any SQL statements in a stored procedure, except the following: Create Default, Create Procedure, Create Rule, Create Trigger, Create View. A stored procedure works much like any HLL procedure—it can have input and output parameters, local variables, numeric and character computations and assignments, database operations (both DDL and DML), and logic to control the execution flow. Here's a simple example of creating a stored procedure:

```
Create Procedure ListCustWithDiscount
    @MinDiscount Dec( 5, 3 )
  As
    Select  *
      From  Customer
      Where Discount >= @MinDiscount
```

A stored procedure is always created in the current database. To execute this procedure, you would use a statement such as the following:

```
Execute ListCustWithDiscount .1
```

NOTE: When you're using the Query Analyzer or OSQL, the Execute keyword is optional if the stored procedure call is the only statement to be executed or the first statement in a batch of statements.

The maximum run-time call depth of nested stored procedures is 32. The @@NestLevel built-in function provides the current nesting level.

When you define a stored procedure, the procedure name follows the Create Procedure keywords and parameter declarations follow the procedure name. The As keyword indicates the beginning of the procedure body, which is one or more SQL statements. Stored procedures can optionally return an integer status value (similar to the way an HLL function returns a value), and you can define output parameters to return data to the caller. We'll cover these topics shortly.

NOTE: Transact-SQL lets you optionally identify a procedure using a name and number (for example, ListCust;1). When you execute a procedure that's been created with a number, you must include the number as well. Although this approach lets you delete all procedures with the same name (and different numbers) on a single Drop Procedure statement, it's a poor naming practice. We recommend you use unique descriptive names (without numbers) for all your stored procedures.

Altering and Deleting Stored Procedures

The Alter Procedure statement lets you change the code for a stored procedure without changing the permissions that have been granted to the procedure. The Alter Procedure statement has similar syntax to the Create Procedure statement. The following example shows how you might revise the ListCustWithDiscount procedure:

```
Alter Procedure ListCustWithDiscount
    @MinDiscount Dec( 5, 3 )
  As
    Select  *
      From  Customer
      Where Status     = 'Active'
        And Discount >= @MinDiscount
```

You can rename a stored procedure with the sp_rename system stored procedure, which takes three arguments: old name, new name, and object type ('object' is the object type for stored procedures). The following example renames the ListCustWithDiscount procedure:

```
sp_rename 'ListCustWithDiscount', 'ListCustomerWithDiscount', 'object'
```

SQL Server automatically compiles and optimizes a stored procedure whenever a table used by the procedure changes or when the procedure is first run after SQL Server is started. If you add a new index and want to force a recompilation to take advantage of the index, use the sp_recompile system stored procedure, as in the following example:

```
sp_recompile 'ListCustWithDiscount'
```

This example marks the ListCustWithDiscount procedure so it's recompiled the next time it's called.

You can delete a stored procedure with the Drop Procedure statement:

```
Drop Procedure ListCustWithDiscount
```

Displaying Information About Stored Procedures

There are three system stored procedures that display information about stored procedures:

▼ **sp_help** *procedure-name*   Displays the procedure's owner and when it was created

■ **sp_helptext** *procedure-name*   Displays source code for the procedure

▲ **sp_depends** *procedure-name*   Displays a list of objects that the procedure references

The sp_helptext system stored procedure is especially useful if you've lost the original source code used to create a stored procedure.

STORED PROCEDURE PARAMETERS

A stored procedure can have up to 1,024 parameters. Each parameter declaration has this basic form:

@parameter-name datatype

A parameter name begins with @, and the subsequent characters can be a Unicode letter, digit, or the @, $, #, or _ symbol. You shouldn't begin parameter names with @@ because SQL Server uses that notation for some built-in functions. A parameter can be any data type allowed for columns (see Chapter 9). If you have multiple parameters, separate the declarations with commas.

You can define a default input value to be used if no argument is supplied when the procedure is called. The previous example could be modified to provide a default that would select all rows with a discount greater than zero, as follows:

```
Create Procedure ListCustWithDiscount
    @MinDiscount Dec( 5, 3 ) = 0.001
  As
    Select  *
      From  Customer
      Where Discount >= @MinDiscount
```

With this definition, you could call the procedure simply using the following statement, which would be equivalent to calling the procedure with .001 as the argument:

```
Execute ListCustWithDiscount
```

All parameters can serve as input parameters. To use a parameter as an output parameter, add the Output keyword to its declaration (after the default value, if any), as in the following example:

```
Create Procedure GetCustDiscount
    @CustId   Int,
    @Discount Dec( 5, 3 ) Output
  As
    Set @Discount =
      ( Select  Discount
          From  Customer
          Where CustId = @CustId )
```

Notice in this example how you can use a scalar subquery to assign a value from a table column. When the procedure returns, the output parameters have their last assigned value. All stored procedure parameters are null-capable; that is, you can pass in and pass back null.

When you call a procedure that has an output parameter, you must supply a variable for the argument and use the Output keyword after the argument on the Execute statement:

```
Execute GetCustDiscount 123789,
                        @CustDiscount Output
```

On the Execute statement, you can use the Default keyword in place of an actual argument as long as the corresponding procedure parameter has a default value declared. You can also omit altogether arguments for parameters at the *end* of the parameter list, as long as *all* parameters for which you don't supply an argument have a default.

> **NOTE:** Because parameters with default values are essentially optional parameters, you may want to place them at the end of the parameter list. This makes it more convenient to omit the corresponding argument when the procedure is called.

An alternative way to specify arguments when you call a stored procedure is to use the corresponding parmeter name as defined in the stored procedure. The following statement illustrates this technique:

```
Execute GetCustDiscount
        @CustId   = 123789,
        @Discount = @CustDiscount Output
```

Using parameter names, as in this example, doesn't require that the arguments be specified in any particular order. The following would also be valid:

```
Execute GetCustDiscount
        @Discount = @CustDiscount Output,
        @CustId   = 123789
```

Transact-SQL lets you specify some arguments (beginning with the first argument) positionally followed by other arguments specified with parameter names. If you use the parameter name technique to specify an argument, you must use also use parameter names to specify any subsequent arguments on the call.

Returning Result Sets

A stored procedure returns a result set for each executed Select statement that isn't used as a scalar subquery (that is, in place of a single value) and that doesn't assign all the columns in the select list to variables or parameters. So, for example, the following stored procedure returns two result sets:

```
Create Procedure ListLowHighDiscCust
  As
    Select  *
      From  Customer
      Where Discount < .01
    Select  *
      From  Customer
      Where Discount > .1
```

The application calling the stored procedure can process the rows in the returned result sets. By default, the Query Analyzer and OSQL utilities display each returned result set.

Status Return Value

A stored procedure can use the Return statement to end execution and set a status value that's returned to the caller, as in the following example:

```
Create Procedure ListCustWithDiscount
    @MinDiscount Dec( 5, 3 ) = 0.001
  As
    If ( @MinDiscount > 1.0 ) Return ( 1 )

    Select  *
      From  Customer
      Where Discount >= @MinDiscount

    Return ( 0 )
```

The return value is optional and can be any integer expression. To get the status return value, you code an assignment on the procedure call:

```
Execute @Status = ListCustWithDiscount .1
```

NOTE: SQL server uses 0 for a successful call and –1 to –99 for system errors on the call (for example, a data conversion error). You can also use 0 for a successful call, but avoid returning status values in the –1 to –99 range.

Fundamental Programming Techniques

You can add comments anywhere in a stored procedure, either following two dashes and running to the end of the current line or spanning multiple lines between /* and */ delimiters:

```
-- This is a comment
/* And so is this
   multiline comment */
```

Unqualified Object Names

Unqualified object names within a stored procedure are implicitly qualified by the stored procedure owner name. Be sure to use explicit qualification for those objects that may be owned by other users.

Local Variable Declarations

All local variables in a stored procedure must be declared before they're used and must have unique names within the stored procedure. The lexical scope of a variable is all lines of code from the point of its declaration to the end of the Create Procedure statement.

NOTE: Although you can use Begin and End statements to create nested blocks in a stored procedure, this has no effect on the scope of a variable.

The format of a variable declaration is similar to that for a parameter:

Declare @*variable-name datatype*

Variable names have the same syntax rules as parameters, and allow the same data types with the exclusion of Text, NText, and Image. You can't declare an initial value for a variable. Here's an example of declaring an integer variable:

```
Declare @RowCnt int
```

Assignment Statements

You can use the Set statement to assign a value to a parameter or variable:

```
Set @RowCnt = 1
```

Although you can assign values to input parameters as well as output parameters within a procedure, changing an input parameter's value has no effect on the caller's data.

You can also add an assignment expression to *all* elements in a single-row Select statement's selection list, as in the following example:

```
Create Procedure GetCustNameAndDiscount
    @CustId    Int,
    @Name      VarChar( 30 ) Output,
    @Discount Dec( 5, 3 )    Output
  As
    Select  @Name     = Name,
            @Discount = Discount
      From  Customer
      Where CustId = @CustId
```

This form of multiple assignment may improve performance by avoiding multiple executions of nearly identical queries. Be careful, though, that you use it only for queries that are guaranteed to return a single row.

Statement Blocks

Wherever a single SQL statement is allowed in a stored procedure, you can use a statement block, delimited by Begin and End statements. So, for example, the following block of three statements will be treated as a single, compound statement:

```
Begin
  Set @DeletedRowCnt = 0
  Delete From Customer
    Where CustId = @CustId
  Set @DeletedRowCnt = @@RowCount
End
```

Statement blocks are important for coding the alternative actions of an If...Else statement and for coding the body of a While loop.

Displaying Messages

The Print statement lets you return any string expression, including literals, character parameters and variables, and functions to the caller's message handler:

```
Print Cast( @CustCount As VarChar(10) ) + ' rows'
```

The string to be returned can be up to 1,024 characters.

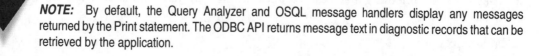

NOTE: By default, the Query Analyzer and OSQL message handlers display any messages returned by the Print statement. The ODBC API returns message text in diagnostic records that can be retrieved by the application.

Conditional Execution

You can use If...Else statements in stored procedures similar to how you use this control structure in HLL programs. Following the If keyword is a condition that evaluates to true, false, or unknown, as described in the section "Conditions and Subqueries," earlier in this chapter. When the condition is true, the statement following the condition is executed; when the condition is false or unknown, the statement following the Else keyword (if specified) is executed. Here's an interesting example to highlight the importance of considering null when you write stored procedures:

```
Create Procedure TestNull As
  Declare @x int
  Set @x = Null
  If ( ( @x = 0 ) Or ( @x <> 0 ) )
    Print 'True'
  Else
    Print 'Unknown'
```

With ANSI-standard behavior, this procedure will print "Unknown" because of SQL's three-valued logic rules. (Recall that the result of any comparison with Null is always unknown, and the result of Or'ing two unknowns is also unknown.)

You can nest If...Else control structures and you can code multiple SQL statements on a single line, so a clean way to express a multiway condition is using an Else If structure, such as the following:

```
If ( @CustCount = 0 ) Begin
    Print 'No rows'
End
Else If ( @CustCount = 1 ) Begin
    Print '1 row'
End
Else Begin
    Print Cast( @CustCount As VarChar(10) ) + ' rows'
End
```

Several programming practices can avoid problems and make your code easier to read. Use parentheses to enclose the condition on the If statement, and use nested parentheses to explicitly show the intended order of evaluation for compound Boolean expressions. Also, use Begin and End blocks for all code under an If or Else branch, even if there's only one statement in the block. If you don't consistently use Begin...End blocks, it's easy to code something that *looks like* a multistatement Else branch but, in fact, is not, as in this example:

```
If ( @CustCount = 0 )
  Print 'No rows'
Else
```

```
Delete From Customer Where Discount Is Null
Print Cast( @CustCount As VarChar(10) ) + ' rows'
```

Without defining a block for the Else branch, the last line is *always* executed because it's not part of the If...Else statement.

While Loops

You can use a While statement in a stored procedure to define an execution loop. After the While keyword, you code a condition that controls execution of the loop. Before each execution of the While statement's body (a simple or block statement), the condition is tested. If true, the body is executed; if false or unknown, control passes to the statement following the While statement. Here's a simple example of a While loop:

```
Create Procedure TestWhile As
  Declare @Count int
  Declare @Limit int
  Set @Count = 0
  Set @Limit = 10
  While ( @Count < @Limit ) Begin
    Print Cast( @Count As VarChar(10) ) + ' iteration'
    Set @Count = @Count + 1
  End
```

You can alter the execution flow within a While loop using Continue and Break statements. The Continue statement transfers control to the beginning of the While loop (the condition test) and the Break statement immediately exits the loop.

GoTo Statement and Labels

SQL has a GoTo statement and statement labels, although using GoTo is not a recommended programming technique. To code a label, use an identifier followed by a colon. A label is coded on a GoTo statement *without* the colon, as in the following code fragment:

```
SkipNextStep:
...
GoTo SkipNextStep
```

WaitFor Statement

To pause execution for a specific duration or until a specified time, you can use the WaitFor statement. There are two forms, as shown here:

```
WaitFor Delay '00:10:30'
or
WaitFor Time '14:30'
```

The first example uses the Delay keyword to specify a time interval of 10 minutes and 30 seconds. You can use any valid datetime format, *without* a date part, so the maximum delay is 24 hours. The second example uses the Time keyword to wait until 2:30 P.M.

Using Cursors

SQL *cursors* provide a way to loop across a result set, reading each row individually. In stored procedures, cursors provide a useful technique to implement complex calculations that aren't easily expressed with the Select statement syntax. Updateable cursors also provide a means for selectively updating or deleting rows within a result set, based on complex conditions. To use a cursor, there are five basic steps:

1. Declare the cursor.
2. Open the cursor.
3. Repeatedly fetch (read) rows from the cursor, optionally updating or deleting a fetched row.
4. Close the cursor.
5. Deallocate the cursor when you no longer need it.

The following example shows the steps to use a cursor to list customer IDs and names:

```
Create Procedure ListCust As
  Declare @CustId   Int
  Declare @CustName VarChar( 30 )
  Declare CustCursor Cursor For
    Select  CustId, Name
      From  Customer
      Order By CustId
      For   Read Only
  Open CustCursor
  While ( 0 = 0 ) Begin
    Fetch Next
      From CustCursor
      Into @CustId, @CustName
    If ( @@Fetch_Status <> 0 ) Break
    Print Cast( @CustId As VarChar(10) ) + ' ' + @CustName
  End
  Close CustCursor
  Deallocate CustCursor
```

The cursor name is coded between the Declare and Cursor keywords, and is the name used to reference the cursor on subsequent statements. The core of a cursor declaration is a Select statement, which can include all the clauses discussed earlier except the Compute clause. In particular, the Select statement can have an Order By clause to sequence the order in which rows are fetched. Importantly, the Select statement can also use parameters and variables in the Where clause (as well as other places where a scalar value is allowed). Thus, you can define a cursor so that the result set depends on execution-time values. The result set defined by the Select statement is *not* actually produced when the Declare Cursor statement is executed; rather, the result set is produced when the Open statement is executed for the cursor. This lets you change the value of any variables used in the cursor's Where clause before you open (or reopen) a cursor to determine which rows get included in the result set.

The first Fetch Next statement reads the first selected row and places each value from the select list into the variable or parameter specified in the corresponding position of the Into clause. Subsequent Fetch Next statements read the next row, as long as there's at least one unread row remaining in the result set.

NOTE: Although the Into clause is optional, there's no practical use for a Fetch that doesn't retrieve values into variables or parameters.

After a Fetch, SQL Server sets the @@Fetch_Status built-in function to return 0 (successful), –1 (no more unread rows), or –2 (the row has been deleted prior to the Fetch operation). You can test @@Fetch_Status to control the loop, as shown in this example. Be aware that @@Fetch_Status returns the status of the most recent Fetch for *any* cursor used by the connection, so you should assign the @@Fetch_Status value to a local variable if you need to use it later in your procedure.

Once you've finished fetching rows, you should close the cursor. You can reopen a cursor to reprocess the same result set from the beginning or to process a different result set based on a new value for a local variable used in the cursor declaration. When you no longer need a cursor, you should deallocate it to free system resources.

Scrollable Cursors

By default, the only type of Fetch operation is Fetch Next. For more-flexible operations, you can add the Scroll keyword before the Cursor keyword:

```
Declare CustCursor Scroll Cursor For
    Select  CustId, Name
      From  Customer
      Order By CustId
      For   Read Only
```

A scrollable cursor allows a variety of Fetch operations, using the keywords shown in Table 10-6.

Keyword	Positions Cursor (and Reads Row)
Next	On the next row after the current row
Prior	On the row before the current row
First	On the first row
Last	On the last row
Absolute n	$n > 0$ Positions to nth row from the beginning
	$n = 0$ No row is returned
	$n < 0$ Positions to nth row before the end
Relative n	$n < -1$ Positions to nth row before current
	$n = -1$ Same as Prior keyword
	$n = 0$ Positions to (and rereads) current row
	$n = 1$ Same as Next keyword
	$n > 1$ Positions to nth row after current

Table 10-6. Fetch Statement Positioning Keywords

Insensitive Cursors

By default most cursors are *dynamic*; that is, as other processes update rows included in the cursor's result set, subsequent Fetch operations get the *new* values. If you want the set of rows to be fixed at the time you open the cursor, add the Insensitive keyword after the cursor name. This causes SQL server to make a temporary copy of the rows in the result set, and to return rows from this temporary copy for subsequent Fetch statements. Even without the Insensitive keyword, SQL Server treats a cursor as if the keyword had been specified when the cursor's Select statement has the Distinct, Union, Group By, or Having keywords.

Updateable Cursors

If you want to update or delete a row that's fetched via a cursor, you can declare the cursor with the For Update clause rather than the For Read Only clause. (You can't use the For Update clause on an insensitive cursor, as described above.) The For Update clause also allows an optional list of columns, which has the effect of limiting the Update statement's Set clause to the listed columns. The following example shows an updateable cursor, a sample Fetch (which is the same as for a read-only cursor), and the form of Update and Delete statements on the current row:

```
Declare @CustId   Int
Declare @Discount Dec( 5, 3 )
Declare CustCursor Cursor For
    Select  CustId, Discount
      From  Customer
      Order By CustId
      For   Update Of Discount
Open CustCursor
...
Fetch Next
  From CustCursor
  Into @CustId, @Discount
If ( @@Fetch_Status = 0 ) Begin
  If ( @Discount = 0.0 ) Begin
    Delete From Customer
      Where Current of CustCursor
  End
  Else If ( @Discount > .5 ) Begin
    Update Customer
      Set Discount = .5
      Where Current of CustCursor
  End
End
...
Close CustCursor
Deallocate CustCursor
```

Notice how the Where clause for both the Update and Delete statements uses the Current of *cursor-name* phrase to specify which row to update or delete in the underlying table. These two types of statements are known as *positioned update* and *positioned delete*.

Additional Cursor Options

SQL Server has an extended form of the Declare Cursor statement that offers additional options, as shown in Table 10-7. To use any of these options, you can't use the Insensitive or Scroll keywords before the Cursor keyword. Instead, you code one or more of the keywords shown in the first column of Table 10-7, following the Cursor keyword. If you code more than one keyword, code them in the order of the rows in Table 10-7.

With the extended form of the Declare Cursor statement, you can also code a For Update clause to limit which columns can be updated. You can't use a For Read Only clause because that option is provided by the Read_Only keyword.

NOTE: The nonextended form of the Declare Cursor statement is the ANSI-standard form. Unless you need an option available only with the extended form, we recommend you use it.

Extended Cursor Keyword	Effect
Local Global	Local specifies that the cursor scope is the stored procedure in which it's defined. Global specifies that the cursor is scoped to the connection and can be used by any stored procedure. When neither is specified, the default is Global unless the database "default to local cursor option" has been set on with the sp_dboption system stored procedure. (Local cursors are recommended to avoid unintended side effects from accessing the same cursor in multiple procedures.)
Forward_Only Scroll	Forward_Only specifies that the only available Fetch option is Fetch Next. Scroll specifies that the Fetch options listed in Table 10-6 are available. The default is Scroll if the Dynamic, Static, or Keyset options are specified, or Forward_Only otherwise.
Dynamic FastForward Static Keyset	Dynamic specifies that the result set is dynamic, as described above. FastForward specifies that the cursor is Forward_Only and Read_Only and has performance optimizations enabled. Static specifies the cursor is insensitive, as described above. Keyset specifies that the set of rows and their order in the result set will not change while the cursor is open; however, any changes to nonkey columns are reflected as rows are fetched.
Read_Only Scroll_Locks Optimistic	Read_Only is equivalent to the For Read Only clause discussed earlier. Scroll_Locks specifies that the cursor is updateable, and row locks are held on each row that's fetched, thus guaranteeing that the row can be updated or deleted. Optimistic specifies that the cursor is updateable, but row locks are not held on each row that's fetched; instead, SQL Server determines whether to allow the update based on whether another process has changed the row since it was fetched.
Type_Warning	Specifies that a warning message is emitted if the cursor is implicitly converted from one type to another.

Table 10-7. Extended Cursor Options

Cursor Parameters and Variables

In addition to scalar parameters and local variables, as discussed earlier, you can declare cursor output parameters and variables, as in the following example:

```
Create Procedure OpenGoodCust
    @GoodCustCursor Cursor Varying Output,
    @MinDiscount Dec( 5, 3 ) = .2
  As
  Set @GoodCustCursor = Cursor For
    Select  CustId, Name
      From  Customer
      Where Discount >= @MinDiscount
      Order By CustId
      For   Read Only
  Open @GoodCustCursor
```

To declare a cursor parameter, follow the parameter name with Cursor Varying Output (all three keywords are required). You can then set the parameter (or a cursor variable) using the form of the Set statement shown in this example. You can call this procedure and use the returned cursor with the following statements:

```
Declare @CustCursor Cursor
Declare @CustId     Int
Declare @CustName   VarChar( 30 )

Execute OpenGoodCust @CustCursor Output, .3

While ( 0 = 0 ) Begin
  Fetch Next
    From @CustCursor
    Into @CustId, @CustName
  If ( @@Fetch_Status <> 0 ) Break
  Print Cast( @CustId As VarChar(10) ) + ' ' + @CustName
End
Close @CustCursor
Deallocate @CustCursor
```

Notice that a cursor can only be passed *back* to a caller, not supplied as an argument on a procedure call. One use of a cursor parameter would be to use logic in the called procedure to select which of several cursors to open and pass back, thus simplifying the calling procedure's processing.

Sending Error Messages

If your stored procedure encounters a problem for which you want to send an error message to the caller, you can use the RaisError statement (note the misspelling of this keyword). Here's an example of sending an ad hoc message with a substitution parameter for the discount value:

```
Create Procedure ListCustWithStatus
    @Status VarChar( 10 )
  As
    If ( ( @Status <> 'Active'   ) And
         ( @Status <> 'Inactive' ) And
         ( @Status <> 'Deleted'  ) ) Begin
      RaisError( 'Invalid status: %s.', 16, 1, @Status )
      Return
    End
    Select *
      From  Customer
      Where Status = @Status
```

The basic syntax for a RaisError statement to send an ad hoc message is

RaisError(*message, severity, state, substitution1, ...*)

The message can be a string up to 8,000 characters and can include up to 20 substitution parameters, each indicated by a percent (%) symbol and a format specification. The format specification can be %s for character strings or %d for integers; floating point and decimal substitution parameters aren't supported. (See the Transact-SQL documentation for the RaisError statement for additional information on format specifications.)

The severity value is an integer between 0 and 25; values 20 and higher cause the current connection to be terminated. The state value is an integer between 1 and 127, and has whatever application-specific meaning you want.

For each substitution parameter in the string, you must supply a literal, parameter, or variable. This value will be merged with the message string sent to the caller.

Predefined Messages

Instead of a message string, you can use a message ID (an integer between 50001 and 2147483647) that identifies a message string you've previously added to the sysmessages table, using a call to the sp_addmessage system stored procedure:

```
sp_addmessage 60001, 16, 'Invalid status: %s.'
```

In this example, the first argument is the message ID, the second is the severity, and the third is the message string. Here's how you'd use this predefined message:

```
RaisError( 60001, 16, 1, @Status )
```

To replace an existing message in the sysmessages table, use a statement such as the following:

```
sp_addmessage 60001, 16, 'Invalid status: %s.', Null, False, Replace
```

To delete an existing message in the sysmessages table, use a statement such as the following:

```
sp_dropmessage 60001
```

By default, the @@Error built-in function is set to 0 for messages with a severity of 10 or less and to the error number for a severity over 10. (Ad hoc messages have an implicit message ID of 50000.) You can add the With SetError option to specify that @@Error be set to the message ID regardless of the message's severity:

```
RaisError( 60001, 16, 1, @Status ) With SetError
```

Other options that you can specify on the With clause are these:

▼   **Log**   Log the error in the server error log and the event log. This option is required for messages with a severity level of 19 or higher.

▲   **NoWait**   Send the message immediately to the client

A stored procedure that calls another stored procedure that sends an error message can check for the most recent error by testing the @@Error function:

```
If ( @@Error > 0 ) Begin
   ... handle error
End
```

Be careful when testing @@Error because it's reset on each operation. The following code shows a safe way to preserve and test the value:

```
Declare @ProcError int
...
Execute MyProc
Set @ProcError = @@Error
...
If ( @ProcError > 0 ) Begin
   ... handle error
End
```

TRIGGERS

A trigger is a special type of stored procedure that's executed when an Insert, Update, or Delete statement updates one or more rows in a table. Because SQL Server calls a trigger for *every* specified operation on a particular table, you can use triggers to extend SQL Server's built-in integrity and data manipulation features.

> **NOTE:** Unlike the Delete statement, the Truncate Table statement does *not* invoke a trigger. A WriteText statement also doesn't invoke a trigger.

You create a trigger by using a Create Trigger statement such as the following:

```
Create Trigger TrackCustomerUpdates
    On   AppDta.dbo.Customer
    For Update
  As
    Insert Into AppDta.dbo.CustUpdLog
            ( CustId,
              Action,
              UpdUser,
              UpdDateTime )
        Select CustId,
              'Update',
              Current_User,
              Current_TimeStamp
          From inserted )
```

This example shows the essential elements of a trigger definition. The trigger name follows the Create Trigger keywords. The On clause specifies a single base table with which the trigger is associated. (You can't create triggers on a view.) The For clause specifies for which actions the trigger is "fired" (that is, invoked); you can use one or more of the Insert, Update, or Delete keywords. Then following the As keyword, you code a stored procedure as explained previously. In this example, the trigger consists of single Insert statement that adds rows to a table that tracks updates to the Customer table.

Once this trigger is created, SQL Server automatically invokes the trigger's stored procedure once for each Update statement that's executed on the Customer table. Within a trigger's stored procedure, you can use the inserted identifier to refer to a temporary, memory-resident table that contains all the *new* row values for the affected table.

> **NOTE:** You don't need to create a table named inserted for use in triggers. SQL Server manages the memory-resident tables used by triggers automatically.

In this example, the CustId values from the updated rows in the Customer table are part of the new rows inserted in the user-defined CustUpdLog table. The other three columns in the CustUpdLog table hold the type of action (i.e., Update), the user performing the action, and the timestamp. To also track Insert and Delete operations, you could use the following two Create Trigger statements in addition to the previous one:

```
Create Trigger TrackCustomerInserts
    On  AppDta.dbo.Customer
    For Insert
  As
    Insert Into AppDta.dbo.CustUpdLog
            ( CustId,
              Action,
              UpdUser,
              UpdDateTime )
        Select CustId,
              'Insert',
              Current_User,
              Current_TimeStamp
          From inserted


Create Trigger TrackCustomerDeletes
    On  AppDta.dbo.Customer
    For Delete
  As
    Insert Into AppDta.dbo.CustUpdLog
            ( CustId,
              Action,
              UpdUser,
              UpdDateTime )
        Select CustId,
              'Delete',
              Current_User,
              Current_TimeStamp
          From deleted
```

The second of these two triggers uses the deleted identifier, which refers to a temporary, memory-resident table that contains all the *old* row values for the affected table.

NOTE: The temporary tables referenced by the inserted and deleted keywords have the same column structure as the base table on which the trigger is defined.

As an alternative to creating one trigger for each type of operation, you can create a single trigger for all three operations and use programming techniques to handle each type of operation appropriately. The following example lists all three types of statements in the For clause and uses conditional statements to insert the appropriate tracking values into the CustUpdLog table:

```
Create Trigger TrackCustomerUpdates
    On  AppDta.dbo.Customer
    For Insert, Update, Delete
  As
    Declare @InsertedCount Int
    Declare @DeletedCount  Int
    Set @InsertedCount = ( Select Count(*) From inserted )
    Set @DeletedCount  = ( Select Count(*) From deleted  )
    If ( @InsertedCount > 0 ) Begin
      Insert Into AppDta.dbo.CustUpdLog
                ( CustId,
                  Action,
                  UpdUser,
                  UpdDateTime )
            Select CustId,
                  Case
                    When ( @DeletedCount > 0 ) Then
                            'Update'
                    Else  'Insert'
                  End,
                  Current_User,
                  Current_TimeStamp
              From inserted
    End
    Else If ( @DeletedCount > 0 ) Begin
      Insert Into AppDta.dbo.CustUpdLog
                ( CustId,
                  Action,
                  UpdUser,
                  UpdDateTime )
            Select CustId,
                  'Delete',
                  Current_User,
                  Current_TimeStamp
              From deleted
    End
```

As this example illustrates, the inserted temporary table has rows whenever an Insert or Update statement affects one or more rows, and the deleted temporary table has rows whenever a Delete or Update statement affects one or more rows. For an Update statement, the deleted temporary table has the *old* row value(s) and the inserted temporary table has the *new* row value(s). This example also reflects another important aspect of triggers—a trigger for an Update or Delete operation on a table is invoked even if no rows are affected by the statement (that is, because no rows satisfy the Where clause). The stored procedure for a trigger should anticipate this possibility.

Checking for Specific Column Changes

For an Insert or Update trigger, you can immediately follow the As keyword with an If Update(*column-name*) clause to test whether the Insert or Update statement explicitly listed one or more particular columns. The following example shows how to use this test:

```
Create Trigger TrackDiscountUpdates
    On  AppDta.dbo.Customer
    For Update
  As
    If Update( Discount )
      Insert Into AppDta.dbo.DiscountLog
             ( CustId,
               Action,
               Discount,
               UpdUser,
               UpdDateTime )
        Select CustId,
               'Update',
               Discount,
               Current_User,
               Current_TimeStamp
          From inserted
```

You can use And and Or logical operators in the If clause to combine tests, as in the following examples:

```
Create Trigger TrackCustomerUpdates
    On  AppDta.dbo.Customer
    For Update
  As
    If Update( Name ) And Update( Discount ) ...
```

```
Create Trigger TrackCustomerUpdates
    On  AppDta.dbo.Customer
    For Update
  As
    If Update( Name ) Or Update( Discount ) ...
```

For an Update statement, the Update(*column-name*) test is true if the column is listed in a Set expression. SQL Server does *not* check whether the new value is different than the old value. For an Insert statement, the Update(*column-name*) test is true if the Insert statement has no column list (which implicitly means "all columns") or if the column is explicitly listed in the column list. The rules for the Update(*column-name*) test apply whether you use a literal, an expression, or the Null or Default keywords to assign a new or changed value.

Another variation of the test for specific columns uses the Columns_Updated function which returns a bitmap that indicates which columns were specified in the SQL Insert or Update statement. The first column in the table is represented by the lowest order position in the bitmap, the second column by the next higher order position in the bitmap, and so on. The following statement tests whether any one of the first, third, or fourth columns were specified:

```
Create Trigger TrackCustomerUpdates
    On   AppDta.dbo.Customer
    For Update
  As
    If ( Columns_Updated() & 13 ) > 0 ...
```

In this example, the mask value of 13 is the sum of the three bitmap values that represent the columns: 1, 4, and 8. You can use any bitwise operation to mask the Columns_Updated function value and then use any logical comparison to test the masked value. We suggest you use this bitmap technique sparingly because it's dependent on the columns' relative positions in the table. The Update(*column-name*) test is a preferable technique because it isn't dependent on column position.

Altering and Deleting Triggers

To change a trigger definition, you can either delete and re-create the trigger or use the Alter Trigger statement. To delete a trigger, use a Drop Trigger statement such as the following:

```
Drop Trigger TrackCustomerUpdates
```

The Alter Trigger statement has the same structure as the Create Trigger statement other than the first keyword.

Working with Triggers

Not only can you create multiple triggers for a table, you can create multiple triggers for the same SQL statement (for example, Update) for a table. Each new Create Trigger statement adds the trigger to those that already exist for the specified table and statement. If there are multiple triggers associated with the same database operation for a table, there's no predictable order to the trigger invocations. This means you shouldn't create multiple triggers for the same operation on a table that depend on a particular execution sequence. This characteristic of triggers doesn't cause any particular problems because you can always implement various actions as regular stored procedures and call them in the required sequence from a single trigger.

A trigger is always created in the same database as the table with which it is associated, and each trigger must have a unique name within the database. You can optionally qualify a trigger name with an owner name like dbo.TrackCustomerUpdates, which should be the same as the table owner.

> **NOTE:** Although a trigger is always associated with a base table in the same database, a trigger can reference objects in other databases. This capability provides a way to implement referential integrity between two tables in different databases, something the Create Table foreign key support doesn't allow.

Even though a trigger is a type of stored procedure, you can't call it with the Execute statement. If you have code you want to share between triggers and regular stored procedures, just put the shared code in a stored procedure and call it from the trigger.

Nested and Recursive Triggers

If a trigger updates a table, these updates may cause either another trigger or the same trigger to fire. By default, SQL Server allows this type of nested trigger invocation to a depth of 32 levels. Although we recommend you allow nested and recursive triggers, you can use system stored procedures to disallow them. The following statement prevents recursive triggers in the specified database:

```
sp_dboption AppDta, 'recursive triggers', 'false'
```

To prevent nested trigger calls (including recursive calls) in *all* databases, you can use the following statement:

```
sp_configure 'nested triggers', 0
```

Displaying Information About Triggers

There are three system stored procedures that display information about triggers:

- ▼ **sp_help** *trigger-name*   Displays the trigger's owner and when it was created
- ■ **sp_helptext** *trigger-name*   Displays source code for the trigger
- ▲ **sp_depends** *trigger-name*   Displays list of objects that the trigger references

The sp_helptext system stored procedure is especially useful if you've lost the original source code used to create a trigger.

Trigger Programming

In general trigger programming is like stored procedure programming; however, there are several considerations that apply to triggers. For one thing, you can't use these statements in a trigger:

Alter Database	Create Trigger	Drop View
Alter Procedure	Create View	Grant
Alter Table	Deny	Load Database
Alter Trigger	Disk Init	Load Log
Alter View	Disk Resize	Reconfigure
Create Database	Drop Database	Restore Database
Create Default	Drop Default	Restore Log
Create Index	Drop Index	Revoke
Create Procedure	Drop Procedure	Truncate Table
Create Rule	Drop Rule	Update Statistics
Create Schema	Drop Table	
Create Table	Drop Trigger	

A trigger should also not return result sets to the caller, which means you shouldn't code free-standing Select statements in a trigger. It's fine to use a scalar subquery to assign a value to a variable because this type of statement doesn't create a result set. You may also want to code a Set NoCount On statement at the beginning of a trigger to prevent SQL Server from sending the messages that indicate how many rows were affected by each statement in a stored procedure.

NOTE: If you use a Set statement within a trigger (or regular stored procedure), the Set option values are restored to their original values when the trigger completes execution.

One of the purposes of a trigger is to add additional integrity checking beyond what's possible with primary and foreign key or check constraints. After checking a condition in a trigger, you can cancel the entire transaction by executing a Rollback statement. The following example shows how to code a trigger that makes sure the user assigning a customer a discount has been approved to offer discounts:

```
Create Trigger CheckDiscountUpdates
    On  AppDta.dbo.Customer
    For Insert, Update
```

```
As
  -- Check only if Discount column is explicitly set
  If Update( Discount ) Begin
    Declare @User VarChar( 256 )
    Set NoCount On
    -- Check only if an actual discount is being assigned
    If ( Exists ( Select *
                    From  inserted
                    Where Discount > 0 ) ) Begin
      -- Make sure this user has approval to assign discounts
      If ( Not Exists ( Select  *
                          From  Employee
                          Where UserName = Current_User And
                                DiscountAuthority = 'Y' ) ) Begin
        -- Send message and abort the transaction
        Set @User = Current_User
        RaisError( 'User %s not approved to assign discounts.',
                  16, 1, @User )
        Rollback
      End
    End
  End
```

A trigger is invoked once for each Insert, Update, or Delete statement, and is invoked only if the statement satisfies all primary key, foreign key, and check constraints. At the time the trigger is invoked, the effects of the SQL statement are reflected in the target database table (and in the memory-resident inserted and deleted tables), but are not yet committed.

The fact that a statement must satisfy all constraints *before* the trigger is called means you can't use a trigger to make database updates to satisfy a constraint. For example, suppose you have a foreign key constraint that prevents deleting a row from the Customer table if there are Sale rows with a matching customer ID value. You might consider creating a trigger for Delete operations on the Customer table so that deleting a Customer row also deletes all dependent Sale rows, thus avoiding "orphan" Sale rows that violate the foreign key constraint. In SQL Server 7, this won't work because the foreign key constraint is checked before the trigger is called, and when there are orphan rows at the time the constraint is checked, the trigger doesn't get called.

A trigger can manipulate the target table, which means you can do additional operations on rows that have been inserted or updated by the SQL statement that fires the trigger. If you use this capability, be sure to avoid or handle recursive firing of triggers.

DML CODING SUGGESTIONS

As with any language, it helps to follow certain coding practices and conventions so your SQL code is more maintainable. Listed here are a few suggestions that we've found helpful.

▼ For DML statements that you'll use repeatedly:

- Create a stored procedure that includes them and/or store them in a source file that can be recalled from Query Analyzer or run in batch with OSQL.

- Place comments at the beginning of your SQL source to describe the action taken.

- Use spaces, blank lines, and separator line comments to improve the readability of your source code.

- Indent the From, Where, Group By, and Having clauses under the Select clause.

- Align the beginning and continuation of each clause (for example, the select list, the from table list, the search condition).

- Align column names, expressions, compound search conditions, and so on on multiline statements for readability.

- Use an As clause to give a meaningful column name to an expression or function in the select list.

- Consider using the SubString scalar function to shorten long character fields for Select statements entered with Query Analyzer. Also, consider using the Cast scalar function to return only meaningful parts of numeric fields. These techniques can make the results easier to view.

- Use meaningful table correlation names (that is, aliases) such as CurCust, not C1.

- Consider null-capable columns when specifying expressions, functions, or search conditions.

- Be sure that a subquery used in a basic condition or in place of a scalar value in an expression can never have more than one row in the result table.

- Be careful to use the proper Any or All keyword in quantified conditions.

- Generally, when a Group By clause is specified, include all grouping columns in the select list so that each row in the result table has the identifying information for the group.

- Use an explicit list of columns in the Insert statement to make clear which column each new value corresponds to.

- Be careful to include a Where clause in an Update or Delete statement unless you intend to update or delete all rows in the table.

■ Be sure to consider the effect of primary, unique, and foreign key constraints when updating a primary, unique, or foreign key column or when deleting a row in a table referenced by a foreign key.

■ Be sure to consider the potential for conflicting access by other processes when you execute multirow retrieval or update statements. Consider table hints on DML statements or other SQL Server facilities to prevent conflicts.

▲ Use commitment control when you need to guarantee all-or-none execution of a multirow transaction.

CONCLUSION

Transact-SQL's Data Manipulation Language (DML) is an essential facility for accessing SQL Server databases. As a developer, you may use DML statements in an ad hoc manner with tools such as the Query Analyzer; but most important is that most applications you build over a SQL Server database require some programmatic use of DML. The introductions and programming advice in this chapter will help you code maintainable and well-performing SQL.

ADDITIONAL RESOURCES

▼ Groff, James R., and Paul N. Weinberg. *LAN Times Guide to SQL.* Berkeley, CA: Osborne/McGraw-Hill, 1994.
   A practical tutorial on SQL that includes lots of examples. This book covers many of the SQL-92 features that are implemented in SQL Server 7.

▲ The Additional Resources listed at the end of Chapter 9 are valuable for working with SQL DML, as well as SQL DDL.

CHAPTER 11

Developing SQL Server Database Applications with Access

Microsoft Access is both a stand-alone database platform and a powerful database development tool that can be used to develop custom client/server database applications. Access contains a rich set of database development tools that allow you to create custom database applications. While Access is primarily intended as a stand-alone database, in this chapter you'll see how Access can also be used to develop SQL Server database applications.

As a database platform, Access uses the Microsoft Jet Database Engine to handle its storage and query functions. Native Access databases are stored in .mdb (Microsoft Database) files that are typically located on the PC's hard drive or a network share. While the Jet engine is primarily designed to handle single-user databases, it can also be used for small multiple-user applications. The Jet engine used by Access contains a full-featured query processor that responds to Jet SQL statements. The syntax of Jet SQL is similar but not identical to SQL Server's Transact-SQL. As you would expect from a database system, Access's query processor is able to perform queries, retrieve result sets, join files, and perform action queries much like SQL Server's more robust multiple-user database.

In addition to its database capabilities, Access provides a visual database development environment. It provides a visual database design tool that allows you to quickly create databases and contains a visual forms builder that can be used to create data-entry screens as well as a graphical report design tool. Access's primary visual development tools are shown in Table 11-1.

In addition to these primary components, Access includes more than 30 wizards that can be used to perform many common tasks such as creating forms, tables, reports, and queries. Figure 11-1 presents a high-level overview of the Access environment. As you

Component	Description
Table Designer	Used to create or link tables and views
Query Designer	Used to create database queries
Forms Designer	Used to create data entry forms
Report Designer	Used to create database reports
Macro Creator	Used to build database macros that can be used to automate simple actions
VBA Editor	Used to create Visual Basic for Applications scripts that can be used for more complex programming tasks

Table 11-1.   Access's Rapid Development Tools

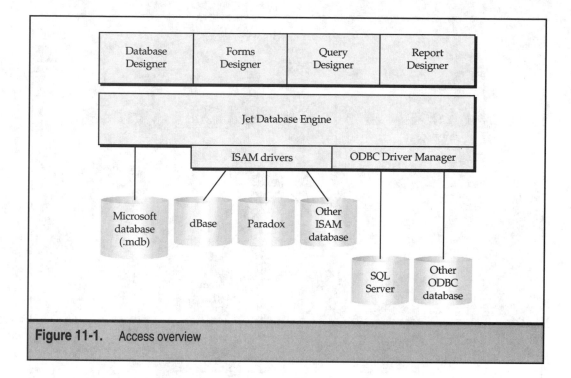

Figure 11-1. Access overview

can see, the core of Access is its local query processor, otherwise known as the Microsoft Jet (Joint Engine Technology) Database Engine. The Jet engine natively accesses data stored in a local .mdb (Microsoft Database) file. However, using external database drivers, the Jet engine is also able to access data stores in other databases like Paradox, dBase, and ODBC data sources. Access's front-end development tools are coupled to the different databases through the Jet engine.

In this chapter, you'll learn how to use Microsoft Access's powerful database design and development features to build client/server applications that take advantage of SQL Server's high-performance, multiple-user database.

THE DIFFERENCE BETWEEN MULTIPLE-USER ACCESS AND SQL SERVER DATABASE IMPLEMENTATIONS

While Access is able to handle multiple users, there is a big difference in the way Access and SQL Server handle multiple users. With Access, each individual system contains its own query processor, and there's no centralized control or optimization over concurrent database access. Figure 11-2 illustrates a multiple-user Access application.

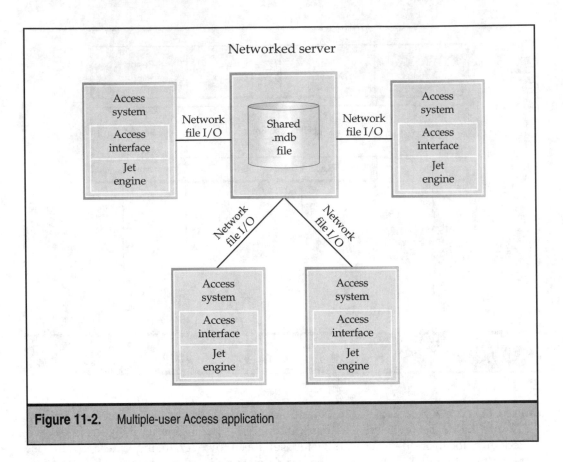

Figure 11-2.　Multiple-user Access application

In a typical multiple-user Access application, the database is essentially an operating system file that's shared and accessed by multiple-client systems running Access. In each case, the query processor is located on the networked client systems—not with the database itself. There is no central mechanism available to optimize concurrent access, nor is there any central resource to handle locking of other resource contention issues. The Access database coordinates multiple users through system tables that are also subject to the same type of multiple-user contention issues as the database tables themselves. In addition, to satisfy queries and other database requests, the client systems must perform network file reads across the network to supply the local query engine with data. Even in a fast network, reading data across the network is many times slower than accessing it using the local hard drive.

Even so, for a small number of users these issues are manageable, and Access can be effectively used to build departmental or other smaller-scale, multiple-user applications. However, when the data access requirements grow, Access just doesn't scale to meet those requirements. The lack of optimization, lack of resource management, and the requirement for network I/O cause the performance and reliability of multiple-user Access applications to decline drastically when dealing with a large number of users or a small number of heavy database users.

In contrast, SQL Server is designed expressly for multiple-user database access. With SQL Server, the database and the query processor reside in a central database server. There is no local query processor on the client systems. Instead, the database application on the client system sends a database request to the SQL Server system. The SQL Server query processor takes in all of the incoming requests, accesses the data store, and returns the results of each request back to each of the client systems. Figure 11-3 presents an overview of a multiple-user database access using SQL Server.

In a multiple-user SQL Server implementation, the database and the query engine are located on the central SQL Server system. The client applications communicate to the

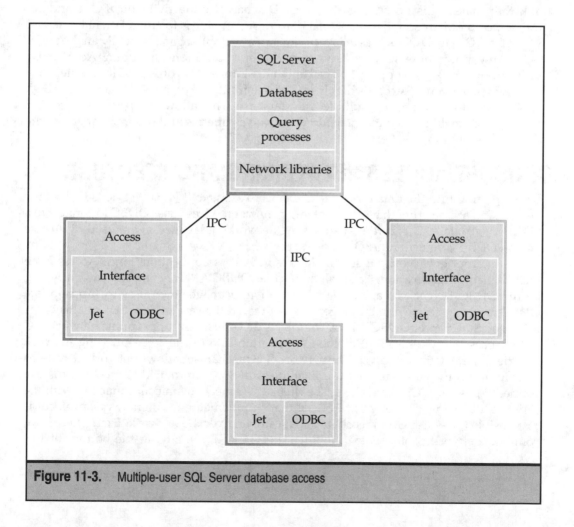

Figure 11-3. Multiple-user SQL Server database access

server using the network protocol and a network communications library. The SQL Server query processor handles all of the incoming requests and can analyze the requests and apply optimizations in how the requests are processed. Since the query engine and the database are physically located on the same system, all locking and data access is fast and efficient. This client/server architecture allows SQL Server to scale upward and deal with hundreds or thousands of clients.

USING ACCESS AS A FRONT-END DEVELOPMENT TOOL

While Access is primarily designed to create stand-alone, single-user database applications, it can also be used as a client/server application development tool. The same graphical development features that make it a productive personal database development tool also make it a powerful tool for developing SQL Server database applications. The missing link that makes this possible is the Open Database Connectivity (ODBC) standard. Developed by Microsoft, the ODBC standard provides access to any relational database via an ODBC driver. ODBC has enjoyed widespread adoption, and virtually all the major database vendors now support it. Many end-user applications, including Access, also include built-in ODBC support. You can find more information on ODBC in Chapter 13.

ODBC can connect Access's highly productive front-end database tools with the SQL Server's high-performance, multiple-user database. This allows you to use Access to quickly and easily build data entry forms, as well as queries and reports that access the databases stored in SQL Server.

MICROSOFT ACCESS NETWORKING ARCHITECTURE

Before getting into the details of how to connect Access to SQL Server, let's look at the networking architecture that's brought into play when Access uses ODBC to connect to a SQL Server database. Figure 11-4 shows the networking layers that are used by Access and an ODBC connection to SQL Server.

At the top level, you can see the Microsoft Access application. Since Access is an ODBC-enabled application, it can call the various ODBC API functions that are provided by the ODBC Driver Manager. The ODBC Driver Manager then uses the appropriate ODBC driver to connect to the target data source. In the case of SQL Server, this is the Microsoft SQL Server ODBC driver. The ODBC driver uses the appropriate network IPC (interprocess communication) method to communicate to the corresponding network libraries on the database server. The network IPC mechanism allows networked systems to communicate with one another. Examples of two common IPC mechanisms are Named Pipes and TCP/IP Sockets. The client's IPC mechanism communicates with the server's IPC using the network protocol that's implemented. The network protocol is responsible for sending and receiving a data stream over the network. Examples of two common network protocols are NetBEUI and TCP/IP. Finally, at the bottom of this

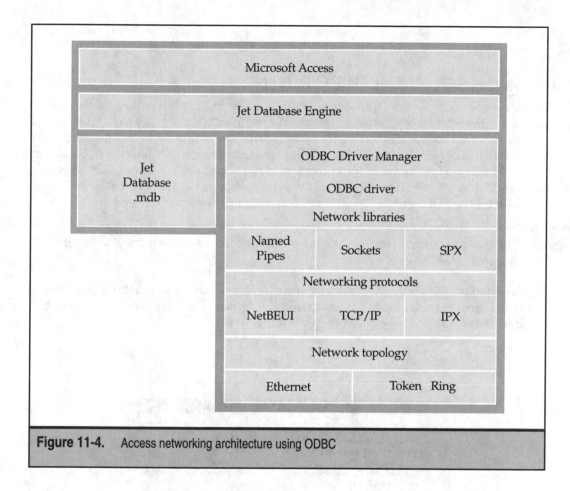

Figure 11-4.   Access networking architecture using ODBC

communications stack is the physical network. The physical network defines the hardware required to physically connect the client and the server systems. The physical network includes the adapter cards, hubs, and cabling that are used to network the distributed client and server systems. Ethernet and Token Ring are examples of two of the most common network topologies.

CONNECTING TO SQL SERVER

Three main requirements must be met in order to connect to SQL Server from Access. The first is rather obvious: you must be able to log in to SQL Server from the system that's running Access. This requires that you have a networked connection between the Access system and the SQL Server system, plus a login to the SQL Server system. Next, the SQL Server ODBC driver must be installed on the Access system and a data source for the target SQL Server system must be created. Finally, you must create a set of linked tables in Access that use the ODBC connection to access SQL Server tables.

Installing the SQL Server ODBC Driver

The Microsoft SQL Server ODBC driver is optionally installed by either the Microsoft Office or Microsoft Access Setup programs. As you would expect, if you have acquired Access as a part of the Microsoft Office suite, then you will need to run the Microsoft Office Setup program. If you are using the stand-alone version of Microsoft Access, then you will need to run Access's Setup program. However, the SQL Server ODBC driver is not installed by default. If you installed Access or Office using the "Typical" installation option, then the SQL Server ODBC driver will not be present on your system.

NOTE: You can also install the SQL Server ODBC driver by installing the SQL Server Client Management utilities on your system.

To install the SQL Server ODBC driver for an existing Access installation, you need to rerun the Access or Office Setup program. The Office 97 Professional Edition Setup program displays the dialog box shown in Figure 11-5.

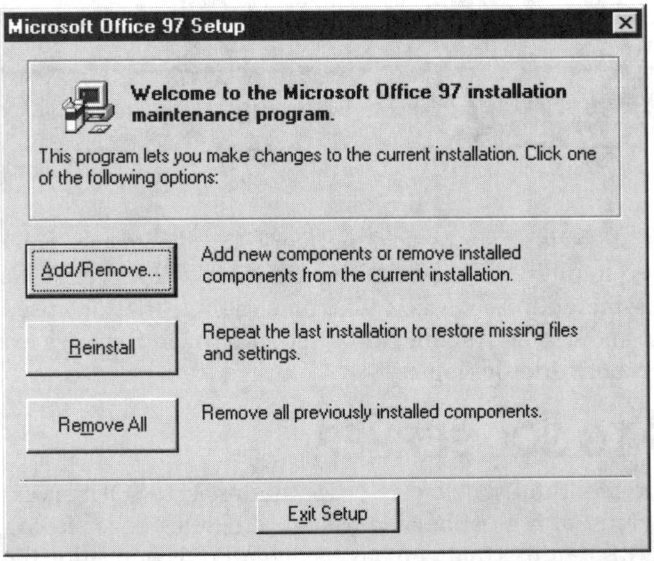

Figure 11-5. Office 97 Professional Edition Setup dialog box

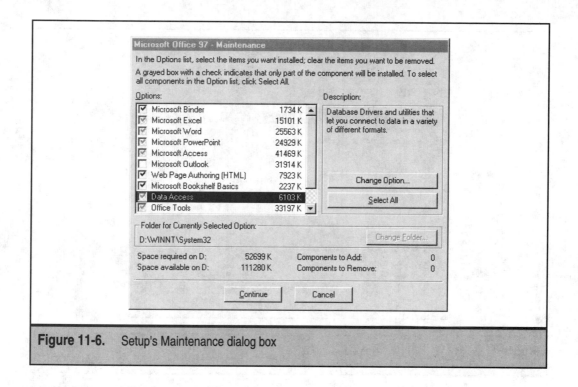

Figure 11-6. Setup's Maintenance dialog box

To install the Microsoft SQL Server ODBC driver to an existing Access installation, first click Add/Remove in this dialog box to display the Maintenance dialog box, shown in Figure 11-6. Select the Data Access check box, and then click Change Option to display the Data Access options dialog box shown in Figure 11-7.

In the Data Access options dialog box, select the Database Drivers check box and then click Change Option to display the Database Drivers dialog box shown in Figure 11-8. Select the Microsoft SQL Server Driver check box and then click OK. The Office 97 Professional Edition Setup program then installs the Microsoft SQL Server ODBC driver on your system.

TIP: After the SQL Server ODBC driver has been installed, it can be used by all of the various Office programs to access SQL Server databases.

Configuring a Data Source

Just installing the SQL Server ODBC driver by itself is not enough to begin using ODBC from Access. You also need to create a data source. To create an ODBC data source for SQL Server, you need to run the ODBC Administrator from the Windows 95 or Windows NT Control Panel. Opening the ODBC Administrator icon displays the ODBC Data Source Administrator dialog box shown in Figure 11-9.

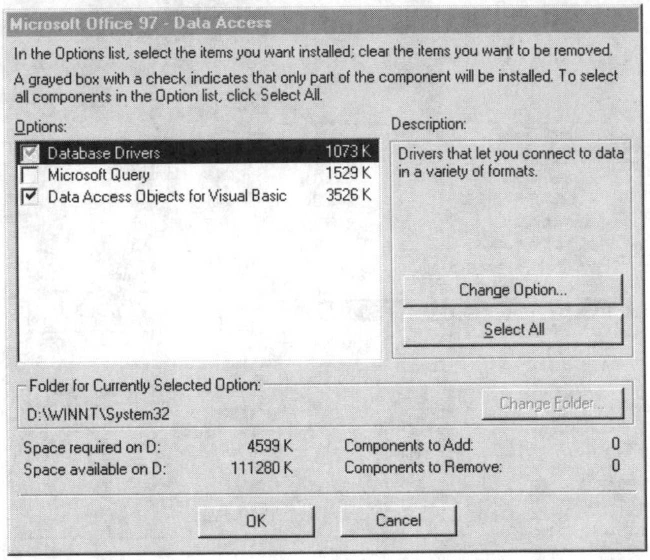

Figure 11-7. Setup's Data Access dialog box

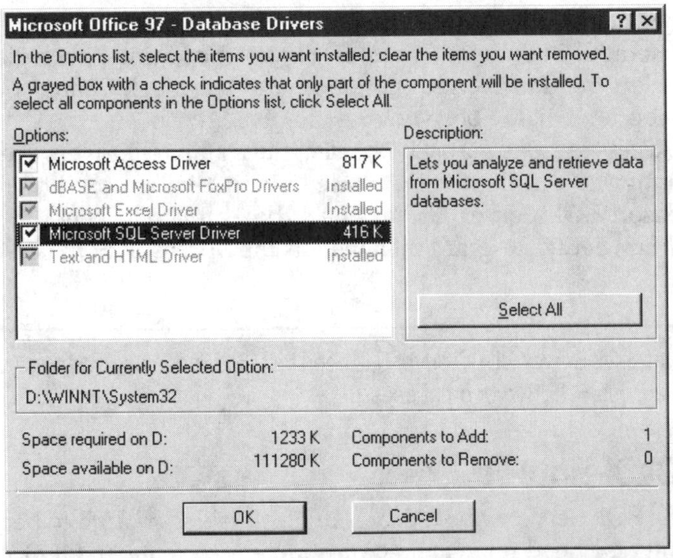

Figure 11-8. Setup's Database Drivers dialog box

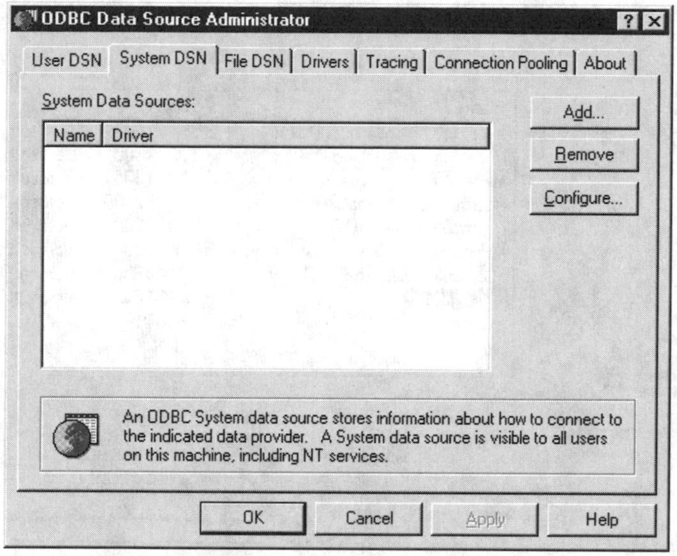

Figure 11-9.   Adding a data source with the ODBC Data Source Administrator

NOTE: For more detailed information about the options presented by the ODBC Administrator, you can refer to Chapter 13.

You can add a new data source in either the User DSN tab, the System DSN tab, or the File DSN tab. Choose the User DSN tab if the data source will be used only by the current user. Choose the System DSN tab if the data source can be used by all users of the system. The File DSN tab allows you to create a File DSN that can be shared by other users. To configure a new system data source, select the User DSN tab, and then click Add. The Create New Data Source dialog box shown in Figure 11-10 will display.

All of the ODBC drivers that are currently installed on the system will be listed in this dialog box. To install the SQL Server ODBC driver, select the SQL Server driver from the list and then click Finish. The SQL Server DSN Configuration Wizard shown in Figure 11-11 will display.

Enter the data source name in the first text box of the wizard. This name can be anything that you choose; its main purpose is to provide a meaningful name to the ODBC data source. The Description field allows you to further identify the data source. Next, from the drop-down combo box, select the name of the SQL Server system that you want this data source to connect to. All of the SQL Server systems on your network will be listed in the combo box. The name "local" is used for ODBC connections that are on the

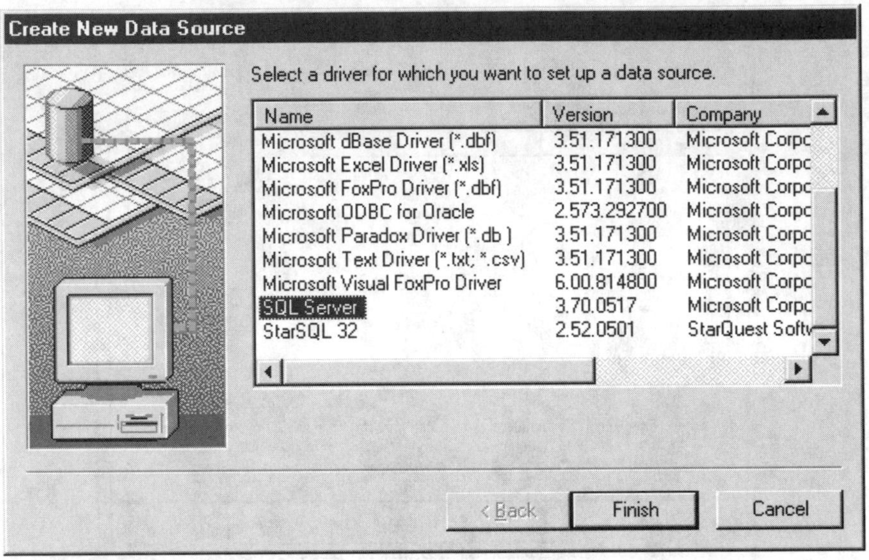

Figure 11-10. Selecting an ODBC driver

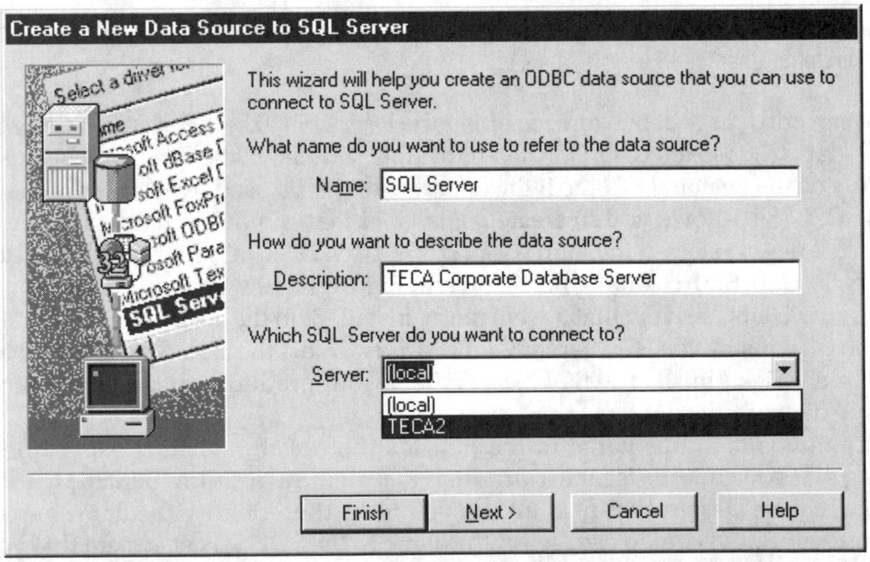

Figure 11-11. Choosing a SQL Server DSN data source name

same system as SQL Server itself. Typically, instead of "local," you would want to select the system name of a networked SQL Server system from the drop-down box. Clicking Next displays the authentication dialog box shown in Figure 11-12.

This authentication allows you to specify the SQL Server security authentication that will be performed. If you're using integrated security, select the option to use Windows NT authentication, which means that your NT password will be used to connect to the SQL Server system. If you're using SQL Server authentication, then you will need to log in to SQL Server using the SQL Server specific ID. For more information about integrated security and standard security, refer to Chapter 3. Clicking Next initiates a connection with SQL Server and displays the connection defaults dialog box shown in Figure 11-13.

The check box at the top of the dialog box allows you to set the default database specified in the SQL Server login. In this example, you can see that the SQL Server example database named pubs has been selected as the default database. For a SQL Server 7 connection, you can leave the other entries at their default values and click Next to display the next SQL Server DSN Configuration Wizard dialog box, shown in Figure 11-14.

This dialog box allows you to set the language, character set, and regional variable that the SQL Server ODBC driver will use. The default settings are acceptable for most North American installations. Clicking Finish completes the data source configuration. Following this, a series of optional dialog boxes allow you to test the newly created data source.

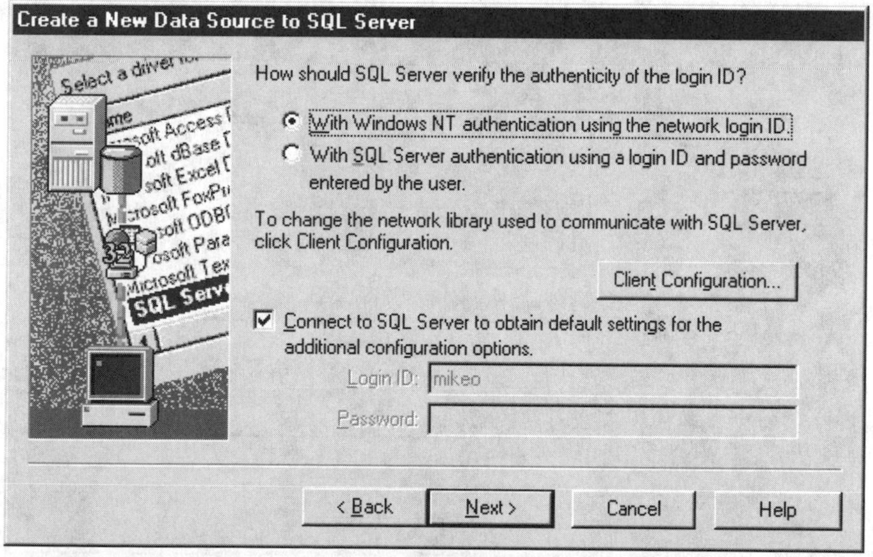

Figure 11-12. Specifying the SQL Server DSN authentication

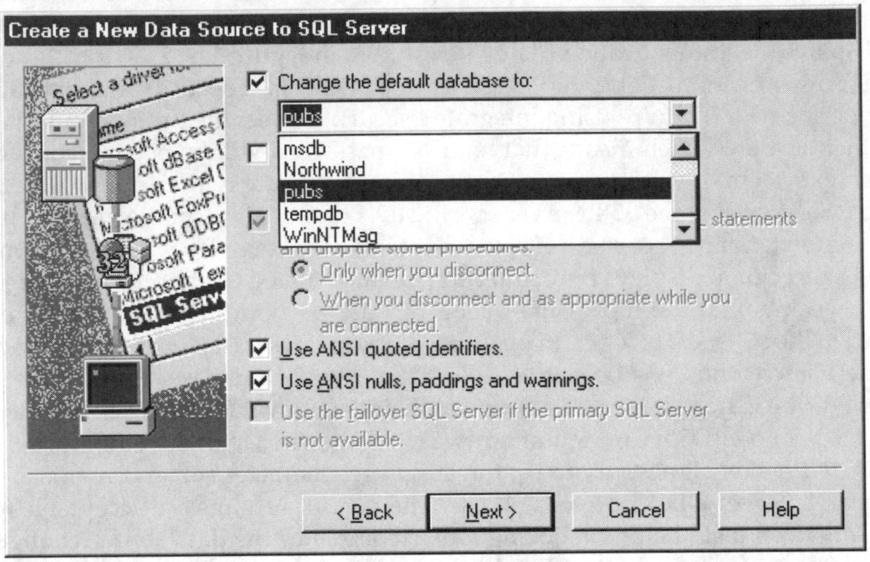

Figure 11-13. Setting the SQL Server DSN default database

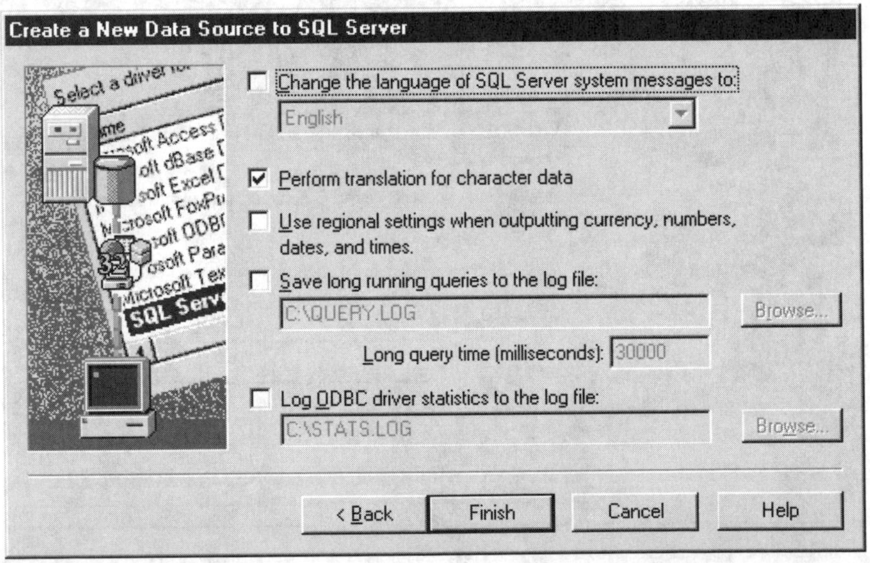

Figure 11-14. Setting the language, character set, and regional variable

After the SQL Server ODBC driver has been installed and a data source has been configured using the ODBC Administrator, you're ready to make the connection to SQL Server from Access.

Linking Tables

Access always begins by opening a local .mdb (Microsoft Database) file. The .mdb file is normally located on a local hard drive, but it can also be located on a network shared drive. The .mdb file contains all of the Access database objects like tables, views, queries, and report definitions. As you might expect from a database system, Access's core database component is a table. All of the other database objects are built based on the database schema that's defined in the Access tables. In a typical single-user implementation, the Access tables contain all of the actual data that comprise the database, but that's not the case when you use Access as a front end to SQL Server. In this scenario, the SQL Server database contains all of the tables and the data. At first, this might seem to be a problem. However, Access provides a mechanism known as *linked tables*, which enable a local Access table to be connected to the remote database table using ODBC. All the Access's interface, query, and report-building components can use linked tables exactly as if they were local tables. In the following section, you'll see how to create a set of local Access tables that are linked to the tables in SQL Server's example pubs database.

Creating a database is the first step in building an Access database application. Building an Access application that uses a SQL Server database is no different. In Figure 11-15,

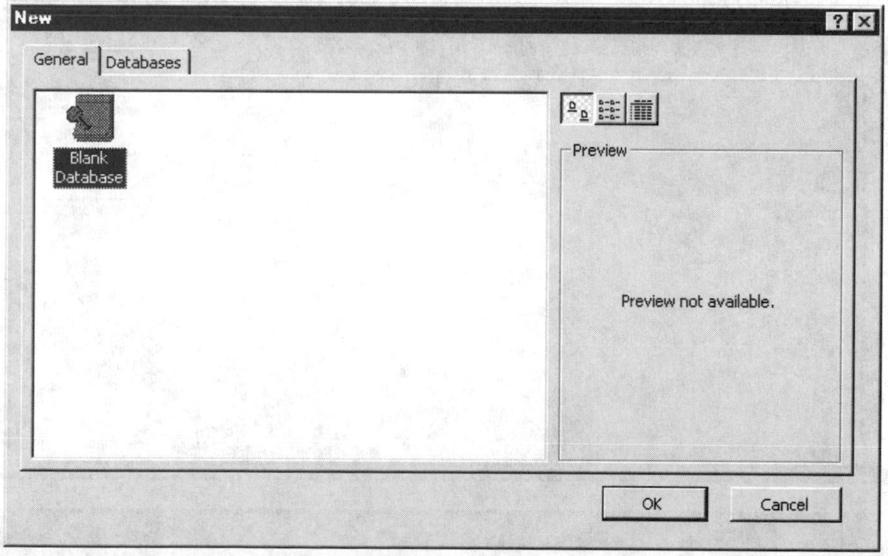

Figure 11-15. Creating a new Access database

you can see the New dialog box, which allows Access to create a new database. Click the Blank Database icon, and then click OK to create a new database that will use tables linked to SQL Server.

NOTE: For simplicity, this example illustrates creating a new Access database that will contain the tables that are linked to the tables in SQL Server's pubs database. However, that's not required. You can also add linked tables to an existing Access database.

Access displays a dialog box that allows you to enter the name and location of the Access database that will be linked to the SQL Server database. After specifying the database name and path, Access creates a new .mdb file and displays the main Access database window shown in Figure 11-16. In this example, the Access database name used is AccessPubs. As you might expect, this database is stored in a file called AccessPubs.mdb.

The New button on the main Access database window shown in Figure 11-16 allows you to create new Access database objects. The first tab enables the creation of tables, and the other tabs permit you to create new queries, forms, reports, macros, and code modules. To create a linked table, select the Tables tab, and then click New. The pop-up dialog box shown in Figure 11-17 will be displayed.

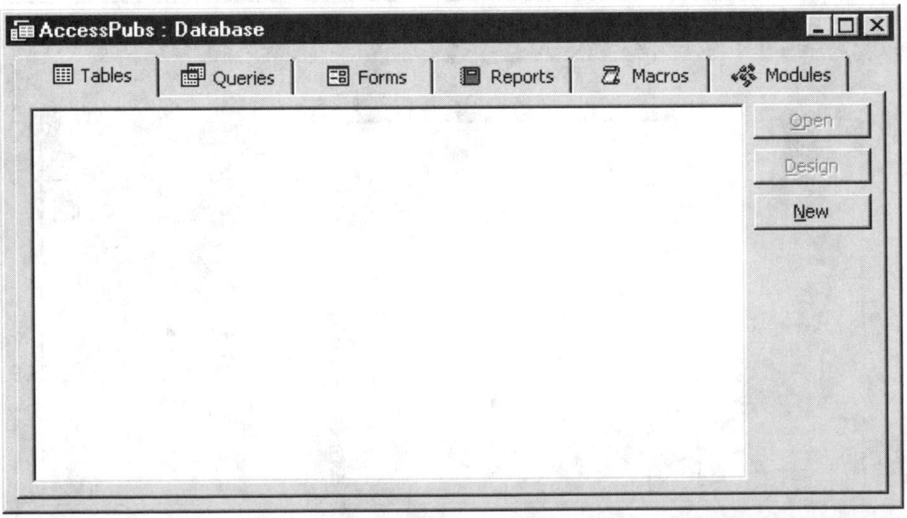

Figure 11-16.   Creating a new Access table

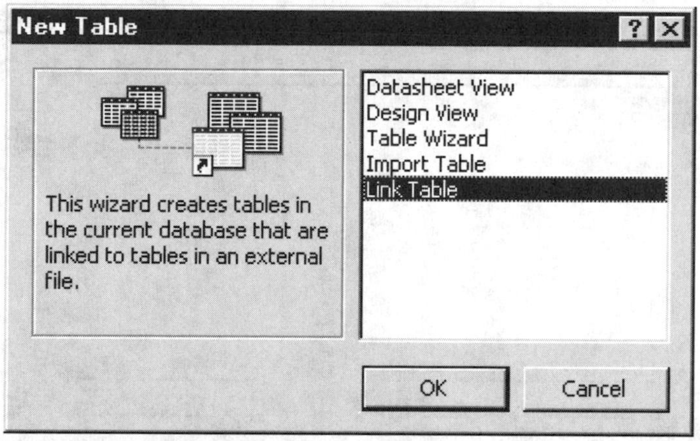

Figure 11-17.   Selecting the Access table type

This dialog box allows you to select the type of Access table to be created. When designing a local Access table, you would typically choose either the Datasheet View, Design View, or Table Wizard to launch Access's local database design utilities. If you want to copy in the table structure and data from another source like an Excel spreadsheet, you would select the Import Table option. This option can also be used to import data from an ODBC data source like SQL server. However, there is a big difference between using the Import Table option versus using the Link Table option. The Import Table option makes a snapshot copy of the imported data in the local Access database. Any subsequent Access operations will only affect the local copy of the data. The original data source will remain unchanged. The Link Table option creates an ODBC connection that will be used to access the data stored in the remote data source. No local copy of the data is performed. All database operations are performed on the remote database table. To create a new Access table that's linked to a SQL Server table, select the Link Table option from the list, and then click OK. The Access Table Link Wizard, shown in Figure 11-18, will be displayed.

This dialog box allows you to select the data source that will be used for the linked tables. To create a link from an Access table to a SQL Server table, you must click the Files of type drop-down box and then select ODBC Databases from the list. After selecting the file type ODBC, the Link button will be enabled. Clicking Link initiates the ODBC Driver Manager, which presents a list of the data sources that have been created using the ODBC Administrator. The ODBC Driver Manager's Select Data Source dialog box is shown in Figure 11-19.

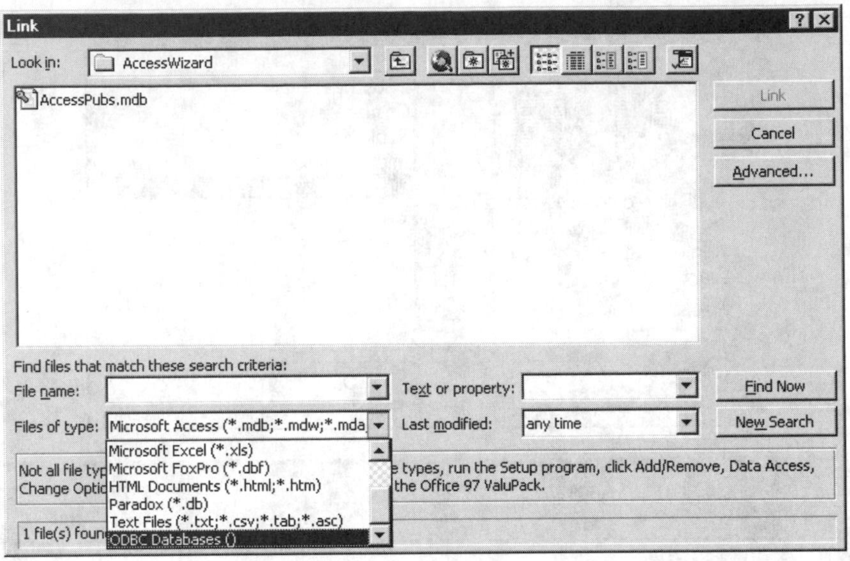

Figure 11-18. Selecting the linked-table source

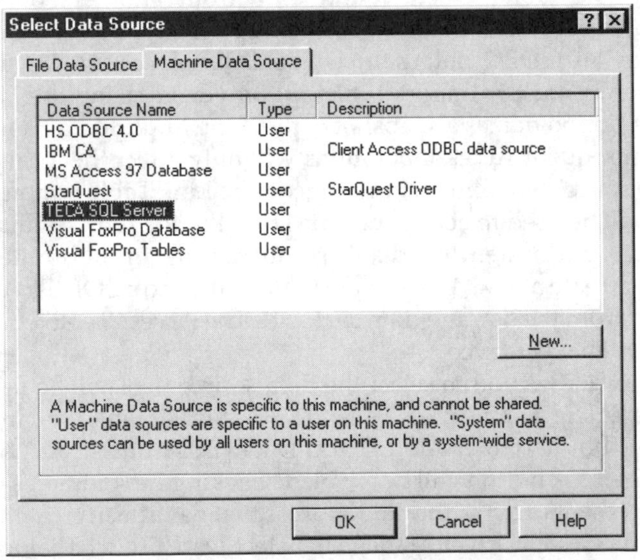

Figure 11-19. Selecting the SQL Server data source

From here, you must select the name of the ODBC data source that is using the SQL Server ODBC driver. Then click OK. The ODBC Driver Manager will load the SQL Server ODBC driver and start a connection to SQL Server. If you're using mixed security, the ODBC Driver Manager prompts you to enter a SQL Server login. The ODBC Driver Manager will make a connection to the SQL Server database that was specified when the data source was created. However, you can override this during the login process. After the connection to SQL Server has been established, a list of tables in the SQL Server database is listed. In Figure 11-20, you can see the list of SQL Server tables in the pubs database.

Access always identifies linked tables using the owner prefix. Therefore, all of the tables listed begin with the prefix dbo followed by the table name. You can select individual tables by highlighting them on the list, or you can select all of the tables in the SQL Server database by clicking Select All.

NOTE: When linking to files on SQL Server 7, it's best to individually select the files that you want to link. Selecting all also includes the SQL Server system files. These are not application files, and they should generally not be included in your Access database.

Linking an Access table to a SQL Server table creates an Access table definition in the local Access database. In the examples in this chapter, the linked tables are created in the AccessPubs.mdb database. The linked table definitions contain the table schema plus the ODBC driver and login information required to make the connection to SQL Server. Having a local copy of the table schema allows Access's design tools to provide excellent responsiveness while creating queries, forms, and reports. However, while the linked table contains a copy of all of the table and column information, it does not contain the actual data. The base table remains in the SQL Server database.

Unlike SQL Server, Access requires that all updateable tables have a unique column identifier. This is due to the fact the Jet engine uses an optimistic recording locking scheme, in which each row to be updated is retrieved before the update based on the unique column value. Then the Jet engine checks the column values to ensure that no other user has modified the row. Although SQL Server does not require this, any tables updated by Access do. If the linked table does not have a unique column identifier, the wizard displays the Select Unique Record Identifier dialog box, shown in Figure 11-21, which prompts you to select a column that can be used as a unique record identifier.

You can select a column in the SQL Server table that will act as a unique identifier for a row. After selecting the appropriate column or columns, clicking OK creates the link for the table, and the Access Table Wizard proceeds to the next selected table. You can also skip selecting columns that can be used as a unique index; but, if you do, Access will view these tables as read-only and will not allow updates to them.

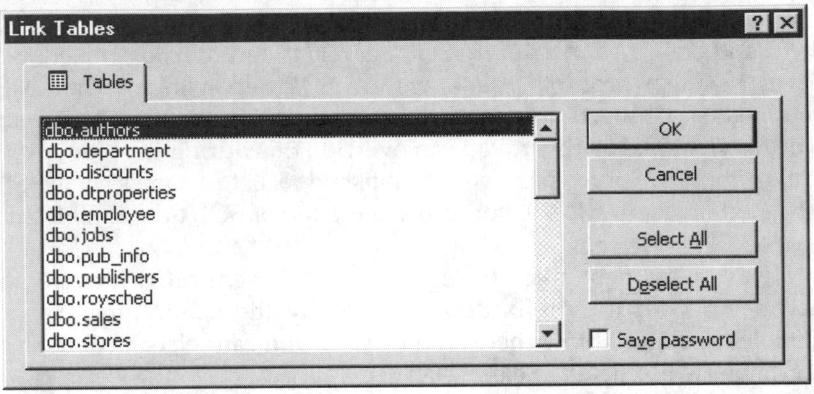

Figure 11-20. Selecting SQL Server tables to be linked

 NOTE: Before linking SQL Server tables, make sure you have an understanding of the table schema for all of the tables that will be linked. Not only is this knowledge required for creating your database applications, it will also make dealing with the Select Unique Row Identifier dialog box much easier. If you do make a mistake during this process, however, you can always delete the table from the Access database and then link the table again. Deleting a linked table from Access does not delete the table from the SQL Server database. It only deletes the local linkage.

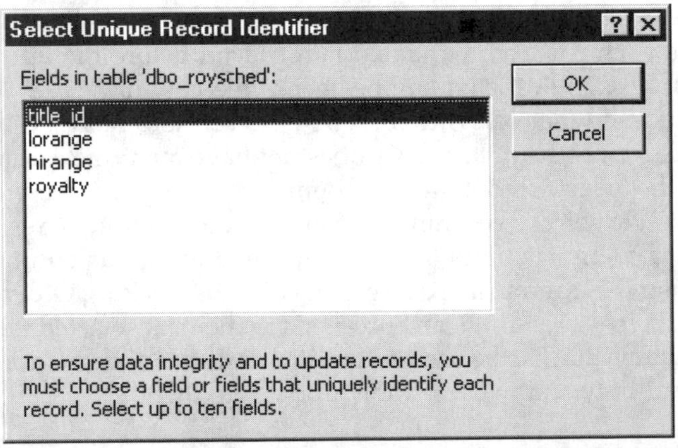

Figure 11-21. Selecting unique record identifiers

After all the desired tables have been linked, the tables will appear in the Access table list, as shown in Figure 11-22.

In Access, all linked tables are associated with the ODBC globe icon rather than the small table icon used for local Access tables. In Figure 11-22, you can see that all of the tables from the pubs database have been linked to corresponding access tables.

After all of the required SQL Server tables have been linked, you can begin to use Access's interface tools to build data entry forms, queries, and reports that use the data from the SQL Server tables. Access provides a rich development environment that includes tools for rapidly generating data entry forms, custom queries, and reports, as well as tools for performing complex programming tasks using VBA. In the next section of this chapter, you'll see the basic steps required to use each of Access's primary data access tools with SQL Server tables.

USING THE QUERY DESIGNER

The Query Designer in Access allows you to very quickly create queries using its graphical query builder interface. Like Access's other database tools, the Query Designer can be used with linked SQL Server tables just as easily as native Access tables. Access queries can be used as stand-alone tools, or they can be used as the basis for Access forms or reports. To create a new query using Access's query builder, first select the Queries tab from the main Access dialog box. Initially the Queries dialog box will be empty for a new database, as shown in Figure 11-23.

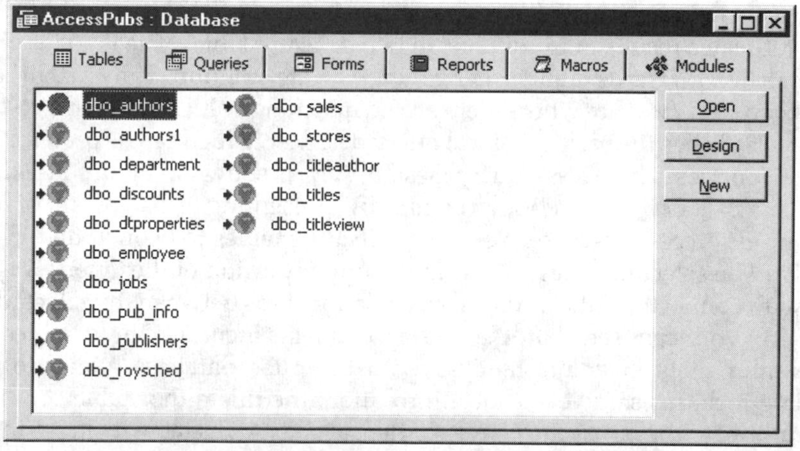

Figure 11-22. List of linked tables

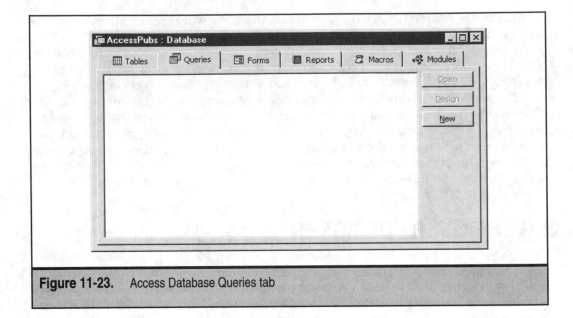

Figure 11-23.   Access Database Queries tab

To build a new query that uses the linked SQL server tables, click New. This will start Access's Query Wizard. The Access Query Wizard allows you to build several different types of queries. The Query Wizard can start the Query Design View, the Simple Query Wizard, the Crosstab Query Wizard, the Find Duplicates Query Wizard, or the Find Unmatched Query Wizard. The Simple Query Wizard steps you through building a simple query with no row selection. The Crosstab Wizard steps you through building a crosstab query that tabulates results from columns in two different tables. The Find Duplicates and Find Unmatched Wizards build queries that locate column values that are either duplicated between tables or where there are no matching values between two tables. The Design View launches the basic graphical query designer, which can be used for both basic and complex queries. The Access Query Design View is shown in Figure 11-24.

The Access Query Design View begins by presenting a list of all of the tables contained in the Access database. You then select the tables to be included in the query from the list. The selected tables appear in the upper portion of the Query Design View, complete with connections that indicate any relationships between the selected tables. In Figure 11-24, you can see that the example query includes three tables: authors, titleauthor, and titles. If you're familiar with the pubs database, you know that the authors table includes sample author information, the titleauthor table provides a link from the authors to the books they have written, and the titles table includes information about each book title.

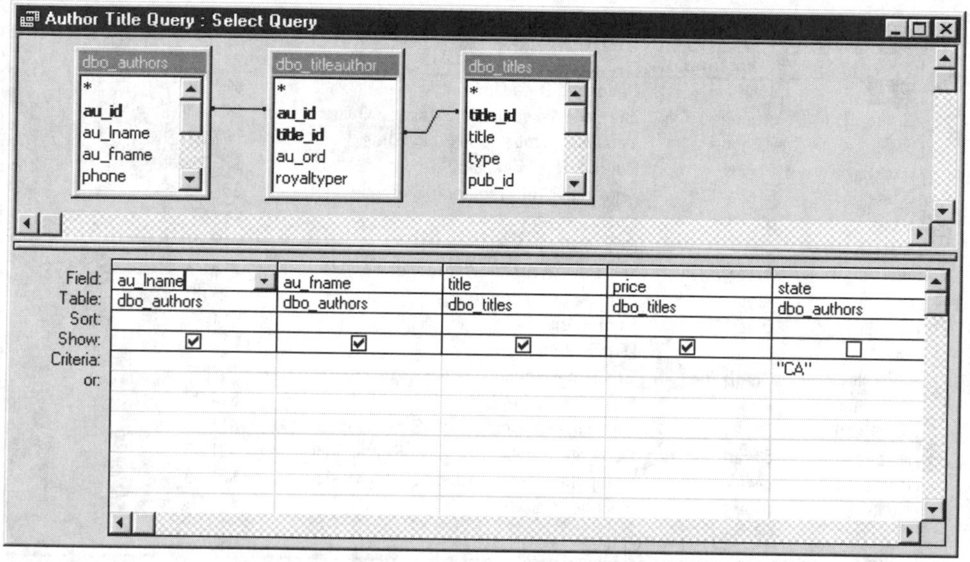

Figure 11-24.   Access Query Design View

TIP: Powerful tools like Access's Query Design View can be fantastic time-savers for quickly designing queries and reports, but they are no substitute for a knowledge of the underlying database schema. No matter what tool you use, you must understand the database tables and relationships to effectively use the tool.

The columns are selected by dragging and dropping them from the table windows to the design grid in the lower portion of the screen. In this example, you can see that the au_lname, au_fname, title, price, and state columns have been selected to be included in the query. All of the columns except the state column will be visible in the result set. The state column is included to allow row selection based on the column value of "CA". This will include only those rows in the query where the author is from California. Clicking the exclamation point button executes the query and displays the results window shown in Figure 11-25.

The results of using the Access Query Designer clearly show the power of Access to quickly and easily produce results. In this example, the Access Query Designer set up a three-file join that included row selection criteria using just a few interactive actions. There was no need to directly enter any SQL in order to produce this result. Access took care of building all of the required SQL behind the scenes. Using the pop-up menu that's displayed when you right-click the results window allows you to see the SQL statement that Access generated to produce its results.

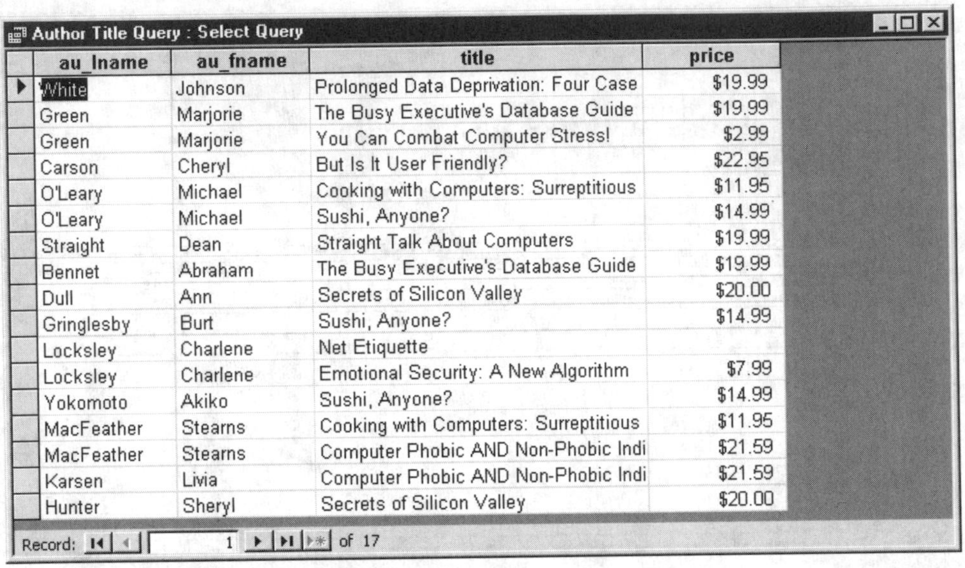

Author Title Query : Select Query

au_lname	au_fname	title	price
White	Johnson	Prolonged Data Deprivation: Four Case	$19.99
Green	Marjorie	The Busy Executive's Database Guide	$19.99
Green	Marjorie	You Can Combat Computer Stress!	$2.99
Carson	Cheryl	But Is It User Friendly?	$22.95
O'Leary	Michael	Cooking with Computers: Surreptitious	$11.95
O'Leary	Michael	Sushi, Anyone?	$14.99
Straight	Dean	Straight Talk About Computers	$19.99
Bennet	Abraham	The Busy Executive's Database Guide	$19.99
Dull	Ann	Secrets of Silicon Valley	$20.00
Gringlesby	Burt	Sushi, Anyone?	$14.99
Locksley	Charlene	Net Etiquette	
Locksley	Charlene	Emotional Security: A New Algorithm	$7.99
Yokomoto	Akiko	Sushi, Anyone?	$14.99
MacFeather	Stearns	Cooking with Computers: Surreptitious	$11.95
MacFeather	Stearns	Computer Phobic AND Non-Phobic Indi	$21.59
Karsen	Livia	Computer Phobic AND Non-Phobic Indi	$21.59
Hunter	Sheryl	Secrets of Silicon Valley	$20.00

Record: 1 of 17

Figure 11-25. Query results window

Generating the query isn't a one-time process. You can alternate between the results window and the design window using the pop-up menu that's displayed when you right-click the results window. The ability to quickly view the query results and then switch back to design mode to fine-tune the query criteria allows very rapid development of complex queries.

When you've finished designing the query, you click the Save button to save the query specification. Closing the Query Design View window also prompts you to save your query specifications.

USING THE FORMS DESIGNER

Access's Forms Designer allows you to quickly create simple data entry forms using either a Visual Basic–like form designer or through a set of wizards. Like the other Access database tools, the Forms Designer can be used just as effectively with linked SQL Server tables as it can with local Access tables. To start the Access Forms Designer, click the Forms tab from the Access Database window and then click New. The New Form dialog box, shown in Figure 11-26, will be displayed.

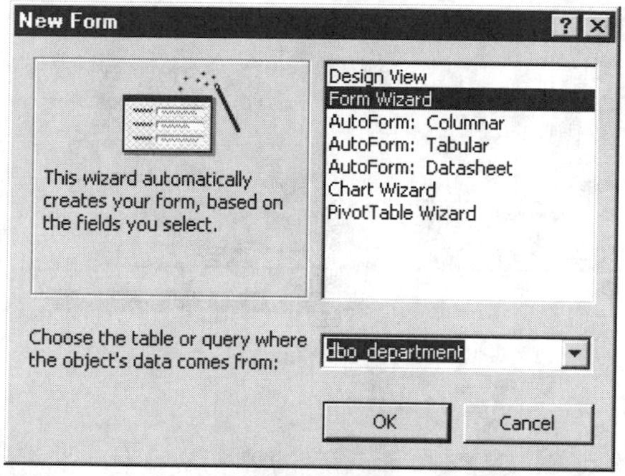

Figure 11-26.   New Form dialog box

This dialog box provides several options for building data-entry forms. The Design View option starts a Visual Basic–like graphical forms designer that is suitable for designing custom forms that can access one or more tables. The Form Wizard builds simple forms based on a single table or query. The AutoForm options allow you to build forms that use a columnar, tabular, or datasheet layout. As their names suggest, the columnar layout presents one row at a time, with the data displayed in two columns. The tabular layout displays multiple rows and columns, while the datasheet layout displays multiple rows in a data-bound grid. The Chart Wizard creates a form that can display several types of graphical charts. The PivotTable Wizard creates a form containing an Excel PivotTable. Selecting the Form Wizard displays the window shown in Figure 11-27.

Much like the Query Wizard presented earlier, the Form Wizard allows you to select multiple tables and columns to be included on the form. In this example, you can see that this particular form is based on the department table, and both of the columns contained in the department file have been included on the form.

NOTE: Access data-entry forms operate on the data in SQL Server's tables. Any changes made using these forms are written to the SQL Server database. To keep the tables in the pubs database in their original state, this example uses a user-created table named department. The department table is not a part of the original pubs database; it is created to demonstrate Forms input and updating without modifying the original pubs tables. The department table has two columns: Dep_ID is an integer data type that is also the table's unique key, while Dep_Name is a 25-character column.

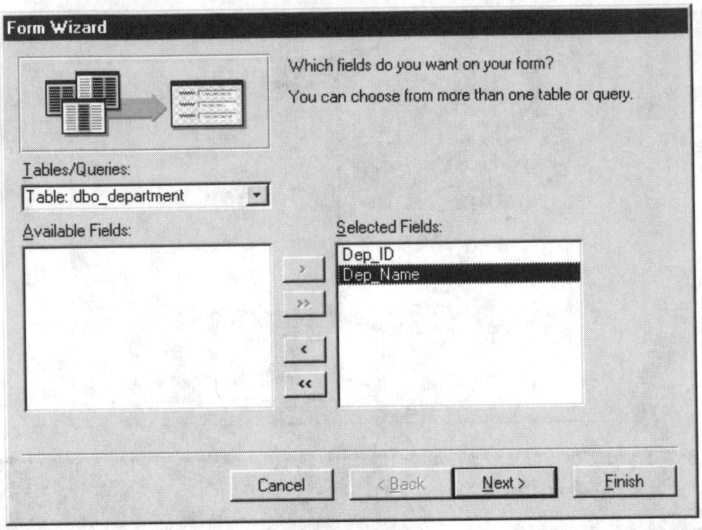

Form Wizard

Which fields do you want on your form?

You can choose from more than one table or query.

Tables/Queries:

Table: dbo_department

Available Fields:

Selected Fields:

Dep_ID
Dep_Name

Cancel   < Back   Next >   Finish

Figure 11-27.   Form Wizard window

After selecting the tables and columns to include on the form, clicking Finish generates the data entry form shown here:

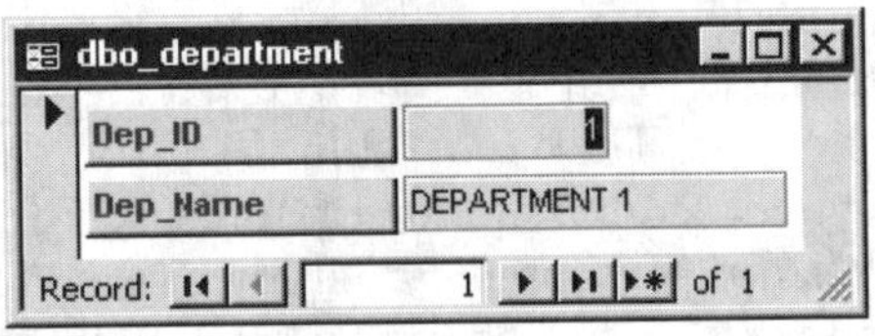

dbo_department

| Dep_ID | 1 |
| Dep_Name | DEPARTMENT 1 |

Record: |◀ ◀   1   ▶ ▶| ▶* of 1

This stock data entry form shows the ability of Access to rapidly generate data entry forms that work with SQL Server tables. This data entry form was generated in just a couple of minutes and required no coding. The form allows the user to enter, update, or delete rows from the department table. The data navigation bar at the bottom of the window allows you to scroll forward and backward through the rows in the SQL Server table.

NOTE: Access data entry forms and action queries are capable of performing an action that the end user has the database permission to perform. Implementing a secure database access plan is a must before allowing end users access to corporate data stored in SQL Server databases.

USING THE REPORT DESIGNER

The Access Report Designer allows you to quickly create reports either by using the graphical report designer interface or by selecting one of Access's stock report wizards. Like Access's other database tools, the Report Designer works with linked SQL Server tables exactly as it works with native Access tables. When you are designing reports, you can either include the table and row selection criteria within the report itself, or you can base the report upon an existing query. In the next section, you'll see how you can create a new Access report using a predefined Access query.

Unlike the Access Query Designer, which can automatically determine the relationships between tables, the Access Report Designer cannot determine the relationships between different tables—even if the column names are the same. However, like the Forms Designer, the Report Designer is able to use an existing query as input. This enables you to design queries that can also do double duty as report selection criteria. In Figure 11-28, you can see a sample query of the three tables in the SQL Server pubs database shown in the Query Designer.

As you might have gathered, this sample query creates a result set that lists the sales by store. The stores table is linked to the sales table by the stor_id column; and, in order get the book title information, this query also joins the sales table to the titles table using the title_id column. This query is then saved using the name Sales by Stores. After the query that defines the report criteria has been defined, you can use the query as input in the Access Report Designer.

To create a new report using Access's Report Designer, first select the Reports tab from the main Access database dialog box. Initially, the Reports dialog box will be empty for a new database. To create a new report, click New, and the New Report dialog box shown in Figure 11-29 will be displayed.

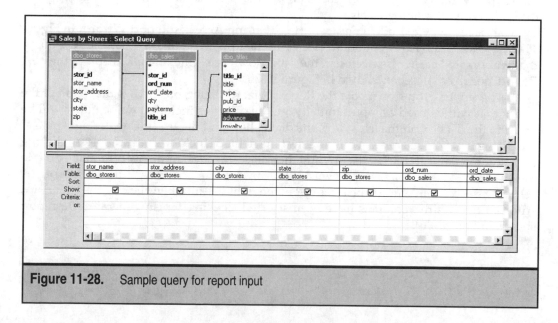

Figure 11-28. Sample query for report input

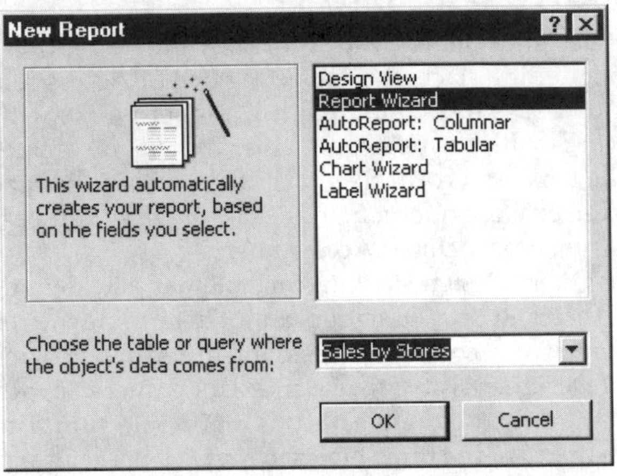

Figure 11-29. New Report dialog box

The Report Wizard option starts a visual report designer that enables you to manually lay out a report. The Report Wizard steps you through a series of dialog boxes that assist in the creation of several common reports. The AutoReport options allow you to build reports that use a columnar or a tabular layout. The Columnar layout presents one row at a time with the data output in two columns. The Tabular layout displays multiple rows and columns on a single page. The Chart Wizard creates a report that can displays several types of graphical charts, while the Label Wizard is used to print different types of mailing labels.

The easiest way to build a new report is by using Access's Report Wizard. In Figure 11-29, the Report Wizard option is selected in the upper list, and the name of the query that was created earlier is selected in the drop-down box. Clicking OK displays the next Report Wizard dialog box, shown in Figure 11-30.

In the upper drop-down box, the Report Wizard dialog box shows the name of the query that will be used as input. Initially, all the columns included in the query will be listed in the list box on the left side of the dialog box, and the list box on the right side of the dialog box will be empty. You can select the fields to include in the report by clicking each column name in the left list box and then clicking the right-arrow button to add it to the list in the right list box. Likewise, you can remove columns from the report by selecting the column name to be removed in the right list and then clicking the left arrow. After all the desired columns have been selected, clicking Finish generates the report shown in Figure 11-31.

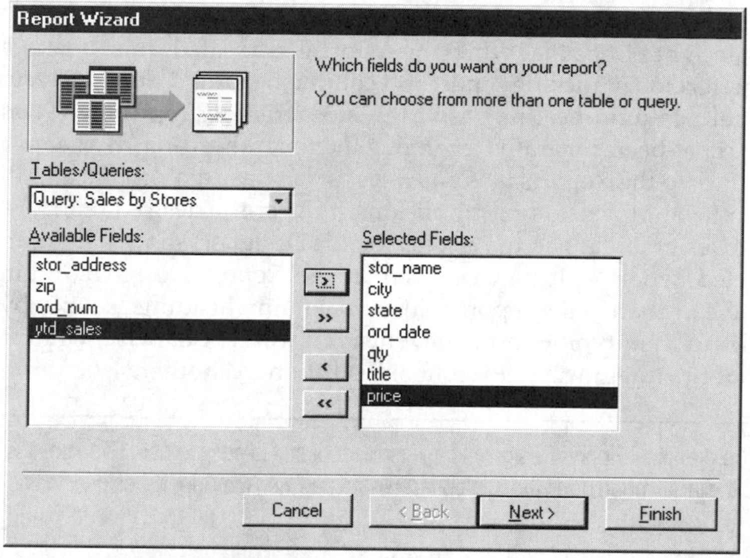

Figure 11-30.   Report Wizard column selection dialog box

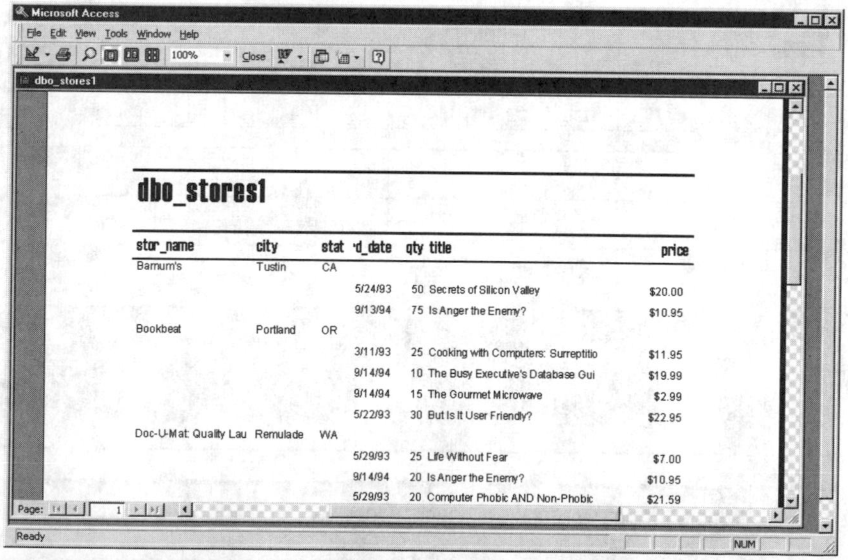

Figure 11-31.   An Access report

This report further illustrates Access's rapid database development power. Using a prebuilt query as input, this Access report performs a three-file join and can be created in minutes. You might notice that while the report was created quickly and easily, it also didn't do a perfect job of picking report and column headings. Obviously, using the SQL Server table and column headings isn't the most friendly reporting layout. However, once the report has been generated, changing the report headings is a snap. To customize the report, bring up the Reports tabs on Access's database dialog box, and then select the report that you want to customize by clicking it. After the desired report is highlighted, you can click Design to launch the Access Report Designer, shown in Figure 11-32.

The selected report will be displayed in the Report Designer. From the Report Designer, you can change the report's title and column headings simply by clicking the desired field and then typing in the new heading value. Likewise, you can change the report's layout by dragging a field from one position to another.

TIP: The graphical Report Designer is a versatile tool that is easy to use. Even so, it is usually better to generate the initial report using the appropriate wizard and then the Report Designer to fine-tune the report.

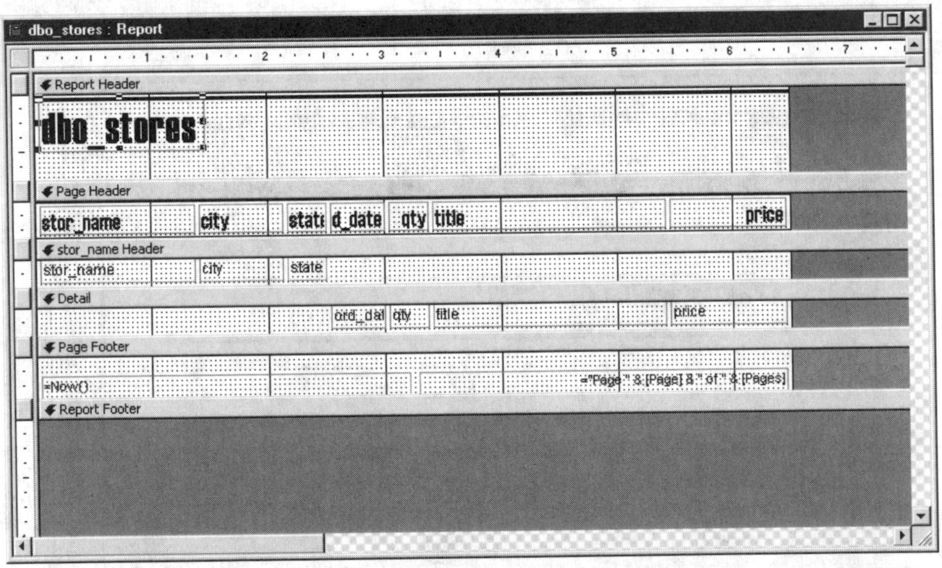

Figure 11-32. Customizing the report with Report Designer

USING MACROS

Access macros allow you to automate repetitive operations or group together batches of related operations. For instance, you can use Access macros to run a series of queries or reports, display a predetermined sequence of data-entry forms, or copy and rename all of the tables in an Access database. While macros do not provide the fine granular level of control that VBA (Visual Basic for Applications) code provides, they are still a powerful automation tool. To create a new Access macro, you must first select a macro on the Macros tab in the main Access database dialog box and then click New. The macro editor shown in Figure 11-33 will display.

In the macro editor, you can see a macro named QueryBatch. This macro groups together two queries and one report. The Action column controls the specific action that each step will perform in the macro, while the Comment column is simply a description that documents the action being performed. As you might have surmised, the OpenQuery action runs an existing query, while the OpenReport action runs an existing report. The text fields in the lower half of the window specify the database objects that the action will apply to. In Figure 11-33, you can see that the OpenReport action will open the saved report named dbo_stores, and the View field indicates that the output will be directed to the printer.

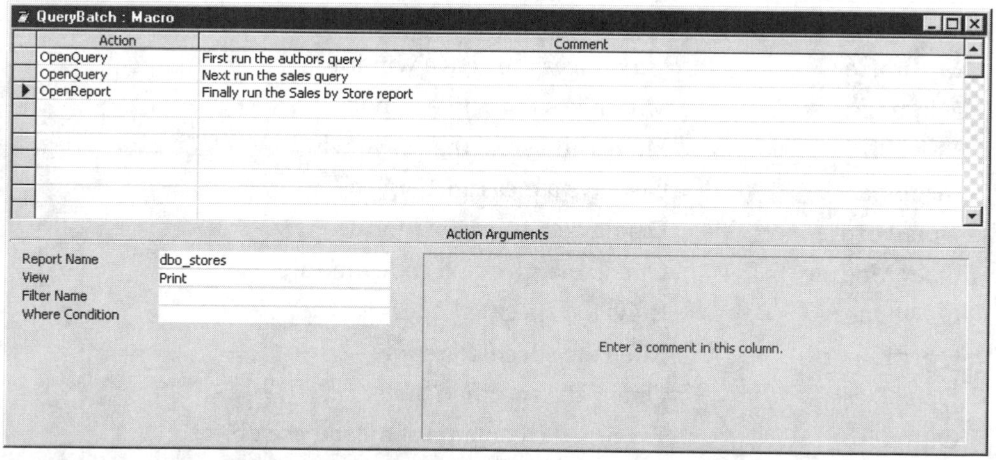

Figure 11-33. Access macro to run a batch of reports

Access supports a wide variety of actions in addition to OpenQuery and OpenReport. Table 11-2 lists the different macro actions supported by Access.

Action	Description
AddMenu	Creates a custom menu
ApplyFilter	Restricts data
Beep	Issues a beep
CancelEvent	Cancels the event that caused the macro to run
Close	Closes the specified window
CopyObject	Copies the specified object
DeleteObject	Deletes the specified object
Echo	Displays text on the screen
FindNext	Finds the next record matching the FindRecord criteria
FindRecord	Finds the first record matching the search criteria
GoToControl	Sets the focus on the specified control on a form
GoToPage	Moves to the specified page in an active form
GoToRecord	Moves to the specified record
Hourglass	Toggles the mouse pointer
Maximize	Maximizes the active window
Minimize	Minimizes the active window
MoveSize	Moves and sizes the active window
MsgBox	Displays a message box
OpenForm	Displays the specified form
OpenModule	Opens the specified code module
OpenQuery	Runs the specified query
OpenReport	Runs the specified report
OpenTable	Opens the specified table
OutputTo	Exports the contents of a database object
PrintOut	Prints the contents of a database object
Quit	Quits Access
Rename	Renames the specified database object

Table 11-2. Access Macro Commands

Action	Description
RepaintObject	Refreshes a specified screen object
Requery	Refreshes a query
Restore	Restores the current window to its previous appearance
RunApp	Executes a Windows application
RunCode	Executes a VBA function
RunCommand	Executes an Access menu command
RunMacro	Executes an Access macro
RunSQL	Executes a SQL statement
Save	Saves the specified object
SelectObject	Selects the specified object
SendKeys	Issues keystrokes
SendObject	Sends an object via e-mail
SetMenuItem	Sets the state of a menu item
SetValue	Sets the value of a control or database field
SetWarnings	Toggles the display of system messages
ShowAllRecords	Removes all filters
ShowToolbar	Displays the specified toolbar
StopAllMacros	Stops the execution of all running macros
StopMacro	Stops the current macro
TransferDatabase	Imports or exports data from a database
TransferSpreadsheet	Imports or exports data from a spreadsheet
TransferText	Imports or exports an ASCII text file

Table 11-2.   Access Macro Commands (*continued*)

As you can see, Access macros can be constructed quickly, and they provide a wide range of functionality. You can use macros to prototype VBA applications, and you can save macros as Visual Basic modules. To save an existing macro as a Visual Basic module, right-click the macro name and then select the Save As option from the pop-up menu. The macro Save As dialog box shown in Figure 11-34 will be displayed. Select the Save as Visual Basic Module radio button and then click OK to convert the macro to VBA code.

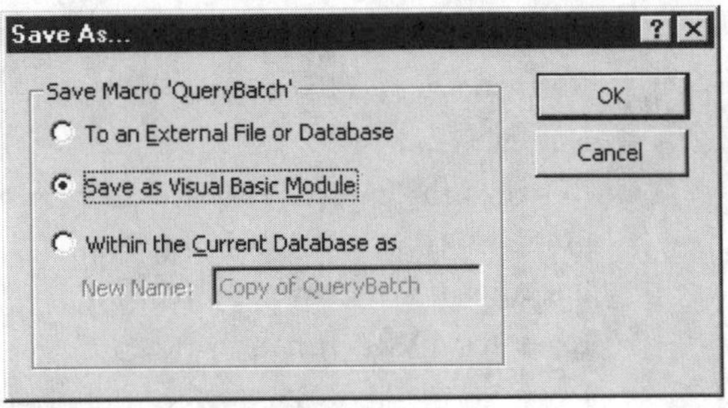

Figure 11-34.   Saving a macro as a Visual Basic module

USING VBA CODE MODULES TO BUILD SQL SERVER APPLICATIONS

While macros are a good tool for automating common tasks and prototype applications, they do not offer the same level of application control as VBA code. VBA is a close cousin to the Visual Basic programming language, and the Access implementation provides many of the same productivity tools that Visual Basic has. For instance, like Visual Basic, the Access Module editor supports color-coded keywords, statement completion, syntax checking, and integrated debugging. VBA is well suited to complex tasks, and it can also be used to manipulate other objects outside of Access, such as standard operating system files. In addition, VBA code provides a level of error handling that is not present in Access modules.

Access provides the DAO (Data Access Objects) object framework as a programming interface to the Jet engine. You can use VBA and DAO to build database applications that can work with either local Access databases or SQL Server databases.

The next section of this chapter illustrates some of the common VBA coding techniques that you can use to access a SQL Server database from Access. The first example illustrates how to use DAO to perform a simple query. The next example demonstrates how to build and execute a parameterized query, and the third example shows how to call a SQL Server stored procedure using SQL Passthrough. You can find more detailed coverage of DAO in Chapter 12.

To create a new Access code module, select the Module tab from the main Access database dialog box and then click New. The Access code editor will be displayed. When the code editor is displayed, you create VBA functions or subroutines to perform customized database access.

TIP: When writing VBA code in Access, it's best to create functions rather than subroutines—even if the code module doesn't need to return any values. VBA subroutines are not visible to the Access Macro Builder or the Switchboard Add-in, while functions are.

Using a DAO Recordset

A DAO Recordset object represents the results of a query. A Recordset object is created using the OpenRecordset method of a DAO Database object. As you might expect, the DAO Database object represents an Access database. The following DAOQuery function illustrates how to create a new recordset from the current database and then access all of the rows and columns contained in that recordset.

```
Private Function DAOQuery()

    Dim db As Database
    Dim rs As Recordset
    Dim fld As Field

    Set db = CurrentDb
    Set rs = db.OpenRecordset("Select * From dbo_authors",
                              dbOpenDynaset)

    Do Until rs.EOF

        For Each fld In rs.Fields
            Debug.Print fld
        Next

        rs.MoveNext
    Loop

    rs.Close


End Function
```

In the beginning of this subroutine, several DAO object type variables are declared to hold the DAO Database, Recordset, and Field objects. Next, the db Database object variable is assigned the value of the current database. The CurrentDB object is an Access object that represents the current database. In this example, the variable db is an instance of the AccessPubs.mdb database that contains the set of tables that are linked to the SQL Server pubs database.

Next, the Database object's OpenRecordset method is used to create a new recordset object named rs. The OpenRecordset method takes two parameters. The first is a SQL statement that defines the result set that will be returned, and the second parameter is a constant that specifies the type of Recordset that will be created. In this case, the SQL Select statement retrieves all of the rows and columns from the table named dbo_authors, which is linked to the SQL Server authors table in the pubs database. The constant dbOpenDynaset indicates that this will be a Dynaset type of Recordset, which supports updating as well as forward and backward scrolling. More information about the DAO Recordset type can be found in Chapter 12. Executing the OpenRecordset function sends a SQL request to SQL Server, which then returns the result set that satisfies the request.

The contents of the Recordset object are accessed using a Do Until loop. Inside the loop, the rs Recordset object's MoveNext method is executed to advance the current cursor position within the Recordset object. This loop is performed until the Recordset object's EOF property becomes true, which indicates that all of the rows in the Recordset have been read. Within the Do Until loop, a For Each loop is used to process each of the row's Field objects. In DAO parlance, a Field object represents a column.

After all of the rows and columns in the Recordset object have been read, the Close method is called to discard the Recordset object and reclaim the resources that it used.

Using Parameterized Queries

The previous DAO example illustrated creating a Recordset using a dynamic SQL statement. While it's quite easy to construct and execute dynamic SQL statements, these statements must also be parsed and an execution plan must be created each time the SQL statement is executed. While this is fine for ad hoc query type of applications, which seldom repeat the same SQL statements, it's not the best for online transaction processing (OLTP) type applications, which execute the same SQL statements many times. OLTP-type applications get the best performance using prepared SQL statements. Unlike dynamic SQL statements that must create a new execution plan each time the statement is run, with prepared SQL the execution plan is created once, at the time the SQL statement is prepared. All subsequent executions use the existing access plan, and there is no need to create a new plan. This gives repeated execution of prepared SQL statements a significant performance advantage over dynamic SQL.

If a prepared SQL statement needed to maintain exactly the same SQL statement and selection criteria each time it was executed, it wouldn't be very flexible and you would need a completely different SQL statement for each query that your application needed to perform. Luckily, prepared SQL has the ability to use parameter markers, which in essence are placeholders for data values. Parameters allow you to reuse the same SQL statement with different data values.

Access supports parameterized queries via Query Definition objects. You can create a parameterized query in Access using VBA code or by creating the query with the Query Designer. In Figure 11-35, you can see an Access Query Definition that uses an input parameter.

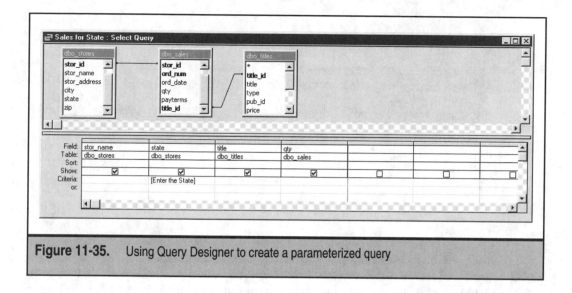

Figure 11-35. Using Query Designer to create a parameterized query

The query definition performs a three-file join of the SQL Server stores, sales, and titles tables. This particular query retrieves the store name, store state, book title, and quantity sold columns from the input files. Unlike the simpler queries that were presented earlier in this chapter, this query prompts for a matching value of the state column before executing the query. The [Enter the State] clause in the criteria row tells Access to prompt for the column value before running the query. This Access query definition is saved under the name of Sales for State. If this query is run directly from Access, a dialog box appears, prompting you to enter a state code. The following QueryParm function shows how you can execute a parameterized query using VBA and DAO.

```
Function QueryParm()

    Dim db As Database
    Dim qd As QueryDef
    Dim rs As Recordset
    Dim fld As Field
    Dim sStateCode As String

    Set db = CurrentDb

    sStateCode = InputBox("Enter the state code")
    Set qd = db.QueryDefs("Sales for State")
    qd![Enter the State] = sStateCode
    Set rs = qd.OpenRecordset()
```

```
Do Until rs.EOF

    For Each fld In rs.Fields
        Debug.Print fld
    Next

    rs.MoveNext
Loop

rs.Close


End Function
```

Like the previous DAO example, this function begins by declaring variables for the DAO objects, as well as a string variable that will contain the user-supplied state code. The db Database object is assigned to the current database using the CurrentDb object. Then a simple InputBox is used to get the state code from the user. The state code is stored in the sStateCode string. Then the qd QueryDef object is set to the name of the query definition that was created earlier using the Query Designer.

Next, the input state code contained in the sStateCode variable is assigned to the query's input parameter. The query's input parameter uses the name of [Enter the state] (including the braces), which was the same as the name of the input parameter that was set up in the Query Designer. After assigning the input parameter, the query is executed by the OpenRecordset function. Then the contents of the result set returned by the query are displayed in the Access Debug window.

Using SQL Server Stored Procedures

Using parameterized queries can provide a performance boost to Access applications that need to perform repetitive SQL statements. However, the best performance for Access-to-SQL Server applications is achieved using stored procedures. Much like prepared SQL, the execution plan for a stored procedure is created before the stored procedure is executed. However, while a prepared statement must be prepared each time the application runs, the execution plan for a stored procedure is prepared once, at the time the stored procedure is created. Since there is no need to parse the incoming SQL statement or prepare an execution plan, stored procedures offer the highest performance mechanism for accessing SQL Server databases.

SQL Server stored procedures are also capable of performing multiple operations (called batches) within the stored procedure and potentially returning multiple result sets. The following CallSP function illustrates how to use Access VBA and DAO to call a SQL Server stored procedure that returns multiple results sets.

```
Function CallSP()

    Dim db As Database
    Dim qd As QueryDef
    Dim rs As Recordset
    Dim fld As Field


    Set db = CurrentDb

    On Error Resume Next
    db.QueryDefs.Delete ("Pubs_Report_1")

    On Error GoTo ErrorHandler

    Set qd = db.CreateQueryDef("Pubs_Report_1")
    qd.Connect = "ODBC;DSN=TECA SQL Server;UID=sa;PWD=;DATABASE=pubs"
    qd.ReturnsRecords = True
    qd.SQL = "reptq1"


    Set rs = qd.OpenRecordset()

    On Error Resume Next
    db.TableDefs.Delete "TempResults"
    db.TableDefs.Delete "TempResults1"
    db.TableDefs.Delete "TempResults2"
    db.TableDefs.Delete "TempResults3"
    db.TableDefs.Delete "TempResults4"
    db.TableDefs.Delete "TempResults5"
    db.TableDefs.Delete "TempResults6"


    On Error GoTo ErrorHandler

    'Now process the next result set using a Jet table
    Set qd = db.CreateQueryDef("")
    qd.SQL = "Select Pubs_Report_1.* Into TempResults
            From Pubs_Report_1"
    qd.Execute
    Set rs = db.OpenRecordset("TempResults")

    Debug.Print "Recordset 1"
    Do Until rs.EOF
```

```
        For Each fld In rs.Fields
            Debug.Print fld
        Next

        rs.MoveNext
Loop
Set rs = db.OpenRecordset("TempResults1")

Debug.Print "Recordset 2"
Do Until rs.EOF

    For Each fld In rs.Fields
        Debug.Print fld
    Next

        rs.MoveNext
Loop

Set rs = db.OpenRecordset("TempResults2")

Debug.Print "Recordset 3"
Do Until rs.EOF

    For Each fld In rs.Fields
        Debug.Print fld
    Next

        rs.MoveNext
Loop

Set rs = db.OpenRecordset("TempResults3")

Debug.Print "Recordset 4"
Do Until rs.EOF

    For Each fld In rs.Fields
        Debug.Print fld
    Next

        rs.MoveNext
Loop

Set rs = db.OpenRecordset("TempResults4")
```

```
    Debug.Print "Recordset 5"
    Do Until rs.EOF

        For Each fld In rs.Fields
            Debug.Print fld
        Next

        rs.MoveNext
    Loop

    Set rs = db.OpenRecordset("TempResults5")

    Debug.Print "Recordset 6"
    Do Until rs.EOF

        For Each fld In rs.Fields
            Debug.Print fld
        Next

        rs.MoveNext
    Loop

    Set rs = db.OpenRecordset("TempResults6")

    Debug.Print "Recordset 7"
    Do Until rs.EOF

        For Each fld In rs.Fields
            Debug.Print fld
        Next

        rs.MoveNext
    Loop

    qd.Close
    rs.Close
    Exit Function


ErrorHandler:
    DisplayDAOError


End Function
```

The CallSP function begins by declaring the object variables needed for DAO Database, Recordset, QueryDef, and Field objects, and then it assigns the db Database object to the current Access database using the CurrentDb object.

Next, VBA error handling is enabled using the On Error statement. In this example, the On Error Resume Next statement is used to allow processing to continue if the following QueryDelete method fails. The QueryDelete method is used to delete any existing instances of the query definition named Pubs_Report_1. Deleting any old query definitions enables the CallSP function to be rerun without encountering errors.

Next, the db Database object's CreateQueryDef method is used to create a new query definition named Pubs_Report_1. Since this is a new database object, the SQL Server connection information must be assigned to the Query Definition's Connect property. Then the ReturnRecords property is set to True, informing DAO that this Query Definition will return a result set. Next, the SQL property is set to the name of reptq1, the name of an existing stored procedure in the pubs database. The following listing shows the Transact-SQL statements that comprise the reptq1 stored procedure.

```
Create Procedure reptq1 As
Select pub_id, title_id, price, pubdate
From titles
Where price is Not Null
Order By pub_id
Compute Avg(price) By pub_id
Compute Avg(price)
```

The By clause in the Compute statement caused this stored procedure to produce seven result sets when run against the pubs database. In order to deal with multiple result sets, Access must create multiple temporary tables where each table holds a separate result set. The next section of code uses the TableDef.Delete method to delete any existing old temporary work tables.

Next, a new QueryDef is created that uses the Pubs_Report_1 query as input and then outputs multiple temporary tables where each table contains a different result set. The DAO object framework automatically numbers each different result set. In this instance, the first result set will be TempResults, the second result set will be TempResults1, and so on. The multiple result sets are processed at the time the qd Query Definition's Execute method is run. Afterward, the contents of each of the different results sets is output to the Access Debug window using the same techniques presented earlier.

Error Handling

One significant difference between the CallSP function and the other VBA functions that were presented earlier is the use of error handling. Using the On Error statement allows Access to trap and respond to run-time errors that would otherwise generate applications errors.

The previous CallSP function used error handling in two different ways. First, the On Error Resume Next statement was used where a known error was expected to occur. In the event that the error was encountered, the program execution continued without interruption to the next statement. Additionally, the On Error Goto ErrorHandler statement was used to trap and respond to unknown errors. Unknown errors are not expected; therefore, program execution should not continue normally if an unexpected error is encountered. In this case, the error handler executes the DisplayDAOError function to inform the user about the error that was encountered. The DisplayDAOError subroutine is presented next.

```
Private Sub DisplayDAOError()

    Dim er As Error

    For Each er In Errors
        MsgBox "Number: " & er.Number & vbCrLf & _
        "Source: " & er.Source & vbCrLf & _
        "Text: " & er.Description
    Next

End Sub
```

The DisplayDAOError subroutine begins by declaring a variable to contain a DAO Error object. Next, a For Each loop is used to iterate through the DAO Errors collection. A loop is needed because the Errors collection can contain multiple error members, where each member maintains information about a different error condition. Within the For Each loop, a MsgBox is created for each message that displays the basic information about the error condition. In this example, the error message number, source line, and a text description are displayed.

TIPS

You can apply a few common sense tips to any client/server type of database application development that you perform with Access. When you use Access to connect to tables in an external database, here are some suggestions:

▼ *Use linked tables rather than the OpenDatabase method.* Linked tables store the database schema locally, which allows Access to avoid retrieving it each time the table is opened.

■ *Be sure to retrieve only the data needed.* Local Access database applications often retrieve more data than they need and then perform extraneous functions to find the data that is really required. Limiting the data returned from SQL Server by using the SQL Select statement's Where clause can radically reduce the disk I/O required at the server, as well as the network bandwidth required to send the results to Access.

- *Use forward-only Recordsets when possible.* Forward-only Recordsets are by far the best performing type of Recordset. They also use fewer local resources.

- *Use updateable Recordsets only when your application really needs the ability to update the Recordset.* Updateable Recordsets are more capable but also more expensive resource-wise than read-only Recordsets.

- *Use stored procedures whenever possible.* SQL server stored procedures provide the fastest possible access to the data stored in SQL Server.

- ▲ *Avoid heterogeneous joins.* Heterogeneous joins are one of the strengths of Access and DAO in that they allow joining tables from Access with tables found in other data sources. However, this almost always requires the creation of one or more temporary tables. It also requires the local Jet engine to perform the actual join, which moves the load from the high-powered server to the usually lower-powered client.

CONCLUSION

The rapid database development tools found in Access can be used to quickly create client/server database applications that connect to SQL Server databases. Access is a great tool for rapid application development, and it can be used to quickly generate custom data entry forms, queries, and reports. Access is hard to beat for generating quick reports and ad hoc queries. However, despite its productivity benefits, Access is limited in scope and flexibility. For complete control over custom application development, you'll need to look into full-blown application programming environments like Visual Basic and Visual C++. The remaining chapters in Part 2 will show you how you development custom SQL Server database applications using Visual Basic. In addition, you can find more detailed information on DAO database development in Chapter 12. Most of the coding techniques presented in that chapter are equally applicable to DAO development with Access.

CHAPTER 12

Developing SQL Server Database Applications with DAO and ODBCDirect

This chapter shows you how to develop SQL Server database applications using Visual Basic and DAO (Data Access Objects). First, you'll find a brief overview of DAO and an explanation of the object hierarchy that's used by DAO. DAO uses the Microsoft Jet Engine and ODBC to access SQL Server. Then you'll see illustrations of the basic DAO programming techniques that can be used to access SQL Server databases. The second part of this chapter covers ODBCDirect, a DAO extension that was introduced with DAO 3.5 to provide high-performance access to ODBC data sources. Like Remote Database Objects (RDO), DAODirect does not use the Microsoft Joint Engine Technology (JET) Engine. Instead, it provides a thin object wrapper over ODBC. This enables DAODirect to provide much better performance going to ODBC data sources. The second part of this chapter provides an overview of ODBCDirect and then presents the essential ODBCDirect coding techniques.

DAO is Visual Basic's default data access method. DAO has been part of Visual Basic since DAO 1 was released with Visual Basic 3. DAO was primarily intended to provide Visual Basic applications with data access to local Access databases, but it can also be used to provide access to a number of other databases, such as dBase, Paradox, and even ODBC databases like Oracle and SQL Server. This flexibility is one of DAO's strong points. DAO and the Jet engine can access a number of different databases using the same code. Being a local query processor, the Microsoft Jet Database Engine gives DAO certain capabilities that are not found in most other client/server data access mechanisms. For instance, DAO and Jet provide the ability to perform heterogeneous joins on data from separate and dissimilar databases. While DAO is very flexible, this flexibility carries a price. The Jet engine is resource intensive and tends to perform poorly when it is used with ODBC data sources such as SQL Server. The ODBCDirect extension that you will see later in this chapter was designed to address these problems. DAO is delivered as a standard part of a number of different Microsoft development products, including the following:

- ▼ Visual Studio 97 and Visual Studio 6
- ■ Visual Basic Enterprise Edition 4, 5, and 6
- ■ Visual Basic Professional Edition 4, 5, and 6
- ■ Visual C++ Enterprise Edition 4, 5, and 6
- ■ Visual C++ Professional Edition 4, 5, and 6
- ▲ Microsoft Access 95 and 97

When accessing ODBC data sources, DAO uses a layered architecture that insulates the DAO object layer from the underlying network protocols and topology. Figure 12-1 illustrates the relationship of DAO, ODBC, and PC networking support.

The top level in Figure 12-1 shows the Visual Basic DAO application that creates and uses the various DAO objects. The DAO object layer works in conjunction with the Microsoft Jet Database Engine. If the database is a local Access database or other ISAM (Indexed Sequential Access Method) type of database, then the Jet engine loads the

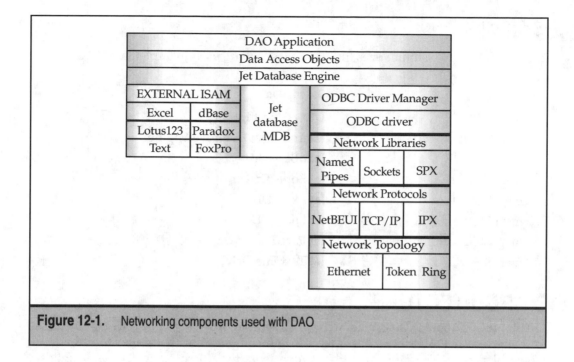

Figure 12-1. Networking components used with DAO

appropriate database driver. If Jet is using a remote database, then the engine loads the ODBC Driver Manager and makes ODBC calls to access the remote ODBC database. The ODBC Driver Manager handles loading the appropriate ODBC driver. The ODBC driver typically uses a network interprocess communication (IPC) method like Named Pipes, TCP/IP Sockets, or SPX to communicate to a remote IPC server that provides access to the target database. The network protocol is responsible for sending and receiving the IPC data stream over the network. Common networking protocols include NetBEUI, TCP/IP, and IPX. Finally, at the bottom of this stack is the physical network topology. The physical network includes the adapter cards and cabling that are required to make the actual connections between the networked systems. Ethernet and Token Ring are examples of two of the most common network topologies.

NOTE: Unlike RDO, where there is a very close correspondence between the RDO calls and the resulting ODBC calls, DAO and the Jet engine have no such close relationship. Like SQL Server, the Jet engine contains its own query processor, and it creates a series of ODBC calls that fulfill its own internal requirements. For instance, one of the first things that the Jet engine does is to query the target database and create its own internal database schema. While this step doesn't usually cause any serious delays for local databases, it can result in lengthy delays for remote databases.

DAO FILES

The following table summarizes the client files that are used to implement DAO:

File	Description
dao35.dll	DAO Object Library
msjet35.dll	Microsoft Jet Database Engine
msxb3032.dll	Jet dBase Driver
msld3032.dll	Jet Lotus Driver
msxl3032.dll	Jet Excel Driver
msxb3032.dll	Jet FoxPro Driver
mspx3032.dll	Jet Paradox Driver
mstx3032.dll	Jet Text File Driver

DAO ARCHITECTURE

DAO is implemented using a hierarchical object framework. In Figure 12-2, you can see an overview of DAO's object hierarchy. The DBEngine is at the top level of the DAO object hierarchy. The DBEngine object represents the Microsoft Jet Database Engine. Only one DBEngine object can be created per application. All of the other DAO objects are contained within the DBEngine object.

The Workspaces and Errors object collections are at the second level of the DAO framework. The Workspaces object collection contains a set of Workspace objects. Each Workspace object represents a database session. The Workspace object is used to control database login security and transaction scope. Each Workspace object contains a collection of Database objects.

The Database object is the central object in the DAO object hierarchy. Like its name suggests, each Database object represents a local or remote database. A Database object is added to the Databases collection when the Jet engine opens a local or remote database. The Database object contains the other primary DAO object collections that are used when accessing SQL Server: TableDef objects, Recordset objects, and QueryDef objects. In addition, the Database object contains Relations and Containers collections that are used for local Jet databases.

Each TableDef object contains a description of one table in the database along with its columns and indexes. The TableDef object contains a collection of Field objects and Index objects where each Field object corresponds to a column in a database table and each Index object corresponds to an index for the table. The Index object itself contains a collection of Field objects that comprises the columns that are used by the particular index. The TableDef object is populated with the appropriate database schema information when the TableDef object is first referenced or attached.

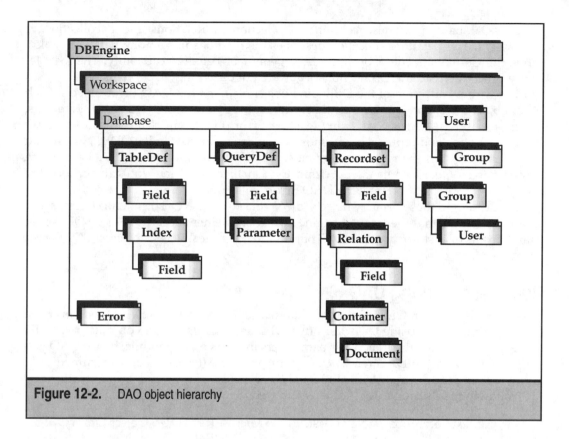

Figure 12-2.   DAO object hierarchy

The collection of Recordset objects within the Database object represents a set of data that satisfies one or more database queries. The Recordset object also defines the type of cursor that will be supported. Jet supports table, dynaset, and snapshot types of Recordset objects. The different types of Recordset objects essentially control how the results of a query will be processed by the Jet engine. The differences and implementation of these different cursor types will be covered later in this chapter. Each Recordset object contains a collection of Field objects. Like the Fields collection that is contained by the TableDef object, each Field object within a Recordset object represents a data column in the Recordset object.

The collection of QueryDef objects represents a set of stored query definitions. A QueryDef is stored in a Jet database and it is roughly equivalent to a SQL Server stored procedure or a SQL action query. Each QueryDef object contains a collection of Parameter objects, as well as a collection of Field objects. Each Parameter object describes a parameter that is passed to a QueryDef object. Like the Fields collection that is contained by the TableDef and Recordset objects, the Fields collection of the QueryDef objects represents the data columns contained by the QueryDef object.

The Database object also contains a collection of Relations and a collection of Containers. The Relations collection describes the relationships among database tables, while the Containers collection provides a generic object store capability. The local Jet query processor uses these collections. They are not used for SQL Server access.

The Errors collection of the DBEngine object contains the DAO Error objects. Each Error object corresponds to an error that is generated by one of the Jet engine operations. When a new DAO error occurs, any existing Error objects are cleared from the DAO Errors collection and replaced by the most recent Error objects. Unlike ODBC, where you must manually test the return code of each ODBC function for errors, DAO errors fire Visual Basic's On Error handler. Within the On Error handler, you can retrieve the specific error information from the DAO Errors collection.

In addition to these primary objects, the Workspace object also contains Groups and Users collections that the local Jet engine uses to implement security. Since SQL Server maintains its own security, these DAO objects are not typically used to access SQL Server databases.

An Overview of Using DAO

DAO is built using an OLE foundation that makes it easy to access DAO functions from Visual Basic. Unlike using ODBC or other DLL-based APIs where you must manually declare all of the functions and their parameters in a .bas or .cls module, to use DAO you only need to add the DAO reference to your project. After that, you can immediately begin creating the desired objects in Visual Basic code.

Following is a summary of the steps required to use DAO from Visual Basic:

1. Make a reference in Visual Basic to the Microsoft DAO 3.5 Object Library.

2. Open a Workspace object.

3. Open a Database object.

   ■ Linked tables connect to SQL Server via a TableDef's Connect property.

   ■ The OpenDatabase method connects to SQL Server using an ODBC connection string.

4. Open a Recordset or QueryDef object.

5. Access the SQL Server database via the Recordset or QueryDef object.

6. Close the Recordset or QueryDef object.

7. Close the Database object.

8. Close the Workspace object.

9. Set the DBEngine object to nothing.

ADDING THE DAO 3.5 REFERENCE TO VISUAL BASIC

The files that provide the basic support for DAO 3.5 are installed on the system when you first install the Professional Edition of Visual Basic or any of the other products that were previously listed. However, even though the files are installed, before you can use them you need to set a reference to the DAO OLE Type Library in Visual Basic's development environment. To set the reference in Visual Basic 5 or 6, first select the Project | References option from the menu to display the References dialog box that you can see in Figure 12-3.

Scroll through Visual Basic's References dialog box until you see Microsoft DAO 3.5 Object Library. Clicking the check box and then clicking the OK button adds the DAO Object Library to Visual Basic's Interactive Development Environment (IDE). Unlike adding ActiveX Controls, adding a reference to Visual Basic's IDE doesn't create any visual objects in the Visual Basic Toolbox. In order to see the DAO properties and methods, you must use Visual Basic's Object Browser, as shown in Figure 12-4.

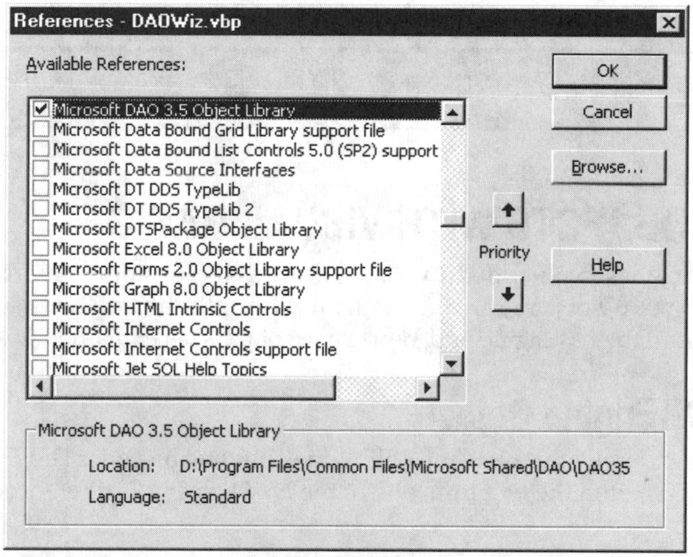

Figure 12-3.   Setting a reference to the DAO 3.5 Type Library

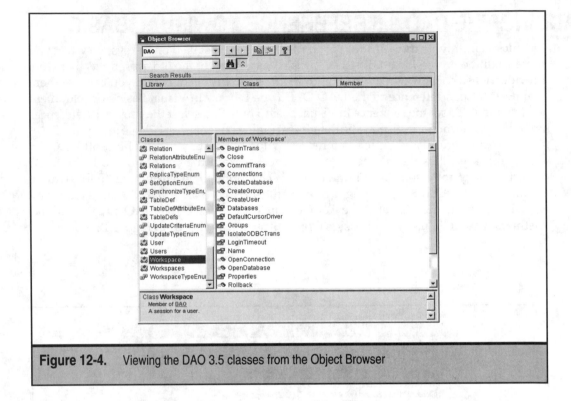

Figure 12-4. Viewing the DAO 3.5 classes from the Object Browser

USING DAO OBJECTS WITH VISUAL BASIC

After a reference has been added to Visual Basic's development environment, you're ready to use the DAO objects in your Visual Basic applications. The first steps in using DAO are to create the DBEngine and Workspace objects, as explained next.

Creating the DBEngine Object

You don't need to explicitly create the DBEngine object using code. The DBEngine object is automatically created the first time one of the DAO objects is referenced.

Creating the Workspace Object

As with the DBEngine, you typically don't need to explicitly create the DAO Workspace object. If a Workspace object doesn't exist, an instance of the Workspace is created automatically the first time your applications use one of the DAO functions. However, there may be times you want to manually create a Workspace object. To do this, you can call the CreateWorkspace method or set a reference to the DBEngine's default Workspace. The following code illustrates how you can create a Workspace object using the CreateWorkspace method:

```
Set ws = CreateWorkspace ("MyWs", "MyId", "MyPwd")
```

The following code illustrates how you can set a reference to the default Workspace object:

```
Set ws = Workspaces(0)
```

The Workspace object is automatically destroyed when you end the Jet engine. You also can manually close a Workspace object using the Close method, as shown in the following example:

```
ws.Close
```

Connecting to SQL Server

DAO supports two different methods of opening SQL Server tables: using linked (or attached) tables or direct connections using the DAO OpenDatabase method. With linked tables, a local Access table contains a link to a target SQL Server table and your Visual Basic application opens the database exactly as it would any other local Access database. Setting up a linked table does not download the information to the local Jet database. The data remains in the SQL Server database. With a direct connection, the OpenDatabase method is used to open a connection to SQL Server. While at first you may think this method would provide the best performance, that's not usually the case. When the Jet engine opens a table using the OpenDatabase method, it must always query the database to determine the table's schema and other attributes. This process adds a considerable startup delay to your application, each time your application runs the OpenDatabase method. Linked tables avoid this overhead by storing the vital database attribute information in the locally linked table. This enables Jet to retrieve the information it needs from the local table without querying the remote data source across the network connection, usually resulting in a considerable reduction of startup time.

Setting Up Linked Tables

Links to tables located on ODBC data sources are usually made when the table is first created, but they can also be created dynamically by your application. When a link is created, database schema and attribute information are permanently stored in the local portion of the linked table. When the Jet engine opens the table, Jet automatically retrieves the locally stored schema and attribute information that it requires and then proceeds to make a connection to the target data source using ODBC.

USING THE VISUAL DATA MANAGER   You can create an Access database that contains linked tables by using a variety of different development tools, such as Access, Visual Studio's Visual Database Tools, or the Visual Data Manager that's included with Visual Basic. In the following section, you'll see how to create an Access database that contains tables that are linked to tables in SQL Server's pubs database. This example illustrates how to create these links using the Visual Data Manager that's provided with Visual Basic 5 and 6.

The Visual Data Manager, shown in Figure 12-5, is started using the Visual Data Manager option from Visual Basic's Add-Ins menu. To create a new Access database, you need to select the File | New | Microsoft Access | Version 7.0 MDB option from the Visual Data Manager's menu.

After the option to create a new database has been selected, the Visual Data Manager displays an open dialog box that enables you to select where you want the local database to be created. You can select any local directory or network share and then enter the name that you want to assign to the local Access database. After the local .mdb file has been created, you can then use the Attachments option from Visual Data Manger's Utilities menu to create links to the tables in the SQL Server database. Figure 12-6 illustrates the Visual Data Manager window used to add new table links.

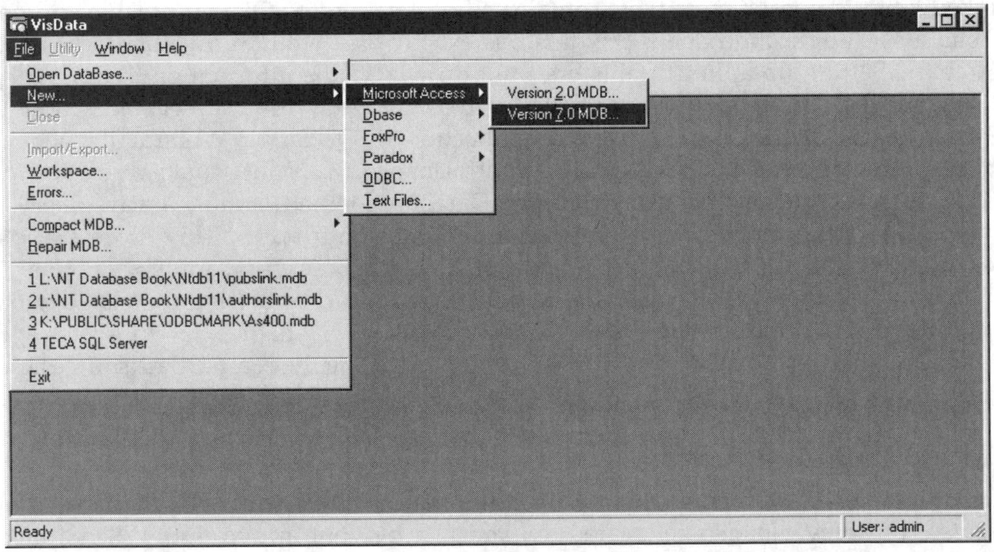

Figure 12-5.   Visual Data Manager

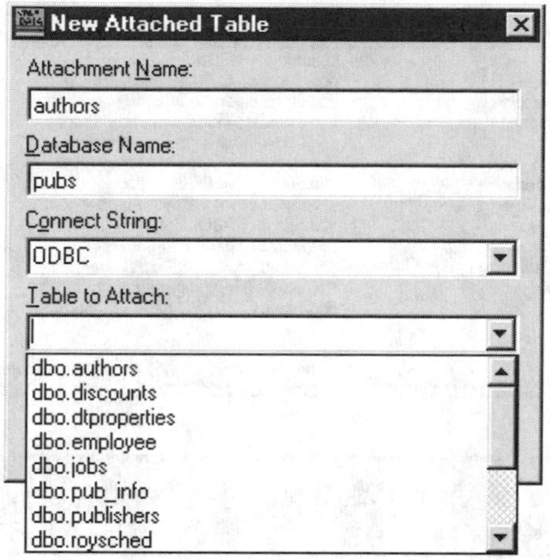

Figure 12-6.   New Attached Table dialog box

The first field that you can see in Figure 12-6 allows you to enter the name of the local table. This is the name that your application uses when it opens and queries the table. In the next field, you enter the name of the SQL Server database that contains the table. In this example, the linked table is found in the sample pubs database. The Connect String prompt allows you to specify the type of link that you are creating. The drop-down box allows you to choose from a variety of different connections, including Access, Excel, and ODBC. To set up a link to a SQL Server table, you need to select the Connect String value of ODBC. The Tables to Attach prompt allows you to identify the SQL Server table that is the target of the link. You can either type in the table name or you can click the drop-down list to display a list of the tables in the target database. Clicking the drop-down list causes the Visual Data Manager to display the ODBC Administrator, where you can select the appropriate data source for the link.

To connect to SQL Server, you must either select an existing ODBC data source that uses the SQL Server ODBC driver or you must take the options available in the ODBC Administrator to create a new data source that uses the SQL Server ODBC driver. After the connection is established, the drop-down list that you can see in Figure 12-6 is displayed, containing the qualified names of all of the tables in the specified database. You must click the appropriate target table and then click the Attach button to create the link. After this process has been repeated for all of the tables in the pubs database, Visual Data Manager's Attachments window will appear, as you see it in Figure 12-7.

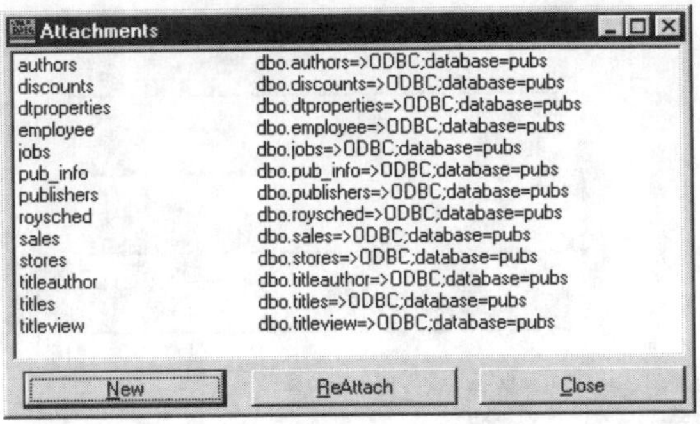

Figure 12-7. Visual Data Manager Attachments dialog box

> **TIP:** It's important to note that DAO treats linked tables the same as local tables. This allows your application to freely mix data from local tables with data from linked tables. The Jet engine's local query processor makes using heterogeneous data possible—even easy.

When all of the tables have been linked to the appropriate target tables, your DAO application can then open, query, and update the tables exactly as if they were local Access tables. The Jet engine takes care of making all of the underlying ODBC calls that are needed to actually read and modify the tables on the remote SQL Server system. The following code shows how you can connect to the authors table in SQL Server's pubs database using a linked table:

```
Set db = OpenDatabase("pubslink.mdb")
Set rs = db.OpenRecordset("Select * From authors")
```

In this section of code, you can see that the OpenDatabase method is used to connect to the SQL Server table. After the OpenDatabase method opens the linked table, the linked table can be processed just like a local table. In the preceding example, a simple query creates a recordset that contains all of the rows and columns from the linked authors table.

> **TIP:** When using linked tables, you must use Jet's SQL syntax rather than SQL Server's Transact-SQL syntax. This is because the Jet engine parses all of the SQL statements except when the SQL PassThrough option is used.

You might notice that none of the typical connection information is used in the previous code example. For instance, this code does not specify a data source nor does it need to supply the database name, or the login ID and password. All of the required connection values are stored in the TableDef object that the Visual Data Manager created for the linked table. In Figure 12-8, you can see the stored connection information that the linked table uses to connect. This information came from the values that were entered when the link was created using the Visual Data Manager.

SETTING UP LINKED TABLES DYNAMICALLY USING DAO While using Access or another interactive tool like the Visual Data Manager is certainly the easiest way to set up a linked table, this approach is not very dynamic and there are times when you might need to create these links on the fly. Luckily, DAO allows you to do just that. The following code illustrates how to create a database and add a linked table using DAO code:

```
Set ws = DBEngine.Workspaces(0)
'Create the database
Set db = ws.CreateDatabase _
    ("newlink.mdb", dbLangGeneral, dbVersion30)
'Create the table def
Set td = db.CreateTableDef("authors")
td.Connect = "ODBC;DSN=Teca SQL Server;UID=;PWD=;DATABASE=pubs;"
td.SourceTableName = "dbo.authors"
db.TableDefs.Append td
Set rs = db.OpenRecordset("Select * From authors")
```

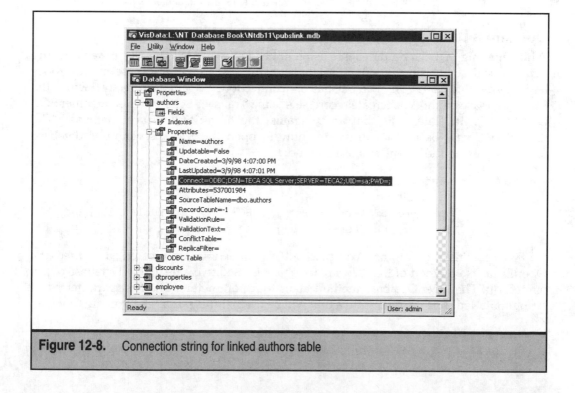

Figure 12-8.   Connection string for linked authors table

In the preceding example, you can see where an instance of the DBEngine. Workspaces object is created and named ws. Next, the CreateDatabase method of the ws workspace object is called to create a new Jet database named newlink.mdb. The second parameter of the CreateDatabase method sets the language version of the Jet database to English, and the third parameter identifies the database version. The value of dbVersion30 creates a Jet database that is compatible with both DAO version 3 and the newer DAO version 3.5.

After the database has been created, you can create a new TableDef object using the CreateTableDef method of the Database object. Next, the table linkage information is set using the Connect and SourceTableName properties. The Connect property of the td TableDef object sets the appropriate connection string. More information about the details of the connection string is given in the following section, "Opening a Database with the OpenDatabase Method." The SourceTableName property sets the qualified name of the SQL Server table. Finally, the new TableDef object is added to the newly created database using the TableDefs.Append method of the db Database object.

After creating the database and linked table with the appropriate DAO objects and methods, you can use the linked table just as you would a local Jet table. In the previous example, you can see where a simple record set is created that contains all of the columns and rows from the dbo.authors table that's found in SQL Server's pubs database.

TIP: If you change the structure of a SQL Server table that is linked to a Jet table, then you must either relink the table or use the RefreshLink method to reset the Jet database schema information.

Opening a Database with the OpenDatabase Method

While opening SQL Server databases using linked tables tends to be faster than opening databases directly using the OpenDatabase method, the OpenDatabase method does have other advantages. For instance, connections opened directly with the OpenDatabase method can create record sets using Transact-SQL and execute other SQL DDL and DML statements that work against the target SQL Server database. The following Visual Basic code illustrates how to open the SQL Server pubs database directly by using the OpenDatabase method:

```
Set ws = Workspaces(0)
Set db = ws.OpenDatabase _
        ("", dbDriverComplete, False, "ODBC;UID=;PWD=;DATABASE=pubs")
Set rs = db.OpenRecordset("Select * From authors")
```

First, an instance of the Workplace object named ws is created, and then the OpenDatabase method of that Workplace object is used to create a new Database object named db. The OpenDatabase method takes four parameters. The first parameter is a string that identifies the data source that will be used. If this parameter contains a value, that value must match one of the data source names found in the ODBC Administrator. If this parameter is blank and the second parameter is set to the value of dbDriverComplete, the ODBC Driver Manager prompts you at run time for all of the information that's required to connect to the target data source. For ODBC connections, the second parameter controls how the ODBC Driver Manager responds to the information provided in the different parameters of the OpenDatabase method. Table 12-1 lists the valid values for this parameter.

The third parameter of the OpenDatabase method is a Boolean data type that specifies if the database will be read-only. The value of False specifies that the database is updateable.

The fourth parameter of the OpenDatabase method is a string that contains ODBC connection information. The string must contain a set of predefined keywords. Table 12-2 presents the valid connection string keywords.

Constant	Description
dbDriverNoPrompt	The ODBC Driver Manager can use only the information provided by the OpenDatabase method. If insufficient information is supplied, the connection fails.
dbDriverPrompt	The ODBC Driver Manager always displays the information provided by the OpenDatabase method.
dbDriverComplete	The ODBC Driver Manager determines if all of the required connection information has been supplied by the OpenDatabase method. If all of the required information is supplied, the connection is made without further prompting. If any of the required information is missing, then the ODBC Driver Manager prompts the user for the missing information.
dbDriverCompleteRequired	This option behaves like dbDriverComplete, except that any prompts containing information that has already been supplied are disabled.

Table 12-1.   Options for the OpenDatabase Method

Keyword	Description
ODBC	Required
DSN	The name of an existing data source created by the ODBC Administrator
DRIVER	The name of an existing ODBC driver
SERVER	The name of an existing SQL Server system
UID	The login ID for the data source
PWD	The password associated with the login ID
DATABASE	The SQL Server target database name

Table 12-2. Connection String Keywords

If the UID, PWD, or DATABASE parameters are blank, then the ODBC Driver Manager must be able to prompt for the remaining information that's required to connect to SQL Server.

After the OpenDatabase method successfully completes, there will be an open connection to SQL Server. You can then query the database or perform other operations. In the previous code example, you can see that a simple record set object named rs is created that will contain all of the rows and columns from the table named authors that is located in the pubs database.

Opening a Database with the DSN-less Connection

The previous example showed how to use the OpenDatabase method in conjunction with the dbDriverComplete parameter to cause the ODBC Driver Manager to prompt the user to select an existing data source name (DSN). However, DAO 3.5 also supports DSN-less connections in which you can connect to an ODBC data source without requiring a preconfigured DSN. The following code illustrates how to establish a DSN-less connection using the OpenDatabase method:

```
Set ws = CreateWorkspace
Set db = ws.OpenDatabase("", dbDriverNoPrompt, False, _
    "ODBC;DRIVER=SQL Server;UID=" & sLoginID & _
    ";PWD=" & sPassword & _
    ";SERVER=" & sServer & _
    ";DATABASE=pubs")
Set rs = db.OpenRecordset("Select * From authors")
```

First, an instance of the Workplace object named ws is created using the CreateWorkspace method. Then the OpenDatabase method of the ws Workplace object is used to create a new Database object named db. However, in this example, the ODBC connection string used in the fourth parameter of the OpenDatabase method contains the DRIVER and SERVER keywords. Using these keywords in the ODBC connection string allows you to directly specify the name of the ODBC driver that you want to use—bypassing the need to have a preconfigured data source.

Closing a Database

Before ending your application, you can close any open databases using the Database object's Close method. An example of the Close method follows:

```
db.Close
```

Alternatively, you can close the connection by setting the Database object to nothing, as follows:

```
Set db = Nothing
```

Using the Close method is preferable because it is more self-explanatory and easier to understand than setting the instance of the object to nothing.

Retrieving Data with DAO

After a Database object has been instantiated using either a direct connection or linked tables, you can use the Database object to create a TableDef object, a QueryDef object, or a Recordset object. In this next section, you'll see how to retrieve data using DAO's Recordset object. You'll learn about the different types of Recordset objects and see how to traverse the Recordset object and use its Fields collection to work with the column values of the target table.

Using the Recordset Object

A Recordset object represents the results of a query. A Recordset object is created using the Database object's OpenRecordset method. You can choose the type of Recordset object you want to create using the type argument of the OpenRecordset method. If you don't specify the type of Recordset, DAO automatically uses a Recordset object with the most functionality. DAO starts with the table-type Recordset object. If the table type isn't available, DAO attempts to use a dynaset Recordset object; followed by a snapshot Recordset object; and, finally, a forward-only Recordset object.

TABLE-TYPE RECORDSETS   A table-type Recordset object is a representation of a local Jet table. As you might expect, this type of Recordset can only be used with Jet workspaces. Table-type Recordset objects can be used to open more than one base table, and they also can be used for ISAM data sources. You cannot use table-type Recordset objects with an ODBC data source or with a linked table. Therefore, table-type Recordset objects are not used to develop SQL Server applications.

DYNASET RECORDSETS   DAO's dynaset Recordset object is analogous to ODBC's keyset cursor. The dynaset type supports forward and backward movement through the

Recordset object, as well as updating of the Recordset object. When a dynaset Recordset object is opened, the Jet engine builds a local set of keys where each key is associated with a row in the Recordset object. When your application accesses rows in the Recordset object, the local index value for the row is used to retrieve the corresponding row's data from the data source. Dynaset Recordset objects are fully updateable but they do not dynamically reflect changes that other users make in the data source. For ODBC data sources, dynaset Recordset objects use optimistic record locking to support concurrency. Dynaset Recordset objects are relatively resource intensive, because the client system must maintain the keys for the entire record set and a buffer that contains the data from the populated result set.

SNAPSHOT RECORDSETS   Snapshot Recordset objects are analogous to ODBC's static cursor. A snapshot Recordset object provides a frozen copy or snapshot of the data source at the time the Recordset object was opened. Snapshot Recordset objects are not updateable, and they do not reflect any changes that are made to the data source unless the Recordset object is closed and reopened. Because of their static nature, snapshot Recordset objects are generally less resource intensive than dynaset Recordset objects. Because snapshot Recordset objects make a local copy of the data, however, you need to be careful about using this type of object with inclusive SQL statements that may return large amounts of data.

FORWARD-ONLY RECORDSETS   The forward-only Recordset object is analogous to ODBC's forward-only cursor. The forward-only Recordset object provides the best performance and the least overhead of any of the other DAO Recordset objects, but it is also less capable than either the dyanset or snapshot Recordset objects. As their name suggests, forward-only Recordsets only support one-way forward movement through the Recordset object. Forward-only result sets are updateable, but they can only update the current row. Any changes in the data source are not reflected in a forward-only Recordset object.

DYNAMIC RECORDSETS   Dynamic Recordsets are analogous to the ODBC dynamic cursor. Dynamic Recordsets are the most powerful type of Recordset object that can be used with an ODBC data source. However, they are also the most resource intensive. Like a dynaset Recordset, a dynamic Recordset object uses a local set of indexes that correspond to each row in the data source. Also like dynaset Recordsets, dynamic Recordsets are fully updateable. However, dynamic Recordsets offer additional functionality beyond the dynaset Recordsets. Dynamic Recordsets automatically reflect all of the changes that are made to the original data source. In other words, if another user updates a row that is contained in a dynamic Recordset object, that user's change is propagated to the dynamic Recordset object. No application code is required to update the values in the dynamic Recordset object. To dynamically maintain the Recordset object, the Jet engine must periodically compare the contents of the Recordset object and the data source and then update the local Recordset object with all of the changes in the data source. This constant maintenance is resource intensive and must be performed by the local Jet engine. Dynamic Recordsets are only available using ODBCDirect, which is discussed in the second part of this chapter.

Creating and Traversing a Dynaset Recordset

Several of the previous code examples presented in the chapter have already shown how to create simple record sets. The following code illustrates how to create a little more complex dynaset Recordset object. This code uses the MSFlexGrid ActiveX control to display the object's contents.

> *TIP:* The MSFlexGrid control isn't displayed in the default view of the Visual Basic Toolbox. To add the control to Visual Basic's Toolbox, select the Components option from Visual Basic's Projects menu. This displays the Components dialog box, which contains a list of all of the ActiveX controls that are installed on the system. Find the Microsoft Flex grid 5.0 control in the list and click its check box to add it to Visual Basic's Toolbox.

```
Private Sub DAOQuery()

    Dim ws As Workspace
    Dim rs As Recordset
    Dim fld As Field
    Dim nRow As Integer

    Screen.MousePointer = vbHourglass

    Set ws = Workspaces(0)
    Set db = ws.OpenDatabase _
        ("", dbDriverComplete, False, "ODBC;UID=" & sLoginID & _
        ";PWD=" & sPassword & ";Database=pubs")
    Set rs = db.OpenRecordset("SELECT * FROM authors", dbOpenDynaset)

    ' Setup the grid
    Grid.Cols = rs.Fields.Count
    Grid.Rows = 1
    Grid.Row = 0

    'Setup the Grid headings
     For Each fld In rs.Fields
        Grid.Col = fld.OrdinalPosition
        Grid.Text = fld.Name
    Next fld

    rs.MoveLast
    Grid.Rows = rs.RecordCount + 1
    Grid.Row = 0
    rs.MoveFirst

    ' Move through each row in the record set
```

```
    Do Until rs.EOF

        Grid.Row = Grid.Row + 1

        'Loop through all fields
        For Each fld In rs.Fields
            Grid.Col = fld.OrdinalPosition
            Grid.Text = fld.Value
        Next fld

        rs.MoveNext
    Loop

    rs.Close

    Screen.MousePointer = vbDefault

End Sub
```

In the previous code example, you can see where the Workspaces object called ws is created. Then the OpenDatabase method of the ws Workspaces object is used to create a new Database object. The first parameter of the OpenDatabase method is an empty string, which means that no data source has been previously defined. The value of dbDriverComplete specifies that the ODBC Driver Manager will prompt the user for any of the required connection values that are not supplied with the OpenDatabase method. Since the first parameter identifying the data source is empty, the ODBC Driver Manager must at least prompt for this information. The value of False in the third parameter specifies that the database will be updateable. The connection string that's used in the fourth parameter passes in the SQL Server user ID and password and sets the database to pubs.

Next, the OpenRecordset method of the db Database object is used to create a new Recordset object. The OpenRecordset method takes four parameters. The first parameter is required and the last three parameters are optional. In this case, the first parameter contains a SQL Select statement that defines the row set. Instead of a SQL statement, this parameter could also contain the name of an existing QueryDef object or a table. The second parameter of the OpenRecordset method specifies the type of Recordset object that will be opened. Table 12-3 lists each of the DAO constants that specify a type of Recordset object.

Using the constant dbOpenDynaset specifies that a Dynaset Recordset object will be opened that allows both forward and backward movement, as well as updating. The third and fourth parameters of the OpenRecordset method are not used in this example. However, it is still important to understand their use. The third parameter sets the options that control the behavior of the Recordset object. Table 12-4 lists the constants that are allowed for the third parameter.

DAO Constant	Recordset Type
dbOpenTable	Table
dbOpenDynamic	Dynamic
dbOpenDynaset	Dynaset
dbOpenForwardOnly	Forward-only
dbOpenSnapshot	Snapshot

Table 12-3.   OpenRecordset Types

OpenRecordset Options Constant	Description
dbAppendOnly	Rows can be appended to the Recordset, but no rows can be updated or deleted.
dbSQLPassThrough	The SQL statement will not be processed by the Jet engine. Instead, the SQL statement will be sent on to the server. This can only be used with snapshot Recordsets.
dbSeeChanges	Generates a DAO error if the Jet engine detects that a row contained in a dynamic or dynaset Recordset has been updated by the application. This is only for local Jet engine databases.
dbDenyWrite	Prevents other users from updating any rows that are contained in the Recordset. This is only for local Jet engine databases.
dbDenyRead	Prevents other users from reading a table-type Recordset (for local Jet engine databases).
dbForwardOnly	Creates a forward-only Recordset. (Note: This option only exists for backward compatibility. Instead of using the dbForward option in the third parameter of the dbOpenRecordset method, use the newer dbOpenForwardOnly constant in the second parameter of the OpenRecordset method to create a forward-only Recordset.)

Table 12-4.   OpenRecordset Options

OpenRecordset Options Constant	Description
dbReadOnly	Prevents the user from changing the Recordset. This is only for local Jet engine databases.
dbReadAsync	Submits SQL to create the Recordset asynchronously.
dbExecDirect	Executes a dynamic SQL statement on the database server. This is only for ODBCDirect connections.
dbInconsistent	Allows an update of a multitable join to write inconsistent one-to-many updates. This is only for local Jet engine databases.
dbConsistent	Ensures that all one-to-many table updates of a multitable join are written consistently. This is only for local Jet engine databases.

Table 12-4.   OpenRecordset Options (*conintued*)

The fourth parameter of the OpenRecordset method sets the type of locking that the Jet engine will use to control the concurrency of data in the Recordset object. Table 12-5 lists the values that are valid for the fourth parameter of the OpenRecordset method.

DAO Locking Constant	Description
dbReadOnly	Sets the Recordset to read-only. No updates are allowed. You can use dbReadOnly in either the options argument or the lockedits argument, but not both. If you use it for both arguments, a run-time error occurs.
dbPessimistic	Sets the Recordset to use *pessimistic locking,* in which the page or record containing the edited row is locked until the Update method is executed.

Table 12-5.   OpenRecordset Lock Types

DAO Locking Constant	Description
dbOptimistic	Sets the Recordset to use *optimistic locking,* in which the page or record containing the edited row is not locked until the Update method is executed, based on a unique index.
dbOptimisticValue	Sets the Recordset to use optimistic locking based on the row values. This is only for ODBCDirect workspaces.
dbOptimisticBatch	Sets the Recordset object to use ODBC *batch updating,* in which sets of local updates are sent to the server in blocks or batches. This is only for ODBCDirect workspaces.

Table 12-5.   OpenRecordset Lock Types (*continued*)

After the Recordset object has been created, the next section of code sets up a grid that is sized according to the values that were returned in the rs Recordset object. First, the number of columns in the grid are set with the number of columns that were contained in the Count property of the Fields collection of the rs Recordset object. Next, the column headings of the Recordset are retrieved using a For Each loop to iterate through the Fields collection of the rs Recordset object. For each fld object contained in the Fields collection, the OrdinalPosition property is used to put it into a unique column of the grid and then the column name is retrieved from the fld.Name property.

Next, to get the number of rows that the grid will use, the Recordset object is populated using the MoveLast method. Following the MoveLast method, the RecordCount property of the Recordset object will contain the number of rows that are contained in the Recordset. The number of grid rows is set with this property plus one additional row that will be used to display column headings. After the grid has been set up, the cursor is repositioned to the first row of the Recordset object using the MoveFirst method.

After the grid's column headings have been set up with the column names from the Recordset object, a Do Until loop is used to read through all of the rows in the Recordset. When the end of the Recordset object is reached, the rs.EOF property becomes True and the code drops out of the read loop. To list all of the Recordset's column values in the grid, a For Each loop is used to iterate through the Fields collection. Again, the OrdinalPosition of each column assigns the Recordset column value to the appropriate column in the grid. The Value property then retrieves the actual column data where it is assigned to the grid's Text property. After all of the data values from the row have been moved to the appropriate location in the grid, the rs.MoveNext method positions the cursor to the next row in the Recordset object.

FINDING RECORDS IN A RECORDSET   DAO supports several different methods for locating records within a Recordset object. The DAO methods that are available for locating records in a Recordset are Seek, FindFirst, FindLast, FindNext, and FindPrevious. The Seek method is primarily targeted for use with table-type Recordsets, which aren't used with SQL Server connections. The various Find methods are compatible with dynamic, dynaset, and snapshot Recordsets.

> **TIP:** While you can use the DAO Find methods to locate specific records within a Recordset when accessing SQL Server databases, it's almost always better to create a Recordset object that is restricted to just the desired rows. You can restrict the size of the Recordset by using the Where clause in the SQL statement that's used in the first parameter of the OpenRecordset method. However, the Find methods can be appropriate when the application needs to perform several subsequent subqueries on the rows contained in the Recordset or when the application may need to frequently present the data in a different order than the data in the Recordset.

The following code illustrates using the FindFirst method with a dynaset Recordset:

```
Private Sub DAORecordSetFindFirst(db As Database)
    Dim rs As Recordset
    Dim fld As Field
    Dim sCriteria As String

    Screen.MousePointer = vbHourglass

    'Use the open Database object named db
    Set rs = db.OpenRecordset("Select * From authors", dbOpenDynaset)

    'Set up the find criteria
    sCriteria = "state = 'CA'"

    ' Populate the Recordset
    rs.MoveLast
    ' Find the first matching record
    rs.FindFirst sCriteria
    If rs.NoMatch Then
        MsgBox "No records found for " & sCriteria
        Screen.MousePointer = vbDefault
        Exit Sub
    End If
    ' Set up the grid
    Grid.Cols = rs.Fields.Count
    Grid.Rows = 2
    Grid.Row = 0

    'Set up the Grid headings
    For Each fld In rs.Fields
```

```
        Grid.Col = fld.OrdinalPosition
        Grid.Text = fld.Name
    Next fld


    Grid.Row = Grid.Row + 1


    'Display one row in the grid
    For Each fld In rs.Fields
        Grid.Col = fld.OrdinalPosition
        Grid.Text = fld.Value
    Next fld


    rs.Close


    Screen.MousePointer = vbDefault

End Sub
```

In this example, the DAO Workspace and Database objects are instantiated and the connection to the SQL Server pubs database is made when the OpenDatabase method is executed. Then the OpenRecordset method of the rs Recordset object is used to create a Recordset object that contains all of the rows and columns of the authors table in the pubs database. The dbOpenDynaset constant specifies that the Jet engine will create a dynaset Recordset object. After the Recordset object has been created, a string variable named sCriteria is assigned the search criteria that will be used to locate the row in the Recordset object. In this case, the string "state = 'CA'" instructs the Jet engine to find the row where the state column contains the value of CA.

TIP: The search criteria string is formatted in the same manner as Jet's SQL Where clause. However, when using the Find methods, you do not specify the literal "Where"—it is assumed.

The Recordset object must be populated before you can successfully use the Find methods to locate data in the Recordset. Using the MoveLast method of the Recordset object will populate the Recordset. Next, the rs Recordset object's FindFirst method uses the string containing the search criteria to locate the first occurrence of the row that matches the search string. If the row isn't found in the Recordset object, the Recordset object's NoMatch property is set to True, a message box will be displayed, and this subroutine will be exited. If a matching row is found in the Recordset object, then a grid is sized to contain the appropriate number of columns and two rows, which is enough to display the column headings along with the first row that was found using the FindFirst method. Next, each column in the first row in the grid is assigned the column heading using the Name property of each fld object (a field object corresponds to a column). After the grid's column headings have been set up, the data values from the found row are assigned to the appropriate grid columns.

The other Find methods operate much like the FindFirst method. For instance, in the following code, you can see how the FindNext method can be used to locate the next occurrences of the rows in the Recordset object where the value of the state column is equal to CA.

```
Private Sub DAORecordSetFindNext(db As Database)
    Dim rs As Recordset
    Dim fld As Field
    Dim sCriteria As String

    Screen.MousePointer = vbHourglass

    'Use the open Database object named db
    Set rs = db.OpenRecordset("Select * From authors", dbOpenDynaset)

    ' Set up the grid
    Grid.Cols = rs.Fields.Count
    Grid.Rows = 1
    Grid.Row = 0

    'Set up the Grid headings
     For Each fld In rs.Fields
        Grid.Col = fld.OrdinalPosition
        Grid.Text = fld.Name
    Next fld

    'Set up the find criteria
    sCriteria = "state = 'CA'"

    ' Find the first matching record
    rs.FindFirst sCriteria

    Do While rs.NoMatch = False
        'Display the current record in the grid
        Grid.Rows = Grid.Rows + 1
        Grid.Row = Grid.Rows - 1

        For Each fld In rs.Fields
            Grid.Col = fld.OrdinalPosition
            Grid.Text = fld.Value
        Next fld
        rs.FindNext sCriteria
    Loop

    Screen.MousePointer = vbDefault

End Sub
```

Again, a Recordset object named rs is created from the authors table in the pubs database. Next, the MSFlexGrid is set up for the number of columns in the grid along with one initial row that contains the grid headings. The grid headings are added to rows using a For Each loop that iterates through the rs object's Fields collection.

After the Recordset is opened and the MSFlexGrid is initialized, a string is set up containing the search criteria of "state = 'CA'". This search criteria instructs the Jet engine to locate the next row in the Recordset object that contains the value of CA in the state column. Then the FindFirst method is used to locate the first row in the Recordset that matches the search criteria. Next, the FindNext method is used within a Do While loop to find all of the subsequent matching rows in the Recordset object that match the specified search criteria. The search begins from the cursor's current location in the Recordset object. If the previous operation positioned the cursor at the first row in the Recordset object that contained the value of CA in the state column, then this search begins with the next row in the Recordset. When no more matches are found, the NoMatch property of the rs Recordset object becomes True, ending the search loop. Within the Do loop, the column values of each row that match the search criteria are assigned to the appropriate columns in the grid.

In the previous example, you saw how the FindFirst and FindNext methods can be used to locate a subset of the rows contained in a Recordset object. In that example, the FindFirst method was used to locate the first matching value of a row with the search criteria, and then the FindNext method was used to search forward for the next matching rows in the Recordset. You can also use the FindLast and FindPrevious methods to move backward through a Recordset object. This can be useful in cases where you may occasionally want to work with data in a different order than it is maintained in the Recordset object.

The following code shows how you can use the FindLast method in conjunction with the FindPrevious method to traverse the Recordset in reverse order:

```
Private Sub DAORecordsetFindLast(db As Recordset)
    Dim fld As Field
    Dim sCriteria As String

    Screen.MousePointer = vbHourglass

    ' Set up the grid
    Grid.Cols = rs.Fields.Count
    Grid.Rows = 1
    Grid.Row = 0

    'Set up the find criteria
    sCriteria = "state = 'CA' And city = 'Oakland'"

    ' Find the first matching record
    ' Use the open recordset named rs
    rs.FindLast sCriteria
```

```
    If rs.NoMatch Then
        MsgBox "No records found for " & sCriteria
        Screen.MousePointer = vbDefault
        Exit Sub
    End If

    ' Find the first matching records in the open recordset
    Do While rs.NoMatch = False
        'Display the current record in the grid
        If rs.NoMatch = True Then Exit Do

        Grid.Rows = Grid.Rows + 1
        Grid.Row = Grid.Rows - 1

        For Each fld In rs.Fields
            Grid.Col = fld.OrdinalPosition
            Grid.Text = fld.Value
        Next fld
        rs.FindPrevious sCriteria
    Loop

    rs.Close

    Screen.MousePointer = vbDefault

End Sub
```

In this example, you can see that the FindLast and FindPrevious methods are used very much like the FindFirst and FindNext methods. First, you set up the desired search criteria. Then you use the appropriate Find method to position the cursor within the Recordset object. In both cases, you first want to be sure that the Recordset object is fully populated before using the Find methods. In this example, a little more sophisticated search string is used. Here the search string is set to locate a row in the Recordset object where the value of the state column is equal to CA and the city is equal to Oakland. Next, the FindLast method is used to locate the last occurrence of a row that matches this search criteria. If no matching row is found, the NoMatch property of the rs Recordset object is set to True, a message box will be displayed, and the subroutine will be exited. If a matching row was found, the values in the row will be assigned to the appropriate columns in the grid. Then the FindPrevious method will be used within a Do While loop to populate the grid with the data from the other rows in the Recordset object that match the specified search criteria. When no more rows in the rs Recordset object match the search criteria, the Do Until loop will be exited.

▼

TIP: While this example uses the same string as the search criteria for both the FindFirst and FindNext methods and the FindLast and FindPrevious methods, you can set a new search value before executing any of these methods.

Limiting Data in a Recordset

While the Find methods can be used to locate specific rows within a Recordset object, over ODBC connections these methods are generally not as efficient as using the SQL Select statement to limit the size of the Recordset object to just the desired results. You can limit the number of rows contained in the Recordset object by using the SQL Where clause. This technique has several advantages. Limiting the size of the Recordset object reduces the I/O required by the server, reduces the network traffic that is required to send the results back to the client, and simplifies the processing required by the application to access the desired data.

The following code shows how to use the SQL Select statement's Where clause to limit the number of rows in the Recordset to those rows in which the state column is equal to CA and the value in the city column is equal to Oakland:

```
Private Sub DAOLimitedRecordSet()

    Dim ws As Workspace
    Dim db As Database
    Dim rs As Recordset
    Dim fld As Field
    Dim nRow As Integer
    Dim sSQL As String

    Screen.MousePointer = vbHourglass

    sSQL = "Select * From authors " _
        & "WHERE state = 'CA' AND city = 'Oakland'"

    Set ws = Workspaces(0)
    Set db = ws.OpenDatabase("", dbDriverNoPrompt, False, _
        "ODBC;Driver=SQL Server;UID=" & sLoginID & _
        ";PWD=" & sPassword & _
        ";Server=" & sServer & _
        ";Database=pubs")
    Set rs = db.OpenRecordset(sSQL, dbOpenDynaset)

    DisplayDynasetGrid rs, Grid, 1

    rs.Close
    db.Close
    ws.Close

    Screen.MousePointer = vbDefault

End Sub
```

In this example, you can see where the string named sSQL is assigned a SQL Select statement that uses the Where clause. Next, a new Workspace object named ws and a new Databases object named db are created. The OpenRecordset method then uses the SQL statement contained in the sSQL string variable to create a new Recordset object that only consists of the rows of the authors table that contain the value of CA in the state column and the value of Oakland in the city column.

Limiting the rows in the Recordset object typically performs better over an ODBC connection, because it moves the select logic from the application to SQL Server. The application program does not need to first retrieve a larger set of rows and then perform additional searches for new row selections.

After the rs Recordset object has been created, the contents of the Recordset object are displayed in a grid using the DisplayDynasetGrid subroutine, and the rs Recordset object is closed. The DisplayDynasetGrid subroutine is a generic subroutine that can be used to display the contents of a Recordset object in an MSFlexGrid. The DisplayDynasetGrid subroutine uses three parameters: the name of a DAO Recordset object, the name of an MSFlexGrid object, and an integer value that controls the direction in which the data will be displayed. The contents of the DisplayDynasetGrid subroutine are shown in the following code:

```
Private Sub DisplayDynasetGrid _
(rs As Recordset, Grid As MSFlexGrid, nDirection As Integer)

    Dim fld As Field
    Dim nForward As Integer
    Dim nReverse As Integer
    On Error Resume Next

    nForward = 1
    nReverse = 2

    ' Set up the grid
    Grid.Cols = rs.Fields.Count
    rs.MoveLast
    Grid.Rows = rs.RecordCount + 1
    Grid.Row = 0
    Grid.Col = 0
    Grid.FixedRows = 1
    Grid.Clear

    'Set up the Grid headings
    For Each fld In rs.Fields
        If rs.EOF = False Then
            Grid.ColWidth(Grid.Col) = _
                TextWidth(String(fld.FieldSize + 4, "a"))
        End If
        Grid.Col = fld.OrdinalPosition
```

```
            Grid.Text = fld.Name
            Grid.ColAlignment(Grid.Col) = 1
    Next fld


    If nDirection = nForward Then

        rs.MoveFirst

        ' Move through each row in the record set
        Do Until rs.EOF

            ' Set the position in the grid
            Grid.Row = Grid.Row + 1
            Grid.Col = 0

            'Loop through all fields
            For Each fld In rs.Fields
                Grid.Col = fld.OrdinalPosition
                Grid.Text = fld.Value
            Next fld

            rs.MoveNext
        Loop

    Else

        rs.MoveLast

        ' Move through each row in the record set
        Do Until rs.BOF

            ' Set the position in the grid
            Grid.Row = Grid.Row + 1
            Grid.Col = 0

            'Loop through all fields
            For Each fld In rs.Fields
                Grid.Col = fld.OrdinalPosition
                Grid.Text = fld.Value
            Next fld

            rs.MovePrevious

        Loop
```

```
        End If

End Sub
```

   The parameters used by the DisplayDynasetGrid subroutine allow it to be reused by many different Recordset and grid objects. At the beginning of this subroutine, two Integer variables are declared and assigned values. These variables are just used to improve the readability of a later section of the code. The section of code immediately following these variables sets up the grid. The number of grid columns is set using the Count property of the Recordset object's Fields collection. Next, the grid's Rows property is set up to have at least one row, which will contain the column heading information. Then the grid's Row and Col properties are used to set the current grid cell at row 0 column 0 (the upper left-hand corner of the grid). Then the grid's Clear method is used to make sure that any old data is deleted from the grid.

   Once the grid's initial number of rows and columns have been set, the heading values and sizes for each of the grid's columns are set up. Every column in the result set will have a corresponding Field object in the Recordset object's Fields collection. A For Each loop iterates through all of the field objects contained in the Fields collection. The first action within the For Each loop sets the column width of the grid using the grid's ColWidth property. In order to set the width of the correct column, the ColWidth property requires the index of the current grid column that is supplied by the grid's Col property. The ColWidth property must be assigned a value in twips, so Visual Basic's TextWidth method is used to return the number of twips required for each Field object. (A *twip* is a unit of screen measurement equal to one twentieth of a printer's point. There are 72 points per logical inch.) The correct number of twips is determined by creating a placeholder string using the Field object's FieldSize property plus four extra characters that help to prevent the grid columns from appearing too crowded. Next, the Field object's OrdinalPosition and Name properties are used to set the headings for the grid columns. Then the grid's ColAlignment property for each column is set to left-justify the cell text in the column.

   Next, the value of the nDirection parameter is checked. A value of 1 causes the data to be listed in forward order; a value of 2 causes the Recordset data to be listed in backward order. If nDirection is equal to nForward (1), then the code in the first part of the If statement will be executed, where a Do Until loop is used to read through all of the columns in the Recordset object. The Do Until loop continues until the Recordset's EOF (End of File) property becomes True, which indicates that all of the rows in the Recordset have been read. Inside the Do Until loop, the grid column is set to the first column and a For Each loop is used to move the data values contained in the Fields collection to the grid columns. After all of the Field values have been processed, the Recordset object's MoveNext method is used to move the cursor to the next row in the Recordset object.

   The code in the second part of the If statement is similar in structure, but it functions in reverse. The Recordset object's MoveLast method is used to position the cursor to the last row in the Recordset. Then the Do loop and the Recordset object's MovePrevious method are used to read through the Recordset from the back to the front. Again, a For Each loop is used to extract the value from each Field object in the Fields collection.

Closing a Recordset

Before ending your application, you can close any open Recordsets using the Recordset object's Close method. An example of the Close method follows:

```
rs.Close
```

Alternatively, you can close the connection by setting the Recordset object to nothing as follows:

```
Set rs = Nothing
```

Using the Close method is preferable because it is more self-explanatory and easier to understand than setting the instance of the object to nothing.

Executing Dynamic SQL Using SQLPassThrough

While the DAO methods allow you to access the SQL Server database in a variety of ways, DAO does not allow you to perform all of the database operations that are possible using SQL. To further complicate this, since the Jet engine is itself a query processor, Jet expects all of the SQL statements that are sent to it to conform to Jet SQL syntax, which is not identical to the Transact-SQL syntax used by SQL Server. Luckily, DAO provides the SQLPassThrough option that allows the Jet engine to pass a SQL statement on to the target data source to be processed.

Creating Database Objects Using Dynamic SQL and SQLPassThrough

The following code listing illustrates how you can use DAO's Database object's SQLPassThrough option to create a table in a SQL Server database.

```
Private Sub CreateTable(db As Database)

    Dim sSQL As String
    On Error Resume Next

    Screen.MousePointer = vbHourglass

    sSQL = "Drop Table department"
    db.Execute sSQL, dbSQLPassThrough

    On Error GoTo 0
    sSQL = "Create Table department _
    (Dep_ID Char(4) Not Null, Dep_Name Char(25), _
     Primary Key(Dep_ID))"
    db.Execute sSQL, dbSQLPassThrough

    Screen.MousePointer = vbDefault

End Sub
```

In this example, you can see where the Execute method of the db Database object is used in conjunction with the dbSQLPassThrough constant to drop and then re-create the department table in the pubs database. Near the beginning of this code, you can see where the Resume Next option of Visual Basic's error handler is used to skip over any errors that may be generated if the table does not exist on the target database when the SQL Drop Table statement is executed. The Database object's Execute method is used to process dynamic SQL statements and the dbSQLPassThrough constant instructs the Jet engine not to process the statement but instead to pass it on to a target data source. After the Drop Table statement has been executed, Visual Basic's error handler is turned off using the GoTo 0 option. This causes any errors that may occur during the Create Table statement to surface to the user. In both cases, it's important to note that the SQL statements that are used follow the Transact-SQL syntax.

NOTE: The Department table is not a part of the original pubs database. It is created in order to demonstrate updating tables without modifying the original tables in the pubs database.

Modifying Data Using Recordsets and SQLPassThrough

In addition to retrieving the data to satisfy SQL queries, Recordset objects can be used to update data. However, as you might have guessed after seeing the various parameters of the OpenRecordset method, not all Recordset objects are updateable. The ability to update a Recordset depends on the type of Recordset that is opened and the options that were used with the OpenRecordset method. A summary of the Recordset object types and their ability to support data update methods is listed in Table 12-6.

Inserting Data in a Recordset

The AddNew method in combination with the Update method of the Recordset object can be used to add rows to an updateable DAO Recordset object. The following code

Result Set	Updateable
dbOpenForwardOnly	Yes (current row only)
dbOpenSnapshot	No
dbOpenDynaset	Yes
dbOpenDynamic	Yes
dbOpenTable	Yes

Table 12-6.   Updateable Recordset Types

illustrates how you can add rows to a result set that was created as a dynaset Recordset.

```
Private Sub AddUsingRecordset(db As Database)

    Dim rs As Recordset
    Dim i As Integer
    Dim sSQL As String

    Screen.MousePointer = vbHourglass

    ' Make sure no records are retrieved on the Select
    sSQL = "Select Dep_ID, Dep_name From department Where 1 = 2"

    'Use the open Database object
    Set rs = db.OpenRecordset(sSQL, dbOpenDynaset)

    ' Insert 50 records
    For i = 1 To 50
        rs.AddNew
        rs!Dep_ID = i
        rs!Dep_Name = "Department " & CStr(i)
        rs.Update
    Next

    ' Display the added records
    DisplayDynasetGrid rs, Grid, 1

    rs.Close

    Screen.MousePointer = vbDefault

End Sub
```

In this example, the OpenRecordset method is used to create a new Recordset object named rs. The first parameter of the OpenRecordset method accepts a string that contains a SQL statement that defines the Recordset object. In this case, the Recordset consists of the Dep_ID and the Dep_Name columns from the department table in the pubs database.

TIP: Since this Recordset is used exclusively to insert rows, the Where 1 = 2 clause is used to ensure that no data is actually sent across the network. This technique can improve the performance of your DAO applications.

The second parameter of the OpenRecordset method uses the dbOpenDynaset constant to specify that the Recordset object will be an updateable, dynaset Recordset. After the Recordset object has been created, a For Next loop is used to add a series of rows to the result set. Within the For Next loop, the AddNew method is called to create a new row buffer for the row that will be added to the Recordset object.

After the AddNew method has been executed, the value of each column is assigned. The value of the Dep_ID column is set using the unique integer supplied by the loop counter variable (i), while the Dep_Name column is assigned the value of a string that is formed by concatenating the literal "Department" and the string representation of the loop counter. After the new row values have been set, the Update method is called to add the row to the Recordset object, which also results in the update of the base department table. Finally, the rows that were inserted in the Recordset are displayed using the DisplayDynasetGrid subroutine and the Close method is used to close the rs Recordset object.

Updating Data in a Recordset

The Edit and Update methods of the Recordset object can be used to update rows in an updateable Recordset. The following code illustrates how you can update the rows in a dynaset Recordset:

```
Private Sub UpdateUsingRecordset(db As Database)

    Dim rs As Recordset
    Dim i As Integer
    Dim sTemp As String

    Screen.MousePointer = vbHourglass

    'Open an updateable record set
    ' using the existing Database object db
    Set rs = db.OpenRecordset _
        ("Select Dep_ID, Dep_name From department", dbOpenDynaset)

    ' Update all of the rows in the department table
    Do Until rs.EOF
        rs.Edit
        ' Jet returns blank filled strings.
    ' Truncate at the first blank
        sTemp = RTrim(rs!Dep_Name)
        rs!Dep_Name = "Updated " & sTemp
        rs.Update
        rs.MoveNext
    Loop

    ' Display the updated records
```

```
DisplayDynasetGrid rs, Grid, 1

rs.Close

Screen.MousePointer = vbDefault
```

End Sub

In this example, the OpenRecordset method is used to create a new Recordset object named rs. The first parameter of the OpenRecordset method is a string that defines that the Recordset object will consist of the Dep_ID and the Dep_Name columns from the sample department table in the pubs database. The dbOpenDynaset constant in the second parameter indicates that the Recordset object will be updateable. After the Recordset object has been created, a Do Until loop is used to read through all of the rows contained in the record set. The loop is ended when the EOF property of the Recordset object becomes True. Within the Do loop, the Edit method is used to put each row into edit mode. Next, because Jet returns string values and all trailing blanks, the nonblank data value of the Dep_Name column is moved into a temporary string variable. This prevents the updated column value from exceeding the length of the column. Next, the value of the Dep_Name column is set to the new string value that begins with the literal "Updated". You might note that the Dep_ID field is not updated because it is the table's primary key. After the new values in the Dep_Name column have been assigned, the Update method is called to update the row in both the result set object and the data source. Then the MoveNext method of the rs result set object is used to move to the next row in the Recordset object. After all of the rows have been updated, the Recordset object in displayed using the DisplayDynasetGrid subroutine and the Close method is used to close the record set.

Deleting Data in a Recordset

The Delete method of the Recordset object is used to remove rows in an updateable DAO Recordset. The following code illustrates how you can delete rows in a dynaset Recordset object:

```
Private Sub DeleteUsingRecordset(db As Database)

    Dim rs As Recordset
    Dim i As Integer

    Screen.MousePointer = vbHourglass

    'Open an updateable recordset using an existing Database object
    Set rs = db.OpenRecordset _
        ("Select * From department", dbOpenDynaset)

    ' Delete all of the rows in the department table
    Do Until rs.EOF
```

```
        rs.Delete
        rs.MoveNext
Loop

' Display the empty records
DisplayDynasetGrid rs, Grid, 1

rs.Close

Screen.MousePointer = vbDefault

End Sub
```

Like the previous examples, the OpenRecordset method is used to create a new Recordset object that contains all of the columns from the department table in the pubs database. The value of dbOpenDynaset in the second parameter of the OpenResultset specifies that the Recordset object is updateable. After the Recordset object has been created, a Do Until loop is used to read through all of the rows of the Recordset. Each row is deleted using the Delete method, and then the MoveNext method is used to position the cursor to the next row in the result set. Finally, the empty Recordset is displayed in a grid and the Close method is used to close the result set object.

> **TIP:** There are faster methods to remove all of the rows in a table. For instance, using the SQL Truncate Table or an unqualified Delete statement provides better performance for mass row deletions. An example using an unqualified Delete statement is presented later in this chapter in the section titled "Deleting Data with SQLPassThrough."

Inserting Data with SQLPassThrough

In the previous example, you saw how to use the Database object's Execute method in conjunction with a Transact-SQL statement and the SQLPassThrough option to execute a SQL DDL (Data Definition Language) statement on the SQL Server. The SQL DDL used in the previous example created a new table. You can also use SQLPassThrough to execute SQL DML (Data Manipulation Language) statements that are capable of modifying the data in an ODBC data source like SQL Server.

> **TIP:** Using SQLPassThrough in conjunction with dynamic SQL DML statements can allow your DAO applications to get around a couple of Jet limitations. For instance, a snapshot Recordset object is not normally updateable. However, using the Database object's Execute method and the SQLPassThrough option, you execute SQL Insert, Update, and Delete statements against the server's database. This can allow your application to take advantage of the low resource requirements of a snapshot Recordset and yet still provide data update capabilities. Similarly, you can use SQL DML in conjunction with SQLPassThrough to update tables that do not have a unique key. This can circumvent Jet's need to enforce optimistic row locking, which requires a unique key, on all tables that will be updated.

In the following code, you can see how to use the SQL Insert statement to add rows to a table on the SQL Server database:

```
Private Sub AddUsingInsert(db As Database)

    Dim i As Integer
    Dim sSQL As String
    On Error GoTo Errorhandler

    Screen.MousePointer = vbHourglass

    ' No recordset is needed
    For i = 1 To 50
        sSQL = "Insert Into department " & _
            "Values('" & CStr(i) & "','DEPARTMENT " & CStr(i) & "')"
        db.Execute sSQL, dbSQLPassThrough
        sSQL = vbNullString
    Next

    Screen.MousePointer = vbDefault
    Exit Sub

Errorhandler:
    DisplayDAOError

    Screen.MousePointer = vbDefault

End Sub
```

In this example, a For Next loop is used to add 50 rows to the department table. Within the For Next loop, the string variable named sSQL is assigned a SQL Insert statement. This string is built by concatenating the SQL Insert statement with two other strings—one for each column in the department table. The first column will be set to a string representation of the loop counter and the second column will be set with a text string that combines the literal 'DEPARTMENT' with a loop counter. The actual insert statement that will be used the first time this For Next loop is executed will appear as follows:

```
Insert Into department Values('1','DEPARTMENT 1')
```

The next time this loop is executed, the sSQL string will contain this value:

```
Insert Into department Values('2','DEPARTMENT 2')
```

You might notice that the column data to be inserted evaluates to a literal value surrounded by a single quote mark ('). This meets the Transact-SQL requirements for an Insert statement that adds character data. The need to format the Values clause of the Insert statement makes this method somewhat unwieldy when you are dealing with many columns.

After the string containing the Insert statement has been built, it is passed as the first parameter of the Database object's Execute method. The dbSQLPassThrough constant in the second parameter of the Execute method causes the Jet engine not to parse this statement but instead to send it as is to SQL Server. The SQL Insert statement doesn't return a result set. After it has successfully completed, a new row will be added to the department table.

Updating Data with SQLPassThrough

In addition to adding new rows with the Insert statement, you can use SQL DML and DAO's SQLPassThrough option to update rows in a base table using the SQL Update statement. The following code illustrates how you can use a single Update to update all of the rows in the department table:

```
Private Sub UpdateUsingUpdate(db As Database)

    Dim sSQL As String
    On Error GoTo Errorhandler

    Screen.MousePointer = vbHourglass

    sSQL = "Update department " & _
        "Set Dep_Name = 'UPDATE' + Substring(Dep_Name, 7, 25)"

    db.Execute sSQL, dbSQLPassThrough

    Screen.MousePointer = vbDefault
    Exit Sub

Errorhandler:
    DisplayDAOError

    Screen.MousePointer = vbDefault

End Sub
```

This example is quite a bit different from the earlier update example that updated the department table using an updateable dynaset Recordset object. In the previous example, each row in the Recordset object was individually updated. This example takes advantage of SQL's set-at-a-time processing to update all of the rows in the department table using a single SQL statement.

> **TIP:** SQL's set-at-a-time processing can often provide performance benefits by shifting the workload to the server query processor and reducing the data flows between the server and the client.

Near the beginning of this example, you can see where the sSQL string variable is assigned the SQL Update statement. This Update statement is issued without a Where clause, which would cause it to update all of the rows in the department table. In addition, you can see that the Set clause assigns the column Dep_Name with the concatenation of the literal value "UPDATE" (6 characters) plus a substring that contains the remaining 19 characters of the Dep_Name column ($6 + 19 = 25$). In effect, this Update statement will overlay the first 6 characters of the Dep_Name column with the value "UPDATE". You can learn more about constructing SQL statements in Chapter 10.

> **NOTE:** Exercise caution when using the SQL Update statement without a Where clause. If this powerful technique is used incorrectly, it could inadvertently update more rows than you intend to.

Deleting Data with SQLPassThrough

The SQL Delete statement can be used with SQLPassThrough to delete one or more rows in a data source. In the following example, you can see how to use the SQL Delete statement in combination with the Execute method to delete all of the rows in a table:

```
Dim sSQL As String

sSQL = "Delete department"
db.Execute sSQL, dbSQLPassThrough
```

Like the previous Update example, this example uses SQL's ability to work with sets of data to delete all of the rows in the department table using a single SQL statement. In this example, the sSQL string variable is assigned the SQL Delete statement. Like the Update statement, when the Delete statement is issued without a Where clause it will delete all of the rows in a table—effectively clearing the table. Obviously, care needs to be taken when working with these types of unqualified SQL statements. However, as you can see, when they are used correctly, SQL statements can be a powerful data manipulation tool that can be leveraged for big performance gains in a client/server environment.

Working with QueryDefs

Like its name suggests, a DAO QueryDef object is essentially a query definition that's stored in a Jet database. QueryDef objects don't perform any actions by themselves. Instead, they store a SQL statement that can be executed against either a local Jet database or an ODBC data source. The SQL statement stored in a QueryDef object either can return a result set like a SQL Select statement or can be an action query like a SQL Insert, Update, or Delete statement. The SQL that's stored in a QueryDef object must either conform to the Jet SQL syntax or, in the case of QueryDef objects that use SQLPassThrough, the SQL syntax that's used by the ODBC data source. As you have probably guessed, the SQL used by a SQLPassThrough QueryDef object that accesses SQL Server must use SQL Server's Transact-SQL syntax.

Being stored in the database, QueryDef objects are most useful for performing SQL statements that will be executed repeatedly, queries that will be shared between users, and specialized tasks like calling stored procedures that return multiple result sets.

> **NOTE:** At first it might seem that QueryDef objects are the same as SQL Server stored procedures, but they are actually quite different. While both QueryDef objects and SQL Server stored procedures are maintained within their respective databases, that's about the limit of their similarity. A QueryDef object can only contain a single SQL statement, while a SQL Server stored procedure can contain complex logic with many SQL statements. Stored procedures can also return output parameters or multiple result sets. QueryDef objects cannot.

In the following section, you'll see how to build a QueryDef object that uses a parameterized query to perform a flexible query using a linked table. Then you'll see how to use a SQLPassThrough type of QueryDef object to perform a complex query. The last section shows you how to call a SQL Server stored procedure using a QueryDef object.

Using Parameterized QueryDefs

All of the previous examples in this chapter have illustrated how to build queries using SQL statements that are constructed using Visual Basic string variables, which the Jet engine passes to the ODBC data source to be executed as dynamic SQL statements. While functional, manually building each SQL statement can be cumbersome, especially for SQL statements that are complex or statements that are executed repeatedly. Using the QueryDef object's Parameters collection is one way you can address this problem. Although DAO doesn't support the use of parameters with QueryDef objects that are based on a Database object that was opened using the OpenDatabase method, you can use the Parameters collection with QueryDef objects that are created using linked tables. The following example illustrates how you can create a QueryDef object that uses a parameterized query.

> **NOTE:** Although DAO is able to use parameters with QueryDef objects based on linked tables, the SQL statements in the QueryDef object are all sent to SQL Server as dynamic SQL. They are not executed as prepared SQL statements created by the ODBC SQLPrepare( ) function—which provide much better performance. However, ODBCDirect does provide the ability to use high-performance static SQL and parameterized queries.

```
Private Sub QueryDefParms()

    Dim db As Database
    Dim qd As QueryDef
    Dim rs As Recordset
    Dim fld As Field
    Dim td As TableDef

    Dim sSQL As String
    On Error GoTo Errorhandler

    Screen.MousePointer = vbHourglass

    sSQL = "Parameters sInputState Text; " _
        & "Select au_lname, au_fname, state From authors" _
        & "Where state = sInputState ;"

    Set db = OpenDatabase("pubslink.mdb")

    Set td = db.TableDefs("authors")
    td.Connect = "ODBC;DRIVER=SQL Server;UID=" & sLoginID & _
        ";PWD=" & sPassword & _
        ";SERVER=" & sServer & _
        ";DATABASE=pubs"


    On Error Resume Next
     db.QueryDefs.Delete ("StateQuery")

    On Error GoTo Errorhandler
    Set qd = db.CreateQueryDef("StateQuery", sSQL)

    qd.Parameters("sInputState") = "OR"

    Set rs = qd.OpenRecordset()

    DisplayDynasetGrid rs, Grid, 1

    rs.Close
    qd.Close
    db.Close

    Screen.MousePointer = vbDefault
    Exit Sub
```

```
Errorhandler:
    DisplayDAOError

    Screen.MousePointer = vbDefault

End Sub
```

Near the beginning of this code listing, you can see where the string sSQL is assigned a SQL Select statement. Since this QueryDef is using linked tables and the Jet engine as a query processor, this SQL statement follows Jet's syntax rules. In this case, the Parameters keyword in the beginning of the string identifies the parameters that will be used with this query. This example uses a single parameter named sInputState that is a DAO Text data type. The semicolon indicates the end of the Parameters section of this query. The remainder of the string contains the Select statement that will be used. This Select statement will create a result set that contains three columns from the authors table: au_lname, au_fname, and state. The Where clause limits the rows in the result set to only those rows where the value of the state column is the same as the value contained in the sInputState parameter. The parameter name used in the Where clause must match the name of the parameter supplied in the Parameters section of the query.

Next, a DAO Jet Database object named db is created using the OpenDatabase method. The name of the Jet database is supplied as a parameter of the OpenDatabase method. After the Database object has been created, a new TableDef object named td is created using the linked authors table in the pubslink.mdb Jet database. The Connect method of the TableDef object is set with a DSN-less connection string that tells the Jet engine how it will connect to SQL Server. After the connection string has been set up, the QueryDefs.Delete method is used to delete any existing QueryDef object in the pubslink database named StateQuery. If the existing QueryDef object isn't deleted, then the CreateQueryDef method that follows will fail when this code is rerun.

TIP: If you know that a given QueryDef will be present in the Jet database, you can open it by name using the QueryDefs(*QueryDefName*) method.

Before attempting to delete the existing QueryDef object using the QueryDefs.Delete method, Visual Basic's error handler is enabled to trap any errors that may be generated if the named QueryDef doesn't exist. The On Error Resume Next statement instructs Visual Basic to ignore any errors that are generated by the following statement and to proceed with the next executable line of code. Following the execution of the Delete method, Visual Basic's error handler is reset to branch to the Errorhandler label if a trappable error is generated. More information about DAO error handling is presented later in this chapter in the section, "Error Handling."

Next, the db Database object's CreateQueryDef method is used to create a new QueryDef object named qd. The CreateQueryDef method uses two parameters to create

Jet QueryDef objects. The first parameter is a string that contains the name of the QueryDef object that will be created. In this example, the QueryDef object is named StateQuery. The second parameter is the sSQL string that contains the Jet SQL statement that will be stored in this QueryDef object.

After the CreateQueryDef method has been executed, a new QueryDef object will be added to the Jet database named publink.mdb. This QueryDef object will have one Parameter object named sInputState. The value of the sInputState QueryDef parameter is then set with a string containing the literal "OR". Then the OpenRecordset method is used to create a new Recordset object that matches the criteria specified in the qd QueryDef object. In this case, the record set will contain all of the rows in the authors table where the state column contains the value of OR. After the StateQuery QueryDef object has been executed, the DisplayDynasetGrid subroutine is used to display the results of the QueryDef in a grid. Before the subroutine exits, the Recordset, QueryDef, and Database objects are all closed.

Using a SQLPassThrough QueryDef

Using a QueryDef object in conjunction with DAO's SQLPassThrough option is one of the techniques that can help increase the performance of your DAO applications. Using SQLPassThrough with a QueryDef object is very similar to the earlier example that used SQLPassThrough with a Recordset object. However, you don't have to explicitly use the dbSQLPassThrough option to use SQLPassThrough with a QueryDef object. In order to use SQLPassThrough with a QueryDef object, you must first set the QueryDef object's Connect property to an ODBC connection string. Then you can set the SQL property to a valid Transact-SQL statement. When the Connect property has been set to an ODBC connection string, the Jet engine knows that the QueryDef object will be using SQLPassThrough and it will bypass parsing the SQL statement. Instead, Jet will send the SQL statement onto the ODBC data source for processing.

> **NOTE:** All Recordset objects that are created using SQLPassThrough are snapshot Recordsets—which are not updateable.

In the following code, you can see how to use a DAO QueryDef object with SQLPassThrough to create a snapshot Recordset object.

```
Private Sub QDSQLPassthru()
    Dim db As Database
    Dim qd As QueryDef
    Dim rs As Recordset
    Dim fld As Field

    Dim i As Integer
    Dim sSQL As String
    On Error GoTo Errorhandler

    Screen.MousePointer = vbHourglass
```

```
        sSQL = "Select au_lname, au_fname, title " _
            & "From authors, titles, titleauthor " _
            & "Where authors.au_id = titleauthor.au_id " _
            & "And titles.title_id = titleauthor.title_id " _
            & "Order By au_lname"

        Set db = OpenDatabase("pubslink.mdb")

        On Error Resume Next
        db.QueryDefs.Delete ("QDPassthru")

        On Error GoTo Errorhandler
        Set qd = db.CreateQueryDef("QDPassthru")
        qd.Connect = "ODBC;DRIVER=SQL Server;UID=" & sLoginID & _
            ";PWD=" & sPassword & _
            ";SERVER=" & sServer & _
            ";DATABASE=pubs"
        qd.SQL = sSQL
        qd.ReturnsRecords = True

        Set rs = qd.OpenRecordset()

        DisplayDynasetGrid rs, Grid, 1

        rs.Close
        qd.Close
        db.Close

        Screen.MousePointer = vbDefault
        Exit Sub

Errorhandler:
    DisplayDAOError

    Screen.MousePointer = vbDefault

End Sub
```

Near the beginning of this example, you can see where the string variable sSQL is assigned with a Transact-SQL Select statement. In this example, the SQL is a little bit more complicated than the simple Select * statement used in the previous examples in this chapter. This Select statement takes advantage of SQL Server's query processor to retrieve the au_lname, au_fname, and titles columns from three joined files in the pubs database. As you would expect, the authors and the titles tables contain the basic information that is pertinent to the authors and their books, while the titleauthor table pairs the authors' IDs with each title ID. Essentially, the titleauthor table lists all of the book titles that belong to each of the sample authors. However, since the titleauthor table contains only the author ID and the title ID columns, if we want to display more meaningful information, like the author's name and each book's title, then we need to join the titleauthor table with the authors and the titles tables. The join conditions are described in the Where clause. In the Where clause you can see that the authors table and the titleauthor table are joined using the au_id column, and the titles table and the titleauthor table are joined using the title_id column. The Order By clause indicates that the result set will be sorted based on the au_lname column (the author's last name).

After the SQL Select statement has been set up, the OpenDatabase method is used to create a new Database object named db. Next, the db Database object's QueryDefs.Delete method is used to delete any existing QueryDef object that is named QDPassthru. Remember that the CreateQueryDef method actually creates a QueryDef object in the Jet database; and, in order to be able to rerun this code, that QueryDef object must not exist when the CreateQueryDef method is executed. If a QueryDef named QDPassthru does exist, then the subsequent CreateQueryDef method will end with an error. Visual Basic's error handler is set to Resume Next, which allows the subroutine to continue processing in the event that the QDPassthru QueryDef object is not present in the publink.mdb database and, therefore, cannot be deleted. Visual Basic's error handler is then reset to capture any errors before executing the CreateQueryDef method. If a run-time error does occur, control will be transferred to the Errorhandler tag. More detailed information on error handling will be presented later in this chapter in the section, "Error Handling."

The CreateQueryDef method creates a new QueryDef object in the Jet database. The first parameter of the CreateQueryDef method contains the name of the QueryDef object.

TIP: If you use an empty string for the QueryDef name, then a temporary QueryDef will be created.

After the QueryDef object has been created, its Connect property is assigned an ODBC connection string. You can see that this example uses a DSN-less connection string because it contains the Driver and Database keywords, as well as the login information. Assigning the ODBC connection string in the Connect property tells Jet that this QueryDef object will be using SQL PassThrough. Next, the QueryDef object's SQL property is assigned the Transact-SQL statement and the ReturnsRecords property is set to True, which identifies this as a QueryDef object that will use a Recordset rather than a SQL action query like an Insert, Update, or Delete statement.

The query is run on the target data source when the OpenRecordset method of the qd QueryDef object is executed. The resulting rs Recordset object is a snapshot type of Recordset object, which means that it will contain a complete copy of the data that was retrieved from the data source. The rs Recordset object is then displayed in a grid using the DisplayDynasetGrid subroutine. When all of the rows in the Recordset object have been read, the Recordset, QueryDef, and Database objects are all closed.

Calling Stored Procedures and Using Multiple Result Sets

Using stored procedures is the best way to develop high-performance, client/server applications using DAO and SQL Server. SQL Server stored procedures are groups of Transact-SQL statements that can contain complex logic. Most database administrators typically create many stored procedures for use in handling routine database administration tasks and performing ad hoc queries and for use in applications. A stored procedure has a precompiled data access plan, which means that there is no need for the SQL Server query engine to parse the SQL and create a new access plan. This precompiled data access plan is what gives stored procedures their high performance. Unlike simple SQL queries or action statements, stored procedures are also capable of returning multiple result sets. This allows you to simplify your application code by letting the higher-performance stored procedure handle several database access tasks with a single procedure call. In addition to their performance characteristics, stored procedures can also provide more secure database access. For instance, you can restrict end-user access for all of the base tables and allow access to the database only through a set of predefined and centrally controlled stored procedures. Since stored procedures can be shared, they also allow multiple developers to utilize a common set of procedure calls.

TIP: While DAO is able to process result sets that are returned by a stored procedure, it's not able to directly work with output parameters that are returned by SQL Server stored procedures. However, you can work around this by wrapping the stored procedure that returns output parameters in another stored procedure that returns a result set. In this way, the calling stored procedure can take any returned output parameters and move them into a result set that can be processed by DAO. ODBCDirect does not have this limitation and can directly access stored procedures' output parameters.

SQL Server's example pubs database contains several sample stored procedures that perform queries using the pubs database. The following code shows the example stored procedure named reptq1:

```
Create Procedure reptq1 As
Select pub_id, title_id, price, pubdate
From titles
Where price Is Not Null
Order By pub_id
Compute Avg(price) By pub_id
Compute Avg(price)
```

This stored procedure retrieves the publication ID, title, price, and data from the titles table. It creates a result set for each different publication ID, as well as a one-record result set that contains the average price for each result set. Executing this stored procedure using the Graphical Query Analyzer produces the results shown in Figure 12-9. You can

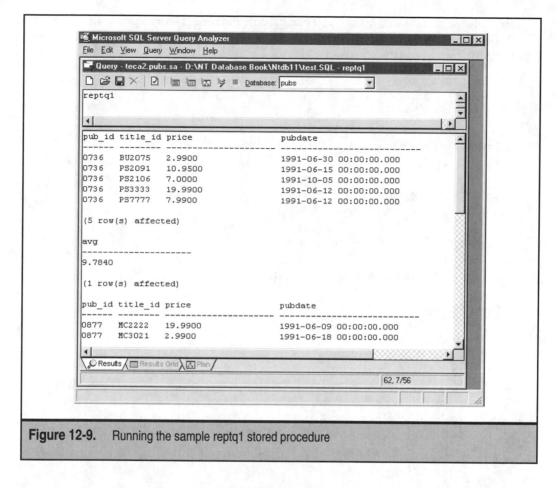

Figure 12-9.   Running the sample reptq1 stored procedure

see how it's possible to use the Graphical Query Analyzer to run the sample reptq1 stored procedure in the pubs database. In the bottom portion of the screen, you can see a portion of the first three result sets that are produced by the stored procedure. The rows for each publication ID are contained in their own result set, and the average price for those rows is computed by the stored procedure and output in a following result set. In total, the reptq1 stored procedure outputs seven result sets using the sample data from the titles table.

Producing this type of output without using the stored procedure would require more programming effort than simply calling the stored procedure. At a minimum, you would need to add the logic in your application to send a Select statement and then process the result set—programmatically keeping track of when the title ID changes and also manually calculating the average price for each publication title.

The following code shows how you can execute the reptq1 stored procedure using the DAO QueryDef object and SQLPassThrough and process the multiple result sets returned by the stored procedure:

```
Private Sub CallQDsp()

    Dim db As Database
    Dim qd As QueryDef
    Dim rs As Recordset
    Dim fld As Field

    Dim sSQL As String
    On Error GoTo Errorhandler

    Screen.MousePointer = vbHourglass

    Set db = OpenDatabase("pubslink.mdb")

    sSQL = "reptq1"

    On Error Resume Next
    db.QueryDefs.Delete ("QDsp")

    On Error GoTo Errorhandler
    Set qd = db.CreateQueryDef("QDsp")
    qd.Connect = "ODBC;DRIVER=SQL Server;UID=" & sLoginID & _
        ";PWD=" & sPassword & _
        ";SERVER=" & sServer & _
        ";DATABASE=pubs"
    qd.SQL = sSQL
    qd.ReturnsRecords = True

    Set rs = qd.OpenRecordset()

    ' Set up the grid
    Grid.Cols = rs.Fields.Count
    Grid.Rows = 1
    Grid.Row = 0

    'Set up the Grid headings
    For Each fld In rs.Fields
        Grid.Col = fld.OrdinalPosition
        Grid.Text = fld.Name
    Next fld
```

```
On Error Resume Next
db.TableDefs.Delete "SPrs"
db.TableDefs.Delete "SPrs1"
db.TableDefs.Delete "SPrs2"
db.TableDefs.Delete "SPrs3"
db.TableDefs.Delete "SPrs4"
db.TableDefs.Delete "SPrs5"
db.TableDefs.Delete "SPrs6"

On Error GoTo Errorhandler

'Now process the next result set using a JET table
Set qd = db.CreateQueryDef("")
qd.SQL = "Select [QDsp].* Into SPrs From [QDsp]"
qd.Execute

Set rs = db.OpenRecordset("SPrs")

rs.MoveLast
Grid.Rows = Grid.Rows + rs.RecordCount
Grid.Row = 0
rs.MoveFirst

' Move through each row in the record set
Do Until rs.EOF

    Grid.Row = Grid.Row + 1

    'Loop through all fields
    For Each fld In rs.Fields
        Grid.Col = fld.OrdinalPosition
        Grid.Text = fld.Value
    Next fld

    rs.MoveNext
Loop

'Get the second result set
Set rs = db.OpenRecordset("SPrs1")

Grid.Rows = Grid.Rows + 1
Grid.Row = Grid.Row + 1
```

```
Grid.Col = 1
Grid.Text = "Average"
Grid.Col = 2
Grid.Text = rs(0).Value

'Now get the 3rd result set
Set rs = db.OpenRecordset("SPrs2")

rs.MoveLast
Grid.Rows = Grid.Rows + rs.RecordCount
rs.MoveFirst

' Move through each row in the record set
Do Until rs.EOF

    Grid.Row = Grid.Row + 1

    'Loop through all fields
    For Each fld In rs.Fields
        Grid.Col = fld.OrdinalPosition
        Grid.Text = fld.Value
    Next fld

    rs.MoveNext
Loop

'Get the 4th result set
Set rs = db.OpenRecordset("SPrs3")

Grid.Rows = Grid.Rows + 1
Grid.Row = Grid.Row + 1

Grid.Col = 1
Grid.Text = "Average"
Grid.Col = 2
Grid.Text = rs(0).Value

'Now process the 5th
Set rs = db.OpenRecordset("SPrs4")

rs.MoveLast
Grid.Rows = Grid.Rows + rs.RecordCount
```

```
    rs.MoveFirst

    ' Move through each row in the record set
    Do Until rs.EOF

        Grid.Row = Grid.Row + 1

        'Loop through all fields
        For Each fld In rs.Fields
            Grid.Col = fld.OrdinalPosition
            Grid.Text = fld.Value
        Next fld

        rs.MoveNext
    Loop

    'Get the 6th result set
    Set rs = db.OpenRecordset("SPrs5")

    Grid.Rows = Grid.Rows + 1
    Grid.Row = Grid.Row + 1

    Grid.Col = 1
    Grid.Text = "Average"
    Grid.Col = 2
    Grid.Text = rs(0).Value

    'Get the 7th result set
    Set rs = db.OpenRecordset("SPrs6")

    Grid.Rows = Grid.Rows + 1
    Grid.Row = Grid.Row + 1

    Grid.Col = 0
    Grid.Text = "Total"
    Grid.Col = 1
    Grid.Text = "Average"
    Grid.Col = 2
    Grid.Text = rs(0).Value

    'Now close up all of the objects
    rs.Close
    qd.Close
    db.Close
```

```
        Screen.MousePointer = vbDefault
        Exit Sub

Errorhandler:
        DisplayDAOError

        Screen.MousePointer = vbDefault

End Sub
```

Like the previous QueryDef example, this example begins by setting the db Database object to the pubslink.mdb Jet database. Then the sSQL string variable is assigned the name of the stored procedure that will be executed—reptq1. Next, to enable this subroutine to be run multiple times, any existing QueryDef object named QDsp is deleted and then the Database object's CreateQueryDef method is executed to create a new QueryDef object in the pubslink database named QDsp. Again, after this method completes, a new QueryDef object will exist in the publink.mdb database.

Next, assigning the Connect property of the QueryDef object with an ODBC connection string sets up the Jet engine to execute this query using SQLPassThrough. As in the previous example, this ODBC connection string uses a DSN-less connection. The SQL property is assigned with the value of the sSQL string, which contains the stored procedure named reptq1.

Next, the ReturnsRecords property is set to True to enable the use of DAO record sets with this QueryDef object. Then the QueryDef object's OpenRecordset method is executed to create a new Recordset object named rs. After the rs Recordset object has been created, the Fields collection is used to set up the grid to display the number of columns that are contained in the Recordset object.

As you can see, to this point, the process of working with stored procedure result sets is very much like working with result sets that are created using dynamic SQL statements and SQLPassThrough. If the stored procedure produces a single result set, you can use the Recordset object exactly as you would with a Recordset object that was produced using a dynamic SQL statement.

The next section of code gives you a glimpse at one of the differences that crop up working with multiple result sets. To process multiple result sets, the Jet engine must create a table in the publink database for each result set. To facilitate rerunning this subroutine, the TableDefs.Delete method is used to delete these existing tables. In this example, you can see that the tables containing the multiple result sets are named SPrs through SPrs6. Before the TableDefs.Delete method is processed, Visual Basic's error handler is set to Resume Next, which allows this subroutine to continue processing in the event that the target tables don't exist.

After any existing table that are in the publink database have been deleted, the CreateQueryDef method is run to create a new QueryDef object. In this case, the QueryDef object is a temporary object and it is not named. The SQL property of this temporary QueryDef object is assigned with a Jet Select Into statement that will create a set of Jet tables named SPrs in the publink database. This Select statement uses the exiting QDsp QueryDef object as input and will output the result set into a Jet table named SPrs. When working with multiple result sets, Jet will automatically name each subsequent result set using sequential numbers. As you might have gathered from the previous Delete code, the seven result sets created by the reptq1 stored procedure will be named SPrs, SPrs1, SPrs2, SPrs3, SPrs4, SPrs5, and SPrs6. The temporary QueryDef is executed using the qd.Execute method.

The subsequent code shows how to open and process each of the TableDef objects that are created in the Jet database. The OpenRecordset method is used to set the rs Recordset object to the Jet table that is named in the first parameter of the OpenRecordset method. Then the grid is expanded according to the number of rows that are contained in the Recordset object. The MoveFirst and MoveNext methods are used to process the Recordset objects that contain multiple rows. Every other Recordset contains a single row that contains the computed average of the price column. Since that Recordset object only consists of a single row, this subroutine retrieves the value of the row directly using the rs(0).Value property. When all of the Recordset objects have been processed, the Recordset, QueryDef, and Database objects are all closed using the Close method.

TIP: If you don't know how many result sets will be created by a stored procedure, you can perform a query to find the tables that were created in the Database object's TableDefs collection.

Error Handling

All of the errors that are generated while executing DAO functions are placed in the DAO Errors collection. When a DAO error occurs, Visual Basic's error handler is fired, which enables you to trap and respond to run-time errors. This tight integration with Visual Basic makes it easy to handle DAO errors. The following ShowError subroutine illustrates how DAO's error handling can be integrated with Visual Basic's On Error function:

```
Private Sub ShowError(db As Database)


    Dim rs As Recordset
    Dim sSQL As String
    On Error GoTo Errorhandler


    sSQL = "Select * From no_such_table"
    Set rs = db.OpenRecordset(sSQL, dbOpenDynaset)
    Rs.close
    Exit Sub


Errorhandler:
    DisplayDAOError


End Sub
```

This subroutine sets up a Select statement to query a nonexistent table appropriately named no_such_table. Before this query is executed, Visual Basic's On Error statement is used to activate error handling for this subroutine. The On Error statement used in this subroutine instructs the program to go to the label named Errorhandler in this subroutine in the event that a trappable error is encountered. If a fatal run-time error occurs and Visual Basic's error handler is not enabled, then the program will terminate at the line where the error was encountered. Table 12-7 lists the various error-handling options that Visual Basic provides.

In the previous example, the error-handling routine will be activated when the program executes the OpenRecordset method using the bogus SQL statement contained in the sSQL variable. When the error is encountered, the program execution will continue with the Errorhandler label and the DisplayDAOError subroutine will be executed. The following code shows how the DisplayDAOError subroutine uses DAO's Error object and Errors collection to display information about a DAO error condition in a simple message box:

```
Private Sub DisplayDAOError
    Dim er As Error

    For Each er In Errors
    MsgBox "Number: " & er.Number & vbCrLf & _
    "Source: " & er.Source & vbCrLf & _
    "Text: " & er.Description
    Next

End Sub
```

Error Handler	Description
On Error Goto *line*	Program execution continues with the line number or label specified. This allows you to trap and programmatically respond to run-time errors.
On Error Resume Next	Program execution continues with the next executable line. This essentially catches and ignores the trappable error condition.
On Error Goto 0	Error handling is disabled.

Table 12-7. Visual Basic's Error-Handling Options

A DAO Error object named er is declared at the beginning of this subroutine. Then a For Each loop is used to iterate through the DAO Errors collection. This is required because some error conditions can have multiple condition and error codes listed in the Errors collection. The Number property of the DAO Error object contains the DAO error message number, while the Source property identifies the source object that fired the error. As you might expect, the Description property contains the error condition's text description. The message box that is displayed by the DisplayDAOError subroutine is shown here:

```
DAOWiz                                                                          ☒

Number: 3078
Source: DAO.Database
Text: The Microsoft Jet database engine cannot find the input table or query 'no_such_table'.  Make sure it exists and that its
name is spelled correctly.

                                       ┌────────┐
                                       │   OK   │
                                       └────────┘
```

ENDING THE JET ENGINE

In some respects, the Jet engine has a mind of its own, and it does not always close all of the connections that it has opened when you end your application. You can manually terminate the Jet engine by setting the DBEngine object to nothing, as follows:

```
Set DBEngine = Nothing
```

Before setting the DBEngine to nothing, be sure to close all of its Database, Recordset, and QueryDef objects.

GENERAL PERFORMANCE TIPS FOR DAO AND ODBC

While DAO is primarily intended to access local Jet databases, its flexibility allows it to be used with ODBC-based data sources like SQL Server as well. DAO also allows—and in some cases requires—combining Jet database operations with SQL Server database operations. In summary, when using standard DAO for SQL Server database access you can get a lot of mileage out of a few general tips:

▼ Take advantage of linked tables. Opening linked tables is generally faster than using the OpenDatabase method, because linked tables use local Jet storage to maintain the database schema information that must otherwise be downloaded by the Jet engine each time the application connects to the SQL Server database.

■ Limit the amount of data returned. A key technique for all database applications, limiting the amount of data through the use of the SQL Select statement reduces the database I/O required by the server, as well as the amount of network traffic. In many instances, it can also make your application logic simpler.

- Use SQLPassThrough—especially for bulk operations. SQLPassThrough allows you to bypass the Jet query engine, which you don't really need when you're developing SQL Server database applications. Allowing SQL Server's query engine to handle the data access provides greater benefits as required workload increases.

- Use snapshots instead of dynasets. While there are exceptions to this tip, using snapshot Recordset objects is less resource intensive and can provide better performance than dynaset Recordset objects, especially when the application only needs to view the data. Snapshot record sets become decidedly less desirable for large Recordsets because they make a local copy of the data. They are also not as easy to use when the data must be updated.

▲ Use stored procedures for maximum performance. Using a precompiled data access plan, stored procedures provide the best performance for SQL Server database applications. Stored procedures are also very flexible. They can be used to perform database updates, configurations, and complex queries that can return multiple result sets.

Using DAO can be a great choice for developing applications that need to access both local Jet or ISAM databases, as well as SQL Server databases. DAO also can provide a good platform for migrating Jet database applications to SQL Server. However, if your database application is primarily intended to access SQL Server, then you would be better off using Jet's close cousin, ODBCDirect, as a basis for building your database applications. The next part of this chapter illustrates the essential techniques for building SQL Server applications using ODBCDirect.

ODBCDIRECT

ODBCDirect was developed to address some of the shortcomings that crop up when using standard DAO to access ODBC-based data sources like SQL Server. ODBCDirect is somewhat of a cross between DAO and RDO. ODBCDirect uses an object model that's very similar to DAO. Like DAO, ODBCDirect makes use of Workspace, Database, Recordset, QueryDef, and Field objects. Like RDO, ODBCDirect is an object layer over ODBC, and it does not use the Microsoft Jet Database Engine. In fact, ODBCDirect can only be used to connect to ODBC data sources; it can't be used to connect to local Jet databases. ODBCDirect also supports most of the advanced ODBC abilities that are provided by RDO. Like RDO, ODBCDirect supports using ODBC cursors, as well as prepared SQL statements, parameterized queries, and stored procedure return parameters. While ODBCDirect is very much like RDO, it offers one very important advantage—ODBCDirect is a part of DAO 3.5 and is available in the lower-cost Visual Basic 6 Professional Edition. RDO is only available as a part of the much higher-priced Visual Basic 6 Enterprise Edition.

ODBCDirect utilizes a layered architecture that more closely resembles RDO than DAO. Figure 12-10 illustrates the relationship of DAO, ODBC, and PC networking support. At the top level, you can see the Visual Basic ODBCDirect application. Like standard DAO, the VB application is responsible for creating and using the various ODBCDirect objects. The ODBCDirect objects are provided using the same files and OLE Type Library as DAO. The ODBCDirect object layer directly loads the ODBC Driver Manager and makes ODBC calls to access the ODBC database. The ODBC Driver Manager handles loading the appropriate ODBC driver. The ODBC driver then takes care of using the appropriate IPC mechanism to communicate to a network library that resides on the target database server. The network protocol transports the IPC data stream over the physical network topology.

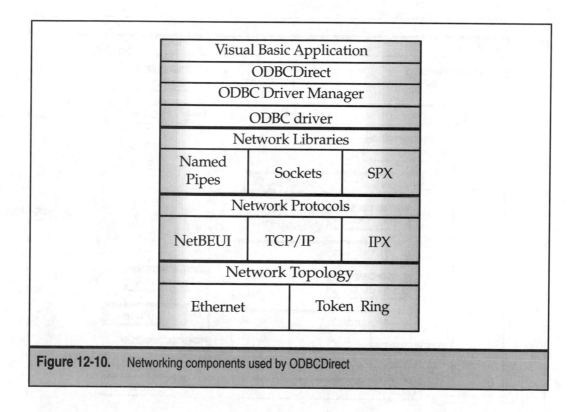

Figure 12-10. Networking components used by ODBCDirect

ODBCDIRECT FILES

The following table presents the run-time DLL used to implement ODBCDirect:

File	Description
dao35.dll	DAO Object Library

ODBCDIRECT ARCHITECTURE

ODBCDirect is implemented using a hierarchical object framework, shown in Figure 12-11, that shares many of the same objects and collections found in the DAO object hierarchy. The DBEngine object is the primary object at the top of the hierarchy, and there is only one DBEngine object per application. The other objects that are common to the DAO object framework are the Workspaces and Errors collections.

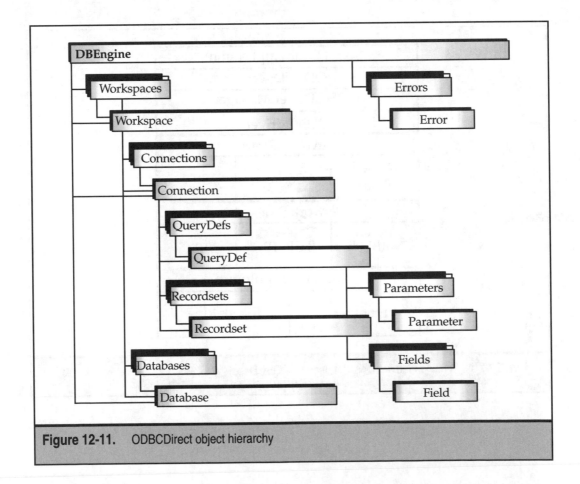

Figure 12-11. ODBCDirect object hierarchy

Like DAO, the ODBCDirect Errors collection contains a set of Error objects in which each Error object maintains information about any errors that are encountered by the object framework. Visual Basic's error handler enables your application to trap and respond to ODBCDirect errors.

The ODBCDirect Workspaces collection contains a set of Workspace objects in which each Workspace represents an ODBC session. A session defines the activities that are performed from the time a user logs in to the time the user logs out. The Workspace object is used to control the application's transaction scope and security. Each Workspace object contains a collection of Connection objects and a collection of Database objects.

The collection of Database objects is identical to DAO's Databases collection. As its name implies, each Database object represents a remote database. The Database object in turn contains a collection of Recordset objects in which each Recordset object contains a result set that's returned from the target data source.

So far, this portion of the ODBCDirect object framework is a lot like regular DAO. However, in addition to these objects that are common to both object hierarchies, ODBCDirect also contains the Connections collection. The Connections collection is not a part of the standard DAO framework. Each Connection object represents an ODBC database connection. The Connection object differs from the Database object in that the Connection object is optimized for ODBC connectivity. The new Connection object allows you to create temporary QueryDef objects for use with stored procedures and prepared SQL statements as well as to perform asynchronous operations. Each Connection object contains a QueryDefs collection and a Recordsets collection. Like their names suggest, the QueryDefs collection consists of QueryDef objects and the Recordsets collection consists of Recordset objects. Each QueryDef object contains a Parameters collection, which represents the parameters that are used by the QueryDef object. Each Recordset object contains a Fields collection, in which each Field object represents a column in the Recordset.

An Overview of Using ODBCDirect

ODBCDirect is implemented using exactly the same OLE object library that DAO uses. This means that ODBCDirect is available with the Visual Basic Professional Edition. This also makes ODBCDirect easy to learn for experienced DAO developers. Like DAO, ODBCDirect's OLE foundation makes it easy to access ODBCDirect methods from Visual Basic without the need to manually declare any of the functions in a .bas or .cls module. The only thing that you need to do before using ODBCDirect in a Visual Basic application is to add a reference to the Microsoft DAO 3.5 Object Library to your Visual Basic project. You can refer to the earlier section in this chapter, "An Overview of Using DAO," for a step-by-step guide to adding the DAO 3.5 Object Library Reference.

Following is a summary of the steps required to use ODBCDirect with Visual Basic:

1. Make a reference in Visual Basic to the Microsoft DAO 3.5 Object Library.

2. Create an ODBCDirect workspace object.

3. Open a Connection or Database object.

4. Create Recordset or QueryDef objects.

5. Use the Recordset or QueryDef methods to work with the data.

6. Close the Recordset or QueryDef object.

7. Close the Connection or Database object.

CREATING THE DBENGINE OBJECT

As with regular DAO, with ODBCDirect you don't need to explicitly create the DBEngine object using code. An instance of the DBEngine object is automatically created the first time one of the DAO objects is referenced.

CREATING AN ODBCDIRECT WORKSPACE OBJECT

After a reference has been added to Visual Basic's development environment, you're ready to use the ODBCDirect objects in your Visual Basic application. The first step in using ODBCDirect is the creation of a Workspace object. The ODBCDirect Workspace object can be explicitly created using the CreateWorkspace method, or DAO will automatically create a Workspace object based on the values in the DBEngine object.

Using the CreateWorkspace Method

The CreateWorkspace method of the DBEngine object can be used to explicitly create a Workspace object. The following code illustrates how to use the CreateWorkspace method to create an ODBCDirect Workspace:

```
'The type parameter sets the workspace to ODBCDirect
Set ws = DBEngine.CreateWorkspace("NewODBCDirectWS", sUser, _
            sPassword, dbUseODBC)
```

The CreateWorkspace method takes four parameters. The first parameter is a string that can be used to identify the Workspace object. If you only need a single Workspace in your application, you can use an empty string. In this example, the ODBCDirect Workspace is named NewODBCDirectWS. The second parameter is a string variable that supplies the login ID, and the third parameter is a string variable that supplies the password. The value of dbUseODBC in the fourth parameter sets this Workspace object as an ODBCDirect Workspace object. If the fourth parameter is omitted or if it contains the constant dbUseJet, then a Jet Workspace object will be created.

Setting the Default Workspace Type

You can also create an ODBCDirect Workspace by setting the DefaultType property of the DBEngine object and then allowing the DAO object framework to create the

Workspace object automatically. The following code illustrates how you can create an ODBCDirect Workspace by setting the DBEngine's DefaultType property to dbUseODBC:

```
'Set the default Workspace type to ODBCDirect
DBEngine.DefaultType = dbUseODBC
'Create the default Workspace as ODBCDirect
Set ws = DBEngine.Workspaces(0)
```

In this example, you can see that the DefaultType property of the DBEngine object is assigned the constant dbUseODBC before the Workspace object is created. Then Visual Basic's Set statement is used to create a new instance of the default Workspace object. The DBEngine.Workspaces(0) code indicates that the first (or default) Workspace object of the DBEngine's Workspaces collection will be used to create the new ws Workspace object.

Connecting to SQL Server

Once an ODBCDirect Workspace object has been created, you can use that object to create a Connection object or a Database object, either of which can be used to access SQL Server. You would typically use a Database object if your application needs to perform simple queries or if it needed Jet compatibility. You would use the Connection object if you want your application to take advantage of the more advanced ODBC capabilities, like creating prepared statements, running asynchronous operations, or calling stored procedures. In the next section of this chapter, you'll see how to connect to SQL Server using the OpenDatabase method followed by the OpenConnection method.

Opening a Connection with the OpenDatabase Method

Connecting to SQL Server using the ODBCDirect's OpenDatabase method is virtually identical to using the OpenDatabase method provided by standard DAO. This code compatibility makes it easy to migrate your existing DAO applications to ODBCDirect. However, using the Database object instead of the newer ODBCDirect Connection object doesn't allow you to take full advantage of all of the capabilities that are present in the newer ODBCDirect Connection object. Even so, the ODBCDirect OpenDatabase object allows you to create leaner and more efficient SQL Server applications because it bypasses the Jet engine. Since the Jet engine contains its own query processor, eliminating it can result in significant resource savings on the PC.

The following code example shows you how to use the OpenDatabase method to connect to an ODBC data source like SQL Server:

```
Private Sub ConnectOpenDatabase()
    Dim ws As Workspace
    Dim db As Database
    Dim sConnect As String

    MousePointer = vbHourglass

    'Set the default Workspace type to ODBCDirect
```

```
        DBEngine.DefaultType = dbUseODBC

        'Create the default Workspace as ODBCDirect
        Set ws = DBEngine.Workspaces(0)
        ws.DefaultCursorDriver = dbUseODBCCursor

        'Setup the Connection String
        sConnect = "ODBC;DSN=;UID=" & sLoginID & _
            ";PWD=" & sPassword & _
            ";Server=" & sServer & _
            ";Database=pubs"

        'Create a new Database object
        Set db = OpenDatabase("", dbDriverComplete, False, sConnect)
        db.Close
        ws.Close

        MousePointer = vbDefault

End Sub
```

If this example looks familiar, it should. Codewise, this technique of connecting to SQL Server is very similar to the standard DAO OpenDatabase method that was presented earlier in the chapter. First a Workspace object is created. The big difference is that the DefaultType parameter is set to dbUseODBC before the Workspace is created. This causes the Workspace to be created as an ODBCDirect Workspace. Next, the Database object is created using the OpenDatabase method. The first parameter of the OpenDatabase method optionally names the Database object. The second parameter tells the ODBC Driver Manager how to react to the ODBC connection string. The value of dbDriverComplete specifies that the ODBC Driver Manager should prompt the user for any connection information that's not supplied. The third parameter sets the read-only attribute to False, and the fourth parameter contains an ODBC connection string. In this case, the ODBC connection string contains login information, but it does not specify the data source name that will be used to make the connection. This means the ODBC Driver Manager will need to prompt the user for the data source name. The biggest difference is that the OpenDatabase method is called from an ODBCDirect Workspace object rather than a DAO Workspace object.

TIP: Your application can dynamically determine the type of Workspace object that is in use by examining the Workspace object's read-only Type property, for example, Workspaces(0).Type. The Type property will contain the value of dbUseODBC for ODBCDirect workspaces and dbUseJet for standard DAO workspaces. You can use this information to allow the same application to be used with Jet or ODBC data sources. If the Type property contains dbUseJet, the application can perform the standard DAO methods. Otherwise, if the Type property contains dbUseODBC, your application can take advantage of the added ODBCDirect functionality.

Closing a Database Connection

Before ending your application, you can close the Database object's connection using the Database object's Close method. An example of the Close method follows:

```
db.Close
```

Alternatively, you can close the connection by setting the Database object to nothing as follows:

```
Set db = Nothing
```

Using the Close method is preferable because it is more self-explanatory and easier to understand than setting the instance of the object to nothing.

Opening a Connection Using the OpenConnection Method

Unlike the Database object, which provides maximum DAO compatibility, the new ODBCDirect Connection object is optimized for remote connectivity. The ODBCDirect Connection object provides the ability to perform asynchronous database operations, as well as the ability to create temporary QueryDef objects that can be used to execute prepared SQL statements and call stored procedures. The following code illustrates how to connect to SQL Server using an ODBCDirect Connection object:

```
Private Sub ConnectOpenConnection()

    Dim sSQL As sConnect
    Dim cn As Connection

    MousePointer = vbHourglass

    sConnect = "ODBC;DSN=;UID=" & sLoginID & _
        ";PWD=" & sPassword & _
        ";Server=" & sServer & _
        ";Database=pubs"

    Set cn = OpenConnection("", dbDriverComplete, False, sConnect)
    cn.Close

    MousePointer = vbDefault

End Sub
```

In this example, you can see that the same ODBC connection string that was used by the Database object is also used by the ODBCDirect Connection object. Again, this example ODBC connection string uses a blank DSN keyword, which means that the ODBC Driver Manger will be required to prompt the user to select the appropriate data source at run time. The UID and PWD keywords supply the required authentication information, and the DATABASE keyword points the ODBC driver to the pubs database. After the ODBC connection string has been set up, the Workspace object's OpenConnection method is used to create a new Connection object named cn. Like the OpenDatabase method, the first parameter of the OpenConnection method can optionally name the Connection object. Naming the object allows it to be selected from the Connections collection by name. Identifying collection members by name can be useful when your application uses multiple Connection objects. The value of dbDriverComplete in the second parameter allows the ODBC Driver Manager to prompt for any missing connection information that's not supplied in the ODBC connection string. In this example, the Driver Manager will prompt for a data source name. The value of False in the third parameter sets this connection to read/write. The fourth parameter contains the ODBC connection string.

Opening a DSN-less Connection Using the OpenConnection Method

The ODBCDirect Connection object also supports DSN-less connections exactly like the DAO Database object that was presented earlier in the DAO portion of this chapter. Using a DSN-less connection removes the requirement of identifying the data source at run time. This simplifies ODBC-based applications, because a data source does not need to exist before your application can connect to the database. A DSN-less connection also eliminates the need to discover the user-configured data source name. The following code illustrates how to establish a DSN-less connection using the ODBCDirect OpenConnection method:

```
Private Sub DSNlessConnectOpenConnection()

    Dim sConnect As String
    Dim cn As Connection

    MousePointer = vbHourglass

    sConnect = "ODBC;Driver=SQL Server;UID=" & sLoginID & _
        ";PWD=" & sPassword & _
        ";Server=" & sServer & _
        ";Database=pubs"

    Set cn = OpenConnection("", dbDriverComplete, False, sConnect)

    MousePointer = vbDefault

End Sub
```

The primary difference between the previous connection and the DSN-less connection that's presented in this example is the ODBC connection string. To establish a DSN-less connection, the ODBC connection string must contain the DRIVER and DATABASE keywords. In this example, the string following the DRIVER keyword shows that the connection will be made using the ODBC driver named SQL Server. Like the standard connection, the UID and PWD keywords supply the database user ID and password information. The values for the UID and PWD keywords are provided by combining the string variables sLoginID and sPassword with the constants already present in the ODBC connection string. The DATABASE keyword specifies that the SQL Server database named pubs will be used.

The connection is actually established when the OpenConnection method is executed. As in the earlier example, the ODBC connection string is supplied as the fourth parameter of the OpenConnection method.

TIP: You can also use a DSN-less ODBC connection string with the ODBCDirect OpenDatabase method.

Ending a Connection

Before ending your application, you can close the Connection object's connection using the Connection object's Close method. An example of the Close method follows:

```
cn.Close
```

Alternatively, you can close the connection by setting the Connection object to nothing, as follows:

```
Set cn = Nothing
```

Retrieving Data with ODBCDirect

After connecting to SQL Server using either a Database object or a Connection object, you can retrieve data using the ODBCDirect Recordset object. In this section, you'll see how to use a Recordset object with the ODBCDirect Database object, as well as a Connection object. In both instances, you'll see how to traverse the rows in the Recordset object, in addition to using the Fields collection to work with the column values contained in the Recordset object.

Using the Database Object's Recordset

Using the ODBCDirect Recordset object with the Database object is virtually identical to using a standard DAO Recordset object. Essentially, there is no difference in the basic coding techniques. However, there is a difference in the type of Recordset objects that are supported. An ODBCDirect-based Recordset object includes support for a dynamic Recordset, but understandably drops support for table-type Recordset objects. A dynamic Recordset object is analogous to an ODBC dynamic cursor in that any changes made to the data in the base table are also reflected in the Recordset object. Unlike the snapshot or dynaset type of Recordset object, when another application or user modifies the column values that are in the base tables, the data in the Recordset is dynamically updated with the changed data values. As you might have gathered, dynamic Recordset objects are more resource intensive than either forward-only or dynaset Recordset objects. Since table-type Recordset objects represent Jet tables, they are not applicable to the ODBC data sources that are used by the ODBCDirect framework. The different types of Recordset objects were summarized in Table 12-3.

The following example illustrates how to use the Recordset object provided by the ODBCDirect Database object:

```
Private Sub DatabaseQuery()

    Dim db As Database
    Dim rs As Recordset
    Dim fld As Field
    Dim sConnect As String

    Screen.MousePointer = vbHourglass

    'Set up the Connection String
    sConnect = "ODBC;DRIVER=SQL Server;UID=" & sLoginID & _
        ";PWD=" & sPassword & _
        ";SERVER=" & sServer & _
        ";DATABASE=pubs"

    'Create a new Database object
    ' use an existing ODBCDirect Workspace
    Set db = OpenDatabase("", dbDriverComplete, False, sConnect)

    'Create a Recordset
    Set rs = db.OpenRecordset("Select * From authors", dbOpenDynaset)

    DisplayDynasetGrid rs, Grid, 1

    Screen.MousePointer = vbDefault

End Sub
```

As you can see from this example, using the Recordset object and the Fields collection of the ODBCDirect database shares the same coding techniques that are used by the standard DAO object framework. However, while the code looks the same, it doesn't perform the same when you're connected to an ODBC data source. The ODBCDirect version connects and retrieves data much faster than the Jet-based DAO version. This performance comes from the more efficient use of the ODBC calls that are generated by the ODBCDirect objects.

Using the Connection Object's Recordset

Using a Recordset object with the ODBCDirect Connections object is conceptually the same as using it with the Database object. In the following code listing, you can see how to query the SQL Server database using a Recordset object based on the ODBCDirect Connection object.

```
Private Sub ConnectionQuery()

    Dim cn As Connection
    Dim rs As Recordset
    Dim fld As Field
    Dim nRow As Integer
    Dim sConnect As String

    Screen.MousePointer = vbHourglass

    sConnect = "ODBC;DRIVER=SQL Server;UID=" & sLoginID & _
        ";PWD=" & sPassword & _
        ";SERVER=" & sServer & _
        ";DATABASE=pubs"

    Set cn = OpenConnection("", dbDriverComplete, False, sConnect)

    Set rs = cn.OpenRecordset _
            ("Select * From employee", dbOpenDynaset)

    DisplayDynasetGrid rs, Grid, 1

    rs.Close

    Screen.MousePointer = vbDefault

End Sub
```

First, this example creates a new Connection object named cn and establishes a DSN-less connection to SQL Server. Next, the Connection object's OpenRecordset method is used to create a dynaset Recordset that contains all of the rows and columns from the employee's table in the pubs database. The main difference between this code example and the prior code example is that in this example the OpenRecordset method is called from the Connection object (cn) rather than the Database object. After the Recordset object has been created, working with it is no different than working with the Recordset that was based on the Database object. The DisplayDynasetGrid subroutine is used to display the contents of the Recordset in a grid, and then the Recordset object is closed.

Using Prepared SQL and the QueryDef Object

While the Connection object's Recordset works the same as the Database object's Recordset, the QueryDef object is quite another story. If you refer back to Figure 12-11, you can see that the QueryDefs collection is contained only in the Connection object. This is because the ODBCDirect QueryDef object is quite different from the standard DAO QueryDef object; therefore, there was no point in attempting to allow shared code as there was with the Recordset object.

> *TIP:*   Unlike DAO, ODBCDirect QueryDef objects are not stored in the database. They are temporary objects.

It's the QueryDef object that really allows the ODBCDirect Connection object to take advantage of the higher-performance coding techniques that are available through ODBC. In the following example, you'll see how to retrieve data using SQL prepared statements and the QueryDef object. Then the following section will illustrate how to update data using prepared SQL and the QueryDef object.

```
Private Sub QueryDefPS(cn As Connection)

    Dim qd As QueryDef
    Dim rs As Recordset
    Dim fld As Field
    Dim nRow As Integer
    Dim sSQL As String

    Screen.MousePointer = vbHourglass

    'Set up the SQL statement
    sSQL = "Select * From authors Where au_id = ?"

    Set qd = cn.CreateQueryDef

    ' Prepare the statement
    With qd
       .SQL = sSQL
       .Parameters(0).Direction = dbParamInput
       .Prepare = dbQPrepare
       .Parameters(0).Value = "712-45-1867"
    End With

    Set rs = qd.OpenRecordset(dbOpenForwardOnly, False)
```

```
' Set up the grid
Grid.Cols = rs.Fields.Count
Grid.Rows = 1
Grid.Row = 0


'Set up the Grid headings
For Each fld In rs.Fields
    Grid.Col = fld.OrdinalPosition
    Grid.Text = fld.Name
Next fld


Grid.Rows = Grid.Rows + 1


'Loop through all fields
For Each fld In rs.Fields
    Grid.Col = fld.OrdinalPosition
    Grid.Text = fld.Value
Next fld


qd.Parameters(0).Value = "238-95-7766"
rs.Requery


Grid.Rows = Grid.Rows + 1
Grid.Row = Grid.Row + 1


'Loop through all fields
For Each fld In rs.Fields
    Grid.Col - fld.OrdinalPosition
    Grid.Text = fld.Value
Next fld



rs.Close

qd.Close



Screen.MousePointer = vbDefault

End Sub
```

Near the beginning of this section of code, you can see where the sSQL string variable is assigned a SQL Select statement. However, notice that this Select statement is a bit different from earlier examples. In this example, all of the columns from the authors table will be selected in which the value of the au_id column is equal to the value represented by the question mark. In SQL, the question mark character represents a replaceable character. These replaceable characters are referred to as *parameters*. When they are used in conjunction with a Select statement, they are typically called *parameterized queries*.

After the SQL statement has been set up, the Connection object's CreateQueryDef method is used to create a new QueryDef object named qd. Next, the Visual Basic With statement is used to set up several of the properties of the QueryDef object.

TIP:　The With statement is Visual Basic shorthand code that executes a series of statements on a single object without requiring you to reference the object repeatedly. The With statement is particularly useful for setting multiple values in an ODBCDirect QueryDef object.

The SQL property is assigned the parameterized query. The Parameters(0) property represents the first parameter (and in this case, the only parameter) that is used by the SQL statement. In the prior example, you can see that the Direction property of the first Parameter in the Parameters collection is assigned the constant value of dbParamInput. This specifies that ODBCDirect will use the parameter as input and no values will be returned in the parameter.

Setting the Prepare property of the QueryDef object to dbQPrepare causes ODBCDirect to execute a SQLPrepare statement. This results in the creation of a temporary data access plan in SQL Server's Procedure Cache. Unlike dynamic SQL statements that cause the SQL Server engine to parse the SQL and create a new access plan for each statement, with prepared SQL statements, the data access plan is created once—when the ODBC SQLPrepare( ) function is executed. Preparing the SQL statement has similar overhead to executing a dynamic SQL statement. However, the big benefit comes from the subsequent execution of the prepared statement. All of the work required to parse the SQL statement and prepare the access plan has already been performed. This results in big performance benefits for SQL statements that are executed multiple times. Were it not for the ability to use parameters, prepared SQL by itself would be rather inflexible. However, the use of parameter marks allows values to be substituted into the prepared statement at run time. This allows the same basic SQL statement to be used multiple times—potentially returning a different result set each time. In this example, the Value property of the first parameter, Parameters(0), is set to the value of 712-45-1876, which results in the creation of the following SQL statement:

```
Select * From authors Where au_id = '712-45-1876'
```

Using parameter markers with the QueryDef object allows different values to be used in the QueryDef's Parameter object's Value property. This allows that same QueryDef (and prepared statement) to be reused to retrieve different data sets.

The OpenRecordset method then executes the prepared SQL statement and places the returned data into a forward-only Recordset object. The Recordset object is then processed using the same techniques that you've seen in other examples in this chapter. The Names property of the Fields collection is used to create the grid headings and then the Value property of each Field object in the Fields collection is used to fill the grid. In this example, no loop is used to traverse the Recordset object because it will only contain a single row.

After the results of the first query have been added to the grid, the Parameters(0).Value property is then assigned the value of 238-95-7766, which results in the creation of the following SQL statement:

```
Select * From authors Where au_id = '238-95-7766'
```

The prepared SQL statement is then reexecuted, using the new parameter value, by the Requery method. The results of the new query are then added to the grid and the Recordset object and QueryDef objects are closed.

Modifying Data with ODBCDirect

You can modify data using ODBCDirect in a number of ways. First, since ODBCDirect supports the Recordset object, you can use the AddNew, Update, and Delete methods to modify the data contained in an updateable Recordset object. Updating data using these Recordset methods is exactly the same as using these methods with DAO. You can refer to the DAO examples presented earlier in this chapter to get a detailed explanation of how these methods work. Also like standard DAO, ODBCDirect supports updating data through the use of SQL statements that are executed using the Database object's Execute method. Again, this technique is extremely similar to using the Execute method under DAO. The earlier DAO section of this chapter provides several examples illustrating how to modify data using direct SQL statements.

Where ODBCDirect differs from DAO is in its ability to update data using prepared SQL via the QueryDef object. Prepared SQL gives your ODBC applications a big performance boost for most online transaction processing (OLTP) type of applications because the data access plan is only created once when the SQL statement is prepared. All subsequent executions of that statement benefit from the existing data access plan. Now you'll see how you can update data using the ODBCDirect QueryDef object.

Inserting Rows with a QueryDef and Prepared SQL

Unlike the QueryDef objects that are used in DAO, ODBCDirect QueryDef objects do not create permanent objects in the database. However, your application can still repeatedly use ODBCDirect QueryDef objects because they create temporary statements that are maintained in SQL Server's Procedure Cache. Executing the CreateQueryDef method or changing the SQL property of an ODBCDirect QueryDef object creates a new prepared statement on the remote data source. Reusing these stored SQL statements results in a significant performance benefit over executing dynamic SQL or updating data using Recordset cursors. The following example shows how you can insert rows into a SQL Server table using a QueryDef object:

```
Private Sub AddUsingQD(cn As Connection)

    Dim qd As QueryDef
    Dim i As Integer
    Dim sSQL As String

    Screen.MousePointer = vbHourglass

    sSQL = "Insert Into department Values(?,?)"

    Set qd = cn.CreateQueryDef("", sSQL)
    qd.Prepare = dbQPrepare

    If qd.Updateable = False Then
        MsgBox "This QueryDef is not updateable", vbOKOnly, App.Title
        Exit Sub
    End If

    For i = 1 To 50
        qd.Parameters(0).Value = CStr(i)
        qd.Parameters(1).Value = "Department " & CStr(i)
        qd.Execute
    Next

    qd.Close

    Screen.MousePointer = vbDefault

End Sub
```

In this example, the sSQL string is assigned with a SQL Insert statement that inserts rows into the department table using two parameter markers in the Values clause. Each parameter marker represents a column value that will be supplied when the statement is executed.

NOTE: Remember, the department table is not a part of the example pubs database. The department table is created in order to illustrate database update techniques without altering the original contents of the pubs database.

Next, a new QueryDef object named qd is created using an existing ODBCDirect connection object's CreateQueryDef method. The CreateQueryDef method takes two parameters. The first parameter optionally supplies a name for the QueryDef object. Naming the QueryDef object is a good idea if you will need to reuse it in different parts of your application. The second optional parameter of the CreateQueryDef method takes the SQL statement that will be prepared on the remote data source. Next, the QueryDef object's Prepare method is used to explicitly tell ODBCDirect that the SQL statement will be prepared on the remote data source. Table 12-8 presents the two available options for the Prepare property.

After the optional Prepare property has been set to prepare the SQL statement, the QueryDef object's Updateable property is examined to determine if the QueryDef object supports updating. In this simple example, if the qd QueryDef object is not updateable, a message box will be displayed and the subroutine will be exited.

The next section contains a For Next loop that's used to insert 50 rows in the department table. Within the loop, the value for each of the two parameters is set using the Value property. The first parameter, qd.Parameters(0), is assigned with the string representation of the integer used as the loop counter and the second parameter, qd.Parameters(1), is assigned the literal "Department" concatenated with the string representation of the loop counter. After the values for each parameter have been added, the QueryDef object's Execute method is used to run the prepared SQL Insert statement adding the row to the department table. When all 50 rows have been added to the department table, the QueryDef object's Close method is used to delete the temporary QueryDef object from SQL Server's buffer.

Updating Data with a QueryDef and Prepared SQL

Updating data using prepared SQL and the ODBCDirect QueryDef object is very similar to inserting data. First, you create the QueryDef object; then you assign the appropriate values to any parameters; and, finally, you execute the prepared SQL statement. The

Constant	Description
dbQPrepare	The QueryDef's SQL statement will be prepared and executed. This is the default value.
dbQUnprepare	The QueryDef object's SQL statements will be executed directly.

Table 12-8.   QueryDef Prepare Values

following code listing illustrates how to update SQL Server tables using a QueryDef object and prepared SQL statements:

```
Private Sub UpdateUsingQD(cn As Connection)
    Dim qd As QueryDef
    Dim i As Integer
    Dim sSQL As String

    Screen.MousePointer = vbHourglass

    sSQL = "Update department Set Dep_Name = ? Where Dep_ID = ?"

    Set qd = cn.CreateQueryDef("", sSQL)
    qd.Prepare = dbQPrepare

    For i = 1 To 50
        qd.Parameters(0).Value = "Updated Department " & CStr(i)
        qd.Parameters(1).Value = CStr(i)
        qd.Execute
    Next

    qd.Close

    Screen.MousePointer = vbDefault

End Sub
```

This example begins by assigning a SQL Update statement to the Visual Basic string named sSQL. This Update statement uses two parameters. The first parameter is used to set the value of the Dep_Name column, and the second parameter is used to select the row that will be updated. In this case, the Dep_ID column is the primary key of the department table, and thus it possesses the Unique attribute. This means that each execution of the Update statement will only update a single row. The SQL DDL used to create the department table follows:

```
Create Table department
    Dep_ID Char(4) Not Null,
    Dep_Name Char(25),
    Primary Key(Dep_ID))
```

Next, a QueryDef object named qd is created by the CreateQueryDef method of an existing Connection object named cn. Like the previous example, the QueryDef object is not named and the prepared SQL statement is passed into the second parameter of the CreateQueryDef method. Then the Prepare property is set to qdQPrepare, which instructs the QueryDef object to prepare and execute SQL statements.

A For Next loop is used to read and update the first 50 rows of the department table. Like the Insert statement that was presented earlier, the Value property of each Parameter object is assigned the appropriate value, and then the SQL statement is executed using the QueryDef object's Execute method. One important difference between this example and the prior Insert example is the order of the parameters. With the Update statement, the first parameter, qd.Parameters(0), sets the value of the Dep_Name column; and the second parameter, qd.Parameters(1), is used to select the row to be updated. After the For Next loop has completed, the QueryDef object is closed.

Deleting Data with a QueryDef and Prepared SQL

Very much like insert and update operations, ODBCDirect QueryDef objects can be used to delete one or more rows in a remote data source. The following code listing illustrates how to delete rows from an ODBC data source using a QueryDef object and prepared SQL statements:

```
Private Sub DeleteUsingQD(cn As Connection)
    Dim qd As QueryDef
    Dim i As Integer
    Dim sSQL As String

    Screen.MousePointer = vbHourglass

    sSQL = "Delete department Where Dep_ID = ?"

    Set qd = cn.CreateQueryDef("", sSQL)
    qd.Prepare = dbQPrepare

    For i = 1 To 50
        qd.Parameters(0).Value = CStr(i)
        qd.Execute
    Next

    qd.Close

    Screen.MousePointer = vbDefault

End Sub
```

Here the sSQL string is assigned with a SQL Delete statement that uses a single parameter marker in the Where clause. As in the previous Update statement, the Where clause is used to select the specified row to be deleted from the department table.

After the SQL statement has been set up, the CreateQueryDef method of an existing Connection object is used to create a new QueryDef object named qd. Again, the new QueryDef is not named and the SQL statement is passed to the CreateQueryDef method's second parameter.

Then a For Next loop is used to read and delete the first 50 rows in the department table. For each row, the parameter value of the prepared SQL Delete statement is assigned a unique key value, and then the Execute method is used to run the Delete statement, which removes the specified row from the department table. At the completion of the For Next loop, the QueryDef object is closed, which results in the removal of the prepared SQL statement from SQL Server's dynamic buffer.

Executing Dynamic SQL with ODBCDirect

Like DAO, ODBCDirect can also be used to execute dynamic SQL statements on the remote database. Dynamic SQL can be used for a variety of data management and data manipulation tasks. However, unlike DAO, since ODBCDirect is already based on an ODBC connection to the data source, it doesn't use a local query engine. Therefore there is no need to specify the dbSQLPassThrough option in order to execute native SQL statements on SQL Server using ODBCDirect. The following code listing illustrates how you can execute a set of dynamic SQL statements that create a SQL Server stored procedure:

```
Private Sub CreateSP(cn As Connection)

    Dim sSQL As String
    On Error Resume Next

    Screen.MousePointer = vbHourglass

    sSQL = "Drop Proc CountStateRows"
    cn.Execute sSQL


    On Error GoTo Errorhandler

    sSQL = "Create Proc CountStateRows" _
        & "(@state char(2), @rows int Output) As " _
        & "Select @rows = Count(*) From authors Where state = @state"

    cn.Execute sSQL
    Screen.MousePointer = vbDefault
    Exit Sub

Errorhandler:
    DisplayDAOError
    Screen.MousePointer = vbDefault

End Sub
```

In the beginning of the CreateSP subroutine shown in this example, the On Error statement is first set to trap any errors and resume subroutine execution with the next statement. Next, the sSQL string is assigned with a SQL Drop Proc statement that will delete the stored procedure named CountStateRows in the pubs database. Then the Execute method of an existing ODBCDirect Connection object is run to dynamically execute the SQL Drop statement. As you might expect, if the CountStateRows stored procedure does not exist, ODBCDirect will report the error and fire Visual Basic's error handler. Setting Visual Basic's error handler to Resume Next will allow the CreateSP subroutine to trap the error and continue processing.

After ensuring that the CountStateRows stored procedure doesn't exist, Visual Basic's error handler is reset to branch to the Errorhandler label if an unexpected run-time error is encountered, where the DisplayODBCError subroutine will display all of the ODBCDirect errors in a message box.

Next, the sSQL string is assigned with a SQL Create Proc statement. This Create Proc SQL DDL defines a stored procedure that uses two parameters. The first parameter is a two-character input variable that will contain a state code, and the second parameter is an integer output variable that will count the number of occurrences the input state is found. The next line shows the simple logic used by the CountStateRows stored procedure. The @rows variable is filled with the results of the count(*) operation, which accumulates the occurrences in which the value of the state column in the authors table is equal to the value supplied in the input parameter. For more information on using Transact-SQL DDL, you can refer to Chapter 9.

After the Visual Basic string with the Create Proc SQL statements has been assigned, the stored procedure is created on the SQL Server system using the ODBCDirect Database object's Execute method. The stored procedure will be created in the database that was identified when the Database object was opened.

> **NOTE:** If the connection to SQL Server was made using a DSN, the stored procedure will be created in the database that is associated with the data source. If a DSN-less connection was used, then the stored procedure will be created in the database that was specified using the DATABASE keyword in the ODBC connection string.

Executing Stored Procedures with QueryDef Objects

Now that you've seen how you can create stored procedures using dynamic SQL and the ODBCDirect Database object's Execute method, let's take a look at how you can call SQL Server stored procedures using the ODBCDirect QueryDef object.

Stored procedures provide the fastest mechanism available for accessing SQL Server data. When a stored procedure is created, a compiled data access plan is added to the SQL Server database. By using these existing data access plans, the application forgoes the need to parse any incoming SQL statements and then create a new data access plan. This results in faster execution of queries or other data-manipulation actions. In addition, using stored procedures allows you to restrict all direct access to SQL Server tables and only allow execute permission to the stored procedures. Being centrally controlled and administrated, the stored procedures can provide a firewall between network nodes and the database.

```
Private Sub CallQDsp(cn As Connection)

    Dim qd As QueryDef

    Dim sSQL As String
    On Error GoTo Errorhandler

    Screen.MousePointer = vbHourglass

    sSQL = "{ Call CountStateRows (? ,?) }"

    Set qd = cn.CreateQueryDef("", sSQL)

    qd.Parameters(0) = "UT"
    qd.Parameters(1).Direction = dbParamOutput

    qd.Execute

    Label_Mid.Caption = "Number of rows:"
    Text_Mid.Text = qd.Parameters(1)

    qd.close

    Screen.MousePointer = vbDefault
    Exit Sub

Errorhandler:
    DisplayDAOError

    Screen.MousePointer = vbDefault

End Sub
```

In this example, the string sSQL is assigned with an ODBC Call statement that will invoke the CountStateRows stored procedure. Two parameter markers are used in the Call statement: one for each parameter used by the stored procedure. The first parameter will be used to input the state code, and the second parameter will return the number of occurrences that the state code was found in the authors table.

Next, the CreateQueryDef method of an existing ODBCDirect Connection object is used to create a new QueryDef object. The first parameter is left as an empty string, which means the QueryDef is not named. The second parameter contains the ODBC Call statement. Before the QueryDef object is used to call the CountStateRows stored procedure, the parameters must be set up. In this example, you can see that the first parameter, qd.Parameters(0), is set to the value of UT. The Direction property of the second parameter, qd.Parameters(1), is set to the value of dbParamOutput. Table 12-9 lists the ODBCDirect parameter constants and their meanings.

After the Parameter objects have been set up, the Execute method of the QueryDef object is used to invoke the stored procedure and pass it the input parameter. When the stored procedure has completed, the value of the output parameter will be immediately available to your application. In the previous example, you can see where the value of the qd.Parameters(1) object is assigned to a text box named Text_Mid. In addition, the string "Number of rows:" is assigned to a Label control named Label_Mid. These controls are both displayed on a Visual Basic form.

TIP: In most instances, your applications will probably need to reuse the QueryDef object that's used to call the stored procedure. To facilitate rerunning the stored procedure, be sure to leave the QueryDef object open until the QueryDef is no longer needed. This will make subsequent calls faster.

Error Handling

ODBCDirect errors are handled in the same way that standard DAO errors are handled. Basic error handling involves using Visual Basic's error handler to trap errors and then branch to a section of error-handling code. The ODBCDirect error handler would typically declare an Error object and then iterate through the Errors collection. The example DisplayDAOError subroutine that was presented earlier in this chapter can be used unchanged for ODBCDirect errors.

Parameter Constant	Description
dbParamInput	Sets the parameter as input only. This is the default.
dbParamOutput	Sets the parameter as output only.
dbParmInOut	Sets the parameter as both input and output.

Table 12-9.   QueryDef Parameter Direction Constants

ADVANCED DATABASE FUNCTIONS USING ODBCDIRECT

In the previous portion of this chapter, you've seen how to use the basic ODBCDirect functions to query the SQL server database, as well as ways to perform various database update operations. In the next part of this chapter, you'll see how to use ODBCDirect for some more advanced functions, such as managing multiple result sets, performing asynchronous queries, and controlling transactions.

Working with Multiple Result Sets

ODBCDirect's ability to process multiple result sets allows it to be used to send multiple SQL Select statements in a single Recordset object, as well as using a QueryDef object to call stored procedures that return multiple result sets. In order to submit multiple SQL Select statements, the ODBCDirect Workspace must first be set to use a local ODBC cursor rather than the default server-side cursor. The following code illustrates one way to direct the ODBCDirect Workspace object to use a local ODBC cursor:

```
'Set the default Workspace type to ODBCDirect
DBEngine.DefaultType = dbUseODBC

'Create the default Workspace as ODBCDirect
Set ws = DBEngine.Workspaces(0)
ws.DefaultCursorDriver = dbUseODBCCursor
```

In this example, you can see that the ODBCDirect Workspace is created normally using the dbUseODBC constant, which specifies that the Workspace object is an ODBCDirect Workspace rather than a Jet Workspace. The key point in configuring the Workspace to use a local ODBC cursor is setting the DefaultCursorDriver property with the constant dbUseODBCCursor. This changes the ODBCDirect Workspace object from using the default server-side cursors to local ODBC cursors. If the DefaultCursorDriver property is not set to dbUseODBCCursor and your application attempts to open multiple result sets, an ODBCDirect error will be generated. It is important to note that the DefaultCursorDriver property of the ODBCDirect Workspace object must be changed before the Connection object and its dependent Recordset object are created.

Once the ODBCDirect Workspace object is set to use a local ODBC cursor, the application is able to send multiple SQL Select statements to the data source. The following example illustrates how to send three different SQL Select statements to SQL Server and process the multiple results that are generated:

```
Private Sub MultipleRS(cn As Connection)

    Dim rs As Recordset
    Dim fld As Field
    Dim sSQL As String
    Dim i As Integer
```

```
    Screen.MousePointer = vbHourglass

    'Set up the 3 Select statements
    sSQL = "Select au_lname, au_fname From authors; "
    sSQL = sSQL & "Select title From titles; "
    sSQL = sSQL & "Select stor_name From stores "

    Set rs = cn.OpenRecordset(sSQL)

    ' Set up the grid
    Grid.FixedRows = 0
    Grid.Cols = 2
    Grid.Rows = 1
    Grid.Row = 0
    i = 1

    Do
        Grid.Col = 0
        Grid.CellBackColor = &HC0C0C0
        Grid.Text = "Recordset"
        Grid.Col = 1
        Grid.CellBackColor = &HC0C0C0
        Grid.Text = "Number: " & i


        While rs.EOF = False
            Grid.Rows = Grid.Rows + 1
            Grid.Row = Grid.Row + 1
            'Loop through all fields
            For Each fld In rs.Fields
                Grid.Col = fld.OrdinalPosition
                Grid.Text = fld.Value
            Next fld
            rs.MoveNext
        Wend

        i = i + 1

    Loop Until rs.NextRecordset = False

    rs.Close

    Screen.MousePointer = vbDefault

End Sub
```

In this example, you can see that the sSQL string containing the SQL statements is quite a bit different than the SQL statements that were used in the other examples in this chapter. In this case, the sSQL string variable contains a compound SQL statement that actually consists of three separate SQL Select statements, separated by semicolons. The first Select statement returns the last and first names from the authors table. The second Select statement returns the title column from the titles table, and the third Select statement returns a result set that consists of the stor_name column from the stores table. This combination of SQL Select statements will return three distinctly different result sets.

Next, a new Recordset object named rs is created using the Connection object's OpenRecordset method. The first parameter of the OpenRecordset method contains the compound SQL statement. After the three Select statements have completed, this next section of code sets up the grid to contain all of the data values from all three result sets. In this case, we know that the maximum number of columns that will be returned is two, so the Grid.Cols property is set to 2, which instructs the grid to only display two columns. While the number of columns in these queries is a known quantity, the number of rows is not. To accommodate a variable number of rows, the grid is initially sized to contain a single row. The grid must then be dynamically expanded as each row is read from the Recordset object.

A Do loop is then used to process the multiple result sets. The Do loop continues until the NextRecordset method of the rs Recordset object returns a value of False, which indicates that there are no more result sets available. The first action performed within the Do loop is setting up a grid row to indicate the beginning of each result set. A heading value containing the literal "Recordset Number" is combined with the loop counter to produce column headings. Setting the CellBackColor property of the Grid object to &HC0C0C0 displays the grid cell containing the Recordset heading in gray rather than the default grid color.

Then a While loop is used to read through all of the rows in each result set. The grid is dynamically expanded to accommodate each row by adding 1 to the Grid.Rows property. Then the current row in the grid is incremented using the Grid.Row property. The Field object values are extracted for each row and moved to the grid using a For Each loop, and the MoveNext method is used to read the next row in the rs Recordset object. The EOF property of the rs Recordset object is set to True when the end of the current record set is reached. After all of the rows in the current result set have been read, the NextRecordset method moves to the next available result set.

Asynchronous Operations

One of the other advanced ODBC functions provided by the ODBCDirect object framework is the ability to perform asynchronous operations. Asynchronous operations allow the application to remain responsive even though it may need to execute long-running database operations. The ODBCDirect Connection object has the capability of asynchronously executing Recordset and QueryDef objects, as well as dynamic SQL using the Execute method. The following example illustrates how to perform an asynchronous query using a Recordset object:

```
sSQL = "Select * From employee "

'Start the Async query and move on
Set rs = cn.OpenRecordset(sSQL, dbOpenDynaset, dbRunAsync)
```

Here, the sSQL string is set up using a simple SQL Select statement. Then the OpenRecordset method is used to create a Recordset object named rs. It is important to note the value of dbRunAsync in the third parameter of the OpenRecordset. The dbRunAsync constant specifies that the Recordset object will be created asynchronously. Unlike Recordset objects that are created synchronously, the program execution does not wait for the OpenRecordset method to complete before processing the next code statement. Instead, when the dbRunAsync option is used, the OpenRecordset method immediately returns control to the application.

> **TIP:** The dbRunAsync option can also be used with the Connection object's Execute method. This can allow asynchronous execution of dynamic SQL statements. You can't use the dbRunAsync option with a Database object.

As you might have guessed, even though program control is returned immediately, this doesn't mean that the result set is immediately available. For very small result sets, the Recordset object may be available almost instantly, but large result sets or complex queries may take several minutes. The following code shows how you can test for the completion of an asynchronous query:

```
Private Sub AsyncFinish(rs as Recordset)

    Dim fld As Field

    Screen.MousePointer = vbHourglass

    If rs.StillExecuting = False Then

        ' Set up the grid
        Grid.Cols = rs.Fields.Count
        Grid.Rows = 1
        Grid.Row = 0

        'Set up the Grid headings
        For Each fld In rs.Fields
            Grid.Col = fld.OrdinalPosition
            Grid.Text = fld.Name
        Next fld
```

```
        Grid.Rows = rs.RecordCount
        Grid.Row = 0

        'Move the results to a grid
        While Not rs.EOF
           Grid.Row = Grid.Row + 1
           'Loop through all fields
           For Each fld In rs.Fields
              Grid.Text = fld.Value
           Next fld
           rs.MoveNext
        Wend

        rs.Close

    End If

    Screen.MousePointer = vbDefault

End Sub
```

The StillExecuting property allows you to test for the completion of an asynchronous operation. If the StillExecuting property is True, the asynchronous operation is still being processed. When the StillExecuting property becomes False, then the operation has finished. In the previous example, you can see where the StillExecuting property of the rs Recordset object is tested for False. If the StillExecuting property is False, then the query has finished and data is available in the Recordset object. After this point, processing the Recordset object is exactly the same as processing a standard synchronous Recordset object. The data is retrieved from the Fields collection and the MoveNext method allows your application to traverse the Recordset.

TIP: The Cancel method can be used to terminate an asynchronous operation. However, to ensure database integrity, you can wrap any database update operations within a Transaction. Using a Transaction allows you to roll back any potentially unfinished updates that might result from canceling a database update before it has completed.

Using Transactions

Transactions are an important database feature that can be used to ensure database integrity. Transactions enable you to group together multiple operations that can be performed as a single unit of work. In many instances, a single logical operation may be comprised of a group of database operations. If one of the database operations fails, then the database integrity will be compromised. For instance, transferring funds from your savings account to your checking account involves several database operations, and the transfer cannot be considered complete unless all of the operations are completed. A transfer from your savings account to your checking account requires both a withdrawal from your savings account and a deposit to your checking account. If either operation fails, the transfer is not completed. Therefore, both of these functions would be considered part of the same logical transaction. In other words, Transactions are mechanisms that allow the database to treat a group of related operations as a single entity. Using Transactions allows an all-or-nothing approach to the group of related operations. If one member of the group fails, then any action performed by the preceding group member will be backed out of the database.

Committing Transactions

When a transaction is successfully completed, it is committed (written) to the database. In the following example, you'll see how to use ODBCDirect to begin a transaction and then commit that transaction to the SQL Server database:

```
'Check to be sure the data source supports transactions
 If cn.Transactions = True Then

    sSQL = "Insert Into department Values(?,?)"

    Set qd = cn.CreateQueryDef("", sSQL)
    qd.Prepare = dbQPrepare

    'Start a transaction and execute the SQL
    BeginTrans

    For i = 1 To 50
        qd.Parameters(0).Value = CStr(i)
        qd.Parameters(1).Value = "Department " & CStr(i)
        qd.Execute
    Next

    'Commit the transaction and update the table
    CommitTrans

    qd.Close
 End if
```

Near the beginning of this example, you can see where the Transactions property of the cn Connection object is checked to see if the connection to the remote data source supports transactions. If the Transactions property is True, then the data source supports transactions. Next, the sSQL string is assigned an Insert statement that inserts a row containing two columns into the department table. Then the sSQL statement is prepared using a QueryDef object. After the qd QueryDef object has been created, the BeginTrans method is used to signal the beginning of a transaction. In this example, the transaction consists of inserting 50 rows. The QueryDef object's Execute method is used within a For Next loop to add 50 rows. All 50 Insert operations are part of the same transaction. When the transaction has completed, the CommitTrans method permanently updates the target database with the transaction.

Rolling Back Transactions

If a transaction doesn't successfully complete, it can be rolled back from the database using the RollBack method. Essentially, the rollback operation restores the database to the state that it was in before the transaction occurred.

TIP: SQL Server maintains database modifications in a transaction log file, which contains a serial record of all of the modifications that have been made to a database. The transaction log contains both before and after images of each transaction.

In the following example, you can see how the RollBack method can be used to roll back a transaction:

```
'Check to be sure the data source supports transactions
If cn.Transactions = True Then

    'Set up the SQL
    sSQL = "Update department Set Dep_Name = 'NO UPDATE'"

    'Start a transaction and execute the SQL
    BeginTrans
    cn.Execute sSQL

    'Now Rollback the transaction - the table is unchanged
    Rollback
End If
```

Here again, the Transactions property of the cn Connections object is tested to determine if the database supports transactions. If it does, then the sSQL string is assigned a SQL Update statement. Since this particular Update statement doesn't contain a Where clause, its execution will update the Dep_Name column in all of the rows in the department table.

Next, the BeginTrans method is used to signal the beginning of a transaction. In this example, the transaction consists of a single Update statement, which is run using the Connection object's Execute method. After the Execute method has finished, you can see how the transaction can be rolled back using the RollBack method. It's important to note that although this transaction consists of a single statement, that statement updates all of the rows of the department file. Therefore, the RollBack method must restore all of the rows in the department file with the values that they contained before the Execute method was issued.

> **NOTE:** The BeginTrans, CommitTrans, and RollBack methods are all contained in the Workspace object. If you need to execute transactions along with other SQL statements that are not part of the transaction, you will need two separate Workspace objects.

CONCLUSION

DAO provides a single object framework that can be used to work with both local databases and SQL Server databases. DAO provides the flexibility to use a single set of code that can be used for both local and client/server applications. However, if you only need to build SQL Server database operations, you'll find that the ODBC-specific features that are provided by ODBCDirect offer significant performance benefits without sacrificing DAO's easy coding.

All of the code listings presented in this chapter are also contained in the DAO Wizard and ODBCDirect Wizard example programs that are on the CD-ROM accompanying this book.

ADDITIONAL RESOURCES

For more information about using DAO and Visual Basic, you can refer to the following Microsoft publications:

- ▼ *Guide to Building Client/Server Applications with Visual Basic.* Microsoft Corporation, 1998.

- ■ Haught, Dan, and Ferguson, Jim. *Microsoft Jet Database Engine Programmer's Guide.* Redmond, WA: Microsoft Press, 1997.

- ▲ Vaughn, William R. *Hitchhiker's Guide to Visual Basic & SQL Server,* Sixth Edition. Redmond, WA: Microsoft Press, 1998.

CHAPTER 13

Developing
NT Database
Applications with
the ODBC API

In this chapter, you'll see how to develop SQL Server database applications using the Visual Basic and the ODBC (Open Database Connectivity) application programming interface (API). The first part of the chapter provides a brief overview of ODBC, and then covers some of the concepts you'll need to know in order to use ODBC effectively. The second half of this chapter illustrates the basic ODBC API programming techniques that can be used to access SQL Server databases.

ODBC is a database access standard that was defined by Microsoft. ODBC was designed to provide a standard method of desktop database access for SQL databases on different platforms. An ODBC application can be used to access data that's on a local PC database, but it is more really intended to access databases on heterogeneous platforms like SQL Server, Oracle, or DB2. Although ODBC originated as a Windows standard, it has also been implemented on several other platforms, including OS/2 and UNIX.

ODBC is essentially a database access API. The ODBC API is database independent and it is based on the SQL/CLI (SQL/Call Level Interface) specifications that were developed by X/Open and ISO/IEC. The ODBC 3.0 standard is comprised of 76 functions, which are documented in Microsoft's three-volume *ODBC 3.0 Reference and SDK Guide*. While, on the surface, the ODBC API consists of a set of function calls, the heart of ODBC is SQL. The primary purpose of the ODBC functions is to send SQL statements to the target database and then process the results of those SQL statements. Obviously, the server must be able to support SQL in order to be accessed through ODBC.

While ODBC is implemented through a set of standard function calls, one of the biggest benefits of ODBC is the fact that it is a widely adopted desktop standard. You don't have to know or understand those functions in order to use ODBC—all of the code required to use ODBC is built into ODBC-enabled applications like Microsoft Access, Word, Excel, or even Visual Basic. ODBC has become a widely adopted database access standard for desktop applications and over 180 different desktop applications are ODBC enabled. You only need to know how to use the application; the underneath layer of the application has been coded to use the ODBC API. This feature applies to end-user applications like Word or Excel, as well as many client/server development tools. You can write ODBC-based client/server applications without really understanding the ODBC API. For example, Visual Basic, PowerBuilder, Delphi, and Visual C++ all provide their own layer of code that encapsulates the ODBC functions—giving the programmer access to ODBC functionality without requiring a direct understanding of the ODBC functions.

Both the Visual Basic Data Access Objects (DAO) functions discussed in Chapter 12 and the Visual Basic Remote Database Objects (RDO) function discussed in Chapter 14 use the ODBC API to access SQL Server databases. While it's possible to use ODBC through the built-in data access functions provided by the various client/server development tools, like most technical things, the better you understand what goes on underneath the application, the more effectively you will be able to use ODBC.

Since ODBC was primarily intended to connect PCs to different client/server database systems, it typically uses a number of network components. Figure 13-1 shows the communications layers used by an ODBC connection. At the top level, you can see the ODBC-enabled application, which makes calls to the various ODBC API functions provided by the ODBC CLI.

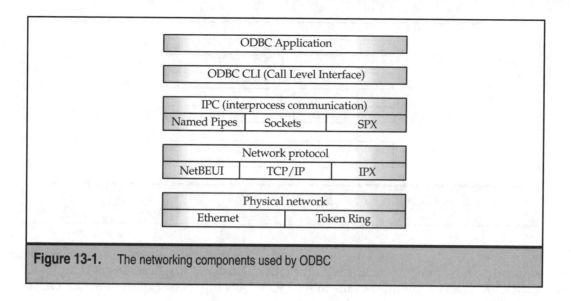

Figure 13-1.   The networking components used by ODBC

Beneath the ODBC CLI is the network interprocess communication (IPC) mechanism, which enables different network processes to communicate with one another. Examples of different IPC mechanisms are Named Pipes and TCP/IP Sockets. The actual IPC mechanism used depends on the network protocol found at the next lower level, the network protocol level.

The network protocol is responsible for sending and receiving a data stream over the network. Examples of different network protocols include NetBEUI and TCP/IP.

At the bottom of this communications stack is the physical network. The physical network includes the adapter cards and cabling required to make the actual connections between the networked systems. Ethernet and Token Ring are examples of two of the most common network topologies.

ODBC ARCHITECTURE

Before getting into the details of how to code an ODBC application, let's take a quick look at the different ODBC components. This will help you understand how your application relates to the ODBC architecture and see the path that it uses to connect to an ODBC-compliant database. Figure 13-2 illustrates the layered architecture used by ODBC.

The ODBC Application

The ODBC application can be either an off-the-shelf application like Word, Excel, or Visual Basic, or it can be a custom ODBC application you've written using Visual Basic, Visual C++, or some other PC development platform. The ODBC application is either

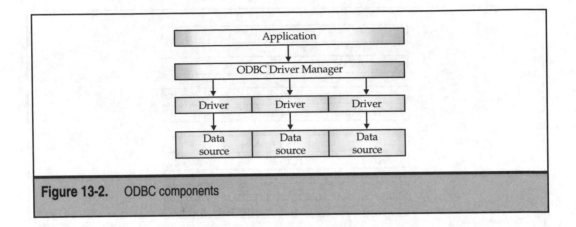

Figure 13-2. ODBC components

statically or dynamically linked with the ODBC Driver Manager (ODBC32.DLL), and the ODBC application makes calls to the ODBC API functions exported by the ODBC Driver Manager.

The ODBC Driver Manager

An ODBC-enabled application like Visual Basic makes calls to the ODBC Driver Manager, the ODBC.DLL for 16-bit applications, or the ODBC32.DLL for 32-bit applications. It's important to note that the application does not make calls directly to the ODBC drivers. The application calls the functions contained in the ODBC Driver Manager, and the ODBC Driver Manager in turn makes calls to the appropriate ODBC driver. This ensures that the ODBC functions are always called in the same way, whether you are connecting to SQL Server or another database platform like Oracle. This layered architecture also allows multiple ODBC drivers to coexist and be active simultaneously.

The ODBC Driver Manager is responsible for loading the appropriate ODBC drivers into memory and routing subsequent requests to the correct ODBC driver. When the ODBC Driver Manager loads an ODBC driver, the ODBC Driver Manager builds a table of pointers to the functions that are in the ODBC driver. The ODBC Driver Manager uses an identifier called a *connection handle* to identify the function pointers for each loaded ODBC driver.

The ODBC Driver

The ODBC driver is responsible for sending SQL requests to the relational database management system (RDBMS) and returning the results to the ODBC Driver Manager, which in turn passes them on to the ODBC client application. Each ODBC-compatible database has its own ODBC driver. For instance, the SQL Server ODBC driver communicates exclusively with SQL Server, and it can't be used to access an Oracle database. Likewise, the Oracle ODBC driver can't be used to access a SQL Server database. For some systems, the ODBC driver may reformat the SQL requests into the correct SQL syntax that's required by the target RDBMS.

The ODBC driver processes the ODBC function calls passed to it from the ODBC Driver Manager. The functions in each ODBC driver are called via function pointers that are maintained by the ODBC Driver Manager.

The Data Source

The data source is created with a program called the ODBC Administrator. The data source insulates the user from the underlying mechanics of an ODBC connection by associating a target relational database and ODBC driver with a user-created name. The user then accesses the database by using the meaningful data source name without needing to know the technical details about the ODBC driver or relational database.

When the ODBC application first connects to a target database, it passes the data source name to the ODBC Driver Manager. The ODBC Driver Manager then uses the data source to determine which ODBC driver to load. The ODBC Driver typically requires the relational database login ID and password to connect to the target database.

On 16-bit Windows 3.1 systems, the ODBC data source information is stored in the ODBC.INI file. On 32-bit Windows 95 and Windows NT systems, the ODBC data source information is stored in the registry, in one of two different registry keys. User data sources are stored under the HKEY_CURRENT_USER key; system data sources are saved under the HKEY_LOCAL_MACHINE key. The user data sources are unique to each current user while the system data sources are available to all users of the system. Figure 13-3 illustrates the registry keys for a sample user data source.

CONFIGURING AN ODBC DATA SOURCE

Before you can begin using ODBC, you must have installed an ODBC driver and configured a data source. The Microsoft SQL Server ODBC driver is typically installed when you install any of the Microsoft ODBC-enabled applications on your system. For instance, the SQL Server ODBC driver is optionally installed when you install any of the following Microsoft products:

Microsoft Office 95 or Office 97
Microsoft Word 95 or Word 97
Microsoft Excel 95 or Excel 97
Microsoft Access 95 or Access 97
Visual Studio 97
Visual Basic Professional Edition 4, 5, or 6
Visual Basic Enterprise Edition 4, 5, or 6
Visual C++ Professional Edition 4, 5, or 6
Visual C++ Enterprise Edition 4, 5, or 6

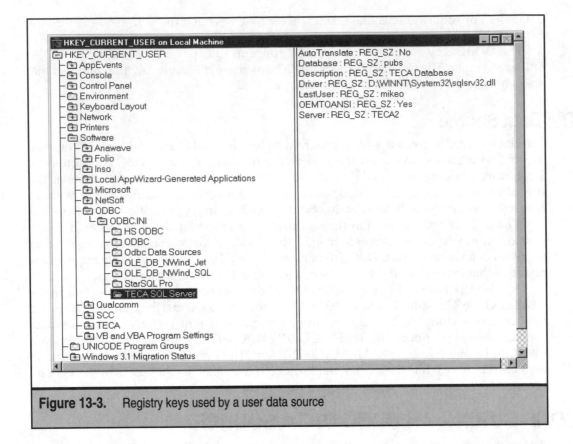

Figure 13-3. Registry keys used by a user data source

Just installing the SQL Server ODBC driver by itself is not enough to begin using ODBC. You also need to create a data source. To create an ODBC data source, you need to run the ODBC Administrator that's found in the Windows 95 or Windows NT Control Panel.

Opening the ODBC Administrator icon displays a window like the one shown in Figure 13-4. The ODBC Administrator program displays all the currently installed data sources. The different tabs allow you to work with the different types of data sources. The User DSN tab displays a list of the data sources for the currently logged on user. The System DSN tab displays a list of the system data sources available to all users of the system. The File DSN tab displays a list of data sources that allow you to connect to a file provider. The ODBC Drivers tab displays all of the different ODBC drivers currently installed on the system. The Tracing tab allows you to trace all the activity for a given ODBC driver. The About tab displays a list of the DLLs and their versions that are used by the ODBC Administrator.

To configure a new user data source, you must click on the User DSN tab. If this is the first time you've run the ODBC Administrator, the list will be blank. If you've already

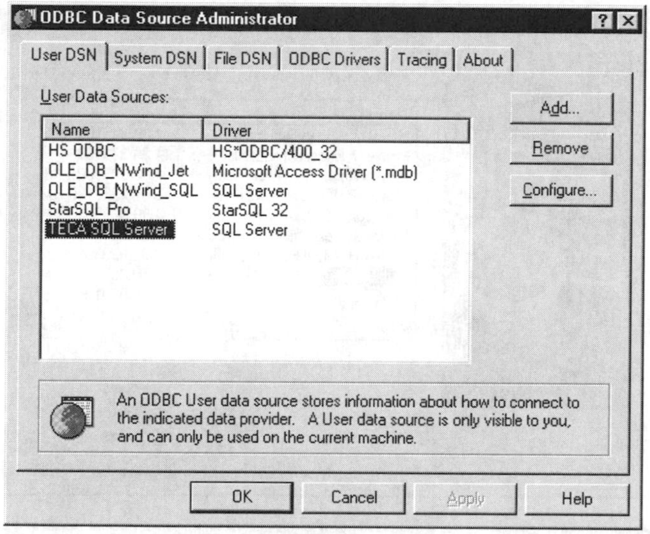

Figure 13-4. Adding a data source with the ODBC Administrator

installed other ODBC drivers and set up data sources, they will appear in either the list of User DSNs or the list of System DSNs.

To add a new data source for SQL Server, select the Add button from the ODBC Administrator dialog box. This action displays the Create New Data Source dialog box shown in Figure 13-5. All of the ODBC drivers currently installed on the system will be listed in this dialog box. You select the ODBC driver you want to use with the new data source by clicking on the name of the ODBC driver and then clicking the Finish button.

The next dialog box displayed varies with the ODBC driver selected. Selecting the SQL Server ODBC driver displays the Microsoft SQL Server DSN Configuration Wizard shown in Figure 13-6. In this text box, you enter the data source name, which can be anything you choose; its main purpose is to associate a meaningful name with the ODBC driver and target RDBMS. This name is used when an ODBC application first attempts to connect to the data. The application must either specify the data source name, or the ODBC Driver Manager will display a dialog box that allows the user to select a data source from a list of all configured data sources.

The Description is a text field that you can use to help identify the data source. The data source description is really only used in the ODBC Administrator.

Finally, from the drop-down combo box, you can select the SQL Server system you want this data source to connect to. All of the SQL Server systems on your network will be

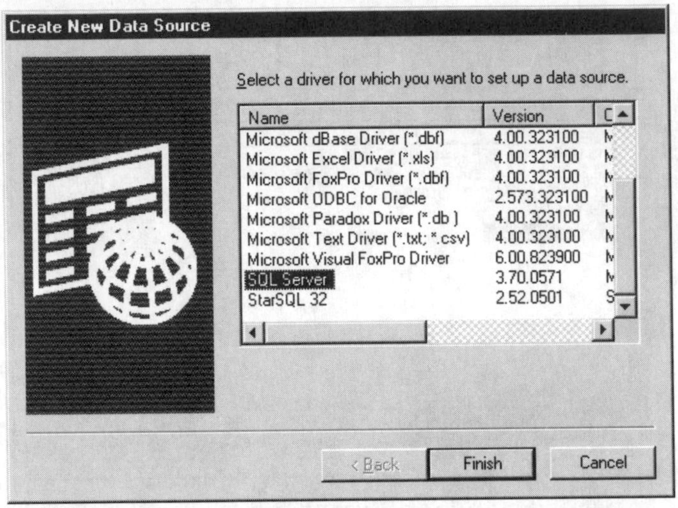

Figure 13-5. Select an ODBC driver

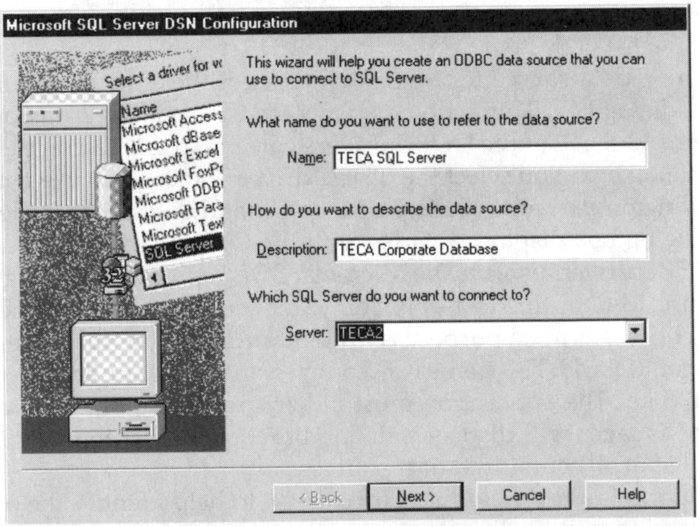

Figure 13-6. SQL Server DSN Configuration Wizard (screen 1)

listed in the combo box. If you're configuring this data source on the SQL Server system itself, you can enter the name of "(local)." This will connect the data source to a SQL Server that's running on the same physical system.

Clicking the Next button displays the next dialog box, shown in Figure 13-7. The second screen of the SQL Server DSN Configuration Wizard allows you to specify the SQL Server security authentication that will be performed. The radio buttons at the top of the window allow you to select between using the Windows NT logon or a SQL Server login. Logging in to SQL Server using the Windows NT logon ID requires a trusted connection and an implementation of Windows NT Authentication Mode or Mixed Security. Using SQL Server's authentication does not require a trusted connection but it does require that a login ID and password are entered by the user. For more information about Windows NT Authentication Mode or Mixed Security, refer to Chapter 3.

The Client Configuration button in screen 2 allows you to change the Network Library that's used to connect to SQL Server. This typically doesn't need to be changed.

Selecting the "Connect to SQL Server to obtain default settings..." check box indicates that the default settings for the remaining steps are to be retrieved from the SQL Server system.

Finally, if you selected SQL Server authentication, you need to enter the login ID and password you'll use to connect to SQL Server.

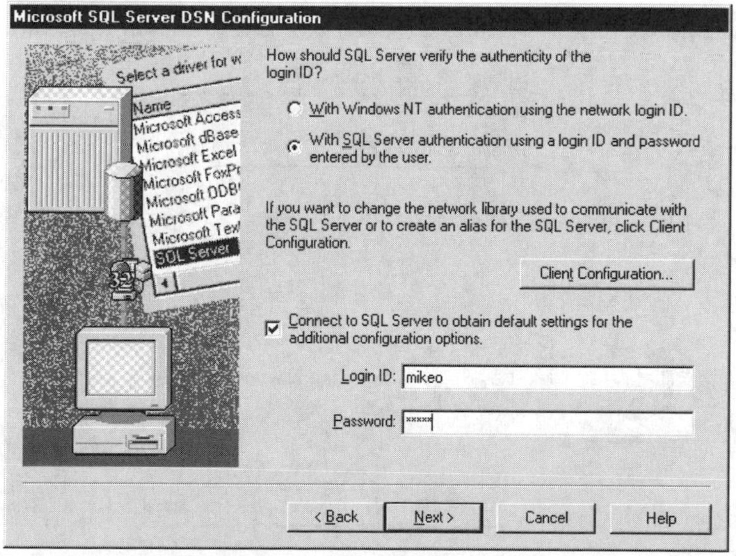

Figure 13-7.   SQL Server DSN Configuration Wizard (screen 2)

Clicking the Next button initiates a connection with SQL Server and displays the window shown in Figure 13-8. The check box at the top of the SQL Server DSN Configuration Wizard allows you to override the default database that's specified in the SQL Server login. Leaving this check box blank specifies that the default database that's entered in SQL Server's login ID will be used.

The "Attach database filename" check box allows you to specify the name of an attachable database that will be used as the default database for the connection.

Checking the "Create temporary stored procedures for prepared SQL statements..." check box causes a temporary stored procedure to be created when the SQLPrepare function is used. This option will only be enabled for SQL Server 6.5 databases. SQL Server 7 databases create a shared plan in SQL Server's Procedure Cache for prepared SQL statements. Generally, checking this option for SQL Server 6.5 databases improves the performance of ODBC applications that use prepared statements. After this check box, two radio buttons appear. With these, you determine when the temporary stored procedures will be dropped. Checking the first of these radio buttons causes the temporary stored procedures to be deleted when you disconnect. Checking the second radio button causes the temporary stored procedures to be dropped when a subsequent SQLPrepare is issued for the same statement handle, when the SQLFreeStmt function is issued or when the ODBC application disconnects.

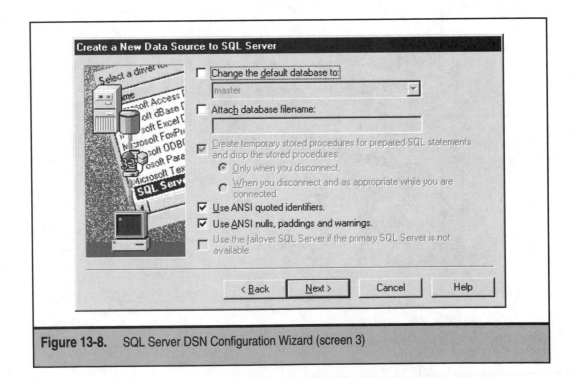

Figure 13-8. SQL Server DSN Configuration Wizard (screen 3)

Checking the "Use ANSI quoted identifiers" check box causes the SQL Server ODBC driver to enforce ANSI rules for quotation marks in SQL statements. Checking the "Use ANSI nulls, paddings, and warnings" check box causes the SQL Server ODBC driver to enforce ANSI rules for handling null columns, padding trailing blanks on varchar fields, and issuing warnings on ANSI rule violations.

Finally, the "Use the failover SQL Server..." check box allows you to indicate a backup SQL Server system in case of the failure of a primary SQL Server system. If a Failover server has been defined for the primary SQL Server system and the "Use the failover SQL Server..." option has been enabled, when the ODBC driver connects to the primary server, it also retrieves the information needed to connect to the failover server. In the event that the connection to the primary SQL Server is lost, the ODBC driver ends the current transaction and then attempts to reestablish a connection to the Failover server.

Clicking the next button displays the SQL Server DSN Configuration Wizard dialog box shown in Figure 13-9. It specifies the language, character set, regional settings, and log files that will be used by the SQL Server ODBC driver. The first check box specifies which language will be used to display ODBC messages. This check box and its associated drop-down combo box will not be available if there is only one language installed on the connected SQL Server.

The next check box controls how the ODBC driver performs character set translation. Selecting the "Perform translation for character data" check box specifies that the ODBC

Figure 13-9. SQL Server DSN Configuration Wizard (screen 4)

driver will use Unicode to convert ANSI strings sent between the ODBC client and the SQL Server system. If this option is not selected, ANSI data is sent directly to SQL Server, which requires that the client and the SQL Server system use the same code page.

The "Use regional settings when outputting currency, numbers, dates and times" check box allows you to override the default settings that are specified in the SQL Server login information.

The "Use regional settings when outputting currency, numbers, dates and times" check box allows you to override the default settings specified in the SQL Server login information.

The next two check boxes allow you to set a maximum time in milliseconds for long-running queries and control whether the SQL Server ODBC driver will record driver statistics. If these options are enabled, they will record their activity in the files that are specified in the text boxes. The default settings disable both of these options.

Clicking the Finish button completes the SQL Server data source configuration and displays the confirmation dialog box shown in Figure 13-10. The next SQL Server DSN Configuration Wizard dialog box presents all the options that were selected during the data source configuration process. Clicking the OK button creates the new data source. If any of the values displayed on the confirmation windows are incorrect, you can click the Cancel button to display the prior SQL Server DSN Configuration Wizard screen. From there you can move through the series of dialog boxes by clicking the Next and Back buttons.

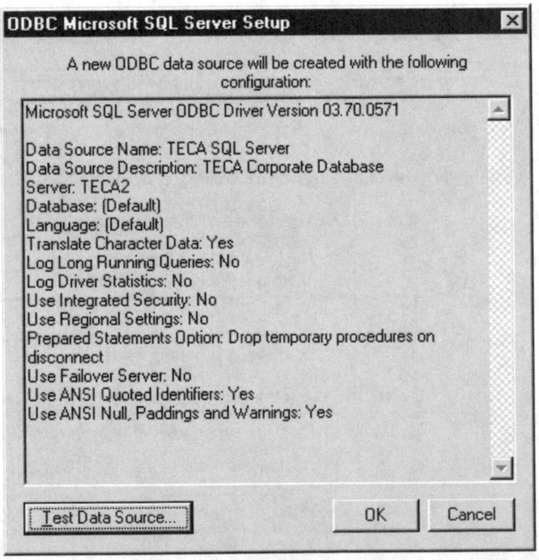

Figure 13-10. SQL Server DSN Configuration Wizard (screen 6)

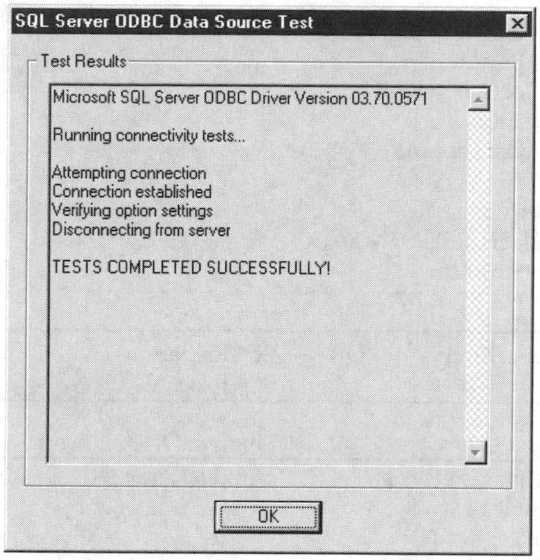

Figure 13-11. SQL Server DSN Configuration Wizard (screen 7)

Clicking the Test Data Source button makes a connection to the SQL Server and verifies the options settings. If the connection is not successful, an error message displays, identifying the error condition. Otherwise, if the connection is successful, the dialog box shown in Figure 13-11 is displayed.

After the SQL Server ODBC driver has been installed and a data source has been configured using the ODBC Administrator, you're ready to run off-the-shelf ODBC applications or to build your own custom ODBC client/server database applications.

Basic Use of the ODBC API

Using the ODBC API is more complicated than using the data control in conjunction with Visual Basic's built-in DAO methods. This is mainly due to the fact that you're calling functions in an external DLL. However, the performance improvements that can be achieved using the ODBC API usually make it worth the effort. When your application is using the ODBC API directly, it will be calling the functions contained in the ODBC Driver Manager (either the ODBC.DLL for 16-bit applications or the ODBC32.DLL for 32-bit applications). In order to use the ODBC API, you need to follow a certain order when calling the ODBC API functions. Figure 13-12 presents an overview of the ODBC API usage.

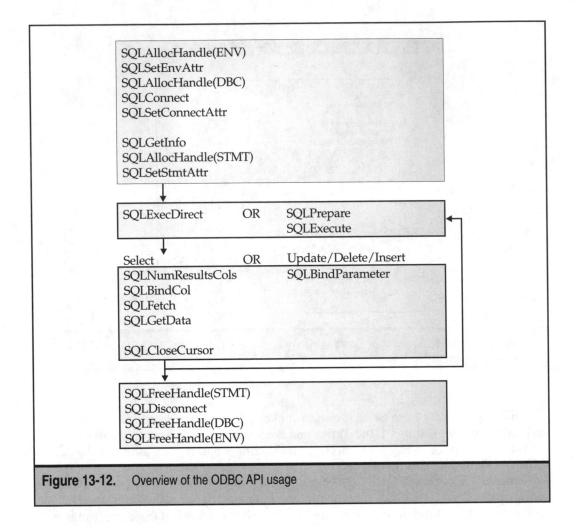

Figure 13-12. Overview of the ODBC API usage

It is important to realize that all ODBC applications must follow the same general ODBC API usage as that shown in Figure 13-12. This is true for both shrink-wrapped desktop applications like Word, Excel, and other ODBC-enabled applications, as well as for the ODBC client/server applications you write. Even though it may not be obvious, Word, MS Query, Excel Access, and all the other ODBC-enabled applications are making this same series of ODBC API calls as your own custom Visual Basic applications.

In Figure 13-12, as you can see, the first thing that must occur in all ODBC applications is calling the SQLAllocHandle function to create an environment handle. The environment handle is used by the ODBC Driver Manager to keep track of each ODBC connection and its state.

Next, the ODBC application must make a call to the SQLSetEnvAttr function. This function registers which version of the ODBC API is being used. If this function is not called, the ODBC driver assumes the application will be using the ODBC 2.0 calling conventions. If the SQLSetEnvAttr function is called using the SQL_ATTR_ODBC_VERSION environment attribute set to SQL_OV_ODBC3 (a value of 3), the ODBC driver knows the application will be using the ODBC 3.*x* calling conventions.

After the environment options have been set, all ODBC applications next must call the SQLAllocHandle function to create a database connection handle. When allocating a database connection handle, the SQLAllocHandle function associates the new database connection handle with the environment handle that was created earlier. The database handle is used to identify the driver that's used in a database connection.

Next, the SQLConnect function is used to start an ODBC connection to the database using the database handle that was returned by the previous SQLAllocHandle function. The SQLConnect function must supply the data source name and the login information required to connect to the target database. Either the SQLDriverConnect function or the SQLBrowseConnect function can be substituted for the SQLConnect function. The SQLDriverConnect function prompts the end user for the required data source connection information; the SQLBrowseConnect function returns a string to your application that identifies the missing connection information. The SQLDriverConnect function is typically used when the application doesn't provide all the required data source login information. The SQLBrowseConnect function is typically used to build custom login dialog boxes.

The last piece of ODBC initialization code is the call to the SQLAllocHandle function to create a statement handle. The statement handle is used to process SQL requests. After the statement handle has been allocated, the ODBC Driver Manager uses the statement handle to manage the state information of the ODBC connection. For instance, your application cannot fetch data before a select operation has been performed. It's the statement handle that allows the ODBC Driver Manager to know the current state of the ODBC statement and therefore also know the valid operations that can be performed at any given time.

After the statement handle has been assigned, your ODBC application can begin to use that statement handle to process SQL requests. This is where the real work of an ODBC application gets done. A typical ODBC application will process many SQL requests using the statement handle and then retrieve and process the results of those requests. The SQLExecute or SQLExecDirect functions are used to send SQL statements to the connected database. The SQLExecute function is used to execute prepared SQL or static SQL statements; the SQLExecDirect function is used for ad hoc or dynamic SQL statements. The SQLPrepare function must be used before the SQLExecute function can be used. The SQLExecute is typically used for SQL statements that will be performed repeatedly. The SQLExecDirect function is normally used for SQL statements that will only be performed once.

The SQLExecute and SQLExecuteDirect functions can process any SQL statement that's valid on the host database. If the SQL request is a Select operation, it will usually create a result set that contains the information that satisfies the SQL query. The result set is accessed using the SQLFetch function. For more information on building SQL statements, refer to Chapters 9 and 10.

When an ODBC application is ready to end, it must also perform cleanup steps to release the memory that was reserved for the various ODBC handles and then close the conversations that were started. As you have probably already guessed, there is a corresponding cleanup statement for each initialization statement. For instance, when an ODBC application terminates, it must first perform the SQLFreeHandle function for each statement handle that has been opened. Then, it must call the SQLDisconnect function for each open connection. Next, it must call the SQLFreeHandle function to release the memory reserved by each database connection handle. And, finally, the ODBC application must call the SQLFreeHandle function to release the memory reserved for the ODBC environment.

While at first this may seem somewhat complicated, these ODBC initialization and cleanup functions are very similar for all ODBC applications. Once you have defined them, you can basically cut and paste them into other ODBC applications.

ODBC Initialization Functions

Now that you've seen the basic rules of how to use the ODBC API, let's take a more detailed look at how to call the ODBC functions from Visual Basic.

ALLOCATING THE ENVIRONMENT   The SQLAllocHandle function is the first function that must be called by an ODBC 3.*x* application. As you can see in the following listing, the SQLAllocHandle function takes three parameters.

```
iResult% = SQLAllocHandle(SQL_HANDLE_ENV, SQL_NULL_HANDLE, henv&)
If iResult% <> SQL_SUCCESS Then
    'Error Handling
End If
```

The first parameter is a flag that identifies the type of handle being allocated. The SQL_HANDLE_ENV constant specifies that an ODBC environment handle will be allocated. The second parameter is used to identify the parent handle. Since the ODBC environment is the most basic ODBC handle, it has no parent handle and the SQL_NULL_HANDLE constant is used to specify a null handle. The third parameter is a long variable that contains the environment handle returned by the SQLAllocateHandle function.

The SQLAllocateHandle function returns an integer that indicates the success or failure of the function. A value of SQL_SUCCESS (0) indicates that the function call completed successfully; any other value indicates that there was an error.

FREEING THE ENVIRONMENT   The SQLFreeHandle function must be called to free the environment handle before the ODBC application terminates. The SQLFreeHandle function releases the memory and the handle that was allocated by the earlier SQLAllocateHandle function. The following code shows how to free an ODBC environment handle:

```
iResult% = SQLFreeHandle(SQL_HANDLE_ENV, ByVal henv&)
If iResult% <> SQL_SUCCESS Then
    'Error Handling
End If
```

The first parameter of the SQLFreeHandle function identifies the type of handle that will be freed. The SQL_HANDLE_ENV constant specifies that an ODBC environment handle will be freed. The second parameter is a long variable that contains the value of the ODBC environment handle that will be freed.

The SQLFreeHandle function returns an integer that indicates the status of the function call. A value of SQL_SUCCESS indicates that the call completed successfully.

Setting the Environment Attributes

After an ODBC environment has been allocated, the SQLSetEnvAttr function must be called to specify that you will be working with the ODBC 3.*x* API or the ODBC 2.*x* API. If you don't use the SQLSetEnvAttr function to explicitly set the environment to ODBC 3.*x*, the environment will default to the ODBC 2.*x* API set. This is to ensure maximum compatibility with existing ODBC applications that conform to the ODBC 2.*x* API. In addition to controlling the ODBC API level that the application will use, the SQLSetEnvAttr function can be used to set up connection pooling. Connection pooling is primarily intended to be used with middle-tier applications. It enables the ODBC connection to be kept open and later reused. This can improve the connection time required for subsequent applications. The following code shows how to set the environment attributes to support the ODBC 3.*x* API:

```
iResult% = SQLSetEnvAttr(henv&, SQL_ATTR_ODBC_VERSION, SQL_OV_ODBC3, 0)
If iResult% <> SQL_SUCCESS Then
'Error Handling
End If
```

The first parameter of the SQLSetEnvAttr function is a long variable that contains the environment handle. The second parameter contains a constant that specifies the type of environment attribute that will be set. The SQL_ATTR_ODBC_VERSION constant specifies that an ODBC version will be set. The third parameter is a constant that contains the version that will be used. The SQL_OV_ODBC3 constant specifies that ODBC API 3.*x* will be used. Finally, the last parameter specifies the length of the third parameter. It is only required when the third parameter contains a string. If it contains a numeric value, as the prior example shows, you can set the last parameter to 0.

Allocating a Database Connection Handle

After the ODBC environment handle has been created and the ODBC environment attributes have been set, the ODBC application can create a database connection handle using the SQLAllocHandle function. The following example shows how to create a database connection handle.

```
iResult% = SQLAllocHandle(SQL_HANDLE_DBC, ByVal henv&, hdbc&)
If iResult% <> SQL_SUCCESS Then
    'Error Handling
End If
```

Like the ODBC environment handle, the database connection handle is created using the SQLAllocHandle function. To create a database connection handle, you must set the first parameter of the SQLAllocHandle to the SQL_HANDLE_DBC constant. The next parameter contains the parent handle. In this case, the parent handle is the environment handle that was previously created. Finally, the third parameter returns the database connection handle that is created.

Again, the SQLAllocHandle function returns an integer that indicates the success or failure of the SQLAllocHandle function. If the SQL_SUCCESS constant is returned, the function is successful.

If the ODBC application needs to connect to multiple data sources, then multiple database connection handles can be created.

Freeing a Database Connection Handle

Every database connection handle created by an ODBC application must be freed before the application terminates. The following code illustrates how to free a database connection handle:

```
iResult% = SQLFreeHandle(SQL_HANDLE_DBC, ByVal hdbc&)
```

The first parameter of the SQLFreeHandle function indicates the type of handle that will be freed. The SQL_HANDLE_DBC constant specifies that a database connection handle will be freed. The second parameter contains the value of the database connection handle to be freed.

Connecting to a Data Source

After an ODBC application has created a database connection handle, the application can use that handle to make the physical connection to a data source. The most common methods of establishing a connection to an ODBC data source are using the SQLConnect or SQLDriverConnect functions. Both functions connect your application to a data source. The main difference is that the SQLConnect function is responsible for supplying all the information needed to make the connection, while the SQLDriverConnect function turns over the task of getting the connection information to the ODBC driver.

USING SQLCONNECT   The following code shows how to call the SQLConnect function to connect to a data source:

```
Dim sDSN As String, sUID As String, sPWD As String
sDSN = "TECA SQL Server"
sUID = "sa"
sPWD = "sapwd"
```

```
iResult% = SQLConnect(ByVal hdbc&, sDSN, Len(sDSN), sUID, Len(sUID), _
                    sPWD, Len(sPWD))
If iResult% <> SQL_SUCCESS And iResult% <> SQL_SUCCESS_WITH_INFO Then
    'Error Handling
End If
```

The first parameter of the SQLConnect function takes the database connection handle that was created earlier using the SQLAllocHandle function. The next set of parameters supplies the required login information. The second parameter is a string that contains the name of the data source that the application will use, and the third parameter is an integer that contains the length of the string containing the data source name. If the second parameter contains a valid data source name, the ODBC Driver Manager loads the corresponding driver and passes it the other connection parameters. If the data source parameter is a null pointer, invalid, or contains the name "DEFAULT," the ODBC Driver Manager uses the default data source defined in the ODBC Administrator. If a default data source does not exist, the SQLConnect function returns SQL_ERROR. The fourth parameter is a string that contains the user ID, and the fifth parameter is an integer containing the length of the user ID string. The sixth and seventh parameters are a string containing a password and an integer indicating the length of the password.

The SQLConnect function returns the value of SQL_SUCCESS or SQL_SUCCESS_WITH_INFO if a connection with the data source is successfully established.

USING SQLDRIVERCONNECT As you saw in the previous example, the SQLConnect function identified the data source and supplied the necessary login information. If your ODBC application isn't able to supply these values, you can use the SQLDriverConnect function to cause the ODBC driver to prompt for this information at run time. The following example shows how to call the SQLDriverConnect function.

```
Dim sInConnect, sOutConnect As String
sInConnect$ = "DSN="
sOutConnect$ = String$(1024, 0)
iResult% = SQLDriverConnect(ByVal hdbc&, ByVal hwnd&, _
    ByVal sInConnect$, Len(sInConnect$), ByVal sOutConnect$, _
    Len(sOutConnect$), iOutConnectLen%, _ SQL_DRIVER_COMPLETE)
If iResult% <> SQL_SUCCESS And iResult% <> SQL_SUCCESS_WITH_INFO Then
    'Error Handling
End If
```

Like the SQLConnect function, the first parameter of the SQLDriverConnect function is the database connection handle. The second parameter contains the Windows handle of the calling application or a null pointer if the window handle is not known. The third parameter contains a connection string.

The connection string can be empty, which causes the ODBC driver to prompt for all the connection information, or it can contain any or all of the connection information. If the connection string is supplied, it takes the following form:

```
keyword1=value;keyword2=value;keyword3=value
```

The following table lists the valid keywords for an ODBC 3.*x* connection string:

Keyword	Description
DSN	Name of a data source
FILEDSN	Name of a file data source (.dsn)
DRIVER	Name of a specific ODBC driver
UID	Login ID
PWD	Password for the login ID
SAVEFILE	Name of a file data source that will contain the saved connection information

An example connection string that would supply all the required login information for SQL Server could be as follows:

```
DSN=MySQLServer;UID=MyLoginID;PWD=MyPwd
```

The DSN keyword points to the value of a data source name that has been previously configured using the ODBC Administrator. The UID keyword identifies the login ID that will be used when the data source connection is established. The PWD keyword precedes the password associated with the login ID. If the values for these keywords are omitted, as they were in the previous code example, or they are invalid, the ODBC driver displays a dialog box that prompts the user for the required connection information.

The fourth parameter of the SQLDriverConnect function is an integer that contains the length of the connection string. The fifth parameter is a string that contains the completed connection string that's returned by the ODBC driver following a successful connection. This string should be sized to a minimum of 1,024 to contain the completed connection string. The sixth parameter is an integer that contains the length of the completed connection string. The seventh is returned by the SQLDriverConnect function and is a pointer to the length of the completed connection string. The last parameter is an integer that specifies if the ODBC driver is to prompt for additional connection information. The SQL_DRIVER_COMPLETE constant indicates that if the information contained in the connection is not adequate to make a connection, the driver will display a dialog box to collect the required connection information.

Disconnecting from a Data Source

Your ODBC application must disconnect from each connected data source before the application terminates. The following code illustrates how to disconnect from a data source using the SQLDisconnect function:

```
iResult% = SQLDisconnect(hdbc&)
```

The SQLDisconnect function takes as input the database connection handle and returns an integer indicating the success or failure of the function call.

Allocating a Statement Handle

After the ODBC environment and database connection handles have been allocated and the data source is connected, allocating a statement handle is the last required ODBC initialization code. The following example shows how to create an ODBC statement handle using the SQLAllocHandle function:

```
iResult% = SQLAllocHandle(SQL_HANDLE_STMT, ByVal hdbc&, hstmt&)
If iResult% <> SQL_SUCCESS Then
    ' Error Handling
    End
End If
```

The first parameter of the SQLAllocHandle function takes a constant that indicates the type of handle that will be allocated. The SQL_HANDLE_STMT constant specifies that an ODBC statement handle will be allocated. The second parameter identifies the parent handle. For an ODBC statement handle, the parent handle is the database connection handle. Finally, the last parameter is the statement handle associated with the ODBC statement handle.

The SQLAllocHandle function returns an integer that indicates the success or failure of the SQLAllocHandle function. If the SQL_SUCCESS constant is returned, the function is successful.

Freeing a Statement Handle

Like the environment handle and the database connection handle, all the ODBC statement handles allocated by an ODBC application must be free before the application terminates. However, unlike the environment handle and the database connection handle, which both use the SQLFreeHandle function, to free a statement handle you can use either the SQLFreeHandle or the SQLFreeStmt function.

USING SQLFREESTMT The SQLFreeStmt function can close a cursor that's used by a statement handle, it can unbind the parameters associated with a given statement handle, or it can free all the resources used by an ODBC statement handle. The following code shows you an example of calling the SQLFreeStmt function:

```
iResult% = SQLFreeStmt(hstmt&, SQL_CLOSE)
```

The first parameter of the SQLFreeStmt function is the statement handle that was created earlier by the SQLAllocHandle function. The second parameter is an integer that controls the type of free statement operation that is performed. The SQL_CLOSE constant closes an open cursor that's associated with a statement handle. Other commonly used constants are SQL_UNBIND, SQL_RESET_PARAMS, and SQL_DROP. The SQL_UNBIND constant frees all the columns that have been bound using the SQLBindParameter function. The SQL_RESET_PARAMS constant releases all the parameters that have been bound to a statement handle using the SQLBindParameter function. The SQL_DROP constant causes the SQLFreeStmt function to free all the resources associated with the statement.

USING SQLFREEHANDLE   The SQLFreeHandle function can also be used to free an ODBC statement handle. The SQLFreeHandle function doesn't have the same degree of control offered by the SQLFreeStmt function. Essentially, the SQLFreeHandle function is equivalent to the SQLFreeStmt function using the SQL_DROP constant. Using the SQLFreeHandle function is the preferred method of freeing all the resources used by an ODBC statement handle. This function is typically used as a part of the process that terminates your application. The added flexibility offered by the SQLFreeStmt option makes it a better choice for other uses. The following code example shows how to call the SQLFreeHandle function to free a statement handle:

```
iResult% = SQLFreeHandle(SQL_HANDLE_STMT, ByVal hstmt&)
```

The first parameter of the SQLFreeHandle function indicates the type of handle that will be freed. The SQL_HANDLE_STMT constant specifies that a statement handle will be freed. The second parameter is the handle of the statement to be freed.

> **TIP:** Most ODBC applications also make use of the SQLGetInfo function call during initialization. While the SQLGetInfo function is not a required function, it can be useful to retrieve information about the capabilities of the ODBC driver. In addition, the SQLTables and SQLColumns functions are often used to retrieve information about the tables and columns in a database.

Retrieving Data Using the ODBC API

The previous section covered the ODBC initialization and termination functions required by all ODBC applications. In this next section, you'll see some of the basic ODBC data access functions used to retrieve, insert, and update information from an ODBC data source.

SQL is at the heart of ODBC data access. SQL statements are sent from the ODBC application to the data source using a statement handle that was previously created using the SQLAllocHandle function. An ODBC application can send any valid SQL command to the host database. SQL Statements are executed by an ODBC application using either dynamic SQL statements or prepared SQL statements. Dynamic SQL is executed by using the SQLExecDirect function; prepared SQL is executed by using a combination of the SQLPrepare and SQLExecute functions.

Retrieving Data with Dynamic SQL with SQLExecDirect

Dynamic SQL is executed using the SQLExecDirect function. The SQLExecDirect function evaluates the SQL statement and builds the data access path at the time the SQLExecDirect function is executed.

The SQL Select statement is probably the most fundamental SQL operation, so retrieving information from an ODBC data source using the SQL Select statement is the first type of ODBC data access that this chapter covers. One of the biggest strengths of ODBC lies in its ability to perform ad hoc queries, joining multiple files and retrieving dynamic sets of data. The SQL Select statement is the workhorse of these types of ad hoc queries. The following code example shows how you can use the SQLExecDirect function to issue a SQL Select statement to retrieve a specific set of rows from a table:

```
sSQL$ = "Select * from authors where state = 'OR'"
iResult% = SQLExecDirect(hstmt&, sSql$, Len(sSql$))
If iResult% <> SQL_SUCCESS Then
        ' Error Handling
End If
```

First, the SQL Select statement is assigned to a string variable. In this case, the string assigned to the variable sSQL$ selects all the rows in the table named "authors," where the value of the column named "state" is equal to the OR constant. Next, the SQLExecDirect function executes this SQL statement on the host database. The first parameter of the SQLExecDirect function is an ODBC statement handle that was created earlier using the SQLAllocHandle function. Following the statement handle, the next parameter contains the SQL statement and the third parameter is an integer that contains the length of the SQL statement that will be executed.

> **NOTE:** SQL statements that are run using SQLExecDirect do not include variables. All data selection criteria is coded in the SQL string using literals. For instance, in the preceding example, only the rows where the state column contains the literal value OR will be selected. If you wanted to select a set of rows where the state column contained a different value, you would need to reformulate a new string containing a SQL Select statement that used a different literal value. Then you would issue a new SQLExecDirect statement.

The SQLExecDirect function returns an integer that reports the success or failure of the operation. If the SQLExecDirect function was successfully executed on the host database, a result set containing the data that satisfied the SQL Select operation is created and the SQLExecDirect function returns SQL_SUCCESS (0). You can see how to process the result set a little later in this chapter. If the function failed because the SQL was invalid, because the user did not have authorization to the requested objects, or for some other reason, the SQLExecDirect function usually returns SQL_ERROR (-1). Your application can use the return code and the SQLGetDiagRec function to determine the cause of various errors. ODBC error handling and the SQLGetDiagRec function are also discussed later in this chapter.

Using Prepared SQL Statements with SQLExecute

The ability to dynamically build and execute SQL statements gives ODBC applications tremendous flexibility. However, the price you pay for that flexibility is performance.

Evaluating the SQL statement and building the required data access path each time the SQLExecDirect function is executed means that the application must wait for all of these operations to complete before the results can be returned to the end user. For ad hoc query situations where the SQL statements vary significantly for each database query, there really isn't a whole lot that your ODBC application can do to improve this. However, for applications that perform a predefined set of SQL statements or for applications that perform repeated SQL statements, the SQLPrepare and SQLExecute functions offer a powerful combination of flexibility and performance. The SQLPrepare function takes care of much of the overhead that's required to execute a SQL statement on the host database. The SQL statement is evaluated and the cursor is opened when the SQLPrepare function is called. This leaves the SQLExecute function the task of just running the already prepared SQL statement.

Using the SQLPrepare and SQLExecute combination doesn't offer significant gains for SQL statements that are issued only once. The time required to execute a single SQLExecDirect function and one iteration of the SQLPrepare and SQLExecute functions is roughly equivalent because both methods must perform the same steps. However, the combination of SQLPrepare and SQLExecute offers very significant performance improvements for SQL statements that are issued multiple times. The SQLPrepare statement only needs to be issued once, which takes care of the overhead of parsing the SQL statement and opening a cursor. Later, the faster SQLExecute statement can be run as many times as it needs to be. Moving the overhead of the cursor open to the SQLPrepare statement makes repeated execution of the SQLExecute statement much faster than repeated execution of the SQLExecDirect function.

The following example shows how to issue the SQLPrepare and SQLExecute functions in Visual Basic:

```
sSql$ = "Select * from authors where state = ?"
'Prepare the SQL statement
iResult% = SQLPrepare(hstmt&, sSql$, Len(sSql$))
If iResult% <> SQL_SUCCESS Then
        'Error Handling
End If
'Bind the parameter
iResult% = SQLBindParameter(ByVal hstmt&, 1, SQL_PARAM_INPUT, _
    SQL_C_CHAR, SQL_CHAR,  4, 0, sState, 4, lState)
If iResult% <> SQL_SUCCESS Then
    'Error Handling
End If

 'Run the prepared SQL statement using the statement handle
iResult% = SQLExecute(hstmt&)
If iResult% <> SQL_SUCCESS Then
        'Error Handling
End If
```

Using the combination of the SQLPrepare and SQLExecute functions is quite similar to the SQLExecDirect function you saw earlier. First, a SQL statement is assigned to a string variable. Next, the SQLPrepare function is executed. The SQLPrepare statement takes exactly the same parameters that the SQLExecDirect function requires. The first parameter is the ODBC statement handle. The second parameter is the string containing the SQL to be executed, and the third parameter is the length of the SQL string. However, it's important to note that the SQLPrepare statement doesn't actually run the SQL statement against the data source. It just does all the work to get the SQL statement ready to be run.

> **NOTE:** SQL Statements executed with SQLPrepare and SQLExecute can include variables—otherwise known as *parameters*. Parameters are associated with the SQL statements using the SQLBindParameter function.

Next, in the preceding example you can see that the SQL uses a question mark (?) instead of a literal OR. After the SQLPrepare function has successfully completed, the SQLExecute function can be called to actually perform the SQL statement. The SQLExecute function only takes a single parameter, the ODBC statement handle. This must be the same ODBC statement handle that was used with the earlier SQLPrepare function. After the SQLExecute function has successfully completed, a result set containing the data to satisfy the SQL request will be available to the ODBC applications.

Working with Result Sets

Now that you've seen how to issue SQL Select requests to the data source, the next step is to retrieve the result sets created by the SQL requests back to your application. The SQLFetch function is the basic ODBC function that allows you to traverse a results set. There are two different ways of retrieving the data in a result set: you can either work with each element of the result set individually using the SQLGetData function, or you can use the SQLBindCol function to bind selected columns to program variables.

USING UNBOUND COLUMNS AND SQLGETDATA   After the SQL statement that generates a result set has been executed using either the SQLExecDirect or the SQLPrepare and SQLExecute pair, a result set containing data is returned to your application. Using unbound columns and the SQLGetData function is probably the most straightforward method of working with a result set in Visual Basic because you don't have to deal with any of Visual Basic's memory management issues. However, as you'll see as you go through the next two examples, using the SQLGetData function requires more code and isn't quite as clean a solution as using bound parameters. The following example illustrates how you can use a combination of SQLFetch and SQLGetData to retrieve the data from an ODBC result set:

```
'Determine the number of columns in the result set
iResult% = SQLNumResultCols(hstmt&, iNbrColumns%)
```

```
If iResult% <> SQL_SUCCESS Then
     'Error handling
End If

'Fetch all the rows in the result set
Do While SQLFetch(hstmt&) <> SQL_NO_DATA_FOUND
sRecord$ = ""
    'Loop through all of the columns in the result set
    For i% = 1 To iNbrColumns%
        iResult% = SQLGetData(ByVal hstmt&, i%, SQL_CHAR, sBuffer, _
            Len(sBuffer), lBufferLen&)
        ' Add each column to the sRecord string separated by Tabs
        sRecord$ = record$ & Chr$(9) & Left$(buffer, bufferLen&)
    Next i%
```

To retrieve the data in an unbound result set, the first ODBC function you would need to call is the SQLNumResultCols function that, as the name suggests, returns the number of columns in the result set. The SQLNumResultCols function takes two parameters. The first parameter is the statement handle that was used by the earlier SQLExecDirect or SQLExecute function. The second parameter is an integer that contains the number of columns in the result set. Again, like virtually all of the other ODBC functions, the SQLNumResultCols function returns an integer that indicates the success or failure of the function call.

Next, the SQLFetch function is used to retrieve each row of the result set. Each successful call of the SQLFetch function retrieves one row of the result set. The SQLFetch function uses the statement handle that was used in the earlier SQLExecDirect or SQLExecute functions. For each successful call, the SQLFetch function returns the value of SQL_SUCCESS. When the SQLFetch function has retrieved the last row from the result set, the SQLFetch function returns the value SQL_NO_DATA_FOUND (100).

In the preceding example, you can see that following each SQLFetch function, the SQLGetData function is called in the middle of a For-Next loop. The SQLGetData function is performed for each column in the result set. The SQLGetData function takes the value of a given column and moves it into a program value. The SQLGetData function takes six parameters. Like the other ODBC data retrieval functions, the first parameter of the SQLGetData function is the statement handle. This must be the same statement handle that was used by the SQLFetch operation. The second parameter is an integer that contains the value of the column from which the SQLGetData function will extract the data.

TIP: When using the SQLGetData function, the column numbering in the result set starts at 1. In addition, the result set columns must generally be accessed in ascending order.

The third parameter indicates the SQL data type of the column. The fourth parameter is a buffer that contains the column value following the successful completion of the SQLGetData function. The fifth parameter is an input parameter that contains the length of the fourth parameter, and the sixth parameter is an output parameter that will contain the length of the data that's retrieved by the SQLGetData function.

USING BOUND COLUMNS AND SQLBINDCOL   While working with unbound columns is a bit more straightforward in Visual Basic, working with bound columns requires less coding and is usually a preferred method of retrieving the data from the columns returned in a result set. However, Visual Basic's limited ability to deal with pointers makes this solution a bit trickier than using SQLGetData with unbound columns. As you'll see in the following example, the SQLBindCol function takes a pointer to a variable as one of its parameters, and it expects the location in memory of the variable to remain the same from the time the SQLBindCol function is executed and the later SQLFetch is performed. For C applications this isn't a problem; however, Visual Basic takes the liberty of moving string variables in memory, which means that their location may change, causing the SQLBindCol function to fail. One way to address this problem is to use a Byte array in the SQLBindCol function instead of a string variable. The following code shows how to use the SQLBindCol function with a byte array to retrieve the data from a result set.

```
Dim bBuffer(256) As Byte
Dim lBufferLen As Long

iResult% = SQLBindCol(hstmt&, 1, SQL_C_CHAR, bBuffer(0), _
    256, lBufferLen)

Do While SQLFetch(ByVal hstmt&) <> SQL_NO_DATA_FOUND
        List1.AddItem ByteArray2String(bBuffer())
Loop
```

As you can see, the parameters for the SQLBindCol function are very similar to the parameters that were used on the SQLGetData function. The first parameter of the SQLBindCol function is the statement handle. This must be the same statement handle that was used on the earlier SQLExecDirect or SQLExecute statement. The second parameter is the number of the column in the result set. The third parameter is the column data type. The fourth parameter is a pointer to the buffer that will contain the column data. This is passed as the first element of the byte array.

TIP: When passing byte arrays as parameters to an external function, always pass the function the first element of the array using the (0) index.

The fifth parameter is an input parameter that contains the length of the buffer, and the sixth parameter is an output parameter that will contain the actual length of the data returned when the SQLFetch is completed.

You can see in this example that there's no need to explicitly move the data after each SQLFetch function. The SQLBindCol function automatically performs the specified data conversion and fills the bound variable—in this case a byte array—with the values from the specified column.

However, there is one additional consideration when working with byte arrays. Visual Basic stores the byte array in Unicode format, and you will probably need to convert the Unicode byte array to a Visual Basic string before your ODBC application can use the character data. The ByteArray2String function that was called in the previous example is shown here:

```
Private Function ByteArray2String(bArray() As String

    Dim sString As String
    Dim nStringLen As Integer

    'Convert the string to Unicode
    sString = StrConv(bArray(), vbUnicode)
    nStringLen = InStr(sString, Chr(0)) - 1

    'Return the Unicode string
    ByteArray2String = Left(sString, nStringLen)

End Function
```

This function takes the byte array as input and uses the Visual Basic StrConv function to convert the Unicode byte array to ASCII. The resulting string is then searched for the Null character (which is the C language string termination character) and then truncates the returned string at the Null character.

Updating Data Using ODBC

Just as you can perform SQL Select statements using either dynamic or static SQL, you can also use the same SQLExecDirect or SQLPrepare and SQLExecute functions to perform other SQL statements. You choose between the SQLExecDirect, and SQLPrepare and SQLExecute functions using the same criteria that applied to the Select statement. If the SQL statement is performed only once, you would typically want to use the SQLExecDirect function. If the SQL statement is issued multiple times and/or you want to pass in different parameters to the SQL statement, you would want to use the SQLPrepare and SQLExecute statements. In the following section you see how to issue some basic SQL statements to insert, update, and delete rows using prepared statements and an open cursor.

Inserting Rows

The ODBC API code for inserting rows is conceptually very similar to the code that was used to retrieve data. First, your ODBC application must have performed all the required ODBC initialization steps, including allocating a statement handle. Next, the SQL statement is prepared using the SQLPrepare function, and any parameters used by the statement are bound using the SQLBindParameter statement. Finally, the SQL statement is executed using the SQLExecute function. The primary difference is in the SQL statement itself. Instead of using the Select statement, you use an Insert statement. The following code example shows how you can insert data using ODBC:

```
'Prepare the Insert statement
 sSql$ = "Insert into department values (?, ?)"
 iResult% = SQLPrepare(hstmt&, sSql$, Len(sSql$))
 If iResult% <> SQL_SUCCESS Then
   'Error Handling
 End If


'Bind the parameters
 iResult% = SQLBindParameter(ByVal hstmt&, 1, SQL_PARAM_INPUT, _
     SQL_C_LONG, SQL_DECIMAL, 4, 0, Dep_ID, 4, lpLenDep_ID)
 If iResult% <> SQL_SUCCESS Then
   'Error Handling
 End If
 iResult% = SQLBindParameter(ByVal hstmt&, 2, SQL_PARAM_INPUT, _
     SQL_C_CHAR, SQL_CHAR, 25, 0, bDep_Name, 25, lpLenDep_Name)
 If iResult% <> SQL_SUCCESS Then
    'Error Handling
 End If
' Now Execute the Insert statement
 iResult% = SQLExecute(ByVal hstmt&)
 If iResult% <> SQL_SUCCESS Then
    'Error Handling
 End If
```

The first step to insert data using the ODBC API is to assign a SQL Insert statement to a string. Not surprisingly, the SQL statement for inserting rows is an Insert statement. Again, you can refer to Chapters 9 and 10 for more information about writing SQL statements. The important thing to notice about this Insert statement is the two parameter markers used as placeholders for the variables that will be passed into this statement when it is executed.

Next, the SQLBindParameter is used to bind each of the two parameters to program variables. The SQLBindParameter function is very much like the SQLBindCol function you saw earlier. The first parameter is the statement handle that was used in the SQLPrepare function. The next parameter is the parameter number of the SQL statement where 1 indicates the first parameter, 2 indicates the second parameter, and so on. The third parameter is an integer that indicates whether the parameter is an input, output, or input/output parameter. The fourth parameter specifies the PC data type of the parameter used in the ODBC application, and the fifth parameter specifies the SQL data type used in the database. The ODBC driver is responsible for converting the parameter data between these two data types when the SQLExecute function is called. The sixth parameter is an integer that specifies the column size of the data. The seventh parameter indicates the number of decimal digits. As you might expect, this should always be 0 for character parameters or for parameters that contain whole numbers. The eighth parameter is a pointer to a buffer that contains the data that will be used in the parameter. The ninth parameter is an input parameter that contains the length of the parameter data used in the eighth parameter. Finally, the tenth parameter is a pointer to the length of the data buffer.

TIP: The parameter markers that are bound to an ODBC statement handle remain in effect until the statement is closed using the SQLFreeStmt with the SQL_DROP option or the statement parameters are reset using the SQL_RESET_PARAMS option.

You need to run a SQLBindParameter statement for each parameter marker that's used in the SQL statement. In the preceding example, the SQL Insert statement uses two parameter markers; therefore, the application needs to run the SQLBindParameter function twice—once for each parameter. After all the required parameter markers have been bound, you can execute the SQL statement using the SQLExecute function and insert the data into the database.

Deleting Rows

Deleting rows from an ODBC data source using prepared SQL follows exactly the same sequence of events you just saw for the Insert statement. First, the SQL statement plus any parameter markers are put into a string. Then the parameters are bound to program variables using the SQLBindParameter statement. Finally, the SQL statement is executed using the SQLExecute command. The following code sample shows how you can delete rows using ODBC:

```
'Prepare the Delete statement
sSql$ = "Delete from department where Dep_ID = ?"
iResult% = SQLPrepare(hstmt&, sSql$, Len(sSql$))
If iResult% <> SQL_SUCCESS Then
    'Error Handling
End If
'Bind the parameters
iResult% = SQLBindParameter(ByVal hstmt&, 1, SQL_PARAM_INPUT, _
           SQL_C_LONG, SQL_CHAR, 4, 0, Dep_ID, 4, lpLenDep_ID)
If iResult% <> SQL_SUCCESS Then
    'Error Handling
End If
iResult% = SQLExecute(ByVal hstmt&)
If iResult% <> SQL_SUCCESS Then
    'Error Handling
End If
```

As you can see, the ODBC functions used to perform the delete operation are virtually identical to the ODBC functions that were used to perform the insert operation. The primary difference is in the SQL statement itself. In this example, the Delete statement takes a single parameter—which in this example happens to be the primary key of the department file. Since there is only one parameter marker used with this SQL Delete statement, the code only needs to use a single SQLBindParameter function. Again, the actual delete operation is performed when the SQLExecute function is called.

> **TIP:** Use multiple statement handles for SQL statements that use different parameters. If the ODBC API application needs to perform a variety of different SQL statements, where each statement requires a different set of parameters, one of the easiest ways to handle this is to use multiple statements. In this scenario each statement would have its own set of parameter bindings.

Updating Rows

Updating rows using ODBC-prepared statements and a cursor uses the same set of ODBC functions you saw in the earlier insert and delete operations. Again, the primary difference is in the SQL statement itself and the parameters that must be bound. The following example shows how you can update a set of columns using the ODBC API:

```
'Prepare the Update statement
sSql$ = "update DEPARTMENT Set Dep_Name = ? where Dep_ID = ?"
result% = SQLPrepare(hstmt&, sql$, Len(sql$))
If result% <> SQL_SUCCESS Then
     'Error handling
End If


'Assign the parameter values
nDep_ID = CLng(Text_DeptNumber.Text)
'Convert the string to a byte array for parameter binding
String2ByteArray bDep_Name, Text_DeptDesc.Text

' Setup the binding lengths
lpLenDep_ID = 4
lpLenDep_Name = 25


'Bind the parameters
result% = SQLBindParameter(ByVal hstmt&, 1, SQL_PARAM_INPUT, _
    SQL_C_CHAR, SQL_CHAR, 25, 0, bDep_Name(0), 25, lpLenDep_Name)
If result% <> SQL_SUCCESS Then
    'Error Handling
End If
```

```
result% = SQLBindParameter(ByVal hstmt&, 2, SQL_PARAM_INPUT, _
    SQL_C_LONG, SQL_DECIMAL, 4, 0, nDep_ID, 4, lpLenDep_ID)
If result% <> SQL_SUCCESS Then
    'Error Handling
End If

result% = SQLExecute(ByVal hstmt&)
If result% <> SQL_SUCCESS Then
    'Error handling
End If
```

The SQL Update statement updates the column named Dep_Name with the value of the first parameter marker, where the value of the column named Dep_ID is equal to the value that's used in the second parameter marker. In this case, since the column Dep_ID is a unique key, the SQL statement updates only one record. However, the Update statement has the potential to update any number of rows that meet the selection criteria specified in the Where clause.

In an earlier example in this chapter, you saw how the ByteArray2String function was used to extract the contents of a Byte Array returned in a parameter and place the value into a String variable. The parameterized Update example illustrated here has exactly the opposite requirement. The contents of a String variable must be moved into a Byte Array before the Update operation is performed. The String2ByteArray helper function performs that task. The following code listing shows the source code of the String2ByteArray function:

```
Private Function String2ByteArray(bArray() As Bytem, sString As String)

    Dim nStringLen As Integer
    Dim i As Integer

    'Move each element of sString to bArray
    For i = 0 To Len(sString) - 1
        bArray(i) = Asc(Mid(sString, i + 1, 1))
    Next i

    'Zero out all remaining array items
    For i = Len(sString) To UBound(bArray)
        bArray(i) = 0
    Next i

End Function
```

Like the insert and delete operations that were covered earlier, the update function first prepares the statement using the SQLPrepare function. Then the SQLBindParameter statement is called twice, once for each parameter marker. Finally, the Update statement is executed when the SQLExecute function is called. Like the previous examples, it's important that the statement handle that's used in the SQLPrepare matches the statement handle that's used in the later SQLBindParameter and SQLExecute operations.

Data Concurrency

Data concurrency is one of the primary issues that's raised when updating multiuser databases like SQL Server. When a row is retrieved by a SQLFetch operation, there is typically no lock placed on the selected row. If multiple users are concurrently updating a database, it's possible that more than one user can simultaneously retrieve the same row for update. If this situation occurs with no mechanism to enforce data concurrency, the first user's updates will be wiped out by any updates made by the second user. There are two primary methods of implementing data concurrency using SQL Server 7. You can either use a data-coding technique known as *optimistic record locking*, or you can take advantage of the new row-locking feature of SQL Server 7.

OPTIMISTIC RECORD LOCKING   One common method of ensuring data concurrency is through the use of optimistic record locking. Optimistic concurrency is implemented by checking column values for updated values before allowing the update operation. For example, consider the following simple SQL Update operation:

```
Update department Set Dep_Name = ? Where Dep_ID = ?
```

This Update statement has no provisions for data concurrency, and the Dep_Name column will always be set by the user who was the last one to execute the Update statement. Using optimistic concurrency, this SQL Update operation might be changed as follows:

```
Update department Set Dep_Name = ? Where Dep_ID = ? And Dep_Name = ?
```

In this example, the And clause provides a mechanism for checking if the Dep_Name column has been modified since the time the data was retrieved. The value that's used in the And clause would be the value of the Dep_Name column as it was originally retrieved. If another user updated the Dep_Name column of this particular row, this Update statement would fail because the Dep_Name field is no longer equal to the value that was retrieved earlier. While implementing optimistic data concurrency using the And clause seems like a good solution for this problem, not all Update operations are as simple as this example. It doesn't take much imagination to see what would happen to this Update statement if it needed to deal with 40 or 50 columns. This solution would quickly turn unwieldy.

One alternative solution to this problem is to add a timestamp column to your tables. Using the timestamp to implement optimistic concurrency would require a SQL Update statement like the following:

```
Update department Set Dep_Name = ? Where Dep_ID = ? And Time_Stamp = ?
```

With this type of implementation, it doesn't matter how many columns are updated—your SQL Update statement only needs to add a single And clause. However, implementing optimistic record locking using timestamps requires the ability to alter your table structure, and not all ODBC applications have this luxury.

Calling Stored Procedures

Calling stored procedures is very much like executing prepared SQL statements. However, unlike using ODBC–prepared statements that are essentially made when the program executes, stored procedures must exist before they are called. You can create SQL Server stored procedures using just a simple text editor; however, the most common way to make them is using the Microsoft SQL Server Query Analyzer.

Figure 13-14 illustrates how to create a simple stored procedure to insert records using the Query Analyzer. The spInsert stored procedure inserts rows into the table called "department." This stored procedure takes two parameters. The first is an integer that corresponds to the first column in the table, and the second is a 25-byte character field that corresponds to the second column in the table.

Unlike Insert, Update, and Delete, prepared statements using ODBC cursors that were covered earlier, a SQL Server stored procedure is compiled the first time it is run and a stored procedure object is maintained in the database. Also, unlike ODBC

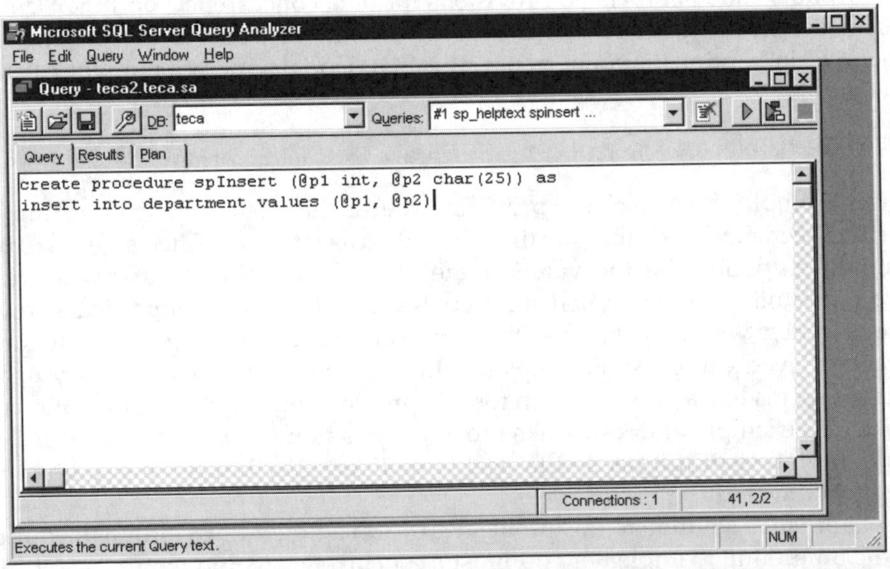

Figure 13-13. Creating a stored procedure to insert records

statements that were created using prepared statements, stored procedures continue to exist in the database after the client program terminates.

TIP: You can use the SQL Server–supplied sp_stored_procedures stored procedure to list the stored procedures for a given database. In addition, you can use the sp_helptext stored procedure to see the Transact-SQL source code of an existing stored procedure.

While the sequence of ODBC function calls required to execute stored procedures are very similar to the ODBC function calls required for an ODBC cursor, there are differences. The following example illustrates the Visual Basic code required to prepare an ODBC statement handle that will be used to call the stored procedure named spInsert.

```
result% = SQLAllocStmt(ByVal dbHandle&, hstmt2&)
If result% <> SQL_SUCCESS Then
    'Error Handling
End If


'Prepare the SP statememt handle
sql$ = "{Call spInsert (?, ?)}"
result% = SQLPrepare(hstmt&, sql$, Len(sql$))
If result% <> SQL_SUCCESS Then
    'Error Handling
End If
```

As you can see, the process to allocate and prepare the ODBC statement follows the same pattern you saw earlier in the example that used an ODBC cursor. The primary difference is in the SQL statement that is prepared. The SQL Call statement is used to invoke the stored procedure. The name of the stored procedure follows the Call keyword. Then, parameter markers are used for all the parameters used by the stored procedure.

TIP: The user of the ODBC client application must have EXECUTE rights on the stored procedure in order to be able to perform the SQL Call statement.

The Visual Basic code that's required to bind the parameters and execute the statement is virtually the same as the code you saw used earlier with ODBC prepared statements.

```
Dim lDep_ID As Long
Dim bDep_Name(25) As Byte

Dim lpLenDep_ID As Long
Dim lpLenDep_Name As Long

'Assign the parameter values
lDep_ID = 0
lDep_ID = CLng(Text_DeptNumber.Text)
```

```
'convert the string to a byte array for parameter binding
StringToByteArray bDep_Name, Text_DeptDesc.Text

' Setup the binding lengths
lpLenDep_ID = 4
lpLenDep_Name = 25

'Bind the parameters
result% = SQLBindParameter(ByVal hstmt&, 1, SQL_PARAM_INPUT, _
    SQL_C_LONG, SQL_INTEGER, 4, 0, lDep_ID, 4, lpLenDep_ID)
If result% <> SQL_SUCCESS Then
    'Error Handling
End If

result% = SQLBindParameter(ByVal hstmt&, 2, SQL_PARAM_INPUT, _
    SQL_C_CHAR, SQL_CHAR, 25, 0, bDep_Name(0), 25, lpLenDep_Name)
If result% <> SQL_SUCCESS Then
    'Error Handling
End If

result% = SQLExecute(ByVal hstmt&)
If result% <> SQL_SUCCESS Then
    'Error Handling
End If
```

The ODBC functions required to bind local variables and execute the SQL Call statement are virtually the same as the functions required to execute a standard prepared statement. In the previous example, you can see that the local variables are declared in the beginning of the code section. Again, a byte string is used for the string variables to get around Visual Basic's predisposition to move string variables in memory. Next, since the spInsert stored procedure uses two parameters, the SQLBindParameter function is called twice. Finally, after the parameters have been bound, the spInsert stored procedure is actually called when the SQLExecute function is called.

ODBC Error Handling and SQLGetDiagRec

The first place that ODBC errors are reported is in the return code that's issued by each of the different ODBC functions. However, the return code by itself doesn't offer a lot of information. Instead, the primary source of additional information about ODBC errors is the SQLGetDiagRec function. ODBC applications would typically call the SQLGetDiagRec function when an ODBC function call doesn't return the value of SQL_SUCCESS (0). The following code shows how to call the SQLGetDiagRec function:

```
Function DisplayODBCError(hstmt&) As Integer
    Dim sSqlState$
    Dim sSqlErrorMsg$
    Dim iSqlErrorMsgLen%
    Dim lSqlErrorCode&
    Dim sSqlErrorStr$
    Dim iResult%
    Dim iResponse%

    sSqlState$ = String$(16, 0)
    sSqlErrorMsg$ = String$(SQL_MAX_MESSAGE_LENGTH - 1, 0)

    Do
iRecNbr = iRecNbr + 1
iResult% = SQLGetDiagRec(SQL_HANDLE_STMT, hstmt&, iRecNbr%,
            sSqlState$, lSqlErrorCode&, sSqlErrorMsg$, _
            Len(sSqlErrorMsg$), isqlErrorMsgLen)

If iResult% = SQL_SUCCESS Or iResult% = SQL_SUCCESS_WITH_INFO Then
        If iSqlErrorMsgLen% = 0 Then
            MsgBox "No additional information", vbOKOnly
        Else
            MsgBox sSqlErrorStr$ & Left$(sSqlErrorMsg$, _
                            iSqlErrorMsgLen%), vbOKOnly
        End If
    End If
    Loop Until result <> SQL_SUCCESS

End Function
```

This example illustrates how to build a generic ODBC error-handling function in Visual Basic. The DisplayODBCError function uses the SQLGetDiagRec function to retrieve all the ODBC errors associated with a given ODBC statement handle and then displays those errors in a message. This function relies on the calling routine to pass in the appropriate statement handle.

The first part of this function declares the working variables used in the function. Next, a Visual Basic DO loop is used to execute the SQLGetDiagRec function until all the errors have been retrieved. As you might have guessed, it's possible for multiple error conditions to be associated with a given statement handle. The first parameter of the SQLGetDiagRec function is an integer that identifies the type of handle the SQLGetDiagRec function will use. The value of SQL_HANDLE_STMT indicated that the function will be working with an ODBC statement handle. The next parameter is the handle that will be used. The third parameter is an integer that's used as input to indicate the error record that will be retrieved. The error record numbers start at 1. If this parameter is set to the value of a record number that doesn't exist, the SQLGetDiagRec function returns the value of SQL_NO_DATA. The fourth parameter is an output parameter that contains the SQLSTATE code. The fifth parameter is a pointer to the output buffer that contains the native data source error code. The sixth parameter is an output string that contains the error text. The seventh parameter is an input parameter that contains the number of bytes available in the error message string used in the sixth parameter. Finally, the eighth parameter is a pointer to a buffer that contains the total number of bytes actually returned in the error message string.

The SQLGetDiagRec function can continue to be called as long as the function returns SQL_SUCCESS. A return code of SQL_NO_DATA indicates that no more error records are available.

CONCLUSION

ODBC is a powerful and flexible data access standard. In this chapter you saw how to set up an ODBC data source for SQL Server, as well as how to use the ODBC API to perform all of the basic data manipulation operations. With this information you're ready to begin building your own ODBC API applications using Visual Basic. Although coding ODBC applications is more complex than using the data control and/or Data Access Objects (DAO), the performance gains you can achieve usually make it worth the extra effort.

All of the code listings presented in this chapter are also contained in the ODBC Wizard example program on the CD-ROM accompanying this book.

ADDITIONAL RESOURCES

The ODBC API is very rich in functionality, and there's a lot more to ODBC than can be presented in one chapter. For more detailed information on ODBC, there's no better place to go than the *Microsoft ODBC 3.0 Software Development Kit and Programmer's Reference* (Redmond, WA: Microsoft Press, 1997).

CHAPTER 14

Developing NT Database Applications with RDO

In this chapter, you'll see how to develop SQL Server database applications using Visual Basic and Remote Database Objects (RDO). In the first part of this chapter, you'll get an overview of RDO, illustrating the RDO object hierarchy. The second half of this chapter presents basic RDO programming techniques and shows you how you can put RDO to work in your own database applications.

RDO combines the ease of programming offered by Data Access Objects (DAO) with the high performance offered by the ODBC API. Whereas DAO is an object layer over the Microsoft Jet Engine, RDO is an object layer that encapsulates the ODBC API. The absence of the high-overhead Jet Engine, combined with RDO's close relationship to ODBC, give it a decided performance advantage over DAO when accessing ODBC-compliant databases like SQL Server. Closely related to RDO is the Microsoft RemoteData control. Whereas RDO is a set of functions, the RemoteData control is a data source control that can be dragged and dropped onto a Visual Basic form. The RemoteData control provides the ability to host other data-bound controls like text, boxes, list boxes, and grid controls. RDO and the RemoteData control provide programmatic access to ODBC-compatible databases without the overhead of a local query processor like the Microsoft Jet Engine. RDO provides access to virtually all of the capabilities provided by the ODBC API but it is significantly easier to use. RDO eliminates the need to manually declare all of the functions in a .bas or .cls file. Instead, RDO's OLE implementation gives it seamless integration into the Visual Basic development environment.

RDO does not come with either the Standard or the Professional Edition of Visual Basic. Since RDO is intended to provide access to enterprise-level databases like SQL Server, RDO is only provided as a part of the Enterprise Edition of the Microsoft developer's products. RDO is provided as a part of the following Microsoft products:

▼ Visual Studio 97 Enterprise Edition

■ Visual Basic Enterprise Edition 4 or 5

▲ Visual C++ Enterprise Edition 4, 5, and 6

Like ODBC, RDO is intended to be used over network connections, with various network protocols and topologies. To achieve network independence, RDO is implemented using a layered architecture. Figure 14-1 illustrates the relationship of RDO to ODBC and the PC's networking support.

At the top level in Figure 14-1, you can see the Visual Basic RDO application, which instantiates and uses the various RDO objects. The RDO object layer converts the RDO calls into their equivalent ODBC API function calls that the RDO object layer makes to the ODBC Driver Manager on behalf of the Visual Basic application. The ODBC Driver Manager is responsible for loading the appropriate ODBC driver, which uses a network Interprocess Communications (IPC) method to communicate to a corresponding server on the target database. Examples of some of the different IPC mechanisms are Named Pipes, TCP/IP Sockets, and SPX. Beneath the IPC layer, the network protocol is responsible for sending and receiving the IPC data stream over the network. Various

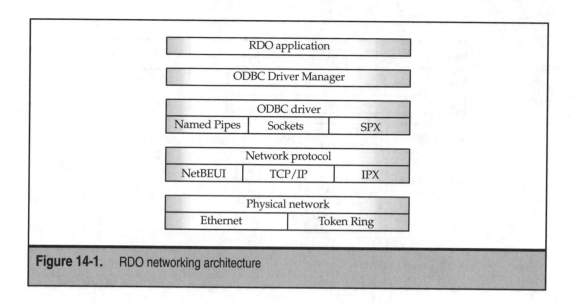

Figure 14-1.   RDO networking architecture

popular networking protocols include NetBEUI, TCP/IP, and IPX. Finally, at the bottom of this stack is the physical network topology. The physical network includes the adapter cards and cabling that are required to make the actual connections between the networked systems. Ethernet and Token Ring are examples of two of the most common network topologies.

RDO FILES

The following table summarizes the client files that comprise RDO:

File	Description
MSRDO20.DLL	RDO Object Library
MSRDO20.OCX	Microsoft RemoteData Control

RDO ARCHITECTURE

RDO is built out of a framework of objects and collections of objects. If you've read Chapter 12, then you'll notice that there is a lot of similarity between RDO's object hierarchy and ODBC. The RDO object model closely parallels ODBC's architecture. Figure 14-2 illustrates the RDO object model.

At the top of the RDO object framework is the rdoEngine. The rdoEngine represents the remote data source. All RDO applications must have an instance of the rdoEngine

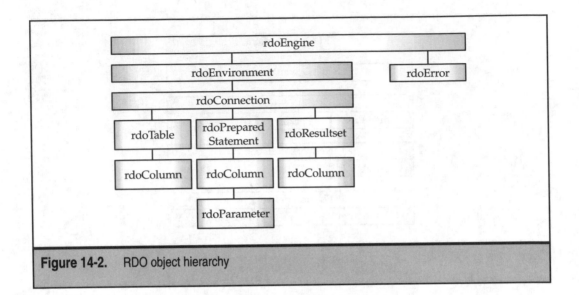

Figure 14-2.   RDO object hierarchy

object. The rdoEngine object is unique in that it is always instantiated as a single object. All of the other RDO objects are contained in collections.

The rdoEnvironment collection is at the next level beneath the rdoEngine. The rdoEnvironment is mainly used to set the user ID and password values and the transaction scope that will be used by a given database connection. The user ID and password are used to authenticate the connection; the transaction scope governs when transactions are committed to the database. Since the rdoEnvironment is a collection, you can have multiple rdoEnvironments for the rdoEngine object. Each rdoEnvironment can use a different user ID, password, and transaction scope.

At the next level of the RDO object hierarchy is the rdoConnection object. The rdoConnection object is responsible for establishing a connection to a data source. The rdoConnection starts a host connection by using the OpenConnection method. The rdoConnection object can supply all of the connection information, such as the data source name, user ID, and password, or it can leave these values blank, which enables the ODBC driver to prompt you for the connection information.

Each rdoConnection object can have collections of rdoTable objects, rdoPreparedStatement objects, or rdoResultset objects. Like their names imply, each rdoTable object represents a database table, each rdoPreparedStatement object represents a prepared SQL statement, and each rdoResultsSet object represents the data set returned by a SQL Select statement. All of these objects can contain rdoColumn objects. For an rdoTable object, each rdoColumn object represents a column in the table. For an rdoResultset object, the rdoColumn object represents one of the columns that was returned by a SQL query. The rdoPreparedStatement object uses both rdoColumn and rdoParameter objects. For an rdoPreparedStatement object, the rdoColumn object is typically used for binding the columns of a result set to local variables. The rdoParameter objects are used to exchange data between local program variables and parameterized queries or stored procedures. The rdoError object contains the any errors that are generated by any of the underlying ODBC operations. Unlike ODBC where you must manually test the return code of each ODBC function for errors, RDO errors fire Visual Basic's On Error handler. Within the On Error handler you can you can use retrieve the specific error information from the rdoErrors collection.

AN OVERVIEW OF USING RDO

RDO is built using an OLE foundation that makes it easy to access RDO functions from Visual Basic. Unlike ODBC where you must manually declare all of the functions and their parameters in a .BAS or .CLS module, to use RDO from Visual Basic you simply need to add the RDO Reference to your project and then create the required RDO objects. Following is a summary of the steps required to use RDO from Visual Basic.

▼ Include the Microsoft Remote Data Object 2.0 Type Library.

■ Create an RDO Engine object.

■ Create an RDO Environment object.

■ Create an RDO Connection object and associate it with a data source.

■ Use RDO Connection object methods to send a SQL statement to the data source.

■ Close the RDO Connection object.

▲ Set the RDO Objects to Nothing.

ADDING RDO 2.0 OBJECTS TO VISUAL BASIC

Before you can begin to use RDO from Visual Basic, you must set a reference to the RDO Type Library. The files that provide the basic support for RDO 2.0 are copied to your PC when you first install the Enterprise Edition of Visual Basic 5 or 6. However, you still need to set a reference to them in Visual Basic's development environment to enable their use from Visual Basic. To add the RDO 2.0 Reference to Visual Basic 5 or 6, you must select the References option from the Project menu, which will display the References dialog box that you can see in Figure 14-3.

Scroll through Visual Basic's References dialog box until you see the "Microsoft Remote Data Object 2.0." Clicking the check box adds the MSRDO20.DLL file to Visual Basic's Interactive Development Environment (IDE). When you add a reference to Visual Basic's IDE, no visual objects are added to the Visual Basic Toolbox, as would happen in

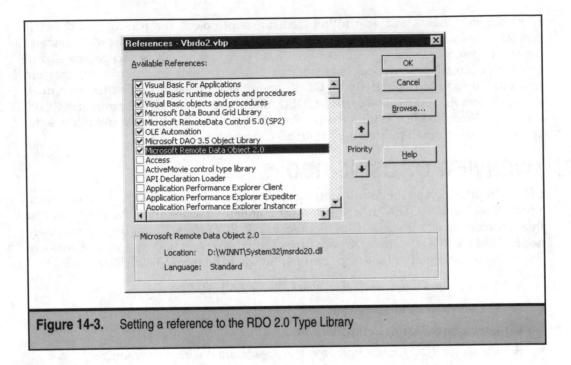

Figure 14-3.   Setting a reference to the RDO 2.0 Type Library

adding ActiveX Controls. In order to see the RDO 2.0 properties and methods, you must use Visual Basic's Object Browser, shown in Figure 14-4.

USING THE RDO OBJECTS WITH VISUAL BASIC

After a reference has been added to Visual Basic's development environment, you can begin to use the RDO objects in your Visual Basic applications. The first step in using RDO is to create an instance of the rdoEngine object. However, you don't need to explicitly add any code to create an instance of the rdoEngine object, because an instance is automatically created the first time any RDO object is referenced in code.

Creating the RDO Engine and Environment

The rdoEngine represents the remote data source; and, being the top-level object in the Remote Data Objects hierarchy, the rdoEngine object contains all of the other RDO objects. The rdoEngine object has several properties that are used as default values when new rdoEnvironment, rdoConnection, or rdoResultset objects are created. Table 14-1 shows the rdoEngine initialization default properties.

The rdoDefaultCursor property specifies whether the connection will use a local (ODBC) cursor or a server-side cursor. The default value of rdUseIfNeeded specifies that local ODBC cursors will be used. More information about cursors will be presented later in the chapter.

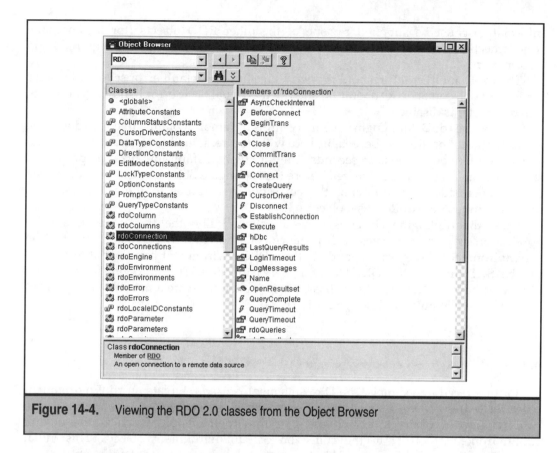

Figure 14-4.   Viewing the RDO 2.0 classes from the Object Browser

The rdoDefaultPassword property and the rdoDefaultUser can supply a login ID and password that are used when making a connection to the remote data source. An empty string is the default value for both of these parameters. This means that the required login

Property	Default	Description
rdoDefaultCursor	rdUseIfNeeded	ODBC cursor
rdoDefaultPassword	""	Database password
rdoDefaultUser	""	Database login ID
rdoDefaultErrorThreshold	–1	Fatal error severity level
rdoDefaultLoginTimeout	15	Login time out limit

Table 14-1.   Default rdoEngine Initialization Properties

information must be supplied by one of the other RDO objects (for instance, the rdoConnection object), or the ODBC driver will prompt the user for the required login information.

The rdoDefaultErrorThreshold property specifies the default error severity level for errors that will end an RDO operation and fire the Visual Basic error handler. By default, this parameter is disabled.

Finally, the rdoDefaultLoginTimeout controls the amount of time that the rdoEngine waits for a connection to be established with the remote data source. The default connection timeout value is 15 seconds. The rdoEngine default initialization properties shown in Table 14-1 can be changed before the rdoEngine object is instantiated, or they can be overridden by supplying the corresponding values to the rdoConnection, rdoEnvironment, or rdoResultset object.

Since the rdoEngine object is created automatically, the first code in a RDO application typically creates an instance of the rdoEnvironment object. The rdoEnvironment closely corresponds to the ODBC environment handle that's returned by the SQLAllocHandle(SQL_HANDLE_ENV) function. The following code listing illustrates how you can use Visual Basic's Set function to create a new rdoEnvironment object (and by default an rdoEngine object):

```
Dim en As rdoEnvironment

Set en = rdoEngine.rdoEnvironments(0)
```

In the preceding example, the Dim statement is used to create an rdoEnvironment object called en. Next, Visual Basic's Set statement is used to set a reference to the rdoEnvironment object called using rdoEnvironments(0), which is the default rdoEnvironement object in the collection of rdoEnvironment objects. This initial reference to the rdoEnvironment object automatically creates the rdoEngine object.

If your application requires multiple login contexts or it must support multiple transaction scopes (the transaction scope controls when pending transactions are written to the database), then you will need to create additional rdoEnvironments by using the rdoCreateEnvironment function. Your application might use multiple logins if you need to simultaneously access multiple databases that have different security information.

TIP: The default transaction scope of the rdoEnvironment immediately commits pending transactions to the data source. The BeginTrans, CommitTrans, and RollBackTrans methods are used to manage pending transactions within an rdoEnvironment.

The following code listing shows how to create an additional rdoEnvironment:

```
Dim en2 As rdoEnvironment

Set en2 = rdoCreateEnvironment("ENV2", "mylogin", "mypassword")
```

In this example, the Dim statement is used to create an rdoEnvironment object called en2. Next, the Set statement is used to set a reference to a new rdoEnvironment object called en2 using the rdoCreateEnvironment method. The first parameter of the rdoCreateEnvironment method specifies a unique name that will be used to identify the new rdoEnvironment within the collection of rdoEnvironments. If you don't want the new rdoEnvironment object appended to the collection of rdoEnvironments, you can specify this name as a zero-length string. The second and third parameters of the rdoCreateEnvironment method specify the user name and password that will be used to connect the new rdoEnvironment to the remote data source.

Closing the rdoEnvironment

The rdoEnvironment Close method terminates an rdoEnvironment object. Terminating an rdoEnviroment removes it from the rdoEnvironments collection and closes all of the rdoConnection objects that were established by that rdoEnvironment object. The following code listing illustrates how to use the Close method to end an rdoEnvironment.

```
En2.Close
```

In this example, the rdoEnvironment object named en2 is terminated by the Close method.

Working with RDO Connections

After the rdoEnvironment object has been created, you can use the rdoConnection object to start a connection to the data source. The rdoConnection object corresponds to the SQLConnect and SQLDriverConnect functions provided by the ODBC API. After creating an rdoConnection object, you must use the OpenConnection method to establish the physical link to the remote data source. The following code example illustrates how to use the rdoConnection object:

```
Dim cn As rdoConnection
Dim sConn As String

Set cn = en.OpenConnection("", rdDriverComplete, False, sConn)
```

The OpenConnection method accepts up to four parameters. The first parameter is required and the three remaining parameters are optional. The first parameter of the OpenConnection method is a string that contains the name of the data source that your RDO application will connect to. Using a blank string in this parameter causes the ODBC driver to use the data source name that's specified in the connection string that's supplied in the fourth parameter. If no data source name is specified in either parameter, the ODBC Driver Manager prompts you at run time for the name of the data source that you want to use. The second parameter is an integer that controls the level of prompting that will be performed by the ODBC driver. The value of rdDriverComplete specifies the ODBC driver that is responsible for collecting all of the information it needs to make a connection to the data source. This means that the ODBC Driver Manager will prompt for any information that it requires to connect to the remote data source. A value of rdDriverNoPrompt prevents the ODBC Driver Manager from prompting for any login information that is not supplied by the OpenConnection method. When the OpenConnection method shown previously is executed, the ODBC Driver Manager displays a dialog box that prompts the user for the data source, as well as the user ID and password. The optional third parameter of the OpenConnection method is a Boolean variable that controls whether updates to the data source will be allowed. A value of True forces the connection to use a read-only mode; a value of False enables the connection to update the target data source. The fourth optional parameter is a string that contains connection information. The previous example uses an empty string; however, you can also supply the connection information using a string as follows:

```
sConn = "DSN=My SQL Server;UID=mylogin;PWD=mypwd"
```

This connection string indicates to the rdoConnection object that it should use the data source named My SQL Server, and it also supplies the login ID of mylogin with the password mypwd.

You might have noticed that the connection string used a set of predefined keywords. Table 14-2 presents the valid connection string keywords.

After the OpenConnection method has made a successful connection to the remote data source, you can use the rdoConnection object ("cn") to create prepared statements or

Keyword	Description
DSN	The name of a registered data source
DRIVER	The name of an installed ODBC driver
SERVER	The name of the database server
UID	The login ID for the data source
PWD	The password associated with the login ID
APP	The name of your application
WSID	The network name of the source computer
DATABASE	The SQL Server target database name
LANGUAGE	The SQL Server language

Table 14-2.   Connection String Keywords

execute SQL statements. Examples of using the rdoConnection object appear a little later in this chapter.

DSN-less Connections

Using the OpenConnection method as illustrated in the prior example requires the existence of a registered data source before the connection can be made. Creating a data source using the ODBC Administrator was illustrated in Chapter 12. However, as you might have guessed from the keywords presented in Table 14-2, RDO also provides the ability to connect to a data source without requiring a preexisting data source. The following code example illustrates how to make a DSN-less connection to SQL server.

```
Dim cn2 s rdoConnection
Dim sConn As String

sConn = _
  "Driver=SQL Server;SERVER=teca2;UID=mikeo;PWD=mypwd;DATABASE=teca"
Set cn2 = en.OpenConnection("", rdDriverNoPrompt, False, sConn)
```

In this example, the Driver keyword identifies an ODBC driver that's installed on the system. The use of the Driver keyword is the primary difference between a DSN connection and a DSN-less connection. Directly identifying the appropriate driver is the key to making a DSN-less connection. For SQL Server connections, the SERVER and the DATABASE keywords identify the remote SQL Server system and the default database that will be used. Like the earlier DSN connection, the UID and PWD keywords specify the login ID and password that will be used to connect to the target database. These values comprise the essential parts of the data source configuration, and the ability to supply them in the connection string allows you to forego the process of creating a data source before connecting to the database.

Closing an RDO Connection

The rdoConnection Close method terminates the link to a target database. Using the Close method on the rdoConnection object destroys any subordinate objects like rdoResultset or rdoQuery objects. However, unlike the Close for an rdoEnvironment object, using the Close method for an rdoConnection object does not remove it from the rdoConnections collection contained in the rdoEnvironment object. The following code shows you how to use the Close method to close an rdoConnection:

```
cn.Close
```

Retrieving Data Using RDO

Once an rdoConnection object has been created, you can use it to query the target database, as well as execute stored procedures, and dynamic and static SQL statements. The primary RDO object that is used to query a data source is the rdoResultset object. The rdoResultset object is responsible for executing a query on the remote data source and then creating a result set. The way in which your application can work with the result set depends on the type of cursor that was used when the application was created.

Cursors

A *cursor*, in this context, defines the mechanism for working with the rows contained in a result set. A cursor allows your application to move through the rows contained in a result set much like reading through the records of a standard file. RDO supports several different cursor types and each type has different attributes. The different cursor types supported by RDO are forward-only cursors, static cursors, keyset cursors, and dynamic cursors.

FORWARD-ONLY CURSORS   The forward-only cursor is the default cursor used by RDO. The forward-only cursor provides the best performance and the least overhead of any of the RDO cursor types, but it is less capable than other RDO cursors. Forward-only result sets are updateable, but they can only update one row at a time. Any changes in the data source are not reflected in a forward-only cursor.

STATIC CURSORS   A static cursor provides a frozen copy or snapshot of the data source at the time the cursor was opened. Result sets created using static cursors are not updateable, and they do not reflect any changes that are made to the data source until the cursor is closed and reopened. Because of their static nature, result sets created by static cursors are generally less resource intensive than the result sets created by keyset or dynamic cursors. However, since the static cursor makes a local copy of the data, you need to be careful about using this type of cursor with large result sets.

KEYSET CURSORS   When a keyset cursor opens a result set, it builds a local set of keys where each key is associated with a row in the result set. When your application accesses rows in the result set, the local keyset is used to retrieve the corresponding row from the data source; the row is then used to populate the result set. Result sets built using keyset cursors are updateable; but after they are fully populated, they do not dynamically reflect changes that other users make in the data source. Keyset cursors are relatively resource intensive because the client system must maintain both the keys for the entire result set and a buffer that contains a block of the actual data values.

DYNAMIC CURSORS   Dynamic cursors are the most powerful type of RDO cursors, but they are also the most expensive. Like a keyset cursor, a result set that is created using a dynamic cursor uses a local set of keys that correspond to each row in the result set. Also like a keyset cursor, a result set created by dynamic cursors is fully updateable. However, unlike a keyset cursor, the result set that's created using a dynamic cursor dynamically reflects any changes that are made to the data source. In order to dynamically maintain the result set, RDO continually checks the result set and the data source, automatically updating the local result set with any data source changes. The local system is responsible for this constant maintenance of the result set.

TIP: The performance advantages and low resource requirements offered by forward-only cursors often make them the best option for most uses.

Working with RDOResult Sets and Dynamic SQL

A result set is created using the OpenResult method of the rdoConnection object. The following code illustrates using the OpenResultset method:

```
Dim rs As RDOQuery
Set rs = cn.OpenResultset _
        ("Select au_lname, au_fname From authors", rdOpenForwardOnly)
```

The OpenResultset method creates a new instance of an rdoResultset object named rs. Creating the new rdoResultset object retrieves the data from the data source and populates the result set. When used with an rdoConnection object, the OpenResultset method takes four parameters. The first parameter is required, and the last three are optional.

The first parameter is a string that contains the SQL statement that will be used to create the result set. In the example just given, the SQL Select statement is used to retrieve the au_lname (last name) and au_fname (first name) columns from the authors table in the pubs database. In addition to a string containing a SQL statement, the first parameter of the OpenResultset method can also contain the name of an rdoTable object or an rdoQuery object.

The second parameter is an integer that specifies that type of result set. The value of rdOpenForwardOnly specifies that the result set will only support forward scrolling. This is the simplest type of result set, and it is also the best-performing option. The following table presents the RDO constants that are used to specify the type of cursor that an rdoResultset object will use:

RDO Constant	Cursor Type
rdForwardOnly	Forward-only cursor (default)
rdOpenStatic	Static cursor
rdOpenKeyset	Keyset cursor
rdOpenDynamic	Dynamic cursor

The third parameter of the OpenResultset method is an integer that is used to indicate the type of concurrency control that is in place. The default value indicates that the result set will be read-only. The following table presents the concurrency control options that are supported by the RDO OpenResultset method:

Lock Type	Description
rdConcurReadOnly	Read-only (default)
rdConcurLock	Pessimistic locking
rdConcurRowVer	Optimistic locking using row ID
rdConcurValues	Optimistic locking using row values
rdConcurBatch	Optimistic locking using batch mode updates

If the fourth parameter is not specified, as was the case with the previous example, then the default value of rdConcurReadOnly will be used, making the cursor read-only. More information about data concurrency is presented in the section "Managing Data Concurrency," later in this chapter.

The last optional parameter of the OpenResultset method controls whether the result set will be created synchronously or asynchronously. The following table presents the different options for the fourth parameter of the OpenResultset method:

Option	Description
rdAsyncEnabled	Create the result set asynchronously
rdExecDirect	Create the result set using dynamic SQL

Creating the result set asynchronously frees the application to perform other tasks while the result set is populated. By default, the result set will be created synchronously, which means that your application will not proceed until the OpenResultset method has completed. More information about using asynchronous result sets is presented in the "Advanced Topics" section, later in this chapter.

After the rdoResultset object has been created, you can use the MoveNext method of the rdoResultset object to traverse the result set. An example of the MoveNext method is shown here:

```
Do

        sTextLine = ""
        For Each cl In rs.rdoColumns
    sTextLine = sTextLine & cl.Value & vbTab
        Next
        List1.AddItem sTextLine
        DoEvents

        rs.MoveNext

    Loop Until rs.EOF = True
```

In this example, a Do-Loop is used in conjunction with the MoveNext method to move through the forward-only result set. Since this result set was created using a forward-only cursor, only the MoveNext method is valid. Other methods to control the cursor within the result set are not supported. The EOF property is checked after each MoveNext operation to determine when the program has reached the end of the result set. For each row in the result set, a For-Each loop is used to retrieve the values of the columns collection (cl). The actual data contained by each column is accessed through the value property of the column object (cl.value). The column values variables are then concatenated into a string that will be displayed in the list named List1.

Closing the Result Set

The rdoResultset Close method closed the cursor that was used to open the result set. Using the Close method on the rdoResultset object also destroys any subordinate rdoColumn objects. The following code shows how to close an rdoResultset object.

```
rs.Close
```

Working with RDOResultsets and Prepared Statements

The ability to use prepared statements and parameter markers is one of the characteristics that gives RDO its good performance. As the earlier chapter covering ODBC pointed out, using prepared statements in your applications is one of those small changes that can result in big performance gains. Using prepared statements with SQL Server allows the SQL statements to be stored in SQL Server's database as stored procedures. The preparation of the SQL statement is performed once when the stored procedure is first created. Subsequent calls using the prepared statement are fast because the compiled stored procedure is already in place. When dynamic SQL without prepared statements is used, the SQL statement must be reevaluated each time you execute the statement. The following code example shows how to create an RDO query using prepared statements:

```
Private Sub RDOQueryPS(cn2 As rdoConnection)

    Dim ps As rdoPreparedStatement
    Dim rs As rdoResultset
    Dim cl As rdoColumn
    Dim sSQL As String
    Dim sTextLine As String

    Screen.MousePointer = vbHourglass
    List1.Clear

    sSQL = "Select au_lname, au_fname, state From authors Where state = ?"

    Set ps = cn2.CreatePreparedStatement("", sSQL)
    ps.rdoParameters(0).Direction = rdParamInput
    ps.rdoParameters(0) = Text_Mid.Text
```

```
Set rs = ps.OpenResultset(rdOpenKeyset, rdConcurRowVer)

For Each cl In rs.rdoColumns
    sTextLine = sTextLine & cl.Name & vbTab
Next

List1.AddItem sTextLine
DoEvents

While Not rs.EOF
    sTextLine = rs!au_lname & vbTab & rs!au_Fname & vbTab & rs!state
    List1.AddItem sTextLine
    rs.MoveNext
Wend

rs.Close

Screen.MousePointer = vbDefault

End Sub
```

In this example, the rdoResultset object named rs is created using the prepared statement contained in the rdoPreparedStatement object named ps. The SQL statement that will be prepared is contained in the sSQL string variable. Unlike the dynamic SQL that you saw used in the earlier RDO query, the SQL that is used with rdoPreparedStatements uses parameter markers for replaceable characters. Inside the sSQL string you can see the parameter marker is indicated by the question mark character ("?").

In this case, before the SQL SELECT statement is executed, the replaceable character (?) in the WHERE clause will be filled in with the appropriate value. This value is supplied to the rdoPreparedStatement object using the rdoParameter object. However, before you can execute the static SQL statement, you must create an instance of the rdoPreparedStatement object using Visual Basic's Set statement. The Set statement makes a reference to the rdoPreparedStatement object that is created using the CreatePreparedStatement method.

The CreatePreparedStatement method takes two parameters. The first parameter is a string that can be used to uniquely name the prepared statement. Specifying an empty string simply adds the statement to the collection of rdoPreparedStatements. The second parameter is a string variable that contains the SQL statement that will be prepared.

TIP: While the SQL statements used with the CreatePreparedStatement method usually contain parameter markers, parameter markers are not required. You can create rdoPreparedStatements using any valid SQL statement. However, the real strength of the rdoPreparedStatement shows for SQL statements that are executed multiple times. SQL statements using parameter markers are more versatile and therefore more likely to be reused than SQL statements that are constructed using literals.

The next step sets the direction of the parameter using the rdoParameter.Direction property. Since the rdoParameter object was not named, it must be referred to using its ordinal position within the collection of the rdoParameters. In this example, there is only one parameter and its ordinal value is found at rdoParameter(0). Parameters used in rdoPreparedStatement can be input, output, or both input and output. The default parameter direction is input. The following table lists the allowable parameter directions.

Direction Value	Description
rdParamInput	Input parameter (default)
rdParamOutput	Output parameter
rdParamInputOutPut	Input and Output Parameter
rdParamReturnValue	Output of the return status

Next, the value of the parameter is set with the contents of the text box named Text_Input. Since the default property for the rdoParameter object is the value property, this property doesn't need to be specifically entered in the code. In this case, the state code value that is entered into the Text_Input text box will be assigned to the first rdoParameter object in the collection of rdoParameters.

After the parameter has been set with the value of the state code that was entered in the Text_Input text box, a result set is created using the OpenResultset method. Using the OpenResultset method with an rdoPreparedStatement is different than using it with dynamic SQL. Instead of using the OpenResultset method with the rdoConnection object, the OpenResultset method is used with the rdoPreparedStatement object. This can be seen in the previous example as ps.OpenResultset. The parameter usage of the OpenResultset method is also different. Creating a result set with an rdoPreparedStatement only requires a single parameter that specifies the type of cursor that will be used. The previous example used a keyset cursor.

TIP: Omitting a specific reference to the default value property is a common shorthand coding technique.

After the result set has been created, a While-Loop is used in conjunction with the MoveNext method to move through the result set. Using the While-Loop as illustrated in the previous example allows the EOF property to be checked before referencing the other properties of the result set. This construct allows you to bypass the processing that is contained within the While block when there are no rows in the result set. This was not really a concern with the dynamic SQL example where both the query and the data source were known quantities. However, in the rdoPreparedStatement example, the contents of the result set depend on what the user enters into the Text_Input text box. It's possible that the user could construct a query that had no match in the data source—in which case the result set would be empty. Following the OpenResultset method and attempting to reference data properties in an empty result set can be a source of run-time errors.

TIP: When the size of the result set varies based on the user's input you may want to limit the size of the result set that can be returned. You can use the MaxRows property of the rdoPreparedStatement object to limit the number of rows that will be returned by a query. In addition to restricting the number of rows, you can limit the amount of time that a query requires by setting the QueryTimeout property of the rdoPreparedStatement object.

The contents of the While block also illustrate another method of accessing the data values contained by a result set. This example uses what is referred to as the Bang notation to reference the columns contained in the result set. The Bang notation gets its name from the use of the exclamation point, and it consists of the result set object name (rs) followed by the Bang (!) and then the column name that's used in the data source (au_lname, au_fname, and state). These column values are then concatenated into a string that will be displayed in the list named List1. The last action within the While block is the use of the MoveNext method to move to the next row of the result set. Since this result set was created using a keyset cursor, the full range of cursor movement methods are valid. Finally, at the end of this example, you can see where the result set is closed.

TIP: You can use the Refresh method of the rdoPreparedStatement to requery the data source using a new parameter value.

Using Dynamic SQL and RDO Execute

In addition to performing queries, RDO can execute SQL DDL (Data Definition Language) statements to create tables, indexes, and views. RDO's Execute method can be used to dynamically execute any valid SQL statement. Unlike the OpenResultset method that is used for queries, the Execute method is not intended to return a result set. The following code illustrates how you can use the Execute method of the rdoConnection object to execute dynamic SQL statements:

```
Dim sSQL as String
On Error Resume Next

    sSQL = "Drop Table department"
    cn.Execute sSQL
    sSQL = "Create Table department _
            (Dep_ID CHAR(4) not null, Dep_Name CHAR(25), primary
key(Dep_ID))"

    cn.Execute sSQL
```

In this example, first the SQL Drop Table statement is used to delete the department table. The Drop Table statement ensures that the department table does not exist before the next SQL statements are executed. If the department table does not exist, Visual

Basic's error handler traps the error, and the execution of the subroutine continues with the next statement. Next, the Create Table statement uses standard SQL DDL (Data Defintion Language) to create a file called department. The department file has two fields: Dep_ID is a 4-byte character field, and Dep_Name is a 25-byte character field. The department file will be keyed on the Dep_ID field. In each case, after the SQL statement has been put into the string variable, sSQL, the Execute method of the cn connection object is used to run the SQL statement. More information about using the Execute method with SQL DML statement is presented a little later in this chapter.

Modifying Data with RDO Cursors

In addition to retrieving the data to satisfy SQL queries, the rdoResultset object can be used for updating data. However, not all rdoResultset objects are updateable. The ability of the rdoResultset object to support updates is governed by parameters that were used when the result set was created by the OpenResultset method. The two most important parameters with respect to the ability to update the result set are the type and the lock-type parameters. As its name suggests, the type parameter of the OpenResultset method specifies the type of cursor that is supported by the result set. A summary of the rdoResultset types and their ability to support data update methods is listed in the following table:

Result Set	Updateable
rdOpenForwardOnly	Yes (current row only)
rdOpenStatic	No
rdOpenKeyset	Yes
rdOpenDynamic	Yes

The RDO cursor types shown previously work in conjunction with the RDO lock-type parameter. The lock-type parameter specifies the type of record locking that will be used for the result set. The valid lock-type values were shown earlier in the section "Working with RDOResult Sets and Dynamic SQL." Concerning the ability to support updates, the lock-type parameter takes precedence over the type parameter. For instance, if the lock-type parameter of the OpenResultset is set to rdConcurReadOnly (read-only), then the result set will not be updateable no matter which cursor type is used. To enable updating, the lock-type parameter must be set to one of the following values: rdConcurLock (pessimistic locking), rdConcurRowVer (optimistic locking using the row ID), rdConcurValues (optimistic locking using row values), or rdConcurBatch (optimistic locking using batch mode updates).

TIP: Using cursors to update data makes more sense for some cursor types than others. Using cursors to update result sets works best for Keyset and Dynamic result sets. While the rdOpenForwardOnly cursor supports an updateable cursor, its narrow scope (one row) limits its usefulness. When using forward-only cursors, you're normally better off performing any required data updates using stored procedures or rdoPreparedStatements and direct SQL.

More information on the lock-type parameter of the OpenResultset method can be found earlier in this chapter in "Working with RDOResult Sets and Dynamic SQL." In addition, more detailed information on RDO and data concurrency can be found later in this chapter in "Managing Data Concurrency."

Inserting Rows Using the AddNew Method

The AddNew method in combination with the Update method of the Resultset object can be used to add rows to an updateable RDO result set. The following code illustrates how you can add rows to a result set that was created using a keyset cursor:

```
Private Sub AddUsingCursor(cn As rdoConnection)

    Dim rs As rdoResultset
    Dim i As Integer

    Screen.MousePointer = vbHourglass
    Set rs = cn.OpenResultset _
            ("Select Dep_ID, Dep_name From department", _
            rdOpenKeyset, rdConcurRowVer)

    For i = 0 To 50
        rs.AddNew
        rs!Dep_ID = i
        rs!Dep_Name = "Department " & CStr(i)
        rs.Update
    Next

    rs.Close

    Screen.MousePointer = vbDefault

End Sub
```

In this example, the OpenResultset method is used to create a new result set object named rs. The first parameter of the OpenResultset method accepts a string that contains a SQL statement that defines the result set. In this case, the result set consists of the Dep_ID and the Dep_Name columns from the department table in the pubs database. The third parameter of the OpenResultset method uses the rdOpenKeyset constant to specify that the result set will use a keyset cursor. The third parameter contains the value rdConcurRowVer, which indicates that this result set is updateable and will use optimistic record locking based on the row ID.

After the result set has been opened, a For-Next loop is used to add a series of rows to the result set. Within the For-Next loop, the AddNew method is called to create a row buffer that will be used to contain the row values to be added. The value of the Dep_ID column is set using a unique integer value for each row. The Dep_Name column is set using the string that is formed by concatenating the literal "Department" and the string representation of the loop counter. Next, the new values are moved into the Dep_ID and Dep_Name columns in the result set. After the row values have been set, the Update method is called to add the row to the result set object and the data source. Finally, the Close method is used to close the result set object.

Updating Rows Using the Update Method

The Edit and Update methods of the Resultset object can be used to update rows in an updateable RDO result set. The following code illustrates how you can update the rows in a result set that was created using a keyset cursor:

```
Private Sub UpdateUsingCursor(cn As rdoConnection)

    Dim rs As rdoResultset
    Dim i As Integer

    Screen.MousePointer = vbHourglass
    Set rs = cn.OpenResultset _
            ("Select Dep_ID, Dep_name From department", _
            rdOpenKeyset, rdConcurRowVer)

    Do Until rs.EOF
        rs.Edit
        rs!Dep_Name = "Updated " & rs!Dep_Name
        rs.Update
        rs.MoveNext
    Loop

    rs.Close

    Screen.MousePointer = vbDefault

End Sub
```

Again, the OpenResultset method is used to create a new result set object named rs. The first parameter of the OpenResultset method is a string that specifies the result set consists of the Dep_ID and the Dep_Name columns from the department table in the pubs database. The rdOpenKeyset and rdConcurRowVer constants used in the second and third parameters indicate that the result set will be created with an updateable keyset cursor that uses optimistic record locking based on the row ID. After the result set has been opened, a Do-Until loop is used to read through all of the rows contained in the result set until the EOF property of the rs rdoResultset object becomes true. Within the Do loop, the Edit method is used to put each row into edit mode. Next, the value of the

Dep_Name column is set to a new string value that begins with the literal "Updated". After the Dep_Name row values have been set, the Update method is called to update the row in both the result set object and the data source. Then the MoveNext method of the rs result set object is used to position the cursor to the next row. Finally, the Close method is used to close the result set object.

Deleting Rows Using the Delete Method

The Delete method of the Resultset object is used to remove rows in an updateable RDO result set. The following code illustrates how you can delete rows in a keyset type of result set:

```
Private Sub DeleteUsingCursor(cn As rdoConnection)

    Dim rs As rdoResultset
    Dim i As Integer

    Screen.MousePointer = vbHourglass
    Set rs = cn.OpenResultset _
            ("Select Dep_ID, Dep_name From department", _
            rdOpenKeyset, rdConcurRowVer)

    Do Until rs.EOF
        rs.Delete
        rs.MoveNext
    Loop

    rs.Close

    Screen.MousePointer = vbDefault

End Sub
```

Like the previous examples, the OpenResultset method is used to create a new rdoResultset object that contains the Dep_ID and the Dep_Name columns from the department table in the pubs database. The second and third parameters of the OpenResultset method contain the rdOpenKeyset and rdConcurRowVer constants to specify that the result set will use a keyset cursor that supports updates using optimistic record locking based on the row ID. After the result set has been opened, a Do-Until loop is used to read through all of the rows contained in the result set. Within the Do-Until loop, the rdoResultset's Delete method is used to delete the row, and then the MoveNext method positions the cursor to the next row in the result set. Finally, the Close method is used to close the result set object.

Modifying Data with RDO Using SQL

In the previous section you saw how to update data using cursors. However, the high overhead incurred by using cursors makes them unsuitable for all uses. Fortunately, you can also update the data in a data source using direct SQL statements. RDO can be used to issue direct SQL data manipulation statements in a manner that's very similar to using the ODBC API. You can often construct a leaner and meaner application using fast forward–only cursors and still retain the ability to perform sophisticated updates using direct SQL Insert, Update, and Delete statements. In this next section you'll see how you can use SQL statements and rdoPreparedStatements in combination with the Execute method to modify the data contained in a remote data source.

TIP: You can use SQL statements to modify the rows in a data source that was used to generate a forward-only result set. However, the changes in the data source will not be reflected in the result set until the cursor is closed and reopened.

Inserting Rows with the SQL INSERT Statement

The SQL Insert statement is used to add rows to a data source. The following code example shows how you can use the SQL Insert statement in combination with the rdoPreparedStatement object:

```
Private Sub AddUsingInsert(cn As rdoConnection)

    Dim ps As rdoPreparedStatement
    Dim sSQL As String
    Dim i As Integer

    Screen.MousePointer = vbHourglass

    sSQL = "Insert Into department Values( ?, ?)"

    Set ps = cn.CreatePreparedStatement("Insert", sSQL)

    For i = 0 To 50
        With cn.rdoPreparedStatements!Insert
            .rdoParameters(0).Value = i
            .rdoParameters(1).Value = "INSERTED Department " & CStr(i)
        End With
        cn.rdoPreparedStatements!Insert.Execute
    Next

    Screen.MousePointer = vbDefault

End Sub
```

In this example, the CreatePreparedStatement method of the rdoConnection object was used to create an Insert statement using parameter markers. The CreatePreparedStatement method makes an instance of a new rdoPreparedStatement object called ps. The CreatePreparedStatement method takes two parameters. The first parameter is an optional string that can be used to uniquely identify the statement. Using a unique statement name allows you to refer to the prepared statement by name, which is particularly useful if your application uses multiple rdoPreparedStatement objects. In this example, the rdoPreparedStatement is named Insert. The second parameter of the CreatePreparedStatement method is a string that contains the SQL statement. The SQL statement itself is an Insert statement that is contained in the sSQL string variable. This Insert statement uses two parameter markers, one for each column that will be inserted into the table. Next, a For-Next loop is used to add 50 rows to the table. Within the For-Next loop, the parameter values used by the rdoPreparedStatement are set. The Bang (!) notation is used to preface the name of the rdoPreparedStatement, which, in this case, refers to the rdoPreparedStatement named Insert in the rdoConnection object named cn.

TIP: The With statement is Visual Basic shorthand code that executes a series of statements on a single object without requiring you to repeatedly reference the object. The With statement is particularly useful for setting multiple values in an rdoPreparedStatement.

Inside a With block, the value property of each of the parameters is set to the appropriate data value. In this example, the different parameters are referred to using their ordinal numbers. In other words, rdoParameter(0) refers to the first parameter marker, which is used for the Dep_ID column, while rdoParameter(1) refers to the second parameter marker, which is used for the Dep_Name column. Like the earlier example that added rows using a cursor, the Dep_ID column is assigned a unique integer value based on the loop counter, while the Dep_Name column is assigned a string that contains the literal "Inserted Department" in conjunction with a string representation of the loop counter. After setting the parameter values, the prepared statement is executed using the Execute method. Here again, you can see that the Bang notation is used to preface the name of the rdoPreparedStatement that will be executed.

Updating Rows

The SQL Update statement is used to update columns in a data source. The following code example shows how you can use the SQL Update statement in combination with the rdoPreparedStatement object to update all of the rows in the department table.

```
Private Sub UpdateUsingUpdate(cn As rdoConnection)

    Dim ps As rdoPreparedStatement
    Dim sSQL As String

    Screen.MousePointer = vbHourglass
```

```
sSQL = "Update department Set Dep_Name = " _
       & "'UPDATE' + Substring(Dep_Name, 7, 25)"

Set ps = cn.CreatePreparedStatement("Update", sSQL)

cn.rdoPreparedStatements!Update.Execute

Screen.MousePointer = vbDefault
```

End Sub

In this example, the CreatePreparedStatement method of the rdoConnection object is used to create a prepared statement to perform the SQL Update statement. You might notice that this example is quite a bit different from the earlier update example that used a result set and an updateable cursor to update all of the rows in a result set. In the previous cursor update example, each row in the result set was individually updated. In contrast, this example takes advantage of SQL's set-at-a-time processing to update all of the rows in the department table using a single SQL statement.

TIP: SQL's set-at-a-time processing can often provide performance benefits by shifting the workload to the server query processor and reducing the data flows between the server and the client.

Near the beginning of this example, you can see where the sSQL string variable is assigned the SQL Update statement. This Update statement is issued without a Where clause, so that all the rows in the department table will be updated. In addition, you can see that the SET clause assigns the Dep_Name column with the concatenation of the literal value "UPDATE" plus a substring that contains the last 19 characters of the Dep_Name column. In effect, this Update statement will overlay the first 6 characters of the Dep_Name column with the value "UPDATE". You can learn more about constructing SQL statements in Chapter 10.

NOTE: Exercise caution when using the SQL UPDATE statement without a WHERE clause. If this powerful technique is used incorrectly, it could inadvertently update more rows than you intend to.

Next, the CreatePreparedStatement method makes an instance of a new rdoPrepared-Statement object called ps. The first parameter of the CreatePreparedStatement method is used to give the prepared statement a unique name that can later be used for referring to that statement. The second parameter of the CreatePreparedStatement method takes the sSQL string variable that contains the SQL UPDATE statement. After the CreatePreparedStatement method has completed, the Execute method is used to run the SQL Update statement, which then updates all of the rows in the department table.

Deleting Rows

The SQL Delete statement is used to delete one or more rows in a data source. In the following example, you can see how to use the SQL Delete statement in combination with the rdoPreparedStatement object to delete all of the rows in a table:

```
Private Sub DeleteUsingDelete(cn As rdoConnection)

    Dim ps As rdoPreparedStatement
    Dim sSQL As String

    Screen.MousePointer = vbHourglass

    sSQL = "Delete department"

    Set ps = cn.CreatePreparedStatement("Delete", sSQL)

    cn.rdoPreparedStatements!Delete.Execute

    Screen.MousePointer = vbDefault

End Sub
```

Like the previous direct SQL examples, the CreatePreparedStatement method of the rdoConnection object is used to create a prepared statement that will be used to perform the SQL Delete statement. Like the Update example, this example uses SQL's ability to work with sets of data to delete all of the rows in the department table, using a single SQL statement.

TIP: Since neither the SQL Update nor Delete examples presented used parameter markers, they could have also been executed by simply calling the Execute method of the rdoConnection object and passing it a string containing the appropriate SQL statement. This would be a bit simpler because it allows you to forego creating the rdoPreparedStatement object. This method would be preferable if your application only needs to call the particular statement on an ad hoc basis. However, if your application needs to perform the SQL statement repeatedly, using an rdoPrepredStatement will generally provide better performance.

Near the beginning of this example, you can see where the sSQL string variable is assigned the SQL Delete statement. Like the Update statement that was presented in the prior example, when the Delete statement is issued without a Where clause, the statement will delete all of the rows in a table—effectively clearing the table. Obviously, care needs to be taken when working with these types of unqualified SQL statements. However, as you can see, when they are used correctly SQL statements can reduce the amount of code that you need to write as well as speed up your applications.

Next, the CreatePreparedStatement method creates an instance of a new rdoPrepared-Statement object called ps. The first parameter of the CreatePreparedStatement method names the rdoPreparedStatement "Delete." The second parameter of the CreatePrepared-Statement method accepts the string variable that holds the SQL Delete statement. Finally, the Execute method is used to actually perform the delete operation that is associated with the rdoPreparedStatement named Delete.

Using Stored Procedures

To get the best possible performance from your SQL Server database application, you'll find that stored procedures are the way to go. Unlike dynamic SQL statements, which call SQL Server's Query Analyzer to build an execution plan before running each SQL statement, a stored procedure's execution plans are compiled when it is created and then saved within the database. Executing stored procedures bypasses the need to call SQL Server's Query Analyzer before executing the queries or other SQL statements in the stored procedure.

Using stored procedures also has some other important benefits. First, since stored procedures are stored with the database, they can be shared by multiple developers. This allows multiple developers to get a productivity boost by leveraging the same code. Next, stored procedures can be used to perform a variety of SQL Server administrative functions that are not possible using just SQL DDL or SQL DML statements. Finally, stored procedures can also provide an additional layer of security. Businesses that need to restrict general database access yet still provide controlled data access can use stored procedures to accomplish this goal by permitting end-user access to just the stored procedures and restricting general database access. This database access scheme is very secure since it funnels all database access through the set of centrally created and maintained stored procedures, and it shuts down any unauthorized data access.

Calling stored procedures using RDO is very similar to using SQL Select, Insert, Update, and Delete statements that contain parameter markers. The biggest difference is that it is common for stored procedures to pass a return value and/or output parameters back to the calling application.

> **TIP:** Unlike executing dynamic or static SQL statements, the stored procedure must exist in the database before it can be called.

The following code illustrates how to use RDO to call a SQL Server stored procedure, pass it an input parameter, and then retrieve the value returned in an output parameter.

```
Private Sub CallSP(cn As rdoConnection)

    Dim ps As rdoPreparedStatement
    Dim sSQL As String

    Screen.MousePointer = vbHourglass
```

```
    sSQL = "{ Call CountStateRows (? ,?) }"

    Set ps = cn.CreatePreparedStatement("", sSQL)

    ps.rdoParameters(0).Direction = rdParamInput
    ps.rdoParameters(0).Value = Text_Mid.Text
    ps.rdoParameters(1).Direction = rdParamOutput

    ps.Execute

    Text_Bot.Text = ps.rdoParameters(1)

    Screen.MousePointer = vbDefault

End Sub
```

Near the beginning of this example, the sSQL string variable is set using the ODBC CALL syntax. The ODBC CALL statement should always be encapsulated within french braces { }. Following the CALL keyword, you can see the name of the stored procedure and any parameters that it uses. This example executes the stored procedure CountStateRows that's contained in the pubs database. The CountStateRows stored procedure is shown here:

```
Create Procedure CountStateRows
(
    @state Char(2),
    @rows Int Output
)
As
Select @rows = Count(*) From authors Where state = @state
Go
```

The CountStateRows stored procedure uses two parameters: the first parameter is an input parameter that contains the state code, and the second parameter is an integer that will return the number of rows in the author database that contain that state code.

After the contents of the sSQL string variable are set with the appropriate Call statement, the CreatePreparedStatement method of cn (the rdoConnection object) is used to create a prepared statement named ps. Like the other prepared statements that you've seen in this chapter, the first parameter of the CreatePreparedStatement method contains a string that can be used to uniquely identify the prepared statement. Using an empty string simply adds the prepared statement to the rdoPreparedStatements collection. The second parameter passes in the sSQL string that contains the SQL Call statement. Next, the direction and value of the parameters used by the ps rdoPreparedStatement object are set. In this example, each parameter of the rdoPreparedStatement object named ps is referred to using its ordinal number. Therefore, ps.rdoParameters(0) refers to the first parameter, and ps.rdoParameters(1) refers to the second parameter. The first parameter is an input-only parameter that contains the value that comes from the text box named Text_State. The second parameter is an output parameter that will be returned by the stored procedure.

After the direction and value of the rdoPreparedStatement are set, the Execute method is used to call the stored procedure. After the stored procedure has been executed, the value returned in the second parameter is used to set the text property of the Text_Rows text box.

Error Handling

All of the errors that are generated while executing RDO functions are placed in the rdoErrors collection. Depending on the severity level, RDO errors can also fire Visual Basic's error handler. This tight integration with Visual Basic makes it easy to handle RDO errors. The following DisplayRDOError subroutine illustrates how you can retrieve error descriptions from the rdoErrors collection and display them in a simple message box:

```
Private Sub DisplayRDOError()

    Dim er As rdoError

    For Each er In rdoErrors
        MsgBox "Number: " & er.Number & vbCrLf & _
            "SQL State: " & er.SQLState & vbCrLf & _
            "Text: " & er.Description
    Next

End Sub
```

The DisplayRDOError subroutine uses RDO's rdoError object to retrieve the error number (er.Number), SQL State (er.SQLState), and descriptive text (er.Description), and then display them using a message box. Since it possible for the rdoErrors collection to return multiple messages, Visual Basic's For-Each loop is used to iterate through the collection of rdoError objects.

When an RDO operation generates an error that exceeds the value set in the rdoDefaultErrorThreshold property of the rdoEngine object, a trapable Visual Basic error event is generated. The following code illustrates how you can use Visual Basic's error handler in conjunction with the DisplayRDOErrors subroutine:

```
Private Sub ShowError()

    Dim sSQL As String
    On Error GoTo RDOError

    sSQL = "Drop Table no_such_table"
    cn.Execute sSQL
    Exit Sub

RDOError:
    DisplayRDOError

End Sub
```

In this example, Visual Basic's error handler is enabled by the On Error statement. When a trapable error is generated, the Visual Basic error handler will transfer control to the RDOError label. Immediately following the RDOError label, the DisplayRDOError subroutine is executed. This displays the error number, SQL state code, and the error description in a message box.

ADVANCED TOPICS

While the beginning of this chapter provided a broad foundation for developing NT database applications using RDO and SQL Server 7, the last part of the chapter drills down a little deeper into a few other important database capabilities provided by RDO 2.0. In this advanced section, you'll see how to work with multiple result sets and learn how you might use them in your applications. Next, you'll see how asynchronous queries can be used to allow your application to perform other tasks while it waits for long-running queries to complete. Then you'll see an example of how to implement SQL Server's server-side cursors to shift the burden of managing result sets from the client to the SQL Server system. Finally, this section ends by taking a closer look at some techniques for managing data concurrency using RDO.

Working with Multiple Result Sets

While the query examples shown in the beginning of this chapter all worked with a single result set, RDO also has the ability to manage multiple result sets. You might want to take advantage of RDO's multiple result set support for tasks like running stored procedures that return multiple result sets or simply as a shorthand way of filling multiple combo boxes or list boxes that are on the same window. The following code shows how you can use RDO and multiple result sets:

```
Private Sub MultipleRS(cn As rdoConnection)

    Dim ps As rdoPreparedStatement
    Dim rs As rdoResultset
    Dim sSQL As String
```

```
    Screen.MousePointer = vbHourglass

    'Setup the two SELECT statements
    sSQL = "Select au_lname From authors; "
    sSQL = sSQL & "Select stor_name From stores "

    Set ps = cn.CreatePreparedStatement("MultiRS", "")
    ps.SQL = sSQL
    ps.RowsetSize = 1

    'Open the first RS
     Set rs = ps.OpenResultset _
            (rdOpenForwardOnly, rdConcurReadOnly)

    While Not rs.EOF
        List1.AddItem rs(0)
        DoEvents
        rs.MoveNext
    Wend


    'The end of the first RS was reached
    ' Now open the 2nd RS

    rs.MoreResults

    While Not rs.EOF
        List1.AddItem rs(0)
        DoEvents
        rs.MoveNext
    Wend

    rs.Close

    Screen.MousePointer = vbDefault

End Sub
```

Near the beginning of this example, the string variable, sSQL, is assigned two different Select statements. When setting up the string to be used to produce multiple result sets, it's important to separate each SQL statement with a semicolon. While this example shows how to use multiple Select statements, you can also use other SQL action queries like Insert, Update, and Delete. After the sSQL string has been assigned with the appropriate SQL statement, the CreatePreparedStatement method of the connection object is used to create a new rdoPreparedStatement object named MultiRS. Next, the properties of the ps rdoPreparedStatement object are set. First, the SQL property is set using the sSQL string variable, and then the RowsetSize property is set to 1.

> **NOTE:** Using its default connection and prepared statement settings, RDO is unable to process multiple result sets using the SQL Server ODBC driver. In order to work with multiple result sets, you must set the RowsetSize property of the rdoPreparedStatement object to 1. In addition, the rdoResultset's cursor type must be set to rdOpenForwardOnly, and the lock type must be rdConcurReadOnly. Alternatively, when you open a new rdoConnection object you can set the CursorDriver property to rdUseODBC.

After the properties of the rdoPreparedStatement object are set, the OpenResultset method is used to open the result set using a forward-only cursor that's set to read-only. It's important to note that the result set attributes that are set when the OpenResultset method is called apply to all of the subsequent result sets that are opened. After the first result set is opened, a While loop is used to read through the result set. Within the While loop, you can see where the value of the first column, rs(0), is added to the list named List1. The first result set is processed until the EOF property becomes true, which indicates that the end of the result set has been reached.

After the first result set has been processed, the MoreResults method of the rs rdoResultset object is used to access the next result set where another While loop is used to read through the second result set. Again, the value in the first (and in this case only) column is added to the list named List2. When the end of the second result set is reached, the While loop terminates and the result set is closed.

Asynchronous Queries

The ability to asynchronously execute queries is another important RDO feature. Asynchronous query execution enables the application to perform other tasks while it waits for a long-running query to complete. This prevents the user from having to wait for the query to complete before any other operation can be performed. Using asynchronous queries and RDO is accomplished by setting the options that are used on the OpenResultset method. The following code shows how to open an asynchronous query:

```
Private Sub AsynchRSStart(cn As rdoConnection)

    Dim sSQL As String

    Screen.MousePointer = vbHourglass

    sSQL = "Select * From authors "
```

```
'Start the Async query and move on
Set rsA = cn.OpenResultset(sSQL, rdOpenForwardOnly, _
            rdConcurReadOnly, rdAsyncEnable)

Screen.MousePointer = vbDefault

End Sub
```

After the SQL statement in the string variable, sSQL, is set up, the OpenResultset method is used to execute the query. The first three parameters of the OpenResultset method should be familiar. The first parameter is a string containing the SQL statement, the second parameter sets the result set type to forward-only, and the third parameter sets the lock type to read-only. It's the fourth parameter that differs from the other query examples presented earlier in this chapter. The value of rdAsyncEnable in the fourth parameter indicates that the result set object should execute the query asynchronously. Instead of waiting for the query to be completed, the application can immediately perform other tasks—including other data queries or update actions. Periodically, the application can check for the completion of the query by using the rdoResultset's StillExecuting property, as shown here:

```
Private Sub AsynchRSFinish(cn As rdoConnection)

    Dim sTextLine As String
    Dim cl As rdoColumn

    Screen.MousePointer = vbHourglass

    If rsA.StillExecuting = False Then

        Do
            sTextLine = ""
            For Each cl In rsA.rdoColumns
                If (Len(cl.Value) <= 7) Then
                    sTextLine = sTextLine & cl.Value & vbTab & vbTab
                Else
                    sTextLine = sTextLine & cl.Value & vbTab
                End If
            Next

            List1.AddItem sTextLine
            DoEvents

            rsA.MoveNext
```

```
         Loop Until rsA.EOF = True

         rsA.Close

     End If

     Screen.MousePointer = vbDefault

End Sub
```

If the StillExecuting property of the rsA result set object is false, then the asynchronous query has completed and the result set is ready to be processed. A Do loop is used to read through all of the rows in the result set. For each row, all of the column values are concatenated together and the resulting string is added to a list. Since this particular query uses the Select * to include all of the columns in the table, a For Each loop is used to access each member of the rdoColumns collection. The Do loop is ended when the end of the result set is reached and then the result set is closed.

Server-Side Cursors

Server-side cursors shift the responsibility for maintaining the cursor from the client system to the SQL Server system. RDO handles both client-side and server-side cursors on your behalf by making the appropriate ODBC API calls to the ODBC Driver Manager. Using server-side cursors can result in application performance improvements by reducing the amount of network input/output (I/O) that's required to maintain the cursor. Additionally, in many instances, the SQL Server system is a much more powerful system than the typical client workstation and is better able to manipulate large cursor keysets. However, like most performance techniques, there is a trade-off. Using server-side cursors requires more server resources than client-side cursors, and the server resource requirements are multiplied by the number of client systems that open up server-side cursors.

Setting the CursorDriver property of the rdoEnvironment object enables your application to use server-side cursors. The following code illustrates setting the rdoEnvironment object and processing a result set using a server-side cursor:

```
Private Sub SSCursor(cn As rdoConnection)

    Dim rs As rdoResultset
    Dim cl As rdoColumn
    Dim sTextLine As String

    Screen.MousePointer = vbHourglass
```

```
' Use Server side cursor
en.CursorDriver = rdUseServer

Set rs = cn.OpenResultset _
    ("Select au_lname, au_fname From authors", rdOpenKeyset)

For Each cl In rs.rdoColumns
    sTextLine = sTextLine & cl.Name & vbTab
Next

List1.AddItem sTextLine
DoEvents

Do Until rs.EOF
    sTextLine = ""
    For Each cl In rs.rdoColumns
        sTextLine = sTextLine & cl.Value & vbTab
        End If
    Next

    List1.AddItem sTextLine
    DoEvents

    rs.MoveNext

Loop

Screen.MousePointer = vbDefault

End Sub
```

As you can see, from a coding standpoint, using server-side cursors is virtually identical to using client-side cursors. The big difference is behind the scenes. Setting the CursorDriver property of the environment object to rdUseServer tells RDO to open a server-side cursor when the OpenResultset method is called. When the OpenResultset method is executed a keyset cursor is created on the server. Moving through the result set and closing the result set is coded exactly the same as using a client-side cursor.

Managing Data Concurrency

Most NT database applications need to support multiple users, and whenever multiple users are updating the same tables you need to implement some mechanism to ensure that the data integrity of each user's update is maintained. From the application developer's standpoint, there are two basic methods for implementing data concurrency: optimistic record locking and pessimistic record locking. Pessimistic record locking is the simplest of these two schemes. With pessimistic record locking, the rows in the current rowset are exclusively locked when the cursor is opened, and they remain locked until the cursor is moved past the rowset boundary. Pessimistic record locking is easy to implement because the application developer relies on the database to enforce the lock conditions. However, pessimistic record locking can be extremely user unfriendly because one or more rows can remain locked indefinitely.

Optimistic record locking is much more user friendly but it also tends to be more difficult to implement. Optimistic record locking is basically built around the premise that no other users will be attempting to update the same row that you are. With optimistic record locking, no exclusive locks are placed on the rows in a result set. Instead, the application is responsible for ensuring that no other users have updated a row before your application performs an update operation. An application generally implements optimistic record locking by either testing the rows' data values or checking a special timestamp column.

RDO has several built-in options that can help you manage data concurrency. The LockType option of the rdoResultset is RDO's primary setting for controlling the type of row locking that will be implemented when an rdoResultset is created. The lock-type property of the OpenResultset method supports the following options:

- ▼ **rdConcurLock** This option supports pessimistic row locking. If SQL Server is using page locking then the current data page is locked when the Edit or AddNew method is executed and the lock is held until the Update method has completed. If SQL Server is using row locking, then only the current row in the result set is locked.

- ■ **rdConcurRowVer** This option supports optimistic row locking based on the row version that is created using the row ID.

- ■ **rdConcorValues** This option supports optimistic row locking based on the data values of all of the columns contained in the result set.

- ■ **rdConcurBatchOnly** This option supports optimistic batch mode record locking.

- ▲ **rdConcurReadOnly** This option does not lock any rows and no updates to the result set are allowed.

If one of these lock methods fails, then RDO generates a trapable error.

TIP: If an update operation fails because of a locking error, you can use the Move 0 method to refresh the current row. (The Move 0 method rereads the current row.) After the row is refreshed, you can reissue the AddNew or Edit method followed by the Update method to complete the update operation.

CONCLUSION

As you have seen throughout this chapter, developing SQL Server database applications with RDO combines the best of DAO and ODBC programming. RDO offers the same ease of use as DAO, and yet it also provides the high performance that's available with the ODBC API.

All of the code listings presented in this chapter are also contained in the RDO Wizard example program that's on the CD-ROM accompanying this book.

ADDITIONAL RESOURCES

RDO provides very close to the same extensive data access functions as the ODBC API that it is based on. For more information about using RDO and Visual Basic, you can refer to the following Microsoft publications:

▼ *Guide to Building Client/Server Applications with Visual Basic*

▲ Vaughn, William R. *Hitchhiker's Guide to Visual Basic and SQL Server*, Sixth Edition. Redmond, WA: Microsoft Press, 1998.

CHAPTER 15

Developing SQL Server Database Applications with OLE DB and ADO

In this chapter, you'll see how to develop SQL Server database applications using Visual Basic and ActiveX Data Objects (ADO). In the first part of this chapter, you'll get a brief overview of OLE DB, with a look at the OLE DB architecture and the basic relationship between OLE DB and ADO. The second part of this chapter will illustrate the basic ADO database programming techniques that are used to build SQL Server database applications.

OLE DB and ADO are the most recent data access programming interfaces developed by Microsoft. Both OLE DB and ADO 2 are delivered as a part of SQL Server 7. Microsoft has positioned OLE DB as the successor to ODBC. Considering the widespread success of ODBC, this leaves OLE DB with some big shoes to fill. The ODBC API has enjoyed near universal acceptance. In addition to providing database support for thousands of custom database applications, most shrink-wrapped desktop applications like Microsoft Office support the ODBC API. ODBC drivers exist for virtually all of the major database systems. However, ODBC was primarily designed to handle relational data. The ODBC API is based upon SQL; and, while it works very well for relational database access, it was never intended to work with other nonrelational data sources.

Like ODBC, OLE DB provides access to relational data but OLE DB extends the functionality provided by ODBC. OLE DB has been designed as a standard interface for all types of data. In addition to relational database access, OLE DB provides access; to a wide variety of data sources, including tabular data like Excel spreadsheets, ISAM files like dBase, e-mail, the new NT 5 Active Directory, and even IBM host DB2 data. Using OLE DB, you can access many different and diverse data sources using a single interface.

OLE DB AND UNIVERSAL DATA ACCESS

As its name implies, OLE DB is built on an OLE foundation. Unlike ODBC, which provides a DLL call-level interface, ADO provides a COM interface for OLE DB that allows it to be called from other OLE-compliant applications. OLE DB is the foundation for Microsoft's data access strategy known as Universal Data Access. Essentially, Universal Data Access refers to a set of common interfaces that are used to represent data contained from any data source. OLE DB is the technology that makes Universal Data Access a reality. Universal Data Access and OLE DB stand at the opposite end of the spectrum from the notion that all objects should be maintained within the database. Instead of attempting to move all of the different bits of data required by a business into an object-oriented database, OLE DB has been created with the understanding that business data is maintained in a variety of diverse data sources. OLE DB provides a similar interface to all sorts of data. OLE DB can be used to access any data that can be represented in a basic row and column format.

OLE DB ARCHITECTURE OVERVIEW

Applications that use OLE DB are typically classified either as OLE DB providers or as OLE DB consumers. Figure 15-1 illustrates the relationship between OLE providers and OLE consumers.

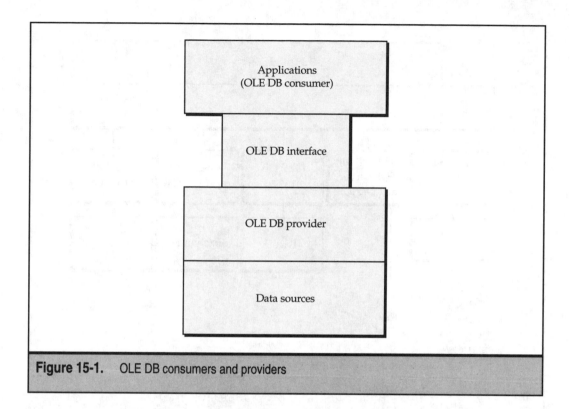

Figure 15-1. OLE DB consumers and providers

As you can see, OLE DB consumers are nothing more than applications that are written to use the OLE DB interface. In contrast, OLE DB providers are responsible for accessing data sources and supplying data to OLE consumers via the OLE DB interface. More specifically, there are actually two types of OLE DB providers: data providers and service providers. Data providers simply expose the data from a data source, while service providers both transport and process data. Service providers typically provide more advanced functions that extend the basic data access found in OLE DB data providers. Microsoft Query is an example of an OLE DB service provider while the Microsoft OLE DB provider for SQL Server is an example of a data provider.

As you would expect from its ODBC roots, OLE DB provides different levels of functionality based on the capabilities of the different OLE DB providers. While all OLE DB drivers support a common interface, each individual driver is able to extend the basic level of OLE DB functionality. Very similar to ODBC, each different OLE DB source uses its own OLE DB provider. Figure 15-2 illustrates how different OLE DB providers are required to access multiple data sources. In the figure, you can see a high-level overview of how a Visual Basic application might use OLE DB to access several heterogeneous data sources. With the exception of ODBC databases, each different data source is accessed using a different OLE DB provider. For example, SQL Server databases are accessed using SQLOLEDB, Microsoft's SQL Server's OLE DB provider; data contained in

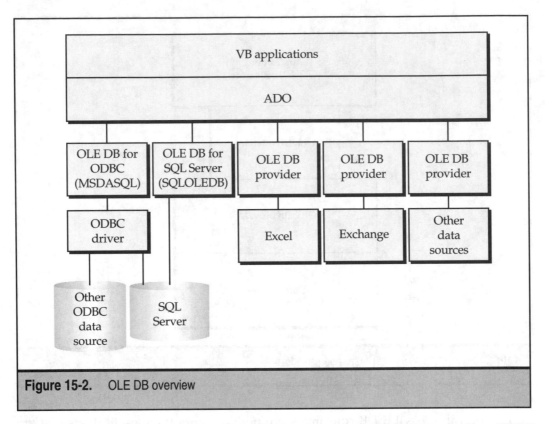

Figure 15-2. OLE DB overview

Microsoft Excel or Exchange is accessed using their respective OLE DB providers. ODBC is an exception to this one OLE DB provider-per-data-source rule. To provide maximum compatibility with existing ODBC data sources, Microsoft developed MSDSSQL, the OLE DB provider for ODBC. Unlike most OLE DB providers, which provide direct database access, the MSDASQL OLE DB provider for ODBC accesses data using existing ODBC drivers. The MSDASQL OLE DB provider for ODBC maps OLE DB calls into their equivalent ODBC calls. As you have probably guessed, the capabilities provided by the OLE DB provider for ODBC are dependent on the underlying ODBC driver. The OLE DB provider for ODBC 1.1 that ships with SQL Server 7 is compatible with the following Microsoft ODBC drivers:

▼ ODBC 3.7, which ships with SQL Server 7

▲ ODBC 2.65, which ships with SQL Server 6.5

Each OLE DB provider delivers data access and reflects its capabilities through its exposed COM interfaces. However, the OLE DB COM interface is a low-level interface that requires support for pointers, data structures, and direct memory allocation. As a result, the direct use of OLE DB providers is unsuitable for development environments that do not provide support for low-level functions like pointers, such as Visual Basic,

VBA, VBScript, Java, JScript, JavaScript, and several others. This is where ADO fits in. ADO allows OLE DB providers to be accessed by interactive and scripting languages that need data access but do not support low-level memory access and manipulation.

ADO (ACTIVEX DATA OBJECTS)

ADO is essentially an OLE DB consumer that provides application-level access to OLE DB data sources. ADO is an OLE automation server that most OLE-compliant development and scripting environments can access. You can download ADO from Microsoft's Web site at the following address:

http://www.microsoft.com/data/ado/download.htm.

ADO is also delivered as a standard part of a number of different Microsoft development products, including

▼ Visual Studio Enterprise Edition 1 and 6

■ Visual Basic Enterprise Edition 4, 5, and 6

■ Visual InterDev 6

▲ SQL Server 7

As you saw in Figure 15-2, OLE DB provides two distinctly different methods for accessing SQL Server data—the OLE DB for SQL Server provider and the OLE DB provider for ODBC. ADO is able to work with both of these OLE DB providers. ADO takes advantage of a multilevel architecture that insulates the applications using the ADO object framework from the underlying network protocols and topology. Figure 15-3 illustrates the relationship of ADO, OLE DB, ODBC, and the PC's networking support.

At the top of the figure, you can see the Visual Basic ADO application. The Visual Basic application creates and uses the various ADO objects. The ADO object framework makes calls to the appropriate OLE DB provider. If the ADO application is using the OLE DB provider for ODBC, then the MSDASQL OLE DB provider will be used. If the ADO application is using the OLE DB for SQL Server provider, then the SQLOLEDB provider will be used. When using the OLE DB provider for ODBC, ADO loads the file msdasql.dll, which in turn loads the ODBC Driver Manager. The OLE DB provider for ODBC maps the OLE DB calls made by ADO into ODBC calls, which are passed on to the ODBC Driver Manager.

The ODBC Driver Manager handles loading the appropriate ODBC driver. The ODBC driver typically uses a network interprocess communication (IPC) method like Named Pipes, TCP/IP Sockets, or SPX to communicate to a remote IPC server that provides access to the target database. The native OLE DB provider for SQL Server doesn't use any additional middle layers. When using the OLE DB provider for SQL Server, ADO loads the sqloledb.dll, which directly loads and uses the appropriate network IPC method to communicate with the database. The IPC client component

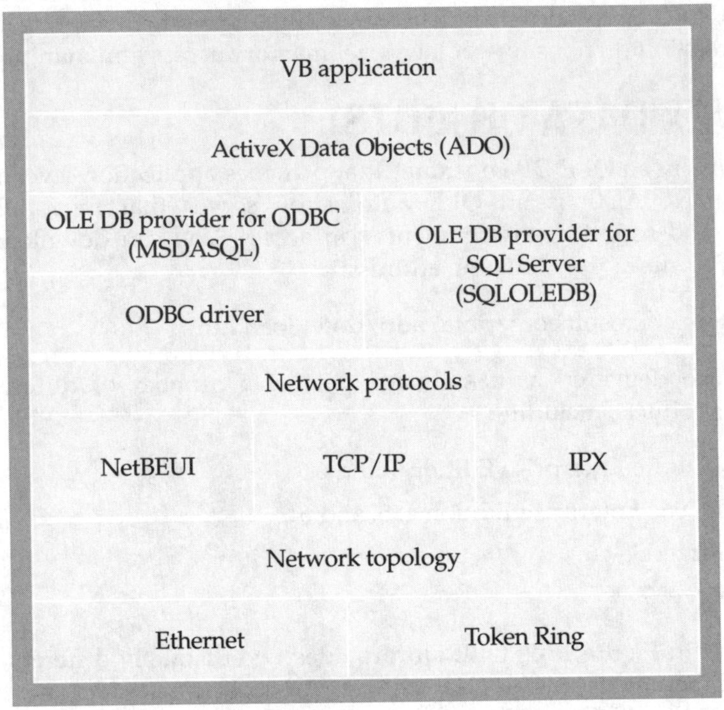

VB application
ActiveX Data Objects (ADO)

OLE DB provider for ODBC (MSDASQL)	OLE DB provider for SQL Server (SQLOLEDB)
ODBC driver	

Network protocols

NetBEUI	TCP/IP	IPX

Network topology

Ethernet	Token Ring

Figure 15-3. Network components that ADO uses

establishes a communications link with the corresponding server IPC through the networking protocol in use. The network protocol is responsible for sending and receiving the IPC data stream over the network. Common networking protocols include NetBEUI, TCP/IP, and IPX. Finally, at the bottom of this stack is the physical network topology. The physical network includes the adapter cards and cabling that make the actual connections between the networked systems. Ethernet and Token Ring are examples of two of the most common network topologies.

OLE DB AND ADO FILES

Here is a summary of the client files that are used to implement ADO:

File	Description
msdasql.dll	OLE DB provider for ODBC
sqloledb.dll	OLE DB provider for SQL Server
msado15.dll	ADO Object Library

ADO ARCHITECTURE

As with several of the other data access object models, ADO is implemented using a hierarchical object framework. However, the ADO object model is simpler and flatter than either Data Access Objects (DAO) or Remote Database Objects (RDO) frameworks. In Figure 15-4, you can see an overview of ADO's object hierarchy.

The Connection, Recordset, and Command objects are the three primary objects in the ADO object model. The Connection object represents a connection to the remote data source. In addition to establishing the connection to a data source, Connection objects can be used to control the transaction scope. A Connection object can be associated with either a Recordset object or a Command object.

The Recordset object represents a result set that is returned from the data source. An ADO Recordset object can either use an open Connection object or it can establish its own connection to the target data source. Recordset objects allow you to both query and modify data. Each Recordset object contains a collection of Field objects where each Field object represents a column of data in the Recordset.

The Command object is used to issue commands and parameterized SQL statements. Command objects can be used for both action SQL statements and SQL queries that return recordsets. Like the ADO Recordset object, the Command object can either use an

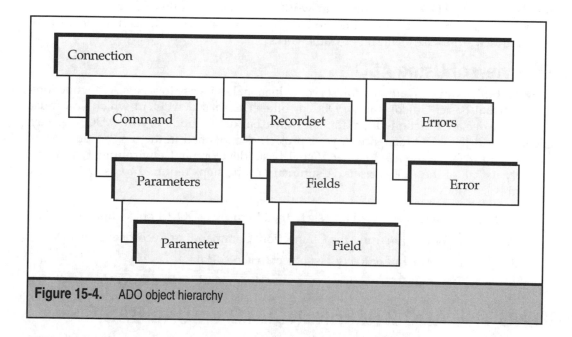

Figure 15-4.   ADO object hierarchy

active Connection object or establish its own connection to the target data source. The Command object contains a Parameters collection in which each Parameter object in the collection represents a parameter that the Command object uses. In a case in which a Command object executes a parameterized SQL statement, each Parameter object would represent one of the parameters in the SQL statement.

Directly beneath the Connection object is the Errors collection. Each Error object contained in the Errors collection contains information about an error that was encountered by one of the objects in the ADO object framework.

In addition to the main objects shown in Figure 15-4, the Connection, Command, Recordset, and Field objects all have a Properties collection, which consists of a set of Property objects. Each Property object can be used to get or set the various properties associated with the object.

While at first glance the ADO framework may seem just as hierarchically structured as DAO and RDO, that's not really the case. Unlike the other data access object frameworks, all of the ADO objects—except the Errors, Fields, and Properties objects— can be created on their own without needing to be accessed through a higher-level object. This makes the ADO object framework much flatter and more flexible than the other object models. For instance, the ADO object framework allows a Recordset object to be opened and accessed without first requiring an instance of the Connection object. The ability to directly use each object without first instantiating any higher-order objects tends to make ADO a bit simpler to work with than the other object frameworks. However, as you'll see in some of the code examples, ADO is not always as straightforward in use as the other frameworks.

An Overview of Using ADO

ADO is built as an OLE automation server, which makes it easy to access ADO functions from Visual Basic. Unlike using ODBC or other DLL-based APIs, in which you must manually declare functions and parameters in a .bas or .cls module, with ADO you only need to add the ADO reference to your project, as explained in the next section. After adding the ADO reference to your Visual Basic development environment, you can readily use all of the ADO objects. A summary of the steps required to use ADO from Visual Basic follows:

1. Make a reference in Visual Basic to the Microsoft ADO 2.1 object library.

2. Open a connection using the Connection, Command, or Recordset object.

3. Use the Command or Recordset object to access data.

4. Close the connection to the Connection, Command, or Recordset object.

ADDING THE ADO 2 REFERENCE TO VISUAL BASIC

Before you can use ADO from Visual Basic, you must set a reference to the ADO type library, also known as the ADO automation server. The files that provide the basic support for ADO 2.1 are installed on the system when you first download the ADO support from the Microsoft Web site or when you install one of the products containing ADO that were listed previously in the section "ADO (ActiveX Data Objects)." Before you

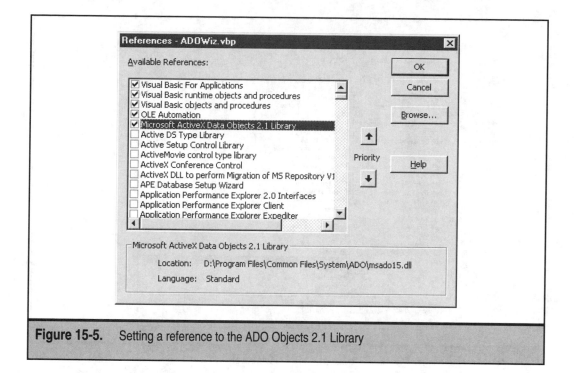

Figure 15-5.   Setting a reference to the ADO Objects 2.1 Library

can begin using ADO in your Visual Basic projects, however, you need to set a reference to the ADO OLE type library in Visual Basic's development environment. To add a reference to the ADO Objects 2.1 Library in Visual Basic 5 or 6, start Visual Basic, and then select Project | References to display the References dialog box shown in Figure 15-5.

In the References dialog box, scroll through the Available References list until you see the "Microsoft ActiveX Data Objects 2.1 Library" option. Clicking in the check box and then clicking the OK button adds the ADO Objects Library to Visual Basic's IDE (Interactive Development Environment). Unlike ActiveX Controls, adding a reference to Visual Basic's IDE doesn't create any visual objects in Visual Basic's Toolbox. In order to see the ADO objects, properties, and methods, you need to use Visual Basic's Object Browser. Figure 15-6 displays the ADO Objects Library using Visual Basic's Object Browser.

USING ADO OBJECTS WITH VISUAL BASIC

After adding a reference to the ADO 2.1 Library to the Visual Basic development environment, you're ready to create Visual Basic applications using ADO. Unlike the DAO or RDO object models, ADO has no top-level object that must be created before you

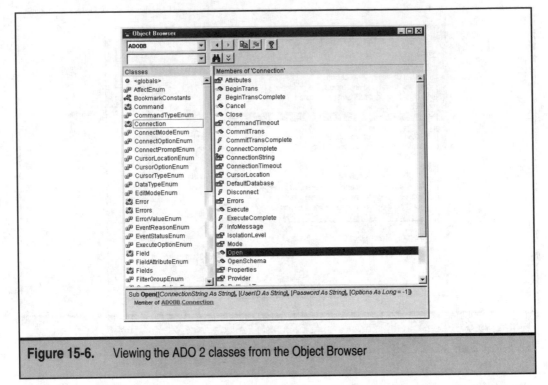

Figure 15-6. Viewing the ADO 2 classes from the Object Browser

establish a connection to a data source. Using ADO, the first action that your application takes is to open a connection using the Connection, Command, or Recordset object.

Connecting to SQL Server

ADO can connect to SQL Server using either the MSDASQL OLE DB provider for ODBC or the SQLOLEDB OLE DB provider for SQL Server. The MSDASQL provider allows the ADO object framework to be used with existing ODBC drivers, while the SQLOLEDB OLE DB provider connects directly to SQL Server. Both of these OLE DB providers can be used with the ADO Connection, Command, and Recordset objects. In the following section, you'll see how to establish a connection with SQL Server using both the OLE DB provider for ODBC and the OLE DB provider for SQL Server. You will also see how to connect to SQL Server using the ADO Connection object, as well as directly through the ADO Recordset object.

Opening a Connection with the OLE DB Provider for ODBC

If you are familiar with the DAO or RDO object frameworks, using the ADO Connection object with the OLE DB provider for ODBC to establish a connection to a SQL Server system is probably the most familiar starting point for beginning to build an ADO application. Like DAO and RDO, the MSDASQL OLE DB provider for ODBC uses an ODBC driver to access SQL Server. This means that the system running the application must either have an existing ODBC driver for SQL Server, and a Data Source Name (DSN) for SQL Server in the ODBC Administrator or the application must use a DSN-less connection string.

The following code illustrates how to use the ADO Connection object and the MSDASQL provider to prompt the user to select an existing DSN that will be used to connect to SQL Server:

```
Dim cn As New ADODB.Connection


' DSN Connection using the OLE DB provider for ODBC - MSDASQL
cn.ConnectionString = "DSN=" & _
    ";DATABASE=pubs;UID=" & sLoginID & _
    ";PWD=" & sPassword

' Prompt the user to select the DSN
cn.Properties("Prompt") = adPromptComplete
cn.Open
cn.Close
```

In the beginning of this code example, you can see where a new instance of the ADO Connection object named cn is created. Since ADO objects do not rely on upper-level objects, each object must generally have a Dim statement that uses Visual Basic's New keyword. Next, the ConnectionString property of the cn Connection object is assigned an ODBC connection string. Like the normal ODBC connection string, the connection string used in the ADO ConnectionString property must contain a set of predefined keywords where each keyword and its associated value is separated by semicolons. Because ADO is based upon OLE DB rather than just ODBC, the keywords used in the connection string are a bit different than the keywords used in a standard ODBC connection string. Table 15-1 presents the valid OLE DB connection string keywords.

After the OLE DB connection string is assigned to the Connection object's ConnectionString property, the Connection object's Prompt property is assigned the constant value of adPromptComplete. This value specifies that the ODBC Driver Manager should prompt for any required connection information that's not supplied in the connection string.

The Prompt property controls how the ODBC Driver Manager responds to the keyword and values contained in the connection string. Table 15-2 lists the valid values for the Prompt property.

Keyword	Description
PROVIDER	This optional keyword can be used to identify the name of the OLE DB provider that will be used. If no provider name is supplied, the connection will use the MSDASQL provider.
DSN	The name of an existing data source created by the ODBC Administrator.
DRIVER	The name of an existing ODBC driver.
SERVER	The name of an existing SQL Server system.
UID	The login ID for the data source.
PWD	The password associated with the login ID.
DATABASE	The SQL Server target database name.

Table 15-1. OLE DB Connection String Keywords

TIP: The Properties collection of the ADO Connection, Command, and Recordset objects allows you to get and set property values using named items in the properties collection. In fact, some ADO properties like the Prompt property are not exposed directly through the object framework and can only be accessed through the Properties collection. While this dynamic Properties collection gives the ADO object model more flexibility than DAO or RDO, it also hides properties making it more difficult to find and work with properties than the more straightforward DAO or RDO object models. If you can't find an ADO property that you think should exist, try searching for it by iterating through the Properties collection.

In this example, the connection string doesn't use the PROVIDER keyword, so the OLE DB provider for ODBC, MSDASQL, is used by default. This means that the connection to SQL Server takes place via an ODBC driver. In addition, the connection string does not specify a value for the DSN keyword. This means that the connection string must either use the DRIVER keyword to make a DSN-less connection or the ODBC Driver Manager must prompt the user for the Data Source Name (DSN) in order to make a connection to SQL Server. In this example, the DRIVER keyword is not used and the value of adPromptComplete is specified in the Prompt property. This allows the ODBC Driver Manager to prompt the user to select an existing ODBC data source.

After the user has responded to the ODBC Driver Manager prompt, the cn Connection object's Open method connects to SQL Server. The Connection object's Open method takes three optional parameters:

▼ The first optional parameter accepts a string that contains an OLE DB connection string. This parameter performs exactly the same function as the Connection object's ConnectionString property, and you can use this parameter as an alternative to setting the ConnectionString property.

Constant	Description
adPromptNever	The ODBC Driver Manager can only use the information provided by the connection string to make a connection. If sufficient information is not supplied, the connection will fail.
adPromptAlways	The ODBC Driver Manager will always display the ODBC Administrator to prompt for connection information.
adPromptComplete	The ODBC driver determines if all of the required connection information has been supplied in the connection string. If all of the required information is present, the connection is made without further prompting. If any of the required information is missing, the ODBC Administrator prompts the user for the missing information.
adPromptCompleteRequired	This option behaves like adPromptComplete, except that any prompts containing information that has already been supplied are disabled.

Table 15-2.   ADO MSDASQL Prompt Constants

- ■ The second optional parameter accepts a String variable that contains a valid login ID for the target data source.
- ▲ The third optional parameter accepts a String variable that can contain the password for the target data source.

TIP: While both OLE DB connection strings and the second and third parameters of the Open method allow you to specify login information, do not use both at the same time. Since you normally need to use the OLE DB connection string to supply the name of the OLE DB provider anyway, it is usually simpler to just supply the login information as a part of the OLE DB connection string.

In this example, there is no other processing, so the Close method ends the connection.

Opening a DSN-less Connection with the OLE DB Provider for ODBC

The previous example illustrated how to establish a SQL Server connection using the MSDASQL provider and an existing DSN. However, there are instances where your application may need to make an ODBC-based connection and it can't rely on a DSN being preconfigured. Luckily, the MSDASQL OLE DB provider also supports using DSN-less connections. Using a DSN-less connection removes the requirement of needing an existing data source.

The following code illustrates how to use the ADO Connection object and the MSDASQL provider to make a DSN-less connection to SQL Server:

```
Dim cn As New ADODB.Connection

' DSNless Connection using the OLE DB provider for ODBC - MSDASSQL
cn.ConnectionString = "DRIVER=SQL Server" & _
    ";SERVER=" & sServer & _
    ";UID=" & sLoginID & _
    ";PWD=" & sPassword & _
    ";DATABASE=pubs"
cn.Open
cn.Close
```

Creating a new ADO Connection object named cn is the first action that takes place in this code example. Next, the ConnectionString property of the cn Connection object is assigned a connection string. As you might expect, since this connection string is intended to establish a DSN-less connection, it is quite a bit different than the connection string that was presented in the previous example. Since the PROVIDER keyword is not used, the MSDASQL provider for ODBC will be used as the default. As you might guess, the DSN keyword is not needed to establish a DSN-less connection. Instead, the DRIVER keyword has the value of "SQL Server" to indicate that the SQL Server ODBC driver should be used.

NOTE: The value used by the DRIVER keyword can optionally be enclosed in { }, as in {SQL Server}, but this is not a requirement.

In addition to specifying the ODBC driver that will be used, a DSN-less ODBC connection string must indicate the server and database that will be used. These values are supplied by the SERVER and DATABASE keywords. Finally, the UID and PWD keywords, described in Table 15-1, supply the required SQL Server login information.

After setting the ConnectionString property with a DSN-less ODBC connection string, the Connection object's Open method starts a connection to the SQL Server system. Then the Connection object's Close method ends the connection.

Opening a Connection with the OLE DB Provider for SQL Server

The OLE DB provider for ODBC is primarily intended to enable ADO applications to access ODBC-compliant databases when there is no native OLE DB provider available. While ODBC is certainly the established database access standard and is supported by virtually all popular databases, that's not the case with OLE DB, being a new technology. There aren't nearly as many native OLE DB providers available, and most of those have come out of Microsoft. SQL Server 7 is one of the first databases to have a native OLE DB provider. SQL Server 7 includes the OLE DB provider for SQL Server that is supplied in the sqloled.dll file.

Using the OLE DB provider for SQL Server is very similar to using the OLE DB provider for ODBC. Because the OLE DB provider for SQL Server does not use ODBC, there is no requirement for using a data source or an existing ODBC driver. However, you do need to specify the name of the OLE DB provider.

The following example illustrates how to make a connection to SQL Server using the ADO Connection object and the OLE DB provider for SQL Server:

```
Dim cn As New ADODB.Connection

' Connect using the OLE DB provider for SQL Server - SQLOLEDB
cn.ConnectionString = "PROVIDER=SQLOLEDB" & _
    ";SERVER=" & sServer & _
    ";UID=" & sLoginID & _
    ";PWD=" & sPassword & _
    ";DATABASE=pubs"
cn.Open
'Perform processing here
cn.Close
```

As in the previous examples, an instance of the ADO Connection object is created. Then the ConnectionString property of the ADO Connection object is assigned an OLE DB connection string. This connection string uses the PROVIDER keyword to specify that the SQLOLEDB provider is utilized. Specifying the PROVIDER keyword is required in order to use the OLE DB provider for SQL Server. If you omit this keyword, the provider defaults to the value of MSDASQL. In addition, the SERVER and DATABASE keywords are also required. The SERVER keyword specifies the name of the SQL Server system that will be connected to; the DATABASE keyword identifies the database that will be used. The UID and PWD keywords provide the authentication values required to log in to SQL Server.

After setting the ConnectionString property, the Open method starts the connection. Once the connection has been established other database access can be performed. In this example, there is no additional work so the connection is closed using the Close method.

Ending a Connection

As the previous examples illustrated, before ending your application you should use the Connection object's Close method to end the database connection. An example of the Close method follows:

```
Dim cn As New ADODB.Connection
'Perform work with the connect and then end it
cn.Close
```

Retrieving Data with the ADO Recordset

ADO allows you to retrieve data using either the Recordset or the Command object. Both of these objects can be used with an active Connection object, or they can open their own connections. In the following section ("Using a Forward-Only Recordset Object"), you'll see how to retrieve data from SQL Server using the Recordset object. You'll learn about the differences between the various types of ADO Recordset objects and how to traverse Recordset objects and work with column values using the ADO Fields collection.

ADO Recordset Types

Like the Recordset object found in DAO or RDO's Resultset object, the ADO Recordset object represents a result set that's returned from a database query. ADO Recordset objects support several different types of cursors that correspond to the different types of ODBC cursors. ADO provides support for forward-only, static, keyset, and dynamic Recordset objects. The type of cursor used in an ADO Recordset object must be set before the Recordset is opened. If you don't specify the type of Recordset object that you want to use, ADO automatically uses a forward-only cursor.

FORWARD-ONLY CURSORS   As a default, ADO uses the forward-only cursor. This cursor provides the best performance and the least overhead of any of the ADO cursor types; however, it is also less capable than other ADO cursors. ADO Recordset objects that use forward-only cursors are updateable, but you can modify only the current row. Any changes in the base table that other users make are not reflected in the Recordset object.

STATIC CURSORS   A static cursor provides a snapshot of the data at the time the cursor was opened. ADO Recordset objects that use static cursors are not updateable, and they do not reflect any changes that are made in the base tables unless the cursor is closed and reopened. Because of their static nature, Recordset objects created by static cursors are generally less resource intensive than Recordset objects that use keyset or dynamic cursors. However, since the static cursor makes a local copy of the data, you need to be careful about using this type of cursor with large result sets.

KEYSET CURSORS   Keyset cursors build a local set of keys where each key is an index to a row in the result set. When your application accesses a Recordset object that uses a keyset cursor, the key value from the local keyset retrieves the corresponding row from the base table. Recordset objects that use keyset cursors are updateable, but after they are fully populated they do not dynamically reflect changes that other users make in the base table. Keyset cursors are very capable, but they are also relatively resource intensive because the client system must maintain the keys for the entire result set as well as a buffer that contains a block of the actual data values.

DYNAMIC CURSORS   Dynamic cursors are the most powerful and capable type of ADO cursor, but they are also the most resource intensive. Dynamic cursors are very similar to keyset cursors. Both use a local set of keys that correspond to each row in the result set, and both are fully updateable. However, unlike Recordset objects that use a keyset cursor, Recordset objects that use dynamic cursors are able to reflect automatically any changes that other applications make to the base tables. In order to dynamically maintain the result set, ADO Recordset objects that use dynamic cursors must continually refresh the result set, automatically updating the local result set with any changes. Obviously, this is an intensive process.

Using a Forward-Only Recordset Object

The ADO Recordset object either can be used with an existing Connection object or it can optionally open a connection to the target data source on its own.

> *TIP:*   When an ADO Recordset object opens its own Connection object, the ADO object framework automatically creates a Connection object, but that object is not associated with a Visual Basic program variable. This makes using the Recordset object quick and easy, but it also adds the overhead required for creating the Connection object for each new Recordset object. If your application needs to create multiple Recordset objects that use the same database, it's much more efficient to use a Connection object and then associate each new Recordset object with the existing Connection object.

The following code listing illustrates how to use a Recordset object with an ADO Connection object:

```
Private Sub ForwardOnlyRecordset(cn As ADODB.Connection)

    Dim rs As New ADODB.Recordset

    Screen.MousePointer = vbHourglass

    ' Associate the Recordset with the Connection object named cn
    rs.ActiveConnection = cn

    'Use the open method
    rs.Open "Select * From stores", , , , adCmdText
```

```
DisplayForwardGrid rs, Grid

rs.Close

Screen.MousePointer = vbDefault

End Sub
```

Before using the ADO Recordset object, you need to assign it to a Visual Basic variable. The Dim statement at the beginning of this subroutine creates a new ADO Recordset object named rs. Next, the ActiveConnection property of the rs Recordset object is set to an active Connection object. The Connection object must be created and connected to SQL Server, as illustrated in the previous examples. The ADO Connection object either could use the OLE DB provider for ODBC, or it could use the OLE DB provider for SQL Server. The ADO coding for both OLE DB providers is the same. Assigning the rs object's ActiveConnection property with an active Connection object associates the new Recordset object with the connected SQL Server system.

After the ActiveConnection property is set, a forward-only cursor is opened using the Recordset object's Open method. The Recordset object's Open method takes five optional parameters.

The first parameter is a Variant data type and, like you might think, it can accept a number of different values—such as the name of an existing Command object, a SQL statement, a table name, or the name of a stored procedure. In the preceding example, the first parameter contains a simple SQL Select statement that will create a result set that consists of all of the rows and columns that are contained in the stores table.

The Open method's optional second parameter can be used to associate the Recordset object with an ADO Connection object. This parameter performs exactly the same function as the Recordset object's ActiveConnection property, and you can use this parameter as an alternative to setting the ActiveConnection property. This parameter can accept either a String that contains an OLE DB connection string or it can accept a Variant that contains the name of an active ADO Connection object. If you specify an OLE DB connection string rather than the name of a Connection object, then ADO will implicitly create a Connection object and use it to establish a link to the target data source.

The third optional parameter of the Open method specifies the cursor type that the Recordset object will use. If this parameter is not designated, then the cursor type will be set to forward-only by default, which is the simplest and also the best-performing option. Table 15-3 presents the ADO constants used to specify the cursor type that an ADO Recordset object will use.

The fourth optional parameter specifies the type of locking that the OLE DB provider will use. If this parameter is not designated, then the lock type will be set to read-only by default. Table 15-4 presents the ADO constants used to specify the lock type that an ADO Recordset object will use.

ADO Constant	Cursor Type
adOpenForwardOnly	Forward-only cursor (default)
adOpenStatic	Static cursor
adOpenKeyset	Keyset cursor
adOpenDynamic	Dynamic cursor

Table 15-3.   ADO Recordset Cursor Types

The fifth optional parameter specifies the options of the Open method. The options parameter explicitly tells ADO how to handle the first parameter if the first parameter does not contain the name of an ADO Command object.

TIP: While it may seem a bit innocuous, specifying a value for the fifth parameter can result in improved performance because ADO does not need to test the data source to determine what type of value was supplied in the first parameter of the Open method. However, if you specify a constant for the fifth parameter that doesn't match the value supplied in the first parameter, then ADO will generate an error.

Table 15-5 presents the ADO constants that are used to specify the options that will be used by an ADO Recordset object.

After the Open method completes, the data in the Recordset object is available for processing. In the previous example, the DisplayForwardGrid subroutine is called to display the contents of the rs Recordset object in a grid. In the next section of code, you'll see how to move through the rows in the Recordset object, as well as how to access the

Lock Type	Description
adLockReadOnly	Read-only (default)
adLockPessimistic	Pessimistic locking
adLockOptimistic	Optimistic locking
adLockBatchOptimistic	Optimistic locking using batch mode updates

Table 15-4.   ADO Recordset Lock Types

column information in the Fields collection. The DisplayForwardGrid subroutine is shown here:

```
Private Sub DisplayForwardGrid _
            (rs As ADODB.Recordset, Grid As MSFlexGrid)

    Dim fld As ADODB.Field

    ' Set up the grid
    Grid.Cols = rs.Fields.Count
    Grid.Rows = 1
    Grid.Row = 0
    Grid.Col = 0

    'Set up the Grid headings
    For Each fld In rs.Fields
        Grid.ColWidth(Grid.Col) = _
          TextWidth(String(fld.ActualSize + 4, "a"))
        Grid.ColAlignment(Grid.Col) = 1
        Grid.Text = fld.Name
        If Grid.Col < rs.Fields.Count - 1 Then
          Grid.Col = Grid.Col + 1
        End If
    Next fld


    ' Move through each row in the record set
    Do Until rs.EOF

        ' Set the position in the grid
        Grid.Rows = Grid.Rows + 1
        Grid.Row = Grid.Rows - 1
        Grid.Col = 0

        'Loop through all fields
        For Each fld In rs.Fields
            Grid.Text = fld.Value
            If Grid.Col < rs.Fields.Count - 1 Then
                Grid.Col = Grid.Col + 1
            End If
        Next fld

        rs.MoveNext
    Loop
End Sub
```

Option	Description
adCmdUnknown	The source is unknown and ADO must test for it (default).
adCmdFile	The source is the name of a file.
adCmdStoredProc	The source is the name of a stored procedure.
adCmdTable	The source is the name of a table.
adCmdText	The source is a command (or SQL statement).

Table 15-5.   Recordset Source Options

At the very beginning of this subroutine, you can see where an instance of the ADO Recordset object named rs is passed as the first parameter, and an instance of the MSFlexGrid object is passed as the second parameter of the DisplayRSGrid subroutine. This allows the same subroutine to be reused with many different Recordset and Grid objects. The Dim statement in this subroutine creates an instance of an ADO Field object named fld.

NOTE: Unlike the previous ADO examples, there was no need to use the New keyword to declare either the ADO Recordset object or the ADO Field object because both of these variables are referring to an instance of a Recordset object that was already created.

After the ADO objects have been declared, the next portion of the subroutine DisplayForwardGrid sets up the grid to display the Recordset object. First, the number of grid columns is set using the Count property of the Recordset object's Fields collection. Next, the grid's Rows property is set up to have at least one row that will contain the column heading information. Then the grid's Row and Col properties are used to set the current grid cell at row 0 column 0 (the upper left-hand corner of the grid).

Once the grid's initial number of rows and columns have been set, the heading values and sizes for each of the grid's columns are set up. Every column in the result set will have a corresponding Field object in the Recordset object's Fields collection. A For Each loop iterates through all of the Field objects contained in the Fields collection. The first action within the For Each loop sets the column width of the grid using the grid's ColWidth property. In order to set the width of the correct column, the ColWidth property requires the index of the current grid column that is supplied by the grid's Col property. The ColWidth property must be assigned a value in twips (one twentieth of a printer's point); Visual Basic's TextWidth function is used to return the number of twips required for each Field object.

The correct number of twips is determined by creating a placeholder string using the Field object's ActualSize property plus four extra characters that help to prevent the grid columns from appearing too crowded. Next, the grid's ColAlignment property for each column is set to left-justify the cell text. Then the Field object's Name property is used as heading text for the grid columns. Finally, the current column is incremented using the grid's Col property. An If statement ensures that the Col property is not assigned a value that is greater than the maximum number of grid columns.

> **NOTE:** Since the ADO object framework doesn't support an OrdinalPosition property like the DAO and RDO frameworks, you have to add code to manually track the current column position.

Next, a Do Until loop reads through all of the columns in the Recordset object. The Do Until loop continues until the Recordset's EOF (End of File) property is becomes true—which indicates that all of the rows in the Recordset have been read. Inside the Do Until loop, the grid's Rows property is incremented to expand the size of the grid, and Row property is incremented to move the current position to the new grid row. Then the current grid column is set to the first column, and a For Each loop moves the data values contained in the Fields collection to the grid columns. Again, an If test ensures that the code doesn't attempt to access an invalid grid column. After all of the Field values have been processed, the Recordset object's MoveNext method moves the cursor to the next row in the Recordset object.

Using a Keyset Recordset Object

The previous code example illustrated how to use ADO to create a simple Recordset object that uses a forward-only cursor. The forward-only cursor is fast and efficient. However, it's not as capable as the other cursor types. For instance, while the forward-only cursor can only make a single pass through a Recordset in forward order, a keyset cursor allows multiple passes, as well as forward and backward scrolling.

The following code illustrates how to use an ADO Recordset object that uses a keyset cursor:

```
Private Sub KeysetRecordset(cn As ADODB.Connection)

    Dim rs As New ADODB.Recordset

    Screen.MousePointer = vbHourglass
```

```
' Associate the Recordset with the open connection
rs.ActiveConnection = cn
rs.Source = "Select * From employee"


' Pass the Open method the SQL and Recordset type parameters
rs.Open , , adOpenKeyset, adLockReadOnly

' Display the grid -- use a 1 to display in forward order
DisplayKeysetGrid rs, Grid, 1

rs.Close

Screen.MousePointer = vbDefault

End Sub
```

In this example, a new ADO Recordset object named rs is created. Then the ActiveConnection property of the rs Recordset object is set to cn, which is the name of an existing ADO Connection object that has an active database connection. Next, the Recordset object's Source property is assigned a simple SQL Select statement that will return all of the rows and columns from the employee table.

> **NOTE:** For publication purposes, several of the examples in this chapter use simple unqualified SQL Select statements. However, unless you know that the target tables are relatively small, you should try to keep your own result sets as small as possible by utilizing the SQL Select statement's Where clause.

Next, the Open method executes the source SQL statement on the target database. In this example, the first two parameters of the Open method don't need to be specified because they were already set using the Source and ActiveConnection properties of the Recordset object. The value of adOpenKeyset in the third parameter indicates that this Recordset object will use a keyset cursor. The value of adLockReadOnly in the fourth parameter makes the Recordset read-only.

After the Open method has executed the query, the DisplayKeysetGrid subroutine displays the contents of the rs Recordset object in a grid. The DisplayKeysetGrid subroutine uses three parameters: the name of an ADO Recordset object, the name of an MSFlexGrid object, and an integer value that controls the direction in which the data will be displayed. Since the capabilities of the keyset cursor are greater than the forward-only cursor, this subroutine contains a couple of enhancements that can take advantage of those capabilities. The code for the DisplayKeysetGrid subroutine is shown here:

```
Private Sub DisplayKeysetGrid _
    (rs As ADODB.Recordset, Grid As MSFlexGrid, nDirection As Integer)
```

```
Dim fld As ADODB.Field
Dim nForward As Integer
Dim nReverse As Integer

nForward = 1
nReverse = 2

' Set up the grid
Grid.Cols = rs.Fields.Count
rs.MoveLast
Grid.Rows = rs.RecordCount + 1
Grid.Row = 0
Grid.Col = 0

'Set up the Grid headings
 For Each fld In rs.Fields
     Grid.ColWidth(Grid.Col) = _
       TextWidth(String(fld.ActualSize + 4, "a"))
     Grid.ColAlignment(Grid.Col) = 1
     Grid.Text = fld.Name
     If Grid.Col < rs.Fields.Count - 1 Then
        Grid.Col = Grid.Col + 1
     End If
Next fld


If nDirection = nForward Then

    rs.MoveFirst

    ' Move through each row in the record set
    Do Until rs.EOF
        ' Set the position in the grid
        Grid.Row = Grid.Row + 1
        Grid.Col = 0

        'Loop through all fields
        For Each fld In rs.Fields
            Grid.Text = fld.Value
            If Grid.Col < rs.Fields.Count - 1 Then
                Grid.Col = Grid.Col + 1
            End If
```

```
        Next fld

        rs.MoveNext
    Loop

  Else

    rs.MoveLast

    ' Move through each row in the record set
    Do Until rs.BOF
        ' Set the position in the grid
        Grid.Row = Grid.Row + 1
        Grid.Col = 0

        'Loop through all fields
        For Each fld In rs.Fields
            Grid.Text = fld.Value
            If Grid.Col < rs.Fields.Count - 1 Then
                Grid.Col = Grid.Col + 1
            End If
        Next fld

        rs.MovePrevious

    Loop

  End If

End Sub
```

As in the DisplayForwardGrid subroutine that was presented earlier, the parameters used by the DisplayKeysetGrid subroutine allow it to be reused by many different Recordset and Grid objects. However, since this subroutine is intended to be used with keyset cursors, which support both forward and backward scrolling, it uses an additional parameter that can control the direction that the data will be listed. The internals of this subroutine are also a bit different than the DisplayForwardGrid subroutine because of the different capabilities of the Keyset Recordset object.

At the beginning of this subroutine, two Integer variables are declared and assigned values. These variables are just used to improve the readability of a later section of the code. The section of code immediately following these variables sets up the grid. This section is very similar to the DisplayForwardGrid that was shown earlier. However, there is one notable difference. Since keyset cursors support backward movement, this subroutine is able to use the Recordset object's MoveLast method to move to the end of the Recordset. This populates the Recordset object, which can then be used to size the grid to the appropriate number of rows. In this example, the grid is sized using the value from the Recordset's RecordCount property plus one additional row for the column headings.

Next, the grid columns are sized and the column headings are set to the database column names for each Field object in the Recordset object's Fields collection. While this code is identical to the ForwardOnlyGrid subroutine, the next section of code after that illustrates how the keyset cursor's ability to scroll forward and backward is used. The value passed in to the third parameter of the DisplayKeysetGrid subroutine controls the direction that the Recordset data will be listed in the grid. A value of 1 causes the data to be listed in forward order, while a value of 2 causes the Recordset data to be listed in backward order. The If test compares the value of the nDirection variable to the value of the Integer variable named nForward. If the value is equal, then the code in the first part of the If statement will be executed. This section of code is essentially the same as the code in the previous DisplayForwardGrid subroutine. A Do loop, in conjunction with a MoveNext method, reads all of the rows in the Recordset object. A For Each loop copies each row's data from the Fields collection to the grid.

The code in the second part of the If statement is similar in structure, but it functions in reverse. The Recordset object's MoveLast method positions the cursor to the last row in the Recordset. Then the Do loop and the Recordset object's MovePrevious method read through the Recordset from the back to the front. Again, a For Each loop extracts the value from each Field object in the Fields collection.

While the DisplayKeysetGrid subroutine has the capability of displaying the data in the Recordset object in either forward or backward order, the previous example only displayed the data in a forward fashion. The following subroutine illustrates how the DisplayKeysetGrid subroutine can be used with a Keyset type of Recordset to display the Recordset data in reverse order:

```
Private Sub KeysetRecordsetReverse()

    Dim rs As New ADODB.Recordset

    Screen.MousePointer = vbHourglass

    ' Pass the Open method the SQL and Recordset type parameters
    rs.Open "Select * From employee", _
        cn, adOpenKeyset, adLockReadOnly, adCmdText

    ' Display the grid -- use a 2 to display in reverse order
    DisplayKeysetGrid rs, Grid, 2

    rs.Close

    Screen.MousePointer = vbDefault

End Sub
```

The example demonstrates a couple of significant differences from the previous examples. In addition to using the DisplayKeysetGrid subroutine to display the Recordset in reverse order, this subroutine shows how to use the first and second parameters of the Recordset object's Open method to pass in the source and connection information. Using the first and second parameters of the Open method is an alternative to explicitly assigning values to the Recordset object's ActiveConnection and Source properties. The first parameter sets the Source property to the simple SQL Select statement that will retrieve all of the rows from the employee table. The second parameter sets the ActiveConnection to an existing Connection object named cn. The third parameter specifies a keyset cursor. The fourth parameter sets the lock type to read-only, and the fifth parameter identifies the first ("source") parameter as a command text.

After the Open method completes, the DisplayKeysetGrid function is called. The name of the open Recordset object is passed into the first parameter, the name of an existing grid is used in the second parameter, and the value of 2 is used in the third parameter to set the display order to backward.

Closing a Recordset

Before ending your application, close any open Recordset objects using the Recordset object's Close method. Here is an example of the Close method.

```
rs.Close
```

Alternatively, you could close the connection by setting the Recordset object to nothing, as follows:

```
Set rs = Nothing
```

Using Prepared SQL and the Command Object

The ability to use prepared SQL statements and parameter markers is one of the features that enables ADO to be used in developing high-performance database applications. As the earlier chapters covering ODBC and RDO pointed out, using prepared statements in your database applications is one of those small changes that can result in big performance gains. Dynamic SQL statements must be parsed and a data access plan must be created each time the Dynamic SQL statement is executed—even if the exact same statement is reused.

Although dynamic SQL works well for ad hoc queries, it isn't the best for executing the type of repetitive SQL statements that make up online transaction processing (OLTP)–type applications. Prepared SQL—or *static SQL*, as it is sometimes called—is better suited to OLTP applications, in which there is a high degree of SQL statement reuse. With prepared SQL, the SQL statement is parsed and the creation of the data access plan is only performed once. Subsequent calls using the prepared statements are very fast because the compiled data access plan is already in place.

TIP: Unlike SQL Server 6.5, which created temporary stored procedures in the tempdb database for prepared SQL statements, SQL Server 7 creates data access plans in its Procedure Cache. The Procedure Cache is a part of SQL Server's buffer cache, which is an area of working memory used by SQL Server 7. Although data access plans stored in the Procedure Cache are shared by all users, each user has a separate execution context. In addition, the access plans created for ad hoc SQL statement queries can also be stored in SQL Server 7's Statement Cache. However, they are only stored if the cost to execute the plan exceeds a certain internal threshold, and they are only reused under "safe" conditions. You can't rely on these being maintained like the data access plans created for prepared SQL statements.

The following code example shows how to create an ADO query that uses a prepared SQL statement:

```
Private Sub CommandPS()

    Dim cmd As New ADODB.Command
    Dim rs As New ADODB.Recordset

    Screen.MousePointer = vbHourglass

    With cmd
        'Use a global Connection object -- cn
        .ActiveConnection = cn
        ' Set up the SQL statement
        .CommandText = "Select * From sales Where stor_id = ?"
        ' Add the parameter (optional)
        .CreateParameter , adChar, adParamInput, 4
        'Set the parameter value
        .Parameters(0).Value = "7131"
    End With

    'Set up the input parameter
    Set rs = cmd.Execute

    DisplayForwardGrid rs, Grid

    rs.Close

    Screen.MousePointer = vbDefault

End Sub
```

In the beginning of this subroutine, a new ADO Command object named cmd is created along with an ADO Recordset object named rs. The Command object will be used to create and execute the prepared SQL statement, while the Recordset object will be used to hold the returned result set.

Next, the Visual Basic With block works with a group of the Command object's properties. The first line of code in the With block sets the Command object's ActiveConnection property to the name of an active ADO Connection object named cn. Then the CommandText property is assigned a string containing the SQL statement that will be executed. This SQL statement will return all of the columns in the sales table where the value of the stor_id column equals a value that will be supplied at run time. The question mark (?) is a parameter marker. Each replaceable parameter must be indicated using a question mark. This example SQL statement uses a single parameter in the Where clause, so only one parameter marker is needed. Next, the CreateParameter method defines the attribute of the parameter.

The CreateParameter statement accepts four parameters. The first optional parameter accepts a string that can be used to give the parameter a name. The second parameter accepts a Long variable, which identifies the data type that will be used with the parameter. In the previous example, the value of adChar indicates that the parameter will contain character data. The third parameter of the CreateParameter statement specifies whether the parameter will be used as input, output, or both. The value of adParamInput shows that this is an input-only parameter. Table 15-6 lists the allowable values for this parameter.

The third parameter specifies the length of the parameter. In the previous example, a value of 4 indicates that the parameter is four bytes long.

After the parameter characteristics have been specified, the value 7131 is placed into the Value property of the first (and in this case only) Parameter object in the Parameters collection. Parameters(0) corresponds to the ? parameter marker that was used in the SQL Select statement. Assigning 7131 to the Parameter object's Value property essentially causes the SQL statement to be evaluated as

```
Select * From sales Where stor_id = "7131"
```

Next, the Command object's Execute method runs the Select statement on SQL Server. Since this SQL Select statement returns a result set, the output of the cmd object is assigned to an ADO Recordset object. The rs Recordset object is then passed into the DisplayForwardGrid subroutine, which will display the contents of the Recordset object. Finally, the Recordset object is closed using the Close method.

If this cmd object were only executed a single time, there would be no performance benefits over simply using the ADO Recordset object to execute the query. However, executing this Command object multiple times will result in improved performance because the SQL statement and access plan have already been prepared. To execute a Command object multiple times, you would simply assign a new value to the Parameter object's Value property and then rerun the Command object's Execute method.

ADO Direction Constant	Description
adParamInput	The parameter is input-only.
adParamOutput	The parameter is an output parameter.
adParamInputOutput	The parameter will be used for both input and output.
adParamReturnValue	The parameter will contain the return value from a stored procedure. This is typically only used with the first parameter (Parameters(0)).

Table 15-6.   ADO Parameter Direction Constants

Executing Dynamic SQL with the ADO Command Object

ADO can also be used to execute dynamic SQL statements on the remote database. Dynamic SQL can be used for a variety of both data management as well as data manipulation tasks. The following example illustrates how you can create a table named department in the pubs database:

```
Private Sub CreateTable(cn As ADODB.Connection)

    Dim sSQL As String
    On Error Resume Next

    Screen.MousePointer = vbHourglass

    'Make certain that the table is created by dropping the table
    ' If the table doesn't exist the code will move on to the
    ' next statement
    sSQL = "Drop Table department"
    cn.Execute sSQL

    'Reset the error handler and create the table
    ' If an error is encountered it will be displayed
    On Error GoTo ErrorHandler
    sSQL = "Create Table department " _
        & "(Dep_ID Char(4) Not Null, Dep_Name Char(25), " _
        & "Primary Key(Dep_ID))"
    cn.Execute sSQL
```

```
        Screen.MousePointer = vbDefault
        Exit Sub

ErrorHandler:
        DisplayADOError
        Screen.MousePointer = vbDefault

End Sub
```

This CreateTable subroutine actually performs two separate SQL action queries. The first statement deletes a table, and the second statement re-creates the table. The SQL Drop statement ensures that the table doesn't exist prior to running the SQL Create statement.

Near the beginning of the subroutine, Visual Basic's On Error statement enables error handling for this subroutine. In this first instance, the error handler is set up to trap any run-time errors and then resume execution of the subroutine with the statement following the error. This method traps the potential error that could be generated by executing the SQL Drop statement when there is no existing table.

Using the ADO Connection object's Execute method is the simplest way to perform dynamic SQL statements. In this example, an existing Connection object that is currently connected to SQL Server issues the SQL statement. The first parameter of the Execute method takes a string that contains the command that will be issued. The first instance uses the SQL Drop Table statement that will delete any existing instances of the table named department.

Next, Visual Basic's error handler is reset to branch to the ErrorHandler label if any run-time errors are encountered. This allows any errors encountered during the creation of the department table to be displayed by the DisplayADOError subroutine. For more details about ADO error handling, see the "Error Handling" section, later in this chapter. The SQL Create Table statement is then performed using the Connection object's Execute method.

NOTE: The department table is not a part of the example pubs database. The department table is created in order to illustrate database update techniques without altering the contents of the original tables in the pubs database.

Modifying Data with ADO

You can modify data with ADO in a number of ways. First, ADO supports updateable Recordset objects that can use the AddNew, Update, and Delete methods to modify the data contained in an updateable Recordset object. ADO also supports updating data using both dynamic and prepared SQL. In the next part of this chapter, you'll see how to update SQL Server data using an ADO Recordset object, followed by several examples that illustrate how to update data using prepared SQL and the ADO Command object.

Updating Data with the ADO Recordset Object

In addition to performing queries, Recordset objects can be used to update data. However, as you have probably surmised after seeing the various parameters of the Recordset object's Open method, not all ADO Recordset objects are updateable. The ability to update a Recordset depends on the type of cursor the Recordset object uses, as well as the locking type that is used. Both of these factors can be specified as parameters of the Open method or by setting the Recordset object's CursorType and LockType properties before the Recordset is opened.

Both the CursorType and LockType properties influence the ability to update a Recordset object. Table 15-7 summarizes the Recordset object cursor and lock types and their ability to support data update methods.

The lock type parameter takes precedence over the cursor type parameter. For instance, if the lock type is set to adLockReadOnly, then the result set will not be updateable no matter which cursor type is used.

INSERTING ROWS IN A RECORDSET OBJECT   You can use the Recordset object's AddNew method in combination with the Update method to add rows to an updateable ADO result set. The following code illustrates how you can add rows to a Recordset object that was created using a keyset cursor:

```
Private Sub CursorAdd(cn As ADODB.Connection)

    Dim rs As New ADODB.Recordset
    Dim i As Integer

    Screen.MousePointer = vbHourglass

    'Pass in the SQL, Connection, Cursor type, lock type and
    'source type
    rs.Open "Select Dep_ID, Dep_Name From department", _
            cn, adOpenKeyset, adLockOptimistic, adCmdText

    'Add 50 rows to the department table
    ' Note that the Bang ! notation is used to specify column names
    For i = 1 To 50
        rs.AddNew
        rs!Dep_ID = i
        rs!Dep_Name = "Department " & CStr(i)
        rs.Update
    Next

    'Display the new rows in a grid
    DisplayKeysetGrid rs, Grid, 1
```

```
    rs.Close

    Screen.MousePointer = vbDefault

End Sub
```

The first parameter of the Recordset object's Open method accepts a string containing a SQL statement that defines the result set. In this case, the result set consists of the Dep_ID and the Dep_Name columns from the department table created in the earlier dynamic SQL example. The second parameter of the Open method contains the name of an active Connection object named cn. The third parameter uses the constant adOpenKeyset to specify that the Recordset object will use a keyset cursor. The fourth parameter contains the value adLockOptimistic. These two parameters indicate that this Recordset object set is updateable and that it will use optimistic record locking. After the result set has been opened, a For Next loop is used to add 50 rows to the Recordset object. Within the For Next loop, the AddNew method is called to create a row buffer that will contain the new row values. Unlike the earlier examples in this chapter that accessed columns by iterating through the Fields collection, this example illustrates how to access individual columns using the column name and Bang (!) notation.

TIP: This notation is case sensitive. When using the Bang notation, you must specify the column names exactly as they appear in the database. Otherwise, a run-time error will be generated.

Recordset Cursor Type	Updateable?
adOpenForwardOnly	Yes (current row only)
adOpenStatic	No
adOpenKeyset	Yes
adOpenDynamic	Yes
Recordset Lock Type	**Updateable?**
adLockReadOnly	No
adLockPessimistic	Yes
adLockOptimistic	Yes
adLockBatchOptimistic	Yes

Table 15-7.   ADO Recordset Cursor and Lock Types and Updates

The value of the Dep_ID column is set using a unique integer value that is obtained by using the loop counter. The Dep_Name column is set using the string that is formed by concatenating the literal "Department" and the string representation of the loop counter. After the row values have been set, the Update method is called to add the row to the Recordset object and the data source. Next, the DisplayKeysetGrid subroutine is called, which will display the new row values in a grid. Finally, the Close method is used to close the Recordset object.

UPDATING ROWS WITH THE RECORDSET OBJECT   The Recordset object's Update method can be used to update rows in an updateable ADO result set. The following code illustrates how you can update the rows in an ADO Recordset object that was created using a keyset cursor:

```
Private Sub CursorUpdate(cn As ADODB.Connection)

    Dim rs As New ADODB.Recordset
    Dim i As Integer
    Dim sTemp As String

    Screen.MousePointer = vbHourglass

    ' Pass in SQL, Connection, cursor type, lock type and source type
    rs.Open "Select Dep_ID, Dep_Name From department", _
            cn, adOpenKeyset, adLockOptimistic, adCmdText

    Do Until rs.EOF
        'Trim off the blanks because ADO doesn't truncate the data
        sTemp = Trim(rs!Dep_Name)
        rs!Dep_Name = "Updated " & sTemp
        'Update the row
        rs.Update
        rs.MoveNext
    Loop

    'Display the updated rows in a grid
    DisplayKeysetGrid rs, Grid, 1

    rs.Close

    Screen.MousePointer = vbDefault

End Sub
```

Again, the Recordset object's Open method is used to create a new ADO Recordset object named rs. The first parameter of the Open method accepts a string that specifies the result set. In this case, Recordset object consists of the Dep_ID and the Dep_Name columns from the department table. An active Connection object named cn is used in the second parameter. The adOpenKeyset and asLockOptimistic constants used in the third and fourth parameters indicate that the Recordset object will use an updateable keyset cursor and optimistic record locking.

After the Recordset object set has been created, a Do Until loop reads through all of the rows in the Recordset object. The loop ends when the Recordset object's EOF property is set to true. Within the Do loop, the value of the Dep_Name column is set to a new string value that begins with the literal "Updated" that is concatenated with the current column value. Then the Update method is called to update the row Recordset object, and the MoveNext method positions the cursor to the next row. After all of the rows in the Recordset have been updated, the DisplayKeysetGrid function displays the contents of the updated department table. Finally, the Close method closes the Recordset object.

DELETING ROWS FROM A RECORDSET OBJECT   The Recordset object's Delete method removes rows in an updateable ADO Recordset object. The following code illustrates how you can delete rows in a forward-only result set:

```
Private Sub CursorDelete(cn As ADODB.Connection)

    Dim rs As New ADODB.Recordset
    Dim i As Integer

    Screen.MousePointer = vbHourglass

    'Pass in the SQL, Connection, cursor type, lock type and source
    'type. Note that this is a forward-only cursor but it can update
    ' the current row.
    rs.Open "Select Dep_ID, Dep_name From department", _
            cn, adOpenForwardOnly, adLockOptimistic, adCmdText

    'Delete all of the rows
    Do Until rs.EOF
        rs.Delete
        rs.MoveNext
    Loop

    'Display the empty Recordset in a grid
    DisplayForwardGrid rs, Grid

    rs.Close
```

```
        Screen.MousePointer = vbDefault

End Sub
```

As in the previous examples, the Open method is used to create a new ADO Recordset object named rs that contains the Dep_ID and Dep_Name columns from the department table. The second parameter contains the name of an active Connection object named rs. The third and fourth parameters contain the constants adOpenForwardOnly and adLockOptimistic, which specify that the result set will use a forward-only cursor that supports updates using optimistic record locking.

TIP: Forward-only record sets are often thought of as read-only because they do not support the same type of capabilities as keyset cursors. However, forward-only Recordset objects do support updating the current row, and in ADO they provide much better performance than keyset or dynamic cursors. Any changes made to the data source will not be reflected in a forward-only Recordset object until it is refreshed.

After the Recordset object has been created, a Do Until loop reads through all of the rows contained in the Recordset object. The rs Recordset object's Delete method deletes each row, and the MoveNext method positions the cursor on the next row in the result set. After all of the rows have been deleted, the DisplayForwardGrid subroutine displays the (now empty) department table. Finally, the Close method closes the Recordset object.

Updating Data with the ADO Command Object

The previous section showed how to update SQL Server databases using Recordset objects and cursors. However, while updating data using Recordset objects is easy to code for, this method is not usually optimal in terms of performance. Using prepared SQL statements to update data usually provides better performance—especially in OLTP-type applications where the SQL statements have a high degree of reuse. Next, you'll see how you can use prepared SQL statements and the ADO Command object's Execute method to insert, update, and delete data in a SQL Server table.

INSERTING ROWS WITH A COMMAND OBJECT AND PREPARED SQL   The SQL Insert statement adds rows to a table. The following example illustrates how to use the Insert statement with an ADO Command object:

```
Private Sub PreparedAdd(cn As ADODB.Connection)

    Dim cmd As New ADODB.Command
    Dim rs As New ADODB.Recordset
    Dim i As Integer
```

```
Screen.MousePointer = vbHourglass

'Set up the Command object's Connection, SQL and parameter types
With cmd
    .ActiveConnection = cn
    .CommandText = "Insert Into department Values(?,?)"
    .CreateParameter , adChar, adParamInput, 4
    .CreateParameter , adChar, adParamInput, 25
End With

'Execute the prepared SQL statement to add 50 rows
For i = 1 To 50
    cmd.Parameters(0) = CStr(i)
    cmd.Parameters(1) = "Department " & CStr(i)
    cmd.Execute
Next

'Create a recordset to display the new rows
rs.Open "Select * From department", cn, , , adCmdText
DisplayForwardGrid rs, Grid

rs.Close

Screen.MousePointer = vbDefault

End Sub
```

In this example, you create new ADO Command and Recordset objects. Then the ActiveConnection property of the Command object receives the name of an active Connection object named cn. Next, the CommandText property is assigned a SQL Insert statement that uses two parameter markers. The CreateParameter method is then used to specify the characteristics of each parameter. The first parameter contains a character value that is 4 bytes long, and the second parameter contains a character value that is 25 bytes long. As you would expect with an Insert statement, both parameters are input-only.

A For Next loop adds 50 rows to the table. Within the For Next loop, the values used by each parameter are assigned. The cmd.Parameter(0) object refers to the first parameter marker, while the cmd.Parameter(1) object refers to the second parameter marker. As in the earlier example that added rows using a cursor, the first parameter (the Dep_ID column) has a unique integer value based on the loop counter. The second parameter (the Dep_Name column) has a string that contains the literal "department" in conjunction with a string representation of the loop counter. After you set the parameter values, the prepared statement executes using the Execute method. The DisplayForwardGrid subroutine displays the contents of the department table in a grid, and then the Recordset closes.

UPDATING DATA WITH A COMMAND OBJECT AND PREPARED SQL The SQL Update statement updates columns in a table. The following example illustrates using the SQL Update statement with an ADO Command object to update all of the rows in the department table:

```
Private Sub PreparedUpdate(cn As ADODB.Connection)

    Dim cmd As New ADODB.Command
    Dim rs As New ADODB.Recordset
    Dim i As Integer

    Screen.MousePointer = vbHourglass

    'Set up the Command object's Connection, SQL and parameter types
    With cmd
        .ActiveConnection = cn
        .CommandText = _
          "Update department Set Dep_Name = ? Where Dep_ID = ?"
        .CreateParameter , adChar, adParamInput, 25
        .CreateParameter , adChar, adParamInput, 4
    End With

    ' Execute the prepared SQL statement to update 50 rows
    For i = 0 To 50
        cmd.Parameters(0).Value = "Updated Department " & CStr(i)
        cmd.Parameters(1).Value = CStr(i)
        cmd.Execute
    Next

    ' Create a recordset to display the updated rows
    rs.Open "Select * From department", cn, , , adCmdText
    DisplayForwardGrid rs, Grid

    rs.Close

    Screen.MousePointer = vbDefault

End Sub
```

As in the previous insert example, new ADO Command and Recordset objects are created in the beginning of the subroutine. The ActiveConnection property method of the

Command object has the name of an active Connection object named cn. Here, the CommandText property has a SQL Update statement that uses two parameter markers. In this case, the first parameter refers to the Dep_Name column, and the second parameter refers to the Dep_ID column. Then the CreateParameter method specifies the characteristics of each parameter.

A For Next loop updates each of the 50 rows in the department table. Within the For Next loop, the values used by each parameter are assigned and the Update statement is run using the Command object's Execute method. After the updates are finished, a Recordset object is created and displayed in a grid using the DisplayForwardGrid subroutine.

DELETING DATA WITH A COMMAND OBJECT AND PREPARED SQL   As with Insert and Update operations, ADO Command objects can be used to delete one or more rows in a remote data source. The following code listing illustrates how to delete rows from a SQL Server database using a prepared SQL Delete statement and a Command object:

```
Private Sub PreparedDelete(cn As ADODB.Connection)

    Dim cmd As New ADODB.Command
    Dim rs As New ADODB.Recordset
    Dim i As Integer

    Screen.MousePointer = vbHourglass

    'Set up the Command object's Connection and SQL command
    With cmd
        .ActiveConnection = cn
        .CommandText = "Delete department"
    End With

    'Execute the SQL once (that's all that is needed)
    cmd.Execute

    'Create a recordset to display the empty table
    rs.Open "Select * From department", cn, , , adCmdText
    DisplayForwardGrid rs, Grid

    rs.Close

    Screen.MousePointer = vbDefault

End Sub
```

Thanks to SQL's set-at-time functionality, this example is a bit simpler than the previous insert and update examples. SQL's ability to manipulate multiple rows with a single statement allows one SQL Update to be used to update all 50 rows in the table. As in those examples, first, new ADO Command and Recordset objects are created, and then the ActiveConnection property method of the Command object gets the name of an active Connection object. Next, a SQL statement is assigned to the Command object's CommandText property. In this case, the SQL Delete statement does not use any parameters. Since no Where clause is contained in this statement, the Delete operation will be performed on all rows in the department table when the Execute method is run.

NOTE: It's a good idea to use caution when using a SQL action statement without a Where clause. This powerful technique can easily inadvertently modify more rows than you intend to.

After the updates are complete, a Recordset object is created and displayed in a grid using the DisplayForwardGrid subroutine and the Recordset object is closed.

Executing Stored Procedures with Command Objects

Stored procedures provide the fastest mechanism available for accessing SQL Server data. When a stored procedure is created, a compiled data access plan is added to the SQL Server database. By using this existing data access plan, the application foregoes the need to parse any incoming SQL statements and then create a new data access plan. This results in faster execution of queries or other data manipulation actions. SQL Server automatically shares stored procedures among multiple users.

Stored procedures can also be used to implement a more robust database security than you can achieve by setting permissions directly on target files. For example, you can restrict all direct access to SQL Server tables and only permit access to the stored procedures. When centrally controlled and administrated, the stored procedures can provide complete control over SQL Server database access.

Using ADO, stored procedures are called in much the same way as are prepared SQL statements. The Command object calls the stored procedure, and a question mark denotes each stored procedure's input and output parameters. The following example is a simple stored procedure that accepts one input parameter and returns one output parameter:

```
Create Procedure CountStoreQty
(
    @stor_id Char(4),
    @qty Int Output
)
As
Select @qty = Select Sum(qty) From sales Where stor_id = @stor_id
GO
```

The CountStoreQty stored procedure in this example accepts a character argument containing the stor_id as input and returns an integer value containing the total of the qty column for all of the rows in the sales table that matched the supplied stor_id. In this example, the SQL Select sum( ) function is used to sum up the values contained in the qty column.

> **NOTE:**   The variable names used in the stored procedure don't need to match the column names in the source table.

The following code example shows how you can call the CountStoreQty stored procedure using an ADO Command object:

```
Private Sub CallSP()

    Dim cmd As New ADODB.Command
    Dim parm0 As New ADODB.Parameter
    Dim parm1 As New ADODB.Parameter
    Dim sSQL As String
    On Error GoTo ErrorHandler

    Screen.MousePointer = vbHourglass

    'Use the global cn Connection object
    cmd.ActiveConnection = cn
    cmd.CommandType = adCmdStoredProc
    cmd.CommandText = "CountStoreQty"

    parm0.Direction = adParamInput
    parm0.Type = adChar
    parm0.Size = 4
    cmd.Parameters.Append parm0

    parm1.Direction = adParamOutput
    parm1.Type = adInteger
    parm1.Size = 4
    cmd.Parameters.Append parm1

    parm0.Value = "7067"
    cmd.Execute

    Label_Mid.Caption = "Total Qty:"
    Text_Mid.Text = parm1.Value
```

```
    Screen.MousePointer = vbDefault

ErrorHandler:
    DisplayADOError cn

    Screen.MousePointer = vbDefault

End Sub
```

In the beginning of this subroutine, you can see where an ADO Command object named cmd and two ADO Parameter objects named param0 and parm1 are created. Using Parameter objects is an alternative to using the CreateParameter method illustrated earlier in this chapter in the section "Using Prepared SQL and the Command Object." Both techniques can be used to specify the characteristics of a parameter marker, and either method can be used to execute prepared SQL as well as stored procedures.

Next, the ActiveConnection property of the Command object is assigned the name of an existing Connection object named cn. This associates the Command object with a target data source. Then the Command object's CommandType property is assigned the value of adCmdStoredProc, and the CommandText property is assigned the name of the stored procedure that will be executed. Since the CommandType property tells ADO that this Command object is used to call a stored procedure, there is no need to set up a SQL string that contains an ODBC Call statement.

The next section of code shows how Parameter objects are initialized. For each Parameter object, the Direction, Type, and Size properties are set. Then the Append method of the Parameters collection is used to add the Parameter object to the Parameters collection.

NOTE: You must add each Parameter object to the Parameters collection in the same order as the parameter is used by the stored procedure or prepared SQL statement. In other words, you must use the Append method for the first Parameter object, which represents the first parameter, before you execute the Append method for the second Parameter object, which represents the second parameter.

After the Parameter objects have been added to the Command object's Parameters collection, the Value property of the first parameter is assigned a string that contains a valid stor_id value. This value will be passed to the first parameter of the CountStoreQty stored procedure. Then the Command object's Execute method is used to call the stored procedure. When the call to the stored procedure has completed, the value of the output parameter will be available in the Value property of the second Parameter object (parm1). In the previous example, this value is assigned to a text box to be displayed.

Error Handling

Run-time errors that are generated using the ADO object framework are placed in the ADO Errors collection. When an ADO run-time error occurs, Visual Basic's error handler is fired, enabling you to trap and respond to run-time errors. This tight integration with Visual Basic makes it easy to handle ADO errors. The following ShowError subroutine illustrates how ADO's error handling can be integrated with Visual Basic's On Error function:

```
Private Sub ShowError(cn As ADODB.Connection)

    Dim rs As New ADODB.Recordset
    On Error GoTo ErrorHandler
    Screen.MousePointer = vbHourglass

    rs.Open "Select * From no_such_table", cn
    rs.Close

    Screen.MousePointer = vbDefault
    Exit Sub

ErrorHandler:
    DisplayADOError cn
    Screen.MousePointer = vbDefault

End Sub
```

The ShowError function attempts to open a Recordset object against a nonexistent table. At the beginning of this function, the On Error statement enables Visual Basic's error handler. In this case, the On Error statement causes the program to branch to the ErrorHandler label when a trappable error is encountered.

Executing the Open method with a nonexisting table causes the ADO object framework to generate a run-time error, which in turn causes the program execution to resume with the first statement following the label. In this example, the Display-ADOError subroutine will be executed following the invalid Open attempt.

The following listing shows how the DisplayDAOError subroutine uses DAO's Error object and Errors collection to display information about a DAO error condition in a simple message box:

```
Private Sub DisplayADOError(cn As ADODB.Connection)

    Dim er As ADODB.Error

    For Each er In cn.Errors
        MsgBox "Number: " & er.Number & vbCrLf & _
```

```
        "Source: " & er.Source & vbCrLf & _
        "Text: " & er.Description
    Next

End Sub
```

In this subroutine, an ADO Connection object is passed in as a parameter. Unlike the RDO and DAO object frameworks, in which the Errors collection is maintained by the base engine object, the ADO Errors collection is contained in the Connection object. Next, a new ADO Error object named er is declared, and a For Each loop iterates through the ADO Errors collection. The loop is required because the ADODB.Errors collection can contain multiple Error objects, each representing a different error condition. With the For Each loop, the values of the Number, Source, and Description properties are displayed in a message box. The Number property of the ADO Error object contains the ADO error message number, while the Source property identifies the source object that fired the error. As you might expect, the Description property contains the error condition's text description. The message box that the DisplayADOError subroutine displays is shown here:

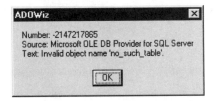

ADVANCED DATABASE FUNCTIONS USING ADO

You've now seen how to use the basic ADO Connection, Recordset, and Command objects to query and update the SQL Server database. In this section, you'll see how to use some of the more advanced ADO functions, such as how to perform updates with batch cursors, perform code queries that produce multiple result sets, commit and roll back transactions, and work with binary image data.

Batch Updates

Batch updates allow all of the changes made to a Recordset object to be written back to the data source all at once. Batch updates are most useful when you are working with disassociated Record sets such as you might use in Web-based applications. With batch updates, the Recordset object is updated using the normal AddNew, Update, and Delete methods. After all of the changes have been made to the Recordset object, the BatchUpdate method is used to post the entire batch of changes to the database. The client Batch cursor library generates a SQL query to synchronize the local Recordset object and the data on the remote SQL Server system. The following example illustrates how to use the ADO Recordset object's BatchUpdate method.

```
Private Sub BatchUpdate(cn As ADODB.Connection)

    Dim rs As New ADODB.Recordset
    Dim i As Integer

    Screen.MousePointer = vbHourglass

    'Pass in the SQL, Connection, Cursor type,
      lock type and source type
    rs.Open "Select Dep_ID, Dep_Name From department", _
            cn, adOpenKeyset, adLockBatchOptimistic, adCmdText

    'Add 50 rows to the department table
    For i = 1 To 50
        rs.AddNew
        rs!Dep_ID = i
        rs!Dep_Name = "Add Batch Department " & CStr(i)
        rs.Update
    Next

    rs.UpdateBatch

    'Display the new rows in a grid
    DisplayKeysetGrid rs, Grid, 1

    rs.Close

    Screen.MousePointer = vbDefault


End Sub
```

This code is very much like the standard ADO cursor update example presented in the section "Updating Rows with the Recordset Object," earlier in this chapter. However, there are a couple of important differences. First, the Recordset object's lock type parameter is assigned the constant adLockBatchOptimistic. This tells ADO that the Recordset object will use a batch cursor. After the Recordset object is opened, the AddNew and Update methods are used to add 50 rows to the local Recordset. It's important to note that unlike a standard keyset cursor, which immediately propagates the new rows to the data source, the batch cursor does not update the data source until the UpdateBatch method executes. Then all of the updated rows are written to the base tables.

TIP: The CancelBatch method can be used to cancel all of the pending changes that would be performed by a BatchUpdate operation.

Working with Multiple Result Sets

ADO's ability to process multiple result sets allows it to send multiple SQL Select statements in a single Recordset object, as well as call SQL Server stored procedures that return multiple result sets. In order to submit multiple SQL Select statements, the ADO Recordset object must use a local cursor rather than a server-side cursor. The following code illustrates how to use the ADO Recordset object to work with multiple result sets:

```
Private Sub MultipleRS(cn As ADODB.Connection)

    Dim rs As New ADODB.RECordset
    Dim fld As Field
    Dim sSQL As String
    Dim i As Integer
    Dim nFldCount As Integer

    Screen.MousePointer = vbHourglass

    'Set up the three Select statements
    sSQL = "Select au_lname, au_fname From authors; "
    sSQL = sSQL & "Select title from titles; "
    sSQL = sSQL & "Select stor_name from stores "

    rs.Open sSQL, cn

    ' Set up the grid
    Grid.FixedRows = 0
    Grid.Cols = 2
    Grid.ColWidth(0) = _
      TextWidth(String(rs.Fields(0).DefinedSize + 2, "a"))
    Grid.ColWidth(1) = _
      TextWidth(String(rs.Fields(1).DefinedSize + 2, "a"))
    Grid.Rows = 1
    Grid.Row = 0
    i = 1

    Do
        Grid.Col = 0
        Grid.CellBackColor = &HC0C0C0
        Grid.Text = "Recordset Number: " & i
```

```
        Grid.Col = 1
        Grid.CellBackColor = &HC0C0C0
        Grid.Text = ""

        Do Until rs.EOF
            Grid.Rows = Grid.Rows + 1
            Grid.Row = Grid.Row + 1
            nFldCount = 0
            'Loop through all fields
            For Each fld In rs.Fields
                Grid.Col = nFldCount
                Grid.Text = fld.Value
                nFldCount = nFldCount + 1
            Next fld
            rs.MoveNext
        Loop

        i = i + 1
        Set rs = rs.NextRecordset
    Loop Until rs.State = adStateClosed

    Screen.MousePointer = vbDefault

End Sub
```

In this multiple-result-set example, you can see that the sSQL string contains a compound SQL statement that actually consists of three separate SQL Select statements seperated by semicolons. The first Select statement returns the last and first names from the authors table. The second Select statement returns the title column from the titles table, and the third Select statement returns a result set that consists of the stor_name column from the stores table. Executing this compound SQL statement returns three different result sets.

The compound SQL statement is executed by the ADO Recordset object's Open method. The first parameter of the Open method contains the compound SQL statement, while the second parameter of the Open method contains the name of an active ADO Connection object named cn. The next section of code following the Open method sets up the grid to contain all of the data values from the three result sets. In this case, the number of columns in these queries is a known quantity, so the Grid.Cols property is set to 2. However, the number of rows is not known. To accommodate a variable number of rows, the grid is initially sized to contain a single row. The grid must then be dynamically expanded by incrementing the Grid.Rows property as each row is read from the Recordset object.

A Do loop processes the multiple result sets. It continues until the State property of the rs Recordset object equals adStateClosed, which indicates that no more result sets are available. Within the Do loop, the current grid row is set up to indicate the beginning of each result set. A heading value containing the literal "Recordset Number" is combined with the result set number and placed in the column heading of the first row. In addition, the CellBackColor property of the current cell is set to &HC0C0C0, which displays the Recordset heading in gray rather than in the default grid color.

Next, a Do Until loop reads through all of the rows in each result set. The grid is dynamically expanded to accommodate each row by adding one to the Grid.Rows property. The current row in the grid is incremented using the Grid.Row property. Then the Field object values are extracted for each row and moved to the grid using a For Each loop, and the MoveNext method is used to move to the next row in the current Recordset object. The Do Until loop ends when the EOF property of the rs Recordset object becomes true. After all of the rows in the current result set have been read, the NextRecordset method sets the rs Recordset object to the next available result set.

Using Transactions

Transactions enable you to group together multiple operations that can be performed as a single unit of work. This helps to ensure database integrity. For instance, transferring funds from your savings account to your checking account involves multiple database operations, and the transfer cannot be considered complete unless all of the operations are successfully completed. A typical transfer from your savings account to your checking account requires two separate but related operations: a withdrawal from your savings account and a deposit to your checking account. If either operation fails, the transfer is not completed. Therefore, both of these functions would be considered part of the same logical transaction. In this example, both the withdrawal and the deposit would be grouped together as a single transaction. If the withdrawal operation succeeded but the deposit failed, the entire transaction could be rolled back, restoring the database to the condition it was in before the withdrawal operation was attempted. SQL Server supports transactions, but not all databases do.

Rolling Back Transactions

In ADO, transactions are enabled in the Connection object. The Connection object's RollbackTrans method can be used to restore the database to the state it was in before the transaction occurred. The following example shows how to use the RollbackTrans method:

```
Private Sub TransRollBack(cn As ADODB.Connection)

    Dim rs As New ADODB.Recordset

    Screen.MousePointer = vbHourglass

    'Start a transaction using the existing Connection object
```

```
cn.BeginTrans

'Execute SQL to delete all of the rows from the table
cn.Execute "Delete department"

'Now Roll back the transaction - the table is unchanged
cn.RollbackTrans

'Create a recordset to display the unchanged table
rs.Open "Select * From department", cn, , , adCmdText
DisplayForwardGrid rs, Grid
rs.Close

Screen.MousePointer = vbDefault

End Sub
```

In this example, executing the BeginTrans method of the Connection object named cn signals to the database that a transaction is about to begin. Then the Connection object's Execute method is used to issue a SQL Delete statement that deletes all of the rows in the department table. However, instead of committing that change to the database, the Connection object's RollbackTrans method is used to undo the transaction, restoring the original contents of the department table. A Recordset object is created and displayed to illustrate that the table's contents were unchanged after the RollBackTrans method.

TIP: SQL Server maintains database modifications in a transaction log file, which contains a serial record of all of the modifications that have been made to a database. The transaction log contains both before and after images of each transaction.

Committing Transactions

When a transaction is successfully completed, the Connection object's CommitTrans method writes the transaction to the database. In the following example, you'll see how to use ADO to begin a transaction and then commit that transaction to the SQL Server database:

```
Private Sub TransCommit(cn As ADODB.Connection)

    Dim rs As New ADODB.Recordset

    Screen.MousePointer = vbHourglass

    'Start a transaction using the existing Connection object
    cn.BeginTrans
```

```
'Execute SQL to delete all of the rows from the table
cn.Execute "Delete department"

'Commit the transaction and update the table
cn.CommitTrans

'Create a recordset to display the empty table
rs.Open "Select * From department", cn, , , adCmdText
DisplayForwardGrid rs, Grid
rs.Close

Screen.MousePointer = vbDefault

End Sub
```

Again, executing the BeginTrans method of the Connection object signals to the database that a transaction is about to begin, and the Execute method is used to issue a SQL Delete statement. However, this time the changes are committed to the database using the Connection object's CommitTrans method. Finally, a Recordset object is opened to illustrate that the table's contents were deleted following the CommitTrans method.

Storing Binary Data

So far, this chapter has presented a variety of methods for working with standard text and numeric data types that are stored in a SQL Server database. However, many modern database applications need to handle both graphic and sound data as well. There's really nothing all that different about graphic and sound data. Both are really just specially formatted binary data normally referred to as *BLOBs (binary large objects)*. However, as the acronym BLOB suggests, this type of data can be quite large.

SQL Server can store binary image data in tables using the Image or LongVarBinary data type. The ADO Field object provides the GetChunk and AppendChunk methods, which are used to access the binary data stored in SQL Server columns. The GetChunk and AppendChunk methods are required in order to manage the potential size of the binary objects. Unlike standard text and numeric data that can be set and retrieved in a single operation, binary data can be several megabytes in size. This requires that the data be accessed a bit at a time or in chunks. The GetChunk and AppendChunk methods do exactly that. The GetChunk method retrieves a chunk of binary data from an ADO Field object, while the AppendChunk method adds a chunk of data to a Field object. The following subroutine is an example of using the GetChunk method to retrieve and display binary data contained in a SQL Server table:

```
Private Sub BinaryData(cn As ADODB.Connection)
    Dim rs As New ADODB.Recordset
    Dim fld As ADODB.Field

    Screen.MousePointer = vbHourglass

    rs.Open "Select pub_id, logo From pub_info", _
        cn, , , adCmdText

    ' Set up the grid
    Grid.Redraw = False
    Grid.Cols = rs.Fields.Count
    Grid.Rows = 1
    Grid.Row = 0
    Grid.Col = 0
    Grid.Clear
    'Size the grid columns bigger than normal
    Grid.ColWidth(0) = _
      TextWidth(String(rs.Fields(0).ActualSize + 4, "a"))
    Grid.ColWidth(1) = _
      TextWidth(String(200, "a"))
    Grid.RowHeightMin = Grid.RowHeight(0) * 3

    'Set up the headings
     For Each fld In rs.Fields
        Grid.Text = fld.Name
        If Grid.Col < rs.Fields.Count - 1 Then
           Grid.Col = Grid.Col + 1
        End If
    Next fld


    ' Move through each row in the record set
    Do Until rs.EOF

        ' Set the position in the grid
        Grid.Rows = Grid.Rows + 1
        Grid.Row = Grid.Rows - 1
        Grid.Col = 0

        'Loop through all fields
        For Each fld In rs.Fields
            If fld.Type = adLongVarBinary Then
                'Store the image into a temp bitmap file
```

```
                    BintoFile "tempbmp.bmp", fld
                    Grid.CellPictureAlignment = flexAlignLeftCenter
                    'Load the temporary bitmap into the grid
                    Set Grid.CellPicture = LoadPicture("tempbmp.bmp")
                Else
                    'Treat the column as regular data
                    Grid.Text = fld.Value
                End If
                If Grid.Col < rs.Fields.Count - 1 Then
                    Grid.Col = Grid.Col + 1
                End If
            Next fld

            rs.MoveNext
        Loop
        Grid.Redraw = True

        rs.Close

        Screen.MousePointer = vbDefault

End Sub
```

Using ADO to work with binary data is a lot like working with standard character data, but there are differences. This example subroutine begins by creating an ADO Recordset object that contains the pub_id and logo columns from the pub_info table in the pubs database. So far, this seems pretty standard. However, in this case, the logo column is an Image data type, and it contains a graphical image for each publisher's logo.

TIP: Exercise caution when accessing binary objects. While their use is generally fine for local database access, lower-speed WAN links to remote databases can cause performance problems for large binary objects.

After the Recordset object has been opened, the grid that will be used to display the data is initialized. Here, the ColWidth property of the two grid columns is used to set the initial column size. Since the first column is a standard character data type, the Field object's ActualSize property is used to specify the column width. However, since the second column contains graphical data, the ActualSize property will not reflect the length required to display the data. To ensure that the column is large enough, the second column is sized for 200 characters. Next, the grid's RowHeightMin property is used to increase the height for all of the rows in the grid. In this case, the original row height is tripled. After the grid is set up, the column headings for the grid are assigned, using a For Each loop to iterate through the Fields collection. The column headings used for binary data types are no different than the column headings for standard character columns.

Next, a Do Until loop reads all of the rows in the Recordset object. For every row, a For Each loop retrieves the column data and puts it into the grid. Since binary data must be handled differently than text data, the Type property of each Field object is checked before moving the data to the grid. If the Field object contains binary data, the Field object's Type property will equal the constant adLongVarBinary, and data will be converted using the BintoFile subroutine and placed into the grid's CellPicture property. Otherwise, the data will be treated as standard text data, and the Field object's Value property will be assigned to the grid.Text property.

The BintoFile subroutine assembles the contents of a binary column into a byte array and then writes that array to a temporary file bitmap. This bitmap file can then be assigned to the CellPicture property using the LoadPicture function. The code for the BintoFile subroutine is listed here:

```
Private Sub BintoFile(sFileName As String, fld As ADODB.Field)
    Dim bBuffer() As Byte
    Dim nLenLeft As Long
    Dim nChunkSize As Long

    ' Remove any existing destination file
    If Len(Dir$(sFileName)) > 0 Then
       Kill sFileName
    End If

    'Re-create a new file
    Open sFileName For Binary As #1

    'Use a 32K initial chuck size
    nChunkSize = 32768
    nLenLeft = fld.ActualSize

    If nLenLeft < nChunkSize Then
        nChunkSize = nLenLeft
    End If

    'Retrieve the binary data in chunks
    Do
        ReDim bBuffer(nChunkSize - 1)
        bBuffer = fld.GetChunk(nChunkSize)

        nLenLeft = nLenLeft - nChunkSize
        If nLenLeft < nChunkSize Then
            nChunkSize = nLenLeft
        End If
```

```
        Loop Until nLenLeft <= 0

        'Write the data to the file
        Put #1, , bBuffer
        Close #1
End Sub
```

The BintoFile subroutine accepts a String variable containing the name of a temporary data file in the first parameter and an ADO Field object in the second parameter. Next, this subroutine checks for the existence of the file named in the first parameter. If the file is found, the Kill statement is used to delete the file. Then a new temporary file is created using the Open statement. It is important to note that this file is opened in binary mode.

After the temporary output file is created, the chunk size is set to a maximum of 32K and the ActualSize property of the ADO Field object is checked. If the data in the Field object is smaller than the maximum chunk size, the chunk size is adjusted. If the data is larger than 32K, the binary data will be retrieved in 32K chunks. A Do loop is used to extract each chunk of binary data and place it into a byte array. After all of the binary data has been copied into the byte array using the GetChunk method, the Put statement is used to write the binary data to the open file, and the file is closed. The binary data contained in the temporary file can then be accessed by other functions.

CONCLUSION

As you've seen in this chapter, ADO provides very similar functionality to both DAO and RDO; however, ADO's more-flexible object model allows it to be used effectively for a wider range of applications. While the DAO object model was primarily designed around the Jet engine and the RDO object model was primarily designed for ODBC data access, the ADO object model was built around OLE DB. Unlike Jet and ODBC, which are both geared toward database access, OLE DB is intended to provide heterogeneous data access to a number of different data sources. In addition to accessing relational databases such as SQL Server, OLE DB provides access to a variety of other data sources, including Excel spreadsheets, Active Directory, and Exchange. While DAO and RDO are not going away any time soon, ADO and OLE DB are clearly Microsoft's future data access technologies.

All of the code listings presented in this chapter are also contained in the ADO Wizard example program on the CD-ROM accompanying this book.

ADDITIONAL RESOURCES

For more information about using ADO, you can refer to the following publication:

▼   Vaughn, William R. *Hitchhiker's Guide to Visual Basic and SQL Server*, Sixth Edition. Redmond, WA: Microsoft Press, 1998.

CHAPTER 16

Developing Database Applications with DB-Library

This chapter illustrates how you can develop SQL Server database applications using the DB–Library for Visual Basic that's shipped with SQL Server. In the first part of this chapter, you'll find an overview of the DB-Library. In the second half of this chapter, you'll learn about basic DB-Library programming techniques and how you can use them to develop your own SQL Server database applications.

The DB-Library is the original native SQL Server data access technology provided by Microsoft. The DB-Library for Visual Basic is a subset of the DB-Library for C; both are included with SQL Server. Originating as a 16-bit Visual Basic VBX Custom Control, the 32-bit DB-Library is not implemented as an OLE Automation server like most other modern data access technologies. Using the DB-Library for SQL Server application development most resembles using the ODBC API. Like ODBC, the DB-Library consists of a set of DLL functions that are all called using Visual Basic function declarations. However, unlike ODBC, which is a generic database access standard that can be used to access a wide variety of the different databases, the DB-Library is SQL Server specific. This means that database applications that are developed using DB-Library only work with SQL Server. To facilitate application development, DB-Library includes a Visual Basic .bas module that contains all of the DB-Library constant and function declarations. Having this module supplied with DB-Library makes application development a bit easier than using the ODBC API, which requires you to supply your own function declarations.

While it is still fully supported, Microsoft halted active development of the DB-Library after the product was ported to 32-bit. Instead, Microsoft has stabilized the DB-Library and opted to put all of the new data access enhancements into the COM-based data access APIs like DAO, RDO, and ADO. Since the DB-Library was stabilized at SQL Server release level 6.5, it does not provide support for the recent SQL Server 7 developments. For instance, the DB-Library doesn't support UNICODE and the new ntext, nvarchar, and nchar data types. Since it is no longer being enhanced, DB-Library isn't the best choice for new application development. It is best used when you need to support legacy applications or when you need to port existing 16-bit DB-Library applications to 32-bit. Considering that there is still a large number of existing DB-Library applications, it is important to know how to use the DB-Library to support and maintain those applications.

Like ODBC, the DB-Library is intended to be used over a network connection with various network protocols and topologies. To achieve network independence, DB-Library is implemented using a layered architecture. Figure 16-1 illustrates the layered networking architecture used by DB-Library.

A DB-Library–enabled application makes calls to the various DB-Library functions that are exposed by the vbsql.ocx dynamic link library. The DB-Library in turn uses the client network library to establish a communications session to SQL Server. Each client network library uses the appropriate network interprocess communication (IPC) mechanism for the type of network that connects the client systems to the SQL Server system. The network IPC mechanism enables different network processes to communicate with one another. For example, if the NetBEUI protocol is being used,

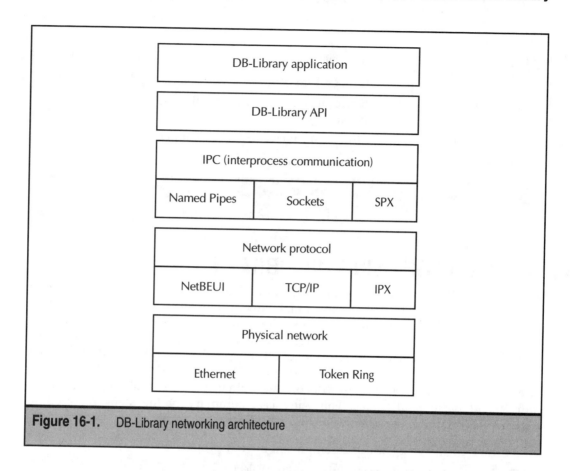

Figure 16-1.   DB-Library networking architecture

then the IPC used by the DB-Library would be Named Pipes. Likewise, if the connection is taking place over a TCP/IP network, then the IPC mechanism will be sockets. The network protocol is responsible for sending and receiving the IPC communication data stream over the network. NetBEUI, TCP/IP, and IPX are all network protocols. As you would expect, both the client system and the server system must support and use the same network IPC mechanism and protocol. Finally, at the bottom of this communications stack is the physical network. The physical network includes the adapter cards and cabling that are required to make the physical connections between the networked systems. Ethernet and Token Ring are examples of two of the most common network topologies.

Table 16-1 summarizes the client files that comprise the DB-Library for Visual Basic.

File	Description
vbsql.ocx	OLE custom control
vbsql.bas	Source module containing DB-Library function declarations
ntwdblib.dll	DB-Library for Win32 (C developement)
dbnmpntw.dll	Network library for Win 32

Table 16-1.   DB-Library Files Included with SQL Server

AN OVERVIEW OF USING DB-LIBRARY

SQL Server's DB-Library is built using a standard Windows dynamic link library (DLL) foundation, which means that you must manually declare all of its functions and their parameters in a .bas or .cls module to use them from a Visual Basic application. To facilitate its use from Visual Basic, Microsoft provided the vbsql.bas module with the DB-Library. To use the DB-Library for Visual Basic, you first need to add the vbsql.ocx OLE Control and the vbsql.bas function declaration module to your Visual Basic project. After these steps have been performed, you can begin using the DB-Library functions in your Visual Basic applications. Following is a summary of the steps required to implement DB-Library applications using Visual Basic.

1. Include the vbsql.ocx OLE component in your project.
2. Include the vbsql.bas module in your project.
3. Initialize the DB-Library.
4. Open a connection handle to SQL Server.
5. Send SQL commands to SQL Server and process the results.
6. Close the connection handle.
7. End the DB-Library.

ADDING VBSQL.OCX TO VISUAL BASIC

The DB-Library is not installed as a part of the default SQL Server client installation option. To install the DB-Library, you must select the Development Tools option using SQL Server's Custom installation option.

Although the files that provide the basic support for the DB-Library are copied to your system when you install the DB-Library, before you can use the DB-Library in a

Visual Basic application you must first add the vbsql.ocx OLE Custom Control to your Visual Basic project's component list. To add the vbsql.ocx control to Visual Basic 5 or 6, you select the Components option from Visual Basic's Project menu. This displays the Components dialog box that you see in Figure 16-2.

The vbsql.ocx file is not included in the initial list of components. You must first select the Browse button and then point the Open dialog box to the directory in which you installed the SQL Server Development Tools. Selecting the vbsql.ocx choice in the Open dialog box and clicking the OK button adds the VBSQL OLE control to Visual Basic's list of components. Next, scroll through Visual Basic's Components dialog box until you see the choice called Vbsql OLE Custom Control Module. Clicking in the adjacent check box followed by the OK button adds the vbsql.ocx file to Visual Basic's IDE (Interactive Development Environment). Adding the new component also results in a new icon being added to the Visual Basic Toolbox. Figure 16-3 shows the Visual Basic Toolbox with the newly added DB-Library.

Next, the vbsql.bas module must be added to your Visual Basic project. To add the vbsql.bas module, right-click the Visual Basic Project window. Then select the Add option from the pop-up menu. Selecting the Add option displays a submenu that lists the different Visual Basic file types. Selecting the Module option from the Add submenu displays the Add Module dialog box shown in Figure 16-4.

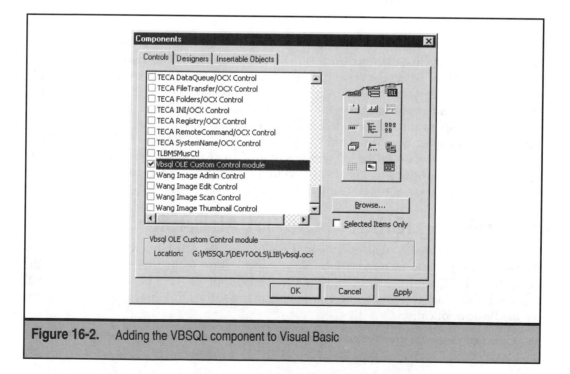

Figure 16-2. Adding the VBSQL component to Visual Basic

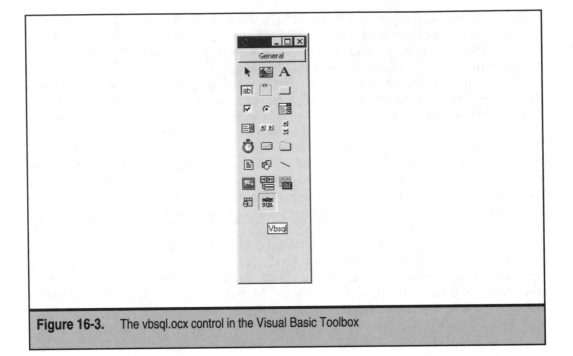

Figure 16-3. The vbsql.ocx control in the Visual Basic Toolbox

Next, point the Add Module dialog to the \Include directory under SQL Server Development Tools installation directory. The vbsql.bas file will be displayed in the Add Module dialog box. Select the vbsql.bas file from the list, and then click the OK button to add the module to your project. After the vbsql.bas module has been installed, the DB-Library is ready to be used in your Visual Basic application.

You can display the function declarations contained in the vbsql.bas module using Visual Basic's Object Browser. To display the function declarations, select the VBSQL class from the Classes list on the left window of the Object Browser. The VBSQL constants and function declarations will be displayed in the right window. Figure 16-5 shows the DB-Library functions displayed using the Object Browser.

USING THE DB-LIBRARY FOR VISUAL BASIC

Now that you've seen a basic overview of how to use the DB-Library, let's take a more detailed look at how to build a DB-Library application from Visual Basic. After the vbsql.ocx OLE Custom Control and the vbsql.bas modules have been added to Visual Basic's development environment, you can begin to use the DB-Library functions in your Visual Basic applications.

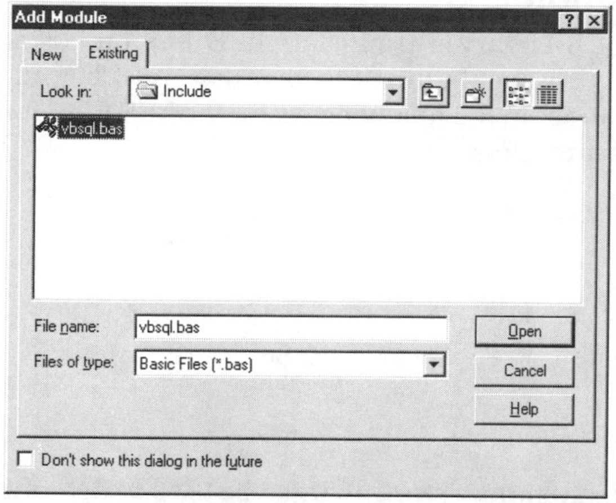

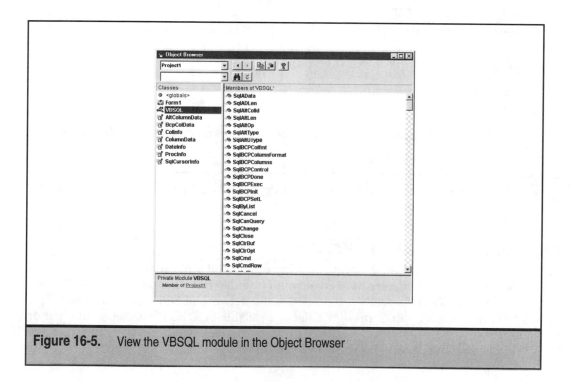

Figure 16-4.   Adding the vbsql.bas code module

Figure 16-5.   View the VBSQL module in the Object Browser

DB-Library Initialization

The first step in using DB-Library is to initialize the DB-Library using the SqlInit function. The SqlInit function is always the first function that must be called in the DB-Library application. As you can see in the following example, the SqlInit function is quite simple and doesn't use any parameters.

```
Dim sVersion As String

sVersion = SqlInit()
If sVersion = vbNullString Then
    MsgBox "The DB-Library could not be initialized"
    Exit Sub
End If
```

The SqlInit function returns a string that can be used to determine if the function has been successfully executed. If the SqlInit function is successful, the string will contain the version identification of the DB-Library. If the SqlInit function fails, the string is set to a null.

Ending the DB-Library

When your DB-Library application ends, the SqlWinExit subroutine must be called to release the memory that was allocated by the earlier SqlInit function. The following code shows how to call the SqlWinExit subroutine.

```
'End the DB-Library
SqlWinExit
```

The SqlWinExit subroutine doesn't take any parameters, and it doesn't return anything.

TIP: You can still use the DB-Library after running the SqlWinExit function, but you must first rerun the SqlInit function.

Enumerating SQL Server Systems

While the DB-Library is on the brink of being obsolete, it still provides an efficient and capable interface that offers features that aren't found in the other data access APIs. One example is DB-Library's ability to enumerate the networked SQL Server systems. This handy ability allows you to present a list of available SQL Server systems in a list or combo box. The following ListServers subroutine shows how you can use the SQlServerEnum function to list the connected servers.

```
Private Sub ListServers()

    Dim sServerList As String * 4097
    Dim nRC As Integer
    Dim nNumberServers As Long
    Dim n As Integer
    Dim nStart As Integer

    MousePointer = vbHourglass

    'Enumerate the SQL Server systems
    nRC = SqlServerEnum _
            (NETSEARCH + LOCSEARCH, sServerList, nNumberServers)

    'Add the SQL Server names to a List or ComboBox
    nStart = 1

    Do While nNumberServers > 0
        n = InStr(nStart, sServerList, Chr$(0))
        ComboBox.AddItem Mid(sServerList, nStart, n - 1)
        nStart = n + 1
        nNumberServers = nNumberServers - 1
    Loop

    MousePointer = vbDefault

End Sub
```

The SQlServerEnum function returns a string of the available SqL Server names separated by null characters. The first parameter of the SQlServerEnum function is a constant that defines the search mode. The following constants can be used in the first parameter of the SQlServerEnum function.

Constant	Description
LOCSEARCH	Search the servers listed in the win.ini file.
NETSEARCH	Search the servers on the network using the installed network libraries

As you would expect, using both the NETSEACH and LOCSEARCH constants cause the SQlServerEnum function to search both the win.ini file and the network.

The second parameter of the SQlServerEnum function is a string that will contain the list of SQL Server systems. On input, this parameter must be sized large enough to hold the entire list of system names. Otherwise, the function will return an error. On output, the string will hold a list of the SQL Server names. Each name will be separated by a null character.

The third parameter of the SQlServerEnum function returns the number of SQL Server systems that are returned. You can use this number to know how many system names to extract from the sServerList string returned in the second parameter.

After the SqlServerEnum function has completed, a Do While loop is used to pull the SQL Server names out of the sServerList variable and add them to a combo box. This loop is performed for the number of SQL Server names that were returned by the SqlServerEnum function. The first line within the Do While loop uses Visual Basic's InStr function to locate the first null character in the sServerList string. This delimits the end of the end of the first SQL Server name. Next, the Mid function is used in conjunction with two variables that track the starting and ending positions of the SQL Server name within the string to extract the name from the string and add it to the combo box. Then the nStart variable, which holds the SQL Server name starting position, is set to begin the next search at the beginning of the next SQL Server name in the sListServers string.

Connecting to SQL Server

After the SqlInit function has been successfully executed, the DB-Library can be connected to SQL Server. The DB-Library provides two functions that can be used to establish a connection to SQL Server: SqlOpen and SqlOpenConnection. The SqlOpen function provides a bit more capability but it is also more difficult to use. The SqlOpenConnection function is more straightforward and is a bit easier to use. It only requires a single function call. The follow section describes how to use the SqlOpen and SqlOpenConnection functions to connect to SQL Server.

Connecting to SQL Server Using SqlOpenConnection

Using the SqlOpenConnection function is quite straightforward, and it can be implemented using a single function call. While the SqlOpenConnection function doesn't allow you to set all of the possible SQL Server connection options, it does allow you to set the most common ones. The following code example illustrates how to use the SqlOpenConnection function.

```
Private Sub DBOpenConnection()

    Dim hConn As Long
    Dim sComputerName As String

    MousePointer = vbHourglass

    'Get the system name
    sComputerName = GetSystemName
```

```
'Open the connection and put the connection handle in hConn
hConn = SqlOpenConnection(sServer, sLoginID, sPassword, & _
        sComputerName, App.EXEName)

SqlClose (hConn)

MousePointer = vbDefault

End Sub
```

In the beginning of this example, a long variable named hConn is declared. This variable is used as a connection handle. It is assigned a value following a successful call to the SqlOpenConnection function. The connection handle is then used by the other DB-Library functions. Next, a string variable that will contain the local computer name is declared.

After these initial declarations, the GetSystemName function is called to retrieve the name of the local computer and assign it to the sComputerName variable. As you will see shortly, the name of the local computer system is used as one of the parameters of the SqlOpenConnection function. The code for the GetSystemName function is shown next.

```
Function GetSystemName() As String

    Dim nLength As Long
    Dim sComputerName As String
    Dim nRC As Long

    'Maximum Computer Name length
    nLength = 15
    sComputerName = Space(nLength + 1)

    'Call the Win32 API
    nRC = GetComputerName(sComputerName, nLength)

    'Return the name

    GetSystemName = Mid$(sComputerName, 1, nLength)

End Function
```

At the heart of the GetSystemName function is the Win32 API function GetComputerName. The Visual Basic declaration of the GetComputerName function follows.

```
Declare Function GetComputerName _
        Lib "kernel32" Alias "GetComputerNameA" _
        (ByVal lpBuffer As String, nSize As Long) As Long
```

The first parameter of the GetComputerName function is a string that will contain the name of the local system as seen in the system's Network Control Panel. The variable used in this parameter must be sized large enough to hold the value of the returned computer name; otherwise, the call to the GetComputerName function will fail. The maximum length for this parameter is 15. On input, the second parameter contains the length of the first string variable used in the first parameter. On output, the second parameter contains the length of the computer that was actually returned.

Before the GetComputerName function is called, the Space function is used to size the sComputerName variable so it is large enough to contain the output of the GetComputerName API. Following the call to the GetComputerName API, Visual Basic's Mid$ statement is used with the returned length to strip out the trailing null and blank characters.

After the GetSystemName function has been used to retrieve the name of the local computer system, the DB-Library SqlOpenConnection function is called to establish a connection to SQL Server. The first parameter of the SqlOpenConnection function is a string variable that contains the name of the target SQL Server system. The second parameter is a string variable that contains the user's login ID. Likewise, the third parameter is a string variable that contains the user's password. The fourth parameter is a string variable that contains the name of the local computer system. In this case, it will contain the value returned from the GetSystemName function. Finally, the last parameter is a string that contains the name of the client application. The EEName property of Visual Basic's App object contains the name of the executable program.

> **TIP:** The fourth parameter of SqlOpenConnection doesn't have to contain the actual name of the local computer system. It can contain any value you want to use to identify this application. The value used in this parameter can be seen in the hostname column output of SQL Server's sp_who stored procedure. However, having a unique identifier for each client can make troubleshooting easier.

Finally, at the end of this example, you can see where the SQL Server connection is closed using the SqlClose function.

Connecting to SQL Server Using SqlOpen

Using the SqlOpen function is a bit more difficult than the SqlOpenConnection function. The SqlOpen function must be implemented using a combination of the SqlLogin function followed by the SqlOpen function. While it is a bit more difficult to implement, the SqlOpenConnection function also allows you to set the full range of the DB-Library connection options. The following listing shows how to initiate a connection to SQL Server using the SqlOpen function.

```
Private Sub DBOpen()

    Dim hConn As Long
    Dim nLoginRec As Long
    Dim nRC As Long

    MousePointer = vbHourglass

    'Init the login structure
    nLoginRec = SqlLogin()

    'Set up the structure members
    nRC = SqlSetLUser(nLoginRec, sLoginID)
    nRC = SqlSetLPwd(nLoginRec, sPassword)
    nRC = SqlSetLHost(nLoginRec, GetSystemName)
    nRC = SqlSetLApp(nLoginRec, App.EXEName)

    'Open the connection and put the connection handle in hConn
    hConn = SqlOpen(nLoginRec, sServer)

    SqlClose (hConn)
    SqlFreeLogin (nLoginRec)

    MousePointer = vbDefault

End Sub
```

This example begins by declaring three long variables. The first, hConn, will be used as a connection handle. The second, nLoginRec, is a pointer to the DB-Library login structure that contains the connection parameters used by the SqlOpen function. The third, nRC, is used to hold any error codes that may be returned by the SqlOpen function.

Next, the DB-Library Login structure is initialized using the SqlLogin function. The SqlLogin function returns a handle to the DB-Library Login structure. This handle is then used by the following set of DB-Library functions that are used to set the values in the structure. The SqlSetLUser function sets the user ID that will be used to connect to SQL Server. The SqlSetLPwd function sets the password that will be used. The SqlSetLHost function sets the name of the local client system. In this example, you can see that the local computer name is assigned using the GetSystemName function that was presented earlier. Then the SqlSetLapp function is used to set the local application name using the App.EXEName property.

After the required values have been set in the DB-Library Login structure, the SqlOpen function is called to make the connection to the SQL Server system. The first parameter of the SqlOpen function contains the handle to the Login structure, while the second parameter is a string that identifies the target SQL Server system.

In this code example, the SQL Server connection is immediately closed using the SqlClose function. Then the memory allocated for the DB-Library login structure is released using the SqlFreeLogin function.

Closing a Connection Library

The SqlClose function ends a single connection that was allocated by an earlier SqlOpen or SqlOpenConnection function. The following code shows how to call the SqlClose function.

```
'Close the hConn connection
SqlClose(hConn)
```

The SqlClose function takes a single argument, the connection handle that was associated with the open connection. If multiple connections are opened and each connection uses a different connection handle, only the connection associated with the hConn handle will be closed. The other connections will remain active.

Closing All Connections

The SqlExit subroutine ends all active connections. The following code shows how to call the SqlExit subroutine.

```
'Close the hConn connection
SqlExit
```

SqlExit is a subroutine, not a function, and it accepts any arguments. All DB-Library connections will be terminated after running SqlExit.

Retrieving Data with DB-Library

The DB-Library has two basic methods for sending SQL queries to SQL Server and then retrieving the result sets. The DB-Library can use the SqlSendCmd function to send single SQL statements to SQL Server, or it can use a combination of the SqlCmd and SqlExec functions to send one SQL statement or a batch of SQL statements to SQL Server. In the following section, you'll see how to retrieve data from SQL Server using the SqlSendCmd function. Then the next section, will illustrate how you can retrieve data using the SqlCmd and SqlExec functions.

Performing Queries Using SqlSendCmd

Using the SqlSendCmd function is both simple and straightforward. To retrieve data from SQL Server using the SqlSendCmd function, you pass a string containing the SQL statement to the SqlSendCmd function. Then you can use the SqlNextRow statement to retrieve each row in the result set. The following example shows how to use the

SqlSendCmd function to send a simple SQL Select statement to SQL Server and then process the result set.

```
Private Sub DBQuery()

    Dim sSQL As String
    Dim hConn As Long
    Dim nRC As Long
    Dim sComputerName As String

    MousePointer = vbHourglass

    'Get the system name
    sComputerName = GetSystemName

    'Open the connection and put the connection handle in hConn
    hConn = SqlOpenConnection(sServer, sLoginID, sPassword, _
            sComputerName, App.EXEName)

    'Set the default database
    nRC = SqlUse(hConn, "pubs")

    'Construct the SQL string
    sSQL = "Select * From authors"

    'Execute the query
    nRC = SqlSendCmd(hConn, sSQL)

    'Display the results in the MSFlex Grid
    DisplayDBGrid hConn, Grid

    MousePointer = vbDefault


End Sub
```

The DBQuery subroutine just shown illustrates the entire process of connecting to the SQL Server system, as well as submitting a simple query using the SqlSendCmd, function. In the beginning of this function, you can see where three working variables are declared. The sSQL string variable is used to hold the SQL Select statement that will be sent to SQL Server. The hConn long variable is used to hold the DB-Library connection handle. The nRC long variable is used to hold the return code issued by the SqlSendCmd function, and the sComputerName string variable is used to hold the name of the local

PC. Next, the GetSystemName function that was presented earlier is used to retrieve the local computer name and assign it the sComputerName variable.

After all of the working variables have been set up, the SqlOpenConnection function is called to establish a connection to the SQL Server system that is named in the first parameter of the SqlOpenConnection function. When the SqlOpenConnection function has completed, the hConn variable will contain a connection handle that must be used in the subsequent DB-Library functions.

The next step after connecting to the SQL Server system is setting up the default database with the SqlUse function. The default database is the database that will be used to locate all unqualified tables that are specified in the SQL requests that are processed by the DB-Library. Setting the default database is optional, but using it allows you to avoid qualifying the tables used in your queries. In this case, the first parameter of the SqlUse function contains the hConn connection handle that was returned by the previous SqlOpenConnection function. The second parameter is a string that contains the name of the database that will be set as the default database. In this instance, the pubs database is set as the default database.

Next, a simple SQL Select statement that will return all of the rows and columns from the authors table is assigned to the sSQL string variable. Then the SQL statement is executed using the SqlSendCmd function. The SqlSendCmd function takes two parameters. The first parameter is a long variable that contains the connection handle returned by the SqlOpen or SqlOpenConnection function. The second parameter is a string that contains the SQL statement to be executed.

If the SqlSendCmd function is a success, then the result set will be processed and displayed in a grid. The DisplayDBGrid subroutine shown next reads the result set and displays it in the MSFlexGrid object.

```
Private Sub DisplayDBGrid(hConn As Long, Grid As MSFlexGrid)

    Dim nRC As Long
    Dim i As Integer

    ' Set up the grid
    Grid.Redraw = False
    Grid.Cols = SqlNumCols(hConn)
    Grid.Rows = 1
    Grid.Row = 0
    Grid.Col = 0
    Grid.Clear

    'Set up the Grid headings
    For i = 1 To Grid.Cols
        Grid.ColAlignment(Grid.Col) = 1
        Grid.Text = SqlColName(hConn, i)
        If Grid.Col < Grid.Cols - 1 Then
```

```
                Grid.Col = Grid.Col + 1
        End If
    Next i


    ' Move through each row in the record set
    Do Until NOMOREROWS = SqlNextRow(hConn)

        ' Set the position in the grid
        Grid.Rows = Grid.Rows + 1
        Grid.Row = Grid.Rows - 1
        Grid.Col = 0

        'Loop through all fields
        For i = 1 To Grid.Cols
            If i = 1 Then
                Grid.ColWidth(Grid.Col) = _
                    TextWidth(String(SqlDatLen(hConn, i), "a"))
            End If
            Grid.Text = SqlData(hConn, i)
            If Grid.Col < Grid.Cols - 1 Then
                Grid.Col = Grid.Col + 1
            End If
        Next i

    Loop

    Grid.Redraw = True
End Sub
```

The DisplayDBGrid subroutine accepts two parameters. The first parameter is the connection handle returned by the SqlOpenConnection function. The second parameter is the name of the MSFlexGrid object. The grid is set up near the beginning of this subroutine. First, the grid's redraw property is set to False, which eliminates the screen repainting that occurs as the grid is being filled. Then the gird is sized with the appropriate number of columns. The SqlNumCols function returns the number of columns contained in the result set. The SqlNumCols function accepts a long variable containing the connection handle. Next, the grid is set up to begin with one row that will initially contain the column headings. Finally, the grid is cleared of any old entries and is sized with the appropriate number of columns

Next, the grid's column headings are assigned using the column headings from the result set. A For Next loop is used to read through all of the columns in the result set. The For Next loop begins at 1 and continues until the counter reaches the number of columns contained in the result set.

> **NOTE:** The DB-Library column index begins at 1 rather than 0. Therefore, the For Next loop is set to begin with the value of 1 rather than 0.

Setting the column alignment to left justification is the first action that happens in the For Next loop. Next, the SqlColName function is used to retrieve the result set column names and assign them to the current grid row. Then the current gird column is incremented. An If test is used to prevent the current grid column from being incremented past the total number of columns assigned to the grid.

After the grid is set up, the SqlNextRow function is used with a Do Until loop to retrieve the contents of the result set.

> **NOTE:** Despite its name, the SqlNextRow function is also used to retrieve the first row in the result set.

The SqlNextRow function accepts a long variable containing the connection handle as a parameter. The function returns the DB-Library SUCCESS constant when it has successfully retrieved a row. When all of the rows in the result set have been retrieved, the function returns the constant NOMOREROWS. Each time the SqlNextRow function is executed, the cursor is positioned to the next row in the result set.

Within the Do Until loop, the number of rows in the gird is incremented using the Grid.Rows property, and the current grid row is incremented using the Grid.Row property. Then the current column position is set to 0 (the first column) and the For Next loop is used to retrieve the values of the columns in the row. Inside the For Next loop, the column width is set using the actual data length in the first row.

> **NOTE:** Sizing the gird bases on the values in the first row is best suited to tables where the size of the column values does not vary a great deal. For tables where the first column's data may not be representative of the other columns, you would want to implement a more sophisticated method. For instance, your application could track the maximum size of each column and resize the column whenever a larger data value is encountered. Alternatively, you could size the grid columns using the SqlColLen function, which returns the maximum size of the column; but for text and char fields, this generally leaves a lot of unused space in the grid.

The SqlDatLen function is used to return the actual data length of the column, and it accepts two parameters. The first parameter is a long variable that contains the connection handle, and the second parameter is an integer that specifies the column in the result set.

Next, the SqlData function is used to retrieve the data value and assign it to a cell in the grid. Like the SqlDatLen function, the SqlData function also takes two parameters. The first parameter contains the connection handle and the second parameter specifies the result set column. After assigning the column value to the grid, the current column is incremented by adding one to the Grid.Col property.

After all of the rows and columns in the result set have been processed, the grid's redraw property is set to True, which causes the grid to repaint with all of the new result set values.

Performing Queries Using SqlCmd, SqlExec, and SqlResults

Using the SqlCmd and SqlExec functions is not quite as easy as using the single SqlSendCmd function. However, the SqlCMD function is a bit more flexible in that it allows you to send a batch of SQL commands to SQL Server. To retrieve data from SQL Server using the SqlCmd function, you pass one or more strings containing SQL statements to the SqlCmd function. After all of the desired SQL statements have been added to the SqlCmd function, you can use the SqlExec function to execute those statements. Then you can use the SqlResults statement to retrieve the result sets generated by the SQL statements. The following DBExecQuery subroutine shows how to use the SqlCmd, SqlExec, and SqlResults functions.

```
Private Sub DBExecQuery(hConn As Long, sServer As String, _
                     sLoginID As String, sPassword As String)

    Dim sSQL As String
    Dim nRC As Long

    Dim sComputerName As String

    MousePointer = vbHourglass

    'Get the system name
    sComputerName = GetSystemName

    'Open the connection and put the handle in hConn
    hConn = SqlOpenConnection(sServer, sLoginID, _
sPassword, sComputerName, App.EXEName)

    'Construct the SQL string
    sSQL = "SELECT * FROM stores"

    'Set the default database
    nRC = SqlUse(hConn, "pubs")

    'Build the Command
    nRC = SqlCmd(hConn, sSQL)

    'Send the SQL statement
    nRC = SqlExec(hConn)
```

```
'Get the Result set
Do Until NOMORERESULTS = SqlResults(hConn)

    'Display the results in the MSFlex Grid
    DisplayDBGrid hConn, Grid

Loop

MousePointer = vbDefault


End Sub
```

The previous DBExecQuery subroutine shows how to connect to SQL Server and how to submit a query using the SqlCmd, SqlExec, and SqlResults functions. In the beginning of this function, you can see where three working variables are declared. The sSQL string variable is used to hold the SQL Select statement that will be sent to SQL Server. The hConn long variable is used to hold the DB-Library connection handle. The nRC long variable is used to hold the return code issued by the SqlSendCmd function, and the sComputerName string variable is used to hold the name of the local PC. After the variables have been declared, the GetSystemName function is used to retrieve the local computer name and assign it to the sComputerName variable.

Then the SqlOpenConnection function is called to open a connection to the SQL Server. The hConn variable will contain a connection handle when the SqlOpen-Connection function has completed.

Then the default database is set to pubs using the SqlUse function, and the SQL Select statement is set up using the SqlCmd function. The SqlCmd function takes two arguments. The first is a long variable that contains the connection handle, and the second is a string variable that contains the SQL statement that will be executed. Next, the SQL Select statement is executed using the SqlExec function. The SqlExec function accepts a single parameter—the connection handle. The success or failure of the SqlExec function can be checked using its return code. More information about DB-Library error handling will be presented later in this chapter in the section "Error Handling."

NOTE:　While this example uses a single command, you can call the SqlCmd function multiple times, and each call can assign a different SQL statement. When the subsequent SqlExec function, is called, the entire batch of SQL statements will be executed.

After the SQL Select statement has completed, the SqlResults function is used to retrieve the first—and in this case only—result set. Then the contents of the result set can be accessed using the SqlNextRow function. In this example, the DisplayDBGrid subroutine that was presented earlier uses the SqlNextRow function to retrieve the contents of the result set and display them in an MSFlexGrid.

▼ *TIP:* The DB-Library doesn't permit you to perform another SqlExec function until the SqlResults function has returned NOMORERESULTS or the SqlCanQuery function is called.

Executing Dynamic SQL

In addition to performing queries, the DB-Library can also execute dynamic SQL action queries on SQL Server. For instance, you can use the SqlSendCmd or the SqlCmd and SqlExec functions to create databases, tables, views, and even stored procedures. In the following CreateTable subroutine, you'll see how to create a new table in the pubs database using dynamic SQL and the DB-Library SqlSendCmd function.

```
Private Sub CreateTable(hConn As Long)

    Dim nRC As Long
    Dim sSQL As String

    Screen.MousePointer = vbHourglass

    'Make certain that the table is created by dropping the table
    ' If the table doesn't exist the code will move on to the next
    ' statement
    sSQL = "Drop Table department"
    'Execute the query
    nRC = SqlSendCmd(hConn, sSQL)

    'Reset the error handler and create the table
    ' If an error is encountered it will be displayed
    sSQL = "CREATE TABLE department " _
        & "(Dep_ID INT not null, Dep_Name CHAR(25), primary _
        key(Dep_ID))"
    'Execute the query

    nRC = SqlSendCmd(hConn, sSQL)

Screen.MousePointer = vbDefault

End Sub
```

In the beginning of this subroutine, you can see where two working variables are declared. The variable nRC is a long data type that's used to hold any return codes generated by the SqlSendCmd function. The sSQL variable is a string data type that's used to contain the SQL statements that will be sent to the SQL Server system.

The first SQL statement that's sent to the SQL Server system is a Drop Table statement. Executing a Drop Table statement ensures that the department table doesn't exist before the subsequent Create Table statement is issued. The department table will be deleted when the SqlSendCmd function is executed with this SQL statement in the second parameter. If the department table is successfully deleted, the SqlSendCmd function will return SUCCESS (1). If it fails, the function will return FAIL (0).

Next, the sSQL variable is assigned a Create Table statement that will create the department table. In this previous example, you can see that the department table will have two columns: one integer column named Dep_ID and one 25-byte character column named Dep_Name. The primary key of the new department table is the Dep_ID column. When the SqlSendCmd function is executed with the sSQL string variable in the second parameter, the department table will be created in the database that's assigned to the hConn connection handle.

Modifying Data with Dynamic SQL

In addition to executing SQL DDL type statements like the Create Table statement that was shown in the previous example, the DB-Library can also execute SQL DML action queries that can insert, update, and delete data contained in a SQL Server database. The following set of examples illustrates how you can modify SQL Server data using dynamic SQL and the DB-Library SqlSendCmd function.

Inserting Rows

You can insert data into a SQL Server table by using the SQL Insert statement. The following SqlAdd subroutine illustrates how you can use the SQL Insert statement with the DB-Library SqlSendCmd function.

```
Private Sub SQLAdd(hConn As Long)

    Dim i As Integer
    Dim nRC As Long
    Dim sSQL As String

    Screen.MousePointer = vbHourglass

    ' No recordset is needed
    For i = 1 To 50
        sSQL = "Insert Into department " & _
            "Values('" & CStr(i) & "','DEPARTMENT " & CStr(i) & "')"

        nRC = SqlSendCmd(hConn, sSQL)
    Next

    'Construct the SQL string
    sSQL = "Select * From department"
```

```
'Execute the query
nRC = SqlSendCmd(hConn, sSQL)

'Display the results in the MSFlex Grid
DisplayDBGrid hConn, Grid

Screen.MousePointer = vbDefault
Exit Sub


End Sub
```

The For Next loop is the core of the SqlAdd subroutine. As you can see in the previous code, this For Next loop will be repeated 50 times. Building the SQL Insert statement is the first action that occurs within the For Next loop. In this example, the Insert statement will insert two columns into the department table. The first column is an integer value that is assigned the value of the loop counter. The second column is a character data type that is assigned the string "DEPARTMENT" plus the string representation of the loop counter. For example, the first time this loop executes, the Insert statement will appear as follows:

```
Insert Into department Values('1', 'DEPARTMENT 1')
```

NOTE: The department table is not a part of the standard pubs database. It was built using the code illustrated in the previous Create Table example.

After the sSQL variable has been set with the SQL Insert statement, the DB-Library SqlSendCmd function is executed to insert the row in the department table. As you saw in the previous examples, the first parameter of the SqlSendCmd is a connection handle that was assigned using the SqlConnection function. The second parameter contains the SQL statement—in this case the SQL Insert statement—that will be executed on the SQL Server system.

After the For Next loop has completed, a Select statement is used with the SqlSendCmd function to retrieve all of the rows that were just added to the department table. The results of the Select statement are then displayed in a grid.

Updating Rows

Updating rows with dynamic SQL is very much like inserting rows. You can update columns in a SQL Server table by using the SQL Update statement. The following SqlUpdate subroutine illustrates how you can use the SQL Update statement to update all of the rows in the department table.

```
Private Sub SQLUpdate(hConn As Long)

    Dim nRC As Long
    Dim sSQL As String

    Screen.MousePointer = vbHourglass

    sSQL = "Update department " & _
        "Set Dep_Name = 'UPDATED ' + Substring(Dep_Name, 1, 25)"

    nRC = SqlSendCmd(hConn, sSQL)

    'Construct the SQL string
    sSQL = "Select * From department"

    'Execute the query
    nRC = SqlSendCmd(hConn, sSQL)

    'Display the results in the MSFlex Grid
    DisplayDBGrid hConn, Grid


    Screen.MousePointer = vbDefault


End Sub
```

The SqlUpdate subroutine illustrates how you can update all of the rows in the department table using a single SQL Update statement. While this same action could have been performed using a SQL Update statement that contains a Where clause, there was no need to do so. The Where clause is used to specify individual rows. Instead, this example is intended to update all of the rows in the department table, so the Where clause has been omitted. This causes the Update statement to act on all of the rows in the department table. Since this technique shifts all of the processing to the server, it also performs much better than updating individual rows because the network I/O is substantially reduced.

In the Update statement, the Set clause identifies the columns that will be updated. In this example, the Dep_Name column will be updated using the literal UPDATE in conjunction with the results of the SQL Substring function, which returns the first 25 characters of the Dep_Name column.

After the Update statement has been built, the SqlSendCmd statement is used to execute it on the SQL Server system. Again, the value of an existing connection handle is used in the first parameter of the SqlSendCmd function, while a string containing the SQL Update statement is used in the second parameter.

Near the end of the SqlUpdate subroutine, you can see where a Select statement is used with the SqlSendCmd function to retrieve all of the rows that were just updated. The results of the Select statement are then displayed in a grid.

Deleting Rows

You can also use dynamic SQL and the DB-Library SqlSendCmd function to delete rows. You can delete rows in a SQL Server table using the SQL Delete statement. The following SqlDelete subroutine shows how to use the SQL Delete statement to delete all of the rows in the department table.

```
Private Sub SQLDelete(hConn As Long)

    Dim sSQL As String
    Dim nRC As Long

    Screen.MousePointer = vbHourglass

    sSQL = "Delete department"

    nRC = SqlSendCmd(hConn, sSQL)

   'Construct the SQL string
    sSQL = "Select * From department"

    'Execute the query
    nRC = SqlSendCmd(hConn, sSQL)

    'Display the results in the MSFlex Grid
    DisplayDBGrid hConn, Grid


    Screen.MousePointer = vbDefault

End Sub
```

Much like the previous Update example, this Delete example takes advantage of SQL's set-at-a-time processing to delete all of the rows in the department table by executing a single SQL statement. In this example, the SQL Delete statement is assigned to the sSQL string and then the string is passed to the SqlSendCmd function. When the SqlSendCmd function is executed, all of the rows in the department table will be deleted.

After the Delete statement has completed, a Select statement is used with the SqlSendCmd function to retrieve the contents of the department table, which should be empty.

Working with Cursors

In addition to supporting entire result sets and dynamic SQL statements, the DB-Library also provides support for cursors. Cursors essentially provide your application with a subset of the rows in a result set. Unlike a standard result set, cursors also permit operations on individual rows. For instance, you can use a cursor to move forward or backward through the rows in a result set, or you can use a cursor to update individual rows in the result set. Cursors can also be a handy mechanism for implementing user interface elements like list boxes that can page through a result set using a set number of rows. Figure 16-6 presents an overview of a simple cursor.

In Figure 16-6, you can see a conceptual overview showing the different elements of a sample keyset cursor. The keyset cursor is a subset of the result set, and it can contain all of the rows of the result set or just a portion of the rows. When a keyset cursor is opened, a set of keys is created where each key is a pointer to a row in the base table. For client-side cursors, the keyset is maintained on the local PC, while a server-side cursor will maintain

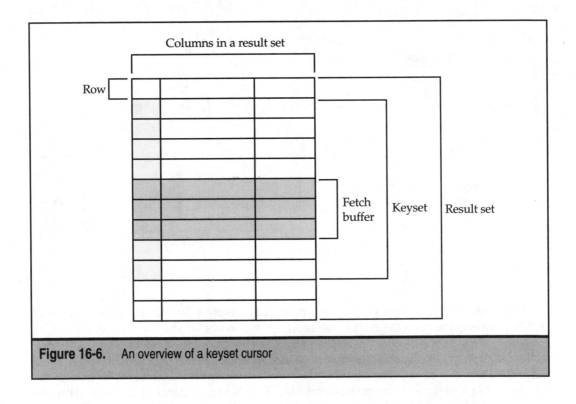

Figure 16-6. An overview of a keyset cursor

the keyset on the server. The fetch buffer is the number of rows in the cursor that have been fetched into client memory. The fetch buffer is a subset of the keyset and can be the same size as the keyset or some portion of the keyset. You can refer to Chapter 10 for more information about cursors.

TIP: The fetch buffer is useful for situations like displaying a fixed number of rows on the screen. In this scenario, you set the fetch buffer to the number of rows to be displayed on the screen. Then subsequent fetches can be used to scroll forward or backward through the result set.

Table 16-2 lists the types of cursors that are supported by the DB-Library. As you can see, DB-Library cursors can be used for both traversing a result set and updating rows within a result set. In the following section, you'll see how you can use cursors to insert, update, and delete rows in a result set.

NOTE: The DB-Library does not support static or snapshot cursors, but you can approximate them by performing a SQL Select Into statement to create a temporary table. Then you can query the temporary table.

Cursor Type	Description
Forward	Dynamic forward-only cursor. This cursor type is updateable, and it reflects other users' changes in the result set. But it only supports forward scrolling.
Keyset	Keyset cursor. This cursor type is updateable, but it doesn't reflect changes made by other users. Both forward and backward scrolling are supported.
Dynamic	Dynamic cursor. This cursor type is updateable, and it reflects changes made by other users. Both forward and backward scrolling are supported.

Table 16-2.   Cursor Types Supported by DB-Library

Inserting Rows

To insert rows using a DB-Library cursor, you must first open the cursor. After the cursor is open, you can modify the values that are contained in the fetched buffer and the modifications that you make will be written back to the base table. As you have probably guessed, you can only modify data that's contained in a single table. You cannot update a result set that's based on a join. The following CursorAdd subroutine illustrates how you can open a cursor and use it to insert 50 rows in a table.

```
Private Sub CursorAdd(hConn As Long)

    Dim nRC As Long
    Dim sSQL As String
    Dim hCursor As Long
    Dim i As Long

    Screen.MousePointer = vbHourglass

    sSQL = "Select Dep_ID, Dep_Name From department"

    hCursor = SqlCursorOpen(hConn, sSQL, CURDYNAMIC, CUROPTCCVAL, 50)

    'Add 50 rows to the department table
    For i = 1 To 50
      sSQL = "Values('" & CStr(i) & "','DEPARTMENT " & CStr(i) & "')"
      nRC = SqlCursor(hCursor, CRSINSERT, i, "", sSQL)
    Next

    'Display the new rows in a grid
    DisplayCursorGrid hCursor, Grid

    SqlCursorClose hCursor

    Screen.MousePointer = vbDefault

End Sub
```

Near the beginning of this subroutine, you can see where the sSQL string variable is assigned a SQL Select statement. This Select statement is used to define the result set. In this case, the result set will consist of all of the Dep_Id and Dep_Name columns from the sample department table.

TIP: If you know that the cursor will only be used to insert rows, you can add a Where clause to the Select statement. The clause will ensure that the result set will not return any rows. For instance, you could use the following SQL: Select * From department Where 1 = 2. Since the condition 1=2 will never be true, this ensures that no rows will be returned in the result set. Even though no rows are in the result set, you can still use it to insert new rows.

Next, the SqlCursorOpen function is used to create the cursor. The SqlCursorOpen function is similar in concept to the SqlOpenConnection function in that it returns a handle that will be used by the following cursor functions. In this case, the handle that is contained in the hCursor variable is a cursor handle. The SqlOpenCursor function takes five parameters. The first parameter is a long data type that contains a valid connection handle that was established by an earlier SqlOpenConnection or SqlOpen function. The second parameter of the SqlCursorOpen function contains the Sql Select statement that defines the result set. The third parameter specifies the type of cursor that will be opened. The following table presents the values that can be used in this parameter.

Constant	Cursor Type
CURDYNAMIC	Dynamic scrollable cursor
CURKEYSET	Keyset cursor
CURFORWARD	Dynamic forward-only cursor
CURINSENSITIVE	Keyset read-only cursor that generates a temporary table

In this example, the value of CURDYNAMIC indicates that a dynamic cursor that will reflect all changes in the base table will be used.

The fourth parameter of the SqlCursorOpen function specifies the type of data concurrency that will be used by the cursor. The concurrency option parameter accepts the following values:

Constant	Description
CUREADONLY	The cursor will only support read operations. Updated will not be allowed.
CURLOCKCC	The cursor places an exclusive lock on each row as it is fetched. The lock is released after the next fetch operation or after the transaction is closed.
CUROPTCC	The cursor will use optimistic record locking based on timestamps or row values if no timestamp is available.
CUROPTCCVAL	The cursor will use optimistic record locking based on row values.

The fifth parameter of the SqlCursorOpen function specifies the size of the fetch buffer. In this example, the fetch buffer is sized at 50 rows.

After the cursor is opened, a For Next loop is used to add 50 rows to the department table. The first action that occurs within the For Next loop is the assignment of the Values clause of a SQL Insert statement to the sSQL string variable. While the SqlCursor function can accept the entire Insert statement, the function only really needs the Values clause. Note that the keyword Values and the parentheses must be present. In this example, the Values clause sets values in the two columns in the department table. The first assignment sets the Dep_ID column using the value of the loop counter. The second column, Dep_Name, is assigned the literal DEPARTMENT concatenated with the value of the loop counter.

Next, the SqlCursor function is called to perform the insert operation. The SqlCursor function takes five parameters. The first parameter is a long value that contains the cursor handle that was opened earlier using the SqlCursorOpen function. The second parameter is a long variable that contains a constant that controls the action performed by the SqlCursor function. The following table presents the DB-Library constants that can be used.

Constant	Description
CRSDELETE	Deletes the row identified in the third parameter.
CRSINSERT	Inserts the row values specified in the fifth parameter.
CRSLOCKCC	Puts an exclusive lock on the row identified in the third parameter.
CRSREFRESH	Refreshes the row values identified in the third parameter.
CRSUPDATE	Updates the row using the row values specified in the string in the fifth parameter.

The third parameter is a long data type that identifies the row number from the fetch buffer that will be acted on. In this example, the loop counter is used to identify the row. The fourth parameter is a string that can contain a SQL Server table name. For an insert operation, this parameter should be an empty string. The fifth parameter of the SqlCursor function is a string that contains SQL that will be performed. For an Insert statement, this can be either a full Insert statement or just the Insert statement Values clause.

Displaying Cursor Data

After 50 rows have been inserted using the cursor, the DisplayCursorGrid subroutine is used to display the contents of the cursor's current fetch buffer in an MSFlexGrid. The DisplayCursorGrid subroutine is quite similar to the DisplayDBGrid subroutine that was presented earlier; however, there are some important differences. The code for the DisplayCursorGrid subroutine is shown in the following example.

```
Private Sub DisplayCursorGrid(hCursor As Long, Grid As MSFlexGrid)

    Dim nRC As Long
    Dim nColumns As Long
    Dim nRows As Long
    Dim sColumnName As String
    Dim nColType As Long
    Dim nColLen As Long
    Dim nUsertype As Long
    Dim nCurrentRow As Long
    Dim nCurrentColumn As Long
    Dim nRowStatus As Long

    ' Set up the grid
    Grid.Redraw = False
    nRC = SqlCursorInfo(hCursor, nColumns, nRows)
    Grid.Cols = nColumns
    Grid.Rows = 1
    Grid.Row = 0
    Grid.Col = 0
    Grid.Clear

    'Set up the Grid headings
     For nCurrentColumn = 1 To Grid.Cols
         Grid.ColAlignment(Grid.Col) = 1
         nRC = SqlCursorColInfo(hCursor, nCurrentColumn, _
                  sColumnName, nColType, nColLen, nUsertype)
         Grid.Text = sColumnName
         If Grid.Col < Grid.Cols - 1 Then
            Grid.Col = Grid.Col + 1
         End If
     Next nCurrentColumn

  nCurrentRow = 0

  nRC = SqlCursorFetch(hCursor, FETCHFIRST, 0)

  If nRC = SUCCEED Then

      ' Move through each row in the record set
      Do

          'Set the current row
          nCurrentRow = nCurrentRow + 1
```

```
nRC = SqlCursorRowStatus _
        (hCursor, nCurrentRow, nRowStatus)

If nRowStatus = FTCSUCCEED Or nRowStatus = 9 Then

' Set the position in the grid
Grid.Rows = Grid.Rows + 1
Grid.Row = Grid.Rows - 1
Grid.Col = 0

'Loop through all fields
For nCurrentColumn = 1 To Grid.Cols
    If Grid.Row = 1 Then
        Grid.ColWidth(Grid.Col) = TextWidth(String(Len( _
        SqlCursorData _
          (hCursor, nCurrentRow, nCurrentColumn)) + 4, "a"))
    End If
    Grid.Text = SqlCursorData _
                (hCursor, nCurrentRow, nCurrentColumn)
    If Grid.Col < Grid.Cols - 1 Then
        Grid.Col = Grid.Col + 1
    End If
Next nCurrentColumn

End If

Loop While nRowStatus = FTCSUCCEED

End If


Grid.Redraw = True


End Sub
```

The DisplayCursorGrid subroutine uses the cursor handle that was returned by the SqlOpenCursor function as its first parameter and the name of an MSFlexGrid object in the second parameter. Next, a set of variables that are used by the different DB-Library cursor functions are declared. Then the grid is sized to contain the appropriate number of columns by using the SqlCursorInfo function. The SqlCursorInfo function takes the cursor handle as input and then returns the number of columns and rows in the cursor in the second and third parameters.

After the grid is sized, the column headings are assigned by using a For Next loop and the SqlCursorColInfo function. The For Next loop is repeated once for each column in the grid. The SqlCursorInfo accepts six parameters. The first parameter contains the cursor handle that was passed into the DisplayCursorGrid subroutine. The second parameter is a long variable that identifies the grid column. The third parameter is a string variable that will return the column name. The fourth parameter is a long variable that will return the column data type. The fifth parameter is a long variable that contains the defined column length, and the sixth parameter is used to return the type code for user-defined data. In this example, only the string containing the column name is used. The name of each column in the result set is placed in the first row of the grid. The For Next loop then increments the nCurrentColumn value, which will be used to retrieve the next set of column information.

After the Grid has been sized and the column headings have been assigned, the SqlCursorFetch function is used to retrieve the fetch buffer. The SqlCursorFetch function takes three parameters. The first parameter contains the cursor handle. The second parameter contains a constant that controls the type of fetch operation that will be performed. The following table lists the DB-Library constants that can be used in the second parameter of the SqlCursorFetch function.

Constant	Description
FETCHFIRST	Fetches the first set of rows from the cursor.
FETCHNEXT	Fetches the next sequential set of rows from the cursor.
FETCHPREV	Fetches the previous set of rows from the cursor. Not valid with forward-only cursors.
FETCHRANDOM	Fetches a set of rows from a keyset cursor beginning with a specified row number.
FETCHRELATIVE	Fetches a set of rows from a keyset cursor beginning with a specified number of rows from the current row number.
FETCHLAST	Fetches the last set of rows from the cursor. Not valid with forward-only cursors.

If the SqlCursorFetch function was successful, then a Do loop is used to read through the rows in the fetch buffer. First, the current row position is assigned to the nCurrent row variable. Then the SqlCursorRowStatus function is called to ensure that the row in the fetched buffer is valid. A row can be invalid if it is deleted.

The SqlCursorRowStatus function uses three parameters. The first parameter is the cursor handle. The second is a long variable that contains the current row number, and the third is a long variable that returns the status of the current row. The value of the nRowStatus variable is then examined to determine if the row is valid. If the row is a valid row, then a For Next loop is used to move all of the row's column values to the grid.

Within this For Next loop, a check is made to determine if the first row of data is being used. If this is the first row, the results of the SqlCursorData function is used in conjunction with the TextWidth function to size each of the grid columns.

NOTE: Like the column-sizing technique used in the DisplayDBGrid function presented earlier, this technique is best suited to rows that have fairly consistent data.

After the grid columns have been sized, the SqlCursorData function is used within a For Next loop to extract the column values and move them into the grid cells. The SqlCursorData function returns a Visual Basic string data type and uses three input parameters. Like the other cursor functions, the first parameter is the cursor handle. The second parameter is a long data type that identifies the row number. The third parameter is a long variable that identifies the current column number. After the data values have been assigned to a grid cell, the current column is incremented and the For Next loop retrieves the next column in the row.

NOTE: In this case, the size of the fetch buffer matched the size of the result set so no further fetches were needed. However, if the fetch buffer had been smaller than the result set size, then a SqlCursorFetch function with the FETCHNEXT constant would have been required to get the next fetch buffer contained in the cursor.

After the contents of the cursor have been moved to the MSFlexGrid, the SqlCursorClose function is called to close the cursor. The SqlCursorClose function accepts a single parameter that identifies the cursor handle to be closed.

UPDATING ROWS   Just as you can insert rows using a cursor, you can also update column values using a cursor. The following CursorUpdate subroutine shows how you can open a cursor and then update the column values exposed in the cursor.

```
Private Sub CursorUpdate(hConn As Long)

    Dim nRC As Long
    Dim sSQL As String
    Dim hCursor As Long
    Dim i As Long
    Dim sTemp As String

    Screen.MousePointer = vbHourglass

    sSQL = "Select Dep_ID, Dep_Name From department"

    hCursor = SqlCursorOpen(hConn, sSQL, CURDYNAMIC, CUROPTCCVAL, 50)
    nRC = SqlCursorFetch(hCursor, FETCHFIRST, 0)
```

```
For i = 1 To 50
    sSQL = "Set Dep_Name = " _
                & "'UPDATED DEPARTMENT " & CStr(i) & "'"
    nRC = SqlCursor(hCursor, CRSUPDATE, i, "", sSQL)
Next

'Display the new rows in a grid
DisplayCursorGrid hCursor, Grid

SqlCursorClose hCursor

Screen.MousePointer = vbDefault

End Sub
```

Before you can update data with a cursor, the cursor must first be opened and the fetch buffer must be populated. Like the earlier Insert example, the SqlCursorOpen function is used to open a cursor. As you would expect, the first parameter contains the cursor handle and the second parameter contains the SQL Select statement that defines the result set. Again, the values of CURDYNAMIC and CUROPTCCVAL in the third and fourth parameters make this a dynamic cursor that uses optimistic locking to enforce data concurrency. The fifth parameter specifies the size of the fetch buffer.

NOTE: Using a dynamic cursor allows all of the modifications to the cursor's row values to be immediately available to both the current application and other applications that may be using the department table.

Next, the fetch buffer is populated using the SqlCursorFetch function and the For Next loop is used to update all of the rows in the fetch buffer. Similar to the earlier Insert example, updating columns uses just the Set clause of a SQL Update statement. The entire Update statement can be used, but the Set clause is all that is needed. In this case, the Dep_Name column will be set to the literal UPDATED DEPARTMENT plus the string representation of the loop counter. After the appropriate Set clause has been constructed, the SqlCursor function is used to perform the update. In the case of an update action, the second parameter must contain the constant CRSUPDATE. The third parameter identifies the row that will be updated, and the fifth parameter is a string that contains the Set clause.

After the update operation has completed, the contents of the cursor are displayed using the DisplayCursorGrid function, and then the SqlCursorClose function is called to close the cursor.

DELETING ROWS　As you have probably guessed, you can also delete the rows contained in a DB-Library cursor. The following CursorDelete subroutine shows how you can open a cursor and then update the column values exposed in the cursor.

```
Private Sub CursorDelete(hConn As Long)

    Dim nRC As Long
    Dim sSQL As String
    Dim hCursor As Long
    Dim i As Integer
    Dim sTemp As String

    Screen.MousePointer = vbHourglass

    sSQL = "Select Dep_ID, Dep_Name From department"

    hCursor = SqlCursorOpen(hConn, sSQL, CURDYNAMIC, CUROPTCCVAL, 50)
    nRC = SqlCursorFetch(hCursor, FETCHFIRST, 0)

    For i = 1 To 50
        nRC = SqlCursor(hCursor, CRSDELETE, i, "", "")
    Next

    'Display the new rows in a grid
    DisplayCursorGrid hCursor, Grid

    SqlCursorClose hCursor

    Screen.MousePointer = vbDefault
```

Deleting rows using a DB-Library cursor is very much like updating rows. First, the cursor must be opened using the SqlCursorOpen function. Then the fetch buffer must be populated using either the SqlFetch or the SqlFetchEx functions. After the fetch buffer is populated, you can use the SqlCursor function to delete the rows in the cursor. To delete a row using the SqlCursor function, you need to use the CRSDELETE constant in the second parameter along with an identifying row number in the third parameter. Unlike the Insert and Update examples shown earlier, there's no need to supply a SQL statement to delete the row. DB-Library uses the row number supplied in the third parameter to locate the row in the fetch buffer.

Executing Stored Procedures

DB-Library can have SQL Server execute stored procedures two ways: by using the SqlSendCmd function with an Execute statement or by using the SqlRpcInit and SqlRpcSend functions. If the stored procedure returns a result set, then your application will need to perform the SqlResults and SqlNextRow functions to retrieve all of the rows and result sets generated by the stored procedure. Both methods can be used to call stored procedures that return result sets. However, if your application needs to access parameter values returned from the stored procedure, then it needs to use the SqlRpcInit function. In the following example, you'll see how to use the SqlRPCInit and SqlRpcInit function to call the SQL Server stored procedure called SumStateQty. The SumStateQty stored procedure is shown here:

```
Create Procedure SumStateQty
(
    @state Char(2),
    @rows Int Output
)
As
Select @rows = Sum(qty) From sales Inner Join stores On _
 sales.stor_id = stores.stor_id
Where state = @state
Go
```

The SumStateQty has one input parameter and one output parameter. The input parameter accepts a two-character state code, and the output parameter returns the total quantity for all stores that are in the specified state. The stored procedure calculates the total quantity by joining the sales and the stores tables in the pubs database, and then uses the Sum function to total the contents of the qty column for the supplied state code.

The following CallSP subroutine illustrates how to use stored procedure parameters by executing the SumStateQty stored procedure. This subroutine passes the stored procedure a state code as an input parameter and then retrieves the output parameter generated by the stored procedure.

```
Private Sub CallSP(hConn As Long)

    Dim nRC As Long
    Dim sSQL As String
    Dim nMaxLen As Long
    Dim nDataLen As Long
```

```
    Screen.MousePointer = vbHourglass

    'Initiate the stored procedure
    nRC = SqlRpcInit(hConn, "SumStateQty", 0)

    'Add the two parameters
    nDataLen = Len("CA")
    nMaxLen = -1
    nRC = SqlRpcParam _
          (hConn, "@state", 0, SQLCHAR, nMaxLen, nDataLen, "CA")

    nDataLen = -1
    nMaxLen = -1
    nRC = SqlRpcParam _
          (hConn, "@qty", SQLRPCRETURN, SQLINT4, nMaxLen, nDataLen, "")

    'Now execute the stored procedure
    nRC = SqlRpcSend(hConn)
    nRC = SqlOk(hConn)

    ' Get the data returned in the output parameter
    Label_Mid.Caption = "Total Qty for State CA"
    Text_Mid.Text = SqlRetData(hConn, 1)

    Screen.MousePointer = vbDefault


End Sub
```

Calling the SqlRpcInit function to initial the DB-Library support for stored procedures is the first step in calling a stored procedure with DB-Library. The SqlRpcInit function takes three parameters. The first parameter is the connection handle that was returned by an earlier call to the SqlOpen or SqlOpenConnection functions. The second parameter is a string that contains the name of the SQL Server stored procedure to be called. The name used in this parameter must match the name of the SQL Server stored procedure. In this example, the stored procedure named SumStateQty will be executed. The third parameter contains a bit mask that sets the options used by the SqlRpcInit function. The following table lists the valid DB-Library constants that are used in the options parameter.

Constant	Description
SQLRPCRECOMPILE	The Stored procedure will be recompiled before it is executed.
SQLRPCRESET	Cancels an executing stored procedure.

After the SqlRpcInit function has been executed to initialize the stored procedure, the SqlRpcParam function must be called for each parameter that's used by the stored procedure. The SumStateQty stored procedure uses two parameters: one for input and the other for output. Therefore, in this example, the SqlRpcParam function must be called twice. The SqlRpcParam function accepts several parameters. Like almost all of the DB-Library functions, the first parameter is the connection handle. The second parameter is a string that contains the name of the parameter. This is an optional parameter. If it's not used, the parameters are identified using the order in which the SqlRpcParameter function is called. In other words, if the parameter name is blank the first time the SqlRpcParameter function is executed, it sets the attributes of the first parameter used by the stored procedure. The second time it is executed, it will set the attributes of the second parameter, and so on. The third parameter sets the input/output options for the parameter. A value of 0 indicates the parameter is used for input only, while a value of SQLRPCRETURN indicates that the parameter will contain returned values. In the previous CallSP subroutine, you can see that the first instance of the SqlRpcParam function sets this value to 0, indicating that it is used for input. Then the second instance of the SqlRpcParam function sets this parameter to SQLRPCRETURN, indicating that it is an output parameter. The fourth parameter of the SqlRpcParameter function identifies the data type used in the parameter. This parameter must contain one of the following constants.

SQLAOPANY	SQLCHAR	SQLINT2
SQLAOPAVG	SQLDATETIM4	SQLINT4
SQLAOPCNT	SQLDATETIME	SQLINTN
SQLAOPMAX	SQLDATETIMN	SQLMONEY
SQLAOPMIN	SQLDECIMAL	SQLMONEY4
SQLAOPNOOP	SQLFLT4	SQLMONEYN
SQLAOPSUM	SQLFLT8	SQLNUMERIC
SQLARRAY	SQLFLTN	SQLTEXT
SQLBINARY	SQLIMAGE	SQLVARBINARY
SQLBIT	SQLINT1	SQLVARCHAR

The fifth parameter sets the maximum length of the parameter. The maximum length must be set for variable-length parameters. Fixed-length parameters can contain the value of –1. The sixth parameter of the SqlRpcParam function sets the data length of the parameter. This parameter must be set for variable-length parameters but can be –1 for fixed-length parameters like integers. The sixth parameter is a string that contains the value that will be passed as input to the stored procedure. As you have probably surmised, this value must be supplied for input parameters. It can be an empty string for output parameters. In the previous example, the value of CA is passed in as input using the first parameter of the SumStateQty stored procedure.

After the stored procedure parameters have been defined, the combination of the SqlRpcSend and SqlOk functions are used to send the command to execute the stored procedures on the SQL Server system.

> **NOTE:** The SqlRpcExec function can also be used to execute a stored procedure. The primary difference between the SqlRpcExec function and the SqlRpcSend function is that the SqlRpcExec function blocks until the stored procedure has completed.

The data from the output parameter is available immediately after the SumStateQty stored procedure has been executed. The SqlRetData function is used to access the data returned by the output parameter of the stored procedure. The SqlRetData function returns a string data type, and it accepts two parameters. The first parameter is the connection handle, and the second parameter is a long data type that specifies the number of the returned parameter.

> **NOTE:** The returned parameter number value used in the second parameter of the SqlRetData function only counts returned parameters, and the count begins with one. The previous example used two parameters. The first parameter was an input parameter, and the second parameter was an output parameter. Since there was only one output parameter, the number of the parameter used by the SqlRetData function is 1.

In this example, the value from the returned parameter is moved into a text box named Text_Mid.

Error Handling

DB-Library error handling is activated by including two predefined subroutines in your Visual Basic project. If you used default name for vbsql.ocxr, then these subroutines must be named Vbsql1_Error and Vbsql1_Message. Otherwise, the "Vbsql1" portion must match the custom name that you have applied to vbsql.ocx.

You don't need to manually write the declarations for these functions. Visual Basic can automatically add these function declarations to your project. Selecting the VBSQL1 object from the object drop-down box in Visual Basic's code-editing window and then clicking the Error and Message procedures in the procedure window automatically adds the function declarations for the Vbsql1_Error and Vbsql1_Message functions.

These subroutines will then be automatically executed when the DB-Library encounters a runtime error. Typically, most applications need to evaluate the error and take some type of action. The Vbsql1_Error message reports about DB-Library errors, while the Vbsql1_Message function reports the errors that SQL Server encounters while executing SQL statements. The following examples show using the Error and Message functions to display a message box that contains additional information about each error condition.

```
Private Sub Vbsql1_Error(ByVal SqlConn As Long, ByVal Severity As Long, _
            ByVal ErrorNum As Long, ByVal ErrorStr As String, _
            ByVal OSErrorNum As Long, ByVal OSErrorStr As String, _
            RetCode As Long)

    Select Case ErrorNum
        Case 10007   'Ignore these informational errors
        Case Else
            MsgBox "Severity: " & Severity & vbCrLf _
                & "Error Number: " & ErrorNum & vbCrLf _
                & "Text: " & ErrorStr, vbOKOnly, App.EXEName
    End Select

End Sub
```

The Vbsql1_Error subroutine ignores all informational type errors that have an error code of 10007. The severity, error number, and message text for all other errors are displayed in a message box.

```
Private Sub Vbsql1_Message(ByVal SqlConn As Long, ByVal Message As Long, _
            ByVal State As Long, ByVal Severity As Long, _
            ByVal MsgStr As String, ByVal ServerNameStr As String, _
            ByVal ProcNameStr As String, ByVal Line As Long)

    Select Case Message
        Case 5701: ' Ignore these informational messages
        Case Else
            MsgBox "Message: " & Message & vbCrLf _
                & "State: " & State & vbCrLf _
                & "Severity: " & Severity & vbCrLf _
                & "Text: " & MsgStr, vbOKOnly, App.EXEName
    End Select

End Sub
```

The Vbsql1_Message subroutine ignores all information messages that have a message number of 5701. For all other errors, the message number, state, severity, and message text are displayed in a message box.

After these two subroutines have been added to your Visual Basic project, DB-Library will automatically execute one or both of these subroutines when it encounters a trappable error. The following subroutine generates an error that is trapped and displayed by the DB-Library error-handling functions.

```
Private Sub ShowError(hConn As Long)

    Dim sSQL As String
    Dim nRC As Long

    Screen.MousePointer = vbHourglass

    sSQL = "Select * From no_such_table"

    'Execute the query
    nRC = SqlSendCmd(hConn, sSQL)

    Screen.MousePointer = vbDefault

End Sub
```

This subroutine attempts to query a nonexistent table appropriately named no_such_table. When the SqlSendCmd function is executed, the SQL Select statement is sent to SQL Server, which attempts to execute the query. The SQL Server error then causes the Vbsql1_Message subroutine to be executed, and the message box shown here will be displayed:

```
DBLIBWiz                            [X]

Message: 208
State: 1
Severity: 16
Text: Invalid object name 'no_such_table'.

              [ OK ]
```

ADVANCED TECHNIQUES

In addition to all of the basic functions presented in the beginning of this chapter, DB-Library is capable of performing many advanced functions. Now you'll see how to use DB-Library to work with multiple result sets, as well as commit and roll back transactions.

Using Multiple Result Sets

Multiple result sets can be generated either by issuing a batch of SQL Select statements using the SqlCmd and SqlExec functions or by calling a stored procedure that produces multiple result sets. The method for processing multiple result sets is essentially the same, no matter how the result sets were created. In both cases, the DB-Library SqlResults function is used to process each result set, and the SqlNextRow function is used to retrieve the rows contained by each result set. The following code example shows how to generate multiple result sets using the SqlCmd and SqlExec functions and then process all of the result sets.

```
Private Sub MultipleRS(hConn As Long)

    Dim sSQL As String
    Dim nRC As Long
    Dim i As Integer
    Dim nFldCount As Integer

/   Screen.MousePointer = vbHourglass

    'Set up s batch of three Select statements
    nRC = SqlCmd(hConn, "Select au_lname, au_fname From authors ")
    nRC = SqlCmd(hConn, "Select title_id, title From titles ")
    nRC = SqlCmd(hConn, "Select stor_name, state From stores ")

    'Send the SQL statements
    nRC = SqlExec(hConn)

    ' Set up the grid
    Grid.Redraw = False
    Grid.FixedRows = 0
    Grid.Cols = 2
    Grid.Rows = 1
    Grid.Row = 0
    i = 1

    'Get the Result set
    Do Until NOMORERESULTS = SqlResults(hConn)
        Grid.Col = 0
        Grid.CellBackColor = &HC0C0C0I
        Grid.Text = "Recordset Number: " & i
        Grid.Col = 1
        Grid.CellBackColor = &HC0C0C0
        Grid.Text = ""
```

```
        Do Until NOMOREROWS = SqlNextRow(hConn)
            Grid.Rows = Grid.Rows + 1
            Grid.Row = Grid.Row + 1
            nFldCount = 0
            'Loop through all fields
            For i = 1 To Grid.Cols
                If Grid.Row = 1 Then
                    Grid.ColWidth(0) = TextWidth(String(20, "a"))
                    Grid.ColWidth(1) = TextWidth(String(30, "a"))
                End If
                Grid.Col = nFldCount
                Grid.Text = SqlData(hConn, i)
                nFldCount = nFldCount + 1
            Next i
        Loop

        i = i + 1
        nRC = SqlResults(hConn)
    Loop

    Grid.Redraw = True

    Screen.MousePointer = vbDefault

End Sub
```

Near the beginning of this subroutine, you can see where the SqlCmd function is executed three times and each instance uses a different SQL Select statement. The first Select statement retrieves the author last name and first name from the authors table. The second Select statement retrieves the title ID and title name from the titles table. The third Select statement retrieves the store name and state for the stores table.

TIP: When building a batch of SQL statements, it's important to allow a space at the end of each SQL statement. This allows DB-Library to properly separate the statements.

After all of the Select statements have been built into a batch using the SqlCmd function, the SqlExec function executes the batch. When the SqlExec function has completed, all three result sets are available to the application.

The next section of this subroutine sets up the grid to contain the query results, and then a loop is performed that uses the SqlResults function to retrieve each of the different result sets. The loop continues until the SqlResults function returns a value of NOMORERESULTS, which indicates that there are no more result sets. The rest of the code that processes the contents of each result set is essentially the same as the code that's used to process a single result set. Within the loop, a grid heading is assigned for each result set. This heading identifies the current result set and is displayed in the grid using a gray background color. Then the SqlNextRow function is used with a Do loop to retrieve all of the rows in the result set. The Do loop continues until the SqlNextRow function returns a value of NOMOREROWS. Within the Do loop, the SqlData function is used to retrieve the data for each of the columns returned in the result set.

Using Transactions

DB-Library also provides support for transactions. A transaction is a database feature that is used to ensure database integrity. Transactions essentially allow you to group together multiple database actions as a single unit of work. If any individual part of a transaction fails, then the entire transaction can be rolled back, leaving the database in the same state that it was in before the transaction was attempted. If all of the steps that comprise the transaction succeed, then the transaction can be committed and all modifications will be written to the database. The following code example illustrates how to use transactions with DB-Library.

```
Private Sub CommitRollBack(hConn As Long)

    Dim sSQL As String
    Dim nRC As Long

    Screen.MousePointer = vbHourglass

'Turn Transactions On
    sSQL = "Set Implicit_Transactions On"
    nRC = SqlSendCmd(hConn, sSQL)

'Execute SQL to delete all of the rows from the table
    sSQL = "Insert Into department Values('1','DEPARTMENT 1')"
    nRC = SqlSendCmd(hConn, sSQL)

    'Now Commit the transaction - the table is updated
    sSQL = "Commmit Transaction"
    nRC = SqlSendCmd(hConn, sSQL)

    'Execute SQL to delete all of the rows from the table
    sSQL = "Delete department"
    nRC = SqlSendCmd(hConn, sSQL)

    'Now Rollback the transaction - the table is unchanged
    sSQL = "Rollback Transaction"
```

```
    nRC = SqlSendCmd(hConn, sSQL)

'Turn Transactions Off
 sSQL = "Set Implicit_Transactions Off"
 nRC = SqlSendCmd(hConn, sSQL)

 'Create a result set to display the table
 sSQL = "Select * From department"
 nRC = SqlSendCmd(hConn, sSQL)

 DisplayDBGrid hConn, Grid


 Screen.MousePointer = vbDefault

End Sub
```

The Transact-SQL statement Set Implicit_Transactions On can be used to turn on support for transactions in a DB-Library application. This SQL statement can be sent to SQL Server using the SqlSendCmd function just like a SQL Select or Insert statement. After beginning the transaction, a SQL Insert statement is constructed that inserts a single row into the department file. Next, the Transact-SQL statement Commit Transaction is used with the SqlSendCmd function to commit the transaction to the database.

After committing the Insert to the database, a Delete operation is constructed that will delete all of the rows in the department table. Then the Delete statement is executed using the SqlSendCmd function. However, this time, instead of committing the changes to the database, the Rollback Transaction statement is sent to SQL Server to undo the delete operation. Then support for transactions is turned off using the Set Implicit_Transactions Off statement.

Finally, at the end of this subroutine, a Select statement is issued to query the contents of the department table. Following this series of transactions, there will be one row in the department table—the Insert transaction that was written using the Commit Transaction statement.

CONCLUSION

In addition to the core functionality illustrated in this chapter, DB-Library is able to perform more advanced functions. For instance, there is a set of functions that enables it to deal with binary image data. There are Browse functions for accessing more than a single row at a time, and there is also access to utility functions like Bulk Copy Program (BCP). As you've seen in this chapter, DB-Library provides rich functionality for accessing SQL Server databases. However, DB-Library doesn't possess an OLE implementation and object framework like DAO, RDO, or ADO. DB-Library is clearly not Microsoft's preferred direction for future database application development. Even so, it's a sure thing that many of the existing DB-Library applications will continue in production for some time. A solid understanding of how to access SQL Server using the DB-Library for Visual Basic will certainly help if it's up to you to maintain those applications.

All of the code listings presented in this chapter are also contained in the DB-Library Wizard example program that is on the CD-ROM accompanying this book.

ADDITIONAL RESOURCES

For more information about using DB-Library, you can refer to the following publications:

▼ *Building SQL Server Applications*, Microsoft Corporation.
▲ Vaughn, William R. *Hitchhiker's Guide to Visual Basic and SQL Server*, Sixth Edition. Redmond, WA: Microsoft Press, 1998.

CHAPTER 17

Web Integration and ASP Development

Database integration with the Web is one of today's hottest development trends. Many businesses are taking the information that's stored in their corporate databases and publishing it for internal use on their intranets, as well as for external use via their corporate Web sites. Static Web sites that are not integrated with any type of database are limited to providing the same information to all users. In addition, static Web pages do not allow remote users to run Web-based applications because there is no back-end database available to store the required user input.

Coupling database information with the Web provides the ability to make Web sites much more dynamic and responsive to user requests. Different users can perform their own individual queries, which enables your Web pages to be more flexible and responsive to the needs of each user. Integrating Web development with corporate database information can also provide remote users with the ability to perform dynamic database queries as well as to run online transaction processing (OLTP) applications. In this scenario, instead of a custom Visual Basic or Visual C++ application, a browser connected to your Web site via TCP/IP can be used as an application platform.

This chapter describes two of the primary ways that you can integrate SQL Server with your Web pages. The first part of this chapter discusses the use of the Web Assistant Wizard that's supplied with SQL Server. The Web Assistant Wizard guides you through the steps that are required to set up a SQL Server query and then output the query results as an HTML document, which can then be linked to your Web site. The SQL Server Web Assistant Wizard is a useful tool that can provide you with a basic level of Web-database integration very quickly; but, as you'll see later in this chapter, it does not provide for dynamic Web-database integration. Instead, the queries created using the Web Assistant Wizard are intended to be run periodically and can even be scheduled by the SQL Server Agent. However, they are static and cannot produce dynamic Web output.

The second part of this chapter discusses ActiveX Server Pages (ASP) for dynamic Web-database integration. ASPs are essentially standard Web pages that include embedded VBScript or JavaScript code that is run by the Internet Information Server (IIS). These scripts provide full program control over user input and database operations. The combination of ASP and SQL Server can be used to perform custom queries and create custom OTLP applications.

WEB INTEGRATION USING THE WEB ASSISTANT WIZARD

The SQL Server Web Assistant Wizard is a tool that generates HTML documents that contain the results of a SQL Server query or stored procedure. The HTML documents created by the SQL Server Web Assistant Wizard can be viewed by any Web Browser, such as Microsoft's Internet Explorer or Netscape's Navigator. Using the Web Assistant Wizard, you can generate queries that are run once or that can be scheduled to run at predetermined intervals.

Building a Simple Web Wizard Query

The SQL Server Web Assistant Wizard can be started from the SQL Server Enterprise Manager by right-clicking the Web Assistant Jobs entry in the list of SQL Server objects displayed in the left pane of the SQL Server Enterprise Manager. Any existing Web Assistant jobs will be displayed in the right pane. Figure 17-1 shows the pop-up menu that's used to start the SQL Server Web Assistant.

To run the SQL Server Web Assistant Wizard, select the New Web Assistant Job option from the pop-up menu. This displays the SQL Server Web Assistant Welcome dialog box shown in Figure 17-2.

The SQL Server Web Assistant Welcome page provides a brief introduction to the Web Assistant and provides you with the opportunity to cancel the wizard in the event that you've inadvertently selected the wrong option.

To begin creating a new Web page using the Web Assistant Wizard, click the Next button. This displays the Web Assistant dialog box shown in Figure 17-3.

This dialog box allows you to select the SQL Server database you want to use to generate the Web page. All of the user databases are displayed in the Databases list box. Highlight the database that you want to use and then click the Next button. In Figure 17-3, you can see that the pubs database has been selected.

Click Next to display the Web Assistant dialog box shown in Figure 17-4.

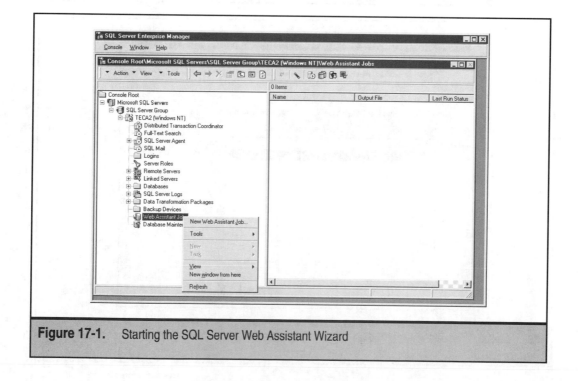

Figure 17-1.   Starting the SQL Server Web Assistant Wizard

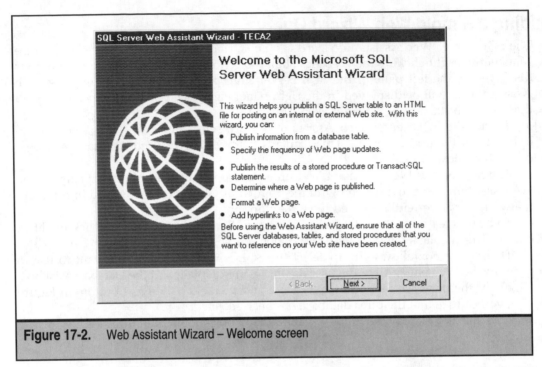

Figure 17-2. Web Assistant Wizard – Welcome screen

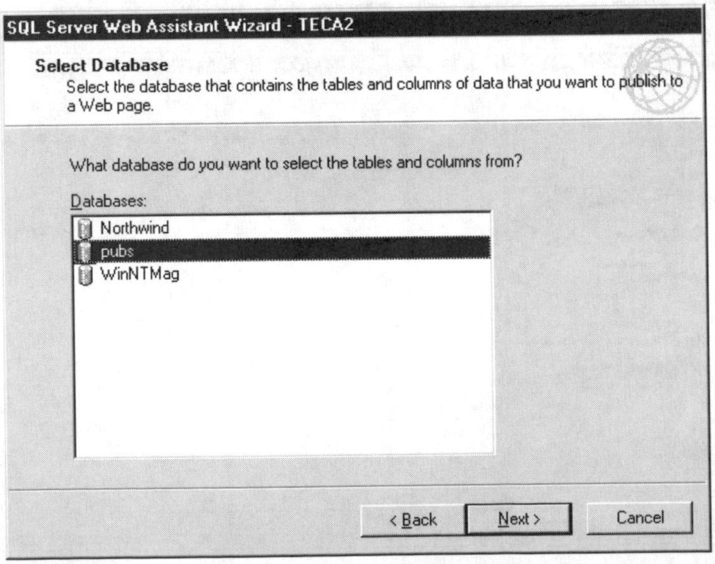

Figure 17-3. Web Assistant Wizard – selecting the database

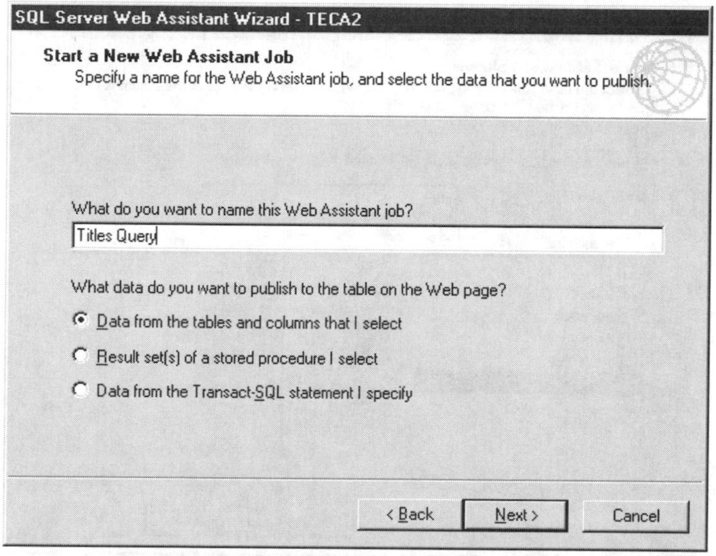

Figure 17-4.   Web Assistant Wizard – titling the Web page

This Web Assistant Wizard dialog box allows you to assign a title to this Web Assistant job. This title will also be used on the Web page that's generated. In addition, you can specify how the data will be retrieved for the SQL Server database. The radio buttons in the center of the screen allow you to select the tables and columns using the Web Assistant Wizard, to select an existing stored procedure, or to manually enter a Transact-SQL statement that will be used to generate a result set. In the example in Figure 17-4, the Web Assistant Wizard will select the tables and columns that will be used.

Click Next to display the Web Assistant dialog box shown in Figure 17-5.

You use the Available tables drop-down list at the top of the screen to select the tables that you want to use with the Web Assistant Wizard. When interactively prompting for the tables and columns, the Web Assistant Wizard allows the selection of only a single table. If you need to present information contained in multiple tables where you must join the tables, then you need to use either a stored procedure or a Transact-SQL statement to retrieve the data.

In this example, which uses the Web Assistant to select the table, the titles table has been selected from the pubs database. Selecting the table in the drop-down list causes the table's columns to be displayed in the Table columns list box on the left side of the dialog box. To include columns from the tables on the Web page, you must highlight the columns that you want to include in the table columns list and then click Add. This will cause the column names to be placed in the Selected columns list on the right side of the

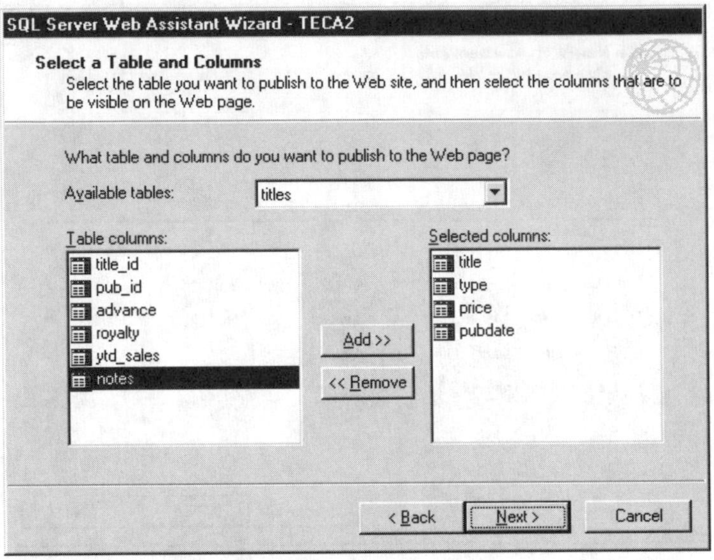

Figure 17-5. Web Assistant Wizard – select Table and columns

dialog box. In Figure 17-5, you can see that the title, type, price, and pubdate columns have been selected for inclusion on the Web page that will be generated by the Web Assistant Wizard.

When all of the desired columns have been included, click Next to display the Web Assistant dialog box shown in Figure 17-6. This dialog box allows you to specify the row selection criteria that you want to use. The dialog box allows you to use the drop-down lists to specify the selection criteria for up to two columns, or you can enter more complex selection criteria using a T-SQL Where clause in the text box at the bottom of the screen. The example shown in Figure 17-6 does not use any row selection criteria, which means that all of the rows in the titles table will be included in the Web page.

After specifying the row selection criteria, click the Next button to display the job scheduling dialog box presented in Figure 17-7. This dialog box allows you to specify when the Web Assistant Wizard job will be run. You can choose to run the Web Assistant job as a one-time job when the wizard has finished, or you can save the job specifications so they can be run later on demand. You can also schedule the Web Assistant job to run automatically either at a scheduled time or whenever the data in the base tables is changed.

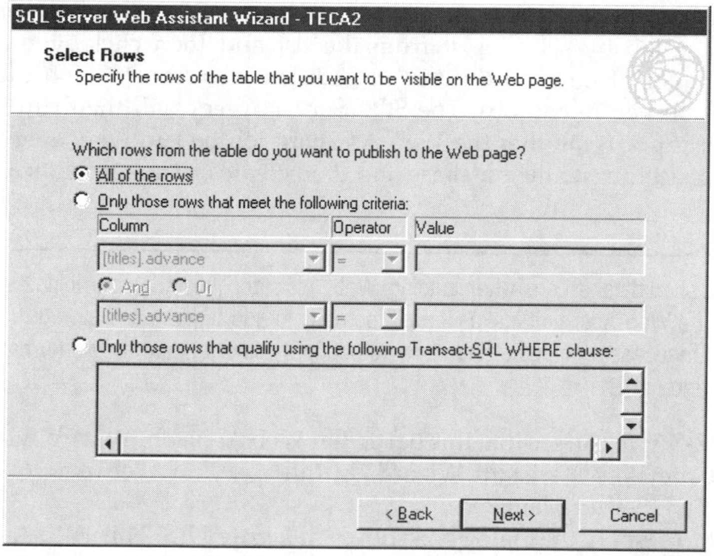

Figure 17-6.   Web Assistant Wizard – select row criteria

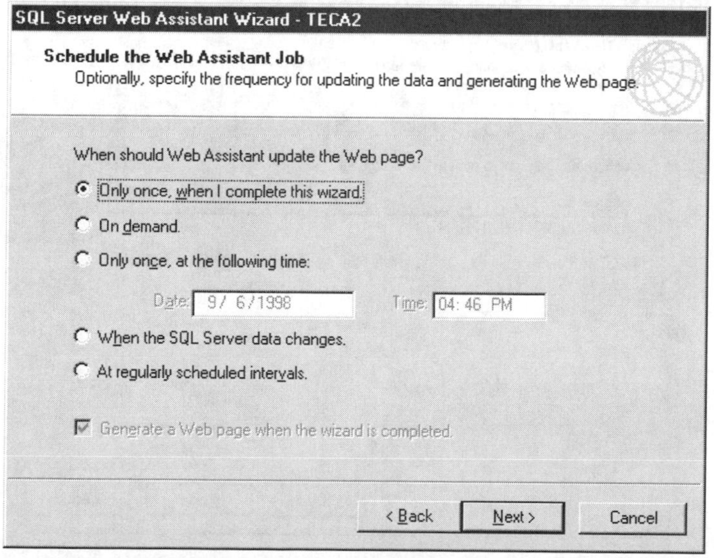

Figure 17-7.   Web Assistant Wizard – schedule the Web Assistant job

When a Web Assistant job is set up to be run on demand, a new Web Assistant job is added to the right pane of the Web Assistant view in the SQL Server Enterprise Manager. You can run the job by selecting it from the list and then clicking the SQL Server Enterprise Manager's Run Wizard icon. A scheduled Web Assistant job adds an entry to the list of SQL Server Agent jobs. The SQL Server Agent will then run the job at the appointed time. Specifying that the Web Assistant job be run whenever data changes adds a stored procedure to the database and then creates a trigger that's attached to the target table.

TIP: You should take care when adding Web Assistant jobs that are initiated whenever data changes. The Web Assistant makes it a bit too easy to add triggers and stored procedures to your database. Unnecessary triggers and stored procedures can degrade the performance of your SQL Server system.

In Figure 17-7, you can see that this particular Web Assistant Wizard will be run at the completion of the Web Assistant Wizard. In this case, no Web Assistant job will be created in the SQL Server Manager.

Click Next to display the dialog box shown in Figure 17-8. This Web Assistant dialog box allows you to specify the output directory where the Web Assistant Wizard will write

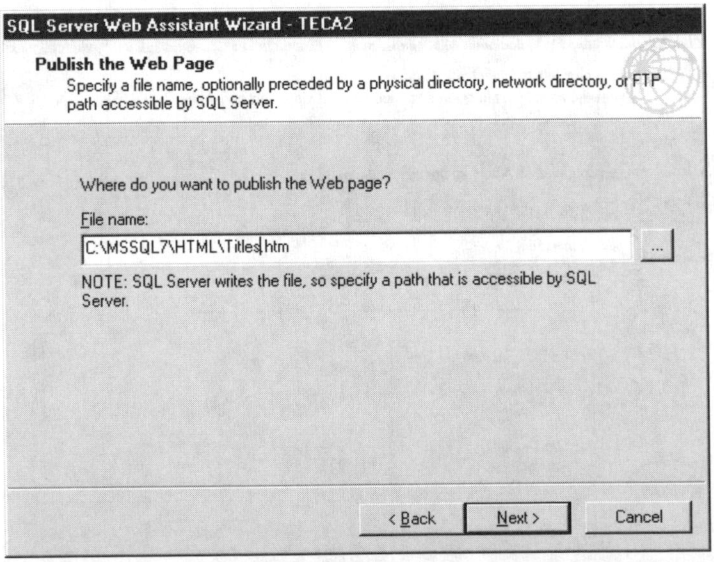

Figure 17-8. Web Assistant Wizard – output directory

the Hypertext Markup Language (.html) file that contains the results of the query. By default, this path points to the MSSQL7\HTML directory, but you can change this to any path or network share that is accessible to SQL Server.

After the HTML file output path has been entered, click Next to display the Web Assistant titles dialog box shown in Figure 17-9. This dialog box allows you to title both the Web page that will be generated and the HTML tables that will display the results of the SQL Server query. As you can see, this dialog box also allows you to set the font that will be used for the titles and to specify whether a date and time stamp are added to the Web page generated by the Web Assistant Wizard. In Figure 17-9, you can see that this Web page will be titled Pubs Titles Query, the HTML table will be titled Query Results, and a date and time stamp will be included on the page.

Click Next to display the next Web Assistant Wizard dialog box, shown in Figure 17-10. This dialog box allows you to control the display of the HTML table that contains the query data. As you can see in Figure 17-10, the Web Assistant's Format a Table dialog box lets you set up column names as column headings, specify the font that is used in the table, and specify whether the table has a visible border.

After setting up the HTML table display options, click Next to display the dialog box shown in Figure 17-11.

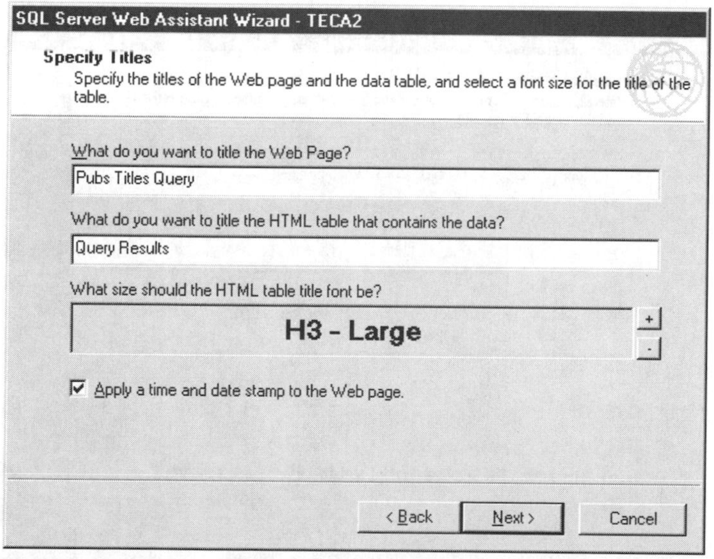

Figure 17-9. Web Assistant Wizard – specify titles

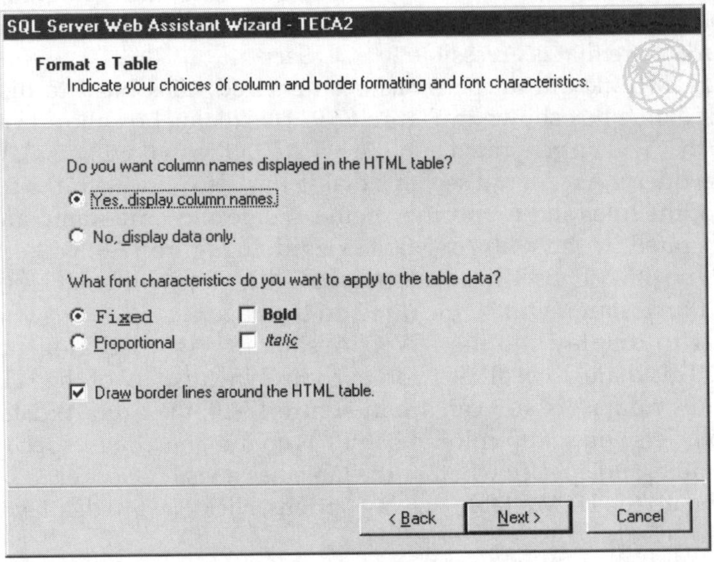

Figure 17-10. Web Assistant Wizard – format a table

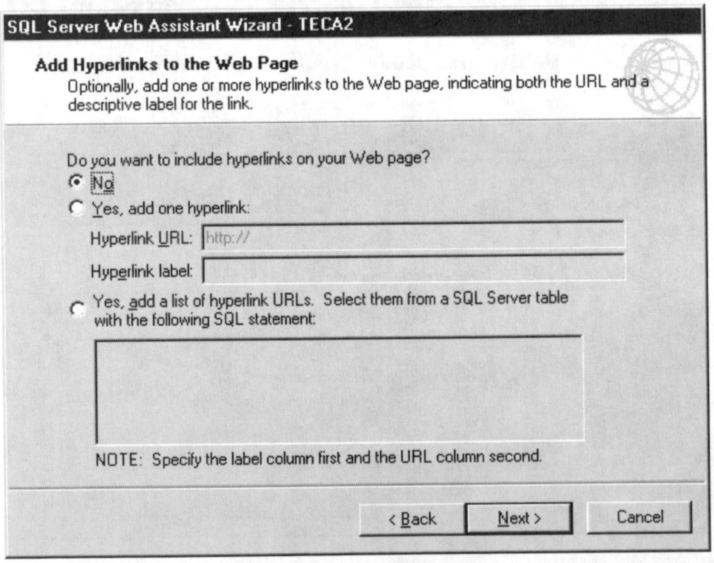

Figure 17-11. Web Assistant Wizard – add hyperlinks to the Web page

The SQL Server Web Assistant's hyperlinks dialog box allows you to add one or more hyperlinks to the Web page generated. The individual hyperlinks are referenced by entering either their URLs or their labels. The Web Assistant also allows you to include a list of hyperlinks on the generated Web page from a SQL Server table by executing a SQL Select statement or stored procedure. The Web Assistant example shown in Figure 17-11 doesn't include any hyperlinks.

Click Next to display the Limit Rows dialog box shown in Figure 17-12. This dialog box is the last setup dialog box displayed by Web Assistant Wizard. The Limit Rows dialog box allows you to control the number of rows displayed in the HTML table. You can truncate the data after a certain number of rows, or you can set the table size to a given number of rows. If the table is sized to hold a specific number of rows, the additional radio buttons that you can see in Figure 17-12 allow you to control the way additional rows are handled. The Limit Rows dialog box gives you the option of either putting all of the data into one scrolling table or generating multiple Web pages. When multiple Web pages are generated, each page will have an HTML table that is sized to the number of rows entered on the Web Assistant Wizard's Limit Rows dialog box. All of the Web pages that are generated can optionally be linked together using hyperlinks.

After configuring the number of rows that will be displayed in the table, click Next to generate the sample Web page shown in Figure 17-13.

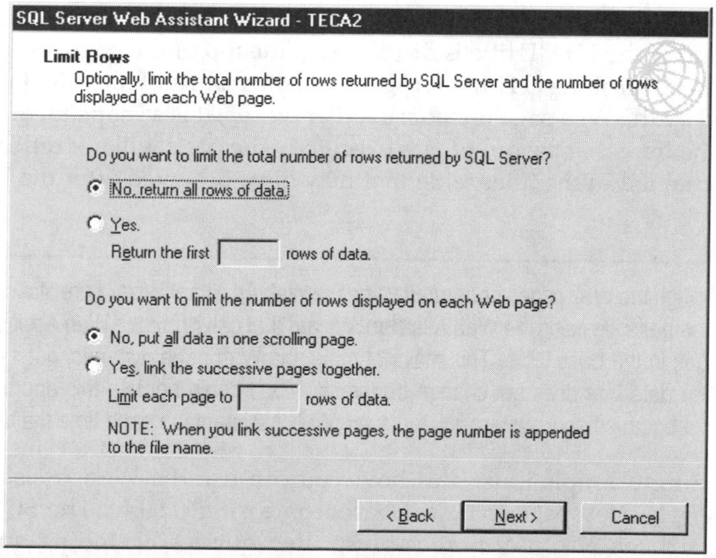

Figure 17-12.   Web Assistant Wizard – limit rows

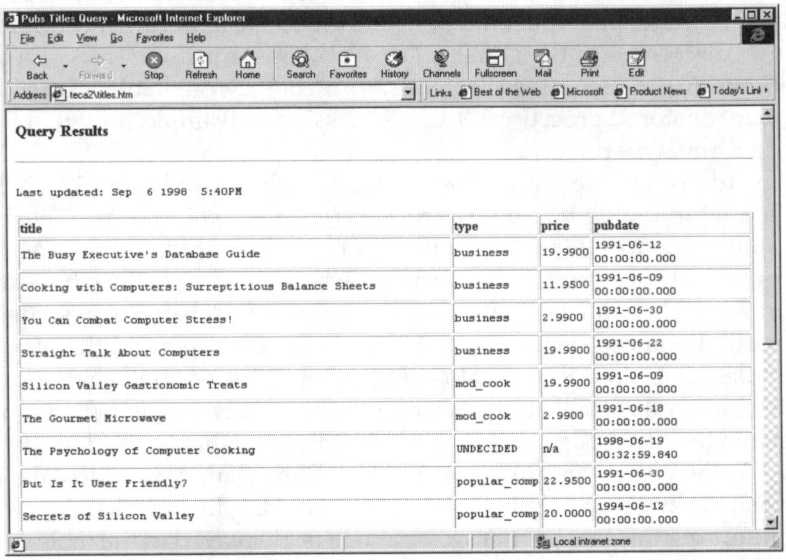

Figure 17-13.   Static Web page generated by the Web Assistant Wizard

The title of the Web page, Pubs Titles Query, is displayed in the Web browser's title bar, and the title of the HTML title is displayed at the top of the page just above the date and time stamp. A scrolling HTML table contains the results of the titles table query. The data displayed by the Web page is static; in other words, it is a snapshot of the data in the titles table at the time that the query was executed. The page will not reflect any changes to the data contained in the titles table that may have occurred after the Web page was generated.

TIP: Although the Web pages generated using the Web Assistant Wizard are static, you can create a trigger on the base file using the Web Assistant Wizard that can rerun the Web Assistant job whenever data changes in the base table. This may not make the Web page dynamic, but it can be a suitable approach for data that does not change frequently. You should not use this approach with a highly volatile table because your system will rerun the Web Assistant job each time the table changes.

The preceding example illustrates how you can use the Web Assistant Wizard to generate a sample Web page that was based on a single table. The SQL Server Web Assistant Wizard can also use more sophisticated queries, including queries that call stored procedures and even pass them input parameters. The next example in this chapter shows you how to call a stored procedure using the Web Assistant Wizard and then display the results of the stored procedure in a Web page.

Calling a Stored Procedure with the Web Wizard

To build a Web Assistant job that calls a SQL Server stored procedure, you first start the SQL Server Web Assistant Wizard by right-clicking the Web Assistant Jobs entry in the SQL Server Enterprise Manager. When the Web Assistant Wizard begins, you respond to the initial dialog boxes as described previously in this chapter. Click Next to move past the Welcome dialog box. Then, on the database selection dialog box, select the database that contains the stored procedure that you want to call and click Next. This displays the Web Assistant Wizard dialog box shown in Figure 17-14.

You can see that this Web page is titled Sales by State. So far this is just like the simple table query that you saw earlier. However, the next part of the screen shows the beginning of the differences. In this example, the Result set(s) of a stored procedure I select option is marked for selection. Selecting this option causes the Web Assistant Wizard to display the set of dialog boxes that allow you to identify and call an existing SQL Server stored procedure.

After selecting the stored procedure option, click Next to display the Web Assistant dialog box shown in Figure 17-15. This dialog box lists all of the stored procedures that are found in the database that was selected using the previous database selection dialog box. On this screen, you select the stored procedure that you want to execute. In Figure 17-15, the stored procedure called StateSales has been selected.

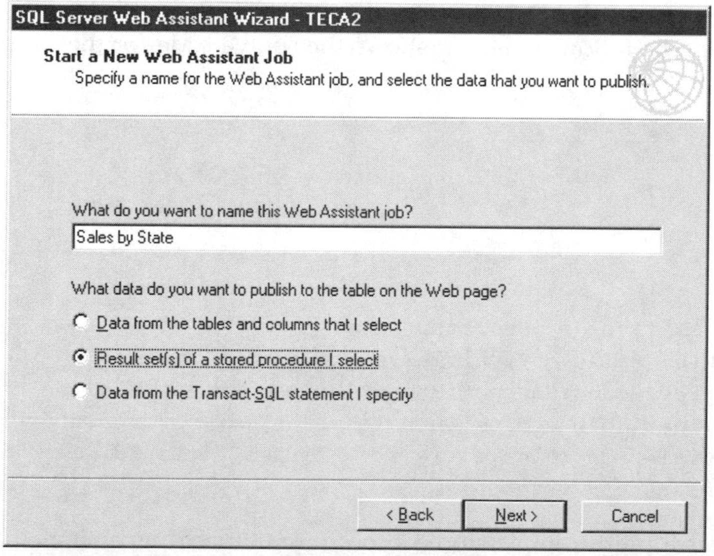

Figure 17-14.   Web Assistant Wizard – titling the Web page

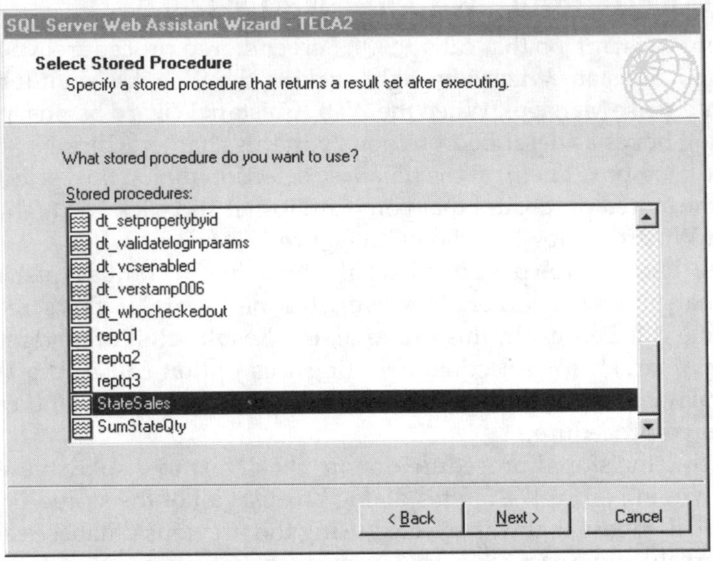

Figure 17-15. Web Assistant Wizard – select stored procedure

The StateSales stored procedure is a user-written stored procedure that accepts a state code as an input parameter and then returns a result set that contains all of the sales for the given state. The following listing shows the source code for the sample StateSales stored procedure:

```
Create Procedure StateSales
(
    @state Char(2)
)
as

Select stores.state, stores.stor_name,
  titles.title, sales.qty, titles.price,
  extendedprice=Round(Convert(Money, sales.qty * titles.price), 2)
From sales Inner Join stores On sales.stor_id = stores.stor_id
Inner Join titles On sales.title_id = titles.title_id
Where stores.state = @state
```

StateSales is a pretty simple stored procedure that accepts a single parameter that contains a two-character state code. Then a SQL Select statement is used to retrieve a set of columns from the stores, titles, and sales tables. This Select statement also computes a column called extendedprice, which is the product of the sales quantity multiplied by the individual title price. As you have probably gathered, the tables used in this Select statement are all related. The sales and stores tables are joined on the stor_id column, and the sales and titles tables are joined on the title_id column. The Where clause limits the row selection to just the rows in which the value of the state column in the stores table is equal to the value supplied in the input parameter.

After selecting the stored procedure that you want the Web Assistant Wizard to execute, click Next to display the Web Assistant screen presented in Figure 17-16. This dialog box allows you to supply values to any input parameters that are used by the stored procedure. All of the input parameters used by the stored procedure are listed on the left side of the list box. You can then supply values for each parameter on the right side of the list box. In Figure 17-16, you can see that the Web Assistant Wizard correctly determined that the StateSales stored procedure used one input parameter: @state. In this example, a value of CA is supplied for the @state parameter. When the Web Assistant job executes the StateSales stored procedure, the value of CA will be passed to the stored procedure.

The other Web Assistant dialog boxes are the same as the ones presented earlier in the simple table query example. Like the Web Assistant job that was created earlier in this chapter, the next steps the Web Assistant Wizard guides you through allow you to schedule the Web Assistant job, select the directory for the HTML output, title the table, select the table format, add hyperlinks, and control the size of the returned result set.

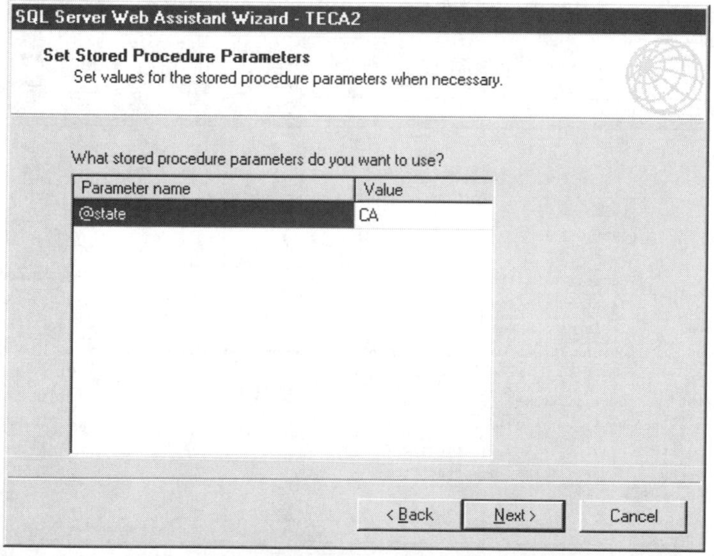

Figure 17-16.   Web Assistant Wizard – set stored procedure parameters

After the Web Assistant job is set up, it will be run according to the options that were set using the wizard. Figure 17-17 presents the Web page that was generated by running the StateSales stored procedure using the Web Assistant Wizard.

In the figure, you can see that the Sales by State Web Page contains only data for the sales that occurred in the state with the code CA. As before, the Web page title, table title, and page format were all controlled by the choices that were made using the Web Assistant Wizard. Again, the data shown on this page is static, and it won't reflect any changes made to the base tables unless the Web Assistant job is rerun.

The first part of this chapter illustrated how you can use SQL Server's Web Assistant Wizard to quickly generate static pages using the tables and stored procedures from SQL Server databases. Although the Web Assistant Wizard is easy to use, the pages generated are not dynamic, and they are not very interactive. Fortunately, you can also integrate SQL Server with the Web using ActiveX Server Pages (ASP). ASP allows you to create interactive pages that can provide data-driven Web pages and are also suitable for creating Web-based database applications. The second half of this chapter shows how you can create Web pages that use ASP to access SQL Server.

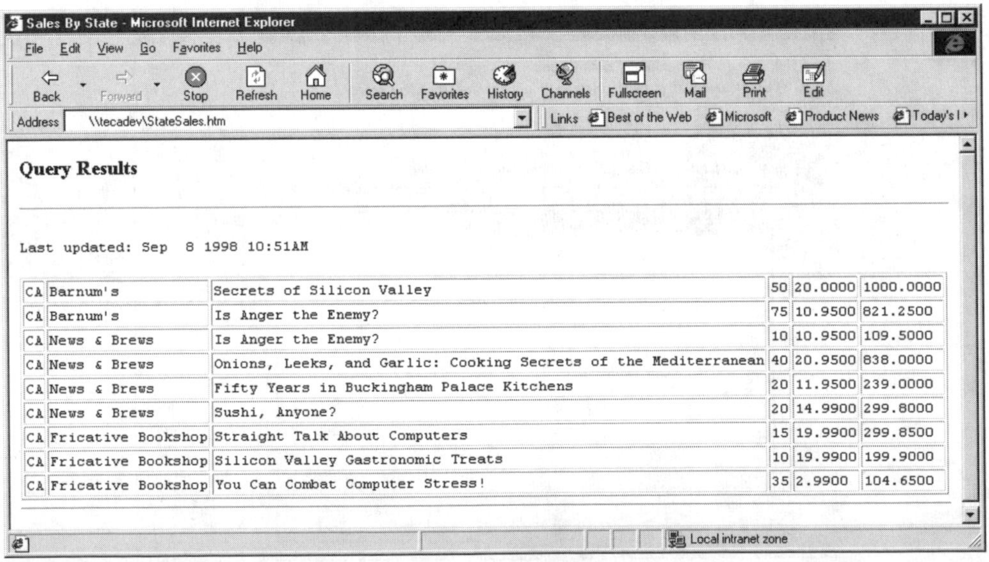

Figure 17-17. Sales by State Web page generated using the Web Assistant Wizard

WEB AND DATABASE INTEGRATION USING ASP

ActiveX Server Pages (ASP) provides server-side scripting for Microsoft Internet Information Server (IIS) Web servers. Introduced in IIS 3.0 and carried forward into IIS 4.0, ASP is based on VBScript, and it enables flexible and dynamic creation of Web pages. Active Server Pages are written using a combination of HTML and embedded VBScript. IIS includes an OLE automation server that executes the VBScript and sends the output of the script to a browser-based client in the form of HTML. Since ASP scripts are executed on the server, they will work with any browser. The Web browser only receives a stream of HTML.

Figure 17-18 shows how ASP combines HTML and ActiveX Script to produce dynamic HTML. As you can see, ASP scripting is quite different from browser-based scripting. With traditional browser-based scripting, an HTML page containing JavaScript or VBScript is sent from the Web server to the browser-based client. The client's browser is responsible for executing the script. Client-based scripting places an increased burden on the client and can also be plagued by incompatibilities that stem from differences in the browser client's ability to execute the script.

ASP server-based scripting is entirely different. An ASP page is executed on the IIS Web server. As the server executes the page, it prepares an HTML stream that will be sent to the client. Any HTML or client scripts contained in the ASP page are passed directly to the client. When the server encounters ASP server scripts, it executes the script on the server and then sends any output generated by the script to the client in the form of HTML. To the browser-based client, there is no difference between the HTML stream created by an ASP script and the HTML stream that's sent from a static Web page.

As you can see, ASP's server-side scripting essentially produces Web pages as the scripts execute. This allows ASP to produce dynamic Web pages that can be very

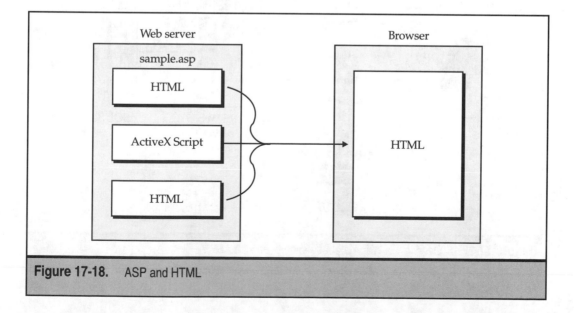

Figure 17-18. ASP and HTML

responsive to the different clients. ASP scripts can also be combined with ActiveX Data Objects (ADO) to integrate SQL Server database information into the HTML stream that is sent to the client systems.

Figure 17-19 illustrates the use of ASP to integrate IIS Web pages with data from a SQL Server database. You can see that the Web clients connect to the IIS Web server using TCP/IP and the HTTP protocol. These connections can be made either over the Internet or on a local intranet. When a Web client requests an ASP page, the IIS Web server will execute the ActiveX scripts contained on the page. To access a SQL Server database, the ActiveX script must instantiate an ADO Connection and Recordset object, which in turn sends a data access request to SQL Server. The SQL Server system can be running on the same system as the IIS Web server; but, for performance reasons, it's almost always better to install SQL Server on a separate system from your Web server and then make the connection over the local network.

When the SQL Server system finishes processing the request, it sends the results back to the ADO object in the ASP script. IIS then reformats the ASP output into HTML that it sends back to the client.

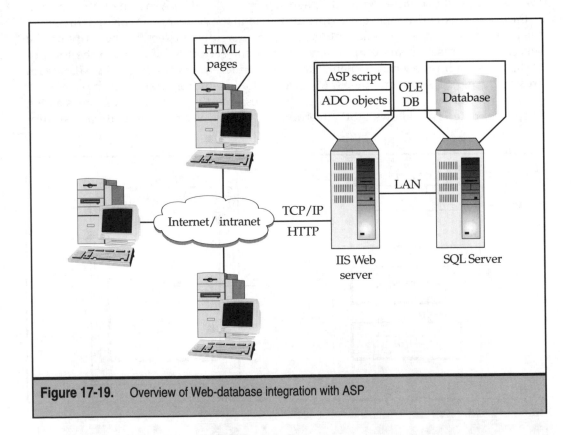

Figure 17-19.   Overview of Web-database integration with ASP

Typically, there must be a network connection between the IIS Web server and the SQL Server database system, but they can also be run on the same system. In addition, the Web server must have an OLE DB provider installed, as well as the ADO run-time DLLs. Figure 17-20 presents the network layers that are used by ASP applications to connect the IIS Web server to the SQL Server database system.

At the top of the figure, you can see the ASP application. The ASP application creates and uses ADO objects to access SQL Server. In turn, the ADO object framework makes calls to the appropriate OLE DB provider. To access SQL Server 7, the ASP application uses the native OLE DB provider for SQL Server. To access SQL Server 6.5 or some other ODBC-compliant database, the ASP application uses the OLE DB provider for ODBC.

Depending on which data access mechanism is used, either the OLE DB provider or the ODBC driver uses the client's network libraries to communicate with the network libraries found on the SQL Server system. These network libraries use a network interprocess communication (IPC) method such as Named Pipes or TCP/IP Sockets.

The network protocol manages the data stream that is sent between the client (in this case, the Web server) and the SQL Server system. TCP/IP and NetBIOS are the most common network protocols in use on NT networks.

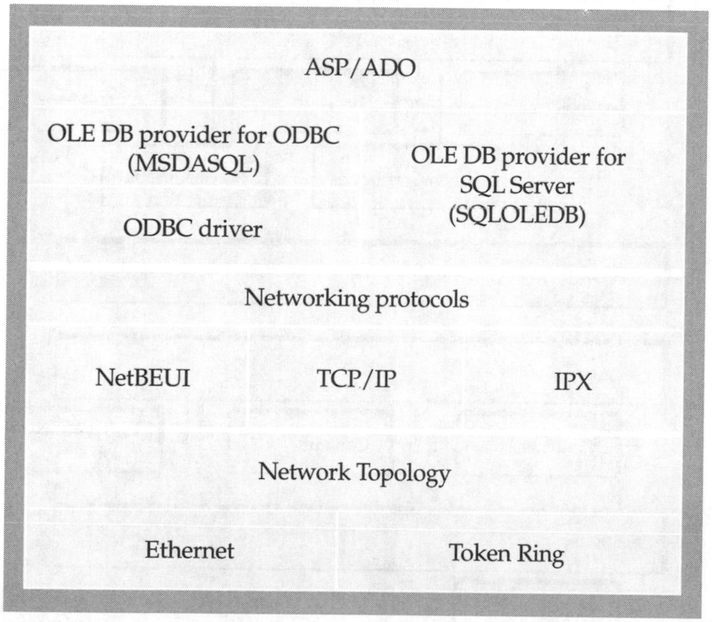

Figure 17-20.   Network components used by ASP and ADO

At the bottom of this stack, you can see that the physical network is used to connect the IIS Web server and the SQL Server system. Ethernet is the most common network topology.

The ASP Object Model

IIS provides its own object model to implement ASP. ASP is implemented as an OLE automation server, and it has a hierarchical object framework. Figure 17-21 presents the ASP object model.

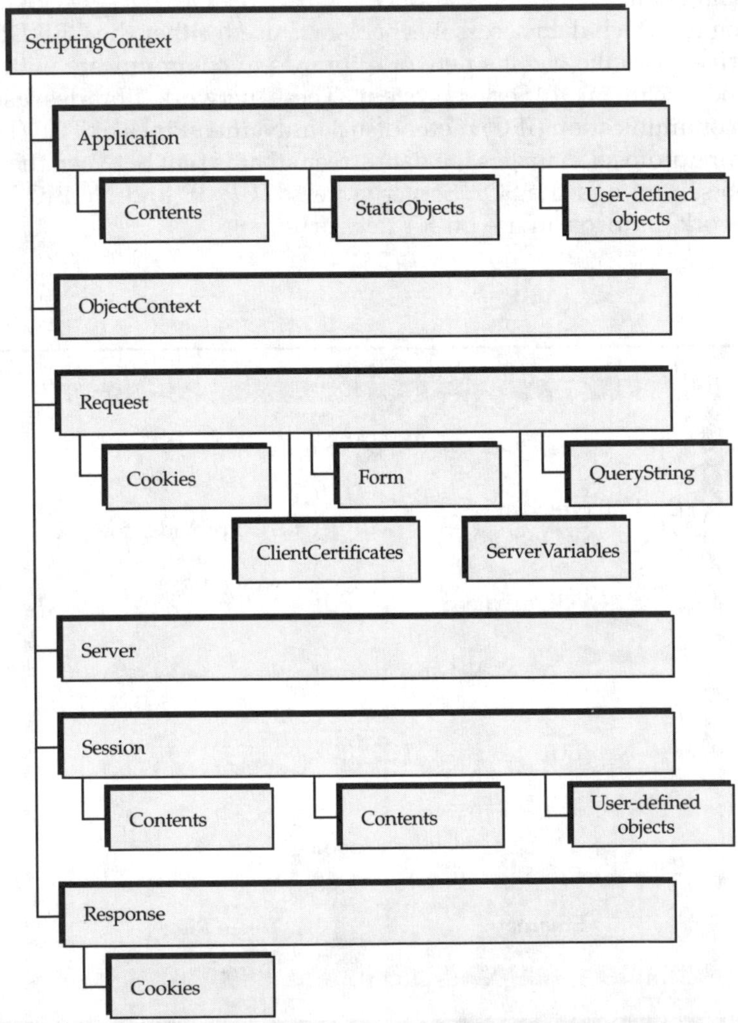

Figure 17-21. The ASP object model

The primary object in the ASP programming model is the ScriptingContext object. The ScriptingContext object exposes the interaction of the client browser. The ScriptingContext object is always available to ASP applications, and you do not need to create references to it. The ScriptingContext object contains the six primary ASP objects, five built-in objects, and the ObjectContext object. The five built-in objects are the Application object, the Request object, the Server object, the Session object, and the Response object.

The Application object is shared by all active Web sessions, and it is used to manage the state for all of the instances of the Web application. It can also be used to store information about multiple users who are connected to the Web. The Application object contains the Contents collection and the StaticObjects collection. Each Contents object in the Contents collection contains all of the items that have been added to the Web application using ActiveX script commands, and each StaticObjects collection contains all of the objects added to the Web application using the HTML <OBJECT> tag. In addition, the Application object can contain user-defined objects that are created by the Web application and can be shared by multiple users.

The Request object receives requests from the Web clients. The Request object can receive all of the data on the form plus information about the current user. The Request object contains several other collections, each of which represents different sets of information that can be returned for the Web client. Each ClientCertificate object in the ClientCertificate collection represents a certificate field returned from the Web client that identifies the client. The Cookies collection contains a set of Web cookies, where each cookie contains a small amount of information about the Web user. The Form collection contains a set of Form objects, where each object represents an HTML form. The QueryString collection contains a set of added URL arguments, and the ServerVariables collection contains a set of server environment variables.

The Server object is used to create other OLE objects that your Web application will use. For instance, the Server object's CreateObject method is used to create the ADO Connection and Recordset objects that are used to access SQL Server.

The Session object maintains information that relates to the current Web session. The Session object is very much like the Application object. However, while the Application object pertains to all Web users, the Session object refers to only the current Web session. The collection of Contents objects contained in the Session object contains all of the items that have been added to the Web session using script commands.

The ObjectContext object provides access to the current object's context. It is typically used to instantiate Microsoft Transaction Server (MTS) objects or to control database transactions.

ASP Basics

The preceding part of this chapter presented the big picture of ASP. You saw how ASP works in conjunction with HTML and how ASP can use ADO and OLE DB to connect to SQL Server as well as the ASP object framework. In the next part of this chapter, you'll explore some of the ASP programming basics and the specific scripting techniques that are used to access SQL Server databases from ASP scripts.

ASP scripting is based on VBScript or JScript. Using VBScript makes it very easy for Visual Basic programmers to quickly get up to speed. VBScript is a subset of the Visual Basic language, sharing the same syntax and object naming conventions as its more capable sibling. However, as you have probably gathered, ASP pages are more than just listings of VBScript. ASP pages are built using a combination of VBScript and HTML. In ASP pages, the VBScript is inserted into the HTML within special script tags. The following listing shows the shorthand form of the tag format used to denote VBScript in ASP pages:

```
<HEAD>
<TITLE>
Sample ASP tags
</TITLE>
</HEAD>
<BODY>
<%
    'Script goes here
%>
</BODY>
```

No doubt because of its economy, this has become the preferred format for script tags. However, you can also use the long form that is shown in the following example. Both forms work exactly the same.

```
<HEAD>
<TITLE>
Sample ASP tags
</TITLE>
</HEAD>
<BODY>
<SCRIPT FOR=Session EVENT=OnEnd LANGUAGE=VBSCRIPT RUNAT=Server>
    'Script goes here
</SCRIPT>
</BODY>
```

The manner in which output is generated is also a bit different for ASP scripts. Output is directed to the user with either the = symbol or by using the Response object's Write method. The following listing illustrates how you can direct output to the browser from an ASP script:

```
<%
Dim sLine3

= "This writes line one"
Response.Write("This writes line two")
```

```
sLine3 = "This writes line three")
=sLine3
%>
```

Another basic ASP programming technique enables you to capture the input from an HTML form and then use that input in your ASP scripts. The following code shows two simple HTML text boxes that allow the Web client to enter a user ID and password:

```
<P>User ID</P>
<INPUT id=text_userid name=userid size=20>
<P><LABEL>Password</LABEL></P>
<INPUT id=text_password name=password size=20 type=password>

<FORM NAME="frm1" METHOD="post" ACTION="loginrsp.asp"
OnSubmit="return validatePassword()">
    <INPUT NAME="btnSubmit" TYPE="submit" VALUE="Submit">
    <INPUT NAME="btnReset" TYPE="reset" VALUE="Reset">
</FORM>
```

Not surprisingly, the name of the User ID field is userid, and the name of the Password field is password. After filling in these fields, the Web user clicks the Submit button, which submits the form to its form handler. In this case, the form handler is an ASP page named loginrsp.asp. The source code for loginrsp.asp contains the following VBScript:

```
<%
Dim sUser
Dim sPwd
 'Retrieve form information
sUser = Request.Form("userid")
sPwd = Request.Form("password")
%>
```

> **TIP:** Unlike standard Web pages that typically end with the extension .htm or .html, ASP pages must end with the extension .asp.

First, the Dim keyword is used to declare two VBScript variables that will contain the contents of the HTML text fields. Then the Request object's Form method is used to assign the contents of the HTML userid text field to the sUser variable. Likewise, the contents of the password field are assigned to the sPwd variable.

You should now know the basics of building Web pages by combining the ASP object model with HTML and VBScript. The "Additional References" section, later in this chapter, contains a list of resources that can help you learn more about general ASP Web building techniques. In the next section of this chapter, you will see how you can access SQL Server databases using ASP and ADO.

Using ADO Objects with ASP

Using ADO, the first action that your application takes is to open a connection to SQL Server using the Connection, Command, or Recordset object. After the connection has been established, your ASP application can then issue exactly the same sort of ADO commands that a standard VB application can perform. It can open and traverse a record set; insert, update, and delete data; and execute stored procedures. In the following sections, you'll see how you can perform all of these types of basic SQL Server operations from an ASP page.

Connecting to SQL Server

ADO can connect to SQL Server from an ASP page using either the OLE DB provider for ODBC or the OLE DB provider for SQL Server. As you saw in Chapter 15, the OLE DB provider for ODBC allows the ADO object framework to be used with existing ODBC drivers, whereas the OLE DB for SQL Server is used only to connect to a SQL Server database. Either of these OLE DB providers can be used with the ADO Connection, Command, or Recordset object. The following script shows how you can establish a connection with SQL Server using the OLE DB provider for ODBC:

```
<HTML>
<HEAD>

<H4> </H4>
<H4>Simple ADO Connection</H4>
<BODY>
<%
Dim sServer
Dim sLoginID
Dim sPassword

Dim cn

'Get the Server and Login information from form1
sServer = Request.Form("txtServer")
sLogin = Request.Form("txtLogin")
sPassword = Request.Form("txtPassword")

'Create a connection object
Set cn = Server.CreateObject("ADODB.Connection")
```

```
'Open a connection; the string refers to the DSN
cn.ConnectionString = "DRIVER=SQL Server" & _
    ";SERVER=" & sServer & _
    ";UID=" & sLoginID & _
    ";PWD=" & sPassword & _
    ";DATABASE=pubs"

cn.Open
%>
```

This sample ASP page begins with the standard HTML tags <HTML> and <HEAD> that begin most Web pages. Next, the page heading is displayed, and the <BODY> section of the page begins. Within the body, you can see where the <% marker denotes the beginning of the ASP script.

This sample script is written in VBScript. The script's first action is to declare three variables that will contain the name of the SQL Server system and the SQL Server authentication information. Next, the cn variable to be used for the ADO Connection object is declared.

After the working variables have been declared, the values are assigned to those variables using the ASP Request object's Form method. The Form method takes a single parameter that contains a string that must match the name of the HTML Input object that was used on the input page. It returns the value that was entered in the named object.

NOTE: To use the Request object's Form method, this ASP page must be the form handler from an initial page that allowed the Web client to enter the values of txtServer, txtLogin, and txtPassword.

Next, the ASP Server object's CreateObject method is used to create a new ADO Connection object and assign that object to the cn variable that was created earlier. The CreateObject method is used to instantiate OLE objects. Although this example illustrates how to create an instance of an ADODB.Connection object, it can also be used with other OLE object frameworks such as SQL-DMO or Active Directory.

Next, the cn Connection object's ConnectionString property is assigned an OLE DB connection string that can be used to establish a DSN-less connection. Since no OLE DB provider was specified by using the PROVIDER keyword, the OLE DB provider for ODBC will be used by default. The DRIVER keyword identifies the driver that will be used. The SERVER keyword specifies the name of the SQL Server system to connect to. The UID and PWD keywords provide the login information, and the DATABASE keyword sets the default database as pubs.

After the ConnectionString property has been assigned with a connection string, the Connection object's Open method is used to open a connection to the SQL Server system identified using the SERVER keyword.

> **NOTE:** For more information about OLE DB providers and the ADO object framework, refer to Chapter 15.

Ending a Connection

Before ending your application, you should use the Connection object's Close method to end the database connection. An example of the Close method is presented here:

```
<%
cn.Close
%>
```

To close the Connection object named cn, this Script must be executed from the same page where the cn variable was declared.

Retrieving Data with the ADO Recordset Object

Using ADO, you can retrieve data with either the Recordset or Command object. The ADO Recordset and Command objects both can be used with an active Connection object, and they can also open their own connections. Each time an ADO Recordset or Command object establishes its own connection, a new communication session is started with SQL Server. If your application needs to perform multiple operations, it's almost always better to open the connection using a Connection object and then use that Connection object with your other Recordset and Command objects. This allows the same communication session to be reused, which is almost always more efficient.

In the previous sections, you saw how to start and stop an ADO connection from an ASP script. Next, you'll see how to combine the ADO Connection and Recordset objects created in the ASP scripts with the HTML required to format the output on a Web page. The following code presents an ASP page that sends a simple query to SQL Server and then outputs the result of that query in an HTML table:

```
<HEAD>
<META NAME="GENERATOR" Content="Microsoft Visual Studio 6.0">

<H4> </H4>
<H4>Simple ADO Query</H4>
<BODY>
<%
Dim sServer
Dim sLoginID
Dim sPassword

Dim cn
Dim rs
```

```
'Get the Server and Login information from form1
sServer = Request.Form("txtServer")
sLoginID = Request.Form("txtLogin")
sPassword = Request.Form("txtPassword")

'Create a connection object
Set cn = Server.CreateObject("ADODB.Connection")
Set rs = Server.CreateObject("ADODB.Recordset")

'Open a connection; the string refers to the DSN
cn.ConnectionString = "DRIVER=SQL Server" & _
    ";SERVER=" & sServer & _
    ";UID=" & sLoginID & _
    ";PWD=" & sPassword & _
    ";DATABASE=pubs"
cn.Open

' Associate the Recordset with the open connection
rs.ActiveConnection = cn

'Use the open method
rs.Open "Select * From stores", , , , adCmdText
%>

<TABLE CellPadding=1 CellSpacing=1 Cols=5>
    <TBODY>

<TR VALIGN=top ALIGN=left>
<TH BGCOLOR=#c0c0c0 BORDERCOLOR=#000000 >
<FONT SIZE=2 FACE="Arial" COLOR=#000000>StoreID</FONT></TH>
<TH BGCOLOR=#c0c0c0 BORDERCOLOR=#000000 >
<FONT SIZE=2 FACE="Arial" COLOR=#000000>Name</FONT></TH>
<TH BGCOLOR=#c0c0c0 BORDERCOLOR=#000000 >
<FONT SIZE=2 FACE="Arial" COLOR=#000000>Address</FONT></TH>
<TH BGCOLOR=#c0c0c0 BORDERCOLOR=#000000 >
<FONT SIZE=2 FACE="Arial" COLOR=#000000>City</FONT></TH>
<TH BGCOLOR=#c0c0c0 BORDERCOLOR=#000000 >
<FONT SIZE=2 FACE="Arial" COLOR=#000000>State</FONT></TH>
<TH BGCOLOR=#c0c0c0 BORDERCOLOR=#000000 >
<FONT SIZE=2 FACE="Arial" COLOR=#000000>Zip</FONT></TH>
</TR>

<TBODY>
<%
```

```
Do Until rs.EOF
%>

<TR VALIGN=top ALIGN=left>
<TD BORDERCOLOR=#c0c0c0 ><FONT SIZE=2 FACE="Arial" COLOR=#000000>
<%=Server.HTMLEncode(rs.Fields("stor_id").Value)%><BR></FONT></TD>
<TD BORDERCOLOR=#c0c0c0 ><FONT SIZE=2 FACE="Arial" COLOR=#000000>
<%=Server.HTMLEncode(rs.Fields("stor_name").Value)%><BR></FONT></TD>
<TD BORDERCOLOR=#c0c0c0 ><FONT SIZE=2 FACE="Arial" COLOR=#000000>
<%=Server.HTMLEncode(rs.Fields("stor_address").Value)%><BR></FONT></TD>
<TD BORDERCOLOR=#c0c0c0 ><FONT SIZE=2 FACE="Arial" COLOR=#000000>
<%=Server.HTMLEncode(rs.Fields("city").Value)%><BR></FONT></TD>
<TD BORDERCOLOR=#c0c0c0 ><FONT SIZE=2 FACE="Arial" COLOR=#000000>
<%=Server.HTMLEncode(rs.Fields("state").Value)%><BR></FONT>
<TD BORDERCOLOR=#c0c0c0 ><FONT SIZE=2 FACE="Arial" COLOR=#000000>
<%=Server.HTMLEncode(rs.Fields("zip").Value)%><BR></FONT></TD>

</TR>

<%
    rs.MoveNext
Loop

rs.Close
cn.Close

%>

</TABLE>
</BODY>
</HTML>
```

In the first part of this ASP page, you can see the typical HTML tags that are found at the beginning of most Web pages. You might also notice in the <META NAME> tag that this ASP page was created using Visual InterDev. The Visual InterDev product has several features that assist in the process of developing ASP applications. More information about using Visual InterDev for Web-database integration is presented later in this chapter in the section "Web-Database Development with Visual InterDev."

The first section of VBScript code begins immediately following the beginning of the Body section of the ASP page. The first part of this script begins much like the simple connection example that was presented earlier. The working variables are declared and then assigned using the Response.Form method. Then an ADO Connection object is created followed by an ADO Recordset object. Next, the connection string is assigned to the ADO Connection object, and then the Open method is called to start the connection to SQL Server.

Next, the ActiveConnection property of the rs Recordset object is set to the active Connection object, named cn. Then the Recordset object's Open method is executed. The first parameter of the Open method contains a simple SQL statement that selects all of the columns and rows from the stores table in the pubs database.

After the results of the query are returned to the ASP page, the ASP page processes the following section of HTML code. In this case, the HTML code creates a table that is sized to contain five columns. Then the column headings and the font for the table headings are assigned. In this example, all of the column headings are built using standard HTML.

The table body section begins with the <TBODY> tag. Immediately following the beginning of the HTML table body, the next section of VBScript sets up the beginning of a Do Until loop. This loop is used to process the contents of the rs Recordset object. When the end of the Recordset object is reached, the rs.EOF property becomes true, and the loop will end.

Within the Do Until loop, a separate <TD> tag is used for each column in the HTML table. The BORDERCOLOR, FONT SIZE, and COLOR tags set up the appearance of each column, and the next portion of the <TD> tag uses an embedded ASP script to assign the value of each column based on a column in the ADO Recordset object. The HTMLEncode method of the ASP Server object repackages the value that is returned from the rs Recordset object's Fields collection. In this example, each specific item in the Fields collection is identified using the actual column name that originates from the stores table.

NOTE: In this example, you can clearly see how ASP allows you to freely mix HTML code with ASP script.

After the data from the current row in the rs Recordset object has been added to the HTML table, the next portion of VBScript code performs a MoveNext method to move to the next row in the Recordset object. Then the Loop statement transfers control back to the top of the Do Until loop. When the last row in the Recordset object has been read, the loop ends, and the rs Recordset and cn Connection objects are closed. Then the HTML tags at the bottom of the ASP page are processed. You can see the results of the ASP page in Figure 17-22.

Closing a Record Set

Before ending your application, you should close any open Recordset objects using the Recordset object's Close method. An example of the Close method follows:

```
<%
rs.Close
%>
```

In this example, the Recordset object named rs is closed using the Close method.

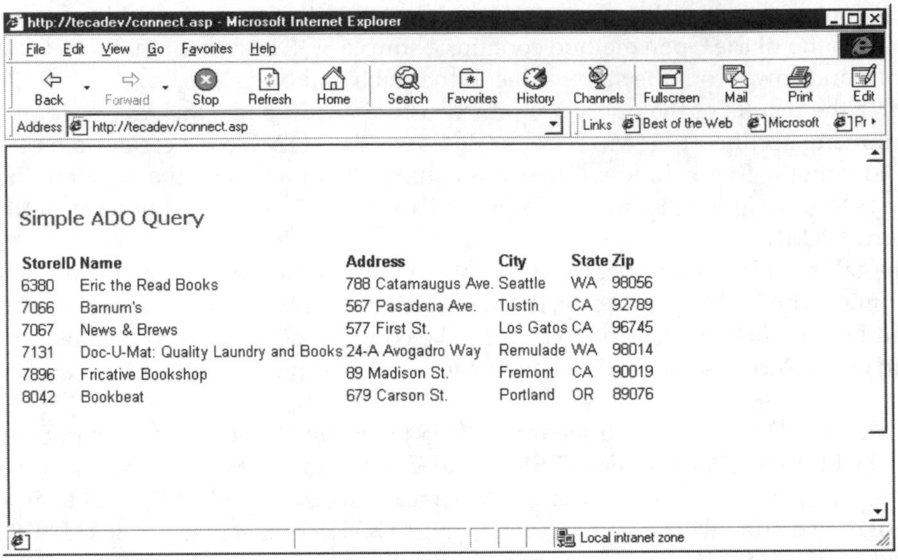

Figure 17-22.   ASP page using an ADO Recordset object

Session Scoped Connections

In the previous sections, you saw how to establish a connection and perform a simple query all on the same page. However, establishing a connection to a remote database is one of the more expensive operations. In the next example, you'll see how you can use the ASP Session object to contain a Connection object that can be used across multiple Web pages.

The ASP object model has two objects that can be globally accessed from multiple Web pages: the Application object and the Session object. While all Web users share the Application object, the Session object is unique to each Web client. If you refer back to Figure 17-21, you'll see that the Session object can hold user-defined objects as well as its own built-in collections. The following example shows how you can add an ADO Connection object to the ASP Session object as a user-defined object:

```
<%@ Language=VBScript %>
<HTML>
<HEAD>
<META NAME="GENERATOR" Content="Microsoft Visual Studio 6.0">
```

```
<LINK REL="stylesheet" TYPE="text/css"
  HREF="_Themes/sumipntg/THEME.CSS" VI6.0THEME="Sumi Painting">
<LINK REL="stylesheet" TYPE="text/css"
  HREF="_Themes/sumipntg/GRAPH0.CSS" VI6.0THEME="Sumi Painting">
<LINK REL="stylesheet" TYPE="text/css"
  HREF="_Themes/sumipntg/COLOR0.CSS" VI6.0THEME="Sumi Painting">
<LINK REL="stylesheet" TYPE="text/css"
  HREF="_Themes/sumipntg/CUSTOM.CSS" VI6.0THEME="Sumi Painting">
</HEAD>

<P> </P>
<H4>This page establishes an ASP Session Level Connection</H4>

<BODY>
<HR>
<%

Dim sServer
Dim sLoginID
Dim sPassword

Dim cn

'Get the Server and Login information from form1
sServer = Request.Form("txtServer")
sLoginID = Request.Form("txtLogin")
sPassword = Request.Form("txtPassword")


'Create a connection object
Set cn = Server.CreateObject("ADODB.Connection")

'Connect using the OLE DB provider for SQL Server - SQLOLEDB
cn.ConnectionString = "PROVIDER=SQLOLEDB" & _
    ";SERVER=" & sServer & _
    ";UID=" & sLoginID & _
    ";PWD=" & sPassword & _
    ";DATABASE=pubs"

cn.Open

Response.Write("Connected to: " & sServer & " as: " & sLoginID)
```

```
'Assign the Open Connection object to the Session object
Set Session("Connection") = cn
Session("Server") = sServer
Session("LoginID") = sLoginID
Session("Password") = sPassword


%>
<HR>

<A HREF="http://tecadev/SimpleConnectQuery.asp">
Click here to run a simple query</A> </P>

</BODY>
</HTML>
```

Like the previous example, this ASP page has been set up as the form handler for another Web page that prompts the user to enter a SQL Server system name and a login ID and password. The first part of this Web page uses the standard HTML tags to set up the header of the Web page and apply a design theme called "Sumi Painting" to the page.

The real action starts at the beginning of the VBScript. The first part of the script declares three working variables that are used to hold the essential SQL Server connection information. Next, the Request object's Form method is used to retrieve the connection information that was supplied on the previous page and assign it to the three variables that were declared earlier. Then the ASP Server object's CreateObject method is used to create a new instance of an ADO Connection object.

After the ADO Connection object is instantiated, its Connection string property is assigned an OLE DB connection string. Unlike the previous example, which used the OLE DB for ODBC provider, this example uses the OLE DB provider for SQL Server. Specifying the PROVIDER=SQLOLEDB keywords in the ConnectionString property directs ADO to use the OLE DB provider for SQL Server. The link to SQL Server is established when the cn Connection object's Open method is executed.

After the link to SQL Server is opened, the login variables and the ADO Connection object are stored in the ASP Session object. As you can see, you can store both OLE objects and standard variables in the Session object. Objects are stored using the VBScript Set statement, and standard variables are stored simply by making an assignment. There's no need to do anything special to create the new properties in the Session object. The properties are automatically created using the name specified in the parentheses. In the preceding example, four new properties are created and assigned in the ASP Session object. The first property is named Connection, and it is an instance of the ADO Connection object. The next three properties are named Server, LoginID, and Password. These properties contain the SQL Server connection information that was passed to this ASP page.

Using Prepared SQL and the Command Object

ADO can be used within ASP scripts to execute both dynamic SQL statements and prepared SQL statements. You have already seen how you can use dynamic SQL to create an ADO Recordset object that is displayed on a Web page. Dynamic SQL statements are conducive to ad hoc queries that are not repeated very often. Since each ad hoc query tends to be different from the previous queries, the overhead required to parse the SQL statement and create a data access plan cannot be avoided. However, many database applications consist of the same basic SQL statements repeated numerous times using different values. These OLTP types of applications can benefit from the use of prepared SQL statements because the SQL statement parsing and data access plan needs to be created only once, when the statement is prepared. ASP and ADO can take advantage of prepared SQL to build OLTP Web applications

Figure 17-23 shows a Web page that uses a drop-down box to specify the data that will be retrieved from a SQL Server table. The contents of the drop-down combo box are dynamically loaded from the values that are found in the stores table in the SQL server pubs database.

Selecting a Store ID from the drop-down combo box and then clicking the Submit button sends a query to the SQL Server system to retrieve the row information for the given Store ID. In this case, the same basic SQL statement will be executed for each different Store ID that will be queried. The repeated use of the same basic SQL statement makes this example a good candidate for prepared SQL. When the row information has been returned to the Web client, it will be displayed in an HTML table, as you can see in Figure 17-24.

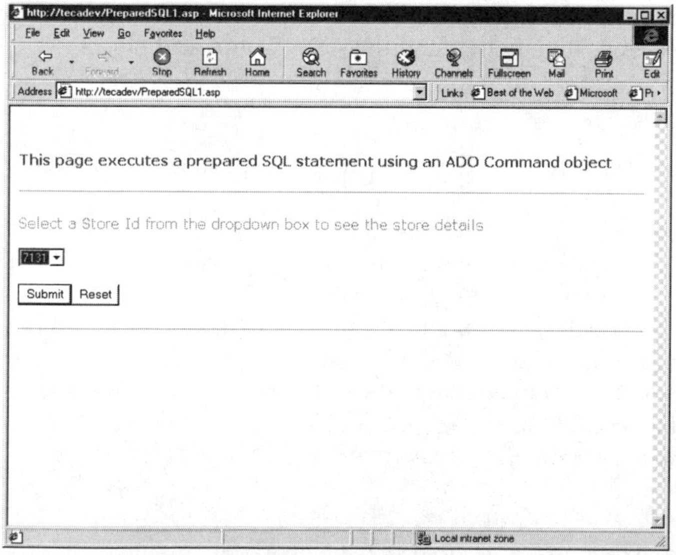

Figure 17-23. ASP and ADO prepared statement demonstration, page 1

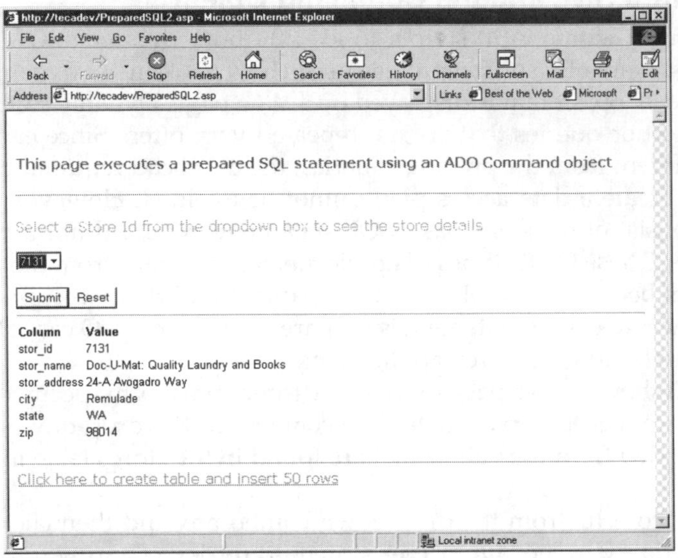

Figure 17-24. ASP and ADO prepared statement demonstration, page 2

Now that you have an overview of how this type of Web page works, take a closer look at how these pages are built. The following example shows how you can dynamically load an HTML drop-down box using an ADO Recordset object and then create a prepared SQL statement using the ADO Command object.

```
<HTML>
<HEAD>
<META NAME="GENERATOR" Content="Microsoft Visual Studio 6.0">

<LINK REL="stylesheet" TYPE="text/css"
   HREF="_Themes/sumipntg/THEME.CSS" VI6.0THEME="Sumi Painting">
<LINK REL="stylesheet" TYPE="text/css"
   HREF="_Themes/sumipntg/GRAPH0.CSS" VI6.0THEME="Sumi Painting">
<LINK REL="stylesheet" TYPE="text/css"
   HREF="_Themes/sumipntg/COLOR0.CSS" VI6.0THEME="Sumi Painting">
<LINK REL="stylesheet" TYPE="text/css"
   HREF="_Themes/sumipntg/CUSTOM.CSS" VI6.0THEME="Sumi Painting">

<P> </P>
<H4>This page executes a prepared SQL statement</H4>
</HEAD>
```

```
<BODY>
<HR>

<form NAME="ps1" METHOD="post" ACTION="PreparedSQL2.asp" >

<P>Select a Store ID from the drop-down box to see the details</P>

<SELECT id=select1 NAME="selectID">
    <%
     Dim cn
     Dim rs

     Set cn = Session("Connection")
     Set rs = cn.Execute("Select stor_id From stores")
     Do While Not rs.EOF
    %>

    <OPTION VALUE=<%=Server.HTMLEncode(rs.Fields("stor_id").Value)%>>
<%=Server.HTMLEncode(rs.Fields("stor_id").Value)%>

    <%
     rs.MoveNext
     Loop
     rs.Close
    %>
</SELECT>

<P></P>

<INPUT type="submit" value="Submit" id=submit1 name=submit1>
<INPUT type="reset" value="Reset" id=reset1 name=reset1>


</form></P>

<%
Dim cmd
Dim pm

'Create a connection object
Set cmd = Server.CreateObject("ADODB.Command")

'Use a session level connection object -- cn
```

```
Set cmd.ActiveConnection = cn

'Set up the SQL statement that uses one parameter marker
cmd.CommandText = "Select * From stores Where stor_id = ?"

'Specify the parameter characteristics
Set pm = cmd.CreateParameter("parm1", 3, 1, 4 ,0)
cmd.Parameters.Append pm

Set Session("PS1") = cmd

%>

<HR>

</BODY>
</HTML>
```

This page begins like a standard HTML page with the normal heading and theme tags. However, one difference between this and the earlier examples is that this page uses the <FORM> tag to indicate that there will be a form handler for this page. The first page allows the user to select the Store ID and also handles the preparation of the SQL statement. The form handler takes the Store ID selected on the first page and actually executes the SQL statement and displays the results in an HTML table. The ACTION keyword identifies the ASP page named PreparedSQL2.asp that will handle the user input.

The <SELECT> tag marks the beginning of the creation of the drop-down combo box. Remember that ASP allows you to freely mix HTML and VBScript to dynamically create Web pages. Here, the <SELECT> tag begins like a standard HTML drop-down box. However, immediately after the <SELECT> tag, VBScript code is executed that creates an ADO Recordset object that contains all of the values from the stor_id column in the stores table. In this example, an ADO Connection object that was stored in the ASP Session object is used to set the active connection. Just as the Set statement is used to store the ADO Connection object in the ASP Session object, the VBScript Set statement is also used to assign that session-level Connection object to the local variable named cn.

Next, the Connection object's Execute method is used to send the SQL Select statement to SQL Server. The values in each of the HTML <OPTION> tags that build up the items in the combo box are assigned within the Do While loop that reads through the rs Recordset object.

After the ASP script has completed filling in the <OPTION> tags that add the items to the combo box, two <INPUT> tags are used to add Submit and Reset buttons to the form.

Next, another section of ASP script is executed to prepare the SQL statement that will be used to retrieve the data from the stores table. In this ASP script, two working variables are declared, and then the Server object's CreateObject method is used to create a new instance of an ADO Command object named cmd.

Next, the cmd object's ActiveConnection property is set with the Connection object that was previously returned from the Session object. Then the CommandText method of the ADO Command object is assigned the parameterized SQL statement. Following the ODBC standard, the question mark character is used as a parameter marker—a placeholder—for a value that will be substituted at run time. This Select statement will retrieve all of the columns from the stores table, where the Store ID equals the value supplied in the parameter.

Next, the ADO Command object's CreateParameter method is used to create a new ADO Parameter object named parm1. The first parameter indicates the data type. Since this is VBScript, there is no OLE Reference library that automatically supplies constants. A value of 3 indicates that this parameter is an integer. The following table presents all of the ADO parameter values:

SQL Server Data Type	ADO Data Type
Binary	adBinary (128)
Varbinary	adVarBinary (204)
Char	adChar (129)
Varchar	adVarChar (200)
Datetime	adDBTimeStamp (135)
Smalldatetime	adDBTimeStamp (135)
Decimal	adNumeric (131)
Numeric	adNumeric (131)
Float	adDouble (5)
Real	adSingle (4)
Int	adInteger (3)
Smallint	adSmallInt (2)
Tinyint	adUnsignedTinyInt (17)
Money	adNumeric (131)
Smallmoney	adNumeric (131)
Bit	adBoolean (11)
Timestamp	adBinary (128)
Text	adLongVarChar (201)
Image	adLongVarBinary (205)

The third parameter specifies whether the parameter is an input value, output value, or both. The following table presents the values using the direction parameter:

Direction Value	Description
adParamInput (1) (Default)	Passes data to the procedure
adParamOutput (2)	Passes data from the procedure
adParamInputOutput (3)	Bidirectional parameter
adParamReturnValue (4)	Return value

The fourth parameter indicates the data length, and the fifth parameter supplies an initial value.

The CreateParameter method specifies the attributes of a given parameter, but it does not actually add the parameter to the ADO Command object. After the ADO Parameter object has been created, you can add it to the Parameters collection of the Command object using the Append method.

This is all that you need to do to set up the prepared statement using ASP and ADO. The next line in the ASP script assigns the ADO Command object that contains the prepared statement to the ASP Session object and names it PS1.

Selecting an item from the drop-down list and then clicking the Submit button evokes the ASP form handler that was specified in the <FORM> tag. The following listing shows the source code for the PreparedSQL2.asp page:

```
<%@ Language=VBScript %>
<HTML>
<HEAD>
<META NAME="GENERATOR" Content="Microsoft Visual Studio 6.0">

<LINK REL="stylesheet" TYPE="text/css"
  HREF="_Themes/sumipntg/THEME.CSS" VI6.0THEME="Sumi Painting">
<LINK REL="stylesheet" type="text/css"
  HREF="_themes/sumipntg/graph0.css" vi6.0theme="sumi painting">
<LINK REL="STYLESHEET" TYPE="TEXT/CSS"
  HREF="_THEMES/SUMIPNTG/COLOR0.CSS" VI6.0THEME="SUMI PAINTING">
<LINK REL="stylesheet" TYPE="text/css"
  HREF="_Themes/sumipntg/CUSTOM.CSS" VI6.0THEME="Sumi Painting">
<P> </P>
<H4>This page executes a prepared SQL statement</H4>
</HEAD>

<BODY>
<HR>

<FORM NAME="ps2" METHOD="post" ACTION="PreparedSQL2.asp" >

<P>Select a Store ID from the drop-down box to see the details</P>
```

```
<SELECT id=select1 NAME="selectID">
   <%
     Dim cn2
     Dim rs2

     Set cn2 = Session("Connection")
     Set rs2 = cn2.Execute("Select stor_id From stores")
     Do While Not rs2.EOF
   %>

  <OPTION VALUE=<%=Server.HTMLEncode(rs2.Fields("stor_id").Value)%>>
<%=Server.HTMLEncode(rs2.Fields("stor_id").Value)%>

     <%
       rs2.MoveNext
       Loop
       rs2.Close
     %>
</SELECT>

<P></P>

<INPUT type="submit" value="Submit" id=submit1 name=submit1>
<INPUT type="reset" value="Reset" id=reset1 name=reset1>

<HR>
<%
Dim cn
Dim rs
Dim cmd
Dim pm
Dim fld

Dim sStor_ID

'Get the Server and Login information from form1
sStor_Id = Request.Form("selectID")

'Get the ADO Command object from the Session object
set cmd = Session("PS1")
'Set the parameter value
cmd.Parameters("parm1").Value = sStor_ID

'Set up the input parameter
Set rs = cmd.Execute
```

```
'Next display the results in a table

%>

<TABLE CellPadding=1 CellSpacing=1 Cols=2>
<TBODY>

<TR VALIGN=top ALIGN=left>
<TH BGCOLOR=#c0c0c0 BORDERCOLOR=#000000>
<FONT SIZE=2 FACE="Arial" COLOR=#000000>Column</FONT></TH>
<TH BGCOLOR=#c0c0c0 BORDERCOLOR=#000000>
<FONT SIZE=2 FACE="Arial" COLOR=#000000>Value</FONT></TH>

<%
For Each fld in rs.Fields
%>

<TR VALIGN=top ALIGN=left>
<TD BGCOLOR=#c0c0c0 BORDERCOLOR=#000000>
<FONT SIZE=2 FACE="Arial" COLOR=#000000>
          <%=Server.HTMLEncode(fld.Name)%><BR></FONT></TD>
<TD BORDERCOLOR=#c0c0c0><FONT SIZE=2 FACE="Arial" COLOR=#000000>
          <%=Server.HTMLEncode(fld.Value)%><BR></FONT></TD>
</TR>

<%
Next

rs.Close

%>

</TABLE>

</FORM>
</P>

<HR>

<A HREF="http://tecadev/CreateInsert.asp">
Click here to create table and insert 50 rows</A>

</BODY>
</HTML>
```

Near the beginning of the PreparedSQL2.asp ASP page, you can see where the HTML <FORM> tag is used to set up a form handler for the PreapredSQL2.asp page. However, this example is noteworthy in that the PreparedSQL2.asp page serves as its own form handler. This allows the drop-down combo box to be used to search for Store IDs from this same page, so there is no need to drop back and display the original search page.

Next, at the <SELECT> tag, you can see where the combo box is loaded from the contents of the ADO Recordset object. This code is essentially the same as the code that was used in the previous ASP page.

The main difference between this page and the previous page surfaces in the following section of VBScript code. After the working variables used in this section of script are declared, the ASP Request object's Form method is used to retrieve the contents of the drop-down combo box that was named selectID.

NOTE: For this same form handler to work with both pages, the drop-down combo box used on each of the different pages must have the same name.

After the value of the Store ID has been retrieved from the combo box, the Set statement assigns the local cmd variable with the ADO Command object that was created on the previous page and then stored in the ASP Session object. Since this is an input parameter, the next line of code sets the value that will be used in the ADO Parameter object. In this example, the ADO Parameter is identified by name in the Parameters collection of the ADO Command object. Setting the parm1 parameter's Value property supplies the value that the will be used at run time in the prepared SQL statement.

The prepared statement is sent to SQL Server when the Command object's Execute method is run. Here, the single-row result set that's generated by the prepared SQL statement is assigned to an ADO Recordset object named rs.

The next section of HTML code creates the HTML table that will be used to display the contents of the ADO Recordset object. The table will consist of two columns. The first column will be used to list the column names, and the second column will contain the column values. The HTML <TR> tag sets up the new table row, and the <TH> tag sets up each table heading column.

Once the table headings have been set up, a VBScript For Each loop is used to process the column information contained in the rs Recordset object. Within the For Each loop, the HTML <TR> sets up each new row in the HTML table while the <TD> tags are set up. The column heading names are supplied to the HTML column using the Server.HTMLEncode(fld.Name) code, and the column values are supplied using ServerHTMLEncode(fld.Value) code. When the For Each loop has read through the collection of ADO Field objects, the rs Recordset object is closed, and the remaining HTML on the ASP page is processed.

Modifying Data with ADO

In addition to dynamically creating Web pages, ASP and ADO can also be used to create data-entry Web pages. This enables you to create Web-based database applications that support the same range of database capabilities as are found in standard client/server database applications. You can modify data using the combination of ASP and ADO in a number of ways. First, you can build ASP pages that support updateable ADO Recordset objects that can use the AddNew, Update, and Delete methods to modify the data contained in SQL Server databases. You can also use ADO to perform both dynamic and prepared SQL data update operations. For a more complete view of the database update capabilities provided by ADO, refer to Chapter 15. In the next part of this chapter, you'll see how to update SQL Server data using an ADO Recordset object.

INSERTING ROWS IN A RECORDSET OBJECT   The ability to update a Recordset object depends on the type of cursor that the Recordset object uses and on the locking type. For example, a Keyset type of Recordset object can be updated, but a Static type of Recordset object cannot be. For a more complete explanation of the various types of ADO Recordset objects and their ability to support updates, refer to Chapter 15.

Once you've opened an updateable ADO Recordset object, that Recordset object's AddNew method can be used in conjunction with the Update method to insert rows in a database table. The following code illustrates how you can add rows to a Recordset object that was created using a keyset cursor:

```
<%@ Language=VBScript %>


<%  Option Explicit      %>

<!--#include file="adovbs.inc"-->

<HTML>
<HEAD>
<META NAME="GENERATOR" Content="Microsoft Visual Studio 6.0">

<LINK REL="stylesheet" TYPE="text/css"
  HREF="_Themes/sumipntg/THEME.CSS" VI6.0THEME="Sumi Painting">
<LINK REL="stylesheet" TYPE="text/css"
  HREF="_Themes/sumipntg/GRAPH0.CSS" VI6.0THEME="Sumi Painting">
<LINK REL="stylesheet" TYPE="text/css"
  HREF="_Themes/sumipntg/COLOR0.CSS" VI6.0THEME="Sumi Painting">
<LINK REL="stylesheet" TYPE="text/css"
  HREF="_Themes/sumipntg/CUSTOM.CSS" VI6.0THEME="Sumi Painting">
</HEAD>
<H4>This page creates the department table an inserts 50 rows
using an ADO Recordset cursor</H4>
<BODY>

<HR>
```

```
<%
Dim cn
Dim sSQL
Dim i
Dim rs
Dim fld

On Error Resume Next

Set cn = Session("Connection")

'Make certain that the table is created by dropping the table
' If the table doesn't exist then the next statement will be executed
sSQL = "Drop Table department"
cn.Execute sSQL

'Reset the error handler and create the table
On Error GoTo 0
sSQL = "Create Table department " _
& "(Dep_ID Integer Not Null, Dep_Name Char(25), Primary Key(Dep_ID))"
cn.Execute sSQL

Set rs = Server.CreateObject("ADODB.Recordset")

' Associate the Recordset with the session level connection object
Set rs.ActiveConnection = cn

'Pass in the SQL, Connection, Cursor type, lock type and source type
rs.Open "Select Dep_ID, Dep_Name From department Where 1=2", _
        cn, adOpenKeyset, adLockOptimistic, adCmdText

'Add 50 rows to the department table
For i = 1 To 50
   rs.AddNew
   rs("Dep_ID").Value = i
   rs("Dep_Name").Value = "Department " & CStr(i)
   rs.Update
Next

'Display the new rows in a table
rs.MoveFirst

%>
```

```
<TABLE CellPadding=1 CellSpacing=1 Cols=2>
<TBODY>

<TR VALIGN=top ALIGN=left>
<%
For Each fld in rs.Fields
%>
<TH BGCOLOR=#c0c0c0 BORDERCOLOR=#000000>
<FONT SIZE=2 FACE="Arial" COLOR=#000000>
<%=Server.HTMLEncode(fld.Name)%>
</FONT></TH>

<%
Next
%>

</TR>

<%



Do Until rs.EOF
%>

<TR VALIGN=top ALIGN=left>

<%
    For Each fld in rs.Fields
%>



<TD BORDERCOLOR=#c0c0c0><FONT SIZE=2 FACE="Arial" COLOR=#000000>
            <%=Server.HTMLEncode(fld.Value)%><BR></FONT></TD>
<%
    Next
    rs.MoveNext
%>

</TR>

<%
Loop
%>
```

```
</TABLE>

<%
rs.Close
%>
<HR>

<A HREF="http://tecadev/Update.asp">Click here to update 50 rows</A>

</BODY>
</HTML>
```

This Web page introduces some new ASP Web building techniques. First, near the top of the Web page, the VBScript Option Explicit statement is used to ensure that all of the variables in the VBScript code are explicitly declared. Like standard Visual Basic, VBScript can automatically use new variables without first declaring them. While at first this may seem like a handy feature, it really isn't. In fact, this is actually a very effective way of introducing insidious and difficult-to-find bugs into your ASP applications. When you specify the Option Explicit statement, VBScript requires all variables to be explicitly declared before they can be used.

Next, an #include statement is used to include a file named adovbs.inc. Like a C header file, using the #include provides a convenient method of copying commonly used constants into the ASP pages. In this case, the adovbs.inc file includes all of the constants that are commonly used in by the ADO object framework. Using this include file allows you to use constants such as adChar and adKeyset in your ADO method calls rather than the actual values that these constants represent.

NOTE: As an alternative to using the include file, you can declare the ADO type library in your application. To declare a type library, you use the <METADATA> tag in your global.asa page. For example, use the following statements:

```
<!--METADATA TYPE="typelib"
FILE="c:\program files\common files\system\ado\msado15.dll"
-->
```

Unlike include files that are scoped to a given page, you can use ADO constants in any script in the same application as the global.asa file. However, the <METADATA> tag requires a hard-coded path name to the OLE type library, and this may not be possible if your application will be deployed on multiple Web servers.

The VBScript that you can see on this page first drops and then re-creates a table called department in the pubs database. Then it uses an ADO Recordset object to insert 50 rows in the table. Finally, the contents of the table are displayed on the Web page in an HTML table.

The first action that occurs within the VBScript is the initialization of the VBScript error handler. In this example, the On Error statement is used to trap any errors that may be generated by attempting to drop the department table if it appears not to exist in the target database. More detailed information about using the error handler is presented in the section titled "Error Handling," later in this chapter.

Next, the ADO Connection object that is stored in the ASP Session object is assigned to the local variable named cn. The Connection object's Execute method is then used to execute two dynamic SQL statements. The first drops the table named department, and the second creates the department table.

After the department table has been created, the ActiveConnection property of the rs Recordset object is set to the Connection object. Then the Recordset object's Open method is use to create an updateable Recordset object. The constant adOpenKeyset indicates that this will be an updateable Keyset type of Recordset object, and the adLockOptimistic constant indicates that optimistic record locking will be used.

TIP: Since this Recordset object will initially be used simply to insert rows, the SQL Where clause 1=2 ensures that no extraneous data is returned to the Web client.

A For Next loop is used to insert 50 rows into the department table. Within the For Next loop, the AddNew method is used to create a buffer to hold the new row. Then the values of the ADO Field objects are assigned. Each object in the Fields collection is identified using its column name. The Dep_ID column is set to the value of the loop counter, and the Dep_Name column is assigned the literal Department combined with the string representation of the loop counter. The new row is then inserted in the base table when the Recordset object's Update method is executed.

After the 50 rows have been inserted into the department table, the MoveFirst method is used to reposition the cursor to the beginning of the Recordset object. Then the contents of the Recordset object are displayed in an HTML table using the same technique that was presented in the earlier query examples. First, a For Each loop is used to extract the column names and add them to the heading of the HTML table. Then a Do Until loop is used to read through all of the rows in the Recordset object. For every row, a For Each loop is used to display each ADO Field object in a cell of the HTML table. When all of the rows in the rs Recordset object have been read, the Recordset object is closed using the Close method.

In Figure 17-25, you can see the resulting Web page that was created by running this ASP page.

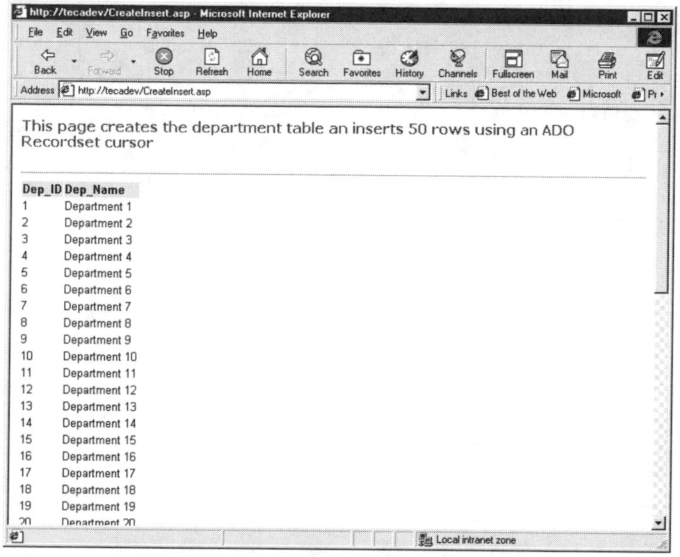

Figure 17-25. ASP Web page showing the inserted contents of the Recordset object

UPDATING ROWS WITH THE RECORDSET OBJECT You can also use ASP to update the rows in a SQL Server table using an ADO Recordset object. After the Recordset object has been opened, the ADO Recordset object's Update method can be used to update the rows in the result set. The following ASP Web page illustrates how you can use the update method to update rows in a SQL Server table:

```
<%@ Language=VBScript %>
<% Option Explicit      %>


<!--#include file="adovbs.inc"-->


<HTML>
<HEAD>
<META NAME="GENERATOR" Content="Microsoft Visual Studio 6.0">

<LINK REL="stylesheet" TYPE="text/css"
  HREF="_Themes/sumipntg/THEME.CSS" VI6.0THEME="Sumi Painting">
<LINK REL="stylesheet" TYPE="text/css"
  HREF="_Themes/sumipntg/GRAPH0.CSS" VI6.0THEME="Sumi Painting">
<LINK REL="stylesheet" TYPE="text/css"
```

```
  HREF="_Themes/sumipntg/COLOR0.CSS" VI6.0THEME="Sumi Painting">
<LINK REL="stylesheet" TYPE="text/css"
  HREF="_Themes/sumipntg/CUSTOM.CSS" VI6.0THEME="Sumi Painting">
</HEAD>
<H4>This page updates 50 rows in the department</H4>
<BODY>

<HR>

<%
Dim cn
Dim sSQL
Dim i
Dim rs
Dim fld

Set cn = Session("Connection")

Set rs = Server.CreateObject("ADODB.Recordset")

' Associate the Recordset with the session level connection object
Set rs.ActiveConnection = cn

'Pass in the SQL, Connection, Cursor type, lock type and source type
rs.Open "Select Dep_ID, Dep_Name From department", _
        cn, adOpenKeyset, adLockOptimistic, adCmdText

rs.MoveFirst
i = 1

Do Until rs.EOF
'Update all the rows in the department table
   rs("Dep_Name").Value = "Updated Department " & CStr(i)
   rs.Update
   i = i + 1
   rs.MoveNext
Loop

'Display the new rows in a table
rs.MoveFirst

%>

<TABLE CellPadding=1 CellSpacing=1 Cols=2>
```

```
<TBODY>

<TR VALIGN=top ALIGN=left>
<%
For Each fld in rs.Fields
%>
<TH BGCOLOR=#c0c0c0 BORDERCOLOR=#000000>
<FONT SIZE=2 FACE="Arial" COLOR=#000000>
<%=Server.HTMLEncode(fld.Name)%></FONT></TH>

<%
Next
%>

</TR>

<%


Do Until rs.EOF
%>

<TR VALIGN=top ALIGN=left>

<%
    For Each fld in rs.Fields
%>

<TD BORDERCOLOR=#c0c0c0><FONT SIZE=2 FACE="Arial" COLOR=#000000>
            <%=Server.HTMLEncode(fld.Value)%></FONT></TD>
<%
    Next
    rs.MoveNext
%>

</TR>

<%
Loop
%>

</TABLE>

<%
```

```
rs.Close
%>
<HR>

<A HREF="http://tecadev/Delete.asp">Click here to update 50 rows</A>

</BODY>
</HTML>
```

This example is similar to the previous insert example. The ASP page begins by using the Option Explicit statement and the #include directive to pull in the ADO constants. Next, the page theme is set, and then the ASP script begins by creating a local instance of the ADO Connection object as well as an instance of an ADO Recordset object. Then the Recordset object's Open method is used to retrieve all of the rows from the department table.

After the Recordset object has been opened, a Do Until loop is used to read through all of the rows in the object. Inside the Do Until loop, the ADO Field object named Dep_Name is reassigned a new value, and then the Update method is executed to update the row.

When all of the rows in the ADO Recordset object have been updated, the cursor is repositioned at the beginning of the rs Recordset object, and the updated contents of the Recordset object are displayed in an HTML table. Figure 17-26 shows the Web page generated by the ASP script.

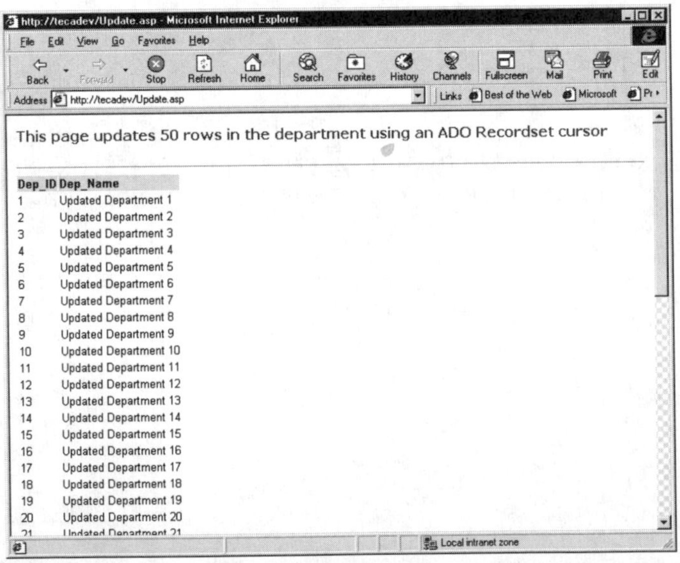

Figure 17-26.   ASP Web page showing the updated Recordset object

DELETING ROWS FROM A RECORDSET OBJECT   The previous examples illustrated how to insert and update the SQL Server database using ASP and ADO. The next example shows how the Recordset object's Delete method can remove rows using an updateable ADO Recordset object:

```
<%@ Language=VBScript %>
<%  Option Explicit       %>

<!--#include file="adovbs.inc"-->
<HTML>
<HEAD>
<META NAME="GENERATOR" Content="Microsoft Visual Studio 6.0">

<LINK REL="stylesheet" TYPE="text/css"
  HREF="_Themes/sumipntg/THEME.CSS" VI6.0THEME="Sumi Painting">
<LINK REL="stylesheet" TYPE="text/css"
  HREF="_Themes/sumipntg/GRAPH0.CSS" VI6.0THEME="Sumi Painting">
<LINK REL="stylesheet" TYPE="text/css"
  HREF="_Themes/sumipntg/COLOR0.CSS" VI6.0THEME="Sumi Painting">
<LINK REL="stylesheet" TYPE="text/css"
  HREF="_Themes/sumipntg/CUSTOM.CSS" VI6.0THEME="Sumi Painting">
</HEAD>

<H4>This page deletes 50 rows in the department</H4>
<BODY>

<HR>

<%
Dim cn
Dim sSQL
Dim rs

Set cn = Session("Connection")

Set rs = Server.CreateObject("ADODB.Recordset")

' Associate the Recordset with the session level connection object
Set rs.ActiveConnection = cn
```

```
'Pass in the SQL, Connection, Cursor type, lock type and source type
rs.Open "Select Dep_ID, Dep_Name From department", _
        cn, adOpenKeyset, adLockOptimistic, adCmdText


Do Until rs.EOF
'Delete all the rows in the department table
    rs.Delete
    rs.MoveNext
Loop

rs.Close

%>
All of the rows in the department table have been deleted
<HR>

<A HREF="http://tecadev/storedproc1.asp">
Click here to create a stored procedure</A>
</BODY>
</HTML>
```

As you can see, this example is similar to the update example that was presented previously. Both use the session-level ADO Connection object to connect the local Recordset object to SQL Server. In addition, in both cases, the ADO Recordset object is an updateable Keyset type of record set that uses optimistic record locking. The primary difference is that within the Do Until loop, this example uses the Recordset object's Delete method to delete each row in the Recordset object.

Executing Stored Procedures with Command Objects

ASP scripts can also be used to execute SQL Server stored procedures. Stored procedures are the fastest mechanism available for accessing SQL Server data. When a stored procedure is created, a compiled data access plan is added to the SQL Server database. When the stored procedure is later executed by an application, there's no need to parse the SQL statements or create a new data access plan. This results in faster execution of queries and other data manipulation actions. Stored procedures can consist of a single SQL statement, or they can be quite complex—complete with their own logic and containing many different SQL statements.

Using stored procedures from ASP Web pages is very much like using prepared SQL. Stored procedures have the ability to accept input parameters, plus they can return a result set or they can return values using output parameters. However, stored procedures differ from prepared SQL in one important aspect: they are persistent. After a stored procedure is created, a new object is added to the SQL Server database. Prepared SQL statements do not add new objects to the SQL Server database.

Figure 17-27 shows a Web page that uses a drop-down box to select a Store ID that will be passed to a SQL Server stored procedure as an input parameter. As in the earlier prepared statement example, the contents of the drop-down combo box are dynamically loaded from the values that are found in the stores table in the SQL server pubs database.

Selecting a Store ID from the drop-down combo box and then clicking the Submit button executes a SQL Server stored procedure that sums the Quantity column of sales table in the pubs database. The total amount for the given Store ID is then returned to the ASP Web page via an output parameter. When the summary information has been returned to the Web client, it is displayed in an HTML table, as shown in Figure 17-28.

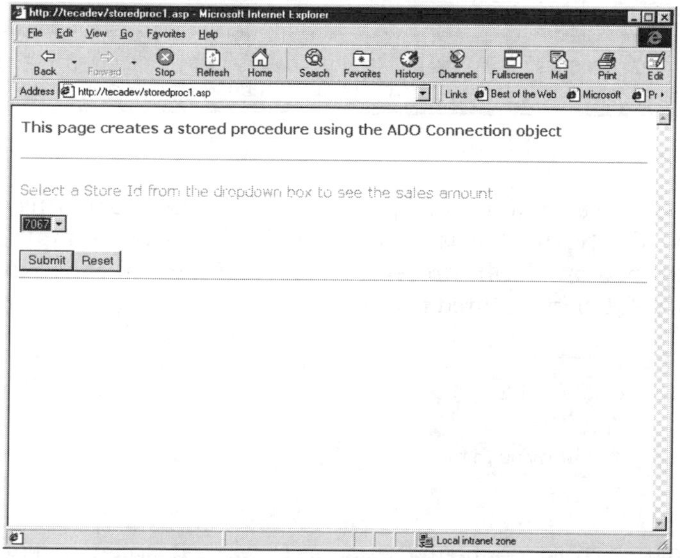

Figure 17-27.   Executing a stored procedure using the ADO Command object (page 1)

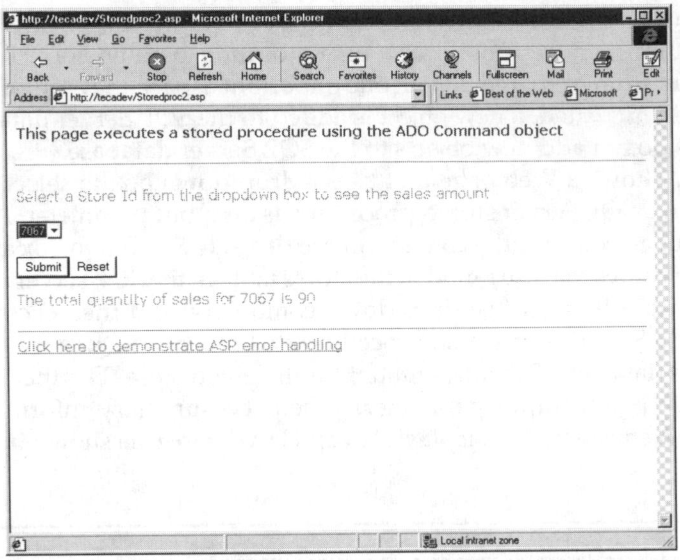

Figure 17-28. Executing a stored procedure using the ADO Command object (page 2)

Now that you've seen how a stored procedure can be used to return output to an ASP page, look at how this type of ASP is constructed. The following example shows how you can dynamically load an HTML drop-down box and then create an ADO Command object that calls a SQL Server stored procedure:

```
<%@ Language=VBScript %>
<%  Option Explicit      %>

<!--#include file="adovbs.inc"-->
<HTML>
<HEAD>
<META NAME="GENERATOR" Content="Microsoft Visual Studio 6.0">

<LINK REL="stylesheet" TYPE="text/css"
   HREF="_Themes/sumipntg/THEME.CSS" VI6.0THEME="Sumi Painting">
<LINK REL="stylesheet" TYPE="text/css"
   HREF="_Themes/sumipntg/GRAPH0.CSS" VI6.0THEME="Sumi Painting">
<LINK REL="stylesheet" TYPE="text/css"
   HREF="_Themes/sumipntg/COLOR0.CSS" VI6.0THEME="Sumi Painting">
<LINK REL="stylesheet" TYPE="text/css"
```

```
     HREF="_Themes/sumipntg/CUSTOM.CSS" VI6.0THEME="Sumi Painting">
</HEAD>

<H4>This page creates a stored procedure</H4>

<BODY>
<HR>
<form NAME="sp1" METHOD="post" ACTION="Storedproc2.asp" >

<P>Select a Store ID from the drop-down box to see the sales amount</P>

<SELECT id=select1 NAME="selectID">
   <%
     Dim cn
     Dim rs

     Set cn = Session("Connection")
     Set rs = cn.Execute("Select stor_id From stores")
     Do While Not rs.EOF
   %>

<OPTION VALUE=<%=Server.HTMLEncode(rs.Fields("stor_id").Value)%>>
<%=Server.HTMLEncode(rs.Fields("stor_id").Value)%>

   <%
     rs.MoveNext
     Loop
     rs.Close
   %>
</SELECT>

<P></P>

<INPUT type="submit" value="Submit" id=submit1 name=submit1>
<INPUT type="reset" value="Reset" id=reset1 name=reset1>

<HR>

<%

Dim sSQL
Dim cmd
Dim parm0
Dim parm1
```

```
'Enable Error handling to skip PS not found errors
On Error Resume Next
sSQL = "Drop Proc CountStoreQty"
cn.Execute sSQL

' Disable error handling
On Error GoTo 0

sSQL = "Create Proc CountStoreQty" _
    & "(@stor_id Char(4), @qty Int Output) as " _
    & "Select @qty = Sum(qty) From sales Where stor_id = @stor_id"

cn.Execute sSQL

'Create a connection object
Set cmd = Server.CreateObject("ADODB.Command")
Set parm0 = Server.CreateObject("ADODB.Parameter")
Set parm1 = Server.CreateObject("ADODB.Parameter")

'Use a session-level connection object -- cn
Set cmd.ActiveConnection = cn

cmd.CommandType = adCmdStoredProc
cmd.CommandText = "CountStoreQty"

parm0.Direction = adParamInput
parm0.Type = adChar
parm0.Size = 4
cmd.Parameters.Append parm0

parm1.Direction = adParamOutput
parm1.Type = adInteger
parm1.Size = 4
cmd.Parameters.Append parm1

Set Session("SP1") = cmd

%>
</form></P>

</BODY>
</HTML>
```

This sample ASP page is constructed similarly to the prepared SQL example that was presented earlier. First, a form handler is added using the <FORM> tag. In this case, the form handler specifies that the ASP page named storedproc2.asp will take the input from this page. Next, the combo box is dynamically loaded using the value of the Store ID column in the stores table. The technique used to load the combo box is the same as in the previous prepared statement example.

Next, a stored procedure named CountStoreQty is dropped and then re-created in the pubs database. The CountStoreQty stored procedure uses two parameters. The first is an input parameter that contains a Store ID. The second is an output parameter that returns the total quantity of sales for the given Store ID. Error handling is enabled to avoid a possible run-time error if the stored procedure is not present when the Drop Proc operation is performed.

To execute the stored procedure, an ADO Command object and two ADO Parameter objects are instantiated using the CreateObject method of the ASP Server object. Then the ActiveConnection property of the Command object is set using the session-level Connection object. Next, the CommandType property is set with the constant adCmdStoredProc, which indicates that the ADO Command object will execute a stored procedure. The name of the stored procedure is then assigned to the CommandText property. After the properties of the ADO Command object have been set, the attributes of the two ADO Parameter objects are assigned, and the Parameter objects are appended to the ADO Command object's Parameters collection.

> **NOTE:** Setting up all of the ADO parameter attributes is not required, but doing so can result in improved application performance. If you do not manually set the parameter attributes, ADO will query the database to discover them.

After the ADO Command object has been set up, it is added to the ASP Session object and given the name SP1.

Selecting an item from the drop-down list and then clicking the Submit button evokes the ASP form handler that was specified in the <FORM> tag. In the following listing you can see the source code for the storedproc2.asp page:

```
<%@ Language=VBScript %>
<% Option Explicit      %>

<!--#include file="adovbs.inc"-->
<HTML>
<HEAD>
<META NAME="GENERATOR" Content="Microsoft Visual Studio 6.0">

<LINK REL="stylesheet" TYPE="text/css"
  HREF="_Themes/sumipntg/THEME.CSS" VI6.0THEME="Sumi Painting">
<LINK REL="stylesheet" TYPE-"text/css"
```

```
   HREF="_Themes/sumipntg/GRAPH0.CSS" VI6.0THEME="Sumi Painting">
<LINK REL="stylesheet" TYPE="text/css"
   HREF="_Themes/sumipntg/COLOR0.CSS" VI6.0THEME="Sumi Painting">
<LINK REL="stylesheet" TYPE="text/css"
   HREF="_Themes/sumipntg/CUSTOM.CSS" VI6.0THEME="Sumi Painting">
</HEAD>

<H4>This page executes a stored procedure</H4>

<BODY>
<HR>
<form NAME="sp1" METHOD="post" ACTION="Storedproc2.asp" >

<P>Select a Store ID from the drop-down box to see the sales</P>

<SELECT id=select1 NAME="selectID">
   <%
     Dim cn
     Dim rs

     Set cn = Session("Connection")
     Set rs = cn.Execute("Select stor_id From stores")
     Do While Not rs.EOF
   %>

<OPTION VALUE=<%=Server.HTMLEncode(rs.Fields("stor_id").Value)%>>
%=Server.HTMLEncode(rs.Fields("stor_id").Value)%>

   <%
     rs.MoveNext
     Loop
     rs.Close
   %>
</SELECT>

<P></P>

<INPUT type="submit" value="Submit" id=submit1 name=submit1>
<INPUT type="reset" value="Reset" id=reset1 name=reset1>

<HR>
```

```
<%
Dim cmd
Dim pm
Dim fld

Dim sStor_ID

'Get the Server and Login information from form1
sStor_Id = Request.Form("selectID")

set cmd = Session("SP1")
'Set the parameter value

cmd.Parameters(0).Value = sStor_ID

'Set up the input parameter
cmd.Execute

'Display the returned value
%>

The total quantity of sales for <%=sStor_Id %> is
<%=cmd.Parameters(1).Value %>

</FORM>
</P>

<HR>
<A HREF="http://tecadev/error.asp">
Click here to demonstrate ASP error handling</A>

</BODY>
</HTML>
```

As in the previous prepared SQL example, the <FORM> tag at the beginning of the page sets up this page as its own form handler. This allows the drop-down combo box to be used to enter new Store IDs without the need to display the original search page. Next, the combo box is dynamically loaded from the contents of the stores table.

After the page is set up, the VBScript code retrieves the Store ID that was selected on the previous page and then uses it to execute the SQL Server stored procedure. The ASP Request object's Form method is used to retrieve the contents of the drop-down combo box named selectID. The contents of the combo box are then assigned to the local variable named sStor_Id.

After the value of the Store ID has been retrieved from the combo box, the Set statement is used to assign the local cmd variable with the ADO Command object named SP1 that was stored in the ASP Session object. The next line of code sets the value of the first ADO Parameter object using the sStor_Id variable. In this example, the ADO Parameter is identified by its ordinal number in the ADO Command object's Parameters collection.

The Command object's Execute method is then used to execute the SQL Server stored procedure. After the stored procedure has completed execution, the returned value can be extracted from the second ADO Parameter object. In this example, the value contained in the cmd.Parameters(1) object is displayed as an ASP output string.

Error Handling

Error handling in ASP scripts is implemented using the VBScript On Error statement. Trapping run-time errors is important. If your Web application generates an untrapped error, the Web application will run into a humbling error message and then cease to function. Unfortunately, the VBScript the On Error statement is not quite as robust as the standard Visual Basic error handler. While the standard Visual Basic error handler allows you to branch to a specific error-handling code section, the VBScript On Error statement only allows you to resume processing at the next operation or disable error handling. It does not support branching to different sections of code. VBScript allows the following two statements:

Statement	Function
On Error Resume Next	Trap the error and continue with the next statement.
On Error Goto 0	Disable error handling.

The VBScript On Error statement allows you to capture run-time errors and can save your application from generating unpleasant errors. In addition, the run-time errors that are encountered using the ADO object framework are placed in the ADO Errors collection. You can process the ADO Errors collection to gather additional information about any errors that your ASP Web application encounters. The following code illustrates how to use the VBScript error handler, as well as how to get error information from the ADO Errors object:

```
<%@ Language=VBScript %>
<HTML>
<HEAD>
<META NAME="GENERATOR" Content="Microsoft Visual Studio 6.0">

<LINK REL="stylesheet" TYPE="text/css"
  HREF="_Themes/sumipntg/THEME.CSS" VI6.0THEME="Sumi Painting">
```

```
<LINK REL="stylesheet" TYPE="text/css"
  HREF="_Themes/sumipntg/GRAPH0.CSS" VI6.0THEME="Sumi Painting">
<LINK REL="stylesheet" TYPE="text/css"
  HREF="_Themes/sumipntg/COLOR0.CSS" VI6.0THEME="Sumi Painting">
<LINK REL="stylesheet" TYPE="text/css"
  HREF="_Themes/sumipntg/CUSTOM.CSS" VI6.0THEME="Sumi Painting">
</HEAD>

<H4>This page demonstrates ASP error handling</H4>
<BODY>
<HR>
<%
Dim cn
Dim rs
Dim er

On Error Resume Next

Set cn = Session("Connection")

Set rs = cn.Execute("Select * From no_such_table")
rs.Close

If cn.Errors.Count > 0 Then

    For Each er In cn.Errors
        Response.Write("Number: " & er.Number)
%>
<P></P>
<%
        Response.Write("Source: " & er.Source)
%>
<P></P>
<%
        Response.Write("Text: " & er.Description)
    Next

End If

%>
<HR>
<A HREF="http://tecadev/finish.asp">
Click here to finish the ASP demonstration</A>
```

```
</BODY>
</HTML>
```

Near the beginning of this VBScript, you can see where the On Error statement is used to enable error handling. Next, a local ADO Connection object is created using the ADO Connection object that was stored in the ASP Session object. Then the Execute method of the ADO Command object is used with an invalid table name. If error handling was not active, a run-time error would occur, and the ASP application would end. However, since error handling is enabled, the program flow continues with the next statement following the Execute method.

Your VBScript code can check for ADO error information by looking at the Count property in the Errors collection. If the Count value is greater than zero, then the ADO object framework encountered some type of run-time error. Your application can extract the ADO error information by iterating through the Error collection. In the preceding example, you can see that a For Each loop is used to process all of the elements in the Errors collection contained in the ADO Connection object. The Number, Source, and Description properties are then displayed as HTML text output.

Figure 17-29 shows the resulting Web page that was generated by the preceding error-handling example.

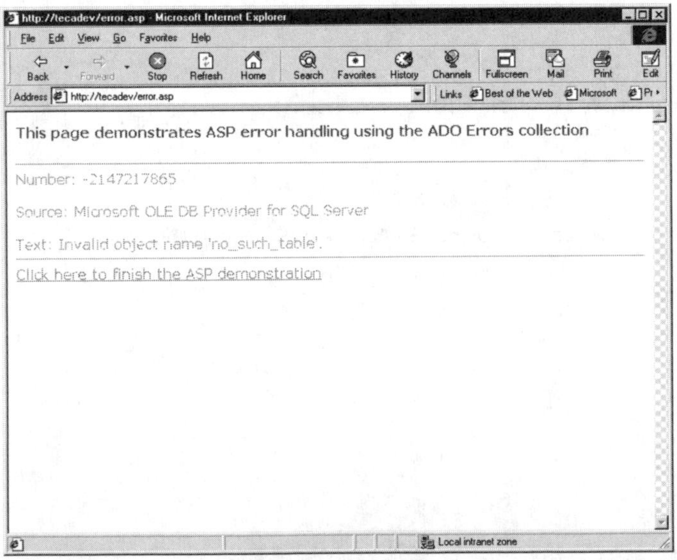

Figure 17-29. ASP and ADO error handling

WEB-DATABASE DEVELOPMENT WITH VISUAL INTERDEV

Although ASP application development can be performed with a generic Web building tool like FrontPage 98 or even a simple text editor, Microsoft's Visual InterDev is the leading tool for ASP application development. At the time of this writing, Visual InterDev 6 is the latest release of the product. This latest release of Visual InterDev includes a new database interface, as well as design-time data-bound controls that can be used to build data-driven Web pages. Like Visual Basic, Visual InterDev provides a VB-like development environment that includes a WYSIWYG Web page builder, a color-coded editor, a full-featured debugger, and a host of HTML and ActiveX tools that can help you build Web applications. Visual InterDev 6 is a sophisticated product, and complete coverage would require a book in itself. This chapter gives you a brief introduction to the features of Visual InterDev and how to use this product to build Web pages that connect to a SQL Server database. Figure 17-30 shows the Visual InterDev development environment

In the center of the screen, you can see two different development windows. One of the windows is in WYSIWYG design mode, and the other window shows the Visual InterDev code editor. The Visual InterDev Toolbox appears on the left side of the

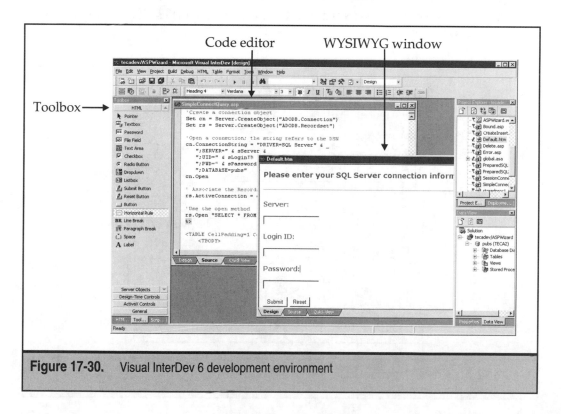

Figure 17-30. Visual InterDev 6 development environment

window. The Visual InterDev Toolbox has four sets of tabs that you can use to build Web pages. In Figure 17-30, the Toolbox shows the HTML elements. You can add these items to your Web pages simply by dragging and dropping them onto either the Visual InterDev design editor or the code editor.

On the right side of the screen are the Visual InterDev Project menu and Data View windows. The Project menu contains a list of all of the source files in the Visual InterDev project. It also allows you to deploy the project on a target Web server. The Data View window lists the databases that are connected to the Visual InterDev design environment.

Creating a new Data Connection is the first step in linking a Visual InterDev Web page with your SQL Server database. To create a Data Connection. you first right-click the global.asa item in the Visual InterDev Project window and then select Add Data Connection from the pop-up menu. The ODBC Administrator will be displayed, which allows you to either select an existing data source or create a new data source that you can use to connect to SQL Server.

TIP: In design mode, Visual InterDev connects to SQL Server directly from the system running the Visual InterDev application. At run time, the ASP application connects directly from the Web server—not the client system.

After the data source is selected, the Connection Properties dialog box shown in Figure 17-31 is displayed.

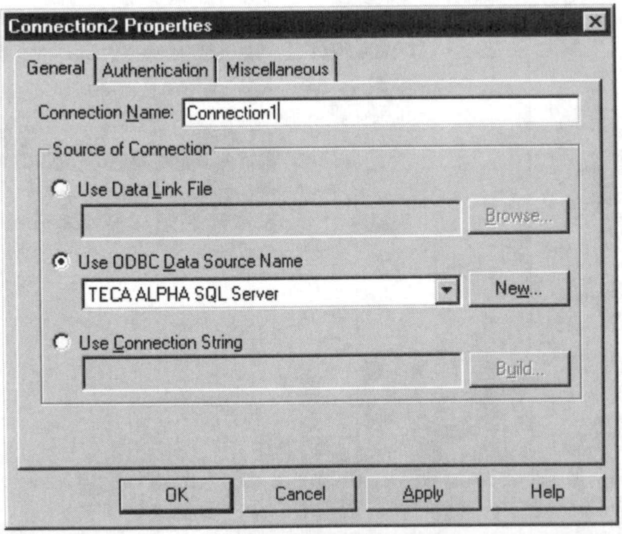

Figure 17-31.   Visual InterDev Connection Properties dialog box

In this dialog box, you can name the connection as well as select how you want to connect to the database. By default, the Connection dialog box is set to use an ODBC driver. However, you can also instruct it to use an OLE DB Provider by selecting the Use Connection String radio button and then selecting the OLE DB provider from the list that's displayed.

After the Connection is created, you can create a Visual InterDev Command object by right-clicking the Connection object and selecting Add Data Command from the pop-up menu.

NOTE: If these Visual InterDev objects seem familiar, they should. The Visual InterDev design-time objects are based on the ADO objects that were discussed earlier in this chapter.

The Command object's properties are shown in Figure 17-32. The Command dialog box allows you to name the Command object and associate it with an existing Visual InterDev Connection object. In Figure 17-32, you can see that the Command object will create a simple record set that's based on the authors table in the pubs database.

After adding the Command object to your project, Visual InterDev will automatically add all of the column names in the record set to the Visual InterDev project menu. You can then add them to your Web page simply by dragging and dropping the column objects from the Project windows onto either the Visual InterDev design or code window.

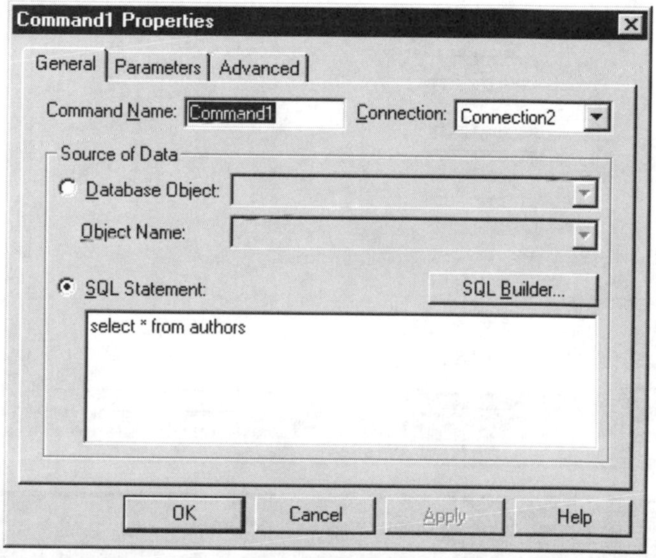

Figure 17-32.   Visual InterDev Command Properties dialog box

Figure 17-33 shows the Visual InterDev design window populated by the columns that were selected in the Command object. All of the fields that were added will automatically be bound to the design-time record set control near the top of Figure 17-33. Near the bottom of the design window, you can see the design-time record set navigation control that was dropped onto the Web page from the Visual InterDev Server objects toolbox.

NOTE: To execute Visual InterDev applications that use the design-time controls, FrontPage 98 Extensions must be installed on the Web Server.

That's all you need to do to build a simple data-driven Web page using Visual InterDev. Visual InterDev is a powerful tool that can simplify the Web creation process and reduce the amount of ASP coding required to link your Web applications to a SQL Server database.

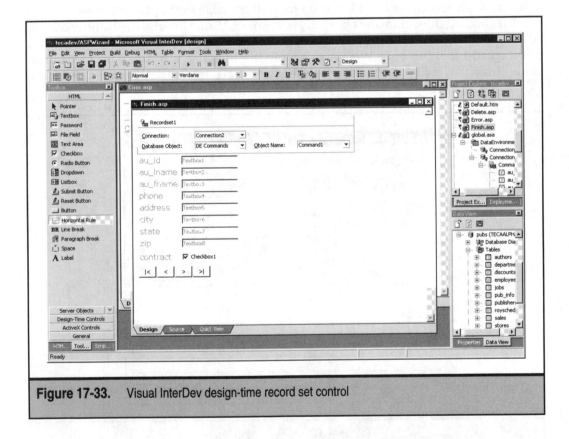

Figure 17-33. Visual InterDev design-time record set control

CONCLUSION

As you've seen in this chapter, you can integrate SQL Sever and the Web in a number of different ways. As usual, in the end, the best method to use depends on the requirements of your own Web application. For Web pages that require only static data, you can use SQL Server Web Assistant Wizard to quickly and easily copy and format SQL Server database information to an HTML Web page. For truly interactive applications that can dynamically list and update data, you can use the combination of ASP and ADO to connect your SQL Server database to the Web.

ADDITIONAL REFERENCES

For more information about using ASP and ADO, refer to the following publications:

▼   O'Neil, Joseph. *Visual InterDev 6 from the Group Up.*
     Berkeley, CA: Osborne/McGraw-Hill, 1998.

▲   Miller, Ken, ed., et al. *Inside Microsoft Visual InterDev.*
     Redmond, WA: Microsoft Press, 1997.

PART III

Appendixes

APPENDIX A

Migrating from SQL Server 6.x to 7

The changes to SQL Server 7's internal database structures make it incompatible with the prior releases of SQL Server. So in order to migrate to SQL Server 7, you must reload all of your existing data and database objects. Database migration data is both time-consuming and somewhat risky. Moving your data from one database to another requires having the available media storage either online or on tape to handle any duplicated data as well as having the processor time required to perform the necessary data conversion. In addition, anytime you move data there is a possibility of data loss. To help make the migration to SQL Server 7 as easy as possible, Microsoft has included a Version Upgrade Wizard that is able to migrate all of your existing 6.*x* database objects to 7. The Version Upgrade Wizard can migrate both SQL Server 6 and 6.5 databases to SQL Server 7.

MIGRATION OVERVIEW

The Version Upgrade Wizard is both easy to use and quite flexible. It allows the migration process to be handled in a couple of different ways. Using the Version Upgrade Wizard, you can perform the migration process on a single system or you can migrate from one system to another. You can also select how much of your database you want to migrate at a time. The Version Upgrade Wizard allows you to migrate all your databases at once, or you can select specific databases to migrate.

There are two basic migration strategies to choose from: side-by-side or computer-to-computer. Side-by-side migration refers to the process of migrating from Server 6.*x* to 7 on the same computer—where SQL Server 7 is running alongside an existing SQL Server 6.*x* installation. The computer-to-computer installation refers to performing the migration by running SQL Server 7 on a separate system from 6.*x*.

There are several factors that influence the migration that you will use. Obviously, the computer-to-computer method requires that you have an available server to run SQL Server 7. Using a separate system allows both SQL Server 6.*x* and SQL Server 7 to be active at the same time. With the side-by-side installation, both SQL Server 6.*x* and 7 are installed on the same system but only one version of SQL Server can be used at a time. To facilitate switching between the different versions, SQL Server 7 provides a very handy Switch feature that allows you to quickly change between SQL Server 6.5 and 7.

In addition to choosing where SQL Server 7 will be installed, you will also need to choose how to move the data from SQL Server 6.*x* to 7. You can transfer the database objects either using the direct pipeline method or by using the media storage method. The direct pipeline method refers to sending the data via a Named Pipes connection while the media storage method refers to storing the data on a tape or network share and then using the storage media to restore the database objects on the SQL Server 7 system. The direct pipeline method uses a custom OLE DB provider that was built expressly for performing this migration. The pipeline method takes the database objects directly from your existing 6.5 databases and converts them straight into 7 format. While the migration speed is certainly dependent on your hardware, Microsoft has reported that the Direct pipeline method can produce throughput that is greater than 1GB per hour and that they have migrated an 80GB SAP database in about 14.5 hours. The media storage method takes longer, but it can also be used in situations where there isn't enough disk space to support the direct pipeline method.

PREREQUISITES

First, the Version Upgrade Wizard will only run on SQL Server version 6 or 6.5. It can not use used directly from a SQL Server 4.x or any earlier release. If you need to convert a SQL Server 4.x system to SQL Server 7, you will first need to upgrade the system to SQL Server 6.5. Then, you can run the Version Upgrade Wizard to convert the system to SQL Server 7. In addition, the Version Upgrade Wizard requires that Service Pack 3 be installed on the SQL Server 6.5 system as well as Windows NT Service Pack 2.

Next, before you run the Version Upgrade Wizard you should be sure that there is enough disk space. Microsoft recommends that there be at least 200MB of free disk storage and that Tempdb on the SQL Server 6.5 system be sized to at least 25MB. SQL Server 7 includes a Database Information Utility that can be used to estimate the disk space required for each type of upgrade. After the upgrade process is finished and the new SQL Server 7 installation has been verified, you can remove the old SQL Server 6.5 installation to reclaim the available disk space.

Finally, prior to running the Version Upgrade Wizard, you should be sure to make a backup of your current SQL Server 6.x installation.

Using the Version Upgrade Wizard

Before running the Version Upgrade Wizard, you should shut down all the applications that are dependent on SQL Server as well as all the SQL Server services, such as replication. The MSSQLService itself can be running or stopped. In addition, Microsoft recommends that the administrator's default database be set to master. After all the prerequisites have been taken care of and an upgrade method has been selected, you are ready to run the Version Upgrade Wizard. The following section of this appendix will describe how to use the Version Upgrade Wizard in an example side-by-side upgrade.

In a side-by-side installation, SQL Server 7 must first be installed on the SQL Server 6.x system that will be upgraded. During the installation, the Version Upgrade Wizard is added to the Microsoft SQL Server - Switch (Common) submenu that's available from the system's Start menu. When the Version Upgrade Wizard is started, it first displays a brief welcome screen. Clicking the Next button displays the first real Version Upgrade Wizard screen, which is shown in Figure A-1.

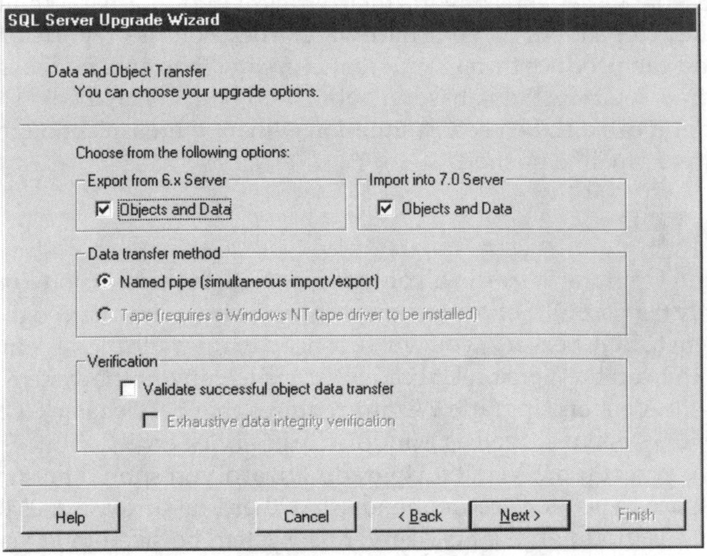

Figure A-1. The Version Upgrade Wizard Data and Object Transfer screen

The Version Upgrade Wizard screen shown in Figure A-1 allows you to select the types of objects that will be migrated from SQL Server 6.x to SQL Server 7. You can choose to migrate database objects, data, or both. In addition, this Wizard screen allows you to select the data transfer option that will be used. In Figure A-1 you can see that the options in the Wizard are set to transfer both database objects and data. In addition, the transfer will use Named Pipes for a direct pipeline type of transfer. The verification options allow you to choose the level of database validation that will be performed during the upgrade process. Selecting the verification option causes the DBCC (Database Consistency Checker) to be run for each object transferred. After all the data transfer options have been set, clicking the Next button displays the server logon windows shown in Figure A-2.

The Logon screen of the Version Upgrade Wizard allows you to enter the authentication information for the sa administrator's logon. The logon information entered in the top portion of the screen is used for the source SQL Server 6.x system, while the logon information in the lower portion of window is used for the target SQL Server 7 system. In both cases, the logon is used for the sa account. In addition, since the Version Upgrade Wizard starts each of the SQL Server systems, this screen also includes the ability to pass startup parameters to both the SQL Server 6.x and 7 systems.

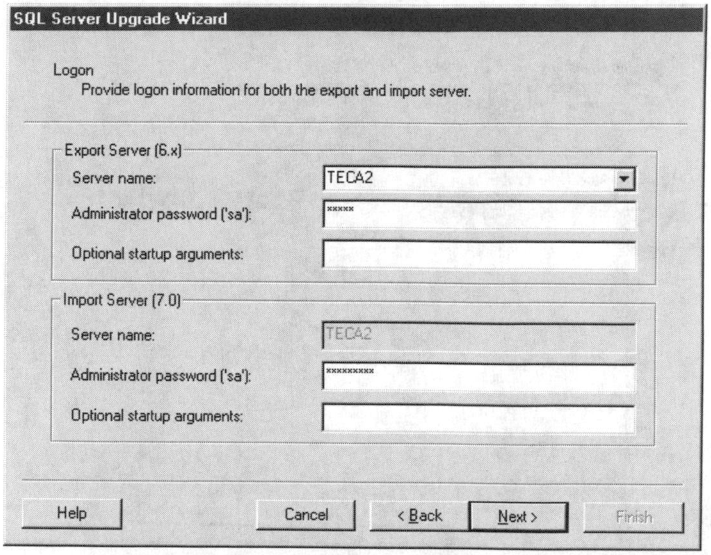

Figure A-2.   The Logon screen

After entering the logon information, clicking the Next button automatically switches to the SQL Server 6.x system and displays the switching message box shown here:

While the switching message is displayed, the Version Upgrade Wizard starts the SQL Server 6.x system and checks for the required service pack level. After the system has successfully started, the database selection window shown in Figure A-3 is displayed.

By default, all of the databases on the SQL Server 6.x system will be automatically included in the list of databases to be converted. If you want to convert all the databases at once, you would then just click the Next button to proceed to the next Version Upgrade

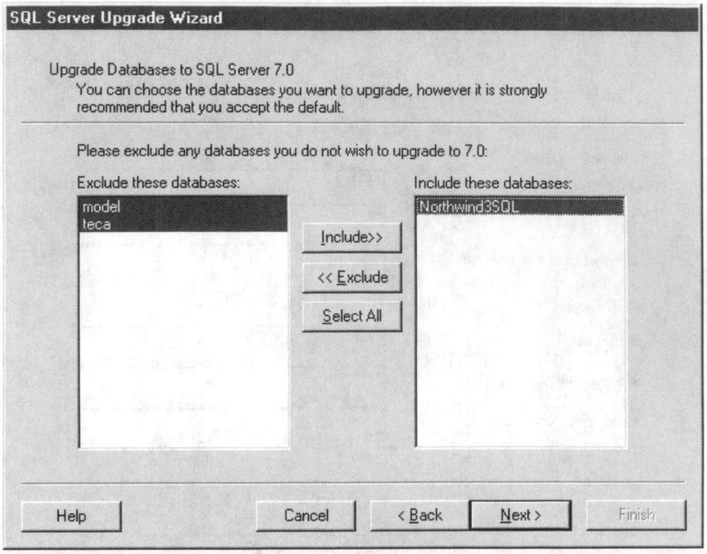

Figure A-3. The database selection screen

Wizard screen. If don't want to convert all your databases at once, you can highlight the databases that you don't want to convert from the list on the right and then click the Exclude button. The selected databases will be removed from the list on the right and moved into the list of excluded databases on the left. In Figure A-3 you can see that the sample Northwind database has been selected for migration. After selecting the SQL Server 6.x database to migrate, clicking the Next button displays the Database Creation screen shown in Figure A-4.

The next screen presented by the Version Upgrade Wizard controls how the databases will be created on the SQL Server 7 system. The default option maintains the same database names and objects that were used on the SQL Server 6.x system. You can also choose to migrate the SQL Server 6.x database objects and data into an existing SQL Server 7 database, or you can run a custom SQL script to convert the data. Each time the Version Upgrade Wizard is run, it generates several SQL scripts that control the conversion process. These scripts are saved in the \Mssql7\Upgrade directory. Although it isn't necessary for the vast majority of migrations, you can manually modify these scripts to customize the migration process. Clicking the Next button displays the Version Upgrade Wizard's System Configuration screen, shown in Figure A-5.

The System Configuration screen governs the migration of your system configuration objects. The top portion of the screen allows you to migrate your server configuration objects, your replication objects, and any existing SQL Executive settings that are

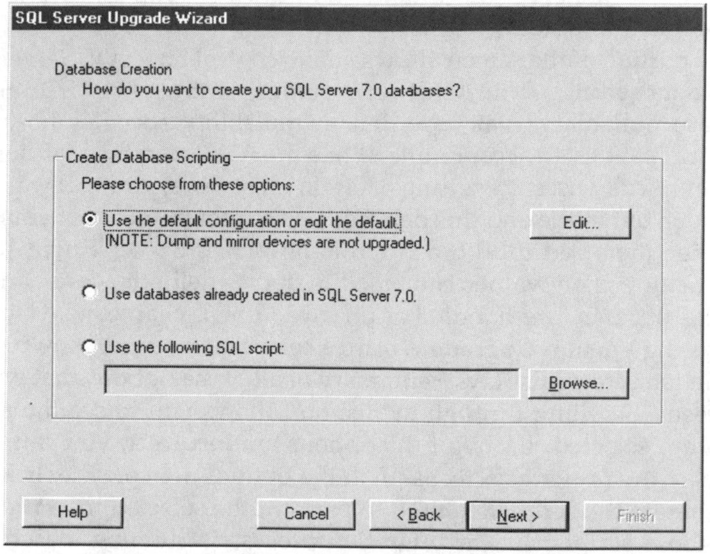

Figure A-4.   The Database Creation screen

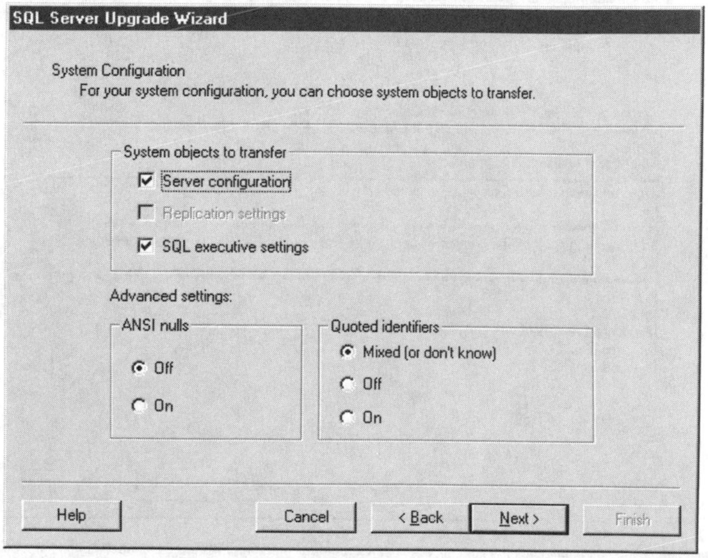

Figure A-5.   The System Configuration screen

configured in your SQL Server 6.*x* system. In most cases, you will want to migrate all these setting to the new system.

The bottom portion of the screen allows you to control how SQL Server 7 will handle the advanced data settings. The ANSI nulls setting controls how SQL Server 7 treats default database nullability. Database default nullability specifies how the database handles a column's ability to accept nulls. While the ANSI standard for this setting is on, SQL Server 6.*x* typically uses the setting of off. In most cases, you will want to accept the default off setting, but in the end this depends on the requirements of your applications. The Quoted identifiers radio button controls how SQL Server 7 will handle quoted strings. If this setting is on, values contained in quotes delimiters are handled as string variables. If it is off, they are handled as an invalid SQL characters. Clicking the Next button displays the Version Upgrade Wizard's completion screen shown in Figure A-6.

The completion screen displays a summary of all of the options that were selected in the earlier screens. Scrolling through the list box allows you to see the entire range of options that were selected. If any of the options are incorrect, you can click the Back button to display the previous screens. If all the options are correct, clicking the Finish button will generate the scripts required to perform the selected migration options and then execute those scripts. As the migration process is running, its current status is displayed in the screen presented in Figure A-7.

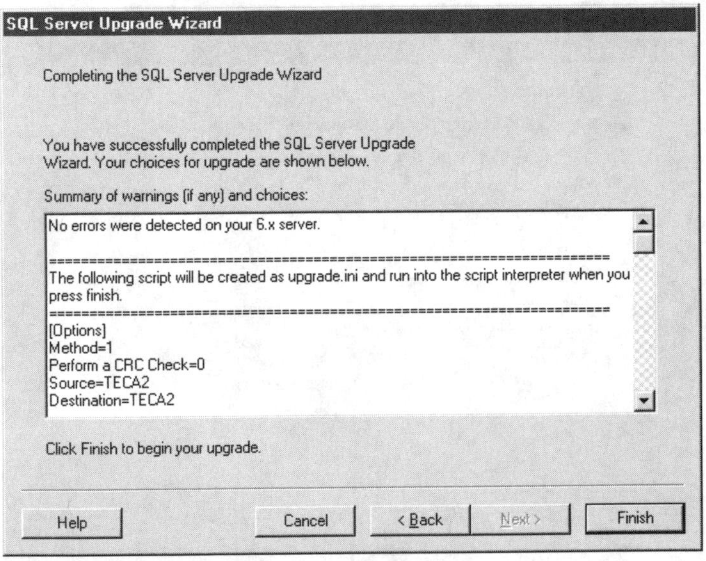

Figure A-6.   The completion screen

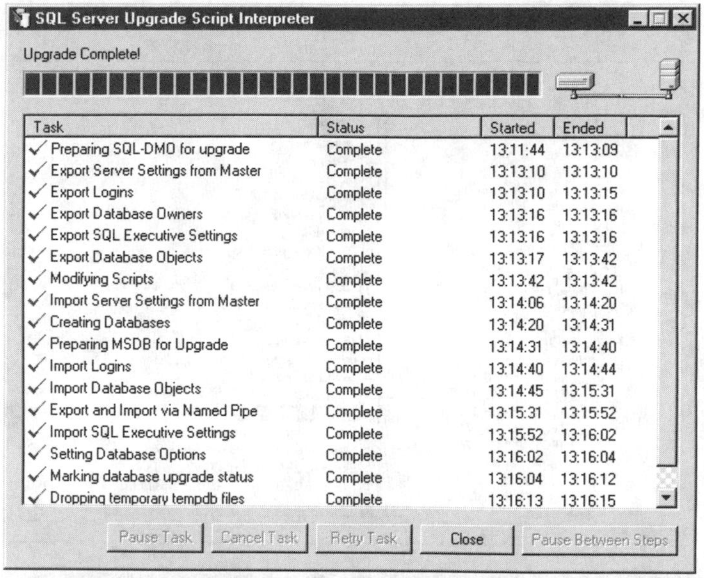

Figure A-7.   The migration status screen

All of the completed steps are presented with a check mark next to the task's description. The currently executing task is identified with a stoplight icon. For a typical migration process, the number of tasks will typically fill the entire list shown in the migration status screen.

Each time the Version Upgrade Wizard is run, a new directory is created under the \Mssql7\Ugrades directory. The new directory is created using a concatenation of the name of the SQL Server system combined with a date and time stamp. Figure A-8 displays the contents of the \Mssql7\Upgrade directory following several runs of the Version Upgrade Wizard.

The Explorer view of the \Mssql7\Upgrade directory in Figure A-8 shows the Version Upgrade Wizard output following five different migration runs. A subdirectory for each database migrated is listed under the time-stamped subdirectory.

The migration actions performed and the results of those actions are all recorded in the various .out files that are contained in the migration subdirectory. You can use these

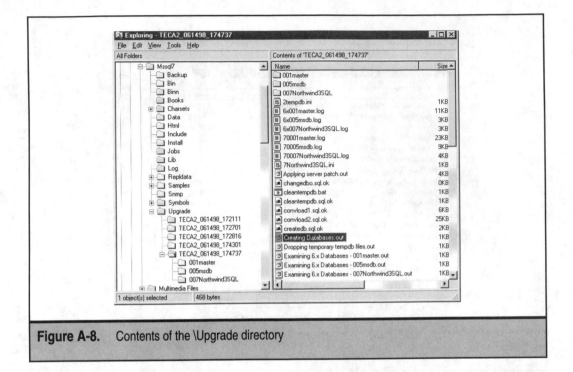

Figure A-8. Contents of the \Upgrade directory

files to help diagnose conversion errors or to create custom scripts. The following listing shows an example of the Create Databases.out script:

```
Initializing SQL/DMO...

Running with QuotedIdentifiers = Mixed

Reading script file as Unicode file

Connecting to server...

ANSI NULLS = 0
Running script statements...
UNICODE byte order mark detected. All i/o will be UNICODE...


=====================================================================
 EXECStmt Summary
=====================================================================
Statements Executed:   5
Passed:    5
Failed:    0
```

CONCLUSION

While reloading databases is never fun, the Version Upgrade Wizard goes a long way toward helping to make this necessary task faster and easier. The default settings used by the Version Upgrade Wizard will be adequate for most migrations. However, being script driven, the upgrade process is pretty flexible and can also support custom upgrade scenarios.

APPENDIX B

Maximum Capacities

The tables in this appendix summarize the maximum capacities and numbers for the various SQL Server 7 database objects and Transact-SQL.

DATABASE CAPACITIES

Databases

Category	Capacity
Database size	1,048,516 terabytes
Files per database	32,767
File size (data)	32 terabytes
File size (log)	4 terabytes
Objects in a database	2,147,483,647
Identifier length	128

Tables

Category	Capacity
Tables per database	Limited by the number of objects in a database
Rows per table	Limited by available storage
Primary Key constraints per table	1
Foreign Key constraints per table	63
Foreign Key table references per table	63
Triggers per table	Limited by the number of objects in a database
Clustered indexes per table	1
Nonclustered indexes per table	250
Constraints per table	250
Unique constraints per table	250 nonclustered, 1 clustered

Columns

Category	Capacity
Columns per index	16
Columns per primary key	16
Columns per foreign key	16
Columns per table	1,024
Index key size (in bytes)	900
Bytes per character or binary column	8,000
Bytes per text, ntext, or image column	2GB
Bytes per row	8,060
Bytes per index	900
Bytes per primary key	900
Bytes per foreign key	900

SQL CAPACITIES

Category	Capacity
Batch size	128 × network packet size
Tables per Select statement	32
Bytes in source text of a stored procedure	Batch size
Parameters per stored procedure	1,024
Nested subqueries	64
Nested trigger levels	32
Columns per Select statement	4,096
Columns per Insert statement	1,024
Bytes per Group By statement	8,060
Bytes per Order By statement	8,060

Index

Note: Page numbers in *italics* refer to illustrations or charts.

Numbers and Symbols

1NF (first normal form), relational database model, 358, *359*

2NF (second normal form), relational database model, 361

3NF (third normal form), relational database model, 361–362

4NF (fourth normal form), relational database model, 362

5NF (fifth normal form), relational database model, 363–364

% (percent sign), Like conditions and SQL Select statements, 491–492

* (asterisk), SQL Select statements, 446, 447, 452, 493

@ (at sign), stored procedures, 521

#include statements, ADO and ASP, 903

▼ A

Access. *See* Microsoft Access

Access methods counters, Performance Monitor, *270–271*

ActiveConnection property (ADO)
    ASP and, 895
    ForwardOnly-Recordset objects, 775
    KeysetRecordset objects, 780
    prepared SQL statements and Command objects, 786

ActiveX Data Objects. *See* ADO

Add Data Connection command, Visual InterDev, 922

Add Hyperlinks to Web Page dialog box, Web Assistant Wizard, 867–869

Add Log File clause, Transact-SQL DDL, 400

Add to Alert dialog box, Performance Monitor alert view, 284, *285*

Add to Chart dialog box, Performance Monitor chart view, *279*

Add to Log dialog box, Performance Monitor log view, 285, *287*

Add to Report dialog box, Performance Monitor report view, 288–289

AddNew method
    inserting rows with RDO, 738–739
    SQLPassThrough (DAO), 624–626

administration, 27–116
    Enterprise Manager, 19–22, 39–116
    SQL Server installations, 28–39

administrative components, 19–26
  command-line utilities, 26
  Distributed Transaction
    Coordinator, 22
  DTS (Data Transformation
    Services), 24–25
  Enterprise Manager, 19–22,
    39–116
  Query Analyzer, 22–23
  SQL Performance Monitor,
    23–24, *25*
  SQL Server Profiler, 23, *24*
  SQL-DMO (Distributed
    Management Objects), 25,
    317–344
  wizards, 22
Administrator, ODBC API, 685,
  686–687
Administrator user name, security,
  126
ADO (ActiveX Data Objects),
  762–811
  adding 2.1 reference to Visual
    Basic, 765–766
  advanced database functions,
    801–811
  architecture overview,
    764–765
  batch updates, 801–803
  Command objects, 764–765,
    784–788, 793–799
  connecting to SQL Server,
    767–773
  Connection objects, 764,
    767–775, 805–807
  error handling, 800–801
  Errors collection, 765
  modifying data with, 788–797
  multiple result sets, 803–805
  network components, 762,
    763
  object hierarchy, *764*
  ODBC Driver Manager,
    762–763
  OLE DB and, 759–762
  OLE DB files and, 763
  overview, 762–763
  Properties collection, 765
  Recordset objects, 764,
    773–784, 789–793
  storing binary data, 807–811
  transactions, 805–807
  updating data with Recordset
    objects, 789–793

Visual Basic applications,
    766–801
  See also DAO (Data Access
    Objects)
ADO (ASP and), 882–920
  ActiveConnection property,
    895
  Close method, 884, 887
  Command objects and
    prepared SQL statements,
    891–899
  connecting to SQL Server,
    882–884
  Connection objects, 883, 894
  CreateObject method, 883
  CreateParameter method,
    895–896
  deleting rows from Recordset
    objects, 909–910
  error handling, 918–920
  executing stored procedures
    with Command objects,
    910–918
  <FORM> tags, 894
  #include statements, 903
  inserting rows in Recordset
    objects, 900–904
  modifying data with, 899–910
  OLE DB providers and,
    882–883
  On Error statements, 904,
    918–920
  Option Explicit statements,
    903, 908
  parameters, 895–896
  PreparedSQL2.asp source
    code, 896–899
  Recordset objects, 884–887,
    900–910
  <SELECT> tags, 894, 899
  Session object, 888–890
  session scoped connections,
    888–890
  updating rows with
    Recordset objects, 905–908
advanced ADO database functions,
  801–811
  batch updates, 801–803
  multiple result sets, 803–805
  storing binary data, 807–811
  transactions, 805–807
advanced ODBCDirect database
  functions, 672–679

advanced RDO topics, 748–754
  asynchronous queries,
    750–752
  managing data concurrency,
    753–754
  multiple result sets, 748–750
  server-side cursors, 752–753
Agent. *See* SQL Server Agent
Agent History option, Push
  Subscription Wizard (merge
  replication), 219, *220*
aggregate functions, SQL Select
  statements, 471–473
Alert Options dialog box,
  Performance Monitor alert view,
  283, *284*
Alert Properties dialog box, SQL
  Server Agent, 97–99
Alert System tab, SQL Server
  Agent, 92, *93*
alert view (Performance Monitor),
  282–285
  Add to Alert dialog box, 284,
    285
  Alert Options dialog box,
    283, *284*
  deleting alerts, 284
  log files, 283
  saving alerts, 284
alerts, creating with SQL Server
  Agent, 96–98
algebraic operations (relational
  database model), 367–376
  commutative operations, 370
  derived attributes, 375, *376*
  difference, 367, *368*
  direct attributes, 375
  division, 370
  equijoin, 373
  inner join, 373–374
  intersection, 367, *368*
  join, 370, 373
  natural join, 373
  outer join, 374
  product, 367, *368*
  projection, 370
  relational calculus, 374
  selection, 370
  set operations examples,
    369–370
  special operations examples,
    371–373
  theta-join, 373
  union, 367, *368*
  union compatibility, 370

Venn diagrams, *368*
view relations, 374–376
virtual attributes, 375, *376*
aliases, table, 482–483
allocation (ODBC API)
    database connection
        handles, 697–698
    environments, 696
    statement handles, 701
Alter Database statements, 400–401
Alter Procedure statements, stored
    procedures, 520
Alter Table statements, 416–418
    columns, 417–418
    constraints, 416–417
Alter Trigger statements, 540
ANSI SQL-92 standard
    setting maximal
        compatibility, 71–72
    SQL statements and, 397
Application objects, ASP, 879
application roles, permissions, 167
applications, database. *See*
    database applications
applications development, Visual
    InterDev, 921–924
architecture
    client/server, 6–7
    DAO, 594–596
    database. *See* database
        architecture
    networking. *See* networking
        architecture
    ODBC API, 683–685
    ODBCDirect, 650–652
    OLE DB, 759–762
    RDO, 721–723
    SQL Server, 4–7
archival backups, 185
articles
    Create Publication Wizard
        (merge replication), *209*
    replication, 202
As clause
    Grant statements, 436
    table hints, 312
ASP (ActiveX Server Pages),
    875–920
    ADO objects and, 882–920
    Application objects, 879
    network components, *877*
    object model, 878–879
    overview, 875–881
    Request objects, 879
    ScriptingContext objects, 879

Server objects, 879
Session objects, 879
VBScript and, 875, 880–881
Web-database integration,
    876
See also Web Assistant
    Wizard
assignment statements
    relational database model,
        367
    stored procedures, 524–525
associations, ERD (Entity
    Relationship Diagram), 382–384
asynchronous operations,
    ODBCDirect, 674–676
asynchronous queries, advanced
    RDO topics, 750–752
Attachments dialog box, Visual
    Data Manager, *602*
attribute integrity, relational
    database model, 365
attributes
    relational database model,
        354–355, 356–357
    retrieving column
        (SQL-DMO), 341–343
authentication modes, 127
    See also security
average response time, database
    performance, 234

▼ B

backup device counters,
    Performance Monitor, *271*
Backup Device Properties dialog
    box, restoring backed-up
    databases, *189*
backups, 173–197
    archival, 185
    backup copies and retention
        periods, 185–187
    Backup Database statements,
        180
    Backup Log statements, 182
    database, 178–180
    Database Maintenance Plan
        Wizard dialog box,
        112–113, *114*
    database objects and,
        175–188
    DBCC statements and,
        177–178
    default filegroups and, 175

devices, 176–177
    differential, 180
    events requiring system
        database, 183–184
    events requiring user
        database, 184
    master database, 183–184
    New Device dialog box, *177*
    organizing, 183–188
    overview, 174–175
    periodic, 184–185
    reasons for, 174–175
    restoring databases, 188–196
    retention periods of backup
        copies, 185–187
    scheduling, 182
    server options, 196–197
    SQL Server Backup dialog
        box, 178, *179*
    SQL Server Properties dialog
        box, 196, *197*
    standby servers and,
        197–198
    striped, 180
    striped in restore operations,
        188
    transaction logs and,
        175–176, 181–183, 188
    truncating transaction logs,
        182–183
    user database, 184
    user-defined filegroups and,
        175
Bang notation, rdoResultsets and
    prepared SQL statements, 736
base tables, Transact-SQL DDL,
    392
Basic conditions, SQL Select
    statements, 487–489
batch updates, advanced ADO
    database functions, 801–803
Between conditions, SQL Select
    statements, 489
binary data, storing via advanced
    ADO database functions,
    807–811
BintoFile subroutine, storing
    binary data, 810–811
BLOBs (binary large objects),
    storing binary data, 807
blocks, stored procedure
    statement, 525
Books Online tool, described, *30*
bound columns and SQLBindCol
    function, ODBC API, 707–708

buffer manager counters, Performance Monitor, 272
Bulk Copy tool, described, *30*
business intelligence, data warehousing, 221

▼ C

cache manager counters, Performance Monitor, *272–273*
calling stored procedures
    DAO QueryDef objects, 638–645
    ODBC API, 714–716
calling stored procedures with Web Assistant Wizard, 871–874
    Select Stored Procedure dialog box, *872*
    Set Stored Procedure Parameters dialog box, *873*
    titling page, *871*
candidate keys, data integrity (relational database model), 366
Cascade keyword, permissions, 437
Case structures, SQL Select statements, 497–498
catalog, SQL, 438–439
categories
    Enterprise Manager Current Activity, 289–292
    event, 244, *245–252*
character strings, SQL scalar functions, 456–458
chart view (Performance Monitor), 277–282
    Add to Chart dialog box, *279*
    Chart Options dialog box, *280*
    Data From dialog box, *281*
    deleting counters from, 280
    exporting charts, 281
    histogram, *278*
    Input Log File Timeframe dialog box, *282*
    line graph, *277*
    log files, 281–282, 283
    saving, 280–281
Check constraints, 17, 414–415
    column-level, 414
    table-level, 415
classes, event, 244, *245–252*
Client Configuration tool, described, *31*

client files
    DAO, 594
    SQL-DMO, 327
client/server architecture, 6–7
Close method
    ADO and ASP, 884, 887
    ADO Connection objects, 773
    ADO Recordset objects, 784–787
    connecting DAO to SQL Server, 607
    connecting ODBCDirect to SQL Server, 655, 657
    DAO Recordset objects, 623
    RDO, 727, 729, 733
    See also disconnecting from data sources
closing all connections, SQLExit subroutine, 824
closing Jet engine, 647
clustered indexes, 15, *16*, 431
coding suggestions, DML, 544–545
collection objects (SQL-DMO), 332–335
    iterating through, 334
    referencing specific, 334–335
column attributes (SQL-DMO), retrieving, 341–343
column data types, Transact-SQL DDL, *405–408*
column definitions
    Showplan_All command, *302–303*
    Transact-SQL DDL, 404–412
column filters, Profiler Filters tab, *260–261*
column-level Check constraints, 414
column-level permissions, 164–165, 437
columns, 14–15
    Alter Table statements, 417–418
    bound and SQLBindCol function, 707–708
    capacities, 943
    computed, 411–412
    constraints, 15–18
    default values, 18
    defined, 14
    derived, 426–427
    Global Unique Identifier (GUIDs), 408–409
    listing (SQL-DMO), 339–341
    manipulating, 417–418

Profiler Data Columns tab, 253–260
    reordering and renaming, 426
    unbound and SQLGetData function, 705–707
ColWidth property, ADO ForwardOnlyRecordset objects, 778–779
Command objects (ADO), 764–765, 784–799
    ASP and prepared SQL statements, 891–899
    ASP and stored procedures, 910–918
    CreateTable function and dynamic SQL statements, 787–788
    deleting data with prepared SQL statements and, 796–797
    dynamic SQL statements and, 787–788
    executing dynamic SQL statements with, 787–788
    executing stored procedures with ASP and, 910–918
    executing stored procedures with, 797–799
    inserting rows with prepared SQL statements and, 793–795
    prepared SQL statements and, 784–787, 795–796, 891–899
    stored procedures and, 797–799, 910–918
    Visual InterDev and, 923–924
Command Properties dialog box, Visual InterDev, *923*
command-line utilities, administrative components, 26
CommandPS subroutine, prepared SQL statements and ADO Command objects, 785–786
Commit statements, transaction integrity, 516–518
CommitRollBack function, DB-Library transactions, 855–856
committing transactions
    ADO, 806–807
    ODBCDirect, 677–678
commutative operations, relational database model, 370

complex SQL Select statements, 479–487
 correlation names, 482–483
 equijoins, 482
 inner joins, 483
 multiple tables in From clause, 479–485
 outer joins, 483–485
 sample retrieving using cross product, *479–481*
 table aliases, 482–483
 Union keyword, 485–487
 Where clause, 482
compound conditions, views, 425–426
Compute clause, SQL Select statements, 505–506
computed columns, Transact-SQL DDL, 411–412
computer-to-computer migrations, Version Upgrade Wizard, 928
concurrency, data. *See* data concurrency
concurrent updates and table locks (DML), 515–518
 Commit and Rollback statements, 516–518
 exclusive locks, 515
 explicit transactions, 516, 518
 implicit transactions, 516–517
 shared locks, 515
 table hints, 515
 transaction integrity, 516–518
conditional execution, stored procedures, 526–527
conditions and subqueries, SQL Select statements, 487–497
conditions and three-valued logic, SQL Select statements, 450–451
configuring data sources, connecting Microsoft Access to SQL Server, 555–561
Connect method, SQL-DMO, 330–331, 336–337
Connect property, DAO QueryDef objects, 637, 644
connecting ADO and ASP to SQL Server, 882–884

connecting ADO to SQL Server, 767–773
 Close method, 773
 Connection objects, 767–770
 MSDASQL OLE DB provider, 767, 768–770
 MSDASQL prompt constants, 768, *770*
 ODBC, 767–772
 OLE DB connection string keywords, *769*
 OLE DB providers, 767–772
 opening connections with OLE DB provider for SQL Server, 772
 opening DSN-less connections with OLE DB provider for ODBC, 771
 Properties collection, 769
 SQLOLEDB OLE DB provider, 767
connecting DAO to SQL Server, 599–607
 Close method, 607
 DSN-less connections, 606–607
 linked tables, 599, 601–604
 OpenDatabase method, 602, 604–606
 overview, 599
 Visual Data Manager, 600–603
connecting DB-Library to SQL Server, 820–824
 closing connection libraries, 824
 GetComputerName function, 822
 GetSystemName function, 821–822
 SQLClose function, 824
 SQLOpen function, 822–824
 SQLOpenConnection function, 820–822
connecting Microsoft Access to SQL Server, 553–567
 configuring data sources, 555–561
 Create New Data Source dialog box, *558*
 Create a New Data Source to SQL Server dialog box, *558, 559, 560*

installing SQL Server ODBC driver, 554–555
 linking tables, 561–567
 ODBC Data Source Administrator, *557*
 requirements, 553–554
connecting ODBCDirect to SQL Server, 653–657
 Close method, 655, 657
 DSN-less connections, 656–657
 OpenConnection method, 655–657
 OpenDatabase method, 653–654
Connection objects (ADO), 764, 767–784, 805–807
 ASP and, 883, 894
 connecting ADO to SQL Server, 767–770
 ForwardOnlyRecordset objects and, 774–775
 opening connections with OLE DB Provider for SQL Server, 772–773
 opening DSN-less connections with OLE DB Provider for ODBC, 771
 Recordset objects and, 773–784
 transactions, 805–807
Connection objects (ODBCDirect), 659
 asynchronous operations, 674–676
Connection Properties dialog box, Visual InterDev, 922
connection string keywords
 OLE DB, *769*
 OpenDatabase method, *606*
 RDO OpenConnection method, *728*
Connection tab, SQL Server Agent, 93, *95*
ConnectionQuery function, ODBCDirect, 659
connections
 closing all with SQLExit subroutine, 824
 DSN-less. *See* DSN-less connections
Connections tab, SQL Server Properties dialog box, 59–62

constants, SQL Select statements and, 453–454

constraints, 15–18, 412–415
- Alter Table statements, 416–417
- Check, 17, 414–415
- disabling for replication, 415
- DRI (Declarative Referential Integrity), 16
- extended stored procedures, 19
- Foreign Key, 16
- key, 412–414
- manipulating, 416–417
- Not Null, 17
- Primary Key, 16
- referential integrity, 16
- rules and, 18
- stored procedures, 18–19
- Unique Key, 17

consumers and providers, OLE DB, 759, 760

core object hierarchy, SQL-DMO, 319–321

correlated references, SQL Select statements Exists conditions, 493

correlated subqueries, SQL Select statements Exists conditions, 493

correlation names, complex SQL Select statements, 482–483

counters, Performance Monitor, 270–276

CountStoreQty stored procedure, executing with ADO Command objects, 797–799

Create Database command, 398

Create Index statements, 429–433
- options, 431–433

Create a New Data Source to SQL Server dialog box, connecting Microsoft Access to SQL Server, 558, 559, 560

Create New Index dialog box, table tasks, 78

Create Procedure statements, stored procedures, 519

Create Publication Wizard (merge replication), 205–211
- articles, 209
- Choose Distributor dialog box, 206, 207
- Choose Publication Name and Description dialog box, 209, 210

Choose Publication Type dialog box, 207
- Completion screen, 211
- Distributors, 206
- master databases, 206
- Specify Articles dialog box, 209
- Specify Subscriber Types dialog box, 208
- Subscribers, 208
- Use Default Properties of the Publication dialog box, 210, 211
- Welcome screen, 206

Create Rule statements, named rules, 415

Create Schema statements, 416

Create Table statements, 401–403, 404, 415
- Niladic functions, 411

Create Trace Wizard
- Index Tuning Wizard and, 293
- Profiler, 266–267, 268

Create Trigger statements, 536–539

Create View statements, 418–419
- With Check option, 424–425

CreateObject method, ADO and ASP, 883

CreateParameter method
- ADO and ASP, 895–896
- prepared SQL statements and ADO Command objects, 786

CreatePreparedStatement method, rdoResultsets and prepared SQL statements, 734

CreateQueryDef method
- DAO QueryDef objects, 637, 644–645
- parameterized DAO QueryDef objects, 634–635
- retrieving data with ODBCDirect, 662

CreateTable function
- dynamic SQL, 831–832
- dynamic SQL statements and ADO Command objects, 787–788

CreateWorkspace method, ODBCDirect, 652

Cube Wizard (data warehousing), 226–231
- Completion screen, 228, 229
- Cube Editor, 432–433

dimensions, 228, 229
- measures, 226, 228
- Select Dimensions dialog box, 228, 229
- Select Fact Table dialog box, 226, 227
- Select Measures dialog box, 226, 228
- Welcome screen, 226, 227

Current Activity categories (Enterprise Manager), 289–292
- Locks/Object category, 291, 292
- Locks/Process ID category, 290
- object lock modes, 291
- object lock types, 290
- Process Details dialog box, 291, 292
- Process Info category, 289–290

CursorDelete subroutine, deleting rows with cursors (DB-Library), 846

cursors, 528–533
- ADO Recordset objects, 773–774
- Fetch statement positioning keywords, 529, 530
- insensitive, 530
- options, 531–532
- overview, 528–529
- parameters and variables, 533
- RDO, 730–731, 737–740
- scrollable, 529
- server-side and RDO, 752–753
- stored procedures and, 528–533
- updateable, 530–531

cursors (DB-Library), 836–846
- CursorAdd subroutine, 838
- deleting rows, 846
- DisplayCursorGrid function, 840–843
- displaying data, 840–844
- fetch buffer, 836, 837
- inserting rows, 838–840
- keyset overview, 836
- overview, 836–837
- SQLCursor function, 840
- SQLCursorClose function, 844
- SQLCursorFetch function, 843

SQLCursorInfo function, 842
SQLCursorOpen function,
  839–840
SQLCursorRowStatus
  function, 843
types of, *837*
updating rows, 844–845
CursorUpdate subroutine,
  updating rows with cursors
  (DB-Library), 844–845

▼ **D**

Damaged databases, restoring,
  188–194
DAO (Data Access Objects),
  591–648
    architecture, 594–596
    client files, 594
    connecting to SQL Server,
      599–607
    creating DBEngine objects,
      598
    creating Workspace objects,
      598–599
    database objects, 594, 596
    DBEngine objects, 594, 596,
      598
    DisplayDAOError
      subroutine, 646–647
    error handling, 645–647
    Errors collections, 596,
      646–647
    Errors objects, 594, 646–647
    installing version 3.5
      reference to Visual Basic,
      597, *598*
    Jet engine, 592–593
    networking components,
      592–593
    object hierarchy, 594–596
    ODBCDirect and, 648–679
    On Error statements,
      645–646
    overview, 592–596
    performance tips, 647–648
    QueryDef objects, 595,
      631–645
    Recordset objects, 595,
      607–623
    retrieving data with, 607–618
    ShowError subroutine,
      645–646

SQLPassThrough, 623–631
TableDef objects, 594
Workspace objects, 594,
  598–599
See also ADO; ODBC;
  ODBCDirect
DAO Recordsets, VBA code
  modules and Microsoft Access,
  581–582
Data Columns tab (Profiler),
  253–260
    available trace data columns,
      253–256
    event-specific data column
      contents, *256–259*
    Selected data list, 260
    Trace Properties dialog box,
      253
data concurrency
    advanced RDO topics,
      753–754
    ODBC API, 713–714
Data Cube Service, Microsoft Data
  Warehousing Framework, 223
Data Definition Languages. *See*
  DDLs
data explosions, data warehousing,
  221
Data From dialog box
    Performance Monitor chart
      view, *281*
    Performance Monitor log
      view, 288
data integrity (relational database
  model), 365–367
    attribute integrity, 365
    candidate keys, 366
    entity integrity, 365–366
    foreign keys, 366–367
    primary keys, 366
    referential integrity, 366–367
Data Manipulation Language. *See*
  DML
data manipulation (relational
  database model), 367–377
    algebraic operations,
      367–376
    assignment operation, 367
data marts, data warehousing, 221
Data and Object Transfer dialog
  box, Version Upgrade Wizard,
  930
Data Source Names. *See* DSN
  Configuration Wizard; DSN-less
  connections

data sources
    connecting Microsoft Access
      to SQL Server, 555–561
    linking Microsoft Access
      tables to SQL Server,
      563–565
    ODBC API, 685–693, 698–700
data structures, relational database
  model, 354–357
Data in Table dialog box, 83–85
Data Transformation Services. *See*
  DTS
data type conversion, scalar
  functions (SQL), 455
Data View window, Visual
  InterDev, 922
data warehousing, 221–231
    business intelligence, 221
    Cube Wizard, 226–231
    data explosions, 221
    data marts, 221
    dimensions, 221
    DSS Analysis Server, 224
    installing OLAP Services,
      225
    measures, 221
    Microsoft Data Warehousing
      Framework, 222–223
    OLAP (OnLine Analytical
      Processing), 221–223
    OLAP Manager, 225–226
    OLAP services, 224–225
    overview, 200, 221
    PivotTable Service, 223, 225
    SQL Server components for,
      224–225
database applications
    developing with DB-Library,
      811–857
    developing with Microsoft
      Access, 547–590
    developing NT . *See* RDO
      (Remote Database Objects)
    developing with OLE DB
      and ADO, 757–811
database architecture, 9–19
    database objects, 12–19
    default databases, *11*
    master database, 10
    model database, 10
    msdb database, 11
    Northwind database, 12
    pubs database, 11
    servers, 9–10
    tempdb database, 11

database connection handles, ODBC API, 697–698

Database Creation screen, Version Upgrade Wizard, *933*

database development, Visual InterDev, 921–924

Database Diagrammer tool, described, *31*

database folders, Enterprise Manager, 74

database functions, advanced ADO, 801–811

Database Maintenance Plan Wizard dialog box, 110–115
    backups, 112–113, *114*
    history data, 113, *115*
    integrity checks, 112
    optimization, 110–112
    reports, 113, *114*
    transaction logs, 113

database management systems. *See* DBMSs

Database object, DAO, 594

database object hierarchy, SQL-DMO, 321–323

database objects, 12–19
    alternatives to SQL statements for creating, 397
    backups, 175–188
    columns, 14–15
    constraints, 15–18
    DAO, 594, 596
    indexes, 15, *16*
    managing. *See* managing databases and database objects

Database objects, retrieving data with ODBCDirect, 657–658

database objects
    tables, 12–13
    views, 15

database owner, security, 126

database owners, user security setup, 129–130

database performance, 233–315
    average response time, 234
    Current Activity categories (Enterprise Manager), 289–292
    DBCC statements, 306–307
    Index Tuning Wizard, 292–299, *300*
    measuring, 235
    miscellaneous tools, 306–309

overview, 234–235

Query Analyzer index analysis, 308

response time, 234

Showplan, 299–305

SQL Server Performance Monitor, 268–289

SQL Server Profiler, 238–268

SQL statement hints, 310–315

throughput, 234

tools, 235–315

tools overview, 235–236, *236–238*

trace flags, 307–308

Transact-SQL functions and stored procedures, 308–309

Database Properties dialog box
    General tab, *66*
    options, *68–69*
    Options tab, *68*
    Permissions tab, *72, 73*
    statement permissions, *162*
    Transaction Log tab, *67*

Database Restore dialog box, restoring backed-up databases, *191*

Database Role Properties dialog box
    managing database users, *153*
    user security setup, *144*

Database Selection screen, Version Upgrade Wizard, *932*

Database Settings tab, SQL Server Properties dialog box, 64–65

Database User Properties dialog box
    managing database users, *154*
    user security setup, *146, 150*

databases
    backups, 173–197
    capacities, 942-943
    creating and modifying, 65–71
    creating with SQL statements, 397–401
    diagrams, 88
    Edit Diagram dialog box, *88*
    file locations and sizes, 398–399
    fixed roles, *125*
    installing SQL Server, 28–30
    listing (SQL-DMO), 338
    management systems. *See* DBMSs

managing. *See* managing databases and database objects

managing users. *See* managing database users

performance. *See* database performance

relational. *See* relational database model

remote objects. *See* RDO (Remote Database Objects)

replication. *See* replication

security, 117–171

user security setup, 141–143

user-defined roles. *See* user-defined database roles

Web integration. *See* ASP; Web Assistant Wizard

See also DBMSs; ODBC

databases counters, Performance Monitor, 273

date, scalar functions (SQL), 460–462

date and time arithmetic (SQL Select statements), 469–471

DB-Library, 811–857
    advanced techniques, 852–856
    building applications, 816–852
    connecting to SQL Server, 820–824
    cursors, 836–846
    dynamic SQL and, 831–835
    enumerating SQL Server systems, 818–820
    error handling, 850–852
    files included with SQL Server, *814*
    initializing, 818
    multiple result sets, 853–855
    networking architecture, *813*
    overview, 812–814
    retrieving data with, 824–831
    SQLInit function, 818
    SQLServerEnum function, 819–820
    SQLWinExit subroutine, 818
    stored procedures, 847–850
    transactions, 855–856
    vbsql.bas module, 815, *817*
    vbsql.ocx for Visual Basic, 814–816
    Visual Basic and, 814–816

DBCC statements, 306–307
    backups and, 177–178
    described, 238
    PinTable command, 307
    Show_Statistics command, 306
    UpdateUsage command, 307
DBEngine objects
    DAO, 594, 596, 598
    ODBCDirect, 652
DBExecQuery subroutine, retrieving data with DB-Library, 829–830
DBMSs (database management systems), 348–353
    database models, 353
    DDLs (Data Definition Languages), 350–351
    DMLs (Data Manipulation Languages), 352
    history of, 348–349
    integrity constraints, 351–352
    traditional file systems comparison, 349–350
    See also managing databases and database objects
dbo user name, database owner, 126
DBQuery subroutine, retrieving data with DB-Library, 825
DDLs (Data Definition Languages)
    coding suggestions, 439–441
    DBMSs (database management systems), 350–351
    Transact-SQL. See Transact-SQL DDL
Declarative Referential Integrity (DRI), constraints, 16
Declare Cursor statements, 528–533
default databases, NT Server groups, 134
default filegroups, backups and, 175
Default Properties dialog box, default tasks, 86, 87
default values, Transact-SQL DDL, 410–411
default Workspace types, ODBCDirect, 652–653
defaults, column, 18
DefaultType property, ODBCDirect, 652–653

Delete statements
    DML, 513–515
    RDO, 740
    RDO and SQL, 744–745
    SQLPassThrough (DAO), 627–628, 631
    triggers and, 536–543
deleting
    alerts, 284
    counters from Performance Monitor chart view, 280
    data with ADO Command objects and prepared SQL statements, 796–797
    data with QueryDef objects and prepared SQL statements (ODBCDirect), 667–668
    NT Server groups, 150
    SQL Server user-defined database roles, 150–151
    stored procedures, 520
    triggers, 540
deleting rows
    from ADO Recordset objects, 792–793
    from ADO Recordset objects (ASP and), 909–910
    DB-Library cursors, 846
    dynamic SQL, 835
    ODBC API, 710–711
    with RDO Delete method, 740
    with RDO and SQL Delete statements, 744–745
denying permissions and permission states, 165–166, 434–485
Dependencies dialog box, table tasks, 81
derived attributes, relational database model, 375, 376
derived columns, 426–427
Design Table dialog box, 76
Design View, Microsoft Access Query Designer, 568, 569
diagrams
    Edit Diagram dialog box, 88
    Entity Relationship. See ERDs
difference operations, relational database model, 367, 368
differential backups, 180
    restoring backed-up databases, 193–194

dimensions
    Cube Wizard (data warehousing), 228, 229
    data warehousing, 221, 228, 229
    OLAP Manager, 226
direct attributes, algebraic operations, 375
direct pipeline method, Version Upgrade Wizard, 928-929
directories, installing SQL Server, 28–30
disabling users, user security setup, 151
disconnecting from data sources
    ODBC API, 700–701
    See also Close method
DisplayADOError subroutine, ADO error handling, 800–801
DisplayCursorGrid function, DB-Library cursors, 840–843
DisplayDAOError subroutine, DAO error handling, 646–647
DisplayDBGrid subroutine, retrieving data with DB-Library, 826–827
DisplayDynasetGrid subroutine, limiting data in DAO Recordset objects, 620–622
DisplayForwardGrid subroutine, ADO ForwardOnlyRecordset objects, 776–778
displaying
    DB-Library cursor data, 840–844
    stored procedure data, 520–521
    stored procedure messages, 525
    trigger data, 541
DisplayKeysetGrid subroutine, ADO KeysetRecordset objects, 780–783
DisplayRDOError subroutine, RDO error handling, 747–748
Distributed Management Framework, SQL-DMF, 318–319
Distributed Management Objects. See SQL-DMO
Distributed Transaction Coordinator, administrative components, 22
Distributors (replication), 202
    Create Publication Wizard, 206

vision operations, relational
database model, 370
DML (Data Manipulation
Language), 443–545
  coding suggestions, 544–545
  concurrent updates and table
    locks, 515–518
  DBMSs (database
    management systems), 352
  Delete statements, 513–515
  Insert statements, 507–510
  modifying table data,
    507–518
  overview, 444–445
  programming suggestions,
    544–545
  SQL Select statements,
    445–507
  stored procedures, 519–543
  Truncate statements, 514
  Update statements, 510–513
DMO (Distributed Management
  Objects). *See* SQL-DMO
Do Until loops
  ADO ForwardOnlyRecordset
    objects, 779
  limiting data in DAO
    Recordset objects, 622
domains
  defined, 118
  relational database model,
    356–357
DRI (Declarative Referential
  Integrity), constraints, 16
Driver Manager, ODBC API, 684
Drop Procedure statements, 520
Drop statements, Transact-SQL
  DDL, 433
Drop Trigger statements, 540
Drop_Existing option, Create Index
  statement, *432*
DSN Configuration Wizard, ODBC
  API, 688–693
DSN-less connections
  connecting DAO to SQL
    Server, 606–607
  connecting ODBCDirect to
    SQL Server, 656–657
  opening with OLE DB
    provider for ODBC, 771
  RDO, 729
DSS Analysis Server, data
  warehousing, 224

DTS (Data Transformation Services)
  administrative components,
    24–25
  described, *31*
  Microsoft Data Warehousing
    Framework, 222
dump devices, backups, 176–177
dynamic cursors
  ADO Recordset objects, 774
  retrieving data with RDO,
    730–731
dynamic Recordsets, retrieving data
  with DAO, 608–609
dynamic SQL statements, 831–835
  CreateTable function,
    831–832
  CreateTable function and
    ADO Command objects,
    787–788
  deleting rows, 835
  executing, 831–832
  executing with ADO
    Command objects, 787–788
  executing with ODBCDirect,
    668–669
  inserting rows, 832–833
  modifying data with, 832–835
  RDO Execute method and,
    736–737
  rdoResult sets and, 731–733
  SQLAdd subroutine, 832–833
  SQLDelete function, 835
  SQLPassThrough (DAO)
    and, 623–624, 628
  SQLSendCmd function,
    831–832
  SQLUpdate subroutine,
    833–835
  updating rows, 833–835
dynaset Recordset objects (DAO),
  608, 609–618
  creating and traversing,
    609–613
  FindFirst method, 614–615
  finding records in, 613–618
  FindLast method, 617–618
  FindNext method, 615–617
  FindPrevious method,
    617–618
  MoveLast method, 613
  OpenRecordset method,
    610–613
  Workspace objects, 610

▼ **E**

Edit Diagram dialog box, database
  tasks, *88*
Edit Job Schedule dialog box, SQL
  Server Agent, 103, *104*
Edit Job Step dialog box, SQL
  Server Agent, 101–105
Edit method
  SQLPassThrough (DAO),
    626–627
  updating rows with RDO
    Update method, 739–740
Edit Recurring Job Schedule dialog
  box
  Push Subscription Wizard,
    215, *216*
  SQL Server Agent, 103, *104*
encrypted view definitions, 425
Enterprise Manager, 19–22, 39–116
  as alternative to SQL
    statements, 397
  continuing servers, 47–48
  Create Publication Wizard,
    205–211
  Current Activity categories,
    289–292
  database folders, 74
  described, *31*, 237
  displaying event logs,
    105–106
  Index Tuning Wizard and,
    294
  managing databases and
    database objects, 65–115
  miscellaneous facilities, 115
  mixed mode security, 21–22
  New Login Properties dialog
    box, 20, *21*
  pausing servers, 47–48
  Properties dialog box, 40, *41*
  registering and unregistering
    servers, 41–46
  security, 20–22
  setting properties, 39–41
  setting server properties,
    48–65
  SQL Server Service Manager
    dialog box, 47
  starting/stopping servers,
    47–48
  Windows NT authentication,
    21
  See also SQL-DMO

entity integrity, relational database model, 365–366
Entity Relationship Diagrams. *See* ERDs
entity subtypes, ERDs, 384–386
enumerating SQL Server systems, 818–820
environments
    creating RDO, 724–727
    freeing ODBC API, 696–697
    Microsoft Access, *549*
    ODBC API allocation, 696
    ODBC API attribute, 697
equijoins
    algebraic operations, 373
    complex SQL Select statements, 482
ERDs (Entity Relationship Diagrams), 377–388
    adding properties to, 380–381
    associations, 382–384
    concepts and symbols, 377–380
    entity subtypes, 384–386
    exclusive relationships, 384
    intersection entities, 383
    multivalued properties, 381–382
    overview, 377
    regular entities, 384
    weak entity notation, 382, 384
    when to use, 386–388
error handling
    ADO, 800–801
    ADO and ASP, 918–920
    DAO, 645–647
    DB-Library, 850–852
    ODBC API and SQLGetDiagRec function, 716–717
    ODBCDirect, 671
    RDO, 747–748
    SQL-DMO, 343–344
    VBA code modules and Microsoft Access, 588–589
    Visual Basic, *646*
error messages, stored procedures and, 534–535
Errors collections
    ADO, 765
    DAO, 596, 646–647
Errors objects, DAO, 594
event logs, displaying, 105–106

Event Viewer, NT Server, *106*
event-specific data column contents, Profiler Data Columns tab, *256–259*
Events tab (Profiler), 244–252
    event categories, 244, *245–252*
    event classes, 244, *245–252*
    Trace Properties dialog box, *245–251*
exclusive locks (DML), concurrent updates and table locks, 515
exclusive relationships, ERDs, 384
Execute method
    dynamic SQL and RDO, 736–737
    dynamic SQL and SQLPassThrough (DAO), 624
    prepared SQL statements and ADO Command objects, 786–787
execution plans, Showplan, 299–300
Exists conditions (SQL Select statements), 492–495
    * (asterisks), 493
    correlated references, 493
    correlated subqueries, 493
    subqueries, 494–495
explicit transactions (DML), concurrent updates and table locks, 516, 518
exporting charts, Performance Monitor chart view, 281
exporting and importing trace definitions, 262
expressions, SQL Select statements and, 453–454
extended stored procedures
    constraints, 19
    Profiler, *239–241*

▼ F

fetch buffer, DB-Library cursors, *836*, 837
Fetch statement positioning keywords, cursors, 529, *530*
Field objects, ADO ForwardOnlyRecordset objects, 778–779
fifth normal forms (5NF), relational database model, 363–364

filegroups
    creating tables on specific, 415–416
    restoring backed-up databases, 195
    Transact-SQL DDL, 400–401
FillFactor = x option, Create Index statement, *432*
Filters tab (Profiler), 260–262
    column filters, *260–261*
    ID value filters, 260
    Include/Exclude filters, 260
    Range filters, 260
    Trace Properties dialog box, 262
    types of filters, 260
FindFirst method, DAO dynaset Recordset objects, 614–615
finding records in, DAO dynaset Recordset objects, 613–618
FindLast method, DAO dynaset Recordset objects, 617–618
FindNext method, DAO dynaset Recordset objects, 615–617
FindPrevious method, DAO dynaset Recordset objects, 617–618
first normal forms (1NF), relational database model, 358, *359*
fixed database roles, *125*
fixed server roles, *124*
flags, trace, 238, 307–308
folders, Enterprise Manager database, 74
For Each loops
    ADO ForwardOnlyRecordset objects, 778–779
    limiting data in DAO Recordset objects, 622
For Update clause, updateable cursors, 530–531
foreign keys
    constraints, 16, 413–414
    data integrity, 366–367
<FORM> tags
    ADO and ASP, 894
    executing stored procedures with ADO Command objects, 917
Formatting tab, Generate SQL Scripts dialog box, 80, *82*
formatting tables, Web Assistant Wizard, 867, *868*
forms, normal. *See* normal forms

Forms Designer (Microsoft Access), 570–572
    Form Wizard window, 571, *572*
    New Form dialog box, 570, *571*
forward-only cursors, RDO, 730
forward-only Recordsets, DAO, 608
ForwardOnlyRecordset objects (ADO), 773, 774–779
    ActiveConnection property, 775
    ColWidth property, 778–779
    Connection objects and, 774–775
    DisplayForwardGrid subroutine, 776–778
    Do Until loops, 779
    Field objects, 778–779
    For Each loops, 778–779
    Open method, 775–776
fourth normal forms (4NF), relational database model, 362
freeing database connection handles, ODBC API, 698
freeing environments, ODBC API, 696–697
freeing statement handles, ODBC API, 701–702
From clauses
    complex SQL Select statements and multiple tables, 479–485
    using SQL Select statements in, 499–500
full backups, restoring backed-up databases, 193–194
full-text catalog tasks, 89–90
Full-Text Indexing tool, described, *31*
functions
    advanced ADO database, 801–811
    SQL scalar, 455–469
    Transact-SQL, *238*
    Transact-SQL and database performance, 308–309

G

general statistics counters, Performance Monitor, *274*

General tab
    Database Properties dialog box, *66*
    SQL Server Agent, 94–96
General tab (Profiler), 242–244
    Source Server dialog box, 243, *244*
    Trace Properties dialog box, 242, *243*
General tab (SQL Server Properties dialog box), 51–55
    sqlservr.exe program parameters, *53–55*
    Startup Parameters dialog box, *53*
Generate SQL Scripts dialog box, 80–84
    Formatting tab, 80, *82*
    General tab, 80, *81*
    Object Scripting Preview dialog box, 80, *82*
    Options tab, 83
GetComputerName function, connecting DB-Library to SQL Server, 822
GetSystemName function, connecting DB-Library to SQL Server, 821–822
global groups, NT Server, 123
Global Unique Identifier Columns (GUIDs), SQL row, 408–409
GoTo statements and labels, stored procedures, 527
"grandfather" rotation, retention periods of backup copies, 185, *186–187*
Grant statements
    As clause, 436
    object permissions, 434–437
graphical Showplan, Query Analyzer, 304–305
Group By clause (SQL Select statements), 474–475
    With Cube option, 502–504
    With Rollup option, 502–504
Group Memberships dialog box, user security setup, *139, 148*
Group Properties dialog box, user security setup, *149*
groups
    New Local Group dialog box, *137*

NT Server. *See* NT Server groups
    security and, 123
guest user name, security, 127, 140
GUIDs (Global Unique Identifier Columns), SQL row, 408–409

H

Hash keyword, join hints, 311–312
Having clause
    SQL Select statements, 475–477
    Where clause comparison, 477
hints. *See* SQL statement hints
histograms, Performance Monitor chart view, 277
history data, Database Maintenance Plan Wizard dialog box, 113, *115*
HOLAP (Hybrid OnLine Analytical Processing), 222
HTML files, Web Assistant Wizard, 866–867
hyperlinks, Add Hyperlinks to Web Page dialog box, 867–869

I

ID value filters, Profiler Filters tab, 260
identifiers, user security setup, 129
identity columns, Transact-SQL DDL, 408
If...Else statements, stored procedures, 526–527
Ignore_Dup_Key option, Create Index statement, 432
image functions, SQL scalar functions, 458
implicit transactions (DML), concurrent updates and table locks, 516–517
importing and exporting trace definitions, 262
In conditions, SQL Select statements, 489–490
#include statements, ADO and ASP, 903
Include/Exclude filters, Profiler Filters tab, 260
index analysis, Query Analyzer, 308

index hints, table hints, *313*
Index Tuning Wizard, 292–299, *300*
    advanced options, *296*
    Create Trace Wizard
      and, 293
    Enterprise Manager and, 294
    overview, 292–293
    Profiler and, 294
    Recommendations dialog
      box, *298*
    reports, 298, *299*
    running, 294–299
    selecting servers and
      databases, *294*
    SQL Scripts and, 293, *300*
    table specifications, *297*
    workloads, 293, *295*
indexes, 428–433
    clustered, 431
    clustered and nonclustered,
      15, *16*
    Create Index statements,
      429–433
    Create New Index dialog
      box, *78*
    Manage Indexes dialog
      box, 77
Indexing Tuning Wizard,
    described, *237*
initialization functions, ODBC API,
    696–702
Initialize Subscription dialog box,
    Push Subscription Wizard,
    216, *217*
inner joins
    algebraic operations,
      373–374
    complex SQL Select
      statements, 483
Input Log File Timeframe dialog
    box, Performance Monitor chart
    view, *282*
input parameters, stored
    procedures, 521
insensitive cursors, 530
Insert statements
    DML, 507–510
    If Update clause, 539–540
    RDO and SQL, 741–742
    SQLPassThrough (DAO),
      628–630
    Transact-SQL DDL, 393
    triggers, 536–543

inserting rows
    with ADO Command objects
      and prepared SQL
      statements, 793–795
    into ADO Recordset objects,
      789–791
    into ADO Recordset objects
      (ASP), 900–904
    into DAO Recordset objects
      (SQLPassThrough),
      624–626
    with DB-Library cursors,
      838–840
    with dynamic SQL
      statements, 832–833
    with ODBC API, 708–710
    with QueryDef objects and
      prepared SQL statements
      (ODBCDirect), 663–665
    with RDO AddNew method,
      738–739
    with RDO and SQL Insert
      statements, 741–742
installing OLAP Services, 225
installing SQL Server, 28–39
    directories and databases,
      28–30
    tools, 30–37
    wizards, 37–39
installing SQL Server ODBC
    driver, connecting Microsoft
    Access to SQL Server, 554–555
integrity, data. *See* data integrity
integrity checks, Database
    Maintenance Plan Wizard dialog
    box, 112
integrity constraints, DBMS,
    351–352
InterDev. *See* Visual InterDev
intersection entities, ERDs, 383
intersection operations, relational
    database model, 367, *368*
Into clause, SQL Select statements,
    506–507

J

Jet engine
    closing, 647
    DAO and, 592–593
    Microsoft Access and, 548
Job Properties dialog box, SQL
    Server Agent, *100*, 103, *105*

Job System tab, SQL Server Agent,
    92–93, *94*
jobs
    creating with SQL Server
      Agent, 98–105
    defined, 8
JobServer object hierarchy,
    SQL-DMO, 324–326
join hints, 310–312
    Hash keyword, 311–312
    Loop keyword, 311–312
    Merge keyword, 311–312
joining tables, 421–423, 427–428
    relational database model,
      370, 373

K

key constraints, 412–414
    foreign keys, 413–414
    primary keys, 413
    unique keys, 413
keyset cursors, RDO, 730
KeysetRecordset objects (ADO),
    773–774, 779–784
    ActiveConnection property,
      780
    DisplayKeysetGrid
      subroutine, 780–783
    KeysetRecordsetReverse
      subroutine, 783–784
    Open method, 780
KeysetRecordsetReverse
    subroutine, ADO
    KeysetRecordset objects, 783–784
Kill Process button, Process Details
    dialog box, 291

L

labels and GoTo statements, stored
    procedures, 527
libraries. *See* DB-Library
Like conditions, SQL Select
    statements, 491–492
Limit Rows dialog box, Web
    Assistant Wizard, *869*
limiting data in DAO Recordset
    objects, 619–622
    DisplayDynasetGrid
      subroutine, 620–622
    Do Until loops, 622

For Each loops, 622
performance tips, 647
twips, 622
Where clause (Select
statements), 619–620
line graph, Performance Monitor
chart view, 277
linked servers, 108–110
linked tables
connecting DAO to SQL
Server, 599, 601–604
performance tips, 647
linking Microsoft Access tables to
SQL Server, 561–567
creating new databases,
561–563
data sources, 563–565
list of linked tables, 567
Select Unique Record
Identifier dialog box,
565, 566
links, Add Hyperlinks to Web Page
dialog box, 867–869
listing columns, SQL-DMO,
339–341
listing databases, SQL-DMO, 338
listing tables, SQL-DMO, 338–339
Local Group Properties dialog box,
user security setup, 139
local groups, NT Server, 123
local variable declarations, stored
procedures, 524
lock granularity hints, table hints,
313–314
lock modes, object, 291
lock types
ADO Recordset object, 775,
777
object, 290
OpenRecordset method,
612–613
Locks/Object category, Enterprise
Manager, 291, 292
Locks/Process ID category,
Enterprise Manager, 290
log files
Performance Monitor alert
view, 283
Performance Monitor chart
view, 281–282
transaction. See transaction
logs
Log On clause, Transact-SQL
DDL, 399

log view (Performance Monitor),
285–288
Add to Log dialog box, 285,
287
Data From dialog box, 288
Log Options dialog box, 286
saving log definition files,
287
Start/Stop button, 287
logging on to NT Server, 118–119
logging in to SQL Server, 119–123
NT Server security
terminology comparison,
119–122
user accounts, 122–123
logical roles
implementing nested for NT
Server groups, 133–134
user security setup, 130
login names, user security setup,
143–147
logins, managing database users,
152
Logins and Server Roles containers,
managing database objects, 90
Logon screen, Version Upgrade
Wizard, 930, 931
Loop keyword, join hints, 311–312

▼ M

macros (Microsoft Access), 577–580
listing, 578–579
QueryBatch, 577
saving, 579, 580
maintenance plans, Database
Maintenance Plan Wizard dialog
box, 110–115
Manage Indexes dialog box, table
tasks, 77
Manage SQL Server Messages
dialog box, 107
Management Objects, Distributed.
See SQL-DMO
managing database users, 151–158
Database Role Properties
dialog box, 153
Database User Properties
dialog box, 154
logins, 152
roles, 153
SQL Server Login Properties
dialog box, 152
stored procedures, 154–157

Transact-SQL functions,
157–158
user names, 153–154
managing databases and database
objects, 65–115
ANSI SQL-92 compatibility
(setting maximal), 71–72
creating and modifying
databases, 65–71
Database Maintenance Plan
Wizard dialog box,
110–115
displaying event logs,
105–106
Enterprise Manager database
folders, 74
General tab (Database
Properties dialog box), 66
linked servers, 108–110
Logins and Server Roles
containers, 90
maintenance plans, 110–115
miscellaneous operations, 73
New Table dialog box, 74–75
NT Server Event Viewer, 106
Options tab (Database
Properties dialog box), 68
Permissions tab (Database
Properties dialog box), 72,
73
sp_dboption options, 70–71
SQL Server Agent, 90–105
tables, 74–85
tasks, 85–90
Transaction Log tab
(Database Properties
dialog box), 67
viewing and creating
messages, 106–108
See also databases; DBMSs;
SQL-DMO
mapping functions, relational
database model, 357
master databases
backups, 183–184
Create Publication Wizard,
206
database architecture, 10
restoring backed-up
databases, 194–195
mathematical functions, SQL scalar
functions, 458–460
.mdb files, linking Microsoft Access
tables to SQL Server, 561–567

measures
  Cube Wizard (data
    warehousing), 226, *228*
  data warehousing, 221,
    226, *228*
  OLAP Manager, 226
measuring database performance,
  235
memory manager counters,
  Performance Monitor, *274–275*
Memory tab, SQL Server
  Properties dialog box, 55–56
Merge keyword, join hints,
  311–312
merge replication, 203–221
  Create Publication Wizard,
    205–211
  Push Subscription Wizard,
    212–221
messages, viewing and creating
  database, 106–108
Messages tab, Manage SQL Server
  Messages dialog box, *107*
Microsoft Access, 547–590
  connecting to SQL Server,
    553–567
  environment, *549*
  Forms Designer, 570–572
  as front-end development
    tool, 552
  Jet engine and, 548
  macros, 577–580
  multiple-user applications,
    549–552
  networking architecture,
    552–553
  ODBC and, 552
  overview, 548–549
  Query Designer, 567–570
  Rapid Development Tools,
    548
  Report Designer, 573–576
  tips, 589–590
  VBA code modules, 580–589
Microsoft Data Warehousing
  Framework, 222–223
  Data Cube Service, 223
  DTS (Data Transformation
    Services), 222
  PivotTable Service, 223
Microsoft English Query tool,
  described, *32*
Microsoft Management Console,
  described, *32*

Microsoft Management Console
  (MMF), SQL-DMF (Distributed
  Management Framework), 318
migrating from version 6.*x* to 7. *See*
  Version Upgrade Wizard
Migration Status screen, Version
  Upgrade Wizard, *935*
mixed authentication mode,
  security, 127
mixed mode security, SQL Server
  Enterprise Manager, 21–22
MMF (Microsoft Management
  Console), SQL-DMF (Distributed
  Management Framework), 318
model databases, database
  architecture, 10
Modify File clause, Transact-SQL
  DDL, 400
MOLAP (Multidimensional
  OnLine Analytical Processing),
  222
monitoring performance with trace
  data
  Profiler, 267
  See also Performance
    Monitor
MoveLast method, DAO dynaset
  Recordset objects, 613
MSDASQL OLE DB provider,
  connecting ADO to SQL Server,
  767, 768–770
MSDASQL prompt constants,
  connecting ADO to SQL Server,
  768, *770*
msdb databases, database
  architecture, 11
MSDTC tool, described, *32*
Multidimensional OnLine
  Analytical Processing (MOLAP),
  222
multiple result sets
  ADO, 803–805
  DAO (QueryDef objects),
    644–645
  DB-Library, 853–855
  ODBCDirect, 672–674
  RDO, 748–750
multiple tables, DML Update
  statements, 512–513
multiple tables in From clauses,
  complex SQL Select statements,
  479–485
multiple-user applications,
  Microsoft Access, 549–551

multiple-user database access, SQL
  Server, 551–552
multivalued properties, ERDs,
  381–382

▼ N

named rules, Create Rule
  statements, 415
names
  login. *See* login names
  unqualified object, 524
  user. *See* user names
naming conventions, Transact-SQL
  DDL, 403–404
natural joins, algebraic operations,
  373
nested logical roles, implementing
  for NT Server groups, 133–134
nested triggers, 541
Network Library Configuration
  tool, described, *32*
networking architecture
  DB-Library, *813*
  Microsoft Access, 552–553
  overview, 4–7
networking components
  ADO, 762, *763*
  ASP and ADO, *877*
  DAO, 592–593
  ODBC API, *683*
  ODBCDirect, *649*
New Attached Table dialog box,
  Visual Data Manager, *601*
New Device dialog box, backups,
  177
New Form dialog box, Forms
  Designer, 570, *571*
New Full-Text Catalog Properties
  dialog box, tasks, 89–90
New Local Group dialog box, user
  security setup, *137*
New Login Properties dialog box,
  SQL Server Enterprise Manager,
  20, *21*
New Report dialog box, Report
  Designer, 573, *574*
New SQL Server Message dialog
  box, *108*
New Table dialog box, 74–75
New User dialog box, user security
  setup, *138*
Niladic functions, Create Table
  statements, *411*

nonclustered indexes, 15, *16*
normal forms (relational database model), 358–365
  fifth (5NF), 363–364
  first (1NF), 358, *359*
  fourth (4NF), 362
  normalization, 358
  redundancy, 358–361
  second (2NF), 361
  third (3NF), 361–362
  types of, 361–365
Northwind database, database architecture, 12
Not logical operator, SQL Select statements, 450
Not Null constraints, 17
Notifications tab, SQL Server Agent, *96, 105*
NT database applications, developing. *See* RDO (Remote Database Objects)
NT Server
  Event Viewer, *106*
  logging on to, 118–119
  SQL Server security terminology comparison, *119–122*
  user security setup, 137–140
NT Server groups, 123
  default databases, 134
  deleting, 150
  implementing nested logical roles, 133–134
  membership, 134
  New Local Group dialog box, *137*
  SQL Server role membership, 134
  user security setup, 131–137
NT User Manager window, *136*
Null conditions, SQL Select statements, 489
null and not null columns, Transact-SQL DDL, 409

O

Object Browser
  viewing RDO classes with, *725*
  viewing SQL-DMO library, *329*
object collections, SQL-DMO, 332–335

object counters, Performance Monitor, *270–276*
object hierarchy
  DAO, 594–596
  ODBCDirect, *650*
  SQL-DMO, 318–327
object lock modes, Current Activity categories, *291*
object lock types, Current Activity categories, *290*
object model, ASP, 878–879
object names, unqualified, 524
object permissions, 162–166, 434–436
  column-level, 164–165
  Deny statements, 434–485
  denying permissions and permission states, 165–166
  Grant statements, 434–437
  managing, 163–164
  Object Properties dialog box, *164, 165*
  Revoke statements, 434–485
  Select statements, 162
  With Grant Option clause, 163, 436–437
Object Properties dialog box, object permissions, *164, 165*
Object Scripting Preview dialog box, Transact-SQL scripts, 80, *82*
object types, Performance Monitor, 268–269, *269–270*
objects
  ActiveX Data. *See* ADO
  Data Access. *See* DAO
  database. *See* database objects
  ownership chain, 168–169
  Remote Database. *See* RDO
ODBC connection strings, DAO QueryDef objects, 644
ODBC Data Source Administrator, connecting Microsoft Access to SQL Server, *557*
ODBC driver, installing SQL Server, 554–555
ODBC Driver Manager
  ADO, 762–763
  RDO, 728
ODBC (Open Database Connectivity) API, 681–718
  Administrator, 685, 686–687
  allocating database connection handles, 697–698
  allocating environments, 696

allocating statement handles, 701
applications, 683–684
architecture, 683–685
basic use of, 693–696
bound columns and SQLBindCol function, 707–708
calling stored procedures, 714–716
configuring data sources, 685–693
connecting ADO to SQL Server, 767–772
connecting to data sources, 698–700
data concurrency, 713–714
data sources, 685–693, 698–700
deleting rows, 710–711
disconnecting from data sources, 700–701
driver, 684–685
Driver Manager, 684
error handling and SQLGetDiagRec function, 716–717
freeing database connection handles, 698
freeing environments, 696–697
freeing statement handles, 701–702
initialization functions, 696–702
inserting rows, 708–710
Microsoft Access and, 552
networking components, *683*
opening DSN-less connections with OLE DB provider, 771
optimistic record locking, 713–714
overview, 682–683
prepared SQL statements and SQLExecute function, 703–705
Query Analyzer, 714
reference resources, 718
Registry keys for data sources, *686*
retrieving data, 702–708
setting environment attributes, 697

SQL Select statements,
702–703
SQL Server DSN
Configuration Wizard,
688–693
SQLAllocHandle function,
696, 697–698, 701
SQLBindCol function,
707–708
SQLBindParameter function,
709–710
SQLConnect function,
698–699
SQLDisconnect function,
700–701
SQLDriverConnect function,
699–700
SQLExecDirect function,
702–703
SQLExecute function,
703–705
SQLFetch function, 705–706
SQLFreeHandle function,
696–697, 698, 702
SQLFreeStmt function,
701–702
SQLGetData function,
705–707
SQLGetDiagRec function,
716–717
SQLNumResultCols
function, 706
SQLPrepare function,
704–705
SQLSetEnvAttr function, 697
unbound columns and
SQLGetData function,
705–707
updating data, 708–714
updating rows, 711–713
See also ODBCDirect
ODBCDirect, 648–679
advanced database
functions, 672–679
architecture, 650–652
asynchronous operations,
674–676
connecting to SQL Server,
653–657
CreateQueryDef
method, 662
CreateWorkspace
method, 652
creating DBEngine
objects, 652

creating Workspace objects,
652–653
DBEngine objects, 652
default Workspace types,
652–653
DefaultType property,
652–653
deleting data with QueryDef
objects and prepared SQL
statements, 667–668
dynamic SQL statements,
668–669
error handling, 671
executing dynamic SQL
statements with, 668–669
executing stored procedures
with QueryDef objects,
669–671
files, 650
inserting rows with
QueryDef objects and
prepared SQL statements,
663–665
modifying data with,
663–668
multiple result sets, 672–674
networking components, 649
object hierarchy, 650
overview, 592–593, 648–652
performance tips, 647–648
retrieving data with, 657–663
stored procedures, 669–671
transactions, 676–679
updating data with
QueryDef objects and
prepared SQL statements,
665–667
Workspace objects, 652–653
See also ODBC API
Office 97 Professional Edition
Setup dialog box, installing SQL
Server ODBC driver, 554–555
OLAP (OnLine Analytical
Processing), 221–223
Microsoft Data Warehousing
Framework, 222–223
multidimensional, 222
overview, 221
types of, 222
OLAP Manager, 225–226
dimensions, 226
measures, 226
partitions, 226
OLAP services, data warehousing,
224–225

OLE DB, 759–762
ADO files and, 763
architecture overview,
759–762
connection string keywords,
769
consumers and providers,
759, 760
Universal Data Access, 759
See also ADO
OLE DB providers
ADO and ASP, 882–883
connecting ADO to SQL
Server, 767–772
On clause, Transact-SQL DDL, 398
On Error statements
ADO and ASP, 904, 918–920
DAO, 645–646
OnLine Analytical Processing. See
OLAP
Open method
ADO
ForwardOnlyRecordset
objects, 775–776
ADO KeysetRecordset
objects, 780
OpenConnection method
connecting ODBCDirect to
SQL Server, 655–657
RDO, 727–729
OpenDatabase method
connecting DAO to SQL
Server, 602, 604–606
connecting ODBCDirect to
SQL Server, 653–654
connection string keywords,
606
DAO QueryDef objects, 634,
637
options, 605
parameterized DAO
QueryDef objects, 634
OpenRecordset method
DAO dynaset Recordset
objects, 610–612
DAO QueryDef objects, 637,
644
lock types, 612–613
ODBCDirect, 662–663
options, 611–612
OpenResultset method (RDO)
inserting rows with
AddNew method, 739
modifying data with
cursors, 738

rdoResultsets and prepared SQL statements, 735
retrieving data with, 731–733
Update method, 740
operators
creating with SQL Server Agent, 93–96
SQL Select statements and, 454
optimistic record locking, ODBC API, 713–714
optimization, Database Maintenance Plan Wizard dialog box, 110–112
optimization hints, table hints, *313*
Option Explicit statements, VBScript, 903, 908
Options tab
Database Properties dialog box, *68*
Generate SQL Scripts dialog box, 83
Order By clause, SQL Select statements, 478, 501
organizing backups, 183–188
archival backups, 185
backup copies and retention periods, 185–187
events requiring system database backups, 183–184
events requiring user database backups, 184
periodic backups, 184–185
striped backups in restore operations, 188
OSQL batch facility
described, 32
Transact-SQL DDL, 395–396
outer joins
algebraic operations, 374
complex SQL Select statements, 483–485
output parameters, stored procedures, 521–522
ownership chain of objects, security, 168–169

P

Pad_Index option, Create Index statement, *432*

parameterized DAO QueryDef objects, 632–635
CreateQueryDef method, 634–635
direction constants, *671*
OpenDatabase method, 634
QueryDefs.Delete method, 634
Select statements and, 634
parameterized queries
defined, 662
VBA code modules and Microsoft Access, 582–584
parameters
ADO and ASP, 895–896
defined, 662
partitions, OLAP Manager, 226
performance, monitoring with Profiler trace data, 267
Performance Monitor, 268–289
access methods counters, *270–271*
administrative components, 23–24, 25
alert view, 282–285
backup device counters, *271*
buffer manager counters, *272*
cache manager counters, *272–273*
chart view, 277–282
counters, 270–276
database counters, *273*
described, *32*, 237
general statistics counters, *274*
log view, 285–288
memory manager counters, *274–275*
object counters, *270–276*
object types, 268–269, *269–270*
overview, 268–276
replication agents counters, *275*
replication distribution counters, *275*
replication logreader counters, *275*
replication merge counters, 275–276
replication snapshot counters, *276*
report view, 288–289

running, 276–277
SQL statistics counters, *276*
statistics counters, 274, *276*
user settable counters, *276*
views, 277–289
performance tips, DAO and ODBC, 647–648
periodic backups, 184–185
permissions, 158–168, 433–438
As clause, 436
Cascade keyword, 437
column-level, 164–165, 437
denying, 165–166
object, 162–166, 434–436
overview, 433–434
restricted statements, 159–161
role, 167
SQL table, *435*
statement, 161–162, 438
stored procedures and, 168
types of, 158
With Grant option, 436–437
Permissions dialog box, table tasks, 78, 79
Permissions tab, Database Properties dialog box, 72, 73
persistence, executing stored procedures with ADO Command objects, 911
physical data independence, relational database model, 356
PinTable command, DBCC statements, 307
pipeline method, Version Upgrade Wizard, 928-929
PivotTable Service
data warehousing, 225
Microsoft Data Warehousing Framework, 223
planning
Database Maintenance Plan Wizard dialog box, 110–115
Showplan, 299–305
user security setup, 128–135
.pml files. *See* log files
Prepare property, retrieving data with ODBCDirect, 662
prepare values, QueryDef object, *665*
prepared SQL statements
ADO Command objects and, 784–787

ADO Command objects and
ASP, 891–899
deleting data with ADO
Command objects and,
796–797
deleting data with QueryDef
objects and, 667–668
inserting rows with ADO
Command objects and,
793–795
inserting rows with
QueryDef objects and,
663–665
rdoResultsets and, 733–736
retrieving data with
ODBCDirect and
QueryDef objects and,
660–663
updating data with prepared
QueryDef objects and,
665–667
updating rows with ADO
Command objects and,
795–796
PreparedSQL2.asp source code,
ADO and ASP, 896–899
primary files, Transact-SQL
DDL, 398
primary keys
attributes, 355
constraints, 16, 413
data integrity, 366
Print statements, stored
procedures, 525
privileges. *See* permissions
Procedure Cache, prepared SQL
statements and ADO Command
objects, 785
procedures, stored. *See* stored
procedures
Process Details dialog box, Current
Activity categories, 291, *292*
Process Info category, Current
Activity categories, 289–290
processes, Kill Process button, 291
Processor tab, SQL Server
Properties dialog box, 57–58
product operations, algebraic
operations, 367, *368*
Profiler, 238–268
administrative components,
23, *24*
Create Trace Wizard,
266–267, *268*
Data Columns tab, 253–260

described, *33, 236*
Events tab, 244–252
extended stored procedures,
239–241
Filters tab, 260–262
General tab, 242–244
importing and exporting
trace definitions, 262
Index Tuning Wizard
and, 294
monitoring performance
with trace data, 267
overview, 236–239
replaying traces, 265–266
Run Traces command,
263–264
SQL Scripts and, 264–265
stored procedures, *239–241*
trace defaults, 264
trace definitions, 242–263
trace window, *263*
programming
DML, 544–545
stored procedures, 524–528
triggers, 542–543
Project menu, Visual InterDev, 922
projection operations, algebraic
operations, 370
prompt constants, MSDASQL, *770*
Prompt property, connecting ADO
to SQL Server, 768, *770*
properties
adding to ERDs, 380–381
Linked Server Properties
dialog box, *109, 110*
multivalued ERD, 381–382
relational database model,
354–355
setting server, 48–65
SQL Server Agent, 90–93
SQL-DMO, 331–332
Table Properties dialog
box, 76
Trigger Properties dialog
box, 79
Properties collections
ADO, 765
connecting ADO to SQL
Server, 769
SQL-DMO, 332–335
Properties dialog box
Enterprise Manager, *40, 41*
SQL Server Agent, 90–93
providers and consumers, OLE
DB, 759, *760*

publications
Create Publication Wizard,
205–211
replication, 202
Publishers, replication, 200, 202
pubs databases, database
architecture, 11
pull replication, 200
push replication, 200
Push Subscription Wizard (merge
replication), 212–221
Agent History option, 219,
220
Choose Destination
Database dialog box, *214*
Choose Subscribers dialog
box, *213, 214*
Completion screen, 218, *219*
Create and Manage
Publications screen, *212*
Edit Recurring Job Schedule
dialog box, 215, *216*
Initialize Subscription dialog
box, 216, *217*
Set Merge Agent Schedule
dialog box, *215*
Set Subscription Priority
dialog box, 216, *217*, 218
Start Required Services
dialog box, 218
subscription completion
message, 219, *220*
Welcome screen, *213*

Q

Quantified conditions, SQL Select
statements, 495–497
queries
asynchronous RDO, 750–752
DB-Library, 824–831
parameterized Microsoft
Access, 582–584
query analysis, SQL Server
Profiler. *See* Profiler
Query Analyzer
administrative components,
22–23
described, *33, 238*
graphical Showplan, 304–305
index analysis, 308
ODBC API, 714
SQL statements, 394–395

query builds, Web Assistant
Wizard, 861–870
Query Designer (Microsoft Access),
567–570
    Design View, 568, *569*
    parameterized queries,
    582–584
    Queries tab, 567, *568*
    Queries Wizard, 568
    results windows, 569, *570*
query hints, SQL statements,
310, *311*
QueryBatch, Microsoft Access
macros, 577
QueryDef objects (DAO), 595,
631–645
    calling stored procedures,
    638–645
    Connect property, 637, 644
    CreateQueryDef method,
    637, 644–645
    deleting data with prepared
    SQL statements and,
    667–668
    executing stored procedures
    with ODBCDirect and,
    669–671
    inserting rows with prepared
    SQL statements and,
    663–665
    multiple result sets, 644–645
    ODBC connection
    strings, 644
    OpenDatabase method, 637
    OpenRecordset method,
    637, 644
    overview, 631–632
    parameter direction
    constants, *671*
    parameterized, 632–635
    prepare values, *665*
    QueryDefs.Delete method,
    634, 637
    reptq1 stored procedure,
    638–644
    retrieving data with
    ODBCDirect and prepared
    SQL statements, 660–663
    SQL statements and, 631–632,
    663–668
    SQLPassThrough and,
    635–637
    TableDefs.Delete
    method, 644

title IDs, 637
updating data with prepared
SQL statements and,
665–667

R

RaisError statements, stored
procedures, 534
Range filters, Profiler Filters tab,
260
Rapid Development Tools,
Microsoft Access, *548*
RDO (Remote Database Objects),
719–753
    adding version 2.0 objects to
    Visual Basic, 723–724
    advanced topics, 748–754
    architecture, 721–723
    asynchronous queries,
    750–752
    Close method, 727, 729, 733
    connection string keywords,
    728
    CreatePreparedStatement
    method, 734
    creating rdoEngine and
    environment, 724–727
    cursors, 730–731, 737–740
    data concurrency, 753–754
    default rdoEngine
    initialization properties,
    725
    deleting rows with Delete
    method, 740
    deleting rows with SQL
    Delete statements, 744–745
    DisplayRDOError
    subroutine, 747–748
    DSN-less connections, 729
    dynamic SQL statements and
    Execute method, 736–737
    dynamic SQL statements and
    rdoResultsets, 731–733
    error handling, 747–748
    files, 721
    inserting rows with AddNew
    method, 738–739
    inserting rows with SQL
    Insert statements,
    741–742
    modifying data with cursors,
    737–740

modifying data with SQL
statements, 741–747
multiple result sets, 748–750
ODBC Driver Manager, 728
OpenConnection method,
727–729
OpenResultset method,
731–733, 738, 739, 740
overview, 720–723
prepared SQL statements and
rdoResultsets, 733–736
rdoConnection objects,
727–729
rdoCreateEnvironment
property, 727
rdoDefaultCursor property,
724
rdoDefaultErrorThreshold
property, 726
rdoDefaultLoginTimeout
property, 726
rdoDefaultPassword
property, 725–726
rdoDefaultUser property,
725–726
rdoErrors collection, 747–748
rdoResultsets and cursors,
737–740
rdoResultsets and dynamic
SQL statements, 731–733
rdoResultsets and prepared
SQL statements, 733–736
reference resources, 755
retrieving data with, 729–736
server-side queries, 752–753
stored procedures and,
745–747
updating rows with SQL
Update statements,
742–743
updating rows with Update
method, 739–740
viewing classes with Object
Browser, 725
read-only views, 423–424
Recordset objects (ADO), 764,
773–784, 789–793
    ASP and, 884–887
    batch updates, 801–803
    Close method, 784
    cursors, 773–774, 776
    deleting rows from, 792–793
    deleting rows from (ASP),
    909–910

dynamic cursors, 774
forward-only cursors, 773, 774–779
inserting rows into, 789–791, 900–904
keyset cursors, 773–774, 779–784
lock types, 775, 777
retrieving data with, 773–784
source options, 776, 778
static cursors, 773
types of, 773–774, 776
updating rows with, 789–793, 905–908
Recordset objects (DAO), 595, 607–623
Close method, 623
creating and traversing dynaset, 609–613
limiting data in, 619–622
modifying data with SQLPassThrough, 624–631
retrieving data with, 607–618
retrieving data with ODBCDirect, 657–659
recursive triggers, 541
redundancy, normal forms, 358–361
referential integrity constraints, 16
relational database model, 366–367
registering and unregistering servers, Enterprise Manager, 41–46
Registry Backup/Restore tool, described, 33
regular entities, ERDs, 384
relational calculus, algebraic operations, 374
relational database model, 347–388
attributes, 354–355, 356–357
components of, 354–355
data integrity, 365–367
data manipulation, 367–377
data structures, 354–357
DBMSs and, 348–353
domains, 356–357
ERDs, 377–388
history of, 354
mapping functions, 357
mathematical relations comparison, 357, 358

normal forms, 358–365
physical data independence, 356
primary key attributes, 355
properties, 354–355
rows, 355
tuples, 355
Relational OnLine Analytical Processing (ROLAP), 222
remote database objects. See RDO
renaming stored procedures, 520
replaying traces, Profiler, 265–266
replication, 200–221
articles, 202
components, 201–202
Create Publication Wizard, 205–211
disabling constraints for, 415
Distributors, 202
merge, 203–221
overview, 200–201
publications, 202
Publishers, 200, 202
pull, 200
push, 200
Push Subscription Wizard, 212–221
site autonomy, 200–201
snapshot, 203
Subscribers, 200, 202
transactional consistency, 200–201
transactional with immediate-updating Subscribers, 203
types of, 202–204
replication agent counters, Performance Monitor, 275
Replication Conflict Viewer, described, 33
Replication Distribution Agent, described, 34
replication distribution counters, Performance Monitor, 275
Replication Log Reader Agent, described, 34
replication logreader counters, Performance Monitor, 275
Replication Merge Agent, described, 34
replication merge counters, Performance Monitor, 275–276

Replication object hierarchy, SQL-DMO, 326–327
Replication Snapshot Agent, described, 35
replication snapshot counters, Performance Monitor, 276
Report Designer (Microsoft Access), 573–576
customizing reports, 576
New Report dialog box, 573, 574
Report Wizard, 574, 575
sample query, 573
report view (Performance Monitor), Add to Report dialog box, 288–289
reports
Database Maintenance Plan Wizard dialog box, 113, 114
Index Tuning Wizard, 298, 299
reptq1 stored procedure, DAO QueryDef objects, 638–644
Request object, ASP, 879
Response tab, SQL Server Agent, 98, 99
response time, database performance, 234
restore operations, striped backups, 188
restoring backed-up databases, 188–196
backing up transaction logs, 188
Backup Device Properties dialog box, 189
from backup devices, 196
damaged databases, 188–194
Database Restore dialog box, 191
differential backups, 193–194
files or filegroups, 195
full backups, 193–194
limiting transactions recovered, 192
master databases, 194–195
options, 191–192
reentering uncommitted operations, 192
Restore Database dialog box, 189, 190, 196

Restore Database statement, 192–193, 195

transaction log backups, 193–194

View Backup Media dialog box, 189, *190*

restricted statements, permissions, 159–161

result sets

multiple. *See* multiple result sets

stored procedures and, 522–523

result tables, Transact-SQL DDL, 392

results windows, Microsoft Access Query Designer, 569, *570*

retention periods of backup copies, 185–187

"grandfather" rotation, 185, *186–187*

retrieving column attributes, SQL-DMO, 341–343

retrieving data with ADO Recordset objects, 773–784

retrieving data with DAO, 607–618

dynamic Recordsets, 608–609

dynaset Recordsets, 608, 609–618

forward-only Recordsets, 608

Recordset objects, 607–609

snapshot Recordsets, 608

table Recordsets, 607

retrieving data with DB-Library, 824–831

DBExecQuery subroutine, 829–830

DBQuery subroutine, 825

DisplayDBGrid subroutine, 826–827

SQLCmd command, 829–830

SQLData function, 828

SQLDatLen function, 828

SQLExec command, 829–831

SQLNextRow function, 828

SQLNumCols function, 827

SQLOpenConnection function, 826

SQLResults command, 829–831

SQLSendCmd function, 824–829

SQLUse function, 826

retrieving data with ODBCDirect, 657–663

Connection objects, 659

ConnectionQuery function, 659

Database objects, 657–658

QueryDef objects and prepared SQL statements, 660–663

Recordset objects, 657–659

retrieving data with RDO, 729–736

Close method, 733

cursors, 730–731

OpenResultset method, 731–733

prepared SQL statements and rdoResultsets, 733–736

retrieving data from views, SQL Select statements, 451–452

Return statements, stored procedures, 523

Revoke statements, object permissions, 434–485

ROLAP (Relational OnLine Analytical Processing), 222

role permissions, application roles, 167

Role Properties dialog box, user security setup, *149*

roles, 124–125

fixed database, 124, *125*

fixed server, 124

managing database users, 153

user security setup, 130

user-defined database, 125, 143, 150–151

RollBack method, ODBCDirect transactions, 678–679

Rollback statements, transaction integrity, 516–518

rolling back transactions, ADO, 805–806

row GUIDs (Global Unique Identifier Columns), Transact-SQL DDL, 408–409

row lock type hints, table hints, *313*

RowGuidCol keyword, Transact-SQL DDL, 408–409

rows

deleting from ADO Recordset objects, 792–793

deleting from ADO Recordset objects (ASP and), 909–910

deleting with DB-Library cursors, 846

deleting duplicate with SQL Select statements, 452–453

deleting with dynamic SQL statements, 835

deleting with ODBC API, 710–711

deleting with RDO Delete method, 740

deleting with RDO and SQL Delete statements, 744–745

inserting with ADO Command objects and prepared SQL statements, 793–795

inserting into ADO Recordset objects, 789–791

inserting into ADO Recordset objects (ASP and), 900–904

inserting with DB-Library cursors, 838–840

inserting with dynamic SQL, 832–833

inserting with ODBC API, 708–710

inserting with QueryDef objects and prepared SQL statements, 663–665

inserting with RDO AddNew method, 738–739

inserting with RDO and SQL Insert statements, 741–742

inserting through views, 509–510

relational database model, 355

retrieving from views with SQL Select statements, 451–452

retrieving with SQL Select statements, 445–448

updating with ADO Recordset objects, 791–792

updating with ADO Recordset objects (ASP and), 905–908

updating with DB-Library cursors, 844–845

updating with dynamic SQL statements, 833–835

updating with ODBC API, 711–713
updating with RDO and SQL Update statements, 742–743
updating with RDO Update method, 739–740
RTrim function, SQL scalar functions, 468–469
rules
    constraints, 18
    Create Rule statements, 415
    named, 415
    Rules Tasks icon, 86
Run Traces command, Profiler, 263–264

▼ S

sa user name, system administrator, 126
saving
    log definition files, 287
    Microsoft Access macros, 579, 580
    Performance Monitor alerts, 284
    Performance Monitor chart views, 280–281
scalar functions (SQL), 455–469
    character string, 456–458
    data type conversion, 455
    date, time, and timestamp, 460–462
    image, 458
    mathematical, 458–460
    miscellaneous, 463–468
    RTrim, 468–469
    text, 458
    user, 462–463
Schedules tab, SQL Server Agent, 103
scheduling backups, 182
scheduling jobs, Web Assistant Wizard, 864, 865
schemes, Create Schema statements, 416
ScriptingContext object, ASP, 879
scripts
    ASP, 875–920
    Generate SQL Scripts dialog box, 80–84
    Profiler and, 264–265
    Transact-SQL, 80–85

scrollable cursors, 529
search conditions, SQL Select statements, 448–450
Search tab, Manage SQL Server Messages dialog box, 107
second normal forms (2NF), relational database model, 361
secondary files, Transact-SQL DDL, 398
security, 117–171
    Administrator user name, 126
    database owner, 126
    groups (NT Server), 123
    guest user name, 127
    logging on to NT Server, 118–119
    logging in to SQL Server, 119–123
    managing database users, 151–158
    mixed authentication mode, 127
    modes, 127
    overview, 118–127
    ownership chain of objects, 168–169
    permissions, 158–168
    principles and guidelines, 170
    roles (SQL Server), 124–125
    SQL Server Enterprise Manager, 20–22
    system administrator, 126
    user objects, 118
    user setup, 128–151
    Windows NT authentication mode, 127
Security tab, SQL Server Properties dialog box, 58–59
security-related SQL Server stored procedures, 155–157
security-related Transact-SQL functions, 157–158
<SELECT> tags, ADO and ASP, 894, 899
Select Dimensions dialog box, Cube Wizard (data warehousing), 228, 229
Select Fact Table dialog box, Cube Wizard (data warehousing), 226, 227
Select Measures dialog box, Cube Wizard (data warehousing), 226, 228

Select statements (SQL DML), 445–507
    * (asterisks), 446, 447, 452
    aggregate functions, 471–473
    Basic conditions, 487–489
    Between conditions, 489
    Case structures, 497–498
    complex, 479–487
    Compute clause, 505–506
    concurrent updates and table locks, 515–518
    conditions and subqueries, 487–497
    conditions and three-valued logic, 450–451
    constants, functions, and expressions, 453–469
    date and time arithmetic, 469–471
    defining views, 419–420
    eliminating duplicate rows, 452–453
    Exists conditions, 492–495
    in From clauses, 499–500
    Group By clause, 474–475, 502–504
    Having clause, 475–477
    In conditions, 489–490
    Into clause, 506–507
    Like conditions, 491–492
    Not logical operator, 450
    Null conditions, 489
    object permissions, 162
    ODBC API, 702–703
    operators, 454
    Order By clause, 478, 501
    overview, 445–447
    parameterized DAO QueryDef objects, 634
    Quantified conditions, 495–497
    retrieving rows from views, 451–452
    retrieving rows with, 445–448
    scalar functions, 455–469
    search conditions, 448–450
    SQL conditions and three-valued logic, 450–451
    structure of, 445
    subqueries as scalar values, 498–499
    Top clause, 500–501
    Where clause, 448–449

Select Stored Procedure dialog box, Web Assistant Wizard, *872*

Select Unique Record Identifier dialog box, linking Microsoft Access tables to SQL Server, 565, *566*

Selected data list, Profiler Data Columns tab, 260

selection operations, algebraic operations, 370

sending error messages, stored procedures and, 534–535

Server object, ASP, 879

server properties, 48–65
    sp_configure system stored procedure options, *48–51*
    SQL Server Properties dialog box, 51–65

Server Settings tab, SQL Server Properties dialog box, 62–64

server-side cursors, advanced RDO topics, 752–753

servers
    database architecture, 9–10
    fixed roles, *124*
    linked, 108–110
    registering and unregistering, 41–46
    standby for backups, 197–198
    stopping, starting, pausing, and continuing, 47–48

Service Manager, described, *35*

Session objects
    ADO and ASP, 888–890
    ASP, 879

session scoped connections, ADO and ASP, 888–890

Set Merge Agent Schedule dialog box, Push Subscription Wizard, *215*

Set statements
    Showplan and, 301–303
    SQL-DMO properties, 331
    stored procedures, 524–525

Set Stored Procedure Parameters dialog box, Web Assistant Wizard, *873*

Set Subscription Priority dialog box, Push Subscription Wizard, 216, *217, 218*

Setup tool, described, *35*

shared locks
    concurrent updates and table locks (DML), 515
    table hints, 312

ShowError subroutines
    ADO error handling, 800
    DAO error handling, 645–646

Showplan, 299–305
    described, 237
    execution plans, 299–300
    graphical, 304–305
    overview, 299–300
    Query Analyzer, 304–305
    Set statements and, 301–303
    Showplan_All commands, 301–303
    Showplan_Text commands, 301–302

Show_Statistics command, DBCC statements, 306

side-by-side migrations, Version Upgrade Wizard, 928, 929

site autonomy, replication, 200–201

skip rows table hints, *314*

snapshot Recordsets
    DAO, 608
    performance tips, 648

snapshots, replication, 203

source options, ADO Recordset objects, 776, *778*

Source Server dialog box, Profiler General tab, 243, *244*

sp_addtype stored procedure, creating user-defined data types, 410

sp_configure system stored procedure options, setting server properties, *48–51*

sp_dboption options, managing databases and database objects, *70–71*

Specify Articles dialog box, Create Publication Wizard, *209*

Specify Subscriber Types dialog box, Create Publication Wizard, *208*

SQL (Structured Query Language). *See* Transact-SQL DDL

SQL catalog, 438–439

SQL Mail tool, described, *35*

SQL Maintenance Utility, described, *36*

SQL Performance Monitor. *See* Performance Monitor

SQL Scripts
    Index Tuning Wizard and, 293, *300*
    Profiler and, 264–265

SQL Server
    administration, 27–116
    administrative components, 19–26
    ADO and, 762–811
    architecture, 4–7
    ASP and, 875–920
    backups, 173–197
    basic components, 7–8
    client/server architecture, 6–7
    components overview, 7–8
    connecting ADO to, 767–773
    connecting DB-Library to, 820–824
    connecting Microsoft Access to, 553–567
    DAO and, 591–648
    data warehousing, 221–231
    database architecture, 9–19
    database performance, 233–315
    database replication, 200–221
    DB-Library and, 811–857
    deleting user-defined database roles, 150–151
    DML and, 443–545
    Enterprise Manager, 19–22
    enumerating systems with DB-Library, 818–820
    installing, 28–39
    logging in to, 119–123
    logins (user security setup), 140–141
    Microsoft Access and, 547–590
    migrating from version 6.*x* to 7. *See* Version Upgrade Wizard
    multiple-user database access, 551–552
    networked architecture, 4–7
    NT Server security terminology comparison, *119–122*
    ODBC API and, 681–718
    ODBCDirect and, 648–679
    OLE DB and, 759–762
    overview, 4–26
    Performance Monitor, 268–289
    permissions, 158–168
    Profiler, 238–268
    RDO and, 719–753

relational database model,
347–388
replication, 200–221
roles, 124–125
security, 117–171
security-related stored
procedures, *155–157*
Showplan, 299–305
SQL-DMO, 317–344
tools, 30–37
Transact-SQL DDL, 8–9,
389–442
Version Upgrade Wizard,
927-937
Web Assistant Wizard,
860–874
SQL Server Agent, 90–105
Alert Properties dialog box,
97–99
Alert System tab, 92, *93*
Connection tab, 93, *95*
creating alerts, 96–98
creating jobs, 98–105
creating operators, 93–96
described, *36*, 90
Edit Job Schedule dialog
box, 103, *104*
Edit Job Step dialog box,
101–105
Edit Recurring Job Schedule
dialog box, 103, *104*
General tab, 94–96
Job Properties dialog box,
100, 103, *105*
Job System tab, 92–93, *94*
Notifications tab, *96*, *105*
Properties dialog box, 90–93
Response tab, 98, *99*
Schedules tab, *103*
Steps tab, 99, *100*
SQL Server application databases
developing with DB-Library,
811–857
developing with Microsoft
Access, 547–590
user security setup, 141–143
SQL Server DSN Configuration
Wizard, ODBC API, 688–693
SQL Server Login Properties
dialog box
managing database
users, *152*
user security setup, *146*
SQL Server Profiler. *See* Profiler

SQL Server Properties dialog box,
51–65
backup options, 196, *197*
Connections tab, 59–62
Database Settings tab, 64–65
General tab, 51–55
Memory tab, 55–56
Processor tab, 57–58
Security tab, 58–59
Server Settings tab, 62–64
user security setup, *136*
SQL Server Service Manager
dialog box, server functions, *47*
SQL statement hints, 310–315
described, *238*
join hints, 310–312
overview, 310
query hints, 310, *311*
table hints, 312–315
types of, 310
SQL statements
prepared. *See* prepared SQL
statements
See also Transact-SQL DDL
SQL statistics counters,
Performance Monitor, *276*
SQL-DMF (Distributed
Management Framework),
SQL-DMO, 318–319
SQL-DMO (Distributed
Management Objects), 317–344
accessing, 327–332
administrative components,
25
client files, 327
Connect method, 330–331,
336–337
core object hierarchy,
319–321
database object hierarchy,
321–323
error handling, 343–344
iterating through collections,
334
JobServer object hierarchy,
324–326
listing columns, 339–341
listing databases, 338
listing tables, 338–339
MMF (Microsoft
Management Console),
318
Object Browser and, *329*
object collections, 332–335
object hierarchy, 318–327

overview, 318–319
properties, 331–332
property collections, 332–335
referencing specific
collection objects, 334–335
Replication object hierarchy,
326–327
retrieving column attributes,
341–343
sample application, 335–344
Set statements, 331
SQL-DMF (Distributed
Management Framework),
318–319
SQL-NS (Namespace), 319
SQLDMOError function,
343–344
SQLServer object hierarchy,
321
SQLServer objects, 329–330,
336–337
table objects, 324
Visual Basic and, 327–329
See also Enterprise Manager
SQL-NS (Namespace), SQL-DMF
(Distributed Management
Framework), 319
SQLAdd subroutine, inserting
rows with dynamic SQL,
832–833
SQLAllocHandle function, ODBC
API, 696, 697–698, 701
SQLBindCol function, ODBC API,
707–708
SQLBindParameter function,
ODBC API, 709–710
SQLClose function, closing
connection libraries, 824
SQLCmd command, retrieving
data with DB-Library, 829–830
SQLConnect function, ODBC API,
698–699
SQLCursor function, inserting
rows with DB-Library cursors,
840
SQLCursorClose function,
displaying DB-Library cursor
data, 844
SQLCursorFetch function,
displaying DB-Library cursor
data, 843
SQLCursorInfo function,
displaying DB-Library cursor
data, 842

SQLCursorOpen function, inserting rows with DB-Library cursors, 839–840

SQLCursorRowStatus function, displaying DB-Library cursor data, 843

SQLData function, retrieving data with DB-Library, 828

SQLDatLen function, retrieving data with DB-Library, 828

SQLDbCreator groups, user security setup and, 138

SQLDelete function, deleting rows with dynamic SQL, 835

SQLDisconnect function, ODBC API, 700–701

SQLDMOError function, SQL-DMO, 343–344

SQLDriverConnect function, ODBC API, 699–700

SQLExec command, retrieving data with DB-Library, 829–831

SQLExecDirect function, ODBC API, 702–703

SQLExecute function, ODBC API, 703–705

SQLExit subroutine, closing all connections, 824

SQLFetch function, ODBC API, 705–706

SQLFreeHandle function, ODBC API, 696–697, 698, 702

SQLFreeStmt function, ODBC API, 701–702

SQLGetData function, ODBC API, 705–707

SQLGetDiagRec function, ODBC API, 716–717

SQLInit function, initializing DB-Library, 818

SQLNextRow function, retrieving data with DB-Library, 828

SQLNumCols function, retrieving data with DB-Library, 827

SQLNumResultCols function, ODBC API, 706

SQLOLEDB OLE DB provider, connecting ADO to SQL Server, 767

SQLOpen function, connecting DB-Library to SQL Server, 822–824

SQLOpenConnection function connecting DB-Library to SQL Server, 820–822

retrieving data with DB-Library, 826

SQLPassThrough (DAO), 623–631
AddNew method, 624–626
Delete method, 627–628
Delete statements, 631
dynamic SQL and, 623–624, 628
Edit method, 626–627
Execute method, 624
Insert statements, 628–630
performance tips, 648
QueryDef objects and, 635–637
Recordset objects and, 624–631
Update method, 626–627
Update statements, 630–631

SQLPrepare function, ODBC API, 704–705

SQLResults function
multiple DB-Library result sets, 853–855
retrieving data with DB-Library, 829–831

SQLRetData function, executing stored procedures with DB-Library, 850

SQLRpcExec function, executing stored procedures with DB-Library, 850

SQLRpcInit function, executing stored procedures with DB-Library, 848–849

SQLRpcParam function, executing stored procedures with DB-Library, 849–850

SQLSendCmd function
dynamic SQL statements, 831–832
retrieving data with DB-Library, 824–829

SQLServer object hierarchy, SQL-DMO, 321

SQLServer objects, SQL-DMO, 329–330, 336–337

SQLServerEnum function, enumerating SQL Server systems with DB-Library, 819–820

sqlservr.exe program parameters, General tab (SQL Server Properties dialog box), 53–55

SQLSetEnvAttr function, ODBC API, 697

SQLUpdate subroutine, updating rows with dynamic SQL, 833–835

SQLUse function, retrieving data with DB-Library, 826

SQLWinExit subroutine, ending DB-Library applications, 818

standby servers, backups and, 197–198

Start Required Services dialog box, Push Subscription Wizard, 218

Start/Stop button, Performance Monitor log view, 287

Startup Parameters dialog box, General tab (SQL Server Properties dialog box), 53

statement blocks, stored procedures, 525

statement handles
allocating ODBC API, 701
freeing ODBC API, 701–702

statement permissions, 161–162
Database Properties dialog box, 162
Grant statements, 438

static cursors
ADO Recordset objects, 773
RDO, 730

statistics collections, DBCC Show_Statistics command, 306

statistics counters, Performance Monitor, 274, 276

Statistics_NoRecompute option, Create Index statement, 432

status return value, stored procedures, 523

Steps tab, SQL Server Agent, 99, 100

Stored Procedure Tasks icon, 86

stored procedures
@ (at signs), 521
Alter Procedure statements, 520
assignment statements, 524–525
blocks, 525
calling. See calling stored procedures
conditional execution, 526–527
constraints, 18–19
Create Procedure statements, 519
cursors, 528–533
deleting, 520

displaying information about, 520–521
displaying messages, 525
Drop Procedure statements, 520
error messages, 534–535
executing with ADO Command objects, 797–799
executing with Command objects, 910–918
executing with DB-Library, 847–850
executing with QueryDef objects and ODBCDirect, 669–671
extended. *See* extended stored procedures
GoTo statements and labels, 527
If...Else statements, 526–527
input parameters, 521
local variable declarations, 524
managing database users, 154–157
output parameters, 521–522
overview, 519
parameters, 521–523
performance tips, 648
permissions and, 168
predefined error messages, 534–535
Print statements, 525
Profiler, *239–241*
programming techniques, 524–528
RaisError statements, 534
RDO and, 745–747
renaming, 520
result sets, 522–523
Return statements, 523
sending error messages, 534–535
Set statements, 524–525
statement blocks, 525
status return value, 523
Transact-SQL, *238*
Transact-SQL and database performance, 308–309
triggers, 536–543
unqualified object names, 524
VBA code modules and Microsoft Access, 584–588

WaitFor statements, 527–528
While loops, 527
storing binary data, advanced ADO database functions, 807–811
striped backups, 180
restore operations, 188
subqueries
conditions and SQL Select statements, 487–497
DML Update statements, 511–512
Exists conditions (SQL Select statements), 494–495
as scalar values, 498–499
Subscribers
Create Publication Wizard, *208*
replication, 200
subscription completion message, Push Subscription Wizard, 219, *220*
SumStateQty stored procedure, DB-Library, 847–848
system administrators
security overview, 126
user security setup, 129
System Configuration screen, Version Upgrade Wizard, *933*

▼ T

table aliases, complex SQL Select statements, 482–483
table hints, 312–315
As clause, 312
DML concurrent updates and table locks, 515
index hints, *313*
lock granularity hints, *313–314*
optimization hints, *313*
overview, 312
row lock type hints, *313*
shared locks, 312
skip rows hints, *314*
transaction isolation level hints, *314*, 315
With clause, 312
table objects, SQL-DMO, 324
table Recordsets, DAO, 607
table specifications, Index Tuning Wizard, *297*
table-level Check constraints, 415

TableDef objects, DAO, 594
TableDefs.Delete method, DAO QueryDef objects, 644
tables, 12–13, 74–85
aliases, 482–483
Alter Table statements, 416–417
capacities, 942
constraints, 15–18
Create New Index dialog box, *78*
creating on specific filegroups, 415–416
Data in Table dialog box, 83–85
defined, 12
Dependencies dialog box, *81*
Design Table dialog box, *76*
Generate SQL Scripts dialog box, 80–84
joining, 370, 373, 421–423, 427–428
linking DAO to SQL Server, 599, 601–604
linking Microsoft Access to SQL Server, 561–567
listing (SQL-DMO), 338–339
Manage Indexes dialog box, *77*
New Table dialog box, 74–75
Object Scripting Preview dialog box, 80, *82*
permissions, 433–438
Permissions dialog box, *78, 79*
SQL catalog, *439*
SQL permissions, *435*
Table Properties dialog box, *76*
Transact-SQL DDL, 392, 401–403
Trigger Properties dialog box, *79*
views, 15
views spanning multiple, 420–423
tasks, 85–90
Default Properties dialog box, 86, *87*
Edit Diagram dialog box, *88*
full-text catalog, 89–90
Rules Tasks icon, 86
Stored Procedure Tasks icon, 86

User-Defined Data Type
Properties dialog box,
86, *87*
View Tasks icon, 85
tempdb databases, database
architecture, 11
text functions, SQL scalar
functions, 458
theta-joins, algebraic
operations, 373
third normal forms (3NF),
relational database model,
361–362
three-valued logic, SQL conditions
and, 450–451
throughput, database
performance, 234
time functions, SQL scalar
functions, 460–462
TimeStamp columns, Transact-SQL
DDL, 404–405
timestamp functions, SQL scalar
functions, 460–462
title IDs, DAO QueryDef
objects, 637
titling page, Web Assistant Wizard,
863, 867, 871
tools
database performance,
235–315
installing SQL Server, 30–37
Microsoft Access Rapid
Development, *548*
tools overview, database
performance, 235–236, *236–238*
Top clause, SQL Select statements,
500–501
trace definitions
exporting and importing, 262
Profiler, 242–263
trace flags
database performance,
307–308
described, *238*
Trace Properties dialog box
(Profiler)
Data Columns tab, *253*
Events tab, *245–251*
Filters tab, *262*
General tab, 242, *243*
trace window, Profiler, 263

traces
Create Trace Wizard,
266–267, *268*
replaying, 265–266
See also Profiler
Transact-SQL DDL (Data Definition
Language), 8–9, 389–442
Add Log File clause, 400
Alter Database statements,
400–401
Alter Table statements,
416–417
alternatives for creating
database objects, 397
ANSI SQL-92 standards
and, 397
base tables, 392
benefits of, 393–394
capacities, 943
Check constraints, 414–415
column data types, *405–408*
column definitions, 404–412
column manipulation,
417–418
computed columns, 411–412
constraints, 412–415
constraints manipulation,
416–417
Create Database command,
398
Create Schema statements,
416
Create Table statements,
401–403, 404, 415
creating tables on specific
filegroups, 415–416
creating views, 418–428
Current Connection Options
dialog box, *396*
cursors, 528–533
DAO QueryDef objects and,
631–632, 663–668
Data Manipulation
Language. *See* DML
database creation, 397–401
database file locations and
sizes, 398–399
DDL coding suggestions,
439–441
default values, 410–411
defining filegroups, 400–401
Drop statements, 433

dynamic statements. *See*
dynamic SQL statements
entering statements, 394–397
Enterprise Manager as
alternative to, 397
example, 392–393
filegroups, 400–401
functions, *238*
hints. *See* SQL statement
hints
identity columns, 408
indexes, 428–433
Insert statements, 393
key constraints, 412–414
Log On clause, 399
managing database users,
157–158
Modify File clause, 400
naming conventions, 403–404
Niladic functions, *411*
null and not null
columns, 409
On clause, 398
OSQL batch facility, 395–396
overview, 390
permissions, 433–438
prepared statements. *See*
prepared SQL statements
primary files, 398
Query Analyzer, 394–395
RDO and, 741–747
result tables, 392
row GUIDs, 408–409
RowGuidCol keyword,
408–409
scripts, 80–85
secondary files, 398
Select statements. *See* Select
statements (SQL DML)
sp_addtype stored
procedure, 410
stored procedures, *238*,
519–543
stored procedures and
database performance,
308–309
tables, 392, 401–403
TimeStamp columns, 404–405
user-defined data types,
409–410
views, 393, 418–428

transaction integrity, Commit and
    Rollback statements, 516–518
transaction isolation level hints,
    table hints, *314*, 315
Transaction Log tab, Database
    Properties dialog box, *67*
transaction logs
        backing up exclusively,
            181–182, 188
        backups and, 175–176
        Database Maintenance Plan
            Wizard dialog box, 113
        restoring backed-up
            databases, 193–194
        truncating, 182–183
transactional consistency,
    replication, 200–201, 203
transactions
        DB-Library, 855–856
        DML concurrent updates
            and table locks, 516–518
transactions (ADO), 805–807
        committing, 806–807
        rolling back, 805–806
transactions (ODBCDirect),
    676–679
        commiting, 677–678
        RollBack method, 678–679
Trigger Properties dialog box, table
    tasks, *79*
triggers, 536–543
        Alter Trigger statements, 540
        Create Trigger statements,
            536–539
        defined, 536
        deleting, 540
        displaying information
            about, 541
        Drop Trigger statements, 540
        If Update clause, 539–540
        nested, 541
        overview, 536–539
        programming, 542–543
        recursive, 541
        static Web pages and, 870
Truncate statements, DML, 514
truncating transaction logs,
    backups, 182–183
Tuning Wizard. *See* Index Tuning
    Wizard
tuples, relational database model,
    355
twips, limiting data in DAO
    Recordset objects, 622

U

unbound columns and
    SQLGetData function, ODBC
    API, 705–707
Uninstall tool, described, *36*
union compatibility, algebraic
    operations, 370
Union keyword, complex SQL
    Select statements, 485–487
union operations, algebraic
    operations, 367, *368*
unique identifiers, user security
    setup, 129
unique keys, constraints, 17, 413
Universal Data Access, OLE DB,
    759
unqualified object names, stored
    procedures, 524
Update statements
        If Update clause, 539–540
        RDO, 739–740
        RDO and SQL, 742–743
        SQLPassThrough (DAO),
            626–627, 630–631
        triggers, 536–543
Update statements (DML), 510–513
        concurrent updates and
            table locks, 515–518
        multiple tables, 512–513
        subqueries, 511–512
updateable cursors, 530–531
updateable views, 424
UpdateUsage command, DBCC
    statements, 307
updating rows
        ADO Command objects,
            793–797
        ADO Command objects and
            prepared SQL statements,
            795–796
        ADO Recordset objects,
            791–792
        ADO Recordset objects (ASP
            and), 905–908
        DB-Library cursors, 844–845
        dynamic SQL statements,
            833–835
        ODBC API, 708–714
        QueryDef objects and
            prepared SQL statements
            (ODBCDirect), 665–667
        RDO and SQL Update
            statements, 742–743

RDO Update method,
    739–740
Upgrade directory, Version
    Upgrade Wizard, 932, 935, *936*
Use Default Properties of the
    Publication dialog box, Create
    Publication Wizard, 210, *211*
user accounts, logging in to SQL
    Server, 122–123
user databases, backups, 184
user names, 118–119
        defined, 118
        managing database users,
            153–154
        multiple, 119
user objects, 118
user scalar functions, SQL, 462–463
user security setup, 128–151
        database owners, 129–130
        Database Role Properties
            dialog box, *144*
        Database User Properties
            dialog box, *146, 150*
        deleting NT Server
            groups, 150
        deleting SQL Server
            user-defined database
            roles, 150–151
        disabling users, 151
        Group Memberships dialog
            box, *139, 148*
        Group Properties dialog
            box, *149*
        guest user name, 140
        identifiers, 129
        Local Group Properties
            dialog box, *139*
        logical roles, 130
        login names, 143–147
        modes, 135
        New Local Group dialog
            box, *137*
        New User dialog box, *138*
        NT Server groups, 131–137
        NT Server users, 137–140
        NT User Manager
            window, *136*
        planning, 128–135
        removing users, 148–151
        Role Properties dialog
            box, *149*
        roles, 130
        SQL Server application
            databases, 141–143

SQL Server Login Properties dialog box, *146*
SQL Server logins, 140–141
SQL Server Properties dialog box, *136*
SQLDbCreator groups and, 138
summary, 147–148
system administrators, 129
unique identifiers, 129
updating login names, 145–147
user-defined database roles, 143
user settable counters, Performance Monitor, *276*
User-Defined Data Type Properties dialog box, tasks, 86, *87*
user-defined data types, Transact-SQL DDL, 409–410
user-defined database roles, 125
deleting SQL Server, 150–151
user security setup, 143
user-defined filegroups, backups and, 175
users, managing database. *See* managing database users
utilities, command-line, 26

▼ V

variables
cursor, 533
local declarations, 524
VBA code modules and Microsoft Access, 580–589
DAO Recordsets, 581–582
error handling, 588–589
parameterized queries, 582–584
SQL Server stored procedures, 584–588
VBScript
ASP and, 875, 880–881
Option Explicit statements, 903, 908
Vbsql1_Error and Vbsql1_Message subroutines, DB-Library error handling, 850–852
vbsql.bas module, DB-Library, 815, *817*
vbsql.ocx, adding to Visual Basic for DB-Library, 814–816
Version Switch tool, described, *37*

Version Upgrade Wizard, 927-937
Completion screen, *934*
computer-to-computer migrations, 928
Data and Object Transfer dialog box, *930*
Database Creation screen, *933*
Database Selection screen, *932*
described, *37*
direct pipeline method, 928-929
Logon screen, 930, *931*
Migration Status screen, *935*
overview, 928-929
prerequisites, 929
side-by-side migrations, 928, 929
System Configuration screen, *933*
types of migration strategies, 928
Upgrade directory, 932, 935, *936*
View Backup Media dialog box, restoring backed-up databases, 189, *190*
view relations, algebraic operations, 374–376
View Tasks icon, 85
viewing RDO classes with Object Browser, *725*
views, 418–428
compound conditions, 425–426
Create View statements, 418–419
defined, 15, 393
defining contents of, 419–423
derived columns, 426–427
encrypted definitions, 425
examples, 425–428
inserting rows through, 509–510
joining tables, 427–428
Performance Monitor, 277–289
permissions, 433–438
read-only, 423–424
reordering and renaming columns, 426
retrieving rows with SQL Select statements, 451–452
select expressions, 419–420

spanning multiple tables, 420–423
updateable, 424
With Check option, 424–425
virtual attributes, algebraic operations, 375, *376*
Visual Basic
adding ADO 2.1 reference to, 765–766
adding DAO 3.5 reference to, 597, *598*
adding RDO 2.0 reference to, 723–724
creating applications with ADO, 766–801
DB-Library and, 814–816
error-handling options, *646*
SQL-DMO and, 327–329
Visual Data Manager
Attachments dialog box, *602*
connecting DAO to SQL Server, 600–603
New Attached Table dialog box, *601*
Visual InterDev, 921–924
Add Data Connection command, 922
Command objects, 923–924
Command Properties dialog box, *923*
Connection Properties dialog box, *922*
Data View window, 922
design-time recordset control, *924*
Project menu, 922

▼ W

WaitFor statements, stored procedures, 527–528
warehousing. *See* data warehousing
weak entity notation, ERDs, 382, 384
Web Assistant Wizard, 860–874
Add Hyperlinks to Web Page dialog box, 867–869
calling stored procedures with, 871–874
database selection, *862*
formatting tables, 867, *868*
HTML files, 866–867
Limit Rows dialog box, *869*
output directory, *866*

overview, 860
query builds, 861–870
scheduling jobs, 864, *865*
selecting row criteria,
   864, *865*
selecting tables and
   columns, 863, *864*
titling pages, *863, 867, 871*
triggers and static Web
   pages, 870
Welcome screen, *862*
See also ASP
Web integration. *See* ASP; Web
Assistant Wizard
Where clause
   complex SQL Select
      statements, 482

Having clause comparison,
   477
limiting data in DAO
   Recordset objects, 619–620
SQL Select statements,
   448–449, 482
While loops
   rdoResultsets and prepared
      SQL statements, 735–736
   stored procedures, 527
Windows NT authentication, 127
   Enterprise Manager, 21
With Check option, Create View
   statements, 424–425
With clause, table hints, 312
With Cube option, Group By
   clause (SQL Select statements),
   502–504

With Grant Option clause, object
   permissions, 163, 436–437
With Rollup option, Group By
   clause (SQL Select statements),
   502–504
wizards
      administrative components,
         22
      installing SQL Server, 37–39
workloads, Index Tuning Wizard,
   293, *295*
Workspace objects
      DAO, 594, 598–599
      DAO dynaset Recordset
         objects, 610
      ODBCDirect, 652–653